SIPRI Yearbook 2023
Armaments, Disarmament and International Security

www.sipriyearbook.org

**STOCKHOLM INTERNATIONAL
PEACE RESEARCH INSTITUTE**

SIPRI is an independent international institute dedicated to research into conflict, armaments, arms control and disarmament. Established in 1966, SIPRI provides data, analysis and recommendations, based on open sources, to policymakers, researchers, media and the interested public.

The Governing Board is not responsible for the views expressed in the publications of the Institute.

GOVERNING BOARD

Stefan Löfven, Chair (Sweden)
Dr Mohamed Ibn Chambas (Ghana)
Ambassador Chan Heng Chee (Singapore)
Jean-Marie Guéhenno (France)
Dr Radha Kumar (India)
Dr Patricia Lewis (Ireland/United Kingdom)
Dr Jessica Tuchman Mathews (United States)
Dr Feodor Voitolovsky (Russia)

DIRECTOR

Dan Smith (United Kingdom)

Dr Ian Davis, *Executive Editor*
Ms Joey M. Fox, *Managing Editor*

Editors
John Batho, Frank Esparraga, Dr Linda Nix,
Annika Salisbury and Emma Zetterström

**STOCKHOLM INTERNATIONAL
PEACE RESEARCH INSTITUTE**

Signalistgatan 9
SE-169 72 Solna, Sweden
Telephone: + 46 8 655 9700
Email: sipri@sipri.org
Internet: www.sipri.org

SIPRI Yearbook 2023

Armaments, Disarmament and International Security

**STOCKHOLM INTERNATIONAL
PEACE RESEARCH INSTITUTE**

OXFORD UNIVERSITY PRESS
2023

Great Clarendon Street, Oxford OX2 6DP,
United Kingdom

Oxford University Press is a department of the University of Oxford.
It furthers the University's objective of excellence in research, scholarship,
and education by publishing worldwide. Oxford is a registered trade mark of
Oxford University Press in the UK and in certain other countries

© SIPRI 2023

The moral rights of the authors have been asserted

All rights reserved. No part of this publication may be reproduced,
stored in a retrieval system, or transmitted, in any form or by any means,
without the prior permission in writing of SIPRI, or as expressly permitted
by law, or under terms agreed with the appropriate reprographics rights
organizations. Enquiries concerning reproduction outside the scope of the
above should be sent to
SIPRI, Signalistgatan 9, SE-169 72 Solna, Sweden

You must not circulate this book in any other form
and you must impose the same condition on any acquirer

Published in the United States of America by Oxford University Press
198 Madison Avenue, New York, NY 10016, United States of America

British Library Cataloguing in Publication Data
Data available

Library of Congress Cataloging in Publication Data
Data available

ISBN 978-0-19-889072-0

Typeset and originated by SIPRI
Printed in the UK by
Bell & Bain Ltd., Glasgow

SIPRI Yearbook 2023 is also published online at
<http://www.sipriyearbook.org>

Links to third party websites are provided by Oxford in good faith and
for information only. Oxford disclaims any responsibility for the materials
contained in any third party website referenced in this work.

Contents

Preface	xvii
Abbreviations and conventions	xix
SIPRI Yearbook online	xxii

1. Introduction: International stability and human security in 2022   3
DAN SMITH

    I. *Food and geopolitics*   5
    II. *Great power relations*   8
    III. *Arms control and nuclear non-proliferation*   13
    IV. *Climate change and environmental diplomacy*   16
    V. *The course of the war in Ukraine*   18
    VI. *Unanswered questions*   26

Part I. Armed conflict and conflict management, 2022

2. Trends in armed conflict   29

    Overview   29
    RICHARD GOWAN

    I. *Global and regional trends and developments in armed conflicts*   31
    RICHARD GOWAN

    Global trends in armed conflict—Regional conflict dynamics

    Table 2.1. Estimated conflict-related fatalities by region, 2018–22   32
    Table 2.2. Estimated conflict-related fatalities in the Americas, 2018–22   34
    Table 2.3. Estimated conflict-related fatalities in Asia and Oceania, 2017–22   36
    Table 2.4. Estimated conflict-related fatalities in Europe, 2018–22   44
    Table 2.5. Estimated conflict-related fatalities in the Middle East and North Africa, 2017–22   46
    Table 2.6. Estimated conflict-related fatalities in sub-Saharan Africa, 2017–22   48

    II. *International conflict management and peace processes*   53
    RICHARD GOWAN

    Geopolitics and international cooperation—Peace processes

    III. *Table of armed conflicts active in 2022*   61
    IAN DAVIS

    Figure 2.1. Armed conflicts by number of estimated conflict-related deaths, 2022   62
    Table 2.7. Categories of conflict-related violence, 2020–22   62
    Table 2.8. Armed conflicts active in 2022   63

3. Multilateral peace operations 69

Overview 69
CLAUDIA PFEIFER CRUZ AND TIMO SMIT

I. *Global trends and developments in peace operations* 71
CLAUDIA PFEIFER CRUZ AND TIMO SMIT

New multilateral peace operations—Multilateral peace operations that closed in 2022—Personnel deployments—The main troop- and police-contributing countries

Figure 3.1. Number of multilateral peace operations, by type of conducting organization, 2013–22 72

Figure 3.2. Number of multilateral peace operations, by region, 2013–22 73

Figure 3.3. Number of personnel in multilateral peace operations, by region, 2013–22 80

Figure 3.4. Largest multilateral peace operations as of 31 December 2022 81

Figure 3.5. Main contributors of military and police personnel to peace operations as of 31 December 2022 82

Table 3.1. Number of multilateral peace operations and personnel deployed, by region and type of organization, 2022 74

II. *Organizations conducting multilateral peace operations* 84
CLAUDIA PFEIFER CRUZ AND TIMO SMIT

United Nations—Regional organizations and alliances—Ad hoc coalitions—Other multilateral operations

Figure 3.6. Number of personnel in multilateral peace operations, by type of conducting organization, 2013–22 85

Figure 3.7. Fatalities among international personnel in United Nations peace operations, 2013–22 90

Figure 3.8. Fatality rates for uniformed personnel in United Nations peace operations, 2013–22 91

Figure 3.9. Hostile death rates for uniformed personnel in three key United Nations peace operations, 2013–22 92

III. *The way forward for multilateral peace operations* 98
CLAUDIA PFEIFER CRUZ

Geopolitical rivalries—Relations with host countries—The regionalization of peace operations

IV. *Table of multilateral peace operations, 2022* 101
CLAUDIA PFEIFER CRUZ

Table 3.2. Multilateral peace operations, 2022 102

4. Private military and security companies in armed conflict 105

Overview 105
ORI SWED, MARINA CAPARINI AND SORCHA MACLEOD

I. *The global growth of private military and security companies: Trends, actors and issues of concern* 107
ORI SWED

Introduction—Issues of concern—Key definitional and legal issues—Efforts at mapping PMSCs—Deployment of PMSCs to territorial states in conflict zones—Key actors: Home states and leading companies—Conclusions

Figure 4.1. Total number of private military and security companies, 1980–2020 114

II. *Private military and security companies in sub-Saharan Africa* 126
MARINA CAPARINI

Shifting geopolitical trends and continental dynamics—Russian PMSCs—Chinese PMSCs—Recent PMSC activity in selected conflict-affected sub-Saharan African states—Conclusions

III. *The current regulatory landscape for private military and security companies* 143
SORCHA MACLEOD

International humanitarian law and proxy actors—Regulation at the United Nations—Recent case law—Conclusions

Part II. Military spending and armaments, 2022

5. Military expenditure and arms production 157

Overview 157
DIEGO LOPES DA SILVA

I. *Global developments in military expenditure, 2022* 159
DIEGO LOPES DA SILVA, NAN TIAN, LUCIE BÉRAUD-SUDREAU, LORENZO SCARAZZATO AND XIAO LIANG

The impact of the war in Ukraine on military expenditure in Central and Western Europe—Trends in military expenditure, 2013–22—The largest military spenders in 2022

Box 5.1. Global inflation and its impact on military spending 164
Figure 5.1. Military expenditure by region, 2013–22 160
Figure 5.2. Rates of growth in military expenditure in Central and Western Europe, 2022 162
Figure 5.3. Difference between relative changes in military expenditure in current and constant values in Central and Western Europe, 2022 165
Table 5.1. Military expenditure by region, 2013–22 170

Table 5.2. Key military expenditure statistics by region, 2022 — 166
Table 5.3. The 15 countries with the highest military expenditure in 2022 — 168

II. *Regional developments in military expenditure, 2022* — 172
NAN TIAN, XIAO LIANG, LUCIE BÉRAUD-SUDREAU,
DIEGO LOPES DA SILVA, LORENZO SCARAZZATO AND
ANA CAROLINA DE OLIVEIRA ASSIS

Africa—The Americas—Asia and Oceania—Europe—Middle East

Figure 5.4. Changes in military expenditure by subregion, 2013–22 and 2021–22 — 174
Table 5.4. Components of US military expenditure, fiscal years 2018–22 — 176
Table 5.5. US military aid to Ukraine, 2014–21 — 178

III. *Arms-producing and military services companies, 2021* — 195
XIAO LIANG, ANA CAROLINA DE OLIVEIRA ASSIS, ANASTASIA CUCINO,
MADISON LIPSON AND SANEM TOPAL

Regional and national developments in the Top 100 for 2021—Notable developments outside the Top 100—Supply chain disruptions, the war in Ukraine and demand for arms

Table 5.6. Trends in arms sales of companies in the SIPRI Top 100, 2012–21 — 196
Table 5.7. Regional and national shares of arms sales for companies in the SIPRI Top 100, 2020–21 — 197

6. International arms transfers — 207

Overview — 207
SIEMON T. WEZEMAN

I. *Global trends in arms transfers, 2018–22* — 209
SIEMON T. WEZEMAN AND PIETER D. WEZEMAN

Key developments in 2022 related to arms transfers—Conflicts, tensions and arms transfers—Estimates of future arms transfers based on known orders

Box 6.1. Definitions and methodology for SIPRI data on international arms transfers — 211
Figure 6.1. The trend in international transfers of major arms, 1950–2022 — 210
Figure 6.2. The trend in international transfers of major arms, imports by region, 1983–2022 — 212
Table 6.1. Selected major arms on order or chosen for future orders from the 10 largest arms suppliers, for delivery after 2022 — 222

II. *Developments among the suppliers of major arms, 2018–22*   224
SIEMON T. WEZEMAN AND PIETER D. WEZEMAN

The United States—Russia—France—Other major exporters

Box 6.2. Financial aspects of arms transfers   232

Table 6.2. The 25 largest exporters of major arms and their main recipients, 2018–22   226

Table 6.3. The 10 largest suppliers of major arms and their recipients, by region, 2018–22   227

Table 6.4. Deliveries by arms category by the 10 largest suppliers of major arms, 2018–22   228

III. *Developments among the recipients of major arms, 2018–22*   233
SIEMON T. WEZEMAN AND PIETER D. WEZEMAN

Africa—The Americas—Asia and Oceania—Europe—The Middle East

Table 6.5. The 40 largest importers of major arms and their main suppliers, 2018–22   234

Table 6.6. Imports of major arms, by region and subregion, 2013–17 and 2018–22   236

7. World nuclear forces   247

Overview   247
HANS M. KRISTENSEN AND MATT KORDA

Table 7.1. World nuclear forces, January 2023   248

I. *United States nuclear forces*   249
HANS M. KRISTENSEN AND MATT KORDA

The role of nuclear weapons in US military doctrine—Warhead production—Strategic nuclear forces—Non-strategic nuclear forces

Table 7.2. United States nuclear forces, January 2023   250

II. *Russian nuclear forces*   260
HANS M. KRISTENSEN AND MATT KORDA

Russian compliance with New START—The role of nuclear weapons in Russian military doctrine—Strategic nuclear forces—Non-strategic nuclear forces

Table 7.3. Russian nuclear forces, January 2023   262

III. *British nuclear forces*   274
HANS M. KRISTENSEN AND MATT KORDA

The role of nuclear weapons in British military doctrine—Sea-based missiles

Table 7.4. British nuclear forces, January 2023   276

IV. *French nuclear forces* — 279
HANS M. KRISTENSEN AND MATT KORDA

The role of nuclear weapons in French military doctrine—Aircraft and air-delivered weapons—Sea-based missiles

Table 7.5. French nuclear forces, January 2023 — 280

V. *Chinese nuclear forces* — 284
HANS M. KRISTENSEN AND MATT KORDA

The role of nuclear weapons in Chinese military doctrine—Aircraft and air-delivered weapons—Land-based missiles—Sea-based missiles

Table 7.6. Chinese nuclear forces, January 2023 — 286

VI. *Indian nuclear forces* — 294
HANS M. KRISTENSEN AND MATT KORDA

The role of nuclear weapons in Indian military doctrine—Aircraft and air-delivered weapons—Land-based missiles—Sea-based missiles—Cruise missiles

Table 7.7. Indian nuclear forces, January 2023 — 296

VII. *Pakistani nuclear forces* — 300
HANS M. KRISTENSEN AND MATT KORDA

The role of nuclear weapons in Pakistani military doctrine—Aircraft and air-delivered weapons—Land-based missiles—Sea-based missiles

Table 7.8. Pakistani nuclear forces, January 2023 — 302

VIII. *North Korean nuclear forces* — 306
HANS M. KRISTENSEN AND MATT KORDA

The role of nuclear weapons in North Korean military doctrine—Fissile material and warhead production—Land-based missiles—Sea-based missiles

Table 7.9. North Korean forces with potential nuclear capability, January 2023 — 319

IX. *Israeli nuclear forces* — 323
HANS M. KRISTENSEN AND MATT KORDA

The role of nuclear weapons in Israeli military doctrine—Military fissile material production—Aircraft and air-delivered weapons—Land-based missiles—Sea-based missiles

Table 7.10. Israeli nuclear forces, January 2023 — 324

X. *Global stocks and production of fissile materials, 2022*   328
MORITZ KÜTT, ZIA MIAN AND PAVEL PODVIG

    Table 7.11. Global stocks of highly enriched uranium, 2022   330
    Table 7.12. Global stocks of separated plutonium, 2022   332
    Table 7.13. Significant uranium-enrichment facilities and capacity worldwide, 2022   334
    Table 7.14. Significant reprocessing facilities worldwide, 2022   336

Part III. Non-proliferation, arms control and disarmament, 2022

8. Nuclear disarmament, arms control and non-proliferation   339

Overview   339
TYTTI ERÄSTÖ, WILFRED WAN AND VITALY FEDCHENKO

I. *Bilateral and multilateral nuclear arms control involving China, Russia and the United States*   341
WILFRED WAN

The Russian–United States strategic stability dialogue—New START—Engagement with China—Conclusions

Table 8.1. Russian and United States aggregate numbers of strategic offensive arms under New START, as of 5 February 2011 and 1 September 2022   344

II. *The 10th review conference of the Non-Proliferation Treaty*   349
WILFRED WAN

Proceedings of the conference—Selected issues—The impact of the Russian invasion of Ukraine—Outlook

III. *The first meeting of states parties to the Treaty on the Prohibition of Nuclear Weapons*   360
TYTTI ERÄSTÖ

The lead-up to the meeting—Decisions taken at the first meeting of states parties—The Vienna Action Plan—The declaration—The positions of 'umbrella' states on the TPNW—Outlook

IV. *The Joint Comprehensive Plan of Action on Iran's nuclear programme*   368
TYTTI ERÄSTÖ

Diplomatic efforts to revive the JCPOA—Key developments in Iran's nuclear programme relevant to the JCPOA—Outstanding issues under Iran's Comprehensive Safeguards Agreement—Looking ahead

V. *Attacks on nuclear installations in Ukraine and the response* 378
missions of the International Atomic Energy Agency
VITALY FEDCHENKO, IRYNA MAKSYMENKO AND POLINA SINOVETS

Events at Ukrainian nuclear installations in 2022—The IAEA
response and its assistance missions to Ukraine—Conclusions

Box 8.1. Attacks on nuclear installations prior to 2022 379
Box 8.2. IAEA General Conference resolutions and decisions on 384
attacks against nuclear installations, 1983–2009

9. Chemical, biological and health security threats 391

Overview 391
FILIPPA LENTZOS AND UNA JAKOB

I. *Health security* 393
FILIPPA LENTZOS

Update on the Covid-19 pandemic—Studies into the origins of
SARS-CoV-2—A pandemic treaty—An outbreak of mpox

II. *Biological weapon allegations* 397
FILIPPA LENTZOS

Allegations in the context of Russia's invasion of Ukraine—
A formal consultative meeting—An unprecedented request for
an investigation of non-compliance with the BWC—Conclusions

III. *Biological weapon disarmament and non-proliferation* 406
FILIPPA LENTZOS

The 2022 preparatory committee—The First Committee of
the UN General Assembly—The ninth review conference—
Conclusions and outlook

IV. *Allegations of and reactions to chemical weapon use* 413
UNA JAKOB

Chemical weapon disarmament and investigations in Syria—
Aftermath of the poisoning of Alexei Navalny—Allegations of
illegal chemical activities in Ukraine

Table 9.1. Overview of ad hoc mechanisms of the Organisation 414
for the Prohibition of Chemical Weapons to address the issue of
chemical weapons in Syria

V. *Chemical weapon control and disarmament* 425
UNA JAKOB

Chemical weapon destruction—Developments in the OPCW—
Preparations for the fifth CWC review conference—Outlook

10. Conventional arms control and regulation of new weapon technologies   435

    Overview   435
    IAN DAVIS

   I. *The Russia–Ukraine War and conventional arms control in Europe*   437
     IAN DAVIS

     Prelude to the Russian invasion—The final build-up—The outlook for European conventional arms control

     Box 10.1. The European conventional arms control architecture   438

  II. *Multilateral regulation of inhumane weapons and other conventional weapons of humanitarian concern*   444
    IAN DAVIS AND GIOVANNA MALETTA

     Incendiary weapons—Explosive weapons in populated areas—Cluster munitions—Landmines, improvised explosive devices and explosive remnants of war—Small arms and light weapons—The open-ended working group on conventional ammunition—Conclusions

     Table 10.1. Meetings of the Certain Conventional Weapons Convention in 2022   445

 III. *Intergovernmental efforts to address the challenges posed by autonomous weapon systems*   463
    VINCENT BOULANIN

     The impact of the Russia–Ukraine War on an already weakened GGE process—Overview of the proposals discussed by the 2022 group of governmental experts—The outcome and way ahead

     Table 10.2. Written proposals presented by states to the 2022 Group of Governmental Experts on Emerging Technologies in the Area of Lethal Autonomous Weapons Systems   466

 IV. *International transparency in arms procurement and military expenditure as confidence-building measures*   471
    PIETER D. WEZEMAN AND SIEMON T. WEZEMAN

     The United Nations Register of Conventional Arms—The United Nations Report on Military Expenditures—Regional transparency mechanisms—Conclusions

  V. *The Hague Code of Conduct against Ballistic Missile Proliferation*   479
    KOLJA BROCKMANN AND LAURIANE HÉAU

     Current trends in ballistic missile proliferation—The 21st annual regular meeting—Outreach activities—United Nations General Assembly resolutions in support of the HCOC—Conclusions

Table 10.3. The voting record for United Nations General Assembly resolutions in support of the Hague Code of Conduct against Ballistic Missile Proliferation	482

11. Space and cyberspace — 483

Overview — 483
NIVEDITA RAJU AND LORA SAALMAN

I. *The space–cyber nexus* — 485
NIVEDITA RAJU AND LORA SAALMAN

Box 11.1. Some types of malware used in cyberattacks — 486

II. *Space attacks and cyberattacks in Ukraine* — 489
NIVEDITA RAJU AND LORA SAALMAN

Cyberattacks on space assets—Cyberattacks on government and industry—Cyberattacks on telecommunications—Cyberattacks on power facilities—Conclusions

III. *Developments in space governance and the impact of the war in Ukraine* — 495
NIVEDITA RAJU

The open-ended working group on reducing space threats—Banning destructive anti-satellite tests—Cooperation between governments and companies—Conclusions

IV. *Developments in governance of cyberspace and the impact of the war in Ukraine* — 501
LORA SAALMAN

The second United Nations open-ended working group on ICT security—International cooperation with Russia—International cooperation with Ukraine—Conclusions

12. Dual-use and arms trade controls — 511

Overview — 511
MARK BROMLEY

I. *The Arms Trade Treaty* — 513
GIOVANNA MALETTA AND LAURIANE HÉAU

Introduction—Treaty implementation—Transparency and reporting—Treaty universalization and international assistance—The financial situation of the ATT—Conclusions

Table 12.1. Arms Trade Treaty numbers of ratifications, accessions and signatories, by region, December 2022 — 520

II. *Multilateral arms embargoes* 525
PIETER D. WEZEMAN

United Nations arms embargoes: Developments and implementation issues—Conclusions

Table 12.2. Multilateral arms embargoes in force during 2022 532

III. *The role and impact of multilateral trade restrictions on Russia and Belarus* 535
MARK BROMLEY

EU trade restrictions—US trade restrictions—Impact of the trade restrictions—Conclusions

IV. *The multilateral export control regimes* 541
KOLJA BROCKMANN

The Australia Group—The Missile Technology Control Regime—The Nuclear Suppliers Group—The Wassenaar Arrangement—Conclusions

Table 12.3. The four multilateral export control regimes 542

V. *Developments in the European Union's dual-use and arms trade controls* 550
KOLJA BROCKMANN, MARK BROMLEY AND GIOVANNA MALETTA

The EU dual-use regulation—The EU foreign direct investment screening regulation—European and United States cooperation on export controls—The EU common position on arms exports—Conclusions

Table 12.4. Submissions of information to the European Union annual report on arms exports, 2011–21 556

Annexes

Annex A. Arms control and disarmament agreements 561

I. *Universal treaties* 562
II. *Regional treaties* 586
III. *Bilateral treaties* 597

Annex B. International security cooperation bodies 601

I. *Bodies with a global focus or membership* 601
II. *Bodies with a regional focus or membership* 610
III. *Strategic trade control regimes* 625

Annex C. Chronology 2022 629

About the authors 639
Index 645

Preface

It has been a turbulent year. In 2022, humanity faced the existential threats of nuclear war, climate change and a pandemic. The toxic effects of this combination were further compounded by a mix of inequality, extremism, nationalism, gender violence and shrinking democratic space. Devastating war raged in the Horn of Africa and in Europe and armed conflicts endured in far too many other places, often without an adequate level of international response or even much awareness of them. Russia's invasion of Ukraine was met with efforts to protect refugees, investigate war crimes and impose sanctions. Much less international attention was devoted to the civil war in Ethiopia, despite two years of atrocities and tens of thousands of deaths.

Accompanying the visible darkening of the horizon of international security—charted in successive editions of this Yearbook—have been the rise of authoritarianism and the erosion of democracy. President Biden made promoting democracy over autocracy a key tenet of his foreign policy and has often framed the US rivalries with China and Russia in those terms. But addressing climate change, resolving the crisis in nuclear arms control, and managing and peacefully settling local and regional conflicts all require collaborative approaches among the great powers. In contrast to that requirement, the international context in 2022 was shaped by deep geopolitical divisions. It remains unclear whether coalitions of other international actors are ready and able to step up to the plate with ideas for re-energizing the ailing international body politic (chapter 1).

Part I of the Yearbook covers armed conflicts and conflict management in 2022. Chapter 2 focuses on armed conflicts and peace processes, and briefly surveys diverging regional trends in both, as well as the performance of the international conflict management system in a year of geopolitical stress. Active armed conflicts occurred in at least 56 states in 2022, five more than in 2021. Outside Europe, most wars continued to take place within states—or in clusters of states with porous borders—and to involve non-state armed groups. The number of personnel deployed to multilateral peace operations globally increased in 2022, breaking a trend of declining personnel numbers between 2016 and 2021 (chapter 3). The use of private military and security companies has widely increased over the last two decades and chapter 4 highlights the risks and the potential for misconduct in the industry, especially when deployed to combat zones or fragile states.

Much of the Institute's research on armaments and disarmament is based on original, rigorous data collection that forms the foundation of SIPRI's databases. Part II is devoted to military spending and armaments, including comprehensive assessments of recent trends in military expenditure and arms production (chapter 5), international arms transfers (chapter 6), and world nuclear forces, including the nuclear modernization programmes current in all the nuclear-armed states (chapter 7). Global military spending rose in 2022 for the eighth consecutive year to reach an estimated $2240 billion, but the volume of global arms transfers again saw a slight drop. However, with tensions increasing in many regions, it seems highly likely that there will be more demand for major arms in the coming years and accordingly an increase in the level of trade in major weapons.

Part III covers non-proliferation, arms control and disarmament. It was another difficult year for nuclear arms control (chapter 8) with the suspension of US-Russian strategic stability dialogue and the second consecutive NPT review conference ending without a substantive consensus outcome. On a positive note, the International Atomic Energy Agency undertook multiple missions of technical experts to Ukraine in 2022, and subsequently established a permanent presence at all four nuclear power plants that were subject to unprecedented attacks during the year. Chapter 9 explores allegations of chemical and biological weapon use and other developments in chemical and biological security threats. Chapter 10 includes a round-up of the multilateral regulation of inhumane weapons and other conventional weapons of humanitarian concern in 2022—and here, there was one welcome sign that thinking about the common good has not completely disappeared. After three years of negotiation, 83 countries agreed the first international compact against using explosive weapons in towns and cities.

The space and cyberspace domains featured prominently in the war in Ukraine in 2022, illustrating a growing space–cyber nexus (chapter 11), while chapter 12 reports on efforts to strengthen controls on the trade in conventional arms and dual-use items, including efforts to impose international trade restrictions on Russia.

This is the 54th edition of the SIPRI Yearbook. It features contributions from 38 authors. Its content has been refereed extensively and a dedicated editorial team ensures that it conforms to the highest publishing standards. The communications, library, operations and IT staff at SIPRI all contribute in different ways to the Yearbook's production and distribution. I would like to take this opportunity to express my gratitude to everybody involved, within SIPRI and beyond—especially our external reviewers, whose insights and suggestions always lead to material improvements in the content.

The common systems and structures needed to provide security, are frequently undermined or violated by misinformation. The Yearbook's focus and SIPRI's commitment to authenticating the facts means that the volume remains an indispensable global public good. This will continue to be the case as the Institute helps to chart a course for emerging from a period of increasing insecurity and war into a more secure world with more equitable, resilient and sustainable societies.

Dan Smith
Director, SIPRI
Stockholm, April 2023

Abbreviations and conventions

ABM	Anti-ballistic missile	CTBTO	Comprehensive Nuclear-Test-Ban Treaty Organization
ACLED	Armed Conflict Location & Event Data Project		
AG	Australia Group	CW	Chemical weapon/warfare
AI	Artificial intelligence	CWC	Chemical Weapons Convention
ALCM	Air-launched cruise missile		
APC	Armoured personnel carrier	DDR	Disarmament, demobilization and reintegration
APM	Anti-personnel mine		
ASAT	Anti-satellite	DPRK	Democratic People's Republic of Korea (North Korea)
ASEAN	Association of Southeast Asian Nations		
ATT	Arms Trade Treaty	DRC	Democratic Republic of the Congo
AU	African Union		
AWS	Autonomous weapon systems	ECOWAS	Economic Community of West African States
BCC	Bilateral Consultative Commission (of the Russian–US New START treaty)	EDF	European Defence Fund
		EPF	European Peace Facility
		ERW	Explosive remnants of war
		EU	European Union
BWC	Biological and Toxin Weapons Convention	EWIPA	Explosive weapons in populated areas
CAR	Central African Republic	FFM	Fact-finding mission
CBM	Confidence-building measure	FMCT	Fissile material cut-off treaty
CBW	Chemical and biological weapon/warfare	FY	Financial year
		G7	Group of Seven (industrialized states)
CCM	Convention on Cluster Munitions		
		GDP	Gross domestic product
CCW	Certain Conventional Weapons (Convention)	GGE	Group of governmental experts
CD	Conference on Disarmament		
CFE	Conventional armed forces in Europe (Treaty)	GLCM	Ground-launched cruise missile
CFSP	Common Foreign and Security Policy (of the EU)	HCOC	Hague Code of Conduct
		HEU	Highly enriched uranium
CSBM	Confidence- and security-building measure	IAEA	International Atomic Energy Agency
CSDP	Common Security and Defence Policy (of the EU)	ICBM	Intercontinental ballistic missile
CSTO	Collective Security Treaty Organization	ICC	International Criminal Court
CTBT	Comprehensive Nuclear-Test-Ban Treaty	ICJ	International Court of Justice

IED	Improvised explosive device	OSCC	Open Skies Consultative Commission
IGAD	Intergovernmental Authority on Development	OSCE	Organization for Security and Co-operation in Europe
IHL	International humanitarian law	P5	Five permanent members of the UN Security Council
IMF	International Monetary Fund	PAROS	Prevention of an arms race in outer space
INF	Intermediate-range Nuclear Forces (Treaty)	PMSC	Private military and security company
ISAF	International Security Assistance Force	POA	Programme of Action to Prevent, Combat and Eradicate the Illicit Trade in Small Arms and Light Weapons in All its Aspects (UN)
ISU	Implementation Support Unit		
ITI	International Tracing Instrument		
JCPOA	Joint Comprehensive Plan of Action	R&D	Research and development
LEU	Low-enriched uranium	SADC	Southern African Development Community
MENA	Middle East and North Africa	SALW	Small arms and light weapons
MIRV	Multiple independently targetable re-entry vehicle	SAM	Surface-to-air missile
MRBM	Medium-range ballistic missile	SLBM	Submarine-launched ballistic missile
MTCR	Missile Technology Control Regime	SLCM	Sea-launched cruise missile
		SORT	Strategic Offensive Reductions Treaty
NAM	Non-Aligned Movement	SRBM	Short-range ballistic missile
NSAG	Non-state armed group	START	Strategic Arms Reduction Treaty
NATO	North Atlantic Treaty Organization		
NGO	Non-governmental organization	TPNW	Treaty on the Prohibition of Nuclear Weapons
NNWS	Non-nuclear weapon state	UAE	United Arab Emirates
NPT	Non-Proliferation Treaty	UAV	Unmanned aerial vehicle
NSG	Nuclear Suppliers Group	UN	United Nations
NWS	Nuclear weapon state	UNHCR	UN High Commissioner for Refugees
OAS	Organization of American States	UNMILEX	UN Report on Military Expenditures
OECD	Organisation for Economic Co-operation and Development	UNODA	UN Office for Disarmament Affairs
OEWG	Open-ended working group	UNROCA	UN Register of Conventional Arms
OHCHR	Office of the UN High Commissioner for Human Rights	WA	Wassenaar Arrangement
		WHO	World Health Organization
OPCW	Organisation for the Prohibition of Chemical Weapons	WMD	Weapon(s) of mass destruction

Conventions

. .	Data not available or not applicable
–	Nil or a negligible figure
( )	Uncertain data
b.	Billion (thousand million)
kg	Kilogram
km	Kilometre (1000 metres)
m.	Million
th.	Thousand
tr.	Trillion (million million)
$	US dollars
€	Euros

Geographical regions and subregions

Africa	Consisting of North Africa (Algeria, Libya, Morocco and Tunisia, but excluding Egypt) and sub-Saharan Africa
Americas	Consisting of North America (Canada and the USA), Central America and the Caribbean (including Mexico), and South America
Asia and Oceania	Consisting of Central Asia, East Asia, Oceania, South Asia (including Afghanistan) and South East Asia
Europe	Consisting of Eastern Europe (Armenia, Azerbaijan, Belarus, Georgia, Moldova, Russia and Ukraine) and Western and Central Europe (with South Eastern Europe)
Middle East	Consisting of Egypt, Iran, Iraq, Israel, Jordan, Kuwait, Lebanon, Syria, Türkiye and the states of the Arabian peninsula

Note: The boundaries, names and designations used in the maps in this volume do not imply any endorsement or acceptance by SIPRI of claims or stances in disputes over specific territories.

SIPRI Yearbook online

www.sipriyearbook.org

The full content of the SIPRI Yearbook is also available online. With the SIPRI Yearbook online you can

- access the complete SIPRI Yearbook on your desktop or handheld device for research on the go
- navigate easily through content using advanced search and browse functionality
- find content easily: search through the whole SIPRI Yearbook and within your results
- save valuable time: use your personal profile to return to saved searches and content again and again
- share content with colleagues and students easily via email and social networking tools
- enhance your research by following clearly linked references and web resources

How to access the SIPRI Yearbook online

Institutional access

The SIPRI Yearbook online is available to institutions worldwide for a one-time fee or by annual subscription. Librarians and central resource coordinators can contact Oxford University Press to receive a price quotation using the details below or register for a free trial at <http://www.oxfordonline.com/freetrials/>.

Individuals can recommend this resource to their librarians at <http://www.oup.com/library-recommend/>.

Individual subscriptions

The SIPRI Yearbook online is available to individuals worldwide on a 12-month subscription basis. Purchase details can be found at <http://www.oup.com/>.

Contact information

Customers within the Americas

Email: oxfordonline@oup.com
Telephone: +1 (800) 624 0153
Fax: +1 (919) 677 8877

Customers outside the Americas

Email: institutionalsales@oup.com
Telephone: +44 (0) 1865 353705
Fax: +44 (0) 1865 353308

Introduction

Chapter 1. Introduction: International stability and human security in 2022

1. Introduction: International stability and human security in 2022

DAN SMITH

Global security in 2022 showed a marked deterioration compared to a decade ago. The problem is not only the Russian invasion of Ukraine in February 2022 and the ensuing war, though that has inevitably and rightly claimed a great deal of international attention. Worldwide, there is more war, with open armed conflict in 56 countries in 2022 compared to fewer than 30 in 2010.[1] There is more military spending, with the total now standing at US$2.2 trillion in 2022, registering an increase for the eighth successive year.[2] Acute food insecurity increased to over 200 million and by some estimates up to 345 million people needed emergency food assistance.[3] As a result of climate change, heatwaves, drought and flooding affected millions of people, with major human and economic costs.[4] In addition, respect for international law has declined, confrontation has increased and arms control has become less effective.

The background is equally troubling, revealing a wide range of factors that press in the direction of insecurity. The Covid-19 pandemic has weakened the economic health of most countries since it first struck in early 2020. As health and economic recovery began in many countries, there were inevitably some countries that lagged behind. The impact of the war in Ukraine on global supplies of food, fertilizers and fuel has now burdened vulnerable communities with surging energy prices and rising costs of staple foods. While the burden is heaviest in the poorest countries, the increase in food and energy prices led to a widespread increase in the cost of living, including in richer countries. In China, the world's major exporter of manufactured goods, political and social restrictions to implement the 'zero Covid' strategy hampered production and trade through much of 2022.[5] In a significant

---

[1] Uppsala University, Department of Peace and Conflict Research, Uppsala Data Conflict Program. See chapter 2, section III, in this volume.
[2] See chapter 5, section I, in this volume.
[3] Food and Agriculture Organization of the United Nations (FAO) et al., *The State of Food Security and Nutrition in the World 2021: Transforming Food Systems for Food Security, Improved Nutrition and Affordable Healthy Diets for All* (FAO: Rome, 2021), p. xiv; and Beasley, D., 'The Ukraine war could leave hundreds of millions hungry around the world', *Washington Post*, 7 Mar. 2022.
[4] World Meteorological Organization, 'Eight warmest years on record witness upsurge in climate change impacts', Press release, 6 Nov. 2022.
[5] 'China's failing Covid strategy leaves Xi Jinping with no good options', *The Economist*, 3 Dec. 2022.

SIPRI Yearbook 2023: Armaments, Disarmament and International Security
www.sipriyearbook.org

number of countries, the pressures were multiplied by extreme weather: a once-in-500-years drought in Europe; the severest drought on record in China, affecting half the country; the inundation of 35 per cent of Pakistan; and floods in some parts of the Greater Horn of Africa (Sudan and South Sudan) and drought in others (Somalia, Ethiopia, Djibouti, Uganda).[6]

International stability was also under pressure from the war in Ukraine and from intensifying confrontation between the great powers—not only about Ukraine but also, and not least, between China and the United States over Taiwan. These tensions, disputes and confrontations resulted directly and indirectly in further pressure on an already weakened set of arrangements in bilateral arms control between Russia and the USA, while the previously postponed five-year review conference of the Nuclear Non-Proliferation Treaty delivered no results.

Given the economic and environmental background and the geopolitical and strategic turbulence of 2022, it is no surprise that the Bulletin of the Atomic Scientists once again moved its 'Doomsday Clock' closer to midnight, the metaphorical hour of the apocalypse. This 10-second adjustment in response to the global situation in 2022 continued a three-decade transition from the relative comfort of 1991, when the clock was put at 17 minutes to midnight, to its current position just 90 seconds from the hour of destruction, the closest that the clock has been since it was instituted in 1947.[7] While the *Bulletin*'s assessment of the danger is, like anybody's, subjective, the reasoning behind it is both serious and transparent. A heightened perception of deepening risk was shared by many observers and actors on the international political stage. There can be no pretence in this hour of danger that there have not been abundant warnings.

This, the 54th edition of the *SIPRI Yearbook*, explores and records in detail many of the germane elements of global insecurity in 2022. The reader will unfortunately find a wealth of evidence to support the contention that the current period is among the few most dangerous times—if not, as the analysts for the Bulletin of the Atomic Scientists conclude, *the* most dangerous moment—of the era since World War II. This chapter offers an introductory overview of some aspects of this disquieting picture, including the impact of the war on Ukraine. It places the war in the context of the broader global picture of conflict and geopolitics, including China–USA relations and nuclear arms control, and the impact of climate change.

---

[6] See, respectively, Toreti, A. et al., *Drought in Europe August 2022*, Joint Research Centre Report no. JRC130493 (Publications Office of the European Union: Luxembourg, 2022); Celis, N., 'Half of China hit by drought in worst heatwave on record', Phys.org, 25 Aug. 2022; UN Children's Fund (UNICEF), 'Devastating floods in Pakistan', 31 Jan. 2023; and World Health Organization, 'Greater Horn of Africa food insecurity and health grade 3 emergency: Situation report as of 23 August 2022', 28 Aug. 2022.

[7] 'A time of unprecedented danger: It is 90 seconds to midnight', *Bulletin of the Atomic Scientists*, 24 Jan. 2023.

I. Food and geopolitics

The broader significance of the war in Ukraine does not lie in its scale. Tens of thousands of people have been killed and injured on both sides and millions of Ukrainians were forced to flee their homes. But the most deadly of recent wars is almost certainly that in the Tigray province of Ethiopia, which started in November 2020; there, estimates of civilian deaths alone over the two years range from 300 000 to 600 000, significantly more than the uncertain numbers thought to have perished in Ukraine during 2022 (see below).[8] Nor does the Ukraine war's significance lie in a common perception in Europe that it signifies war returning to the continent. In fact, there have been armed conflicts and wars in Europe in every decade since the 1960s, though only in the Western Balkans and North Caucasus has the violence been at the level seen in Ukraine in 2022.

The broader impact and significance of the war in Ukraine are generated by two factors. One is that the two combatant countries are both major food producers and the war, especially because of its impact on Ukrainian agriculture, has therefore exacerbated the problem of world hunger. The second is that Russia is one of the world's three great powers, and faces an adversary supported by the USA, which is still the largest economy and has the most powerful armed forces in the world. Great powers clashing in this way has a major geopolitical impact. If China were also to involve itself in the conflict, beyond seeking to exert political influence on its outcome, this would only magnify the impact.

Food

For many governments, the war in Ukraine was not the most important event of 2022. It featured primarily because of its impact on the domestic availability and prices of food, fuel and fertilizer. In better-off countries this means a cost-of-living crisis, while in poorer countries it means hunger and food insecurity.

The impact of the war comes in the wake of the Covid-19 pandemic, exacerbating an existing trend of steadily increasing world hunger since 2017.[9] One effect of the pandemic was to generate a major spike in world food prices in 2021, which may have moderated in 2022 but looks set to carry on in 2023. It is the third price spike this century—the earlier two were in 2007–2008 and

---

[8] Abraha, M., 'Think the war in Ukraine is the world's deadliest conflict? Think again', *The Guardian*, 28 Dec. 2022; and Naranjo, J., 'Ethiopia's forgotten war is the deadliest of the 21st century, with around 600,000 civilian deaths', *El País*, 27 Jan. 2023.

[9] Food and Agriculture Organization of the United Nations (FAO) et al., *The State of Food Security and Nutrition in the World 2022: Repurposing Food and Agricultural Policies to Make Healthy Diets More Affordable* (FAO: Rome, 2022), sections 2.1 and 2.2, tables 1 and 2, and figure 2.

2010–11. As a result of these three spikes, the real cost of food this century has more than doubled.[10] The latest spike is associated with a worsening of the layered indicators of world hunger revealed by the annual report from five United Nations agencies, *The State of Food Security and Nutrition in the World*. In the first two years of the pandemic, the percentage of the world population that was undernourished rose from 8.4 to 9.8 per cent, an estimated 702–828 million people. The number of people who could not afford a healthy diet was around 3 billion in 2021. Of that total, 2.37 billion lacked access to enough food, and 923 million did not know where their next meal was coming from.[11] The number of people in need of emergency food assistance in 2021 was 205 million, an increase of almost 30 million extremely hungry people.[12]

Russia and Ukraine are both major producers of staple foods, accounting for more than half the global production of sunflower oil, 19 per cent of barley and 14 per cent of wheat.[13] In addition, Ukraine has in recent years been the source of about half the wheat used by the World Food Programme to support vulnerable people.[14] Thus, at each layer of the problem of world hunger—from limits on food availability to acute food insecurity—interruption of food exports from Russia and Ukraine has had a major global impact.

By the end of 2022, the armed conflict had rendered a quarter of Ukraine's farmland unproductive.[15] Sanctions against Russia led to a reduction in food and fertilizer exports, even though the sanctions system was intended to allow those exports to continue.[16] Russian action to mine and blockade Ukraine's Black Sea ports severely restricted trade in the first half of 2022. In July, the Black Sea Grain Initiative brokered by the UN and Türkiye allowed exports of Ukrainian grain and Russian food and fertilizers to start up again.[17] However, the agreement is fragile as well as temporary, and there is a constant diplomatic back and forth about whether to renew and how to continue it.[18]

---

[10] Headley, D. and Ruel, M., 'The global food price crisis threatens to cause a global nutrition crisis: New evidence from 1.27 million young children on the effects of inflation', International Food Policy Research Institute (IFPRI) Blog, 14 Dec. 2022.

[11] FAO et al. (note 3).

[12] Food Security Information Network (FSIN) and Global Network Against Food Crises, *2022 Global Report on Food Crises: Joint Analysis for Better Decisions, Mid-Year Update* (FSIN: Rome, Sep. 2022), p. 6.

[13] Delgado, C., 'War in the breadbasket: The ripple effects on food insecurity and conflict risk beyond Ukraine', SIPRI Commentary, 1 Apr. 2022.

[14] Beasley (note 3).

[15] World Food Programme, 'Ukraine transitional interim country strategic plan (2023–2024)', 13 Dec. 2022.

[16] Glauber, J., Laborde, D. and Mamun, A., 'Food export restrictions have eased as the Russia Ukraine war continues, but concerns remain for key commodities', IFPRI Blog, 23 Jan. 2023.

[17] United Nations, Black Sea Grain Initiative, Joint Coordination Centre, 'Beacon on the Black Sea'.

[18] Roth, A., 'Putin threatens to tear up fragile Ukraine grain deal in bellicose speech', *The Guardian*, 7 Sep. 2022; and 'Grain export deal back on as Russia rejoins in unexpected U-turn', *Daily Sabah*, 2 Nov. 2022.

Geopolitics

The UN Security Council risks being hobbled once again, as it was during the cold war. While the basis of divergence and antagonism between Russia and the USA and its allies is different from the foundations of US–Soviet confrontation in the cold war, the effect on the Security Council can be the same because of the voting system, in which any one of the five permanent members can veto any resolution.

However, much of the rest of the UN continued to function effectively in 2022. For example, the UN special envoy for Yemen led a mediation effort producing a truce in April 2022.[19] UN peace operations continued to function and had their mandates renewed by the Security Council. Meanwhile, the UN agencies continued to drive their work forward. There were inefficiencies and wasted opportunities, as well as successes, but the contribution to knowledge, communication and well-being that UN agencies made in various ways was significant and probably indispensable. Protecting this framework of global institutions should be an important goal of government policies in poor and rich countries alike, because without it, human security and well-being will suffer further.

For Europe, the war in Ukraine had a profound effect. The annual ministerial meeting of the Organization for Security and Co-operation in Europe (OSCE) in December 2022 did not adopt any decisions, not even a budget; as host, the Polish government refused to allow Russia's foreign minister, Sergey Lavrov, to attend, although the Russian ambassador to the OSCE did participate.[20] There must be doubt about the OSCE's continuing role as an operational organization that sends missions to monitor ceasefires and elections, and facilitates conflict management and resolution. For several years, Russia has systematically sidelined it over key issues such as Crimea, eastern Donbas and the reignition of war between Armenia and Azerbaijan in 2020. The OSCE's future role may lie in a return to its origins in the cold war as the *Conference on* Security and Cooperation in Europe, from which the OSCE emerged in the period from November 1990 to December 1994.[21]

One aspect of the deepening of division and distance between Russia and the West is economic. When the cold war came to an end, Russia began to move much closer to the Western economic and trading system. Russian raw materials fed Europe's appetite for energy, while Western investment finance and consumer goods were available in Russia. Economic sanctions enacted by the West together with some retaliatory measures implemented by Russia have interrupted trading and economic relations, severing them in

---

[19] Armed Conflict Location & Event Data Project, 'Yemen Truce Monitor', Status as of 7 Oct. 2022.
[20] Hernandez, G. H., 'OSCE in crisis over Russian war on Ukraine', *Arms Control Today*, Jan./Feb. 2023.
[21] Organization for Security and Co-operation in Europe (OSCE), 'History'.

some cases, seriously denting them in others.[22] The effectiveness of sanctions is measured first in the extent to which they weaken the target economy and, second and consequently, whether they lead to a change in the target government's behaviour. On these measures, the record of sanctions achieving political impact is poor.[23] Nonetheless, the termination of trading and financial links could be lasting. The dimensions of this effect are hard to discern as yet but, for example, it seems unlikely that Western brand names will be as popular and permitted in Russia for some time to come and Europe's appetite for Russian energy supplies, though it may return, will probably never be as whole-hearted again.

Contention and confrontation in global geopolitics diminish the capacity for managing and helping resolve local and regional conflicts. Although the war in Ukraine stands out for many reasons, it is worth recalling that Ukraine was only one of 56 countries that experienced armed conflict in 2022.[24] In many cases, conflicts have been protracted and violence has become endemic; in others, conflicts were reigniting, like the conflict in Palestine where violence during 2022 escalated to levels not experienced since the second intifada ended in 2005.[25] The risk for these countries and their regions lies partly in the absence of a decisive international capacity to mitigate and manage violent conflicts, which was at its strongest when the UN Security Council was freed from the burden of cold war division in the 1990s and in the first five years of this century.[26]

II. Great power relations

Chinese–Russian alignment?

In February 2022 the Chinese and Russian leaders avowed that their friendship had no limits, with no areas where cooperation was off the table.[27] Not quite three weeks later, Russian forces invaded Ukraine.

---

[22] Demertzis, M. et al., 'How have sanctions impacted Russia?', Bruegel Policy Contribution no. 18/22, Oct. 2022; and Snegovaya, M. et al., 'Russia sanctions at one year: Learning from the cases of South Africa and Iran', Center for Strategic and International Studies (CSIS), Feb. 2023. On the impact of trade restrictions on Russia, see chapter 12, section III, in this volume.

[23] Mulder, N., *The Economic Weapon: The Rise of Sanctions as a Tool of Modern War* (Yale University Press: New Haven, CT, 2022); and Staibano, C. and Wallensteen, P. (eds), *International Sanctions: Between Wars and Words* (Routledge: London, 2005).

[24] See chapter 2, sections I and II, in this volume.

[25] 'UN envoy reports "sharp increase" in violence this year in Israel–Palestine conflict', UN News, 19 Dec. 2022; and United Nations, 'With 2022 deadliest year in Israel–Palestine conflict, reversing violent trends must be international priority, middle east coordinator tells Security Council', UN Meetings Coverage, Security Council SC/15179, 18 Jan. 2023.

[26] Mack, A. et al., *Human Security Report 2005* (Oxford University Press: Oxford, 2005).

[27] Putin, V. and Xi, J., Joint statement of the Russian Federation and the People's Republic of China on the international relations entering a new era and the global sustainable development, 4 Feb. 2022.

There is a tendency in the West to treat China and Russia as a single bloc, and to develop that into a vision of a global contest between democracy and autocracy, as articulated by US President Joe Biden in his 2022 State of the Union Address, and picked up thereafter by European Commission President Ursula von der Leyen.[28] This narrative oversimplifies the reality of China's support for Russia's military action.[29] China was one of 35 states that abstained in the UN General Assembly vote in March 2022 on a resolution condemning the invasion of Ukraine. Its position both respected Ukraine's sovereignty and criticized enlargement of the North Atlantic Treaty Organization (NATO), which Russia has argued is a justification for its actions against Ukraine.[30] The world's most populous democracy, India, also abstained in the March 2022 vote. It has criticized Russia but avoided aligning with the West, and insists, like China, that disputes be settled by peaceful means.[31] While frustrating for Western government leaders and diplomats who want more forthright support from other countries, this is a widely held view. Refusing to condemn Russia is not in itself evidence of alignment with Moscow.

There are further grounds for scepticism about how closely China and Russia are aligned. One lies in the very limited practical support that China has offered, in the form of equipment parts and, reportedly, continuing sales of drones.[32] This is hardly comparable with either the volume or form of Western assistance to Ukraine; no transfers from China to Russia of complete weapon systems or lethal aid have yet been recorded.[33] China has bought Russian energy, as has India, but at prices that are discounted by as much as 40 per cent.[34] What the USA and the European Union (EU) may see as China and India sabotaging their sanctions on Russia can just as easily look like exploiting Russia's need for foreign earnings by insisting on bargain prices.

Another reason for scepticism derives from the differences between Chinese and Russian histories, cultures, current world positions and interests. China is a major manufacturing power that has experienced economic

---

[28] See, respectively, Biden, J., State of the Union address, White House Briefing Room, 1 Mar. 2022; and De Camaret, C. and Baillard, D., '"Democracy is standing up against autocracy" in Ukraine, EU's von der Leyen says', France 24, 18 Mar. 2022.

[29] De la Fuente, R. A., Gibson, T. and Gowan, R., 'UN votes reveal a lot about global opinion on the war in Ukraine', *World Politics Review*, 21 Feb. 2023.

[30] 'China says it respects Ukraine's sovereignty and Russia's security concerns', Reuters, 25 Feb. 2022.

[31] Roy, A., 'Japan's Kishida and India's Modi discuss response to Ukraine crisis', Reuters, 19 Mar. 2022.

[32] Garcia, N., 'Trade secrets: Exposing China–Russia Defense trade in global supply chains', C4ADS, 15 July 2022; and Mozur, P., Krolik, A. and Bradsher, K., 'As war in Ukraine grinds on, China helps refill Russian drone supplies', *New York Times*, 21 Mar. 2023.

[33] Vergun, D., 'DOD official says US not yet seeing China giving lethal aid to Russia', US Department of Defense News, 22 Feb. 2023.

[34] Kimani, A., 'China and India are buying Russian crude at a 40% discount', Oilprice.com, 29 Nov. 2022; and Sor, J., 'China is snapping up Russian oil at the steepest discount in months as EU scrambles to keep a lid on Moscow's energy income', Markets Insider, 7 Dec. 2022.

growth averaging 10 per cent a year for four decades, albeit slowing recently.[35] It continues to need markets in the rich West. Even the 'trade war' that the USA initiated in 2018 has not changed this.[36] Much higher tariffs have become the new normal, but trade between the two countries has flourished.[37] Russia is not in that position. Its major export to the West was energy; in 2022 Europe had to find energy from other sources and did so. Other, less wealthy countries, unable to switch as easily as Europe, will likely become more important to Russia in coming years. In these circumstances, Russia has both less incentive and less capacity than China does to temper competition and confrontation with cooperation.

Finally, as world powers, China is rising while Russia is declining. Russia has proven in the last 15 years (approximately, since its incursion into Georgia in 2008) to be willing to use force, and agile in the ways it does so. However, the course of the war in Ukraine has revealed a massive overestimation of Russian military capability by Western (and presumably also Russian) analysts in previous years.[38] Paradoxically, in 2022, while the Russian military underperformed compared to Western expectations, the Russian economy showed a degree of resilience that many Western analysts had not expected.[39] Nonetheless, while China's economy is second only to the USA's by one measure (the exchange rate) and larger than it by another (purchasing power parity), Russia was the 11th largest economy in the world at the end of 2021.[40] Russia remains the third largest military spender in the world, but it spends less than one-third of what China does and not much over a tenth of what the USA spends.[41] In other words, China looms over Russia only somewhat less than the USA does. An alliance between China and Russia cannot be an alliance of equals; the rising power will surely expect to be the dominant partner in the relationship as it unfolds over the years ahead, regardless of the outcome of Russia's war in Ukraine.

---

[35] Hirst, T., 'A brief history of China's economic growth', World Economic Forum, 30 July 2015.

[36] Wong, D. and Koty, A. C., 'The US–China trade war: A timeline', China Briefing, 25 Aug. 2020.

[37] Bown, C. P., 'US–China trade war tariffs: An up-to-date chart', Peterson Institute for International Economics (PIIE) Charts, 16 Mar. 2021; and Gordon, N., 'For all the "decoupling" rhetoric, US–China trade is booming', *Fortune*, 23 July 2021.

[38] Dougherty, C., 'Strange debacle: Misadventures in assessing Russian military power', War on the Rocks, 16 June 2022.

[39] Lipsky, J., 'Why Russia's economy is more resilient than you might think', New Atlanticist Blog, 30 June 2022; and Bhan, A., 'The Ukraine war, sanctions, and the resilient Russian economy', Observer Research Foundation, 26 Feb. 2023.

[40] Allison, G., Kiersznowski, N. and Fitzek, C., *The Great Economic Rivalry: China vs the US* (Harvard Belfer Center: Cambridge, MA, 23 Mar. 2022); and Statista, 'Economy of Russia: Statistics & facts', 16 Jan. 2023.

[41] See chapter 5, table 5.3, in this volume.

China and the USA

The differences between China and the USA are deep and significant. The deterioration of their relations during the past 10–15 years is different from what has happened between Russia and the USA over the same years. While China can often make rhetorical common cause with Russia, it also pursues its own strategy for power and influence. And while China does not want to see Russia eviscerated by the war with Ukraine, that is largely because it does not want to face a stronger and more confident American adversary; it is not in itself evidence of a Chinese sentiment of solidarity with Russia. As the rising power, China chafes at the US assumption of superiority, at the global military reach the USA continues to display, and at many aspects of US behaviour.[42] But its leaders are most unlikely to want to share global stature with Russia.

China has increased its military spending for each of the last 28 years, and is now engaged in what may be a quite ambitious programme of modernization and enhancement of its nuclear forces, with a potential capacity to increase its warhead numbers from 410 to 1500 by 2035.[43] It has also provided military aid, though in much smaller amounts than the USA, to gain political influence and strategic position, such as in a new arrangement with the Solomon Islands.[44] China has also invested heavily in economic development projects (some $840 billion this century, almost all in the form of loans) that provide it with considerable soft power, albeit at the cost of the beneficiaries becoming indebted.[45]

Taiwan

In the USA, opposition to China's rise to global prominence is bipartisan in a national political scene otherwise characterized by sharp partisan divisions. This was demonstrated not least when US Speaker of the House Nancy Pelosi led a congressional delegation to visit Taiwan in August 2022, which also underlined that the USA's regional policy is likely to include more forthright support for Taiwan.[46] Ever since China became a full member of the UN and

---

[42] See e.g. Yi, W., 'The right way for China and the United States to get along in the new era', Chinese foreign minister's speech at the Asia Society, New York, 22 Sep. 2022.

[43] See chapter 5, section II, and chapter 7, section V, in this volume.

[44] Beachamp-Mustafaga, N., 'China's military aid is probably less than you think', The RAND Blog, 26 July 2022; Liang, X., 'What can we learn from China's military aid to the Pacific?', SIPRI Commentary, 20 June 2022; and Cave, D., 'China and Solomon Islands draft secret security pact', New York Times, 24 Mar. 2022.

[45] Malik, A. A. et al., *Banking on the Belt and Road: Insights from a New Global Dataset of 13,427 Chinese Development Projects* (AidDATA: Williamsburg, VA, 29 Sep. 2021); and 'Did China's debt-trap destroy Sri Lankan economy', *International Finance*, 15 Jan. 2023.

[46] Spegele, B., 'Nancy Pelosi's trip reflects growing US bipartisan support for Taiwan', *Wall Street Journal*, 2 Aug. 2022.

Taiwan was excluded, the USA has maintained a studiedly ambiguous policy, acknowledging that Chinese leaders regard Taiwan as part of 'One China', yet also offering Taiwan support, which, though largely tacit, included sales of advanced weapon systems. Half a century on, however, the USA is edging towards a different approach; in 2022, President Biden repeated earlier statements that the USA would defend Taiwan if China attacked, though US diplomats have also qualified the commitment.[47]

Speaker Pelosi's visit to Taiwan was followed by hastily announced Chinese military exercises and the suspension of cooperation with the USA on a range of issues, not least climate change.[48] China exerts military pressure on Taiwan via naval manoeuvres and intrusions by Chinese aircraft into Taiwan's air defence identification zone (ADIZ).[49] China intensified this form of pressure dramatically during 2022, almost doubling the number of aircraft intruding into Taiwan's ADIZ to 1727 over the year, including, in December, the largest single incursion of 71 combat aircraft.[50]

North East Asia

All this serves as a reminder that North East Asia is the frontline in an increasingly tense and risk-heavy relationship between China and the USA plus its allies. Japanese military spending is increasing and has surpassed the self-imposed limit of 1 per cent of gross domestic product (GDP).[51] The region is further troubled by the continuing missile development programme of the Democratic People's Republic of Korea (DPRK, North Korea). After a four-month pause in missile tests, in early March 2022 North Korea conducted the first of over 90 missile test-firings it undertook in the year.[52] These tests sent more than one missile on a trajectory over Japan or close to it. The tests

---

[47] Wong, T., 'Biden vows to defend Taiwan in apparent US policy shift', with R. Wingfield-Hayes, 'Analysis', BBC News, 23 May 2022; and Ruwitch, J., 'Biden, again, says US would help Taiwan if China attacks', NPR, 19 Sep. 2022.

[48] Ni, V., 'China halts US cooperation on range of issues after Pelosi's Taiwan visit', The Guardian, 5 Aug. 2022.

[49] An ADIZ is effectively a buffer zone around sovereign air space, in which the state unilaterally claims the right to identify and monitor aircraft that enter the zone, normally civil aircraft. ADIZs are far from universal; upwards of 12 countries have established them. See Bakhtiar, H. S. et al., 'Air defence identification zone (ADIZ) in international law perspective', Journal of Law, Policy and Globalization, vol. 56 (2016).

[50] AFP, 'China's warplane incursions into Taiwan air defence zone doubled in 2022', The Guardian, 2 Jan. 2023; and Lee, Y., 'Taiwan reports China's largest incursion yet to air defence zone', Reuters, 26 Dec. 2022.

[51] See chapter 5, section II, in this volume.

[52] Choe S-H., 'Tracking North Korea's missile launches', New York Times, 13 Mar. 2023. See also chapter 7, section VIII, in this volume.

included both ballistic and cruise missiles and both intercontinental and shorter range tactical weapons.[53]

In March, as missile testing began, reports surfaced suggesting North Korea might be preparing to recommence nuclear weapons testing after a five-year gap.[54] That did not happen but the reports and concerns re-emerged in September 2022 when North Korea enacted a law that permits the country's armed forces to use nuclear weapons not only to defend and retaliate against invasion but also to make a pre-emptive strike in case of an imminent attack.[55]

There is, unfortunately, no reason to suppose that the escalation in tensions and increased military deployments will decelerate any time soon. Apart from the UN, there is no forum in which the countries of the region can jointly discuss their security dilemmas, including territorial disputes in the South China and East China seas. Mutual security and confidence-building measures are lacking. The regional powers are all strengthening their armed forces and external powers such as the USA, the United Kingdom, India and Australia are deploying naval forces in the region.[56] With these deployments, the risk of naval incidents rises and the importance of managing them safely when they occur increases commensurately.[57] The evidence of 2022, however, does not reveal an appetite on any side to change course that is likely to hinder the development of even modest confidence-building measures.

III. Arms control and nuclear non-proliferation

The year began with a bright moment. The five permanent members (P5) of the UN Security Council—China, France, Russia, the UK and the USA—issued a joint statement on the need to prevent nuclear war. Essentially repeating the epochal joint statement by the Soviet and US leaders Mikhail Gorbachev and Ronald Reagan in 1985, the P5 statement, issued on 3 January 2022, affirmed that 'nuclear war cannot be won and must never be fought'.[58] The logic flowing from that statement implies that its five signatories would steer away from behaviour that might lead to nuclear weapons use by design or accident. It is not in logic possible to both forswear nuclear war and be

---

[53] McCurry, J., 'North Korea says missile tests simulated striking South with tactical nuclear weapons', The Guardian, 10 Oct. 2022.

[54] Reuters, 'North Korea: Satellite images suggest building work at nuclear site for first time since 2018', The Guardian, 8 Mar. 2022.

[55] 'Kim Jong-un says new law guarantees North Korea will never give up nuclear weapons', The Guardian, 9 Sep. 2022.

[56] Mahadzir, D., '6 naval task groups from US, UK, India, Japan and Australia underway in Pacific', USNI News, 30 Aug. 2022.

[57] Anthony, I., Saalman, L. and Su, F., 'Naval incident management in Europe, East Asia and South East Asia', SIPRI Insights on Peace and Security no. 2023/03, Mar. 2023.

[58] Joint Soviet–United States statement on the summit meeting in Geneva, Ronald Reagan Presidential Library & Museum, 21 Nov. 1985; and Joint statement of the leaders of the five nuclear-weapon states on preventing nuclear war and avoiding arms races, 3 Jan. 2022.

willing to start one. Yet of all the P5, only China has a policy affirming it will only use nuclear weapons to retaliate to a nuclear attack—a 'no first use' policy. Equally, the statement included the wish to avoid a nuclear arms race among the five signatories, which must raise questions about the path of nuclear modernization and upgrades on which all are set.[59]

The mounting crisis over Russia's invasion of Ukraine, and the implicit and explicit threats about using nuclear weapons that came from Russian officials and media figures close to the Russian government, quickly sucked the life out of the P5 statement. Rather than the era of arms reduction and improved relations that the 1985 Gorbachev–Reagan statement presaged, the year that followed the P5 statement saw more dangers, more risky behaviour, and more concern and anxiety among ordinary citizens about the prospect of nuclear war. And arms control took another backward step in February 2022 when the US administration suspended US–Russian strategic stability talks.[60]

The P5 statement was aimed at the review conference (RevCon) of the Nuclear Non-Proliferation Treaty (NPT), which had been deferred several times since 2020 and was by then rescheduled for January 2022. By the time the P5 statement was issued, the RevCon had been deferred again to August, when it finally happened. That further postponement might have offered breathing space during which the P5 could work towards outlining practical measures to act on the logic of their statement. The opportunity was not taken and the RevCon came to an end without any agreement on next steps—and even the draft outcome document outlining rather modest steps was eventually blocked by Russia due to disagreements over Ukraine.[61]

The Iran nuclear deal

The Iran nuclear deal agreed in 2015—formally, the Joint Comprehensive Plan of Action (JCPOA)—showed signs of breaking down irrecoverably in 2022. Iran's development of nuclear technology has long been controversial in the West and Middle East. The country does not possess nuclear weapons and is a party to the NPT, meaning it has forsworn developing, producing or owning them. Yet suspicions of Iran's intentions have long been widespread, and between 2006 and 2010 the UN Security Council passed six resolutions demanding an end to the country's uranium enrichment programme, five of which had sanctions attached.[62] The JCPOA sought to block the country's

---

[59] Gibbons, R. D., 'Five nuclear weapon states vow to prevent nuclear war while modernizing arsenals', *Bulletin of the Atomic Scientists*, 17 Jan. 2022.

[60] Detch, J. and Gramer, R., 'Biden halts Russian arms control talks amid Ukraine invasion', *Foreign Policy*, 25 Feb. 2022. See also chapter 8, section I, in this volume.

[61] See chapter 8, section II, in this volume.

[62] Arms Control Association, 'UN Security Council resolutions on Iran', Fact sheet, Jan. 2022.

path to developing nuclear weapons until at least 2030.[63] The administration of Donald J. Trump, however, announced in 2018 that the USA would pull out of its JCPOA obligations even though the International Atomic Energy Agency confirmed that Iran was fully implementing its own obligations.[64] In 2019 Iran responded by starting to breach the JCPOA limits on its various activities. Negotiations on restoring the deal began in 2021, even though the Iranian government changed in June of that year, but progress was slow.[65] As 2022 proceeded, Iran's support for Russia inevitably complicated negotiations on renewing the JCPOA. By the end of 2022, its prospects did not look encouraging.[66]

US nuclear posture

While campaigning for the US presidency in 2020, Joe Biden expressed his view that 'the sole purpose' of nuclear weapons is for deterrence, and retaliation if deterrence fails.[67] While not quite being a 'no first use' policy, it is close to it; the difference is that 'no first use' is an unqualified limitation on when to use nuclear weapons, while 'sole purpose' is a statement of intent, which could arguably change if circumstances demanded.[68]

In October 2022, the Biden administration produced its Nuclear Posture Review (NPR), which explicitly rejected both 'no first use' and 'sole purpose', arguing that either one would result in 'an unacceptable level of risk in light of the range of non-nuclear capabilities . . . that could inflict strategic-level damage'.[69] Overall, the NPR did not articulate any significant change in US posture, strategy and forces, avoiding commitments either to reductions or increases in force levels. Perhaps, in view of the global political climate and the state of US relations with both China and Russia, it would have been unrealistic to expect any other outcome. Apart from the decision not to proceed with the development of a nuclear-armed cruise missile, which was envisaged in the 2018 NPR, the 2022 NPR was rather disappointing from the perspective of arms control and disarmament.

---

[63] Rauf, T., 'Resolving concerns about Iran's nuclear programme', *SIPRI Yearbook 2016*, pp. 673–88; and Rauf, T., 'Implementation of the Joint Comprehensive Plan of Action in Iran', *SIPRI Yearbook 2017*, pp. 505–10.

[64] International Atomic Energy Agency (IAEA), 'Verification and monitoring in the Islamic Republic of Iran in light of United Nations Security Council Resolution 2231 (2015)', Report by the director general, GOV/2018/24, 24 May 2018.

[65] Abadi, C., 'The Iran nuclear deal's long year of negotiations and uncertainty', *Foreign Policy*, 24 Dec. 2021.

[66] See chapter 8, section IV, in this volume.

[67] Biden, J. R., 'Why America must lead again', *Foreign Affairs*, 23 Jan. 2020.

[68] Panda, A. and Narang, V., 'Sole purpose is not no first use: Nuclear weapons and declaratory policy', War on the Rocks, 22 Feb. 2021.

[69] US DOD, *2022 Nuclear Posture Review*, 27 Oct. 2022, p. 9.

IV. Climate change and environmental diplomacy

The unfolding environmental crisis was addressed by two major intergovernmental meetings in 2022: the 27th conference of parties (COP27) of the UN Framework Convention on Climate Change (UNFCCC) in November, and the 15th conference of parties (COP15) of the UN Convention on Biological Diversity (CBD), held in October and December.[70]

There are numerous other international agreements on environmental deterioration—the EU lists 29 more—and, in March 2022, representatives of over 190 governments met in the UN Environmental Assembly and agreed to draft a new legally binding treaty on plastic pollution, to be ready by the end of 2024.[71] Nonetheless, the UNFCCC, under which the Paris Agreement of 2015 was reached, and the CBD are the two key agreements so far. The COPs are very large events. COP27 on climate, held in Sharm el-Shaikh, Egypt, was attended by more than 100 heads of government among a total of over 35 000 people (about 5000 fewer than COP26), if attendance by non-governmental participants at all the side events is counted.[72] COP15 on biodiversity was held in Montreal, Canada, with a preliminary meeting in October, held in Kyunming, China, and online; the Montreal gathering had 10 000 registered participants.[73] Both conferences were held against a background of unfulfilled promises. The world is not on track to stay below 1.5°C warming, which was agreed to be the preferred target in Paris in 2015, nor even below 2°C warming, which was agreed to be the essential target.[74] Likewise, when government representatives met in Montreal to agree a new action plan on protecting biodiversity, they were setting out to replace the Aichi framework agreed in 2010 at COP10 in Nagoya, Japan.[75] None of the Aichi targets (due to be met by 2020) was achieved.[76]

A generally shared view of COP27 is that the new agreement to set up a 'loss and damage' fund is a significant yet vague step.[77] It will change the terms of

---

[70] United Nations Framework Convention on Climate Change (UNFCCC), opened for signature 9 May 1992, entered into force 21 Mar. 1994, UN Treaty Collection; and UN Convention on Biological Diversity (CBD), opened for signature 5 June 1992, entered into force 29 Dec. 1993.

[71] 'Nations sign up to end global scourge of plastic pollution', UN News, 2 Mar. 2022; and United Nations, Environment Assembly, 'End plastic pollution: Towards an internationally legally binding instrument', Resolution, UNEP/EA.5/Res.14, 2 Mar. 2022. For the list of environmental treaties see European Commission, 'International issues: Multilateral environmental agreements'.

[72] United Nations, 'COP27: Delivering for people and planet'.

[73] Convention on Biological Diversity, 'Conference of the parties (COP)'; and Shanahan, M., 'Explainer: COP15, the biggest biodiversity conference in a decade', China Dialogue, 1 Dec. 2022.

[74] 'Countries' climate promises still not enough to avoid catastrophic global warming: UN report', UN News, 26 Oct. 2022.

[75] Convention on Biological Diversity, 'Aichi biodiversity targets', 18 Sep. 2020.

[76] Convention on Biological Diversity, Secretariat, *Global Biodiversity Outlook 5: Summary for Policymakers*, Aug. 2020.

[77] UNFCCC Secretariat, 'COP27 reaches breakthrough agreement on new "loss and damage" fund for vulnerable countries', Press release, 20 Nov. 2022.

discussion on the costs of climate change for poorer countries, which have historically done least to create the problem yet face the heaviest burden from its consequences. The loss and damage agreement is aimed at righting that wrong. However, many key issues have not yet been agreed, including what constitutes loss and damage from the impact of climate change.[78] Is the focus on compensation after natural disasters or on the costs of readiness? Would the fund cover the costs of building new infrastructure? It is also not yet agreed how to pay into the fund, nor how to pay out.[79] These issues are to be discussed by a transitional committee that COP27 established, which is to report with recommendations to COP28 in December 2023. The agreement in Sharm el-Sheikh, in other words, is not the end of the story.

Despite this achievement, doubts remained about the firmness of commitments to resolving the challenges that global warming and climate change present. While optimists could point to the agreement on loss and damage, sceptics could note that, as at every previous COP, there was no formal agreement to reduce the use of fossil fuels, which all experts agree is necessary to slow global warming.[80] Notably in that context, over 600 lobbyists from fossil fuel industries were present and accredited to the conference.[81]

COP15 in Montreal successfully adopted a new framework for action to halt biodiversity loss.[82] It has four long-range goals and 23 more detailed targets to be achieved by 2030. There can be no objection in principle to this outcome. Biodiversity loss is in part connected to climate change but also to other aspects of social and economic development, especially changes in land use and soil depletion. The sixth mass extinction of species to occur in the planet's history is well under way, at a rate of extinction that is between tens and hundreds of times higher than it has averaged over the past 10 million years. There is no rational case for delaying action to address the biodiversity crisis but the question, of course, is whether the will is there to make the changes that are required to protect the natural foundations on which humanity depends.[83] Generating the energy and collective action needed for

---

[78] European Parliamentary Research Service (ERPS), 'Understanding loss and damage: Addressing the unavoidable impacts of climate change', ERPS Briefing, July 2022; and Liao, C. et al., 'What is loss and damage?', Chatham House Explainer, 6 Dec. 2022.

[79] Najam, A., 'COP27's "loss and damage" fund for developing countries could be a breakthrough—or another empty climate promise', The Conversation, 21 Nov. 2022.

[80] McGuire, B., 'The big takeaway from COP 27? These climate conferences just aren't working', The Guardian, 20 Nov. 2022.

[81] Global Witness, '636 fossil fuel lobbyists granted access to COP 27', 10 Nov. 2022.

[82] Convention on Biodiversity, 'COP15: Nations adopt four goals, 23 targets for 2030 in landmark UN biodiversity agreement', Press release, 19 Dec. 2022.

[83] See e.g. Kolbert, E., *The Sixth Extinction: An Unnatural History* (Henry Holt & Co: New York, 2014); Cowie, R. H., Bouchet, P. and Fontaine, B., 'The sixth mass extinction: Fact, fiction or speculation?', *Biological Reviews*, vol. 97, no. 2 (2022); and Intergovernmental Science-Policy Platform on Biodiversity and Ecosystem Services (IPBES), *Global Assessment Report on Biodiversity and Ecosystem Services* (IPBES: Bonn, 2019).

such change is never likely to be easy; in the current international setting, it is particularly difficult.

V. The course of the war in Ukraine

War facts and figures

Russia first invaded Ukraine in 2014, seizing Crimea and much of the eastern provinces of Donetsk and Luhansk, and triggering a continuing armed conflict in eastern Ukraine.[84] Following a systematic build-up of its forces near the border during 2021, Russia invaded Ukraine for the second time on 24 February 2022. Full-scale war ensued. Whereas the 2014 action was carried out in part by stealth, the 2022 invasion was an open act of aggression. As in 2014, the February 2022 action had no justification in the form of a Ukrainian attack or threat of one. The invasion breached Ukraine's national sovereignty, the UN Charter and the 1994 Budapest Memorandum, in which Russia undertook, along with the UK and the USA, to uphold Ukraine's territorial sovereignty.[85]

Russia's military build-up in 2021 assembled an invasion force variously estimated by agencies in the West as up to 190 000 strong.[86] On 24 February 2022, Russia launched missiles against multiple targets and initiated ground offensives, from Belarus in the north towards Kyiv, from Russia towards Kharkiv, from Donetsk and Luhansk, which Russia had formally recognized as independent states on 21 February, and from Crimea, which Russia annexed in 2014.[87] Before 24 February 2022, Russian-occupied areas accounted for just under 6.5 per cent of Ukraine's territory. By the end of March, Russian forces occupied some 24 per cent of Ukraine, though control was incomplete and contested in many areas. Russia still occupied 16.6 per cent of Ukraine's territory at the end of 2022, a third down on its peak but well over twice what it held before the invasion.[88]

---

[84] For a discussion on the initial causes of the conflict in Ukraine see Wilson, A., 'External intervention in the Ukraine conflict: Towards a frozen conflict in the Donbas', *SIPRI Yearbook 2016*, pp. 143–57; and Clem, R. S., 'Clearing the fog of war: Public versus official sources and geopolitical storylines in the Russia–Ukraine conflict', *Eurasian Geography and Economics*, vol. 58, no. 6 (2017). On the various armed groups fighting in the early phases of the conflict see Galeotti, M., *Armies of Russia's War in Ukraine* (Osprey Publishing: Oxford, 2019).

[85] Memorandum on security assurances in connection with Ukraine's accession to the Treaty on the Non-Proliferation of Nuclear Weapons, 7 Dec. 1994.

[86] Wintour, P., 'Russia has amassed up to 190,000 troops on Ukraine's borders, US warns', *The Guardian*, 18 Feb. 2022.

[87] President of Russia, 'Address by the president of the Russian Federation', English transcript, 21 Feb. 2022; and Jones, S. G., 'Russia's ill-fated invasion of Ukraine: Lessons in modern warfare', CSIS Brief, June 2022.

[88] Breteau, P., 'War in Ukraine: Russia now controls only 16% of Ukrainian territory', *Le Monde*, 6 Jan. 2023.

As in many wars, data on the scale of human suffering is patchy and unreliable. The UN regards its own estimates of approximately 8000 Ukrainian civilians killed in the first year of war as significant underestimates.[89] In addition, harrowing accounts of atrocities emerged early in the war and throughout the year.[90] Numbers of refugees and internally displaced persons (IDPs) fluctuate, as some people flee fighting and danger but return when there is some degree of safety in doing so; by early 2023 there were some 8 million Ukrainian refugees in other countries in Europe and 5.35 million IDPs (down from 6.5 million in March 2022).[91]

Figures for combatant casualties are uncertain, as is usually the case in wartime.[92] Russian Defence Minister Sergey Shoigu said in September 2022 that Russian forces had suffered 5937 combat deaths and put Ukrainian combat deaths at 61 207.[93] These figures are completely at odds with Western estimates and Ukrainian statements. In February 2023 the British Defence Intelligence announced an estimate of Russian combat casualties of 175 000 to 200 000 personnel, including private military contractors such as the Wagner Group and regular Russian forces, and including 40 000 to 60 000 deaths.[94] These figures appear to be generally used in the West, though the Ukrainian Ministry of Defence claimed the Russian death toll after one year of war was over 130 000.[95]

Russian attacks on civilian centres have been a feature of the renewed war. Missile attacks on energy infrastructure have had a heavy short-term impact, though Ukrainian authorities have improved protection of the electricity grid and can repair it quickly.[96] Artillery and missile bombardment destroyed many urban areas—a foreseeable aspect of the war, given Russian

---

[89] 'UN rights chief deplores Ukraine death toll one year after Russian invasion', UN News, 21 Feb. 2023; and Farge, E. and Tétrault-Farber, G., 'UN says recorded civilian toll of 8,000 in Ukraine is "tip of the iceberg"', Reuters, 21 Feb. 2023.

[90] Human Rights Watch, 'Ukraine: Apparent war crimes in Russia-controlled areas', 3 Apr. 2022; 'As Russian soldiers retreat, they leave evidence of war crimes', *The Economist*, 8 Apr. 2022; UN Office of the High Commissioner for Human Rights, 'UN report details summary executions of civilians by Russian troops in northern Ukraine', Press release, 7 Dec. 2022; and Biesecker, M. and Kinetz, E., 'Evidence of Russian crimes mounts as war in Ukraine drags on', AP News, 30 Dec. 2022.

[91] UN High Commissioner for Refugees, Operational Data Portal: Ukraine Refugee Situation; International Organization for Migration, Global Data Institute, 'Ukraine—Internal displacement report: General population survey, round 12', 23 Jan. 2023; and Filo, E. and Parrish, F., 'Conflict in Ukraine: What do we know about internal displacement so far?', International Displacement Monitoring Centre, Mar. 2022.

[92] Crawford, N. C., 'Reliable death tolls from the Ukraine war are hard to come by—the result of undercounts and manipulation', The Conversation, 4 Apr. 2022.

[93] 'Russia calls up 300,000 reservists, says 6,000 soldiers killed in Ukraine', Reuters, 21 Sep. 2022; and 'Russia reveals military losses in Ukraine', RT, 21 Sep. 2022.

[94] British Ministry of Defence (@DefenceHQ), Twitter, 17 Feb. 2023. <https://twitter.com/DefenceHQ/status/1626472945089486848>.

[95] McDonald, S., 'Russian death toll soars past 130,000 as war nears 1-year mark: Ukraine', *Newsweek*, 4 Feb. 2023.

[96] 'Russia has destroyed 30 percent of Ukraine's power stations: Kyiv', Al Jazeera, 18 Oct. 2022; and 'How Ukraine tamed Russian missile barrages and kept the lights on', *The Economist*, 12 Mar. 2023.

force structure and doctrine.[97] There will likely also be negative health and environmental impacts arising from the destruction of hospitals, sewage systems and water supplies, as well as from the release into the atmosphere of pulverized cement, metals and industrial compounds from destroyed buildings.[98] Further concerns about long-term health and safety arose because of the proximity of fighting to major nuclear installations, including the long-disused Chornobyl Nuclear Power Plant and the Zaporizhzhia Nuclear Power Plant.[99]

Russia's goals

Russian leaders have stated Russia's goals in overlapping forms. President Vladimir Putin has both emphasized the aim of replacing the Ukrainian leadership, depicted as 'criminals' and 'neo-Nazis', and invoked more ambitious aims, envisaging the end of the Ukrainian state, on the grounds that it has no historical right to exist.[100] Such thinking draws on grandiose and largely polemical theorizing about a historical and geopolitical Russian mission to be a great power, dominant in Eurasia.[101] He also depicts the war as an existential struggle against the West.[102] Yet some presentations have articulated the war aims in more limited terms that swing on the need to protect Russians living in the provinces of Donetsk and Luhansk.[103] These goals are not logically incompatible with each other but they are distinct, which could imply different strategic paths for reaching them and give rise to different political narratives. In one narrative, Russia is a victim of the West and of neo-Nazism in Ukraine; in another, Russia is a generous protector

---

[97] Cranny-Evans, S., 'The role of artillery in a war between Russia and Ukraine', RUSI, 14 Feb. 2022.

[98] Roberts, L., 'Surge of HIV, tuberculosis and COVID feared amid war in Ukraine', *Nature*, 15 Mar. 2022; and Garrity, A., 'Conflict rubble: A ubiquitous and under-studied toxic remnant of war', Conflict and Environment Observatory, 10 July 2014.

[99] Steavenson, W. and Rodionova, M., 'The inside story of Chernobyl during the Russian occupation', *The Economist*, 10 May 2022; Liou, J., 'Situation at Zaporizhzhya Nuclear Power Plant "untenable," protection zone needed, IAEA's Grossi tells Board', IAEA, 12 Sep. 2022; and IAEA, 'IAEA director general statement on situation in Ukraine', Update no. 138, 30 Dec. 2022. See also chapter 8, section V, in this volume.

[100] See e.g. speeches by Putin in the Kremlin: President of Russia (note 87); President of Russia, 'Address by the president of the Russian Federation', English transcript, 24 Feb. 2022; and President of Russia, 'Article by Vladimir Putin "On the historical unity of Russians and Ukrainians"', 12 July 2021.

[101] See e.g. Dugin, A., *Last War of the World-Island: The Geopolitics of Contemporary Russia* (Arktos: London, 2015).

[102] Faulconbridge, G., 'Putin casts war as a battle for Russia's survival', Reuters, 21 Feb. 2023; and Maçães, B., '"Russia cannot afford to lose, so we need a kind of a victory": Sergey Karaganov on what Putin wants', *New Statesman*, 24 Feb. 2023.

[103] See e.g. 'Russia had "no choice" but to launch "special military operation" in Ukraine, Lavrov tells UN', UN News, 24 Sep. 2022. Some passages on Russians in the two provinces were part of the argument for recognizing the independence of Donetsk and Luhansk, advanced by President Putin three days before the invasion. President of Russia (note 87).

of all Russians, even those who live in other states; in a third, Russia has a destiny to fulfil.

Many Western experts have argued that Russian leaders did not have a properly worked out strategic plan, but a 'delusional strategy' with 'arrogant and haphazard planning', and a 'shockingly bad' invasion plan.[104] After six months of war, analysts saw repetition of the same mistakes.[105] One analysis identified a key weakness as the absence of a backup plan, when Russian forces were unable to take Kyiv in the first 10 days.[106] Another argued that even if that operation were successful, Russia would need a full-scale military occupation to control Ukraine, for which it lacked sufficient forces.[107] Putin's announcement of a call-up of 300 000 reservists, while presaging the annexation of four provinces of Ukraine (including Donetsk and Luhansk, which had previously been recognized as independent), could be regarded as evidence to support this latter view.[108]

Overall, Western analysis contains considerable emphasis on seeing the war as a whole as an ill-considered mistake. By the end of 2022, the war's outcome was, of course, still undecided, meaning that conclusive judgements about mistakes, failures and successes need to wait.

The West's involvement

The West, broadly defined, has been a participant in the Ukraine crisis, though not a combatant in the war, since before the renewed war started. The impetus for this has come from both sides. The USA and its allies helped Ukraine strengthen its armed forces in the wake of the 2014 annexation of Crimea and effective occupation of parts of eastern Donbas by Russia. When the 2022 invasion occurred, the assistance was steadily stepped up.

Aid to Ukraine and sanctions against Russia

The first year of aid commitments to Ukraine totalled €143 billion, including humanitarian and general financial aid as well as military assistance.[109] That total, which reflects promises made, not actual spending, is not far short of the €174 billion that members of the Organisation for Economic Co-operation

---

[104] Freedman, L., 'The fight for Ukraine', Comment is Freed, 27 Feb. 2022; and Kagan, F. W. and Clark, M., 'How not to invade a nation', *Foreign Affairs*, 29 Apr. 2022.
[105] Massicot, D., 'Russia's repeat failures', *Foreign Affairs*, 15 Aug. 2022.
[106] Zabrodskyi, M. et al., *Provisional Lessons in Contemporary Warfighting from Russia's Invasion of Ukraine: February–July 2022* (RUSI: London, Nov. 2022), pp. 1, 12, 48.
[107] Freedman, L., 'A reckless gamble', Comment is Freed, 25 Feb. 2022.
[108] President of Russia, 'Address by the president of the Russian Federation', English transcript, 21 Sep. 2022; and President of Russia, 'Signing of treaties on accession of Donetsk and Lugansk people's republics and Zaporozhye and Kherson regions to Russia', 30 Sep. 2022.
[109] Trebesch, C. et al., *The Ukraine Support Tracker: Which Countries Help Ukraine and How?*, Kiel Working Paper no. 2218, Feb. 2023, pp. 1–2. See also chapter, 5, section II, in this volume.

and Development spent in total on official development assistance in 2021.[110] The financial aid to Ukraine has been essential to the government's continued ability to meet basic functions and the military aid has been indispensable for its war effort.

In addition, the West, led by the EU and the USA, has emphasized supporting Ukraine by enforcing a range of sanctions—including sectoral sanctions, banking restrictions, road and maritime transport bans, travel bans, asset freezes, arms embargoes and trade restrictions—against Russia and Belarus. Already in March 2022, the sanctions that had been imposed on Russia were regarded as the most comprehensive ever put together against a major power since the end of World War II.[111] EU and US assessments indicate that these sanctions have impacted Russia's economic growth and reduced its ability to source components for its military equipment.[112] Yet there are grounds for doubt about the long-term efficacy of sanctions. However hard the designers and enforcers of economic sanctions work to make them technically sound and effective in their own right—such as by interrupting and limiting trade, financial transfers and the assets and travel of key individuals in the intended manner—the track record of sanctions for achieving their intended policy goals is decidedly mixed.[113] Sanctions are an effective means of virtue signalling but often little more, and are sometimes counterproductive.[114] The statistical record in the 20th century was that only one in three uses of sanctions was 'at least partially successful' in achieving its political goals.[115]

Russia and NATO

The West is also involved in the Ukraine crisis by featuring in the Russian narrative that presents the invasions of Ukraine in 2014 and 2022 as forced on Russia by NATO's incorporation of eastern European states in the years after the cold war.[116] These were former members of the Warsaw Pact (Bulgaria, Czechia, Hungary, Poland, Romania, Slovakia) and three former Soviet republics (Estonia, Latvia, Lithuania). NATO described these additions to its membership as a process of *enlargement*, resulting from democratic decisions

---

[110] Organisation for Economic Co-operation and Development, 'Official development assistance (ODA)'.

[111] Hufbauer, G. C. and Hogan, M., 'How effective are sanctions against Russia?', PIIE Blog, 16 Mar. 2022. On the trade restrictions on Russia see chapter 12, section III, in this volume.

[112] See European Council, 'Infographic: Impact of sanctions on the Russian economy', 17 Mar. 2023; and US Department of State, Office of the Spokesperson, 'The impact of sanctions and export controls on the Russian Federation', Fact sheet, 20 Oct. 2022.

[113] Staibano, C. and Wallensteen, P. (eds), *International Sanctions: Between Wars and Words* (Routledge: London, 2005); and Biersteker, T. J., Eckert, S. E. and Tourinho, M. (eds), *Targeted Sanctions: The Impacts and Effectiveness of United Nations Action* (Cambridge University Press: Cambridge, 2016).

[114] Haass, R. N., 'Economic sanctions: Too much of a bad thing', Brookings Policy Brief, 1 June 1998.

[115] Mulder, N., *The Economic Weapon: The Rise of Sanctions as a Tool of Modern War* (Yale University Press: New Haven, CT, 2022) p. 295.

[116] President of Russia (note 100).

by the new member states, while Russia and critics of NATO tend to use the term *expansion*, depicting a power play.

The Russian argument includes the assertion that, as the cold war came to an end, NATO undertook not to take in new members from east of the former German Democratic Republic (East Germany). This quite widely accepted view appears to be based on a misunderstanding that simplifies a nuanced situation. There was no formal undertaking that NATO would not incorporate new members to its east. In that sense there was no promise, which means NATO did not break faith when enlargement/expansion happened. In the final years and months of the Soviet Union's existence, however, statements were made to Soviet leaders that there would be no eastward enlargement.[117] Among several examples, the German foreign minister at the time, Hans Dietrich Genscher, said in January 1991 that NATO would not grow to the east, and his US counterpart, James Baker, a few days later during a visit to Moscow, offered 'ironclad guarantees that NATO's jurisdiction or forces would not move eastward', a position he modified in subsequent remarks.[118] As the exchanges on this issue unfolded, there were remarks from the Soviet side acknowledging the principle that states are free to choose their allies, implying that NATO might well accept new applicants into its membership.[119] And in 1993, Russian President Boris Yeltsin agreed with Polish President Lech Walesa that Poland had the right to join NATO.[120] Indeed, the NATO–Russia Founding Act signed in 1997 includes explicit reference to 'new members' of NATO, indicating all parties' acceptance of that prospect.[121]

The Russian view focuses on the assurances that were offered while the NATO view focuses on the absence of formal agreement. Perhaps NATO could and should have handled these issues differently.[122] This is certainly a discussion worth having. But it is hard to see moral equivalence between, on the one hand, what may have been diplomatic errors by the USA and its allies in the 1990s and, on the other hand, open aggression, systematic attacks on civilian targets, large-scale urban destruction and, if UN-collected evidence is borne out, abundant war crimes.[123]

---

[117] 'NATO expansion: What Gorbachev heard', National Security Archive, 12 Dec. 2017; and McCarthy, B., 'Fact-checking claims that NATO, US broke agreement against alliance expanding eastward', PolitiFact, 28 Feb. 2022.

[118] Baker, P., 'In Ukraine conflict, Putin relies on a promise that ultimately wasn't', *New York Times*, 9 Jan. 2022.

[119] Neal, J., '"There was no promise not to enlarge NATO"', *Harvard Law Today*, 16 Mar. 2022.

[120] Wintour, P., 'Russia's belief in NATO "betrayal"—and why it matters today', *The Guardian*, 12 Jan. 2022.

[121] Founding Act on Mutual Relations, Cooperation and Security between NATO and the Russian Federation signed in Paris, France, 27 May 1997.

[122] Sarotte, M. E., *Not One Inch: America, Russia, and the Making of Post-Cold War Stalemate* (Yale University Press: New Haven, CT, 2021).

[123] United Nations, Human Rights Council, Report of the Independent International Commission of Inquiry on Ukraine, A/HRC/52/62 (Advance version), 15 Mar. 2023.

In keeping with its view of NATO's culpability, in December 2021 Russia proposed two treaties that would have meant NATO agreeing not to absorb new members and, in particular, not Ukraine.[124] There was no likelihood of NATO accepting this restriction. But it does reflect a genuine Russian view denying the legitimacy of NATO's increase in size.

This only makes the NATO part of the West's response to the war the more striking—and the more galling perhaps for Russia. NATO, which was declared 'brain dead' by French President Emmanuel Macron in 2019, has revived and is in the process of enlarging (or expanding) once again.[125] Finland acted against clearly expressed Russian interests and preferences for the first time since the end of World War II, while Sweden put aside two centuries of not aligning with major powers in a domestic political debate lasting little more than two months. The two countries applied together to join NATO, despite strongly voiced Russian objections and warnings about potential countermeasures.[126] At the end of 2022, Hungary and Türkiye had still to approve the applications, the latter using the occasion to raise long-held concerns about the presence in both countries of politically active Kurds whom it regards as having ties to terrorism.[127]

The nuclear dimension

During 2022, Russian spokespersons repeatedly warned that the use of nuclear weapons in the context of the war in Ukraine had not been ruled out.[128] By the end of the year, there was less concern about this possibility in the headlines in the West, though US officials reportedly believe there are some situations—if President Putin were losing power, or feared NATO forces would directly enter the war, or faced defeat—in which Russia might use a nuclear weapon.[129] Nuclear deterrence theory would propose that such action by Russia would be deterred by the USA's arsenal; however, there

---

[124] Russian Ministry of Foreign Affairs, 'Treaty between the United States of America and the Russian Federation on security guarantees', 17 Dec. 2021; and Russian Ministry of Foreign Affairs, 'Agreement on measures to ensure the security of the Russian Federation and member states of the North Atlantic Treaty Organization', 17 Dec. 2021.

[125] Rose, M., 'France's Macron: I'm not sorry I called NATO brain dead', Reuters, 28 Nov. 2019.

[126] 'Ukraine war: Russia warns Sweden and Finland against NATO membership', BBC News, 11 Apr. 2022; Erlanger, S. and Lemola, J., 'Despite Russian warnings, Finland and Sweden draw closer to NATO', *New York Times*, 13 Apr. 2022; and 'Yle poll: Support for NATO membership hits record high', Yle News, 14 Mar. 2022.

[127] Chatterjee, P., 'Who are "terrorists" Turkey wants from Sweden and Finland?', BBC News, 5 July 2022; and 'Sweden deports man with alleged ties to Kurdish militant group', Reuters, 3 Dec. 2022.

[128] Karmanau, Y. et al., 'Putin puts nuclear forces on high alert, escalating tensions', AP News, 28 Feb. 2022; Sevastopulo, D. and Qinio, A., 'Putin puts world on alert with high-stakes nuclear posturing', *Financial Times*, 7 Mar. 2022; and Faulconbridge, G. and Osborn, A., 'Analysis: Truth or bluff? Why Putin's nuclear warnings have the West worried', Reuters, 28 Sep. 2022.

[129] Barnes, J. E. and Sanger, D. E., 'Fears of Russian nuclear weapons use have diminished, but could re-emerge', *New York Times*, 3 Feb. 2022.

might be room for doubt as to whether the US president would actually authorize nuclear retaliation to a relatively limited Russian strike against a third country, especially one that, like Ukraine, is not a member of NATO. Arguments about nuclear use, the utility of nuclear weapons and what victory in a nuclear war might look like have swirled endlessly for decades.[130] This unresolved debate suggests that the risk of nuclear use is always real but also always low, because the outcome would be uncertain and wholly negative. It is worth noting the report that US war-gaming has identified how, in the event of Russia using nuclear weapons in Ukraine or against other targets, the USA could deliver a devastating blow against Russian forces using conventional weapons only.[131]

Prospects

By the end of 2022, the drift of many commentaries on the war, from both Russia and the West, reflected the expectation of a long war ahead, suggesting that neither side had a clear path towards victory. At the same time, a year in, there was no clear path towards a negotiated peace. In 2022, there were negotiations and agreements on issues such as grain exports and prisoner swaps.[132] On ending the fighting, however, there was no progress since March 2022.[133] In early 2023, the respective positions of Russia and Ukraine remained far apart. The two sides' territorial demands are incompatible; and Russian President Putin denies the legitimacy of the government of Ukraine, while Ukraine President Volodymyr Zelensky does not trust his Russian counterpart at any level.[134] It can be argued that, eventually, co-existence will be necessary, even if it involves two hostile states facing each other across a heavily fortified border. What is not clear, however, is the short- to middle-term process of getting there.

For Russia, if it cannot gain outright victory, the unpleasant prospect looms of Ukraine joining NATO. In late 2021, when Russia proposed treaties ruling out Ukraine's accession to the alliance, that prospect was not imminent.

---

[130] See e.g. Bundy, M., 'To cap the volcano', *Foreign Affairs*, vol. 48, no. 1 (Oct. 1969); Ball, D., 'US strategic forces: How would they be used?', *International Security*, vol. 7, no. 3 (1982–83); Smith, D., 'The uselessness and the role of nuclear weapons: An exercise in pseudo-problems and disconnection', eds J. Gjelstad and O. Njølstad, *Nuclear Rivalry and International Order* (Sage: London, 1996); and Kaplan, F., *The Bomb: Presidents, Generals, and the Secret History of Nuclear War* (Simon & Schuster: New York, 2020).

[131] Kaplan, F., 'Why the US might not use a nuke, even if Russia does', Slate, 7 Oct. 2022.

[132] United Nations, Black Sea Grain Initiative (note 17); and 'Dozens freed in new Ukraine–Russia prisoner swap', Al Jazeera, 15 Dec. 2022.

[133] Seddon, M. et al., 'Ukraine and Russia explore neutrality plan in peace talks', *Financial Times*, 16 Mar. 2022.

[134] President of Russia, 'Presidential address to the Federal Assembly', 21 Feb. 2023; and Simpson, J. and Waterhouse, J., 'Ukraine war: Zelensky rules out territory deal with Putin in BBC interview', BBC News, 16 Feb. 2023.

NATO had declared at its Bucharest summit in 2008 that Ukraine (and Georgia) 'will become members of NATO'.[135] However, following the conflict between Georgia and Russia in 2008, what was already understood to be a sensitive issue was regarded by some member states as particularly difficult to approach.[136] That, together with the lack of a timeline in the Bucharest statement, suggested that while some NATO members strongly supported Ukraine's accession, the decision could be long deferred.[137] After a year of close cooperation between NATO and Ukraine, that has changed. Questions remain about timing and modalities, but Ukraine's closeness to NATO is a practical reality and, unless the country is conquered, its membership of NATO is a probability. Ukraine may move towards EU membership as well; its self-improvement programme of anti-corruption reforms is part of what is required for EU candidacy.[138]

VI. Unanswered questions

The same challenge has been identified in successive recent editions of this yearbook: Can energy and a sense of direction in the UN compensate for the lack of global leadership from the great powers? How might it be possible to achieve a balance in world affairs when the great powers are focused on their rivalries with each other? As the international system reels under the impact of the war in Ukraine, is there any space on the international agenda for action to address even the most shared of problems such as the environmental crisis?

At the end of 2022, these questions had no answer and it seemed unlikely that the uncertainties surrounding many important issues would be cleared up soon. While the great powers squared off, much of the rest of the world was paying attention to other developments. The combined impact on human security and international stability was far from positive.

Yet, as in previous editions, it is worth noting that important international institutions are still functioning effectively. As always, an important issue is whether and how well the political classes in many different countries are able to utilize the strengths of those institutions for the common good. That is perhaps an issue that will hinge on the degree to which political discourse starts to recognize common good and shared interests as key determinants of each country's prosperity and stability.

---

[135] NATO, 'Bucharest Summit declaration', Press release, 3 Apr. 2008.
[136] Lazarevic, D., 'NATO enlargement to Ukraine and Georgia: Old wine in new bottles?', *Connections*, vol. 9, no. 1 (winter 2009).
[137] Bayer, L., 'The West's last war-time taboo: Ukraine joining NATO', Politico, 6 Dec. 2022.
[138] Minakov, M., 'Fighting corruption in wartime Ukraine', Focus Ukraine, 13 Feb. 2023.

Part I. Armed conflict and conflict management, 2022

Chapter 2. Trends in armed conflict

Chapter 3. Multilateral peace operations

Chapter 4. Private military and security companies in armed conflict

2. Trends in armed conflict

Overview

While 2022 was a year of widespread armed conflict globally, the variety and level of violence involved fluctuated significantly between regions. Russia's war on Ukraine dominated discussion of war and peace but it was the sole example of a major interstate war involving standing armies in the course of the year. Outside Europe, most wars continued to take place within states—or in clusters of states with porous borders—and to involve non-state armed groups ranging from transnational extremist jihadist networks and criminal gangs to separatist forces and rebel groups.

The total number of states experiencing armed conflicts was 56, five more than in 2021. Three of these (in Ukraine, Myanmar and Nigeria) were definitely classifiable as major conflicts involving 10 000 or more estimated conflict-related deaths. It is likely that the Ethiopian Civil War also passed this threshold, as tens of thousands of deaths are widely believed to have taken place even though there is no firm data available. In addition, 16 further cases were intensive armed conflicts involving 1000–9999 deaths. The total number of estimated conflict-related fatalities in 2022 was 147 609, slightly below the 2021 figure. This, however, masks significant regional fluctuations in violence. The level of fatalities in some cases of persistent heavy armed conflict, such as Afghanistan and Yemen, dropped considerably. The number of recorded deaths leapt in Ukraine and fatalities almost doubled in Myanmar. Africa remained the region with the most armed conflicts, although many involved fewer than 1000 conflict-related deaths. There were also two successful coups d'état and three unsuccessful coup attempts in Africa during the year, while there were none in any other region.

Russia's war on Ukraine threatened to increase global instability in 2022, through the disruption of food and energy markets and the undermining of international conflict resolution mechanisms. However, the global effects of the war were more muted than initially seemed likely. Nonetheless, economic uncertainty led to a wave of political unrest in many regions. Over 12 000 food- and fuel-related protests were recorded globally in 2022. Yet, while these frequently led to individual incidents of violence, they did not escalate into new civil or regional conflicts.

Russia and the Western powers also avoided allowing their worsening relations over Ukraine to block diplomacy on other conflicts at the United Nations. The UN Security Council continued to produce mandates for peace operations, sanctions regimes and mediation efforts at a similar rate to 2021

SIPRI Yearbook 2023: Armaments, Disarmament and International Security
www.sipriyearbook.org

(see also chapter 3). In some cases, such as Afghanistan, Haiti and Myanmar, its resolutions broke new ground, suggesting that the major powers still see the body as a conduit for some cooperation. The Security Council and the UN system were, however, unable to find decisive solutions in a series of cases—notably a surge of jihadist violence in the Sahel, mounting violence in the Democratic Republic of the Congo and a breakdown of law and order in Haiti, where the UN already had a role in crisis management.

If the UN managed to muddle through 2022, it was more difficult for Russia's and Ukraine's allies to find space for compromise in the Organization for Security and Co-operation in Europe, while the European Union and the North Atlantic Treaty Organization focused increasingly on Ukraine and territorial defence rather than conflict management. Outside Europe, the African Union and subregional African entities—including the Group of Five for the Sahel and the Economic Community of West African States—struggled to deal with the parallel challenges of jihadist violence and coups d'état on the continent. Nonetheless, national and multinational forces did succeed in pushing back against jihadist groups in Somalia and Mozambique. In South East Asia, the Association of Southeast Asian Nations made little progress in its efforts at diplomacy over Myanmar.

Opportunities for peacemaking were limited in 2022. The UN succeeded in arranging a truce in Yemen that lasted from April until October—apparently leading to a decline in fatality rates and improved access to aid, despite ongoing violence—while a combination of United States, Saudi Arabian, UN and African mediators fitfully nudged the military authorities in Sudan to agree a new framework for civilian government following military–civilian turmoil throughout 2021. A new offensive by the Ethiopian military and its allies forced the Tigray People's Liberation Front to sue for a truce in November 2022, which was hurriedly worked out in Pretoria, South Africa, and held reasonably well into 2023. In Colombia, a new left-wing government worked on a peace initiative with a number of armed groups in late 2022, which had made uncertain progress by December.

RICHARD GOWAN

I. Global and regional trends and developments in armed conflicts

RICHARD GOWAN

While 2022 was a year of widespread armed conflict, there were variations in the scale, type and causes of conflict-related violence in different regions. Russia's aggression against Ukraine was the bloodiest war of the year, and the impact on food and energy prices was rapidly felt worldwide. However, it was still a rare, although not unique, example of a classic interstate war between standing armies. The majority of conflicts in 2022 continued to take place within states—or across clusters of states in regions with porous borders, such as the Sahel and the Great Lakes region in Africa—and to involve a mix of non-state armed groups (NSAGs) ranging from transnational jihadist organizations to organized criminal networks. Many countries that suffered from violence faced intersecting forms of instability. Burkina Faso, for example, witnessed both an increase in violence by jihadist groups and two military coups d'état in the course of the year. Given the complexity and diversity of the types of armed conflict between and within different regions, it is hard to generalize about *global* trends in conflict.

The challenge of taking a genuinely global view of conflict has taken on additional moral and political, as well as analytical, weight in 2022 for at least four reasons. First, many observers in the Global South, and some in the United States and Europe, have criticized the global media and Western officials for paying more attention to Russia's actions in Ukraine than fatalities and atrocities elsewhere.[1] Second, the spectre of a new cold war between the Western powers, Russia and perhaps China led many analysts to reassess conflicts in other regions as elements of this broader global competition.[2] The activities of the Wagner Group, a Russian 'private military company' active in Africa and Ukraine, came in for particular scrutiny as possible evidence of Russia's global reach.[3] Third, the global price shocks associated with Russia's aggression, which compounded the after-effects of the Covid-19 pandemic and already high inflation, caused some observers to fear that economic distress could cause conflict elsewhere.[4] Fourth, the obvious failure of the United Nations to prevent Russia from breaching the UN Charter sparked a

---

[1] Ridgwell, H., 'Amnesty cites "double standards" in global response to Russia's war on Ukraine', Voice of America, 28 Mar. 2023.

[2] Burrows, M. and Darnal, A., 'Red cell: Is the West losing the Global South?', Stimson Center, 10 Dec. 2022.

[3] See e.g. 'Russia has made worrying inroads into Africa', *Financial Times*, 4 Sep. 2022; and Tharoor, I., 'Russia deepens its influence in West Africa', *Washington Post*, 24 Oct. 2022. On the Wagner Group, see chapter 4 in this volume.

[4] International Crisis Group, '7 Priorities for the G7: Managing the global fallout of Russia's War on Ukraine', Brussels, 22 June 2022.

Table 2.1. Estimated conflict-related fatalities by region, 2018–22

	2018	2019	2020	2021	2022
Americas	23 290	22 339	20 205	20 582	21 247
Asia and Oceania	49 857	48 786	36 378	58 070	28 204
Europe	1 093	481	7 313	279	29 015
Middle East and North Africa	76 712	53 481	34 245	28 629	18 665
Sub-Saharan Africa	26 532	27 243	38 502	46 193	50 478
Total	**177 484**	**152 330**	**136 643**	**153 753**	**147 609**

Note: Fatality figures are collated from 4 event types: battles; explosions/remote violence; protests, riots and strategic developments; and violence against civilians. Figures include all conflict-related fatalities in the region, irrespective of whether the countries were engaged in armed conflict. See Armed Conflict Location & Event Data Project (ACLED), 'ACLED definitions of political violence and protest', 11 Apr. 2019.

Source: ACLED, 'Dashboard', accessed 27 Jan. 2023.

debate inside and outside the UN system on the flaws of international conflict management.[5]

In this context, the data on armed conflict in this SIPRI Yearbook is valuable as an objective touchpoint in often emotional debates about recent international events (see section III, table 2.8). This section summarizes some of the main global features of armed conflict identifiable from this data and briefly surveys diverging regional trends. The subsection on Asia summarizes conflict dynamics in Myanmar, while the subsection on Europe includes a narrative of Russia's war on Ukraine.

Global trends in armed conflict

Data gathered by the Armed Conflict Location & Event Data Project (ACLED) suggests that at least 56 countries experienced armed conflict in 2022 (see section III, table 2.8), with an estimated 147 609 conflict-related fatalities worldwide. These figures are tentative and it is noteworthy that estimates of fatalities for at least two wars, in Ethiopia and Ukraine, vary considerably.[6] Nonetheless, ACLED's figures are ostensibly similar to those for 2021, when 51 countries in conflict led to 153 753 related deaths. This apparent continuity is deceptive as there were major fluctuations in levels of violence in different regions over the two years (see table 2.1). Two regions—Asia and Oceania, and the Middle East and North Africa—experienced significant declines in conflict-related deaths in 2022. Africa and the Americas saw increases and Europe saw a huge leap tied to Russia's war against Ukraine. The geography

---

[5] Gowan, R., 'The Ukraine war and UN reform', International Crisis Group, 6 May 2022; and Friedman, U., 'How the UN Security Council can reinvent itself', *The Atlantic*, 7 July 2022.

[6] See Pilling, D. and Schipani, A., 'War in Tigray may have killed 600 000 people, peace mediator says', *Financial Times*, 15 Jan. 2023; and Keaten, J., 'The calculus of war: Tallying Ukraine war an elusive task', *The Independent*, 24 Feb. 2023.

of armed conflict judged in terms of deaths rather than conflicts has altered decisively over the past five years. In 2017, Asian and Middle Eastern conflicts accounted for 71 per cent of all recorded conflict-related fatalities worldwide. In 2022, they accounted for just 31 per cent.

This rise and fall in regional death rates, however, is mainly attributable to the de-escalation and escalation of a few specific conflicts. The decline in death rates in Asia is almost entirely attributable to the decline in violence in Afghanistan after the Taliban seized power in 2021, while the slowing of the wars in Iraq and Syria are the main factors in the Middle East figures. Conversely, ACLED's data identifies three countries that experienced 'major wars' in statistical terms, where recorded conflict-related fatalities exceeded 10 000: Ukraine, Myanmar and Nigeria. In addition, reports suggest that ACLED's data under-reports fatalities in Ethiopia's Tigray province in 2022, which should probably also be regarded as a major war. ACLED further identified 16 high-intensity conflicts (1000 to 9999 fatalities) during the year: seven in Africa, four in the Americas, three in the Middle East and two in Asia (see section III, table 2.8).

Despite the major fluctuations in levels of conflict-related fatalities between 2021 and 2022, there were also notable continuities. There were no completely new wars on a significant scale in 2022 (Russia's all-out assault on Ukraine was itself an escalation of a conflict that had been running since 2014).[7] While some bloody conflicts did pause or de-escalate in the course of the year, the resulting peace deals are tentative and easily reversible. As in recent years, most conflicts were classifiable as intrastate armed conflicts (as opposed to interstate), but this definition is of limited utility for two reasons. First, many supposedly intrastate wars are now part of regional conflict formations, such as those in the Sahel and the Great Lakes; and, second, there was a high degree of 'internationalization' of civil wars and other internal conflicts, as outside actors offered direct or indirect support to the combatants.[8] In Africa, in particular, this regionalization and internationalization of conflict is associated with the persistence of transnational extremist jihadist organizations, although interstate competition is also a prominent factor.

Economic shocks, political instability and armed conflict

One global phenomenon that *could* have been associated with conflict trends in 2022 was the global economic turbulence associated with Russia's war on

---

[7] The combined total of conflict-related fatalities in states passing the baseline for 'armed conflict' (25 deaths) in 2022 that had not done so in 2021 was just over 300.

[8] An armed conflict is considered 'internationalized' if there is significant involvement by a foreign entity that is clearly prolonging or exacerbating the conflict, such as armed intervention in support of—or the provision of significant levels of weapons or military training to—one or more of the conflict parties by a foreign government or non-state actor, including private military companies. Multilateral peace operations are another form of internationalization of a conflict (see chapter 3 in this volume).

Table 2.2. Estimated conflict-related fatalities in the Americas, 2018–22

Country	2018	2019	2020	2021	2022
Brazil	6 463	4 909	5 033	5 546	6 434
Colombia	1 473	1 422	1 758	2 135	2 260
El Salvador	941	879	362	402	267
Guatemala	796	1 112	573	661	642
Haiti	229	374	520	584	1 227
Honduras	672	907	662	596	595
Jamaica	223	275	258	275	376
Mexico	9 799	9 362	8 411	8 280	7 793
Puerto Rico	124	144	114[a]	173	202
Trinidad and Tobago	242	178	159	185	275
Venezuela	1 859	2 489	2005	1396	827
Total	22 821	22 051	19 855	20 233	20 898

Notes: Fatality figures are collated from 4 event types: battles; explosions/remote violence; protests, riots and strategic developments; and violence against civilians. See Armed Conflict Location & Event Data Project (ACLED), 'ACLED definitions of political violence and protest', 11 Apr. 2019. A country is treated as being in an armed conflict if there were 25 or more battle-related deaths in a given year. The first available year for data on conflicts in the region in the ACLED database is 2018.

[a] Battle-related deaths were below 25.

Source: ACLED, 'Dashboard', accessed 10–11 Jan. 2023.

Ukraine—and the imposition by Western powers of wide-ranging sanctions on Russia—adding to existing pressures tied to Covid-19 recovery and already rising levels of inflation. Wheat and corn prices reached record highs in the first half of the year as a collapse in Ukrainian and Russian grain and fertilizer exports compounded existing agricultural supply problems.[9] Energy prices also rose sharply, which in turn made food exports more expensive.[10] Many observers feared that this combination of shocks would hit countries that were already experiencing conflict or political instability and were heavily reliant on food imports, such as Somalia and Lebanon, particularly hard.[11] While global food price increases began to level off from the second quarter of 2022, concerns about economic destabilization persisted throughout the year.

In retrospect, it seems safe to say that economic factors did contribute to an increase in political instability in 2022 but that this did *not* translate immediately into a rise in armed conflict. One study based on ACLED data identifies 12 500 food- and fuel-related protests in 150 countries in 2022, with the largest number of such protests in Pakistan, Ecuador, India, Indonesia and

---

[9] 'War and drought drove food prices to a record high in 2022', AP News, 7 Jan. 2023.

[10] Guénette, J-D. and Khadan, J., 'The energy shock could sap global growth for years', World Bank Blogs, 22 June 2022.

[11] See e.g. McGuirk, E. and Burke, M., 'War in Ukraine, world food prices and conflict in Africa', VoxEU, 26 May 2022; and Rahman, F., 'Lebanon is country worst hit by food-inflation crisis', *The National*, 4 Aug. 2022.

Nepal.¹² Although these events sometimes became violent—as when police in Sierra Leone fired on a group of protestors in August 2022, reportedly killing approximately 20 people—they did not generally escalate into larger-scale or prolonged violence.¹³ The most obvious example of this tendency was in Sri Lanka, where economic problems—largely the result of pressures that pre-dated Russia's invasion of Ukraine—led to a wave of protests and the fall of the government in June 2022.¹⁴ These protests did not escalate into sustained violence or the targeting of the country's Tamil or Muslim minorities.

In some cases, such as Haiti, economically motivated protests increased instability in already violent situations, adding to the problem of gang-related violence. Haitian gangs also targeted the country's fuel supply.¹⁵ Furthermore, it is worth noting that persistent economic deprivation and inequality is an established factor in many of the conflicts cited here. The expansion of transnational extremist jihadist groups in the Sahel, for example, is linked to a lack of economic opportunities for young men in the region, who turn to violence as a means of subsistence.¹⁶ In some conflict-affected states, such as Sudan, economic pain and surging inflation placed political actors under additional pressure throughout the year.¹⁷ While the economic fall-out from the Russian–Ukrainian War may have exacerbated these problems, it did not lead *directly* to new wars in 2022.

Regional conflict dynamics

Beneath the broad global trends noted above, a review of ACLED's data highlights that conflict dynamics continued to vary markedly across regions in 2022.

The Americas

The overall level of violence in the Americas remained fairly constant between 2021, with 20 233 conflict-related fatalities, and 2022, with 20 898 (see table 2.2). Most of the violence in the region was linked to organized

---

[12] Hossain, N. and Hallock, J., *Food, Energy and Cost of Living Protests, 2022* (Friedrich Ebert Stiftung: New York, Dec. 2022).

[13] Fofana, U. and Inveen, C., 'Freetown in shock after dozens killed in Sierra Leone protests', Reuters, 11 Aug. 2022.

[14] Keenan, A., 'Sri Lanka's uprising forces out a president but leaves system in crisis', International Crisis Group, 18 July 2022.

[15] Mérancourt, W. and Coletta, A., 'Steep fuel price hikes spark violent protests in Haiti', *Washington Post*, 16 Sep. 2022.

[16] Eizenga, D., 'Long terms trends across security and development in the Sahel', West African Papers no. 29 (Organisation for Economic Co-operation and Development: Paris, 2019).

[17] Oluwole, V., 'Top 10 African countries with the highest inflation rates in 2022', *Business Insider Africa*, 22 June 2022.

Table 2.3. Estimated conflict-related fatalities in Asia and Oceania, 2017–22

Country	2017	2018	2019	2020	2021	2022
Afghanistan	36 956	43 367	41 620	31 359	42 630	3 956
Bangladesh	228	243	382	278[a]	354[a]	308
India	1 418	2 170	1 536	1 341	1 013	905
Indonesia	49[a]	164	212	131	135	247
Kyrgyzstan	..	4[a]	8[a]	2[a]	32[b]	70[b]
Myanmar	1 408	262	1 514	687	11 011	19 357
Pakistan	1 720	1 225	1 157	835	1 409	1 785
Papua New Guinea	..	..	..	..	131	223
Philippines	4 355	2 107	1 704	1 497	1 163	890
Tajikistan	..	64[a]	66[a]	2[a]	20[b]	71[b]
Thailand	93	100	172	102	66	42[a]
Total	46 227	49 706	48 371	36 234	57 964	27 854

.. = Data not available.

Notes: Fatality figures are collated from 4 event types: battles; explosions/remote violence; protests, riots and strategic developments; and violence against civilians. See Armed Conflict Location & Event Data Project (ACLED), 'ACLED definitions of political violence and protest', 11 Apr. 2019. A country is treated as being in an armed conflict if there were 25 or more battle-related deaths in a given year.

[a] Battle-related deaths were below 25.
[b] Combined battle-related deaths exceeded 25.

Source: ACLED, 'Dashboard', accessed 13 Jan. 2023.

crime.[18] Central American governments pursued robust security operations against cartels and gangs. El Salvador declared a state of emergency in March and launched an anti-gang crackdown that made progress in weakening criminal groups but raised concerns about government repression.[19] Mexico also continued to pursue a highly securitized strategy against criminal organizations, claiming progress in reducing crime (ACLED data suggests fatalities in the country fell in 2022) but surges in criminal violence remained common.[20] In Colombia, by contrast, newly elected President Gustavo Petro promised a conciliatory approach to conflict resolution (see section II). The most striking surge in violence in the Americas, however, was in Haiti, where heavily armed gangs took control of swathes of the capital, Port-au-Prince, and its environs.[21] In September, the situation escalated when gang members blockaded the city's fuel terminal, cutting off gas supplies for two months.[22]

---

[18] For a discussion of gang–state violence in the Americas see 'Armed conflict and peace processes in the Americas', *SIPRI Yearbook 2022*, pp. 75–102.
[19] Quintanilla, J. and Phillips, T., 'El Salvador crackdown breaks the gangs: At huge cost to human rights', *The Guardian*, 20 Feb. 2023.
[20] 'Several violent episodes in Mexico suggest a worrying trend', *The Economist*, 1 Sep. 2022.
[21] International Crisis Group, 'Haiti's last resort: Gangs and the prospect of foreign intervention', Crisis Group Latin America and Caribbean Briefing no. 48, Brussels, 14 Dec. 2022.
[22] Isaac, H. and Ellsworth, B., 'Gang blockade cripples Haiti fuel supplies, hospitals prepare to close', Reuters, 27 Sep. 2022.

Asia and Oceania

In Asia, the number of conflict-related fatalities in Afghanistan fell sharply from over 40 000 in 2021 to fewer than 4000 in 2022, as the Taliban imposed its rule on the country (see table 2.3). The Taliban faced ongoing challenges from Islamic State–Khorasan Province (ISKP) and the National Resistance Front (NRF), a group based in the north of the country.[23] ISKP has carried out bombings in Kabul but neither group yet presents a serious threat to Taliban rule. Despite the much reduced level of violence, Afghans faced dire economic conditions throughout 2022. More than 24 million people required humanitarian assistance and the Taliban placed new curbs on women's rights.[24] While the USA and its allies have largely given up on counterterrorist operations in Afghanistan, the USA made an exception when it killed al-Qaeda leader Ayman Zawahiri in Kabul in a drone strike.[25] The number of attacks on Pakistan's security forces on its border with Afghanistan increased, possibly linked to the Afghan Taliban harbouring its Pakistani allies, while Pakistan endured an extended political crisis following the ousting of Prime Minister Imran Khan by parliament.[26]

There were also varying types of instability and armed conflict across other parts of Asia in 2022. In January, widespread protests broke out in Kazakhstan over economic issues. The Collective Security Treaty Organization (CSTO) deployed troops at the request of the government to help maintain order, in an operation that lasted less than two weeks.[27] There were border clashes between Kyrgyz and Tajik forces throughout the year, including a serious flare-up in mid September, but the two sides were able to agree ceasefires before any incidents escalated out of control.[28] In South Asia, there was a spike in violence in Kashmir, as anti-Indian militant groups targeted the region's Hindu minority.[29] China and India continued their long-standing border dispute. Chinese forces entered Indian-administered territory in Arunachal Pradesh in December but there was no flare-up equivalent to

---

[23] International Crisis Group, 'Afghanistan's security challenges under the Taliban', Asia Report no. 326, Brussels, 12 Aug. 2022.

[24] UN Office for the Coordination of Humanitarian Affairs et al., *Humanitarian Needs Overview: Afghanistan*, Humanitarian Programme Cycle 2023, Jan. 2023.

[25] Plummer, R. and Murphy, M., 'Ayman al-Zawahiri: Al-Qaeda leader killed in drone strike', BBC News, 2 Aug. 2022.

[26] See 'Pakistan' in International Crisis Group, 'Ten conflicts to watch in 2023', Global commentary, 1 Jan. 2023.

[27] Hegglin, O., 'The CSTO and its deployment in Kazakhstan', Human Security Centre, 8 Feb. 2022. See also chapter 3, section I, in this volume.

[28] Sultanalieva, S., 'Kyrgyzstan-Tajikistan border clashes prove deadly for civilians', Human Rights Watch, 21 Sep. 2022.

[29] International Crisis Group, 'Violence in Kashmir: Why a spike in killings signals an ominous new trend', 28 June 2022.

the 2020 clash at Galwan, which resulted in fatalities on both sides.[30] China also increased military pressure on Taiwan, doubling the number of its air sorties into the Taiwanese Air Defence Identification Zone in the course of 2022, notably in response to the visit of US House of Representatives Speaker Nancy Pelosi to the island in August.[31] In the Philippines, by contrast, the government made progress in the peace process with the Moro Islamic Liberation Front (MILF) in Mindanao, and the movement engaged in local elections for the first time in May.[32]

Myanmar

The most dramatic surge in violence in Asia took place in Myanmar, where a patchwork coalition of armed groups and militias continued to resist the military regime that took power in a coup d'état in 2021.[33] The military State Administration Council (SAC) and its allies faced a range of opponents, which included civilian protestors, a civil disobedience movement, long-standing ethnic armed organizations (EAOs) and a large number of anti-coup militias, including the People's Defence Forces (PDFs), a loose coalition of armed groups broadly loyal to the anti-junta National Unity Government (NUG). Estimates of the number of PDF groups, which one analysis describes as 'small cells of people who oppose the coup' rather than formed military units, ranged from the hundreds to the thousands in 2022.[34] The NUG's political control or influence over these local forces is limited. Although the NUG declared a 'people's war' against the military in September 2021, the resulting conflict has been fragmented, involving varying coalitions of armed actors in different regions.

Anti-SAC groups carried out bombings and other attacks in urban centres, including the commercial capital Yangon, but the SAC maintained control of these cities.[35] The majority of the violence took place in rural areas, which are home to two-thirds of Myanmar's population. PDF units largely made up of civilians were particularly active in the Dry Zone of central Myanmar, launching ambushes and improvised explosive device attacks against the pro-SAC Pyusawhti militia and the army.[36] While the junta ratcheted up attacks on its

---

[30] Lalwani, S. P., Markey, D. and Singh, V., 'Another clash on the India-China border underscores risks of militarisation', US Institute of Peace, 20 Dec. 2022.

[31] AFP, 'China's warplane incursions into Taiwan air defence zone doubled in 2022', *The Guardian*, 1 Jan. 2023.

[32] Engelbrecht, G., 'Ballots and bullets in Bangsamoro', International Crisis Group, 20 June 2022.

[33] International Crisis Group, 'Myanmar's coup shakes up its ethnic conflicts', Asia Report no. 319, Brussels, 12 Jan. 2022.

[34] Loong, S., 'Post-coup Myanmar in six warscapes', International Institute for Strategic Studies, 10 June 2022.

[35] Robinson, G., 'Yangon's calm masks Myanmar's pain a year after military takeover', *Financial Times*, 9 Feb. 2022.

[36] Loong, S., 'The Dry Zone: An existential struggle in central Myanmar', International Institute for Strategic Studies, 5 July 2022.

opponents in the first quarter of 2022—burning homes, executing detainees and allegedly using children as human shields in at least one incident—its forces failed to reassert full control and resistance attacks continued through the year.[37]

In other parts of the country, existing EAOs continued to play a central role in the conflict. In south-eastern Myanmar, the Karen National Union (KNU) and Karenni National Progressive Party (KNPP) allied with newer post-coup groups and have been politically supportive of the NUG.[38] The military and the SAC responded with similar tactics to those used in the Dry Zone, frequently resorting to air strikes against population centres. In north-eastern Myanmar, by contrast, most EAOs kept their political distance from the NUG, although a few fought independent campaigns against the SAC throughout the year.[39] Shan State also experienced fighting among the EAOs themselves. In Rakhine State, on the border with Bangladesh, the site of the ethnic cleansing of the Rohingya in 2016–17, the Arakan Army (AA) maintained an informal ceasefire with SAC forces throughout the first half of 2022. The AA, which is seeking a quasi-independent enclave inside Myanmar, took advantage of the junta's focus on other areas to consolidate its control in rural areas.[40] However, the AA declined to enter formal peace talks with the SAC in June, and hostilities between the two sides reignited in July when the military launched air attacks on AA bases.[41] The two sides agreed a new informal ceasefire in late November, which held for the remainder of the year, although there is little sign of the AA or the SAC wanting to move to more durable peace talks.[42]

By the end of the year, Myanmar appeared to be locked in an open-ended cycle of conflict and fragmentation. While the NUG and PDFs remained splintered in most regions, they also proved durable, using online fundraising targeted at the diaspora to fund their campaigns.[43] Data gathered by ACLED shows the military becoming more reliant on air strikes across the country, highlighting the SAC's preference for punishment and containment rather

---

[37] Radio Free Asia (RFA), 'Myanmar junta soldiers said to have held preschoolers as "human shields" after raid', RFA Myanmar Service, 28 Feb. 2022.

[38] Loong, S., 'Southeast Myanmar: A shared struggle for federal democracy', International Institute for Strategic Studies, 23 Sep. 2022.

[39] Loong, S., 'Northeast Myanmar: Three axes of conflict', International Institute for Strategic Studies, 16 Aug. 2022.

[40] International Crisis Group, 'Avoiding a return to war in Myanmar's Rakhine State', Asia Report no. 325, Brussels, 1 June 2022.

[41] Hlaing, H. W., 'Insurgents in Rakhine State return to war on the military', US Institute for Peace, 3 Oct. 2022.

[42] Radio Free Asia (RFA), 'Myanmar military, Arakan Army halt hostilities on humanitarian grounds', RFA Burmese, 28 Nov. 2022.

[43] International Crisis Group, 'Crowdfunding a war: The money behind Myanmar's resistance', Asia Report no. 328, 20 Dec. 2022.

than the more difficult task of subduing its opponents—even though it vastly outguns them.[44]

Peacemaking efforts led by the Association of Southeast Asian Nations (ASEAN) and the UN made little progress. Prime Minister Hun Sen of Cambodia, which chaired ASEAN in 2022, visited Myanmar in January but made little impact on the political situation and faced criticism from other members for the initiative.[45] The SAC failed to make any progress on implementation of the Five-Point Consensus agreed with ASEAN in April 2021, and angered the grouping by executing four political opponents in July, despite pleas for clemency from Hun Sen. ASEAN continued its 2021 policy of excluding representatives of the junta from its key meetings, including a summit with US President Joe Biden in May.[46] Although the SAC initiated peace talks with a number of EAOs in mid 2022, most observers dismissed this as window dressing and the EAOs that are actively fighting the regime did not participate.[47] Cambodia's foreign minister and ASEAN special envoy for Myanmar, Prak Sokhonn, announced that the SAC was willing to talk to the NUG in July, but the SAC's terms, which included the NUG renouncing its opposition to military rule, were unrealistic.[48] UN envoy Noeleen Heyzer visited Myanmar in August but her meetings were unproductive and the SAC refused to let her see the jailed civilian leader, Aung San Suu Kyi.[49]

In November, ASEAN leaders agreed at their annual summit to continue to exclude SAC representatives from key meetings but stepped back from imposing further penalties on the junta.[50] The SAC made one positive gesture to the opposition on 17 November, marking Myanmar's National Day by pardoning 6000 prisoners including some high-profile political detainees.[51] However, the SAC began pressing ahead with preparations for national elections in 2023, which many observers fear will be a lightning rod for further violence.[52] In December, the UN Security Council passed its first full resolution on Myanmar (see section II) calling for an end to the violence, a

[44] Head J., 'Myanmar: Airstrikes have become deadly new tactic in the civil war', BBC News, 31 Jan. 2023.
[45] Nachemson, A., 'Misreading the room: Why Hun Sen is failing on Myanmar', Al Jazeera, 30 Mar. 2022.
[46] Widakuswara, P., 'Empty chair for Myanmar in US–ASEAN special summit', Voice of America, 12 May 2022.
[47] 'Myanmar junta seeks to divide and rule in EAO peace talks', Mizzima, 6 June 2022.
[48] Strangio, S., 'ASEAN envoy hails "some progress" on second Myanmar mission', The Diplomat, 7 July 2022.
[49] Peck, G. and Lederer E. M., 'UN envoys tells Myanmar general: End violence, seek democracy', AP News, 17 Aug. 2022.
[50] Association of Southeast Asian Nations, 'ASEAN leaders' review and decision on the implementation of the five-point consensus', Statement, 11 Nov. 2022.
[51] 'Some political prisoners among almost 6000 freed in Myanmar junta amnesty', The Irrawaddy, 17 Nov. 2022. The SAC announced a further mass amnesty for over 7000 prisoners in Jan. 2023.
[52] International Crisis Group, 'A road to nowhere: The Myanmar regime's stage-managed elections', Asia Briefing no. 175, Brussels, 28 Mar. 2023.

return to democracy and cooperation with ASEAN. This was in part meant to be a signal to Indonesia, ASEAN chair in 2023, to push more actively for inclusive dialogue between the key players, including anti-coup forces.

Europe: Russia's war on Ukraine

The situation in Europe dominated international relations throughout the year. Russia's full-scale invasion of Ukraine on 24 February, which was apparently planned as a short operation to oust Ukrainian President Volodymyr Zelensky from office, morphed into the first large-scale war in Europe since the Balkan wars of the 1990s after the initial Russian offensive was repelled in March and April. The war, which increasingly pivoted around large-scale artillery battles as the conflict dragged on, raised fundamental questions about the future of the European and global security orders, including the taboo against nuclear weapon use.

The USA and its allies warned loudly of Russia's military build-up around Ukraine, including in Belarus, throughout the last quarter of 2021 and in the first months of 2022.[53] A series of meetings between Western and Russian officials to discuss European security issues in January bore little fruit.[54] The crisis accelerated on 21 February when the Russian government formally recognized Dontesk and Luhansk (the secessionist regions of eastern Ukraine outside Kyiv's control since 2014) as independent republics and promised to send a 'peacekeeping force' to protect them.[55] This pretext for invasion was not given long to develop. On 24 February, Russia launched a full-scale assault on Ukraine, seizing territory in the south of the country while attacking Kyiv from the north. The offensive on the capital soon stuttered as Ukrainian forces put up unexpectedly stiff resistance and the Russian army was hampered by poor planning and logistics.[56] On 29 March, Russia announced that it was reducing operations on the Kyiv front.[57] Ukrainian forces found evidence of Russian atrocities, including a massacre of hundreds of civilians in the town of Bucha.[58]

The military focus shifted to Ukraine's south-eastern coast as Russian forces attempted to consolidate early gains by capturing the city of Mariupol.[59]

---

[53] For a narrative on pre-war diplomacy see Harris, S. et al., 'Road to war: US struggled to convince allies, and Zelensky, of risk of invasion', *Washington Post*, 16 Aug. 2022.

[54] Pifer, S., 'After US–Russia, NATO-Russia, and OSCE meetings, what next?', Brookings Institution, 13 Jan. 2022.

[55] 'Putin orders Russian forces to "perform peacekeeping functions" in eastern Ukraine's breakaway regions', Reuters, 22 Feb. 2022.

[56] For a detailed analysis of Russia's plans and initial operations, see Zabrodskyi, M. et al., *Preliminary Lessons in Conventional Warfighting from Russia's invasion of Ukraine* (Royal United Services Institute: London, 30 Nov. 2022).

[57] Jack, V. and Gijs, C., 'Russia says that it will reduce Kyiv offensive to "increase trust" for future peace talks', Politico, 29 Mar. 2022.

[58] Human Rights Watch, 'Ukraine: Russian forces' trail of death in Bucha', 21 Apr. 2022.

[59] 'Mariupol: Key moments in the siege of the city', BBC News, 17 May 2022.

The siege of Mariupol, which culminated in fighting in and around the gigantic Azovstal steelworks, ended in May, leaving the city devastated. In parallel, Russia suffered an embarrassing setback at sea when Ukraine sank the flagship of the Black Sea Fleet, the *Moskva*, on 14 April.[60] Russian forces secured additional territory in eastern Ukraine in the months that followed, but the pace of their advance was now grinding.[61] The war increasingly involved massive artillery exchanges, with both sides expending huge quantities of munitions.[62]

Throughout the third quarter of 2022, Ukraine signalled that it was preparing to launch a counteroffensive. Ukrainian forces retook some 12 000 square kilometres of north-eastern Ukraine around Kharkiv in under two weeks, pushing back ill-prepared Russian units.[63] Russia responded by announcing the annexation of the Ukrainian oblasts under its control or partial control in late September, after brief 'referendums' in the regions which the UN General Assembly declared illegal.[64] Ukraine also fought a protracted battle to retake the southern city of Kherson, from which Russian forces withdrew in November.[65]

Russia had been carrying out missile attacks on targets across Ukraine from the first days of the war, but it began more systematic attacks on Ukraine's energy infrastructure in the third quarter of the year.[66] Russia accelerated these attacks after a successful Ukrainian sabotage operation against the Kerch Bridge, which connects Crimea to Russia, in October. Russia's overarching goal appeared to be to break the Ukrainian will to fight by creating widespread power shortages over the winter.[67] In addition to its missile stocks, Russia used Iranian-made drones in this campaign, cementing ties between the two countries.[68] While the Russian campaign caused many temporary blackouts in Ukraine (which would continue into 2023), as well as

---

[60] Russia attributed the sinking to an unexplained fire aboard the ship. Hauser, J., '1 dead and 27 missing after Russian flagship *Moskva* sunk in Black Sea', CNN, 22 Apr. 2022.

[61] See e.g. 'Russia advances in battle for key eastern Ukrainian city', Al Jazeera, 19 June 2022.

[62] De Luce, D., Kube, C. and Lee, C. E., 'Who will win in Ukraine? It could hinge on which side can secure enough artillery ammunition', NBC News, 13 Dec. 2022.

[63] Khurshudyan, I. et al., 'Inside the Ukrainian counteroffensive that shocked Putin and reshaped the war', *Washington Post*, 29 Dec. 2022.

[64] 'Russia annexes four Ukrainian regions', Deutsche Welle, 30 Sep. 2022; and United Nations, 'Ukraine: UN General Assembly demands Russia reverse course on "attempted illegal annexation"', UN News, 12 Oct. 2022.

[65] Rácz, A., 'Russia's withdrawal from Kherson', German Council on Foreign Relations (DGAP), 10 Nov. 2022.

[66] Schlein, L., 'UN: Half of Ukraine's energy infrastructure destroyed by Russian attacks', Voice of America, 13 Dec. 2022.

[67] Glanz, J. and Hernandez, M., 'How Ukraine blew up a key Russian bridge', *New York Times*, 17 Nov. 2022.

[68] Grove, T., 'Russia launches new drone attacks as partnership with Iran deepens', *Wall Street Journal*, 10 Dec. 2022.

significant civilian casualties, there was no sign of a collapse in public morale by December.

Throughout the war, Russian President Vladimir Putin and other Russian officials, backed by voluble media commentators, signalled a willingness to use nuclear weapons in the war if North Atlantic Treaty Organization (NATO) member states intervened directly.[69] While US officials consistently maintained that they saw no sign of Russia preparing for imminent battlefield nuclear weapon use, there was widespread international concern about the risks related to the fighting around the Zaporizhzhia Nuclear Power Plant in southern Ukraine, which Russian troops used as a military base.[70] Russia's warnings of nuclear weapon use disturbed Western decision makers. President Biden warned of a risk of 'Armageddon' in October.[71] Especially around the Group of Twenty (G20) summit in November, the USA and its allies lobbied hard and successfully for China and other major non-Western powers to warn against nuclear weapon use.[72] These efforts and back-channel talks seemed to ease US concerns about Russia's intentions.[73]

While primarily fought on the battlefield, the war was accompanied by a wider 'war of narratives' as both sides used information campaigns to shape global perceptions of the conflict—especially through social media.[74] Russia floated a series of allegations, including in the UN Security Council, that the USA had maintained a biological weapon programme in Ukraine. (The Chinese authorities were also keen to amplify these claims.)[75] In October, Russia claimed that Ukraine was working on a 'dirty bomb' using nuclear materials, although an investigation by the International Atomic Energy Agency (IAEA) helped dispel this allegation.[76] Overall, Ukraine decisively won the battle to shape the public narrative about the war in Europe and the USA throughout 2022; although some Republican politicians continued to oppose the USA investing heavily in support of the Ukrainian government, Russia had more success in selling its narrative to non-Western audiences.[77]

There were few openings for a peaceful end to the war. In the first months of hostilities, Ukrainian and Russian representatives met for talks in Belarus

---

[69] Horovitz, L. and Wachs, L., 'Russia's nuclear threats in the war against Ukraine', German Institute for International and Security Affairs, 20 Apr. 2022.

[70] Bachega, H., 'Russia using Zaporizhzhia Nuclear Power Plant as army base, Ukraine', BBC News, 8 Aug. 2022.

[71] Blake, A., 'Biden's scary invocation of nuclear "Armageddon"', Washington Post, 7 Oct. 2022.

[72] Bugos, S., 'G-20 majority condemns Russian nuclear threats', Arms Control Today, Dec. 2022.

[73] Barnes, J. E. and Sanger, D. E., 'Fears of Russian nuclear weapons use have diminished, but could re-emerge', New York Times, 3 Feb. 2023.

[74] Butcher, E., 'War of narratives: Russia and Ukraine', Royal United Services Institute, 16 May 2022.

[75] Rising, D., 'China amplifies unsupported Russian claim of Ukraine biolabs', AP News, 11 Mar. 2022. See also chapter 9, section II, in this volume.

[76] Borger, D., 'Russia steps up Ukraine "dirty bomb" claim in letter delivered to UN', The Guardian, 25 Oct. 2022.

[77] See e.g. Blankenship, M. and Ordu, A. U., 'Russia's narratives about its invasion of Ukraine are lingering in Africa', Brookings Institution, 27 June 2022.

Table 2.4. Estimated conflict-related fatalities in Europe, 2018–22

Country	2018	2019	2020	2021	2022
Armenia	6[b]	2[a]	27	24[b]	217
Azerbaijan	47[b]	14[a]	7 057	33[b]	68
Russia	121	46	56	26[a]	105[a]
Ukraine	889	403	113	149	28 357[c]
Total	**1 063**	**465**	**7 253**	**232**	**28 747**

Notes: Fatality figures are collated from 4 event types: battles; explosions/remote violence; protests, riots and strategic developments; and violence against civilians. See Armed Conflict Location & Event Data Project (ACLED), 'ACLED definitions of political violence and protest', 11 Apr. 2019. A country is treated as being in an armed conflict if there were 25 or more battle-related deaths in a given year. The first available year for data on conflicts in the region in the ACLED database is 2018.

[a] Battle-related deaths were below 25.
[b] Combined battle-related deaths exceeded 25.
[c] May be a severe underestimate (see table 2.8).

Source: ACLED, 'Dashboard', accessed 18 Jan. 2023.

and Türkiye.[78] Both Russian and Western sources have claimed that a deal seemed close in April—possibly involving a Ukrainian pledge not to join NATO in return for a Russian withdrawal to the lines of 23 February—but the details are unclear.[79] Early on in the war, President Zelensky floated ideas for a new system of security guarantees for Ukraine as part of a peace settlement.[80] As the war continued, however, the public positions of both sides hardened. Russia's purported annexation of Ukrainian territory in September made the prospects for diplomacy even narrower. In November, Zelensky proposed a ten-point peace plan that included ideas—such as Russia paying reparations or the establishment of a tribunal that could in theory try Putin for the crime of aggression—that Russia would be highly unlikely ever to countenance.[81] While the overall lack of progress towards peace did not stop Russia and Ukraine agreeing to some steps to mitigate the effects of the war, most notably the Black Sea Grain Initiative (see section II), both sides appeared resigned to the possibility of a long conflict by the end of 2022.

Other European conflicts

The war in Ukraine also had knock-on effects on other conflicts and vulnerable states in the region (see table 2.4). Western officials were especially concerned that Russia would aim to destabilize Moldova in parallel with

---

[78] 'Ukraine, Russia hold third round of talks', Deutsche Welle, 7 Mar. 2022; and 'Russia, Ukraine fail to make progress at "difficult" Turkey talks', AFP, 10 Mar. 2022.

[79] Hill, F. and Stent, A., 'The world Putin wants', *Foreign Affairs*, Sep./Oct. 2022.

[80] Gijs, C., 'Zelenskyy: Ukraine ready to discuss neutral status to reach Russia peace deal', Politico, 28 Mar. 2022.

[81] 'Explainer: What is Zelenskyy's 10-point peace plan?', Reuters, 28 Dec. 2022.

Ukraine, although the country managed to avoid a major political crisis in 2022 despite the huge economic pressures it faced.[82]

Having scored a significant military victory over Armenia in 2020 in their long-running struggle for Nagorno-Karabakh, Azerbaijan appears to have seen Russia's focus on Ukraine as an opportunity to put more pressure on Armenia. The two sides clashed in July, August and September.[83] Despite mediation efforts by Russia and the European Union (EU), tensions remained high. In December, an unofficial but probably officially blessed group of 'activists' from Azerbaijan blockaded the Lachin corridor linking Nagorno-Karabakh to Armenian-held territory, limiting supplies to civilians.[84]

There were also tensions in the Western Balkans, and particularly in Kosovo, throughout 2022, although these did not escalate into full-scale armed conflict. A dispute over car registration created renewed frictions between the government of Kosovo and the Serb minority in the summer, and in July 2022 some Serbs started to set up roadblocks around their villages.[85] While the USA and the EU mediated a deal to ease the crisis, it escalated again in November, when ethnic-Serb police and officials resigned en masse over the registration issue, and Kosovo Serbs barricaded the main border crossing with Serbia. Serbia put its military on alert and asked NATO for permission to deploy 1000 soldiers inside Kosovo under the terms of UN Security Council Resolution 1244.[86] By the end of the month, there were signs that the crisis was starting to simmer down, and the Kosovo Serbs agreed to dismantle their barricades on 29 December.[87]

Middle East and North Africa

In the Middle East and North Africa, there was a significant increase in conflict-related fatalities in Iraq from 2844 in 2021 to 4483 in 2022 (see table 2.5). A political stand-off over the formation of a new government led to factional violence in Baghdad in August, but the eventual agreement on a new cabinet in October at least temporarily eased the crisis.[88] The most significant decrease in recorded fatalities was in Yemen, where the UN succeeded

---

[82] These concerns increased in Apr. and May following a series of unexplained explosions in the secessionist region of Transnistria. Pronczuk, M., 'Explosions rattle a breakaway region in Moldova, raising fears of a broader war', *New York Times*, 26 Apr. 2022.

[83] International Crisis Group, 'Averting a new war between Armenia and Azerbaijan', Europe Report no. 266, Brussels, 30 Jan. 2023.

[84] 'Tensions rise between Armenia and Azerbaijan over blocked supply corridor', Reuters, 15 Dec. 2022.

[85] 'Kosovo government postpones its plan for volatile north after tensions rise', Reuters, 31 July 2022.

[86] UN Security Council Resolution 1244, 10 June 1999; and Stojanovic, M., 'Serbia considering sending 1000 "security personnel" into Kosovo', Balkan Insight, 9 Dec. 2022.

[87] 'Kosovo: Serbs agree to dismantle barricades after talks', BBC News, 29 Dec. 2022.

[88] Davison, J., 'Iraqi cleric Sadr calls off protests after worst Baghdad violence in years', Reuters, 30 Aug. 2022; and Abdul-Zahra, Q., 'Iraqi Parliament approves new cabinet in long-awaited vote', AP News, 28 Oct. 2022.

Table 2.5. Estimated conflict-related fatalities in the Middle East and North Africa, 2017–22

Country	2017	2018	2019	2020	2021	2022
Egypt	1 540	1 116	1 003	626	264	273
Iraq	32 486	5 676	3 719	2 844	2 844	4 483
Iran	182	254	480	436	221	576
Israel–Palestine	118	412	184	51[a]	383	221
Jordan	35[a]	6[a]	7[a]	7[a]	2[a]	38
Lebanon	391	36[a]	25[a]	48	74	56
Libya	1 735	1 258	2 294	1 560	115	165
Syria	54 574	30 045	15 639	8 211	5 876	5 649
Türkiye	2928	1 940	962	569	310	274
Yemen	17 872	34 348	28 051	19 753	18 404	6 736
Total	**111 861**	**75 091**	**52 364**	**34 105**	**28 493**	**18 471**

Notes: Fatality figures are collated from 4 event types: battles; explosions/remote violence; protests, riots and strategic developments; and violence against civilians. See Armed Conflict Location & Event Data Project (ACLED), 'ACLED definitions of political violence and protest', 11 Apr. 2019. A country is treated as being in an armed conflict if there were 25 or more battle-related deaths in a given year.

[a] Battle-related deaths were below 25.

Source: ACLED, 'Dashboard', accessed 18 Jan. 2023.

in negotiating a humanitarian truce between the UN-backed government and the Houthi forces in April.[89] This formally held until October. Although violence never ceased entirely, the deal allowed an increase in aid deliveries, and the level of violence remained lower even after the formal end of the truce.[90] The level of violence in both Syria and Libya remained fairly consistent with 2021. While Türkiye was widely reported to be planning a military incursion into north-east Syria, targeting Kurdish groups in the region, and Turkish aircraft carried out a series of air strikes in the region in November, it did not launch a ground operation.[91]

Violence between Israeli forces and Palestinians claimed 146 Palestinian lives in the West Bank in the course of 2022, the highest figure since 2004.[92] New Palestinian armed groups unaffiliated with the Palestinian Authority emerged in the West Bank—starting in the city of Jenin—and clashed with Israeli forces.[93] Israel also launched air strikes on Gaza in August targeting the Palestinian Islamic Jihad (PIJ) group, but Hamas—the main force in

---

[89] Office of the Special Envoy of the Secretary-General for Yemen, 'Timeline on the progress of the truce implementation', Updated 3 Apr. 2023.

[90] Armed Conflict Location & Event Data Project, 'Violence in Yemen during the UN-mediated truce, April–October 2022', 14 Oct. 2022.

[91] PBS Newshour, 'What's at stake in Turkey's military escalation in Syria?', AP Beirut, 10 Dec. 2022.

[92] Berger, M., '2022 was the deadliest year for West Bank Palestinians in almost two decades', *Washington Post*, 29 Dec. 2022.

[93] International Crisis Group, 'The new generation of Palestinian armed groups: A paper tiger?', 17 Apr. 2023.

Gaza—did not engage in these hostilities.[94] Palestinian attacks claimed 29 Israeli lives in 2022.[95]

In North Africa, the UN's efforts to forge a unity government in Libya lost steam during the year, although the country's factions largely refrained from violence, despite a flare-up of fighting in Tripoli in August.[96] The Moroccan military and Saharawi forces continued to fight a low-level conflict in Western Sahara.[97]

Sub-Saharan Africa

Sub-Saharan Africa was the continent where the highest number of countries (22 of 53) experienced conflict in 2022. More than half these involved fewer than 1000 conflicted-related deaths (see table 2.6). There was an increase in violence in the Sahel and West Africa, however, linked in part to increasing violence in Burkina Faso, Mali and Niger involving a mix of transnational extremist jihadist groups and local insurgents. The combined number of conflict-related deaths in the three countries approached 10 000—the statistical definition of a major conflict—and a large percentage of these fatalities took place in the tri-border area where they meet. By one estimate, jihadists killed 5000 civilians in this area in 2022, taking advantage of the lack of state control. There was more evidence of jihadist groups spreading violence further into littoral West Africa in 2022, again taking advantage of limited state capacity and porous borders.[98] Jihadist groups attacked and kidnapped civilians in northern Benin and Togo in a series of incidents in 2022, and there were warnings of spillover risks to Ghana.[99]

This expanding violence took place in parallel with a significant reconfiguration of the international security presence in the region. France wound up its regional counterterrorist force, Operation Barkhane, between March and November.[100] The withdrawal followed a breakdown in relations with the post-coup authorities in Mali, which ostentatiously leaned towards Russia as 2022 progressed. Task Force Takuba, a multinational military force in support of Operation Barkhane involving special forces from France's

---

[94] Youssef, H., 'Israel-Gaza conflict: A short confrontation with disproportionate implications', US Institute of Peace, 30 Aug. 2022.

[95] Berger (note 92).

[96] UN News, 'Libya: Political stalemate and lack of progress on elections', 30 Aug. 2022.

[97] Betteridge-Moss, M., 'Western Sahara's "frozen conflict" heats up, but world's attention elsewhere', *New Humanitarian*, 1 Feb. 2023.

[98] Africa Center for Strategic Studies, 'Five zones of militant Islamist violence in the Sahel', 26 Sep. 2022.

[99] Brottem, L., 'Jihad takes root in northern Benin', Armed Conflict Location & Event Data Project, 23 Sep. 2022; and Promediation, *The Jihadist Threat in Northern Ghana and Togo: Stocktaking and Prospects for Containing the Expansion* (Abidjan: Konrad Adenauer Stiftung, Mar. 2022).

[100] Petrini, B., 'Security in the Sahel and the end of Operation Barkhane', International Institute for Strategic Studies, 5 Sep. 2022; and Vincent, E., 'After ten years, France to end military operation Barkhane in the Sahel', *Le Monde* (English edn), 9 Nov. 2022.

Table 2.6. Estimated conflict-related fatalities in sub-Saharan Africa, 2017–22

Country	2017	2018	2019	2020	2021	2022
West Africa	6 519	8 885	10 967	15 187	16 620	21 244
Benin	18[a]	31[a]	37[a]	64	93	180
Burkina Faso	117	303	2 216	2 304	2 374	4 242
Côte d'Ivoire	43[a]	14[a]	46[a]	132	38[a]	45
Ghana	89	25[a]	48[a]	48[a]	38[a]	142
Guinea	47[a]	39[a]	41[a]	145	28[a]	38[a]
Mali	942	1 747	1 875	2 856	1 913	4 795
Niger	240	506	729	1 126	1 498	990
Nigeria	4 979	6 215	5 968	8 499	10 634	10 734
Togo	44[a]	5[a]	7[a]	13[a]	4[a]	78
Central Africa	6 087	6 345	6 300	9 114	10 200	9 032
Angola	66	41[a]	23[a]	74	150[a]	105
Cameroon	745	1 663	1 308	1 767	1 425	1 003
Central African Republic	1 799	1 171	596	446	1 708	839
Chad	296	259	567	738	831	696
Congo, Democratic Republic of the	3 181	3 211	3 806	6 089	6 086	6 389
East Africa	15 147	10 992	9 545	13 722	18 794	19 586
Burundi	290[a]	326	305	331	304	258
Ethiopia	1 347	1 565	670	4 057	9 053	6 663[b]
Kenya	781	410	276	311	393	551
Madagascar	218	142	350	354	304	332
Mozambique	130	224	692	1 785	1 161	928
Somalia	6 156	5 420	4 512	3 255	3 262	6 520
South Sudan	4 846	1 704	1 801	2 382	2 160	1 906
Sudan	1 313	1 055	776	959	1 650	2 065
Uganda	66	146[a]	163	288	507	363
Total	**27 553**	**26 222**	**26 812**	**38 023**	**45 614**	**49 862**

Notes: Fatality figures are collated from 4 event types: battles; explosions/remote violence; protests, riots and strategic developments; and violence against civilians. See Armed Conflict Location & Event Data Project (ACLED), 'ACLED definitions of political violence and protest', 11 Apr. 2019. A country is treated as being in an armed conflict if there were 25 or more battle-related deaths in a given year.

[a] Battle-related deaths were below 25.
[b] Likely to be a severe underestimate (see table 2.8 and section II of this chapter).

Source: ACLED, 'Dashboard', accessed 19–26 Jan. 2023.

European allies, suspended joint operations with Malian forces in February and left Mali in June.[101] There were also significant questions about the viability of the UN Multidimensional Integrated Stabilization Mission in Mali, which faced ongoing guerrilla attacks, losing 15 personnel to malicious acts in 2022, and tense relations with the military authorities. A number of countries, among them Germany, Sweden and the United Kingdom, announced

[101] Swedish Armed Forces, 'Task Force Takuba suspended: New challenges await the special forces', 25 Apr. 2022; and AFP, 'EU's Takuba anti-terror force quits junta-controlled Mali', Euractiv.com, 1 July 2022.

that they would leave the mission.[102] Mali's withdrawal from the Group of Five for the Sahel (G5 Sahel) following a dispute over whether the country's government, which took power in a 2021 coup, could chair the G5 Sahel reduced the group's ability to handle jihadists. West African leaders therefore focused coordination of their struggle with the jihadists through other regional means, such as the Accra Initiative—a framework for intelligence sharing and joint military efforts.[103]

The erosion of established operations in the Sahel was tied to Mali's decision to invite the Wagner Group, a Russian private military company, into the country in late 2021.[104] Western observers were already worried about Wagner's operations in Africa and the Middle East, but the group's direct involvement in Ukraine alongside Russian regular forces throughout 2022 raised further concerns about its activities elsewhere.[105] Wagner had developed a predatory reputation among the populations it was meant to protect in the Central African Republic (CAR), where it was first deployed in 2017.[106] In both CAR and Mali, the presence of Russian private contractors appears to have encouraged the host government to become less cooperative with the UN by, for example, limiting the movements of UN forces in areas where Wagner is undertaking operations. There have also been allegations of human rights abuses.[107] In March 2022, Malian and Wagner forces are alleged to have killed up to 300 civilians in the central Malian town of Moura.[108] In parallel, Russia has supplied arms to both countries and taken their side in UN Security Council debates. (Mali and CAR avoided voting against Russia's interests in UN General Assembly debates on Ukraine throughout 2022.)

Jihadist violence was a major factor in the high level of violence in Nigeria, although by no means the only driver of conflict in the country. Having won a brutal internecine conflict against jihadist rivals in 2021, Islamic State–West Africa Province (ISWAP, a breakaway faction of Boko Haram) continued to terrorize civilians in north-east Nigeria and neighbouring areas of Chad and Niger.[109] The group also organized a high-profile prison break in the capital,

---

[102] There is data on fatalities on the United Nations Peacekeeping website. See also the discussion on MINUSMA in chapter 3, section II, in this volume.

[103] Mensah, K., 'West African leaders seek solutions to curb terrorism from Sahel region', Voice of America, 22 Nov. 2022.

[104] Thompson, J., Doxsee, C. and Bermudez Jnr, J. S., 'Tracking the arrival of Russia's Wagner Group in Mali', Center for Strategic and International Studies, 2 Feb. 2022.

[105] Serwat, L. et al., 'Wagner Group operations in Africa', Armed Conflict Location & Event Data Project, 30 Aug. 2022.

[106] Bax, P., 'Russia's influence in the Central African Republic', International Crisis Group, 3 Dec. 2021.

[107] Druet, D., 'Wagner Group poses fundamental challenges for the protection of civilians by UN peacekeeping operations', IPI Global Observatory, 20 Mar. 2023. On the role of the Wagner Group in CAR and Mali, see chapter 3, section III, and chapter 4, section II, in this volume.

[108] Human Rights Watch, 'Mali: Massacre by army, foreign soldiers', 5 Apr. 2022.

[109] International Crisis Group, 'After Shekau: Confronting jihadists in Nigeria's north-east', Africa Briefing no. 180, Brussels, 29 Mar. 2022.

Abuja, in July, suggesting that its reach is growing.[110] Nigeria faced multiple other sources of violence, including separatism in the south-east of the country and widespread criminality and gang violence, and the authorities have become increasingly reliant on vigilantes to handle threats as substitutes for state security services.[111] This tactic raises concerns about the reliability and discipline of such vigilantes. There were also violent incidents in late 2022 linked to campaigning in Nigeria's February 2023 national elections, although the level of violence appeared to be below that connected to previous polls.[112]

African forces scored some successes in fighting extremist jihadist groups in other regions. There was a decline in the number of conflict-related deaths in Mozambique's Cabo Delgado province—where Rwandan troops and the Southern African Development Community Mission in Mozambique (SAMIM), which helped contain insurgents linked to the Islamic State in 2021, continued to provide security support throughout 2022.[113] In Somalia, the national army and clan militias succeeded in driving al-Shabab out of large parts of the centre of the country in an operation that ran from August to December 2022.[114] While the African Union (AU) retains a large mission in Somalia, it did not take a direct role in this offensive. The UN Security Council and the AU agreed in March 2022 that the mission will close in 2024.[115]

In Central Africa, the March 23 Movement (M23) rebel group—widely alleged to be supported by Rwanda—launched a new offensive against government forces and UN peacekeepers in eastern Democratic Republic of the Congo (DRC) in March 2022.[116] The UN representative in the country, Bintou Keita, warned the Security Council that M23 was a 'conventional army' with the capacity to defeat the UN Organization Stabilization Mission in the DRC (MONUSCO).[117] Public discontent with the UN's response spilled over into violence against the peacekeepers.[118] The Congolese government has invited the East African Community Regional Force in the DRC (EACRF-DRC) to deploy a new security force to quell armed groups in the east, including M23.

---

[110] Samuel, M., 'Kuje prison break: Is Nigeria out of security options?', ISS Today, 11 July 2022.

[111] Okoli, A. C., 'Nigeria insecurity: 2022 was a bad year and points to the need for major reforms', The Conversation, 28 Dec. 2022; and International Crisis Group, 'Managing vigilantism in Nigeria: A near-term necessity', Africa Report no. 308, Brussels, 21 Apr. 2022.

[112] International Crisis Group, 'Mitigating risks of violence in Nigeria's 2023 elections', Africa Report no. 311, Brussels, 10 Feb. 2023.

[113] Cheatham, A., Long, A. and Sheehy, T. P., 'Regional security support: A vital first step for peace in Mozambique', US Institute of Peace, 23 June 2022. Also see chapter 3, section II, in this volume.

[114] International Crisis Group, 'Sustaining gains in Somalia's offensive against Al-Shabaab', Africa Briefing no. 187, Brussels, 21 Mar. 2022.

[115] AFP, 'From Amisom to Atmis: Will new AU mission in Somalia succeed?', The East African, 1 Apr. 2022. See also chapter 3, section II, in this volume.

[116] Armed Conflict Location & Event Data Project, 'Actor profile: The March 23 Movement', 23 Mar. 2023.

[117] Lederer, E. M., 'UN envoys warns Congo's M23 rebels are acting like an army', AP News, 30 June 2022.

[118] On developments with MONUSCO see chapter 3, section II, in this volume.

The first unit deployed in August, but the violence has not subsided, despite rebels withdrawing from some areas temporarily.[119] There was persistent conflict in Cameroon and CAR, although with fewer recorded fatalities than 2021. In Chad, the authorities responded to pro-democracy protestors with deadly violence.

In the Horn of Africa, the Ethiopian Civil War initially eased in the early months of 2022, and the government and the Tigray People's Liberation Front (TPLF) agreed a truce in late March.[120] The government and Eritrea, its ally, launched a new attack on the TPLF in August, however, scoring significant military successes before the AU brokered a peace agreement in Pretoria, South Africa, on 2 November (see section II).[121] In Sudan, protestors frequently took to the streets to demand a reversal of the October 2021 seizure of power by the armed forces, which had participated in a tenuous power-sharing agreement with civilian officials since the overthrow of President Omar al-Bashir in 2019. The security forces frequently used deadly force against protestors, even though the military had promised a return to civilian rule in August.[122] There was also widespread violence in Darfur, West Kordofan and Blue Nile state—all locations of long-running local conflict—that resulted in the displacement of 300 000 people in the course of 2022.[123] In South Sudan, political leaders agreed in August to the extension of a 2018 peace agreement that supposedly marked the end of the country's civil war. As in previous years, however, widespread localized violence persisted in large parts of the country.[124] UN officials and independent analysts noted that shifting weather and flood patterns linked to climate change were increasing displacement and intercommunal friction in South Sudan, exacerbating conflict risks.[125]

There were also three attempted and two successful coups d'état in Africa in 2022.[126] (There were no similar incidents in other regions, although Myanmar faced worsening violence arising from its 2021 coup, as outlined above.) This compares to two attempted and four successful coups or other

---

[119] van de Walle, N., 'East Africa's DR Congo force: A case for caution', International Crisis Group, 25 Aug. 2022. On the deployment of the Eastern African Community Regional Force to the DRC see chapter 3, section I, in this volume.

[120] AFP in Addis Ababa, 'Ethiopia: Tigray rebels agree "cessation of hostilities" after government truce', The Guardian, 25 Mar. 2022.

[121] AFP in Addis Ababa, 'Fighting in Ethiopia shatters months-long truce', The Guardian, 24 Aug. 2022; and International Crisis Group, 'Turning the Pretoria deal into lasting peace in Ethiopia', 23 Nov. 2022.

[122] International Crisis Group, 'A critical window to bolster Sudan's next government', 23 Jan. 2023.

[123] Ochab, E. U., 'Sudan: Between violence, humanitarian crisis and protests', Forbes, 30 Dec. 2022.

[124] Human Rights Watch, 'South Sudan: Use peace deal extension for reforms', Nairobi, 18 Aug. 2022.

[125] de Coning, C. et al., Climate, peace and security fact sheet, 'South Sudan', Norwegian Institute of International Affairs (NUPI), Oslo, Mar. 2022; and International Crisis Group, 'Floods, displacement and violence in South Sudan', Brussels, 27 Oct. 2022.

[126] Mwai, P., 'Are military takeovers on the rise in Africa?', BBC News, 4 Jan. 2023.

unconstitutional attempts to change the government in 2021. The three unsuccessful coup attempts in 2022 were in Gambia, Guinea Bissau and Sao Tome and Principe. Military officers successfully seized power twice in Burkina Faso, first in January and then in September. These coups did not precipitate significant violence in their own right. In the Burkinan case, as previously in Mali, there was support for the removal of elected leaders.[127]

---

[127] Powell, J., 'Burkina Faso coup: Latest sign of a rise in the ballot box being traded for bullets', The Conversation, 25 Jan. 2022.

II. International conflict management and peace processes

RICHARD GOWAN

This section reviews the performance of the international conflict management system in a year of geopolitical stress. It highlights the impact of major power tensions on bodies such as the United Nations and argues that the damage caused by Russia's war on Ukraine has been significant but less than seemed likely in February 2022. It also discusses the state of peacemaking in this difficult environment, highlighting the different dynamics in Yemen, Sudan, Ethiopia and Colombia.

Geopolitics and international cooperation

The collapse of major power relations tied to Russia's war on Ukraine had the potential to weaken international cooperation over conflict management more generally. The current panoply of conflict management mechanisms—both UN frameworks and regional alternatives—evolved in a period of limited major power competition after the cold war. The intensification of major power tensions prior to Russia's full-scale invasion of Ukraine was already associated with a degradation of multilateral cooperation and an increase in direct competition, most obviously in the handling of the war in Syria.[1] As of February 2022, it seemed possible that the spike in friction between Russia and the Western powers would further undercut, or just halt, diplomacy in forums like the UN.[2]

The UN institutions

One of the striking features of 2022 was how far the major powers managed to maintain a degree of cooperation over conflict management in many cases. While the UN Security Council held 50 rancorous meetings (including formal and informal events) on Ukraine in 2022, it still managed to maintain business as usual on other issues. Russia only used its veto twice on issues other than Ukraine in the course of the year—once with China to block new sanctions on North Korea and once as a tactical gambit in a debate on cross-border aid to Syria—although it did abstain on a growing number of texts that it disliked.[3] China appears to have been active behind the scenes

---

[1] On escalating regional conflicts and hotspots and declining capacity or willingness to manage them, see the discussions in Smith, D., 'The international system and law', *SIPRI Yearbook 2020*, pp. 19–23; and Smith, D., 'International cooperation', *SIPRI Yearbook 2021*, pp. 24–25.

[2] Gowan, R., 'The UN is another casualty of Russia's war: Why the organization might never bounce back', *Foreign Affairs*, 10 Mar. 2022.

[3] Steube, A., 'Voting wrap-up of the UN Security Council in 2022: Bitterness mixed with agreements', PassBlue, 9 Jan. 2023.

lobbying Russia not to be more obstructionist.[4] In some cases, the Security Council was only able to agree technical rollovers of existing mandates, but it did manage to innovate on a number of occasions. Among these were a new mandate for the UN Assistance Mission in Afghanistan in March, imposing new sanctions on Haitian gang members in October and agreeing the first full Security Council resolution on Myanmar in December.[5] The Council also unanimously agreed new provisions applying humanitarian 'carve-outs' to all UN sanctions regimes in December, something for which aid workers and non-governmental organizations had long been lobbying.[6] It appears that all the major powers concluded that it is still in their interests to work through the UN on some crises, and that Russia sees the Council as a space for residual compromise on conflicts with the West.

Russia also proved willing to work with UN Secretary-General António Guterres on a limited number of initiatives to mitigate the fall-out from the war in Ukraine. Guterres visited Moscow and Kyiv in April and helped to finalize an agreement, initially worked out by the International Committee of the Red Cross, on the evacuation of civilians trapped in the siege of the Azovstal steelworks in Mariupol.[7] In the following months, he worked closely with Turkish officials to persuade Ukraine and Russia to sign up to the Black Sea Grain Initiative. Under the initiative, which was agreed in July, Russia agreed to allow Ukrainian exports of foodstuffs from Odesa and other ports, reducing upward pressures on global food prices.[8] This agreement held for the rest of the year, despite a brief period in October when Russia suspended its involvement after Ukraine attacked the Black Sea Fleet in Sevastopol.[9] The UN reported that 17.8 million tonnes of grain and other food products had been shipped out of Ukraine between August 2022 and mid January 2023, although Ukraine's overall grain exports were still well below the previous year's.[10] While a number of UN member states, notably Mexico, called on Guterres to build on this success by launching a peace initiative

[4] See 'The Ukraine war's impact on the UN' in International Crisis Group, '10 Challenges for the UN in 2022–23', Special Briefing no. 8, Brussels, 14 Sep. 2022.

[5] See UN Security Council Resolution 2626, 17 Mar. 2022; UN Security Council Resolution 2653, 21 Oct. 2022; and UN Security Council Resolution 2669, 21 Dec. 2022. On the arms embargo imposed on Haitian gang members, see chapter 12, section II, in this volume. On discussions in the UN Security Council about the potential deployment of an international specialized force to Haiti, see chapter 3, section I, in this volume.

[6] UN Security Council Resolution 2664, 9 Dec. 2022.

[7] Lederer, E. M., 'UN chief and Russia's Putin agree on key Ukraine evacuation', AP News, 26 Apr. 2022.

[8] Ignatov, O. et al., 'Who are the winners in the Black Sea grain deal?', International Crisis Group, 3 Aug. 2022.

[9] Tanis, F., 'Russia rejoins UN deal to ship grain from Ukraine, easing food insecurity concerns', NPR, 2 Nov. 2022.

[10] United Nations, Secretary-General, 'Note to correspondents: Update on the Black Sea Grain Initiative', New York, 18 Jan. 2023; and Braun, K., 'Column: More to Ukraine's recent grain exports success than meets the eye', Reuters, 19 Oct. 2022.

between Russia and Ukraine, the secretary-general argued the time was not ripe for this.[11]

If Russia's war on Ukraine did not entirely derail international conflict management efforts, major power competition did complicate efforts to address some specific conflicts. Following a pattern set in 2020 and 2021, for example, China and Russia refused to let the Security Council—and, by extension, the UN system—play a significant role in resolving Ethiopia's civil war.[12] While China and Russia did acquiesce to the Council resolution on Myanmar noted above, both continued to provide material support to the military junta and insisted that the Security Council should not threaten Myanmar's generals with any concrete penalties.[13] In parallel, China and Russia also became increasingly firm in defending North Korea's interests at the UN in 2022.[14] While major power cooperation over armed conflicts and other disputes is still possible, this is on a case-by-case basis.

Regional organizations

Maintaining cooperation was less easy in the Organization for Security and Co-operation in Europe (OSCE). The OSCE Special Monitoring Mission (SMM) in Ukraine withdrew from the country in some disorder following Russia's offensive, and the Russian government refused any extension of the mission's mandate.[15] The war inevitably dominated debates at the organization's headquarters in Vienna, and the chair, Poland, took every opportunity to put diplomatic pressure on Russia. Russia also blocked adoption of the OSCE budget throughout the year, forcing it to operate on a month-by-month financial basis, thereby disrupting the planning and management of its missions.[16] Nonetheless, Russia did not block renewal of the mandates for OSCE presences other than the SMM, which allowed the organization to continue to operate in the Balkans and Central Asia.

While the OSCE struggled, the European Union (EU) and the North Atlantic Treaty Organization (NATO) shifted their focus from conflict management to the defence of Ukraine and their own security. NATO had already refocused its attention to territorial defence prior to 2022, but the

---

[11] de la Fuente, J. R. and Olabuenaga, P. A., 'Mexico's initiative for dialogue and peace in Ukraine', *Just Security*, 23 Sep. 2022.

[12] Worley, W., 'Exclusive: Russia, China foiled UN meetings on Tigray famine, says Lowcock', Devex, 21 June 2022.

[13] International Crisis Group, 'Coming to terms with Russia's Myanmar embrace', Asia Briefing no. 173, Brussels, 4 Aug. 2022; and 'Myanmar: Vote on draft resolution', Security Council Report, 21 Dec. 2022.

[14] Lederer, E. M., 'China and Russia defend North Korea vetoes in first at UN', AP News, 9 June 2022.

[15] Miller, C. and Liechtenstein, S., 'Inside the OSCE's botched withdrawal from Ukraine', Politico, 10 June 2022. On the closure of the OSCE SMM see also chapter 3, section I, in this volume.

[16] International Crisis Group, 'Seven priorities for preserving the OSCE in a time of war', Special Briefing no. 9, Brussels, 29 Nov. 2022. On OSCE multilateral peace operations in 2022, see chapter 3, section II, in this volume.

challenge in Ukraine led the EU to rethink the use and goals of its conflict management tools. The EU repurposed the European Peace Facility (EPF), designed to support security operations worldwide, to prioritize military assistance to Ukraine.[17] The EU also innovated in October in response to the deteriorating situation between Armenia and Azerbaijan by launching a two-month 'monitoring capacity', involving 40 civilian experts, to patrol the Armenian side of the international border.[18] When this closed on schedule in December, the Armenian government asked the EU to deploy a larger civilian Common Security and Defence Policy (CSDP) mission. The European Council responded positively in January 2023.[19]

Beyond Europe, regional organizations also contended with difficult questions about how to handle conflicts largely separate from events in Europe. In South East Asia, the Association of Southeast Asian Nations made little progress in dealing with the worsening civil war in Myanmar (see section I). In Africa, the African Union (AU) and subregional formations including the Economic Community of West African States (ECOWAS) and the Group of Five for the Sahel (G5 Sahel)—Burkina Faso, Chad, Mali, Mauritania and Niger—were divided over how to address the spate of coups d'état on the continent.[20] The Malian government pulled out of the G5 Sahel, which has coordinated a counterterrorist force in the Sahel since 2014, albeit to limited effect. This was a response to the other G5 members' refusal to allow the country's military authorities, which took power in a 2021 coup, to take on the presidency of the grouping.[21] By contrast, at a December summit, ECOWAS leaders frustrated at their inability to deal with coups in cases such as Burkina Faso, proposed a regional force that could respond to future military takeovers.[22]

Overall, the multilateral and regional organizations dealing with armed conflicts muddled through 2022 better than seemed likely in the first months of the year. Major power tensions complicated but did not wreck cooperative mechanisms. Nonetheless, debates over other challenges, such as peace enforcement and peacemaking, also tested these bodies (see below).

---

[17] Foy, H., 'Arming Ukraine: How war forced the EU to rewrite defence policy', *Financial Times*, 27 Feb. 2023.

[18] EEAS Press Team, 'Q&A: EU monitoring capacity to Armenia', Brussels, 20 Oct. 2022.

[19] Council of the European Union, 'Armenia: EU launches a civilian mission to contribute to stability in border areas', Press release, 20 Feb. 2023. See also chapter 3, section II, in this volume.

[20] On AU debates on unconstitutional changes of government, see 'Bolstering the AU's institutional capacity' in International Crisis Group, 'Eight priorities for the African Union in 2023', Crisis Group Africa Briefing no. 186, Nairobi/Brussels, 14 Feb. 2023.

[21] 'Mali's withdrawal from G5 Sahel effective from June 30', Africanews, 17 June 2022. On the Joint Force of the G5 Sahel, see also chapter 3, section II, in this volume.

[22] Onuah, F., 'West African leaders plan force to counter "coup belt" reputation', Reuters, 5 Dec. 2022. On existing ECOWAS peace missions, see chapter 3, sections I and II, in this volume.

Peace processes

There were few successful peace processes in 2022. Edinburgh University's Peace Agreement Database recorded 18 agreements of different types signed in the course of the year.[23] These included four concerning the Democratic Republic of the Congo and its neighbours on restoring stability in the east of the country, and two between Armenia and Azerbaijan. Nonetheless, armed conflicts continued in both cases. Even where there was progress, as in Ethiopia and Sudan, the results were fragile. Mediators and diplomats noted that the main goal of their efforts in 2022 was to mitigate the fall-out from conflict rather than resolve it.[24] This was true of the UN's engagement in Ukraine, but also of the organization's efforts to continue to engage with the Taliban in Afghanistan to ensure access to aid. In the case of Syria, despite disputes with Russia, the UN Security Council focused for much of 2022 on preserving the Council-mandated mechanism for delivering assistance to opposition-held north-west Syria.[25]

Some peace processes did make progress in 2022, however, and four—in Yemen, Sudan, Ethiopia and Colombia—offer different insights on the possibility of peacemaking in a challenging period.

Yemen

The UN's most notable humanitarian initiative in 2022 concerned Yemen. The UN had made multiple efforts to foster peace talks in Yemen since the country's descent into civil war in 2014, so there was surprise when Special Envoy Hans Grundberg announced that the internationally recognized government of President Abdrabbuh Mansur Hadi and the Houthis (the official name is Ansar Allah) had signed a humanitarian truce.[26] The truce probably reflected the fact that some of the main external actors supporting the UN-backed government—notably Saudi Arabia and the United Arab Emirates (UAE)—were keen for a lull in an exhausting war. President Hadi stood down on 7 April, apparently at the instigation of his former regional supporters. Moreover, battlefield dynamics were significant. The Houthis had incurred military setbacks but had also increased their attacks on Saudi Arabian and UAE territory, not least in a series of highly publicized drone attacks on Abu Dhabi in January 2022.[27] Both sides had reasons to ease the conflict. Nonetheless, the terms of the initial deal were relatively narrow, centred on easing a fuel embargo on Houthi-held territory and permitting a

---

[23] University of Edinburgh, Peace Agreements Database, updated Jan. 2023.
[24] Mediators and diplomats, Private discussions with author, 5 Nov. 2022.
[25] Gowan, R., Khalifa, D. and Pradhan, A., 'A vital humanitarian mandate for Syria's north-west', International Crisis Group, 5 July 2022.
[26] Salisbury, P., 'Behind the Yemen truce and presidential council announcements', International Crisis Group, 8 Apr. 2022.
[27] 'Timeline: UAE under drone, missile attacks', Al Jazeera, 3 Feb. 2022.

limited number of commercial flights in and out of the Houthi-held capital, Sanaa. All involved underlined that this was not a full ceasefire and violence continued throughout the year, albeit at a significantly lower level than in 2021.[28] The rate of aid deliveries also increased in this period, suggesting that the truce achieved its baseline goals.

The two sides renewed the truce every two months in 2022 until October and the UN suggested renewal should be moved to a six-monthly basis. However, tensions began to rise over a further aspect of the deal—an offer by the Houthis to open road access to the city of Taiz, a key transport hub in central Yemen which the Houthis had all but surrounded since 2015.[29] The Hadi government had initially wanted this to be part of the truce but settled for talks on the matter. The technicalities of which roads to open proved complex, however, while the Houthis demanded that the government should commit to paying the salaries of civil servants and military personnel in the areas under Houthi control to keep the deal alive. With the two sides linking these issues and the post-Hadi government in a state of internal confusion, no progress was made on easing access to Taiz in the run-up to a 2 October deadline for renewing the truce and the deal formally collapsed. Elements of the truce continued in practice, however, as commercial flights to and from Sanaa continued to operate and there was an ongoing decrease in fighting. By the end of the year, the Houthis were in direct discussions with Saudi Arabia, suggesting that the truce had at least bought time for diplomatic options to open up. Nonetheless, the political scene in Yemen grew more fragmented throughout the year, following internecine fighting on the anti-Houthi side. This process of fragmentation is likely to further complicate achieving a political settlement.

Sudan

A second notable peace process in 2022, in Sudan, demonstrated very different dynamics.[30] The focus of this process was on restoring military–civilian power-sharing in Khartoum, which had collapsed when the military seized full power in 2021. The talks took place against a backdrop of street protests, violence against protestors by the security forces and economic crisis. All this was further complicated by the sheer number of actors attempting to mediate a way out of the impasse. The UN Integrated Transition Assistance Mission in Sudan (UNITAMS), which was mandated to assist the move to civilian rule in 2019, began inclusive discussions on a way forward in

---

[28] Armed Conflict Location & Event Data Project (ACLED), 'Violence in Yemen during the UN-mediated truce: April to October 2022', 14 Oct. 2022.

[29] International Crisis Group, 'A moment of truth for Yemen's truce', 30 Sep. 2022; and International Crisis Group, 'How Huthi–Saudi negotiations will make or break Yemen', Middle East & North Africa Briefing no. 89, Brussels, 29 Dec. 2022.

[30] Boswell, A., 'A breakthrough in Sudan's impasse?', International Crisis Group, 12 Aug. 2022.

January but made little progress. Other actors then joined. The AU and the Intergovernmental Authority on Development (IGAD) joined the UN in trying to facilitate civilian–military talks in May. Civilian Sudanese leaders refused to join these talks, however, demanding that the military commit to quitting politics. At this point, the United States and Saudi Arabia, which has maintained good links with the military, quietly initiated informal talks to break the deadlock. Although these also became bogged down in civil–military tensions—and annoyed AU and IGAD officials who felt that the second channel was distracting from their own process—General Abdel Fattah al-Burhan unexpectedly announced on 4 July that he was willing to allow civilian leaders to form a government. Suspecting that this was a ruse to placate Saudi Arabia and the USA, civilian political leaders refused to engage with the proposal immediately.

The USA and Saudi Arabia continued to work to get the two sides talking, with support from the United Kingdom and the UAE, while a group of Sudanese lawyers pushed the process forward by tabling a draft constitution outlining how a transition might work.[31] By November, a broad coalition of civilian representatives was ready to sign a framework agreement supporting this path and setting up more detailed talks early in 2023. An agreement to this effect was signed on 5 December, although many critics in Sudan felt that it was too lenient on the military. Street protests and incidents of violence against civilians continued, as the local resistance committees in support of civilian rule sought to keep pressure on the military not to renege on its promises.[32] The outlook at the end of 2022 remained uncertain.

Ethiopia

In contrast to the complex political manoeuvring in Sudan, the process that led to a ceasefire in the Ethiopian Civil War in November 2022 demonstrated the brute force of battlefield dynamics. The conflict between the Ethiopian government and the Tigray People's Liberation Front (TPLF), which began in November 2020, had swung dramatically throughout 2021. Nonetheless, both sides wanted a respite by early 2022 and, as noted above, reached a truce in March when both parties unilaterally declared a pause in hostilities without engaging in any formal negotiations.[33] There then followed a desultory period in which Ethiopia maintained a blockade of TPLF-controlled Tigray region and external actors failed to invest in securing a lasting peace. The truce collapsed on 24 August and government forces and their supporters, including troops from neighbouring Eritrea, waged a campaign against the

---

[31] International Crisis Group, 'A critical window to bolster Sudan's next government', Statement, 23 Jan. 2023.
[32] International Crisis Group (note 31).
[33] AFP in Addis Ababa, 'Ethiopia: Tigray rebels agree "cessation of hostilities" after government truce', *The Guardian*, 25 Mar. 2022.

TPLF. There have been reports that this phase of the war alone claimed 100 000 lives—far more than ACLED can record with confidence, due in part to a highly effective media and internet blackout by Ethiopia.[34] Whatever the actual death toll, TPLF negotiators were desperate to secure a new cessation of hostilities and made major concessions at AU-mediated talks in Pretoria, South Africa, at the start of November, including a promise to lay down their arms in 20 days. Although a hastily agreed deal, it proved unexpectedly durable in the following months. The AU launched a monitoring and verification mission to support the agreement in December.[35] Aid supplies to Tigray gradually improved and Tigrayan forces began to hand over heavy weapons in January.[36] Ethiopian Prime Minister Abiy Ahmed met with TPLF leaders soon after.[37]

The Yemeni, Sudanese and Ethiopian cases offer differing perspectives on options for peacemaking in 2022. The UN's work in Yemen showed that there is still space for the organization to manage successful conflict mitigation efforts, as did the secretary-general's work on the Black Sea Grain deal. By contrast, the Sudanese process demonstrates the mix of mediators and facilitators required to advance more complex peace processes. Finally, the Ethiopian process shows that, even in a complex security environment, battlefield victory and defeat are still key determinants of the political outcome of wars—however they are presented.

Colombia

The year ended with an aspirational attempt at peace in Colombia, when President Gustavo Petro, who assumed office in August, attempted to build on the 2016 peace agreement with the Revolutionary Armed Forces of Colombia (FARC) by starting talks with other armed groups, including the National Liberation Army (ELN), the largest remaining non-state armed group, in the final quarter of the year.[38] Colombia declared a ceasefire with the ELN and four other armed groups on 31 December.[39] This, however, proved difficult to implement as the ELN promptly denied any involvement in a ceasefire and Petro accused other signatories of breaking the deal.[40]

---

[34] International Crisis Group, 'Turning the Pretoria deal into lasting peace in Ethiopia', Statement, 23 Nov. 2022.

[35] On the AU Monitoring, Verification and Compliance Mission (AU-MVCM) in Ethiopia, see chapter 3, section I, in this volume.

[36] Endeshaw, D., 'Tigray forces begin handing over heavy weapons to Ethiopian army', Reuters, 11 Jan. 2023.

[37] 'Ethiopian PM meets Tigray leaders for first time since peace deal', Reuters, 4 Feb. 2023.

[38] Dickinson, E., 'Colombia's last guerrillas make first step toward "total peace"', International Crisis Group, 23 Nov. 2022.

[39] 'Colombia announces ceasefire with five illegal armed groups', Reuters, 1 Jan. 2023.

[40] 'Colombia's Petro accuses armed group of violating ceasefire', Al Jazeera, 13 Mar. 2023.

III. Table of armed conflicts active in 2022

IAN DAVIS

There were active armed conflicts in at least 56 states in 2022, five more than in 2021: 11 in the Americas; 10 in Asia and Oceania; 3 in Europe; 10 in the Middle East and North Africa, one more than in 2021; and 22 in sub-Saharan Africa, four more than in 2021 (see figure 2.1 and table 2.8).[1] As in preceding years, most took place within a single country (intrastate) between government forces and one or more non-state armed groups, or between two or more such groups. Only four were fought between states: the Russia–Ukraine War and low-level border clashes between India and Pakistan, Armenia and Azerbaijan, and Kyrgyzstan and Tajikistan. Two were fought between state forces and armed groups aspiring to statehood: the conflicts between Israel and the Palestinians, and between Türkiye and the Kurds.

According to data from the Armed Conflict Location & Event Data Project (ACLED), there were at least three major armed conflicts (resulting in 10 000 or more estimated conflict-related deaths in the year): in Ukraine (approximately 28 400 reported fatalities), Myanmar (19 400) and Nigeria (10 700). There were also 17 high-intensity armed conflicts (resulting in 1000–9999 estimated conflict-related deaths in the year). However, these categorizations should be considered tentative, as information on fatalities can be unreliable.[2] As noted in table 2.8 and sections I and II, in the cases of Ethiopia and Ukraine they may be quite severe underestimates.

All three major armed conflicts and most of the high-intensity armed conflicts were internationalized, involving foreign actors, which may have led to the conflict being prolonged or exacerbated.

Estimated battle deaths decreased by 19 per cent compared to 2021, while those attributed to 'explosions and remote violence' increased by 28 per cent (see table 2.7). The number of explosive and remote violence events in 2022 almost doubled compared with 2021. In the 'violence against civilians' category both 'events' and 'fatalities' increased for the third consecutive year.

---

[1] A country is treated as being in an armed conflict if there were 25 or more battle-related deaths in a given year.

[2] Armed Conflict Location & Event Data Project (ACLED), 'FAQs: ACLED fatality methodology', 27 Jan. 2020. On casualty counting see also Giger, A., 'Casualty recording in armed conflict: Methods and normative issues', *SIPRI Yearbook 2016*, pp. 247–61; and Delgado, C., 'Why it is important to register violent deaths', SIPRI Commentary, 30 Mar. 2020.

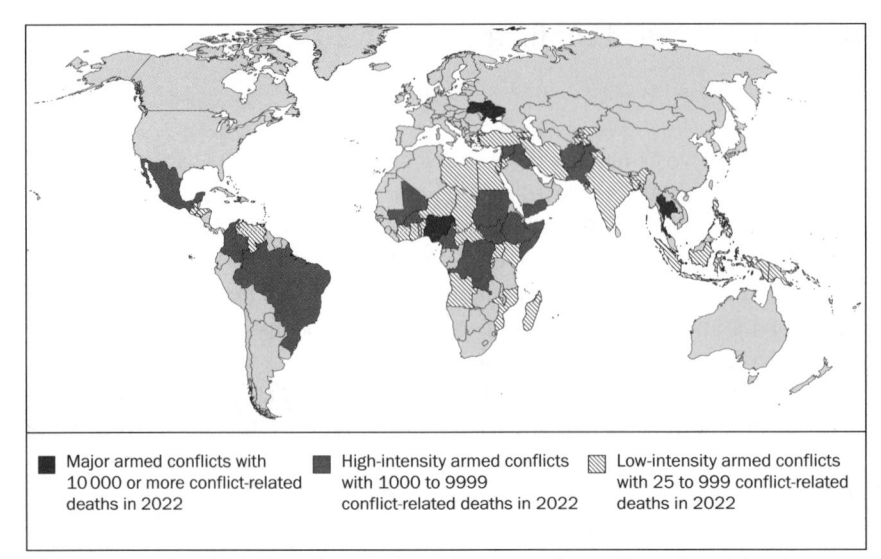

Figure 2.1. Armed conflicts by number of estimated conflict-related deaths, 2022

Table 2.7. Categories of conflict-related violence, 2020–22

	No. of events				Estimated fatalities[b]			
Event type[a]	2020	2021	2022	Change, 2021–22 (%)	2020	2021	2022	Change, 2021–22 (%)
Battles	39 277	34 017	32 582	–4	80 300	89 009	72 176	–19
Explosions/ remote violence	25 834	25 500	50 261	97	21 609	25 615	32 839	28
Protests, riots and strategic developments	170 762	191 523	179 547	–6	3 492	3 961	3 802	–4
Violence against civilians	26 504	29 719	32 144	8	31 242	35 168	38 792	10
Total	262 377	280 759	294 534	5	136 643	153 753	147 609	–4

[a] For definitions of event types, see Armed Conflict Location & Event Data Project (ACLED), 'ACLED definitions of political violence and protest', 11 Apr. 2019.

[b] Includes all conflict-related fatalities, irrespective of whether the countries were engaged in armed conflict.

Source: ACLED, 'Dashboard', accessed 30 Jan. 2023.

Table 2.8. Armed conflicts active in 2022

Location[a]	Type[b]	Internationalized[c] External actors	Peace operation	Key parties/dynamics	Start year[d]	Intensity (2022)[e]	Estimated conflict-related fatalities[f] 2022	Change from 2021 (%)
Americas								
Brazil	Subnational intrastate	No	No	State forces v criminal gangs; inter-gang violence	[g]	High	6 434	16
Colombia	Subnational intrastate	Yes	Yes (UN and OAS)	State forces v NSAGs; inter-NSAG violence; inter-gang violence	1964	High	2 260	6
El Salvador	Subnational intrastate	No	No	State forces v criminal gangs; inter-gang violence	[h]	Low	267	-34
Guatemala	Subnational intrastate	No	No	State forces v criminal gangs; inter-gang violence	[i]	Low	642	-3
Haiti	Subnational intrastate	No	Yes (UN)	State forces v criminal gangs; inter-gang violence	[g]	High	1 227	110
Honduras	Subnational intrastate	No	No	State forces v criminal gangs; inter-gang violence	[g]	Low	595	0
Jamaica	Subnational intrastate	No	No	State forces v criminal gangs; inter-gang violence	[g]	Low	376	37
Mexico	Subnational intrastate	No	No	State forces v cartels; inter-cartel/gang violence	1994	High	7 793	-6
Puerto Rico	Subnational intrastate	No	No	State forces v criminal gangs; inter-gang violence	[g]	Low	202	17
Trinidad and Tobago	Subnational intrastate	No	No	State forces v criminal gangs; inter-gang violence	[g]	Low	275	49
Venezuela	Subnational intrastate	Yes	No	State forces v Colombian NSAGs; inter-gang violence	[g]	Low	827	-41
Asia and Oceania								
Afghanistan	Subnational intrastate (post-civil war)	Yes	Yes (UN)	State forces (Taliban) v anti-Taliban NSAGs	2022	High	3 956	-91
Bangladesh	Subnational intrastate	Yes	No	State forces v NSAGs; inter-NSAG violence (esp. in Rohingya refugee camps and Chittagong Hill Tracts)	2022	Low	308	-13
India	Interstate border and subnational intrastate	Yes	Yes (UN)	Kashmir (LOC); State forces v NSAGs (esp. in north-east, Maoist)	1947	Low	905	-11
Indonesia	Subnational intrastate	Yes	No	States forces v NSAGs (esp. Papua, IS, al-Qaeda)	1962	Low	247	83
Kyrgyzstan	Interstate border	Yes	No	Border clashes (Ferghana Valley)	2021	Low	70[j]	119
Myanmar	Civil war	Yes	No	State forces v NSAGs (ethnic armed groups); State forces v NUG	1948	Major	19 357	76

Location[a]	Type[b]	Internationalized[c] External actors	Peace operation	Key parties/dynamics	Start year[d]	Intensity (2022)[e]	Estimated conflict-related fatalities[f] 2022	Change from 2021 (%)
Pakistan	Interstate border and subnational intrastate	Yes	Yes (UN)	Kashmir (LOC); State forces v NSAGs (esp Taliban and Baloch separatists)	1947	High	1 785	27
Papua New Guinea	Subnational intrastate	No	No	State forces v NSAG (TPNPB-OPM); Inter-communal and clan militia violence	1964	Low	223	70
Philippines	Subnational intrastate	Yes	Yes (ad hoc)[#]	State forces v NSAGs (Moro conflict and NPA); war on drugs	1991	Low	890	−23
Tajikistan	Interstate border	Yes	No	Border clashes (Ferghana Valley)	2021	Low	71[j]	255
Europe								
Armenia	Interstate border	Yes	No	Nagorno-Karabakh conflict	2020	Low	217	804
Azerbaijan	Interstate border	Yes	Yes (OSCE and ad hoc)	Nagorno-Karabakh conflict	2020	Low	68	106
Ukraine	Interstate	Yes	Yes (EU and OSCE[#])	Russian invasion Feb. 2022; Ukraine v NSAGs (Russian-backed separatists)	2014	Major	28 357[k]	18 932
Middle East and North Africa								
Egypt	Subnational intrastate	No	Yes (ad hoc)	State forces v NSAGs (Sinai insurgency)	2011	Low	273	3
Iraq	Subnational intrastate	Yes	Yes (UN, EU and NATO)	Multiple and overlapping: state forces and NSAGs (esp. Iranian-backed militias, IS, PKK)	2013	High	4 483	58
Iran	Subnational intrastate	Yes	No	State forces v NSAGs (PJAK insurgency; Sistan and Baluchestan insurgency)	2004	Low	576	161
Israel–Palestine	Extra-state	Yes	Yes (EU)	Territorial dispute/occupation; State forces v NSAGs (esp. Hamas and PIJ)[l]	1947	Low	221	−42
Jordan	Subnational intrastate	Yes	No	State forces v unidentified NSAGs (local tribal militia and groups from Syria)	2022	Low	38	1 800
Lebanon	Subnational intrastate	Yes	No	Clashes between rival militias; sectarian tensions	2020	Low	56	−24
Libya	Subnational intrastate	Yes	Yes (UN and EU)	Limited clashes between NSAGs (2020 ceasefire largely held)	2011	Low	165	43

Syria	Civil war	Yes	Yes (UN)	Multiple and overlapping: state forces v NSAGs; external state forces v NSAGs; inter-NSAG violence	2011	High	5 649	−4
Türkiye	Extra-state and subnational intrastate	No	No	State forces v Kurdish NSAGs (esp. PKK)	1978	Low	274	−12
Yemen	Civil war	Yes	Yes (UN)	Multiple and overlapping: state forces (backed by Saudi Arabia-led coalition) v NSAGs (esp. the Houthis, AQAP, STC); inter-NSAG violence	2014	High	6 736	−63

Sub-Saharan Africa
West Africa

Benin	Subnational intrastate	No	No	State forces v NSAGs; inter-NSAG violence	2020	Low	180	94
Burkina Faso	Subnational intrastate	Yes	No	State, regional and international forces v NSAGs (esp. Ansarul Islam, Katiba Serma, ISGS and JNIM); inter-communal violence	2016	High	4 242	79
Côte d'Ivoire	Subnational intrastate	No	No	State forces v NSAGs (mainly unidentified groups or ethnic militias); inter-NSAG violence	2022	Low	45	18
Ghana	Subnational intrastate	No	No	State forces v NSAGs (mainly unidentified groups or communal/ethnic militias); inter-NSAG violence	2022	Low	142	274
Mali	Subnational intrastate	Yes	Yes (UN and EU)	State, regional and international forces; Russian PMSCs v NSAGs (esp. Ansarul Islam, Katiba Serma, ISGS and JNIM); inter-NSAG violence; military coup	2012	High	4 795	151
Niger	Subnational intrastate	Yes	Yes (EU)	State, regional and international forces v NSAGs (esp. Boko Haram, ISWAP, Ansarul Islam, Katiba Serma, ISGS and JNIM); inter-NSAG violence	2014	Low	990	−34
Nigeria	Subnational intrastate	Yes	No	State, regional and international forces v NSAGs (esp. Boko Haram and ISWAP; farmer–herder violence; inter-NSAG violence	2009	Major	10 734	1
Togo	Subnational intrastate	Yes	No	State forces v NSAG (JNIM) in northern Savanes region	2022	Low	78	1 850

Central Africa

Location[a]	Type[b]	Internationalized[c] External actors	Internationalized[c] Peace operation	Key parties/dynamics	Start year[d]	Intensity (2022)[e]	Estimated conflict-related fatalities[f] 2022	Change from 2021 (%)
Angola	Subnational intrastate	No	No	State forces v NSAG (separatist insurgency, FLEC, in Cabinda province)	1975	Low	105	-30
Cameroon	Subnational intrastate	Yes	No	State forces v NSAGs: anglophone separatists (south-west and north-west); Boko Haram and ISWAP (far-north)	2014	High	1 003	-30
Central African Republic	Subnational intrastate	Yes	Yes (UN, AU and EU)	State forces, Russian PMSCs and Rwandan forces v NSAGs (esp. CPC-affiliated)	2012	Low	839	-51
Chad	Subnational intrastate	Yes	No	State forces v NSAGs (esp. Boko Haram and Libya-based FACT); intercommunal violence; military coup	2014	Low	696	-16
Congo, Democratic Republic of	Subnational intrastate	Yes	Yes (UN and EAC)	State, Rwandan and Tanzanian forces v multiple NSAGs (domestic and external in eastern provinces); intercommunal violence	2005	High	6 389	5

East Africa

Location[a]	Type[b]	External actors	Peace operation	Key parties/dynamics	Start year[d]	Intensity (2022)[e]	2022	Change from 2021 (%)
Burundi	Subnational intrastate	No	No	State forces v NSAGs	2018	Low	258	-15
Ethiopia	Subnational intrastate	Yes	No	State and Eritrean forces v NSAGs: TPLF (Tigray, Amhara and Afar regions) and (OLA–Oromo conflict)[n]	1973	High	6 663[m]	-26
Kenya	Subnational intrastate	No	No	State forces v NSAGs; localized ethnic-based		Low	551	40
Madagascar	Subnational intrastate	No	No	State forces v rural bandits	2012	Low	332	9
Mozambique	Subnational intrastate	Yes	Yes (EU and SADC)	State and regional forces v NSAGs: Cabo Delgado insurgency; resource conflicts	2013	Low	928	-20
Somalia	Subnational intrastate	Yes	Yes (UN, AU and EU)	State forces, AMISOM and US forces v NSAGs, esp. al-Shabab; clan-based violence	2003	High	6 520	100
South Sudan	Subnational intrastate	Yes	Yes (UN and IGAD)	State forces v NSAGs; intercommunal violence/community-based militias	2011	High	1 906	-12

| Sudan | Subnational intrastate | Yes | Yes (UN) | State forces v NSAGs in Darfur (JEM, SLM/A-AW, SLM/A-MM), Kordofan and Blue Nile (SPLM-North Agar and SPLM/A-N Hilu); military coup | 2003 | High | 2 065 | 25 |
| Uganda | Subnational intrastate | Yes | No | State forces, DRC forces and MONUSCO v NSAG (cross-border ADF insurgency) | 1996 | Low | 363 | –28 |

ACLED = Armed Conflict Location & Event Data Project; ADF = Allied Democratic Forces; AMISOM = African Union Mission to Somalia; AQAP = Al-Qaeda in the Arabian Peninsula; AU = African Union; CPC = Coalition of Patriots for Change; EAC = East African Community; EU = European Union; FACT = Front for Change and Concord in Chad (Front pour l'alternance et la concorde au Tchad); FLEC = Front for the Liberation of the Enclave of Cabinda; IGAD = Intergovernmental Authority on Development; IS = Islamic State; ISGS = Islamic State in the Greater Sahara; ISWAP = Islamic State-West Africa Province; JEM = Justice and Equality Movement; JNIM = Support Group for Islam and Muslims (Jama'at Nasr al-Islam wal Muslimin); LOC = Line of Control; MONUSCO = United Nations Organization Stabilization Mission in the Democratic Republic of the Congo; NPA = New People's Army; NSAG = Non-state armed group; NUG = National Unity Government; OAS = Organization of American States; OLA = Oromo Liberation Army; OSCE = Organization for Security and Co-operation in Europe; PIJ = Palestinian Islamic Jihad; PJAK = Kurdistan Free Life Party (Partiya Jiyana Azad a Kurdistanê); PKK = Kurdistan Workers' Party (Partiya Karkerên Kurdistanê); PMSC = Private military and security company; SADC = Southern African Development Community; SLM/A-AW = Sudan Liberation Movement/Army–Abdul Wahid; SLM/A-MM = Sudan Liberation Movement/Army–Minni Minnawi; SPLM = Sudan People's Liberation Movement; STC = Southern Transitional Council; TPNPB-OPM = West Papua National Liberation Army–Free Papua Movement (Tentara Pembebasan Nasional Papua Barat-Organisasi Papua Merdeka); TPLF = Tigray People's Liberation Front.

Notes: The armed conflicts in the table are listed by location, in alphabetical order, in five geographical regions: the Americas; Asia and Oceania; Europe; the Middle East and North Africa; and sub-Saharan Africa. Armed conflict involves the use of armed force between two or more states or non-state armed groups (NSAGs). There is a threshold of battle-related violence causing 25 or more deaths in a given year. The table draws on data from the Armed Conflict Location & Event Data Project (ACLED).

[a] Location refers to the state in which the government is being challenged by an opposition organization, an NSAG or another state, and/or the geographical location of the fighting.
[b] The types of armed conflict are:

Interstate (international) armed conflict: the use of armed force by one or more states against another state or states;
Intrastate (non-international) armed conflict: usually involves sustained violence between a state and one or more NSAG fighting with explicitly political goals (e.g. to take control of the state or part of its territory) but can also include armed conflict between NSAGs, sometimes with less clear goals. Intrastate armed conflicts can also be classified as: *Subnational armed conflict*, typically confined to particular areas of a sovereign state while economic and social activities in the rest of the country proceed relatively untroubled; *Civil war*, involving most of the country and resulting in at least 1000 conflict-related deaths in a given year; and *Extra-state armed conflict*, which occurs between a state and a political entity that is not widely recognized as a state but has long-standing aspirations of statehood (e.g. the Israeli–Palestinian conflict).

^{c} An armed conflict is considered *internationalized* if there is significant involvement by a foreign entity that is clearly prolonging or exacerbating the conflict, such as armed intervention in support of—or the provision of significant levels of weapons or military training to—one or more of the conflict parties by a foreign government or non-state actor, including private military companies. Multilateral *peace operations* are another form of internationalization of a conflict (see chapter 3 in this volume); # indicates that the mission closed during the year.

^{d} The year when fighting caused at least 25 battle-related deaths for the first time.

^{e} With the caveat that data on conflict-related deaths is often imprecise and tentative, armed conflicts are categorized as *major* (10 000 or more conflict-related deaths in the current year), *high intensity* (1000–9999 conflict-related deaths) or *low intensity* (25–999 conflict-related deaths).

^{f} Estimated fatality figures are collated from four ACLED event types: battles; explosions/remote violence; protests, riots and strategic developments; and violence against civilians. See ACLED, 'ACLED definitions of political violence and protest', 11 Apr. 2019. Once the threshold of 25 battle-related deaths has been crossed, the fatalities from the other three event types are added to give a total number of 'estimated conflict-related fatalities'. Fatality data can be unreliable, since undercounting and manipulation of such data are common in war. The numbers are therefore tentative *estimates* that indicate a trend in a conflict's form and impact. See ACLED, 'FAQs: ACLED fatality methodology', 27 Jan. 2020.

^{g} The first year for which data on conflicts in this country is available in the ACLED database is 2018; it is not possible to verify the situation prior to that date.

^{h} Some armed political and criminal violence continued following the 1979–92 Salvadoran Civil War. The first year for which data on conflicts in El Salvador is available in the ACLED database is 2018; it is not possible to verify the situation prior to that date.

^{i} Some armed political and criminal violence continued following the end of the 1960–66 Guatemalan Civil War. The first year for which data on conflicts in Guatemala is available in the ACLED database is 2018; it is not possible to verify the situation prior to that date.

^{j} Combined battle-related deaths exceeded 25.

^{k} This may be a low estimate of fatalities given that other public sources suggest much higher casualty rates. However, all estimates of the number of fatalities in this armed conflict, both military and civilian, are particularly difficult to verify due to likely undercounting and manipulation of the data. See e.g. Crawford, N. C., 'Reliable death tolls from the Ukraine war are hard to come by: The result of undercounts and manipulation', The Conversation, 4 Apr. 2022.

^{l} Israel describes the conflict as about 'disputed territory', while a range of authoritative bodies such as the United Nations Security Council, the International Court of Justice and the International Committee of the Red Cross define it as an occupation where international humanitarian law applies.

^{m} This may be a low estimate of fatalities given that other public sources suggest much higher casualty rates. See e.g. Pilling, D. and Schipani, A., 'War in Tigray may have killed 600,000 people, peace mediator says', *Financial Times*, 15 Jan. 2023.

^{n} The first available year for data on conflicts in this country in the ACLED database is 1997; it is not possible to verify the situation prior to that date.

Sources: ACLED, 'Dashboard', accessed 10–26 Jan. 2023; various other sources; and author's assessments.

3. Multilateral peace operations

Overview

This chapter describes general developments and trends in multilateral peace operations in 2022. There were 64 active peace operations in 2022—an increase of one compared to the previous year. Five started in 2022: the Collective Security Treaty Organization (CSTO) Collective Peacekeeping Forces to Kazakhstan; the African Union Transition Mission in Somalia; the Economic Community of West African States Stabilisation Support Mission in Guinea-Bissau (SSMGB); the East African Community Regional Force in the Democratic Republic of the Congo (EACRF-DRC); and the African Union Monitoring, Verification and Compliance Mission in Ethiopia (AU-MVCM). Four ended in 2022: the CSTO Collective Peacekeeping Forces to Kazakhstan; the Organization for Security and Co-operation in Europe (OSCE) Special Monitoring Mission to Ukraine (SMM); the African Union Mission in Somalia (AMISOM); and the International Monitoring Team (IMT) in Mindanao.

The number of personnel deployed to multilateral peace operations globally increased in 2022. This breaks a trend of declining personnel numbers between 2016 and 2021. The rise in 2022 mostly reflected variations in personnel deployments to operations in sub-Saharan Africa, which continued to host the most peace operations and personnel. Four of the five new operations in 2022 were launched in the region and all of them by regional organizations, namely the African Union, the East African Community and the Economic Community of West African States. These newly established missions illustrate the increasing regionalization of peace operations and the emphasis on the deployment of uniformed rather than civilian personnel.

Moreover, relations between peace operations and host governments reached a new low in 2022, with the expulsion of United Nations personnel from Mali and the Democratic Republic of the Congo. The erosion of these relations was intensified by demonstrations in which protestors demanded the closure of UN peacekeeping operations in both countries given their alleged ineffectiveness in dealing with the respective conflicts. In Mali and the Central African Republic, these difficult relationships were further complicated by the presence of the Wagner Group, a Russian private military company, which was accused of participating in human rights abuses and disinformation campaigns. Finally, Russia's invasion of Ukraine on 24 February 2022 exacerbated already mounting geopolitical rivalries, particularly between Western countries and Russia. This led to the closure of the OSCE SMM, as well as difficult political dynamics within the UN Security Council.

SIPRI Yearbook 2023: Armaments, Disarmament and International Security
www.sipriyearbook.org

Table 3.2 in section IV provides further details on the different multilateral peace operations and the organizations and alliances deploying them.

CLAUDIA PFEIFER CRUZ AND TIMO SMIT

I. Global trends and developments in peace operations

CLAUDIA PFEIFER CRUZ AND TIMO SMIT

In 2022 the United Nations, regional organizations and alliances, and ad hoc coalitions of states carried out 64 multilateral peace operations in 38 countries/territories across the world—the highest number of operations in the past decade (see figure 3.1). This was one more operation than in 2021.[1] Over the past decade the number of peace operations has remained relatively stable but, more recently, these operations have increasingly taken place in sub-Saharan Africa (see figure 3.2). Of the 64 operations, 24 were located in this region, with 18 in Europe, 14 in the Middle East and North Africa, 5 in Asia and 3 in the Americas (see table 3.1). The Central African Republic (CAR) has continued to be the country hosting the largest number of peace operations, with five operations on its territory, and deploying an average of 16 128 personnel per month in 2022. On 31 December 2022 it deployed 17 487 personnel and ranked second in terms of the number of personnel deployed to peace operations, only behind Somalia (20 685 personnel).

New multilateral peace operations

Five multilateral peace operations started in 2022: the Collective Security Treaty Organization (CSTO) Collective Peacekeeping Forces to Kazakhstan; the African Union Transition Mission in Somalia (ATMIS); the Economic Community of West African States (ECOWAS) Stabilisation Support Mission in Guinea-Bissau (SSMGB); the East African Community Regional Force in the Democratic Republic of the Congo (EACRF-DRC); and the African Union Monitoring, Verification and Compliance Mission (AU-MVCM) in Ethiopia.

Kazakhstan: CSTO Collective Peacekeeping Forces

The CSTO Collective Peacekeeping Forces to Kazakhstan were established on 6 January 2022 at the request of Kazakh President Kassym-Jomart Tokayev, following demonstrations initially driven by rising fuel prices but

---

[1] See also table 3.2. The quantitative analysis draws on data collected by SIPRI to examine trends in peace operations. According to SIPRI's definition, a multilateral peace operation must have the stated intention of: (*a*) serving as an instrument to facilitate the implementation of peace agreements already in place; (*b*) supporting a peace process; or (*c*) assisting conflict prevention or peacebuilding efforts. Good offices, fact-finding or electoral assistance missions, and missions comprising non-resident individuals or teams of negotiators are not included. Since all SIPRI data is reviewed on a continual basis and adjusted when more accurate information becomes available, the statistics in this chapter may not fully correspond with data found in previous editions of the SIPRI Yearbook or other SIPRI publications.

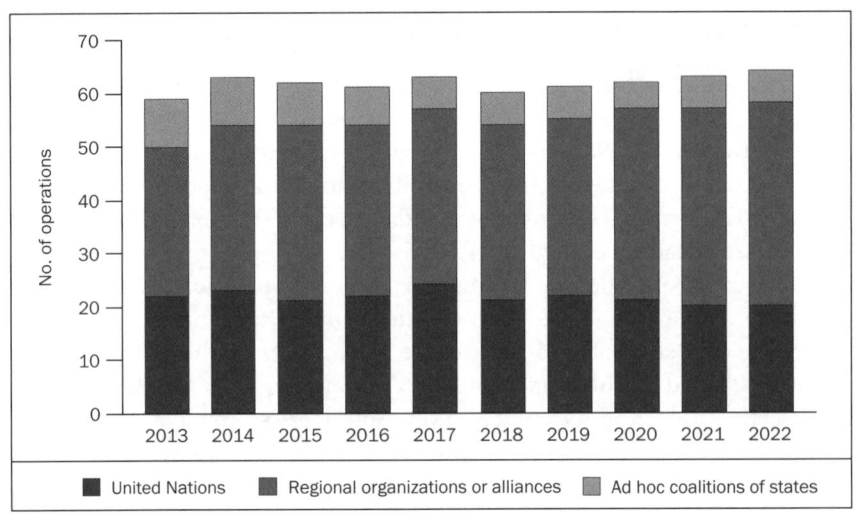

Figure 3.1. Number of multilateral peace operations, by type of conducting organization, 2013–22

that quickly escalated into mass protests with broader political demands.[2] Tokayev argued that 'international terrorist groups' had 'hijacked' the protests and used the alleged attack from these groups as a pretext to appeal to the CSTO to send troops to guard strategic infrastructure facilities and assist law enforcement with stabilization.[3] This was the first time that the CSTO had exercised its peacekeeping provision as envisaged in the 1992 Collective Security Treaty.[4] According to Article 4 of the treaty, the organization can only deploy troops if the territory or sovereignty of a member state is threatened by an external force. Specialists on Central Asia and representatives of governments questioned the existence of an external threat to Kazakhstan and criticized the decision for creating a controversial precedent for authoritarian leaders in the region.[5] The operation, which deployed 3920 officers from Armenia, Belarus, Kyrgyzstan, Russia and Tajikistan, was officially terminated on 19 January 2022, following Tokayev's announcement that the forces had completed their mission.

Somalia: ATMIS

ATMIS replaced the African Union Mission in Somalia (AMISOM) on 1 April 2022, with the mandate to support the national government in the

---

[2] Collective Security Treaty Organization (CSTO), 'The statement by Nikol Pashinyan, the Chairman of the CSTO Collective Security Council—Prime Minister of the Republic of Armenia', 6 Jan. 2022.

[3] Hedenskorg, J. and von Essen, H., 'Russia's CSTO intervention in Kazakhstan: Motives, risks and consequences', Swedish Institute of International Affairs, 14 Jan. 2022.

[4] CSTO, 'Collective Security Treaty', 15 May 1992.

[5] Pannier, B., 'The consequences of inviting Russian-led CSTO troops into Kazakhstan', Radio Free Europe/Radio Liberty, 6 Jan. 2022.

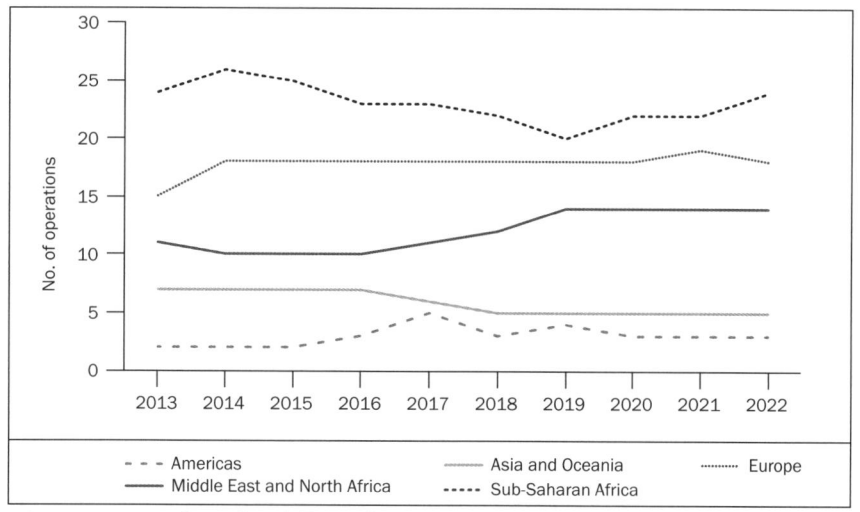

Figure 3.2. Number of multilateral peace operations, by region, 2013–22

fight against al-Shabab and other terrorist groups, provide security, develop the capacity of the security forces, justice and local authorities, and support peace and reconciliation in the country.[6] In recent years, AMISOM had become increasingly unpopular among a section of Somali politicians and its future was also threatened by budget cuts. However, the security situation in the country remained too fragile for a complete withdrawal of AU contingents.[7] The new peace operation is also likely to face some of its predecessor's financial issues, despite the European Union (EU) approving support to ATMIS under the European Peace Facility in July 2022.[8] Moreover, many of the other issues that challenged AMISOM remain a concern under ATMIS, including power struggles among political elites and the ongoing al-Shabab insurgency. An attack by the group in Mogadishu in October 2022, for example, claimed the lives of 100 people and injured more than 300.[9]

The mandate of the new peace operation is expected to last until 31 December 2024, after which its security responsibilities are expected to be handed over to the Somali security forces. Both the mandate and the authorized deployments of ATMIS have changed little from its predecessor. The key difference in the mandate is the inclusion of a transition plan that envisages a four-phased approach to the transfer of responsibilities to the Somali

---

[6] United Nations Security Council Resolution 2628, 31 Mar. 2022.

[7] See e.g. the discussion in Pfeifer Cruz, C., van der Lijn J. and Smit, T., 'Global and regional trends and developments in multilateral peace operations'; and Davis, I., 'Armed conflict and peace processes in East Africa', *SIPRI Yearbook 2022*, pp. 56–58, 232, respectively.

[8] Council of the European Union (EU), 'EU support to the African Union Mission in Somalia: Council approves further support under the European Peace Facility', Press release, 6 July 2022.

[9] Sheikh, A. and Hassani, A., 'Car bombs at busy Somalia market intersection killed at least 100, president says', Reuters, 30 Oct. 2022.

Table 3.1. Number of multilateral peace operations and personnel deployed, by region and type of organization, 2022

Conducting organization	Americas	Asia and Oceania	Europe	Middle East and North Africa	Sub-Saharan Africa	**World**
Operations	3	5	18	14	24	**64**
United Nations	2	2	2	7	7	20
Regional organization or alliance	1	1	13	6	17	38
Ad hoc coalition	0	2	3	1	0	6
Personnel	306	311	7 567	14 206	92 594	**114 984**
United Nations	279	301	1 013	12 362	66 553	80 508
Regional organization or alliance	27	–	5 431	693	26 041	32 192
Ad hoc coalition	–	10	1 123	1 151	–	2 284

– = not applicable.

Notes: Numbers of active operations cover the year 2022, including operations closed during the year. Personnel figures are as of 31 Dec. 2022.

Source: SIPRI Multilateral Peace Operations Database, Apr. 2023.

government.[10] In terms of personnel deployments, during the reconfiguration of the peace operation, both the military and police components maintained AMISOM strength.[11] A drawdown of 2000 ATMIS personnel was expected by the end of 2022 but was postponed to the end of 2023.[12]

Guinea-Bissau: SSMGB

The SSMGB was established by ECOWAS on 3 February 2022, following a coup attempt against Guinea-Bissau President Umaro Sissoco Embaló.[13] The peace operation started to be deployed in April 2022 and resembles the 2012 ECOWAS Mission in Guinea Bissau (ECOMIB), which was deployed following a coup d'état staged by elements of the armed forces.[14] Indeed, General Francis Behanzin, ECOWAS commissioner for political affairs, peace and security, stated that the peace operation launched in 2022 was 'the same mission' as the 2012 ECOMIB in practice, given that the situation in the country had not completely stabilized.[15] The initial mandate is for one year with the possibility of renewal.

---

[10] African Union (AU), 'Communiqué of the 1068th meeting of the Peace and Security Council held on 8 Mar. 2022, on the reconfiguration of the AU Mission in Somalia (AMISOM)', 8 Mar. 2022.

[11] AU (note 10).

[12] UN Security Council Resolution 2670, 21 Dec. 2022.

[13] Economic Community of West African States (ECOWAS), 'Final communiqué of the extraordinary summit of the ECOWAS Authority of Heads of State and Government on the political situation in Burkina Faso, Guinea and Mali', 3 Feb. 2022.

[14] Dansó, I., 'Guiné-Bissau: Debate aceso sobre força militar da CEDEAO' [Guinea-Bissau: Ongoing debate on ECOWAS military force], Deutsche Welle, 4 May 2022.

[15] 'ECOWAS stabilisation force deployed in troubled Guinea Bissau', Africanews, 21 June 2022.

Democratic Republic of the Congo: EACRF-DRC

In the face of the deteriorating situation in the east of the DRC, where the country's armed forces have been fighting a resurgence of rebels from the March 23 Movement (Mouvement du 23 mars, M23), the East African Community (EAC) established its first peace operation on 20 June 2022: the EACRF-DRC.[16] The operation is a Kenyan-led security force with authorized deployments also from Burundi, South Sudan, Tanzania and Uganda. On 15 August 2022 Burundi was the first country to deploy its contingents under the EACRF-DRC.[17] Reportedly, several Burundian troops had already been on the ground in South Kivu since December 2021 in order to fight the armed group Resistance for the Rule of Law in Burundi (Résistance pour un Etat de Droit au Burundi, RED-Tabara), which opposes the Burundian government.[18] Kenya was the second country to deploy troops, doing so on 2 November 2022.[19] While the Uganda People's Defence Force (UPDF) continued to operate in the North Kivu and Ituri provinces under bilateral agreements renewed on 20 September, on 18 November it announced the deployment of one battalion under the EAC regional force.[20] At the end of 2022, Uganda and South Sudan had not yet deployed their forces despite pressure from the EAC, while Tanzania's commitment to deploy forces remained unclear.

The draft concept of operations for the EACRF-DRC is relatively brief and vague in terms of mandate. The mandate states that the joint force should support the maintenance of order in the DRC, humanitarian relief to affected populations and demobilization efforts.[21] In the EAC communiqué that launched the operation, the heads of state 'directed that an immediate ceasefire should be enforced'.[22] In November 2022 the EACRF-DRC's commander, Major General Jeff Nyagah, stated that the operation's immediate plan was to secure the strategic city of Goma from rebels, while two peace initiatives for the Great Lakes region (the Nairobi and Luanda processes) were being developed. Nyagah also emphasized that these political processes were the priorities, and that the disarmament and demobilization of armed groups and the reintegration of displaced persons would be the next steps.[23]

---

[16] East African Community (EAC), 'Communiqué of the Third Heads of State Conclave on the Democratic Republic of Congo', 20 June 2022. On the conflict in DRC, see Davis, I., 'Armed conflict and peace processes in Central Africa', *SIPRI Yearbook 2022*, pp. 221–23.

[17] 'Burundi sends troops into Congo as part of East African Force', Reuters, 15 Aug. 2022.

[18] UN High Commissioner for Refugees (UNHCR), 'UNHCR position on returns to North Kivu, South Kivu, Ituri and adjacent areas in the Democratic Republic of Congo affected by ongoing conflict and violence—Update III', Nov. 2022.

[19] Waita, E., 'Kenya deploys troops to Congo to help end decades of bloodshed', Reuters, 3 Nov. 2022.

[20] AFP, 'Uganda to deploy 1000 troops to Congo to fight rebels', Voice of America, 22 Nov. 2022.

[21] EAC, 'Concept of Operations (CONOPS) for the deployment of the East African Community Regional Force in the Democratic Republic of Congo (EACRF-DRC)', 19 June 2022.

[22] EAC (note 16).

[23] Wambui, M., 'Regional force ready to replace MONUSCO without its mistakes', *East African*, 20 Nov. 2022.

The operation was established amid heightened tensions between the DRC and Rwanda, with the latter reportedly providing support to M23 rebels since their emergence in 2012.[24] The rebel group, which had been dormant for almost a decade, resurged well armed and equipped in November 2021 and made significant territorial gains in 2022.[25] In November 2022, M23 agreed to a temporary ceasefire and, although breaches in the ceasefire have been reported, it handed over strategic positions near Goma in late December 2022.[26]

Ethiopia: AU-MCVM

On 29 December 2022 the AU launched the AU-MVCM in Mekelle, in the Tigray region of Ethiopia. The peace operation is in line with the Permanent Cessation of Hostilities Agreement (COHA) signed on 2 November 2022 between the government of Ethiopia and the Tigray People's Liberation Front (TPLF).[27] Political tensions in Tigray turned into armed conflict in November 2020 and, in the following months, the conflict escalated into a civil war.[28] The monitoring and verification team aims to ensure that the peace agreement is implemented and to prevent ceasefire violations.

Discussions on a peace operation to Haiti

In addition to these deployed operations, discussions in the UN Security Council about the potential deployment of an international specialized force to Haiti took place in 2022.[29] On 7 October 2022, faced with increasing gang violence and mass protests caused by spiralling fuel prices that paralyzed the country, the Haitian interim prime minister, Ariel Henry, called for foreign military support.[30] Although gang violence has been a problem in Haiti for many years, it intensified following the assassination of President Jovenel Moïse in July 2021.[31] At the 17 October UN Security Council meeting, the United States announced that it would work on a resolution authorizing a non-UN international security assistance mission to operate under

[24] Peyton, N. and Holland, H., 'UN experts: Rwanda has intervened militarily in eastern Congo', Reuters, 4 Aug. 2022.
[25] United Nations, Security Council, Record of UN Security Council 9081st meeting, 29 June 2022; and Blanshe, M., 'DRC: M23 rebels capture Bunagana border post, Uganda dismiss accusations of helping them', Africa Report, 13 June 2022.
[26] 'M23 rebels hand over strategic position in eastern DRC', Africanews, 23 Dec. 2022.
[27] AU, 'The African Union launches the African Union Monitoring, Verification and Compliance Mission in Mekelle, Tigray region, Ethiopia', 29 Dec. 2022. On the peace process in Ethiopia, see chapter 2, section II, in this volume.
[28] For details of the armed conflict in 2021, see Davis (note 7), pp. 225–29.
[29] United Nations, Security Council, Record of UN Security Council 9153rd meeting, 17 Oct. 2022; United Nations, Security Council, Record of UN Security Council 9159th meeting, 21 Oct. 2022; and United Nations, Security Council, Record of UN Security Council 9233rd meeting, 21 Dec. 2022.
[30] Coto, D., 'Haiti's leader requests foreign armed forces to quell chaos', AP News, 8 Oct. 2022.
[31] See the discussion in Caparini, M., 'Armed conflict in North America and the Caribbean', *SIPRI Yearbook 2022*, pp. 86–87.

Chapter VII of the UN Charter.[32] However, by the end of 2022, no decision had been taken to deploy such a mission.

Multilateral peace operations that closed in 2022

Four multilateral peace operations ended in 2022: the CSTO Collective Peacekeeping Forces to Kazakhstan; the Organization for Security and Co-operation in Europe (OSCE) Special Monitoring Mission to Ukraine (SMM); AMISOM; and the International Monitoring Team (IMT) in Mindanao.

Kazakhstan: CSTO Collective Peacekeeping Forces

The CSTO Collective Peacekeeping Forces to Kazakhstan (see above) was a short-term operation that was terminated on 19 January 2022, 13 days after it deployed.

Ukraine: OSCE SMM

The OSCE SMM was deployed on 21 March 2014, at the request of the Ukrainian government, to observe and report on the security situation in Ukraine and to facilitate dialogue among parties to the conflict in the east of the country. Prior to 2022, the peace operation's mandate had been consecutively renewed on a yearly basis at the OSCE Permanent Council. However, the SMM officially closed on 31 March 2022 following Russia's refusal to join the consensus on extending its mandate for another year. Instead, Russia demanded immediate closure proceedings.[33] The peace operation's closure was a direct consequence of the war in Ukraine, and Russia claimed that its decision was partly due to the change in the security situation in the country.[34] The Russian decision was criticized by several OSCE participating states.[35] Prior to Russia's invasion of Ukraine, SMM personnel observed and reported ceasefire violations, facilitated dialogue and mediated local truces that allowed, among other things, the repair of critical civilian infrastructure.[36] The SMM was the largest unarmed civilian multilateral peace operation, with 809 international personnel deployed at the time it was discontinued.

---

[32] United Nations, Security Council, Record of UN Security Council 9153rd meeting (note 29).

[33] Liechtenstein, S., 'Russia blocks mandate extension of OSCE Monitoring Mission to Ukraine', *Security and Human Rights Monitor*, 31 Mar. 2022.

[34] Liechtenstein (note 33).

[35] See e.g. British Foreign, Commonwealth and Development Office and Bush, N., 'Russia blocks decision on the mandate extension of OSCE's Special Monitoring Mission to Ukraine: UK statement to the OSCE, 31 Mar. 2022', Speech, 31 Mar. 2022; and United States Mission to the OSCE and Carpenter, M., 'Statement on the mandate extension of the OSCE Special Monitoring Mission to Ukraine', 31 Mar. 2022.

[36] Liechtenstein (note 33).

Somalia: AMISOM

AMISOM was established by the AU Peace and Security Council on 19 January 2007, with the approval of the UN Security Council, and given an initial mandate of six months and an AU authorized strength of 8000 to 9000 personnel.[37] The objectives of the peace operation were to support a national reconciliation congress and to help create security conditions for humanitarian assistance.[38] Over time, and with a deteriorating security situation on the ground, AMISOM's mandate evolved to include reducing the threat posed by the al-Shabab insurgency, supporting the Somali security forces and protecting the political process.[39]

In 2017, AMISOM deployments started to decrease following UN Security Council Resolution 2372, which authorized the gradual transfer of security responsibilities to the Somali security forces.[40] In the same period, AMISOM's main donor, the EU, cut its budget support to the peace operation, partly as a result of the operation's lack of progress in combating al-Shabab.[41] In its early years AMISOM had been relatively successful in ousting the insurgent group from key urban centres, but in its final years the peace operation undertook fewer offensive operations and acted more as a holding force. This was partly because the Somali National Army was unable to hold recaptured areas.[42]

Formal discussions about the discontinuation of AMISOM started to take place in early 2021, when both UN and AU assessments recommended its reconfiguration.[43] Nevertheless, due to disagreements between the AU and the host government regarding the restructuring, decisions on ending the peace operation were deferred. On 21 December 2021, when AMISOM's mandate was close to expiring, the UN Security Council extended it for another three months to allow for further negotiations among the Somali government, personnel contributors and donors.[44] On 1 April 2022 the AU Peace and Security Council replaced AMISOM with ATMIS (see above).[45] From 2015 to its discontinuation, AMISOM had been the largest multilateral peace operation in terms of personnel deployments, a position that ATMIS assumed when established.

---

[37] UN Security Council Resolution 1744, 21 Feb. 2007.
[38] UN Security Council Resolution 1744 (note 37); and Transnational Federal Government of the Somali Republic and the AU, 'Status of Mission Agreement (SOFA)', 6 Mar. 2022.
[39] UN Security Council Resolution 2073, 7 Nov. 2012.
[40] UN Security Council Resolution 2372, 30 Aug. 2017.
[41] Institute for Security Studies, Peace and Security Council (PSC) Report, 'The impact of new funding uncertainties on AMISOM', 7 Mar. 2018.
[42] International Crisis Group, 'Reforming the AU Mission in Somalia', Africa Briefing no. 176, 15 Nov. 2021.
[43] AU, Report of the Independent Assessment Team on the African Union's engagement in and with Somalia post 2021, 30 May 2021.
[44] UN Security Council Resolution 2614, 21 Dec. 2021.
[45] UN Security Council Resolution 2628 (note 6).

The Philippines: IMT

On 30 June 2022 the IMT ended almost two decades of monitoring activities in Mindanao, the Philippines. The peace operation was launched in October 2004 with the objective of monitoring the implementation of a 2003 ceasefire agreement between the Philippine government and the former Moro Islamic Liberation Front (MILF), one of the largest rebel groups in the region. In 2014 MILF signed a peace agreement with the Philippine government that led to the formation of the Bangsamoro Autonomous Region in Muslim Mindanao. In March 2022 Philippine President Rodrigo Duterte stated that the mandate of the IMT would no longer be extended, although MILF was still in the process of gradual disarmament.[46] During its almost two decades of activities, the peace operation received personnel contributions from Brunei, Indonesia, Japan, Libya, Malaysia and Norway. At the time of its discontinuation, the IMT encompassed personnel solely from Brunei and Malaysia.

Personnel deployments

Over the past decade there has been a general trend towards fewer personnel being deployed globally in multilateral peace operations.[47] However, December 2022 saw a modest increase of 2.79 per cent in the number of personnel deployed in multilateral peace operations compared to December 2021, which had registered one of the lowest numbers within the period 2013–22. During 2022 the number of personnel deployed increased from 111 858 to 114 984, with the main variations in personnel numbers taking place in Europe and sub-Saharan Africa. In Europe numbers decreased, due mostly to the closing of the OSCE SMM. In sub-Saharan Africa numbers increased, due to larger deployments to the Southern African Development Community Mission in Mozambique (SAMIM) and the UN Multidimensional Integrated Stabilization Mission in the Central African Republic (MINUSCA) and the establishment of the SSMGB and the EACRF-DRC.

Personnel deployed to multilateral peace operations are concentrated in sub-Saharan Africa (see figure 3.3). On 31 December 2022, 92 594 personnel were deployed to peace operations in the region, which corresponds to 80.5 per cent of all globally deployed personnel (compared to 79 per cent in December 2021). This was the first increase in the number of personnel deployed in sub-Saharan Africa since 2015. Nevertheless, since MINUSCA

---

[46] Stanford University, 'Moro Islamic Liberation Front', Mapping Militant Organizations, accessed 6 Feb. 2023.

[47] The number of personnel deployed in multilateral peace operations, unless otherwise specified, refers exclusively to international personnel and does not include national personnel employed in these operations.

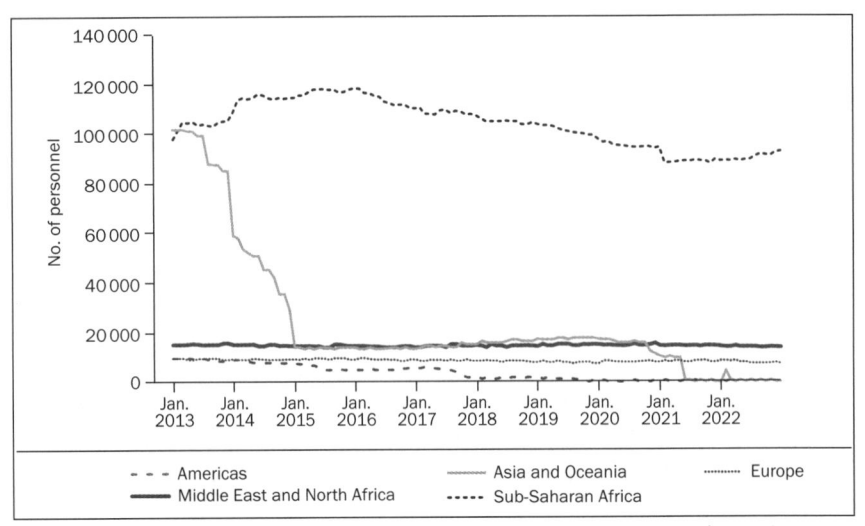

Figure 3.3. Number of personnel in multilateral peace operations, by region, 2013–22

Note: Personnel numbers are based on monthly data, with the last observation from Dec. 2022.

was established in 2014, there has been no new large-scale peace operation deployed to Africa or elsewhere.

In the Americas, Asia and Oceania, and the Middle East and North Africa, the numbers of personnel deployed remained relatively stable during 2022. The exception was Asia in January 2022, which was much higher than in the other months due the creation of the short-lived CSTO Collective Peace-keeping Forces to Kazakhstan.

The main troop- and police-contributing countries

As of 31 December 2022, the 10 largest contributors of military personnel accounted for 53.8 per cent of all military personnel deployed globally in multilateral peace operations. Although Ethiopia had been the largest military personnel contributor since 2019, in 2022 the country's ranking dropped to eighth with 4710 military personnel deployed on 31 December 2022, a decrease of 45.3 per cent compared to 2021 (see figure 3.4). This decline was largely a result of the withdrawal of Ethiopian peacekeepers from the UN Interim Security Force for Abyei (UNISFA) following the escalation of tensions between Ethiopia and Sudan over the al-Fashaga border area, where Ethiopian farmers cultivate land claimed by Sudan. In August 2021 Sudan had demanded the replacement of Ethiopian troops in UNISFA and, following much debate, on 10 April 2022 Ethiopia withdrew its contingent,

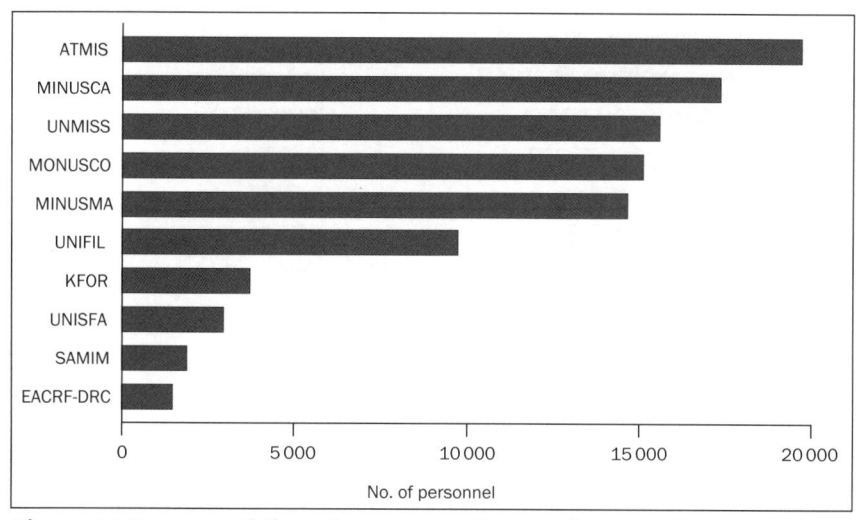

Figure 3.4. Largest multilateral peace operations as of 31 December 2022

ATMIS = African Union Transition Mission in Somalia; EACRF-DRC = East African Community Regional Force in the Democratic Republic of the Congo; KFOR = Kosovo Force; MINUSCA = United Nations Multidimensional Integrated Stabilization Mission in the Central African Republic; MINUSMA = UN Multidimensional Integrated Stabilization Mission in Mali; MONUSCO = UN Organization Stabilization Mission in the Democratic Republic of the Congo; SAMIM = Southern African Development Community Mission in Mozambique; UNIFIL = UN Interim Force in Lebanon; UNISFA = UN Interim Security Force for Abyei; UNMISS = UN Mission in South Sudan.

except for a rear party that would be repatriated later.[48] On 31 December 2021 Ethiopia had 3220 personnel deployed to UNISFA, but on 31 December 2022 the country had no deployments to the peacekeeping operation. Moreover, following the termination of Ethiopian participation in UNISFA, hundreds of military personnel from the war-torn Tigray region sought asylum in Sudan fearing for their safety.[49] Ethiopia continued to be an important contributor to ATMIS and the UN Mission in South Sudan (UNMISS), although the number of its personnel deployed to the latter fell by 44.9 per cent in 2022 compared to the previous year.

Bangladesh was the top military personnel contributor to peace operations with a total of 6728 military personnel deployed on 31 December 2022, an increase of 13.8 per cent compared to December 2021. Since 2017, the country has contributed more than 1000 personnel to each of the four largest UN peace operations: MINUSCA, the UN Multidimensional Integrated Stabilization Mission in Mali (MINUSMA), the UN Organization Stabilization Mission in

---

[48] United Nations, Security Council, 'Situation in Abyei: Report of the secretary-general', 14 Apr. 2022.

[49] 'Ethiopia ex-peacekeepers from Tigray arrive in Sudan for asylum', Africanews, 16 May 2022.

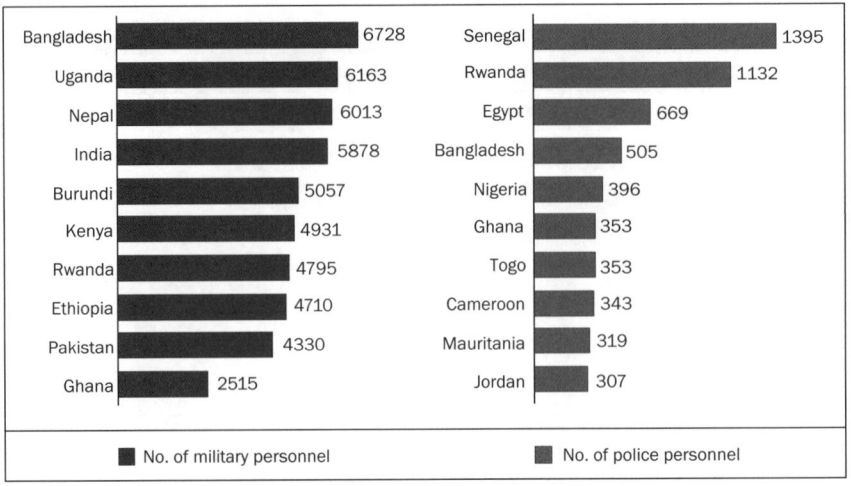

Country	No. of military personnel	Country	No. of police personnel
Bangladesh	6728	Senegal	1395
Uganda	6163	Rwanda	1132
Nepal	6013	Egypt	669
India	5878	Bangladesh	505
Burundi	5057	Nigeria	396
Kenya	4931	Ghana	353
Rwanda	4795	Togo	353
Ethiopia	4710	Cameroon	343
Pakistan	4330	Mauritania	319
Ghana	2515	Jordan	307

Figure 3.5. Main contributors of military and police personnel to peace operations as of 31 December 2022

the Democratic Republic of the Congo (MONUSCO) and UNMISS.[50] Other countries from South Asia—Nepal, India and Pakistan—are also among the largest contributors of military personnel. In December 2022 these countries were important military personnel contributors to MONUSCO, and Pakistan held the largest military contingent within the peacekeeping operation. India and Nepal are also important military personnel contributors to UNMISS, and Nepal and Pakistan are important military personnel contributors to MINUSCA. Moreover, since the withdrawal of the Ethiopian peacekeepers from UNISFA, these four South Asian countries are among the main contributors of military personnel to that peace operation.

With 6 out of the top 10, most of the main contributors to military personnel on 31 December 2022 were from sub-Saharan Africa (see figure 3.5). Uganda was the second main contributor, with 6163 military personnel deployed to peace operations, and its contributions primarily went to ATMIS. Military deployments to ATMIS and the EACRF-DRC put Kenya among the top contributors of military personnel. In addition to ATMIS and the EACRF-DRC, Burundi also deployed substantial military personnel to MINUSCA. Meanwhile, Rwanda was the top troop contributor to MINUSCA and UNMISS, the two largest UN peace operations. Ghana was new to the 2022 list of top 10 contributors, mostly because it became the main troop contributor to UNISFA (with 656 military personnel deployed), followed by Pakistan (585), Bangladesh (509) and India (488). Nevertheless, in December

---

[50] On 31 Dec. 2022 Bangladesh also contributed military personnel to UNISFA, UNIFIL and smaller missions such as MINURSO, UNFICYP, UNMHA and UNSMIL.

2022, as in previous years, most Ghanian peacekeepers were deployed to UNIFIL and UNMISS.

The top 10 contributing countries of police personnel to multilateral peace operations together provided 66.8 per cent of all police personnel deployed as of 31 December 2022. Senegal continued to be the main contributor, with 1395 police personnel, which was an increase of 11.7 per cent compared to December 2021. The country contributes police personnel primarily to MINUSCA, MINUSMA and MONUSCO. The next five top contributors of police personnel in 2022 were the same, and in the same order, as in 2021: Rwanda, Egypt, Bangladesh, Nigeria and Ghana. Jordan was the new addition to the top 10 contributors of police personnel in 2022, replacing Indonesia.

II. Organizations conducting multilateral peace operations

CLAUDIA PFEIFER CRUZ AND TIMO SMIT

The United Nations remains the main organization deploying multilateral peace operations, accounting for about one-third of all operations and 70 per cent of all personnel deployed on 31 December 2022 (see figure 3.6).[1] However, most peace operations were deployed by regional organizations and alliances, which led 38 multilateral peace operations in 2022—one more than in 2021. These took place primarily in sub-Saharan Africa. Ad hoc coalitions of states conducted six multilateral peace operations in 2022, the same as in 2021. In addition to these, there was a series of multilateral operations that aimed to contribute to security and stability but were not classified as multilateral peace operations under SIPRI's definition.

United Nations

In 2022 the UN deployed 20 multilateral peace operations—the same number as in 2021. Over the course of 2022 the number of personnel deployed in UN peace operations increased by 1.47 per cent, from 79 343 to 80 508. This modest increase breaks a trend since 2015 of consecutive year-on-year decreases in UN personnel in peace operations. The increase occurred primarily among uniformed personnel, in which deployments on 31 December 2022 were 1.6 per cent higher in comparison with December 2021. Meanwhile, the number of civilians deployed decreased by 0.68 per cent. On 31 December 2022, uniformed personnel represented 94.4 per cent of the personnel deployed in UN peace operations.

Central African Republic: MINUSCA

On 31 December 2022 the UN Multidimensional Integrated Stabilization Mission in the Central African Republic (MINUSCA) was the largest UN peace operation, deploying 17 321 international personnel. This represents an increase of 20.1 per cent compared to 31 December 2021, when it ranked as the fourth largest UN peace operation, after the UN Mission in South Sudan (UNMISS), the UN Organization Stabilization Mission in the Democratic Republic of the Congo (MONUSCO) and the UN Multidimensional Integrated Stabilization Mission in Mali (MINUSMA), respectively. The increase in MINUSCA personnel reflects a UN Security Council decision to strengthen the peacekeeping operation in response to heightened

---

[1] 'Multilateral peace operations' include both United Nations peacekeeping operations and special political missions.

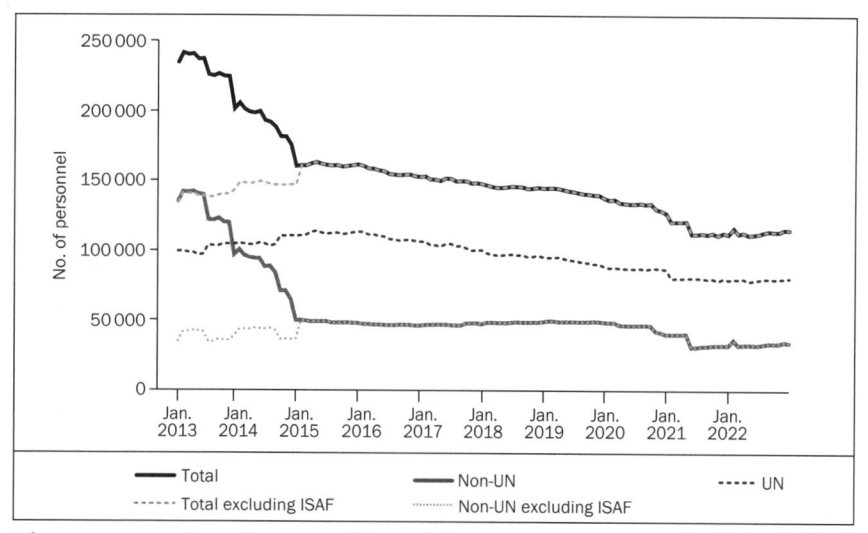

Figure 3.6. Number of personnel in multilateral peace operations, by type of conducting organization, 2013–22

ISAF = International Security Assistance Force; UN = United Nations.

Note: Personnel numbers are based on monthly data, with the last observation from Dec. 2022.

instability and violence in the country.[2] There were disagreements during the negotiations on the renewal of MINUSCA's mandate in 2021, and China and Russia both abstained in the vote. In 2022 disagreements continued and were in part related to the text's reference to 'all parties to the conflict', which would in theory include the Central African Armed Forces (Forces Armées Centrafricaines, FACA) and the Wagner Group, a Russian private military company closely tied to the Russian government and implicated in human rights abuses in the Central African Republic (CAR).[3] In 2022 China and Russia abstained once again in MINUSCA's mandate renewal. However, unlike in previous years, the 2022 mandate excluded 'support for the extension of State authority' from the peacekeeping operation's priority tasks. Supporting state authority over territories was another activity in which the Wagner Group has become increasingly involved in CAR.[4] Following the 2020–21 general elections, Wagner engagement in counteroffensives to reclaim rebel-held territory increased significantly.[5] Moreover, the presence and activities of the Wagner Group was an increasing point of tension between the UN peacekeeping operation and the CAR government in 2022.

---

[2] UN Security Council Resolution 2566, 12 Mar. 2021.
[3] On the role of the Wagner Group in sub-Saharan Africa see chapter 4, section II, in this volume.
[4] UN Security Council Resolution 2659, 14 Nov. 2022.
[5] Serwat, L. et al., 'Wagner Group operations in Africa: Civilian targeting trends in the Central African Republic and Mali', ACLED, 30 Aug. 2022.

South Sudan: UNMISS

UNMISS, which had been the largest UN peace operation since 2019, dropped to second place on 31 December 2022 with 15 579 personnel deployed—a decrease of 3.48 per cent. The security situation in South Sudan remained dire: subnational violence, abductions and revenge killings continued to take place in 2022, as well as an alarming spike in conflict-related sexual violence, which increased by 96 per cent.[6] Nevertheless, the number of killings in South Sudan decreased by 16 per cent in 2022.[7] Since the 2018 Revitalized Agreement on the Resolution of the Conflict in the Republic of South Sudan (R-ARCSS), the total number of violent incidents reported—including killing, injury, abduction and conflict-related sexual violence—has notably decreased.[8] In 2022, it decreased by 27 per cent.[9] While most violent incidents were perpetrated by community-based militias or civil defence groups (54 per cent), subnational violence involving parties to conflict victimized the largest proportion of civilians (48 per cent).[10]

Democratic Republic of the Congo: MONUSCO

With 15 108 deployed personnel, MONUSCO was the third largest UN peace operation on 31 December 2022, which represents a decrease of 1.34 per cent compared to 31 December 2021. During negotiations in December 2022 for its mandate renewal, some UN member states advocated for a reduction in the number of troops deployed in order to progress towards the transition plan for MONUSCO agreed in 2021.[11] However, the final text maintained the peacekeeping operation's strength due to the deteriorating situation in the eastern Democratic Republic of the Congo (DRC) and the resurgence of March 23 Movement (Mouvement du 23 mars, M23, see section I).[12]

Despite the UN decision to continue the peacekeeping operation until the end of 2024, demonstrations among local populations opposing MONUSCO's continuation took place in July 2022 in eastern DRC, where the operation is primarily deployed. MONUSCO's limited achievements in addressing the conflict and the consequent discontent from local populations fuelled anti-MONUSCO sentiment and violent protests. The protests left dozens

---

[6] United Nations, Security Council, 'Situation in South Sudan: Report of the secretary-general', 13 Sep. 2022; and UN Mission in South Sudan (UNMISS), Human Rights Division, 'Annual brief on violence affecting civilians: Jan.–Dec. 2022', 18 Mar. 2023.

[7] UNMISS (note 6). On fatalities related to the conflict in South Sudan see chapter 2, table 2.6, in this volume.

[8] UNMISS Human Rights Division, 'Quarterly brief on violence affecting civilians: Oct.–Dec. 2022', 17 Feb. 2023.

[9] UNMISS (note 6).

[10] UNMISS (note 6).

[11] Security Council Report, 'Democratic Republic of the Congo: Vote on MONUSCO mandate renewal and the 1533 sanctions regime', 19 Dec. 2022.

[12] UN Security Council Resolution 2666, 20 Dec. 2022; and United Nations, Security Council, Record of UN Security Council 9081st meeting, 29 June 2022.

dead, including four UN peacekeepers, and culminated in the operation's intervention brigade opening fire at a border post and killing two civilians.[13] The deterioration in relations between the UN peacekeeping operation and the host country resulted in the Congolese government expelling the spokesperson of MONUSCO and discussing how to speed up the operation's withdrawal. A UN secretary-general report expected by July 2023 is supposed to discuss the potential reconfiguration of the peacekeeping operation, considering the transition plan for MONUSCO and the role of the East African Community Regional Force in the DRC (EACRF-DRC) and other existing initiatives in support of the DRC.[14]

Mali: MINUSMA

MINUSMA was the fourth largest UN peace operation on 31 December 2022, with 14 666 international personnel deployed—a decrease of 1.68 per cent compared to 2021. The peace operation's mandate was renewed for another year on 29 June 2022 by the UN Security Council, but with 'firm opposition' from the Malian representative at the UN to the language in the document allowing freedom of movement of MINUSMA personnel to conduct human rights investigations.[15] Moreover, despite the increased reporting of human rights violations and abuses, the Malian representative affirmed that the country did not intend to implement the mandate's related provisions.[16]

Since MINUSMA's mandate was expanded in 2019 to include supporting the stabilization of central Mali, the peacekeeping operation has been stretched beyond capacity. The withdrawal of French troops and the suspension of most German military operations in Mali in August 2022 put MINUSMA under further stress.[17] According to a UN secretary-general report from 30 March 2022, the withdrawal of the French-led Operation Barkhane and Takuba Task Force would 'undoubtedly create a security gap, with implications for MINUSMA'.[18] The decisions to end these counter-terrorism operations in Mali were partly a result of heightened tensions with the Malian transitional authorities and partly due to the deployment of the Wagner Group in the country since December 2021.[19]

---

[13] United Nations, 'DR Congo: Guterres 'outraged' over peacekeepers' aggression, calls for accountability', UN News, 31 July 2022.

[14] UN Security Council Resolution 2666 (note 12).

[15] United Nations, Security Council, Record of UN Security Council 9082nd meeting, 29 June 2022.

[16] UN Security Council (note 15); and Office of the UN High Commissioner for Human Rights, 'Mali: UN expert gravely concerned by deterioration of security and human rights situation', 15 Aug. 2022.

[17] 'EU's Takuba force quits junta-controlled Mali', France 24, 1 July 2022; and Payen, C. and Garland, C., 'France withdraws last soldiers from Mali amid jihadist resurgence', France 24, 17 Aug. 2022.

[18] United Nations, Security Council, 'Situation in Mali: Report of the secretary-general', 30 Mar. 2022.

[19] On the role of the Wagner Group in Mali see chapter 4, section II, in this volume.

In November 2022, two force-contributing countries (Germany and the United Kingdom) announced their gradual withdrawal from MINUSMA following the activities of the Wagner Group.[20] Earlier in 2022, Sweden and Benin had already declared that they planned to withdraw from the peace operation by the end of 2023.[21] In a clear reference to the Wagner Group, the 2022 UN Security Council resolution that renewed MINUSMA's mandate condemned 'the use of mercenaries and violations of international humanitarian law and human rights abuses perpetrated by them'.[22] In late March 2022 in the town of Moura, an estimated 300 civilians were executed by Malian armed forces and foreign soldiers, with the latter identified by several sources as Russian.[23] Moreover, troop contributors are increasingly reluctant to deploy their personnel to MINUSMA, which has been the deadliest UN peace operation for the past two years (see below).[24]

The UN peacekeeping operation in Mali also experienced increased opposition and hostility from civil society in Bamako and the government in 2022.[25] On 14 July 2022 the Malian authorities suspended MINUSMA's troop rotations after arresting 49 soldiers from Côte d'Ivoire, accusing them of being mercenaries. The soldiers had travelled to Mali to support the German contingent in the peacekeeping operation.[26] The rotations were resumed in August, but at the end of 2022 most of the Ivorian troops, except for three female soldiers who were released as a 'humanitarian gesture', remained in detention.[27] Tensions between MINUSMA and the host country were further escalated when the operation's spokesperson was expelled under accusation of publishing 'false information' about the arrival of the Ivorian troops.[28]

A UN strategic review of MINUSMA with options for its configuration was due to be published in January 2023, as requested by the UN Security Council.[29] In advance of the operation's mandate renewal, UN Secretary-General António Guterres suggested that an AU peace operation with a Chapter VII Security Council mandate could be an alternative to MINUSMA.[30]

---

[20] AFP, 'UK to end deployment of 300 troops to UN mission in Mali', Defense Post, 15 Nov. 2022; 'Ivory Coast to withdraw from Mali peacekeeping force—Letter', Reuters, 15 Nov. 2022; and Köpp, D. and Hairsine, K., 'Germany deliberates pulling out of UN's Mali mission', Deutsche Welle, 17 Nov. 2022.

[21] 'UN says Benin will terminate contribution to peacekeeping mission in Mali', Reuters, 19 May 2022; and 'Sweden announces early pullout of troops from UN Mali mission', Reuters, 3 Mar. 2022.

[22] UN Security Council Resolution 2640, 29 June 2022.

[23] Human Rights Watch, 'Mali: Massacre by army, foreign soldiers', 5 Apr. 2022.

[24] Jezequel, J-H., Nossiter, F. and Maiga, I., 'MINUSMA at a crossroads', International Crisis Group, 1 Dec. 2022.

[25] Dessu, M. K. and Yohannes, D., 'What do protests say about UN peacekeeping in Africa?', Institute for Security Studies, 28 Oct. 2022.

[26] 'Mali authorizes UN troop rotations after standoff', Africanews and AFP, 14 Aug. 2022.

[27] 'Mali releases three women from among 49 detained Ivorian soldiers', Reuters, 4 Sep. 2022.

[28] 'Mali expels UN spokesman adding to growing diplomatic tensions', RFI, 22 July 2022.

[29] UN Security Council Resolution 2640 (note 22).

[30] 'UN chief wants African Union force with tougher mandate for Mali', RFI, 6 May 2022.

Lebanon (UNIFIL) and South Sudan/Sudan (UNISFA)

In addition to the 'big four' UN peace operations, two other UN operations featured significant numbers of deployed personnel: the UN Interim Force in Lebanon (UNIFIL) and the UN Interim Security Force for Abyei (UNISFA). Although the deployments to UNIFIL remained relatively stable in 2022, the deployments to UNISFA had decreased by 17.7 per cent on 31 December 2022 compared to 2021. This decrease to 2970 personnel reflected the UN Security Council decision to reconfigure the peace operation with a slightly reduced troop ceiling.[31] UNISFA's most recent mandate renewal, on 12 May 2022, maintained its new troop ceiling.[32] UNISFA deployments were also affected by Ethiopia's decision to withdraw its contingent (by far the peace operation's largest) by April 2022 following border tensions with Sudan over the al-Fashaga area (see section I).

The Wagner Group and peace operation–host country relations

Developments in UN peace operations in 2022 demonstrated the worsening relations between some peace operations and host governments. In the cases of Mali and CAR, this deterioration was exacerbated by the presence of the Wagner Group, which (*a*) carried out activities within the scope of peace operations, such as the extension of state authority; (*b*) was accused of human rights abuses that national authorities either refused to act on or refused to acknowledge; and (*c*) targeted UN peace operations with disinformation campaigns that inflated anti-UN sentiment and weakened peace operations' relations with host countries.[33] These new challenges faced by UN peace operations were directly affected by the intensification of geopolitical tensions, in particular between Russia and the West and linked to the war in Ukraine.

Fatalities in United Nations peace operations

During 2022, 74 international personnel and 27 local staff died while serving in UN peace operations (see figure 3.7), which was 21 fewer fatalities than in 2021.[34] Of the 74 international personnel fatalities, 53 were military personnel, 13 were international civilian personnel and 8 were police. There was a decrease in the number of fatalities across all categories of personnel compared with 2021, except for police, which had registered 2 deaths in 2021. The fatality rate for uniformed personnel in 2022 was 0.81 per 1000 uniformed personnel (see figure 3.8), 0.04 points lower than in 2021.

---

[31] UN Security Council Resolution 2609, 15 Dec. 2021.
[32] UN Security Council Resolution 2630, 12 May 2022.
[33] Trithart, A., 'Disinformation against UN peacekeeping operations', International Peace Institute, 7 Nov. 2022.
[34] The figures for fatalities in this section do not include the UN's personnel category described as 'other', and they refer to international personnel unless otherwise specified.

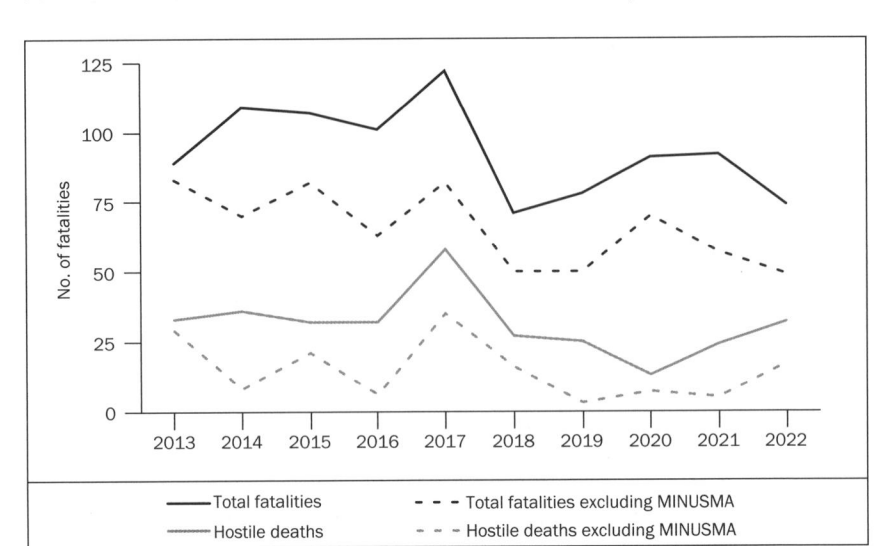

Figure 3.7. Fatalities among international personnel in United Nations peace operations, 2013–22

MINUSMA = United Nations Multidimensional Integrated Stabilization Mission in Mali.

Note: Fatality numbers are represented annually.

Even though the total number of fatalities in 2022 decreased, the number of hostile deaths (i.e. fatalities caused by malicious acts) among international personnel increased from 24 in 2021 to 32 in 2022. In contrast to 2021, when most of the deaths were caused by illness, in 2022 the main cause of peacekeepers' deaths was malicious acts. Military personnel, the category which tends to be most targeted by malicious acts, accounted for most of these deaths (28). In 2022, 22 peacekeepers died from illness, 11 died due to accidents, for 8 the cause of death was undetermined or unknown and 1 death was self-inflicted.

In 2022 MINUSMA continued to be the deadliest peace operation for peacekeepers, with 25 fatalities registered, although this was 10 fewer than in 2021. Of these, 15 were caused by malicious acts, meaning that even though the number of fatalities within the peace operation decreased, the proportion of hostile deaths increased from 54.3 per cent in 2021 to 60 per cent in 2022. These 15 fatalities in MINUSMA accounted for 46.9 per cent of the 32 hostile deaths registered within UN peace operations in 2022 (compared to 79.2 per cent in 2021). Excluding MINUSMA, the number of uniformed personnel fatalities was the lowest number for the past decade (49). In contrast, the rates of hostile deaths excluding MINUSMA reached their highest levels since 2017, mainly due to the high number of hostile deaths within MONUSCO.

The proportion of hostile deaths within MONUSCO increased from 7.69 per cent in 2021 to 61.9 per cent in 2022. This increase was largely due a MONUSCO helicopter that was shot down in March and killed eight

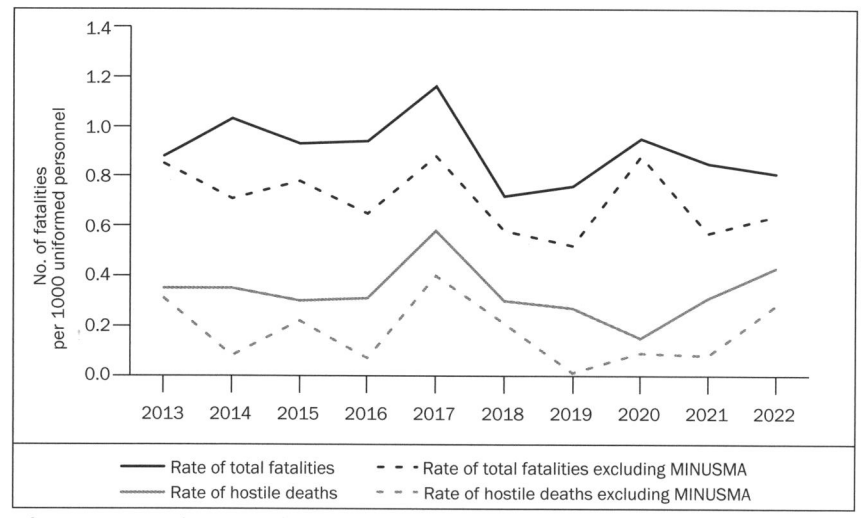

Figure 3.8. Fatality rates for uniformed personnel in United Nations peace operations, 2013–22

MINUSMA = United Nations Multidimensional Integrated Stabilization Mission in Mali.

Note: Fatality numbers are represented annually.

peacekeepers in an area where clashes between M23 and the Armed Forces of the DRC (FARDC) were taking place and due to the killing of four peacekeepers in a week of violent anti-MONUSCO protests.[35] Over the past decade, MINUSMA, MINUSCA and MONUSCO have been the deadliest UN peace operations for peacekeepers, but in 2022 the fatality rates of hostile deaths increased exclusively for MONUSCO (see figure 3.9).

Regional organizations and alliances

All five new operations in 2022 were established by regional organizations or alliances. As of 31 December 2022, multilateral peace operations established by regional organizations or alliances deployed a total of 32 192 personnel, an increase of 6.69 per cent compared to the 30 174 personnel deployed in 2021.

Africa

Five African regional organizations—the African Union (AU), the East African Community (EAC), the Economic Community of West African States (ECOWAS), the Intergovernmental Authority on Development (IGAD) and the Southern African Development Community (SADC)—conducted a total

---

[35] UN Organization Stabilization Mission in the Democratic Republic of the Congo (MONUSCO), 'MONUSCO pays tribute to the blue helmets killed in helicopter crash', 2 Apr. 2022; and 'UN honors five peacekeepers killed in eastern DRC', Africanews, 1 Aug. 2022.

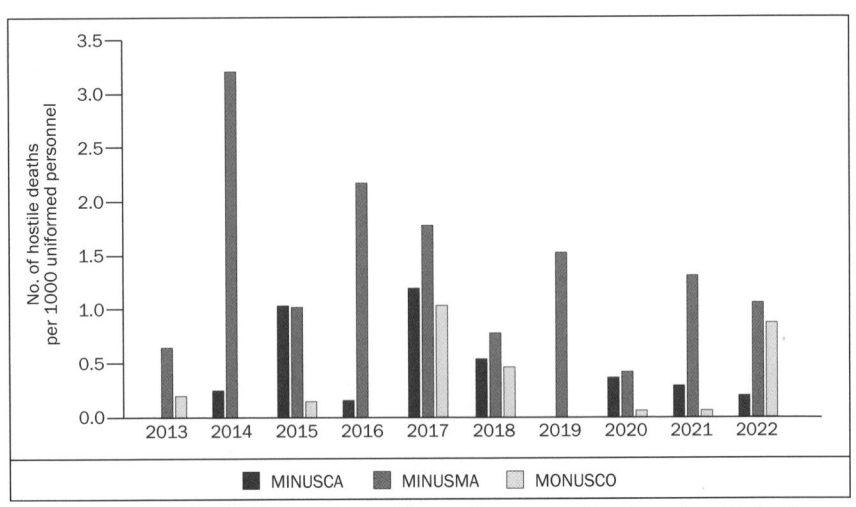

Figure 3.9. Hostile death rates for uniformed personnel in three key United Nations peace operations, 2013–22

MINUSCA = United Nations Multidimensional Integrated Stabilization Mission in the Central Africa Republic; MINUSMA = UN Multidimensional Integrated Stabilization Mission in Mali; MONUSCO = UN Organization Stabilization Mission in the Democratic Republic of the Congo.

of 11 multilateral peace operations in 2022, which was 2 more than in 2021. The total number of personnel increased by 15.2 per cent from 21 562 to 24 840. This increase was primarily due to SADC's additional deployments to the SADC Mission in Mozambique (SAMIM), ECOWAS launching the Stabilisation Support Mission in Guinea-Bissau (SSMGB) and the EAC launching the EACRF-DRC.

The AU was the regional organization conducting most of the African operations and deploying most personnel. This was largely due to the AU Transition Mission in Somalia (ATMIS), the largest multilateral peace operation in 2022, with 19 723 personnel on 31 December 2022. Other AU peace operations, namely the AU Mission for Mali and the Sahel (MISAHEL), the AU Mission for the CAR and Central Africa (MISAC), the AU Mission in Libya, the AU Military Observer Mission to the CAR (MOUACA) and the AU Monitoring, Verification and Compliance Mission (AU-MVCM) are much smaller peace operations.

On 31 October 2022 the AU Peace and Security Council (PSC) requested that the AU Commission initiate the gradual drawdown and closure of MOUACA, and its mandate activities be undertaken by MISAC.[36] The context for this decision was the fragile security situation in CAR and uncertain financial

---

[36] African Union, 'Communiqué of the 116th meeting of the PSC, held on 31 October 2022 on the topic: The situation in the Central African Republic (CAR) and the operations of the African Union Military Observer Mission in Central African Republic (MOUACA)', 31 Oct. 2022.

support to MOUACA. The peace operation's deployment had already been suspended on 31 July 2022 following the end of the European Peace Facility funding, with little prospect of a funding extension.[37] Moreover, the security situation in the country had prevented MOUACA's deployment beyond the capital Bangui, thereby limiting the operation's ability to carry out its mandate.[38] By the end of 2022, the PSC had not yet established a deadline for the closure of MOUACA.

In addition to the SSMGB, ECOWAS also led the ECOWAS Mission in Gambia (ECOMIG), which has been in place since January 2017 to address the constitutional crisis that followed the 2016 national elections. On 4 December 2022 ECOWAS extended ECOMIG's mandate for a further year, instructing a gradual downsizing of the peace operation and the training of Gambian defence and security forces.[39] As of 31 December 2022, it deployed 1001 personnel, primarily military.

IGAD led the Ceasefire and Transitional Security Arrangements Monitoring and Verification Mechanism (CTSAMVM), which has been monitoring compliance with the South Sudan peace agreement since 2018. Prior to that, the peace operation (under different names) successively monitored other ceasefire agreements.

SADC established SAMIM in 2021 to support Mozambique's fight against violent extremism in the province of Cabo Delgado.[40] On 12 April 2022 SADC approved the transition of SAMIM from AU scenario six (rapid deployment capability) to scenario five (multidimensional mission) with a robust mandate.[41] This implied the deployment of civilian, police and correctional service personnel, in addition to military contingents currently on the ground. However, by the end of 2022, none of these additional components had been deployed to Cabo Delgado. In 2022 SAMIM almost doubled its troop deployments from 1077 in December 2021 to 1900 on 31 December 2022, largely due to an increase in the deployments from the South African National Defence Force (SANDF)—the largest contingent of the peace operation.[42] The Joint Force of the Rwanda Defence Force (RDF) and the Rwanda National Police (RNP) also increased its presence in Mozambique from a strength of 1000 to around 2500 personnel. The Joint Force is not a multilateral peace operation, but a single-country contingent deployed through a bilateral agreement with

---

[37] Amani Africa, 'Update on the situation in CAR and the operations of MOUACA', 31 Oct. 2022.
[38] Amani Africa (note 37).
[39] Economic Community of West African States (ECOWAS), 'Final Communique, sixty-second ordinary session of the Authority of Heads of State and Government', 4 Dec. 2022.
[40] Southern Africa Development Community (SADC), 'Communiqué of the Extraordinary Summit of the SADC Heads of State and Government', 23 June 2021.
[41] SADC, 'Communiqué of the Extra-Ordinary Summit of the Organ Troika of the Southern African Development Community (SADC) plus SAMIM personnel contributing countries and the Republic of Mozambique', 12 Apr. 2022.
[42] Cabo Ligado, 'Cabo Ligado Weekly: 28 Mar.–3 Apr. 2022', 5 Apr. 2022.

the government of Mozambique. Finally, on 20 June 2022 the EAC launched the EACRF-DRC.

Europe and North America

Regional organizations and alliances from the northern hemisphere—the European Union (EU), the North Atlantic Treaty Organization (NATO) and the Organization for Security and Co-operation in Europe (OSCE)—conducted 25 multilateral peace operations during 2022, which was 2 less than in 2021. While 2021 saw the closure of the largest NATO multilateral peace operation, namely the Afghanistan-based Resolute Support Mission (RSM), in 2022 the largest OSCE multilateral peace operation, the Special Monitoring Mission to Ukraine (SMM), came to an end. The combined number of personnel deployed by these organizations decreased by 14.7 per cent, from 8588 on 31 December 2021 to 7325 on 31 December 2022.

In 2022 the EU conducted 15 missions and operations in the framework of its Common Security and Defence Policy (CSDP) that met SIPRI's classification of a multilateral peace operation, which was the same number as in 2021. The EU established two military CSDP missions in 2022—the EU Military Partnership Mission in Niger (EUMPM Niger) and the EU Military Assistance Mission in Support of Ukraine (EUMAM Ukraine), which provides military training to the Ukrainian armed forces in Germany and Poland—but neither of these constituted a multilateral peace operation. On 17 October 2022 the Council of the EU amended the mandate of the EU Monitoring Mission in Georgia (EUMM Georgia) to enable the temporary deployment of 40 civilian monitors from that mission to Armenia. This was to monitor the international border with Azerbaijan in order to build confidence between the two countries, following a series of deadly clashes in September 2022.[43] However, the deployment—referred to as the EU Monitoring Capacity to Armenia (EUMCAP)—was not a separate entity and had its tasks carried out by EUMM Georgia. Therefore, it did not constitute a new peace operation. The EU eventually established a fully fledged civilian CSDP mission in Armenia that would succeed EUMCAP, but this decision was not taken until January 2023.[44] The EU Capacity Building Mission in Mali (EUCAP Mali Sahel) and the EU Training Mission in Mali (EUTM Mali) remained in place despite worsening relations between the EU and the Malian authorities, but suspended their training of the Malian armed forces,

---

[43] Council Decision (CFSP) 2022/1970 of 17 Oct. 2022 amending Decision 2010/452/CFSP on the European Union Monitoring Mission in Georgia, EUMM Georgia, *Official Journal of the European Union*, L279/93, 18 Oct. 2022.

[44] Council Decision (CFSP) 2023/162 of 23 Jan. 2023 on a European Union Mission in Armenia (EUMA), *Official Journal of the European Union*, L22/29, 24 Jan. 2023.

national guard and gendarmerie in April 2022 amid concerns over the presence and role of the Wagner Group in Mali.[45]

With the closing of the RSM in 2021, NATO conducted one less multilateral peace operation in 2022. Kosovo Force (KFOR), which has been active since 1999, is now NATO's largest multilateral peace operation with 3747 international military personnel deployed on 31 December 2022. A slight reduction in KFOR personnel explains the decrease of 0.54 per cent in NATO personnel deployed in peace operations to 4247 on 31 December 2022. In February 2021, at the request of the Iraqi government, NATO agreed to expand the NATO Mission in Iraq (NMI).[46] However, by the end of 2022 there were no official reports of an expansion having been carried out.

The OSCE conducted eight multilateral peace operations in 2022, although only seven were active by the end of the year. As of 31 December 2022, the organization had 198 personnel, almost half of them in the OSCE Mission in Kosovo (OMIK). With 87 deployed personnel, OMIK became the largest OSCE peace operation following the closure of the SMM. Also due to the SMM closing, the number of international personnel deployed to OSCE field operations had decreased by 80.8 per cent on 31 December 2022 in comparison with December 2021. Most of the OSCE operations maintained fewer than 30 international personnel during 2022 and have been active since the 1990s. In 2022 the SMM registered one fatality associated with the war in Ukraine, when a national civilian member of the operation died in an attack on Kharkiv.[47]

Ad hoc coalitions

With the closure of the International Monitoring Team (IMT) in Mindanao, five operations conducted by ad hoc coalitions of states were active at the end of 2022. These were the Office of the High Representative (OHR) in Bosnia and Herzegovina; the Joint Control Commission (JCC) Joint Peacekeeping Forces (JPKF) in the disputed Trans-Dniester region of Moldova; the Multinational Force and Observers (MFO) in the Sinai Peninsula; the Neutral Nations Supervisory Commission (NNSC) on the Korean peninsula; and the Russian–Turkish Joint Monitoring Centre (RTJMC) in Azerbaijan. The number of personnel deployed in multilateral peace operations in this category decreased by 2.43 per cent in 2022, from 2341 on 31 December 2021 to 2284 on 31 December 2022.

---

[45] 'EU halts military training in Mali, German foreign minister to hold talks with junta', France 24, 12 Apr. 2022.
[46] North Atlantic Treaty Organization (NATO), 'NATO Mission Iraq', accessed 28 Feb. 2023.
[47] Organization for Security and Co-operation in Europe (OSCE), 'OSCE mourns death of national mission member of the OSCE Special Monitoring Mission to Ukraine', 2 Mar. 2022.

The role of the OHR remained an internationally disputed issue in 2022, since neither China nor Russia recognized the authority of the High Representative Christian Schmid. This led Russia to suspend financial support for the OHR in April 2022.[48] The debate was heightened by the high representative's decision to impose a series of amendments to the constitution of the federation of Bosnia and Herzegovina and to the election law of the country on the eve of the 2 October 2022 general elections.[49] According to the high representative, the measures aimed to improve the functionality of the federation and to ensure timely implementation of the election results.[50] Nevertheless, the action was met with mixed reactions from international stakeholders, with the EU delegation to Sarajevo stressing that the decision was 'of the High Representative alone'.[51]

The war in Ukraine increased tensions in the region and altered the dynamics of the JCC, which comprised 10 Ukrainian observers, and the JPKF, which is made up of military contingents from Moldova, the breakaway region of Trans-Dniester and Russia. Following Russia's invasion of Ukraine, the Ukrainian authorities closed the border with the Trans-Dniester region of Moldova, in part because they considered the Russian contingents stationed in the area (including the peacekeepers within the framework of the JPKF) as a potential threat.[52] Moreover, on 8 March 2022 the Ukrainian government announced the recall of all its peace operation forces, including military observers within the JCC, to return to Ukraine and assist in the war effort.[53]

Other multilateral operations

Multilateral organizations and ad hoc coalitions of states are increasingly deploying operations that aim to contribute to security and stability. These sometimes resemble multilateral peace operations but cannot be classified as such according to the definition applied by SIPRI. Besides EUMAM Ukraine and EUMPMP Niger, the main examples of such operations include the Multinational Joint Task Force (MNJTF) against Boko Haram, officially conducted under the political auspices of the Lake Chad Basin Commission, and

---

[48] Trkanjec, Z., 'Russia suspends financing of high representative in BiH', Euractiv, 20 Apr. 2022.
[49] Sahadžić, M., 'The Bonn Powers in Bosnia and Herzegovina: Between a rock and a hard place', ConstitutionNet and International IDEA, 29 Nov. 2022.
[50] Sahadžić (note 49).
[51] Delegation of the European Union (EU) to Bosnia and Herzegovina and EU Special Representative in Bosnia and Herzegovina, 'EU in BiH on the decision by the high representative to amend the BiH election law and the constitution of the Federation of BiH', 2 Oct. 2022.
[52] Calugareanu, V. and Verseck, K., 'Will the war in Ukraine spell the end of Transnistria?', Deutsche Welle, 12 Jan. 2023.
[53] 'Ukraine to pull troops and equipment from UN missions', Reuters, 9 Mar. 2022. At that time, in addition to the JCC, Ukraine had peacekeepers deployed to MINUSMA, MONUSCO, UNISFA, UNMIK, UNMISS, UNFICYP, KFOR and OM Moldova.

the Joint Force of the Group of Five for the Sahel (JF-G5S). Both are combat operations mandated by the AU and are made up of national contingents operating primarily within, and occasionally across, their own national borders. The MNJTF and the JF-G5S were established in 2015 and 2017, respectively. On 22 November 2022 the member states of the Accra Initiative—a regional security arrangement established in 2017 comprising Benin, Burkina Faso, Côte d'Ivoire, Ghana, Niger and Togo—announced another 10 000-strong military operation with the code name Multinational Joint Task Force/Accra Initiative (MNJTF/AI). The objective of the force is to halt the spread of terrorist and violent extremist groups from the Sahel to the coastal states of West Africa, including by means of joint cross-border military operations.[54]

Whereas some success has been attributed to the MNJTF in terms of its ability to suppress Boko Haram in the Lake Chad Basin, the JF-G5S has not been very successful in reducing the threat from armed groups in its main areas of operation in Burkina Faso, Mali and Niger.[55] In 2022 the JF-G5S was badly affected by the worsening political relations between Mali's transitional authorities and its neighbours, including the other members of the G5 Sahel, and with the European countries that have a military presence in the region, especially France. In May 2022 the Malian government announced its withdrawal from the G5 Sahel, including the JF-G5S, at which point Niger's president declared the joint force 'dead', even though the remaining contingents continued to conduct operations thereafter.[56] Meanwhile, France ended its counterterrorism Operation Barkhane in 2022 and withdrew its military from Mali in August.[57] Task Force Takuba—a multinational task force under the command of Operation Barkhane, comprising special forces from France and several other European countries—also withdrew its forces from the country in July 2022.[58]

[54] Africa Defence Forum, 'Accra Initiative takes aim at extremism's spread', 13 Dec. 2022.
[55] Onuoha, C., Yaw Tchie, A. E. and Llorens Zabalena, M., *A Quest to Win the Hearts and Minds: Assessing the Effectiveness of the Multinational Joint Task Force* (NUPI: Oslo, 2023).
[56] 'Niger president says G5 Sahel force is "dead" after Mali's departure', Reuters, 18 May 2022; and United Nations, Security Council, 'Joint Force of the Group of Five for the Sahel: Report of the secretary-general', S/2022/838, 9 Nov. 2022.
[57] Payen, C. and Garland, C., 'France withdraws last soldiers from Mali amid jihadist resurgence', France 24, 17 Aug. 2022.
[58] UN Security Council (note 56).

III. The way forward for multilateral peace operations

CLAUDIA PFEIFER CRUZ

There were three interconnected developments in 2022 that are likely to affect multilateral peace operations going forward: (*a*) the intensification of geopolitical rivalries between Russia and the West; (*b*) the deterioration in relations between some operations and their host countries; and (*c*) the regionalization of peace operations. These developments are a continuation of trends identified earlier, but during 2022 they were exacerbated by a combination of events, especially the war in Ukraine.

Geopolitical rivalries

The new geopolitical situation, highly influenced by the war in Ukraine, makes the future of several peace operations uncertain. The United Nations Multidimensional Integrated Stabilization Mission in Mali (MINUSMA) is one of them, especially following the decision of several troop-contributing countries to withdraw from the peace operation largely due to the presence of the Wagner Group in Mali. The same chain of events might be experienced in the Central African Republic (CAR), where the Wagner Group is also present. The requirement for consensus to renew or establish Organization for Security and Co-operation in Europe (OSCE) field operations has already led to the termination of the Special Monitoring Mission to Ukraine (SMM), due to the Russian veto, although it is unlikely that the peace operation would have been able to continue even if a mandate extension had been agreed. Moreover, the format of the decision-making process might place the future of other OSCE operations in jeopardy. Within the UN Security Council, all operational mandates were renewed in 2022, despite harder negotiations and disagreements. Although Russia and China abstained in several mandate renewals, such as the UN Multidimensional Integrated Stabilization Mission in the Central African Republic (MINUSCA) and MINUSMA (the latter was voted on without unanimity for the first time since its establishment), they did not veto any mandate extensions.[1] By the same token, CAR and Mali refused to condemn the invasion of Ukraine in UN meetings.[2] In this regard, it is not a coincidence that the deterioration in relations between some peace operations and their host countries and the regionalization of peace

---

[1] Security Council Report, 'Central African Republic: MINUSCA mandate renewal', What's In Blue, 13 Nov. 2022; and Security Council Report, 'Mali: Council vote to renew the mandate of MINUSMA', What's In Blue, 29 June 2022.

[2] United Nations, 'Aggression against Ukraine: Resolution/Adopted by the General Assembly', 2 Mar. 2022; and United Nations, 'Territorial integrity of Ukraine: Defending the principles of the Charter of the United Nations: Resolution/Adopted by the General Assembly', 12 Oct. 2022.

operations continued to unfold against a backdrop of intensified geopolitical rivalries between Russia and the West.

Relations with host countries

The notion that peace operations have not properly addressed protracted conflict-related crises has permeated discussions between these operations and their host governments. This was a constant source of tension during 2022, especially in certain host countries that saw demonstrations against UN peace operations, such as the UN Organization Stabilization Mission in the Democratic Republic of the Congo (MONUSCO) and MINUSMA. This anti-UN sentiment was, to some extent, both inflamed and embraced by the national governments of host countries. Popular discontent with UN peace operations also contributed to strained relationships between MINUSCA and the host government. In addition, local perceptions that UN operations had failed to address the security situation on the ground served as an endorsement of both the CAR and Malian governments bringing in Wagner Group forces. The presence of the Wagner Group and the targeting of UN peace operations with disinformation campaigns have further contributed to undermining the relationship between some peace operations and their host countries (see section II).

This erosion of relations has also hampered the execution of peace operation mandates. The Malian government, for example, denied MINUSMA free movement to investigate alleged human rights abuses—a core part of its mandate. Moreover, such abuse is likely to increase as national armed forces intensify collaboration with the Wagner Group (given the group's record to date).[3] Nevertheless, the activities of Wagner are only one facet of the problem, as challenging relations between some peace operations and their host countries predate the group's deployment. In the Democratic Republic of the Congo (DRC), for instance, where the Wagner Group's presence could not be confirmed by the end of 2022, other issues have worsened the relations between host government and peace operation, such as public demonstrations and the killing of civilians by UN peacekeepers.

The regionalization of peace operations

The five peace operations established in 2022 (see section I) illustrate how such operations have been increasingly launched under the auspices of regional organizations. Regional organizations and alliances have established operations in their own geographical area to address crises experienced by

---

[3] Serwat, L. et al., 'Wagner Group operations in Africa: Civilian targeting trends in the Central African Republic and Mali', ACLED, 30 Aug. 2022.

their member states. Moreover, these newly established operations point to a continued trend of deploying peace operations in sub-Saharan Africa, which has been (and is likely to continue to be) the main host region of peace operations. Since 2019, it has been the region where most of the new operations have been deployed. Four of the five operations established in 2022 were deployed in sub-Saharan Africa, and the other operation—the Collective Security Treaty Organization (CSTO) Collective Peacekeeping Forces to Kazakhstan—was short-term and discontinued soon after being launched. Additionally, apart from the African Union Transition Mission in Somalia (ATMIS), which is largely a continuation of the African Union Mission in Somalia (AMISOM), the newly established operations follow the existing trend of smaller operations with smaller deployments. Since the launch of MINUSCA in 2014, there has been no new large-scale operation.

In this context, regional organizations have launched operations to address crises that have either been neglected by the international community—the rationale for establishing the Southern African Development Community Mission in Mozambique (SAMIM) in 2021—or for which the existing peace operation is considered to have an inadequate mandate—part of the explanation for launching the East African Community Regional Force in the DRC (EACRF-DRC) in 2022. These regional responses have also become increasingly militarized. Combined with the intensification of geopolitical rivalries and the deterioration in relations between peace operations and host countries, the trend towards the regionalization of peace operations might lead to future mandates with less emphasis on human rights, good governance and democratization.

IV. Table of multilateral peace operations, 2022

CLAUDIA PFEIFER CRUZ

Table 3.2 provides data on the 64 multilateral peace operations conducted in 2022, including operations that were either launched or terminated during the year. The table lists operations conducted under the authority of the United Nations, operations conducted by regional organizations and alliances, and operations conducted by ad hoc coalitions of states. UN operations are divided into two subgroups: (*a*) observer and multidimensional peacekeeping operations run by the Department of Peace Operations and (*b*) special political and peacebuilding missions. The table draws on the SIPRI Multilateral Peace Operations Database, which provides information on all UN and non-UN peace operations conducted since 2000, such as location, dates of deployment and operation, mandate, participating countries, number of personnel, budget and fatalities.

Table 3.2. Multilateral peace operations, 2022

Unless otherwise stated, all figures are as of 31 Dec. 2022. Operations that closed in 2022 are shown in italic type and their figures are based on the month of their termination. The figures for closed operations are not included in the aggregate figures.

Operation	Start	Location	Mil.	Pol.	Civ.
UN peacekeeping operations			67 022	7 686	3 443
UNTSO	1948	Middle East	152	–	64
UNMOGIP	1951	India/Pakistan	42	–	21
UNFICYP	1964	Cyprus	799	67	39
UNDOF	1974	Syria (Golan)	1 131	–	48
UNIFIL	1978	Lebanon	9 511	–	232
MINURSO	1991	Western Sahara	224	2	67
MONUSCO	1999	DRC	12 935	1 592	581
UNMIK	1999	Kosovo	9	10	89
UNISFA	2011	Abyei	2 765	50	155
UNMISS	2011	South Sudan	13 198	1 545	836
MINUSMA	2013	Mali	12 342	1 604	720
MINUSCA	2014	CAR	13 914	2 816	591
UN special political missions			1 178	98	1 081
UNAMA	2002	Afghanistan	1	–	237
UNAMI	2003	Iraq	243	–	236
UNSMIL	2011	Libya	237	–	172
UNSOM	2013	Somalia	633	14	151
UNVMC	2017	Colombia	62	54	100
UNMHA	2019	Yemen	2	–	41
BINUH	2019	Haiti	–	8	55
UNITAMS	2021	Sudan	–	22	89
AU			18 606	1 040	77
MISAHEL	2013	Mali	–	–	..
MISAC	2014	CAR	–	–	..
AU Mission in Libya	2020	Libya	–	–	..
MOUACA	2020	CAR	14	–	..
ATMIS	2022	Somalia	18 586	1 040	70
AU-MVCM	2022	Ethiopia	10	–	2
CSTO			–	–	–
CSTO Collective Peacekeeping Forces to Kazakhstan	*2022*	*Kazakhstan*	*3 920*	*–*	*–*
EAC			1 500	–	–
EACRF-DRC	2022	DRC	1 500	–	–
ECOWAS			1 506	125	1
ECOMIG	2017	Gambia	875	125	1
SSMGB	2022	Guinea-Bissau	631	–	–
EU[a]			1 709	–	1 171
EUFOR ALTHEA	2004	Bosnia and Herzegovina	892	–	14
EUBAM Rafah	2005	Palestinian territories	–	–	9
EUPOL COPPS	2005	Palestinian territories	–	–	60
EULEX Kosovo	2008	Kosovo	–	–	230
EUMM Georgia	2008	Georgia	–	–	220
EUTM Somalia	2010	Somalia	179	–	12
EUCAP Sahel Niger	2012	Niger	–	–	128

Operation	Start	Location	Mil.	Pol.	Civ.
EUTM Mali	2013	Mali	429	–	57
EUBAM Libya[b]	2013b	Libya	–	–	55
EUAM Ukraine	2014	Ukraine	–	–	130
EUCAP Sahel Mali	2015	Mali	–	–	126
EUTM RCA	2016	CAR	105	–	2
EUAM Iraq	2017	Iraq	–	–	69
EUAM RCA	2020	CAR	–	–	45
EUTM Mozambique	2021	Mozambique	104	–	14
IGAD			–	–	86
CTSAMVM	2015	South Sudan	–	–	86
NATO			4 247	–	..
KFOR	1999	Kosovo	3 747	–	..
NMI	2018	Iraq	500	–	..
OAS			–	–	27
MAPP/OEA	2004	Colombia	–	–	27
OSCE			–	–	198
OSCE Mission to Skopje	1992	North Macedonia	–	–	34
OSCE Mission to Moldova	1993	Moldova	–	–	12
OSCE PRCIO	1995	Azerbaijan (Nagorno-Karabakh)	–	–	4
OSCE Mission to Bosnia and Herzegovina	1995	Bosnia and Herzegovina	–	–	29
OSCE Presence in Albania	1997	Albania	–	–	15
OMIK	1999	Kosovo	–	–	87
OSCE Mission to Serbia	2001	Serbia	–	–	17
OSCE SMM	*2014*	*Ukraine*	–	–	*809*
SADC			1 900	0	0
SAMIM	2021	Mozambique	1 900	0	0
Ad hoc coalition of states			2 266	0	18
NNSC	1953	South Korea	10	–	–
MFO	1982	Egypt (Sinai)	1 151	–	..
JCC	1992	Moldova (Trans-Dniester)	985	–	–
OHR	1995	Bosnia and Herzegovina	–	–	18
IMT	*2004*	*Philippines (Mindanao)*	*20*	*3*	*3*
RTJMC	2021	Azerbaijan (Nagorno-Karabakh)	120	–	–

– = not applicable; .. = information not available; ATMIS = AU Transition Mission in Somalia; AU = African Union; AU-MVCM = AU Monitoring, Verification and Compliance Mission; BINUH = UN Integrated Office in Haiti; CAR = Central African Republic; Civ. = international civilian personnel; CSTO = Collective Security Treaty Organization; CTSAMVM = Ceasefire and Transitional Security Arrangements Monitoring and Verification Mechanism; DRC = Democratic Republic of the Congo; EAC = East African Community; EACRF-DRC = EAC Regional Force in the DRC; ECOMIG = ECOWAS Mission in the Gambia; ECOWAS = Economic Community of West African States; EU = European Union; EUAM Iraq = EU Advisory Mission in Support of Security Sector Reform in Iraq; EUAM RCA = EU Advisory Mission in the CAR; EUAM Ukraine = EU Advisory Mission for Civilian Security Sector Reform Ukraine; EUBAM Libya = EU Integrated Border Management Assistance Mission in Libya; EUBAM Rafah = EU Border Assistance Mission for the Rafah Crossing Point; EUCAP Sahel Mali = EU Common Security and Defence Policy (CSDP) Mission in Mali; EUCAP Sahel Niger = EU CSDP Mission in Niger; EUFOR ALTHEA= EU Military Operation in Bosnia and Herzegovina; EULEX Kosovo = EU Rule of Law Mission in Kosovo; EUMM Georgia = EU Monitoring Mission in Georgia; EUPOL COPPS = EU

Police Mission for the Palestinian Territories; EUTM Mali = EU Training Mission Mali; EUTM Mozambique = EU Training Mission Mozambique; EUTM RCA = EU Training Mission in the CAR; EUTM Somalia = EU Training Mission Somalia; IGAD = Intergovernmental Authority on Development; IMT = International Monitoring Team; JCC = Joint Control Commission Peacekeeping Force; KFOR = Kosovo Force; MAPP/OEA = Organization of American States Mission to Support the Peace Process in Colombia; MFO = Multinational Force and Observers; Mil. = military personnel (troops and military observers); MINURSO = UN Mission for the Referendum in Western Sahara; MINUSCA = UN Multidimensional Integrated Stabilization Mission in the CAR; MINUSMA = UN Multidimensional Integrated Stabilization Mission in Mali; MISAC = AU Mission for the CAR and Central Africa; MISAHEL = AU Mission for Mali and the Sahel; MONUSCO = UN Organization Stabilization Mission in the DRC; MOUACA = AU Military Observer Mission to the CAR; NATO = North Atlantic Treaty Organization; NMI = NATO Mission Iraq; NNSC = Neutral Nations Supervisory Commission; OAS = Organization of American States; OHR = Office of the High Representative; OMIK = OSCE Mission in Kosovo; OSCE = Organization for Security and Co-operation in Europe; OSCE SMM = OSCE Special Monitoring Mission in Ukraine; Pol. = police; PRCIO = Personal Representative of the Chairman-in-Office on the Conflict Dealt with by the OSCE Minsk Conference; RTJMC = Russian–Turkish Joint Monitoring Centre; SADC = Southern African Development Community; SAMIM = SADC Mission in Mozambique; SSMGB = Stabilisation Support Mission in Guinea-Bissau; UN = United Nations; UNAMA = UN Assistance Mission in Afghanistan; UNAMI = UN Assistance Mission in Iraq; UNDOF = UN Disengagement Observer Force; UNFICYP = UN Peacekeeping Force in Cyprus; UNIFIL = UN Interim Force in Lebanon; UNISFA = UN Interim Security Force for Abyei; UNITAMS = UN Integrated Transition Assistance Mission in Sudan; UNMHA = UN Mission to Support the Hodeidah Agreement; UNMIK = UN Interim Administration Mission in Kosovo; UNMISS = UN Mission in South Sudan; UNMOGIP = UN Military Observer Group in India and Pakistan; UNSMIL = UN Support Mission in Libya; UNSOM = UN Assistance Mission in Somalia; UNTSO = UN Truce Supervision Organization; UNVMC = UN Verification Mission in Colombia.

[a] Figures on international civilian staff may include uniformed police.

[b] EUBAM Libya was established in 2013 but did not qualify as a multilateral peace operation prior to 1 Jan. 2019.

Source: SIPRI Multilateral Peace Operations Database, accessed 13 Apr. 2023. Data on multilateral peace operations is obtained from the following categories of open source: (*a*) official information provided by the secretariat of the organization concerned; (*b*) information provided by the operations themselves, either in official publications or in written responses to annual SIPRI questionnaires; and (*c*) information from national governments contributing to the operation under consideration. In some instances, SIPRI researchers may gather additional information on an operation from the conducting organizations or governments of participating states by means of telephone interviews and email correspondence. These primary sources are supplemented by a wide selection of publicly available secondary sources, including specialist journals, research reports, news agencies, and international, regional and local newspapers.

4. Private military and security companies in armed conflict

Overview

The last 20 years have witnessed the rapid growth of private military and security companies (PMSCs). This chapter begins by presenting an overview of the trend and highlights the issues of concern, the key legal and definitional complexities, and efforts to date to map the proliferation of PMSCs (section I). There is no universally accepted, legally binding, standard definition of a PMSC and the sector often operates in a legal lacuna: the employees of PMSCs are not soldiers or civilians, nor can they usually be defined as mercenaries. The wars in Iraq (2003–11) and Afghanistan (2001–21) reshaped perceptions of the private military and security industry, with the massive deployment of contractors by the United States leading to new market opportunities across the globe.

Today, PMSCs operate in almost every country in the world, for a broad variety of clients, assuming responsibilities for critical state and security functions. The main actors in the sector include both the host countries in which PMSCs are headquartered and key companies within those countries. A handful of home states host the majority of PMSCs: the USA, the United Kingdom, China and South Africa are estimated to collectively host about 70 per cent of the entire sector. Russia, while having a relatively small PMSC sector, has arguably used its contractors for combat more than others.

There are thousands of PMSCs around the world, most of which abide by the law, operate within their mandate, and in general contribute to stabilization and security in the settings where they operate. In the last two decades, however, the rising prominence of several high-profile PMSCs in conflict areas has prompted increased public interest in the industry. The more recent use of PMSCs by Russia in combat roles in Libya, Syria and Ukraine, as well as in several conflicts across sub-Saharan Africa, has intensified concerns. Many of these concerns centre on the activities of the Wagner Group, a Russian PMSC that has become a state proxy, promoting Russian foreign interests across multiple conflict areas. Wagner's activities have been linked with human rights abuses, violations of international humanitarian law, problematic and exploitative contracts, and election meddling. In Ukraine, the Wagner Group has been deployed en masse alongside Russian military units and it has redeployed operators from other conflicts and recruited nationals from Afghanistan, Libya and Syria.

Russia and China appear to be driving the current expansion of PMSC activity in Africa (section II), although earlier waves of activity were led by European former colonial powers or were part of cold war proxy rivalries. The

SIPRI Yearbook 2023: Armaments, Disarmament and International Security
www.sipriyearbook.org

current phase of growing PMSC involvement in Africa has occurred in a context of increased geopolitical rivalry and internationalized armed conflict. Control and extraction of natural resources is a common focal point.

Western PMSCs remain active in Africa, especially in various counterterrorism initiatives, but not in direct combat roles. In contrast, Russian PMSCs, in particular the Wagner Group, engage directly in military operations, typically for governments (and currently juntas or military transition governments) threatened by rebels or insurgents, with payment often in high-value natural resources or mining concessions. The Wagner Group has been the focus of numerous UN reports or investigations for alleged human rights abuses and violations of international humanitarian law in sub-Saharan Africa.

Chinese PMSCs have emerged more slowly and in a more restrained and circumscribed manner, but with a close connection to Chinese investment, infrastructure development and trade expansion. This may portend a more lasting engagement for Chinese interests and actors, including PMSCs, and a greater strategic impact on access to natural resources and, more broadly, sub-Saharan African political dynamics.

While the use of PMSCs in armed conflicts and fragile environments appears to be growing, questions remain about the adequacy of existing international efforts and norms to regulate the sector (section III). One of the key regulatory challenges is the use of PMSCs, particularly by Russia and Türkiye, as proxy actors in armed conflicts. These deployments are often framed as lying outside the international legal definition of a mercenary, so some states have turned to counterterrorism approaches instead; for example, by seeking to impose terrorist designations on the Wagner Group or by sanctioning its leading personnel. Cases attempting to hold mercenaries and PMSC personnel to account under criminal justice regimes are rare.

Regulatory endeavours at the UN have been reinvigorated by the war in Ukraine and the activities of the Wagner Group. A UN intergovernmental working group process has been attempting to address the gaps between the international legal provisions addressing mercenaries and the softer regulatory approaches of multistakeholder initiatives addressing PMSCs, such as the Montreux Document and the International Code of Conduct for Private Security Providers. However, consensus on the necessity of a legally binding instrument, let alone substantive content, remains elusive. Several key issues arose in the working group discussions in 2022: states were still unable to agree on whether the instrument should be binding or non-binding, and there was lack of consensus on its scope, human rights provisions and the content on accountability and remedies for victims. Discussions will continue at the UN in 2023, but whether they will translate into concrete and credible regulatory change remains to be seen.

ORI SWED, MARINA CAPARINI AND SORCHA MACLEOD

I. The global growth of private military and security companies: Trends, actors and issues of concern

ORI SWED

Introduction

The last 20 years have witnessed the rapid growth of the private military and security industry, with security providers increasing their participation in the state execution of military and security functions. This is a rapid change that has transformed a profession often given pariah status into a legitimate industry and a commonplace state proxy. At the same time, this change has introduced new types of security and human rights concerns with the state delegating its capacity to use coercive violence to private for-profit actors.

This section presents an overview of the trend and highlights the issues of concern, the key legal and definitional complexities, and efforts to date to map the proliferation of private military and security companies (PMSCs). It also discusses the deployment of PMSCs to conflict zones in Ukraine and the Middle East and North Africa (MENA), and then identifies the key actors in the sector: both the host countries in which PMSCs are headquartered and the key companies within those countries. This chapter discusses the use of PMSCs in the extractive industries in sub-Saharan Africa (section II) and outlines the specific regulatory challenges associated with PMSCs (section III).

The outsourcing of military and security functions is an old phenomenon, grounded in the tradition of mercenarism. Soldiers for hire were mentioned in biblical battlefields, took part in conflicts across the Hellenic world, were essential in medieval warfare, participated in colonialization enterprises and have taken part in various conflicts in the modern area.[1] The recent trend started at the end of the cold war and gained momentum and renewed legitimacy with the 'global war on terrorism' (an ongoing international counterterrorism campaign initiated by the United States following the 11 September 2001 terrorist attacks) and later the wars in Iraq (2003–11), Afghanistan (2001–21) and the Sahel and Great Lakes regions (2011–present). Across those wars, states used PMSCs to address the high personnel demand in responding to a real or perceived increase in insecurity or war conditions.

Factors contributing to the growth of PMSCs vary by region and state, yet they mostly fit with cost-efficiency calculations, where the sector provides skills and services that states either do not possess or would be too prohibitive to develop. For instance, for many countries, it is more efficient

---

[1] See a review of the history of this phenomenon in Singer, P. W., 'Corporate warriors: The rise of the privatized military industry and its ramifications for international security', *International Security*, vol. 26, no. 3 (2001).

to hire experts in aerial surveillance than to purchase, train and maintain a specialized aerial wing. The skills and services PMSCs offer vary, and governments sometimes use them for reasons of political expediency—such as when regular security forces are mistrusted, or to provide plausible deniability. In Afghanistan and Iraq, for example, the USA reverted to outsourcing to avoid the political and economic implications of a national draft.[2] Privatization was a way to avoid political pressure and to outsource sacrifice.[3] Similarly, China and Russia have also utilized PMSCs to address distinct political needs without involving their armed forces: for Russia, it was the ability to promote the state's foreign policy in a way that is separate from the state, while for China, the aim has been to protect its foreign investments.[4]

However, mostly, outsourcing corresponds with the increased complexity and high specialization within contemporary warfare and national security. Examples include the cyber domain, anti-piracy maritime security, counter-terrorism and surveillance. In short, the greater the specialization (e.g. telecommunication expertise in signal detection of terrorists' communication) the more challenging it is to master and maintain it. Outsourcing provides a shortcut to such security products.

This is a major trend. PMSCs operate today in almost every country in the world, for a broad variety of clients, assuming responsibilities for critical state and security functions such as border security and policing illegal immigration.[5] Their level of integration in many countries is extremely high, taking part in every aspect and stage of the national security supply chain, from arms manufacturing to weapons and facilities maintenance, training, combat support and tactical solutions on the ground.

Since 11 September 2001 the number of PMSCs has been increasing steadily, an indication of their proliferation across the globe.[6] The number of contractors deployed varies dramatically, ranging from a handful of operators that provide a specific service to thousands of contractors that offer a

---

[2] Avant, D., 'The mobilization of private forces after 9/11: Ad hoc response to poor planning', ed. J. Burk, *How 9/11 Changed Our Ways of War* (Stanford University Press: Stanford, CA, 2013).

[3] Taussig-Rubbo, M., 'Outsourcing sacrifice: The labor of private military contractors', *Yale Journal of Law & the Humanities*, vol. 2, no. 1 (2009).

[4] Fasanotti, F. S., 'Russia's Wagner Group in Africa: Influence, commercial concessions, rights violations, and counterinsurgency failure', Brookings Institution, 8 Feb. 2022; Stronski, P., 'Implausible deniability: Russia's private military companies', Carnegie Endowment for International Peace, 2 June 2020; 'China turns to PMCs to protect its workers and BRI investments in Africa', ADF, 5 Jan. 2022; and Legarda, H. and Nouwens, M., 'Guardians of the Belt and Road', Mercator Institute for China Studies, 16 Aug. 2018.

[5] Davotti, D., 'The rise of private military and security companies in European Union migration policies: Implications under the UNGPs', *Business and Human Rights Journal*, vol. 4, no. 1 (2019); and Business & Human Rights Resource Centre, 'USA: Govt. contractors accused of profiting from separation and detention of migrant and asylum seeking families', 26 June 2018.

[6] Swed, O. and Burland, D., 'The global expansion of PMSCs: Trends, opportunities, and risks', Working group on the use of mercenaries as a means of violating human rights and impeding the exercise of the right of peoples to self-determination, Texas Tech University, 2020.

host of services. Many contracts are short, measured in days, while others are long-term and can last years. It is extremely difficult to provide an accurate assessment of the size and scope of the market due to the privacy of contracts, the dual uses of some of the services that PMSCs provide (such as transportation), and the extreme secrecy surrounding the sector. However, PMSCs are used by China, Russia, the USA, the European Union, the North Atlantic Treaty Organization, the United Nations and others, indicating the broad consensus around the practice.

Issues of concern

The PMSC sector's problematic reputation is grounded in several dubious historical incidents. During the 1960s, for example, bands of mercenaries operated across Africa in the service of former colonial powers.[7] In the next decade some of the same groups were involved in several coup attempts in Benin, the Comoros and the Seychelles.[8] Later, Sandline International, a British PMSC, was associated with a scandal in Papua New Guinea (in 1997) and a coup attempt in Equatorial Guinea (in 2004).[9]

In the last two decades, the rising prominence of PMSCs in conflict areas and security settings has prompted increased public interest in the industry. Although secretive, the scale of their deployment has increased their international visibility. In many conflict zones today, PMSCs not only provide physical security for employees or infrastructure but also serve in roles traditionally reserved for the armed forces. For example, they provide logistical or intelligence support for military operations, or training for state and non-state armed groups—and, in some cases, they are involved in combat. As noted above, the USA has led this trend, and in several instances, its deployment of PMSCs has been accompanied by concerns about corruption, fraud and misconduct, and even violations of human rights and international humanitarian

---

[7] Othen, C., *Katanga 1960-63: Mercenaries, Spies and the African Nation that Waged War on the World* (History Press: Cheltenham, 2015); and Francis, D. J., 'Mercenary intervention in Sierra Leone: Providing national security or international exploitation?', *Third World Quarterly*, vol. 20, no. 2 (1999).

[8] Hughes, G., 'Soldiers of misfortune: The Angolan Civil War, the British mercenary intervention, and UK policy towards Southern Africa, 1975–6', *International History Review*, vol. 36, no. 3 (2014); and Francis (note 7).

[9] McCormack, T., 'The "Sandline Affair": Papua New Guinea resorts to mercenarism to end the Bougainville conflict', *Yearbook of International Humanitarian Law*, vol. 1 (Springer/Asser Press: New York/The Hague, Dec. 1998); and Fabricius, P., 'The coup attempt in Equatorial Guinea: Implications for private military companies in Africa', ed. N. Mlambo, *Violent Conflicts, Fragile Peace: Perspectives on Africa's Security Problems* (Adonis & Abbey Publishers Ltd: Abuja, 2008).

law (IHL).[10] Two events that received wide international scrutiny were the involvement of Blackwater in the Nisour Square shooting in 2007, which resulted in 37 civilian casualties, and CACI's involvement in the Abu Ghraib Prison torture scandals in 2004.[11] Other cases of misconduct and contractors shooting at civilians have also been widely reported.[12]

These concerns have become even more acute in the more recent use of PMSCs by Russia in the Syrian Civil War (2011–present), Libya (2014–present) and Ukraine (2014–present), and in several conflicts across sub-Saharan Africa. Many of these concerns have centred on the activities of the Wagner Group, a Russian PMSC that has become a state proxy, promoting Russian foreign policy interests across multiple conflict areas. Wagner's activities have been linked with human rights abuses, problematic and exploitative contracts, and election meddling.[13] In Syria, Wagner was linked to 'violent harassment, intimidation and sexual abuse, against peacekeepers, journalists, humanitarian workers and minorities' in a case in deliberation at the European Court of Human Rights.[14] An analysis of the Wagner Group's involvement in Mali and the Central African Republic (CAR) by the Armed Conflict Location & Event Data Project (ACLED) has pointed out that the group engages in higher levels of civilian targeting compared to local armed forces. In Mali alone over 450 civilians were killed in nine incidents linked to Wagner in 2020–22.[15] Several sources state that Wagner operatives have been harassing and intimidating civilians in CAR.[16] Wagner was also involved in

---

[10] Swed, O. and Materne, A., 'No accounting for bad contracting: Private military and security contracts and ineffective regulation in conflict areas', *Studies in Comparative International Development*, vol. 57, no. 1 (2022); Vine, D., '"We're profiteers": How military contractors reap billions from US military bases overseas', *Monthly Review*, vol. 66, no. 3 (July 2014); Tzifakis, N. and Huliaras, A., 'The perils of outsourcing post-conflict reconstruction: Donor countries, international NGOs and private military and security companies', *Conflict, Security & Development*, vol. 15, no. 1 (2015); and Hurst, L., 'The privatization of Abu Ghraib', *Toronto Star*, 16 May 2004.

[11] Hersh, S. M., 'Torture at Abu Ghraib', *New Yorker*, 10 May 2004.

[12] See e.g. Chatterjee, P., *Halliburton's Army: How a Well-connected Texas Oil Company Revolutionized the Way America Makes War* (Bold Type Books: Mar. 2010); and 'Leaks reveal Blackwater excesses', Al Jazeera, 23 Oct. 2010.

[13] Swerwat, L. et al., 'Wagner Group operations in Africa: Civilian targeting trends in the Central African Republic and Mali', ACLED, 30 Aug. 2022; and Faulkner, C., 'Undermining democracy and exploiting clients: The Wagner Group's nefarious activities in Africa', *CTC Sentinel*, vol. 15, no. 6 (June 2022).

[14] International Federation for Human Rights, 'Wagner in Syria: Appeal to European Court of Human Rights after case dismissed in Russia', Press release, 9 June 2022; and European Parliament, 'Motion for a resolution on human rights violations by private military and security companies, particularly the Wagner Group', B9-0567/2021, 21 Nov. 2021.

[15] Swerwat et al. (note 13).

[16] United Nations Human Rights Office of the High Commissioner, 'CAR: Russian Wagner Group harassing and intimidating civilians—UN experts', 27 Oct. 2021; Cohern, R., 'Putin wants fealty, and he's found it in Africa', *New York Times*, 24 Dec. 2022; and Human Rights Watch, 'Central African Republic: Abuses by Russia-linked forces', 3 May, 2022.

massacres in Aïgbado, CAR, and Moura, Mali, in 2022, resulting in hundreds of casualties.[17]

The Wagner Group was created in 2014 by Yevgeny Prigozhin, a confidant of Russian President Vladimir Putin, yet the connection to the Russian government remains obfuscated.[18] There is no legal framework for PMSCs in Russia and mercenarism is outlawed by the country's criminal code.[19] The government regularly denies any direct link to the group, arguing that it is a private entity that operates in a free market.[20] However, the group's increased involvement in the war in Ukraine—fighting alongside Russian troops, opening recruitment facilities in Russia and using state resources—underscores the strong links with the administration.[21]

These and other incidents involving PMSCs highlight the urgency and importance of addressing the challenges this industry presents. Unregulated and unchecked actors that enjoy state support and are sanctioned to use violence can lead to instability and risk.[22] While the use of PMSCs in armed conflicts and fragile environments appears to be growing, questions remain about the adequacy of existing international efforts and norms to regulate the sector (see section III).

Key definitional and legal issues

Defining PMSCs has been a challenging task for academics, policymakers and legal scholars. There is not a universally accepted, legally binding, standard definition of a 'military company' or a 'security company'. The sector often operates in a legal lacuna given that it does not clearly fit existing jurisprudence, local or international. The employees of PMSCs are not soldiers or civilians, nor can they usually be defined as mercenaries.[23] The 1989 International Convention against the Recruitment, Use, Financing and Training

---

[17] Obaji Jr., P., 'Survivors say Russian mercenaries slaughtered 70 civilians in gold mine massacre', *Daily Beast*, 31 Jan. 2022; and 'UN says investigators prevented access to site of Mali killings', Reuters, 21 Apr. 2022.

[18] Taylor, A., 'What we know about the shadowy Russian mercenary firm behind an attack on US troops in Syria', *Washington Post*, 23 Feb. 2018.

[19] Reynolds, N., 'Putin's not-so-secret mercenaries: Patronage, geopolitics, and the Wagner Group', Carnegie Endowment for International Peace, 8 July 2019.

[20] Sukhankin, S., 'War, business and ideology: How Russian private military contractors pursue Moscow's interests', Jamestown Foundation, 20 Mar. 2019.

[21] Engelbrecht, C., 'Putin ally acknowledges founding Wagner mercenary group', *New York Times*, 26 Sep. 2022.

[22] Bodurtha, M., 'An obligation to regulate: How private military companies embolden conflict with impunity from the Middle East to Central Africa', *The Bulletin—Columbia Journal of Transnational Law*, 1 Apr. 2022.

[23] Chesterman, S. and Lehnardt, C. (eds), *From Mercenaries to Market: The Rise and Regulation of Private Military Companies* (Oxford University Press: Oxford, 2007); and Percy, S. V., 'Mercenaries: Strong norm, weak law', *International Organization*, vol. 61, no. 2 (2007).

of Mercenaries provides a compound definition of who is a mercenary.[24] However, its complexity renders it a weak legal tool, which has never been used to prosecute mercenaries. Hence, while PMSCs are often described as mercenaries in the media, there is no legal standing for this classification. The distinction between PMSCs and mercenaries is important as it affects the scope and application of international law and national regulations (see section III). Without an effective definition there is no effective regulation and accountability.

The 2008 'Montreux Document on pertinent international legal obligations and good practices for states related to operations of PMSCs during armed conflict' (Montreux Document)—the result of an international process launched by the government of Switzerland and the International Committee of the Red Cross to promote respect for IHL and human rights law whenever PMSCs are present in armed conflicts—identifies PMSCs as:

private business entities that provide military and/or security services, irrespective of how they describe themselves. Military and security services include, in particular, armed guarding and protection of persons and objects, such as convoys, buildings and other places; maintenance and operation of weapons systems; prisoner detention; and advice to or training of local forces and security personnel.[25]

The document also sets out three key relationships between states and PMSCs: contracting states (countries that hire PMSCs), territorial states (countries on whose territory PMSCs operate) and home states (countries in which PMSCs are headquartered or based).

Furthermore, the integrated, complex nature of modern warfare and the highly specialized roles it involves (e.g. drone operators, prisoner interrogators, cyber experts and tank mechanics) blur the definition of front lines and combat. The outsourcing of some of those functions, historically executed by soldiers, muddies definitions even more. When contractors are employed to replace soldiers in combat support missions (e.g. monitoring communication as surveillance support, building fortifications instead of the

---

[24] Article 47 of Protocol I Additional to the 1949 Geneva Conventions, applicable in international armed conflicts, describes a mercenary as someone who: (*a*) is especially recruited in order to fight in an armed conflict; (*b*) in fact takes a direct part in hostilities; (*c*) is motivated essentially by the desire of private gain; (*d*) is neither a national of a party to the conflict nor a resident of territory controlled by a party to the conflict; (*e*) is not a member of the armed forces of a party to the conflict; and (*f*) has not been sent by a state which is not a party to the armed conflict on official duty as a member of its armed forces. See Protocol I Additional to the 1949 Geneva Conventions, and Relating to the Protection of Victims of International Armed Conflicts, opened for signature 12 Dec. 1977, entered into force 7 Dec. 1978, Article 47, 'Mercenaries'. For the International Convention's definition see United Nations Human Rights Office of the High Commissioner, International Convention against the Recruitment, Use, Financing and Training of Mercenaries, adopted 4 Dec. 1989 by General Assembly Resolution 44/34.

[25] International Committee of the Red Cross (ICRC) and Swiss Federal Department of Foreign Affairs (FDFA), *The Montreux Document on Pertinent International Legal Obligations and Good Practices for States Related to Operations of PMSCs during Armed Conflict* (ICRC/FDFA: Aug. 2009), preface, para. 9. For further discussion, see section III in this chapter.

engineering corps or transporting captives as part of a mission package) they become an integral part of the mission, even if their role seems to be mundane. In fact, given their significance, across most militaries those functions are still executed by soldiers. Relations become especially complicated in intrastate armed conflicts, which often include significant technical, logistical and development dimensions.[26]

PMSCs are therefore not easily categorized, and the services offered vary dramatically and are not restricted to combat. In fact, most of this sector's activity is located in the range between combat support (e.g. conflict area logistics or communication) and combat service support (e.g. training or rear base maintenance), often making these actors unintelligible to other commercial actors. Their contracts, which may provide clarification on the nature of their activity and proper designation are undisclosed, so much of their activity remains hidden. The convoluted organizational structure and business interactions and practices, where contractors outsource their own services or operate under shell companies, make the sector even harder to monitor, define or measure.

Efforts at mapping PMSCs

In the absence of clear definitions and faced with the challenges of collecting information, much research and analysis of PMSCs is anecdotal—often drawing on notorious incidents (such as the Nisour Square incident and the Abu Ghraib prison abuses, mentioned above) or other criminal episodes that receive widespread media coverage. Yet those represent only a segment of the industry, and this gap in information and data about the sector is reflected in the limited and often skewed research.

In 2007, as a response to high-profile incidents involving contractors and the demand for better oversight, the US Congress passed the Transparency and Accountability in Military and Security Contracting Act of 2007, which started more systematic data collection on contracts and contractors. It allowed the Congress to better monitor the industry and offered a glimpse into the role of PMSCs in the US security apparatus. Over time, and with more information available, several studies used quantitative measures to monitor PMSCs and the implications of their operations and employment. Yet those studies did not use a standardized definition of PMSCs. Instead,

---

[26] Intrastate armed conflicts are the most common form of armed conflict today and usually involve sustained violence between a state and one or more non-state armed groups. For further details, see chapter 2 in this volume.

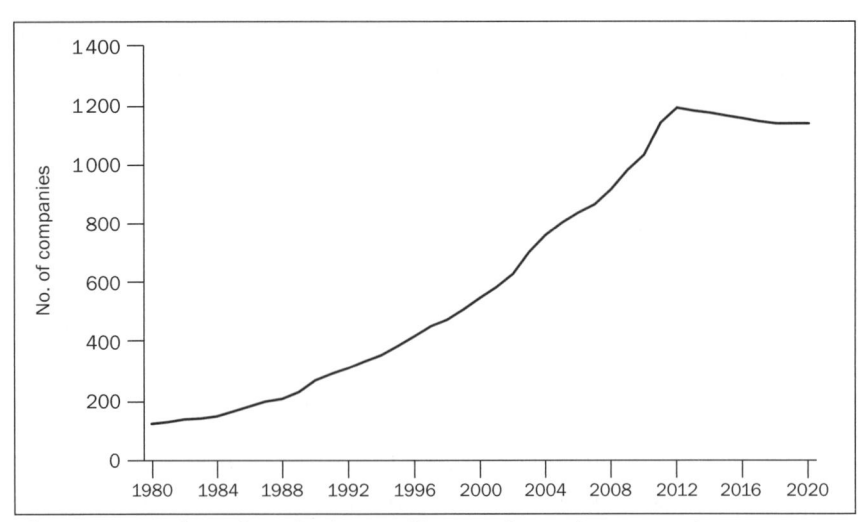

Figure 4.1. Total number of private military and security companies, 1980–2020

Source: Swed, O., The Global Private Military and Security Companies Dataset, Texas Tech University, Peace, War, and Social Conflict Laboratory, 2020.

they either assessed their participation in a conflict in general or used existing state definitions and categorizations.[27]

Furthermore, there have been several attempts to systematically map PMSCs and their activity. Conflict data sets that collect event data, such as the Social Conflict Analysis Database and ACLED, have captured PMSCs' activities in their coverage of conflicts.[28] The Private Security Database built on this coverage and provided a systematic review of contractors' involvement in weak and failed states, looking mostly at security guards.[29] In two different data sets, researchers independently collected data on PMSCs, focusing on contracts.[30] The Private Security Event Dataset, which covered PMSCs' activities across three different regions, also offered a temporal dimension, namely who did what, where and when.[31] Another attempt was

---

[27] Cotton, S. K. et al., 'Hired guns: Views about armed contractors in Operation Iraqi Freedom', RAND Corporation, Jan. 2010; and Tkach, B., 'Private military and security companies, contract structure, market competition, and violence in Iraq', *Conflict Management and Peace Science*, vol. 36, no. 3 (2019).

[28] Salehyan, I. et al., 'Social conflict in Africa: A new database', *International Interactions*, vol. 38, no. 4 (2012); and Raleigh, C. et al., 'Introducing ACLED: An Armed Conflict Location and Event Dataset', *Journal of Peace Research*, vol. 47, no. 5 (2010).

[29] Branović, Ž., *The Privatisation of Security in Failing States: A Quantitative Assessment*, Geneva Centre for the Democratic Control of Armed Forces (DCAF) Occasional Paper no. 24 (DCAF: Geneva, Apr. 2011); and Data on Armed Conflict and Security (DACS), 'Private Security Database', accessed 13 Mar. 2023.

[30] Akcinaroglu, S. and Radziszewski, E., 'Private military companies, opportunities, and termination of civil wars in Africa', *Journal of Conflict Resolution*, vol. 57, no. 5 (2013); and Tkach (note 27).

[31] Avant, D. and Neu, K. K., 'The Private Security Events Database', *Journal of Conflict Resolution*, vol. 63, no. 8 (2019).

conducted with the Commercial Military Actor Database, which focused on civil wars and offered a broader list of companies.[32]

Lastly, in a report to the UN working group on the use of mercenaries, the PMSC data of the Peace, War, and Social Conflict Laboratory at Texas Tech University was used to provide a comprehensive longitudinal review of the sector.[33] This data collection effort focused on companies that operate internationally in conflict areas and deliver services that are mission essential for military operations and that otherwise would be carried out by the armed forces. This definition is also used to frame the discussion of PMSCS in this section of the chapter. Figure 4.1, taken from the UN working group report, illustrates the scope and growth of the sector.

The complexity of the sector, its clandestine nature and the blurred lines between security and military services continue to place limitations on attempts to effectively map it. Thus, this section focuses less on specific companies and more on clients and patrons, and primarily considers PMSCs deployed to armed conflict zones.

Deployment of PMSCs to territorial states in conflict zones

The main locations in which PMSCs are deployed have shifted in the last three decades. During the 1990s, contractors took an instrumental part in several armed conflicts, with the most notable being the Sierra Leone Civil War (1991–2002) and the Kosovo War (1998–99).[34] Overall, however, armed conflicts during that period included relatively limited PMSC capacities, deploying hundreds of operators at best.[35] In Kosovo, Military Professional Resources Incorporated (MPRI) and Brown and Root Industrial Services provided logistics and training services. In Sierra Leone, Executive Outcomes forces, which provided combat solutions, artillery, intelligence and air support, were estimated at a few hundred personnel. The following decade, with the wars in Afghanistan and Iraq, reshaped perceptions of the industry. At its peak, the number of contractors employed by the US-led coalition in Afghanistan alone surpassed 200 000.[36] Those forces provided a comprehensive umbrella of services, which included security, translation, intelligence, logistics,

[32] Petersohn, U. et al., 'The Commercial Military Actor Database', *Journal of Conflict Resolution*, vol. 66, no. 4–5 (2022).

[33] Swed and Burland (note 6).

[34] Howe, H. M., 'Private security forces and African stability: The case of Executive Outcomes', *Journal of Modern African Studies*, vol. 36, no. 2 (June 1998); and Ortiz, C., 'The private military company: An entity at the center of overlapping spheres of commercial activity and responsibility', eds T. Jäger and G. Kümmel, *Private Military and Security Companies* (VS Verlag für Sozialwissenschaften: Wiesbaden, 2007).

[35] Maciąg, M., 'Engagement of Executive Outcomes in Sierra Leone—Utility assessment', *Security and Defence Quarterly*, vol. 27, no. 5 (2019).

[36] Swed, O., 'The Afghanistan War's legacy: The reimagining of the outsourcing of war and security', *Armed Forces & Society* (July 2022).

construction, housing and many others. The conclusion of the two wars then dramatically reduced the number of PMSCs operating in Afghanistan and Iraq. At the same time, the massive deployment of contractors in those wars created new market opportunities across the globe, as clients identified the utility and benefits of outsourcing security and military functions. During 2022, the sector's main areas of operation were in Ukraine and MENA, both discussed below, and in sub-Saharan Africa (see section II).

International PMSCs operating in Ukraine

The armed conflict in Ukraine (2014–present) has been a focal point for PMSC activity.[37] Russian PMSCs participated in the invasion and subsequent annexation of the Crimean peninsula in 2014 and have supported the Donbas pro-Russian separatists since the beginning of the conflict.[38] Open sources have identified several Russian PMSCs operating in Ukraine, among them ENOT Corp (United People's Communal Partnerships), Cossacks, RSB-Group (Russian Security Systems) and the ATK group.[39] The Russian invasion of Ukraine in February 2022 led to even greater involvement of Russian PMSCs in the conflict, especially following significant losses in troops and equipment.[40] The Wagner Group, the most recognized Russian PMSC, has been deployed en masse alongside Russian military units.[41] The estimated number of Wagner contractors in the war is around 50 000.[42] The Wagner Group's overt and extensive involvement internationalized the participation of its contractors.[43] Wagner started redeploying operators from other con-

---

[37] On the armed conflict in Ukraine see chapter 2, section I, in this volume. For a discussion on the initial causes of the conflict see Wilson, A., 'External intervention in the Ukraine conflict: Towards a frozen conflict in the Donbas', *SIPRI Yearbook 2016*, pp. 143–57; and Clem, R. S., 'Clearing the fog of war: Public versus official sources and geopolitical storylines in the Russia–Ukraine conflict', *Eurasian Geography and Economics*, vol. 58, no. 6 (2017). On the various armed groups fighting in the conflict see Galeotti, M., *Armies of Russia's War in Ukraine* (Osprey Publishing: Oxford, 2019).

[38] Sparks, J., 'Revealed: Russia's "Secret Syria mercenaries"', Sky News, 10 Aug. 2016. In Donbas several PMSCs were deployed, including RSB-Group, Antiterror-Orel, MAR and ENOT Corp; see Jones, S. G. et al., *Russia's Corporate Soldiers: The Global Expansion of Russia's Private Military Companies*, Center for Strategic and International Studies (CSIS) (Rowman & Littlefield: Lanham, MD, July 2021).

[39] Information about these Russian PMSCs is very limited. See Gusarov, V., 'Russian private military companies as licensed tool of terror', Inform Napalm, 24 Nov. 2015; and Bristow, J., *Russian Private Military Companies: An Evolving Set of Tools in Russian Military Strategy* (Foreign Military Studies Office: Fort Leavenworth, KS, 2019).

[40] Hernandez, H., 'War in Ukraine: Faced with the Russian group Wagner, "Mozart" supports the Ukrainians', OiCanadian, 25 Sep. 2022.

[41] 'Wagner deployed like normal army units on Ukraine front line: UK', Al Jazeera, 29 July 2022.

[42] DeYoung, K., 'Wagner mercenaries buy North Korean missiles for use in Ukraine war', *Washington Post*, 22 Dec. 2022.

[43] Kemal, L., 'Wagner Group lures foreign mercenaries with bumped-up salaries as Russia suffers losses', Middle East Eye, 6 Oct. 2022.

flicts and recruiting nationals from Afghanistan, Libya and Syria.[44] Western PMSCs also operated in Ukraine in 2022, although the nature of their services and clients was very different. Most of the Western PMSCs' clients were civilians, not governments, and they were hired for extraction missions or VIP protection.[45] Some offered logistics or training services—Mozart Group, Ukrainian Private Military Company, Armed Guardian Services (ARGUS) International, Raytheon Technologies, SEAL, Task Force Yankee Ukraine, European Security Academy—but they did not directly engage in the fighting, and some PMSCs did not even have armed operators in the field.

International PMSCs operating in the Middle East and North Africa

Several conflicts in MENA have involved private contractors. The mobilization of massive numbers of contractors to support, replace and augment coalition forces in Iraq, largely at the initiative of the USA, cemented the role of PMSCs as a legitimate tool for providing security in the region. Other countries in the region also began to contract the services of PMSCs, such as Constellis and G4S, mostly for capacity building, physical security and logistics.

In 2022, PMSCs were heavily active in Iraq and Syria, where various external powers—most notably Iran, Russia, Türkiye and the USA—have sought to assert influence in the complex armed conflicts in those two countries.[46] The USA, for example, has several military bases in Iraq and eastern Syria, and as of October 2022 employed 7908 contractors there. Most of the contractors were not Americans, with 3052 third-country nationals and 2156 locals.[47] The majority of this workforce was used for combat service support (base support, logistics, maintenance, construction and translation) and about 10 per cent of their activity was focused on security.

In contrast, the Russian employment of PMSCs in the region, mostly affiliated with the Wagner Group, has been focused on combat. Russia has employed about 4000 contractors along with Russian standing army units in support of the Syrian government in the civil war (2011–present). The contractors have been hired to train Syrian forces, protect assets and economic interests, and

---

[44] Erteima, M., '1300 Wagner mercenaries sent from Libya to help Russian forces in Ukraine', Anadolu Agency, 25 Mar. 2022; Cafarella, J., Yazici, E. and Coles, Z., 'Russia mobilizes reinforcements from Syria and Africa to Ukraine', Institute for the Study of War, 31 Mar. 2022; Vallortigara, B., 'Mercenary fighters in Libya and Ukraine: How social media are exposing the Russian Wagner Group', Moshe Dayan Center for Middle Eastern and African Studies, 31 May 2022; and AP News, 'Russia recruiting Afghan special forces who fought with US to fight in Ukraine', *The Guardian*, 31 Oct. 2022.

[45] Debusmann, B., 'Private military firms see demand in Ukraine war', BBC News, 9 Mar. 2022.

[46] On the armed conflicts in Iraq and Syria, see Fazil, S., 'Armed conflict and peace processes in Iraq, Syria and Turkey', *SIPRI Yearbook 2022*, pp. 164–74.

[47] US Office of the Assistant Secretary of Defense for Sustainment, 'Contractor support of US operations in the USCENTCOM area of responsibility', CENTCOM, Quarterly Contractor Census Reports, Oct. 2022; and 'Why does the US still have forces in Syria?', Al Jazeera, 24 Aug. 2022.

take part in combat missions.[48] They have worked closely with Syrian forces on the ground while coordinating aerial and artillery support for the Russian contingents in the country. The Russian contractors have been instrumental in securing the Syrian regime's victories against the Islamic State and rebel forces, often leading the attacks alongside Syrian government forces.[49] During 2022, many of those contractors were relocated to Ukraine, leaving an unverified number of Russian contractors in Syria.

Another PMSC that operates in Syria is SADAT International Defense Consultancy, a Turkish company with government ties. SADAT's services differ from those provided by Russian or Western PMSCs, and specialize in establishing proxy local forces through training, arming and sending them to fight on behalf of Türkiye.[50] They do not generally engage directly in combat; instead, they raise local paramilitaries that engage in combat. SADAT has been the main recruiter of Syrian fighters in regional conflicts. These fighters have been deployed in Syria and Libya in the service of Turkish foreign policy and military interventions in those countries.[51]

SADAT International Defense Consultancy was also influential in the second Libyan Civil War (2014–20), working closely with the Government of National Accord (GNA) in western Libya.[52] SADAT formed part of the Turkish military intervention, which included arming and training the GNA and its allies and the active participation of Turkish soldiers in the fighting. SADAT's role was to recruit, arm, train and support brigades of Syrian mercenaries that fought on behalf of the GNA.[53] A 2021 UN panel of experts report on Libya indicated that SADAT was responsible for the supervision and payment of about 5000 Syrian fighters.[54] In 2022 there were still reports of Syrian fighters affiliated with SADAT in Libya.[55]

Russian PMSCs are also heavily involved in Libya in support of the other main party in the conflict: the Libyan National Army (in essence an armed non-state group), headed by Marshal Khalifa Haftar. Some of the Russian

---

[48] Landay, J., Stewart, P. and Hosenball, M., 'Russia's Syria force grows to 4,000, US officials say', Reuters, 4 Nov. 2015; and Fitzpatrick, C., 'How many Russian soldiers have died in Syria?', Daily Beast, 13 Apr. 2017.

[49] Bristow (note 39).

[50] Frantzman, S., 'Mob boss: Turkey diverted aid for Turkmen to "Nusra" linked extremists', *Jerusalem Post*, 30 May 2021. On Türkiye's role in the armed conflicts in Iraq and Syria, see also Fazil (note 46).

[51] Powers, M., 'Making sense of SADAT, Turkey's private military company', War on the Rocks, 8 Oct. 2022.

[52] Andlauer, A., 'Sadat, une société turque de conseil militaire, reviendra-t-elle en Libye?' [Sadat, a Turkish military consulting company, will it return to Libya?], RFI, 2 Jan. 2020.

[53] Lund, A., *The Turkish Intervention in Libya*, Swedish Defence Research Agency (FOI) (FOI: Stockholm, Mar. 2022).

[54] United Nations, Security Council, Letter dated 8 March 2021 from the panel of experts on Libya established pursuant to Resolution 1973 (2011) addressed to the president of the Security Council, S/2021/229, 8 Mar. 2021.

[55] Bozkurt, A., 'Turkey continues to deploy Syrian fighters to Libya', Nordic Monitor, 16 June 2022.

contractors (from the RSB-Group and the Wagner Group) have been involved in the protection of commercial interests, such as the energy terminals and infrastructure in Benghazi, Derna, Sirte and Tobruk, or providing technical support.[56] In addition, the Wagner Group deployed about 3000 contractors who headed the fighting effort, including artillery and air forward control, sniper teams and other combat functions.[57] As of early 2022, the estimated number of contractors stood at 900.[58]

In Yemen, the ongoing civil war (2014–present) has created a massive humanitarian crisis and regional instability.[59] PMSCs have been deployed in support of the participating armies and some have taken part in the fighting. The Saudi Arabian-led coalition has deployed PMSC combat units and targeted killing teams.[60] However, Saudi Arabia had been building up its capacities for decades before this conflict, using Western PMSCs for technical and logistical support. For instance, BAE systems and its forerunners have sold advanced weapons to Saudi Arabia since the 1960s, and even provided former British Royal Air Force pilots who flew for the Royal Saudi Air Force during the North Yemen Civil War (1962–70).[61] By the start of 2000, BAE Systems and related companies employed thousands of staff in the country, delivering weapons system maintenance, training and logistical functions. During the current conflict in Yemen, it is reported that about 6300 British contractors have provided military logistics support to Saudi Arabia.[62] The UAE, a prominent Saudi Arabian partner, has been using contractors to address skilled personnel shortages, using Latin American operators and Westerns pilots.[63] Attracted by potential profits, contractors from different parts of the world have joined pro-Saudi Arabian coalition initiatives to form private armies.[64]

---

[56] Jones et al. (note 38).

[57] Kharief, A., 'Wagner in Libya—Combat and influence', Rosa Luxemburg Stiftung, Jan. 2022; and United Nations (note 54).

[58] Erteima (note 44).

[59] On the armed conflict in Yemen, see also chapter 2, sections I and II, in this volume, and Davis, I., 'Armed conflict and peace processes in Yemen', *SIPRI Yearbook 2022*, pp. 185–91.

[60] Merat, A., '"The Saudis couldn't do it without us": The UK's true role in Yemen's deadly war', *The Guardian*, 18 June 2019; DCAF Geneva Centre for Security Sector Governance, 'Addressing the contemporary use of private military and security companies in Yemen', YouTube, 23 June 2022; 'Mexican, Colombian "Blackwater" mercenaries killed in Yemen', teleSUR, 10 Dec. 2015; and Roston, A., 'A Middle East monarchy hired American ex-soldiers to kill its political enemies. This could be the future of war', BuzzFeed News, 16 Oct. 2018.

[61] Cooper, T., *Hot Skies Over Yemen: Aerial Warfare Over the Southern Arabian Peninsula: Volume 1, 1962–1994* (Helion and Company: Warwick, 2017).

[62] Merat (note 60).

[63] Hager, E. and Mazzetti, M., 'Emirates secretly sends Colombian mercenaries to Yemen fight', *New York Times*, 25 Nov. 2015; and Whitelock, C. and Jones, N., 'UAE relied on expertise of retired US troops to beef up its military', *Washington Post*, 18 Oct. 2022.

[64] Alexander, I., 'From Haiti to Yemen: Why Colombian mercenaries are fighting foreign wars', New Arab, 4 Aug. 2021; and AP News, '2 German ex-soldiers convicted over Yemen mercenary plans', *US News & World Report*, 24 Oct. 2022.

Beyond the continuous logistical and maintenance support in Saudi Arabia and neighbouring countries, a review of PMSCs' activities in Yemen and along its maritime boundaries, which looked at professional organizations such as the International Code of Conduct Association (ICOCA), indicated that in 2022 the sector was mostly employed in maritime security and energy infrastructure security.[65]

Key actors: Home states and leading companies

A handful of home states host the majority of PMSCs: the USA, the United Kingdom, China and South Africa are estimated to collectively host about 70 per cent of the entire sector.[66] Russia, while having a relatively small PMSC sector, has arguably used its contractors for combat more than others. This subsection focuses on the two states that lead the current trend of outsourcing security and war functions—the USA and Russia—and identifies areas of potential concern around some of their deployments.

United States

For the last two decades the USA has been the leading user and facilitator of the PMSC market, principally (but not exclusively) in relation to the deployment of the expeditionary forces to Afghanistan and Iraq.[67] The PMSC market emerged in the USA with the creation of new companies or the diversification of services among existing companies, mostly those that specialized in military services. Although PMSCs have been used in combat capacities in Afghanistan and Iraq, those occasions have been rare. Most US PMSCs are contracted for base support, construction, communication, logistics, management, medical, security, training, translation, transportation and other non-military functions. At the end of 2022, US PMSCs were operating or had business connections in almost every country across the globe.

One of the main US contracting parties is the Department of Defense, with the US Central Command (USCENTCOM) being one of the main employers of PMSCs.[68] Employment of PMSCs in the last decade has declined significantly with the conclusion of the wars in Afghanistan and Iraq. However, at the end of 2022, USCENTCOM still employed about 20 000 contractors—more than the total estimated Wagner deployment in sub-Saharan Africa by Russia. Other US government departments and branches also employ PMSCs. For example, PMSCs, such as the GEO Group or MVM, have been contracted by

---

[65] See the International Code of Conduct Association (ICOCA) website; and job recruitment web pages such as Silent Professionals.
[66] Swed and Burland (note 6).
[67] Swed and Burland (note 6).
[68] US CENTCOM's area of responsibility covers the Middle East (including Egypt in North Africa), Central Asia and parts of South Asia.

the US Immigration and Customs Enforcement (ICE) for border control and immigration management on the southern border of the USA.[69] Similarly, the US State Department has been using PMSCs for a range of functions, including working with Tier 1 Group to provide combat training in Saudi Arabia.[70] US PMSCs generally comprise a core of US employees, complemented by larger numbers of third-country nationals or locals. This means that most of the workforce, especially in big operations, is international or indigenous to the country of operation.[71]

Russia

Since the 1990s, the Russian government has had a complex relationship with private actors that profit from security and military services. The PMSC market in Russia has been mainly associated with patrons and politicians, given that these types of services are considered illegal in Russia and fall under the definition of mercenarism, as noted in the introduction.[72] Yet, regardless of the legal limitations, a few Russian companies have been offering their services since the 1990s, with some taking part in the Second Chechen War (1999–2009) and the Georgian–Russian War (2008).[73] Having identified the potential of PMSCs as state proxies and as an international instrument with plausible deniability, Russia started exploring the greater utility of this sector in 2013, with the deployment of Slavonic Corps in Syria.[74] The Wagner Group is the latest and most successful iteration of this trend. While Russian PMSCs have commercial interests, for the most part they are not independent actors. Instead, according to critical Western states and experts, they are directly linked to government foreign policy.[75]

Russian PMSCs have been used for combat operations in CAR, Libya, Mali, Mozambique, Syria and Ukraine. They have also been used as military proxies, assuming roles that were traditionally conducted by soldiers, among them training local forces of Russian allies in several countries, mostly in sub-Saharan Africa (see section II).[76] They provide different levels of security services, ranging from protester suppression for the government of Alexander Lukashenko in Belarus to commercially focused services such as

---

[69] Business & Human Rights Resource Centre (note 5).
[70] US Government Publishing Office, 'State, Foreign Operations, And Related Programs Appropriations for Fiscal Year 2020', Senate Hearing 116, 9 Apr. 2019.
[71] Swed and Burland (note 6).
[72] Schwartz, A. and Montfort, P., 'Band of brothers: The Wagner Group and the Russian state', CSIS, 21 Sep. 2020.
[73] Bristow (note 39).
[74] Stronski (note 4); and 'The last battle of the "Slavic Corps"', Fontanka, 14 Nov. 2013.
[75] Doxsee, C., 'Putin's proxies: Examining Russia's use of private military companies', CSIS, Statement before the US House Oversite and Reform Subcommittee on National Security, 15 Sep. 2022.
[76] Bristow (note 39).

maritime security and facilities security.[77] Lastly, Russian PMSCs have been associated with cyber and influence operations, attempting to impact public opinion and sway election outcomes. In particular, the Wagner Group has been linked to such operations in sub-Saharan Africa, while the Internet Research Agency (IRA) has sought to influence US and European elections and discourse.[78]

Similar to US PMSCs, Russian PMSCs have been recruiting worldwide, yet most of their employees are Russian nationals.[79] For the period 2014–18, most Wagner Group employees came from within Russia. Since the Russian invasion of Ukraine in February 2022, Russian PMSCs have sought to recruit more employees in Africa, MENA, the former Soviet republics and Afghanistan, but the evidence suggests that most of the recruits are still Russian.[80] The Wagner Group, in particular, has engaged in a massive recruitment drive to address the Russian army's personnel shortage in the war. The recruitment effort has been very different from earlier, more secretive approaches, with Wagner promoting enlistment on billboards and commercials, and opening recruitment offices across the country and at its headquarters in Saint Petersburg.[81] Nevertheless, the main source of recruits appears to be Russian prisons. Although Russian law prohibits prisoners from joining the army, they can join a PMSC. Wagner has approached convicts serving life or long-term prison sentences, offering them their freedom and rights in return for a few months of service.[82] This has been endorsed by the government, which has offered clemency to volunteers.[83] It is estimated that about 40 000 of the total 50 000 Wagner personnel in Ukraine were recruited in this way.[84]

---

[77] Tondo, L. et al., 'Alleged Wagner Group fighters accused of murdering civilians in Ukraine', *The Guardian*, 25 May 2022; Rondeauz, C., 'Decoding the Wagner Group: Analyzing the role of private military security contractors in Russian proxy warfare', *New America*, 7 Nov. 2019; and Marten, K., 'Russia's use of semi-state security forces: The case of the Wagner Group', *Post-Soviet Affairs*, vol. 35, no. 3 (2019).

[78] Grossman, S., Bush, D. and DiResta, R., 'Evidence of Russia-linked influence operations in Africa', Stanford Internet Observatory, 29 Oct. 2019; and Badawy, A. et al., 'Characterizing the 2016 Russian IRA influence campaign', *Social Network Analysis and Mining*, vol. 9, no. 1 (2019).

[79] Weiss, M. et al., 'The fallen mercenaries in Russia's dark army', New Lines Magazine, 19 Dec. 2021.

[80] 'Russia's Wagner fighters suffer 30 000 casualties in Ukraine: US', Al Jazeera, 18 Feb. 2023.

[81] Quinn, A., 'Putin private army's clever new hiring strategy: Billboards!', Daily Beast, 20 July 2022; and AFP, 'Russia's Wagner paramilitary group opens first official HQ in St Petersburg', Euronews, 11 Sep. 2022.

[82] Triebert, C., 'Video reveals how Russian mercenaries recruit inmates for Ukraine war', *New York Times*, 16 Sep. 2022.

[83] Ilyushina, M., 'Putin secretly pardoned convicts recruited by Wagner to fight in Ukraine', *Washington Post*, 10 Jan. 2023.

[84] Ilyushina (note 83).

Other significant home states

Several other countries have developed a vibrant PMSC market, yet their footprint and type of activity are not as substantial as the two countries described above. The UK hosts some of the largest PMSCs, among them G4S, Aegis Defence Services and GardaWorld.[85] Those, as well as others (e.g. Olive Group, Control Risks, Armor Group, 3e Global, Minimal Risk Consultancy and Chesterfield Group) offered a host of support services to the coalition forces and local governments during the wars in Afghanistan and Iraq. At one point there were an estimated 60–80 British PMSCs in Iraq during the war.[86] While the British PMSC market accounts for a significant segment of the global industry, there are no real indications in recent years that it has been involved in direct combat. This could be attributed to the UK's regulation of the industry, which is more rigorous and extensive than in most countries.

The Chinese PMSC market gained momentum after a new legal framework allowing armed services was passed in 2009. Most of its activity has been associated with the security challenges that Chinese companies and personnel face in commercial operations across the Belt and Road Initiative (BRI).[87] The BRI is at the heart of a Chinese strategic plan which aims to shift international economic gravity towards China. It includes the creation of roads, ports and rail transport that will cross Asia, MENA and Europe. Many of these infrastructure projects pass through politically unstable territories and introduce security risks for the project's workforce. For example, in 2012, 29 Chinese workers were kidnapped in Sudan, and in 2016, over 300 workers were evacuated from South Sudan due to security concerns.[88] Reluctant to fully rely on local governments to protect Chinese employees, infrastructure, materials and projects, the Chinese government decided to outsource this function. Within a decade, Chinese PMSCs started providing security services in countries across the BRI projects and beyond (including in Africa, see section II).[89]

Another important home country for PMSCs is South Africa. It is the home of one of the most influential PMSCs, Executive Outcomes, which was involved in several African wars during the 1990s.[90] Building on this legacy,

---

[85] Norton-Taylor, R., 'Foreign Office to propose self-regulation for private military firms', *The Guardian*, 23 Apr. 2009; and Overton, L., Benevilli, E. and Bruun, L., 'Britain is the world centre for private military contractors—and it's almost impossible to find out what they're up to', openDemocracy, 20 Dec. 2018.

[86] Norton-Taylor, R., 'Britain is at centre of global mercenary industry, says charity', *The Guardian*, 3 Feb. 2016.

[87] ADF (note 4); and Legarda and Nouwens (note 4).

[88] Nantulya, P., 'Chinese security firms spread along the African Belt and Road', Africa Center for Strategic Studies, 15 July 2021; and Laessing, U. and Wee, S., 'Kidnapped Chinese workers freed in Sudan oil state', Reuters, 7 Feb. 2012.

[89] Nantulya (note 88); ADF (note 4); and Markusem, M., 'A stealth industry: The quiet expansion of Chinese private security companies', CSIS, 15 Jan. 2022.

[90] Howe (note 34).

South Africa has become a hub for PMSCs that specialize in combat and combat support services. The companies with higher international visibility are Dyck Advisory Group (DAG), which has operated in Mozambique, and STTEP International, which has operated in Nigeria and Uganda.[91]

Israel has several small PMSCs operating in sub-Saharan Africa and Latin America, but its most prominent contribution is in cyber services, such as surveillance and influence tools, which have been widely contracted across the globe.[92] France and Germany also have emerging PMSC markets that operate mostly in sub-Saharan Africa.[93]

Conclusions

The incidents and activities of concern related to PMSCs described in this section represent a very small segment of a large industry. There are thousands of PMSCs around the world, most of which abide by the relevant laws, operate within their mandate, do not commit human rights violations or war crimes, and in general contribute to stabilization and security in the settings where they operate, often working closely with the UN and nongovernmental organizations.[94] The accountability model they present is self-regulation, using industry standards and codes of conduct. Many of the leading companies in the sector are members of professional organizations such as the ICOCA, ASIS International, the British Association of Private Security Companies (BAPSC), MSS Global and the International Stability Operations Association (ISOA).[95] These associations require PMSCs to follow a specific code of conduct and are used as a conduit to provide training and support on legal, human rights, equality and other issues. While self-regulation has limitations, it can assist in monitoring the industry and making it more accountable.[96] Beyond self-regulation, several countries have been addressing existing gaps in regulation of the sector, generating jurisprudence that creates better accountability overall. This includes clearer definitions,

---

[91] Freeman, C., 'South African mercenaries' secret war on Boko Haram', *The Telegraph*, 10 May 2015.
[92] Legziel, K., '"Like in Fauda": How Israeli security guards took over the world', Haaretz, 23 Feb. 2022; and Duhem, V., 'How Israel's defence and intelligence industries are making inroads across Africa', Global Sentinel, 5 Feb. 2022.
[93] Cascias, A. and Koubakin, R., 'Mercenary armies in Africa', Deutsche Welle, 15 Apr. 2022.
[94] Krahmann, E. and Leander, A., 'Contracting security: Markets in the making of MONUSCO peacekeeping', *International Peacekeeping*, vol. 26, no. 2 (2019).
[95] See ICOCA; ASIS International; British Association of Private Security Companies (BASPC); MSS Global; and International Stability Operations Association (ISOA).
[96] De Nevers, R., 'The effectiveness of self-regulation by the private military and security industry', *Journal of Public Policy*, vol. 30, no. 2 (Aug. 2010); and De Nevers, R., 'Private security companies and the laws of war', *Security Dialogue*, vol. 40, no. 2 (2009).

clearer and more specific regulations, better contracts and clearer legal boundaries.[97]

However, regulation is still very weak in many countries, including across many locations in which PMSCs operate. This means that a company that is willing to exploit any gaps can effectively do so.[98] States that increasingly rely on PMSCs as a dispensable or deniable proxy are also able to exploit such regulatory gaps, and arguably pose even greater problems and risks.[99] Within this type of relationship, states tend to ignore their PMSC proxy violations while protecting them in international forums. Lastly, emerging trends in the outsourcing of cyber capacities, which include influence operations that can cause social and political disarray or win elections, and surveillance, which can be used to monitor minorities, activists, opposition and dissidents, introduce new challenges and threats.

---

[97] Human Rights Watch, 'Iraq: Pass new law ending immunity for contractors', 8 Jan. 2008; Leander, A., 'Parsing Pegasus: An infrastructural approach to the relationship between technology and Swiss security politics', *Swiss Political Science Review*, vol. 27, no. 1 (2021); Leander, A., 'Making markets responsible: Revisiting the state monopoly on the legitimate use of force', eds O. Swed and T. Crosbie, *The Sociology of Privatized Security* (Palgrave Macmillan: Cham, 2019); and McNaylor, M., 'Mind the "gap": Private military companies and the rule of law', *Yale Journal of International Affairs*, vol. 5, no. 2 (2010).

[98] Prem, B., 'The regulation of private military and security companies: Analyzing power in multi-stakeholder initiatives', *Contemporary Security Policy*, vol. 42, no. 3 (2021).

[99] See e.g. the Battle of Khasham, when about 300 Russian contractors died in an attack on a US military base in Syria. Gibbons-Neff, T., 'How a 4-hour battle between Russian mercenaries and US commandos unfolded in Syria', *New York Times*, 24 May 2018.

II. Private military and security companies in sub-Saharan Africa

MARINA CAPARINI

As set out in section I of this chapter, private military and security companies (PMSCs) are found in a variety of contexts and fulfil diverse roles that include intelligence and risk advisory services, cybersecurity, (dis)information campaigns, close protection for high-profile individuals, security for property and infrastructure, military and security training, technical and logistical support services to host state and expeditionary forces, and in some cases combat operations. They have also become increasingly involved in providing protective and logistical services to United Nations peacekeeping and humanitarian operations.[1]

This section focuses on the contemporary use of PMSCs in sub-Saharan Africa, especially those with links to armed conflict and natural resource extraction. It discusses several trends shaping the current context of PMSC activities in sub-Saharan Africa, including the incidence and character of political violence and armed conflict, and the intersecting drives for political, military and economic influence of external powers such as China, Europe, Russia and the United States on the African continent. These factors help to explain the recent increase in the presence of PMSCs and the emergence of new actors, some of whom act as proxy forces for their home governments.

While Russia and China appear to be driving the current expansion of PMSC activity in Africa (and are the main focus of this section), both returned relatively late to the continent. From the 1960s onwards Africa experienced foreign mercenary attacks as European powers sought to preserve financial interests and influence during decolonization processes.[2] Mercenaries were also used to bolster and strengthen US influence on local allies in cold war conflicts in Africa and other areas of the Global South, while maintaining plausible deniability.[3] The demise of bipolar rivalry with the end of the cold war resulted in the broad decline of superpower influence and withdrawal of their patronage and support for proxy actors in Africa. Russia became largely

---

[1] Tkach, B. and Phillips, J., 'UN organizational and financial incentives to employ private military and security companies in peacekeeping operations', *International Peacekeeping*, vol. 27, no. 1 (2020); and United Nations Human Rights Council, 'Impact of the use of private military and security services in humanitarian action', Report of the working group on the use of mercenaries as a means of violating human rights and impeding the exercise of the right of peoples to self-determination, A/HRC/48/51, 2 July 2021.

[2] See e.g. French, H., 'The mercenary position', *Transition*, no. 73 (1997).

[3] Voss, K., 'Plausibly deniable: Mercenaries in US covert interventions during the cold war, 1964–1987', *Cold War History*, vol. 16, no. 1 (2016); and Gleijeses, P., '"Flee! The white giants are coming!": The United States, the mercenaries, and the Congo, 1964–5', *Diplomatic History*, vol. 18, no. 2 (spring 1994).

disengaged from the 1990s until 2014 (with the exception of arms sales), while China focused on its internal economic development.[4]

However, with rising instability, insurgencies and civil wars in the early 1990s, unleashed by the end of the cold war and other factors, a proliferation of new private military firms emerged to offer combat services in Africa, including Executive Outcomes (South Africa) and Sandline International (United Kingdom).[5] This was followed by mainly US and British PMSCs offering a broad array of services, as neo-liberal policies to outsource governmental defence- and security-related services gathered pace. The deployment of large numbers of military contractors—to support US forces in Iraq and operations in Afghanistan and to protect private corporations, including extractive firms in conflict-affected regions of the world—provided impetus for an expanding global 'market for force'.[6] The final part of this section briefly examines the latest wave of PMSC activity in selected conflict-affected states.

Shifting geopolitical trends and continental dynamics

The current phase of growing PMSC involvement in Africa has occurred in a context of increased geopolitical rivalry and internationalized armed conflict on the continent compared to the immediate post-cold war period. There has been a significant rise in the number of state-based armed conflicts, with 15 such conflicts occurring in Africa in 2011 and 25 in 2021.[7] There is also a high rate of conflict recurrence.[8] Internal armed conflicts in sub-Saharan Africa are markedly internationalized—an external state or states actively participate in the conflict by rendering support to the government, the opposing side or both—and this tends to make them more severe and protracted. Whereas 12 internationalized internal conflicts were recorded in sub-Saharan Africa between 1991 and 2010, this rose to 27 such conflicts

---

[4] Duursma, A. and Masuhr, N., 'Russia's return to Africa in a historical and global context: Anti-imperialism, patronage, and opportunism', *South African Journal of International Affairs*, vol. 29, no. 4 (2022); Webber, M., 'Soviet policy in sub-Saharan Africa: The final phase', *Journal of Modern African Studies*, vol. 30, no. 1 (Mar. 1992); and Shinn, D. H., 'China–Africa ties in historical context', eds A. Oqubay and J. Yifu Lin, *China–Africa and an Economic Transformation* (Oxford University Press: Oxford, 2019).

[5] Howe, H. M., 'Private security forces and African stability: The case of Executive Outcomes', *Journal of Modern African Studies*, vol. 36, no. 2 (1998).

[6] Singer, P. W., *Corporate Warriors: The Rise of the Privatized Military Industry* (Cornell University Press: Ithaca, NY, 2003); Pelton, R. Y., *Licensed to Kill: Hired Guns in the War on Terror* (Three Rivers Press: New York, 2006); and Avant, D. D., *The Market for Force: The Consequences of Privatizing Security* (Cambridge University Press: Cambridge, 2009).

[7] Palik, J., Obermeier, A. M. and Aas Rustad, S., *Conflict Trends in Africa, 1989–2021*, Peace Research Institute Oslo (PRIO) Paper (PRIO: Olso, 2022), p. 12. 'State-based conflict' is defined here as a conflict in which at least one party is a state, involving armed force that results in at least 25 battle-related deaths in a calendar year; see Palik, Obermeier and Aas Rustad, p. 7.

[8] Jarland, J. et al., 'How should we understand patterns of recurring conflict?', PRIO, Conflict Trends, Mar. 2020.

between 2011 and 2021.[9] According to the Peace Research Institute Oslo (PRIO), the number of 'internationalized' civil wars in Africa increased from 11 in 2018 to 19 in 2020, before falling to 17 in 2021.[10] The continent hosts multilateral peace operations mounted by the UN, the European Union (EU), the African Union and subregional organizations, currently the Eastern African Community (EAC), the Economic Community of West African States (ECOWAS), the Intergovernmental Authority on Development (IGAD) and the Southern African Development Community (SADC).[11] Other intervening forces, public and private, include Western powers (the USA, France and other European states), regional powers such as Kenya and Rwanda, and increasingly China and Russia, and other powers such as Türkiye and Israel. The growth of interference in armed conflicts on the continent strongly suggests the weakening of multilateralism.[12]

Competition between China, the USA and the EU

Heightened geopolitical competition among major powers plays out on the continent in intertwined military, commercial and diplomatic spheres, forming an important backdrop for understanding the development of PMSC presence. China's Belt and Road Initiative (BRI), aimed at building land and sea routes connecting China to key markets globally, has since 2013 provided loans, constructed roads, railways and ports and struck trade accords with developing states, often in exchange for access to natural resource concessions and without the required 'liberal peace' commitments to improve governance or human rights that Western partners have emphasized. However, China has also sought to play a bigger role in peace, security and stability in Africa.[13] Since 2009, when it overtook France, China has been the largest contributor of uniformed personnel to UN peacekeeping missions among the permanent members of the UN Security Council.[14] Since 2018 it has ranked among the top ten contributors of uniformed (troop and police) personnel of all UN member-states.[15] Moreover, it has become increasingly involved in conflict mediation, including recently in the Horn of Africa.[16]

---

[9] International Institute for Strategic Studies (IISS), 'The Armed Conflict Survey 2022: Sub-Saharan Africa Regional Analysis', IISS Analysis, 18 Nov. 2022.

[10] Palik, Obermeier and Aas Rustad (note 7), p. 16.

[11] For a comprehensive picture of multilateral peace operations in Africa, see SIPRI, 'SIPRI map of multilateral peace operations 2022', May 2022; and chapter 3 in this volume.

[12] IISS (note 9).

[13] Ryder, H. and Eguegu, O., 'Africans welcome China's role in peace and security, but are pushing for greater agency and responsibility', ACCORD, Conflict and Resilience Monitor, 10 Feb. 2022.

[14] SIPRI Multilateral Peace Operations Database, accessed 3 Mar. 2023; and International Peace Institute (IPI), 'UN peacekeeping personnel contributions by the P5 (Nov. 1990–Aug. 2017)', Troop contributions, Providing for Peacekeeping database, accessed 20 Mar. 2023.

[15] SIPRI Multilateral Peace Operations Database, accessed 3 Mar. 2023; and United Nations Peacekeeping, 'Troop and police contributors', Country contribution reports, Dec. 2018–22.

[16] Nantulya, P., 'China's diplomacy in the Horn—Conflict mediation as power politics', Africa Center for Strategic Studies, Spotlight, 12 Oct. 2022.

Furthering China–Africa security cooperation (building African capacities and enhancing military, police, counterterrorism and law enforcement cooperation) was also identified as a strategic priority in the China–Africa Action Plan agreed at the eighth ministerial conference of the Forum for China–Africa Cooperation in November 2021.[17]

China's presence has spurred competing commercial and diplomatic efforts by, among others, the USA, Russia, Türkiye, Japan and the United Arab Emirates on the continent.[18] A new US initiative aimed at revitalizing relations with Africa was launched in mid 2022, emphasizing support for traditional priorities of democracy and security, as well as advancing pandemic recovery and economic opportunity, and supporting conservation, climate adaptation and a just energy transition. The strategy notably repeats its objective to counter 'harmful activities' by China, Russia and other actors.[19] A modest EU policy initiative to invest globally in infrastructure development around the world, with a particular emphasis on Africa, has also emerged to counter Russian and Chinese influence.[20]

In the post-cold war era, US, European and South African PMSCs preceded Russian and Chinese companies on the continent, often having close links to the security sectors and assistance programmes of their home states. US and British PMSCs such as Academi (formerly Blackwater and Xe Services LLC), CACI, Military Professional Resources Incorporated (MPRI), Halliburton, G4S, Erinys, Triple Canopy, Amentum (which absorbed DynCorp in 2020), Control Risks, Aegis Defence Services (acquired by GardaWorld in 2015) and Olive Group became prominent actors during the military campaigns in Afghanistan and Iraq.[21] Western PMSCs remain active in Africa, especially in various counterterrorism initiatives.[22] For example, the US company CACI was awarded a six-year US$249 million contract in 2020 to provide operations, planning and training support to the US Africa Command (AFRICOM), assisting its headquarters in Germany and presence across Africa in

---

[17] Chinese Ministry of Foreign Affairs, 'Forum on China–Africa Cooperation Dakar Action Plan', 30 Nov. 2021, para. 6.1.

[18] Wong, E., 'The US wants to counter China's moves in Africa. But American officials try not to mention that', *New York Times*, 14 Dec. 2022; Smith, E., 'Top US, Chinese and Russian officials tour Africa as global charm offensive gathers pace', CNBC, 31 Jan. 2023; 'Turkey is making a big diplomatic and corporate push into Africa', *The Economist*, 23 Apr. 2022; 'Japan vows billions to counter China in Africa', Deutsche Welle, 27 Aug. 2022; and Butt, U., 'UAE: The scramble for the Horn of Africa', Middle East Monitor, 31 Jan. 2021.

[19] White House, 'Fact sheet: US strategy toward sub-Saharan Africa', 8 Aug. 2022; White House, *US Strategy Toward Sub-Saharan Africa* (White House: Washington, DC, Aug. 2022); and Baker, P. and Walsh, D., 'Biden aims to inject new energy into US relations with African nations', *New York Times*, 14 Dec. 2022.

[20] Barbero, M., 'Europe is trying (and failing) to beat China at the development game', *Foreign Policy*, 10 Jan. 2023.

[21] Overton, I., Benevilli, E. and Bruun, L., 'Britain is the world centre for private military contractors—and it's almost impossible to find out what they're up to', openDemocracy, 20 Dec. 2018.

[22] E.g. Priest, D. and Arkin, W. A., 'National Security Inc.', *Washington Post*, 20 July 2010.

'planning and executing peacetime, crisis and contingency operations'.[23] AFRICOM supports counterterrorism efforts by partners in Somalia and the Horn of Africa against al-Shabaab; and in West Africa it supports efforts to limit terrorist expansion in the Sahel and the coastal states.[24] Further, PMSCs play an important role in information or influence operations to counter disinformation.[25] Since 2016 the US Department of Defense has worked with private contracting firms to counter misinformation from US adversaries in the media, including social media, and to 'degrade the ability of adversaries to persuade, inspire and recruit'; in 2021 the department doubled its allocation to the Counter Threat Messaging Support Program through a five-year, $979 million contract with Peraton to support US Central Command in countering misinformation from US adversaries.[26]

Geopolitical rivalry is also reflected in rising public resentment towards the continuing involvement of former European colonial powers in the national security and political affairs of certain African states. For example, anti-French protests have spread through West African states, in particular those where France has conducted counter-insurgency operations that are widely perceived as having failed.[27] France claims that this anti-French sentiment is stoked by Russian disinformation campaigns.[28] Populist sentiments have created fertile ground for the expansion of Russian influence through commercial links, especially over gold and minerals, although Russia's own approach to counterinsurgency has attracted increasing criticism (see below).[29] Trade restrictions and other sanctions imposed on Russia following its invasion of Ukraine have reinforced the growing importance of Russia's economic ties in the region. For example, the Wagner Group's

[23] CACI, 'CACI awarded $249 million task order to provide support to US Africa Command', Press release, 16 Mar. 2020.
[24] US Department of State, 'Special online briefing with General Stephen J. Townsend Commander, US Africa Command (US AFRICOM)', 26 July 2022.
[25] Paul, C. et al., *The Role of Information in US Concepts for Strategic Competition*, RAND Research Report (RAND Corporation: Santa Monica, CA, 2022); and Pecquet, J., 'US looks to expose Russian propaganda in Africa', Africa Report, 25 May 2022.
[26] Hewitt Jones, J., 'DOD awards $1 B contract to Peraton to counter misinformation', Fedscoop, 11 Aug. 2021.
[27] Thomas-Johnson, A., 'Senegal: Anti-French sentiment on the rise as protests continue', Al Jazeera, 12 Mar. 2021; Lorgerie, P., 'Thousands take to the streets of Bamako in anti-French protest', Reuters, 5 Feb. 2022; 'Chad: Hundreds stage anti-French Protest in N'djamena', Africanews, 15 May 2022; Carayol, R., 'Anti-French protests in West Africa spill over into Chad', Mediapart, 1 June 2022; Arslam, F. E., 'Protesters in Niger call for departure of French troops', Andalou Agency, 19 Sep. 2022; Morrow, A., 'Anti-French anger grips Burkina Faso in wake of second military coup', RFI, 2 Oct. 2022; and Melly, P., 'Why France faces so much anger in West Africa', BBC News, 5 Dec. 2021.
[28] Rankin, J., 'Emmanuel Macron accuses Russia of feeding disinformation in Africa', *The Guardian*, 20 Nov. 2022; and Africa Center for Strategic Studies, 'Mapping disinformation in Africa', 26 Apr. 2022.
[29] 'Moscow guns for African gold', *Africa Confidential*, vol. 63, no. 2 (20 Jan. 2022); Felbab-Brown, V., 'Nonstate armed actors in 2023: Persistence amid geopolitical shuffles', Brookings Institution, Order from Chaos Blog, 27 Jan. 2023; and 'French commander accuses Wagner of "preying" on Mali', Arab News, 21 July 2022.

tendency to work for payment in the natural resource sector, including gold and diamonds, reflects not only the high value of those resources but their advantages for circumventing Western sanctions.[30]

Russian PMSCs

The presence of Russian PMSCs has increased globally since around 2015. At least 11 such companies have been identified and a number of them cooperate closely with the Russian Ministry of Defence and/or the Russian Federal Security Service (FSB).[31] The Wagner Group is the PMSC currently attracting the most attention for its presence and activities in conflict zones. It is an informal, semi-state network of overlapping shell companies, natural resource extraction businesses and private military forces financed and led by Yevgeny Prigozhin, a confidant of Russian President Vladimir Putin.[32] Although mercenarism is technically illegal in Russia according to Article 359 of the Criminal Code, and this lack of formal juridical identity has enabled the Russian government to deny association with such groups, Wagner Group and other PMSCs have been used in cooperation with the Russian military and/or private individuals connected to Putin's regime.[33] A distinguishing facet of the Wagner Group is its capacity to shift fluidly—sometimes within the same setting—between being a proxy for the Russian government and being an autonomous, profit-seeking commercial entity engaged by other governments.[34] The Wagner Group operates generally as a light, mobile force. When using heavier equipment, this appears to often occur in cooperation with the Russian military or local forces.[35] Wagner's fluidity was first seen in Syria, linked to its commercial mode of working for foreign governments confronted by insurgency in exchange for ownership shares or profits from the extraction of natural resources.[36]

---

[30] Hunter, M., 'Going for Gold: Russia, sanctions and illicit gold trade', Policy Brief, Global Initiative Against Transnational Organized Crime, Geneva, Apr. 2022; and Keating, J., 'Russia's bright, shiny anti-sanctions weapon: Inside the billion-dollar business of "blood gold"', Grid, 15 July 2022. On trade restrictions on Russia, see chapter 12, section III, in this volume.

[31] Jones, S. G. et al., *Russia's Corporate Soldiers: The Global Expansion of Russia's Private Military Companies*, Center for Strategic and International Studies (CSIS) (Rowman & Littlefield: Lanham, MD, July 2021), p. 15.

[32] Mackinnon, A., 'Russia's Wagner Group doesn't actually exist', *Foreign Policy*, 6 July 2021.

[33] Marten, K., 'Russia's use of semi-state security forces: The case of the Wagner Group', *Post-Soviet Affairs*, vol. 35, no. 3 (2019); and Fasanotti, F. S., 'Russia's Wagner Group in Africa: Influence, commercial concessions, rights violations, and counterinsurgency failure', Brookings Institution, Order from Chaos Blog, 8 Feb. 2022.

[34] Galeotti, M., 'The protean PMC: Learning the lessons of the Wagner Group's ability to be both proxy and autonomous agent', Written evidence submitted to the Foreign Affairs Committee of the British Parliament, May 2022, para. 3.

[35] Faulkener, C. and Plichta, M., 'Win, lose, or draw, the Wagner Group benefits from the war in Ukraine', Lawfare, 23 Oct. 2022.

[36] Galeotti (note 34), para. 10.

Despite the many media and think tank reports that have appeared on Russian PMSCs in recent years, the precise extent of their activities in sub-Saharan Africa remains unclear. According to a report published in 2022 by RAND, Russian PMSCs are highly likely to have conducted at least 35 operations in at least 16 sub-Saharan African states since 2005.[37] The report describes most Russian PMSC activity as resembling that carried out by Western or African PMSCs, with about 60 per cent involving ground or maritime security and 30 per cent training or support services. The remaining 10 per cent consisted of combat or operational tasks, all of which were carried out by the Wagner Group.[38]

Another independent report shows recent Russian PMSC activity as having increased sevenfold globally, from operating in 4 countries in 2015 to 27 in 2021, including in at least 16 sub-Saharan African states between 2016 and 2021.[39] It identifies the Wagner Group as the most prolific, having operated in 14 sub-Saharan African states.[40] Other Russian PMSCs identified include Redut-Antiterror/Centre R and Moran Security Group (Somalia); Moran Security Group (Nigeria); RSB-Group (Russian Security Systems) (the Gulf of Guinea); Patriot (Burundi and the Central African Republic, CAR); and Sewa Security Services (CAR).[41]

The most documented deployments of Wagner personnel concern four states—CAR, Mali, Mozambique and Sudan—where they provided military training or combat services for the governments.[42] The Wagner Group has been the focus of numerous UN reports or investigations for alleged human rights abuses and violations of international humanitarian law, including by the UN Security Council, UN-appointed independent experts on human rights, the UN panel of experts on CAR and the UN Multidimensional Integrated Stabilization Mission in CAR (MINUSCA).[43] The actions of the Wagner Group have also prompted hearings by US and British legislators.[44] The arrival of Russian PMSCs in CAR and Mali followed years of unsuccessful efforts by UN stabilization missions, the EU and France to counter insurgency and stabilize the states. France, the USA and other Western powers

---

[37] Grissom, A. R. et al., *Russia's Growing Presence in Africa: A Geostrategic Assessment*, RAND Research Report (RAND Corporation: Santa Monica, CA, 2022), pp. 16–17.

[38] Grissom et al. (note 37), p. 17.

[39] Jones et al. (note 31), pp. 1, 52.

[40] The 14 sub-Saharan African states are: Botswana, Burundi, Central African Republic, Chad, the Comoros, Congo, Equatorial Guinea, Guinea-Bissau, Madagascar, Mali, Mozambique, Nigeria, South Sudan and Sudan.

[41] Jones et al. (note 31), p. 15.

[42] Stanyard, J., Vircoulon, T. and Rademeyer, J., 'The grey zone: Russia's military, mercenary and criminal engagement in Africa', Global Initiative Against Transnational Organized Crime, Feb. 2023, pp. 12–13.

[43] See the discussions in sections I and III of this chapter.

[44] British Parliament, Foreign Affairs Committee, 'The Wagner Group and beyond: Proxy private military companies', Inquiry, Oral and written evidence, 2022–23.

have alleged Africa-wide disinformation campaigns coordinated by Yevgeny Prigozhin to build and amplify hostility towards them, while promoting influence and support for Wagner and Russia.[45] The situations in CAR and Mali are discussed in more detail below.

When political operations are included, such as disinformation and influence campaigns or politically biased election observation, the number of states involved is larger. According to the US Treasury Department, a front company linked to the Wagner Group has conducted fake election monitoring missions and influence operations in Zimbabwe, Madagascar, the Democratic Republic of the Congo (DRC), South Africa and Mozambique.[46] In Madagascar certain candidates were offered funding by Wagner advisers to run in the 2018 presidential election campaign in return for mining access.[47] Wagner also has a commercial hub in Cameroon, running convoys of natural resources from CAR to the port of Douala, including gold extracted from the mines it controls.[48] Russia signed a military cooperation agreement with Cameroon in April 2022, leading to speculation that it was paving the path to more active Wagner activity in the country.[49]

The Wagner Group, or in some cases affiliates and shell companies considered part of the wider group of entities under the control of Prighozhin, has often been compensated in sub-Saharan Africa through control of local mining assets, which is something that is also claimed to be driving its involvement in areas of Ukraine where lucrative mines are located.[50]

Sanctions against the Wagner Group

The USA has repeatedly imposed sanctions against Yevgeny Prigozhin and individuals and companies connected to him for attempting to influence the 2016 and 2020 US presidential elections, for combat operations in Ukraine and for destabilizing activities elsewhere, including countries in sub-Saharan Africa.[51] On 13 December 2021 the EU imposed a set of 'restrictive measures' against the Wagner Group and eight individuals holding key positions in or linked to it, for sending mercenaries to conflict zones in CAR, Libya, Syria and Ukraine, fomenting violence, committing serious human rights violations and abuses, looting natural resources and intimidating civilians in violation

---

[45] US Department of State, 'Yevgeniy Prigozhin's Africa-wide disinformation campaign', 4 Nov. 2022; and Lederer, E. M., 'US and Russia clash over violent extremism in Africa', AP News, 11 Jan. 2023.

[46] US Department of the Treasury, 'Treasury escalates sanctions against the Russian government's attempts to influence US elections', Press release, 15 Apr. 2021.

[47] Stanyard, Vircoulon and Rademeyer (note 42), p. 13.

[48] Olivier, M., 'CAR–Cameroon: An investigation into the Wagner Group's African financial model', Africa Report, 18 Jan. 2023.

[49] 'Cameroon signs agreement with Russia in further boost to military ties', RFI, 22 Apr. 2022.

[50] Bertrand, N., Liebermann, O. and Marquardt, A., 'Russian artillery fire down nearly 75%, US officials say, in latest sign of struggles for Moscow', CNN, 10 Jan. 2023.

[51] US Department of the Treasury (note 46); and US Department of the Treasury, 'Treasury targets assets of Russian financier who attempted to influence 2018 US elections', Press release, 30 Sep. 2019.

of international law.[52] On 1 June 2022 the European Court of Justice ruled against Prigozhin, who had sought the annulment of EU sanctions against him.[53] Despite years of sanctions levied by the USA and the EU, Prigozhin is estimated to have generated revenues of over one-quarter of a billion dollars from the extraction of oil, gas, diamonds and gold in Africa and the Middle East during the four years leading up to the Russian invasion of Ukraine.[54]

Chinese PMSCs

The international Chinese private security industry has developed more cautiously compared to those in other countries and has certain characteristics that set it apart from Western counterparts. The first Chinese private security contractors, which focused on the protection of infrastructure and personnel from theft and attacks or abduction, began to offer overseas services in 2010.[55] They have been increasingly deployed to areas in sub-Saharan Africa where China has expanded its investments and commercial presence as part of the BRI. Since its inception in 2013, the BRI has brought over 10 000 Chinese companies, including some 2000 state-owned enterprises, and over 1 million Chinese citizens to the continent.[56] The BRI presents clear opportunities for private security firms, as 84 per cent of Chinese BRI investment occurs in medium-high risk areas.[57] Yet despite the existence of over 7000 PMSCs that serve the domestic market and employ around 5 million former military and police personnel in China, observers maintain that only around 20–30 Chinese PMSCs operate internationally, although the numbers employed by these firms are believed to far exceed the 3200 formally reported.[58] Moreover, Chinese PMSCs are not 'private sector' because they are expected to follow government directives and exist either as

---

[52] 'L'Europe sanctionne le groupe russe Wagner pour ses "actions de déstabilisation"' [Europe sanctions Russian Wagner Group for its "destabilizing actions"], *Jeune Afrique*, 14 Dec. 2021; and Council Implementing Decision (CFSP) 2021/2199 of 13 Dec. 2021 implementing Decision 2013/255/CFSP concerning restrictive measures against Syria, *Official Journal of the European Union*, L445I, vol. 65, 13 Dec. 2021, pp. 14–23.

[53] Court of Justice of the European Union, 'The General Court confirms the restrictive measures adopted by the Council against the Russian businessman Yevgeniy Viktorovich Progozhin, in view of the situation in Libya', Press release no. 91/22, 1 June 2022.

[54] Johnson, M., 'Wagner leader generated $250mn from sanctioned empire', *Financial Times*, 21 Feb. 2023.

[55] Ghisellli, A., 'Market opportunities and political responsibilities: The difficult development of Chinese private security companies abroad', *Armed Forces & Society*, vol. 6, no. 1 (2020).

[56] Nantulya, P., 'Chinese security firms spread along the African Belt and Road', Africa Center for Strategic Studies, 15 June 2021.

[57] Devonshire-Ellis, C., '84% of China's BRI investments are in medium-high risk countries', Silk Road Briefing, 2 July 2020.

[58] Nantulya (note 56); Arduino, A., 'China's private army: Protecting the new Silk Road', The Diplomat, 20 Mar. 2018; and Yuan, J., 'China's private security companies and the protection of Chinese economic interests abroad', *Small Wars & Insurgencies*, vol. 33, no. 1–2 (2022), p. 179.

state-owned sole proprietorships or with at least 51 per cent of their capital state-owned.[59]

The Chinese government has been cautious regarding the development of these firms, with ongoing restrictions on their ability to offer armed services, although certain PMSCs operating abroad have been authorized to carry arms.[60] China has been slow to develop adequate legislation and national guidance for PMSCs working abroad, potentially constraining the professionalization of the industry. This has raised concerns that some PMSCs may be using legal grey areas to provide armed security without adequate oversight.[61] These gaps in the regulation of Chinese PMSCs operating abroad increase the risks of serious misconduct and resulting political and reputational damage.[62]

Nevertheless, the Chinese government encourages the use of Chinese PMSCs for its overseas businesses and personnel. Despite having less operational experience than some other PMSCs in high-risk environments, these firms offer certain advantages over well-established Western PMSCs in terms of a common language and culture, greater affordability and greater expected reliability in protecting proprietary information.[63] Based on comments by President Xi Jinping at the 20th Communist Party congress in October 2022 that China will be strengthening its protection of Chinese citizens and legal entities overseas, observers believe that Chinese PMSCs will be enabled to play a larger role in coming years.[64]

Chinese fishing fleets and cargo vessels have encountered piracy, armed robbery and kidnap-for-ransom risks in Somalia and more recently in the hotspot of the Gulf of Guinea, where in 2019 some 73 per cent of kidnappings and 92 per cent of hostage-takings worldwide had occurred.[65] These and other coastal attacks have spurred the development of Chinese maritime security services, notably the company Hua Xin Zhong An (HXZA), which was the first (and by 2020 the only) Chinese PMSC to have obtained permission to conduct armed escort missions abroad, including off the coast of Somalia.[66]

---

[59] Nantulya (note 56).

[60] Yuan (note 58).

[61] Nouwens, V., 'Who guards the "Maritime Silk Road"?', War on the Rocks, 24 June 2020; and Nantulya, P., 'Chinese security contractors in Africa', Carnegie Endowment for International Peace, 8 Oct. 2020.

[62] Legarda, H. and Nouwens, M., 'Guardians of the Belt and Road: The internationalization of China's private security companies', Mercator Institute for China Studies (MERICS), China Monitor Report, 16 Aug. 2018, p. 14.

[63] Sukhankin, S., 'An anatomy of the Chinese private security contracting industry', Jamestown Foundation, 3 Jan. 2023; and Nouwens (note 61).

[64] Honrada, G., 'China private security companies making a BRI killing', Asia Times, 1 Nov. 2022.

[65] 'Seventeen Chinese, Ukrainian seamen kidnapped off Cameroon', France 24, 16 Aug. 2019; 'Crew of Chinese boat freed after ransom payment: Nigerian army', Al Jazeera, 7 Mar. 2021; and International Chamber of Commerce, 'Gulf of Guinea remains world's piracy hotspot in 2021, according to IMB's latest figures', 14 Apr. 2021.

[66] Nouwens (note 61).

It is also the only Chinese PMSC that, as of early 2023, is certified by the International Code of Conduct Association, an international industry self-regulatory body.[67]

Attacks on Chinese personnel and infrastructure within the region have become more common and the Chinese private security industry appears to be developing more capacity to operate in high-risk environments.[68] Haiwei Dui, also known as Overseas Security Guardians (HK) Company, is one of the pre-eminent Chinese PMSCs that have expanded globally, with a presence in 51 countries.[69]

In the eastern DRC, Chinese mining companies have encountered increasing attacks and abductions by rebel groups. In 2020, Frontier Services Group (FSG), a Hong Kong-listed firm first established by former Blackwater founder Erik Prince but now controlled by the China International Trust and Investment Corporation (CITIC), won the contract to protect the Sino Congolaise des Mines (Sicomines) project.[70] Under the controversial $6 billion joint venture, which was originally agreed in 2007, China would provide transport infrastructure in exchange for cobalt and copper mining rights.[71] After Prince resigned from FSG in April 2021, the company became the 'first choice for Chinese firms in Africa'.[72] FSG's contracts with Chinese companies in the DRC and Nigeria resulted in its safety, insurance and infrastructure division doubling its revenue between 2020 and 2021.[73] In the DRC, FSG has provided protection for Chinese diplomats, personnel and property in the mining sector.[74] For example, the Chinese Enterprises Association in the DRC is reported to have hired FSG to provide security training.[75]

---

[67] See International Code of Conduct Association (ICOCA), 'HXZA—Company profile', accessed 20 Mar. 2023.

[68] Clover, C., 'Chinese private security companies go global', *Financial Times*, 26 Feb. 2017; and Pintado, C., 'Chinese mercenaries in Africa', *Small Wars Journal*, 6 May 2021.

[69] Arduino, A., 'The footprint of Chinese private security companies in Africa', China–Africa Research Initiative (CARI) Policy Brief no. 42, John Hopkins University School of Advanced International Studies, 2020, pp. 16–17.

[70] Fisher, M., Shapira, I. and Rauhala, E., 'Behind Erik Prince's China venture', *Washington Post*, 4 May 2018.

[71] 'Erik Prince wins keys security contract from Chinese–Congolese joint venture Sicomines', Africa Intelligence, 1 Dec. 2020.

[72] 'Frontier Services Group becomes first choice for Chinese firms in Africa after DeWe takeover', Africa Intelligence, 5 Oct. 2021.

[73] 'Les recettes de Frontier Services Group, fondé par Erik Prince qui sécurise les mines chinoises en RDC sont passées de 4,3 à 8,6 millions $' [Revenue from Frontier Services Group, founded by Erik Prince, which secures Chinese mines in the DRC, increased from $4.3 million to $8.6 million], Congo Virtuel, 6 Sep. 2021.

[74] Olander, E., 'DRC: Chinese ambassador pays visit to opposition leader Moise Katumbi', Africa Report, 18 Apr. 2022.

[75] 'Chinese miners hire Frontier Services Group for their security training in troubled Kivus', Africa Intelligence, 15 Feb. 2022.

Recent PMSC activity in selected conflict-affected sub-Saharan African states

Burkina Faso

Rumours that the groundwork was being laid for the engagement of the Wagner Group in Burkina Faso began circulating shortly after the military coup in January 2022.[76] Increasingly anti-French and pro-Russian rhetoric appeared in the media, and public demonstrations were organized by groups funded in part by Wagner-related entities through organizations in Mali and CAR. These groups waved Russian flags and called for France to leave and the new authorities to develop closer relations with Russia.[77]

In an atmosphere of increasing Islamic extremist violence and following an attack on a humanitarian assistance convoy by jihadist forces on 30 September 2022—which killed 37 people, including 27 soldiers—Burkina Faso experienced another coup.[78] Soldiers ousted Paul-Henri Damiba, who had seized power from the democratically elected President Roch Marc Kaboré in a coup in January.[79] In December 2022, Ghanaian President Nana Addo Dankwa Akufo-Addo alleged that Burkina Faso's military government had reached an agreement with the Wagner Group for assistance in combating the jihadist violence in exchange for a gold mining concession in the south of the country. The allegations were strongly denied by the Burkinan authorities.[80] Akufo-Addo's comment came shortly after Burkina Faso's prime minister, Apollinaire Joachim Kyélem de Tambèla, travelled to Moscow to strengthen Burkinan–Russian relations.[81]

Central African Republic

Amid a long-running rebellion and insurgency, and in response to the inability of UN peacekeepers to stabilize CAR, President Faustin-Archange Touadéra sought Russian weapons and military instructors to train the Central African Armed Forces (FACA) in 2017.[82] CAR received Russian assistance in the form of weapons and 175 military advisers, although only 5 of the advisers were Russian military, with the other 170 comprising private contractors hired by Lobaye Invest, part of the complex network of companies owned by Yevgeny

---

[76] Roger, B., '[Enquête] Le Burkina Faso dans le viseur de Wagner' [(Investigation) Burkina Faso in Wagner's sights], *Jeune Afrique*, 30 June 2022.

[77] Roger (note 76).

[78] 'Burkina Faso: Recounting the attack on a convoy in Gaskindé days before a second coup', Africanews, 7 Oct. 2022.

[79] 'Burkina Faso's military leader ousted in second coup this year', *The Guardian*, 30 Sep. 2022.

[80] Skrdlik, J., 'Burkina Faso denies hiring Wagner mercenaries', Organized Crime and Corruption Reporting Project, 23 Dec. 2022.

[81] Mednick, S., 'Burkina Faso contracts Russian mercenaries, alleges Ghana', *The Independent*, 15 Dec. 2022.

[82] Bax, P., 'Russia's influence in the Central African Republic', International Crisis Group, Africa Commentary, 3 Dec. 2021.

Prigozhin. Despite the fact that President Touadéra denied any formal contract with the Wagner Group, 1000–2000 Wagner personnel were soon observed in Bangui, the capital of CAR.[83] An elite squad from the Wagner Group also provides security for President Touadéra. Former FSB member Valery Zakharov, overseeing the Russian elements of Touadéra's presidential guard, functions as an adviser for national security, with an office in the presidency.[84]

Moreover, the Wagner Group's arrival coincided with the award of diamond and gold mining licences to Lobaye Invest.[85] The gold is reportedly exported uncontrolled and without the payment of taxes through Bangui M'Poko International Airport.[86] In 2019, three Russian journalists who were in CAR to investigate the link between Russian private military contractors and CAR's gold and mineral resources were killed in an ambush.[87] In 2022, mercenaries working for the Wagner Group were alleged to have launched a series of attacks on artisanal gold mines in the border region between CAR and Sudan, resulting in the deaths of dozens of migrant miners. Rather than securing the mines to extract gold, the attacks appear to have been mainly aimed at violent plundering of the sites.[88] Wagner has also been accused of violently taking control of the diamond industry in CAR through the shell company Diamville, which buys and sells diamonds.[89] Wagner chief Yevgeny Prigozhin denied these allegations.[90]

The Armed Conflict Location & Event Data Project (ACLED) has found Wagner Group forces to have high levels of civilian targeting in their counter-insurgency operations, and since mid 2021 they have increasingly operated independently of FACA.[91] In November 2021, a leaked EU report described most FACA units as 'operating under direct command or supervision by WG [Wagner Group] mercenaries', who exercise strong influence over the general staff and command and control of FACA, and 'who are able unhindered to take

---

[83] Bax (note 82).
[84] Olivier, M., 'CAR: Who are President Touadéra's Russian guardian angels?', Africa Report, 17 Mar. 2021.
[85] Malkova, I. and Baev, A., 'A private army for the president: The tale of Evgeny Prigozhin's most delicate mission', The Bell, 31 Jan. 2019.
[86] Olivier (note 84).
[87] Lister, T. and Shukla, S., 'Murdered journalists were tracked by police with shadowy Russian links, evidence shows', CNN, 10 Jan. 2019.
[88] Burke, J., 'Russian mercenaries accused of deadly attacks on mines on Sudan–CAR border', The Guardian, 21 June 2022.
[89] European Investigative Collaborations, Dossier Center and All Eyes on Wagner, 'CAR: Prigozhin's blood diamonds. A report by the project All Eyes on Wagner', Dec. 2022.
[90] Ilyushina, M. and Ebel, F., 'Russian mercenaries accused of using violence to corner diamond trade', Washington Post, 6 Dec. 2022.
[91] Serwat, L. et al., 'Wagner Group operations in Africa: Civilian targeting trends in the Central African Republic and Mali', ACLED, 30 Aug. 2022.

over command on the spot and thus use FACA for their own operations'.[92] UN experts have also said that Russian PMSCs have been connected to violent attacks in CAR, including mass summary executions, arbitrary detentions, torture and force disappearances. In March 2021, a group of independent human rights experts working for the UN Human Rights Council (including the members of the UN working group on the use of mercenaries, the special rapporteur on torture and other experts in the special procedures of the Human Rights Council) issued a joint statement about their concerns that Russian PMSCs, including Sewa Security Services, Lobaye Invest and the Wagner Group, operating jointly with FACA, were linked to a series of violent attacks following presidential elections in December 2020, as well as grave human rights abuses and violations of international humanitarian law, for which no one had been held accountable.[93]

The independent human rights experts further flagged the presence of Russian military advisers and trainers at MINUSCA bases, including Russian 'trainers' who had been medically evacuated. They warned that the close proximity and coordinated meetings with peacekeepers risked blurring important distinctions between civil, military and peacekeeping operations.[94] A joint statement by the human rights experts issued in October 2021 drew attention to reports of the intimidation and violent harassment of civilians and communities, including peacekeepers, journalists, aid workers and minorities, by Russian 'instructors' working closely with FACA and the police, including in the arrest and detention of individuals. The experts noted widespread reports of rape and sexual violence committed by Wagner personnel, and the lack of accountability of personnel and instructors in this context.[95]

As tensions between the Wagner Group and MINUSCA increased, disinformation about the UN mission appeared on social media, heightening the risks to UN personnel. Some UN personnel were prevented from carrying out their duties in areas controlled by Wagner, including the deputy head of mission, Louise Brown, who was physically threatened while near the border with Chad in May 2021.[96] On 22 February 2022, four French soldiers serving as bodyguards for French General Stéphane Marchenoir, MINUSCA's chief of staff, were arrested at Bangui Airport and accused of planning to assassinate

---

[92] European External Action Service (EEAS), 'Political and strategic environment of CSDP missions in the Central African Republic (CAR)', EEAS(2021) 1213, 15 Nov. 2021, para. 5.
[93] United Nations Office of the High Commissioner for Human Rights (OHCHR), 'CAR: Experts alarmed by government's use of "Russian trainers", close contacts with UN peacekeepers', Press release, 31 Mar. 2021.
[94] OHCHR (note 93).
[95] OHCHR, 'CAR: Russian Wagner Group harassing and intimidating civilians—UN experts', Press release, 27 Oct. 2021.
[96] *Africa Confidential*, 'France and Russia tussle in Bangui', vol. 62, no. 15 (19 July 2021).

the president. The four men were released only after MINUSCA threatened to leave CAR.[97]

Democratic Republic of the Congo

In October 2022, Congolese President Félix Tshisekedi publicly declared that he would not engage Russian mercenaries to assist the government in combating the M23 armed group.[98] Shortly thereafter, the DRC announced the procurement of Russian military combat and transport helicopters.[99] On 21 December 2022 the UN Security Council lifted notification requirements for arms shipments to the DRC, as well as provision of assistance, consultancy services or military training, while maintaining the arms embargo on all non-governmental entities and individuals.[100] Various East European PMSCs are present in the DRC, including Agemira from Bulgaria, which services Russian combat helicopters and aircraft, and Asociatia RALF from Romania, which guards Goma International Airport.[101]

Mali

A widening insurgency in Mali, including the expansion of jihadist groups, and two military coups (in 2020 and 2021) escalated tensions between the military-controlled government and former colonial power France and Western allies. In December 2021 the government invited Russian instructors (widely reported as being part of the Wagner Group) to begin operating in Mali.[102] As a result, France withdrew its counterterrorism troops and the European multinational Task Force Takuba in mid 2022. The Malian government then established a military cooperation agreement with Russia in November, ostensibly to provide military training to local Malian forces. However, during 2022 evidence emerged that the Wagner Group was fighting alongside the Malian armed forces to combat Islamic extremists, often targeting ethnic Fulani communities (perceived to be linked to the insurgents) using tactics associated with Wagner's previous actions in CAR and Libya.[103] According to ACLED, civilian targeting accounted for 71 per cent of Wagner involvement in political violence in Mali in 2022, and over 2000 civilians have been killed since December 2021, one-third of which

---

[97] 'UN clashes with Wagner worsen', *Africa Confidential*, vol. 62, no. 6 (8 Mar. 2022).
[98] Khalaf, R., Pilling, D. and Schipani, A., 'DR Congo leader rules out deploying Russian mercenaries to quell rebels', *Financial Times*, 18 Oct. 2022.
[99] 'DRC: Kinshasa strikes military procurement deal with Moscow', Africa Intelligence, 27 Oct. 2022.
[100] Tasamba, J., 'UN Security Council lifts notification requirements for arms supply to DR Congo', Andalou Agency, 21 Dec. 2022.
[101] Schlindwein, S., 'Are white mercenaries fighting in the DRC conflict?', Deutsche Welle, 17 Jan. 2023.
[102] For developments in Mali in 2021, Baudais, V. and Hickendorff, A., 'Armed conflict and peace processes in West Africa', *SIPRI Yearbook 2022*, pp. 202–12.
[103] Human Rights Watch, 'Mali: Massacre by army, foreign soldiers', 5 Apr. 2022.

were attributable to the Wagner Group. In contrast, 500 civilians were killed in the previous 12 months.[104] Russian-speaking soldiers, believed to have been Wagner personnel, and Malian armed forces are accused of killing around 300 civilian men, including some detained suspected Islamist fighters, in an operation on the village of Moura in central Mali between 27 March and 1 April 2022.[105]

The Wagner Group allegedly provided security services to the Malian government for $10 million per month in early 2022.[106] However, ECOWAS had imposed sanctions against the government for postponing elections and the transition to civilian rule, leaving it unable to meet its obligations to pay Wagner until sanctions were lifted in July 2022, having agreed to hold elections in 2024. One apparent solution to the funding problem was (similar to Wagner's experience in CAR) to seek to get the operating permits of some of the gold mines transferred to the Wagner Group.[107]

Sudan

In November 2017 a new phase in Russia–Sudan cooperation began with several security and economic agreements. These included the establishment of a Russian naval base in Port Sudan on the Red Sea, and concession agreements between the Sudanese Ministry of Minerals and the company M-Invest, a Russia-based entity controlled by Prigozhin, for gold prospecting and mining in Sudan, then the third largest producer of gold in Africa.[108] Afterwards, Wagner Group personnel were deployed to Sudan to provide a range of military and security services, including training Sudanese military and police personnel, transportation of weapons and information operations. According to the US Department of Justice, these forces suppressed local pro-democracy uprisings against the regime of President Omar al-Bashir, who was ultimately deposed. Additionally, social media disinformation campaigns and staged executions were organized by M-Invest. In payment, M-Invest was awarded concession agreements to explore gold mining sites in Sudan.[109] Financial facilitators based in Thailand and Hong Kong supported these activities in Sudan, and were included in US sanctions for having assisted Prigozhin to evade sanctions. The Wagner Group has continued to

---

[104] Serwat et al. (note 91).
[105] Human Rights Watch (note 103); Burke, J. and Akinwotu, E., 'Russian mercenaries linked to civilian massacres in Mali', *The Guardian*, 4 May 2022; and UNOCHR, 'Mali: UN experts call for independent investigation into possible international crimes committed by government forces and "Wagner group"', Press release, 31 Jan. 2023.
[106] AFP, 'Mali paying Wagner Group $10 mn a month, US General says', *Barron's*, 3 Feb. 2022.
[107] Roger, B., 'Mali: Comment Wagner compte faire main basse sur des mines d'or' [Mali: How Wagner plans to get its hands on gold mines], *Jeune Afrique*, 7 Sep. 2022.
[108] Yakoreva, A., '"Putin's Cook" set out to mine gold in Africa', The Bell, 5 June 2018.
[109] US Department of the Treasury, 'Treasury targets financier's illicit sanctions evasion activity', Press release, 15 July 2020.

work with Sudan's military leaders and through the Meroe Gold venture has undertaken joint mining activities with the Rapid Support Force, with gold allegedly smuggled to Russia to build up its reserves before the war in Ukraine.[110]

Conclusions

Recent trends concerning PMSC involvement in sub-Saharan Africa suggest that the ascendant actors have close, symbiotic links to home state interests as instruments of national policy and geopolitical competition. Control and extraction of natural resources is a common focal point. Russian PMSCs, in particular the Wagner Group, engage directly in military operations, typically for governments (and currently juntas or military transition governments) threatened by rebels or insurgents, with payment often in high-value natural resources or mining concessions. Chinese PMSCs have emerged more slowly and in a more restrained and circumscribed manner, but with a close connection to the Chinese state. China has been increasing its economic and political power throughout Africa with a massive injection of investment, infrastructure development and trade expansion. This may portend a more lasting engagement for Chinese interests and actors, including PMSCs, and a greater strategic impact on access to natural resources and, more broadly, sub-Saharan African political dynamics. Regulation and oversight of both Russian and Chinese PMSCs remain grey areas, which is a concern in view of the scope of demand for private security resulting from Chinese investments across Africa and the seemingly upward trajectory of geostrategic competition playing out on the continent.

---

[110] Eltayeb, A. F., 'Sudan: The Wagner–RSF ties that block the path to democratisation', Africa Report, 2 Feb. 2023.

III. The current regulatory landscape for private military and security companies

SORCHA MACLEOD

Russia's invasion of Ukraine in February 2022, and the utilization of the Wagner Group in that conflict, as well as in other ongoing armed conflicts, has firmly refocused international attention on the regulatory gaps around both mercenaries and private military and security companies (PMSCs).[1] While many of the regulatory developments during 2022 are associated with or are a response to the actions of the Wagner Group, it is important to note that other mercenary groups and PMSCs have also been active in armed conflicts, which points to broader systemic issues. In particular, ongoing atrocities by mercenaries and related actors, including grave human rights violations, war crimes and crimes against humanity, with a lack of concomitant accountability, continue to raise significant concerns.[2] Moreover, the increasing trend towards deploying mercenaries and related actors in armed conflicts serves to highlight the fundamental lack of agreement among the international community on how to characterize such actors, and consequently impedes international regulatory and accountability processes and mechanisms.[3] This section briefly examines three main areas of regulatory challenges and developments that emerged or were consolidated during 2022: (*a*) proxy actors in armed conflicts; (*b*) the regulation of PMSCs at the United Nations; and (*c*) case law involving mercenaries or PMSCs.

International humanitarian law and proxy actors

The opaque legal status of some PMSCs has enabled states, particularly Russia and Türkiye, to use them as agents of proxy warfare. It is a relatively recent phenomenon that presents specific regulatory challenges.[4] The

---

[1] See e.g. Rondeaux, C., 'Chasing the Wagner Group: Why it's so hard to get a handle on Putin's ghost army', New America, 13 Feb. 2023; United Nations working group on the use of mercenaries as a means of violating human rights and impeding the exercise of the right to peoples of self-determination, 'Mali', JAL MLI 3/2022, 30 Dec. 2022 (in French); and UN working group on the use of mercenaries, 'Russian Federation', JAL RUS 17/2022, 20 Jan. 2023. See also sections I and II in this chapter.

[2] UN General Assembly, Human Rights Council, Report of the working group on the use of mercenaries, 'Access to justice, accountability and remedies for victims of mercenaries, mercenary-related actors and private military and security companies', A/HRC/51/25, 5 July 2022; and Office of the UN High Commissioner for Human Rights (OHCHR), 'Statement by the UN working group on the use of mercenaries warns about the dangers of the growing use of mercenaries around the globe', 4 Mar. 2022.

[3] On the discussion of definitions of PMSCs and mercenaries see also section I in this chapter.

[4] See e.g. UN, '"Legitimacy crisis" in Libya must be overcome ahead of elections, Special Representative says, briefing Security Council', 15 Nov. 2022; UN General Assembly, Report of the working group on the use of mercenaries, 'The evolving forms, trends and manifestations of mercenaries and mercenary-related activities', A/75/259, 28 July 2020, paras 32–38; and Rondeaux, C., 'Decoding the Wagner Group: Analyzing the role of private military security contractors in Russian proxy warfare', New America, 7 Nov. 2019.

Wagner Group is probably the most well-known proxy actor and, despite denials from the Russian government, its operatives are participating in multiple armed conflicts, including in the Central African Republic (CAR), the Democratic Republic of the Congo, Libya, Mali, Sudan and Ukraine. Similarly, SADAT International Defense Consultancy, a Turkish-registered company, has sent recruits to conflicts in Libya and Nagorno-Karabakh.[5] Both SADAT and the Wagner Group engage in predatory recruitment practices by recruiting individuals from conflict-affected areas, which in some cases could meet the definition of human trafficking due to their coercive and fraudulent character.[6] Additionally, the Wagner Group is recruiting from correctional facilities in Russia. While some prisoners may be willing recruits, others are being recruited 'under threat of punishment or intimidation' and forced to take part in hostilities in Ukraine.[7] Furthermore, these actors are committing human rights abuses—including violations of the right to life, torture, arbitrary detention, and sexual and gender-based violence (SGBV)—which in some instances reach the level of war crimes and crimes against humanity, such as in the widespread and systemic killing of civilian populations.[8]

The presence of mercenaries, and the Wagner Group in particular, is prolonging conflicts and further destabilizing the regions in which they operate. The international community has struggled to react to the challenges presented by such actors and states have applied a multitude of disparate labels, including 'mercenaries' and 'PMSCs', as well as 'terrorists' and 'transnational criminal organizations'.[9] This disjointed response is unsurprising given that there have long been substantial disagreements among states regarding the characterization of these types of actors. Moreover, these reactions make sense when examined within the context of the international legal framework.

Unlike the term PMSC, and others such as private military company (PMC), the term mercenary is legally defined under international humanitarian law

---

[5] See e.g. Syrians for Truth and Justice (STJ), 'Libya: Syrian mercenaries played a key role in recent Tripoli clashes', 14 Sep. 2022; UN working group on the use of mercenaries, 'Türkiye', JAL TUR 7/2020, 10 June 2020; and UN working group on the use of mercenaries, 'Türkiye', JAL TUR 21/2020, 6 Nov. 2020.

[6] STJ and the Syria Justice and Accountability Center (SJAC), 'Mercenarism in Syria: Predatory recruitment and the enrichment of criminal militias', 28 May 2021.

[7] See e.g. OHCHR, 'Russian Federation: UN experts alarmed by recruitment of prisoners by "Wagner Group"', Press release, 10 Mar. 2023; and UN working group on the use of mercenaries, 'Russian Federation' (note 1).

[8] See e.g. UN working group on the use of mercenaries, 'Mali' (note 1).

[9] See e.g. British Ministry of Defence, 'Latest Defence Intelligence update on the situation in Ukraine—09 March 2022', 10 Mar. 2022; US Department of the Treasury, 'Treasury sanctions Russian proxy Wagner Group as a Transnational Criminal Organization', 23 Jan. 2023; and Ross, D. G., Chace-Donahue, E. and Clarke, C. P., 'Understanding the US designation of the Wagner Group as a transnational criminal organisation', International Centre for Counter-Terrorism, 25 Jan. 2023.

(IHL) in Article 47 of Additional Protocol I to the Geneva Conventions.[10] Article 47(1) does not criminalize mercenarism, rather it provides that a person who meets the definition of a mercenary is not a combatant and is therefore not automatically entitled to prisoner of war status and protections. This is one reason why accountability for mercenarism is hard to achieve. It is also generally acknowledged that the cumulative and subjective criteria that form the basis of the definition of a mercenary set out in Article 47(2) are very difficult to fulfil. Article 47(2) provides that:

A mercenary is any person who:
  (a) is specially recruited locally or abroad in order to fight in an armed conflict;
  (b) does, in fact, take a direct part in the hostilities;
  (c) is motivated to take part in the hostilities essentially by the desire for private gain and, in fact, is promised, by or on behalf of a Party to the conflict, material compensation substantially in excess of that promised or paid to combatants of similar ranks and functions in the armed forces of that Party;
  (d) is neither a national of a Party to the conflict nor a resident of territory controlled by a Party to the conflict;
  (e) is not a member of the armed forces of a Party to the conflict; and
  (f) has not been sent by a State which is not a Party to the conflict on official duty as a member of its armed forces.[11]

Russia's use of the Wagner Group in armed conflicts, for example, appears to be a clear attempt to circumvent the provisions of Article 47(2). By concluding bilateral agreements with numerous states to provide 'trainers' or 'instructors' for military and security forces, the Russian government has been able to claim that it has sent Russian security personnel on 'official duty' (see Article 47(2)(f)) and that they therefore do not meet the international legal definition of mercenary. For example, it has stated: 'Some 500 instructors from the Russian Federation are currently in the Central African Republic, at the request of its lawful central leadership, to assist in the training of local military and security forces of the host country. They are unarmed and do not take part in hostilities.'[12] Nevertheless, extensive reports from CAR and other conflict areas do not support this contention, rather they confirm that Wagner operatives are engaged in combat and would appear to meet the Article 47 definition of mercenary.[13] Wagner Group operations in Ukraine

---

[10] Protocol I Additional to the 1949 Geneva Conventions, and Relating to the Protection of Victims of International Armed Conflicts, opened for signature 12 Dec. 1977, entered into force 7 Dec. 1978, Article 47, 'Mercenaries'.

[11] Protocol I (note 10), Article 47(2).

[12] UN working group on the use of mercenaries, 'Information from the Russian Federation in response to the joint enquiry of the special procedures of the Human Rights Council on the alleged activities of Russian private military and security companies in the Central African Republic, JAL RUS 5/2021, 24 March 2021', 28 Apr. 2021.

[13] See e.g. UN Security Council, 'Final Report of the panel of experts on the Central African Republic extended pursuant to Security Council Resolution 2536 (2020)', S/2021/569, 25 June 2021, which reported that the Russian instructors conducted very limited, if any, training of the CAR armed forces.

present a different problem. Russian nationals deployed by Wagner to fight in Ukraine would not meet the definition set out in Article 47, specifically paragraph (2)(c), as they are nationals of a party to the conflict. Conversely, any non-Russian nationals deployed by the Wagner Group in Ukraine would meet the definition.[14]

The definitional challenges around Article 47 partially explain why some states and regional organizations are turning to counterterrorism approaches to counter the activities of the Wagner Group, including imposing terrorist designations and sanctions.[15] Another reason is that only 37 states are party to the International Convention against the Recruitment, Use, Financing and Training of Mercenaries that criminalizes mercenarism.[16] This means that many states do not have specific provisions at the national level to deal with mercenarism, including the requirement to investigate, powers of extradition, and established mechanisms for accountability and remedy. It remains to be seen whether a counterterrorism approach will be effective, not least in dealing with the Wagner Group, but particularly in addressing some of the bigger systemic issues associated with the use of proxy actors.

It should be noted that Article 359 of the Russian Criminal Code broadly reflects IHL, as well as the International Convention on mercenarism, and thus defines a mercenary as 'a person acting with the aim of receiving material remuneration and not being a citizen of the state participating in an armed conflict or hostilities, not permanently residing on its territory, or being a person sent in fulfilment of official duties'.[17] Article 359 further designates mercenarism as a crime punishable by imprisonment, fines and other sanctions, the extent of which were increased in 2022.[18]

The Russian government has consistently denied that the Wagner Group exists, or indeed that it has any link to the organization, citing Article 359 as confirmation.[19] Moreover, the government insists that Russian law does not permit the registration of PMSCs and that 'the unified State register of legal entities maintained by the Federal Tax Service of the Russian Federation does not and, by definition, cannot list such entities, including... the Wagner

---

[14] On the Wagner Group's activities in Ukraine, see section I in this chapter.

[15] See e.g. US Department of the Treasury (note 9); and Ross, Chace-Donahue and Clarke (note 9). The European Union (EU) has also imposed a number of measures, see e.g. Council of the EU, 'EU imposes restrictive measures against the Wagner Group', Press release, 13 Dec. 2022.

[16] OHCHR, International Convention against the Recruitment, Use, Financing and Training of Mercenaries, adopted 4 Dec. 1989 by General Assembly Resolution 44/34.

[17] Criminal Code of the Russian Federation no. 63-FZ, 13 June 1996 (as amended on 14 July 2022), Article 359, 'Mercenary' (in Russian), accessed 24 Apr. 2023.

[18] Criminal Code of the Russian Federation (note 17), Article 359.

[19] See e.g. UN working group on the use of mercenaries, 'Information from the Russian Federation regarding the joint enquiry of the special procedures of the Human Rights Council concerning the extrajudicial execution of (REDACTED) a citizen of the Syrian Arab Republic', JAL RUS 14/2021 of 13 Dec. 2021, 25 Feb. 2022.

Group'.[20] In late 2022, however, a business and management consultancy using the name 'PMC Wagner Centre' registered as a joint-stock company in St Petersburg.[21] In light of this development, it is yet to be determined whether the Russian government will acknowledge the legal existence of, and its connections to, the Wagner Group.

Regulation at the United Nations

The conflict in Ukraine and the escalating operations of the Wagner Group during 2022, particularly in the Sahel region, have reinvigorated regulatory endeavours at the UN. Attempts to address the gaps between the international legal provisions addressing mercenaries and the softer regulatory approaches of multistakeholder initiatives addressing PMSCs, such as the Montreux Document and the International Code of Conduct for Private Security Providers, have a long, chequered and ultimately unfruitful history at the UN.[22] Between 2010 and 2017, states met annually at an open-ended intergovernmental working group (OEIWG I) to consider 'the possibility of elaborating an international regulatory framework on the regulation, monitoring and oversight of the activities of private military and security companies', but were unable to reach consensus on the necessity of a legally binding instrument, let alone substantive content.[23] A second open-ended intergovernmental working group (OEIWG II), established in 2017, has what could be described as a compromise mandate, 'to elaborate the content of an international regulatory framework, without prejudging the nature thereof, relating to the activities of private military and security companies'.[24] It met in May 2022 for its third session to discuss a Revised Zero Draft Instrument on an International Regulatory Framework on the Regulation, Monitoring of and Oversight over the Activities of Private Military and Security

---

[20] UN working group on the use of mercenaries (note 12).
[21] Rusprofile, [JOINT STOCK COMPANY 'PMC Wagner Centre', Date of registration 27.12.2022], accessed 17 Apr. 2023 (in Russian).
[22] International Committee of the Red Cross (ICRC) and Swiss Federal Department of Foreign Affairs (FDFA), *The Montreux Document on Pertinent International Legal Obligations and Good Practices for States Related to Operations of PMSCs during Armed Conflict* (ICRC/FDFA: Aug. 2009), preface, para. 9; International Code of Conduct Association, International Code of Conduct for Private Security Providers, as amended 10 Dec. 2021; and UN Human Rights Council, 'Open-ended intergovernmental working group to consider the possibility of elaborating an international regulatory framework on the regulation, monitoring and oversight of the activities of private military and security companies relating to the activities', accessed 24 Apr. 2023.
[23] United Nations, General Assembly, Human Rights Council, Report of the open-ended intergovernmental working group to consider the possibility of elaborating an international regulatory framework on the regulation, monitoring and oversight of the activities of private military and security companies on its sixth session, A/HRC/36/36, 4 Aug. 2017.
[24] United Nations, General Assembly, Human Rights Council, Resolution adopted by the Human Rights Council on 28 September 2017, Mandate of the open-ended intergovernmental working group to elaborate the content of an international regulatory framework on the regulation, monitoring and oversight of the activities of private military and security companies, A/HRC/RES/36/11, 9 Oct. 2017.

Companies.[25] A revised second draft is expected to be issued in early 2023 based on the discussions at that session. Four key issues arose in the Revised Zero Draft Instrument discussions from a human rights and accountability perspective, as discussed below.

Form and nature

States have been unable to agree on whether the Revised Zero Draft Instrument should be binding or non-binding. The consequence of this is that it contains language applicable to both a binding instrument and a non-binding instrument, making it a sort of Schrödinger's instrument that reflects the complex and highly politicized mandate of the OEIWG II. Yet a decision about the form and nature of the instrument must be taken sooner rather than later because the duality of the current situation is confusing and untenable. Whether a binding or non-binding instrument is adopted, it must add value to the regulatory environment, especially on accountability, and not simply reproduce the provisions of the Montreux Document.

While the continued development of multistakeholder regulatory initiatives such as the Montreux Document, the International Code of Conduct for Private Security Providers and the Voluntary Principles on Security and Human Rights are positive, insufficient numbers of states have committed to them: 58 to the Montreux Document, 7 to the Code of Conduct and 10 to the Voluntary Principles.[26] In addition, while there are important ongoing efforts at the UN to create a binding treaty on business and human rights, there must be acknowledgement of the specificities that differentiate the PMSC industry from other business sectors, such as the right to use force or detain persons.[27] There is a need, therefore, to strengthen the existing frameworks and to fill the normative gaps. At the same time, it is desirable that a PMSC instrument complements, and does not conflict with, overlapping provisions of the draft business and human rights treaty.

Legislative and regulatory frameworks pertaining to PMSCs differ considerably from one country to another, but national laws and regulations often seem to contain few human rights safeguards. In many instances, national laws on PMSCs contain inadequate provisions on licensing, registration, vetting of personnel, training (specifically on human rights and IHL), the scope of permissible and prohibited activities, the use of force, firearms and other weapons, reporting obligations for infractions or violations of

---

[25] OHCHR, Open-ended intergovernmental working group to elaborate the content of an international regulatory framework, without prejudging the nature thereof, relating to the activities of private military and security companies, 'Revised Zero Draft Instrument on an International Regulatory Framework on the Regulation, Monitoring of and Oversight Over the Activities of Private Military and Security Companies', 14 Apr. 2022.

[26] Voluntary Principles Initiative, 'The Voluntary Principles on Security and Human Rights', 2000, accessed 24 Apr. 2023.

[27] OHCHR, 'BHR treaty process: OHCHR and business and human rights', accessed 24 Apr. 2023.

domestic and/or human rights law, accountability, including penal and civil sanctions for human rights abuses, and remedies for victims. Clear legal norms emphasizing national implementation and enforcement can help to prevent violations or, failing that, ensure accountability and provide effective remedies for victims.

Scope

While the scope of the Revised Zero Draft Instrument extends to the extraterritorial provision of PMSC services, it ought to be expanded to include the domestic provision of services given the increase in PMSCs generally and their wide-ranging activities.[28] States will need to take all measures necessary to ensure the legal liability of companies based in or managed from a state party's territory regarding human rights violations as a result of their activities conducted domestically and abroad, or the activities of their subsidiaries or business partners. National legislation will need to contain extraterritorial provisions, which can facilitate the prosecution of PMSCs and their personnel for abuses. For the instrument to be effective, states will need to not only prohibit the outsourcing of activities that constitute direct participation in hostilities or a continuing combat function (CCF), but also further prohibit the provision of for-profit services constituting direct participation in hostilities or CCF by private individuals and companies that are either registered or have their principal place of management in their territories.[29] This prohibition will also need to apply to the export of such services abroad.

Human rights provisions

The Revised Zero Draft Instrument lacks a broad and detailed articulation of applicable human rights and IHL. For example, it could mirror PP2 and other relevant parts of the preamble of the third revised draft of the business and human rights treaty and refer to the nine core international human rights instruments and the eight fundamental conventions adopted by the International Labour Organization.[30] During the second session of the OEIWG II, states and civil society highlighted the importance of the inclusion of gender-responsive and gender-transformative approaches within any

---

[28] Remarks of Dr Sorcha MacLeod, Chair-Rapporteur of the working group on the use of mercenaries, Third session of the open-ended intergovernmental working group to elaborate the content of an international regulatory framework, without prejudging the nature thereof, relating to the activities of private military and security companies, 9 May 2022.

[29] ICRC, 'Interpretive guidance on the notion of direct participation in hostilities', *How Does Law Protect in War?* (online casebook), accessed 24 Apr. 2023.

[30] United Nations, General Assembly, Human Rights Council, Text of the third revised draft legally binding instrument with textual proposals submitted by States during the seventh and the eighth sessions of the open-ended intergovernmental working group on transnational corporations and other business enterprises with respect to human rights, A/HRC/52/41/Add.1, 23 Jan. 2023.

instrument.[31] Essential and concrete gender-transformative provisions are lacking in the Revised Zero Draft Instrument, however. By including them, the instrument would help to ensure, among other things, that states gather gender-disaggregated data, conduct a gender analysis before legislating or regulating, and investigate and prosecute SGBV, while PMSCs would be required to develop and implement gender-transformative approaches in their operations.[32] Additionally, it is important that the instrument adopts inclusive language to expressly acknowledge that PMSCs are in a position to negatively impact persons in vulnerable situations, such as migrants, indigenous persons, racialized persons, older persons, persons with disabilities and the LGBTI+ community. Furthermore, the instrument must take account of the fact that barriers are likely to be higher for these groups when seeking redress for violations by PMSCs.

Accountability and remedies

The Revised Zero Draft Instrument does not include adequate and detailed guidance that will ensure comprehensive accountability, and effective redress and remedies for victims in particular.[33] Adequate regulation, monitoring and enforcement are paramount in light of persistent concerns over the lack of accountability for human rights violations and abuses by PMSCs, especially when operating transnationally. In some cases, victims remain without effective remedy decades after the alleged violations and abuses occurred. Severe challenges to victims seeking access to justice are posed by the lack of judicial infrastructure, qualified members of the judiciary and judicial independence, and by threats of reprisals against members of the judiciary, victims and witnesses. Corruption within legal systems and a lack of trained investigators also pose major challenges. In addition to ensuring an effective legal system, it is important to ensure that local populations that have been adversely impacted by armed conflict or violence have trust and confidence in the system. For that reason, the system itself needs to be easily accessible to vulnerable groups, including women and children. It needs to be able to address mass human rights abuses and provide the necessary protections. In

---

[31] United Nations, General Assembly, Human Rights Council, 'Progress report on the second session of the open-ended intergovernmental working group to elaborate the content of an international regulatory framework, without prejudging the nature thereof, to protect human rights and ensure accountability for violations and abuses relating to the activities of private military and security companies', A/HRC/48/65, 6 July 2021.
[32] MacLeod, S. and Van Amstel, N., 'Private military and security companies and gendered human rights challenges: Oversight or blatant disregard?', *Business and Human Rights Journal*, vol. 7, no. 1 (2022), pp. 181–7; MacLeod, S. and Van Amstel, N., 'Gendered human rights impacts in the private military and security sector', SSRN, 3 Sep. 2020; and United Nations, General Assembly, Report of the working group on the use of mercenaries as a means of violating human rights and impeding the exercise of the right of peoples to self-determination: The gendered human rights impacts of private military and security companies, A/74/244, 29 July 2019.
[33] For a comprehensive discussion on accountability see United Nations, General Assembly (note 2).

order to do so, it should also ensure that complementary support measures are set up, as appropriate, including medical assistance, free legal assistance and psychosocial care.

The OEIWG II will meet again in 2023 to discuss the expected revised second draft of the instrument and has another opportunity to address the gaps around scope, accountability and a victim-centred approach. If states continue to find themselves unable to agree on key provisions that are crucial for an effective regulatory framework, not least whether it ought to be binding or non-binding, the outlook for a credible instrument is gloomy.

Recent case law

Cases attempting to hold mercenaries to account under criminal justice regimes are rare, but in 2022 a judgment was delivered in a complaint lodged in the Russian courts relating to alleged atrocities committed by Wagner Group operatives. In that case, the family of Mohammed Elismail, a Syrian national purportedly tortured, murdered and mutilated in Homs in 2017 by suspected Wagner Group personnel, sought to initiate a criminal investigation into his death with the Investigative Committee of the Russian Federation. The claim was based on multiple alleged violations of the Russian Criminal Code, specifically murder (Article 105(2)), war crimes (Article 356) and mercenarism (Article 359).[34] In February 2022 the Moscow City Court upheld the decision of the Basmanny District Court in not addressing the inaction of the Investigative Committee in relation to the complaint and no investigation took place.[35] The case clearly illustrates the problem of lack of accountability and impunity for such actors, as the family encountered delays, inaction and other difficulties at every stage of the process.[36] Now that domestic remedies have been exhausted, an application has been made to the European Court of Human Rights, which is still outstanding.[37] In any event, even if the case is accepted, the outcome may be moot given Russia's decision to leave the Council of Europe in 2022.[38]

Another case in 2022 illustrates the emerging phenomenon of the instrumentalization of the term 'mercenary' to justify the prosecution and conviction of individuals who do not fulfil the criteria to be defined

---

[34] Criminal Code of the Russian Federation (note 17), Article 359.

[35] International Federation for Human Rights (FIDH), 'Wagner in Syria: Moscow court upholds decision in murder case, obstructing accountability', 9 Feb. 2022; and FIDH, 'Wagner in Syria: Ruling by Russian court entrenches impunity for brutal murder', 18 Jan. 2022.

[36] UN working group on the use of mercenaries, 'Russian Federation', JAL RUS 14/2021, 13 Dec. 2021.

[37] FIDH, 'Wagner in Syria: Appeal to European Court of Human Rights after case dismissed in Russia', Press release, 9 June 2022.

[38] Council of Europe, 'Russia ceases to be a party to the European Convention on Human Rights on 16 Sep. 2022', 23 Mar. 2022.

as a mercenary under IHL.[39] At the same time, it illustrates that suspected mercenaries are entitled to human rights protections, in this particular instance the right to a fair trial and opposition to the imposition of capital punishment. The case involved two British nationals (Shaun Pinner and Aiden Aslin) and a Moroccan national (Brahim Saadoune), who had been officially recruited into the Ukrainian armed forces prior to the Russian invasion of Ukraine in February 2022. They were subsequently captured by Russian forces and held as prisoners of war, and then handed over to the authorities in Donetsk. In June 2022 all three were prosecuted and convicted in Donetsk of: (*a*) forcible seizure of power or retention of power; (*b*) participation in an armed conflict or hostilities as a mercenary; and (*c*) the promotion of training in terrorist activities.

Death sentences were imposed in relation to the attempted seizure of power, and prison terms were imposed for the remaining offences, including mercenarism. Concerns were raised that the tribunal was neither impartial nor independent, and that the trial was expedited (given that it took place over only three days and included sentencing). The lack of both a public hearing and the presumption of innocence raised further concerns. Allegations were also made that the defendants gave coerced testimony, had inadequate legal representation and were denied a right of review by an independent higher tribunal. Given that all three individuals were members of the Ukrainian armed forces, a party to the conflict, the definition of mercenary under Article 47 of Additional Protocol I was not satisfied, and they ought not to have been tried for mercenarism. Furthermore, as combatants they were entitled to the privilege of belligerency and appropriate treatment as prisoners of war.[40] Their convictions were therefore a probable violation of IHL. All three men were subsequently released as part of a prisoner exchange between Ukraine and Russia.[41]

Despite the exponential increase in the use of mercenaries as proxy actors, there has not yet been a corresponding increase in the number of cases brought by victims of their human rights violations or in prosecutions of suspected mercenaries. This is almost certainly due to the difficulty of identifying such actors in conflict and post-conflict environments, combined with the absence of effective investigation and prosecution by states and the lack of routes to accountability for victims.

---

[39] UN working group on the use of mercenaries, 'Mr Denis Vladimirovich Pushilin', JUA OTH 73/2022, 7 July 2022.

[40] ICRC, 'Immunities', *How Does Law Protect in War?* (online casebook), accessed 25 Apr. 2023; and ICRC, 'Unprivileged belligerent', *How Does Law Protect in War?* (online casebook), accessed 25 Apr. 2023.

[41] Sabbagh, D., 'Aiden Aslin among 10 international "prisoners of war" released by Russian authorities', *The Guardian*, 22 Sep. 2022.

Conclusions

In 2022, the atrocities committed by mercenaries and PMSCs received significantly more international attention than in recent years. This is due largely to the international community's belated realization of the dangers posed by mercenaries and PMSCs deployed in armed conflicts as proxy actors, with the threats presented by the Wagner Group being a prominent example. The presence of such actors is prolonging armed conflicts around the world, acting as a destabilizing factor and undermining peace efforts. While some states have responded with counterterrorism approaches, others seem to have been galvanized into paying more attention to the regulatory frameworks around mercenaries and PMSCs. Whether this will translate into concrete and credible regulatory change via the OEIWG II, for example, remains to be seen but it is clear that robust conversations will be had at the UN in the near future. The absence of cases holding mercenary and PMSC personnel criminally liable for atrocities is of particular concern, as is the complete lack of accountability and remedy available to their victims. States must step up and fully realize their obligations to respect, protect and fulfil human rights when mercenaries and PMSCs commit atrocities. Above all, this requires states ensuring that victims have effective routes to accountability and remedy at national and international levels.

Part II. Military spending and armaments, 2022

Chapter 5. Military expenditure and arms production

Chapter 6. International arms transfers

Chapter 7. World nuclear forces

5. Military expenditure and arms production

Overview

In an eighth consecutive year of growth, global military expenditure continued to reach new heights in 2022. The rise of 19 per cent over the decade 2013–22 and of 3.7 per cent in just one year pushed world military expenditure up to an estimated US$2240 billion, the highest level recorded in the SIPRI Military Expenditure Database (see section I). Despite the increase in 2022, the global military burden—world military expenditure as a share of world gross domestic product (GDP)—remained at 2.2 per cent because of a simultaneous growth in the world economy. Governments around the world spent an average of 6.2 per cent of their budgets on the military, or $282 per person.

It may turn out to have been a watershed year, since 2022 brought significant changes in security policies in Europe and in Asia and Oceania (see section II). Germany, whose chancellor defined the invasion of Ukraine as an 'epochal tectonic shift', plans to make additional efforts to spend 2.0 per cent of its GDP on the military. Meanwhile, for the third consecutive year Japan's military spending as a share of GDP surpassed the cap of 1.0 per cent that it had maintained since 1955. Moreover, the government announced plans to increase its total security spending to 2.0 per cent of GDP by 2027. The shift in Japanese security policy is a result of growing regional tensions, especially with China and North Korea.

The war in Ukraine had a major effect on both global and regional military expenditure in 2022. Military expenditure in Europe grew by 13 per cent, with most Central and West European countries—some of which were already among the largest military spenders in the world—responding to the invasion with significant increases in military spending (see section I). They also made plans for future growth, with some increases stretching until 2033. This suggests that the war, and the ensuing rise in European military spending, will exacerbate the ongoing upward trend in global military expenditure. Most of these allocations are for modernization of military equipment and increasing troop numbers. Military aid for Ukraine was another cause of the increase in military expenditure in Central and West Europe and North America: these countries either sent financial military aid to Ukraine or spent more to replenish dwindling stockpiles after sending military equipment. Ukraine's own military spending rose more than sevenfold, amounting to over one-third of the country's economy. Russian military spending also increased, by 9.2 per cent, despite economic sanctions from Western countries. Budget updates during the year showed how the costs of the war had increased compared to Russia's initial plans.

SIPRI Yearbook 2023: Armaments, Disarmament and International Security
www.sipriyearbook.org

The estimated military spending in the Middle East rose for the first time in four years, by 3.2 per cent. Saudi Arabia is the region's largest military spender, and its 16 per cent increase was the main reason for the regional increase. In Israel, the second largest spender, military spending fell 4.2 per cent.

Spending in Asia and Oceania rose by 2.7 per cent in 2022. China's ongoing military modernization and increased spending in India and Japan have been major factors pushing military spending in the region. Military spending by China, the world's second largest spender, rose for the 28th consecutive year, by 4.2 per cent. This narrowed the gap between its spending and that of the United States.

While the USA remained by far the largest military spender in the world, exceptionally high levels of inflation transformed a nominal increase in military spending of 8.8 per cent into a 0.7 per cent real-terms increase. As a consequence, overall military spending in the Americas rose only slightly, by 0.3 per cent.

The only region in which military spending fell was Africa, down by 5.3 per cent. This was the region's first decrease since 2018 and its largest since 2003. Poor economic performance and natural disasters in the region's largest spenders led to the fall in military spending despite ongoing security challenges.

The impact of the war in Ukraine on the global arms industry interacted with the legacy of the Covid-19 pandemic (see section III). The combined arms sales of the 100 largest arms-producing and military services companies (the SIPRI Top 100) totalled $592 billion in 2021 (the most recent year for which data is available), 1.9 per cent higher than in 2020. This continued the upward trend in arms sales since at least 2015 and is likely to continue as the war in Ukraine creates more demand for arms. This growth came despite the continuing effects of the pandemic, most notably the disruption in supply chains, labour shortages and a lack of semiconductors. Arms sales by US companies in the Top 100 decreased by 0.9 per cent in 2021, but the USA continued to dominate the ranking with 40 companies with total arms sales of $299 billion. The eight Chinese arms companies included in the Top 100 in 2021 had aggregated arms sales of $109 billion, 6.3 per cent more than in 2020.

DIEGO LOPES DA SILVA

I. Global developments in military expenditure, 2022

DIEGO LOPES DA SILVA, NAN TIAN, LUCIE BÉRAUD-SUDREAU, LORENZO SCARAZZATO AND XIAO LIANG

Global military expenditure continued to rise in 2022 to reach a total of US$2240 billion.[1] The growth of 3.7 per cent continued an eight-year streak of increases that remained unbroken even amid the Covid-19 pandemic-related economic downturn. Indeed, world military expenditure grew by 19 per cent between 2013 and 2022 (see table 5.1, end of this section). The war in Ukraine was a major driver of global military expenditure in 2022. Most European countries, some of which were already among the world's largest spenders, made increases to military spending in 2022 and announced plans for further rises in 2023 and beyond. Increases in parts of Asia and Oceania also contributed to the global growth in 2022.

World military expenditure rose alongside global gross domestic product (GDP). The world economy continued to recover from the pandemic-related downturn in 2022, with growth in GDP estimated to be 3.4 per cent.[2] As a result, the global military burden—world military expenditure as a share of world GDP—is estimated to have been 2.2 per cent in 2022, the same as in 2021. The growth rate of global military expenditure outpaced population growth once again, resulting in military spending per capita rising for the sixth consecutive year in 2022, to $282. In contrast, average military spending as a share of government expenditure fell by 0.1 percentage points to 6.2 per cent in 2022.

World military expenditure grew in four of the five geographical regions: the Americas, Asia and Oceania, Europe, and the Middle East (see figure 5.1). Of the four, Europe had by far the largest increase, of 13 per cent to reach $480 billion. Estimated military spending in the Middle East in 2022 increased by 3.2 per cent to $184 billion and in Asia and Oceania spending grew by 2.7 per cent to $575 billion. The rate of growth was low in the Americas, at 0.3 per cent, to give a total of $961 billion. In contrast, military expenditure in Africa declined by 5.3 per cent to $39.4 billion.

This section continues by providing an initial assessment of the impact of the war in Ukraine on the military expenditure of Central and West European states. It then describes the global trends in military expenditure

---

[1] All figures for spending in 2022 are quoted in current 2022 US dollars. Except where otherwise stated, figures for increases or decreases in military spending are expressed in constant 2021 US dollars, often described as changes in 'real terms' or adjusted for inflation. Of the 168 countries for which SIPRI attempted to estimate military expenditure in 2022, relevant data was found for 150. See the notes in table 5.1 for more details on estimates in world and regional totals.

[2] International Monetary Fund (IMF), *World Economic Outlook Update: Inflation Peaking Amid Low Growth* (IMF: Washington, DC, Jan. 2023).

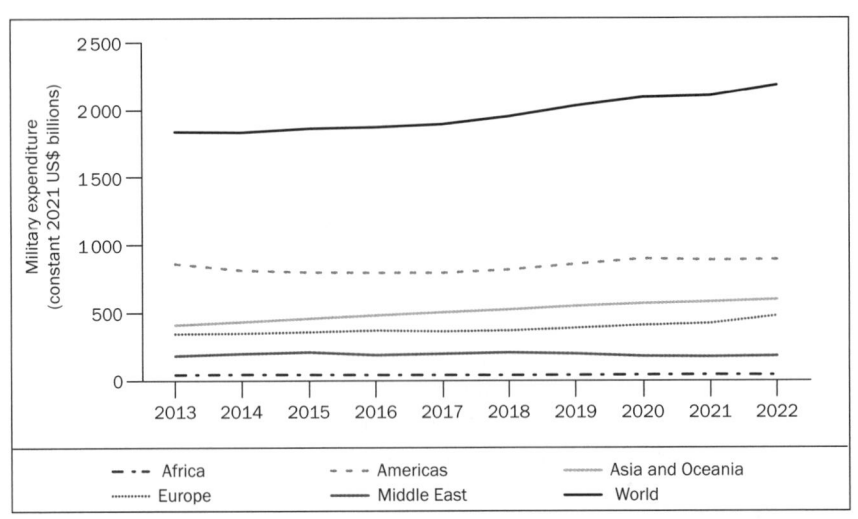

Figure 5.1. Military expenditure by region, 2013–22
Source: SIPRI Military Expenditure Database, Apr. 2023.

over the period 2013–22 before identifying the 15 countries with the highest military spending in 2022. Regional and subregional trends and the spending of individual countries are discussed in section II. It should be borne in mind that military expenditure is an input measure that is not directly related to the output of military activities, such as military capability or military security. Long-term trends in military expenditure and sudden changes in trends may be signs of a change in military output, but such interpretations should be made with caution.[3]

The impact of the war in Ukraine on military expenditure in Central and Western Europe

One immediate consequence of Russia's invasion of Ukraine in February 2022 has been rising military expenditure in Central and Western Europe.[4] Expressing a general sense of urgency, nearby countries were quick to announce major increases in the wake of the invasion, and leaders of the European Union (EU) and the North Atlantic Treaty Organization (NATO) regularly called for increased military spending by their member states.[5]

---

[3] For sources and methods of the SIPRI Military Expenditure Database see SIPRI Military Expenditure Database, 'Sources and methods'.

[4] On other aspects of the war in Ukraine see chapter 1, section V, chapter 2, section I, chapter 8, section V, chapter 10, section I, chapter 11 and chapter 12, section III, in this volume.

[5] Stoltenberg, J., NATO secretary general, Statement at the start of the extraordinary NATO Summit, 24 Mar. 2022; and von der Leyen, U., President of the European Commission, 'On the Commission's proposals regarding REPowerEU, defence investment gaps and the relief and reconstruction of Ukraine', Press statement, 18 May 2022.

General Rajmund Andrzejczak, chief of the general staff of Poland's armed forces, epitomized the sense of urgency when he said that, 'If we really want to live in the peacetime, we have to invest much more'.[6]

The announced increases in military spending, albeit oriented towards the same goal, differed in terms of their timelines, status and targets. The timelines of most increases stretched across several years, but some were meant to take place in 2022. Denmark, for example, plans to gradually increase its military spending to 2.0 per cent of GDP by 2033, whereas Sweden aims to reach this target by 2026.[7] In terms of the status, some increases were approved and signed off by governments in 2022, while others were still being discussed or subject to parliamentary approval. The Lithuanian Parliament, for example, was quick to unanimously approve a mid-year proposal to increase 2022 military spending to 2.5 per cent of GDP.[8] As a result, its military spending was 27 per cent higher than in 2021.

Another important distinction between the various pledges are the targets. Following Russia's annexation of Crimea in 2014, NATO set 2.0 per cent of GDP as the guideline for the military spending of its members.[9] Several countries have thus chosen to formulate their expenditure goals in terms of increasing their military burden, and at least 12 Central and West European countries linked their pledged increase in military spending to increased economic output.[10] However, there are variations in the size of the targeted burdens. Austria, a non-NATO member that has been militarily neutral since 1945, plans to increase spending to 1.0 per cent of its GDP.[11] In contrast, Poland, a NATO member, intends to raise its military burden to 4.0 per cent of its GDP in 2023, with the ultimate goal of eventually reaching 5.0 per cent, considerably higher than the NATO guideline.[12]

The military burden rose most sharply in Lithuania, from 2.0 per cent in 2021 to 2.5 per cent in 2022. In contrast, Portugal's military burden fell by 0.2 percentage points to 1.4 per cent. In total, only eight Central and West European countries had a military burden of 2.0 per cent of GDP or more in 2022. Of the Central and West European countries that announced an

---

[6] Bayer, L., 'Let's not make it official: NATO allies reluctant to increase spending goals', Politico, 19 Jan. 2023.

[7] 'Denmark to boost defence spending and phase out Russian gas', Reuters, 6 Mar. 2022; and 'Sweden's supreme commander says defence spending to reach 2% of GDP by 2026', Reuters, 1 Nov. 2022.

[8] 'Lithuania raises defence spending to 2.52 percent of GDP', LRT, 17 Mar. 2022.

[9] NATO, North Atlantic Council, Wales summit declaration, 5 Sep. 2014, para. 14.

[10] Bergmann, M. et al., 'Transforming European defense', Center for Strategic and International Studies, Aug. 2022; and Tocci, N., 'The paradox of Europe's defense moment', *Texas National Security Review*, vol. 6, no. 1 (winter 2022/23).

[11] Kurmayer, N. J., 'Austria to significantly up military spending', Euractiv, 07 Mar. 2022.

[12] 'Poland to ramp up defense budget to 4% of GDP', Deutsche Welle, 30 Jan. 2023; and Krzysztoszek, A., 'Poland to spend 5% of GDP on defence', Euractiv, 18 July 2022.

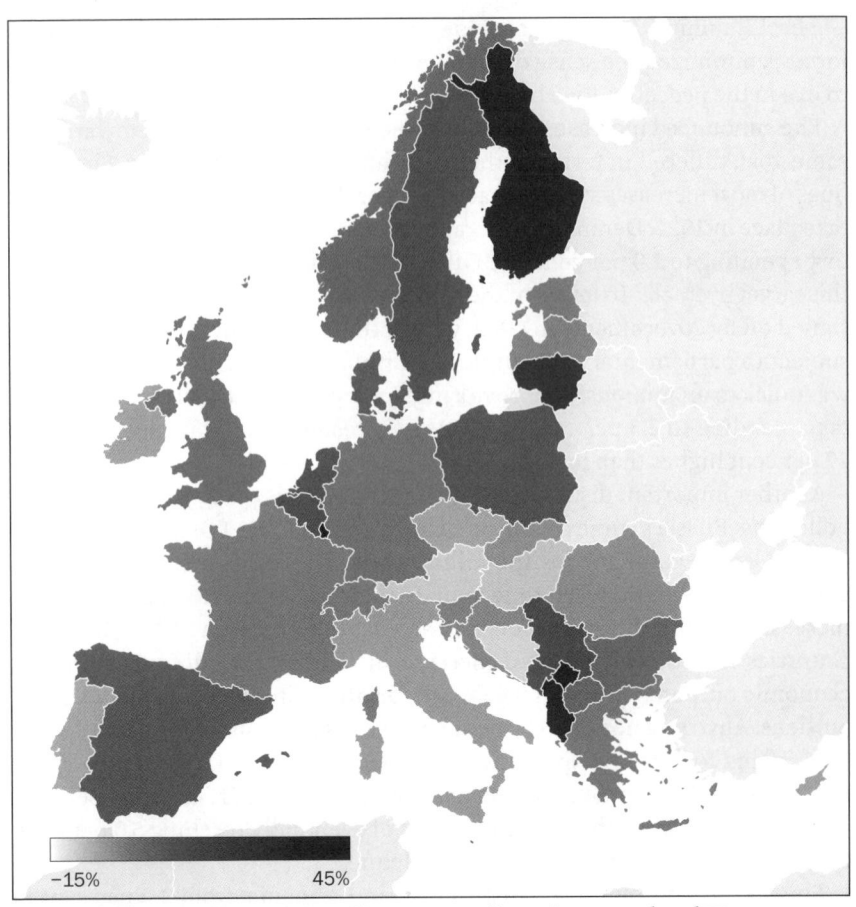

Figure 5.2. Rates of growth in military expenditure in Central and Western Europe, 2022

Source: SIPRI Military Expenditure Database, Apr. 2023.

increase in military spending in 2022, Greece had the highest military burden (3.7 per cent of GDP), while Ireland had the lowest (0.2 per cent).

Despite the numerous announced increases in military spending, the average military burden in Central and Western Europe increased by only 0.1 percentage points, to 1.6 per cent of GDP in 2022. The limited growth was due to simultaneous rises in both military expenditure and GDP. Overall, according to the International Monetary Fund (IMF), economic performance in 2022 was better than expected for numerous economies, including European countries.[13] Thus, even though most Central and West European countries increased military spending by a significant amount, on average the burden of the military on the economy was almost unchanged.

---

[13] International Monetary Fund (note 2), p. 1.

Geographical proximity to Russia and Ukraine is a factor underlying increases in military spending in 2022 (see figure 5.2). Most of the acutest increases took place in countries bordering or close to Russia and Ukraine (e.g. Finland, with a 36 per cent increase) or where other conflict dynamics were evident (e.g. Kosovo, also 36 per cent).

These substantial increases were counterposed by decreases in several countries, of which Bosnia and Herzegovina had the largest, an 11 per cent drop. Most Central and West European countries with falling military expenditure in 2022 pledged to increase their military spending but with longer time frames or later starting dates. Although Bosnia and Herzegovina made no announcements on increasing military spending, Austria (–9.8 per cent), Croatia (–1.5 per cent) and Slovenia (–0.5 per cent) set 2023 as the first year of increases.[14]

Soaring inflation is another factor explaining the differences in military spending changes (see box 5.1). In 2022 inflation among advanced economies reached its highest rate in 40 years. Countries in the eurozone endured 10 per cent inflation.[15] This led to large differences between changes in military spending in constant prices (i.e. in real terms) and in current prices: the gap between the two figures shows the extent of the impact of inflation (see figure 5.3). The average gap was nearly 11 percentage points, but the gap extended to more than 20 percentage points in extreme cases such as Lithuania and Estonia.

For several countries, military spending shrank or barely rose in real terms despite spending significantly more in nominal terms. For example, Latvia's military spending went up by 16 per cent in current prices, but inflation transformed this to a 0.4 per cent decrease in constant prices; and Estonia's nominal growth of 22 per cent produced real-terms growth of only 0.7 per cent. Some countries that announced increases for 2022 were unable to implement them because of rampant inflation. In Czechia, for example, despite a supplementary budget to increase military spending, inflation reduced a 9.6 per cent increase in current prices to a 5.8 per cent decrease in constant prices.

The war is likely to have a lasting effect on military spending in Central and Western Europe. The pledges to increase military spending stretch far into the future and foreshadow years of growth. This, of course, is not the first time that Russia's actions have propelled a wave of rising military spending in the subregion: after the annexation of Crimea in 2014, Central and West European military spending increased substantially. Considering

---

[14] Austrian Federal Ministry of Defence, 'Landesverteidigungs-Finanzierungsgesetz von Nationalrat beschlossen' [National Defence Financing Act passed by the National Council], APA-OTS, 15 Nov. 2022; Croatian News Agency (HINA), 'Croatian Defence Ministry's 2023 budget to increase by €40m', N1, 30 June 2022; and Ralev, R., 'Slovenia to boost defence spending to 2%/GDP by 2030—Minister', SeeNews, 17 Mar. 2022.

[15] International Monetary Fund (IMF), *World Economic Outlook: Countering the Cost-of-Living Crisis* (IMF: Washington, DC, Oct. 2022), p. 1.

Box 5.1. Global inflation and its impact on military spending

Rising prices dominated world economic news in 2022. Although inflation—a measure of the general change in the price level of goods and services in an economy—is an ever-present phenomenon, in 2022 it reached record levels not seen in decades.[a] Inflation in advanced economies reached its highest rate since 1982, while in emerging markets it was at its highest rate since 1999.[b]

The global inflation crisis is the sum of two separate crises

First, the fallout from the Covid-19 pandemic created a supply shortage (caused by supply chain problems and labour shortages) and pent-up consumer demand.[c] Sharp increases in prices reflected this imbalance in supply and demand. How countries responded to the Covid-19 pandemic also affected inflation. In the case of the United States, for example, the government's $2 trillion stimulus package reinforced excessive consumer demand and pushed prices even higher.[d]

Second, Russia's invasion of Ukraine severely disrupted Ukraine's exports of grain.[e] Concurrently, Western sanctions on Russia—the world's largest exporter of wheat, natural gas and oil to global markets—amplified worldwide food and energy prices.[f] This aggravated the already record levels of global inflation.[g]

In the case of military spending, SIPRI collects military data in local currency nominal prices but, for meaningful comparison over time, all country-specific figures are adjusted for inflation using a country-specific consumer price index (CPI) provided by the International Monetary Fund (IMF).[h] High inflation both reduces the military's purchasing power and increases the opportunity cost of holding money. The opportunity cost of holding money refers to the opportunities forgone by holding money and not spending it during high inflation. High inflation will have an impact on the value of a country's currency and this, in turn, will affect the purchasing power of the military on all its spending activities, ranging from operations and maintenance to procurement. In those countries where inflation in 2022 reached record levels, expenditure plans by militaries for late 2022 would have been substantially affected as money held for expected future spending lost a substantial amount of value. In cases where inflation was higher than the nominal increase in military spending, the military would effectively have had less money to spend than in 2021.

[a] International Monetary Fund (IMF), *World Economic Outlook: Countering the Cost-of-Living Crisis* (IMF: Washington, DC, Oct. 2022), chapter 1.

[b] International Monetary Fund (note a).

[c] Lopez, G., 'A global inflation crisis', *New York Times*, 26 July 2022.

[d] Ritz, B., 'What's in the record-breaking $2 trillion stimulus package?', *Forbes*, 25 Mar. 2020; and Tankersley, J. et al., 'A weekslong campaign to sell the stimulus bill to the American public begins tonight', *New York Times*, 12 Mar. 2021.

[e] Council of the European Union, 'Infographic—Ukraine grain exports explained', 17 Jan. 2023.

[f] E.g. International Energy Agency (IEA), *Russian Supplies to Global Energy Markets* (IEA: Paris, 2022).

[g] Lopez (note c); IEA (note f); IEA, 'Energy fact sheet: Why does Russian oil and gas matter?', 21 Mar. 2022; and Rastogi, K. and Ang, C., 'These are the top 10 countries that produce the most wheat', World Economic Forum, 4 Aug. 2022.

[h] IMF, International Financial Statistics Database, Sep. 2022.

---

that the situation in 2022 is worse than in 2014, the response to the fully fledged invasion in terms of spending has been more robust. As a result, it is reasonable to expect an acceleration of the ongoing upward trend in regional and, consequently, global military spending.

MILITARY EXPENDITURE 165

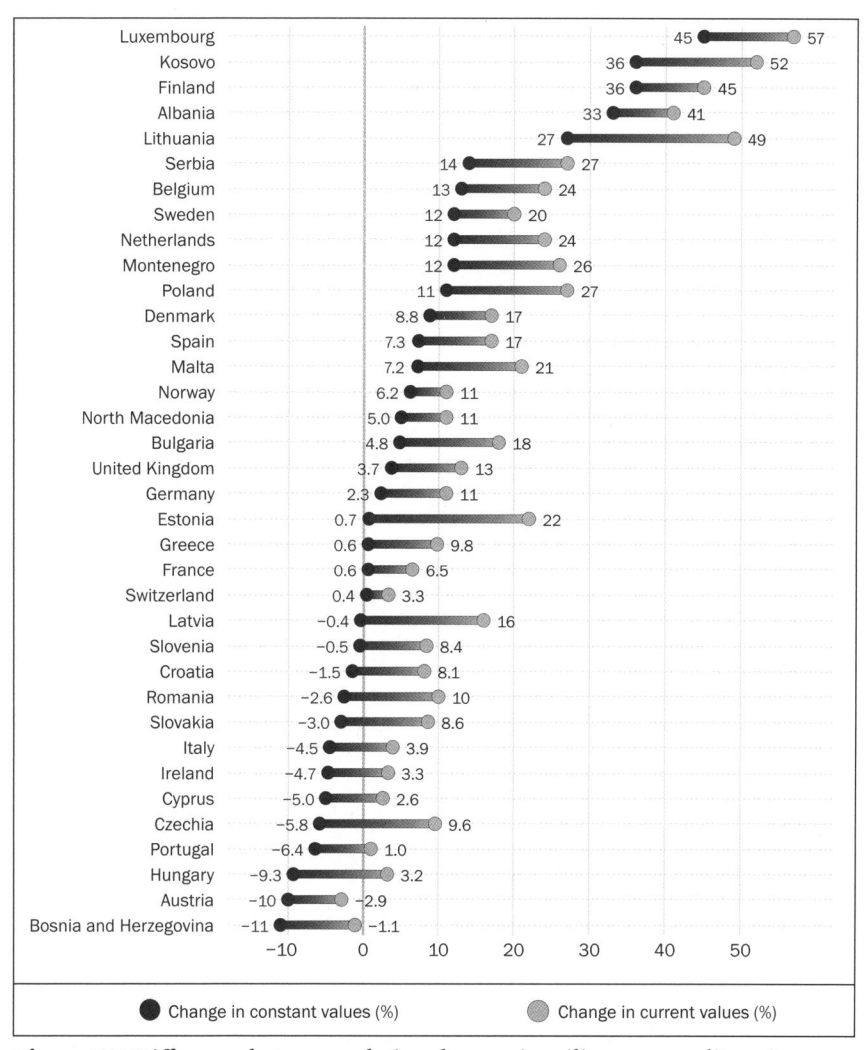

Country	Change in constant values (%)	Change in current values (%)
Luxembourg	45	57
Kosovo	36	52
Finland	36	45
Albania	33	41
Lithuania	27	49
Serbia	14	27
Belgium	13	24
Sweden	12	20
Netherlands	12	24
Montenegro	12	26
Poland	11	27
Denmark	8.8	17
Spain	7.3	17
Malta	7.2	21
Norway	6.2	11
North Macedonia	5.0	11
Bulgaria	4.8	18
United Kingdom	3.7	13
Germany	2.3	11
Estonia	0.7	22
Greece	0.6	9.8
France	0.6	6.5
Switzerland	0.4	3.3
Latvia	−0.4	16
Slovenia	−0.5	8.4
Croatia	−1.5	8.1
Romania	−2.6	10
Slovakia	−3.0	8.6
Italy	−4.5	3.9
Ireland	−4.7	3.3
Cyprus	−5.0	2.6
Czechia	−5.8	9.6
Portugal	−6.4	1.0
Hungary	−9.3	3.2
Austria	−10	−2.9
Bosnia and Herzegovina	−11	−1.1

Figure 5.3. Difference between relative changes in military expenditure in current and constant values in Central and Western Europe, 2022

Note: Changes in current values are calculated from spending denominated in national currencies; changes in constant values are calculated in US dollars at 2021 prices based on the national Consumer Price Index (CPI) with 2021 as the base year.

Source: SIPRI Military Expenditure Database, Apr. 2023.

Trends in military expenditure, 2013–22

Global military spending rose in all but two of the years 2013–22, with a cumulative increase of 19 per cent. After the annual growth rate peaked in 2019, reaching 4.0 per cent, it started to fall mainly because of the Covid-19 pandemic. However, despite the massive economic downturn, world military

Table 5.2. Key military expenditure statistics by region, 2022

Expenditure figures are in US$, at current prices and exchange rates. Changes are in real terms, based on constant (2021) US dollars.

Region/subregion	Expenditure, 2022 (US$ b.)	Change (%) 2021–22	Change (%) 2013–22	Major changes, 2022 (%)[a] Increases		Decreases	
World	2240	3.7	19				
Africa[b]	39.4	–5.3	–6.4	Ethiopia	88	Nigeria	–38
North Africa	(19.1)	–3.2	11	Togo	80	Zimbabwe	–33
Sub-Saharan Africa[b]	20.3	–7.3	–18	South Sudan	51	Mozambique	–20
				Guinea	43	Mali	–18
Americas[c]	961	0.3	3.5	Guatemala	19	Argentina	–32
Central America and the Caribbean[c]	11.2	–6.2	38	Dominican Republic	16	Mexico	–9.7
						Brazil	–7.9
North America	904	0.7	3.7	El Salvador	12	Trinidad and Tobago	–6.8
South America	46.1	–6.1	–5.4	Bolivia	8.7		
Asia and Oceania[d]	575	2.7	45	India	6.0	Kazakhstan	–33
Central Asia[e]	1.4	–29	–28	Japan	5.9	Sri Lanka	–31
East Asia[f]	397	3.5	50	China	4.2	Philippines	–25
Oceania	35.3	0.5	48	Singapore	2.8	Thailand	–11
South Asia	98.3	4.0	46				
South East Asia	43.1	–4.0	13				
Europe	480	13	38	Ukraine	640	Bosnia and Herzegovina	–11
Central Europe and Western Europe	345	3.6	30	Luxembourg	45	Austria	–9.8
Eastern Europe	135	58	72	Kosovo	36	Hungary	–9.3
				Finland	36	Portugal	–6.4
Middle East[g]	(184)	3.2	–1.5	Qatar	27	Türkiye	–26
				Saudi Arabia	16	Lebanon	–14
				Iran	4.6	Kuwait	–11

( ) = uncertain estimate.

[a] These lists shows the countries with the largest increases or decreases for each region as a whole, rather than by subregion. Countries with a military expenditure in 2022 of less than $100 million, or $50 million in Africa, are excluded.

[b] Figures exclude Djibouti, Eritrea and Somalia.

[c] Figures exclude Cuba.

[d] Figures exclude North Korea, Turkmenistan and Uzbekistan.

[e] Figures exclude Turkmenistan and Uzbekistan.

[f] Figures exclude North Korea.

[g] Figures exclude Syria and Yemen.

Source: SIPRI Military Expenditure Database, Apr. 2023.

expenditure still managed to grow. The 3.7 per cent increase in 2022 seems to indicate a return to pre-pandemic growth rates. Given the war in Ukraine and the subsequent pledges to increase military spending, the 2022 increase is likely to forbode a significant upward trend.

World military expenditure is highly concentrated. Just two countries—the United States and China—accounted for 52 per cent of world military expenditure in 2022. Thus, any change in their military spending has a significant effect on the global total. In 2022, a 0.7 per cent rise in US military spending was accompanied by a 4.2 per cent increase in China's military spending. The US and Chinese increases and those by Saudi Arabia (16 per cent), Russia (9.2 per cent) and India (6.0 per cent) were the main contributors to the 3.7 per cent rise in world military expenditure in 2022.

Of the 10 years 2013–22, world military expenditure fell in only two: by 1.7 per cent in 2013 and by 0.3 per cent in 2014. Those declines were largely explained by falls in US military expenditure that were only partly mitigated by increases in the military expenditure of China, India, Russia, Saudi Arabia and the United Kingdom. In contrast, in 2015 the increase in total spending of these five states surpassed the drop in US spending; alongside increases in smaller spenders, this led to an increase in world military expenditure of 1.5 per cent. As US military spending began to rise again in 2018, the growth rate of world military expenditure followed suit: 3.0 per cent in 2018, 4.0 per cent in 2019 and 3.1 per cent in 2020. The pandemic-led economic downturn brought the growth rate down to 0.6 per cent in 2021.

Between 2013 and 2022, regional spending decreased only in Africa (–6.4 per cent) and the Middle East (–1.5 per cent; see table 5.2). The decrease in the Middle East can be attributed to falls in Saudi Arabia (–2.7 per cent), Iraq (–37 per cent), Oman (–39 per cent) and Lebanon (–87 per cent). Military spending in the region is highly correlated with oil prices, and the drop in spending since 2015 is probably connected to a depreciation of oil in international markets.[16]

Spending in the other three regions increased: in the Americas by 3.5 per cent, in Asia and Oceania by 45 per cent, and in Europe by 38 per cent. Among the 12 subregions, the largest increase was in Eastern Europe (72 per cent), mostly due to the 58 per cent rise in 2022—growth between 2013 and 2021 was only 9.0 per cent.

Spending fell in just three of the subregions between 2013 and 2022: Central Asia (–28 per cent), sub-Saharan Africa (–18 per cent) and South America (–5.4 per cent). The decline in military spending in sub-Saharan Africa meant that the gap between spending in sub-Saharan Africa and North Africa narrowed from 40 per cent in 2013 to almost disappear in 2020. Subsequently, sub-Saharan African military spending rose in 2021 but fell once again in 2022, whereas North African military spending dropped in both years. The fall in both subregions in 2022 was driven by declines in each subregion's largest spender: Nigeria (–38 per cent) and Algeria (–3.7 per cent).

---

[16] Tian, N., 'Oil price shocks and military expenditure', *SIPRI Yearbook 2017*, pp. 343–49.

Table 5.3. The 15 countries with the highest military expenditure in 2022

Expenditure figures and GDP are in US$, at current prices and exchange rates. Changes are in real terms, based on constant (2021) US dollars.

Rank[a] 2022	Rank[a] 2021	Country	Military expenditure, 2022 ($ b.)	Change (%) 2021–22	Change (%) 2013–22	Military expenditure as a share of GDP (%)[b] 2022	Military expenditure as a share of GDP (%)[b] 2013	Share of world military expenditure, 2022 (%)
1	1	USA	877	0.7	2.7	3.5	4.0	39
2	2	China	[292]	4.2	63	[1.6]	[1.7]	[13]
3	5	Russia	[86.4]	9.2	15	[4.1]	[3.9]	[3.9]
4	3	India	81.4	6.0	47	2.4	2.5	3.6
5	8	Saudi Arabia	[75.0]	16	–2.7	[7.4]	[9.0]	[3.3]
Subtotal top 5			1 412	..	..	..	..	63
6	4	UK	68.5	3.7	9.7	2.2	2.3	3.1
7	7	Germany	55.8	2.3	33	1.4	1.2	2.5
8	6	France	53.6	0.6	15	1.9	1.8	2.4
9	10	South Korea	46.4	–2.5	37	2.7	2.1	2.1
10	9	Japan	46.0	5.9	18	1.1	0.9	2.1
Subtotal top 10			1 682	..	..	..	..	75
11	36	Ukraine	44.0	640	1 661	[34]	1.6	2.0
12	11	Italy	33.5	–4.5	24	1.7	1.4	1.5
13	12	Australia	32.3	0.3	47	1.9	1.6	1.4
14	13	Canada	26.9	3.0	49	1.2	1.0	1.2
15	14	Israel	23.4	–4.2	26	4.5	5.5	1.0
Subtotal top 15			1 842	..	..	..	..	82
World			**2 240**	**3.7**	**19**	**2.2**	**2.3**	**100**

.. = not applicable; [ ] = estimated figure; GDP = gross domestic product.

[a] Rankings for 2021 are based on updated military expenditure figures for 2021 in the current edition of the SIPRI Military Expenditure Database. They may therefore differ from the rankings for 2021 given in *SIPRI Yearbook 2022* and in other SIPRI publications in 2022.

[b] These figures are based on GDP estimates from International Monetary Fund, World Economic Outlook Database, Oct. 2022; and International Monetary Fund, International Financial Statistics Database, Sep. 2022.

Source: SIPRI Military Expenditure Database, Apr. 2023.

The global military burden—that is, global military spending as a share of global GDP—fell slightly over the decade, from 2.3 per cent in 2013 to 2.2 per cent in 2022. This indicates that world GDP and world military expenditure rose more or less in line with each other. In the first two years of the pandemic (2019–20), as the global economy shrank, the global military burden rose by 0.2 percentage points to reach 2.4 per cent—the highest point since 2015. As the world economy returned to growth—with estimated growth of 3.4 per cent in 2022—and with several countries showing a surprisingly strong recovery from the pandemic-related downturn, the military burden fell back to 2.2 per cent from 2021.[17]

---

[17] International Monetary Fund (note 15), chapter 1.

Middle Eastern countries had the highest average military burden in 2022, at 3.9 per cent of GDP. Europe had the second largest average at 2.5 per cent, a growth of 0.8 percentage points compared to 2021. This rise was largely due to a dramatic growth in Ukraine's military burden—by 30 percentage points in a single year. The average military burdens for countries in Africa (1.7 per cent), the Americas (1.2 per cent), and Asia and Oceania (1.5 per cent) were considerably lower. Between 2013 and 2022, the average military burden only rose in Europe (by 1.0 percentage point). In the Americas, the average military burden fell by 0.3 percentage points from 2013, whereas in Africa and Asia and Oceania the fall was 0.2 percentage points. The largest drop (0.6 percentage points) took place in the Middle East.

The largest military spenders in 2022

The top 15 largest military spenders in the world spent an accumulated $1842 billion in 2022, accounting for 82 per cent of the world total. The war in Ukraine led to two substantial changes in the top 15: Russia became the third largest military spender, and Ukraine ranked 11th after a 640 per cent increase in its military spending (see table 5.3).[18] This is the first time that Ukraine has ranked among the top 15 spenders.

Almost all countries in the top 15 increased their military spending compared to 2013, except for Saudi Arabia, where military spending in 2022 was 2.7 per cent below the level of 2013. By far the largest increase took place in Ukraine (1661 per cent), while the smallest was in the USA (2.7 per cent). Other notable increases took place in China (63 per cent), Canada (49 per cent), and Australia and India (47 per cent each). Excluding Ukraine, the average growth rate over the decade was 27 per cent.

The military burdens of six countries in the top 15 dropped between 2013 and 2022. Among the countries that increased their military burdens, Ukraine stands out once again. The increase of 32 percentage points is the result of a massive economic contraction coupled with a more than sevenfold rise in military spending in 2022. Despite sanctions and a 9.2 per cent growth in military spending, Russia's military burden increased only moderately over the decade, by 0.2 percentage points.

Following Ukraine, the second largest military burden among the top 15 was Saudi Arabia's, at 7.4 per cent of GDP. In total, 8 of the 15 had military burdens above or equal to the world military burden (2.2 per cent). The lowest military burden among top 15 countries was Japan's, at 1.1 per cent of GDP.

---

[18] The United Arab Emirates (UAE) would probably rank as one of the 15 largest spenders, most likely within the ranks 11–15, but a lack of data since 2014 means that no reasonable estimate of its military spending can be made and thus it has been omitted from the top 15 ranking.

Table 5.1. Military expenditure by region, 2013–22

Figures for 2013–22 are in US$ b. at constant (2021) prices and exchange rates. Figures for 2022 in the right-most column, marked *, are in current US$ b. Figures do not always add up to totals because of the conventions of rounding.

	2013	2014	2015	2016	2017	2018	2019	2020	2021	2022	2022*
World total	1 839	1 834	1 864	1 872	1 893	1 950	2 028	2 092	2 104	2 182	2 240
Geographical region											
Africa	40.5	42.4	(40.5)	38.6	37.6	36.3	37.2	39.0	40.0	37.9	39.4
North Africa	16.8	17.9	(18.2)	(18.2)	(17.6)	(17.2)	(18.3)	(19.5)	(19.2)	(18.6)	(19.1)
Sub-Saharan Africa	23.6	24.5	22.3	20.4	20.0	19.1	19.0	19.5	20.8	19.3	20.3
Americas	861	813	798	795	794	817	858	898	888	891	961
Central America and the Caribbean	7.4	7.7	7.4	8.2	7.7	8.4	9.2	11.3	10.9	10.3	11.2
North America	808	759	745	743	740	761	803	840	832	838	904
South America	45.5	46.0	45.5	43.5	45.9	46.9	46.1	45.9	45.9	43.1	46.1
Asia and Oceania	410	432	459	481	503	523	549	568	580	596	575
Central Asia	1.8	1.8	1.7	1.6	1.6	1.7	2.1	1.8	1.8	1.3	1.4
East Asia	277	293	312	325	339	357	375	390	401	415	397
Oceania	24.3	26.3	28.8	31.5	31.6	31.1	32.5	34.0	35.8	36.0	35.3
South Asia	68.1	71.8	73.5	79.9	85.5	89.5	95.0	95.3	95.6	99.4	98.3
South East Asia	39.4	39.1	42.9	43.5	45.0	43.5	44.2	46.6	46.5	44.4	43.1
Europe	345	348	357	369	362	368	387	408	421	477	480
Central and Western Europe	275	273	276	284	292	299	315	333	344	356	345
Eastern Europe	70.0	75.4	81.6	84.9	70.3	69.0	72.8	75.2	76.3	120	135
Middle East	183	198	(209)	(188)	(197)	(206)	(197)	(179)	(175)	(180)	(184)

World military spending per capita (current US$)

246	241	239	237	244	248	258	264	267	282

Military burden (i.e. military spending as a % of gross domestic product, both measured in current US$)[a]

World	**2.3**	**2.2**	**2.4**	**2.3**	**2.3**	**2.2**	**2.3**	**2.4**	**2.2**	**2.2**
Africa	1.9	2.1	1.8	1.8	1.7	1.6	1.6	1.7	1.7	1.7
Americas	1.5	1.4	1.4	1.3	1.4	1.3	1.3	1.4	1.3	1.2
Asia and Oceania	1.7	1.8	1.8	1.7	1.7	1.6	1.6	1.7	1.7	1.5
Europe	1.5	1.5	1.5	1.5	1.5	1.6	1.6	1.8	1.7	2.5
Middle East	4.5	4.6	5.3	5.1	4.9	4.6	4.4	4.5	4.3	3.9

( ) = total based on country data accounting for less than 90% of the regional total.

Notes: The totals for the world and regions are estimates, based on data from the SIPRI Military Expenditure Database. When military expenditure data for a country is missing for a few years, estimates are made, most often on the assumption that the rate of change in that country's military expenditure is the same as that for the region to which it belongs. When no estimates can be made, countries are excluded from the totals. The countries excluded from all totals here are Cuba, Djibouti, Eritrea, North Korea, Somalia, Syria, Turkmenistan, Uzbekistan and Yemen. Totals for regions cover the same groups of countries for all years. The SIPRI military expenditure figures are presented on a calendar-year basis, calculated on the assumption of an even rate of expenditure throughout the financial year. Further detail on sources and methods can be found on the SIPRI website.

[a] World military burden is total world military expenditure as a share of world gross domestic product (GDP). The military burden of each region is the average national military burden for countries in the region for which data is available.

Sources: SIPRI Military Expenditure Database, Apr. 2023; International Monetary Fund, World Economic Outlook Database, Oct. 2022; International Monetary Fund, International Financial Statistics Database, Sep. 2022; and United Nations Department of Economic and Social Affairs, Population Division, 'World population prospects 2022', 2022.

II. Regional developments in military expenditure, 2022

NAN TIAN, XIAO LIANG, LUCIE BÉRAUD-SUDREAU,
DIEGO LOPES DA SILVA, LORENZO SCARAZZATO AND
ANA CAROLINA DE OLIVEIRA ASSIS

Global military expenditure—which rose to an estimated US$2240 billion in 2022—is distributed unevenly around the world. States in the Americas accounted for the largest share of the total, 43 per cent. It was followed by Asia and Oceania with a 26 per cent share, Europe with 21 per cent, and the Middle East with an estimated 8.2 per cent share. Africa accounted for the smallest share, 1.8 per cent of world military spending.[1]

This section reviews the main trends in military expenditure in 2022 and over the decade 2013–22 from a regional perspective. It describes how specific developments have affected national decision-making on military spending, as well as subregional and regional trends. For analysis of global trends see section I.

Africa

Military expenditure in Africa was $39.4 billion in 2022. Spending in the region fell for the first time since 2018, down 5.3 per cent in real terms compared to 2021 and 6.4 per cent lower than in 2013. The fall in 2022 was the largest relative drop in the region since 2003. The 4 countries in North Africa (Algeria, Libya, Morocco and Tunisia) accounted for 48 per cent of Africa's military spending, while the 44 countries in sub-Saharan Africa accounted for the remaining 52 per cent.

North Africa

At $19.1 billion in 2022, military expenditure by North African countries was 3.2 per cent lower than in 2021 but still 11 per cent higher than in 2013 (see figure 5.4). Algeria and Morocco make up most of the military spending in the subregion: together, they accounted for 74 per cent of the total in 2022.

Amid historical rivalries and the ongoing territorial dispute over the Western Sahara, Algeria's military spending fell by 3.7 per cent in 2022, while spending in Morocco fell slightly, by 0.2 per cent.[2] Despite the minor decrease,

---

[1] All figures for spending in 2022 are quoted in current 2022 US dollars. Except where otherwise stated, figures for increases or decreases in military spending are expressed in constant 2021 US dollars, often described as changes in 'real terms' or adjusted for inflation. For sources and methods of the SIPRI Military Expenditure Database, see SIPRI Military Expenditure Database, 'Sources and methods'.

[2] Rachidi, I., 'Morocco and Algeria: A long rivalry', Sada, Carnegie Endowment for International Peace, 3 May 2022; and 'Timeline: Algeria and Morocco's diplomatic disputes', Al Jazeera, 15 Jan. 2023.

Algeria remained the largest spender in the subregion, at $9.1 billion. This is 1.8 times larger than Morocco's military spending, which in 2022 stood at $5.0 billion.

Sub-Saharan Africa

Military expenditure in sub-Saharan Africa was $20.3 billion in 2022, down 7.3 per cent from 2021 and 18 per cent lower than in 2013.[3] The decrease in 2022 was the second largest of all subregions (behind only Central Asia) and occurred after a 6.7 per cent increase in 2021.

The subregion's largest military spender, Nigeria, has had a volatile expenditure pattern in recent years. In 2021 a supplementary budget pushed military spending up by 56 per cent to strengthen the country's military capabilities against a range of security challenges, ranging from banditry and farmer–herder conflict to armed conflicts against non-state armed groups such as Boko Haram and Islamic State–West Africa Province.[4] In 2022, however, Nigeria's military spending fell by 38 per cent to $3.1 billion, mainly because the 2022 supplemental budget made no allocation to the military. In 2022 Nigeria was devastated by the worst seasonal floods in a decade, displacing over 1 million people and destroying farmland.[5] Thus, whereas 73 per cent of the 2021 supplementary budget was for the military, the 2022 supplemental budget focused on rebuilding infrastructure damaged or destroyed by the floods.[6] Furthermore, a debt crisis also strained public finances, including allocations to the military.[7]

Military spending in South Africa, the second largest in the subregion, continued to decline in 2022. At $3.0 billion, spending was down for the second consecutive year; 8.4 per cent lower than in 2021 and 21 per cent lower compared to 2013. In the parliamentary debate on the military budget for 2022, the defence minister, Thandi Modise, acknowledged that poor economic performance had put severe pressure on finances and, as a result, the downward trend in military spending continued.[8]

---

[3] The total for sub-Saharan Africa excludes the Comoros and Sao Tome and Principe, which are not in the SIPRI Military Expenditure Database and are assumed to have low expenditure, and Djibouti, Eritrea and Somalia, for which data is not available.

[4] Nextier, *Nigeria's Security Situation Analysis Report* (Nextier: Abuja, 2022); and George, L., 'Nigeria's oil output at 32-year low as thieves hobble output', Reuters, 9 Sep. 2022. On armed conflict in Nigeria see chapter 2, section I, in this volume.

[5] Onukwue, A., 'Nigeria's worst floods in a decade have displaced over a million people', World Economic Forum, 20 Oct. 2022.

[6] Iroanusi, Q., 'Three days to year-end, Senate passes supplementary budget for 2022', *Premium Times* (Abuja), 28 Dec. 2022; and Nigerian Budget Office of the Federation, 'Supplementary appropriation bill 2021', p. 4.

[7] Clowes, W., 'Debt repayments consume 80% of Nigeria's revenue collection', Bloomberg, 3 Jan. 2023.

[8] Modise, T., 'Minister Thandi Modise: Defence Dept budget vote 2022/23', South African government, 24 May 2022.

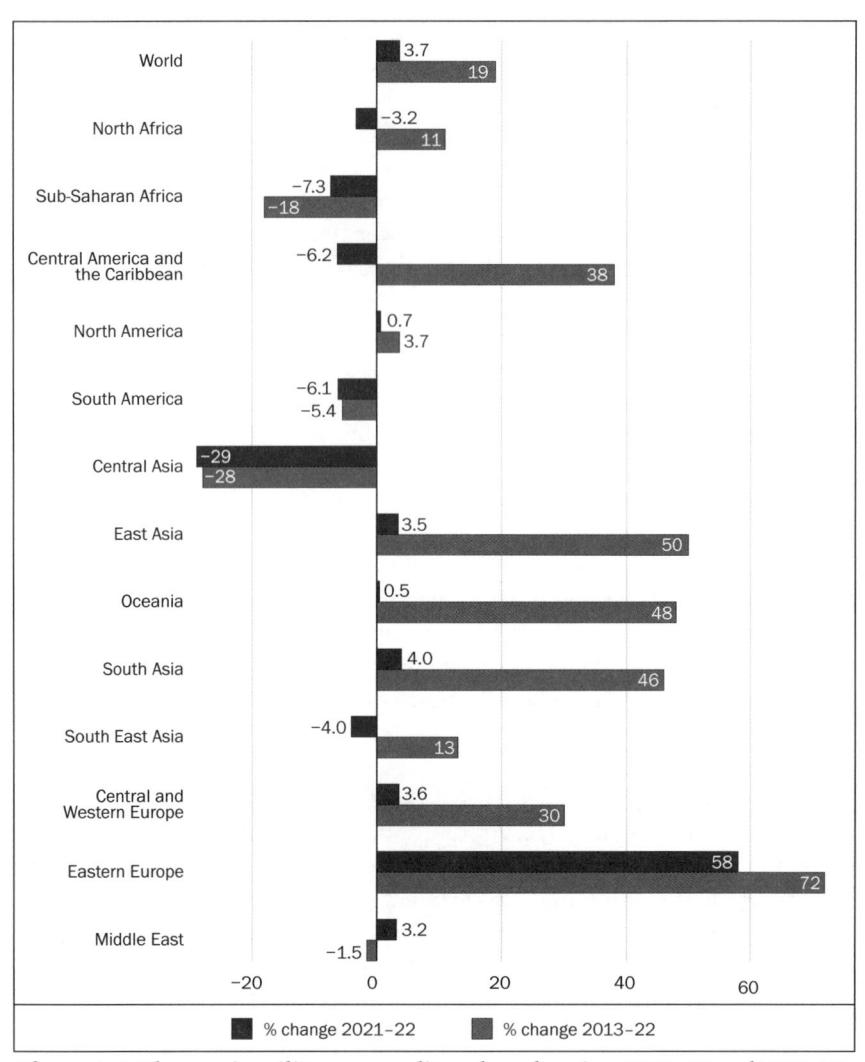

Figure 5.4. Changes in military expenditure by subregion, 2013–22 and 2021–22

Region	% change 2021–22	% change 2013–22
World	3.7	19
North Africa	−3.2	11
Sub-Saharan Africa	−7.3	−18
Central America and the Caribbean	−6.2	38
North America	0.7	3.7
South America	−6.1	−5.4
Central Asia	−29	−28
East Asia	3.5	50
Oceania	0.5	48
South Asia	4.0	46
South East Asia	−4.0	13
Central and Western Europe	3.6	30
Eastern Europe	58	72
Middle East	3.2	−1.5

South Africa's nominal military spending is projected to remain unchanged until 2025 under the country's Medium Term Expenditure Framework (MTEF).[9] With average inflation at around 5.5 per cent, further decreases in military expenditure are expected in the coming years. In response to the MTEF's budgetary constraints, the South African National Defence Force is already planning to reduce its personnel levels by 3000 between 2023 and 2025.[10]

---

[9] South African National Treasury, *Medium Term Budget Policy Statement 2022* (National Treasury: Pretoria, 26 Oct. 2022).

[10] Martin, G., 'SANDF to shed 3000 members over the next three years', DefenceWeb, 4 Aug. 2022.

Despite the general fall in sub-Saharan Africa's military spending, there were substantial increases in Ethiopia and Togo. Ethiopia's military spending rose at the fastest rate of any African country, up 88 per cent to $1.0 billion in 2022. The increase coincided with a government offensive against the Tigray People's Liberation Front (TPLF).[11] Togo's military spending increased by 80 per cent to $337 million in 2022, the second-highest rate of growth in Africa. The increase coincided with the intensification of attacks by violent Islamist militants that began in November 2021.[12] In addition to the government implementing a state of emergency in northern Togo in June 2022, the military conducted military exercises and operations to combat the militants in the region.[13]

The Americas

Military spending by countries in the Americas totalled $961 billion in 2022, 0.3 per cent higher than in 2021 and up by 3.5 per cent from 2013. Spending fell in South America and in Central America and the Caribbean in 2022, but rose in North America, mainly due to the growth in the United States. North American countries (i.e. the USA and Canada) accounted for 94 per cent of total regional spending in 2022, with 4.8 per cent in South America, and 1.2 per cent in Central America and the Caribbean.

North America

North American military spending reached $904 billion in 2022. This was an increase of 0.7 per cent compared to 2021 and 3.7 per cent higher than in 2013. At $26.9 billion, Canada's military spending was 3.0 per cent higher than in 2021 despite historic levels of inflation.[14] Following Russia's invasion of Ukraine in February 2022, Canada announced additional military spending of 8 billion Canadian dollars (US$6.1 billion) over the five financial years 2022/23–2027/28, as well as a new defence policy review.[15]

---

[11] 'Eritreans hunted down as military call-up intensifies over Ethiopia's Tigray war', BBC News, 12 Oct. 2022; Amnesty International, 'Ethiopia: Fears of fresh atrocities loom in Tigray as conflict intensifies', 24 Oct. 2022; and 'Ethiopia govt. says army controls 70 percent of Tigray', Defense Post, 11 Nov. 2022. On the armed conflict and peace process in Tigray see also chapter 2, section II, in this volume.

[12] 'Togo : Attaque terroriste signalée près de la frontière avec le Burkina' [Togo: Terrorist attack reported near the border with Burkina], Togo First, 10 Nov. 2021; and Koffi, M. F., 'Togo extends state of emergency due to militant attacks', Voice of America, 7 Sep. 2022.

[13] Koffi (note 12); 'Facing threat, Togo forces simulate "jihadist" attack', Defense Post, 21 Oct. 2022.

[14] Gordon, J., 'Canada inflation up near 40-year high; calls mount for 75-bps rate hike', Reuters, 22 June 2022.

[15] Canadian Department of National Defence, 'Defence spending: Budget 2022', Appearance before the House of Commons, Standing Committee on National Defence, 27 Apr. 2022; and Canadian Department of Finance, 'Canada's leadership in the world', 7 Apr. 2022.

Table 5.4. Components of US military expenditure, fiscal years 2018–22

Figures are current US$ b. unless otherwise stated. Figures may not add up to the given totals because of the conventions of rounding.

Component	2018	2019	2020	2021	2022
Department of Defense (DOD)	601	654	690	718	742
Military personnel	146	156	161	173	167
Operations and maintenance	257	272	279	286	294
Procurement	113	125	139	141	145
RDT&E	77	89	100	106	119
Other (construction, housing etc.)	8.6	12	11	12	17
Department of Energy, atomic energy military activities	21	23	24	26	29
Other military-related activities	10	9.3	10	11	11
National Intelligence Program, military-related activities	[45]	[45]	[47]	[46]	[49]
Department of State, international security assistance[a]	6.8	6.8	6.7	6.7	6.7
Transfers to fund southern border wall construction	..	−3.6	..	..	..
Supplemental appropriations to the DOD	..	..	..	..	34.4
Supplemental appropriations to the State Department related to Ukraine	..	..	..	..	4.7
Total	**682**	**734**	**778**	**806**	**877**
Military expenditure as share of GDP (%)	*3.3*	*3.4*	*3.7*	*3.5*	*3.5*

.. = not applicable; [ ] = estimated figure; GDP = gross domestic product; RDT&E = research, development, testing and evaluation.

[a] This international security assistance consists of International Military Education and Training (IMET), Foreign Military Finance (FMF), and peacekeeping.

Sources: SIPRI Military Expenditure Database, Apr. 2023; US Department of Defense (DOD), Office of the Under Secretary of Defense (Comptroller), various documents, various years; Federation of American Scientists (FAS), Intelligence Resource Program, 'Intelligence budget data'; US Department of State, *Congressional Budget Justification: Department of State, Foreign Operations and Related Programs*, various years; and McGarry, B. W., 'Department of Defense supplemental funding for Ukraine: A summary', Congressional Research Service (CRS) Insight, 13 Feb. 2023.

The United States. US military spending in 2022 was $877 billion. Despite nominal growth of 8.8 per cent, the real increase in 2022 was a marginal 0.7 per cent. The United States remained by far the largest military spender in the world, allocating three times more than the second largest spender, China. US military expenditure, according to SIPRI methodology, includes spending by the Department of Defense (DOD), the Department of Energy, the Department of State, funding for the National Intelligence Program and supplemental appropriations related to the war in Ukraine among other things (see table 5.4).

The small size of the increase in US military spending in 2022 was primarily due to the highest levels of inflation since 1981.[16] The Covid-related supply chain disruptions, labour shortages and pent-up consumer demand pushed inflation upwards. Russia's war in Ukraine and the resulting increase in food and energy prices further exacerbated it.[17] Between 2021 and 2022, nominal US military expenditure rose by 8.8 per cent, but an inflation rate of 8.1 per cent in the same period meant that expenditure rose by only 0.7 per cent in real terms. The Federal Reserve—the US central bank—expects that inflation will average around 3.5 per cent in 2023.[18] This means that the 4.1 per cent increase in the DOD's budget for fiscal year 2023 proposed by US President Joe Biden may result once more in a marginal real-terms increase in US military spending in 2023.[19]

A major development in 2022 was the military expenditure that the US Congress appropriated in response to Russia's invasion of Ukraine.[20] Although the USA has been a provider of military assistance to Ukraine since at least 2002, the scope and size of the aid drastically increased in 2022. Before Russia's full-scale invasion of Ukraine, US military aid to Ukraine was primarily in the form of Foreign Military Finance (FMF) and International Military Education and Training (IMET) and through the Ukraine Security Assistance Initiative (USAI).[21] Between 2014 and 2021, military aid from these three assistance programmes averaged about $280 million per year, growing from $9.2 million in 2014 to $538 million by 2021 (in constant US dollars; see table 5.5). In 2022, SIPRI estimates that US military aid to Ukraine shot up to $19.9 billion (in current dollars), the largest ever recorded amount of military assistance donated by any country to any recipient in the world in a single year. This was the majority (64 per cent) of the $31.3 billion of military-related supplemental spending related to the war in Ukraine in 2022. In addition to military aid to Ukraine, this expenditure involved supplemental funding to the DOD and the Department of State, expenditure to support the operations

---

[16] Desilver, D., 'In the US and around the world, inflation is high and getting higher', Pew Research Center, 15 June 2022.

[17] Amaglobeli, D. et al., 'Response to high food, energy prices should focus on most vulnerable', IMF Blog, International Monetary Fund (IMF), 7 June 2022; and Smialek, J., 'New inflation developments are rattling markets and economists. Here's why', *New York Times*, 15 Sep. 2022.

[18] Banerji, G., 'Fed officials raise estimates for inflation, unemployment in 2023', *Wall Street Journal*, 14 Dec. 2022.

[19] US Department of Defense, 'The Department of Defense releases the president's fiscal year 2023 defense budget', 28 Mar. 2022.

[20] McGarry, B. W., 'Department of Defense supplemental funding for Ukraine: A summary', Congressional Research Service (CRS) Insight, 13 Feb. 2023.

[21] US Department of State, *Congressional Budget Justification: Department of State, Foreign Operations and Related Programs—Fiscal Year 2023* (Department of State: Washington, DC, 2022); and Arabia, C. L., Bowen, A. S. and Welt, C., 'US security assistance to Ukraine', Congressional Research Service (CRS) Insight, 27 Feb. 2023.

Table 5.5. US military aid to Ukraine, 2014–21

Figures are constant (2021) US$ m.

Programme	2014	2015	2016	2017	2018	2019	2020	2021	2022	Total
FMF	7	54.0	90.0	109	102	74.0	120	115	1 203	1 874
IMET	2.2	2.2	3.2	2.4	2.9	3.1	3.0	3.0	2.8	24.8
PDA	–	–	–	–	–	–	–	–	11 661	11 661
USAI	–	–	257	167	212	229	268	420	5 553	7 106
Other military assistance	0.02	0.02	1.7	0.02	–	–	–	–	–	1.8
Total	9.2	56.2	352	278	317	306	391	538	18 420	20 668

FMF = Foreign Military Finance; IMET = International Military Education and Training; PDA = Presidential Drawdown Authority; USAI = Ukraine Security Assistance Initiative.

Sources: Office of the Under Secretary of Defense (Comptroller), various documents, various years; US Department of State, *Congressional Budget Justification: Department of State, Foreign Operations and Related Programs*, various years; and McGarry, B. W., 'Department of Defense supplemental funding for Ukraine: A summary', Congressional Research Service (CRS) Insight, 13 Feb. 2023.

of the USA and its allies in Europe, and expansion of US arms-industrial production capacity to speed up weapon replenishment (see section III).[22]

The three main assistance programmes and authorities through which military aid was disbursed to Ukraine in 2022 were the Presidential Drawdown Authority (PDA), the USAI and FMF. A fourth category, IMET, was much smaller: only $3 million in 2022.[23]

The 1961 Foreign Assistance Act gives the US president the authority to direct, via a PDA, the secretary of state to transfer 'defense articles and defense services' from existing DOD stocks to a foreign country (i.e. Ukraine) without congressional authorization in response to an unforeseen emergency.[24] Of the $19.9 billion in military aid given to Ukraine, $12.6 billion (63 per cent) was expenditure to replenish US stocks of equipment sent to Ukraine under the various PDAs.[25] While the use of PDAs to provide military assistance is

[22] US House of Representatives, Committee on Appropriations, 'Ukraine Supplemental Appropriations Act, 2022', [10 Mar. 2022]; and US House of Representatives, Committee on Appropriations, 'Additional Ukraine Supplemental Appropriations Act, 2022', [10 May 2022].

[23] Arabia et al. (note 21); and Masters, J. and Merrow, W., 'How much aid has the US sent Ukraine? Here are six charts', Council on Foreign Relations, 22 Feb. 2023.

[24] Yousif, E., 'Ukraine aid strains US defense stockpiles', Stimson, 25 July 2022; US Department of State, Bureau of Political-Military Affairs, 'Use of presidential drawdown authority for military assistance for Ukraine', Fact sheet, 20 Mar. 2023; and Foreign Assistance Act, US Public Law no. 87–195, signed into law 4 Sep. 1961, as amended.

[25] US House of Representatives, 'Ukraine Supplemental Appropriations Act, 2022' and 'Additional Ukraine Supplemental Appropriations Act, 2022' (note 22).

not new, the number and monetary value in 2022 were unprecedented.[26] President Biden directed 27 PDAs to Ukraine in 2022, with values ranging from $100 million to $1 billion.[27]

Military aid under the USAI totalled $6.0 billion in 2022 (30 per cent of US military aid to Ukraine).[28] Unlike the PDAs, under the USAI the US government procures military equipment from the arms industry.[29] Military aid sent to Ukraine via the USAI is generally slower than under the PDA and is designed to strengthen the capabilities of the Ukrainian armed forces over the long term.[30]

Supplemental funding for FMF, which falls under the budget of the State Department, amounted to $4.7 billion in 2022, of which $1.3 billion (6.5 per cent of US military aid to Ukraine) went to Ukraine. The remaining $3.4 billion has been provided to other European allies and partners.[31] FMF, which includes financial assistance and loans, may have been used by European allies and partners that have provided security assistance to Ukraine to replenish their military stocks.[32]

Despite the record levels of military aid that the USA sent to Ukraine in 2022, it amounted to only 2.3 per cent of total US military spending. In comparison, the USA's spending on modernizing and improving its own military capabilities (i.e. procurement and research and development, R&D) totalled $264 billion in 2022, or 30 per cent of total US military spending. The other main spending categories were personnel (19 per cent) and operation and maintenance (34 per cent).

Central America and the Caribbean

Military spending in Central America and the Caribbean fell by 6.2 per cent in 2022 to $11.2 billion. Over the decade, however, military spending rose 38 per cent. The use of military forces to curb armed criminal activity remains the main driver of military spending in the region.[33]

---

[26] White House, 'Drawdown under Section 506(a)(1) of the Foreign Assistance Act of 1961 for France to support its counterterrorism efforts in Mali, Niger, and Chad', Presidential memorandum, 11 Aug. 2014; and Lopez, C. T., 'US provided more than $1 billion in security assistance to Ukraine in past year', US Department of Defense, 4 Mar. 2022.

[27] Arabia et al. (note 21).

[28] US House of Representatives, 'Additional Ukraine Supplemental Appropriations Act, 2022' (note 22).

[29] US Department of Defense, 'Biden administration announces additional security assistance for Ukraine', 3 Feb. 2023.

[30] US Department of Defense (note 29); and White House (note 26).

[31] US Department of State, *Congressional Budget Justification: Department of State, Foreign Operations and Related Programs—Fiscal Year 2024* (Department of State: Washington, DC, 2023), p. 218.

[32] US Department of State, Bureau of Political-Military Affairs, 'US security cooperation with Ukraine', Fact sheet, 24 Feb. 2023.

[33] On armed conflict between state forces and armed gangs in Central America see Caparini, M., 'Armed conflict in North America and the Caribbean', *SIPRI Yearbook 2022*, pp. 82–87.

Military spending in Mexico, the subregion's largest military spender, fell by 9.7 per cent in 2022 to $8.5 billion. Military spending as a share of government expenditure fell from 2.5 per cent in 2021 to 2.2 per cent 2022, with budget allocations favouring health expenditure over the military.[34] Nearly one-fifth of Mexico's military expenditure is spent on the National Guard—a militarized police force created in 2019 to combat organized crime. Since its establishment, its budget has increased by 33 per cent. In 2022 the Mexican Congress approved a set of reforms whereby the operational, administrative and budgetary control of the National Guard was transferred to the defence ministry, the Secretariat of National Defence. The reallocation was criticized by civil society organizations as the use of military forces in public security missions in Mexico has been associated with major violations of human rights.[35] Due to its militarized nature, SIPRI has included spending on the National Guard in Mexico's military expenditure since its creation.

In 2022 the government of El Salvador launched a series of major military operations across several cities in response to rising levels of gang violence.[36] One operation, a siege of the town of Soyapando, engaged over 10 000 troops.[37] This offensive pushed military spending to the highest level since the end of the 1979–92 civil war: a 12 per cent growth to $422 million.

Military expenditure by the Dominican Republic rose by 16 per cent in 2022 to $761 million. The growth can be attributed to a security crisis in neighbouring Haiti: Haitian President Jovenel Moïse was assassinated in unclear circumstances in July 2021, followed a few weeks later by a major earthquake.[38] Since then, instability has ensued, with gang violence and political disarray sending migrants towards the border with the Dominican Republic. The Dominican government responded with more investment in military operations and procurement.[39]

---

[34] Pérez, M., Ramos, R. and Monroy, J., 'Más recursos en salud; menos a Sedena y Comar' [More resources for health; less for the Secretariat of National Defence and the Mexican Commission for Refugee Assistance], *El Economista*, 9 Sep. 2021.
[35] United Nations, Office of the High Commissioner for Human Rights, 'México: El traspaso de la Guardia Nacional a la Secretaría de la Defensa Nacional es un retroceso para la seguridad pública basada en los derechos humanos' [Mexico: The transfer of the National Guard to the Ministry of National Defence is a step backwards for human rights-based public security], Press release, 9 Sep. 2022.
[36] 'Nayib Bukele desplegará policías y militares para cercar las ciudades de El Salvador contra los pandilleros' [Nayib Bukele to deploy police and military to seal off El Salvador's cities from gang members], *El País*, 24 Nov. 2022.
[37] Murphy, M., 'El Salvador: El impresionante despliegue de 10.000 soldados por parte de Nayib Bukele contra las maras en un municipio aledaño a la capital' [El Salvador: Nayib Bukele's massive deployment of 10 000 troops against gangs in a municipality near the capital], BBC News, 4 Dec. 2022.
[38] 'Haiti president's assassination: What we know so far', BBC News, 1 Feb. 2023.
[39] Herrera, J., 'Gobierno de Abinader ha invertido más que sus antecesores en equipos militares para proteger frontera y espacio aéreo' [Abinader's government has invested more than his predecessors in military equipment to protect the border and airspace], Acento, 16 Feb. 2023.

South America

South America's military spending fell by 6.1 per cent in 2022 to $46.1 billion. This was 5.4 per cent lower than in 2013. The 2022 drop was largely due to a decline in Brazilian military expenditure.

A fall of 7.9 per cent in 2022 took military spending in Brazil to $20.2 billion, 14 per cent lower than in 2013. The military burden fell to 1.1 per cent in 2022 from 1.2 per cent in 2021. During his 2019–22 presidency, Jair Bolsonaro built a close relationship with the armed forces, although this did not translate into more funding for the military.[40] Rather, military spending dropped in every year of the Bolsonaro administration, with an overall 16 per cent cut between 2019 to 2022. Simultaneously, however, there was a shift in the composition of expenditure from investment in military equipment to personnel costs. That shift was implemented by a 2019 law that restructured and improved the salary conditions and benefits for military personnel.[41] After its enactment, spending on personnel rose from 72 per cent of total military expenditure in 2019 to 77 per cent in 2022.

Plans to modernize Argentina's armed forces have faced setbacks. In 2020 Argentina created the National Defence Fund (Fondo Nacional de la Defensa, Fondef) to finance arms acquisitions and reverse previous failures in military procurement practices.[42] However, the country's poor economic performance has been a major obstacle to the implementation of Fondef. In 2022 military expenditure fell by 32 per cent to $2.6 billion. The decline was mainly due to soaring inflation, at 72 per cent in 2022.

Asia and Oceania

The combined military expenditure in Asia and Oceania was $575 billion in 2022, an increase of 2.7 per cent from 2021 and of 45 per cent from 2013. This continued an uninterrupted upward trend dating back to at least 1989, the earliest year for which SIPRI has an estimate for regional military spending.[43] The regional increase in 2022 was due primarily to China, India and Japan, which collectively accounted for 73 per cent of total regional spending in 2022. Five of the top 15 global spenders in 2022 are in Asia and Oceania: China

---

[40] Hunter, W. and Vega, D., 'Populism and the military: Symbiosis and tension in Bolsonaro's Brazil', *Democratization*, vol. 29, no. 2 (2022).

[41] Brazilian Law no. 13 954 of 16 Dec. 2019, *Diário Oficial da União*, 17 Dec. 2019 (in Portuguese).

[42] 'Fondo Nacional de la Defensa' [National Defence Fund], Law no. 27 565, enacted 17 Sep. 2020, *Boletín Oficial de la República Argentina*, 1 Oct. 2020. See also Tian, N. et al., 'Regional developments in military expenditure, 2020', *SIPRI Yearbook 2021*, pp. 260–61.

[43] No data is available for North Korea, Turkmenistan or Uzbekistan for 2013–22 and they are not included in the totals for Asia and Oceania. Data for Viet Nam is not available for the years 2019–22 and for Afghanistan for 2022. Incomplete data for Tajikistan, which indicates an increase, is included in the total.

(ranked 2nd), India (ranked 4th), the Republic of Korea (South Korea, ranked 9th), Japan (ranked 10th) and Australia (ranked 13th).

Of the 26 states in Asia and Oceania for which data was available, 13 increased their military spending in 2022. Despite this, strong economic recovery in the region meant that the military burden fell in all but four countries. At the same time, several countries in the region recorded significant decreases in military spending in 2022: the largest by Kazakhstan (–33 per cent), followed by Sri Lanka (–31 per cent) and the Philippines (–25 per cent).

Central Asia

Military expenditure by the three countries in Central Asia for which data is available fell by 29 per cent in 2022 to $1.4 billion. This was the steepest annual subregional decline. Over the decade, military spending fell by 28 per cent. The decrease, however, hardly affected estimates for Asia and Oceania because Kazakhstan, Kyrgyzstan and Tajikistan accounted for only 0.2 per cent of regional spending.

The subregional decline was principally the result of a 33 per cent spending cut by Kazakhstan, by far the largest spender in the subregion, to $1.1 billion. This marked its third consecutive year of decreasing military spending, in line with the 2020–22 multi-year budget, which included efforts to reduce personnel costs.[44] At 0.5 per cent of GDP, Kazakhstan had the second lowest military burden in Asia and Oceania (after only Papua New Guinea at 0.3 per cent).

East Asia

Military expenditure in East Asia increased by 3.5 per cent in 2022, reaching a total of $397 billion. Over the decade 2013–22 military spending in the subregion grew by 50 per cent, representing the highest increase in Asia and Oceania and globally second only to Eastern Europe. The increase in 2022 also marked the 28th consecutive year of rising spending in East Asia. The three major spenders in the subregion were China, which accounted for 74 per cent of the total, followed by South Korea and Japan, representing 12 per cent each. Spending by Taiwan made up 3 per cent of the subregional total.

Military spending by China, the world's second largest spender, reached an estimated $292 billion in 2022, an increase of 4.2 per cent since 2021 and of 63 per cent since 2013. China's military spending has increased for 28 consecutive years, the longest streak by any country in the SIPRI Military Expenditure Database. However, the growth rate in 2022 was the second

---

[44] Ashimov, A., 'Kazakhstan to modernise armed forces' weaponry in defence-spending plan', Caravanserai, 14 Feb. 2020; and Kazinform, 'Defense spending to fall in Kazakhstan in 2020', Strategy 2050, 5 Feb. 2020.

lowest annual growth since 1995, only higher than the increase of 2.6 per cent in the previous year. China's military burden remained unchanged from 2021 at 1.6 per cent of GDP.

The consistent increase in China's military spending reflects the ongoing modernization of its armed forces, the People's Liberation Army (PLA). The current spending priorities follow the guiding principles for the PLA under the 14th five-year plan (for 2021–25), with a focus on boosting the arms-industrial base and promoting emerging military technologies, including military applications of artificial intelligence (AI).[45] These priorities were reaffirmed by the 20th congress of the Communist Party of China, held in October 2022.[46]

SIPRI's military expenditure data for China differs from the official national defence budget: the SIPRI figure for 2022 is 33 per cent, or 489 billion yuan ($73 billion), higher than the figure published in the official state budget. The annually published national defence budget excludes important elements of what SIPRI defines as military expenditure, some of which are listed in other sections of the official state budget. Since 2020, SIPRI's estimate of Chinese military expenditure has included six components.[47] Official information is available for four of the components: national defence, the People's Armed Police, pension payments to demobilized and retired soldiers, and additional military construction spending. Together, these four categories accounted for 91 per cent of China's total spending in 2022. Estimates are made for the two remaining components: the China Coast Guard and additional funding for military research, development, testing and evaluation. The combined share of these two components was 8.7 per cent of the total in 2022.

Japan allocated $46.0 billion to its military in 2022, up by 5.9 per cent from 2021 and by 18 per cent from 2013. Japan's military policy is undergoing a significant shift, abandoning its post-World War II era cap on military spending of 1.0 per cent of GDP. At 1.1 per cent of GDP, the Japanese military burden in 2022 exceeded the cap for the third consecutive year and was the highest since 1960. The latest National Security Strategy, published in December 2022, aims to increase the country's security spending to 2.0 per cent of GDP by 2027.[48] As well as the military budget, the target covers the budgets for the Japan Coast Guard, public security infrastructure and other civil defence costs.

---

[45] Xinhua, [(Two Sessions authorized for release) Draft planning outline: Accelerate the modernization of national defence and the military to achieve unity of a prosperous country and a strong military], 3 May 2021 (in Chinese).

[46] Xi, J., 'Hold high the great banner of socialism with Chinese characteristics and strive in unity to build a modern socialist country in all respects', Report to the 20th National Congress of the Communist Party of China, 16 Oct. 2022.

[47] Tian, N. and Su, F., *A New Estimate of China's Military Expenditure* (SIPRI: Stockholm, Jan. 2021).

[48] Japanese Ministry of Defense (MOD), 'National security strategy of Japan', Dec. 2022.

Also in December 2022, the Japanese government presented its 2023 budget which includes a 26 per cent nominal increase in the budget for the armed forces, the Japanese Self-Defense Forces (JSDF).[49] To fund these announced increases, the Japanese government proposed a combination of spending cuts in other areas, tax increases and the use of non-tax revenues such as government construction bonds.[50] The Japanese government cites a deteriorating security environment as the main rationale for increasing the country's military spending. It identifies three primary security threats for Japan: China's growing assertiveness, the unpredictable military activities of the Democratic People's Republic of Korea (DPRK, or North Korea) and Russian aggression, exemplified by the invasion of Ukraine.[51]

Military expenditure in South Korea fell by 2.5 per cent to $46.4 billion in 2022, ending a 22-year streak of real-terms increases. The decline was largely a result of inflation, with the military budget having a nominal increase of 2.9 per cent. South Korea's military expenditure is mainly driven by the perceived nuclear and conventional missile threat from North Korea.[52] South Korean President Yoon Suk-yeol, who took office in May 2022, has adopted a harsher stance towards North Korea compared to the policy of rapprochement and dialogue under the previous administration.[53] In 2022 North Korea conducted a record-breaking total of over 90 missile tests.[54] In response, President Yoon proposed higher military spending in 2023 to improve capabilities for air defence and pre-emptive and retaliatory strikes by the armed forces.[55]

Oceania

In 2022 total military expenditure in Oceania totalled $35.3 billion, 0.5 per cent more than in 2021. Spending rose by 48 per cent over the decade 2013–22.

The increases were mainly due to growth in military spending by Australia, which accounted for 92 per cent of the subregion's total in 2022. Its spending of $32.3 billion was 0.3 per cent higher than in 2021 and 47 per cent higher than in 2013. Australia continues to perceive growing geopolitical threats in its neighbourhood and globally, from China's military modernization to Russia's

---

[49] Japanese Ministry of Defense, [Defence programs and budget of Japan (draft): 2023 budget summary], Dec. 2022 (in Japanese).

[50] Watanabe, K., [Key points of FY2023 defence-related budget], Japanese Ministry of Finance, Dec. 2022 (in Japanese).

[51] Liang, X. and Tian, N., 'The proposed hike in Japan's military expenditure', SIPRI Commentary, Jan. 2023.

[52] On North Korean nuclear forces see chapter 7, section VIII, in this volume.

[53] Yeung, J., Hancocks, P. and Seo, Y., 'South Korea's new leader says age of appeasing North Korea is over', CNN, 28 May 2022.

[54] Choe, S., 'Tracking North Korea's missile launches', *New York Times*, 23 Dec. 2022.

[55] Kim, J., 'Yoon Suk-yeol seeks record defense budget to counter North Korean threats', NK News, 30 Aug. 2022.

invasion of Ukraine.[56] Following a change of government after elections in May 2022, the new Labor government reaffirmed the goal of spending at least 2.0 per cent of GDP on the military.[57] Included in this figure is the 475 million Australian dollars (US$329 million) in military aid that Australia provided to Ukraine during 2022, making it the largest donor of military assistance to Ukraine in Asia and Oceania.[58]

South Asia

In 2022 military expenditure in South Asia rose to $98.3 billion, representing a 4.0 per cent increase from 2021 and a 46 per cent increase from 2013. Following the Taliban takeover in August 2021, information on military expenditure for Afghanistan was not available for 2022.

Changes in South Asia's expenditure were primarily the result of increases by India, its biggest spender, which accounted for 83 per cent of the sub-regional total in 2022. Despite increasing its military spending by 6.0 per cent in 2022 to $81.4 billion, India dropped from being third to fourth largest spender in the world. Its military spending in 2022 was 47 per cent higher than in 2013.

India's military spending growth reaffirms the government's commitment to military modernization amid border tensions with China and Pakistan.[59] This is supported by a continued rise in expenditure on capital outlays (23 per cent of total spending). This budget line funds equipment upgrades for the armed forces, as well as construction of more infrastructure along India's disputed border with China, where border clashes broke out again in December 2022.[60] Personnel expenses (e.g. salaries and pensions) remained the largest expenditure category in the Indian military budget, accounting for half of all spending.

In line with efforts to encourage self-reliance in arms development and production, 68 per cent of the capital outlays budget was earmarked for domestic equipment procurement in 2022, up from 64 per cent in 2021.[61] To support privately owned arms companies, 25 per cent of military R&D costs were allocated to the such companies, and the Indian Ministry of Defence

---

[56] Kassam, N., *Lowy Institute Poll 2022* (Lowy Institute: Sydney, June 2022).

[57] Australian Department of Defence, 'Delivering on our commitment to keep Australians safe', Media release, 25 Oct. 2022.

[58] Australian Department of Defence, 'Additional support for Ukraine', Press release, 27 Oct. 2022.

[59] On India's border tensions see Davis, I. and Yuan, J., 'Armed conflict and peace processes in South Asia', *SIPRI Yearbook 2022*, pp. 120–24.

[60] Indian Ministry of Defence, 'Defence gets Rs 5.94 lakh crore in Budget 2023-24, a jump of 13% over previous year', Press release, 1 Feb. 2023.

[61] Indian Ministry of Defence, 'Self reliance in defence sector', Press release, 19 Dec. 2022.

also established a Technology Development Fund (TDF) to finance indigenous production by small and medium-sized enterprises and start-ups.[62]

At $10.3 billion, Pakistan's military spending in 2022 was 2.0 per cent lower than in 2021 but 46 per cent higher than in 2013. The real-terms decline can be mostly attributed to inflation.[63] Notably, Pakistan spent the highest share of total government expenditure on the military (18 per cent) in Asia and Oceania.

Grappling with a deep economic crisis and high inflation of 48 per cent, Sri Lanka reduced its military spending by 31 per cent in 2022 to $1.1 billion. As a result, its military burden fell from 1.9 per cent in 2021 to 1.4 per cent. The spending reductions are expected to continue in the coming years, as the government has announced cuts to the number of armed personnel of one-third by 2023 and one-half by 2030.[64]

South East Asia

The military spending by the nine countries in South East Asia with available data decreased by 4.0 per cent in 2022 to $43.1 billion, continuing the decline since 2020. Over the decade 2013–22 spending increased by 13 per cent. The subregion is home to the two countries with the highest military burden in Asia and Oceania: Myanmar (3.0 per cent) and Singapore (2.8 per cent). Military spending information has not been publicly available for Laos since 2014 and for Viet Nam since 2019.

Singapore, South East Asia's largest military spender, increased its spending by 2.8 per cent in 2022 to reach $11.7 billion. The increase was mainly attributed to resumption of projects affected by the Covid-19 pandemic.[65] Military spending in Indonesia, the subregion's second largest spender, grew by 1.3 per cent to $9.0 billion after a decrease of 9.0 per cent in 2021. Indonesia had the lowest military burden in the subregion (at 0.7 per cent of GDP), casting doubt on its ability to fund its military modernization programmes, including the procurement of submarines and combat aircraft from South Korea.[66]

Increases in Singapore and Indonesia were offset by substantial reductions by the subregion's third and fourth spenders, Thailand and the Philippines, which cut spending by 11 per cent and 25 per cent, respectively. This was the second consecutive year of decrease in Thailand's spending, prompted by the

---

[62] Indian Ministry of Defence, 'Funding under Technology Development Fund scheme of DRDO enhanced to Rs 50 crore per project from Rs 10 crore', Press release, 19 Dec. 2022.

[63] 'As Pakistani rupee drops to record low, FM blames politics', Al Jazeera, 20 July 2022.

[64] 'Sri Lanka to slash military by a third to cut costs', Al Jazeera, 13 Jan. 2023.

[65] Singaporean Ministry of Finance (MOF), *Revenue and Expenditure Estimates for the Financial Year 2022/2023* (MOF: Singapore, 2022), pp. 63–76.

[66] Indonesian Cabinet Secretariat, 'Gov't issues regulation on 2020–2024 National Defense Policy', 24 Jan. 2021; and Smith, J., '"No going back" for S. Korea, Indonesia defence cooperation after jet funding dispute', Reuters, 17 Feb. 2023.

continued economic impact of the Covid-19 pandemic. The sharp decline in Philippine military spending followed two consecutive years of increases.

Europe

Total military spending in Europe in 2022 amounted to $480 billion, 13 per cent higher than in 2021, and marking a 38 per cent increase from 2013. Six of the top 15 global spenders in 2022 are in Europe: Russia (ranked 3rd), the United Kingdom (ranked 6th), Germany (ranked 7th), France (ranked 8th), Ukraine (ranked 11th) and Italy (ranked 12th). Russia's invasion of Ukraine in February 2022 was undoubtedly the main driver of the high year-on-year increase across the whole region.

Central and Western Europe

Military expenditure in Central and Western Europe increased by 3.6 per cent to $345 billion in 2022, the highest figure since the end of the cold war. Over the decade 2013–22, the countries of Central and Western Europe increased their overall military expenditure by 30 per cent. Countries in Western Europe accounted for 90 per cent of the subregional total throughout the decade.

The United Kingdom's military expenditure reached $68.5 billion in 2022, up by 3.7 per cent from 2021 and by 9.7 per cent since 2013. This was the sixth consecutive year of increase. The rise in British spending in 2022 was primarily due to its military aid to Ukraine—the second largest after the USA—which was estimated to have totalled $2.5 billion in 2022. The country's military burden remained stable at 2.2 per cent of GDP.

The short-lived administration led by Prime Minister Elizabeth Truss made a commitment to raise military spending to 3 per cent of GDP by 2030.[67] However, given the financial constraints facing the country, the commitment was subsequently deferred by her successor, Rishi Sunak, until 2023.[68] The final decision will now follow a reassessment of the 2021 Integrated Review of Security, Defence, Development and Foreign Policy.[69]

With an increase of 2.3 per cent, Germany's military expenditure reached $55.8 billion in 2022—this meant that it overtook France to become the second largest spender in Central and Western Europe, after the UK. SIPRI's

---

[67] Truss, L., British Prime Minister, Speech at the UN General Assembly, 22 Sep. 2022.
[68] British Treasury, *Autumn Statement 2022* (His Majesty's Stationery Office: London, Nov. 2022), p. 34.
[69] British government, *Global Britain in a Competitive Age: The Integrated Review of Security, Defence, Development and Foreign Policy* (Her Majesty's Stationery Office: London, Mar. 2021); and Chuter, A., 'UK refuses to make defense spending commitments amid strategy review', *Defense News*, 17 Nov. 2022.

estimate includes military aid to Ukraine, totalling around $2 billion in 2022, making Germany the second highest European donor.

Soon after the Russian invasion of Ukraine, Chancellor Olaf Scholz declared the event a *Zeitenwende* or 'epochal tectonic shift' for Germany. He stated that the country would aim for a military burden of 2.0 per cent of its GDP by 2025, up from 1.4 per cent in 2022.[70] To meet that goal, he also announced the establishment of an extra-budgetary fund of €100 billion ($105 billion) aimed at increasing the military capabilities of the armed forces, to be spent over five years.[71] The fund was left untouched in 2022, but from 2023 onwards it will cover major procurement programmes: 38 per cent will go to air systems, 21 per cent to land systems and 12 per cent to naval systems. Command and control systems will receive 27 per cent, and the remaining 2 per cent will be split between personal equipment and R&D on AI.[72]

Military spending by Poland reached $16.6 billion in 2022, the highest figure to date, marking an 11 per cent increase compared to 2021 and a 95 per cent increase over the decade 2013–22. The military burden was 2.4 per cent, the country's highest since 1993 and the third highest in Central and Western Europe, after Greece and Lithuania.

In March 2022 the Polish government passed the Homeland Defence Act to reorganize its national defence policy and raise the military burden to 3.0 per cent in 2023.[73] This target was later revised to 4.0 per cent of GDP.[74] Among the measures in the new law is a plan to increase the number of soldiers (professionals and reservists) from 143 500 to around 300 000 in order to respond to 'the increasingly difficult geopolitical situation in the region'.[75] This troop increase would provide Poland with one of the largest land armies in the European Union (EU).[76] The act also includes a new fund to support the modernization of the armed forces. The fund is to be financed through the issuing of new debt and aims to provide resources to sustain the procurement

---

[70] Nienaber, M. and Kowalcze, K., 'Germany to hike defense budget by up to €10 billion in 2024', Bloomberg, 15 Feb. 2023; and Morris, L., Brady K. and Stern. D. L., 'Germany pledged a military revamp when Ukraine war began. Now it's worse off', *Washington Post*, 17 Feb. 2023.

[71] Marksteiner, A., 'Explainer: The proposed hike in German military spending', SIPRI Commentary, 25 Mar. 2022; and von der Burchard, H. and Rinaldi, G., 'Germany backtracks on defense spending promises made after Ukraine invasion', Politico, 5 Dec. 2022.

[72] German Federal Chancellery, 'Entwurf eines Gesetzes über die Feststellung des Bundeshaushaltsplans für das Haushaltsjahr 2023' [Draft law on the determination of the Federal budget plan for the financial year 2023], German Bundesrat, Drucksache no. 20/3100, 5 Aug. 2022.

[73] Ustawa z dnia 11 marca 2022 r. o obronie Ojczyzny [Act of 11 March 2022 on homeland defence], *Dziennik Ustaw Rzeczypospolitej Polskiej*, 23 Mar. 2022 (in Polish). See also Adamowski, J., 'Europe goes on shopping spree to fill capability gaps', *Defense News*, 6 Sep. 2022.

[74] 'Poland to ramp up defense budget to 4% of GDP', Deutsche Welle, 30 Jan. 2023.

[75] Polish Prime Minister's Chancellery, 'More troops and more money for defence—The Council of Ministers adopted a draft Homeland Defence Act', 22 Feb. 2022.

[76] Polish Prime Minister's Chancellery (note 75).

effort. It is unclear what sum the fund aims to raise, and the auction of the first batch of issued bonds was cancelled without explanation.[77]

In 2022 Finnish military expenditure reached $4.8 billion, an increase of 36 per cent compared to 2021—Finland's highest annual increase since 1962. This raised Finland's military burden from 1.3 per cent to 1.7 per cent. The country shares a 1300-kilometre border with Russia, and the decision to allocate extra funding to military expenditure came after the invasion of Ukraine, which 'brought about fundamental changes in Finland's security environment' and led to it applying to join the North Atlantic Treaty Organization (NATO).[78] The increase was mainly assigned to procurement, which constituted roughly one-third of total military expenditure.

The European Union established the European Defence Fund (EDF) in 2017 to foster military R&D collaboration among companies across its member states. In July 2022 the European Commission announced the results of its 2021 call for proposals, with $1.2 billion ($1.3 billion) being split among 61 projects.[79] This sum is included in the total military expenditure of the subregion for 2022, and effectively makes the EU the 25th largest military spender in Central and Western Europe.

The European Peace Facility (EPF) was established in 2021 as an off-budget mechanism alongside the EU's Multiannual Financial Framework 2021–27.[80] Countries' contributions to the fund are included in estimates of national military spending. The EPF replaced and expanded the scope of pre-existing mechanisms, allowing for the financing of military action under the EU's Common Foreign and Security Policy (CFSP). During 2022 it was mainly used to fund and coordinate military aid to Ukraine, which amounted to $3.2 billion.[81]

Eastern Europe

Military spending in Eastern Europe increased by 58 per cent in 2022 to $135 billion. This upsurge was due to Russia's war against Ukraine, which unsurprisingly drove the military spending of both states upwards. Between 2013 and 2022, East European military expenditure grew by 72 per cent.

---

[77] Ciślak, J., 'Odwołano sprzedaż obligacji na rzecz Funduszu Wsparcia Sił Zbrojnych' [Bond sale the Armed Forces Support Fund cancelled], Defence24, 24 Oct. 2022 (in Polish).

[78] Finnish Ministry of Defence, 'Supplementary budget strengthens defence capability', 20 May 2022; and Finnish Ministry of Defence, 'Finland and NATO'. On the NATO applications of Finland and Sweden see chapter 1, section V, in this volume.

[79] European Commission, Directorate-General for Defence Industry and Space, 'Results of the EDF 2021 calls for proposals: EU invests €1.2 billion in 61 defence industrial cooperation projects', 20 July 2022.

[80] Council of the EU, 'Timeline—European Peace Facility', 24 Mar. 2023.

[81] European External Action Service, 'The European Peace Facility', Strategic Compass, Jan. 2023.

Russia. In 2022 Russia's estimated total military expenditure reached $86.4 billion, a 9.2 per cent increase over 2021 and 15 per cent over 2013. This was equivalent to 4.1 per cent of Russia's GDP in 2022, up from 3.7 per cent in 2021. Figures for Russia's military expenditure in 2022 are highly uncertain given the increasing opaqueness of Russian financial authorities since the invasion of Ukraine.[82] The 2022 estimate of Russia's total military expenditure is based on two documents: budgetary execution documents as of 1 August 2022, which were released on 1 September but are no longer available on the Russian Treasury website;[83] and an audit of the 2023–25 Budget Law by the Russian Accounts Chamber issued in October 2022.[84]

Despite the limited available information, some analysis is possible. For instance, available data shows how the costs of the war increased compared to initial plans. In the 2022–24 Budget Law, voted at the end of 2021, the 'national defence' budget line (which accounts for almost 80 per cent of Russia's total military expenditure) was initially planned to be 3502 billion roubles ($50.1 billion).[85] The estimated actual spending, based on October 2022 documents, was 4679 billion roubles ($67.0 billion), a 34 per cent nominal increase from the first budget.[86] This growth rate was above Russia's estimated inflation rate of 14 per cent in 2022.[87]

Within this overall spending figure, some key spending categories increased during the year.[88] The increases concerned mainly classified spending under the budget category 'armed forces of the Russian Federation', which rose by 52 per cent in nominal terms from the initial budget for 2022 to 2316 billion roubles ($33.2 billion). This classified spending is generally assumed to include procurement of military equipment and maintenance—two spending categories likely to have required additional resources due to the war. Classified spending dedicated to military R&D also increased, as did expenditure for the troops of the national guard, Rosgvardiya, which was up by 23 per cent from the initial budget to 349 billion roubles ($5.0 billion). These paramilitary troops are also deployed in Ukraine, alongside the regular armed forces.[89] Another interesting line item is 'mobilization and extra forces

---

[82] See e.g. Cooper, J., 'Implementation of the Russian Federal Budget during January–July 2022 and spending on the military', SIPRI Background Paper, Oct. 2022.

[83] Russia Federal Treasury, [Budget execution report as of 1 August 2022: Federal budget], 1 Sep. 2022 (in Russian). As of Feb. 2023, data from 1 Jan. 2022 remained accessible, but no more recent information.

[84] Russian Accounts Chamber, [Opinion of the Accounts Chamber of the Russian Federation on the draft federal law 'On the federal budget for 2023 and for the planning period 2024 and 2025' (main provisions)] (Accounts Chamber: Moscow, 2022), p. 20 (in Russian).

[85] Russian Ministry of Finance, [On the federal budget for 2022 and for the planning period of 2023 and 2024], Dec. 2021, p. 49.

[86] Russian Accounts Chamber (note 84), p. 20.

[87] International Monetary Fund, World Economic Outlook Database, Oct. 2022.

[88] Cooper (note 82), table 5.

[89] 'Putin orders $81,500 payment to families of National Guards who die in Ukraine', Reuters, 6 June 2022.

training'. The revised budget for the period up to 1 August 2022 lists spending under this category as 17.1 billion roubles ($245 million), up 106 per cent in nominal terms from actual spending in 2021.[90]

By the end of 2022, Western sanctions had not yet significantly hampered Russia's economy and its financial capacity.[91] After almost a full year of sanctions, the Russian economy appeared to have resisted better than anticipated by some Western commentators at the start of the war, suggesting that Russia still had sufficient resources to sustain its war effort.[92] Indeed, whereas in April 2022 the International Monetary Fund (IMF) had initially predicted an 8.5 per cent contraction in Russia's GDP in 2022, by January 2023 this had been revised to a smaller contraction of 2.2 per cent.[93] However, these figures rely on official Russian statistics that may not be reliable. Furthermore, GDP data would include the increase in production of military equipment.

A key factor when it comes to the resilience of Russia's economy and funding the war has been revenue from commodity exports. Russia is the largest exporter of oil to global markets.[94] Just as for the trade in goods, Russia has established new trading patterns for its oil exports to circumvent sanctions. Although Russia sells its oil at lower prices than other producers, it has increased exports significantly to countries that were not previously among its main customers, such as China, India and Türkiye.[95] Nonetheless, in January 2023 revenue from oil exports was down 40 per cent compared to January 2022, which will make Russia's budgeting harder.[96] Despite this, oil and gas revenue is still expected to account for 34 per cent of total government income in the 2023 budget.[97]

The gradual loss of revenue from commodity exports means that the Russian government will increasingly need to resort to other sources of income to cover budgetary deficits. The Russian Ministry of Finance has identified the main sources for financing the federal budget deficit for the coming years as the National Wealth Fund (NWF) and state loans.[98] As a consequence, the value of the NWF—the country's sovereign wealth fund, which was

---

[90] Russia Federal Treasury (note 83).

[91] On the impact of trade restrictions on Russia see chapter 12, section III, in this volume.

[92] 'How new sanctions could cripple Russia's economy', *The Economist*, 27 Feb. 2022.

[93] International Monetary Fund (IMF), *World Economic Outlook: War Sets Back the Global Recovery* (IMF: Washington, DC, Apr. 2022), p. 6; and International Monetary Fund (IMF), *World Economic Outlook Update: Inflation Peaking Amid Low Growth* (IMF: Washington, DC, Jan. 2023), p. 4.

[94] International Energy Agency (IEA), 'Oil market and Russian supply', Feb. 2022.

[95] 'Russia sanctions: What impact have they had on its oil and gas exports?', BBC News, 26 Jan. 2023; and Kurmanaev, A. and Reed, S., 'How Russia is surviving the tightening grip on its oil revenue', *New York Times*, 7 Feb. 2023.

[96] Zhdannikov, D., Aizhu C. and Verma, N., 'Lost Russian oil revenue is bonanza for shippers, refiners', Reuters, 8 Feb. 2023.

[97] Russian Ministry of Finance, [Budget for citizens 2023–2025: Draft Federal Law on the Federal Budget for 2023 and for the planning period 2024 and 2025], Nov. 2022, p. 4 (in Russian).

[98] Russian Ministry of Finance (MOF), [Budget for citizens to the Federal Law on the Federal Budget for 2023 and for the planning period 2024 and 2025] (MOF: Moscow, 2022), p. 10 (in Russian).

established in 2008 during the global financial crisis—is expected to decrease significantly, from 13 546 billion roubles ($184 billion) at the start of 2021 to 5947 billion roubles ($75.4 billion) at the start of 2025.[99] In addition, the Russian government can count on a large foreign reserve, which stood at around $580 billion at the end of 2022—among the largest in the world.[100] Russia could also sell some of this foreign currency or gold reserves. However, around $300 billion of its foreign assets have been frozen by sanctions.[101] Additionally, some costs of the war may be extra-budgetary. For example, some oblasts may have taken on the responsibility to compensate the families of dead or wounded soldiers, while some regions have also paid for volunteer military battalions.[102]

Ukraine. In 2022 Ukraine's estimated total military expenditure reached $44.0 billion, a growth of 640 per cent since 2021. As a consequence, while Russia's military spending was 11 times larger than Ukraine's in 2021, this ratio narrowed to just 2:1 in 2022. Its spending over the decade 2013–22 increased by 1661 per cent.

In addition to its own military spending, Ukraine has also received substantial financial and equipment-related military assistance from several countries. Financial military aid to Ukraine is estimated to have totalled at least $30 billion in 2022, excluding the value of military equipment stocks donated to Ukraine. Direct financial military assistance is accounted for in the SIPRI estimates of military spending of the donor countries. In addition, general financial support and loans sustaining Ukraine's public finances could contribute indirectly to Ukraine's military budgeting.

Ukraine's total military expenditure represented 34 per cent of its GDP in 2022, up from 3.2 per cent in 2021. This made Ukraine the country with the largest military burden in the world by far. The increase in military burden was due to a combination of the huge rise in military spending with a severe economic contraction. According to IMF estimates, Ukraine's GDP declined by 35 per cent in 2022.[103] Nonetheless, the IMF considered that Ukraine's economy remained resilient despite the ongoing war.[104]

---

[99] Raymond, H., 'Sovereign Wealth Funds as domestic investors of last resort during crises', *Economie Internationale*, vol. 123, no. 3 (2010); and Russian Ministry of Finance (note 98), p. 11.

[100] Bank of Russia, 'International reserves of the Russian Federation (end of period)', 17 Feb. 2023; and Bank of Finland Institute for Emerging Economies (BOFIT), 'Russia's foreign currency and gold reserves hit record high', BOFIT Weekly, 21 Jan. 2022.

[101] 'Sanctions have frozen around $300 bln of Russian reserves, FinMin says', Reuters, 13 Mar. 2022.

[102] Cooper (note 82), p. 7.

[103] International Monetary Fund (note 87).

[104] McMahon, M. and Liboreiro, J., 'IMF praises Ukraine's economic resilience as "astonishing" while country pushes for $15-billion loan', Euronews, 21 Feb. 2023.

Middle East

Estimated military expenditure in the Middle East rose by 3.2 per cent to $184 billion in 2022. This was 1.5 per cent lower than in 2013.[105] The regional rise in 2022 was largely due to 16 per cent growth in military spending by Saudi Arabia, the largest spender in the region and the fifth in the world.

Six of the 10 largest military burdens are in the Middle East: Saudi Arabia (7.4 per cent), Qatar (7.0 per cent), Oman (5.2 per cent), Jordan (4.8 per cent), Israel (4.5 per cent) and Kuwait (4.5 per cent). The military burden fell in almost all countries in the region in 2022, except for Qatar (0.5 percentage points increase), Iran (0.4 percentage points increase) and Jordan (unchanged at 4.8 per cent). While Qatar's military burden increased because military spending rose at a faster pace than the economy, Iranian military spending increased amid economic contraction.

Military spending in Israel fell for the first time since 2009. The 4.2 per cent decrease left military spending at $23.4 billion in 2022, but still 26 per cent higher than in 2013. Expenditure in 2022 did not follow the approved budget, which had projected a significant rise.[106] Nor did it meet the 3–4 per cent growth projections of the 2030 Security Concept adopted in 2018.[107] Israel has been cutting public expenditure since mid 2021 to reduce its deficit, and in December 2022 it finally achieved a budget surplus of 0.5 per cent of GDP.[108] The reduction in military spending took place despite growing clashes between the Israeli military forces and Palestinian militants, as well as intensified strikes on Syria.[109]

Saudi Arabia continued to lead a military coalition against Houthi forces in Yemen. The eight-year-long conflict worsened again in 2022, as missile and air strikes by both sides intensified.[110] Saudi Arabia's military spending grew by 16 per cent in 2022 to reach an estimated $75.0 billion. However, Saudi Arabian military expenditure has been very volatile. The increase in 2022 was the first since 2018, and spending has been on an overall downward trend since the start of the country's involvement in the conflict in Yemen, in 2015: spending fell by 23 per cent between 2015 and 2022. Both the decline since

---

[105] This total excludes Syria and Yemen, for which it was impossible to make a reliable series of estimates for inclusion in the regional total.

[106] Ahronheim, A., 'Israel finally has a budget, and so does the IDF—Analysis', *Jerusalem Post*, 4 Nov. 2021.

[107] Israeli Prime Minister's Office, 'PM Netanyahu presents "2030 Security Concept" to the Cabinet', 15 Aug. 2018.

[108] Israeli Ministry of Finance, 'Estimated execution of the state budget: January–December FY2022', 11 Jan. 2023.

[109] Al Tahhan, Z. and Humaid, M., 'Six major developments that shaped 2022 for Palestinians', Al Jazeera, 26 Dec. 2022; and Al-Khalidi, S., 'Israeli attacks squeeze Iranian aerial supplies to Syria, sources say', Al Jazeera, 2 Sep. 2022. On the conflicts involving Israel see chapter 2, section I, in this volume.

[110] Robinson, K., 'Yemen's tragedy: War, stalemate, and suffering', Council on Foreign Relations, 21 Oct. 2022. See also chapter 2, section II, in this volume.

2015 and the 2022 rise can be at least partly attributed to variations in oil prices in the international market.

In 2022 Türkiye's military spending fell for the third straight year, to $10.6 billion, a decrease of 26 per cent compared to 2021. Despite a nominal spending increase of 28 per cent, soaring inflation as part of the country's widespread economic woes resulted in the biggest annual real-terms decrease in Turkish military expenditure since at least 1949.

III. Arms-producing and military services companies, 2021

XIAO LIANG, ANA CAROLINA DE OLIVEIRA ASSIS, ANASTASIA CUCINO, MADISON LIPSON AND SANEM TOPAL

The combined arms sales of the world's 100 largest arms-producing and military services companies in 2021 (the SIPRI Top 100 for 2021) totalled US$592 billion.[1] This represented an annual increase of 1.9 per cent in these companies' arms sales.[2] Arms sales by the Top 100 have been on an upward trajectory since at least 2015 (the first year for which SIPRI included Chinese firms in its ranking) and increased by 19 per cent in real terms between 2015 and 2021 (see table 5.6).

This section reviews developments in the arms production and military services industry in 2021 (the most recent year for which consistent data on arms sales of the Top 100 is available) and 2022. It first outlines regional and national developments in the SIPRI Top 100 for 2021 and notable developments outside the Top 100. It then assesses the compounded effects on the industry and its supply chains of the disruptions caused by the Covid-19 pandemic and the Russian Federation's invasion of Ukraine, and the surge in demand caused by that war. 'Arms sales' are defined as sales of military goods and services to military customers domestically and abroad.[3]

Regional and national developments in the Top 100 for 2021

North America: Mergers, acquisitions and the rise of private equity

North America is the region with the largest presence in the Top 100, accounting for more than half of the total value of arms sales in 2021 (see table 5.7).

Arms sales by US companies in the Top 100 decreased by 0.9 per cent in 2021, but the USA continued to dominate the ranking with 40 companies and total arms sales of $299 billion. Twenty-five of these companies recorded a year-on-year decline in arms sales in 2021.

The world's five largest arms companies in 2021 were all based in the USA, continuing a pattern that dates back to 2018. Despite a decrease in its arms

---

[1] Unless otherwise stated, all financial figures—including arms sales figures—in this section are presented in nominal (current) 2021 US dollars, while percentage changes and shares are in constant 2021 US dollars (i.e. in real terms). For further detail on the SIPRI Top 100 see the SIPRI Arms Industry Database, Dec. 2022. For a full list of the Top 100 for 2021 as analysed here see Béraud-Sudreau, L. et al., 'The SIPRI Top 100 Arms-producing and Military Services Companies, 2021', SIPRI Fact Sheet, Dec. 2022.

[2] This change of 1.9% refers to the arms sales in 2020 and 2021 of the 100 companies in the Top 100 for 2021. The change of 0.8% in table 8.5 compares the arms sales of the Top 100 for 2021 with the arms sales of the slightly different set of companies in the Top 100 for 2020.

[3] For further details see SIPRI Arms Industry Database, 'Sources and methods'.

Table 5.6. Trends in arms sales of companies in the SIPRI Top 100, 2012–21

Change is the difference (in %) between the total arms sales of the Top 100 of each year and the different set of companies in the Top 100 for the previous year.

	2012	2013	2014	2015	2016	2017	2018	2019	2020	2021
Arms sales in current prices and exchange rates										
Total ($b.)	405	406	398 ‖	446	460	477	505	539	557	592
Change (%)		0.3	−2.1 ‖	..	3.2	3.6	5.8	6.8	3.3	6.3
Arms sales in constant (2021) prices and exchange rates										
Total ($b.)	439	429	415 ‖	497	518	522	538	575	588	592
Change (%)		−2.2	−3.3 ‖	..	4.4	0.8	3.0	6.8	2.2	0.8

‖ = series break.

Note: There is a series break between 2014 and 2015, when Chinese companies were first included in the data set.

Source: SIPRI Arms Industry Database, Dec. 2022.

sales of 0.6 per cent in 2021, Lockheed Martin again topped the ranking with $60.3 billion in arms sales. Raytheon Technologies (ranked 2nd) was the only company in the top five that recorded an increase in arms sales, of 9.1 per cent compared with 2020. The decreases in arms sales reported by Lockheed Martin, Boeing (ranked 3rd) and General Dynamics (ranked 5th) were mainly attributable to inflation, as their arms sales increased in nominal terms between 2020 and 2021.

A continuation of mergers and acquisitions in the US arms industry in 2021 led to the entry of new companies into the Top 100.[4] For example, Peraton (ranked 21st) acquired the information technology (IT) and mission-support services business of Northrop Grumman (ranked 4th) in February 2021 and then in May 2021 it bought Perspecta, another military-related IT services company. In early 2020 Amentum was spun-off from AECOM's management services business, which provided a wide array of services such as consulting, logistics, IT and training to both civilian and military customers. Amentum then bought DynCorp International—an aerospace company—in November 2020. In 2021 Amentum's arms sales reached $5.0 billion and it entered the Top 100 at rank 25.

There will probably be fewer large-scale mergers among the largest US firms in the coming years as a result of an effort by the administration of US President Joe Biden to reduce 'extreme consolidation' within the arms industry.[5] The Biden administration sees the mergers, which reduce competition and leave the USA overly reliant on a small group of suppliers,

---

[4] Marksteiner, A. et al., 'Arms-producing and military services companies, 2020', *SIPRI Yearbook 2022*, pp. 287–96.

[5] White House, 'Department of Defense releases new report on safeguarding our national security by promoting competition in the defense industrial base', Fact sheet, 15 Feb. 2022. See also US Department of Defense (DOD), Office of the Under Secretary of Defense for Acquisition and Sustainment, *State of Competition within the Defense Industrial Base* (DOD: Washington, DC, Feb. 2022).

Table 5.7. Regional and national shares of arms sales for companies in the SIPRI Top 100, 2020–21

Arms sales figures are in constant (2021) US$ and changes between 2020 and 2021 are in real terms, based on constant (2021) US$. Figures for 2020 refer to the companies in the Top 100 for 2021, not the slightly different set of companies in the Top 100 for 2020. Figures may not add up to the given totals because of the conventions of rounding.

No. of companies	Region/Country[a]	Arms sales ($m.) 2021	Arms sales ($m.) 2020	Change in arms sales, 2020–21 (%)	Share of Top 100 sales, 2021 (%)
41	North America	300 460	302 783	−0.8	51
40	United States	299 180	301 780	−0.9	51
1	Canada	1 280	1 003	28	0.2
27	Europe	123 290	118 270	4.2	21
8	United Kingdom	40 430	41 563	−2.7	6.8
5	France	28 750	24 908	15	4.9
4	Germany	9 320	8 826	5.6	1.6
3	Trans-European[b]	18 840	19 805	−4.9	3.2
2	Italy	16 850	14 615	15	2.8
1	Sweden	4 090	3 726	9.8	0.7
1	Poland	1 430	1 445	−1.0	0.2
1	Ukraine	1 330	1 447	−8.1	0.2
1	Norway	1 170	1 013	15	0.2
1	Spain	1 080	924	17	0.2
21	Asia and Oceania	135 550	128 146	5.8	23
8	China	109 140	102 634	6.3	18
4	Japan	9 030	9 161	−1.4	1.5
4	South Korea	7 180	6 932	3.6	1.2
2	India	5 130	4 612	11	0.9
1	Singapore	2 160	1 966	9.8	0.4
1	Taiwan	1 970	1 811	8.8	0.3
1	Australia	940	1 029	−8.6	0.2
6	Russia	17 770	17 701	0.4	3.0
5	Middle East	14 990	14 073	6.5	2.5
3	Israel	11 630	11 294	3.0	2.0
2	Türkiye	3 360	2 779	21	0.6
100	Total	592 060	580 973	1.9	100

[a] Figures for a country or region refer to the arms sales of the Top 100 companies headquartered in that country or region, including those by subsidiaries in another country or region. They do not reflect the sales of arms actually produced in that country or region.

[b] The 3 companies classified as 'trans-European' are Airbus, MBDA and KNDS.

Source: SIPRI Arms Industry Database, Dec. 2022.

as a threat to national security. These mergers could also have knock-on effects on procurement costs and product innovation.[6] This policy is only the latest attempt by a US administration to either encourage or discourage

---

[6] Lopez, C. T., 'DOD report: Consolidation of defense industrial base poses risks to national security', US Department of Defense, 16 Feb. 2022.

consolidation in the US arms industry, with policy shifts dating back at least to the 'last supper' speech in 1993.[7]

Another important development in the US arms industry is the increasingly visible trend for acquisitions of larger arms companies by private equity firms since 2019–20. In addition to the formation of Peraton and Amentum, other notable private equity acquisitions include Advent International's purchase of two British arms-producing companies, Cobham in January 2020 and Ultra Electronics in July 2022, and the purchase in May 2021 of Cubic Corporation by Veritas Capital and Evergreen Coast Capital. Such acquisitions reduce transparency in financial reporting since US private equity firms are not required to report financial results to the public.[8] This makes it increasingly difficult to establish an accurate picture of the size of the arms industry. The growing trend for private equity acquisitions is likely to continue due to the historically strong financial performance of the arms industry and the expected higher demand for arms in the context of heightening geopolitical tensions.

Asia and Oceania: Pursuit of self-reliance

The combined arms sales of the 21 companies in Asia and Oceania included in the Top 100 amounted to $136 billion in 2021—an increase of 5.8 per cent compared with 2020.

Amid rising geopolitical tensions and perceived threats in the region, many governments in Asia and Oceania have implemented policies to support the development of domestic arms-industrial capabilities with the aim of enhancing self-reliance in arm production.[9] There are wide disparities within the region in progress towards this goal.[10] There is generally more self-reliance in arms production in East Asia than in South East Asia and South Asia.

China leads the region in terms of the size of its arms companies. It is the only country in the region that has companies that can produce complex weapon systems in all sectors. Arms companies in Australia, India, Japan, the Republic of Korea (South Korea), Singapore and Taiwan have developed advanced production in niche areas and are also represented in the Top 100. While other countries in Asia and Oceania, such as Indonesia, Malaysia, Pakistan, Thailand and Viet Nam, have domestic arms industries, they

---

[7] See e.g. Dunne, J. P. and Surry, E., 'Arms production', *SIPRI Yearbook 2006*, pp. 399–401; and Jackson, S. T., 'Key developments in the main arms-producing countries', *SIPRI Yearbook 2012*, p. 223.

[8] US Securities and Exchange Commission, 'Private fund', 6 Jan. 2023.

[9] On South East Asia see Bitzinger, R. A., 'Revisiting armaments production in Southeast Asia: New dreams, same challenges', *Contemporary Southeast Asia*, vol. 35, no. 3 (Dec. 2013). On China, India, South Korea and Taiwan see Bitzinger, R. A., *Arming Asia: Technonationalism and its Impact on Local Defense Industries* (Routledge: Abingdon, 2017).

[10] Béraud-Sudreau, L. et al., *Arms-production Capabilities in the Indo-Pacific Region: Measuring Self-reliance* (SIPRI: Stockholm, Oct. 2022), p. 54.

remain limited and are still concentrated in low-technology production and the maintenance, repair and overhaul of foreign systems.[11] None of these countries is represented in the Top 100.

Eight Chinese arms companies appear in the Top 100 for 2021. Their aggregated arms sales reached $109 billion, 6.3 per cent more than in 2020. The growth in arms sales reflects the scale of China's modernization of its military equipment and its objective to become self-reliant in the production of all categories of major arms.[12] Seven of the eight Chinese companies increased their arms sales in 2021. China North Industries Group Corporation (NORINCO, ranked 7th), a land systems specialist, is the largest Chinese arms company. Its arms sales rose by 11 per cent to $21.6 billion in 2021.

There have been signs of consolidation in China's arms industry since the mid 2010s. This marks a reversal of previous structural reforms that aimed to improve productivity and competitiveness by breaking up sector monopolies.[13] In 2021 the two largest shipbuilders in China, China Shipbuilding Industry Corporation (CSIC) and China State Shipbuilding Corporation (CSSC), finalized a merger to form a new entity operating under the name CSSC (ranked 14th). With arms sales of $11.1 billion, CSSC was the largest military shipbuilder in the world in 2021.

The total arms sales of the four companies in the Top 100 based in Japan fell by 1.4 per cent in 2021 to $9.0 billion.[14] Arms sales of Mitsubishi Heavy Industries (ranked 35th), Japan's biggest arms producer, dropped by 5.3 per cent. In contrast, Fujitsu (ranked 77th) recorded strong growth, with an increase in arms sales of 10 per cent in 2021.

At $7.2 billion, the total arms sales of the four South Korean firms in the Top 100 were 3.6 per cent higher in 2021 than in 2020.[15] The growth was largely driven by Hanwha Aerospace (ranked 50th), which saw its arms sales rise by 7.6 per cent to $2.6 billion. Hanwha's arms sales are expected to rise significantly in the coming years, after it signed a major arms deal with Poland in 2022, following the Russian invasion of Ukraine.[16]

The arms sales of the two Indian companies in the Top 100 totalled $5.1 billion in 2021, 11 per cent more than in 2020. The arms sales of Hindustan Aeronautics (ranked 42nd) increased by 6.7 per cent and those of Bharat

---

[11] Béraud-Sudreau et al. (note 10).
[12] Cheung, T. M., *Fortifying China: The Struggle to Build a Modern Defense Economy* (Cornell University Press: Ithaca, NY, 2009), p. 183; and Cheung, T. M., *Innovate to Dominate: The Rise of the Chinese Techno-security State* (Cornell University Press: Ithaca, NY, 2022).
[13] Tian, N. and Su, F., 'Estimating the arms sales of Chinese companies', SIPRI Insights on Peace and Security no. 2020/2, Jan. 2020.
[14] Data on Japanese companies were provided by the Mitsubishi Research Institute.
[15] Data on South Korean companies were provided by the Korea Institute for Industrial Economics and Trade (KIET).
[16] Reuters, 'South Korea and Poland ink $5.8bn contract for tanks, howitzers', Nikkei Asia, 28 Aug. 2022.

Electronics (ranked 63rd) by 20 per cent. Both companies have benefited from major orders placed by the Indian armed forces in recent years. At the same time, the Indian government has lingering concerns over the productivity of Indian arms companies, their dependence on the domestic market and their reliance on foreign resources.[17] Against this background, Indian companies have started to diversify their business into the civilian market and to set up export offices overseas.[18]

For the first time, a Taiwanese firm appears in the Top 100 for 2021: the National Chung-Shan Institute of Science and Technology (NCSIST). NCSIST, which specializes in missiles and military electronics, recorded arms sales of $2.0 billion in 2021, ranking it 60th. The growth of Taiwan's arms industry can be attributed to its specific geopolitical circumstances and limited access to foreign military equipment.[19]

Europe (other than Russia)

In 2021 Europe (excluding Russia) accounted for 27 of the Top 100 arms companies. Their combined arms sales reached $123 billion, up by 4.2 per cent compared with 2020.

With eight firms in the 2021 ranking, the United Kingdom remained the European country hosting the highest number of Top 100 companies. Six of the eight firms recorded decreases in their arms sales in 2021. The arms sales of the biggest, BAE Systems (ranked 6th), fell by 1.0 per cent to $26.0 billion in 2021.

In contrast, all five companies based in France recorded growth in their arms sales in 2021, reaching a total of $28.8 billion in 2021. Arms sales by Dassault Aviation Group (ranked 19th) rose by 59 per cent and reached $6.3 billion. This was driven by deliveries of 25 Rafale combat aircraft to India and Qatar. Significant increases in arms sales were also recorded for Safran (ranked 24) and Naval Group (ranked 29th). While Rheinmetall (ranked 31st) remained the largest arms company in Germany, its arms sales fell by 1.7 per cent in 2021. In Italy, Leonardo (ranked 12th) increased its arms sales by 18 per cent to $13.9 billion, while Fincantieri (ranked 46th) reported year-on-year growth of 5.9 per cent to reach $3.0 billion.

Among the three trans-European companies, Airbus (ranked 15th) recorded the highest arms sales, $10.9 billion in 2021. This was 15 per cent lower than in 2021, which the firm attributed to lower sales in its military aircraft segment. Arms deliveries by MBDA (ranked 27th) increased significantly, by 15 per

---

[17] Indian Department of Defence Production, 'Defence Production Policy 2018', 23 Aug. 2018, p. 4. See also Indian Department of Defence Production, 'Strategy for defence exports'.

[18] E.g. Hindustan Aeronautics Ltd (HAL), *58th Annual Report 2020–21* (HAL: Bengaluru, Oct. 2021), p. 76; and Indian Ministry of Defence (MOD), *Annual Report Year 2018–2019* (MOD: New Delhi, [2019]), p. 59.

[19] Béraud-Sudreau et al. (note 10), pp. 34–36.

cent to $5.0 billion in 2021, as it began the process of catching up on deliveries that had been delayed by the effects of the pandemic. Having merged in 2015, Nexter of France and Krauss-Maffei Wegmann (KMW) of Germany furthered their integration in 2020 and were thus replaced in the Top 100 by KMW+Nexter Defense Systems (KNDS), which ranked 44 in 2021.[20]

The growth in the total arms sales of the European arms industry is likely to continue in 2022 as the demand for arms grows in Europe due to Russia's invasion of Ukraine. To meet this demand and in response to ongoing supply chain challenges and depleting stockpiles (due to military aid to Ukraine), in 2022 the European Union (EU) strengthened existing initiatives and established new ones to boost the arms industry. In February 2022 the European Commission proposed the European Chips Act, which included more than €43 billion ($45 billion) in investment to address semiconductor shortages exacerbated by the Covid-19 pandemic and to increase the EU's share of global production of semiconductors.[21] In an effort to address the fragmentation of the EU arms industry, in May the Commission allocated additional financial incentives to the European Defence Fund (EDF) to support closer cooperation between EU member states and between their national arms industries.[22] In the same month the Commission published a plan aimed at bolstering the EU arms industry through joint procurement to meet the demand arising from the war in Ukraine.[23] In December the European Council agreed a general approach to the proposed European Defence Industry Reinforcement through Common Procurement Act (EDIRPA) for consideration by the European Parliament.[24] EDIRPA is intended to further incentivize joint arms procurement and arms-industrial cooperation within the EU.[25]

Several leading EU arms companies in the Top 100, such as Thales (ranked 6th), Leonardo and Airbus, are expected to benefit from these financial instruments. For example, Thales participated in 41 of the 60 EDF-funded projects in 2021 and Leonardo in 23.[26]

---

[20] French Ministry of Armed Forces, 'Communiqué: Évolution de la gouvernance et poursuite de l'intégration de KNDS, champion européen de l'armement terrestre' [Communiqué: Development of governance and further integration of KNDS, European land armament champion], Press release, 14 Dec. 2020.

[21] European Commission, 'European Chips Act', 8 Feb. 2022.

[22] European Commission, 'European Defence Fund: €1 billion to boost the EU's defence capabilities and new tools for defence innovation', Press release, 25 May 2022.

[23] European Commission, High Representative of the Union for Foreign Affairs and Security Policy, 'Defence investment gaps and measures to address them', Joint Communication to the European Parliament, the European Council and others, JOIN(2022) 24 final, 23 May 2022.

[24] Council of the EU, 'EU defence industry: Council reaches general approach on boosting common procurement', Press release, 1 Dec. 2022.

[25] European Commission, 'Defence industry: EU to reinforce the European defence industry through common procurement with a €500 million instrument', Press release, 19 July 2022.

[26] Foundation for Strategic Research (FRS), 'European Defence Fund (EDF)—Results of the 2021 EDF calls for proposals: A first review', 3 Oct. 2022.

Russia

Six Russian companies appear in the SIPRI Top 100 for 2021. This is three fewer than in 2020 because no data is available for Almaz-Antey, KRET and Russian Electronics. The combined arms sales of the six companies that are included reached $17.8 billion in 2021, which was 0.4 per cent higher than in 2020.

Three of the Russian companies—United Aircraft Corporation (UAC), United Engine Corporation (UEC) and Russian Helicopters—recorded decreases in their arms sales, while the other three—United Shipbuilding Corporation (USC), Tactical Missiles Corporation and UralVagonZavod—recorded increases. The 18 per cent increase registered by Tactical Missiles Corporation (ranked 37th) can be partly attributed to growth in its foreign sales, most likely to India.[27] The estimated arms sales of UAC (ranked 30th) fell to $4.5 billion in 2021, and arms sales as a proportion of its total sales decreased from 82 per cent in 2020 to 70 per cent in 2021. The change most likely stems from the Russian government's 2016 instruction to the arms industry to increase civilian production.[28]

Four of the Russian companies in the Top 100 for 2021—UAC, UEC, Russian Helicopters and UralVagonZavod—belong to the Rostec holding group, which owns numerous Russian arms companies. SIPRI's ranking excludes holding entities with no direct operational activities and therefore does not include Rostec. However, it is worth noting that Rostec's arms sales decreased by 13 per cent between 2020 and 2021 to $15.5 billion.

The Middle East

Taken together, the five companies in the Top 100 based in the Middle East generated $15.0 billion in arms sales in 2021. This was a 6.5 per cent increase compared with 2020 and the highest rate of growth of all regions represented in the Top 100. All five increased their arms sales in 2021. Turkish Aerospace (ranked 84th) recorded the largest increase, at 62 per cent, and Israel Aerospace Industries (IAI, ranked 38th) the lowest, at 1.9 per cent. Most of the five Middle Eastern firms display a relatively high level of specialization in military products: on average, arms sales accounted for 91 per cent of their total sales in 2021.

Edge, a conglomerate based in the United Arab Emirates (UAE) that was among the top 25 arms companies in 2020, has not disclosed any arms sales figures for 2021 and therefore could not be included in the 2021 ranking. However, Edge reported $5.0 billion of orders in 2022, which indicates that

---

[27] 'Tactical Missiles Corporation's export to be over $1 bln in 2021—CEO', TASS, 21 July 2021; and 'Tactical Missiles Corporation to make over 40 aftersales service contracts by 2025', TASS, 14 Feb. 2023.

[28] President of Russia, [Meeting on diversification of civilian production by defence industry organizations], 24 Jan. 2018 (in Russian).

it would almost certainly be in the Top 100 if figures for its arms sales were available.[29]

The aggregated arms sales of the three Israeli companies in the Top 100 were $11.6 billion in 2021, which was 3.0 per cent higher than in 2020. Elbit Systems (ranked 28th) increased its arms sales by 3.6 per cent to $4.8 billion in 2021. Israeli arms companies have taken advantage of the normalization of diplomatic relations with the UAE following the 2020 Abraham Accords.[30] For example, in 2021 Elbit established a subsidiary in the UAE, and IAI and Edge agreed to cooperate in the design of uncrewed weapon systems.[31]

The two Turkish companies in the Top 100 in 2021—Aselsan and Turkish Aerospace—had combined arms sales of $3.4 billion. Aselsan (ranked 56th) recorded a 6.0 per cent increase in its arms sales to reach $2.2 billion. The substantial year-on-year growth by Turkish Aerospace was partly due to the delivery of several Anka-S uncrewed aerial vehicles (UAVs) to the Turkish armed forces. It meant that the company re-entered the ranking in 2021 having been outside the Top 100 in 2020.

Notable developments outside the Top 100

The ongoing growth of arms sales of the Top 100 also means that even companies outside the ranking can be substantial in size and can have profound impact on international and regional security. For example, Brazil, Saudi Arabia and Türkiye all have notable arms companies with significant arms sales that do not rank in the Top 100. These companies are helping their respective states develop indigenous arms-production capabilities through developing niche weapon systems and partnering with leading international firms.

Despite not being in the Top 100, the UAV specialist Baykar is Türkiye's top arms exporter.[32] It recorded arms sales of $789 million in 2021. Its Bayraktar TB2 armed UAV has been used extensively by Ukraine during the war there and Baykar is in the process of building a production facility in Ukraine.[33] Baykar's UAVs have also been deployed in other conflicts, including Türkiye's military operations in Syria, the 2020 Nagorno-Karabakh conflict and the

---

[29] Edge, 'UAE's Edge marks three year anniversary as major global force in advanced technology and defence', Press release, 29 Nov. 2022.

[30] Davis, I., 'The Israeli–Palestinian conflict and peace process', *SIPRI Yearbook 2021*, pp. 162–64.

[31] Elbit Systems, 'Elbit Systems establishes a company in the United Arab Emirates', Press release, 14 Nov. 2021; and Naval News, 'UAE's Edge and Israel's IAI team up for USV development', 20 Nov. 2021.

[32] 'Baykar becomes top exporter in Turkey's defense, aerospace sector', *Daily Sabah*, 15 June 2022.

[33] Sezer, C., 'Turkey's Baykar to complete plant in Ukraine in two years—CEO', Reuters, 28 Oct. 2022.

armed conflict in Tigray.[34] Another Turkish company, Roketsan, produces munitions for the Bayraktar TB2 UAVs. It reported an almost 50 per cent increase in its arms sales in 2021.[35] However, Roketsan could not be included in the final ranking due to a lack of verifiable data.

Embraer is Brazil's largest arms company, with arms sales of $590 million in 2021. It is developing military aircraft in collaboration with foreign companies such as L3Harris (ranked 13th) of the USA and BAE Systems of the UK.[36] In the maritime sector, Embraer works with Germany's Thyssenkrupp (ranked 55th) to deliver frigates for the Brazilian Navy, while Itaguaí Construções Navais (ICN) leads the construction of submarines with technology transfer from France's Naval Group.[37]

Saudi Arabian Military Industries (SAMI) is a state-owned arms company. Its arms sales increased 25-fold between 2020 and 2021 to reach $624 million due to the acquisition in late 2020 of another Saudi Arabian company, Advanced Electronics Company (AEC). It has established joint programmes with many US and European companies, including Lockheed Martin, Boeing and Thales.[38]

Supply chain disruptions, the war in Ukraine and demand for arms

Many arms companies in the SIPRI Top 100 rely on extensive and complex supply chains to function efficiently. For example, Airbus (ranked 15th) and Leonardo (ranked 12th) both rely on vast global supply chains involving, respectively, 21 000 and 11 000 companies.[39] Many thus faced a high risk of disruption from the public health measures implemented worldwide from 2020 to curb the spread of Covid-19. The ripple effects of the pandemic included disruption to international shipping, labour shortages and a lack of semiconductors—a key component of major weapon systems.

The significant regional disparities in the Top 100 in 2021 reflected the impact of the pandemic-related disruptions. Collectively, the arms sales

---

[34] Fazil, S., 'Armed conflict and peace processes in Iraq, Syria and Turkey', *SIPRI Yearbook 2022*, pp. 168–74; Davis, I., 'The interstate armed conflict between Armenia and Azerbaijan', *SIPRI Yearbook 2021*, pp. 127–32; and Davis, I., 'Armed conflict and peace processes in East Africa', *SIPRI Yearbook 2022*, pp. 225–29.

[35] Istanbul Chamber of Commerce, 'Roketsan Roket San. ve Tic. A.Ş.: İSO 500—2021 yili sonuçlari' [Roketsan Rocket Industries and Trade plc: İSO 500—Results for 2021], Istanbul Chamber of Industry (İSO), 2022.

[36] 'Planemaker Embraer, BAE agree on defense partnership; Eve gets order', Reuters, 19 July 2022.

[37] Naval Group, 'Key milestones for the Brazilian submarine program celebrated in Itaguaí', Press release, 11 Dec. 2020.

[38] Saudi Arabian Military Industries (SAMI), 'SAMI Composites LLC signs agreement with Lockheed Martin to develop composites manufacturing center of excellence in Riyadh', 19 July 2022; Saudi Arabian Military Industries (SAMI), 'SAMI announces joint venture agreement with Boeing', 6 Apr. 2022; and Thales, 'Thales in the Kingdom of Saudi Arabia'.

[39] Leonardo, *Annual Report 2021* (Leonardo: Rome, Jan. 2022), p. 132; and Airbus, *Universal Registration Document 2021* (Airbus: Leiden, Apr. 2022), p. 95.

of North American companies fell by 0.8 per cent, largely due to supply chain problems and inflation. Similarly, most of the European companies that specialize in military aerospace reported losses for 2021, which they attributed to supply chain disruption.[40] However, this was offset by strong growth in other regions, particularly in Asia and Oceania, where arms sales rose by 5.8 per cent in 2021.

Russia's invasion of Ukraine in February 2022 added to supply chain problems for arms producers, as Russia is an exporter of raw materials such as aluminium, copper, steel and titanium that are used in the manufacturing of military equipment.[41] With the implementation of Western sanctions on Russia, including the ban by the EU on imports of Russian steel products, and the broader severing of Western countries' economic ties with Russia, European and North American arms companies have had to reorganize their supply chains to procure raw materials from other producers.[42]

At the same time, war in Ukraine has prompted a surge in the demand for arms in Europe and the USA. Following Russia's invasion in February 2022, Western countries supplied Ukraine with large quantities of military equipment from the existing stocks of their armed forces and financial assistance. However, as the war continued, stockpiles diminished.[43] The Ukraine Defense Contact Group (also known as the Ramstein group) is a USA-led group of more than 50 countries and international organizations that have pledged to assist Ukraine. It has been coordinating efforts to boost arms production and replenish stockpiles.[44] For example, as of January 2023 the US government had awarded several contracts to arms companies to replenish the USA's stockpiles.[45] These included a $624 million order with Raytheon Technologies for Stinger missiles; a $663 million order for Javelin anti-tank missiles placed with a joint venture partnership between Lockheed Martin and Raytheon Technologies; and a $624 million order with Lockheed Martin for HIMARS light multiple rocket launchers.

However, increasing arms-production output takes time, especially in the face of supply chain disruptions, and it could be several years before

---

[40] BAE Systems, *Annual Report 2021* (BAE Systems plc: London, 2022), p. 25; Muravska, J. et al., 'Challenges and barriers that limit the productivity and competitiveness of UK defence supply chains', RAND Corp., July 2021; Melrose Industries, *Annual Report 2021* (Melrose Industries plc: Birmingham, 31 Mar. 2022), p. 14; Meggit, *Enabling the Extraordinary: To Fly To Power To Live—Annual Report and Accounts 2021* (Meggit plc: Coventry, 2 Mar. 2022), pp. 6, 9; and Carey, N., 'Analysis: Supply chain snags threaten to slow air industry take-off', Reuters, 21 July 2022.

[41] Pavel, C. C. and Tzimas, E., *Raw Materials in the European Defence Industry* (European Commission, Joint Research Centre: Petten, 2016).

[42] Calhoun, D. L., President and chief executive officer, '2022 address to shareholders', Boeing, 29 Apr. 2022.

[43] Pietralunga, C., 'War in Ukraine is putting Western arms stocks under pressure', *Le Monde*, 23 Nov. 2022.

[44] Garamone, J., 'Momentum builds for Ukraine Defense Contact Group', US Department of Defense, 8 Sep. 2022.

[45] US Department of Defense, 'Ukraine contracting action', 13 Jan. 2023.

arms companies are able to adjust to the new demand created by the war in Ukraine. For example, the joint venture to produce Javelin missiles plans to increase its annual output from 2100 missiles to nearly 4000. However, almost doubling the pace of production could take two years to implement.[46]

Artillery rounds for 155-millimetre howitzers are also among Ukraine's key requirements. By the end of 2022 the USA had supplied over 1 million standard and 4700 precision-guided 155-mm artillery rounds to Ukraine.[47] In September 2022 the pace of production was 14 400 rounds per month; at this rate, it would take more than five years to replenish US stocks to previous levels. The US Department of Defense (DOD) has put plans in place with manufacturers to increase the pace of production to 36 000 rounds per month, which will take three years to implement.[48]

Arms producers in Europe are also anticipating a substantial increase in demand for military equipment because of the war. For example, orders for Rheinmetall's defence division more than doubled between 2021 and 2022 as the result of the need to replenish stockpiles of armoured vehicles sent to Ukraine and of Germany's plans to increase military expenditure (see section II).[49] Similarly, the intake of orders by Swedish arms producer Saab surged in 2022 and the company anticipated further growth based on a projected rise in global military spending.[50]

The need to support Russia's war effort in Ukraine has created growing production pressure for Russian arms companies. Western sanctions have also affected the operations and supply chains of Russian companies. Almaz-Antey, for example, stated in March 2022 that it could not receive payments for some of its arms export deliveries.[51] Some Russian companies are also reported to be facing production difficulties due to reduced access to imported components such as semiconductors.[52]

The war in Ukraine and other violent conflicts, accompanied by rising geopolitical tensions, have thus resulted in surging demand for arms production. At the same time, the supply chain challenges exacerbated by these conflicts and tensions might pose significant hurdles to the industry in meeting this demand. These two major forces could characterize development of the global arms industry in the coming years.

---

[46] Taiclet, J., CEO of Lockheed Martin, Transcript, *Face the Nation*, CBS News, 8 May 2022.
[47] US Department of State, 'US security cooperation with Ukraine', 21 Dec. 2022.
[48] LaPlante, W. A., Under secretary of defense for acquisition and sustainment, and Baker, S. N., Deputy under secretary of defense for policy, Press briefing, US Department of Defense, 9 Sep. 2022.
[49] Rheinmetall, 'Interim report after nine months of 2022', Press release, 10 Nov. 2022.
[50] Saab, *Interim Report Q3* (Saab AB: Stockholm, Oct. 2022), p. 2.
[51] ['Almaz-Antey' reports $1 billion pending for export deliveries], *Kommersant*, 22 Mar. 2022 (in Russian).
[52] US Department of State, 'The impact of sanctions and export controls on the Russian Federation', Fact sheet, 20 Oct. 2022.

6. International arms transfers

Overview

The volume of international transfers of major arms in 2018–22 was 5.1 per cent lower than in 2013–17 and 3.9 per cent higher than in 2008–12. The volume of transfers in 2018–22 was among the highest since the end of the cold war but was still around 35 per cent lower than the totals for 1978–82 and 1983–87, when arms transfers peaked. States' arms acquisitions, often from foreign suppliers, are largely driven by armed conflict and political tensions between states (see section I). There are strong indications that tensions are increasing in most regions, most pronounced in Europe after Russia's invasion of Ukraine in February 2022, and it is thus highly likely that there will be more demand for major arms in the coming years, much of which will be fulfilled by international transfers.

SIPRI has identified 63 states as exporters of major arms in 2018–22, but most are minor exporters. The 25 largest suppliers accounted for 98 per cent of the total volume of exports, and the 5 largest suppliers in the period—the United States, Russia, France, China and Germany—accounted for 76 per cent of the total volume of exports (see section II). Since 1950, the USA and Russia (or the Soviet Union before 1992) have consistently been by far the largest suppliers. However, in 2018–22 the USA's position became more dominant and the gap with Russia larger. In 2018–22 the USA's arms exports were 14 per cent higher than in 2013–17 and its share of the global total increased from 33 to 40 per cent. In contrast, Russia's arms exports decreased by 31 per cent and its share of the global total dropped from 22 to 16 per cent. Exports by France, the third largest supplier, grew by 44 per cent between 2013–17 and 2018–22, while exports by China and Germany decreased by 23 per cent and 35 per cent respectively. Known plans for future deliveries strongly indicate that the gap between the USA and Russia will increase. These plans also suggest that in a few years Russia may no longer be the second largest exporter of major arms, at least partly as a result of some of its main clients becoming more capable of producing their own locally designed major arms but also partly due to pressure from the USA and others not to buy Russian arms.

SIPRI has identified 167 states as importers of major arms in 2018–22. The five largest arms importers were India, Saudi Arabia, Qatar, Australia and China, which together accounted for 36 per cent of total arms imports (see section III). The region that received the largest volume of major arms supplies in 2018–22 was Asia and Oceania, accounting for 41 per cent of the total, followed by the Middle East (31 per cent), Europe (16 per cent), the Americas (5.8 per cent) and

SIPRI Yearbook 2023: Armaments, Disarmament and International Security
www.sipriyearbook.org

Africa (5.0 per cent). Between 2013–17 and 2018–22, the flow of arms to Europe (47 per cent) increased, while flows to Africa (–40 per cent), the Americas (–21 per cent), the Middle East (–8.8 per cent), and Asia and Oceania (–7.5 per cent) decreased. Asia and Oceania has been the region with the highest share of global arms imports since 1988–92, and the share of the Middle East, despite the decrease in imports, remained among the highest since 1988–92. While Africa's share decreased significantly, the level of imports in 2018–22 was higher than between 1988 and 2007. In contrast, the level of imports to states in the Americas was the lowest since 1983–87.

Many of the 167 importers are directly involved in armed conflict or in tensions with other states in which the imported major arms play an important role. Many of the exporters are direct stakeholders or participants in at least some of the conflicts and tensions, which partly explains why they are willing to supply arms, even when the supply seems to contradict their stated arms export policies.

SIEMON T. WEZEMAN

I. Global trends in arms transfers, 2018–22

SIEMON T. WEZEMAN AND PIETER D. WEZEMAN

The volume of international transfers of major arms in 2018–22 was 5.1 per cent lower than in 2013–17, but was 3.9 per cent higher than in 2008–12 and 27 per cent higher than in 1998–2002 when arms transfers were at their lowest volume for any successive five-year period since 1958–62 (see figure 6.1 and box 6.1).[1] However, the total volume in 2018–22 was still around 35 per cent lower than the peak reached in the periods 1978–82 and 1983–87, at the height of the cold war.[2]

Despite a 7.5 per cent drop in imports of major arms by states in Asia and Oceania between 2013–17 and 2018–22, it remained the region with the highest volume of arms imports, as has been the case since 1988–92, and accounted for 41 per cent of the global total (see figure 6.2).[3]

The flow of arms to states in the Middle East also decreased, by 8.8 per cent, between 2013–17 and 2018–22, but the region's share of 32 per cent of the global total remained among the highest of any of the seven successive five-year periods after 1983–87 and almost 80 per cent higher than 2003–2007 and 2008–12.

Arms imports to Africa (–40 per cent) and the Americas (–21 per cent) fell between 2013–17 and 2018–22, and these regions' shares of total global arms transfers decreased. For Africa, however, the level of imports in 2018–22 was still higher than in any of the four successive five-year periods between 1988 and 2007. In contrast, the level of imports by states in the Americas was the lowest of any of the eight successive five-year periods since 1983–87.

Imports of major arms by European states rose by 47 per cent between 2013–17 and 2018–22, largely driven by the perception of an increased threat from Russia among most European states. However, the level of imports in 2018–22 was not much different from levels in the three five-year periods from 1993–97 to 2003–2007. The war in Ukraine had only a limited impact on the total volume of arms transfers in 2018–22, but Ukraine did become a major importer of arms in 2022. In addition, most European states substantially increased their arms import orders in 2022 and announced plans for more

---

[1] In this chapter, the terms 'arms exports' and 'arms imports' are used to refer to international transfers of major arms, as defined by SIPRI. For that definition and a description of how the volume of transfers is measured see box 6.1.

[2] Except where indicated, the information on the arms deliveries and orders referred to in this chapter is taken from the SIPRI Arms Transfers Database. Since year-on-year deliveries can fluctuate, SIPRI compares consecutive multi-year periods—normally 5-year periods. This provides a more stable measure of trends in transfers of major arms. The figures here may differ from those in previous editions of the SIPRI Yearbook because the Arms Transfers Database is updated annually.

[3] For SIPRI's definition of the regions and subregions see SIPRI, 'Regional coverage', SIPRI Databases.

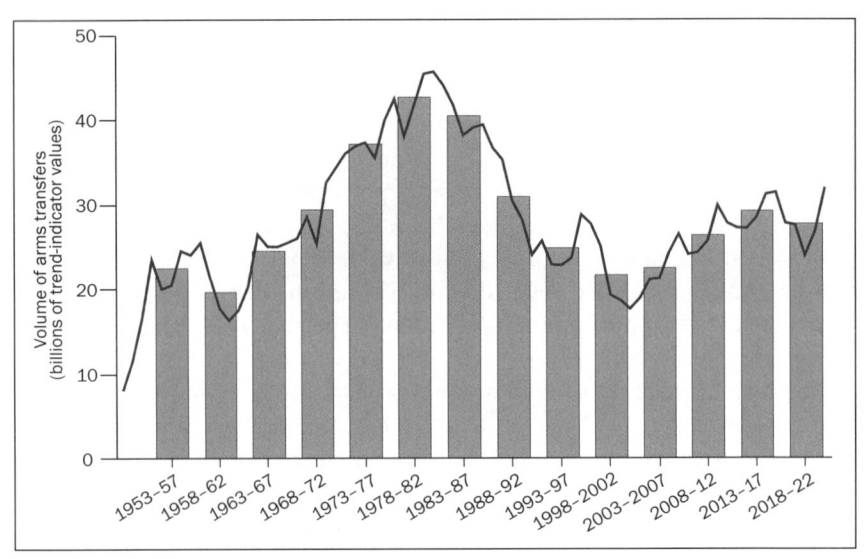

Figure 6.1. The trend in international transfers of major arms, 1950–2022

Note: The bar graph shows the average annual volume of arms transfers for 5-year periods from 1953 and the line graph shows the annual totals since 1950. See box 6.1 for an explanation of the SIPRI trend-indicator value (TIV).

Source: SIPRI Arms Transfers Database, Mar. 2023.

orders in 2023 and the next few years, firmly indicating a further growth of arms imports by states in Europe in the coming decade.

The five largest arms exporters in 2018–22 were the United States, Russia, France, China and Germany, the same as in 2013–17 (see section II). The five states that imported the most arms in the period were India, Saudi Arabia, Qatar, Australia and China (see section III). Three of these were also among the five largest importers in 2013–17, while Qatar and Australia were new to this group.

Increases and decreases, even large ones, in arms exports for individual suppliers measured over five-year periods are not uncommon and are generally a weak indicator of trends, especially for the medium-sized and smaller suppliers. Such changes can often be linked to unpredictable markets with a relatively small group of possible buyers for large volumes of major arms and buyers' willingness to switch between suppliers. Competition within most major arms markets is intense, and winning or losing one or a few large contracts can make a big difference. An example is the 35 per cent decrease in exports by the United Kingdom between 2013–17 and 2018–22, which was largely due to the UK not being able to repeat a major order from Saudi Arabia for Typhoon combat aircraft. Delivery of 48 Typhoon and associated missiles to Saudi Arabia accounted for almost half of all British exports of major arms in 2013–17 but most of the contracts had been fulfilled by the end of 2017.

INTERNATIONAL ARMS TRANSFERS 211

Box 6.1. Definitions and methodology for SIPRI data on international arms transfers

The SIPRI Arms Transfers Database contains information on deliveries of major arms to states, international organizations and non-state armed (i.e. rebel) groups from 1950 to 2022. A new set of data is published annually, replacing the data in earlier editions of the SIPRI Yearbook or other SIPRI publications.

Definitions

SIPRI's definition of 'transfer' includes sales, manufacturing licences, aid, gifts, and most loans or leases. The item must have a military purpose: the recipient must be the armed forces or paramilitary forces or intelligence agency of another country, a non-state armed group, or an international organization.

The SIPRI Arms Transfers Database only includes 'major arms', which are defined as (*a*) most aircraft, including uncrewed aerial vehicles; (*b*) air defence missile systems and larger air defence guns; (*c*) air refuelling systems; (*d*) most armoured vehicles; (*e*) artillery over 100 millimetres in calibre; (*f*) engines for combat-capable aircraft and other larger aircraft, for combat ships and larger amphibious and support ships, and for most types of armoured vehicles; (*g*) guided missiles, torpedoes, and most types of guided bombs and shells; (*h*) larger sensors (radars, sonars and many passive electronic sensors); (*i*) most ships; (*j*) larger ship-borne weapons (naval guns, missile launch systems and anti-submarine weapons); (*k*) reconnaissance satellites; and (*l*) most gun or missile-armed turrets for armoured vehicles.

In cases where an air refuelling system, engine, sensor, naval gun or other ship-borne system, or turret (items c, f, h, j and l) is fitted on a platform (vehicle, aircraft or ship), the transfer only appears as a separate entry in the database if the item comes from a different supplier from that of the platform.

The SIPRI trend-indicator value

SIPRI has developed a unique system for measuring the volume of transfers of major arms using a common unit, the trend-indicator value (TIV). The TIV is intended to represent the transfer of military resources. Each weapon has its own specific TIV but similar systems have similar TIVs. Second-hand arms, and second-hand but significantly modernized arms, are given a reduced TIV. SIPRI calculates the volume of transfers by multiplying the weapon-specific TIV with the number of arms delivered in a given year. SIPRI TIV figures do not represent the financial values of arms transfers.

Source: SIPRI, 'Sources and methods', SIPRI Arms Transfers Database.

Discussions on a new order for 48 Typhoons had been going on at least since 2008 and seemed to be at an advanced stage in 2020.[4] However, by the end of 2022 there had been no further public discussion about the proposed order. France, meanwhile, has succeeded in gaining large orders for Rafale combat aircraft against competing designs (including the Typhoon) from other supplying states that had previously been more successful (see section II).

[4] BAE Systems, *Half-yearly Report 2020*, 30 July 2020, p. 32.

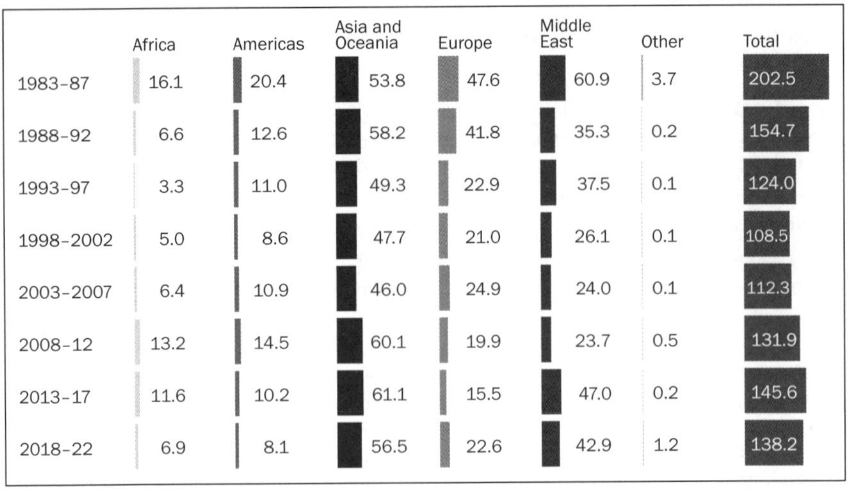

	Africa	Americas	Asia and Oceania	Europe	Middle East	Other	Total
1983–87	16.1	20.4	53.8	47.6	60.9	3.7	202.5
1988–92	6.6	12.6	58.2	41.8	35.3	0.2	154.7
1993–97	3.3	11.0	49.3	22.9	37.5	0.1	124.0
1998–2002	5.0	8.6	47.7	21.0	26.1	0.1	108.5
2003–2007	6.4	10.9	46.0	24.9	24.0	0.1	112.3
2008–12	13.2	14.5	60.1	19.9	23.7	0.5	131.9
2013–17	11.6	10.2	61.1	15.5	47.0	0.2	145.6
2018–22	6.9	8.1	56.5	22.6	42.9	1.2	138.2

Figure 6.2. The trend in international transfers of major arms, imports by region, 1983–2022

Note: Figures are billions of SIPRI trend-indicator values (TIVs). See box 6.1 for an explanation of TIVs.

Source: SIPRI Arms Transfers Database, Mar. 2023.

Key developments in 2022 related to arms transfers

Supply chain disruptions

By 2022 the worst impacts of the Covid-19 pandemic that started in early 2020 were largely over. During the pandemic, several exporters, importers and producers reported delays in some arms programmes, as supply chains were disrupted, deliveries were rescheduled due to travel restrictions, or funding priorities changed. However, the data on transfers of major arms from 2020 onwards shows that the pandemic and the resulting global economic downturn had only marginal direct and indirect effects on production, deliveries and orders for major arms.[5]

The main problems encountered seemed to be in supply chains and the most enduring effect will likely be an awareness of the importance of reliable supply chains, all the way down to minor components and raw materials. This may lead states to rethink their dependence on foreign suppliers for major arms and to increase efforts to strengthen their national industrial

---

[5] See also Wezeman, S. T., Kuimova, A. and Wezeman, P. D., 'International arms transfers and developments in arms production', *SIPRI Yearbook 2021*; and Wezeman, S. T., Kuimova, A. and Wezeman, P. D., 'International arms transfers', *SIPRI Yearbook 2022*.

base for arms production.[6] Many of the larger arms-importing states were already moving towards more local production and design, and the pandemic is likely to accelerate this trend.[7] Moreover, the sudden pressure on arms production capabilities and supply chains due to the war in Ukraine in 2022 will likely have led to further efforts to reduce dependence on foreign suppliers.[8] These factors seem to suggest that acquisition of major arms from national production (in the form of indigenous designs or designs resulting from cooperation between several states that are long-standing allies) will become increasingly important. In turn, this may result in fewer major arms imports by more developed states.

How the war in Ukraine is affecting military technology choices

The full-scale, high-intensity war in Ukraine that began with Russia's invasion in February 2022 has already started to have a major impact on global arms transfers. Aside from the significant supplies to Ukraine, it also has dramatically increased tensions in Europe resulting in increased acquisitions of major arms by many states in the region (see below). Moreover, the war has also divided world opinion, with ramifications in other parts of the world.[9] Many states will be drawing lessons from full-scale warfare between two large and modern armed forces, including evaluations of the performance of specific weapons and technologies.[10] Together, the increased tensions, the global political schism and the technical lessons from the war in Ukraine are likely to have a profound impact on arms transfers in the near future.

In the first months of the war, Russia lost large numbers of tanks from short-range, light, cheap and easy-to-use anti-tank weapons employed by Ukraine, including thousands supplied by Western states as aid and integrated within weeks in the Ukraine forces.[11] Ukraine also used armed uncrewed aerial vehicles (UAVs), supplied by Türkiye before and during the war, with great

---

[6] For examples of such rethinking see Lopez, C. T., 'DOD addresses supply chain resiliency with Lone Star State industry', US Department of Defense (DOD) News, 22 June 2022; Wirth, A. J. et al., 'Keeping the defense industrial base afloat during COVID-19', RAND Corporation Research Report no. RR-A1392-1, 2021; and Australian Industry Group, 'Defence industry development: Australian defence industry policy post COVID-19', Aug. 2020.

[7] For examples in Asia and Oceania see Béraud-Sudreau, L. et al., *Arms-production Capabilities in the Indo-Pacific Region: Measuring Self-reliance* (SIPRI: Stockholm, Oct. 2022).

[8] European Defence Agency (EDA), 'EDA study analyses defence industrial strategies', EDA News, 11 Oct. 2022; and European Commission, High Representative of the Union for Foreign Affairs and Security Policy, 'Defence investment gaps and measures to address them', Joint Communication to the European Parliament, the European Council and others, JOIN(2022) 24 final, 23 May 2022.

[9] On the global divisions over the war in Ukraine, see chapter 1, section V, in this volume.

[10] 'What weapons are significant for current and future warfare? Lesson learned from recent conflicts', Panel session at SIPRI Stockholm Security Conference, 8 Nov. 2022, YouTube, 12 Dec. 2022; Venckunas, V., 'Eight lessons air forces are learning from the war in Ukraine', AeroTime, 8 Jan. 2023; and Philip, S. A., 'How "graveyard" of Russian tanks in Ukraine is upending armour doctrines worldwide & for India', *The Print*, 30 Oct. 2022.

[11] Cranny-Evans, S., 'How anti-tank weapons shaped the early phase of the Ukraine war', Army Technology, 17 June 2022.

effect in the first months, while crewed combat aircraft used by both sides have been rather less effective throughout 2022.[12] There was widespread use of artillery, which was most effective when using guided rockets and shells, and in combination with advanced fire controls, while air defence systems supplied by the West proved themselves capable of defending Ukraine against most Russian missiles and aircraft.[13] Due to the rapidly changing battlefield dynamics, however, it is difficult to learn lessons from the war on exactly which types of major arms are likely to be most useful in future warfare. This lack of clarity is reflected in the diversity of arms acquisitions announced in 2022 in Ukraine and elsewhere. Armed UAVs that had already shown their use in other recent wars, such as the 44-day Azerbaijan–Armenia War in 2020 over the Nagorno-Karabakh region, were much in demand by many states, as were smart munitions for artillery and aircraft.[14] Japan even announced in late 2022 that it will replace all of its combat and observation helicopters with uncrewed systems.[15] Other states, however, remained confident about combat helicopters, with Poland, for example, ordering up to 96 combat helicopters and Australia 29 from the USA in late 2022. And despite the seemingly poor showing of tanks in the war in Ukraine, there was renewed interest in them in Europe, most notably in the large Polish order in 2022 for almost 1300 tanks, the largest European order for tanks since the 1980s, and the supply of hundreds of tanks to Ukraine (see below).

Conventional weapons and nuclear weapons

The spectre of the use of nuclear weapons has become more of a concern as several states, most recently Russia in 2022, have threatened or hinted such weapons could be used.[16] Several conventional arms acquisition orders and decisions in recent years have links to nuclear weapons as potential dual-capable delivery systems or as a nuclear weapon proliferation concern. Germany, for example, ordered 35 F-35 combat aircraft from the USA in late 2022, following orders for the same aircraft by Italy (2006), the Netherlands (2008) and Belgium (2018). In each of the four states, one of the roles of the F-35 combat aircraft will be to function as delivery systems for US tactical nuclear bombs stored in the state, replacing existing aircraft that perform

---

[12] Gordon, C., 'Russian Air Force "has lot of capability left" one year on from Ukraine invasion', *Air and Space Forces Magazine*, 15 Feb. 2023; Peck, M., 'Ukraine war proves big guns are back', *National Defense*, 16 Sep. 2022; and Chapple, A., 'The drones of the Ukraine war', RFE/RL, 17 Nov. 2022.

[13] Szondy, D., 'Invasion of Ukraine shows artillery still rules the battlefield', *New Atlas*, 20 Nov. 2022; and Garamone, J., 'US, allies work to supply Ukraine air defense needs', US Department of Defense News, 29 Nov. 2022.

[14] Shabazov, F., 'Tactical reasons behind military breakthrough in Karabakh conflict', *Eurasia Daily Monitor*, vol. 17, no. 155 (3 Nov. 2020).

[15] Yeo, M., 'Japan to replace attack, observation helicopters with drone fleet', *Defense News*, 9 Feb. 2023.

[16] On Russian nuclear doctrine in 2022 see chapter 1, section V, and chapter 7, section II, in this volume.

this task.[17] In 2022 Russia delivered a small number of Iskander-M surface-to-surface missiles (with a range of 500 kilometres) to Belarus. Announcing the deal in June 2022, President Vladimir Putin specifically mentioned that the missiles were nuclear-capable.[18] As at the end of 2022, there was growing speculation that Russia might instigate a nuclear 'sharing' arrangement with Belarus, with the nuclear warheads to be placed in Belarus but remaining under Russian control—the first such arrangement for Russia, which Putin later confirmed.[19]

As part of a new trilateral security partnership between Australia, the UK and the USA (called AUKUS) created in 2021, which is widely seen as a counter to China in the Indo-Pacific region, the USA and the UK will supply Australia with up to eight nuclear-powered submarines. The selection of specific designs and decisions about orders are expected in 2023, although delivery of the submarines is not expected to start before at least the 2030s.[20] The submarines are likely to use highly enriched uranium (HEU) in their nuclear reactors, following the practice for reactors in British and US submarines. HEU can be used in nuclear weapon programmes and these would be the first transfers of HEU reactors and their fuel to full control by a non-nuclear weapon state.[21] Australia has said that, as a signatory to the 1968 Treaty on the Non-Proliferation of Nuclear Weapons, which includes strict safeguards to prevent diversion of HEU, it will neither seek nuclear weapons nor produce the HEU or process it after use.[22] However, concerns remain that other states might use the Australian case as a precedent for acquiring their own nuclear-powered submarines with an unsafeguarded HEU fuel capability, which may then be used for a nuclear weapon programme. AUKUS would be less of a

---

[17] On the US nuclear 'sharing' role in Europe see chapter 7, section I, in this volume.

[18] At the same time, Putin also announced that Russia will modify Belarusian combat aircraft to be able to carry tactical nuclear weapons. Adamowski, J., 'Russia to provide nuclear-capable missiles and fighter jets to Belarus', *Defense News*, 27 June 2022; and 'Russia to send Belarus nuclear-capable missiles', Deutsche Welle, 26 June 2022.

[19] Drennan, J., 'Possible Russian nuclear deployments to Belarus could shift Europe's nuclear balance', US Institute of Peace, 30 June 2022; 'Russia gave Belarus Iskander system that can carry nuclear weapons, Putin says', TASS, 25 Mar. 2023; and 'Putin says Moscow to place nuclear weapons in Belarus, US reacts cautiously', Euractiv.com, 26 Mar. 2023.

[20] Liptak, K., Atwood, K. and Liebermann, O., 'US is expected to sell Australia at least 4 nuclear-powered submarines', CNN, 8 Mar. 2023.

[21] Kuperman, A. J., 'Fixing a fatal, nuclear flaw in AUKUS', *Breaking Defense*, 7 Mar. 2023. This will not be the first transfer of a nuclear submarine using HEU: In 1988 the Soviet Union delivered one to India, which was at the time not yet in possession of nuclear weapons. However, this was on a time-limited lease. In 2012 Russia delivered a replacement and this will itself be replaced in 2025, in both cases also on lease. Unlike Australia, India is not a party to the Treaty on the Non-Proliferation of Nuclear Weapons (Non-Proliferation Treaty, NPT). For a summary and other details of the NPT see annex A, section I, in this volume.

[22] Wong, P., Australian Minister of Foreign Affairs, 'AUKUS won't undermine Australia's stance against nuclear weapons', *The Guardian*, 23 Jan. 2023. See also Wezeman et al., *SIPRI Yearbook 2022* (note 5), p. 301.

precedent according to some experts if Australia were to instead use low-enriched uranium (LEU) in the submarines.[23]

Conflicts, tensions and arms transfers

Active armed conflicts and increasing tensions between states are arguably the main drivers of arms acquisitions by states. At least 5 of the top 10 importers of major arms in 2018–22 (Egypt, India, Pakistan, Saudi Arabia and the USA) were engaged in armed conflicts in 2022.[24] In some cases the conflicts were within their own state (e.g. Egyptian and Indian state forces against internal non-state armed groups), some were interstate (e.g. Indian state forces against Pakistani state forces), while others were external interventions in support of other states against non-state armed groups (e.g. Saudi Arabia in Yemen, and the USA in Somalia). All these conflicts involved the use of major arms and, except for those used by the USA, most of these arms were imported. Three other members of the top 10—China, Japan and the Republic of Korea (South Korea)—while not engaged in armed conflict, were nonetheless embroiled in interstate tensions in 2022. In those cases, major arms were used as a show of force to indicate resolve: by China in the South China Sea and on its disputed border with India; by Japan and China in the East China Sea; and by Japan and South Korea against the Democratic People's Republic of Korea (DPRK, or North Korea).

The linkages between arms acquisition and conflict or tensions with other states are also visible in many of the other 157 states identified by SIPRI as recipients of major arms in 2018–22. However, it is also clear that there is not necessarily a direct correlation between the level of imports of major arms and the level of conflict or tension. For example, sub-Saharan Africa had numerous armed conflicts, and internal and bilateral tensions in 2018–22, as well as other security concerns, but no state in sub-Saharan Africa was among the top 40 importers in that period. Collectively, arms imports by sub-Saharan Africa states were significantly lower in 2018–22 than in previous years. Arms imports by Ethiopia in 2018–22, for example, were 51 per cent lower than in 2013–17 and the country was the 75th largest arms importer globally—despite

---

[23] Kuperman, A. J., 'Fixing a fatal, nuclear flaw in AUKUS', *Breaking Defense*, 7 Mar. 2023; Kuperman, A. J., Interview with H. Lemahieu, Lyndon B. Johnson School of Public Affairs, Texas, 14 Mar. 2022; Pabelliña, K. M., 'The gamble of AUKUS: Eroding the rules of nuclear non-proliferation?', Asia-Pacific Leadership Network (APLN) Policy Brief no. 84, Sep. 2022; Supriyanto, R. A., 'AUKUS and Southeast Asia's non-proliferation concerns', BASIC, 5 July 2022; Center for Arms Control and Non-Proliferation, 'Uranium enrichment: For peace or for weapons', Fact Sheet, 26 Aug. 2021; and Rauf, T., 'Driving nuclear submarines through IAEA safeguards', InDepthNews, 25 Nov. 2021. See also Wezeman et al., *SIPRI Yearbook 2022* (note 5), p. 301.

[24] For a list of all the states or territories involved in armed conflict in 2022, see chapter 2, table 2.8, in this volume.

the 2020–22 war in Ethiopia causing some of the highest casualty rates in the world during those years.[25]

Generally, the major arms imported by states in sub-Saharan Africa have involved relatively small quantities of older or relatively unsophisticated designs, with a low economic or military value. However, these arms are essential for the military operations of states, for example in fighting non-state armed groups. For instance, both Nigeria and Uganda imported only small numbers of combat aircraft and combat helicopters in recent years but, according to their air forces, those imported arms were instrumental in winning their wars against rebel forces.[26] In another case, limited supplies of major arms played an important role in supporting peacekeeping operations in Africa.[27] The five countries that contributed troops to the African Union Transition Mission in Somalia (ATMIS) in 2022—Burundi, Djibouti, Ethiopia, Kenya and Uganda—together accounted for 0.4 per cent of global arms imports in 2018–22. However, some of the major arms they received, in particular 80 light armoured vehicles specifically supplied for ATMIS, were important to sustaining their role in ATMIS.

In other cases, there are concerns about the misuse of major arms supplied to militaries, even when supplied in small volumes, such as those used in military coups or abuses of international humanitarian law and human rights.[28] A military coup in Burkina Faso in 2021 led the USA in 2022 to reassess and then halt its military assistance to the country; the withdrawn assistance was the finance of the supply of light armoured vehicles from South Africa to Burkina Faso for delivery in 2021–22.[29] In 2022 France reportedly halted the supply of four light armoured vehicles to Gabon because of the risk that they could be used in potential violence by the military during the planned Gabonese presidential election in 2023.[30]

The relationship between arms transfers and conflicts or tensions is further highlighted by the pattern of transfers to the other regions of the world (see section III). The only region relatively free from major interstate tensions, and where the three armed conflicts in 2022 were mainly centred

---

[25] On the armed conflict in Ethiopia see chapter 2, sections I and II, in this volume; and Davis, I., 'Armed conflict and peace processes in East Africa', *SIPRI Yearbook 2022*, pp. 225–29.

[26] Martin, G., 'Nigerian Air Force confirms additional air assets are on the way', defenceWeb, 27 Mar. 2023; and 'Russian attack helicopters turned the tide against the LRA: UPDF', defenceWeb, 28 Mar. 2023.

[27] 'ATMIS 24 APCs better off', defenceWeb, 8 Aug. 2022.

[28] See e.g. Maletta, G. and Héau, L., 'Funding arms transfers through the European peace facility: Preventing risks of diversion and misuse', SIPRI Commentary, June 2022, pp. 14–15.

[29] Savell, S., 'US security assistance to Burkina Faso laid the groundwork for a coup', *Foreign Policy*, 3 Feb. 2022; Mohammed, A. and Pamuk, H., 'US halts nearly $160 million aid to Burkina Faso after finding military coup occurred', Reuters, 19 Feb. 2022; and Arieff, A., 'Burkina Faso: Conflict and military rule', Congressional Research Service In Focus no. IF10434, 17 Oct. 2022.

[30] 'Paris refuse de livrer des blindés à la Garde républicaine du Gabon' [Paris refuses to deliver tanks to the Republican Guard of Gabon], Gabonactu.com, 3 Oct. 2022.

on gang-related violence, is South America, where SIPRI data shows a significant decrease in arms imports by states in recent years.

Arms-exporting states are often direct or indirect participants in the conflicts or tensions affecting the states to which they supply major arms. This partly explains why some arms exporters are willing to supply arms (sometimes as military aid) even when the supply seems to contradict the exporter's stated arms export policies (see section II for several examples).

The war in Ukraine as a driver of arms transfers in 2022

Ukraine imported very few major arms in the period from its independence in 1991 until the end of 2021. This changed after the Russian invasion of Ukraine in February 2022, as the USA, Canada, Australia and at least 23 European states began to send large quantities of military aid to Ukraine.[31] As a result, it became the third largest importer of major arms in 2022, after Qatar and India, accounting for 8.3 per cent of total global arms imports. In the five-year period 2018–22, Ukraine accounted for 2.0 per cent of total global arms imports and was the 14th largest importer. Of the 29 states that supplied major arms to Ukraine in 2022, the main suppliers were the USA, which accounted for 35 per cent of total Ukrainian arms imports during the year, Poland (17 per cent), Germany (11 per cent), the UK (10 per cent) and Czechia (4.4 per cent). Many of the arms supplied in 2022 were second-hand items from existing stocks, including 228 artillery pieces and an estimated 5000 guided artillery rockets from the USA, 280 tanks from Poland and over 7000 anti-tank missiles from the UK. Some newly produced arms were also supplied, such as air defence systems from Germany, Poland, the UK and the USA.

In many cases, the supply of arms by one state was financed by other states or by the European Union (EU) through the European Peace Facility. For example, by the end of 2022, the EU had made €3.1 billion (US$3.2 billion) available to pay for military equipment that EU member states supplied to Ukraine.[32] In other cases, states cooperated to pay for weapons supplied by third countries. For example, the Netherlands and the USA paid for 90 tanks originating from Morocco to be delivered to Ukraine after upgrades by a company in Czechia.[33] Within the North Atlantic Treaty Organization (NATO), member states also supplied NATO-standard weapons to other

---

[31] On military assistance to Ukraine in 2022 see also chapter 1, section V; chapter 5, section II; and chapter 12, section V, in this volume.

[32] Council of the European Union, 'Ukraine: Council agrees on further support under the European Peace Facility', Press release, 17 Oct. 2022; and Bilquin, B., 'European Peace Facility: Ukraine and beyond', European Parliamentary Research Service, At a Glance no. PE738.221, Nov. 2022. On the European Peace Facility see also chapter 5, section II, and chapter 12, section V, in this volume.

[33] Vergun, D., 'Aid package to Ukraine includes T-72B tanks', US Department of Defense News, 4 Nov. 2022; and 'Le Maroc offre ses chars à l'Ukraine' [Morocco offers its tanks to Ukraine], MENA Defense, 22 Jan. 2023.

member states, which in turn supplied their older Soviet-standard weapons to Ukraine. These weapons could usually be more easily absorbed by the Ukrainian armed forces since they were similar to existing Ukrainian stocks. For example, Germany supplied NATO-standard Leopard-2 tanks to Czechia after the latter had given other major arms to Ukraine.[34]

Ukraine did not receive all the types of arms it asked its supporters to provide and, at different stages during 2022, there were different views among states about what should be supplied. For example, while Poland and Czechia delivered tanks to Ukraine in the first half of 2022, Germany, the UK and the USA only indicated their willingness to do so in late 2022, for delivery in 2023.[35] Other states that supplied weapons remained opposed to supplying tanks. For example, Italy maintained throughout 2022 that it would not supply tanks or other 'offensive' weapons.[36] Despite a growing willingness among states to send a wider variety of arms to Ukraine, at the end of 2022 suppliers were still not prepared to deliver arms with a long-range strike capability, such as combat aircraft and long-range land-attack missiles.

Since April 2022 many of the Western supplies of military assistance to Ukraine have been coordinated through the USA-led Ukraine Defense Contact Group.[37] Nonetheless, government motives—often expressed in short statements without in-depth explanations—for delaying the supply of weapons or not supplying certain types of weapons, have continued to vary. The motives included assessments of what equipment would fit best to the Ukrainian military's capability, for fast absorption and effective use; a reluctance to deplete national arsenals; caution about the risk that certain weapons could be used by Ukraine to attack Russian territory; and concerns that the supply of certain weapons could lead to a direct confrontation with Russia. For example, the USA refused to supply ATACMS ballistic missiles with a range of 300 km as requested by Ukraine, with the main reported reasons being that it would be too aggressive a move and that it would deplete US missile stockpiles.[38] Similarly, the German government throughout 2022 refused to supply tanks (or to authorize other states to re-export

---

[34] Zimmermann, V. N., 'Die Tschechische Republik erhält aus Deutschland 14 Leopard-Panzer' [The Czech Republic receives 14 Leopard tanks from Germany], *Frankfurter Allgemeine*, 29 Aug. 2022.

[35] Sabbage, D. and Harding, L., 'Ukraine confident UK will send Challenger 2 tanks to help war effort', *The Guardian*, 13 Jan. 2023; and Debusmann Jr, B., Wright, G. and Radford, A., 'Germany confirms it will provide Ukraine with Leopard 2 tanks', BBC News, 25 Jan. 2023.

[36] 'Italy will not be sending "offensive weapons" to Ukraine', Technology Org, 30 Jan. 2023.

[37] Ismay, J., 'A new US-led international group will meet monthly to focus on aiding Ukraine', *New York Times*, 26 Apr. 2022; and US Department of State, 'Special online briefing with Ambassador Julianne Smith, US permanent representative to NATO', Special Briefing, 13 Feb. 2023.

[38] Kube, C. and De Luce, D., 'US military leaders are reluctant to provide longer-range missiles to Ukraine', NBC News, 16 Sep. 2022; Gordon, M. R. and Lubold, G., 'US altered Himars rocket launchers to keep Ukraine from firing missiles into Russia', *Wall Street Journal*, 5 Dec. 2022; and McLeary, P., Seligman, L. and Ward, A., 'US tells Ukraine it won't send long-range missiles because it has few to spare', Politico, 13 Feb. 2023.

German-made tanks from their arsenals) on the grounds that such a move might escalate the war or could draw Germany directly into the war, and that Ukraine did not yet have the capability to deploy the tanks.[39] However, after months of pressure from allied capitals, Germany confirmed in early January 2023 that it would supply 14 Leopard-2A6 tanks to Ukraine, and gave other states permission to also supply tanks of German origin.[40]

The arms supplied to Ukraine in 2022 were vital for the Ukrainian effort to halt the Russian offensive in February and March; continued to play a major role in Ukraine's defence and counter-offensives against Russia throughout the rest of 2022; and are a necessity for its future survival. Russia, in contrast, relied almost exclusively on domestically produced arms—although from around August 2022 it did import UAVs and many hundreds of flying bombs from Iran. While Iran acknowledged a small number of supplies of such arms to Russia before 2022, it has denied any arms supplies since the start of the war, despite overwhelming evidence to the contrary.[41]

As the war progressed in 2022, artillery gained in importance for both sides.[42] In 2022 many states supplied Ukraine with a total of 532 guns with a calibre of 105 millimetres or more, as well as 55 multiple-rocket launchers, and promised more for delivery in 2023. In addition, the war also emphasized the importance of ammunition for artillery and lighter weapons.[43] Such ammunition has seen very intensive use, to the extent that both sides have reportedly started to run out of stocks and Ukrainian use also outstripped new production of its suppliers.[44] A constant supply of ammunition formed

---

[39] Metzger, N., 'Warum Deutschland keine Leopard 2 liefert' [Why Germany does not deliver Leopard 2s], ZDF Heute, 19 Oct. 2022.

[40] 'Deutschland liefert Leopard-Panzer an Ukraine' [Germany supplies Leopard tanks to Ukraine], ZDFheute, 24 Jan. 2023; Debusmann et al. (note 35); and Oltermann, P. and Roth, A., 'Germany announces it will supply Leopard 2 tanks to Ukraine', *The Guardian*, 25 Jan. 2023.

[41] The flying bombs are often referred to as 'suicide drones' or 'loitering munitions' but are essentially slow, simple, one-way micro aircraft with a pre-set flight path and target. 'Iran says it shipped drones to Russia before Ukraine war', Reuters, 5 Nov. 2022; and 'Ukraine war: US says Iranian drones breach sanctions', BBC News, 18 Oct. 2022. The import of the UAVs and the flying bombs is banned under UN Security Council Resolution 2231, which placed an embargo on imports from Iran of UAVs and missiles with a range of 300 km or more without specific prior approval by the Security Council. See UN Security Council Resolution 2231, 20 July 2015. On the embargo under Resolution 2231 see chapter 12, section II, in this volume.

[42] Peck (note 12); 'US Army chiefs stress importance of artillery as key lesson of Ukraine war', *Military Watch Magazine*, 14 May 2022; and Cancian, M. F. and Anderson, J., 'Expanding equipment options for Ukraine: The case of artillery', Center for Strategic and International Studies, 23 Jan. 2023.

[43] These types of ammunition are largely not included in the SIPRI data on major arms. This is partly because transparency in ammunition transfers is very low; e.g. they are not included in various multilateral arms transparency mechanisms. They are included here to underline that transfers of ammunition can have a major impact. For the definition of 'major arms' see box 6.1; and on transparency mechanisms see chapter 10, section IV, in this volume.

[44] Rettman, A., 'EU figures show intensity of Russia–Ukraine artillery war', EUobserver, 16 Mar. 2023; Zalan, E., 'EU leaders agree 1m artillery shells for Ukraine', EUobserver, 23 Mar. 2023; Kube, C., 'Russia and Ukraine are firing 24,000 or more artillery rounds a day', NBC News, 11 Nov. 2022; 'Ukraine updates: NATO warns of donor ammunition shortages', Deutsche Welle, 13 Feb. 2023; and Baily, R. et al., 'Russian offensive campaign assessment, December 31', Institute for the Study of War, 31 Dec. 2022.

a significant part of the military aid provided to Ukraine. The USA alone had by the end of 2022 committed to sending Ukraine over 1.5 million artillery shells and artillery rockets, and over 100 million rounds of small arms ammunition.[45]

Russia was also apparently running low on missiles and other ammunition, and the USA and allies at various times in 2022 alleged that Russia was importing artillery shells from North Korea and that it was trying to acquire ballistic ground-to-ground missiles from Iran.[46] North Korea denied any such supplies or plans, while Iran gave conflicting information about the missiles.[47] By the end of 2022 there was no clear evidence of North Korean supplies reaching Russia, whereas the Iranian ballistic missile option seemed thwarted by US and European warnings to Iran of the consequences if it did supply the missiles. In addition, Russia may have been deterred from importing the Iranian missiles on the grounds that it would likely open the door for long-range US missiles to be supplied to Ukraine.[48]

Arms imports and naval build-up in the eastern Mediterranean

Amid ongoing maritime disputes in the eastern Mediterranean, states in the region continued to increase their naval capabilities in 2018–22, with the help of supplies of major arms by other states.[49] In 2018–22 Egypt received four submarines and the first of four frigates on order from Germany, two of three frigates on order from France, and two frigates from Italy. Israel received the first two of four frigates on order from Germany and placed an order for three submarines, in addition to one planned for delivery in 2023.

Greece ordered three frigates and six Rafale combat aircraft, including for use in an anti-ship role, from France in 2022, after it had ordered 18 Rafales in 2021. These deals were closely linked to a 2021 mutual defence agreement between Greece and France. France stressed that the agreement was not directed against Türkiye, but that it aimed to strengthen European sovereignty, including in the eastern Mediterranean, where France and Greece

---

[45] US DOD, 'Fact sheet on US security assistance to Ukraine', Press release, 21 Dec. 2022.
[46] US Department of State, 'Department press briefing—November 1, 2022', Press briefing, 1 Nov. 2022; and Nicholls, M., 'Russia trying to get ballistic missiles from Iran, says Britain', Reuters, 10 Dec. 2022. On Resolution 2231, which bans imports from Iran of missiles with a range of 300 km or more without specific prior approval by the UN Security Council, see note 41 and chapter 12, section II, in this volume.
[47] 'Iran agrees to ship missiles, more drones to Russia', Reuters, 19 Oct. 2022; and 'Iran denies plan to send missiles to Russia for Ukraine war', Defense Post, 21 Oct. 2022.
[48] Rathbone, J. P. et al., 'Russia and Iran hesitate over co-operation as West warns of costs', *Financial Times*, 6 Mar. 2023; Nicholls (note 46); and 'Ukraine warns of threat from Belarus, US says Iran helped Russia operate drones from Crimea', France 24, 20 Oct. 2022. Any such missiles supplied to Russia would also still be against the UN sanctions on Iran. For more on the UN embargo see chapter 12, section II, in this volume.
[49] On tensions in the eastern Mediterranean see Davis, I., 'Key general developments in the region', *SIPRI Yearbook 2022*, pp. 147–48.

Table 6.1. Selected major arms on order or chosen for future orders from the 10 largest arms suppliers, for delivery after 2022

Figures are units of major arms.

Supplier	Combat aircraft[a]	Helicopters[b]	Major surface warships[c]	Submarines	SAM systems[d]	Tanks	Other armoured vehicles	Artillery
USA	1 371	496	5	–	40	634	2 658	401
Russia	84	..	4	1	13	444	55	–
France	210	252	16	5	6	–	552	176
China	94	–	13	9	1	717	–	128
Germany	–	–	11	18	25	85	1 389	137
Italy	115	195	9	–	1	–	1 703	–
UK	20	1	26	–	–	14	2	30
Spain	–	–	2	–	–	..	608	10
South Korea	136	–	3	3	..	990	23	1 232
Israel	18	–	–	–	26	19	69	87

.. = data not available; – = no orders; SAM = surface-to-air missile.

[a] Combat aircraft here include combat helicopters, combat/trainer aircraft and anti-submarine warfare aircraft.
[b] Excluding light helicopters.
[c] Major warships here include aircraft carriers, corvettes, destroyers and frigates.
[d] SAM systems here include only land-based systems and exclude systems for portable/very short-range SAMs.

Source: SIPRI Arms Transfers Database, Mar. 2023.

have crucial interests. Türkiye said the arms deals and the defence agreement threatened regional peace and stability.[50]

Türkiye is able to produce most types of warships, but it remains dependent on imports for certain naval assets such as submarines and helicopters, as well as key components for ships such as engines. However, deteriorating relationships with some of its long-term arms suppliers, mainly with the USA, have jeopardized Türkiye's access to military naval technology.[51] Within the EU there was some debate in 2020 about the possibility of imposing arms export restrictions on Türkiye. Germany, in particular, opposed such restrictions.[52] In 2022 work continued on six submarines ordered by Türkiye from Germany in 2011 for delivery in 2023–27. Türkiye also has an amphibious assault ship on order from Spain for delivery in 2023. Türkiye had planned to equip the ship with F-35B combat aircraft from the USA. However, as part of

---

[50] 'Greek parliament approves defence pact with France', Reuters, 7 Oct. 2021; and 'Greece approves arms deal with France amid Turkey tensions', *Daily Sabah*, 15 Feb. 2022.
[51] Işık, Y., 'CAATSA sanctions are hurting Turkey's military readiness at a time when NATO can't afford it', Middle East Institute, 6 May 2021; and Özberk, T., 'Turkey develops sanction-busting systems to secure naval helicopters', Shephard, 6 Feb. 2023.
[52] Wezeman, P. D., 'Multilateral arms embargoes', *SIPRI Yearbook 2021*, p. 575.

strained relations between the two states, the USA cancelled a planned deal for such aircraft (see section II).[53] Instead, the ship will now be equipped with armed UAVs produced by Türkiye, to become the first aircraft carrier with an uncrewed air strike force.[54]

Cyprus, which has overlapping maritime claims with other states in the eastern Mediterranean, remains a very minor importer of major arms: in 2018–22 it was the 95th largest globally. It did not acquire any warships or combat aircraft, nor has it announced plans for them, but it did import a limited number of anti-ship missiles from France to double the range of its coastal defence systems to around 180 km.[55]

Estimates of future arms transfers based on known orders

While many states have recently placed orders for major arms or plan to make such orders soon, publicly available information remains limited in most cases. It is extremely difficult, therefore, to provide even rudimentary predictions of global trends in arms acquisitions, no matter whether these are near- or long-term forecasts. Nonetheless, there are indications—especially the perception among many states that security threats are increasing (which acts as a driver of arms transfers) and the continued growth in military spending (which acts as an enabler)—that there will be more, rather than less, demand for major arms in the coming years.[56] Much of this demand will be met by arms imports, as many states are still unable to produce domestically all the major arms they believe they need.

While it is difficult to make predictions about future trends in arms transfers, data on orders can give a rough indication of which states will be among the largest exporters in coming years. The data on combat aircraft and major warships, which have a high military value, is particularly telling. The USA will almost certainly continue to be, by far, the largest exporter of major arms beyond 2022 (see table 6.1), especially as it will supply around 60 per cent of all combat aircraft currently on order. Russia, which was the second largest arms exporter in the world in 2018–22, has a relatively low number of pending deliveries.

---

[53] 'Türkiye'nin ilk milli uçak gemisi görüntülendi' [Türkiye's first national aircraft carrier displayed], TRT Haber, 24 Mar. 2018.

[54] Suorsa, O. P. and Cannon, B. J., 'Turkey's future drone carriers', War on the Rocks, 20 Nov. 2022.

[55] Hazou, E., 'Cyprus said to be close to selecting new defensive weapons systems', *Cyprus Mail*, 27 Jan. 2022.

[56] On military spending trends see chapter 5 in this volume.

II. Developments among the suppliers of major arms, 2018–22

SIEMON T. WEZEMAN AND PIETER D. WEZEMAN

SIPRI has identified 63 states as exporters of major arms in 2018–22. The five largest exporters of arms during that period—the United States, Russia, France, China and Germany—accounted for over three-quarters (76 per cent) of all arms exports (see table 6.2). US and French arms exports rose between 2013–17 and 2018–22, while Russian, Chinese and German arms exports fell. The top 25 arms exporters accounted for 98 per cent of the world's arms exports in 2018–22. States in North America and Europe together accounted for 87 per cent of all arms exports in the period. The five largest exporters in Western Europe—France, Germany, Italy, the United Kingdom and Spain—supplied around one-quarter (24 per cent) of total global arms exports in 2018–22.

The United States

The USA's arms exports grew by 14 per cent between 2013–17 and 2018–22 and its share of total global arms exports rose from 33 per cent to 40 per cent. The USA delivered major arms to 103 states in 2018–22, almost as many as the next two biggest exporters combined. Its total arms exports in 2018–22 were 148 per cent higher than those of Russia—the second largest exporter—compared with 50 per cent higher in 2013–17.

Exports to the Middle East accounted for 41 per cent of total US arms exports in 2018–22 (see table 6.3), down from 49 per cent in 2013–17. Partly on account of its policies aimed at containing Iranian influence, the USA exported large volumes of advanced major arms to states in the region.[1] Four Middle Eastern states were among the top 10 importers of US arms in 2018–22: Saudi Arabia accounted for 19 per cent of US arms exports, Qatar 6.7 per cent, Kuwait 4.8 per cent and the United Arab Emirates (UAE) 4.4 per cent.

States in Asia and Oceania received 32 per cent of total US arms exports in 2018–22, roughly the same proportion as in 2013–17 (33 per cent). Three major US allies in the region were among the 10 largest importers of US arms in 2018–22: Japan accounted for 8.6 per cent of total US arms exports, Australia 8.4 per cent and the Republic of Korea (South Korea) 6.5 per cent.

---

[1] Lopez, C. T., 'US, Gulf nations assess the same threats in the Middle East', US Department of Defense, 13 Feb. 2023. On US–Iranian tensions see Smith, D., 'Introduction: International stability and human security in 2020', *SIPRI Yearbook 2021*, pp. 11–12; Davis, I., 'Key general developments in the region', *SIPRI Yearbook 2021*, pp. 141–43; and Davis, I. and Fazil, S., 'Armed conflict and peace processes in Iraq, Syria and Turkey' and Davis, I., 'The Israeli–Palestinian conflict and peace process', *SIPRI Yearbook 2022*, pp. 158–59 and 160–61, respectively.

Taiwan was the 4th largest importer of US arms in 2013–17, but only the 19th largest in 2018–22. However, by the end of 2022 it had several large orders in place for major arms from the USA, including 66 combat aircraft. The USA has been providing military support to Taiwan since 1950 and in recent years this support has been growing in importance again with increased concerns (in both the USA and Taiwan) about the possibility of a Chinese invasion of Taiwan. In 2022 the US Congress passed the Taiwan Enhanced Resilience Act, which authorized the US government to provide Taiwan with up to US$2 billion a year in military aid and up to $2 billion in loans for military purchases from the USA through to 2027. However, if or when the grants and loans will be used remained undecided at the end of 2022.[2]

A total of 23 per cent of US arms exports went to states in Europe in 2018–22, up from 11 per cent in 2013–17. The rise in US arms exports to the region is because many European North Atlantic Treaty Organization (NATO) states started rearming due to growing tensions with Russia in 2022. Three of the USA's NATO partners in the region were among the 10 largest importers of US arms in 2018–22: the UK accounted for 4.6 per cent of US arms exports, the Netherlands 4.4 per cent and Norway 4.2 per cent. Particularly important among the arms delivered to these countries were 78 F-35 combat aircraft for all three (16 to the UK, 32 to the Netherlands and 30 to Norway) and 14 P-8A anti-submarine warfare (ASW) aircraft for Norway (5) and the UK (9). However, due to increasingly strained bilateral relations, the USA's arms exports to its NATO ally Türkiye were at a lower level in 2018–22, such that Türkiye dropped from being the 7th largest recipient of US arms in 2013–17 to the 27th largest in 2018–22. Of particular importance was the cancellation by the USA of a programme for up to 100 F-35 combat aircraft to Türkiye after the latter imported two Russian S-400 air defence systems in 2019.[3] In 2022 the US government considered the possibility of allowing Türkiye to acquire less advanced F-16 combat aircraft, reportedly on the grounds of maintaining NATO unity and capabilities, as well as US national security, economic and commercial interests. However, within Congress there were significant doubts about such a deal due to continuing political and economic relations between Türkiye and Russia, Türkiye stalling its support for Swedish and Finnish NATO accession, Turkish–Greek disputes and concerns about human rights.[4]

The volume of US exports of major arms to Ukraine increased sharply in 2022 (see section I). Nevertheless, as the supplies to Ukraine involved

[2] Lawrence, S. V. and Campbell, C., 'Taiwan: Political and security issues', Congressional Research Service (CRS) In Focus no. IF10275, 17 Feb. 2023.
[3] Jennings, G., 'US, Turkey continue to settle F-35 dispute', Janes, 24 Jan. 2023.
[4] Zanotti, J. and Thomas, C., 'Turkey (Türkiye): Possible US F-16 sale', Congressional Research Service (CRS) Insight no. IN2111, 16 Feb. 2023.

Table 6.2. The 25 largest exporters of major arms and their main recipients, 2018–22

Rank 2018–22	Rank 2013–17[a]	Exporter	Share of total global exports (%) 2013–17	Share of total global exports (%) 2018–22	Change in volume (%) from 2013–17 to 2018–22	Main recipients and their share of exporter's total exports (%), 2018–22						
1	1	USA	33	40	14	Saudi Arabia	19	Japan	8.6	Australia	8.4
2	2	Russia	22	16	-31	India	31	China	23	Egypt	9.3
3	3	France	7.1	11	44	India	30	Qatar	17	Egypt	8.0
4	4	China	6.3	5.2	-23	Pakistan	54	Bangladesh	12	Serbia	4.5
5	5	Germany	6.1	4.2	-35	Egypt	18	South Korea	17	Israel	9.5
6	9	Italy	2.5	3.8	45	Qatar	24	Egypt	23	Türkiye	12
7	6	UK	4.7	3.2	-35	USA	20	Qatar	16	Saudi Arabia	7.7
8	8	Spain	2.5	2.6	-4.4	Australia	35	Saudi Arabia	19	Belgium	12
9	12	South Korea	1.3	2.4	74	Philippines	16	India	13	Thailand	13
10	7	Israel	2.6	2.3	-15	India	37	Azerbaijan	9.1	Philippines	8.5
11	10	Netherlands	2.1	1.4	-39	USA	27	Mexico	11	Tunisia	7.4
12	15	Türkiye	0.6	1.1	69	Qatar	20	UAE	17	Oman	13
13	14	Sweden	0.9	0.8	-16	USA	25	Pakistan	24	Brazil	15
14	13	Switzerland	1.0	0.7	-34	Australia	21	Denmark	14	Spain	13
15	20	Australia	0.3	0.6	64	Canada	35	Chile	31	USA	13
16	17	Canada	0.6	0.5	-9.4	Saudi Arabia	49	UAE	22	USA	4.9
17	11	Ukraine	1.7	0.5	-70	China	48	Saudi Arabia	13	Thailand	7.5
18	19	UAE	0.4	0.4	-5.8	Egypt	28	Jordan	27	Algeria	15
19	30	Poland	0.1	0.4	168	Ukraine	95	Nepal	1.2	Ecuador	0.6
20	18	Belarus	0.5	0.3	-37	Serbia	33	Viet Nam	25	Uganda	14
21	22	South Africa	0.3	0.3	6.7	UAE	27	USA	21	India	15
22	16	Norway	0.6	0.3	-55	USA	27	Ukraine	15	Lithuania	14
23	24	Brazil	0.2	0.3	35	France	25	Nigeria	15	Chile	12
24	33	Belgium	0.1	0.2	212	Saudi Arabia	35	Canada	28	Pakistan	21
25	25	Jordan	0.2	0.2	14	USA	61	Egypt	26	Armenia	7.0

UAE = United Arab Emirates.

Notes: Percentages below 10 are rounded to one decimal place; percentages over 10 are rounded to whole numbers.

[a] The rank order for exporters in 2013–17 differs from that published in SIPRI Yearbook 2018 because of subsequent revision of figures for these years.

Source: SIPRI Arms Transfers Database, Mar. 2023.

Table 6.3. The 10 largest suppliers of major arms and their recipients, by region, 2018–22

Figures are the percentage shares of the supplier's total volume of exports of major arms delivered to each recipient region in 2018–22.

	USA	Russia	France	China	Germany	Italy	UK	Spain	South Korea	Israel
Africa	2	12	3.5	9.5	4.3	5.5	0.2	1.5	0.2	1.0
Americas	1.5	–	7.2	<0.05	7.6	8.9	31	13	7.9	13
Asia and Oceania	32	65	44	80	32	11	22	37	63	59
Europe	23	5.9	6.6	4.8	20	6.9	13	17	28	26
Middle East	41	17	34	5.6	36	68	30	31	0.9	–

– = no deliveries; <0.05 = between 0 and 0.05.

Notes: Percentages below 10 are rounded to one decimal place; percentages over 10 are rounded to whole numbers. Figures may not always add up to 100% because of the conventions of rounding and because some suppliers exported small volumes of major arms to unidentified recipients or to international organizations that cannot be linked to a particular region.

Source: SIPRI Arms Transfers Database, Mar. 2023.

relatively less advanced and mainly second-hand military equipment from US stocks, the level of US arms exports to Ukraine in 2022 was still below the levels sent to four other states that year—Kuwait, Saudi Arabia, Qatar and Japan—because they received advanced new weapons, such as combat aircraft and air defence systems.

The USA has many pending arms export deliveries (see table 6.1 in section I). In 2022 alone 13 states ordered a total of 376 combat aircraft and combat helicopters from the USA, with the largest order from Canada for 88 combat aircraft. Other major orders agreed in 2022 included 96 combat helicopters and 394 tanks for Poland; 24 transport aircraft, 29 combat helicopters and 40 transport helicopters for Australia; 35 combat aircraft and 60 heavy transport helicopters for Germany; and 20 combat aircraft and 18 heavy transport helicopters for South Korea.

Russia

In 2018–22 Russia delivered major arms to 47 states and accounted for 16 per cent of total global arms exports. Russian arms exports remained stable between 2008–12 and 2013–17, but fell by 31 per cent between 2013–17 and 2018–22. The annual volumes of arms exports in 2018 and 2019 were at similar levels to or higher than those in each of the previous 20 years, but were significantly lower in 2020, 2021 and 2022.

States in Asia and Oceania received 65 per cent of total Russian arms exports in 2018–22, while Middle Eastern and African states received 17 per cent and 12 per cent respectively. Just under two-thirds of Russian arms exports went to three states in 2018–22: India (31 per cent), China (23 per cent) and

Table 6.4. Deliveries by arms category by the 10 largest suppliers of major arms, 2018–22

Figures are the percentage shares of each category of major arms in the exports of the 10 largest suppliers in 2018–22.[a]

Arms category	USA	Russia	France	China	Germany	Italy	UK	Spain	South Korea	Israel	World total
Aircraft	64	44	59	29	11	39	32	44	7.0	7.8	48
Combat aircraft and helicopters	53	40	45	21	1.5	24	23	4.5	6.6	2.8	37
Air defence systems	3.6	6.9	2.2	5.3	4.1	–	0.1	0.2	–	17	3.8
Armoured vehicles	9.6	12	1.7	20	15	6.2	1.3	0.9	4.0	0.4	10
Artillery	0.3	0.1	0.9	3.7	1.6	1.5	4.3	0.7	23	2.5	1.5
Engines	2.2	20	4.6	0.3	13	0.1	15	–	–	–	6.1
Missiles	16	13	11	17	10	3.8	17	0.1	1.0	39	13
Naval weapons	0.9	0.6	0.3	–	–	2.3	–	–	–	0.9	0.7
Satellites	–	0.2	0.7	–	–	–	–	–	–	–	0.1
Sensors	3.3	1.0	3.4	2.3	9.2	3.9	1.6	1.5		22	3.8
Ships	0.5	3.1	16	22	36	42	8.5	53	65	6.7	12
Major surface warships	–	0.8	2.8	16	11	39	–	45	27	–	5.4
Submarines	–	2.3	10	0.4	20	–	–	–	9.0	–	2.6
Other	–	–	–	<0.05	–	0.6	21	0.1	–	4.6	1.0

– = no deliveries; <0.05 = between 0 and 0.05.

Notes: Percentages below 10 are rounded to 1 decimal place; percentages over 10 are rounded to whole numbers.

[a] On SIPRI's categories of major arms see box 6.1 in section I of this chapter.

Source: SIPRI Arms Transfers Database, Mar. 2023.

Egypt (9.3 per cent). India was also the largest recipient of Russian arms in 2013–17, but exports to India decreased by 37 per cent between the two periods. In contrast, exports increased to China (by 39 per cent) and Egypt (by 44 per cent) within the same time frame. However, Russia made no deliveries to Egypt in 2021–22 and the volume of deliveries to China in 2020–22 was at a much lower level than in 2018–19. It is likely that order volumes from these two states will reduce in the coming years. Egypt, for example, cancelled a large order for combat aircraft in 2022, probably due to pressure from the USA, while China is becoming less reliant on Russian imports as it develops domestic alternatives. Exports to the other 7 of the 10 largest recipients of Russian arms in 2018–22 decreased, by 59 per cent on average.

The low volume of pending deliveries of major arms from Russia indicates that its arms exports are likely to continue to drop in the coming years. Combat aircraft (including combat helicopters) have been among Russia's main arms exports since 1992. It delivered 328 of these in 2018–22, which accounted for 40 per cent of Russian arms exports in the period (see table 6.4). However, by the end of 2022, it had pending deliveries for only

84 combat aircraft. Russia's invasion of Ukraine will probably put additional constraints on Russia's ability to export arms, as it is likely to prioritize the production of arms for its own military over those for export. The multilateral sanctions, including wide-ranging trade restrictions, imposed on Russia, coupled with pressure from the USA and its allies on states not to acquire Russian arms, will also hamper its efforts to export arms.[5]

France

French arms exports accounted for 11 per cent of the global total in 2018–22 and were 44 per cent higher than in 2013–17. One important reason for the increase was the 284 Rafale combat aircraft ordered from France since 2015, of which 92 were delivered in 2018–22. These aircraft accounted for 33 per cent of the total French arms exported in that period. After previously losing export orders to competitors, the series of major orders for the aircraft since 2015 was labelled a 'success story' by the French government.[6] Arms exports are an important foreign policy tool for the French government and essential for maintaining a French arms industry that allows strategic autonomy in arms procurement.[7] Among the methods used to promote arms exports, the French government has sold 'combat proven' equipment from national stocks that can be delivered fast to fulfil urgent foreign demand.[8] In 2021, for example, France sold 24 Rafales from its own air force inventory to Greece and Croatia (12 each) and will restock its inventory with new aircraft in the near future.

Most of France's arms exports in 2018–22 went to states in Asia and Oceania (44 per cent) and the Middle East (34 per cent). It delivered major arms to 62 states in 2018–22, but the three largest recipients—India, Qatar and Egypt—together received 55 per cent of French arms exports in that period. This was largely due to the supply of a total of 108 combat aircraft to these states (India received 62, Qatar 36 and Egypt 10), along with 4 submarines to India and 3 frigates to Egypt. With a 30 per cent share of exports, India was by far the largest recipient of French arms in 2018–22, replacing Egypt, which occupied that position in 2013–17 (see section III).

The most notable French arms export agreement signed in 2022 was with Indonesia, for 42 Rafale combat aircraft. By the end of 2022, France had far more major arms on order for export than Russia.

---

[5] On the trade restrictions on Russia see chapter 12, section III, in this volume.
[6] French Ministry of the Armed Forces (MAF), *Rapport au Parlement sur les exportations d'armament de la France* [Report to Parliament on French arms exports] (MAF: Paris, 2022), p. 49.
[7] French Ministry of the Armed Forces (note 6), pp. 16–17.
[8] French Ministry of the Armed Forces (note 6), p. 50.

Other major exporters

China

China accounted for 5.2 per cent of total global arms exports in 2018–22, although its arms exports decreased by 23 per cent compared to 2013–17. Most Chinese arms exports (80 per cent) went to states in Asia and Oceania. China delivered major arms to 46 states in 2018–22, but over half of its arms exports (54 per cent) went to just one state—Pakistan, which has become highly dependent on China for its arms procurement since the USA reduced its military aid to Pakistan in 2011 and from 2018 largely stopped supplying it with arms.[9] Given that China still has orders to deliver 700 tanks, 2 frigates, 8 submarines and 72 combat aircraft to Pakistan, the country will remain the largest recipient of Chinese arms in the near future. In 2022, for the first time since the mid 1970s, when Albania was one of China's top arms importers, there were substantial Chinese arms exports to a European state—Serbia, which received two surface-to-air missile (SAM) systems. However, Serbia accounted for only 4.5 per cent of Chinese arms exports in 2018–22.

Germany

Exports of major arms by Germany made up 4.2 per cent of the global total in 2018–22. Despite a decrease in exports of 35 per cent compared to 2013–17, Germany remained the fifth largest exporter of major arms in 2018–22. States in the Middle East received the largest share of German arms exports in 2018–22 (36 per cent), followed by Asia and Oceania (32 per cent) and Europe (20 per cent). One explanation for the decrease in German arms exports is the delay in deliveries of one submarine each to Israel, Singapore and Türkiye. These were planned to be delivered by the end of 2022 as part of a total of 14 submarines ordered from Germany by these three states.

Italy

Italy accounted for 3.8 per cent of the world's arms exports in 2018–22. Italian arms exports were 45 per cent higher in 2018–22 than in 2013–17 and the highest for any five-year period since 1981–85. Two-thirds (67 per cent) of Italian arms exports in 2018–22 went to the Middle East. Three states accounted for 59 per cent of Italian arms exports: Qatar (24 per cent), Egypt (23 per cent) and Türkiye (12 per cent).

United Kingdom

Arms exports by the UK decreased by 35 per cent between 2013–17 and 2018–22. By the end of 2022 existing orders for British arms indicated its

---

[9] Filseth, T., 'US resumes arms sales to Pakistan with $450 million F-16 deal', *National Interest*, 8 Sep. 2022; and Kronstadt, K. A., 'Pakistan–US relations', Congressional Research Service (CRS) In Focus no. IF11270, 8 July 2021.

exports were unlikely to increase soon. A total of 29 frigates on order by Australia, Canada, Indonesia and Poland have a considerable arms export value, but deliveries of these ships are planned over a long period, from the mid 2020s to 2044.

Spain

Arms exports by Spain decreased by 4.4 per cent between 2013–17 and 2018–22. Spain's exports of major arms in 2018–22 were almost entirely ships (53 per cent of the total volume) and transport aircraft (39 per cent). Most significant were the deliveries of two large destroyers to Australia and three smaller frigates to Saudi Arabia.

South Korea

Arms exports by South Korea increased by 74 per cent between 2013–17 and 2018–22, giving it a 2.4 per cent share of the global total. Most South Korean arms exports (63 per cent) went to states in Asia and Oceania, but demand for the country's arms is also growing in other regions, as demonstrated by the large orders that Poland and Egypt placed in 2022 (see section III). Important aspects in South Korean efforts to gain orders are its ability to deliver quickly, at comparatively low prices, and to offer licensed or joint production.[10] The fast delivery seemed especially important to Poland as it sees Russia as an imminent threat. The first Korean tanks and artillery pieces were delivered to Poland in 2022, only months after the orders were signed.[11] South Korea has stated that it aims to become the fourth largest arms exporter by 2027 (after the USA, Russia and France), touted arms exports as an important economic export growth engine, and announced major investments of public funds to develop exportable military technology and promote exports.[12] While South Korea has built up a large order book in recent years, with substantial pending deliveries, even the high values of orders for major arms placed recently are only a fraction of the value of South Korea's total exports (see box 6.2).

Israel

Arms exports by Israel decreased by 15 per cent between 2013–17 and 2018–22, but there were significant pending deliveries by the end of 2022. Particularly important are a series of long-standing orders for air defence systems by India, which has been a major recipient of Israeli arms since the early 2000s, and an increase in orders for air defence systems in Europe. There were also

---

[10] Lendon, B. and Bae, G., 'President Yoon wants South Korea to become one of world's top weapons suppliers', CNN, 17 Aug. 2022.

[11] Palowski, J., 'K9A1 howitzers and K2 main battle tanks delivered to Poland', Defence24.com, 6 Dec. 2022.

[12] Lendon and Bae (note 10); and Park, Y., 'South Korea to invest $1.16 billion in defense industry by 2027 to boost exports', *Aju Business Daily*, 16 Feb. 2023.

Box 6.2. Financial aspects of arms transfers

Arms exports are often pursued for economic reasons either to gain income directly from foreign trade or to reduce domestic procurement costs. In the latter case, increased production runs for arms exports can lead to reduced unit costs for domestic arms acquisitions. For some states, economic benefits of arms exports are important, especially for the smaller producers, while larger producers may be in a position where the economic benefits are outweighed by other considerations that may limit arms exports. To support better understanding of such economic drivers, SIPRI collects and publishes data on the financial value of the arms trade in addition to the SIPRI arms transfers trend-indicator values.

The governments of most of the main arms-exporting states publish financial data on arms exports. According to SIPRI's statistics on arms transfers, states that produce official data on the financial value of their arms exports accounted for over 90 per cent of the total volume of deliveries of major arms. There are significant limitations in using this data. For example, there is no internationally agreed definition of what constitutes 'arms' and governments thus use different lists; some states report on export licences issued or used and other states report actual exports; and these methodologies may change over time. However, the data can be used to obtain rough indications of the relative importance of arms exports for a national economy and globally.[a]

The estimate of the financial value of the global international arms trade for 2021—the latest year for which relevant data is available—was at least US$127 billion. The data suggests a significant real-terms increase over time from at least $95 billion in 2012 (in constant 2021 US dollars).

Despite the increase, the estimated value of the global arms trade remains only a fraction of the total trade in all products and services: for 2012 it was less than 0.4 per cent and for 2021 less than 0.5 per cent of the value of total global trade.[b]

On a state level, there are vast differences in arms exports as a share of total exports. In 2021, for example, arms exports accounted for 2.7 per cent of all Russia's exports, and only 0.8 per cent of Sweden's.[c] For states that publish only data on the value of licences or orders, which often result in actual exports spread over several years, such shares cannot be calculated. However, even for South Korea, which reported very high increases in arms export orders in 2021 and 2022, the value of those orders in 2021 was still only 0.9 per cent of total actual exports in 2021.[d]

[a] For an explanation of SIPRI's methodology for this data set, the various issues with official financial data on arms exports, and data for the period 1994–2021, see SIPRI, 'Financial value of the global arms trade', SIPRI Databases.

[b] The value of the total global trade in all products and services in 2021 was $27.3 trillion. World Trade Organization (WTO), *World Trade Statistical Review 2021* (WTO: Geneva, 2022), p. 11.

[c] World Bank, 'Exports of goods and services (current US$)—Russian Federation', World Bank Open Data; and World Bank, 'Exports of goods and services (current LCU)—Sweden', World Bank Open Data.

[d] World Bank, 'Exports of goods and services (current US$)—Korea, Rep.', World Bank Open Data.

orders in 2022 for Israeli air defence systems by Colombia and Morocco. Since the normalization of relations between Israel and the UAE and Bahrain in 2020, new potential markets have been opened for Israeli arms.

III. Developments among the recipients of major arms, 2018–22

SIEMON T. WEZEMAN AND PIETER D. WEZEMAN

SIPRI has identified 167 states as importers of major arms in 2018–22. The top five arms importers—India, Saudi Arabia, Qatar, Australia and China—received 36 per cent of total global arms imports in the period (see table 6.5). States in Asia and Oceania accounted for 41 per cent of all arms imports in 2018–22, followed by the Middle East (31 per cent), Europe (16 per cent), the Americas (5.8 per cent) and Africa (5.0 per cent).

In addition to the 167 importing states, 2 international organizations—the North Atlantic Treaty Organization (NATO) and the African Union—and non-state armed groups in Libya, Sudan (Darfur), Syria and Yemen received major arms in 2018–22. Of these, only NATO received a significant volume (0.5 per cent of the global total).

This section reviews significant developments among the main recipients of arms in each region.

Africa

Imports of major arms by African states in 2008–12 were at their highest level since the end of the cold war (1988–92), but decreased by 12 per cent between 2008–12 and 2013–17 and by 40 per cent between 2013–17 and 2018–22 (see table 6.6).[1] This brought the African share of total global imports of major arms down to 5.0 per cent in 2018–22, compared to 8.0 per cent in 2013–17 and 10 per cent in 2008–12. The main suppliers to Africa in 2018–22 were Russia, accounting for 40 per cent of African imports of major arms, the United States (16 per cent), China (9.8 per cent) and France (7.6 per cent). Russia has been the main supplier to Africa since the end of the cold war, with China, the USA and France being the other main suppliers for the most part.

Changing import patterns for Algeria and Morocco have dominated the general trend for Africa in the post-cold war period. For both 2013–17 and 2018–22 they were by far the largest importers in the region but, despite continuing and seemingly growing tensions between the two, their imports decreased significantly between the periods: Algeria by 58 per cent and Morocco by 30 per cent.[2] The decrease may be temporary since both have recently made some significant orders for major arms for delivery in the near future. Morocco has 24 combat aircraft, 24 combat helicopters and 56 tanks on

---

[1] Note that Africa does not include Egypt, which SIPRI includes in the Middle East.
[2] Rachidi, I., 'Morocco and Algeria: A long rivalry', *Sada*, 3 May 2022; and 'Timeline: Algeria and Morocco's diplomatic disputes', Al Jazeera, 15 Jan. 2023.

Table 6.5. The 40 largest importers of major arms and their main suppliers, 2018–22

Rank 2018–22	Rank 2013–17[a]	Importer	Share of total global imports (%) 2013–17	Share of total global imports (%) 2018–22	Change in volume (%) from 2013–17 to 2018–22	1st		2nd		3rd	
1	1	India	12	11	−11	Russia	45	France	29	USA	11
2	2	Saudi Arabia	10	9.6	−8.7	USA	78	France	6.4	Spain	4.9
3	20	Qatar	1.5	6.4	311	USA	42	France	29	Italy	14
4	7	Australia	3.6	4.7	23	USA	73	Spain	19	Switzerland	3.0
5	4	China	4.2	4.6	4.1	Russia	83	France	8.1	Ukraine	5.6
6	3	Egypt	4.5	4.5	−5.3	Russia	34	Italy	19	France	19
7	13	South Korea	2.2	3.7	61	USA	71	Germany	19	France	7.9
8	9	Pakistan	3.0	3.7	14	China	77	Sweden	5.1	Russia	3.6
9	24	Japan	1.2	3.5	171	USA	97	UK	1.9	Sweden	0.3
10	14	United States	2.0	2.7	31	UK	24	Netherlands	13	France	11
11	6	UAE	4.1	2.7	−38	USA	66	Türkiye	7.4	Russia	5.4
12	28	Kuwait	0.9	2.4	146	USA	78	Italy	10	France	9.0
13	18	United Kingdom	1.7	2.3	31	USA	81	South Korea	13	Israel	2.8
14	116	Ukraine	<0.05	2.0	8 631	USA	34	Poland	17	Germany	11
15	43	Norway	0.5	2.0	285	USA	86	South Korea	8.2	Italy	3.5
16	16	Israel	1.8	1.9	2.9	USA	79	Germany	20	Italy	0.2
17	46	Netherlands	0.4	1.9	307	USA	95	Germany	3.9	Finland	0.6
18	5	Algeria	4.1	1.8	−58	Russia	73	Germany	10	France	5.2
19	12	Türkiye	2.4	1.3	−49	Italy	35	Spain	20	Russia	19
20	21	Singapore	1.4	1.3	−14	France	52	USA	26	UK	7.6
21	29	Thailand	0.9	1.0	−1.1	South Korea	33	China	14	USA	10
22	37	Brazil	0.6	0.9	48	France	39	UK	14	Sweden	13
23	39	Philippines	0.5	0.9	64	South Korea	42	Israel	22	USA	15
24	11	Indonesia	2.7	0.9	−69	South Korea	32	USA	26	France	12
25	19	Bangladesh	1.6	0.9	−48	China	74	UK	5.8	Türkiye	4.5
26	42	Poland	0.5	0.9	64	USA	56	South Korea	17	Germany	6.5

27	10	Viet Nam	2.8	−72	Russia	55	Israel	16	Belarus	10
28	23	Italy	1.3	−41	USA	92	Israel	4.4	France	2.0
29	25	Morocco	1.1	−30	USA	76	France	15	China	6.8
30	34	Myanmar	0.8	−3.0	Russia	42	China	29	India	14
31	112	NATO[b]	<0.05	2 700	France	66	USA	18	UK	15
32	32	Afghanistan	0.8	−11	USA	96	Brazil	2.6	Belarus	1.4
33	26	Canada	1.1	−36	USA	32	Australia	27	Spain	15
34	30	Greece	0.9	−26	France	48	USA	29	UK	12
35	31	Kazakhstan	0.8	−22	Russia	94	China	2.6	South Africa	1.8
36	50	Belarus	0.3	55	Russia	100	China	0.1	..	..
37	85	Serbia	0.1	743	China	43	Russia	31	Belarus	20
38	53	Chile	0.3	56	UK	38	Australia	36	USA	10
39	33	Jordan	0.8	−39	USA	40	UAE	20	Russia	17
40	70	Bahrain	0.1	380	USA	83	UK	7	Italy	4.1

.. = data not available or not applicable; <0.05 = between 0 and 0.05; NATO = North Atlantic Treaty Organization; UAE = United Arab Emirates.

Notes: Percentages below 10 are rounded to one decimal place; percentages over 10 are rounded to whole numbers.

[a] The rank order for importers in 2013–17 differs from that published in *SIPRI Yearbook 2018* because of subsequent revision of figures for these years.
[b] The data is for imports by the organization itself, not the total imports by NATO member states.

Source: SIPRI Arms Transfers Database, Mar. 2023.

Table 6.6. Imports of major arms, by region and subregion, 2013–17 and 2018–22

Figures for volume of imports are SIPRI trend-indicator values (TIVs).[a]

Recipient region	Volume of imports (TIV) 2013–17	Volume of imports (TIV) 2018–22	Change in volume (%) from 2013–17 to 2018–22	Share of total imports (%) 2013–17	Share of total imports (%) 2018–22
Africa	11 626	6 923	–40	8.0	5.0
North Africa	8 003	4 120	–49	5.5	3.0
Sub-Saharan Africa	3 619	2 799	–23	2.5	2.0
Americas	10 160	8 071	–21	7.0	5.8
Central America and the Caribbean	1 410	410	–71	1.0	0.3
North America	4 430	4 769	7.7	3.0	3.5
South America	4 295	2 832	–34	3.0	2.0
Asia and Oceania	61 100	56 511	–7.5	42	41
Central Asia	2 209	1 562	–29	1.5	1.1
East Asia	13 945	16 836	21	9.6	12
Oceania	5 467	6 844	25	3.8	5.0
South Asia	25 223	22 949	–9.0	17	17
South East Asia	14 258	8 321	–42	9.8	6.0
Europe	15 450	22 659	47	11	16
Central Europe	1 603	3 556	122	1.1	2.6
Eastern Europe	3 338	4 579	37	2.3	3.3
Western Europe	10 510	14 514	38	7.2	11
Middle East	47 039	42 877	–8.8	32	31
Other[b]	180	1 157	543	0.8	0.7
Total	**145 576**	**138 198**	**–5.1**		

Notes: Percentages below 10 are rounded to one decimal; percentages over 10 are rounded to whole numbers.

[a] The SIPRI TIV is an indicator of the volume of arms transfers and not their financial value. The method for calculating the TIV is described in box 6.1 in section I of this chapter.

[b] 'Other' refers to unidentified recipients or to international organizations that cannot be linked to a particular region.

Source: SIPRI Arms Transfers Database, Mar. 2023.

order from the USA, all for delivery by the end of 2025. It also has 2 surface-to-air missile (SAM) systems and 30 self-propelled guns on order from France, and in 2022 signed a US$500 million deal with Israel for several long-range SAM systems.[3] The Algerian orders are less clear as Algeria and some of its suppliers are not very transparent on orders or planned orders for arms. It is known to have 22 combat aircraft on order from Russia, and there are reports of an order for 14 more, as well as for an unknown number of tanks.[4] However, any planned deliveries from Russia may be affected by the fallout

---

[3] Zaken, D., 'IAI agrees $500m missile defense systems deal with Morocco', Globes, 13 Feb. 2022.

[4] BMPD, [Algeria received a new batch of T-90SA tanks], LiveJournal, 10 Aug. 2022 (in Russian); and Genty-Boudry, Y., 'Algérie : Su-34 contre le Maroc?' [Algeria: Su-34 against Morocco?], *Air & Cosmos*, 23 Mar. 2021.

from the war in Ukraine, including US pressure on Algeria to reconsider arms deals with Russia, and possible diversion by Russia of weapons produced for export to its own forces.[5] Algeria also has at least one and possibly up to six frigates on order from China for delivery from 2023.[6]

Sub-Saharan Africa

States in sub-Saharan Africa accounted for 2.0 per cent of total global imports of major arms in 2018–22. Despite numerous armed conflicts, internal and bilateral tensions, and other security concerns in sub-Saharan Africa, arms imports to the subregion decreased 23 per cent between 2013–17 and 2018–22, reaching their lowest level in two decades.[7]

Several arms-exporting states are competing for influence in sub-Saharan Africa. Russia overtook China to become the largest supplier to the subregion in 2018–22. Its share of arms imports to sub-Saharan Africa rose from 21 per cent in 2013–17 to 26 per cent in 2018–22, while China's fell from 29 per cent to 18 per cent. Until 2013–17 Russia's deliveries to the subregion had been larger than China's for all periods since at least the end of the cold war. France increased its share from 4.8 per cent to 8.3 per cent, making it the third largest arms supplier to sub-Saharan Africa in 2018–22.

Arms import volumes vary significantly over time for most states in sub-Saharan Africa and these states often have a diverse range of suppliers—as exemplified by the three largest sub-Saharan importers in 2018–22: Angola, Nigeria and Mali.

Angola's imports in 2018–22 were 57 per cent higher than in 2013–17 and almost 1000 per cent higher than in 2008–12, when almost no major arms were imported. Russia accounted for over 55 per cent of all supplies in both 2018–22 and 2013–17. However, Angola received major arms from at least 10 other suppliers in both periods, including Belarus, Brazil, China, France, Israel, Lithuania, South Africa and the USA. Neither Russia nor China supplied major arms to Angola in the decade before 2013.

Nigeria has had a relatively more stable trend in total imports in the last two decades: imports in 2018–22 were 9.4 per cent lower than in 2013–17, and the biggest variation was the 147 per cent increase between 2003–2007 and 2008–12. In 2013–17 Russia was the largest arms supplier to Nigeria, but in both 2008–12 and 2018–22 it was China. However, neither accounted for more than 38 per cent of total Nigerian imports in the last decade, and in both 2013–17 and 2018–22 they shared the Nigerian arms market with at least

---

[5] Rubio, M. (US Senator for Florida), 'Rubio calls for sanctions on Algerian purchase of Russian weapons', Press release, 15 Sep. 2022; and Malyasov, D., 'Russia uses T-90S tanks originally bound for export customers', Defence Blog, 4 Oct. 2022.

[6] Martin, G., 'Algerian navy takes delivery of Chinese-built corvette', defenceWeb, 3 Apr. 2023.

[7] On armed conflict in sub-Saharan Africa see 'Armed conflict and peace processes in sub-Saharan Africa', *SIPRI Yearbook 2022*, pp. 193–239; and chapter 2 in this volume.

11 other suppliers, including Brazil, Czechia, France, Germany, Ukraine and the USA.

Mali's imports increased by 210 per cent between 2013–17 and 2018–22. Russia was its main supplier in both periods, but Mali also received major arms from Brazil, China, France, South Africa, Spain, Türkiye, the United Arab Emirates (UAE) and the USA. After the coups in Mali in 2020 and 2021, France and the USA became far more reluctant to supply arms to the country. Russia, in contrast, increased its arms exports to Mali in 2021–22 with supplies of three combat helicopters and two light combat aircraft. These arms deliveries are widely assumed to be part of Russian efforts to expand its presence and influence in Mali and were combined with the deployment of the Wagner Group, a Russian private military and security company (PMSC).[8] Similar use by Russia of a combination of arms deliveries and deployment of Russian PMSCs has been previously observed in Libya and the Central African Republic.[9]

The Americas

Arms imports by states in the Americas decreased by 21 per cent between 2013–17 and 2018–22. The USA and Brazil were the largest importers of major arms in the region in 2018–22, accounting for 47 per cent and 16 per cent of the regional total, respectively. Of the US imports, 24 per cent came from the United Kingdom, mainly in the form of large gas turbines for USA-produced warships and air-refuelling systems for USA-produced tanker aircraft. Another 21 per cent was accounted for by 110 second-hand combat aircraft from several states (including Australia, France, Israel and Jordan), acquired by several US companies to train US forces and in some cases also those of US allies.

Imports of major arms by South American states decreased by 34 per cent between 2013–17 and 2018–22. Despite ongoing intrastate violence in South America, tensions between states in the region are few.[10] Nevertheless, some states, including Brazil and Chile, have significant ongoing arms import programmes. Brazil's arms imports were 48 per cent higher than in 2013–17 and accounted for 44 per cent of the subregional total in 2018–22. Chile's arms

---

[8] The exact status of the Wagner Group is unclear, but it appears to be operating on behalf of the Russian state rather than as non-state 'mercenaries'. Racz, A., 'Band of brothers: The Wagner Group and the Russian state', Center for Strategic and International Studies, 21 Sep. 2020.

[9] On the role of the Wagner Group in Mali and the Central African Republic see chapter 4, section II, in this volume. See also Lindén, K., 'Russia's relations with Africa: Small, military-oriented and with destabilising effects', Swedish Defence Research Agency (FOI) Studies in African Security, Memo no. 8090, Jan. 2023.

[10] On armed gang violence and other armed violence in parts of South America see chapter 2, section I, in this volume.

imports rose by 56 per cent between the two periods, giving it a 24 per cent share of total South American arms imports.

Asia and Oceania

Imports of major arms by states in Asia and Oceania decreased by 7.5 per cent between 2013–17 and 2018–22. However, arms imports by states in Oceania alone increased by 25 per cent between 2013–17 and 2018–22, with Australia by far the largest arms importer. Six of the world's 10 largest arms importers in 2018–22 were in Asia and Oceania: India, Australia, China, the Republic of Korea (South Korea), Pakistan and Japan. The USA (31 per cent) accounted for the largest share of arms exported to states in the region, followed by Russia (26 per cent) and France (12 per cent).

India and Pakistan

India and Pakistan have been among the largest arms importers for decades. Their demand for arms is mainly driven by tensions with each other and, in the case of India, with China. For the 30-year period 1993–2022, India was the largest importer of major arms globally, while Pakistan was the eighth largest, and both have major ongoing arms import programmes.

With an 11 per cent share of total global arms imports, India was the world's biggest importer of major arms in 2018–22. It retained this position even though its arms imports dropped by 11 per cent between 2013–17 and 2018–22. The decrease can be attributed to several factors, including India's slow and complex arms procurement process, efforts to diversify its arms suppliers, and attempts to replace imports with major arms that are designed and produced domestically.

Russia was the largest supplier of arms to India in both 2013–17 and 2018–22, but its share of total Indian arms imports fell from 64 per cent to 45 per cent. Russia's position as India's main arms supplier is under pressure due to strong competition from other supplier states (including France, Israel, South Korea, the UK and the USA), increased Indian arms production and, since 2022, the constraints on Russia's arms exports related to its invasion of Ukraine (discussed in section II).

India's arms imports from France, which included 62 combat aircraft and 4 submarines, increased by 489 per cent between 2013–17 and 2018–22, and thus France displaced the USA as the second largest supplier to India.

Imports of major weapons by Pakistan increased by 14 per cent between 2013–17 and 2018–22 and accounted for 3.7 per cent of the global total. China supplied over three-quarters (77 per cent) of Pakistan's arms imports in 2018–22. The long-standing reactive armament dynamic between India and Pakistan was illustrated by Pakistan's import in 2022 of 14 J-10C combat aircraft, out of a total of 36 ordered from China. Pakistani Prime Minister

Imran Khan referred to the procurement as being needed to counter efforts 'to create an imbalance in the region', while earlier the Pakistani interior minister stated that the procurement was aimed at countering the Indian purchase of Rafale combat aircraft from France.[11]

East Asia

Imports of major arms by states in East Asia increased by 21 per cent between 2013–17 and 2018–22. China, Japan and South Korea were among the top 10 importers of major arms globally in 2018–22. All three have expanded their military capabilities and continue to do so but with different levels of dependency on arms imports. China is rapidly moving towards self-reliance in major arms, while Japan and South Korea, despite their well-developed arms industries, remain reliant on arms imports in some key weapon categories, especially long-range strike capabilities such as advanced combat aircraft and missiles.[12] Both Japan's and South Korea's arms acquisitions are largely driven by tensions with the Democratic People's Republic of Korea (DPRK, or North Korea) and, in the case of Japan, with China. The USA, a treaty ally of Japan and South Korea, and itself experiencing tense security relations with North Korea and China, has been their main supplier since 1950.

Arms imports by China grew by 4.1 per cent and accounted for 4.6 per cent of the global total in 2018–22. Most Chinese arms imports (83 per cent) came from Russia. Russian deliveries to China in the last three years of the period (2020–22) consisted almost entirely of helicopters and aircraft engines, which are the last few types of major arms that China has seemingly had difficulties in developing.

Japan increased its arms imports between 2013–17 and 2018–22 by 171 per cent. The USA delivered 29 F-35 combat aircraft to Japan, amounting to one-third (33 per cent) of Japanese arms imports. Japan has pending deliveries of 118 F-35 combat aircraft from the USA, and in 2022 decided to order up to 400 long-range (at least 1600 kilometres) Tomahawk land-attack missiles from the USA for use on Japanese naval ships as a 'counterstrike capability'. The Tomahawks provide a new capability for Japan and are a quick off-the-shelf order as Japan's own long-range land-attack missiles are still being developed.[13] Until now, only the UK has received Tomahawks from the USA, with 195 delivered between 1997 and 2016.

---

[11] Press Trust of India, 'Pakistan gets China-made J-10C fighter jets to "counter India's Rafale"', NDTV, 11 Mar. 2022; and 'Six China-made J-10C jets inducted into PAF', *Dawn*, 12 Mar. 2022.

[12] Béraud-Sudreau, L. et al., *Arms-production Capabilities in the Indo-Pacific Region: Measuring Self-reliance* (SIPRI: Stockholm, Oct. 2022).

[13] Nemoto, R., 'Japan seeks to buy 400 US Tomahawk missiles, Kishida says', Nikkei Asia, 28 Feb. 2023; and Kosuke, T., 'PM Kishida announces Japan will acquire 400 Tomahawk missiles from US', The Diplomat, 28 Feb. 2023.

South Korea increased its arms imports between 2013–17 and 2018–22 by 61 per cent. The USA delivered 40 F-35 combat aircraft to South Korea in 2018–22, which accounted for 43 per cent of South Korean arms imports in the period. South Korea has 20 F-35 combat aircraft on order from the USA.

Australia

As a key ally of the USA, Australia is also building up its long-range strike capabilities based on a perceived heightened threat from China.[14] Australia increased its arms imports by 23 per cent between 2013–17 and 2018–22. With a 4.7 per cent share of global arms imports, it was the fourth largest arms importer in the world in 2018–22. The delivery of 64 combat aircraft from the USA accounted for 62 per cent of Australian arms imports in the period. Substantial orders for major arms have been placed in recent years for delivery after 2022, further expanding Australian military capabilities. These include at least 510 ship-, air- and land-launched land-attack missiles with ranges between 300 and at least 1600 km—a new capability for Australia.

South East Asia

Although most South East Asian states continued to be affected by tensions in the South China Sea, mainly with China, arms imports by states in the subregion fell by 42 per cent between 2013–17 and 2018–22. The decrease is at least partly because many of those states are still in the process of incorporating the substantial volumes of major arms delivered before 2018 into their armed forces. Nevertheless, states in the subregion are continuing to build up their military capabilities. The Philippines, for example, increased its arms imports by 64 per cent between 2013–17 and 2018–22. Imports of two frigates from South Korea in 2020–21 provided the Philippines with its first two modern major combat ships, and two more frigates are on order. Singapore expects to take delivery of four submarines from Germany within the next few years. During the period 2018–22, Indonesia placed orders for 42 Rafale combat aircraft from France, doubling its current inventory, as well as 3 submarines from South Korea and 6 frigates from Italy and 2 from the UK.

Europe

Arms imports by European states were 47 per cent higher in 2018–22 than in 2013–17. The biggest European arms importer in 2018–22 was the UK, which was the 13th largest arms importer in the world, followed by Ukraine (see section I) and Norway, ranked 14th and 15th respectively. For all three, the

---

[14] Shugart, T., 'Australia and the growing reach of China's military', Lowy Institute Analysis, Aug. 2021; and Grady, J., 'Australia developing new defense strategy in response to China, says deputy prime minister', USNI News, 12 July 2022.

USA was the largest supplier and in total the USA accounted for 56 per cent of arms imports by European states in 2018–22, a significant increase over the previous three five-year periods (covering 2003–17) when the US share was 33–35 per cent. These increasing imports from the USA both contrast with and are a driver for efforts since 2013 by the European Union (EU) to promote an EU defence technological and industrial base that can provide more EU autonomy in military technology.[15] Russia accounted for 5.8 per cent of European arms imports in 2018–22 (mainly to Belarus) and Germany 5.1 per cent.

European NATO states

Largely in response to the deteriorating security environment in the region, NATO states in Europe increased their arms imports by 65 per cent between 2013–17 and 2018–22. The USA accounted for 65 per cent of total arms imports by European NATO member states and by NATO itself in 2018–22. The next biggest suppliers were France (8.6 per cent) and South Korea (4.9 per cent). Based on existing programmes, the arms imports of European NATO states are expected to continue to rise in the coming years. This includes orders placed before the February 2022 Russian invasion of Ukraine and several large orders announced since, some of which were the result of accelerated procurement processes implemented in response to the war, for example by Poland, Germany, the Netherlands and the Baltic states.

In the first four years of the period (2018–21), Poland's most notable arms import orders included 32 combat aircraft and 4 missile and air defence systems from the USA. In 2022, however, Poland announced new orders for 394 tanks, 96 combat helicopters and 12 missile and air defence systems from the USA; 48 combat aircraft, 1000 tanks, 672 self-propelled guns and 288 multiple-rocket launchers from South Korea; and 3 frigates from the UK.

As a direct reaction to the 2022 invasion of Ukraine, Germany introduced new legislation to allow faster decisions and procurement processes for new arms.[16] The largest German arms import order was for 35 F-35 combat aircraft from the USA, a deal signed in late 2022 after an accelerated procurement process.[17] This was the first time since the late 1970s that Germany has ordered combat aircraft from a foreign supplier.

---

[15] European Commission, 'Commission unveils significant actions to contribute to European defence, boost innovation and address strategic dependencies', 15 Feb. 2022; and Csernatoni, R., 'The EU's defense ambitions: Understanding the emergence of a European defense technological and industrial complex', Carnegie Europe Working Paper, 6 Dec. 2021.

[16] German Ministry of Defence, 'Parlamentsbeschluss: Beschaffung für die Bundeswehr wird beschleunigt' [Parliament resolution: Procurement for the Bundeswehr will be accelerated], 8 July 2022.

[17] The F-35 will replace the Tornado aircraft in Germany's nuclear strike role within NATO. For further detail see section I of this chapter and chapter 7, section I, in this volume.

The Netherlands ordered six additional F-35s in 2022 to ensure that it would not be left behind in the growing queue for this aircraft model.[18] Similarly, Estonia, Latvia and Lithuania each decided to acquire from the USA HIMARS multiple-rocket launchers and 300 km range ATACMS missiles for use with the HIMARS.

The Middle East

Arms imports by states in the Middle East were 8.8 per cent lower in 2018–22 than in 2013–17. Three of the top 10 arms-importing states in 2018–22 were in the Middle East: Saudi Arabia, Qatar and Egypt. The USA accounted for 54 per cent of Middle Eastern arms imports. The next largest suppliers were France (12 per cent), Russia (8.6 per cent) and Italy (8.4 per cent).

Arms transfers continued to play a major role in security developments in the Gulf region in 2018–22, where various tensions persisted, including those between Iran and most other Gulf states. Imported arms also play a major role in the war in Yemen where Saudi Arabia and the UAE have since 2015 actively supported the government against Houthi forces who are supported by Iran.[19]

Saudi Arabia

The world's second largest arms importer in 2018–22 was Saudi Arabia, which received 9.6 per cent of all arms imports. The USA supplied 78 per cent of Saudi Arabian arms imports in the period, which included the delivery of 91 combat aircraft with hundreds of land-attack missiles and over 20 000 guided bombs. Saudi Arabia has used US aircraft delivered since 2016 in its heavily criticized air attacks in Yemen, which continued in 2022 at least up until the six-month truce between the Saudi Arabia-led coalition and the Houthi forces that started in April 2022.[20] Since US President Joe Biden took office in January 2021, his administration has put restrictions on new licences for exports of what it described as 'offensive weapons' to Saudi Arabia, without specifying what defined 'offensive'. Discussions of further US restrictions on arms exports to Saudi Arabia continued in the US Congress during 2022 but in December 2022 the Biden administration made clear it

---

[18] Dutch Ministry of Defence, 'Defence accelerates purchases of F-35s and MQ-9 Reapers', 24 June 2022.
[19] On the armed conflict and peace process in Yemen see chapter 2, section II, in this volume.
[20] 'Saudi-led airstrikes in Yemen have been called war crimes. Many relied on US support', *Washington Post*, 4 June 2022; 'Biden ends support for Saudi's Yemen war in foreign policy shift', Al Jazeera, 4 Feb. 2021; and United Nations, Security Council, 'Final report of the panel of experts on Yemen established pursuant to Security Council Resolution 2140 (2014)', S/2023/130, 21 Feb. 2023.

would continue to supply arms to Saudi Arabia.[21] At the end of 2022, Saudi Arabia still had 41 combat aircraft on order from the USA.

Saudi Arabia also acquired air defence systems from the USA during 2018–22, partly to defend against missile attacks from the Houthi forces in Yemen, and partly to deal with a perceived missile threat from Iran.[22] In particular, Saudi Arabia imported 2 Patriot SAM systems and over 400 Patriot missiles from the USA, to add to much larger numbers supplied before 2018, and in 2018 ordered 7 THAAD anti-ballistic missile (ABM) systems for delivery from 2023.

Qatar

With an increase in arms imports by 311 per cent between 2013–17 and 2018–22, Qatar became the third largest arms importer in the world. Its main suppliers in 2018–22 were the USA, which accounted for 42 per cent of Qatari arms imports, France (29 per cent) and Italy (14 per cent). Qatar's arms imports in 2018–22 included 36 Rafale combat aircraft from France, 26 F-15QA combat aircraft from the USA and 8 Typhoon combat aircraft from the UK, as well as 3 frigates from Italy. By the end of 2022, Qatar also had 22 F-15QAs on order from the USA and 16 Typhoons from the UK.

United Arab Emirates

The UAE's arms imports in 2018–22 were 38 per cent lower than in 2013–17, and it was the 11th largest arms importer globally. The USA was its main supplier, accounting for 66 per cent of the UAE's total arms imports. Notable US deliveries in 2018–22 included hundreds of SAMs and over 20 000 guided bombs. More US missiles are on order and the UAE also has substantial volumes of major arms on order from other suppliers, including 80 Rafale combat aircraft and 2 frigates from France, 4 corvettes from Singapore, and over 30 armed uncrewed aerial vehicles (UAVs) from China, South Africa and Türkiye.

Kuwait

Arms imports by Kuwait increased by 146 per cent between 2013–17 and 2018–22. This was mainly due to the delivery of 28 combat aircraft and 218 tanks from the USA and 6 combat aircraft from Italy (with 22 more still on order at the end of 2022).

---

[21] Blanchard, C. M., 'Saudi Arabia', Congressional Research Service (CRS) In Focus no. IF10822, 10 Mar. 2023; Abramson, J., 'Biden urged to halt arms sales to Saudi Arabia', *Arms Control Today*, Nov. 2022; and Widakuswara, P., 'White House defends support for Saudis in Yemen war', Voice of America, 16 Dec. 2022.
[22] United Nations, S/2023/130 (note 20), p. 8.

Iran

Arms imports by Iran have been at a very low level relative to those of other arms importers in the Gulf since around 1993. Its imports of major arms in 2018–22 were close to zero. In 2022 Iran placed an order for 24 Su-35 combat aircraft from Russia, its first significant procurement of combat aircraft since the early 1990s and the first procurement of major arms after the expiration in 2020 of the UN embargo on such supplies to Iran.[23]

Egypt

Egypt's arms imports decreased by 5.3 per cent between 2013–17 and 2018–22, and it dropped from third largest to sixth largest arms importer in the world. Egypt has a very diversified group of suppliers and in 2018–22 imported major arms from nine states. Russia was Egypt's largest arms supplier during that period, accounting for 34 per cent of total Egyptian arms imports. However, Russia has dropped away as a supplier to Egypt—it delivered no major arms in 2021–22 and there are no known expected deliveries, or plans for new Egyptian orders, from Russia. A major deal for 24 Su-35 combat aircraft from Russia planned for delivery in 2021–22 was cancelled by Egypt in 2022, reportedly after pressure on Egypt from the USA.[24]

In 2018–22 France and Italy each accounted for 19 per cent of Egyptian arms imports and both are likely to remain important suppliers to Egypt. At the end of 2022 Egypt still had 30 Rafale combat aircraft and 1 frigate on order from France, while Italy was negotiating a $10–12 billion arms deal for 24 Typhoon combat aircraft, 20 trainer aircraft, 4 large frigates, 20 patrol craft, 20–24 helicopters and a satellite.[25] The USA accounted in 2018–22 for 6.9 per cent of Egypt's arms imports but in 2020 approved an order for up to 43 combat helicopters and in 2022—probably as compensation for Egypt's cancellation of the Su-35 from Russia—offered to supply Egypt F-15 combat aircraft.[26]

Before 2022 South Korea had only once supplied major arms to Egypt (a second-hand corvette as a gift in 2017). After 2022 it is set to become a new major supplier after signing an order for at least 200 self-propelled guns. It was also by the end of 2022 close to gaining an Egyptian order for possibly over 100 advanced trainer/light combat aircraft.[27]

---

[23] Bromley, M. and Wezeman, P. D., 'Multilateral arms embargoes', *SIPRI Yearbook 2022*, p. 601.

[24] 'Will Iran get the Su-35?', Scramble, 5 Jan. 2022; and Lake, J., 'Egypt grows its modern family', Times Aerospace, 18 Jan. 2023.

[25] 'Egypt close to completing $3bn arms deal with Italy', Middle East Eye, 6 June 2022; and Lake (note 24).

[26] O'Brien, C., 'US plans to sell F-15 fighters to Egypt amid human rights dispute', Politico, 15 Mar. 2022; and Lake (note 24).

[27] Jung, M., 'KAI to focus on Egypt project after FA-50 export deal with Malaysia', *Korea Times*, 2 Mar. 2023; and Nh, J., 'Egypt aims for local production of South Korean trainer aircraft', *Asian Military Review*, 19 Jan. 2023.

7. World nuclear forces

Overview

At the start of 2023, nine states—the United States, the Russian Federation, the United Kingdom, France, China, India, Pakistan, the Democratic People's Republic of Korea (DPRK, or North Korea) and Israel—together possessed approximately 12 512 nuclear weapons, of which 9576 were considered to be potentially operationally available. An estimated 3844 of these warheads were deployed with operational forces (see table 7.1), including about 2000 that were kept in a state of high operational alert—the same number as the previous year.

Overall, the number of nuclear warheads in the world continues to decline. However, this is primarily due to the USA and Russia dismantling retired warheads. Global reductions of operational warheads appear to have stalled, and their numbers are rising again. At the same time, both the USA and Russia have extensive and expensive programmes under way to replace and modernize their nuclear warheads, their missile, aircraft and submarine delivery systems, and their nuclear weapon production facilities (see sections I and II).

China is in the middle of a significant modernization and expansion of its nuclear arsenal (see section V). Its nuclear stockpile is expected to continue growing over the coming decade and some projections suggest that it will deploy at least as many intercontinental ballistic missiles (ICBMs) as either Russia or the USA in that period. However, China's overall nuclear warhead stockpile is still expected to remain smaller than that of either of those states.

The nuclear arsenals of the other nuclear-armed states are even smaller (see sections III–IV, VI–IX), but all are either developing or deploying new weapon systems or have announced their intention to do so. India and Pakistan also appear to be increasing the size of their nuclear weapon inventories, and the UK has announced plans to increase its stockpile. North Korea's military nuclear programme remains central to its national security strategy and it may have assembled up to 30 nuclear weapons and could produce more. Israel continues to maintain its long-standing policy of nuclear ambiguity, leaving significant uncertainty about the number and characteristics of its nuclear weapons.

The availability of reliable information on the status of the nuclear arsenals and capabilities of the nuclear-armed states varies considerably. In some cases, estimates can be based on the amount of fissile material—plutonium and highly enriched uranium (HEU)—that a country is believed to have produced (see section X) and on observations of missile forces.

HANS M. KRISTENSEN AND MATT KORDA

SIPRI Yearbook 2023: Armaments, Disarmament and International Security
www.sipriyearbook.org

Table 7.1. World nuclear forces, January 2023

All figures are approximate and are estimates based on assessments by the authors. The estimates presented here are based on public information and contain some uncertainties, as reflected in the notes to tables 7.1–7.10.

Country	Year of first nuclear test	Warhead stockpile[a] Deployed[b]	Stored[c]	Total	Retired warheads	Total inventory
United States	1945	1 770[d]	1 938[e]	3 708	1 536[f]	5 244
Russia	1949	1 674[g]	2 815[h]	4 489	1 400[f]	5 889
United Kingdom	1952	120	105	225	–[i]	225[j]
France	1960	280	10	290	..	290
China	1964	–	410	410	–	410
India	1974	–	164	164	..	164
Pakistan	1998	–	170	170	..	170
North Korea	2006	–	30	30	..	30[k]
Israel	..	–	90	90	..	90
Total		**3 844**	**5 732**	**9 576**	**2 936**	**12 512**

.. = not applicable or not available; – = nil or a negligible value.

Notes: SIPRI revises its world nuclear forces data each year based on new information and updates to earlier assessments. The data for Jan. 2023 replaces all previously published SIPRI data on world nuclear forces.

[a] Some states, such as the USA, use the official term 'stockpile' to refer to this subset of warheads, while others, such as the UK, often use 'stockpile' to describe the entire nuclear inventory. SIPRI uses the term 'stockpile' to refer to all deployed warheads as well as warheads in central storage that could potentially be deployed after some preparation.

[b] These are warheads placed on missiles or located on bases with operational forces.

[c] These are warheads in central storage that would require some preparation (e.g. transport and loading on to launchers) before they could be deployed.

[d] This figure includes c. 1370 warheads deployed on ballistic missiles and c. 300 stored at bomber bases in the USA, as well as c. 100 non-strategic (tactical) nuclear bombs thought to be deployed across 6 airbases in 5 North Atlantic Treaty Organization member states (Belgium, Germany, Italy, the Netherlands and Türkiye). These non-strategic bombs remain in the custody of the USA.

[e] This figure includes c. 100 non-strategic nuclear bombs stored in the USA. The remainder are strategic nuclear warheads.

[f] This figure refers to retired warheads that have not yet been dismantled.

[g] This figure includes c. 1474 strategic warheads deployed on ballistic missiles and c. 200 deployed at heavy bomber bases.

[h] This figure includes c. 999 strategic and c. 1816 non-strategic warheads in central storage.

[i] SIPRI previously estimated that the UK had c. 45 retired warheads awaiting dismantlement; however, SIPRI's assessment as of Jan. 2023 is that these warheads are likely to be reconstituted to become part of the UK's growing stockpile over the coming years (see note j).

[j] The British government declared in 2010 that its nuclear weapon inventory would not exceed 225 warheads. It is estimated here that the inventory remained at that number in Jan. 2023. A planned reduction to an inventory of 180 warheads by the mid 2020s was ended by a government review published in 2021. The review introduced a new ceiling of 260 warheads.

[k] Information about the status and capability of North Korea's nuclear arsenal comes with significant uncertainty. North Korea might have produced enough fissile material to build 50–70 nuclear warheads; however, it is likely that it has assembled fewer warheads, perhaps c. 30.

I. United States nuclear forces

HANS M. KRISTENSEN AND MATT KORDA*

As of January 2023 the United States maintained a military stockpile of approximately 3708 nuclear warheads, the same number as the previous year. Approximately 1770 of these—consisting of about 1670 strategic and roughly 100 non-strategic (tactical) warheads—were deployed on ballistic missiles and at bomber bases. In addition, about 1938 warheads were held in reserve and around 1536 retired warheads were awaiting dismantlement (184 fewer than the previous year's estimate), giving a total inventory of approximately 5244 nuclear warheads (see table 7.2).

The US stockpile is expected to continue to decline slightly over the next decade as nuclear modernization programmes consolidate some nuclear weapon types. Although the US Department of Energy indicated in early 2022 that the USA was currently 'on pace to completely dismantle the weapons that were retired at the end of [fiscal year (FY)] 2008 by the end of FY 2022', that schedule appears to have slipped.[1]

The estimates presented here are based on publicly available information regarding the US nuclear arsenal and assessments by the authors.[2] While in 2021 the USA briefly restored a policy of declassifying the size of its nuclear stockpile and the annual number of dismantled warheads, this practice was not repeated in 2022.[3]

In 2022 the USA remained in compliance with the final warhead limits prescribed by the 2010 Russian–US Treaty on Measures for the Further Reduction and Limitation of Strategic Offensive Arms (New START), which places a cap on the numbers of US and Russian deployed strategic nuclear forces.[4] The most recent exchange of treaty data, from September 2022, lists the USA as having 1420 warheads attributed to 659 deployed ballistic missiles and heavy bombers.[5] Just as with Russia, many of the USA's strategic delivery systems carry fewer warheads than their maximum capacity in order to meet the limits of New START. If the USA chose to no longer comply with the treaty, or if the treaty were to expire without a follow-on agreement, the

---

[1] US Department of Energy (DOE), National Nuclear Security Administration (NNSA), *Fiscal Year 2022 Stockpile Stewardship and Management Plan*, Report to Congress (DOE: Washington, DC, Mar. 2022), pp. 2-15–2-16. US fiscal years end on 30 Sep. of the named year.

[2] Kristensen, H. M. and Korda, M., 'Estimating world nuclear forces: An overview and assessment of sources', SIPRI Commentary, 14 June 2021.

[3] US Department of State, 'Transparency in the US nuclear weapons stockpile', Fact sheet, 5 Oct. 2021.

[4] For a summary and other details of New START see annex A, section III, in this volume. On related developments in 2022 see chapter 8, section I, in this volume.

[5] US Department of State, Bureau of Arms Control, Verification and Compliance, 'New START Treaty aggregate numbers of strategic offensive arms', Fact sheet, 1 Sep. 2022. See also table 8.1 in chapter 8, section I, in this volume.

* The authors wish to thank Eliana Johns for contributing invaluable research to this publication.

Table 7.2. United States nuclear forces, January 2023

All figures are approximate and some are based on assessments by the authors.

Type	Designation	No. of launchers	Year first deployed	Range (km)[a]	Warheads x yield	No. of warheads[b]
Strategic nuclear forces		746				3 508[c]
Aircraft (bombers)		107/66[d]				788[e]
B-52H	Stratofortress	87/46	1961	16 000	20 x AGM-86B ALCMs 5–150 kt[f]	500[g]
B-2A	Spirit	20/20	1994	11 000	16 x B61-7, -11, B83-1 bombs[h]	288
Land-based missiles (ICBMs)		400				800[i]
LGM-30G Minuteman III						
	Mk12A	200	1979	13 000	1–3 x W78 335 kt	600[j]
	Mk21 SERV	200	2006	13 000	1 x W87-0 300 kt	200[k]
Sea-based missiles (SLBMs)		14/280[l]				1 920[m]
UGM-133A Trident II D5LE						
	Mk4	..	1992	>12 000	1–8 x W76-0 100 kt	–[n]
	Mk4A	..	2008	>12 000	1–8 x W76-1 90 kt	1 511
	Mk4A	..	2019	>12 000	1 x W76-2⁰ 8 kt	25
	Mk5	..	1990	>12 000	1–8 x W88 455 kt	384
Non-strategic nuclear forces						200[p]
F-15E	Strike Eagle	..	1988	3 840	5 x B61-3, -4	80
F-16C/D	Falcon	..	1987	3 200[q]	2 x B61-3, -4	60
F-16MLU	Falcon[r]	..	1985	3 200	2 x B61-3, -4	30
PA-200	Tornado[r]	..	1983	2 400	2 x B61-3, -4	30
Total stockpile						3 708
Deployed warheads						1 770
Reserve warheads						1 938
Retired warheads awaiting dismantlement						1 536[s]
Total inventory						5 244[t]

.. = not available or not applicable; – = nil or a negligible value; ALCM = air-launched cruise missile; ICBM = intercontinental ballistic missile; kt = kiloton; SERV = security-enhanced re-entry vehicle; SLBM = submarine-launched ballistic missile.

[a] For aircraft, the listed range is for illustrative purposes only; actual mission range will vary according to flight profile, weapon payload and in-flight refuelling.

[b] These figures show the total number of warheads estimated to be assigned to nuclear-capable delivery systems. Only some of these warheads have been deployed on missiles and at airbases, as described in the notes below.

[c] Of these strategic warheads, c. 1670 were deployed on land- and sea-based ballistic missiles and at bomber bases. The remaining warheads were in central storage. This number differs from the number of deployed strategic warheads counted by the 2010 Russian–US Treaty on Measures for the Further Reduction and Limitation of Strategic Offensive Arms (New START) because the treaty attributes 1 weapon to each deployed bomber, even though bombers do not carry weapons under normal circumstances. Additionally, the treaty does not count weapons stored at bomber bases and, at any given time, some nuclear-powered ballistic missile submarines (SSBNs) are not fully loaded with warheads and are thus not counted under the treaty.

[d] The first figure is the total number of bombers in the inventory; the second is the number of bombers that are counted as nuclear-capable under New START. The USA has declared that it will deploy no more than 60 nuclear bombers at any given time but normally only c. 50 are deployed, with the remaining aircraft in overhaul.

[e] Of the c. 788 bomber weapons, c. 300 (200 ALCMs and 100 bombs) were deployed at the bomber bases; all the rest were in central storage. Many of the gravity bombs are no longer fully active and are slated for retirement after deployment of the B61-12 is completed in the mid 2020s.

[f] The B-52H is no longer configured to carry nuclear gravity bombs.

[g] In 2006 the US Department of Defense decided to reduce the number of ALCMs to 528 missiles. Burg, R., Director of Strategic Security in the Air, Space and Information Operations, 'ICBMs, helicopters, cruise missiles, bombers and warheads', Statement before the US Senate, Armed Services Committee, Subcommittee on Strategic Forces, 28. Mar. 2007, p. 7. Since then, the number has probably decreased gradually to c. 500 as some missiles and warheads have probably been expended in destructive tests.

[h] Strategic gravity bombs are assigned to B-2A bombers only. The maximum yield of strategic bombs is 360 kt for the B61-7, 400 kt for the B61-11 and 1200 kt for the B83-1. However, all these bombs, except the B-11, have lower-yield options. Most B83-1s have been moved to the inactive stockpile and B-2As rarely exercise with the bomb.

[i] Of the 800 ICBM warheads, only 400 were deployed on the missiles. The remaining warheads were in central storage.

[j] Only 200 of these W78 warheads were deployed, as each ICBM has had its warhead load reduced to carry a single warhead; all of the remaining warheads were in central storage.

[k] SIPRI estimates that another 340 W87 warheads might be in long-term storage outside the stockpile for use in the W87-1 warhead programme to replace the W78.

[l] The first figure is the total number of SSBNs in the US fleet; the second is the maximum number of missiles that they can carry. However, although the 14 SSBNs can carry up to 280 missiles, 2 vessels are normally undergoing refuelling overhaul at any given time and are not assigned missiles. The remaining 12 SSBNs can carry up to 240 missiles, but 1–2 of these vessels are usually undergoing maintenance at any given time and may not be carrying missiles.

[m] Of the 1920 SLBM warheads, c. 970 were deployed on submarines as of Jan. 2023; all the rest were in central storage. Although each D5 missile was counted under the 1991 Strategic Arms Reduction Treaty (START I) as carrying 8 warheads and the missile was initially flight-tested with 14, the US Navy has reduced the warhead load of each missile to an average of 4–5 warheads. D5 missiles equipped with the new low-yield W76-2 are estimated to carry only 1 warhead each.

[n] It is assumed here that all W76-0 warheads have been replaced by the W76-1.

[o] According to US military officials, the new low-yield W76-2 warhead will normally be deployed on at least 2 of the SSBNs on patrol in the Atlantic and Pacific oceans.

[p] Of the 200 non-strategic bombs, c. 100 are thought to be deployed across 6 airbases in 5 North Atlantic Treaty Organization (NATO) member states (Belgium, Germany, Italy, the Netherlands and Türkiye), although the weapons remain in the custody of the US Air Force. The other c. 100 bombs were in central storage in the USA. Older B61 versions will be dismantled once the B61-12 is deployed. The maximum yields of non-strategic bombs are 170 kt for the B61-3 and 50 kt for the B61-4. All have selective lower yields. The B61-10 was retired in 2016.

[q] Most sources list an unrefuelled ferry range of 2400 kilometres, but Lockheed Martin, which produces the F-16, lists 3200 km.

[r] These dual-capable aircraft are operated at airbases outside the USA by other members of NATO.

[s] Up until 2018, the US government published the number of warheads dismantled each year, but the administration of President Donald J. Trump ended this practice. The administration of President Joe Biden temporarily restored transparency, but publication of the 2018, 2019 and 2020 data showed that far fewer warheads had been dismantled than assumed (e.g. only 184 in 2020). Nonetheless, dismantlement of the warheads has continued, leaving an estimated 1536 warheads in the dismantlement queue as of Jan. 2023.

t In addition to these intact warheads, more than 20 000 plutonium pits were stored at the Pantex Plant, Texas, and perhaps 4000 uranium secondaries were stored at the Y-12 facility at Oak Ridge, Tennessee.

Sources: US Department of Defense, various budget reports and plans, press releases and documents obtained under the Freedom of Information Act; US Department of Energy, various budget reports and plans; US Air Force, US Navy and US Department of Energy, personal communication with officials; *Bulletin of the Atomic Scientists*, 'Nuclear notebook', various issues; and authors' estimates.

USA (like Russia) could add reserve warheads to missiles and bombers and potentially double its number of deployed strategic nuclear weapons.

This section enumerates the USA's holdings of nuclear weapons, both strategic (including those delivered by air, land and sea) and non-strategic. Before doing so, it first outlines the role played by nuclear weapons in US military doctrine and describes the USA's warhead-production capacity.

The role of nuclear weapons in US military doctrine

In 2022 the administration of US President Joe Biden released its long-awaited Nuclear Posture Review (NPR), the principal document outlining US nuclear policy. The 2022 NPR affirmed three roles for US nuclear weapons: 'Deter strategic attacks; Assure Allies and partners; and Achieve US objectives if deterrence fails.'[6] The review states that 'The United States would only consider the use of nuclear weapons in extreme circumstances to defend the vital interests of the United States or its Allies and partners'; however, it does not elaborate on what specifically constitutes 'vital interests', nor does it define the phrase 'Allies and partners'.[7] In contrast to the language about expanding nuclear options against non-nuclear attacks in the 2018 NPR issued by the administration of President Donald J. Trump, the 2022 NPR appears to reduce the emphasis on this role.[8] Even so, the NPR acknowledges 'the range of non-nuclear capabilities being developed and fielded by competitors that could inflict strategic-level damage', and the USA retains a wide range of options against nuclear and non-nuclear attacks.[9]

The USA under the Biden administration continued to implement the large-scale nuclear weapon programmes initiated under the 2009–17 administration of President Barack Obama and accelerated and expanded by the 2017–21 Trump administration. These modernization programmes cover all three legs of the nuclear triad (see below). However, the 2022 NPR

[6] US Department of Defense (DOD), *2022 National Defense Strategy of the United States of America* (DOD: Washington, DC, Oct. 2022), p. 7.
[7] US Department of Defense (note 6), p. 9.
[8] US Department of Defense (note 6), p. 7; and US Department of Defense (DOD), *Nuclear Posture Review 2018* (DOD: Washington, DC, Feb. 2018). On the 2018 NPR see Kristensen, H. M., 'US nuclear forces', *SIPRI Yearbook 2019*.
[9] US Department of Defense (note 6), p. 9.

includes two major changes from the previous review: cancelling the sea-launched cruise missile (SLCM-N) proposed by the Trump administration and retiring the B83-1 gravity bomb.

The 2022 NPR concludes that the SLCM-N is no longer necessary given existing capabilities, uncertainty as to whether it would provide leverage to negotiate arms control limits on Russia's non-strategic nuclear weapons, and the estimated cost in the light of other nuclear modernization programmes and defence priorities.[10] At the end of 2022, however, the US Congress continued funding of limited research for the SLCM-N: the FY 2023 National Defense Authorization Act allocated US$25 million for this, in contradiction to the findings of the 2022 NPR.[11] If a new administration after 2024 decides to fully fund the programme, then the new missile could be deployed on attack submarines by the early 2030s. This would go against the US pledge from 1992 not to develop a nuclear sea-launched cruise missile and could potentially result in the first significant increase in the size of the US nuclear weapon stockpile since 1996.[12]

The Biden administration chose to continue the retirement of the B83-1 gravity bomb—the last nuclear weapon with a megaton-level yield in the US nuclear arsenal—which the Trump administration had put on hold. The 2022 NPR states that the B83-1 would be retired 'due to increasing limitations on its capabilities and rising maintenance costs'.[13] It also alludes to an eventual replacement weapon 'for improved defeat' of hard and deeply buried targets.[14]

Warhead production

Since the end of the cold war, the US nuclear weapon-production complex has relied on refurbishment of existing warhead types to maintain the nuclear arsenal. In 2018, however, the USA shifted to a much more ambitious plan focused on new warhead production, which depends heavily on the ability to produce new plutonium pits—the core of a nuclear weapon. Whereas production capacity in 2021 and 2022 was limited to around 10 plutonium pits per year, the National Nuclear Security Administration (NNSA) plans to produce

---

[10] US Department of Defense (note 6), p. 20. On the SLCM-N see US Office of the Under Secretary of Defense for Policy, *Strengthening Deterrence and Reducing Nuclear Risks*, part II, *The Sea-Launched Cruise Missile-Nuclear (SLCM-N)* (US Department of State, Office of the Under Secretary of State for Arms Control and International Security: Washington, DC, 23 July 2020), p. 3.

[11] US Senate, Committee on Armed Services, 'National Defense Authorization Act for Fiscal Year 2023: Report', 18 July 2022; and US House of Representatives, Committee on Armed Services, 'National Defense Authorization Act for Fiscal Year 2023: Report', 1 July 2022.

[12] Bush, G. W., US president, 'Address before a joint session of the Congress on the state of the union', 28 Jan. 1992.

[13] US Department of Defense (note 6), p. 20.

[14] US Department of Defense (note 6), p. 20.

up to 30 pits in 2026 and set an initial target of at least 80 pits per year by 2030 to meet the demands of the US nuclear modernization programmes.[15] In order to fulfil these objectives, the NNSA is modernizing its plutonium-processing facility (PF-4) at Los Alamos National Laboratory in New Mexico and creating a new plutonium-processing facility at the Savannah River Site in South Carolina.[16]

In February 2022 the NNSA confirmed what outside experts had long predicted—that the goal of producing up to 80 pits per year by 2030 would not be possible.[17] Hence, some of the nuclear weapon programmes described below will probably face delays or new delivery systems could be initially deployed with existing warheads.[18]

Strategic nuclear forces

US offensive strategic nuclear forces include heavy bombers, land-based intercontinental ballistic missiles (ICBMs) and nuclear-powered ballistic missile submarines (SSBNs). These forces, together known as the triad, changed little during 2022. SIPRI estimates that a total of 3508 nuclear warheads were assigned to the triad, of which an estimated 1670 warheads were deployed on ballistic missiles and at heavy bomber bases.

Aircraft and air-delivered weapons

As of January 2023 the US Air Force (USAF) operated a fleet of 152 heavy bombers: 45 B-1Bs, 20 B-2As and 87 B-52Hs. Of these, 66 (20 B-2As and 46 B-52Hs) were nuclear-capable and approximately 60 (18 B-2As and 42 B-52Hs) are assigned nuclear missions under US nuclear war plans. The B-2A can deliver gravity bombs (B61-7, B61-11 and B83-1) and the B-52H can deliver the AGM-86B/W80-1 nuclear air-launched cruise missile (ALCM). SIPRI estimates that approximately 788 warheads were assigned to strategic bombers, of which about 300 are deployed at bomber bases and ready for delivery on relatively short notice.[19] The USA is modernizing its nuclear

---

[15] US National Nuclear Security Administration (NNSA), 'Plutonium pit production', Fact sheet, Apr. 2019; and US Government Accountability Office (GAO), *Nuclear Weapons: NNSA Should Further Develop Cost, Schedule, and Risk Information for the W87-1 Warhead Program*, Report no. GAO-20-73 (GAO: Washington, DC, Sep. 2020), pp. 14–15.

[16] US Department of Energy (note 1), p. 8-7.

[17] Demarest, C., '80 pits by 2030 won't happen, NNSA boss reaffirms. But "acceleration" is in the works', *Aiken Standard*, 8 Feb. 2022. See also e.g. US Government Accountability Office (note 15), p. 5; Hunter, D. E. et al., 'Independent assessment of the two-site pit production decision: Executive summary', Institute for Defense Analyses (IDA) document no. NS D-10711, May 2019, p. 4; and Demarest, C., 'Plutonium pit production in SC might happen in 2035. The target was 2030', *Aiken Standard*, 12 June 2021.

[18] US Air Force (USAF), *Report on Development of Ground-Based Strategic Deterrent Weapon*, Report to eight congressional committees (USAF: [Washington, DC,] May 2020), p. 4.

[19] The reduction in bomber weapons compared with *SIPRI Yearbook 2022* is not the result of new cuts but of new stockpile numbers causing a reassessment of the estimate.

bomber force by upgrading nuclear command-and-control capabilities on existing bombers, developing improved nuclear weapons (the B61-12 gravity bomb and the new AGM-181 Long-Range Standoff Weapon, LRSO) and building a new heavy bomber (the B-21 Raider).

The first six B-21s are expected to enter service in 2027; the aircraft will gradually replace the B-1B and B-2 bombers.[20] It is expected that the USAF will procure at least 100 (possibly as many as 145) of the new bombers, with the latest service costs estimated at approximately $203 billion for the entire 30-year operational programme, at an estimated production cost of $550 million per aircraft.[21] As a result of these developments, the number of US bomber bases with nuclear capability is expected to increase from two in 2022 to five by the early 2030s.[22]

The B-21 appears to have a slightly reduced weapons load than the B-2. It will be capable of delivering two types of nuclear weapon: the B61-12 guided nuclear gravity bomb, which is also designed to be deliverable from shorter-range non-strategic aircraft (see below); and the AGM-181 LRSO ALCM, which is in development. The AGM-181 LRSO will replace the AGM-86B ALCM in the early 2030s and will carry the W80-4 nuclear warhead, a modified version of the W80-1 warhead that is used on the AGM-86B. In mid 2022 the NNSA announced that the schedule for the first production unit of the W80-4 had slipped to the end of FY 2027, instead of FY 2025 as originally planned. Production is scheduled to be completed in FY 2031.[23]

Land-based missiles

As of January 2023 the USA deployed 400 LGM-30G Minuteman III ICBMs in 400 silos across three missile wings.[24] Another 50 empty silos are kept in a state of readiness for reloading with stored missiles if necessary. SIPRI estimates that 800 warheads were assigned to the ICBM force, of which 400 were deployed on the missiles. Each Minuteman III ICBM is armed with either a 335-kiloton W78/Mk12A or a 300-kt W87-0/Mk21 warhead. Missiles carrying the W78 can be uploaded with up to two more warheads

---

[20] Tirpak, J. A., 'B-21 Raider first flight now postponed to 2023', *Air Force Magazine*, 20 May 2022; and US Air Force, 'B-21 bomber to be unveiled Dec. 2', 20 Oct. 2022.

[21] Capaccio, A., 'Under-wraps B-21 bomber is seen costing $203 billion into 2050s', Bloomberg, 17 Nov. 2021; and Tirpak, J. A., 'A new bomber vision', *Air Force Magazine*, 1 June 2020.

[22] Dawkins, J. C., Commander, 8th Air Force and Joint-Global Strike Operations Center, Barksdale Air Force Base, 'B21 General Dawkins intro', YouTube, 19 Mar. 2020, 01:35; and Kristensen, H. M., 'USAF plans to expand nuclear bomber bases', FAS Strategic Security Blog, Federation of American Scientists, 17 Nov. 2020.

[23] Leone, D., 'Two-year delay for first LRSO warhead, but NNSA says will still deliver on-time to Air Force', Defense Daily, 4 Aug. 2022.

[24] Willett, E., 'AF meets New START requirements', US Air Force Global Strike Command, Press release, 28 June 2017.

for a maximum of three multiple independently targetable re-entry vehicles (MIRVs). ICBMs with the W87-0 can only be loaded with one warhead.[25]

The USAF has scheduled its next-generation ICBM to begin replacing the Minuteman III in 2028, with full replacement by 2036, although delays to this schedule are expected.[26] Flight-testing of this new ICBM—the LGM-35A Sentinel—is expected to begin in 2023.[27] Each Sentinel will be able to carry up to two warheads, with the USAF planning to produce a significantly modified warhead based on the same design as the W87-0, known as the W87-1. The cost of the W87-1 warhead-modernization programme has been estimated at between $12.2 billion and $14.2 billion, but this excludes the considerable costs of producing the plutonium pits for the warhead.[28] After the NNSA completed a review of the W87-1 in 2021, the programme entered the development engineering phase in 2022, with anticipated completion of the first production unit in FY 2030.[29] However, production of the W87-1 in time to meet the Sentinel's planned deployment schedule depended on the NNSA's projected production rate of at least 80 plutonium pits per year by 2030 (see above). The NNSA's acknowledgement that this objective is unrealistic probably means that the Sentinel will initially be deployed with the existing W87-0 warheads.[30]

Sea-based missiles

The US Navy operates a fleet of 14 Ohio-class SSBNs, of which 12 are normally considered to be operational with the remaining 2 typically undergoing refuelling and overhaul at any given time. Eight of the SSBNs are based at Naval Base Kitsap in Washington state, on the Pacific Ocean, and six at Naval Submarine Base Kings Bay in Georgia, on the Atlantic. The most recent refuelling was completed in 2022, meaning that all 14 boats are now potentially deployable until 2027, when the first Ohio-class submarine is expected to retire.[31]

Each Ohio-class SSBN can carry up to 20 Trident II D5 submarine-launched ballistic missiles (SLBMs). To meet the New START limit on deployed launchers, 4 of the 24 initial missile tubes on each submarine were deactivated so that the 12 SSBNs that are usually operational can carry no

[25] On the warheads and yields see also Kristensen, H. M. and Korda, M., 'United States nuclear forces', *SIPRI Yearbook 2021*, p. 341.
[26] Richard, C. A., Commander, US Strategic Command, Statement before the US Senate, Armed Services Committee, 13 Feb. 2020, p. 9. On the Sentinel see also Kristensen and Korda (note 25), p. 341.
[27] 'LGM-35A Sentinel intercontinental ballistic missile, USA', Airforce Technology, 29 July 2022.
[28] US Department of Energy (note 1), p. 8-32.
[29] Sirota, S., 'NNSA completes requirements review of GBSD's W87-1 warhead', Inside Defense, 22 Apr. 2021; and US National Nuclear Security Administration (NNSA), 'W87-1 modification program', Jan. 2022.
[30] Demarest, '80 pits by 2030 won't happen' (note 17); and US Air Force (note 18).
[31] US Navy, Office of the Chief of Naval Operations, *Report to Congress on the Annual Long-Range Plan for Construction of Naval Vessels for Fiscal Year 2020* (US Navy: Washington, DC, Mar. 2019).

more than 240 missiles.[32] At any given time 8–10 SSBNs are normally at sea, of which 4–5 are on alert in their designated patrol areas and ready to fire their missiles within 15 minutes of receiving the launch order. The US SSBN fleet conducts about 30 deterrence patrols per year.[33]

The Trident II D5 SLBMs carry two basic warhead types: the 455-kt W88 and the W76. The latter exists in two versions: the 90-kt W76-1 and the low-yield W76-2.[34] The NNSA has begun modernizing the ageing W88 warhead, and the first production unit of the W88 Alt 370 was completed on 1 July 2021.[35] Mass production was expected to be authorized by the end of 2022, but appears to have been delayed.[36] Each SLBM can carry up to eight warheads but normally carries an average of four or five. SIPRI estimates that around 1920 warheads were assigned to the SSBN fleet as of January 2023, of which nearly 1000 were deployed on SLBMs.[37]

The newest warhead, the low-yield W76-2, was first deployed in late 2019 and has now been deployed on SSBNs in both the Atlantic and the Pacific.[38] It is a modification of the W76-1 and is estimated to have an explosive yield of 8 kt.[39] The 2022 NPR left open the possibility that the W76-2 warhead might be retired in the medium term as the F-35A combat aircraft and the LRSO are fielded over the coming decade.[40]

Since 2017 the US Navy has been replacing its Trident II D5 SLBMs with an enhanced version, known as the D5LE (LE for 'life extension'), which is equipped with the new Mk6 guidance system. The upgrade is scheduled for completion in 2024.[41] In 2022 the US Navy conducted four flight tests of the D5LE. It will arm Ohio-class SSBNs for the remainder of their service lives (up to 2042) and will also be deployed on the United Kingdom's Trident submarines (see section III). A new class of SSBN, the Columbia class, will initially be armed with D5LE SLBMs, but from 2039 these will

---

[32] US Navy Office of Information, 'Fleet ballistic missile submarines—SSBN', Fact file, 25 May 2021.
[33] See e.g. Kristensen, H., 'US SSBN patrols steady, but mysterious reduction in Pacific in 2017', FAS Strategic Security Blog, Federation of American Scientists, 24 May 2018.
[34] The older W76-0 version has been, or remains in the process of being, retired. On these warheads see also Kristensen and Korda (note 25), pp. 342–43.
[35] US National Nuclear Security Administration (NNSA), 'NNSA completes first production unit of W88 Alteration 370', 13 July 2021.
[36] Leone, D., 'Mass production of refurbished nuclear weapons could begin soon, NNSA says', Exchange Monitor, 15 Sep. 2022.
[37] US Department of State (note 5).
[38] Arkin, W. M. and Kristensen, H. M., 'US deploys new low-yield nuclear submarine warhead', FAS Strategic Security Blog, Federation of American Scientists, 29 Jan. 2020; and US Department of Defense, 'Statement on the fielding of the W76-2 low-yield submarine launched ballistic missile warhead', Press release, 4 Feb. 2020.
[39] US military officials, Private communication with authors, 2019–20.
[40] US Department of Defense (note 6), p. 20.
[41] Wolfe, J., Director of US Strategic Systems Programs, 'US nuclear weapons policy, programs, and strategy in review of the defense authorization request for fiscal year 2020 and the Future Years Defense Program', Statement before the US Senate, Armed Services Committee, Subcommittee on Strategic Forces, 1 May 2019, p. 4.

be replaced with an upgraded SLBM, the D5LE2.[42] The US Navy's FY 2022 budget submission estimated the procurement cost of the first Columbia-class SSBN—the USS *District of Columbia* (SSBN-826)—at approximately $15 billion, followed by a cost of $9.3 billion for the second boat.[43] The USS *District of Columbia* is scheduled to start patrols in 2031.[44]

To arm the D5LE2, the NNSA has begun early design development of a new nuclear warhead, known as the W93. This would be the first new warhead design developed by the USA since the end of the cold war. The W93 warhead will be housed in a new Mk7 re-entry body (aeroshell) that will also be deployed on the UK's new Dreadnought-class submarines (see section III). The W93 appears intended to initially supplement, rather than replace, the W76-1 and the W88. Another new warhead is planned to replace those warheads. The completion of the first production unit of the W93 is tentatively scheduled for 2034–36.[45]

Non-strategic nuclear forces

As of January 2023 the USA had one basic type of air-delivered non-strategic weapon in its stockpile—the B61 gravity bomb, which exists in two versions: the B61-3 and the B61-4.[46] There were an estimated 200 of these bombs in the stockpile.

SIPRI estimates that the USAF has deployed approximately 100 of the B61 bombs outside the USA for potential use by combat aircraft operated by members of the North Atlantic Treaty Organization (NATO), although the weapons remain in USAF custody. They are at six airbases in five NATO member states: Kleine Brogel in Belgium; Büchel in Germany; Aviano and Ghedi in Italy; Volkel in the Netherlands; and İncirlik in Türkiye.[47] The remaining (c. 100) B61 bombs are thought to be stored at Kirtland Air Force Base in New Mexico for potential use by US aircraft, possibly including

---

[42] Wolfe, J., Director of US Strategic Systems Programs, 'FY2021 budget request for nuclear forces and atomic energy defense activities', Statement before the US House of Representatives, Armed Services Committee, Subcommittee on Strategic Forces, 3 Mar. 2020, p. 5.

[43] O'Rourke, R., *Navy Columbia (SSBN-826) Class Ballistic Missile Submarine Program: Background and Issues for Congress*, Congressional Research Service (CRS) Report for Congress R41129 (US Congress, CRS: Washington, DC, 22 Feb. 2022), p. 9.

[44] Wolfe (note 41), p. 8.

[45] US Department of Energy (note 1), p. 2-10.

[46] A third version, the B61-10, was retired in Sep. 2016. US Department of Energy (DOE), National Nuclear Security Administration (NNSA), *Fiscal Year 2018 Stockpile Stewardship and Management Plan*, Report to Congress (DOE: Washington, DC, Nov. 2017), figures 1.1–1.7, p. 1-13.

[47] For detailed overviews of the dual-capable aircraft programmes of the USA and its NATO allies see Kristensen (note 8), pp. 299–300; and Andreasen, S. et al., *Building a Safe, Secure, and Credible NATO Nuclear Posture* (Nuclear Threat Initiative: Washington, DC, Jan. 2018).

in East Asia.[48] USA-based fighter wings for this mission include the 366th Fighter Wing at Mountain Home Air Force Base in Idaho.[49]

To replace all current versions of the B61 (including the non-strategic B61-3 and B61-4), the USA is producing the new B61-12 guided nuclear bomb. A guided tail-kit enables the B61-12 to hit targets more accurately, meaning that it can use lower yields and thus generate less radioactive fallout.[50] Full-scale production of the B61-12 began in late 2022 and is expected to be completed by 2026.[51] Once deployment to the bases outside the USA begins, the B61-3 and B61-4 bombs currently deployed at those bases will be returned to the USA and dismantled.

Operations to integrate the incoming B61-12 on seven types of aircraft operated by the USA or its NATO allies continued in 2022: the B-2A, the new B-21, the F-15E, the F-16C/D, the F-16MLU, the F-35A and the PA-200 (Tornado).[52] The F-35A will replace all Belgian, Dutch and US F-16s and German and Italian Tornado aircraft in the nuclear strike role.

[48] US Department of Defense, *Nuclear Posture Review 2018* (note 8), p. 48.
[49] Heflin, L., '53rd Wing WSEP incorporates NucWSEP, enhances readiness for real world operations', Press release, Air Combat Command, 9 Sep. 2021.
[50] Kristensen, H. M. and McKinzie, M., 'Video shows earth-penetrating capability of B61-12 nuclear bomb', FAS Strategic Security Blog, Federation of American Scientists, 14 Jan. 2016.
[51] Meub, K., 'B61-12 production begins', *Sandia LabNews*, Sandia National Laboratories, 11 Feb. 2022; and Defense Visual Information Distribution Service, 'F-35 dual-capable aircraft team meets goals ahead of schedule, earns prestigious award', F-35 Joint Program Office Public Affairs, 17 Feb. 2022.
[52] US Air Force (USAF), *Acquisition Annual Report Fiscal Year 2018: Cost-effective Modernization* (USAF: Washington, DC, [n.d.]), p. 24.

II. Russian nuclear forces

HANS M. KRISTENSEN AND MATT KORDA*

As of January 2023 the Russian Federation maintained a military stockpile of approximately 4489 nuclear warheads, a slight increase of around 12 warheads compared with the estimate for January 2022. About 2673 of these were strategic warheads, of which roughly 1674 were deployed on land- and sea-based ballistic missiles and at bomber bases. Russia also possessed approximately 1816 non-strategic (tactical) nuclear warheads. All of the non-strategic warheads are assessed to be at central storage sites. An additional 1400 retired warheads were awaiting dismantlement (100 fewer than the previous year's estimate), giving a total estimated inventory of approximately 5889 warheads (see table 7.3).

These estimates are based on publicly available information about the Russian nuclear arsenal and assessments by the authors. Because of a lack of transparency, estimates and analysis of Russia's nuclear weapon developments come with considerable uncertainty, particularly regarding the country's sizable stockpile of non-strategic nuclear weapons. However, it is possible to formulate a reasonable assessment of the progress of Russia's nuclear modernization by reviewing satellite imagery and other forms of open-source intelligence, official statements, industry publications and state media interviews with Russian government officials.[1]

This section enumerates Russia's holdings of strategic and non-strategic air-delivered, land-based and sea-based nuclear weapons. Before doing so, it first considers Russia's compliance with its bilateral arms control obligations and describes the role played by nuclear weapons in Russian military doctrine.

Russian compliance with New START

It was a tumultuous and discouraging year for the last remaining bilateral strategic arms control treaty between Russia and the United States, the 2010 Treaty on Measures for the Further Reduction and Limitation of Strategic Offensive Arms (New START). This treaty places a cap on the numbers of Russian and US deployed strategic nuclear forces and allows for on-site inspections to verify compliance.[2]

At the end of 2022, the USA concluded that it was unable to determine whether or not Russia remained in compliance throughout the year with its

---

[1] Kristensen, H. M. and Korda, M., 'Estimating world nuclear forces: An overview and assessment of sources', SIPRI Commentary, 14 June 2021.

[2] For a summary and other details of New START see annex A, section III, in this volume. On related developments in 2022 see chapter 8, section I, in this volume.

* The authors wish to thank Eliana Johns for contributing invaluable research to this publication.

obligation under the treaty to deploy no more than 1550 strategic warheads.[3] This was due to Russia's decision to indefinitely suspend treaty inspections.[4] The US report was careful to note, however, that 'While this is a serious concern, it is not a determination of noncompliance' and also assessed that Russia's deployed warheads were likely to have been under the New START limit at the end of 2022.[5]

In September 2022 Russia declared that it had 1549 deployed warheads attributed to 540 strategic launchers, thus remaining under the final warhead limits of New START.[6] Just as with the USA, many of Russia's strategic delivery systems carry fewer warheads than their maximum capacity in order to meet the New START limits. If Russia chose to no longer comply with the treaty limits, or if the treaty were to expire without a follow-on agreement, Russia (like the USA) could add reserve warheads to missiles and bombers and potentially double its number of deployed strategic nuclear weapons.[7]

The role of nuclear weapons in Russian military doctrine

Russia's official deterrence policy (last updated in 2020) lays out explicit conditions under which it could launch nuclear weapons: to retaliate against an ongoing attack 'against critical governmental or military sites' by ballistic missiles, nuclear weapons or other weapons of mass destruction (WMD), and to retaliate against 'the use of conventional weapons when the very existence of the state is in jeopardy'.[8] This formulation is largely consistent with previous public iterations of Russian nuclear policy.

In January 2022 Russia joined the four other permanent members of the United Nations Security Council in stating that 'a nuclear war cannot be won and must never be fought'.[9] This statement was reiterated by a member of Russia's delegation to the UN General Assembly in November 2022. He specifically noted how Russia's nuclear doctrine remained unchanged after its invasion of Ukraine in 2022: 'In response to today's absolutely ungrounded accusation that Russia allegedly threat[ened] to use nuclear weapons during

---

[3] US Department of State, 'New START treaty annual implementation report', Report to Congress, 31 Jan. 2023, p. 6.

[4] 'Russia suspends START arms inspections over US travel curbs', Reuters, 8 Aug. 2022; Atwood, K. and Hansler, J., 'Russia postpones nuclear arms control talks with US, State Department says', CNN, 28 Nov. 2022; and US Department of State (note 3), pp. 8–15.

[5] US Department of State (note 3), pp. 5–6.

[6] US Department of State, Bureau of Arms Control, Verification and Compliance, 'New START Treaty aggregate numbers of strategic offensive arms', Fact sheet, 1 Sep. 2022.

[7] Korda, M. and Kristensen, H., 'If arms control collapses, US and Russian strategic nuclear arsenals could double in size', FAS Strategic Security Blog, Federation of American Scientists, 7 Feb. 2023. On the negotiation of the renewal of New START see chapter 8, section I, in this volume.

[8] Russian Ministry of Foreign Affairs, 'Basic principles of state policy of the Russian Federation on nuclear deterrence', Approved by Russian Presidential Executive Order no. 355, 2 June 2020.

[9] Joint statement of the leaders of the five nuclear-weapon states on preventing nuclear war and avoiding arms races, 3 Jan. 2022. See also chapter 8, section I, in this volume.

Table 7.3. Russian nuclear forces, January 2023

All figures are approximate and some are based on assessments by the authors.

Type/ Russian designation (NATO designation)	No. of launchers	Year first deployed	Range (km)[a]	Warheads x yield	No. of warheads[b]
Strategic nuclear forces	567				2 673[c]
Aircraft (bombers)	70[d]				580[e]
Tu-95MS/M (Bear-H)[f]	55	1984/ 2015	6 500– 10 500	6–16 x 200 kt Kh-55 (AS-15A) or Kh-102 (AS-23B) ALCMs	448
Tu-160M1/M2 (Blackjack)	15	1987/ 2021	10 500– 13 200	12 x 200 kt Kh-55 or Kh-102 ALCMs, bombs	132
Land-based missiles (ICBMs)	321				1 197[g]
RS-20V Voevoda (SS-18 Satan)	34	1988	11 000– 15 000	10 x 500–800 kt[h]	340
RS-18 (SS-19 Stiletto)	–	1980	10 000	6 x 400 kt	–[i]
Avangard (SS-19 Mod 4)[j]	7	2019	10 000	1 x HGV	7
RS-12M Topol (SS-25 Sickle)	–[k]	1988	10 500	1 x 800 kt	–
RS-12M1 Topol-M (SS-27 Mod 1/mobile)	18	2006	10 500	1 x [800 kt]	18
RS-12M2 Topol-M (SS-27 Mod 1/silo)	60	1997	10 500	1 x [800 kt]	60
RS-24 Yars (SS-27 Mod 2/mobile)	171	2010	10 500	[4 x 250 kt][l]	684
RS-24 Yars (SS-27 Mod 2/silo)	22	2014	10 500	4 x [250 kt]	88
RS-28 Sarmat (SS-X-29)	..	[2024]	>10 000	[10 x 500 kt]	–
Sirena-M[m]	9	2022	–	Command and control module	–
Sea-based missiles (SLBMs)	11/176[n]				896[o]
RSM-54 Sineva/Layner (SS-N-23 M2/3)[p]	5/80	2007/ 2014	9 000	4 x 100 kt[q]	320[r]
RSM-56 Bulava (SS-N-32)	6/96	2012	>8 050	[6 x 100 kt][s]	576
Non-strategic nuclear forces					1 816[t]
Navy weapons	..				835
Submarines/surface ships/naval aircraft	..		Land-attack cruise missiles, sea-launched cruise missiles, anti-submarine weapons, surface-to-air missiles, depth bombs, torpedoes[u]		835
Air force weapons	266				506
Tu-22M3M (Backfire-C)	60	1974	..	3 x ASMs, bombs	300
Su-24M/M2 (Fencer-D)	70	1974	..	2 x bombs	70[v]
Su-34 (Fullback)	124	2006	..	2 x bombs	124[v]
Su-57 (Felon)	–	[2024]	..	[bombs, ASMs]	..
MiG-31K (Foxhound)	12	2018	..	1 x ALBM	12

Type/ Russian designation (NATO designation)	No. of launchers	Year first deployed	Range (km)[a]	Warheads x yield	No. of warheads[b]
Air, coastal and missile defence	882				385
53T6 (SH-08 Gazelle)	68	1986	30	1 x 10 kt	68
S-300/400 (SA-20/21)	750[w]	1992/ 2007	..	1 x low kt	290
3M55/P-800 Oniks (SS-N-26 Strobile), 3K55/K300-P Bastion (SSC-5 Stooge)	56	2015	>400	1 x [10–100 kt]	23
SPU-35V Redut (SSC-1B Sepal)	8[x]	1973	500	1 x 350 kt	4
Army weapons	170				90
9K720 Iskander-M (SS-26 Stone), 9M728 Iskander-K (SSC-7 Southpaw)	150	2005	350	1 x [10–100 kt]	70[y]
9M729 (SSC-8 Screwdriver)	20	2016	2 350	1 x [10–100 kt]	20[z]
Total stockpile					**4 489**
Deployed strategic warheads					1 674
Reserve warheads					2 815
Strategic					999
Non-strategic					1 816
Retired warheads awaiting dismantlement					**1 400**
Total inventory					**5 889**

.. = not available or not applicable; – = nil or a negligible value; [ ] = uncertain SIPRI estimate; ALBM = air-launched ballistic missile; ALCM = air-launched cruise missile; ASM = air-to-surface missile; HGV = hypersonic glide vehicle; kt = kiloton; ICBM = intercontinental ballistic missile; NATO = North Atlantic Treaty Organization; SLBM = submarine-launched ballistic missile.

[a] For aircraft, the listed range is for illustrative purposes only; actual mission range will vary according to flight profile, weapon payload and in-flight refuelling.

[b] These figures show the total number of warheads estimated to be assigned to nuclear-capable delivery systems. Only some of these warheads have been deployed on missiles and at airbases, as described in the notes below.

[c] Of these strategic warheads, c. 1674 were deployed on land- and sea-based ballistic missiles and at bomber bases. The remaining warheads were in central storage. This number is different from the number of deployed strategic warheads counted by the 2010 Russian–United States Treaty on Measures for the Further Reduction and Limitation of Strategic Offensive Arms (New START) because the treaty attributes 1 weapon to each deployed bomber, even though bombers do not carry weapons under normal circumstances. Additionally, the treaty does not count weapons stored at bomber bases and, at any given time, some nuclear-powered ballistic missile submarines (SSBNs) are not fully loaded with warheads and are thus not counted under the treaty.

[d] All of Russia's long-range strategic bombers are nuclear-capable. Of these, only c. 55 are thought to be counted as deployed under New START. Because of ongoing bomber modernization, there is considerable uncertainty about how many bombers are operational.

[e] The maximum possible payload on the bombers is estimated to be c. 800 nuclear weapons but, given that only some of the bombers are fully operational, SIPRI estimates that only c. 580 weapons have been assigned to the long-range bomber force. Of these, c. 200 might be deployed and stored at the 2 strategic bomber bases. The remaining weapons are thought to be in central storage facilities.

[f] Two types of Tu-95MS aircraft were produced: the Tu-95MS6 (Bear-H6), which can carry 6 Kh-55 (AS-15A) missiles internally; and the Tu-95MS16 (Bear-H16), which can carry a total of 16 missiles, including 10 Kh-55 missiles externally. Both types were being modernized in 2022. The modernized aircraft, the Tu-95MSM, can carry 8 Kh-102 (AS-23B) missiles externally and possibly 6 internally, for a total of 14 missiles.

[g] These ICBMs can carry a total of 1197 warheads, but SIPRI estimates that they have had their warhead load reduced to c. 834 warheads, with the remaining warheads in storage.

[h] It is possible that, as of Jan. 2023, the RS-20Vs carried only 5 warheads each to meet the New START limit for deployed strategic warheads.

[i] It is believed that the remaining RS-18s have been retired, although activities continued at some regiments.

[j] The missile uses a modified RS-18 ICBM booster with an HGV payload.

[k] Although the final division at Vypolzovo had not yet completed its upgrade to the RS-24 by the end of 2022, it is believed that its legacy RS-12M missiles had been removed in preparation for the upgrade.

[l] It is possible that, as of Jan. 2023, the RS-24s carried only 3 warheads each to meet the New START limit on deployed strategic warheads.

[m] The division at Yurya is equipped with the new Sirena-M nuclear command and control missile, which is based on the RS-24 ICBM. The missiles are not nuclear-armed, but rather serve as an emergency launch communication module. They are included in this table because their launchers are counted against the limits permitted under New START.

[n] The first figure is the total number of nuclear-powered ballistic missile submarines (SSBNs) in the Russian fleet; the second is the maximum number of missiles that they can carry. Of Russia's 11 operational SSBNs (as of Jan. 2023), 1–2 are in overhaul at any given time and do not carry their assigned nuclear missiles and warheads (see note o).

[o] The warhead load on SLBMs is thought to have been reduced for Russia to stay below the New START warhead limit. Additionally, at any given time, 1–2 SSBNs are in overhaul and do not carry nuclear weapons. Therefore, it is estimated here that only c. 640 of the 896 SLBM warheads have been deployed.

[p] The current version of the RSM-54 SLBM might be the Layner (SS-N-23 M3), a modification of the previous version—the Sineva (SS-N-23 M2). However, the US Air Force's National Air and Space Intelligence Center (NASIC) did not include the Layner in its 2020 report on ballistic and cruise missile threats, and there is some uncertainty regarding its status and capability.

[q] In 2006 US intelligence estimated that the RSM-54 missile could carry up to 10 warheads, but it lowered the estimate to 4 in 2009. The average number of warheads carried on each missile has probably been limited to 4 multiple independently targetable re-entry vehicles (MIRVs) to meet the New START limits.

[r] SIPRI estimates that, at any given time, only 256 of these warheads are deployed on 4 operational Delta IV submarines, with the fifth boat in overhaul. The actual number may even be lower as 2 boats often undergo maintenance at the same time.

[s] It is possible that, as of Jan. 2023, RSM-56 Bulava (SS-N-32) SLBMs carried only 4 warheads each for Russia to meet the New START limit on deployed strategic warheads.

[t] According to the Russian government, non-strategic nuclear warheads are not deployed with their delivery systems but are kept in storage facilities. Some storage facilities are near operational bases. It is possible that there are more unreported nuclear-capable non-strategic systems.

[u] Only submarines are assumed to be assigned nuclear torpedoes.

[v] These estimates assume that half of the aircraft have a nuclear role.

^{w} As of Jan. 2023 there were at least 80 S-300/400 sites across Russia, each with an average of 12 launchers, each with 2–4 interceptors. Each launcher has several reloads, which are assumed likely to be conventional.

^{x} It is assumed that all SPU-35V Redut units, except for a single silo-based version in Crimea, had been replaced by the K-300P Bastion by Jan. 2023.

^{y} This estimate assumes that around half of the dual-capable launchers have a secondary nuclear role. In its 2020 report, NASIC listed the 9M728 as 'Conventional, Nuclear Possible'.

^{z} This figure assumes that there are 5 9M729 battalions, each with 4 launchers, for a total of 80 missiles. Each launcher is assumed to have at least 1 reload, for a total of at least 160 missiles. Most missiles are thought to be conventional, with 4–5 nuclear warheads per battalion, for a total of c. 20.

Sources: Russian Ministry of Defence, various press releases; US Department of State, START Treaty Memoranda of Understanding, 1990–July 2009; New START aggregate data releases, various years; US Air Force, National Air and Space Intelligence Center (NASIC), *Ballistic and Cruise Missile Threat 2020* (NASIC: Wright-Patterson Air Force Base, OH, July 2020); US Department of Defense (DOD), *2022 National Defense Strategy of the United States of America* (DOD: Washington, DC, Oct. 2022); US Office of the Deputy Assistant Secretary of Defense for Nuclear Matters, *Nuclear Matters Handbook 2020* (DOD: Washington, DC, Mar. 2020); DOD, various Congressional testimonies; BBC Monitoring; Russian news media; Russian Strategic Nuclear Forces website; International Institute for Strategic Studies, *The Military Balance*, various years; Cochran, T. B. et al., *Nuclear Weapons Databook*, vol. 4, *Soviet Nuclear Weapons* (Harper & Row: New York, 1989); *IHS Jane's Strategic Weapon Systems*, various issues; US Naval Institute, *Proceedings*, various issues; *Bulletin of the Atomic Scientists*, 'Nuclear notebook', various issues; and authors' estimates.

the special military operation in Ukraine, we would like to stress once again that Russia's doctrine in this sphere is purely defensive and does not allow any broad interpretation'.[10]

Nonetheless, the invasion of Ukraine has raised questions about Russia's nuclear doctrine, and about where, when and how Russia might use nuclear weapons. Several speeches made by Russian President Vladimir Putin and senior Russian officials and commentators alluding to the potential use of nuclear weapons in the conflict have added to the uncertainty.[11]

A few days after the invasion, Putin placed Russia's nuclear arsenal on 'high combat alert', saying that 'aggressive statements' from the North Atlantic Treaty Organization (NATO) had caused him to increase Russia's nuclear readiness.[12] However, it appears that this order did not involve deployment of additional nuclear systems; it was primarily related to enhancing staffing levels and nuclear command and control. By the end of 2022 none of Russia's nuclear forces had conducted any unusual deployment patterns in the context of the war in Ukraine.

[10] 'Russia's nuclear doctrine is purely defensive, says Russian diplomat', TASS, 9 Nov. 2022.
[11] See e.g. President of Russia, 'Address by the president of the Russian Federation', 24 Feb. 2022; President of Russia, 'Address by the president of the Russian Federation', 21 Sep. 2022; and 'Russia can defend new regions with nuclear weapons: Medvedev', Al Jazeera, 22 Sep. 2022.
[12] President of Russia, 'Meeting with Sergei Shoigu and Valery Gerasimov', 27 Feb. 2022.

Strategic nuclear forces

As of January 2023 Russia had an estimated 2673 warheads assigned for potential use by strategic launchers: heavy bombers, land-based intercontinental ballistic missiles (ICBMs) and submarine-launched ballistic missiles (SLBMs). This is an increase of approximately 108 warheads compared with January 2022 due to fluctuations in the arsenal caused by the deployment of newer ICBMs with multiple independently targetable re-entry vehicles (MIRVs) as well as the introduction of a new nuclear-powered ballistic missile submarine (SSBN).

Aircraft and air-delivered weapons

As of January 2023 the Long-Range Aviation command of the Russian Air Force operated a fleet of approximately 70 operational heavy bombers, comprising 15 Tu-160 (Blackjack) and 55 Tu-95MS (Bear) bombers.[13] Not all of these counted as deployed under New START and some were undergoing various upgrades. The maximum possible payload on the bombers is approximately 800 nuclear weapons. However, since not all of the bombers were fully operational, it is estimated here that the number of assigned weapons was lower—around 580. SIPRI estimates that approximately 200 of these weapons were probably stored at the two strategic bomber bases: Engels in Saratov oblast and Ukrainka in Amur oblast.[14]

Modernization of the bombers—which includes upgrades to their avionics suites, engines and long-range nuclear and conventional cruise missiles—continued throughout 2022 but remained subject to delays.[15] It seems likely that all of the Tu-160s (including at least 10 brand-new Tu-160M2 bombers) and most of the Tu-95s will eventually be upgraded to maintain a bomber force of perhaps 50–60 operational aircraft. These modernized bombers are intended to be a temporary bridge to Russia's next-generation bomber: the PAK-DA, serial production of which is planned to begin in 2028–29.[16] The

---

[13] For the missiles, aircraft and submarines discussed in this section, a designation in parentheses (e.g. Blackjack) following the Russian designation (e.g. Tu-160) is that assigned by the North Atlantic Treaty Organization (NATO). The Tu-95MS exists in two versions: the Tu-95MS16 (Bear-H16) and the Tu-95MS6 (Bear-H6).

[14] Podvig, P., 'Strategic aviation', Russian Strategic Nuclear Forces, 7 Aug. 2021.

[15] President of Russia, 'Meeting with workers of Gorbunov Kazan aviation factory and Tu-160M pilots', 25 Jan. 2018; Ignatyeva, L., 'New Kazan strategic bombardier hits the sky', Realnoe Vremya, 11 Jan. 2023; and President of Russia, 'Заседание коллегии Министерства обороны' [Ministry of Defence Board meeting], 21 Dec. 2022.

[16] 'PAK DA demonstrational model to be ready by 2023—Source', TASS, 2 Aug. 2021; 'Russia begins construction of the first PAK DA strategic bomber—Sources', TASS, 26 May 2020; Lavrov, A., Kretsul, R. and Ramm, A., 'ПАКетное соглашение: новейшему бомбардировщику назначили сроки выхода в серию' [PAKage agreement: The latest bomber assigned a deadline for production], *Izvestia*, 14 Jan. 2020; and 'Russia tests engine for next-generation strategic missile-carrying bomber', TASS, 31 Oct. 2022.

PAK-DA will also eventually replace all bombers deployed with non-strategic forces (see below).[17]

Both the Tu-160 and the Tu-95 strategic bombers currently carry the Kh-55 (AS-15) air-launched cruise missile (ALCM), but this is being replaced on the upgraded bombers by the new Kh-102 (AS-23B) ALCM. In November 2022 the British Ministry of Defence assessed that Russia was 'likely removing the nuclear warheads from ageing [Kh-55] nuclear cruise missiles and firing the unarmed munitions at Ukraine'.[18] Russia has used both types of bomber to conduct attacks on Ukraine. Some of Russia's strategic bombers have thus been damaged; at least two Tu-95 bombers were visibly damaged from a probable Ukrainian strike on Engels Airbase in December 2022.[19]

Land-based missiles

As of January 2023 the Strategic Rocket Forces (SRF)—the branch of the Russian armed forces that controls land-based ICBMs—consisted of 12 missile divisions grouped into 3 armies, deploying an estimated 321 ICBMs of different types and variations (see table 7.3).[20] These ICBMs can carry a maximum of about 1197 warheads, but SIPRI estimates that they have had their warhead load reduced to around 834 warheads to keep Russia below the New START limit for deployed strategic warheads. These ICBMs carry approximately half of Russia's estimated 1674 deployed strategic warheads.

Russia is close to completing the replacement of Soviet-era ICBMs with new types, although this process has taken much longer than expected. In December 2022 Colonel General Sergei Karakaev, commander of the SRF, stated that around 85 per cent of the ICBM force had been modernized.[21] The bulk of the modernization programme has focused on the RS-24 Yars (SS-27 Mod 2), a MIRVed version of the RS-12M1/2 Topol-M (SS-27 Mod 1). SIPRI estimates that, as of January 2023, the number of deployed RS-24s had grown to approximately 193 mobile- and silo-based RS-24 missiles, including five completed mobile divisions (at Barnaul, Irkutsk, Nizhniy Tagil, Novosibirsk and Yoshkar-Ola), with one more in progress (at Vypolzovo—sometimes referred to as Bologovsky).[22] Karakaev

---

[17] 'Russia to test next-generation stealth strategic bomber', TASS, 2 Aug. 2019.

[18] British Ministry of Defence (@DefenceHQ), Twitter, 26 Nov. 2022, <https://twitter.com/DefenceHQ/status/1596389927733927937>.

[19] Cenciotti, D., 'Explosion hits Engels-2 Airbase, Russia, reportedly damaging at least two Tu-95 bombers', The Aviationist, 5 Dec. 2022.

[20] One of these ICBM divisions, the 8th Missile Division at Yurya, Kirov oblast, was being modernized alongside the rest of the ICBM force; however, the division's Sirena-M ICBMs are believed to serve as back-up launch code transmitters and therefore have not been armed with nuclear weapons.

[21] Karakaev, S. V. (Col. Gen.), interviewed in Biryulin, R., Andreev, D. and Reznik, A., 'Ядерный щит России по-прежнему надёжен' [Russia's nuclear shield is still reliable], *Krasnaya Zvezda*, 16 Dec. 2022; and 'Russian TV show announces new ICBM to enter service soon', TRK Petersburg Channel 5, 21 Apr. 2014, Translation from Russian, BBC Monitoring.

[22] Karakaev (note 21); and authors' estimates.

stated that one regiment of the Vypolzovo division had begun combat duty by the end of 2022, and the entire division's upgrade to the RS-24 would be completed in 2023.[23] SIPRI estimates that this division has already been fully disarmed of its older RS-12M Topol (SS-25) ICBMs in preparation for receiving the new RS-24, indicating that the Topol ICBM is now fully out of service across the SRF.[24]

Deployment of the silo-based RS-24s continues at Kozelsk, Kaluga oblast, with one regiment of 10 silos completed in 2018 and the second completed in 2020.[25] The third regiment began combat duty in December 2021 and the regiment's first two missiles were placed into their silos in 2022.[26] However, commercial satellite imagery indicates that the necessary infrastructure upgrades are unlikely to be completed by the 2024 target date.[27] It is likely that the 60 RS-12M2 Topol-M (SS-27 Mod 1) silos at Tatishchevo, Saratov oblast, will eventually also be upgraded to the RS-24.

In December 2021 Russia completed the rearmament of the first of the former RS-20V regiments at Dombarovsky, Orenburg oblast, with six RS-18 (SS-19 Mod 4) missiles equipped with the Avangard hypersonic glide vehicle (HGV) system.[28] Russia has been installing Avangard-equipped missiles at a rate of two per year in upgraded complexes. In 2022 it installed the first missile in the second Avangard regiment at Dombarovsky. The entire regiment's rearmament is scheduled for completion by the end of 2027 with a total of 12 Avangard-equipped missiles.[29]

Russia has also been developing a new 'heavy' liquid-fuelled, silo-based ICBM, known as the RS-28 Sarmat (SS-X-29), as an additional replacement for the RS-20V. After many years of delay, Russia flight-tested its first RS-28 ICBM in April 2022.[30] However, no other RS-28 tests occurred in 2022, further delaying operational deployment of the missile.[31] Despite the lack of tests, in November 2022 the general director of the Makeyeva State

---

[23] Karakaev (note 21).
[24] Karakaev (note 21); and authors' estimates.
[25] 'Два полка РВСН в 2021 году будут перевооружены на ракетные комплексы "Ярс"' [Two regiments of the Strategic Rocket Forces will be re-equipped with 'Yars' missile systems in 2021], TASS, 21 Dec. 2020; Karakaev (note 21); and authors' assessment based on analysis of satellite imagery.
[26] Karakaev, S. V. (Col. Gen.), interviewed in Biryulin, R. and Andreev, D., 'Бесспорный аргумент России' [Russia's indisputable argument], *Krasnaya Zvezda*, 17 Dec. 2021; and Karakaev (note 21).
[27] Authors' assessment based on analysis of satellite imagery.
[28] President of Russia, 'Expanded meeting of the Defence Ministry Board', 21 Dec. 2021.
[29] President of Russia, [Ministry of Defence Board meeting] (note 15); and Karakaev (note 21).
[30] President of Russia, 'Test launch of Sarmat ICBM', 20 Apr. 2022.
[31] 'Russia re-adjusts Sarmat intercontinental ballistic missiles' test-launch program—Source', TASS, 8 Nov. 2021; 'Часть районов Камчатки закроют на время испытания межконтинентальной баллистической ракеты' [Some areas of Kamchatka will be closed for the duration of the test of an intercontinental ballistic missile], Kamchatka-Info, 2 June 2022; and 'Путин: системы ПВО С-500 начали поступать в войска, МБР "Сармат" встанет на боевое дежурство до конца года' [Putin: S-500 air defence systems began to arrive with the troops, the Sarmat ICBM will be on combat duty before the end of the year], Interfax, 21 June 2022.

Rocket Centre stated that the RS-28 had already entered serial production.[32] The first division to receive RS-28 ICBMs will be the ICBM division at Uzhur, Krasnoyarsk krai.[33] Satellite imagery indicates that one regiment's older RS-20Vs have already been removed to prepare for the incoming RS-28 ICBMs, although it is unlikely that any had been loaded into these silos by the end of 2022.

Other reported development programmes for future ICBMs include the Osina-RV (derived from the RS-24) and the Kedr project, which purportedly includes research and development on next-generation missile systems.[34]

Russia reportedly conducted more than 200 small- and larger-scale exercises with road-mobile and silo-based ICBMs during 2022. These included combat patrols for road-mobile regiments, simulated launch exercises for silo-based regiments and participation in command staff exercises.[35] In December 2022 Karakaev noted that Russia plans to conduct eight ICBM flight tests in 2023, double the number of such tests in 2022.[36]

Sea-based missiles

As of January 2023 the Russian Navy had a fleet of 11 operational nuclear-armed SSBNs. The fleet included five Soviet-era Delfin-class or Project 667BDRM (Delta IV) SSBNs and six Borei-class or Project 955 (Dolgorukiy) SSBNs. One new Borei-class SSBN entered service in 2022.[37]

Russia plans to have a total of 10 Borei-class SSBNs, 5 assigned to the Northern Fleet (in the Arctic Ocean) and 5 to the Pacific Fleet, replacing all remaining Delfin-class SSBNs.[38] The three newest are of an improved design, known as Borei-A or Project 955A. After delays due to technical issues during sea trials, the first Borei-A was accepted into the navy in June 2020, the second in December 2021 and the third—the *Generalissimus Suvorov*—in December 2022.[39] A fourth Borei-A was launched in December 2022 and is

---

[32] Emelyanenkov, A., 'Генеральный конструктор Владимир Дегтярь: "Сармат" запущен в серийное производство' [General designer Vladimir Degtyar: 'Sarmat' has entered mass production], *Rossiskaya Gazeta*, 23 Nov. 2022.

[33] Karakaev (note 21).

[34] Karakaev (note 26); Военно-болтовой (@warbolts), Telegram, 15 June 2021, <https://t.me/warbolts/439>; 'Russia develops new-generation Kedr strategic missiles system', TASS, 1 Mar. 2021; and 'Источник сообщил, что работа по созданию ракеты "Кедр" начнется в 2023–2024 годах' [Source says work on 'Kedr' rocket will begin in 2023–2024], TASS, 2 Apr. 2021.

[35] Karakaev (note 21).

[36] Karakaev (note 21).

[37] President of Russia, 'Церемония подъёма флага на поступающих в состав ВМФ кораблях и спуска на воду атомной подлодки «Император Александр III»' [The ceremony of raising the flag on ships entering the Navy and launching the nuclear submarine 'Emperor Alexander III'], 29 Dec. 2022; and 'Russia's nuclear sub successfully tests Bulava missile', TASS, 3 Nov. 2022.

[38] 'Источник: еще две стратегические подлодки "Борей-А" построят на "Севмаше" к 2028 году' [Source: Two more 'Borei-A' strategic submarines to be built at 'Sevmash' by 2028], TASS, 30 Nov. 2020.

[39] Sevmash, 'На Севмаше состоялась церемония вывода из эллинга атомной подводной лодки «Генералиссимус Суворов»' [The commissioning ceremony of the nuclear submarine 'Generalissimus Suvorov' took place at Sevmash], 25 Dec. 2021; and President of Russia (note 37).

likely to be delivered to the navy no earlier than December 2023.[40] The next three Borei-A SSBNs are scheduled for delivery in the mid to late 2020s.[41]

Each of the 11 operational SSBNs can be equipped with 16 ballistic missiles and the Russian SSBN fleet can carry a total of 896 warheads.[42] However, one or two SSBNs is normally undergoing repairs and maintenance at any given time and is not armed. It is also possible that the warhead load on some missiles has been reduced to meet the total warhead limit under New START. As a result, SIPRI estimates that only about 640 of the 896 warheads have been deployed. The Delfin SSBNs are thought to carry RSM-54 SLBMs, either the Sineva (SS-N-23 M2) or a modified version, known as Layner (SS-N-23 M3), while the Borei and Borei-A SSBNs carry newer RSM-56 Bulava (SS-N-32) SLBMs.

In 2022 the Russian Navy continued to develop the Poseidon or Status-6 (Kanyon), a long-range, strategic nuclear-powered torpedo intended for deployment on two new types of special-purpose submarine: the K-329 *Belgorod* or Project 09852—a converted Antei-class or Project 949A (Oscar II) nuclear-powered guided-missile submarine (SSGN); and the Khabarovsk class or Project 09851.[43] Despite an apparent aborted test of the torpedo in November 2022, Russian defence sources indicated that 'the first batch' of Poseidon torpedoes had been produced and would soon be delivered to the *Belgorod*.[44] The official handover of the *Belgorod* to the Russian fleet took place in July 2022.[45] Following its delivery, the submarine was spotted operating in the Barents Sea throughout September 2022.[46] The *Belgorod* and the Khabarovsk submarines will each be capable of carrying up to six Poseidon torpedoes.[47]

---

[40] President of Russia (note 37).

[41] Sevmash, 'На Севмаше заложили атомные подводные крейсеры «Дмитрий Донской» и «Князь Потемкин»' [Nuclear-powered submarine cruisers 'Dmitry Donskoy' and 'Prince Potemkin' laid down at Sevmash], 23 Aug. 2021.

[42] The Delfin-class SSBNs carry RSM-54 Sineva/Layner (SS-N-23 M2/3) SLBMs, while the Borei and Borei-A SSBNs carry RSM-56 Bulava (SS-N-32) SLBMs. Each RSM-54 can carry up to 4 warheads, while each RSM-56 can carry up to 6 warheads. It is assumed that each RSM-56 has had its warhead load reduced to 4 warheads, to meet New START limits.

[43] Sutton, H. I., 'Khabarovsk-class-submarine', Covert Shores, 20 Nov. 2020; and Sutton, H. I., 'Poseidon torpedo', Covert Shores, 22 Feb. 2019.

[44] Sciutto, J., 'US observed Russian navy preparing for possible test of nuclear-powered torpedo', CNN, 10 Nov. 2022; and 'First batch of nuclear-armed drones Poseidon manufactured for special-purpose sub Belgorod', TASS, 15 Jan. 2023.

[45] 'Shipbuilders deliver special-purpose sub with nuclear-powered drones to Russian Navy', TASS, 8 July 2022.

[46] Sutton, H. I., 'New images reveal Russia's "missing" submarine Belgorod in Arctic', Naval News, 5 Oct. 2022.

[47] 'Вторую подлодку-носитель "Посейдонов" планируют спустить на воду весной–летом 2021 года' [Second 'Poseidon' carrier submarine to be launched in spring–summer 2021], TASS, 6 Nov. 2020.

Non-strategic nuclear forces

There is no universally accepted definition of 'tactical', 'non-strategic' or 'theatre' nuclear weapons. These terms generally refer to shorter-range weapons that are not covered by arms control agreements regulating long-range strategic forces. Russia's non-strategic nuclear weapons chiefly serve to compensate for perceived conventional inferiority relative to NATO forces; to provide regional (as opposed to intercontinental) deterrence options; and to maintain overall parity with the total US nuclear force level. There has been considerable debate among Western officials and experts about the role that non-strategic nuclear weapons have in Russian nuclear strategy, including potential first use.[48]

The US Defense Intelligence Agency estimated in 2021 that Russia had 1000–2000 non-strategic warheads.[49] SIPRI estimates that, as of January 2023, Russia had approximately 1816 warheads assigned for potential use by non-strategic forces—around 96 fewer than the previous year due to a reduction in the number of older launchers; however, these estimates come with a high degree of uncertainty. Most Russian delivery systems for non-strategic nuclear weapons are dual-capable, meaning that they can also deliver conventional warheads. They are intended for use by ships and submarines, aircraft, air- and missile-defence systems, and in army missiles.

Navy weapons

The Russian navy is estimated to have 835 warheads assigned for use by land-attack cruise missiles, anti-ship cruise missiles, anti-submarine rockets, depth bombs, and torpedoes delivered by surface ships, submarines and naval aviation.

The nuclear version of the long-range, land-attack Kalibr sea-launched cruise missile (SLCM), also known as the 3M-14 (SS-N-30A), is a significant

---

[48] On this debate see e.g. US Department of Defense, *Nuclear Posture Review 2018* (DOD: Washington, DC, Feb. 2018), p. 30; Kofman, M. and Fink, A. L., 'Escalation management and nuclear employment in Russian military strategy', War on the Rocks, 23 June 2020; Oliker, O., 'Moscow's nuclear enigma: What is Russia's arsenal really for?', *Foreign Affairs*, Nov./Dec. 2018; Stowe-Thurston, A., Korda, M. and Kristensen, H. M., 'Putin deepens confusion about Russian nuclear policy', Russia Matters, Harvard Kennedy School, 25 Oct. 2018; Tertrais, B., 'Russia's nuclear policy: Worrying for the wrong reasons', *Survival*, vol. 60, no. 2 (Apr. 2018); Ven Bruusgaard, K., 'The myth of Russia's lowered nuclear threshold', War on the Rocks, 22 Sep. 2017; and Kaushal, S. and Cranny-Evans, S., 'Russia's nonstrategic nuclear weapons and its views on limited nuclear war', Royal United Services Institute, 21 June 2022.

[49] Berrier, S., Director, US Defense Intelligence Agency, 'Worldwide threat assessment', Statement for the record, US Senate, Armed Services Committee, 26 Apr. 2021.

new addition to the navy's stock of weapons.[50] It has been integrated on numerous types of surface ship and attack submarine, including the new Yasen/Yasen-M or Project 885/885M (Severodvinsk) SSGN.[51] The third boat of this class was delivered to the Pacific Fleet in December 2021 and became operational in 2022.[52] Three additional Project 885M SSGNs are currently being built.

In addition to the 3M-14, the Project 855M SSGNs will be armed with the 3M-55 (SS-N-26) SLCM and the future 3M-22 Tsirkon (SS-NX-33) hypersonic anti-ship missile. Test launches of the latter missile were conducted in October 2022, and it is scheduled to enter service in 2026.[53]

Air force weapons

Approximately 506 non-strategic nuclear weapons are assigned to the Russian Air Force for use by Tu-22M3M (Backfire-C) intermediate-range bombers, Su-24M (Fencer-D) fighter-bombers, Su-34 (Fullback) fighter-bombers and MiG-31K (Foxhound) attack aircraft.[54] The new Su-57 (Felon) combat aircraft is also dual-capable. Deliveries began in 2020 and continued in 2022.[55]

The MiG-31K is equipped with the new 9A-7760 Kinzhal air-launched ballistic missile (ALBM). In 2022 it was operational with the Southern Military District and Northern Fleet and will eventually be integrated into the Western and Central Military Districts by 2024.[56] The first combat use of a conventional Kinzhal took place in March 2022 during the invasion of

---

[50] There is considerable confusion about the designation of what is commonly referred to as the Kalibr missile. The Kalibr designation actually refers not to a specific missile but to a launcher for a family of weapons that, in addition to the 3M-14 (SS-N-30/A) land-attack versions, includes the 3M-54 (SS-N-27) anti-ship cruise missile and the 91R anti-submarine missile. For further detail see US Navy, Office of Naval Intelligence (ONI), *The Russian Navy: A Historic Transition* (ONI: Washington, DC, Dec. 2015), pp. 34–35.

[51] It is important to caution that, although a growing number of vessels are capable of launching the dual-capable 3M-14, it is uncertain how many of them have been assigned a nuclear role.

[52] Manaranche, M., 'Yasen-M class SSGN "Novosibirsk" begins its sea trials', Naval News, 2 July 2021; Sevmash, 'На Севмаше состоялась церемония передачи Военно-морскому флоту двух атомных подводных лодок—"Князь Олег" и "Новосибирск"' [Sevmash held a hand-over to the Navy ceremony of two nuclear submarines—'Prince Oleg' and 'Novosibirsk'], 21 Dec. 2021; and 'Perm sub with Tsirkon hypersonic missiles to enter service with Russian Navy in 2026', TASS, 5 Jan. 2023.

[53] 'Perm sub with Tsirkon hypersonic missiles to enter service' (note 52).

[54] US Department of Defense, 'US nuclear deterrence policy', 1 Apr. 2019, p. 3; International Institute for Strategic Studies, *The Military Balance 2021* (Routledge: London, 2021); and authors' estimates. It is possible that the Su-30SM is also capable of delivering nuclear weapons.

[55] D'Urso, S., 'First serial production Su-57 Felon delivered to the Russian Aerospace Forces', The Aviationist, 30 Dec. 2020; Rob Lee (@RALee85), Twitter, 3 Feb. 2022, <https://twitter.com/RALee85/status/1489302156729593869>; and United Aircraft Corporation (UAC), 'ОАК передала Минобороны очередную партию серийных самолётов пятого поколения Су-57' [UAC handed over another batch fifth-generation Su-57s to the Defence Ministry], 28 Dec. 2022.

[56] President of Russia (note 28); 'Russia's upgraded MiG-31 fighters to provide security for Northern Sea Route', TASS, 26 Nov. 2021; and Kretsul, R. and Cherepanova, A., 'Прибавить гиперзвук: еще один военный округ вооружат «Кинжалами»' [Hypersonic boost: Another military district to be armed with 'Daggers'], *Izvestia*, 7 June 2021.

Ukraine: according to Sergei Shoigu, the Russian minister of defence, it had been used at least three times as of August 2022.[57]

Russia has also begun introducing the nuclear-capable Kh-32 (AS-4A) air-to-surface missile. This is an upgrade of the Kh-22N (AS-4) used on the Tu-22M3.[58]

Air-, coastal- and missile-defence weapons

Russian air-, coastal- and missile-defence forces are estimated to have around 385 nuclear warheads. Most have been assigned for use by dual-capable S-300 and S-400 air-defence forces and the Moscow A-135 missile-defence system. Russian coastal-defence units are believed to have been assigned a small number of nuclear weapons for anti-ship missions.

It is likely that the stock of warheads associated with Russia's air-, coastal- and missile-defence forces will eventually decrease as conventional air-defences improve—including the Nudol and Aerostat systems under development in 2022—and as legacy warheads are retired.

Army weapons

The Russian Army has an estimated 90 warheads to arm 9K720 Iskander-M (SS-26) short-range ballistic missiles (SRBMs) and 9M729 (SSC-8) ground-launched cruise missiles (GLCMs). As of January 2023 the dual-capable Iskander-M had completely replaced the Tochka (SS-21) SRBM in 12 missile brigades.[59] Unconfirmed rumours suggest that the 9M728 (SSC-7) may also have a nuclear capability.

The dual-capable 9M729 GLCM was cited by the USA as its main reason for withdrawing from the 1987 Treaty on the Elimination of Intermediate-range and Shorter-range Missiles (INF Treaty) in 2019.[60] SIPRI estimates that four or five 9M729 battalions have so far been co-deployed with four or five of the Iskander-M brigades. In 2020 and 2021 Russia indicated a willingness to impose a moratorium or a ban on future 9M729 deployments in European territory, subject to conditions.[61]

---

[57] 'Shoigu reveals Kinzhal hypersonic missile was used three times during special operation', TASS, 21 Aug. 2022.

[58] US Department of Defense (note 48), p. 8.

[59] Authors' assessment based on analysis of satellite imagery.

[60] US Department of State, Bureau of Arms Control, Verification and Compliance, 'INF Treaty at a glance', Fact sheet, 8 Dec. 2017. For a summary and other details of the INF Treaty see annex A, section III, in this volume. See also Topychkanov, P. and Davis, I., 'Russian–US nuclear arms control and disarmament', *SIPRI Yearbook 2020*; and Kile, S. N., 'Russian–US nuclear arms control and disarmament', *SIPRI Yearbook 2018*.

[61] President of Russia, 'Statement by Vladimir Putin on additional steps to de-escalate the situation in Europe after the termination of the Intermediate-Range Nuclear Forces Treaty (INF Treaty)', 26 Oct. 2020; and Russian Ministry of Foreign Affairs, 'Agreement on Measures to Ensure the Security of the Russian Federation and Member States of the North Atlantic Treaty Organization: Draft', Unofficial translation, 17 Dec. 2021. See also Kristensen, H. M. and Korda, M., 'Russian nuclear forces', *SIPRI Yearbook 2020*, p. 356.

III. British nuclear forces

HANS M. KRISTENSEN AND MATT KORDA*

As of January 2023 the United Kingdom's nuclear weapon stockpile consisted of approximately 225 warheads (see table 7.4)—an unchanged estimate from the previous year. SIPRI assesses that around 120 of these are operationally available for delivery by Trident II D5 submarine-launched ballistic missiles (SLBMs), with about 40 being carried on a nuclear-powered ballistic missile submarine (SSBN) that is on patrol at all times. The UK is expected to increase the number of warheads it possesses in the coming years.

These estimates are based on open-source information on the British nuclear arsenal and conversations with British officials. The UK has generally been more transparent about its nuclear activities than many other nuclear-armed states. However, it has never declassified the history of its stockpile or the actual number of warheads it possesses, and in 2021 it declared that it will no longer publicly disclose figures for the country's operational stockpile, deployed warheads or deployed missiles.[1]

This section briefly outlines the role played by nuclear weapons in the UK's military doctrine and then describes its sea-based missiles and its nuclear weapon modernization programme.

The role of nuclear weapons in British military doctrine

The British government has stated that it remains 'deliberately ambiguous about precisely when, how and at what scale [it] would contemplate the use of nuclear weapons'.[2] However, British policy also states that the UK 'would consider using ... nuclear weapons only in extreme circumstances of self-defence, including the defence of [North Atlantic Treaty Organization (NATO)] Allies'.[3]

Like the United States, the UK operates its submarines with detargeted missiles, although it would take only moments to load the targeting coordinates. Unlike US SSBNs, which can launch in minutes, the UK says that its submarines 'are at several days' notice to fire'.[4]

---

[1] British Government, *Global Britain in a Competitive Age: The Integrated Review of Security, Defence, Development and Foreign Policy*, CP403 (Her Majesty's Stationery Office: London, Mar. 2021), pp. 76–77. On the challenges of collecting information on world nuclear forces more generally see Kristensen, H. M. and Korda, M., 'Estimating world nuclear forces: An overview and assessment of sources', SIPRI Commentary, 14 June 2021.

[2] 10th NPT review conference, National report of the United Kingdom, NPT/CONF.2020/33, 5 Nov. 2021, para. 13. On the review conference see also 'The 10th review conference of the Non-Proliferation Treaty', chapter 8, section II, in this volume.

[3] British Government (note 1), p. 76.

[4] British Ministry of Defence, 'The UK's nuclear deterrent: What you need to know', 17 Feb. 2022.

* The authors wish to thank Eliana Johns for contributing invaluable research to this publication.

Sea-based missiles

The UK is the only nuclear-armed state that operates a single type of nuclear weapon: the country's nuclear deterrent is entirely sea-based. The UK possesses four Vanguard-class SSBNs, based at Faslane on the west coast of Scotland, each of which can carry up to 16 Trident II D5 submarine-launched ballistic missiles.[5] In a posture known as continuous at-sea deterrence (CASD), which began in 1969, one British SSBN carrying approximately 40 warheads is on patrol at all times.[6] The second and third SSBNs remain in port but could be put to sea in a crisis. The fourth is in overhaul at any given time and is unable to deploy.

In its Integrated Review of Security, Defence, Development and Foreign Policy, published in March 2021, the British government announced a significant increase to the upper limit of its nuclear weapon stockpile, to a maximum of 260 warheads.[7] Until then, it was assumed that the UK's nuclear weapon stockpile had been gradually decreasing towards a goal of 180 warheads by the mid 2020s, as described in the UK's strategic defence and security reviews (SDSRs) of 2010 and 2015.[8] British officials clarified in 2021 that the target of 180 warheads stated in the SDSRs 'was indeed a goal, but it was never reached'.[9] Instead, in its statement submitted to the 10th review conference of the 1968 Treaty on the Non-Proliferation of Nuclear Weapons, held in 2022, the British government stated that the new and higher number of 260 warheads 'is a ceiling, not a target, and it is not our current stockpile number'.[10]

Replacement of the submarines

The UK's four Vanguard-class SSBNs entered service between December 1994 and February 2001, each with an expected service life of 25 years.[11] The

---

[5] Mills, C., *Replacing the UK's Strategic Nuclear Deterrent: Progress of the Dreadnought Class*, Research Briefing no. 8010 (House of Commons Library: London, 28 Sep. 2022), p. 9.

[6] British Ministry of Defence, 'UK's nuclear deterrent (CASD)', 17 Mar. 2021.

[7] British Government (note 1), p. 76. For further detail see Kristensen, H. M. and Korda, M., 'British nuclear forces', *SIPRI Yearbook 2022*, pp. 371–72.

[8] British Government, *Securing Britain in an Age of Uncertainty: The Strategic Defence and Security Review*, Cm 7948 (Her Majesty's Stationery Office: London, Oct. 2010), p. 38; and British Government, *National Security Strategy and Strategic Defence and Security Review 2015: A Secure and Prosperous United Kingdom*, Cm 9161 (Her Majesty's Stationery Office: London, 2015), p. 34. See also Kristensen, H. M. and Korda, M., 'United Kingdom nuclear weapons, 2021', Nuclear notebook, *Bulletin of the Atomic Scientists*, vol. 77, no. 3 (May 2021).

[9] Liddle, A. (@AidanLiddle), British permanent representative to the Conference on Disarmament, Twitter, 16 Mar. 2021, <https://twitter.com/aidanliddle/status/1371912132141445120>. This information was also later confirmed by other officials. British officials, Interviews with the authors, May 2021.

[10] 10th NPT review conference, NPT/CONF.2020/33 (note 2), para. 22.

[11] Mills (note 5), p. 10.

Table 7.4. British nuclear forces, January 2023

All figures are approximate and some are based on assessments by the authors.

Type/designation	No. of launchers	Year first deployed	Range (km)	Warheads x yield	No. of warheads
Sea-based missiles (SLBMs)	4/64[a]				120
Trident II D5	48[b]	1994	>10 000[c]	1–8 x 100 kt[d]	120
Total operationally available warheads					120[e]
Other stored warheads					105[f]
Total stockpile					225[g]

kt = kiloton; SLBM = submarine-launched ballistic missile.

[a] The first figure is the total number of nuclear-powered ballistic missile submarines (SSBNs) in the British fleet; the second is the maximum number of missiles that they can carry. However, the total number of missiles carried is lower (see note b). Of the 4 SSBNs, 1 is in overhaul at any given time.

[b] The 3 operational SSBNs can carry a total of 48 Trident SLBMs. The United Kingdom has purchased the right to 58 missiles from a pool shared with the United States Navy.

[c] The Trident II D5 missiles on British SSBNs are identical to the Trident II D5 missiles on US Navy SSBNs, which have demonstrated a range of more than 10 000 km in test flights.

[d] The British warhead is called the Holbrook, a modified version of the USA's W76 warhead, with a potential lower-yield option.

[e] Of the 120 operationally available warheads, c. 40 are deployed on the single SSBN that is at sea at any given time, with the remaining warheads assigned to the 2 other deployable SSBNs.

[f] This figure includes retired warheads that have not yet been dismantled. It seems likely that they will be reconstituted to become part of the UK's total stockpile over the coming years (see note g). Many of the stored warheads that have not been retired are thought to be undergoing upgrade from the Mk4 re-entry body to the Mk4A.

[g] The British government declared in 2010 that its inventory would not exceed 225 warheads, and that the UK would reduce the number of warheads in its overall nuclear stockpile to no more than 180. Despite these stated intentions, the UK's nuclear stockpile appears to have remained at c. 225 warheads. The UK's Integrated Review of Security, Defence, Development and Foreign Policy, published in 2021, introduced a new ceiling of 260 warheads.

Sources: British Ministry of Defence, white papers, press releases and website; British House of Commons, *Hansard*, various issues; *Bulletin of the Atomic Scientists*, 'Nuclear notebook', various issues; and authors' estimates.

2015 SDSR stated the government's intention to replace the Vanguard-class submarines with four new SSBNs, known as the Dreadnought class.[12]

The new submarines were originally expected to begin entering service by 2028, but this has been delayed until the early 2030s. The service life of the Vanguard-class SSBNs has been commensurately extended to an overall lifespan of about 37–38 years.[13] The work to upgrade the ageing SSBNs has been subject to delays and budget overruns. For example, the UK's lead SSBN, HMS *Vanguard*, completed its refit and rejoined the fleet in July 2022,

[12] British government, Cm 9161 (note 8), para. 4.73.
[13] Mills (note 5), p. 10.

about three years later than expected. The cost of the *Vanguard* upgrade rose from an initial projection of about £200 million (US$307 million) in 2015 to more than £500 million ($688 million) in 2021.[14]

The delay meant that the UK's three other SSBNs had to extend their deterrence patrols. The length of time at sea for British nuclear submarines has reportedly increased from about 60–70 days in the 1970s to over 140 days in recent years, with some reports suggesting that a new record for the Royal Navy of 157 days was set in 2022.[15] These extended patrols were potentially factors contributing to several operating errors, accidents and personnel issues (including low morale and allegations of drug and sexual abuse) that have dogged the UK's nuclear forces over the past five years.[16] Furthermore, a January 2023 inspection revealed that the work on the HMS *Vanguard* was of a poor standard—contractors apparently used superglue to repair critical parts surrounding the nuclear reactor's cooling pipes—and nuclear safety issues prevented the SSBN from going out on deterrence patrol.[17]

The missiles and warhead

Given that the UK draws its SLBMs from a common pool shared with the USA, the UK is benefiting from the US Navy's programme to extend the service life of the Trident II D5 missile. The first and second life-extended versions are known as the D5LE and the D5LE2, respectively; the D5LE will function until the early 2060s and the D5LE2 until the mid 2080s (see section I).[18]

The warhead carried on the Trident II D5 is called the Holbrook, which is produced by the UK but based closely on the USA's W76 warhead design. It is being incorporated into the more effective USA-produced Mk4A re-entry body (aeroshell).[19] It is possible that sufficient Mk4A-upgraded warheads had been produced by the end of 2021 to arm the UK's Vanguard-class SSBNs.[20]

---

[14] British Ministry of Defence, 'British jobs secured through upgrade to nuclear deterrent', 4 Dec. 2015; and Nutt, K., 'Trident submarine refit delay may cost taxpayers £500 million', *The National*, 10 Oct. 2021.

[15] Sabbagh, D. and Edwards, R., 'Safety fears as UK Trident submarines are put to sea for longest-ever patrols', *The Guardian*, 6 Dec. 2022.

[16] Edwards, R., 'Threat to nuclear safety from prolonged Trident patrols', The Ferret, 6 Dec. 2022; and Nicolls, D., 'Royal Navy nuclear-armed submarine forced to abort mission after catching fire', *Daily Telegraph*, 7 Nov. 2022. See also e.g. Lusher, A., 'Nuclear submarine sex and drugs scandal: Nine Trident crew expelled from Navy amid "cocaine" and affairs allegations', *The Independent*, 28 Oct. 2017.

[17] Starkey, J., 'Sub standard: Nuclear security alert after botched attempt to fix Trident submarine with super glue', *The Sun*, 30 Jan. 2023; and Middleton, J., 'Royal Navy orders investigation into nuclear submarine "repaired with glue"', *The Guardian*, 1 Feb. 2023.

[18] Mills (note 5), p. 11.

[19] For detail on how the upgrade improves the weapon's capability see Cullen, D., *Extreme Circumstances: The UK's New Nuclear Warhead in Context* (Nuclear Information Service: Reading, Aug. 2022).

[20] Nukewatch, 'Warhead convoy movements summary 2021', 2021.

In 2020 the British government announced its intention to replace the Holbrook with a new warhead that will use the Mk7 aeroshell being developed for the USA's new W93 warhead (see section I).[21] According to the British Ministry of Defence, the replacement warhead is 'not exactly the same warhead [as the W93] but ... there is a very close connection, in design terms and production terms'.[22]

Although the future of the W93 programme is being debated in the USA, British officials stated in 2021 that the UK's warhead-replacement programme would move forward regardless of the status of the USA's W93 programme.[23] In both the UK and the USA, the decision to introduce new warheads is thought to stem from strong internal political pressure to enhance nuclear infrastructure and capabilities.[24] The UK has not issued an official cost estimate or timeline for its programme, but it is likely that the new warhead will come into service sometime in the late 2030s or early 2040s.[25]

---

[21] Wallace, B., British Secretary of State for Defence, 'Nuclear deterrent', Written statement HCWS125, British House of Commons, 25 Feb. 2020; and Wolfe, J., Director of US Strategic Systems Programs, 'FY2022 budget request for nuclear forces and atomic energy defense activities', Statement before the US Senate, Armed Forces Committee, Subcommittee on Strategic Forces, 12 May 2021, pp. 6–7. For further detail see Kristensen, H. M. and Korda, M., 'British nuclear forces', *SIPRI Yearbook 2021*, pp. 360–61.

[22] Lovegrove, S., Permanent Secretary, Ministry of Defence, Statement, British House of Commons, Defence Committee, Oral evidence: MOD annual report and accounts 2019–20, HC 1051, 8 Dec. 2020, Q31.

[23] Mehta, A., 'UK official: American warhead decision won't impact British nuclear plans', *Defense News*, 13 Apr. 2021.

[24] Cullen (note 19), p. 6.

[25] Cullen (note 19), p. 4.

IV. French nuclear forces

HANS M. KRISTENSEN AND MATT KORDA*

As of January 2023 France's nuclear weapon stockpile consisted of about 290 warheads, the same number as in January 2022. The warheads are allocated for delivery by 48 submarine-launched ballistic missiles (SLBMs) and approximately 50 air-launched cruise missiles (ALCMs) produced for land- and carrier-based aircraft (see table 7.5). However, the 10 warheads assigned to France's carrier-based aircraft are thought to be kept in central storage and are not normally deployed.

The estimate of France's nuclear weapon stockpile is based on publicly available information.[1] France is relatively transparent about many of its nuclear weapon activities and has in the past publicly disclosed the size of its stockpile and details of its nuclear-related operations.[2]

This section begins by outlining the role played by nuclear weapons in France's military doctrine and its nuclear modernization programmes. It then describes its air-delivered and sea-based weapons.

The role of nuclear weapons in French military doctrine

France considers all of its nuclear weapons to be strategic and reserved for the defence of France's 'vital interests'.[3] While this concept has appeared in various governmental white papers and presidential speeches for several decades, what constitutes France's 'vital interests' remains unclear. In February 2020 President Emmanuel Macron announced that 'France's vital interests now have a European dimension';[4] however, in October 2022 he clarified that these interests 'would not be at stake if there was a nuclear ballistic attack in Ukraine or in the region', suggesting that the threshold for nuclear weapon use by France may be higher than previous comments had implied.[5]

In addition, France's report to the 10th review conference of the 1968 Treaty on the Non-Proliferation of Nuclear Weapons, held in 2022, states that 'For deterrence to work, the circumstances under which nuclear weapons would be used are not, and should not be, precisely defined, so as not to enable a

---

[1] Kristensen, H. M. and Korda, M., 'Estimating world nuclear forces: An overview and assessment of sources', SIPRI Commentary, 14 June 2021.

[2] Macron, E., French President, Speech on defence and deterrence strategy, École de Guerre, Paris, 7 Feb. 2020 (in French, with English translation).

[3] Tertrais, B., *French Nuclear Deterrence Policy, Forces and Future: A Handbook*, Recherches & Documents no. 04/2020 (Fondation pour la Recherche Stratégique: Paris, Feb. 2020), pp. 25–29, 62–63.

[4] Macron (note 2). See also Kristensen, H. M. and Korda, M., 'French nuclear forces', *SIPRI Yearbook 2021*.

[5] 'Avec Emmanuel Macron' [With Emmanuel Macron], *L'événement*, France 2, 12 Oct. 2022 (author translation).

* The authors wish to thank Eliana Johns for contributing invaluable research to this publication.

Table 7.5. French nuclear forces, January 2023

All figures are approximate and some are based on assessments by the authors.

Type/designation	No. of launchers	Year first deployed	Range (km)[a]	Warheads x yield	No. of warheads
Land-based aircraft					
Rafale BF3[b]	40	2010–11	2 000	1 x [<300 kt] TNA[c]	40
Carrier-based aircraft					
Rafale MF3[b]	10	2010–11	2 000	1 x [<300 kt] TNA[c]	10[d]
Sea-based missiles (SLBMs)	4/64[e]				240
M51.1	16	2010	>6 000	4–6 x 100 kt TN 75	80
M51.2[f]	32[g]	2016	>9 000[h]	4–6 x 100 kt TNO	160
M51.3[i]	–	[2025]	>[9 000]	[up to 6] x 100 kt TNO	–
Total stockpile					290[j]

– = nil or a negligible value; [ ] = uncertain SIPRI estimate; kt = kiloton; SLBM = submarine-launched ballistic missile; TNA = *tête nucléaire aéroportée* (air-launched nuclear warhead); TNO = *tête nucléaire océanique* (sea-based nuclear warhead).

[a] For aircraft, the listed range is for illustrative purposes only; actual mission range will vary according to flight profile, weapon payload and in-flight refuelling.

[b] The BF3 and MF3 aircraft both carry the ASMPA (*air–sol moyenne portée–améliorée*) air-launched cruise missile (ALCM). Most sources report that the ASMPA has a range of 500–600 kilometres, although some suggest that it might be over 600 km.

[c] There is uncertainty as to the yield of the new TNA warhead. Some non-official sources continue to attribute a yield of 300 kt to the TNA, the same yield as the previous TN81 warhead carried by the original ASMP missile. However, MBDA, the manufacturer of the ASMPA missile that carries the TNA, has stated that the warhead has a 'medium energy' yield, which is thought to be less than 100 kt. The TNA also appears to be based on the same design as the TNO, which is believed to have a yield of 100 kt. In the absence of official or consistent authoritative sources, these numbers should be treated as uncertain estimates.

[d] The 10 warheads assigned to France's carrier-based aircraft are thought to be kept in central storage and are not normally deployed.

[e] The first figure is the total number of nuclear-powered ballistic missile submarines (SSBNs) in the French fleet; the second is the maximum number of missiles that they can carry. However, the total number of missiles carried is lower (see note g). Of the 4 SSBNs, 1 is in overhaul at any given time.

[f] SIPRI estimates that 1 SSBN—*Le Vigilant*—has yet to be upgraded to carry the M51.2 SLBM and its accompanying TNO warhead.

[g] France has 48 SLBMs in service—enough to equip the 3 operational SSBNs.

[h] The M51.2 has a 'much greater range' than the 6000-km range of the M51.1 according to the French Ministry of the Armed Forces.

[i] The M51.3 is under development and has not yet been deployed.

[j] In Feb. 2020 President Emmanuel Macron reaffirmed that the arsenal 'is currently under 300 nuclear weapons'. A few of the warheads are thought to be undergoing maintenance and inspection at any given time.

Sources: Speeches (in French) of French presidents and defence ministers: Macron, E., Speech on defence and deterrence strategy, École de Guerre, Paris, 7 Feb. 2020; Parly, F., French Minister of the Armed Forces, Speech, ArianeGroup, Les Mureaux, 14 Dec. 2017; Hollande, F., Speech on nuclear deterrence, Istres Airbase, 19 Feb. 2015; Sarkozy, N., Speech on the new defence policy, Porte de Versailles, 17 June 2008; Sarkozy, N., Speech on the white paper on national defence and security, nuclear deterrence and the non-proliferation of nuclear weapons, Cherbourg,

21 Mar. 2008; and Chirac, J., Speech on France's defence policy, Île Longue, Brest, 19 Jan. 2006. Other sources: French Ministry of Defence/Ministry of the Armed Forces, various publications; French National Assembly, various defence bills; *Air Actualités*, various issues; *Aviation Week & Space Technology*, various issues; *Bulletin of the Atomic Scientists*, 'Nuclear notebook', various issues; Tertrais, B., *French Nuclear Deterrence Policy, Forces and Future: A Handbook*, Recherches & Documents no. 04/2020 (Fondation pour la Recherche Stratégique: Paris, Feb. 2020); and authors' estimates.

potential aggressor to calculate the risk inherent in a potential attack.'[6] France reserves the right to issue 'a sole, one-time-only nuclear warning', suggesting that it could use a nuclear weapon against a military, political or symbolic target as a signal to a potential adversary.[7]

The Macron administration has strongly reaffirmed a commitment to the long-term modernization and strengthening of France's air- and sea-based nuclear forces.[8] Current plans include the modernization of aircraft and ALCMs and of nuclear-powered ballistic missile submarines (SSBNs, or *sous-marins nucléaires lanceurs d'engins*, SNLEs) and SLBMs (see below). By 2040 France is expected to have fielded a next-generation combat aircraft equipped with a new cruise missile and four new SSBNs equipped with an upgraded ballistic missile.

Aircraft and air-delivered weapons

The airborne component of the French nuclear forces consists of land- and carrier-based aircraft. The French Air and Space Force has 40 deployed nuclear-capable Rafale BF3 aircraft based at Saint-Dizier Airbase in northeast France. The French Naval Nuclear Air Force (*Force aéronavale nucléaire*, FANu) consists of a squadron of 10 Rafale MF3 aircraft for deployment on the aircraft carrier *Charles de Gaulle*. The FANu and its nuclear-armed missiles are not permanently deployed but can be rapidly deployed by the French president in support of nuclear operations.[9]

The Rafale aircraft are equipped with medium-range air-to-surface cruise missiles (*air–sol moyenne portée–améliorée*, ASMPA), which are currently

---

[6] 10th NPT review conference, National report of France, NPT/CONF.2020/42/Rev.1, 1 Aug. 2022, p. 3. On the review conference see also 'The 10th review conference of the Non-Proliferation Treaty', chapter 8, section II, in this volume.
[7] 10th NPT review conference, NPT/CONF.2020/42/Rev.1 (note 6), p. 4.
[8] Macron, E., French President, Speech on the challenges and priorities of defence policy (in French), Toulon, 19 Jan. 2018; and Élysée, 'Transformer nos armées : le Président de la République présente le nouveau projet de loi de programmation militaire' [Transforming our armed forces: The President of the Republic presents the new military programming bill], 20 Jan. 2023.
[9] Pintat, X. et al., 'Rapport d'information fait au nom de la commission des affaires étrangères, de la défense et des forces armées par le groupe de travail "La modernisation de la dissuasion nucléaire"' [Information report made on behalf of the Committee on Foreign Affairs, Defense and the Armed Forces by the working group 'Modernization of nuclear deterrence'], Report no. 560, French Senate, 23 May 2017.

being refurbished.[10] In March 2022 France conducted a second successful flight test of the new version, the *air–sol moyenne portée–amélioré rénové* (ASMPA-R). It subsequently approved the start of serial production of the missiles and midlife refurbishment of the upgraded missile inventory, which will keep the ASMPA in service until 2035.[11] The ASMPA-R missiles are equipped with the same warhead as the ASMPA, the *tête nucléaire aéroportée* (TNA, air-launched nuclear warhead), which the missile's producer (MBDA) says has a 'medium energy' yield.[12]

The Ministry of the Armed Forces has begun developing a successor: a fourth-generation air-to-surface nuclear missile (*air–sol nucléaire de 4e génération*, ASN4G) with enhanced stealth and manoeuvrability to counter potential technological improvements in air defences.[13] The ASN4G is scheduled to reach initial operational capability in 2035 to replace the ASMPA-R.[14] France is also modernizing and expanding its fleet of Rafale aircraft. The French military budget for 2023 includes plans for the delivery of 13 new Rafale aircraft to the armed forces.[15]

Sea-based missiles

The main component of France's nuclear forces is the Strategic Oceanic Force (*Force océanique stratégique*, FOST). It consists of four Le Triomphant-class SSBNs based on the Île Longue peninsula near Brest, north-west France. Each can carry 16 SLBMs; however, at any given time one SSBN is out of service for overhaul and maintenance work and is therefore not armed. France has 48 SLBMs in service—enough to equip the three operational SSBNs.

The French Navy maintains a continuous at-sea deterrence posture with one SSBN on patrol at all times. In March 2022 there were reports that the French Navy had deployed more than one SSBN for the first time since the 1980s, possibly in response to Russia's invasion of Ukraine.[16] It is unclear

---

[10] For further detail see Kristensen and Korda (note 4), p. 366.

[11] Mills, C., *Nuclear Weapons at a Glance: France*, Research Briefing no. 9074 (House of Commons Library: London, 28 July 2022), p. 10; and Scott, R., 'Successful flight test of upgraded ASMPA missile paves way for refurbishment', Janes, 30 Mar. 2022.

[12] MBDA, 'ASMPA: Air-to-ground missile, medium range, enhanced'.

[13] French Ministry of the Armed Forces, 'La dissuasion nucléaire' [Nuclear deterrence], *Actu Défense*, 14 June 2018, p. 1; and Tran, P., 'France studies nuclear missile replacement', *Defense News*, 29 Nov. 2014.

[14] Medeiros, J., '"Faire FAS" : 55 ans de dissuasion nucléaire aéroportée' ['Go FAS': 55 years of airborne nuclear deterrence], *Air Actualités*, Oct. 2019, p. 36.

[15] Jennings, G., 'France begins Rafale F4 flight trials', Janes, 21 May 2021; and French Ministry of the Armed Forces (MAF), *Projet de loi de finances: 2023–LPM 2019–2025 Année 5* [Finance bill: 2023– Miliary Programming Law 2019–2025 year 5] (MAF: Paris, Sep. 2022), p. 41.

[16] Jézéquel, S., 'Pourquoi la France a-t-elle fait appareiller trois sous-marins nucléaires au départ de l'Ile-Longue ?' [Why did France sail three nuclear submarines from Île-Longue?], *Le Télégramme*, 21 Mar. 2022.

whether this practice will continue or whether it was a one-off test of the capability.

France's SLBM, the M51, is undergoing a series of upgrades. The missile is equipped with multiple independently targetable re-entry vehicles (MIRVs) and the first version, the M51.1, can carry up to six 100-kiloton TN 75 warheads. The second version, the M51.2, is armed with a new warhead, the *tête nucléaire océanique* (TNO, sea-based nuclear warhead), which is assumed to have a yield of 100 kt.[17] SIPRI estimates that one of France's four SSBNs, *Le Vigilant*, has yet to be upgraded to carry the M51.2 SLBM and its accompanying TNO warhead. To allow for targeting flexibility, some of the SLBMs carried by France's SSBNs carry fewer warheads than others.[18] France has also commenced design work on another upgrade, the M51.3, which will have improved accuracy. It is due to be operational in 2025.[19]

A production programme for a third-generation SSBN, designated the SNLE 3G, was officially launched in early 2021.[20] The SNLE 3G will eventually be equipped with a further modification of the M51 SLBM, the M51.4.[21] The construction of the first of four submarines in the class is scheduled to begin in 2023 and is expected to be completed by 2035. The other three submarines will be delivered on a schedule of one boat every five years.[22]

---

[17] Groizeleau, V., 'Dissuasion : 25 milliards en cinq ans pour le renouvellement des deux composantes' [Deterrence: 25 billion in five years for the renewal of the two components], Mer et Marine, 2 Oct. 2019; and Groizeleau, V., 'Dissuasion : F. Hollande détaille sa vision et l'arsenal français' [Deterrence: F. Hollande outlines his vision and the French arsenal], Mer et Marine, 20 Feb. 2015.

[18] Tertrais (note 3), p. 57.

[19] French Ministry of the Armed Forces, 'Missiles balistiques stratégiques (MSBS)' [Strategic ballistic missiles], 28 Jan. 2020; and Parly, F., French Minister of the Armed Forces, Speech (in French), ArianeGroup, Les Mureaux, 14 Dec. 2017.

[20] French Ministry of the Armed Forces, 'Florence Parly, ministre des armées, annonce le lancement en réalisation des sous-marins nucléaires lanceurs d'engins de 3e génération (SNLE 3G)' [Florence Parly, minister of the armed forces, announces the launch of the 3rd-generation nuclear-powered ballistic missile submarines (SNLE 3G)], 19 Feb. 2021; and Mackenzie, C., 'France to begin building new ballistic missile subs', *Defense News*, 22 Feb. 2021.

[21] Tertrais (note 3), pp. 56, 60, 65.

[22] French Ministry of the Armed Forces (note 20); Groizeleau, 'Dissuasion : 25 milliards en cinq ans' (note 17); and Mackenzie (note 20).

V. Chinese nuclear forces

HANS M. KRISTENSEN AND MATT KORDA*

As of January 2023 China maintained an estimated total stockpile of about 410 nuclear warheads—around 60 more than SIPRI's estimate for the previous year. China's warheads are assigned to its operational land- and sea-based ballistic missiles and to nuclear-configured aircraft (see table 7.6). Although the Chinese nuclear stockpile is projected to continue growing over the coming decade and the number of Chinese intercontinental ballistic missiles (ICBMs) is likely to reach or even exceed the numbers held by either Russia or the United States, China's overall nuclear warhead stockpile is still expected to remain smaller than that of either of those states.

SIPRI's estimate of 410 warheads relies on publicly available information on the Chinese nuclear arsenal.[1] Since China has never declared the size of its nuclear arsenal, many of the assessments here rely on data from the US Department of Defense (DOD) and must therefore be treated with caution. For example, in its 2022 report to the US Congress on Chinese military and security developments, the US DOD projected that China might field a stockpile of roughly 1500 warheads by 2035.[2] This projection relies, however, on several assumptions about China's future force posture and plutonium production. It remains to be seen how accurate these assumptions are.

This section continues by summarizing the role played by nuclear weapons in China's military doctrine. It then describes the air-delivered, land-based and sea-based nuclear weapons that constitute the three legs of China's nascent nuclear triad.

The role of nuclear weapons in Chinese military doctrine

The Chinese government's declared aim is to maintain China's nuclear capabilities at the minimum level required to safeguard national security, with the goal of 'deterring other countries from using or threatening to use nuclear weapons against China'.[3] The posture is changing significantly, with hundreds of missile silos being built, additional submarines under construction and new nuclear bombers being added to the force.

---

[1] Kristensen, H. M. and Korda, M., 'Estimating world nuclear forces: An overview and assessment of sources', SIPRI Commentary, 14 June 2021.

[2] US Department of Defense, *Military and Security Developments Involving the People's Republic of China 2022*, Annual Report to Congress (Office of the Secretary of Defense: Washington, DC, 29 Nov. 2022), p. 98; and Sokolski, H. D. (ed.), *China's Civil Nuclear Sector: Plowshares to Swords?*, Nonproliferation Policy Education Center (NPEC) Occasional Paper no. 2102 (NPEC: Arlington, VA, Mar. 2021).

[3] Chinese State Council, *China's National Defense in the New Era* (Information Office of the State Council: Beijing, July 2019), chapter 2.

* The authors wish to thank Eliana Johns for contributing invaluable research to this publication.

This development has triggered widespread discussions about long-standing elements of Chinese nuclear doctrine, including its stated nuclear 'no-first-use' (NFU) policy.[4] In its 2022 report the US DOD assessed that China is implementing an 'early warning counterstrike' strategy—akin to a 'launch-on-warning' (LOW) posture—using ground- and space-based sensors to enable rapid launch of missiles before an adversary can destroy them.[5] The US DOD noted that, as of 2022, China had deployed at least three early-warning satellites to facilitate this posture.[6]

Despite the continuing increase in the sophistication and size of China's nuclear arsenal, there is no official public evidence that the Chinese government has deviated from its long-standing core nuclear policies, including its NFU policy.[7] Additionally, in its 2022 report the US DOD stated that China 'probably believes a LOW posture is consistent with its no first use policy'.[8]

The Chinese nuclear posture has traditionally involved procedures for loading warheads on to launchers in a crisis, but with warheads, missiles and launchers kept separate during peacetime.[9] A transition to a LOW posture, where space-based sensors could detect an incoming attack before impact, does not necessarily require China to keep warheads on delivery vehicles under normal circumstances; doing so would constitute a significant change to the country's long-held nuclear custodial practices. Nevertheless, missile brigades do still need training to load warheads. According to the US DOD's 2022 report, the brigades of the People's Liberation Army (PLA) Rocket Force (PLARF) conduct 'combat readiness duty' and 'high alert duty' drills, which 'apparently includes assigning a missile battalion to be ready to launch and rotating to standby positions as much as monthly for unspecified periods of time'.[10] Since at least 2020, the PLARF has also begun to conduct nuclear attack survival exercises that are designed to test troops' readiness to launch nuclear counterattacks in the event of an imminent detonation.[11] This suggests that China is practising launching missiles in a LOW scenario.

---

[4] Chinese Ministry of National Defense, 'China resolutely opposes 2022 Pentagon report on Chinese military: Defense spokesperson', 6 Dec. 2022.

[5] US Department of Defense (note 2), pp. 99–100.

[6] US Department of Defense (note 2), pp. 99–100.

[7] Santoro, D. and Gromoll, R., 'On the value of nuclear dialogue with China', Pacific Forum, *Issues & Insights* (special report), vol. 20, no. 1 (Nov. 2020); and Kulacki, G., 'Would China use nuclear weapons first in a war with the United States?', The Diplomat, 27 Apr. 2020.

[8] US Department of Defense (note 2), p. 99.

[9] Stokes, M. A., *China's Nuclear Warhead Storage and Handling System* (Project 2049 Institute: Arlington, VA, 12 Mar. 2010), p. 8; Li, B., 'China's potential to contribute to multilateral nuclear disarmament', *Arms Control Today*, vol. 41, no. 2 (Mar. 2011); and US Department of Defense (note 2), p. 95.

[10] US Department of Defense (note 2), p. 95.

[11] Baughman, J., 'An assessment of People's Liberation Army Rocket Force survivability training', China Aerospace Studies Institute, 15 Aug. 2022; and Lu, Z., Liu, X. and Yue, X., [The missile was successfully launched, but all the personnel were 'killed'. Is it a victory?], *PLA Daily*, 7 Dec. 2021 (in Chinese).

Table 7.6. Chinese nuclear forces, January 2023

All figures are approximate and some are based on assessments by the authors.

Type/Chinese designation (US designation)	No. of launchers	Year first deployed	Range (km)[a]	Warheads x yield[b]	No. of warheads[c]
Aircraft	20[d]				20
H-6K (B-6)	10	2009	3 100	1 x bomb	10
H-6N (B-6N)	10	2020	3 100	1 x ALBM	10
H-20 (B-20)	–	[2028]	..	..	–
Land-based missiles	382				318
DF-4 (CSS-3)	6[e]	1980	5 500	1 x 3.3 Mt	–
DF-5A (CSS-4 Mod 2)	6	1981	12 000	1 x 4–5 Mt	6
DF-5B (CSS-4 Mod 3)	12	2015	13 000	5 x 200–300 kt	60
DF-5C (CSS-4 Mod 4)	..	[2024]	13 000	[MIRV]	..
DF-15 (CSS-6)	..	1990	600	1 x .[f]	..
DF-17 (CSS-22)	54[g]	2020	>1 800	1 x HGV[h]	..
DF-21A/E (CSS-5 Mod 2/6)	24[i]	2000/2016	>2 100[j]	1 x 200–300 kt	24[k]
DF-26 (CSS-18)	162	2016	>3 000	1 x 200–300 kt	54[l]
DF-27 (..)	–	[2026]	5 000–8 000	1 x 200–300 kt	–
DF-31 (CSS-10 Mod 1)	6	2006	7 200	1 x 200–300 kt	6
DF-31A/AG (CSS-10 Mod 2)[m]	84	2007/2018	11 200	1 x 200–300 kt	84
DF-41 (mobile version) (CSS-20)	28[n]	2020	12 000	3 x 200–300 kt	84
Sea-based missiles (SLBMs)	6/72[o]				72
JL-2 (CSS-N-14)	–	2016	>7 000	1 x 200–300 kt	–
JL-3 (CSS-N-20)	72[p]	2022	>10 000	[Multiple]	72
Total stockpile	**474**				**410**

.. = not available or not applicable; – = nil or a negligible value; [ ] = uncertain SIPRI estimate; ALBM = air-launched ballistic missile; HGV = hypersonic glide vehicle; kt = kiloton; MIRV = multiple independently targetable re-entry vehicle; Mt = megaton; SLBM = submarine-launched ballistic missile.

[a] For aircraft, the listed range is for illustrative purposes only; actual mission range will vary according to flight profile, weapon payload and in-flight refuelling.

[b] Warhead yields are listed for illustrative purposes. Actual yields are not known, except that older and less accurate missiles were equipped with megaton-yield warheads. Newer long-range missile warheads probably have yields of a few hundred kilotons, and it is possible that some warheads have even lower yield options.

[c] Figures are based on estimates of 1 warhead per nuclear-capable launcher, except for the MIRV-capable DF-5B, which can carry up to 5 warheads, and the MIRV-capable DF-41, which is estimated to carry up to 3 warheads. China's warheads are not thought to be deployed on launchers under normal circumstances but kept in storage facilities. All estimates are approximate.

[d] The number of bombers only counts those estimated to be assigned a nuclear role. H-6 bombers were used to deliver nuclear weapons during China's nuclear weapon testing programme (1 test used a fighter–bomber) and models of nuclear bombs are exhibited in military museums. It is thought (but not certain) that a small number of H-6 bombers previously had a secondary contingency mission with nuclear bombs. The United States Department of Defense (DOD) reported in 2018 that the People's Liberation Army Air Force has been reassigned a nuclear mission, which is expected to revolve primarily around China's new dual-capable ALBM.

e The US DOD's 2022 report still listed the old liquid-fuelled DF-4 as an element of China's fixed intercontinental ballistic missile (ICBM) force, but as of Jan. 2023 SIPRI assesses that the DF-4 is in the process of being retired and most likely no longer has an operational nuclear strike role.

f The US Central Intelligence Agency concluded in 1993 that China 'almost certainly' had developed a warhead for the DF-15, but it is unclear whether the capability was fielded. As of Jan. 2023 SIPRI assesses that the DF-15 serves an entirely conventional role.

g This number is based on the assumption that at least 3 DF-17 brigades were operational as of Jan. 2023.

h The DF-17 carries an HGV with an unknown payload. The US DOD's 2021 and 2022 reports to the US Congress noted that the DF-17 is 'primarily a conventional platform' but that it could 'be equipped with nuclear warheads'.

i In 2017 the National Air and Space Intelligence Center of the US Air Force (USAF) reported that China had 'fewer than 50' DF-21A launchers. The DF-21E is thought to be a replacement for the DF-21A.

j The range of the nuclear-armed DF-21 variants, the DF-21A (CSS-5 Mod 2) and the DF-21E (Mod 6), is thought to be greater than the 1750 km reported for the original DF-21 (CSS-5 Mod 1), which has been retired. The USAF has reported the range as 2150 km.

k It is assumed that nuclear launchers do not have any reloads, unlike conventional versions (DF-21C and DF-21D) that are assumed to have 1 reload.

l The DF-26 is a dual-capable launcher. It is thought that its mission is primarily conventional and that only some of the launchers (perhaps up to one-third) are assigned nuclear warheads. Only 1 nuclear warhead is assumed for each of the DF-26's missiles that have been assigned a nuclear mission, with any reloads assumed to be conventional.

m The DF-31AG is thought to carry the same missile as the DF-31A.

n This number assumes that at least 2 brigades were operational as of Jan. 2023.

o The first figure is the total number of operational nuclear-powered ballistic missile submarines (SSBNs) in the Chinese fleet; the second is the maximum number of missiles that they can carry.

p In Nov. 2022 the commander of the US Pacific Fleet stated that China was replacing its deployed JL-2 SLBMs with JL-3 SLBMs, although it is unknown how many have been replaced. Capaccio, A., 'China has put longer-range ICBMs on its nuclear subs, US says', Bloomberg, 19 Nov. 2022. It is thought that the system is also intended to arm the future Type 096 SSBN, which will not be ready for several years.

Sources: US Air Force (USAF), National Air and Space Intelligence Center, *Ballistic and Cruise Missile Threat*, various years; USAF Global Strike Command, various documents; US Central Intelligence Agency, various documents; US Defense Intelligence Agency, various documents; US Department of Defense, *Military and Security Developments Involving the People's Republic of China*, Annual Report to Congress, various years; Kristensen, H. M., Norris, R. S. and McKinzie, M. G., *Chinese Nuclear Forces and US Nuclear War Planning* (Federation of American Scientists/Natural Resources Defense Council: Washington, DC, Nov. 2006); *Bulletin of the Atomic Scientists*, 'Nuclear notebook', various issues; Google Earth satellite imagery; and authors' estimates.

Aircraft and air-delivered weapons

Chinese medium-range bombers were used to conduct more than 12 atmospheric nuclear tests in the 1960s and 1970s.[12] Until 2018 this capability to deliver nuclear weapons using Hong-6 or H-6 (B-6) bombers was not fully operational and was probably a back-up contingency mission.[13] In 2018, however, the US DOD reported that the PLA Air Force (PLAAF) was 'newly re-assigned a nuclear mission'.[14] The H-6N (B-6N) is apparently China's 'first nuclear-capable air-to-air refuelable bomber', and it had been operationally fielded by 2020.[15] In addition, the PLAAF has been developing its first long-range strategic bomber, the H-20 (B-20), with an anticipated range of more than 10 000 kilometres, a stealthy design and dual-capability—that is, able to deliver both conventional and nuclear weapons.[16]

To arm the H-6N, China has been developing two new air-launched ballistic missiles (ALBMs), one of which is assessed by the USA to be potentially nuclear-capable.[17] The US DOD stated in its 2022 report that the PLAAF's operational airborne nuclear capability was still 'developing tactics and procedures' to conduct the nuclear mission and noted that this capability gave China a 'nascent nuclear triad'.[18]

Land-based missiles

China's nuclear-capable land-based ballistic missile arsenal has been undergoing significant modernization as China replaces its ageing silo-based,

---

[12] De Geer, L.-E., 'Detection by Sweden of Chinese nuclear tests in the atmosphere', ed. V. Fedchenko, SIPRI, *The New Nuclear Forensics: Analysis of Nuclear Materials for Security Purposes* (Oxford University Press: Oxford, 2015), table 8A.1.

[13] For the aircraft, missiles and submarines discussed here, a designation in parentheses (in this case B-6) following the Chinese designation (in this case H-6) is that assigned by the USA.

[14] US Department of Defense, *Military and Security Developments Involving the People's Republic of China 2018*, Annual Report to Congress (Office of the Secretary of Defense: Washington, DC, 16 May 2018), p. 75.

[15] US Department of Defense (note 2), pp. 59–60.

[16] US Department of Defense (note 2), p. 83; and US Office of the Deputy Assistant Secretary of Defense for Nuclear Matters, *Nuclear Matters Handbook 2020* (US Department of Defense: Washington, DC, Mar. 2020), figure 1.1, p. 3.

[17] US Department of Defense (note 2), pp. 55–56; Ashley, R., Director, US Defense Intelligence Agency, 'Worldwide threat assessment', Statement for the record, US Senate, Armed Services Committee, 6 Mar. 2018, p. 8; US Air Force, National Air and Space Intelligence Center (NASIC), *Ballistic and Cruise Missile Threat 2020* (NASIC: Wright-Patterson Air Force Base, OH, July 2020), p. 7; and Stewart, V. R., Director, US Defense Intelligence Agency, 'Worldwide threat assessment', Statement for the record, US Senate, Armed Services Committee, 9 Feb. 2016. See also Kristensen, H. M. and Korda, M., 'Chinese nuclear forces', *SIPRI Yearbook 2022*, pp. 384–85.

[18] US Department of Defense (note 2), p. 60.

liquid-fuelled missiles with large numbers of new mobile and silo-based, solid-fuelled models.[19]

Intercontinental ballistic missiles

In 2021 commercial satellite imagery revealed that China had started construction of hundreds of new missile silos across northern China.[20] By January 2023 the number of new silos under construction was approximately 350, spread out among three large fields in northern China and three mountainous areas in east-central China. The northern silo fields are thought to be intended for solid-fuelled Dongfeng (DF) ICBMs—most likely the DF-31A (CSS-10 Mod 2) or the DF-41 (CSS-20)—while the more mountainous sites are expected to be filled with liquid-fuelled DF-5B (CSS-4 Mod 3) ICBMs.[21] By January 2023 silo construction at the northern fields had been largely completed, along with perimeter fences, electrical and radio towers, and air defence systems.[22] Notably, China's new northern silo fields are located deeper inside China than any other known ICBM base, including the new silos in east-central China, making them less vulnerable to long-range conventional strikes.[23]

SIPRI assesses that, as of January 2023, the total number of Chinese ICBM launchers—including training launchers, new launchers under construction and operational launchers—exceeded 450, with approximately 142 of those thought to be operational. It appears that the USA made a similar assessment in December 2022. The US DOD had previously estimated that, as of the end of 2021, China had 300 ICBM launchers with as many missiles in its inventory.[24] This estimate probably included launchers still under construction and missiles in production for them. The jump between the US DOD's assessments of 2021 and 2022 triggered a congressional notification from US Strategic Command that China had surpassed the USA in total ICBM launchers (but not in deployed ICBMs or warheads assigned to ICBMs).[25]

If China eventually fills each of the silos under construction with a single-warhead missile, it would have the capacity to deploy approximately

---

[19] Missile ranges specified here refer to Western definitions. China defines missile ranges differently: short, <1000 kilometres; medium, 1000–3000 km; long, 3000–8000 km; and intercontinental, >8000 km.

[20] Lewis, J. and Eveleth, D., 'Chinese ICBM silos', Arms Control Wonk, 2 July 2021; Korda, M. and Kristensen, H. M., 'China is building a second nuclear missile silo field', FAS Strategic Security Blog, Federation of American Scientists, 26 July 2021; and Lee, R., 'PLA likely begins construction of an intercontinental ballistic missile silo site near Hanggin Banner', China Aerospace Studies Institute, 12 Aug. 2021.

[21] US Department of Defense (note 2), p. 94; and authors' estimates.

[22] Authors' assessment based on analysis of satellite imagery.

[23] Korda and Kristensen (note 20).

[24] US Department of Defense (note 2), p. 167.

[25] Inhofe, J. (@JimInhofe), Twitter, 5 Dec. 2022, <https://twitter.com/JimInhofe/status/1599877030299901952>.

560 warheads on its ICBMs. If each silo were filled with a missile equipped with three multiple independently targetable re-entry vehicles (MIRVs), this number could rise to approximately 1200 warheads. However, as of January 2023 it remained unclear how China ultimately plans to operate the new silos: whether they will all be filled, how many warheads each missile would carry, and whether a portion of them could potentially have conventional strike roles.[26]

China has four basic types of ICBM: the DF-4, the DF-5, the DF-31 and the DF-41, with variants of each type. Most have a single warhead, while a smaller but growing number can deliver multiple warheads.

As of January 2023 SIPRI assesses that China's oldest ICBM system, the DF-4 (CSS-3), is nearing the completion of its gradual retirement from service and probably no longer has an operational nuclear strike role. SIPRI estimates that the number of deployed missiles in the DF-5 (CSS-4) family of ICBMs, the Chinese missiles assumed to have the longest range, has increased slightly as China has probably begun to deploy upgraded versions in the new silos currently under construction in east-central China.

In its 2022 report the US DOD noted that China appeared to be doubling the number of launchers in some mobile ICBM brigades from 6 to 12, although some new bases appear to have only 8 launchers.[27] China is believed to have deployed at least two mobile DF-41 brigades, with a third base nearing completion—totalling around 28 launchers—and appears to be preparing for the integration of additional DF-41 brigades.[28] The US DOD assessed in 2022 that China might ultimately plan to deploy the DF-41 in both road-mobile and silo-based modes, in some or all of China's new missile silo fields, and potentially in a rail-based mode as well.[29]

The US DOD's 2022 report states that China has also begun developing a new missile called the DF-27, which could have a range of 5000–8000 km.[30] However, public information about this new missile is scarce and its purported range can already be covered by China's other ICBMs. This suggests that the DF-27 could eventually be used in a conventional strike role.

After many years of research and development, China has equipped a small number of ICBMs with nuclear MIRVs. The DF-5B can reportedly carry up to five warheads per missile, while the DF-41 can probably carry no more

---

[26] The conventional strike role is based on circumstantial evidence in Lee, R., 'A case for China's pursuit of conventionally armed ICBMs', The Diplomat, 17 Nov. 2021.

[27] US Department of Defense (note 2), p. 65; and Eveleth, D. (@dex_eve), Twitter, 3 Nov. 2021, <https://twitter.com/dex_eve/status/1456009540982374404>.

[28] US Department of Defense (note 2), p. 65; and Lee, R. (@roderick_s_lee), Twitter, 28 Dec. 2021, <https://twitter.com/roderick_s_lee/status/1475885536254599172>.

[29] US Department of Defense (note 2), p. 65.

[30] US Department of Defense (note 2), p. 65.

than three.[31] The DF-5C (CSS-4 Mod 4) that is believed to be in development might also be able to deliver MIRVs.

In 2021 China reportedly conducted a test of what appeared to be a fractional orbital bombardment system (FOBS) equipped with a hypersonic boost-glide system.[32] In its 2022 report the US DOD assessed that the tested system came close to striking its target after flying completely around the world for approximately 40 000 km and over 100 minutes.[33] While details about this new system are scarce, if the initial reporting is accurate, then it may be intended to counter advances in US missile defences.

Intermediate- and medium-range ballistic missiles

In 2016 the PLARF began deploying the dual-capable DF-26 (CSS-18) intermediate-range ballistic missile (IRBM) with an estimated maximum range exceeding 3000 km. The missile can reach targets in India, the South China Sea and the western Pacific Ocean, probably including US bases on Guam.[34] The missile is equipped with a manoeuvrable re-entry vehicle (MaRV) that can be rapidly swapped with another warhead. This theoretically allows the PLARF to switch the missile's mission between precision conventional strikes and nuclear strikes against ground targets—and even conventional strikes against naval targets—relatively quickly.[35] The majority of the DF-26s are thought to serve a conventional mission, with a smaller number (perhaps up to one-third) assigned a nuclear role. In its 2022 report the US DOD noted that, among China's nuclear forces, the DF-26 is the weapon system that is most likely to be fielded with a lower-yield warhead 'in the near-term', although it remains unclear whether very low-yield options have been produced for China's nuclear forces.[36]

The US DOD estimated in its 2022 report that China might have up to 250 DF-26 launchers and 250 or more DF-26 missiles in its inventory.[37] However, this is significantly more than is indicated by the apparent operational base infrastructure; the US DOD's estimate may thus include launchers that are in production or otherwise not yet fully operational. There were sightings of the missile at several PLARF brigade bases during 2022, and SIPRI assesses that five or six DF-26 brigades appear to be operational, with around

---

[31] US Department of Defense (note 2), pp. 65, 94; and Lewis, J. G., 'China's belated embrace of MIRVs', eds M. Krepon, T. Wheeler and S. Mason, *The Lure and Pitfalls of MIRVs: From the First to the Second Nuclear Age* (Stimson Center: Washington, DC, May 2016), pp. 95–99.

[32] Sevastopulo, D., 'China conducted two hypersonic weapons tests this summer', *Financial Times*, 20 Oct. 2021. See also Raju, N., 'Developments in space security', *SIPRI Yearbook 2022*, pp. 573–74.

[33] US Department of Defense (note 2), p. 65.

[34] US Department of Defense (note 2), p. 64.

[35] Pollack, J. H. and LaFoy, S., 'China's DF-26: A hot-swappable missile?', Arms Control Wonk, 17 May 2020; Deng, X., 'China deploys Dongfeng-26 ballistic missile with PLA Rocket Force', *Global Times*, 26 Apr. 2018; and US Department of Defense (note 2), p. 65.

[36] US Department of Defense (note 2), p. 98.

[37] US Department of Defense (note 2), p. 167.

162 launchers in total, although only about one-third of those are assumed to have a nuclear mission.

The US DOD's 2022 report indicates a sizable increase in China's force of medium-range ballistic missiles (MRBMs), from 150 launchers and 150 or more missiles in 2020 to 250 launchers and 500 or more missiles at the end of 2021.[38] These numbers are probably on the higher end of an estimated range and, as with the above IRBM estimate, could also include launchers and missiles in production. The increase in MRBMs—coupled with the corresponding decrease in China's short-range ballistic missiles (SRBMs)—is most likely due to the replacement of many SRBMs with the new DF-17 (CSS-22) MRBM equipped with a hypersonic glide vehicle (HGV). While China's MRBMs are generally dual-capable, most of them are probably assigned conventional payloads.[39] SIPRI estimates that, as of January 2023, around 24 of the PLARF's MRBMs—the DF-21A/E (CSS-5 Mods 2 and 6)—were assigned nuclear weapons.

Sea-based missiles

In 2022 China continued to pursue its strategic goal from the early 1980s of developing and deploying sea-based nuclear weapons. The PLA Navy (PLAN) currently fields six Type 094 (Jin class) nuclear-powered ballistic missile submarines (SSBNs), two of which are Type 094As—upgraded variants of the original design.[40] The US DOD's 2022 report assesses that these six operational SSBNs constitute China's 'first credible, sea-based nuclear deterrent'.[41] China's SSBN fleet is based at Hainan Island in the South China Sea.

Each of China's Type 094 submarines can carry up to 12 three-stage, solid-fuelled Julang (JL) submarine-launched ballistic missiles (SLBMs), which exist in two types: the JL-2 (CSS-N-14) and the JL-3 (CSS-N-20). US reports in late 2022 suggested that China had replaced or was in the process of replacing the JL-2 SLBMs with the longer-range JL-3.[42] The JL-3 is capable of carrying multiple warheads and has an estimated range of more than 10 000 km.[43] Unless the range is significantly more than 10 000 km, the JL-3 would not be able to strike continental USA if fired from the South China Sea.

---

[38] US Department of Defense (note 2), p. 167; and US Department of Defense, *Military and Security Developments Involving the People's Republic of China 2020*, Annual Report to Congress (Office of the Secretary of Defense: Washington, DC, 1 Sep. 2020), p. 166.

[39] US Department of Defense (note 2), p. 65.

[40] Chan, M., 'China's new nuclear submarine missiles expand range in US: Analysts', *South China Morning Post*, 2 May 2021.

[41] US Department of Defense (note 2), p. 53.

[42] Capaccio, A., 'China has put longer-range ICBMs on its nuclear subs, US says', Bloomberg, 19 Nov. 2022.

[43] US Air Force (note 17), p. 33.

There has been considerable speculation about whether the missiles on China's SSBNs are routinely fitted with nuclear warheads. The US DOD stated in its 2022 report that China 'likely began near-continuous at-sea deterrence patrols' in 2021.[44] This wording implies that China may have begun intermittent patrols with nuclear weapons onboard, although it is not definitive and would constitute a significant change to the country's long-held practice of keeping nuclear warheads in central storage in peacetime.

China has probably begun construction of its next-generation SSBN, the Type 096.[45] A potential hull section was visible in commercial satellite imagery in February 2021.[46] Reports vary widely on the design parameters, but the new submarine is expected to be larger and quieter than the Type 094 and could potentially be equipped with more missile-launch tubes. Given the expected lifespans of the current Type 094 and the next-generation Type 096 SSBNs, the PLAN is expected to operate both types concurrently.[47] It remains unclear how many SSBNs the PLAN ultimately intends to operate. Satellite imagery from December 2022 shows that China was nearing completion of two new piers at the Longpo Naval Base. This would raise the total number of potential submarine berths at the base from 8 to 12, although some of these could be intended for attack submarines.

[44] US Department of Defense (note 2), p. 96.
[45] US Department of Defense (note 2), p. 96.
[46] Sutton, H. I., 'First image of China's new nuclear submarine under construction', Naval News, 1 Feb. 2021.
[47] US Department of Defense (note 2), p. 96.

VI. Indian nuclear forces

HANS M. KRISTENSEN AND MATT KORDA*

As of January 2023 India was estimated to have a growing stockpile of about 164 nuclear weapons—a small increase from the previous year (see table 7.7). These weapons were assigned to a maturing nuclear triad of aircraft, land-based missiles and nuclear-powered ballistic missile submarines (SSBNs).

The warhead estimate is based on calculations of India's inventory of weapon-grade plutonium (see section X), the estimated number of operational nuclear-capable delivery systems, India's nuclear doctrine, publicly available information on the Indian nuclear arsenal, and private conversations with defence officials.[1] The Indian government has provided little public information about the size of its nuclear forces, other than conducting occasional parade displays and announcing missile flight tests.

This section starts by outlining the role played by nuclear weapons in Indian military doctrine. It then enumerates India's holdings of nuclear weapons—its aircraft and air-delivered weapons and its land- and sea-based missiles—and assesses the nuclear capability of its cruise missiles.

The role of nuclear weapons in Indian military doctrine

The limited ranges of India's initial nuclear systems meant that, until the early 2010s, their only credible role was to deter Pakistan. However, with the development over the subsequent decade of longer-range missiles capable of targeting all of China, in recent years it appears that India has placed increased emphasis on deterring China.

While India has adhered to a nuclear no-first-use (NFU) policy since 1999, this pledge was qualified by a 2003 caveat (reaffirmed in 2018) that India could also use nuclear forces to retaliate against attacks by non-nuclear weapons of mass destruction (WMD).[2] Doubts about India's commitment to the NFU policy have increased with evidence that some parts of India's nuclear arsenal are being kept at a much higher state of readiness.[3] This has prompted a debate about whether India could be transitioning towards

---

[1] Kristensen, H. M. and Korda, M., 'Estimating world nuclear forces: An overview and assessment of sources', SIPRI Commentary, 14 June 2021.

[2] Indian Ministry of External Affairs, 'The Cabinet Committee on Security reviews [o]perationalization of India's nuclear doctrine', Press release, 4 Jan. 2003; Indian Ministry of External Affairs, 'Draft report of National Security Advisory Board on Indian nuclear doctrine', 17 Aug. 1999; and Indian Prime Minister's Office, 'Prime Minister felicitates crew of INS Arihant on completion of nuclear triad', Press release, 5 Nov. 2018.

[3] For further detail see Kristensen, H. M. and Korda, M., 'Indian nuclear forces', *SIPRI Yearbook 2021*.

* The authors wish to thank Eliana Johns for contributing invaluable research to this publication.

a counterforce nuclear posture to target an adversary's nuclear weapons earlier in a crisis, even before they could be used.[4]

Aircraft and air-delivered weapons

India has several types of combat aircraft with performance characteristics that potentially make them suitable as nuclear-delivery platforms, including the Mirage 2000H, Jaguar IS and Rafale. However, there is no official source that confirms the nuclear-capable role of these aircraft, with one exception: a detailed source describes how the Mirage 2000H was converted for a nuclear strike role in the 1990s.[5] SIPRI estimates that approximately 48 nuclear gravity bombs were assigned to Indian aircraft as of January 2023.

Land-based missiles

The Indian Army's Strategic Forces Command operates five types of mobile nuclear-capable ballistic missile: the short-range Prithvi-II and Agni-I; the medium-range Agni-II; and the intermediate-range Agni-III and Agni-IV. SIPRI estimates that India had around 80 operational missiles as of January 2023. At least two new land-based ballistic missiles were in development: the medium-range Agni-P and the intermediate-range Agni-V; a variant with an intercontinental range, the Agni-VI, was in the design stage of development.[6]

Several of India's land-based ballistic missiles achieved significant milestones in 2022. The Agni-P completed its third test launch in October 2022, following two (one failed and one successful) in 2021. The Indian Army typically requires at least three consecutive successful tests before a missile can be inducted into military service.[7] The Agni-P is described by the Indian Ministry of Defence as a next-generation nuclear-capable ballistic missile. It reportedly incorporates technology developed specifically for the Agni-V programme, including an advanced navigation system and a new mobile canisterized launch system, which will reduce the time required to place the

---

[4] Clary, C. and Narang, V., 'India's counterforce temptations: Strategic dilemmas, doctrine, and capabilities', *International Security*, vol. 43, no. 3 (winter 2018/19); Kaushal, S. et al., 'India's nuclear doctrine: The Agni-P and the stability–instability paradox', Royal United Services Institute (RUSI), 8 July 2021; and Rajagopalan, R., *India and Counterforce: A Question of Evidence*, ORF Occasional Paper no. 247 (Observer Research Foundation: New Delhi, May 2020).

[5] Kampani, G., 'New Delhi's long nuclear journey: How secrecy and institutional roadblocks delayed India's weaponization', *International Security*, vol. 38, no. 4 (spring 2014), pp. 94, 97–98. For further detail see Kristensen, H. M. and Korda, M., 'Indian nuclear forces', *SIPRI Yearbook 2022*, pp. 393–94.

[6] Vikas, S. V., 'Why India may not test Agni 6 even if DRDO is ready with technology', OneIndia, 10 July 2019.

[7] Gupta, S., 'Agni-P missile moves towards induction after user trials', *Hindustan Times*, 23 Oct. 2022; and O'Donnell, F., 'Aim for higher testing standards', *The Pioneer* (Nioda), 27 July 2015.

Table 7.7. Indian nuclear forces, January 2023

All figures are approximate and some are based on assessments by the authors.

Type/designation	No. of launchers	Year first deployed	Range (km)[a]	Warheads x yield[b]	No. of warheads[c]
Aircraft[d]	84				48
Mirage 2000H	32	1985	1 850	1 x 12 kt bomb	32
Jaguar IS	16	1981	1 600	1 x 12 kt bomb	16
Rafale	36	2022	2 000	..	–
Land-based missiles	80				80
Prithvi-II	24	2003	250[e]	1 x 12 kt	24
Agni-I	16	2007	>700	1 x 10–40 kt	16
Agni-II	16	2011	>2 000	1 x 10–40 kt	16
Agni-III	16	2018	>3 200	1 x 10–40 kt	16
Agni-IV	8	2022	>3 500	1 x 10–40 kt	8
Agni-V	..	[2023]	>5 000	1 x 10–40 kt	..
Agni-VI	–	[2027]	>6 000	1 x 10–40 kt [possible MIRV]	–
Agni-P	–	[2025]	1 000–2 000	[1 x 10–40 kt]	–
Sea-based missiles	3/14[f]				16
Dhanush	2	2013	400	1 x 12 kt	4[g]
K-15 (B-05)[h]	12[i]	2018	700	1 x 12 kt	12
K-4	–[j]	[2025]	3 500	1 x 10–40 kt	–
Other stored warheads[k]					[20]
Total stockpile	**178**				**164**[k]

.. = not available or not applicable; – = nil or a negligible value; [ ] = uncertain SIPRI estimate; kt = kiloton; MIRV = multiple independently targetable re-entry vehicle.

[a] For aircraft, the listed range is for illustrative purposes only; actual mission range will vary according to flight profile, weapon payload and in-flight refuelling.

[b] The yields of India's nuclear warheads are not known. The 1998 nuclear tests demonstrated yields of up to 12 kt. Since then, it is possible that boosted warheads have been introduced with a higher yield, perhaps up to 40 kt. There is no open-source evidence that India has developed 2-stage thermonuclear warheads.

[c] Aircraft and several missile types are dual-capable—that is, they can be armed with either conventional or nuclear warheads. This estimate counts an average of 1 nuclear warhead per launcher. All estimates are approximate.

[d] The Rafale is listed as a potential future nuclear delivery platform. It seems likely that it would probably initially replace the Jaguar in that role. However, in the absence of official or authoritative sources, SIPRI has not attributed nuclear weapons to Rafale aircraft in its estimate for Jan. 2023. Other aircraft that could potentially have a secondary nuclear role include the Su-30MKI.

[e] The Prithvi-II's range is often reported as 350 kilometres. However, the United States Air Force's National Air and Space Intelligence Center sets the range at 250 km.

[f] The first figure is the number of operational vessels—2 ships and 1 nuclear-powered ballistic missile submarine (SSBN); the second is the maximum number of missiles that they can carry. India has launched 3 SSBNs, but only 1—INS *Arihant*—was believed to be operational as of Jan. 2023, and it was believed to have only a limited operational capability. The second SSBN—INS *Arighat*—was conducting sea trials throughout 2022 and might become operational in 2023. The third, known as S4, was reportedly launched in Nov. 2021 but, as of Jan. 2023, its status remained unclear.

^{g} Each Sukanya-class patrol ship equipped with Dhanush missiles was thought to have possibly 1 reload.

^{h} The K-15 may have been renamed the B-05. Some sources have referred to the K-15 missile as 'Sagarika', which was the name of the missile-development project, rather than the missile itself.

^{i} Each of India's first 2 SSBNs has 4 missile tubes, each of which can carry 3 K-15 submarine-launched ballistic missiles (SLBMs), for a total of 12 missiles per SSBN. Only 1 SSBN was believed to be operational as of Jan. 2023 (see note f).

^{j} Each of the 8 missile tubes on India's third and fourth SSBNs will be able to carry 3 K-15 SLBMs or 1 K-4 SLBM once the latter missile becomes operational.

^{k} In addition to the c. 144 warheads estimated to be assigned to operational forces, SIPRI estimates that c. 20 warheads might have been produced for missiles nearing operational status, including the Agni-V (c. 8 warheads) and the K-15 (c. 12 warheads for INS *Arighat*), for a total estimated stockpile of c. 164 warheads. India's warhead stockpile is expected to continue to increase.

Sources: Indian Ministry of Defence, annual reports and press releases; International Institute for Strategic Studies, *The Military Balance*, various years; US Air Force (USAF), National Air and Space Intelligence Center, *Ballistic and Cruise Missile Threat*, various years; Indian news media reports; *Bulletin of the Atomic Scientists*, 'Nuclear notebook', various issues; and authors' estimates.

missiles on alert in a crisis.[8] The solid-fuelled Agni-P can reportedly manoeuvre during re-entry, which could allow the missile to evade future missile defences of states in the region (e.g. China and Pakistan). An unidentified government source denied that the Agni-P was intended to replace older Agni missiles.[9]

In 2022 India also conducted test launches of the Prithvi-II, the Agni-III, the Agni-IV and the Agni-V. Notably, the Indian government, for the first time, described the Agni-IV test as 'part of routine user training launches', which is the language typically used to describe tests of Indian missiles already in service.[10] Given the missile's apparent induction in 2014 and subsequent serial production, SIPRI assesses that the Agni-IV became operational in 2022.[11] The three-stage, solid-fuelled Agni-V was test launched for the ninth time in December 2022.[12] Reports on the test suggest that the Indian Defence Research and Development Organisation (DRDO) may have been testing a new solid rocket motor made from lighter composite materials to increase the missile's range.[13]

---

[8] Indian Ministry of Defence (MOD), 'DRDO successfully flight tests new generation Agni P ballistic missile', Press release, 28 June 2021; and Rout, H. K., 'India test fires new generation nuclear capable Agni-Prime missile off Odisha coast', *New Indian Express*, 28 June 2021.

[9] Philip, S. A., 'Agni Prime is the new missile in India's nuclear arsenal. This is why it's special', ThePrint, 30 June 2021; and Zhen, L., 'India's latest Agni-P missile no great threat to China: Experts', *South China Morning Post*, 1 July 2021.

[10] Indian Ministry of Defence, 'Intermediate range ballistic missile, Agni-4, successfully tested', Press release, 6 June 2022; Indian Ministry of Defence, 'Year end review 2022', 17 Dec. 2022; and Wright, T., 'India's test of the Agni-IV', International Institute for Strategic Studies, 27 June 2022.

[11] Subramanian, T. S., 'Agni-IV missile successfully test fired', *The Hindu*, 20 Jan. 2014.

[12] Sharma, A., 'India tests long-range missile for nuclear deterrence', AP News, 15 Dec. 2022; and Gupta, S., 'Has the range of Agni V missile been increased?', *Hindustan Times*, 16 Dec. 2022.

[13] Gupta (note 12).

India is developing a land-based version of the short-range K-15 submarine-launched ballistic missile (SLBM), known as the Shaurya.[14] However, because of the high level of uncertainty about the status of the Shaurya, it is not included in SIPRI's estimate for January 2023.[15]

India is believed to be developing multiple independently targetable re-entry vehicles (MIRVs), but as of January 2023 the status of the programme remained unclear. The technology has reportedly been tested on the Agni-P and could potentially be used on the intercontinental Agni-VI currently in development.[16] The Agni-VI is controversial because its expected range may extend well beyond India's possible regional targets in Pakistan and China.

Sea-based missiles

With the aim of creating an assured second-strike capability, India has continued to develop the naval component of its nascent nuclear triad and to build a fleet of four to six SSBNs.[17] The first of these SSBNs, INS *Arihant*, completed what the Indian government described as its first 'deterrence patrol' in 2018—although it seems unlikely that the missiles were armed with nuclear warheads at the time.[18] A second SSBN, INS *Arighat*, was launched in November 2017 and underwent advanced sea trials in 2021–22 ahead of its expected commissioning into the Indian Navy in 2023.[19] Satellite imagery indicates that each submarine has been equipped with a four-tube vertical-launch system and each could carry up to 12 two-stage, short-range K-15 SLBMs (which may have been renamed the B-05).[20] SIPRI estimates that 12 nuclear warheads have been delivered for potential deployment by INS *Arihant* and another 12 have been produced for INS *Arighat*.

A third submarine, known as S4, was reportedly launched in November 2021, and a fourth is under construction for possible launch in 2023.[21] These

---

[14] See e.g. Press Trust of India, 'India successfully test-fires nuclear capable hypersonic missile Shaurya', *Hindustan Times*, 3 Oct. 2020; and Gupta, S., 'Govt okays induction of nuke-capable Shaurya missile amid Ladakh standoff', *Hindustan Times*, 6 Oct. 2020.

[15] For further detail see Kristensen and Korda (note 5), p. 395.

[16] Rout, H. K., 'India to conduct first user trial of Agni-V missile', *New Indian Express*, 13 Sep. 2021.

[17] Davenport, K., 'Indian submarine completes first patrol', *Arms Control Today*, vol. 48, no. 10 (Dec. 2018).

[18] Peri, D., 'Now, India has a nuclear triad', *The Hindu*, 18 Oct. 2016; Indian Prime Minister's Office (note 2); Davenport (note 17); and Joshi, Y., 'Angels and dangles: Arihant and the dilemma of India's undersea nuclear weapons', War on the Rocks, 14 Jan. 2019.

[19] 'Indian submarine fleet to get fresh impetus by early 2023', *Economic Times* (Mumbai), 21 Oct. 2022.

[20] Indian Defence Research and Development Organisation (DRDO), 'MSS—Achievements', 6 Sep. 2019.

[21] Biggers, C. (@CSBiggers), Twitter, 28 Dec. 2021, <https://twitter.com/CSBiggers/status/1476048094580117509>; and Unnithan, S., 'A peek into India's top secret and costliest defence project, nuclear submarines', *India Today*, 10 Dec. 2017; and Bhattacharjee, S., 'Third Arihant class submarine quietly launched in November', *The Hindu*, 4 Jan. 2022.

submarines are believed to be significantly larger than the first two; satellite imagery indicates that they are approximately 20 metres longer.[22] They will reportedly have eight launch tubes able to hold up to 24 K-15 missiles or 8 K-4 missiles.[23] The K-4 is in development but probably remains several years away from operational capability. Two potential test launches of the K-4 in 2022 were apparently disrupted by the presence of Chinese spy ships.[24]

India's first naval nuclear weapon, the short-range Dhanush missile, is a version of the dual-capable Prithvi-II that can be launched from two Sukanya-class offshore patrol vessels.[25] Given the slow speed and high degree of vulnerability of the Sukanya-class vessels, the system will probably be retired when the SSBN programme with longer-range missiles matures.

Cruise missiles

There have been numerous media claims that some Indian cruise missiles are nuclear-capable. These claims concern the ground- and air-launched Nirbhay subsonic cruise missile and the supersonic air-, ground-, ship- and submarine-launched BrahMos cruise missile.[26] Notably, one of the latter was accidentally launched into Pakistani territory in March 2022 (see section VII).

Although a DRDO poster at an Indian defence exhibition in October 2022 listed the Nirbhay as capable of delivering 'conventional and strategic warheads', as of January 2023 no known official or authoritative source had explicitly attributed nuclear capability to India's cruise missiles.[27] In addition, United States sources list the BrahMos as 'conventional'.[28] The systems are therefore excluded from SIPRI's estimate for January 2023.

---

[22] Sutton, H. I., 'Indian Navy's third ballistic missile submarine doubles missile armament', Covert Shores, 29 Dec. 2021.

[23] Bhattacharjee (note 21). See also Kristensen and Korda (note 5), p. 397.

[24] 'Chinese spy ships may complicate India's missile test plans in Indian Ocean for the second month in a row', Swarajya, 7 Dec. 2022.

[25] 'Nuke-capable Dhanush and Prithvi-II launched', New Indian Express, 12 Mar. 2011; and Indian Ministry of Defence (MOD), Annual Report 2018–19 (MOD: New Delhi, 2019), p. 100.

[26] See e.g. Pandit, R., 'India successfully tests its first nuclear-capable cruise missile', Times of India, 8 Nov. 2017; Gady, F.-S., 'India successfully test fires indigenous nuclear-capable cruise missile', The Diplomat, 8 Nov. 2017; and Mitra, J., 'Nuclear BrahMos: On the anvil?', South Asian Voices, 10 July 2018.

[27] A copy of the DRDO poster is available on Twitter. Alpha Defense (@alpha_defense), Twitter, 19 Oct. 2022, <https://twitter.com/alpha_defense/status/1582584800191590401>.

[28] US Air Force, National Air and Space Intelligence Center (NASIC), Ballistic and Cruise Missile Threat 2017 (NASIC: Wright-Patterson Air Force Base, OH, June 2017), p. 37.

VII. Pakistani nuclear forces

HANS M. KRISTENSEN AND MATT KORDA*

According to SIPRI estimates, Pakistan possessed approximately 170 nuclear warheads as of January 2023—a small increase compared with the previous year (see table 7.8). These weapons were assigned to Pakistan's nascent triad of aircraft, ground-launched ballistic and cruise missiles, and sea-launched cruise missiles. The development of several new delivery systems and Pakistan's growing accumulation of fissile material (see section X) suggest that its nuclear weapon arsenal and fissile material stockpile are likely to continue to expand over the next decade, although projections vary considerably.[1]

The Pakistani government has never publicly disclosed the size of its nuclear arsenal. Limited official public data and exaggerated news stories about Pakistan's nuclear weapons mean that analysing the number and types of Pakistani warheads and delivery vehicles is fraught with uncertainty.[2] The estimates in this section are based on the authors' analysis of Pakistan's nuclear posture, fissile material production, public statements by Western officials and private conversations with Pakistani officials.

This section starts by outlining the role played by nuclear weapons in Pakistan's military doctrine. It then describes Pakistan's air-delivered and land-based weapons and the nascent sea-based capability.

The role of nuclear weapons in Pakistani military doctrine

Pakistan has been pursuing the development and deployment of new nuclear weapons and delivery systems as part of its 'full spectrum deterrence posture' in relation to India.[3] This includes long-range missiles and aircraft as well as several short-range, lower-yield nuclear-capable weapon systems.[4]

---

[1] See e.g. Sundaresan, L. and Ashok, K., 'Uranium constraints in Pakistan: How many nuclear weapons does Pakistan have?', *Current Science*, vol. 115, no. 6 (25 Sep. 2018); Salik, N., 'Pakistan's nuclear force structure in 2025', Regional Insight, Carnegie Endowment for International Peace, 30 June 2016; and Jones, G. S., 'Pakistan's nuclear material production for nuclear weapons', Proliferation Matters, 16 Feb. 2021. See also Berrier, S., Director, US Defense Intelligence Agency, 'Worldwide threat assessment', Statement for the record, US Senate, Armed Services Committee, 26 Apr. 2021. On Pakistan's fissile material stockpile see Kile, S. N. and Kristensen, H. M., 'Pakistani nuclear forces', *SIPRI Yearbook 2019*; and International Panel on Fissile Materials, 'Pakistan', 31 Aug. 2021.

[2] Kristensen, H. M. and Korda, M., 'Estimating world nuclear forces: An overview and assessment of sources', SIPRI Commentary, 14 June 2021.

[3] Kidwai, K., Keynote address and discussion session, 77th South Asian Strategic Stability workshop, 'Deterrence, nuclear weapons and arms control', International Institute for Strategic Studies (IISS) and Centre for International Strategic Studies (CISS), 6 Feb. 2020. For a detailed assessment of Pakistan's nuclear posture see Tasleem, S. and Dalton, T., 'Nuclear emulation: Pakistan's nuclear trajectory', *Washington Quarterly*, vol. 41, no. 4 (winter 2019).

[4] Pakistani Inter Services Public Relations (ISPR), Press release no. PR-94/2011-ISPR, 19 Apr. 2011.

* The authors wish to thank Eliana Johns for contributing invaluable research to this publication.

Pakistan has placed an emphasis on non-strategic (tactical) nuclear weapons specifically in response to India's 'Cold Start' doctrine.[5]

In March 2022 India accidentally launched a conventional BrahMos cruise missile into Pakistani territory during a 'routine maintenance and inspection' exercise.[6] India reportedly did not alert Pakistan during the crisis and only issued a public statement two days after the incident. Pakistan may not have tracked the missile correctly while it was in flight.[7] During the incident, the Pakistan Air Force (PAF) Air Defence Operations Centre is reported to have suspended all military and civilian aircraft for nearly six hours and placed frontline bases and strike aircraft on high alert.[8] The two countries' initial responses to the incident suggest that regional crisis frameworks in South Asia may be far less stable than previously assumed.

In October 2022 United States President Joe Biden commented that Pakistan was 'one of the most dangerous nations in the world' due to the lack of 'cohesion' in its nuclear security and command and control procedures.[9] Pakistan forcefully rebutted this statement.

Aircraft and air-delivered weapons

As of January 2023 Pakistan was estimated to operate a small stockpile of nuclear gravity bombs.

Two versions of the Ra'ad (Hatf-8) air-launched cruise missile (ALCM) were being developed to supplement this stockpile by providing the PAF with a nuclear-capable stand-off capability at ranges of 350–600 kilometres.[10] Neither version had been operationally deployed as of January 2023.

Pakistan has several types of combat aircraft with performance characteristics that make them suitable as nuclear-delivery platforms, including the Mirage III, the Mirage V, the F-16 and the JF-17. However, no official sources have confirmed their nuclear-capable roles. Given this significant uncertainty, SIPRI assesses that the Mirage III and possibly the Mirage V are

---

[5] On the doctrine—under which India looks to maintain the capability to launch large-scale conventional strikes or incursions against Pakistani territory at a level below the threshold at which Pakistan would retaliate with nuclear weapons—see Kidwai (note 3); and Saalman, L. and Topychkanov, P., *South Asia's Nuclear Challenges: Interlocking Views from India, Pakistan, China, Russia and the United States* (SIPRI: Stockholm, Apr. 2021). For a US diplomatic assessment of India's 'Cold Start' strategy see Roemer, T., US Ambassador to India, 'Cold Start: A mixture of myth and reality', Cable New Delhi 000295, 16 Feb. 2010, via WikiLeaks. Although Indian officials had previously denied the existence of the Cold Start doctrine, India's chief of the army staff acknowledged its existence in an interview in 2017. Unnithan, S., '"We will cross again"', *India Today*, 4 Jan. 2017.

[6] Korda, M., 'Flying under the radar: A missile accident in South Asia', FAS Strategic Security Blog, Federation of American Scientists, 4 Apr. 2022.

[7] Korda (note 6).

[8] Bhatt, M., 'The curious case of a misfired missile', *DNA* (Mumbai), 14 Mar. 2022.

[9] Khan, Z., 'Pakistan hits back at Biden's "dangerous nation" comment', AP News, 15 Oct. 2022.

[10] For further detail on the Ra'ad ALCM see Kristensen, H. M. and Korda, M., 'Pakistani nuclear forces', *SIPRI Yearbook 2021*, p. 387.

Table 7.8. Pakistani nuclear forces, January 2023

All figures are approximate and some are based on assessments by the authors.

Type/designation	No. of launchers	Year first deployed	Range (km)[a]	Warheads x yield[b]	No. of warheads[c]
Aircraft[d]	36				36
Mirage III/V	36[e]	1998	2 100	1 x 5–12 kt bomb or Ra'ad ALCM (in development)[f]	36
Land-based missiles	126[g]				126
Abdali (Hatf-2)	10	2002	200	1 x 5–12 kt	10
Ghaznavi (Hatf-3)	16	2004	300	1 x 5–12 kt	16
Shaheen-I/IA (Hatf-4)[h]	16	2003/2022	750/900	1 x 5–12 kt	16
Shaheen-II (Hatf-6)	24	2014	2 000	1 x 10–40 kt	24
Shaheen-III[i]	–	[2023]	2 750	1 x 10–40 kt	–
Ghauri (Hatf-5)	24	2003	1 250	1 x 10–40 kt	24
Nasr (Hatf-9)	24	2013	70	1 x 5–12 kt	24
Ababeel	–	..	2 200	[MRV or MIRV][j]	–
Babur/-1A GLCM (Hatf-7)[k]	12	2014/[early 2020s]	350/450	1 x 5–12 kt	12
Babur-2 GLCM[l]	–	..	900	1 x 5–12 kt	–
Sea-based missiles					
Babur-3 SLCM	–	[2025]	450	1 x 5–12 kt	–
Other stored warheads[m]					[8]
Total stockpile	**162**				**170**[m]

.. = not available or not applicable; – = nil or a negligible value; [ ] = uncertain SIPRI estimate; ALCM = air-launched cruise missile; GLCM = ground-launched cruise missile; kt = kiloton; MIRV = multiple independently targetable re-entry vehicle; MRV = multiple re-entry vehicle; SLCM = sea-launched cruise missile.

[a] For aircraft, the listed range is for illustrative purposes only; actual mission range will vary according to flight profile, weapon payload and in-flight refuelling.

[b] The yields of Pakistan's nuclear warheads are not known. The 1998 nuclear tests demonstrated a yield of up to 12 kt. Since then, it is possible that boosted warheads have been introduced with a higher yield. There is no open-source evidence that Pakistan has developed 2-stage thermonuclear warheads.

[c] Aircraft and several missile types are dual-capable—that is, they can be armed with either conventional or nuclear warheads. Cruise missile launchers (aircraft and land- and sea-based missiles) can carry more than 1 missile. This estimate counts an average of 1 nuclear warhead per launcher. Pakistan does not deploy its warheads on launchers but keeps them in separate storage facilities.

[d] There are unconfirmed reports that Pakistan modified for a nuclear weapon-delivery role some of the 40 F-16 aircraft procured from the United States in the 1980s. However, it is assumed here that the nuclear weapons assigned to aircraft are for use by Mirage aircraft. When the Mirage IIIs and Vs are eventually phased out, it is possible that the JF-17 will take over their nuclear role in the Pakistan Air Force.

[e] Pakistan possesses many more than 36 Mirage aircraft, but this table only includes those that are assumed to have a nuclear weapon-delivery role.

[f] The Ra'ad (Hatf-8) ALCM has a claimed range of 350 km and an estimated yield of 5–12 kt. However, there is no available evidence to suggest that the Ra'ad has been deployed and it is therefore not included in the operational warhead count. In 2017 the Pakistani military displayed

a Ra'ad-II variant with a reported range of 600 km. It was test flown for the first time in 2020 and several additional flights will be needed before it becomes operational.

g Some launchers might have 1 or more missile reloads.

h It is unclear whether the Shaheen-IA has the same 'Hatf-4' designation as the Shaheen-I.

i The designation for the Shaheen-III is unknown.

j The Pakistani military claimed in 2017 that the Ababeel can deliver multiple warheads using MIRV technology, but does not appear to have provided any further information since then.

k Pakistan has been upgrading its original Babur GLCMs to Babur-1As by improving their avionics and target-engagement systems to hit both land and sea targets. The range of the original Babur is listed as 350 km by the US Air Force's National Air and Space Intelligence Center, while Pakistan claims that the range of the improved Babur-1A is 450 km.

l The Babur-2 GLCM is sometimes referred to as the Babur-1B.

m In addition to the *c*. 162 warheads estimated to be assigned to operational forces, SIPRI estimates that *c*. 8 warheads have been produced to arm future Shaheen-III missiles, for a total estimated stockpile of *c*. 170 warheads. Pakistan's warhead stockpile is expected to continue to increase.

Sources: Pakistani Ministry of Defence, various documents; US Air Force (USAF), National Air and Space Intelligence Center, *Ballistic and Cruise Missile Threat*, various years; International Institute for Strategic Studies, *The Military Balance*, various years; *Bulletin of the Atomic Scientists*, 'Nuclear notebook', various issues; and authors' estimates.

the most likely to have a nuclear-delivery role. The Mirage III has been used for developmental test flights of the nuclear-capable Ra'ad ALCM, while the Mirage V is believed to have been given a strike role with Pakistan's small arsenal of nuclear gravity bombs.[11]

At the end of 2022 Pakistan had more than 100 operational JF-17 aircraft and had plans in place to acquire around another 188 JF-17s to replace the ageing Mirage III and Mirage V aircraft.[12] When the Mirage aircraft are eventually phased out, it is possible that the JF-17 will take over their nuclear role in the PAF and that the Ra'ad ALCM will be integrated on to the JF-17.[13]

Land-based missiles

As of January 2023 Pakistan's nuclear-capable ballistic missile arsenal comprised an estimated 126 short- and medium-range systems.

Pakistan has deployed four types of solid-fuelled, road-mobile short-range ballistic missile: the Abdali (also designated Hatf-2), the Ghaznavi (Hatf-3), the Shaheen-I/IA (Hatf-4) and the Nasr (Hatf-9). The dual-capable Ghaznavi was test launched twice in 2021, after which the PAF listed its range

[11] International Institute for Strategic Studies (IISS), *The Military Balance 2022* (Routledge: London, 2022), p. 297; and Dominguez, G., 'Pakistan test-launches longer-range variant of Ra'ad II ALCM', Janes, 19 Feb. 2020. For further detail on the nuclear capability of the F-16s see Kristensen, H. M. and Kile, S. N., 'Pakistani nuclear forces', *SIPRI Yearbook 2020*, p. 370.

[12] Aamir, A., 'Pakistan to boost air strike power with 50 enhanced fighter jets', Nikkei, 6 Feb. 2022.

[13] 'Ra'ad ALCM: The custodian of Pakistan's airborne nuclear deterrence', PakDefense, 6 Dec. 2020; and Pakistan Strategic Forum, 'Update on Pakistan: "JF-17 Thunder's integration with RA'AD II ALCM"', 8 July 2020.

as 290 km.[14] The Shaheen-IA, an extended-range version of the Shaheen-I, was test launched twice in 2021—once to a range of 900 km.[15] While the Shaheen-I was displayed at the 2021 Pakistan Day Parade, it was replaced by the Shaheen-IA at the 2022 parade, potentially indicating the latter system's deployment.[16] Notably, the Abdali—Pakistan's oldest ballistic missile type—was not displayed at the Pakistan Day Parade in either 2021 or 2022 and has not been tested since 2013, perhaps indicating that the missile is being superseded by newer systems.

The arsenal also included two types of operational medium-range ballistic missile: the liquid-fuelled, road-mobile Ghauri (Hatf-5); and the two-stage, solid-fuelled, road-mobile Shaheen-II (Hatf-6).[17] A longer-range variant in development, the Shaheen-III, has been test launched at least three times—in 2015, 2021 and April 2022—but was probably not yet deployed as of January 2023.[18] This missile has a claimed range of 2750 km, making it the longest-range system that Pakistan has tested to date. The Ghauri, Shaheen-II and Shaheen-III were all displayed at the Pakistan Day Parade in 2022. The Pakistani government has claimed that the Ababeel (a variant of the Shaheen-III under development) could deliver multiple warheads, using multiple independently targetable re-entry vehicle (MIRV) technology, but its last test launch was in 2017 and its status remained unclear as of January 2023.[19]

---

[14] Pakistani Inter Services Public Relations (ISPR), 'Pakistan conducted a training launch of surface to surface ballistic missile Ghaznavi', Press release no. PR-141/2021-ISPR, 12 Aug. 2021; and Pakistani Inter Services Public Relations (ISPR), 'Pakistan today conducted a successful training launch of surface to surface ballistic missile Ghaznavi, capable of delivering nuclear and conventional warheads up to a range of 290 kilometers', Press release no. PR-19/2021-ISPR, 3 Feb. 2021.

[15] Pakistani Inter Services Public Relations (ISPR), 'Pakistan conducted successful flight test of Shaheen-1A surface to surface ballistic missile', Press release no. PR-199/2021-ISPR, 25 Nov. 2021; and Pakistani Inter Services Public Relations (ISPR), 'Pakistan conducted successful flight test of Shaheen-1A surface to surface ballistic missile, having a range of 900 kilometers', Press release no. PR-59/2021-ISPR, 26 Mar. 2021.

[16] Pakistani Inter Services Public Relations (ISPR), 'Pakistan Day Parade: 23 March 2022', ISPR Official, YouTube, 24 Mar. 2022; and Pakistani Inter Services Public Relations (ISPR), 'Pakistan Day Parade: March 2021', ISPR Official, YouTube, 25 Mar. 2021.

[17] United States Air Force, National Air and Space Intelligence Center (NASIC), *Ballistic and Cruise Missile Threat 2020* (NASIC: Wright-Patterson Air Force Base, OH, July 2020), p. 25; and Pakistani Inter Services Public Relations (ISPR), 'Pakistan conducted successful training launch of surface to surface ballistic missile Shaheen-II', Press release no. PR-104/2019-ISPR, 23 May 2019.

[18] Pakistani Inter Services Public Relations (ISPR), 'Shaheen 3 missile test', Press release no. PR-61/2015-ISPR, 9 Mar. 2015; Jamal, S., 'Pakistan tests nuclear-capable Shaheen-III ballistic missile', *Gulf News*, 20 Jan. 2021; and ISPR spokesperson (@OfficialDGISPR), Twitter, 9 Apr. 2022, <https://twitter.com/OfficialDGISPR/status/1512710884518359042>.

[19] Pakistani Inter Services Public Relations (ISPR), Press release no. PR-34/2017-ISPR, 24 Jan. 2017. The US Air Force's National Air and Space Intelligence Center also describes the 2017 test as involving 'the MIRV version of the Ababeel'. US Air Force, National Air and Space Intelligence Center (NASIC), *Ballistic and Cruise Missile Threat 2017* (NASIC: Wright-Patterson Air Force Base, OH, June 2017), p. 25. On the Ababeel see also Kile and Kristensen (note 1), p. 335.

In addition to expanding its arsenal of land-based ballistic missiles, Pakistan has continued to develop the nuclear-capable Babur (Hatf-7) ground-launched cruise missile, with an estimated range of 350 km.[20] The Babur has been test launched about 12 times since 2005 and it has been used in army field training since 2011, indicating that the system is probably operational. An upgraded version, with a claimed range of 450 km, is known as the Babur-1A and was featured in the 2022 Pakistan Day Parade.[21] A version known as the Babur-2 (sometimes referred to as the Babur-1B) has a claimed range of 900 km and was tested most recently in December 2021.[22]

Sea-based missiles

As part of its efforts to achieve a secure second-strike capability, Pakistan has sought to create a nuclear triad by developing a sea-based nuclear force. The Babur-3 submarine-launched cruise missile (SLCM) is intended to establish a nuclear capability for the Pakistan Navy's three Agosta-90B diesel–electric submarines.[23] Pakistan test launched the Babur-3 in 2017 and 2018.[24]

---

[20] US Air Force (note 19), p. 37.
[21] Pakistani Inter Services Public Relations, 'Pakistan Day Parade: 23 March 2022' (note 16); and Pakistani Inter Services Public Relations (ISPR), 'Press release no. PR24/2021, Pak conducted successful launch of Babur cruise missile—11 Feb 2021(ISPR)', ISPR Official, YouTube, 11 Feb. 2021.
[22] Pakistani Inter Services Public Relations (ISPR), 'Pakistan conducted a successful test of an enhanced range version of the indigenously developed Babur cruise missile', Press release no. PR-142/2018-ISPR, 14 Apr. 2018; Gupta, S., 'Pakistan's effort to launch 750km range missile crashes', *Hindustan Times*, 23 Mar. 2020; and Pakistani Inter Services Public Relations (ISPR), 'Pakistan conducted a successful test of an enhanced range version of the indigenously developed Babur cruise missile 1B', Press release no. PR-222/2021-ISPR, 21 Dec. 2021.
[23] Pakistani Inter Services Public Relations (ISPR), Press release no. PR-10/2017-ISPR, 9 Jan. 2017; and Panda, A. and Narang, V., 'Pakistan tests new sub-launched nuclear-capable cruise missile. What now?', The Diplomat, 10 Jan. 2017.
[24] Pakistani Inter Services Public Relations (ISPR), 'Pakistan conducted another successful test fire of indigenously developed submarine launched cruise missile Babur having a range of 450 kms', Press release no. PR-125/2018-ISPR, 29 Mar. 2018. Reports of a ship-launched cruise missile test in 2019 might have been for a different missile. Gady, F.-S., 'Pakistan's Navy test fires indigenous anti-ship/land-attack cruise missile', The Diplomat, 24 Apr. 2019.

VIII. North Korean nuclear forces

HANS M. KRISTENSEN AND MATT KORDA*

The Democratic People's Republic of Korea (DPRK, or North Korea) maintains an active but highly opaque nuclear weapon programme. SIPRI estimates that, as of January 2023, North Korea possessed around 30 nuclear weapons (see table 7.9, end of section), but that it probably possessed sufficient fissile material for an approximate total of 50–70 nuclear devices, depending on warhead design.

These estimates are based on calculations of the amount of fissile material—plutonium and highly enriched uranium (HEU)—that North Korea is believed to have produced for use in nuclear weapons (see section X), its nuclear weapon testing history and its observable missile forces. Analysing the numbers and types of North Korean warheads and delivery vehicles is fraught with uncertainty due to limited and untrustworthy public sources. Most of the data presented here is derived from sources outside North Korea, including satellite imagery, United States government reports and statements (which may also be biased), and expert analyses.[1]

North Korea has conducted a total of six nuclear explosive tests: in 2006, 2009, 2013, twice in 2016, and most recently 2017.[2] In January 2020 the North Korean government announced that it would no longer observe the moratorium on conducting nuclear explosive tests or flight tests of intermediate-range and intercontinental ballistic missiles that it imposed upon itself in 2018.[3] It actually ended the moratorium in 2022 by launching a Hwasong-12 (KN17) intermediate-range ballistic missile (IRBM).[4] This publicly acknowledged long-range ballistic missile launch was part of an unprecedentedly busy year of missile testing for North Korea: it conducted more than 90 tests of short-range ballistic missiles (SRBMs), medium-range ballistic missiles (MRBMs), land-attack cruise missiles, hypersonic glide vehicles (HGVs), submarine-launched ballistic missiles (SLBMs), IRBMs and intercontinental ballistic missiles (ICBMs).

In addition, in January 2021 the North Korean leader, Kim Jong Un, announced that North Korea had been able to develop tactical (i.e.

---

[1] Kristensen, H. M. and Korda, M., 'Estimating world nuclear forces: An overview and assessment of sources', SIPRI Commentary, 14 June 2021.

[2] Fedchencko, V., 'Nuclear explosions, 1945–2017', *SIPRI Yearbook 2018*.

[3] Nebehay, S., 'North Korea abandons nuclear freeze pledge, blames "brutal" US sanctions', Reuters, 21 Jan. 2020.

[4] For the missiles and submarines discussed in this section, a designation in parentheses (e.g. KN17 in this case) following the North Korean designation (e.g. Hwasong-12) is the designation assigned by the US Department of Defense.

* The authors wish to thank Eliana Johns for contributing invaluable research to this publication.

non-strategic) nuclear weapons and 'a super-large hydrogen bomb'.[5] The latter claim might refer to a weaponized design of the nuclear device that was tested in 2017 and is suspected to have had a thermonuclear yield.[6] Kim also emphasized the need to 'make nuclear weapons smaller and lighter for more tactical uses', possibly for deployment on some of the new shorter-range missiles that were test launched in 2021–22.[7]

This section continues by summarizing the role played by nuclear weapons in North Korea's military doctrine. It then outlines the country's capabilities for production of fissile material and nuclear warheads before describing its missiles and missile programmes.

The role of nuclear weapons in North Korean military doctrine

North Korea has repeatedly signalled through doctrinal commitments and the testing of new capabilities that it will continue to develop its long- and short-range nuclear capabilities to serve as both a deterrent and potentially a response to any perceived threat.

According to North Korea's 2013 Law on Consolidating the Position of a Self-defence Nuclear Power, the country's nuclear arsenal would only be used 'to repel invasion or attack from a hostile nuclear weapons state and make retaliatory strikes', and nuclear weapons would not be used against non-nuclear states 'unless they join a hostile nuclear weapons state in its invasion and attack on the DPRK'.[8] In a speech in October 2020, Kim Jong Un reiterated North Korea's pledge not to use nuclear weapons 'preemptively'.[9] This does not constitute a no-first-use policy, however, since Kim made it clear that he could turn to nuclear weapons if 'any forces infringe upon the security of our state'.[10]

The development of tactical weapons with lower yields could indicate plans to have the capability to respond on a more limited scale to threats that do not meet the threshold for a full-scale nuclear attack. In 2022 North Korea tested several short-range missiles that state media claimed were meant for deploying tactical nuclear weapons, and it even launched a barrage of missiles that simulated use of its tactical battlefield nuclear weapons to 'hit and

---

[5] Korean Central News Agency, 'On report made by Supreme Leader Kim Jong Un at eighth Party Congress of WPK', KCNA Watch, 9 Jan. 2021.

[6] Fedchencko (note 2), p. 299.

[7] Korean Central News Agency (note 5); and 'Respected comrade Kim Jong Un guides military drills of KPA units for operation of tactical nukes', *Rodong Sinmun*, 10 Oct. 2022.

[8] [Law on Consolidating the Position of a Self-defence Nuclear Power], adopted by the Supreme People's Assembly 1 Apr. 2013, articles 4 and 5 (in Korean). For an English translation see Korean Central News Agency, 'Law on consolidating position of nuclear weapons state adopted', Korea News Service, 1 Apr. 2013.

[9] 'Kim Jong Un's October speech: More than missiles', 38 North, 13 Oct. 2020.

[10] 'Kim Jong Un's October speech' (note 9). On North Korea's nuclear doctrine and likely targets see also Kristensen, H. M. and Korda, M., 'North Korean nuclear forces', *SIPRI Yearbook 2022*, pp. 411–15.

wipe out the set objects'.[11] The eventual deployment of tactical weapons also raises questions about North Korea's nuclear command and control, particularly surrounding whether Kim has pre-delegated nuclear launch authority to his battlefield commanders.

Notably, on 8 September 2022 the North Korean Parliament, the Supreme People's Assembly, passed a law promulgating a new doctrine that specified updated principles and conditions for the use of nuclear weapons.[12] The law, which updated and repealed the 2013 law, requires that North Korea's nuclear forces are 'regularly ready for action'.[13] It also clarifies that nuclear weapons could be used pre-emptively—contradicting the pledge from October 2020—in response to a perceived nuclear or non-nuclear attack on North Korea's leadership or the command structure of its nuclear forces, or other significant attack against a strategic target.[14] It also suggests that North Korea could use nuclear weapons to 'seize the initiative' during wartime.[15] In a speech to the assembly, Kim Jong Un declared that the law codified North Korea's 'irreversible' status as a nuclear-armed state and that it would 'never give up' its nuclear weapons.[16]

Further, in December 2022 the plenary meeting of the Central Committee of the Worker's Party of Korea (WPK) highlighted the importance of 'mass-producing of tactical nuclear weapons' for use against regional targets, in Japan and the Republic of Korea (South Korea).[17] It also noted that the first mission of North Korea's nuclear force is to 'deter war and safeguard peace and stability', but that, if deterrence fails, it will 'carry out the second mission, which will not be for defense'. North Korea's strategy also includes the development of another ICBM system 'whose main mission is quick nuclear counterstrike'.[18] This probably refers to North Korea's planned development of a solid-fuelled ICBM, which would allow launch crews to maintain a higher state of readiness and execute a quicker launch process than a liquid-fuelled ICBM.

---

[11] 'Respected comrade Kim Jong Un guides military drills' (note 7).

[12] [Law on the Nuclear Weapons Policy of the Democratic People's Republic of Korea], adopted by the Supreme People's Assembly 8 Sep. 2022 (in Korean). For an English translation see Korean Central News Agency, 'Law on DPRK's policy on nuclear forces promulgated', DPRK Today, 9 Sep. 2022.

[13] [Law on the Nuclear Weapons Policy] (note 12), Article 7.

[14] [Law on the Nuclear Weapons Policy] (note 12), Article 6.

[15] [Law on the Nuclear Weapons Policy] (note 12), Article 6.

[16] *Rodong Sinmun*, [State administration speech by dear comrade Kim Jong Un at the 7th session of the 14th Supreme People's Assembly of the Democratic People's Republic of Korea 8 September Juche 111 (2022)], KCNA Watch, 9 Sep. 2022 (in Korean, author translation).

[17] 'Report on 6th enlarged plenary meeting of 8th WPK Central Committee', *Minju Choson*, 1 Jan. 2023.

[18] 'Report on 6th enlarged plenary meeting' (note 17).

Fissile material and warhead production

Plutonium-production and -separation capabilities

North Korea's plutonium-production and -separation capabilities for manufacturing nuclear weapons are located at the Yongbyon Nuclear Scientific Research Centre in North Pyongan province.[19] Since its inspectors were required to leave the country in 2009, the International Atomic Energy Agency (IAEA) has monitored North Korea's nuclear programme using open-source information and commercial satellite imagery.[20]

The Yongbyon complex houses an ageing 5-megawatt-electric (MW(e)) graphite-moderated research reactor, from which plutonium can be extracted. Between December 2018 and July 2021 the IAEA found no signs that the reactor had been operational; however, in August 2021 the IAEA reported that there were indications that this had changed.[21] These indications of the reactor's likely operational status were confirmed in September 2022 by the IAEA director general, Rafael Grossi.[22] It remains unclear whether North Korea has resumed construction of the 50-MW(e) reactor at Yongbyon that began in the 1980s. However, various activities observable at the site suggest that construction may have restarted in early 2022.[23]

In July 2022 commercial satellite imagery revealed smoke emitting from the thermal plant at the Yongbyon complex, which supplies steam to the radiochemistry laboratory used for plutonium reprocessing. This suggests that, although the plant may not be operating at full power, it could have been in early stages of preparation for a reprocessing campaign or treatment of radioactive waste.[24] New activity was also observed for the first time since 2016 at Building 500, a facility used to store radioactive and toxic waste produced at the radiochemistry laboratory.[25]

Throughout 2021 and 2022, commercial satellite imagery indicated that North Korea continued construction of a new experimental light

---

[19] For an assessment of North Korea's nuclear weapon production facilities and infrastructure see Hecker, S. S., Carlin, R. L. and Serbin, E. A., 'A comprehensive history of North Korea's nuclear program: 2018 update', Stanford University, Center for International Security and Cooperation, 11 Feb. 2019.

[20] Dixit, A., 'IAEA ready to undertake verification and monitoring in North Korea', International Atomic Energy Agency (IAEA), 4 Mar. 2019.

[21] International Atomic Energy Agency (IAEA), Board of Governors and General Conference, 'Application of safeguards in the Democratic People's Republic of Korea', Report by the director general, GOV/2021/40-GC(65)/22, 27 Aug. 2021, para. 12; and Pabian, F., Town, J. and Liu, J., 'North Korea's Yongbyon nuclear complex: More evidence the 5 MWe reactor appears to have restarted', 38 North, 30 Aug. 2021.

[22] Grossi, R. M., Introductory statement to the Board of Governors, International Atomic Energy Agency (IAEA), 12 Sep. 2022.

[23] Lewis, J., Pollack, J. and Schmerler, D., 'North Korea resuming construction at the Yongbyon 50 MW(e) reactor', Arms Control Wonk, 10 May 2022.

[24] Makowsky, P. et al., 'North Korea's Yongbyon Nuclear Research Center: Plutonium production continues', 38 North, 28 July 2022.

[25] Makowsky et al. (note 24).

water reactor at Yongbyon, which will eventually be capable of producing plutonium for nuclear weapons.[26] Grossi stated in September 2022 that construction of these new buildings may have been completed.[27]

In 2022 the South Korean Ministry of National Defense estimated that North Korea's plutonium stockpile had increased to approximately 70 kilograms, an increase of 20 kg in two years.[28] This is approximately 30 kg more than the estimate used for SIPRI's assessment of North Korea's nuclear weapon holdings (see section X). The latter estimate takes into account reductions to the plutonium stockpile as a result of North Korea's six nuclear tests. In April 2021 Siegfried Hecker—a former senior official in the US nuclear programme who was given unprecedented access to North Korean nuclear facilities over several years—estimated that North Korea's plutonium stocks could increase by up to 6 kg per year at full operation.[29]

Uranium-enrichment capabilities

It is widely believed that North Korea has focused on the production of HEU for use in nuclear warheads to overcome its limited capacity to produce weapon-grade plutonium. However, there is considerable uncertainty about North Korea's uranium-enrichment capabilities and its stock of HEU.

North Korea produces yellowcake—the raw material for reactor fuel rods—at its Pyongsan Uranium Concentrate Plant (Nam-chon Chemical Complex) in North Hwanghae province.[30] The IAEA director general reported in September 2022 that North Korea continued to operate its gas centrifuge enrichment facility after its floor space was expanded by approximately one-third of its original size.[31] These activities were visible on satellite imagery throughout 2021 and 2022.[32]

A classified intelligence assessment by the USA in 2018 reportedly concluded that North Korea probably had more than one covert uranium-enrichment

---

[26] IAEA, GOV/2021/40-GC(65)/22 (note 21), para. 12; and Bermudez, J. S., Cha, V. and Jun, J., 'Yongbyon update: New activity at Building 500 and rising waters', Beyond Parallel, Center for Strategic and International Studies, 11 July 2022.

[27] Grossi (note 22).

[28] South Korean Ministry of National Defense (MND), [2022 defence white paper] (MND: Seoul, 24 Feb. 2023) (in Korean).

[29] 'Estimating North Korea's nuclear stockpiles: An interview with Siegfried Hecker', 38 North, 30 Apr. 2021.

[30] Bermudez, J. S., Cha, V. and Jun, J., 'Current status of the Pyongsan Uranium Concentrate Plant (Nam-chon Chemical Complex) and January Industrial Mine', Beyond Parallel, Center for Strategic and International Studies, 8 Nov. 2021; and Bermudez, J. S., Cha, V. and Kim, D., 'Recent activity at the Pyongsan Uranium Concentrate Plant (Nam-chon Chemical Complex) and January Industrial Mine', Beyond Parallel, Center for Strategic and International Studies, 26 Mar. 2021.

[31] Grossi (note 22).

[32] United Nations, Security Council, Midterm report of the panel of experts submitted pursuant to Resolution 2627 (2022), S/2022/668, 7 Sep. 2022, para. 11; Lewis, J., Pollack, J. and Schmerler, D., 'North Korea expanding uranium enrichment plant at Yongbyon', Arms Control Wonk, 14 Sep. 2021; and Cohen, Z., 'Satellite images reveal North Korea expanding facility used to produce weapons-grade uranium', CNN, 16 Sep. 2021.

plant and that the country was seeking to conceal the types and numbers of production facilities in its nuclear weapon programme.[33] A more recent open-source assessment concludes that the increased production capacity at Pyongsan indicates that North Korea does not require another uranium milling facility of comparable size.[34]

Several non-governmental researchers identified an additional suspected covert uranium-enrichment plant located at Kangson (or Kangsong), to the south-west of Pyongyang, in 2018.[35] A 2021 IAEA report noted that the plant shared 'infrastructure characteristics with the reported centrifuge enrichment facility at Yongbyon'.[36] A report by a UN panel of experts cautioned that access to the plant was required to confirm the nature and purpose of the activities being conducted on-site.[37] Other experts have suggested that the site could be used for manufacturing centrifuge components rather than for enriching uranium.[38]

Analysts agree that North Korea has HEU production capabilities, but there are many unknowns about how much HEU has been produced, especially given the uncertainties around activities at the Kangson site. Hecker estimated in early 2021 that North Korea had produced 600–950 kg of HEU by the end of 2020. The HEU stockpile estimate used for SIPRI's assessment of North Korea's nuclear weapon holdings suggests a wider range of 250–1350 kg as of the beginning of 2022 (see section X).[39]

Nuclear warhead production

It is unclear how many nuclear weapons North Korea has produced with its fissile material, how many have been deployed on missiles and what the military characteristics of the weapons are. As noted above, North Korea has demonstrated a thermonuclear capability (or a nuclear explosive test with suspected thermonuclear yield) once, in 2017.[40] There is no open-source evidence or state intelligence confirming North Korea's capability to deliver an operational nuclear warhead on an ICBM. Moreover, most of North

---

[33] Kube, C., Dilanian, K. and Lee, C. E, 'North Korea has increased nuclear production at secret sites, say US officials', NBC News, 1 July 2018; and Nakashima, E. and Warrick, J., 'North Korea working to conceal key aspects of its nuclear program, US officials say', *Washington Post*, 1 July 2018.

[34] Park, S. et al., 'Assessing uranium ore processing activities using satellite imagery at Pyongsan in the Democratic People's Republic of Korea', *Science and Global Security*, vol. 29, no. 3 (2021).

[35] Panda, A., 'Exclusive: Revealing Kangson, North Korea's first covert uranium enrichment site', The Diplomat, 13 July 2018; and Albright, D. and Burkhard, S., 'Revisiting Kangsong: A suspect uranium enrichment plant', Imagery brief, Institute for Science and International Security, 2 Oct. 2018.

[36] IAEA, GOV/2021/40-GC(65)/22 (note 21), para. 14.

[37] United Nations, Security Council, Midterm report of the panel of experts submitted pursuant to Resolution 2569 (2021), S/2021/777, 8 Sep. 2021, p. 7.

[38] 'Estimating North Korea's nuclear stockpiles' (note 29).

[39] See also Kristensen, H. and Korda, M., 'Nuclear notebook: How many nuclear weapons does North Korea have in 2022?', *Bulletin of the Atomic Scientists*, 8 Sep. 2022.

[40] Fedchencko (note 2), p. 299.

Korea's nuclear tests demonstrated yields in the range of 5–15 kilotons.[41] As a result, SIPRI estimates that North Korea has used only a small portion of its HEU for thermonuclear weapons and has probably used the majority for a larger number of fission-only single-stage weapons deliverable by an MRBM or possibly by an IRBM.[42]

It is unclear whether North Korea is prioritizing the development and production of higher-yield thermonuclear weapons or lower-yield fission-only or boosted single-stage weapons.[43] More powerful warheads with the high yield demonstrated in the 2017 test would consume more fissile material if based on a composite warhead design, or would require special hydrogen fuel if based on a two-stage thermonuclear warhead design. Lower-yield single-stage fission weapon designs would require less fissile material. The choice of assumptions can thus result in very different estimates of the number of nuclear weapons.

For this reason, SIPRI estimates that North Korea could potentially produce 50–70 nuclear weapons with its inventory of fissile material as of January 2023; however, it is likely that the number of operational warheads is smaller, potentially 30.[44] Most of those warheads are likely to be single-stage fission weapons with possible yields of 10–20 kt, similar to those demonstrated in the 2013 and 2016 tests. The SIPRI estimate falls within the range of a July 2020 assessment by the US Army that North Korea had 20–60 bombs.[45] It also falls within the range of a 2018 South Korean intelligence assessment, which estimated that North Korea's nuclear arsenal contained 20–60 weapons.[46]

Assumptions about fissile material production and warhead designs also affect projections of the future size of North Korea's nuclear arsenal. For example, a 2021 study assumed that North Korea might already have 67–116 nuclear weapons and projected that the inventory might reach 151–242 nuclear weapons by 2027.[47] It seems more plausible, however, that North Korea might be capable of adding sufficient fissile material for up to six nuclear warheads per year.[48] This would potentially be sufficient to produce a total of approximately 80–90 weapons by the end of the decade.[49]

---

[41] Fedchencko, V., 'Nuclear explosions, 1945–2016', *SIPRI Yearbook 2017*.

[42] Ballistic missiles are typically divided into 4 range categories: short range (less than 1000 km), medium range (1000–3000 km), intermediate range (3000–5500 km) and intercontinental (>5500 km).

[43] Kristensen and Korda (note 39).

[44] For additional assessments see 'Estimating North Korea's nuclear stockpiles' (note 29).

[45] US Army, *North Korean Tactics*, Army Techniques Publication no. 7-100.2 (Headquarters, US Department of the Army: Washington, DC, July 2020), p. 1-11.

[46] Kim, H., 'Seoul: North Korea estimated to have 20–60 nuclear weapons', AP News, 2 Oct. 2018.

[47] Bennett, B. W. et al., *Countering the Risk of North Korean Nuclear Weapons* (RAND Corp.: Santa Monica, CA, Apr. 2021).

[48] This is in line with the production estimate suggested in US Army (note 45), p. 1-11.

[49] Kristensen and Korda (note 39).

Although North Korea demolished tunnels and facilities at the Punggye-ri nuclear test site in 2018, satellite images since 2021 show that the test tunnel and support buildings have been re-opened.[50] This construction indicates that the site had not been abandoned but kept in caretaker status, potentially allowing nuclear testing to resume in the future.[51]

Land-based missiles

North Korea is increasing both the size and capability of its ballistic missile force, which consists of indigenously produced missile systems with ranges from a few hundred kilometres to more than 12 000 km (see table 7.9).[52] Since 2016, it has pursued development and production of several missile systems with progressively longer ranges and increasingly sophisticated delivery capabilities.[53] There is considerable uncertainty about the operational status of North Korea's IRBMs and ICBMs. According to independent analyses, North Korea may have deployed long-range missiles at several missile bases.[54]

It is unclear which of North Korea's missiles can carry nuclear weapons. The available evidence suggests that some MRBMs and IRBMs are the most likely to have an operational nuclear capability. South Korea's 2022 Defence White Paper notes that, given that North Korea uses uniquely lofted launch angles for its ICBM tests, 'additional confirmation is needed to determine whether North Korea has acquired core ICBM technologies, including the ability to re-enter the atmosphere'.[55]

It must be emphasized that inclusion of a specific North Korean missile in the following overview (and in table 7.9) does not necessarily indicate that it is confirmed as nuclear-capable or as having a nuclear role.

Short-range ballistic missiles

As of January 2023 North Korea had several types of SRBM, including older liquid-fuelled systems, possibly based on Soviet R-17 (Scud) missiles, and newer solid-fuelled missiles of indigenous design. These newer missiles, known by the designations given by the USA as the KN23, the KN24 and the

---

[50] United Nations, S/2022/668 (note 32), paras 4–5.
[51] Lee, C., 'North Korea's saber-rattling rekindles nuclear test site questions', Voice of America, 26 Jan. 2022.
[52] US Air Force, National Air and Space Intelligence Center (NASIC), *Ballistic and Cruise Missile Threat 2020* (NASIC: Wright-Patterson Air Force Base, OH, July 2020).
[53] James Martin Center for Nonproliferation Studies (CNS), CNS North Korea Missile Test Database, Nuclear Threat Initiative, as of 24 Mar. 2022.
[54] Bermudez, J. S. and Cha, V., 'Undeclared North Korea: The Yusang-ni missile operating base', Beyond Parallel, Center for Strategic and International Studies, 9 May 2019; Frank, M., 'Continued construction at Yusang-ni missile base', Open Nuclear Network, 26 July 2021; and United Nations, Security Council, Final report of the panel of experts submitted pursuant to Resolution 2515 (2020), S/2021/211, 4 Mar. 2021, annexes 16–18.
[55] South Korean Ministry of National Defense (note 28), p. 30 (author translation).

KN25—and possibly all known by the common North Korean designation of Hwasong-11 (with different suffixes for each missile)—were tested or launched nearly 50 times, and possibly many more, between the beginning of 2019 and early 2023.[56] Notably, in September 2021 North Korea launched two KN23 SRBMs using a rail-mobile launcher for the first time and carried out two further test launches of the rail-mobile KN23 in January 2022.[57] Rail-mobile launchers would enable North Korea to move missiles around the country rapidly and significantly increase the survivability of its second-strike force. North Korea has also been modernizing its older SRBMs by equipping them with manoeuvrable re-entry vehicles (MaRVs) designed to evade the missile-defence systems of nearby states (particularly South Korea and Japan).[58]

In April 2022 Kim Jong Un announced the launch of two SRBMs, which he called a 'new-type tactical guided weapon' developed to enhance 'the efficiency in the operation of tactical nukes', potentially implying that such warheads have already been deployed with earlier delivery systems.[59] Accompanying images pictured a new type of solid-fuelled SRBM mounted on a road-mobile launcher.[60] As an illustration of this new capability, North Korea test-launched eight SRBMs in June and seven in November 2022.[61] The launches on 2 November were among at least 23 missiles fired that day, the highest number ever launched by North Korea in a single day. North Korean state media said that the missiles were a response to Vigilant Storm 23, a South Korean–US combined military exercise that took place between 31 October and 5 November.[62]

Medium- and intermediate-range ballistic missiles

North Korea has four types of MRBM: the Hwasong-7 (Nodong/Rodong), -8 and -9 (KN04) and the Pukguksong-2 (KN15).[63] All except the Hwasong-8 were probably operational as of January 2023. Assuming that North Korea is able to produce a sufficiently compact warhead, these MRBMs are considered to be its most likely nuclear-delivery systems. All three operational missiles

---

[56] James Martin Center for Nonproliferation Studies (note 53); and Zwirko, C., 'North Korea reveals internal names for several missile systems: Analysis', NK News, 3 Apr. 2023.

[57] 'Firing drill of railway-borne missile regiment held', *Rodong Sinmun*, 15 Jan. 2022.

[58] Panda, A., 'Introducing the KN21, North Korea's new take on its oldest ballistic missile', The Diplomat, 14 Sep. 2017.

[59] 'Respected comrade Kim Jong Un observes test-fire of new-type tactical guided weapon', *Rodong Sinmun*, 17 Apr. 2022.

[60] Van Diepen, V. H., 'North Korea's new short-range ballistic missile', 38 North, 25 Apr. 2022.

[61] Kristensen and Korda (note 39).

[62] 'Report of General Staff of KPA on its military operations corresponding to US–South Korea combined air drill', Uriminzokkiri, 7 Nov. 2022; and US Air Force, '8th Operations Group surges for Vigilant Storm 23', Kunsan Air Base, 7 Nov. 2022.

[63] On the Pukguksong-2 see Kristensen and Korda (note 10), p. 420.

have ranges of 1000–1200 km, meaning that they could reach targets anywhere in South Korea or Japan.[64]

The Hwasong-10 (BM-25/Musudan) IRBM, with an estimated range exceeding 3000 km, has a poor test rate, with no flight tests since 2016–17. It is likely to have been superseded by more sophisticated missile programmes—in particular the Hwasong-12 (KN17).[65] The latter is a single-stage, liquid-fuelled IRBM carried on a road-mobile transporter-erector-launcher (TEL). In January 2022 North Korea launched a Hwasong-12 for the first time in nearly five years, demonstrating a similar trajectory to its previous launches.[66] It remains unknown if the Hwasong-12 has been deployed. North Korea launched a missile that resembled the Hwasong-12 in performance in October 2022, although the images and reports subsequently released by North Korean state media implied that it was a 'new type' of IRBM.[67]

The Hwasong-8, which is another new missile, was first revealed in 2021. It appears to be composed of a modified Hwasong-12 booster and can carry multiple different payloads, including an HGV and a MaRV. The Hwasong-8 variant carrying a MaRV was tested twice in January 2022. During the second test, North Korea claimed that the missile conducted a 'corkscrew' manoeuvre.[68] This reportedly prompted the US civil aviation authority to temporarily pause commercial airline departures along the west coast of the USA for approximately 15 minutes.[69]

Intercontinental ballistic missiles

North Korea has displayed four types of ICBM: the Hwasong-13 (KN08), -14 (KN20), -15 (KN22) and -17 (KN28). It has prioritized building and deploying an ICBM that could potentially deliver a nuclear warhead to targets in the USA. However, there remains considerable uncertainty in assessments of North Korea's long-range missile capabilities. For example, neither the 2019 missile report issued by the US Department of Defense (DOD) nor the 2020 report from the US Air Force listed the Hwasong-13, -14 or -15 as being deployed.[70] The Hwasong-13 and, possibly, the Hwasong-14 are likely to have

---

[64] US Air Force (note 52), p. 25.
[65] James Martin Center for Nonproliferation Studies (note 53).
[66] Japanese Ministry of Defense, [North Korean missiles and other related formation], 30 Jan. 2022 (in Japanese).
[67] Xu, T., *Analysis of the DPRK's Ballistic Missile Launch Campaign in September/October 2022* (Open Nuclear Network: Vienna, 14 Oct. 2022).
[68] *Chongnyon Chonwi*, 'Distinguished feat of WPK in history of leading Juche-based defence industry success in another hypersonic missile test-fire respected comrade Kim Jong Un watches test-fire in field', KCNA Watch, 12 Jan. 2022.
[69] Liebermann, O., Muntean, P. and Starr, B., 'US grounded planes as a "precaution" after a North Korean missile launch', CNN, 11 Jan. 2022.
[70] These publications present the USA's most detailed current public assessments of North Korean long-range nuclear capabilities. The Hwasong-17 was first displayed in Oct. 2020. US Department of Defense (DOD), *2019 Missile Defense Review* (DOD: Washington, DC, 2019), p. 7; and US Air Force (note 52), p. 29.

been superseded by more sophisticated ICBM programmes and, as a result, the Hwasong-13 is excluded from SIPRI's estimate for January 2023.[71]

The Hwasong-15 has a significantly larger second stage and more powerful booster engines than the Hwasong-14.[72] The Hwasong-17 would hypothetically be large enough to accommodate multiple warheads, but such capabilities have not yet been demonstrated.[73] On 24 March 2022 North Korea claimed to have test-launched the Hwasong-17 and said the missile reached an apogee of more than 6200 km and travelled nearly 1100 km over the course of 68 minutes.[74] This suggests a possible range of approximately 15 000 km if flown on a minimum-energy trajectory. However, some analysts believe that the ICBM may have been unsuccessfully tested on 16 March, and that the missile tested on 24 March may instead have been a Hwasong-15.[75] On 18 November North Korea again claimed to have successfully tested the Hwasong-17.[76]

In December North Korea conducted a ground test of a solid-fuelled rocket motor, indicating progress towards capacity for building a solid-fuelled ICBM or SLBM.[77]

Cruise missiles

North Korea has developed at least two land-attack cruise missiles (LACMs) that are explicitly designed to deliver nuclear weapons: the Hwasal-1 and the Hwasal-2. Combined, these two cruise missiles had been tested at least eight times as of the end of 2022. Although North Korea has described these LACMs as 'strategic weapons', it also clarified in October 2022 that the missiles were 'deployed at the units of the Korean People's Army for the operation of tactical nukes'.[78]

---

[71] NK News, 'North Korea military parade 2020: Livestream & analysis', YouTube, 10 Oct. 2020.

[72] Kristensen, H. M. and Korda, M., 'North Korean nuclear forces', *SIPRI Yearbook 2021*, p. 402.

[73] Panda, A. (@nktpnd), Twitter, 13 Oct. 2021, <https://twitter.com/nktpnd/status/1448073861363290124>.

[74] *Pyongyang Times*, 'Striking demonstration of great military muscle of Juche Korea: Successful test-launch of new-type ICBM respected comrade Kim Jong Un guides test launch of ICBM Hwasongpho-17', KCNA Watch, 25 Mar. 2023.

[75] Zwirko, C., 'Imagery casts doubt over North Korea's Hwasong-17 ICBM claims', NK News, 25 Mar. 2022.

[76] 'Military miracles which demonstrated to whole world national prestige and honor of Juche Korea', *Rodong Sinmun*, 18 Nov. 2022.

[77] Van Diepen, V., 'The next big thing? North Korea ground tests ICBM-sized rocket motor', 38 North, 21 Dec. 2022.

[78] Shin, H. and Smith, J., 'N. Korea tests first "strategic" cruise missile with possible nuclear capability', Reuters, 13 Sep. 2021. See also Kristensen and Korda (note 10), pp. 421–22; and 'Respected comrade Kim Jong Un guides test-fire of long-range strategic cruise missiles', Korea Central News Agency, 13 Oct. 2022.

Sea-based missiles

North Korea has continued to develop its family of Pukguksong ('Polaris') solid-fuelled SLBMs as part of an effort to improve the survivability of its nuclear-capable ballistic missile systems.[79]

In October 2021 North Korea unveiled a 'new type' of smaller SLBM with an unknown designation but with characteristics seemingly similar to its newer SRBM designs.[80] This SLBM was reportedly test launched one week later from the port of Sinpo to an approximate range of 590 km, landing in the Sea of Japan.[81] The test's low apogee of 60 km indicated that this new SLBM is likely to have a shorter range than many of the Pukguksong SLBMs.[82] The missile was launched using North Korea's only Gorae-class (Sinpo) experimental submarine, *8.24 Yongung*.[83] The vessel appears to have been damaged during the launch.[84] This submarine can hold and launch only a single SLBM. The same type of missile may have also been tested on 7 May 2022.[85] It is unclear whether the test was successful. It is also possible that the same type of missile was tested on 25 September 2022 from an 'underwater launching ground' inside a reservoir; the North Korean media statement accompanying the launch explicitly stated that the missile was designed to carry a tactical nuclear warhead and implied that it was already operational.[86]

At its April 2022 military parade, North Korea revealed a sixth probable member of the Pukguksong family that is longer and wider than all of North Korea's previously displayed SLBMs.[87] The missile's name has not yet been formally announced.

---

[79] On North Korea's earlier Pukguksong family of missiles see Kristensen and Korda (note 72), p. 403.

[80] Xu, T., *Brief on the Defence Development Exhibition of the Democratic People's Republic of Korea* (Open Nuclear Network: Vienna, 18 Oct. 2021); and Xu, T., 'Brief on the 19 October 2021 submarine-launched ballistic missile test of the Democratic People's Republic of Korea', Open Nuclear Network, 21 Oct. 2021.

[81] Korean Central News Agency, 'Academy of Defence Science succeeds in test-launch of new-type SLBM', KCNA Watch, 20 Oct. 2021.

[82] 'N. Korea fires what seems to be SLBM toward East Sea: S. Korea', Yonhap News Agency, 19 Oct. 2021.

[83] Korean Central News Agency (note 81); Makowsky, P. and Liu, J., 'Sinpho South shipyard: Evidence of the SINPO-class SSBA participation in recent SLBM test', 38 North, 21 Oct. 2021; and Bermudez, J. S. and Cha, V., 'Sinpo South shipyard update: SLBM test launch', Beyond Parallel, Center for Strategic and International Studies, 21 Oct. 2021.

[84] Bermudez, J. S., Cha, V. and Jun, J., 'Sinpo-class submarine damaged during October 19 test launch', Beyond Parallel, Center for Strategic and International Studies, 7 Jan. 2022.

[85] Japanese Ministry of Defense, [North Korean missiles and other related formation], 7 May 2022 (in Japanese).

[86] 'Chairman of Central Military Commission of WPK Kim Jong Un guides military exercises of tactical nuclear operation units of KPA', Voice of Korea, 9 Oct. 2022.

[87] Xu, T., *Emerging Capabilities? The Unflown SLBMs of the DPRK* (Open Nuclear Network: Vienna, 25 July 2022).

In November 2020 the South Korean National Intelligence Service announced that North Korea was building a new ballistic missile submarine.[88] The vessel, designated Sinpo-C by the US DOD, appears to be based on a modified Project-633 (Romeo) diesel–electric submarine and is expected to be fitted with three missile-launch canisters.[89] This Soviet-era submarine has a noisy design and limited underwater range, and thus could encounter operational challenges. According to a 2019 report by North Korean state media, the submarine's operational deployment was 'near at hand', although by the end of 2022 it did not yet appear to be operational.[90]

[88] Bermudez, J. S. and Cha, V., 'Sinpo South shipyard: Construction of a new ballistic missile submarine?', Beyond Parallel, Center for Strategic and International Studies, 28 Aug. 2019; Cha, S., 'North Korea building two submarines, one capable of firing ballistic missiles: Lawmaker', Reuters, 3 Nov. 2020; and Dempsey, J. and Schmerler, D., 'Two halls enter: One sub leaves', Arms Control Wonk, 17 June 2021.

[89] Hotham, O., 'New North Korean submarine capable of carrying three SLBMs: South Korean MND', NK News, 31 July 2019; and Cha (note 88).

[90] 'NK leader inspects new submarine to be deployed in East Sea: State media', Yonhap News Agency, 23 July 2019.

WORLD NUCLEAR FORCES

Table 7.9. North Korean forces with potential nuclear capability, January 2023

All figures are approximate and some are based on assessments by the authors. The inclusion of a missile in this table does not necessarily indicate it is known to have a nuclear role. Systems that are unlikely to have a nuclear or operational role are excluded.

Type/ North Korean designation (US designation)	Year first displayed	Range (km)	Description and status
Land-based missiles			
Hwasong-5/-6 (Scud-B/-C)	1984/1990	300/500	Single-stage, liquid-fuelled SRBMs launched from 4-axle wheeled TEL. NASIC estimates fewer than 100 Hwasong-5 and -6 launchers.
			Operational.
. . (KN18/KN21)	2017	250/450	Hwasong-5 and -6 variants with separating manoeuvrable warhead.
			Flight-tested in May and Aug. 2017 from wheeled and tracked TELs.
			Deployment status unknown; may have been superseded by newer solid-fuelled SRBMs.
Hwasong-11 variants (KN23/KN24[a]/KN25)	2018/2019	380–800	New generation of solid-fuelled SRBMs. Resemble Russia's Iskander-M, South Korea's Hyunmoo-2B and the USA's ATACMS SRBMs.
			Successfully flight-tested at least 50 times, and possibly many more, from wheeled, tracked and rail-based launchers since 2019, including nearly 20 known launches in 2022.
			Deployment status unknown; probably operational.
Hwasong-7 (Nodong/ Rodong)	1993	>1 200	Single-stage, liquid-fuelled MRBM launched from 5-axle wheeled TEL. NASIC estimates fewer than 100 Hwasong-7 launchers.
			Two launched on 18 Dec. 2022.
			Operational.
Hwasong-9 (KN04/ Scud-ER)	2016	1 000	Single-stage, liquid-fuelled Scud extended-range MRBM variant launched from 4-axle wheeled TEL.
			Flight-tested in 2016.
			Probably operational.
Pukguksong-2 (KN15)	2017	>1 000	Two-stage, solid-fuelled MRBM launched from tracked TEL. Land-based version of Pukguksong-1 SLBM.
			Flight-tested in 2017.
			Probably operational.

Type/ North Korean designation (US designation)	Year first displayed	Range (km)	Description and status
Hwasal-1	2021	1 500	Land-attack cruise missile flight-tested multiple times in 2021 and 2022 from wheeled TEL.
			Deployment status unknown; probably operational.
Hwasal-2	2021	2 000	Land-attack cruise missile flight-tested multiple times in 2022 from wheeled TEL.
			Deployment status unknown; probably operational.
Hwasong-8/Unnamed 'hypersonic missile'	2021	>1 000	Two versions of HGV carried by a shortened Hwasong-12 booster.
			Hwasong-8 flight-tested in Sep. 2021 with unknown result; unnamed missile successfully flight-tested twice in Jan. 2022. Both systems displayed at exhibition in Oct. 2021. Suspected flight test with MaRV on 5 and 11 Jan. 2022.
			Under development.
Hwasong-10 (BM-25/ Musudan)	2010	>3 000	Single-stage, liquid-fuelled IRBM launched from 6-axle wheeled TEL. NASIC estimates fewer than 50 Hwasong-10 launchers.
			Several failed flight tests in 2016.
			Deployment status unknown; may have been superseded.
Hwasong-12 (KN17)	2017	>4 500	Single-stage, liquid-fuelled IRBM launched from 8-axle wheeled TEL.
			Flight-tested several times in 2017 with mixed success. Tested again on 30 Jan. 2022.
			Deployment status unknown.
'New type' IRBM	2022	>4 500	Single-stage, liquid-fuelled IRBM launched on 4 Oct. 2022. Strongly resembles existing Hwasong-12 design, but with potential modifications to the nose cone and propulsion system.
			Deployment status unknown.
Hwasong-14 (KN20)	2017	>10 000	Two-stage, liquid-fuelled ICBM launched from 8-axle wheeled TEL. First ICBM.
			Successfully flight-tested twice in 2017.
			Deployment status unknown; may have been superseded.

Type/ North Korean designation (US designation)	Year first displayed	Range (km)	Description and status
Hwasong-15 (KN22)	2017	>13 000	Two-stage, liquid-fuelled ICBM launched from 9-axle wheeled TEL. Successfully flight-tested in Nov. 2017. Displayed at parade in Oct. 2020 and at exhibition in Oct. 2021.
			Possibly launched on 24 Mar. 2022.
			Deployment status unknown.
Hwasong-17 (KN28)[b]	2020	15 000	Two-stage, liquid-fuelled ICBM launched from 11-axle wheeled TEL. Largest ICBM to date, possibly capable of carrying MIRVs and penetration aids.
			Displayed at parade in Oct. 2020 and at exhibition in Oct. 2021. May have been unsuccessfully flight-tested on 16 Mar. 2022, and missile tested on 24 Mar. 2022 may have been a Hwasong-15 instead of a Hwasong-17 as claimed by North Korea. Successful test of Hwasong-17 on 18 Nov. 2022.
			Under development.
Sea-based missiles			
Pukguksong-1 (KN11)	2014	>1 000	Two-stage, solid-fuelled SLBM.
			Flight-tested several times in 2015 and 2016 with mixed success. Displayed at exhibition in Oct. 2021.
			Deployment status unknown; may have been superseded.
Pukguksong-3 (KN26)	2017	1 900–2 500	Two-stage, solid-fuelled SLBM.
			Successfully flight-tested in Oct. 2019.
			Deployment status unknown.
Pukguksong-4	2020	3 500–5 400	Two-stage, solid-fuelled SLBM. Appears wider than Pukguksong-1 and shorter than Pukguksong-3.
			No known flight tests. Displayed at parade in Oct. 2020.
			Deployment status unknown.
Pukguksong-5	2021	..	Two-stage, solid-fuelled SLBM. Roughly same length as Pukguksong-3 with elongated shroud; possibly capable of carrying MIRVs and penetration aids.
			No known flight tests. Displayed at parade in Jan. 2021 and at exhibition in Oct. 2021.
			Deployment status unknown.

Type/ North Korean designation (US designation)	Year first displayed	Range (km)	Description and status
Small 'new type' SLBM	2021	400–600	Appears to deviate from traditional Pukguksong SLBM design, instead bearing similarities to KN23 SRBM.
			Displayed at exhibition in Oct. 2021 and successfully flight-tested a week later.
			Deployment status unknown; possibly operational.
Unknown SLBM	2022	..	Revealed at military parade in Apr. 2022. Name not yet formally announced, but appears to be a member of the Pukguksong family of SLBMs.
Total warheads		30[c]	

.. = not available or not applicable; HGV = hypersonic glide vehicle; ICBM = intercontinental ballistic missile; IRBM = intermediate-range ballistic missile; MaRV = manoeuvrable re-entry vehicle; MIRV = multiple independently targetable re-entry vehicle; MRBM = medium-range ballistic missile; NASIC = US Air Force National Air and Space Intelligence Center; SLBM = submarine-launched ballistic missile; SRBM = short-range ballistic missile; TEL = transporter-erector-launcher.

Notes: Information about the status and capability of North Korea's missiles comes with significant uncertainty. This table includes missiles that could potentially have a nuclear capability, whether or not confirmed as being equipped with nuclear warheads or assigned nuclear missions. Several missiles may have been intended for development of technologies that will eventually become operational on newer missiles. There is no publicly available evidence that North Korea has produced an operational nuclear warhead for delivery by an ICBM.

[a] North Korea refers to the KN24 as the Hwasong-11Na, which could be considered akin to 'Hwasong-11B', as Na (나) is the second letter in the Korean alphabet (Hangul). This indicates that the KN24 is an improvement on or replacement for the original Hwasong-11 (KN02 Toksa) SRBM. Many of North Korea's other new SRBMs also appear to use the official Hwasong-11 designation with different suffixes.

[b] This missile was previously assumed to be designated the Hwasong-16; however, it was revealed at North Korea's Oct. 2021 Defence Development Exhibition that it is called the Hwasong-17.

[c] SIPRI estimates that North Korea might have produced enough fissile material to build 50–70 nuclear warheads; however, it is likely that it has assembled fewer warheads, perhaps c. 30, of which only a few would be thermonuclear warheads and nearly all would be lower-yield single-stage fission warheads.

Sources: US Department of Defense (DOD), *2019 Missile Defense Review* (DOD: Washington, DC, 2019); US Air Force, National Air and Space Intelligence Center, *Ballistic and Cruise Missile Threat*, various years; *IHS Jane's Strategic Weapon Systems*, various editions; Hecker, S., Stanford University, Personal communication, 2020; *Bulletin of the Atomic Scientists*, 'Nuclear notebook', various issues; published expert analyses; and authors' estimates. For the estimated number of warheads see also Hecker, S., 'What do we know about North Korea's nuclear program?', Presentation, Dialogue on DPRK Denuclearization Roadmaps and Verification, Kyung Hee University, Global America Business Institute (GABI) and Natural Resources Defense Council (NRDC), 20 Oct. 2020; 'Estimating North Korea's nuclear stockpiles: An interview with Siegfried Hecker', 38 North, 30 Apr. 2021; and Fedchenko, V. and Kelley, R., 'New methodology offers estimates for North Korean thermonuclear stockpile', *Janes Intelligence Review*, Sep. 2020, pp. 44–49.

IX. Israeli nuclear forces

HANS M. KRISTENSEN AND MATT KORDA*

As of January 2023 Israel was estimated to have a stockpile of around 90 nuclear warheads (see table 7.10), the same number as in January 2022. This estimate is at the lower end of a possible range that other analysts have suggested could reach as high as 300 nuclear weapons.[1]

Israel continues to maintain its long-standing policy of nuclear ambiguity: it neither officially confirms nor denies that it possesses nuclear weapons.[2] This lack of transparency means that there is significant uncertainty about the size of Israel's nuclear arsenal and the yields and characteristics of its weapons.[3] The estimate here is largely based on calculations of Israel's inventory of weapon-grade plutonium (see section X) and the number of operational nuclear-capable delivery systems. The locations of the storage sites for the warheads, which are thought to be stored partially unassembled, are unknown.

This section continues by briefly outlining the role played by nuclear weapons in Israel's military doctrine. It then outlines the country's capabilities for production of fissile material before describing its air-delivered, land-based and sea-based weapons.

The role of nuclear weapons in Israeli military doctrine

Since the late 1960s the Israeli government has repeated that Israel 'won't be the first to introduce nuclear weapons into the Middle East'. However, to accommodate the apparent fact that Israel possesses a significant nuclear arsenal, Israeli policymakers have previously interpreted 'introduce nuclear weapons' as publicly declaring, testing or actually using the nuclear capability, which, according to open-access sources, Israel has not yet done.[4]

Military fissile material production

Declassified United States government documents indicate that Israel may have assembled its first nuclear weapons in the late 1960s, using plutonium

---

[1] See e.g. Luscombe, B., '10 questions: Jimmy Carter', *Time*, 30 Jan. 2012; and Clifton, E., 'Powell acknowledges Israeli nukes', Lobe Log, 14 Sep. 2016.

[2] On Israel's 'strategic ambiguity' policy see also Cohen, A., 'Israel', eds H. Born, B. Gill and H. Hänggi, SIPRI, *Governing the Bomb: Civilian Control and Democratic Accountability of Nuclear Weapons* (Oxford University Press: Oxford, 2010).

[3] Kristensen, H. M. and Korda, M., 'Estimating world nuclear forces: An overview and assessment of sources', SIPRI Commentary, 14 June 2021.

[4] For further detail see Kristensen, H. M. and Korda, M., 'Israeli nuclear forces', *SIPRI Yearbook 2022*, pp. 404–405.

* The authors wish to thank Eliana Johns for contributing invaluable research to this publication.

Table 7.10. Israeli nuclear forces, January 2023

All figures are approximate and some are based on assessments by the authors.

Type/designation	No. of launchers	Year first deployed	Range (km)[a]	No. of warheads
Aircraft	125/50[b]			30
F-16I	100/25	1980	1 600	30
F-15	25/25	1998	4 450	..[c]
Land-based missiles	50			50[d]
Jericho II	25	1990	>1 500	25
Jericho III	25	[2011]	[>4 000]	25[e]
Sea-based missiles	5/20[f]			10
'Popeye' variant SLCM	20	[2002]	[<1 500]	10
Total stockpile	**120**			**90**[g]

.. = not available or not applicable; [ ] = uncertain SIPRI estimate; SLCM = sea-launched cruise missile.

[a] Aircraft range is for illustrative purposes only; actual range will vary according to flight profile, weapon payload and in-flight refuelling.

[b] The first figure is the total number of aircraft in the inventory; the second is the number of aircraft that might be adapted for a nuclear strike mission. It is estimated that aircraft from 2 squadrons might serve a nuclear strike role.

[c] It is not known whether the Israeli Air Force has added nuclear capability to the F-15 aircraft as the United States has done, but one US official has privately described Israel's F-15s as its 'nuclear squadron'.

[d] Commercial satellite images show what appear to be 23 caves or bunkers for mobile Jericho launchers at Sdot Micha Airbase. High-resolution satellite imagery that became available in 2021 indicates that each cave appears to have 2 entrances, which suggests that each cave could hold up to 2 launchers. If all 23 caves are full, this would amount to 46 launchers.

[e] The Jericho III is gradually replacing the older Jericho II, if this has not happened already. A longer-range version with a new solid rocket motor may be under development.

[f] The first figure is the total number of Dolphin-class submarines in the Israeli fleet; the second is the estimated maximum number of missiles that they can carry. In addition to 6 standard 533-millimetre torpedo tubes, the submarines are reportedly equipped with 4 other specially designed 650-mm tubes that could potentially be used to launch larger nuclear-armed SLCMs.

[g] Given the unique lack of publicly available information about Israel's nuclear arsenal, this estimate comes with a considerable degree of uncertainty.

Sources: Cohen, A., *The Worst-kept Secret: Israel's Bargain with the Bomb* (Columbia University Press: New York, 2010); Cohen, A., *Israel and the Bomb* (Columbia University Press: New York, 1998); US National Security Archive, various declassified US government document collections related to Israel's nuclear weapon programme; International Institute for Strategic Studies, *The Military Balance*, various years; IHS Jane's Strategic Weapon Systems, various issues; Fetter, S., 'Israeli ballistic missile capabilities', *Physics and Society*, vol. 19, no. 3 (July 1990); *Bulletin of the Atomic Scientists*, 'Nuclear notebook', various issues; and authors' estimates.

produced by the Israel Research Reactor 2 (IRR-2) at the Negev Nuclear Research Center (NNRC) near Dimona, in southern Israel.[5] This heavy water reactor is not under International Atomic Energy Agency (IAEA) safeguards. There is little publicly available information about its operating history and power capacity (see section X).[6] Commercial satellite imagery has revealed progress on significant construction inside and near to the NNRC site since 2021, although the purpose of this work is unknown.

As of the beginning of 2022 Israel is estimated to have had a stockpile of 740–1090 kilograms of plutonium, depending upon the rate at which the reactor was also used for tritium production (see section X). Based on this estimate and assuming that Israel's warhead arsenal is likely to consist of single-stage, boosted fission weapons, Israel could potentially have built anywhere between 185 and 273 nuclear weapons, assuming approximately 4 kg of plutonium per weapon. However, as with other nuclear-armed states, Israel is unlikely to have converted all of its plutonium into warheads and has probably assigned nuclear weapons to only a limited number of launchers. Moreover, the available tritium required to boost the warheads would represent an additional constraint on the number of weapons Israel could build. As a result, SIPRI estimates that Israel has approximately 90 warheads, rather than several hundred.

Aircraft and air-delivered weapons

Approximately 30 of Israel's nuclear weapons are estimated to be gravity bombs for delivery by F-16I or F-15 aircraft. The status of the F-15 is unclear, but when Israel sent six F-15s from Tel Nof Airbase to the United Kingdom for an exercise in September 2019, a US official privately commented that Israel had sent its 'nuclear squadron'.[7] Nuclear gravity bombs without nuclear cores would probably be stored at protected facilities near one or two air force bases, such as Tel Nof Airbase in central Israel and Hatzerim Airbase in the Negev desert.

Israel is also acquiring 50 F-35 combat aircraft from the USA. These are particularly suitable for deep strike operations, although it is unclear whether Israel would use them for a nuclear mission.[8]

---

[5] For a history of Israel's nuclear weapon programme see Cohen, A., *The Worst-kept Secret: Israel's Bargain with the Bomb* (Columbia University Press: New York, 2010); Burr, W. and Cohen, A., 'Duplicity and self-deception: Israel, the United States, and the Dimona inspections, 1964–65', Briefing Book no. 733, National Security Archive, 10 Nov. 2020; and Cohen, A. and Burr, W., 'How Israel built a nuclear program right under the Americans' nose', *Haaretz*, 17 Jan. 2021. See also Kristensen and Korda (note 4), pp. 405–407.

[6] Glaser, A. and Miller, M., 'Estimating plutonium production at Israel's Dimona reactor', 52nd annual meeting of the Institute of Nuclear Materials Management (INMM), 17–21 July 2011.

[7] US military official, Interview with the author (H. M. Kristensen), Oct. 2019.

[8] Lockheed Martin, 'Israel's 5th generation fighter'.

Land-based missiles

Up to 50 warheads are thought to be assigned for delivery by land-based Jericho ballistic missiles, although the Israeli government has never publicly confirmed that it possesses the missiles. The missiles are believed to be located, along with their mobile transporter-erector-launchers (TELs), in caves or bunkers at Sdot Micha Airbase near Zekharia, about 25 kilometres west of Jerusalem. High-resolution satellite imagery suggests that an upgrade of the bunkers was ongoing during 2022. SIPRI assesses that each of the 23 bunkers might be capable of storing two launchers. Each cluster of bunkers also appears to be coupled with facilities potentially for missile handling and warhead loading. A nearby complex with its own internal perimeter has four tunnels to underground facilities that could be used for warhead storage, although SIPRI assesses that the nuclear cores are probably stored elsewhere.

Israel is upgrading its arsenal of missiles from the solid-fuelled, two-stage Jericho II medium-range ballistic missile to the three-stage Jericho III missile with a longer range, exceeding 4000 km. The latter first became operational in 2011 and might now have replaced the Jericho II.[9] In recent years, Israel has conducted several test launches of what it calls 'rocket propulsion systems'. These could be related to upgrades to its ballistic missile force; it is possible, however, that some of these tests could be related to the development of Israeli space-launch vehicles, which use solid rocket motors.[10]

Sea-based missiles

Israel operates five German-built Dolphin-class (Dolphin-I and Dolphin-II) diesel–electric submarines.[11] It plans to modernize and add to its fleet in the coming years. The home port of Israel's submarines is Haifa on the Mediterranean coast.

There are unconfirmed reports that all or some of the submarines have been equipped to launch an indigenously produced nuclear-armed sea-launched variant of the Popeye cruise missile, giving Israel a sea-based nuclear strike capability.[12] Several former officials of the German Ministry of Defence stated in 2012 that they had always assumed that Israel would use the submarines

---

[9] O'Halloran, J. C. (ed.), 'Jericho missiles', *IHS Jane's Weapons: Strategic, 2015–16* (IHS Jane's: Coulsdon, 2015), p. 53.

[10] Israeli Ministry of Defense (@Israel_MOD), Twitter, 31 Jan. 2020, <https://twitter.com/Israel_MOD/status/1223172528992149504>; and Lewis, J., 'Israeli rocket motor test', Arms Control Wonk, 23 Apr. 2021.

[11] SIPRI Arms Transfers Database, Mar. 2022.

[12] Bergman, R. et al., 'Israel's deployment of nuclear missiles on subs from Germany', *Der Spiegel*, 4 June 2012.

for nuclear weapons.[13] The German government subsequently denied that the submarines have the capability to carry nuclear warheads.[14] If the submarines have been equipped with nuclear missiles, SIPRI assesses that around 10 cruise missile warheads might be available for the submarine fleet.

In early 2022 Israel signed a deal with Germany to procure three new submarines, which will be known as the Dakar class, to replace the three oldest Dolphin-I-class boats.[15] Concept art for the Dakar-class submarines includes an enlarged sail (or fin) that could be fitted with a vertical-launch system that would be capable of launching existing or future missile types.[16]

[13] Bergman et al. (note 12). See also Frantz, D., 'Israel's arsenal is point of contention', *Los Angeles Times*, 12 Oct. 2003; and Sutton, H. I., 'History of Israeli subs', Covert Shores, 20 May 2017.
[14] Fisher, G., 'Israel's German-built submarines are equipped with nuclear weapons, Der Spiegel reports', *Times of Israel*, 3 June 2012.
[15] 'Israel signs $3.4 bln submarines deal with Germany's Thyssenkrupp', Reuters, 20 Jan. 2022.
[16] Newdick, T., 'Our first look at Israel's new Dakar class submarine reveals a very peculiar feature', The Drive, 20 Jan. 2022.

X. Global stocks and production of fissile materials, 2022

MORITZ KÜTT, ZIA MIAN AND PAVEL PODVIG
INTERNATIONAL PANEL ON FISSILE MATERIALS

Materials that can sustain an explosive fission chain reaction are essential for all types of nuclear explosive, from first-generation fission weapons to advanced thermonuclear weapons. The most common of these fissile materials are highly enriched uranium (HEU) and plutonium. This section gives details of military and civilian stocks, as of the beginning of 2022, of HEU (table 7.11) and separated plutonium (table 7.12)—including in weapons—and details of the capacity to produce these materials (tables 7.13 and 7.14). The information in the tables is based on estimates prepared for the International Panel on Fissile Materials (IPFM). The most recent annual declarations on civilian plutonium and HEU stocks to the International Atomic Energy Agency (IAEA) give data for 31 December 2021 (INFCIRC/549).

The production of both HEU and plutonium starts with natural uranium. Natural uranium consists almost entirely of the non-chain-reacting isotope uranium-238 (U-238) and is only about 0.7 per cent uranium-235 (U-235). The concentration of U-235 can be increased through enrichment—typically using gas centrifuges. Uranium that has been enriched to less than 20 per cent U-235 (typically, 3–5 per cent)—known as low-enriched uranium—is suitable for use in power reactors. Uranium that has been enriched to contain at least 20 per cent U-235—known as HEU—is generally taken to be the lowest concentration practicable for use in weapons. However, to minimize the mass of the nuclear explosive, weapon-grade uranium is usually enriched to over 90 per cent U-235.

Plutonium is produced in nuclear reactors when U-238 in the fuel is exposed to neutrons. The plutonium is subsequently chemically separated from spent fuel in a reprocessing operation. Plutonium comes in a variety of isotopic mixtures, most of which are weapon-usable. Weapon designers prefer to work with a mixture that predominantly consists of plutonium-239 (Pu-239) because of its relatively low rate of spontaneous emission of neutrons and gamma rays and the low level of heat generation from alpha decay. Weapon-grade plutonium usually contains more than 90 per cent Pu-239. The plutonium in typical spent fuel from power reactors (reactor-grade plutonium) contains 50–60 per cent Pu-239 but is weapon-usable, even in a first-generation weapon design.

All states that have a civil nuclear industry (i.e. that operate a nuclear reactor or a uranium-enrichment plant) have some capability to produce fissile materials that could be used for weapons. The categories for fissile materials in tables 7.11 and 7.12 reflect the availability of these materials for weapon purposes. Material described as 'Not directly available for weapons' and 'Unsafeguarded' is either material produced outside weapon programmes or weapon-related material that states have pledged not to use in weapons. This material is not placed under international safeguards (e.g. IAEA or Euratom) or under bilateral monitoring. The category 'Safeguarded/monitored' includes material that is subject to such controls. The data presented in tables 7.11 and 7.12 accounts only for unirradiated fissile material, a category that corresponds to the IAEA definition of 'unirradiated direct use material'.

Table 7.11. Global stocks of highly enriched uranium, 2022

All figures are tonnes and are for unirradiated highly enriched uranium (HEU) as of the beginning of 2022. Most of this material is 90–93% enriched uranium-235 (U-235), which is typically considered weapon-grade. Important exceptions are noted. Final totals are rounded to the nearest 5 tonnes.

State	Total stock	In or available for weapons	Not directly available for weapons — Unsafeguarded	Safeguarded/ monitored	Production status
China	14	14 ± 3	–	–	Stopped 1987–89
France[a]	29	25 ± 6	–	3.8	Stopped 1996
India[b]	5	–	4.9 ± 2	–	Continuing
Iran[c]	0.03	–	0.03	–	Continuing
Israel[d]	0.3	0.3	–	–	Unknown
Korea, North[e]	Uncertain	Uncertain	–	–	Uncertain
Pakistan[f]	5	4.9 ± 1.5	–	–	Continuing
Russia[g]	680	672 ± 120	8[h]	–	Continuing[i]
UK[j]	23	22	0.6[k]	–	Stopped 1962
USA[l]	487	361	126.2	–	Stopped 1992
Other states[m]	>3.9	–	–	>3.9	
Total	**1 245**	**1 100**	**140**	**10**	

[a] A 2014 analysis offers grounds for a significantly lower estimate of France's stockpile of weapon-grade HEU (between 6 ± 2 tonnes and 10 ± 2 tonnes) based on evidence that the Pierrelatte enrichment plant may have had both a much shorter effective period of operation and a smaller capacity to produce weapon-grade HEU than previously assumed.

[b] It is believed that India is producing HEU (enriched to 30–45%) for use as naval reactor fuel. The estimate is for HEU enriched to 30%.

[c] The data for Iran is the estimate by the International Atomic Energy Agency (IAEA) as of 19 Feb. 2022. Iran started enriching uranium up to 20% on 4 Jan. 2021 and started enriching HEU up to 60% enrichment level on 17 Apr. 2021.

[d] Israel may have acquired c. 300 kg of weapon-grade HEU illicitly from the USA in or before 1965. Some of this material may have been consumed in the process of producing tritium.

[e] North Korea is known to have a uranium-enrichment plant at Yongbyon and possibly others elsewhere. Independent estimates of uranium-enrichment capability and possible HEU production extrapolated to the beginning of 2022 suggest a potential accumulated HEU stockpile in the range 250–1350 kg.

[f] This estimate for Pakistan assumes total HEU production of 5 tonnes, of which c. 100 kg was used in nuclear weapon tests.

[g] This estimate assumes that the Soviet Union stopped all HEU production in 1988. It may therefore understate the amount of HEU in Russia (see also note i).

[h] This material is believed to be in use in various research facilities, civilian as well as military-related. In addition, this number includes the HEU that was produced for fuel for China's CFR-600 reactor. That fuel was delivered to China in Sep.–Dec. 2022. The fuel contains c. 7.6 tonnes of HEU with enrichments of 21% and 26%, for a total of 2 tonnes of 90% HEU equivalent.

[i] The Soviet Union stopped production of HEU for weapons in 1988 but kept producing HEU for civilian and non-weapon military uses. Russia continues this practice.

[j] The estimate for the UK reflects a declaration of 21.9 tonnes of military HEU as of 31 Mar. 2002, the average enrichment of which was not given.

[k] This figure is from the UK's INFCIRC/549 declaration to the IAEA for the end of 2021. As the UK has left the European Union, the material is no longer under Euratom safeguards.

[l] The amount of US HEU is given in actual tonnes, not 93%-enriched equivalent. In 2016 the USA declared that, as of 30 Sep. 2013, its HEU inventory was 585.6 tonnes, of which 499.4 tonnes

was declared to be for 'national security or non-national security programs including nuclear weapons, naval propulsion, nuclear energy, and science'. This material was estimated to include c. 360.9 tonnes of HEU in weapons and available for weapons, 121.1 tonnes of HEU reserved for naval fuel and 17.3 tonnes of HEU reserved for research reactors. The remaining 86.2 tonnes of the 2013 declaration was composed of 41.6 tonnes 'available for potential down-blend to low enriched uranium or, if not possible, disposal as low-level waste', and 44.6 tonnes in spent reactor fuel. As of the end of 2021 the amount available for use had been reduced to c. 468.2 tonnes, which is estimated to include 92.3 tonnes of HEU in naval reserve and 14.9 tonnes reserved for research reactors. It is estimated that at the end of 2021 the amount of material to be down-blended had been reduced to 19 tonnes.

^{m} The IAEA's 2021 annual report lists 156 significant quantities of HEU under comprehensive safeguards in non-nuclear weapon states as of the end of 2021. Without knowing the exact enrichment levels, that means these states hold at least 3.9 tonnes of HEU since, for HEU, a significant quantity is defined as 25 kg of U-235.

In INFCIRC/912 (from 2017) more than 20 states committed to reducing civilian HEU stocks and providing regular reports. So far, only 2 countries have reported under this scheme. At the end of 2018 (time of last declaration), Norway held less than 4 kg of HEU for civilian purposes. As of 30 June 2019, Australia held 2.7 kg of HEU for civilian purposes.

Sources: International Panel on Fissile Materials (IPFM), *Global Fissile Material Report 2022: Fifty Years of the Nuclear Non-Proliferation Treaty: Nuclear Weapons, Fissile Materials, and Nuclear Energy* (IPFM: Princeton, NJ, 2022). *China*: Zhang, H., *China's Fissile Material Production and Stockpile* (IPFM: Princeton, NJ, 2017). *France*: International Atomic Energy Agency (IAEA), 'Communication received from France concerning its policies regarding the management of plutonium', INFCIRC/549/Add.5/26, 11 Oct. 2022; and Philippe, S. and Glaser, A., 'Nuclear archaeology for gaseous diffusion enrichment plants', *Science & Global Security*, vol. 22, no. 1 (2014). *Iran*: IAEA, Board of Governors, 'Verification and monitoring in the Islamic Republic of Iran in light of United Nations Security Council Resolution 2231 (2015)', Report of the director general, GOV/2022/4, 3 Mar. 2022. *Israel*: Myers, H., 'The real source of Israel's first fissile material', *Arms Control Today*, vol. 37, no. 8 (Oct. 2007), p. 56; and Gilinsky, V. and Mattson, R. J., 'Revisiting the NUMEC affair', *Bulletin of the Atomic Scientists*, vol. 66, no. 2 (Mar./Apr. 2010). *North Korea*: Hecker, S. S., Braun, C. and Lawrence, C., 'North Korea's stockpiles of fissile material', *Korea Observer*, vol 47, no. 4 (winter 2016). *Russia*: Podvig, P. (ed.), *The Use of Highly-Enriched Uranium as Fuel in Russia* (IPFM: Washington, DC, 2017); and IPFM, 'Russia delivers fuel for China's CFR-600 reactor', IPFM Blog, 28 Dec. 2022. *UK*: British Ministry of Defence, 'Historical accounting for UK defence highly enriched uranium', Mar. 2006; and IAEA, 'Communications received from the United Kingdom of Great Britain and Northern Ireland concerning its policies regarding the management of plutonium', INFCIRC/549/Add.8/25, 7 Dec. 2022. *USA*: US Department of Energy (DOE), National Nuclear Security Administration, *Highly Enriched Uranium, Striking a Balance: A Historical Report on the United States Highly Enriched Uranium Production, Acquisition, and Utilization Activities from 1945 through September 30, 1996* (DOE: Washington, DC, Jan. 2001); White House, 'Transparency in the US highly enriched uranium inventory', Fact sheet, 31 Mar. 2016; US DOE, *FY 2021 Congressional Budget Request*, vol. 1, *National Nuclear Security Administration* (DOE: Washington, DC, Feb. 2020), p. 593; and US DOE, *Tritium and Enriched Uranium Management Plan through 2060*, Report to Congress (DOE: Washington, DC, Oct. 2015). *Other states*: IAEA, *IAEA Annual Report 2021* (IAEA: Vienna, 2021), annex, table A4, p. 149; IAEA, 'Communication dated 19 July 2019 received from the Permanent Mission of Norway concerning a joint statement on minimising and eliminating the use of highly enriched uranium in civilian applications', INFCIRC/912/Add.3, 15 Aug. 2019; and IAEA, 'Communication dated 23 January 2020 received from the Permanent Mission of Australia concerning the joint statement on minimising and eliminating the use of highly enriched uranium in civilian applications', INFCIRC/912/Add.4, 5 Mar. 2020.

Table 7.12. Global stocks of separated plutonium, 2022

All figures are tonnes and are for unirradiated plutonium as of the beginning of 2022. Important exceptions are noted. Final totals are rounded to the nearest 5 tonnes.

State	Total stock	In or available for weapons	Not directly available for weapons[a] Unsafeguarded	Safeguarded/ monitored	Military production status
China	3	2.9 ± 0.6	0.04[b]	–	Stopped in 1991
France	91	6 ± 1.0	–	84.9	Stopped in 1992
India	10	0.65 ± 0.15	8.5 ± 4.9[c]	0.4	Continuing
Israel[d]	0.8	0.84 ± 0.1	–	–	Continuing
Japan	45.8	–	–	45.8	–
Korea, North[e]	0.04	0.04	–	–	Continuing
Pakistan[f]	0.5	0.5 ± 0.17	–	–	Continuing
Russia	192	88 ± 8	88.5[g]	15[h]	Stopped in 2010
UK	119.7	3.2	116.5	–	Stopped in 1995
USA[i]	87.8	38.4	46.4	3[j]	Stopped in 1988
Total	**550**	**140**	**260**	**150**	

[a] With the exception of India, figures for civilian stocks are based on INFCIRC/549 declarations to the International Atomic Energy Agency (IAEA). The data for France, Japan, Russia, the UK and the USA is for the end of 2021, reflecting their most recent INFCIRC/549 declaration to the IAEA. Some countries with civilian plutonium stocks do not submit an INFCIRC/549 declaration. Of these countries, the Netherlands, Spain and Sweden store their plutonium abroad, but the total amounts are too small to be noted in the table.

[b] These numbers are based on China's INFCIRC/549 declaration to the IAEA for the end of 2016. As of Mar. 2023, this is the most recent declaration.

[c] India's unsafeguarded civilian material is the plutonium separated from spent power-reactor fuel. While such reactor-grade plutonium can in principle be used in weapons, it is labelled as 'Not directly available for weapons' here since it is intended for breeder reactor fuel. It was not placed under safeguards in the 'India-specific' safeguards agreement signed by the Indian government and the IAEA on 2 Feb. 2009. India does not submit an INFCIRC/549 declaration to the IAEA.

[d] Israel is believed to be operating the Dimona plutonium-production reactor. The estimate assumes partial use of the reactor for tritium production from 1997 onwards. The estimate is for the beginning of 2022. Without tritium production, stockpiles could be as high as 1090 kg.

[e] North Korea reportedly declared a plutonium stock of 37 kg in June 2008. It is believed that it subsequently unloaded plutonium from its 5-MW(e) reactor 3 additional times, in 2009, 2016 and 2018. The stockpile estimate has been reduced to account for the 6 nuclear tests conducted by the country. North Korea's reprocessing facility operated again in 2021 for 5 months.

[f] At the beginning of 2022 Pakistan was operating 4 plutonium-production reactors at its Khushab site. This estimate assumes that Pakistan is separating plutonium from all 4 reactors.

[g] This material includes 63.5 tonnes of separated plutonium declared in Russia's 2022 INFCIRC/549 declaration as civilian. Russia does not make the plutonium it reports as civilian available to IAEA safeguards. This amount also includes 25 tonnes of weapon-origin plutonium stored at the Mayak Fissile Material Storage Facility, which Russia pledged not to use for military purposes.

[h] This material is weapon-grade plutonium produced between 1 Jan. 1995 and 15 Apr. 2010, when the last Russian plutonium-production reactor was shut down. It cannot be used for weapon purposes under the terms of a 1997 Russian–US agreement on plutonium-production reactors. The material is currently stored at Zheleznogorsk and is subject to monitoring by US inspectors.

i In 2012 the USA declared a government-owned plutonium inventory of 95.4 tonnes as of 30 Sep. 2009. In its INFCIRC/549 declaration of stocks as of 31 Dec. 2021, the USA declared 49.4 tonnes of unirradiated plutonium (both separated and in mixed oxide, MOX) as part of the stock identified as excess to military purposes.

j The USA has placed *c.* 3 tonnes of its excess plutonium, stored at the K-Area Material Storage Facility at the Savannah River Site, under IAEA safeguards.

Sources: International Panel on Fissile Materials (IPFM), *Global Fissile Material Report 2022: Fifty Years of the Nuclear Non-Proliferation Treaty: Nuclear Weapons, Fissile Materials, and Nuclear Energy* (IPFM: Princeton, NJ, 2022). *Civilian stocks (except for India)*: International Atomic Energy Agency (IAEA), 'Communication received from certain member states concerning their policies regarding the management of plutonium', INFCIRC/549, various dates. *China*: Zhang, H., *China's Fissile Material Production and Stockpile* (IPFM: Princeton, NJ, 2017). *Israel*: Glaser, A. and de Troullioud de Lanversin, J., 'Plutonium and tritium production in Israel's Dimona reactor, 1964–2020', *Science & Global Security*, vol. 29, no. 2 (2021). *North Korea*: Kessler, G., 'Message to US preceded nuclear declaration by North Korea', *Washington Post*, 2 July 2008; Hecker, S. S., Braun, C. and Lawrence, C., 'North Korea's stockpiles of fissile material', *Korea Observer*, vol 47, no. 4 (winter 2016); and IAEA, Board of Governors and General Conference, 'Application of safeguards in the Democratic People's Republic of Korea', Report by the acting director general, GOV/2019/33-GC(63)/20, 19 Aug. 2019. *Russia*: Russian–US Agreement Concerning the Management and Disposition of Plutonium Designated as No Longer Required for Defense Purposes and Related Cooperation (Plutonium Management and Disposition Agreement), signed 29 Aug. and 1 Sep. 2000, amendment signed 5 Sep. 2006, entered into force 13 July 2011. *USA*: National Nuclear Security Administration (NNSA), *The United States Plutonium Balance, 1944–2009* (NNSA: Washington, DC, June 2012); and Gunter, A., 'K-Area overview/update', US Department of Energy, Savanah River Site, 28 July 2015.

Table 7.13. Significant uranium-enrichment facilities and capacity worldwide, 2022

With the exception of two facilities (marked *) that continue to use gaseous diffusion to enrich uranium in uranium-235 (U-235), all facilities use gas centrifuge isotope-separation technology.

State	Facility name or location	Type	Status	Capacity (thousands SWU/yr)[a]
Argentina[b]	Pilcaniyeu*	Civilian	Uncertain	20
Brazil	Resende	Civilian	Expanding capacity	45–50
China[c]	Lanzhou	Civilian	Operational	2 600
	Hanzhong (Shaanxi)	Civilian	Operational	2 000
	Emeishan	Civilian	Operational	1 050
	Heping*	Dual-use	Operational	230
France	Georges Besse II	Civilian	Operational	7 500
Germany	Urenco Gronau	Civilian	Operational	3 700
India	Rattehalli	Military	Operational	15–30
Iran[d]	Natanz	Civilian	Expanding capacity	22
	Qom (Fordow)	Civilian	Expanding capacity	2.5
Japan	Rokkasho[e]	Civilian	Resuming operation	75
Korea, North	Yongbyon[f]	Uncertain	Operational	8
Netherlands	Urenco Almelo	Civilian	Operational	5 200
Pakistan	Gadwal	Military	Operational	..
	Kahuta	Military	Operational	15–45
Russia	Angarsk	Civilian	Operational	4 000
	Novouralsk	Civilian	Operational	13 300
	Seversk	Civilian	Operational	3 800
	Zelenogorsk[g]	Civilian	Operational	7 900
UK	Capenhurst	Civilian	Operational	4 500
USA	Urenco Eunice	Civilian	Operational	4 900

[a] Separative work units per year (SWU/yr) is a measure of the effort required in an enrichment facility to separate uranium of a given content of U-235 into two components, one with a higher and one with a lower percentage of U-235. Where a range of capacities is shown, the capacity is uncertain or the facility is expanding its capacity.

[b] In Dec. 2015 Argentina announced the reopening of its Pilcaniyeu gaseous diffusion uranium-enrichment plant, which was shut down in the 1990s. There is no evidence of actual production.

[c] Assessments of China's enrichment capacity in 2015 and 2017 identified new enrichment sites and suggested a much larger total capacity than had previously been estimated.

[d] The figures for Iran are for Dec. 2022 and show a significant increase compared with the beginning of 2022, when the Natanz facility had a capacity of 12 000 SWU/yr. Since the USA's withdrawal in 2018 from the Joint Comprehensive Plan of Action (JCPOA), which agreed limits on and made more transparent Iran's nuclear programme, Iran continues to increase enrichment capacities and levels at its Natanz and Fordow facilities.

[e] The Rokkasho centrifuge plant has been in the process of being refitted with new centrifuge technology since 2011. Production since the start of retrofitting has been negligible.

[f] North Korea revealed its Yongbyon enrichment facility in 2010. It appears to be operational as of 2020. It is believed that North Korea is operating at least one other enrichment facility.

[g] Zelenogorsk operates a centrifuge cascade for HEU production of fuel for fast reactors and research reactors.

Sources: Indo-Asian News Service (IANS), 'Argentina president inaugurates enriched uranium plant', *Business Standard* (New Delhi), 1 Dec. 2015; Nuclear Engineering International, 'Brazil's INB launches new centrifuge cascade', 25 Nov. 2021; Zhang, H., 'China's uranium enrichment complex', *Science & Global Security*, vol. 23, no. 3 (2015); Zhang, H., *China's Fissile Material Production and Stockpile* (International Panel on Fissile Materials: Princeton, NJ, 2017); International Atomic Energy Agency (IAEA), Board of Governors, 'Verification and monitoring in the Islamic Republic of Iran in light of United Nations Security Council Resolution 2231 (2015)', Report by the director general, GOV/2022/62, 10 Nov. 2022; Albright, D., Burkhard, S. and Faragasso, S., 'Updated highlights of comprehensive survey of Iran's advanced centrifuges', Institute for Science and International Security, 1 Dec. 2022; and Hecker, S. S., Carlin, R. L. and Serbin, E. A., 'A comprehensive history of North Korea's nuclear program: 2018 update', Stanford University, Center for International Security and Cooperation, 11 Feb. 2019. Enrichment capacity data is based on IAEA, Integrated Nuclear Fuel Cycle Information Systems (iNFCIS); Urenco, 'Global operations'; and International Panel on Fissile Materials (IPFM), *Global Fissile Material Report 2022: Fifty Years of the Nuclear Non-Proliferation Treaty: Nuclear Weapons, Fissile Materials, and Nuclear Energy* (IPFM: Princeton, NJ, 2022).

Table 7.14. Significant reprocessing facilities worldwide, 2022

State	Facility name or location	Fuel	Type	Status	Design capacity (tHM/yr)[a]
China[b]	Jiuquan pilot plant	LWR	Civilian	Operational	50
France	La Hague UP2	LWR	Civilian	Operational	1 000
	La Hague UP3	LWR	Civilian	Operational	1 000
India[c]	Kalpakkam	HWR	Dual-use	Operational	100
	Tarapur	HWR	Dual-use	Operational	100
	Tarapur-II	HWR	Dual-use	Operational	100
	Trombay	HWR	Military	Operational	50
Israel	Dimona	HWR	Military	Operational	40–100
Japan	JNC Tokai	LWR	Civilian	Shut down in 2014[d]	(was 200)
	Rokkasho	LWR	Civilian	Start planned for 2025	800
Korea, North	Yongbyon	GCR	Military	Operational	100–150
Pakistan	Chashma	HWR	Military	Starting up	50–100
	Nilore	HWR	Military	Operational	20–40
Russia	Mayak RT-1, Ozersk	LWR	Civilian	Operational	400
	EDC, Zheleznogorsk[e]	LWR	Civilian	Starting up	250
UK	Sellafield B205	Magnox	Civilian	Shut down in July 2022	1 500
	Sellafield Thorp	LWR	Civilian	Shut down in 2018	(was 1 200)
USA	H-canyon, Savannah River Site	LWR	Civilian	Operational	15

GCR = gas-cooled reactor; HWR = heavy water reactor; LWR = light water reactor.

[a] Design capacity refers to the highest amount of spent fuel the plant is designed to process and is measured in tonnes of heavy metal per year (tHM/yr), tHM being a measure of the amount of heavy metal—uranium in these cases—that is in the spent fuel. Actual throughput is often a small fraction of the design capacity. LWR spent fuel contains c. 1% plutonium; HWR, GCR and Magnox fuel contain c. 0.4% plutonium.

[b] China is building a pilot reprocessing facility near Jinta, Gansu province, with a capacity of 200 tHM/yr, to be commissioned in 2025. A second reprocessing plant of the same capacity is planned for the same site.

[c] As part of the 2005 Indian–US Civil Nuclear Cooperation Initiative, India has decided that none of its reprocessing plants will be opened for International Atomic Energy Agency safeguards inspections.

[d] In 2014 the Japan Atomic Energy Agency announced the planned closure of the head-end of its Tokai reprocessing plant, effectively ending further plutonium-separation activity. In 2018 the Japanese Nuclear Regulation Authority approved a plan to decommission the plant.

[e] Russia continues to construct the 250 tHM/yr pilot Experimental and Demonstration Centre (EDC) at Zheleznogorsk. A pilot reprocessing line with a capacity of 5 tHM/yr was launched in June 2018.

Sources: Kyodo News, 'Japan approves 70-year plan to scrap nuclear reprocessing plant', 13 June 2018; Japan Nuclear Fuel Ltd, 'Provisional operation plans for Rokkasho reprocessing plant and MOX fuel fabrication plant', 10 Feb. 2023; [Rosatom ready to start 'green' processing of spent nuclear fuel], RIA Novosti, 29 May 2018 (in Russian); and Sellafield Ltd and Nuclear Decommissioning Authority, 'Job done: Sellafield plant safely completes its mission', 19 July 2022. Data on design capacity is based on International Atomic Energy Agency, Integrated Nuclear Fuel Cycle Information Systems (iNFCIS); and International Panel on Fissile Materials (IPFM), *Global Fissile Material Report 2022: Fifty Years of the Nuclear Non-Proliferation Treaty: Nuclear Weapons, Fissile Materials, and Nuclear Energy* (IPFM: Princeton, NJ, 2022).

Part III. Non-proliferation, arms control and disarmament, 2022

Chapter 8. Nuclear disarmament, arms control and non-proliferation

Chapter 9. Chemical, biological and health security threats

Chapter 10. Conventional arms control and regulation of new weapon technologies

Chapter 11. Space and cyberspace

Chapter 12. Dual-use and arms trade controls

8. Nuclear disarmament, arms control and non-proliferation

Overview

The importance of arms control agreements and commitments was underlined early in 2022 by a joint statement by the leaders of the five permanent members of the United Nations Security Council (the P5) on 'Preventing nuclear war and avoiding arms races'. However, the full-scale invasion by one of these nuclear weapon states—Russia—of a neighbouring non-nuclear weapon state—Ukraine—led to significant setbacks in bilateral and multilateral engagement on nuclear arms control throughout the rest of the year.

The war presented unprecedented nuclear safety, security and safeguards challenges for the International Atomic Energy Agency (IAEA), the Ukrainian authorities and the personnel of nuclear installations in Ukraine (see section V). Never before had operating nuclear power plants been attacked by shelling or missile strikes by state militaries, nor occupied by military forces. The IAEA undertook multiple missions of technical experts to Ukraine in 2022, and subsequently established a permanent presence at all four nuclear power plants there. The IAEA also put forward a conceptual framework—the 'seven indispensable pillars of nuclear safety and security'—for addressing threats to nuclear installations in wartime.

Although bilateral talks between Russia and the USA continued in early 2022, they found differences between their positions on several key issues to be intractable (see section I). The invasion in February prompted the USA to suspend the dialogue, and there was subsequently only limited bilateral engagement between the two countries. The broader situation also affected the implementation of their 2010 Treaty on Measures for the Further Reduction and Limitation of Strategic Offensive Arms (New START) and negotiations of a potential follow-on framework. Although Russia and the USA continued to implement most elements of New START in 2022, in August Russia notified the USA that it was not ready to resume on-site inspections of its nuclear weapon-related sites. Suspension of the strategic stability dialogue also meant there were no talks on an arms control framework to succeed New START on its expiry in 2026.

In the case of proposed bilateral strategic stability dialogue between China and the USA, there was no movement (see section I). China remained unwilling to engage in arms control talks without preconditions.

Iran's military support to Russia meant that the war in Ukraine even overshadowed the talks on reviving the Joint Comprehensive Plan of Action (JCPOA) on the Iranian nuclear programme. The talks that had started in

SIPRI Yearbook 2023: Armaments, Disarmament and International Security
www.sipriyearbook.org

Vienna in April 2021 continued in 2022, without leading to a solution (see section IV). The talks were further complicated by an IAEA investigation into Iran's past nuclear activities and a government crackdown on protests in the country. Even though it is hard to see any alternative that would address the key concerns of both Iran and the USA as effectively as the JCPOA, voices on both sides continued to question the long-term benefits of reviving it. Instead, the parties seem willing to live with the status quo despite the costs and risks.

Negotiations between the United States and North Korea have proceeded sporadically for decades but have failed to halt the advance of North Korea's nuclear and missile programmes. The last round of denuclearization negotiations collapsed in 2019, and in 2022 North Korea test launched more ballistic missiles than ever before in a single year (see chapter 7).

The international community came close but failed to reach agreement at the 10th review conference of the 1968 Treaty on the Non-Proliferation of Nuclear Weapons (NPT) in August 2022 (see section II). Nearly all states parties were willing to reach consensus on a substantive outcome. A compromise text was produced despite disagreement over issues that have been obstacles at past review conferences (e.g. the 1995 Middle East Resolution) or had been expected to be obstacles at this conference (e.g. the 2021 trilateral security pact between Australia, the UK and the USA, known as AUKUS, and the relationship between the NPT and the 2017 Treaty on the Prohibition of Nuclear Weapons, TPNW). The lack of consensus was largely attributed to Russia, resulting in what has been referred to as 'consensus minus one'. With two consecutive review conferences now having ended without a consensus substantive outcome or recommendations, the parties agreed to establish a working group on further strengthening the NPT's review process in advance of the 2026 review conference.

The first meeting of states parties to the TPNW reached agreement on several key issues (see section III). As well as establishing a Scientific Advisory Group, the parties unanimously adopted a political declaration and an action plan. The latter contains 50 specific actions, including actions on universalization; victim assistance, environmental remediation and international cooperation and assistance; scientific and technical advice in support of implementation; supporting the wider nuclear disarmament and non-proliferation regime; inclusion; and implementation of the treaty's gender provisions. However, since all the nuclear-armed states remain non-parties, the challenges for the treaty's core objective—nuclear disarmament—remain formidable.

Despite these limited successes, by the end of 2022 even the P5 dialogue had been put on hold, with the process reportedly limited to expert-level engagement. Unless diplomatic trends reverse, a new and more dangerous phase in arms control is on the horizon.

TYTTI ERÄSTÖ, WILFRED WAN AND VITALY FEDCHENKO

I. Bilateral and multilateral nuclear arms control involving China, Russia and the United States

WILFRED WAN

Bilateral and multilateral engagement on nuclear arms control suffered significant setbacks in 2022. The beginning of the year was auspicious, with a joint statement by the leaders of the five permanent members of the United Nations Security Council (the P5)—China, France, the Russian Federation, the United Kingdom and the United States—on 'Preventing nuclear war and avoiding arms races' (see section II). This underlined the importance of arms control agreements and commitments and expressed the intention to seek 'bilateral and multilateral diplomatic approaches' including to prevent arms racing.[1] January was also marked by the continuation of the bilateral strategic stability dialogue between Russia and the USA. During these talks, which were intended as a precursor to arms control negotiations, the two sides exchanged security concerns, but they found differences between their positions on several key issues to be intractable.

The Russian invasion of Ukraine in February 2022 upended bilateral relations. The war stopped most communication between Russia and the USA and also affected the implementation of the 2010 Treaty on Measures for the Further Reduction and Limitation of Strategic Offensive Arms (New START) and negotiations of a potential follow-on framework. Meanwhile, there was no movement between China and the USA on strategic stability dialogue. China remained unwilling to engage in arms control talks without preconditions, a position it largely shares with France and the UK.

This section covers these developments, looking in turn at Russian–US strategic stability dialogue, implementation of New START and talks on a follow-on, and engagement with China. It concludes by analysing prospects for progress on any of these fronts.

The Russian–United States strategic stability dialogue

In January 2022 Russia and the USA convened their bilateral strategic stability dialogue, the third session since it was initiated at the June 2021 meeting between US President Joe Biden and Russian President Vladimir Putin. This was termed an 'extraordinary session' because of the lack of preliminary meetings of the two inter-agency expert working groups (on 'principles and objectives for future arms control' and on 'capabilities and actions with

---

[1] 'Joint statement of the leaders of the five nuclear-weapon states on preventing nuclear war and avoiding arms races', 3 Jan. 2022.

strategic effects') that the two sides had agreed to create in September 2021.[2] The dialogue took place against the backdrop of Russia's military build-up near the Ukrainian border.[3]

In advance of the third session, in December 2021 Russia had transmitted to the USA two draft agreements—one between Russia and the USA and one between Russia and the North Atlantic Treaty Organization (NATO)—that relayed its desired security guarantees and were intended as a 'starting point' for talks.[4] The session, held in Geneva and led by Russian and US deputy foreign ministers, Sergey Ryabkov and Wendy Sherman, included the exchange of security concerns on both sides and the discussion of preliminary ideas for reciprocal action.[5] Sherman noted US interest in discussing arms control that would include both strategic and non-strategic nuclear weapons. The USA also indicated its openness to discussion of limits on the size and scope of military exercises and of the placement of missiles, including the future of certain missile systems in Europe formerly covered by the 1987 Intermediate-range Nuclear Forces (INF) Treaty.[6] These reflected some overlap with the Russian draft treaties. For his part, Ryabkov called for quick action on arms control negotiations, noting that any such arrangements would be linked to the joint development of a 'strategic equation' encompassing nuclear and non-nuclear weapons.[7] Both sides cited irreconcilable differences on other key security issues, in particular a Russian proposal for NATO to refrain from further enlargement of its membership, including the accession of Ukraine and other states in Eastern Europe.

The Russian invasion of Ukraine in February 2022 prompted the USA to suspend the bilateral strategic stability dialogue.[8] In April, an official of the Russian Ministry of Foreign Affairs (MFA) confirmed that the process was

---

[2] Joint statement on the outcomes of the US–Russia Strategic Stability Dialogue, Geneva, 30 Sep. 2021. See also Saalman, L., 'Bilateral and multilateral nuclear arms control involving China, Russia and the United States', *SIPRI Yearbook 2022*, pp. 440–41.

[3] On Russia's build-up of forces and subsequent invasion see chapter 1, section V, and chapter 2, section I, in this volume. On the effect on nuclear facilities in Ukraine see section V of this chapter.

[4] Russian Ministry of Foreign Affairs, 'Press release on Russian draft documents on legal security guarantees from the United States and NATO', 17 Dec. 2021.

[5] US Mission to International Organizations in Geneva, 'Deputy Secretary Sherman's participation in an extraordinary session of the strategic stability dialogue with Russian Deputy Foreign Minister Sergey Ryabkov', 10 Jan. 2022.

[6] Sherman, W. R., US Deputy Secretary of State, Briefing on the US–Russia strategic stability dialogue, US Department of State, 10 Jan. 2022. For a summary and other details of the Treaty on the Elimination of Intermediate-Range and Shorter-Range Missiles (INF Treaty) see annex A, section III, in this volume. On the demise of the INF Treaty see Topychkanov, P. and Davis, I., 'Russian–United States nuclear arms control and disarmament', *SIPRI Yearbook 2020*, 399–409.

[7] 'Future Russia–US strategic equation should include nuclear and non-nuclear weapons—Russian deputy FM', Interfax, 30 Nov. 2020.

[8] US Mission to International Organizations in Geneva, US statement to the Conference on Disarmament, Subsidiary Body One on the Cessation of the Nuclear Arms Race and Nuclear Disarmament, 15 Mar. 2022; and Detsch, J. and Gramer, R., 'Biden halts Russian arms control talks amid Ukraine invasion', 25 Feb. 2022.

formally 'frozen' and speculated that the process could be resumed with the completion of what Russia termed its 'special military operation' in Ukraine.[9] Over ensuing months, both sides spoke of their willingness in abstract terms to engage on topics of strategic stability and nuclear arms control, including through separate presidential statements from Biden and Putin delivered at the 10th review conference of the 1968 Non-Proliferation Treaty (NPT) in August 2022 (see section II).[10]

However, there was limited bilateral engagement between Russia and the USA after February. This included the establishment in March 2022 of a military-to-military deconfliction line to reduce the risks of miscalculation amid the war in Ukraine, and telephone calls between the Russian and US defence ministers, Sergey Shoigu and Lloyd Austin, in May and October.[11]

The USA at times demonstrated a willingness to delink the war in Ukraine from other topics, with President Biden stating that 'even as we rally the world to hold Russia accountable [for the war], we must continue to engage Russia on issues of strategic stability'.[12] Several members of the Russian government, including President Putin and Ryabkov, similarly suggested that they were ready to restart the process and awaited a response from the USA.[13] Yet the Russian foreign minister, Sergey Lavrov, also said that it is 'impossible to discuss strategic stability' while ignoring Western involvement in the war.[14] As the year ended, there remained no tangible plans for resumption of the strategic stability dialogue.[15]

New START

The suspension of the Russia–USA strategic stability dialogue meant the disruption of a process that aimed to lay the groundwork for a follow-on treaty to New START.[16] This is the only remaining treaty that sets limits on the size and composition of the Russian and US nuclear arsenals (see table 8.1), but it is set to expire in February 2026.

Russia and the USA continued to implement most elements of New START in 2022 despite the Russian invasion of Ukraine and the accompanying nuclear

---

[9] 'Russia says strategic stability dialogue with US "frozen", TASS reports', Reuters, 30 Apr. 2022.

[10] Biden, J., US president, Statement ahead of the 10th NPT review conference, White House Briefing, 1 Aug. 2022; and Putin, V., Russian president, Greetings on the opening of the 10th NPT review conference, 1 Aug. 2022.

[11] Youssef, N. A., 'US, Russia establish hotline to avoid accident conflict', *Wall Street Journal*, 3 Mar. 2022; and 'Russia's Shoigu holds second call with US defense secretary in three days', Reuters, 23 Oct. 2022.

[12] Biden, J., US president, Message to the Arms Control Association, 2 June 2022.

[13] Kremlin, 'Valdai International Discussion Club meeting', 27 Oct. 2022.

[14] 'Lavrov says Ukraine war affects prospects for nuclear talks', Reuters, 1 Dec. 2022.

[15] Bugos, S., 'Russian–US arms dialogue remains uncertain', *Arms Control Today*, vol. 52, no. 6 (July/Aug. 2022).

[16] For a summary and other details of New START, see annex A, section III, in this volume.

Table 8.1. Russian and United States aggregate numbers of strategic offensive arms under New START, as of 5 February 2011 and 1 September 2022

Category	Treaty limit[a]	Russia Feb. 2011	Russia Sep. 2022	Russia Change	United States Feb. 2011	United States Sep. 2022	United States Change
Deployed ICBMs, SLBMs and heavy bombers	700	521	540	+19	882	659	−223
Warheads on deployed ICBMs, SLBMs and heavy bombers	1550	1537	1549	+12	1800	1420	−380
ICBM and SLBM launchers and heavy bombers	800	865	759	−106	1124	800	−324

ICBM = intercontinental ballistic missile; SLBM = submarine-launched ballistic missile.

[a] The treaty entered into force on 5 Feb. 2011. The treaty limits had to be reached by 5 Feb. 2018.

[b] Each heavy bomber, whether equipped with cruise missiles or gravity bombs, is counted as carrying only one warhead, even though the aircraft can carry larger weapon payloads.

Source: US Department of State, Bureau of Arms Control, Verification and Compliance, 'New START Treaty aggregate numbers of strategic offensive arms', Fact sheet, 1 Sep. 2022.

sabre-rattling—including President Putin's threat that any external interference would have 'such consequences that you have never encountered' and his decision in February 2022 to introduce a 'special combat duty regime' in Russia's deterrence forces.[17] Implementation of the treaty included data exchanges on the status of the two sides' strategic nuclear forces in March and September. In accordance with their obligations, both sides provided notification in advance of launches of treaty-accountable ballistic missiles— including in April as Russia tested its new RS-28 Sarmat (SS-X-29) system, a heavy intercontinental ballistic missile (ICBM) equipped with multiple independently targetable re-entry vehicles (MIRVs).[18]

In August 2022 Russia notified the USA that it was not ready to resume on-site inspections of its nuclear weapon-related sites. The system of verifying compliance with New START had been challenged by the Covid-19 pandemic, with on-site inspections on pause since March 2020 and an imbalanced reliance on notification exchanges and the meetings of the Bilateral Consultative Commission (BCC), the body established to address treaty compliance or implementation concerns.[19] In August 2022 the USA had sent notification of its intention to resume on-site inspections, leading Russia to stop the process. It cited limitations to its rights to conduct inspections on US territory linked to travel restrictions imposed by the USA in response

---

[17] 'Putin orders "special service regime" in Russia's deterrence force', TASS, 27 Feb. 2022.

[18] Vergun, D., 'Russia notified US of ICBM test launch', US Department of Defense, 20 Apr. 2022.

[19] Saalman (note 2), pp. 438–39. For a brief description of the BCC see annex B, section I, in this volume.

to Russia's actions in Ukraine, as well as Covid-19 related circumstances.[20] Russia observed that only with the resolution of these issues would it be 'possible to return to the full application of the verification mechanisms' under New START.[21] In response, the USA declared that it would not consider holding talks on a follow-up treaty until inspections resumed.[22] Despite this, the two sides agreed to insert text in the draft final outcome document of the 10th NPT review conference committing themselves to 'full implementation' of New START and 'to pursue negotiations in good faith on a successor framework . . . in order to achieve deeper, irreversible and verifiable reductions in their nuclear arsenals'.[23] However, Russia objected to the document on other grounds, preventing a consensus outcome with any such substantive content (see section II).

A session of the BCC in Cairo scheduled to begin in late November 2022 would have presented an opportunity for Russia and the USA to discuss the resumption of inspections and other implementation concerns. But Russia decided at the 'political level' and at the last minute to postpone the session, with Ryabkov later citing the situation in Ukraine while also expressing concerns about US implementation of New START.[24] A Russian MFA spokeswoman stressed New START's importance and expressed an expectation that the USA would create the conditions for a session in 2023 with a 'return to the full-format implementation' of treaty provisions.[25]

Engagement with China

In recent years China has played an active role in the dialogue process among the P5, which are also the five states recognized as nuclear weapon states under the NPT.[26] In a press briefing on the P5 leaders' joint statement of January 2022, China expressed the need to strengthen communication

---

[20] 'Russia suspends START arms inspections over US travel curbs', Reuters, 8 Aug. 2022.

[21] Russian Ministry of Foreign Affairs, 'Foreign Ministry statement on the Treaty on Measures for the Further Reduction and Limitation of Strategic Offensive Arms', 8 Aug. 2022.

[22] Lindsay, J. and Lewis, S., 'US–Russia nuclear weapons inspections must resume before new arms talks, says US', Reuters, 2 Sep. 2022.

[23] 10th NPT review conference, 'Draft final document', NPT/CONF.2020/CRP.1/Rev.2, 25 Aug. 2022, para. 17.

[24] 'Russia had no choice but to nix New START treaty talks, says senior diplomat', TASS, 29 Nov. 2022; and Bugos, S., 'Russia delays meeting on New START', *Arms Control Today*, vol. 52, no. 10 (Dec. 2022).

[25] 'Russia expects US to attempt to organize New START commission's session in 2023', TASS, 29 Nov. 2022.

[26] For a summary and other details of the NPT, including the definition of nuclear weapon state, see annex A, section I, in this volume.

among the P5 on strategic stability issues.[27] Fu Cong, director-general of the Chinese MFA's Department of Arms Control, again rejected the idea of China becoming involved in arms control negotiations before Russia and the USA reduced their stockpiles to a level comparable to China's arsenal.[28] Fu also denied US claims of a significant Chinese nuclear build-up, although he acknowledged that China was taking measures to 'modernize' its arsenal as a means to achieve national security.[29]

In the days following the joint P5 statement, Bonnie Jenkins, the US under secretary of state for arms control and international security, indicated that the USA would continue to pursue engagement with China in both the P5 process and bilaterally, highlighting a desire to increase transparency and reduce risk and miscalculation.[30] She observed that the two sides were exploring pathways to start strategic stability discussions, following on from the November 2021 virtual meeting between US President Joe Biden and Chinese President Xi Jinping. At that time, the two agreed—in the words of the US national security advisor, Jake Sullivan—that they 'would look to begin to carry forward discussions on strategic stability'.[31] (Official statements from China were more oblique.)

In February 2022, Russian President Putin visited Beijing to take part in the opening ceremony of the Olympic Winter Games and to hold talks with President Xi. This built on two virtual meetings between the leaders in 2021.[32] In a joint statement dated 4 February 2022, they welcomed the P5 statement and expressed their belief that all nuclear weapon states should, among other things, 'withdraw nuclear weapons deployed abroad, eliminate the unrestricted development of global anti-ballistic missile defense (ABM) system[s], and take effective steps to reduce the risks of nuclear wars and any armed conflicts between countries with military nuclear capabilities.'[33] They chastised the USA for undermining strategic stability and weakening the arms control framework, citing its withdrawal from the INF Treaty and development of intermediate- and shorter-range ground-based missiles in both the Asia-Pacific and Europe. They also called for the USA to 'respond

---

[27] Chinese Ministry of Foreign Affairs, 'Director-general of the Department of Arms Control of the Foreign Ministry Fu Cong holds a briefing for Chinese and foreign media on the joint statement of the leaders of the five nuclear-weapon states on preventing nuclear war', 4 Jan. 2022; and Joint statement (note 1).

[28] On the relative sizes of the Chinese, Russia and US nuclear forces see chapter 7, World Nuclear Forces, table 7.1 and sections I, II and V, in this volume.

[29] Zhao, J., 'Ministry dismisses claims of nuclear capabilities', *China Daily*, 5 Jan. 2022.

[30] 'US looking for ways to reduce nuclear risk with China', Kyodo News, 16 Jan. 2022.

[31] Brookings Institution, 'Readout from the Biden–Xi virtual meeting: Discussion with National Security Advisor Jake Sullivan', Webinar transcript, 16 Nov. 2021, p. 11. See also Saalman (note 2), p. 442.

[32] Chinese Ministry of Foreign Affairs, 'President Xi Jinping had a virtual meeting with Russian President Vladimir Putin', 15 Dec. 2021.

[33] Chinese–Russian joint statement on 'The international relations entering a new era and the global sustainable development', 4 Feb. 2022.

positively to the Russian initiative' in this respect.[34] In December 2022, presidents Putin and Xi held another virtual meeting to discuss the broader China–Russia strategic partnership.[35]

During 2022 US officials raised further alarms about the pace and scale of Chinese nuclear modernization. In March the commander of US Strategic Command, Admiral Charles Richard, described it as a 'strategic breakout'.[36] In September his successor, Anthony Cotton, opined in his confirmation hearing that Chinese expansion of its nuclear forces did not reflect minimal deterrence, and expressed disbelief about the size and short construction time of three new nuclear missile fields in western China.[37] In November a report by the US Department of Defense (DOD) assessed that China had probably accelerated its nuclear expansion, and projected that its stockpile size—estimated to surpass 400 warheads—could reach about 1500 by 2035 if expansion continued at the current pace.[38] The DOD report noted that China was unwilling to engage in nuclear arms control negotiations.[39] The public version of the 2022 US Nuclear Posture Review projects that the USA will face two strategic competitors by 2030, and observes that Chinese nuclear forces would have to be accounted for in future Russian–US arms control negotiations.[40]

China and the USA sought to improve bilateral relation after tensions over Taiwan were inflamed by a visit there by the speaker of the US House of Representatives, Nancy Pelosi, in August 2022 and increased Chinese military activity in the region. Their foreign ministers, Wang Yi and Antony Blinken, met in September 2022 and presidents Biden and Xi met in person for the first time at the 2022 Bali summit of the Group of 20 (G20) in November. Official summaries of the latter meeting suggest that there was only an exchange of views on broader 'issues of strategic importance', with discussion of the nuclear issue confined to Russia's actions in the context of Ukraine, as Biden reaffirmed the message in the P5 joint statement.[41] China, Russia and the

---

[34] Chinese–Russian joint statement (note 33).

[35] Chinese Ministry of Foreign Affairs, 'President Xi Jinping had a virtual meeting with Russian President Vladimir Putin', 30 Dec. 2022.

[36] Richard, C., Statement to hearing on US Strategic Command and US Space Command, US Senate, Committee on Armed Services, 8 Mar. 2022, p. 8.

[37] Cotton, A. J., Statement to nomination hearing, US Senate, Committee on Armed Services, 15 Sep. 2022, p. 18.

[38] US Department of Defense, *Military and Security Developments Involving the People's Republic of China 2022*, Annual report to Congress (DOD: Nov. 2022), p. 94. China's stockpile is estimated to be c. 400 nuclear warheads as of Jan. 2023 in chapter 7, section V, in this volume.

[39] US Department of Defense (note 38), p. 97.

[40] US Department of Defense (DOD), *2022 National Defense Strategy of the United States of America* (DOD: Washington, DC, Oct. 2022). On the US Nuclear Posture Review see also chapter 7, section I, in this volume.

[41] Chinese Ministry of Foreign Affairs, 'President Xi Jinping meets with US President Joe Biden in Bali', 14 Nov. 2022; and White House, 'Readout of President Joe Biden's meeting with President Xi Jinping of the People's Republic of China', 14 Nov. 2022.

USA also endorsed the leaders' declaration of the G20 summit, which states that 'the use or threat of use of nuclear weapons is inadmissible'.[42]

Conclusions

Prospects for bilateral or multilateral nuclear arms control and strategic stability dialogue appeared dim at the end of 2022. Multilateral dialogue had been put on hold, with the P5 process reportedly limited to expert-level engagement. Russia–United States talks on a successor arms control framework had been suspended. Statements by some Russian officials indicated that resolution of some kind in Ukraine may be required before Russia will consider the resumption of that dialogue. Additionally, they suggested that the full implementation of New START—in particular, the resumption of on-site inspections and the convening of the BCC—had also become contingent on addressing the deterioration in relations as a result of the war.

Beyond the immediate effects of Russia's invasion of Ukraine, worsening relations between China and Russia on one side and the USA on the other provide significant impediments to future bilateral or multilateral nuclear arms control. There is a narrowing window of opportunity in which continuity can be ensured before the expiration of New START in 2026. Unless diplomatic trends reverse, a new and more dangerous phase in Russia–USA relations is on the horizon, one with ramifications for global arms control.

---

[42] G20 Bali summit, Leaders' declaration, 15–16 Nov. 2022, para. 4.

II. The 10th review conference of the Non-Proliferation Treaty

WILFRED WAN

The 10th review conference of the parties to the 1968 Treaty on the Non-Proliferation of Nuclear Weapons (NPT) was held from 1 to 26 August 2022 at United Nations Headquarters in New York.[1] The conference had originally been scheduled to take place in 2020, which would have marked the 50th anniversary of the entry into force of what is widely considered to be the cornerstone of the international non-proliferation regime. However, it was delayed four times because of the Covid-19 pandemic.

Despite extensive efforts—which included negotiations into the last day, resulting in the postponement and suspension of the final plenary meeting—the conference came to an end without consensus on the contents of a substantive final outcome document. The invasion of Ukraine in February 2022 pervaded the discussions, and the conference president—Ambassador Gustavo Zlauvinen of Argentina—attributed the lack of consensus on a final outcome document to the position of one delegation: the Russian Federation. The result was a second consecutive review conference without a consensus substantive outcome or recommendations.

This section reviews the proceedings of the review conference, highlighting the most significant and contentious issues. It then assesses the impact on the conference of the Russian invasion of Ukraine before describing the outlook for the NPT.[2]

Proceedings of the conference

The conference marked the regular review of the operation of the NPT across its three pillars: nuclear disarmament, nuclear non-proliferation and peaceful uses of nuclear energy. The groundwork for the 10th review conference had been laid by a preparatory committee, which held three sessions starting in 2017, in a review cycle prolonged by the Covid-19 pandemic.[3] Under its rules of procedure, the conference established three main committees, allocating to each several items of consideration centred on the pillars. Main Committee I considered the implementation of the provisions of the treaty relating to

---

[1] For a summary and other details of the NPT see annex A, section I, in this volume.

[2] On other aspects of the war in Ukraine see chapter 1, section V, chapter 2, section I, chapter 5, section I, chapter 11, section II, and chapter 12, section III, in this volume.

[3] On the work of the preparatory committee see Kile, S. N., 'Developments in multilateral nuclear disarmament and non-proliferation', *SIPRI Yearbook 2018*, pp. 235–36; Erästö, T., 'Other developments related to multilateral treaties and initiatives on nuclear arms control, disarmament and non-proliferation', *SIPRI Yearbook 2019*, pp. 391–93; and Kile, S. N. and Erästö, T., 'Multilateral nuclear arms control and non-proliferation treaties and initiatives', *SIPRI Yearbook 2020*, pp. 430–33.

non-proliferation of nuclear weapons, disarmament and international peace and security. Main Committee II focused on non-proliferation of nuclear weapons, safeguards and nuclear weapon-free zones. Main Committee III considered the inalienable right of all parties to the treaty to conduct research on and to produce and use nuclear energy for peaceful purposes.[4]

The first plenary meeting, on 1 August, decided to establish three subsidiary bodies, one under each main committee, for the duration of the conference.[5] The subsidiary body of Main Committee I examined 'nuclear disarmament and security assurances'; that of Main Committee II examined 'regional issues, including with respect to the Middle East and implementation of the 1995 Middle East resolution';[6] and that of Main Committee III examined 'peaceful uses of nuclear energy and other provisions of the Treaty; and improving the effectiveness of the strengthened review process'.

The formal meetings of the main committees began late in the first week of the conference, following which the closed meetings of the three subsidiary bodies took place. This work also spanned the second and third weeks of the review conference. None of the three main committees or their subsidiary bodies reached consensus on a text. The chair of each subsidiary body then proposed a draft report, under their own authority, that reflected the state of deliberations. In the final meeting of each of the main committees, the chair released a working paper under their own authority to reflect the discussion in both the main committee and the accompanying subsidiary body.[7] These three papers include sections on the operation of all of the elements of the treaty and include forward-looking sections and commitments.

On the basis of the working papers from the three main committee chairs, Zlauvinen produced a draft final outcome document that was publicly shared in the fourth and final week of the conference.[8] He and the national delegates discussed the contents of this draft in closed plenary sessions.[9] At the same time, in the third week of the conference he had invited Ambassador Jarmo Viinanen of Finland to facilitate discussions on the draft among a smaller group of states, including on sections relating to disarmament and non-proliferation, to continue the work of the main committees.[10] These

---

[4] 10th NPT review conference, Preparatory Committee, Final report, NPT/CONF.2020/1, annex V.

[5] 10th NPT review conference, 'Decision on subsidiary bodies', NPT/CONF.2020/DEC.1, 1 Aug. 2022.

[6] 1995 NPT Review and Extension Conference, Resolution on the Middle East, Final document, part I, NPT/CONF.1995/32 (Part I), June 1995, annex.

[7] 10th NPT review conference, Chairs' working papers, Main Committee I, NPT/CONF.2020/MC.I/WP.1, 22 Aug. 2022; Main Committee II, NPT/CONF.2020/MC.II/WP.1, 22 Aug. 2022; and Main Committee III, NPT/CONF.2020/MC.III/WP.1, 22 Aug. 2022.

[8] 10th NPT review conference, 'Draft final document', NPT/CONF.2020/CRP.1, 22 Aug. 2022.

[9] Mukhatzhanova, G., '10th NPT review conference: Why it was doomed and how it almost succeeded', *Arms Control Today*, vol. 52, no. 8 (Oct. 2022).

[10] Zlauvinen, G., in 'Webinar: The NPT review conference', Konrad Adenauer Foundation, 9 Sep. 2022.

discussions—which took place at the Mission of Finland—extended the trend of closed-door presidential consultations from the 2015 review conference; they were again criticized by some for their non-inclusive and non-transparent nature.[11] Other small groups were formed to negotiate issues of particular importance and sensitivity. Meanwhile, consultations on text on the peaceful uses of nuclear energy continued under the chair of Main Committee III. The draft outcome document would be revised twice as a result of these parallel tracks, with the third version presented on the penultimate day of the conference.[12]

Selected issues

Even prior to the Russian invasion of Ukraine, expectations about the outcome of the 10th review conference were muted among states parties given the outcome of the previous review conference, in 2015, and subsequent worsening of the geopolitical context and the nuclear landscape. That the conference continued to the eleventh hour and nearly reached consensus on a substantive outcome—resulting in what has been referred to as 'consensus minus one'—reflects the work that the parties put in over the course of the four weeks in New York. It also indicates that the third draft of the final outcome document was a compromise text that nearly all states parties were willing to come to terms with, including on issues that have been obstacles at past review conferences or had been expected to be obstacles at this conference.

The 1995 Middle East resolution

The failure in 2015 of NPT states parties to reach a substantive conclusion was largely attributed to the discussion around the establishment of a zone free of weapons of mass destruction (WMD) in the Middle East.[13] Agreement to pursue this issue had been part of a package that led to the indefinite extension of the NPT at its 1995 Review and Extension Conference.[14] In contrast to 2015, the text on the Middle East in the draft final outcome document of the 10th review conference seemed amenable to the states parties. Some

---

[11] Rauf, T., 'The 2015 Non-Proliferation Treaty review conference', *SIPRI Yearbook 2016*, p. 698; and 10th NPT review conference, Summary record of the 13th meeting, NPT/CONF.2020/SR.13, 30 Sep. 2022, paras 113, 152.

[12] 10th NPT review conference, 'Draft final document', NPT/CONF.2020/CRP.1/Rev.2, 25 Aug. 2022.

[13] Wan, W., 'Why the 2015 NPT review conference fell apart', United Nations University, Centre for Policy Research, 28 May 2015.

[14] 1995 NPT Review and Extension Conference, Resolution on the Middle East (note 6).

observers suggested that this was facilitated by consultations between Egypt and the United States.[15]

The text underlined the 'essential' nature of the 1995 Resolution on the Middle East and reaffirmed support for its implementation.[16] It also reflected developments in two sessions of the Conference on the Establishment of a Middle East Zone Free of Nuclear Weapons and Other Weapons of Mass Destruction, convened in November 2019 and November 2021.[17] Some analysts suggested that the positive outcome at those sessions—convened despite the opposition of Israel and the USA and without their participation—helped to ease the pressure of the zone issue at the review conference.[18] A third session was held in November 2022 and a fourth is scheduled for November 2023.

At the same time, the text did not assuage all concerns: Lebanon preferred 'a stronger commitment' to establishing the zone, Syria found the text 'weak' as it did not specify obligations for Israel, and Iran expressed its displeasure about its lack of participation in the small-group consultation and drafting process.[19] Yet no state appeared ready to block consensus because of the issue. In the final plenary meeting, Egypt—which the USA had blamed for the outcome at the 2015 conference—observed that it 'would accept the text . . . as the minimum basis for collective efforts to implement the 1995 resolution'.[20]

AUKUS and naval nuclear propulsion

The 2021 trilateral security pact between Australia, the United Kingdom and the United States (AUKUS) lays the groundwork for the transfer of naval nuclear propulsion technology, including naval reactors and, potentially, highly enriched uranium (HEU) as fuel.[21] Any transfer of HEU would, in effect, bypass application of the controls under Australia's Comprehensive Safeguards Agreement with the International Atomic Energy Agency

---

[15] Batsanov, S., Chernavskikh, V. and Khlopkov, A., '10th NPT review conference: The nonproliferation and peaceful uses of nuclear energy pillars', *Arms Control Today*, vol. 52, no. 8 (Oct. 2022).

[16] 10th NPT review conference, NPT/CONF.2020/CRP.1/Rev.2 (note 12), para. 166.

[17] Kile and Erästö (note 3), pp. 433–34; and Erästö, T. and Fedchenko, V., 'Multilateral nuclear arms control, disarmament and non-proliferation treaties and initiatives', *SIPRI Yearbook 2022*, pp. 464–65.

[18] Bino, T., 'A Middle Eastern WMD-Free Zone: Are we any closer now?', *Arms Control Today*, vol. 20, no. 7 (Sep. 2020).

[19] 10th NPT review conference, NPT/CONF.2020/SR.13 (note 11), paras 52, 112, 152.

[20] 10th NPT review conference, Main Committee II, Summary record of the 11th meeting, NPT/CONF.2020/MC.II/SR.11, 25 Oct. 2022, para. 90; and 2015 NPT review conference, Remarks by R. Gottemoeller, Under secretary of state for arms control and international security, US Department of State, 22 May 2015.

[21] On the AUKUS agreement see Tian, N. et al., 'Regional developments in military expenditure, 2021', *SIPRI Yearbook 2022*, pp. 275–76; and Wezeman, S. T., Kuimova, A. and Wezeman, P. D., 'Developments among the recipients of major arms, 2017–21', *SIPRI Yearbook 2022*, pp. 325–26.

(IAEA).²² This is permitted under a so-called loophole that exempts a non-nuclear weapon state's nuclear material from safeguards when it is used in a 'non-proscribed military activity', such as propulsion.²³

The challenge posed by naval propulsion to the NPT has been previously identified. However, the involvement of two nuclear weapon states in AUKUS led some NPT states parties to decry the double standard and underline the negative implications for the regime, with concerns that it could create a new precedent. At the review conference, China characterized the agreement as a 'flagrant violation of the object and purpose of the NPT' and proposed text for the report of Main Committee II on a special committee to deliberate on the transfer of naval nuclear propulsion reactors and HEU.²⁴ Other states raised similar concerns about the need to tighten this aspect of verification and monitoring.²⁵

Despite the strongly held views on the topic, the work of the committee and subsequent small-group negotiation managed to produce agreeable text for the draft final outcome document. The text notes in three concise but broad sentences only that the topic of naval nuclear propulsion 'is of interest' to states parties, the importance of 'transparent and open dialogue' on the topic, and that non-nuclear weapon states pursuing this 'should engage with the IAEA in an open and transparent manner'.²⁶

The Treaty on the Prohibition of Nuclear Weapons

After the adoption of the Treaty on the Prohibition of Nuclear Weapons (TPNW) in 2017, the five permanent members of the UN Security Council (P5) and the North Atlantic Treaty Organization (NATO) had separately issued statements that claimed the TPNW 'contradicts, and risks undermining, the NPT' and 'is at odds with the existing non-proliferation and disarmament architecture'.²⁷ Following the TPNW's entry into force in January

---

²² Agreement between Australia and the International Atomic Energy Agency for the Application of Safeguards in Connection with the Treaty on the Non-Proliferation of Nuclear Weapons, entered into force 10 July 1974, IAEA INFCIRC/217; and Additional Protocol, entered into force 12 Dec. 1997, IAEA INFCIRC/217/Add.1.

²³ Carlson, J., 'Verification of nuclear material in non-proscribed military use by a state with a comprehensive safeguards agreement: Legal and related aspects', Vienna Center for Disarmament and Non-Proliferation (VCDNP), 15 Feb. 2022.

²⁴ 10th NPT review conference, Statement by Li Song, Deputy head of Chinese delegation, on nuclear non-proliferation, 10 Aug. 2022.

²⁵ 10th NPT review conference, 'Nuclear naval propulsion', Working paper submitted by Indonesia, NPT/CONF.2020/WP.67, 25 July 2022; and 10th NPT review conference, Summary record of the 3rd meeting, NPT/CONF.2020/SR.3, 7 Sep. 2022.

²⁶ 10th NPT review conference, NPT/CONF.2020/CRP.1/Rev.2 (note 12), para. 36.

²⁷ Five permanent members of the UN Security Council, Joint statement on the Treaty on the Non-Proliferation of Nuclear Weapons, 24 Oct. 2018; and NATO, North Atlantic Council, Statement on the Treaty on the Prohibition of Nuclear Weapons, 20 Sep. 2017.

2021, there had thus been concern that the new treaty could be a divisive issue at the NPT review conference.[28]

The convening of the first TPNW meeting of states parties (MSP) in June 2022 in Vienna and its adoption of two outcome documents (see section III) appeared as relevant developments in the context of discussions in Main Committee I. Austria, Ireland, Kazakhstan and Mexico submitted a working paper to the 10th review conference exploring the compatibility and complementarity of the TPNW with the NPT.[29] They also sought to include specific language in the outcome document that recognized these aspects, including in the context of implementing Article VI of the NPT (on the obligation to pursue negotiations on nuclear disarmament).[30] But this was not a red line for them.

The draft final outcome document included only a factual acknowledgment of the TPNW and its first MSP, which came despite initial resistance from France. The text did reiterate 'deep concern at the catastrophic humanitarian consequences of the use of nuclear weapons'—language that echoed the outcome document of the 2010 review conference, which had constituted the building blocks of the series of conferences on humanitarian consequences that led to the TPNW.[31] The draft also further cited humanitarian consequences in committing states parties to raise awareness of disarmament and non-proliferation issues among the public, to refrain from inflammatory rhetoric concerning the use of nuclear weapons, and to take further steps to identify, explore and implement risk-reduction measures.[32]

Nuclear risk reduction and disarmament

Risk reduction featured throughout the review cycle and at the review conference, underlining the sense of urgency in addressing the heightened possibility of nuclear weapon use. While the discussion around the topic has been largely constructive, many states have expressed misgivings that the increased focus on risk reduction was a distraction from the nuclear weapon states' lack of progress in nuclear disarmament.[33]

---

[28] For a summary and other details of the TPNW see annex A, section I, in this volume.

[29] 10th NPT review conference, 'Complementarity of the Treaty on the Prohibition of Nuclear Weapons with the existing disarmament and non-proliferation regime', Working paper submitted by Austria, Ireland, Kazakhstan and Mexico, NPT/CONF.2020/WP.76, 26 Aug. 2022.

[30] 10th NPT review conference, NPT/CONF.2020/WP.76 (note 29), paras 34–36.

[31] 10th NPT review conference, NPT/CONF.2020/CRP.1/Rev.2 (note 12), para. 124; 2010 NPT review conference, Final Document, NPT/CONF.2010/50 (Vol. I), May 2010, part I, para. 80 and Conclusions I(A)(v); and Kile, S. N., 'Treaty on the Prohibition of Nuclear Weapons', *SIPRI Yearbook 2018*, pp. 307–11.

[32] 10th NPT review conference, NPT/CONF.2020/CRP.1/Rev.2 (note 12), paras 37–40.

[33] E.g. Mishra, S., 'The nuclear risk reduction approach: A useful path forward for crisis mitigation', Asia-Pacific Leadership Network for Nuclear Non-proliferation and Disarmament (APLN), 27 Jan. 2023.

In recognition of these concerns, the draft final outcome document specifically reaffirmed that 'nuclear risk reduction is neither a substitute nor a prerequisite for nuclear disarmament'.[34] It would also have committed nuclear weapon states to make concrete progress on action 5 of the 2010 Action Plan and to take steps to mitigate the risks of miscalculation, misperception, miscommunication or accident.[35] The document then details a series of measures for those states to pursue, including regular dialogue on nuclear doctrines, development of crisis-prevention and management arrangements, mechanisms and tools, and maintenance of practices de-targeting nuclear weapons and keeping them at the lowest possible alert levels—with the added call to report on these activities at future preparatory committees and the next review conference.

In contrast, there was little in the way of tangible measures on the nuclear disarmament that is prescribed in Article VI of the NPT. While the draft final outcome document reaffirms the validity of disarmament commitments adopted at the 2000 and 2010 review conferences, some delegates viewed the language on these as having been weakened and expressed concern about the discussion around these commitments.[36] The states in the Non-Aligned Movement (NAM) called for greater accountability in the NPT's disarmament pillar through 'concrete, measurable, timebound actions'.[37] Similarly, the states of the New Agenda Coalition lamented the lack of benchmarking, which could help in 'maintaining the credibility of the regime'.[38] The only tangible measures included in the draft final outcome document centred on Russia and the USA committing to pursue negotiations 'in good faith' on a successor framework to New START (see section I).[39]

Issues of risk reduction and disarmament had come up earlier in 2022 in the context of a joint statement on 'Preventing nuclear war and avoiding arms races' issued on 3 January by the leaders of the P5—China, France, Russia, the UK and the USA—which are also the five NPT-recognized nuclear weapon states.[40] The leaders' joint statement echoed the 1985 declaration of US President Ronald Reagan and the Soviet leader, Mikhail Gorbachev, that

---

[34] 10th NPT review conference, NPT/CONF.2020/CRP.1/Rev.2 (note 12), para. 36.

[35] 10th NPT review conference, NPT/CONF.2020/CRP.1/Rev.2 (note 12), para. 37. On the 64-step action plan see 2010 NPT review conference', NPT/CONF.2010/50 (Vol. I) (note 31), pp. 19–29; and Kile, S. N., 'Nuclear arms control and non-proliferation', *SIPRI Yearbook 2011*, pp. 379–80.

[36] 10th NPT review conference, NPT/CONF.2020/SR.13 (note 11), paras 62, 68, 123.

[37] 10th NPT review conference, NPT/CONF.2020/SR.13 (note 11), para. 46. For a list of members and other details of NAM see annex B, section I, in this volume.

[38] 10th NPT review conference, NPT/CONF.2020/SR.13 (note 11), para. 62. The New Agenda Coalition consists of Brazil, Egypt, Ireland, Mexico, New Zealand and South Africa.

[39] 10th NPT review conference, NPT/CONF.2020/CRP.1/Rev.2 (note 12), para. 187.

[40] 'Joint statement of the leaders of the five nuclear-weapon states on preventing nuclear war and avoiding arms races', 3 Jan. 2022.

'a nuclear war cannot be won and must never be fought'.[41] The statement, which followed on from a December 2021 joint communique, was released during what would have been the opening days of the 10th review conference before the decision to postpone it for the fourth time. The leaders' joint statement reaffirms the importance of addressing nuclear threats and complying with bilateral and multilateral agreements, while highlighting their intent to 'continue seeking . . . diplomatic approaches to avoid military confrontations'. However, any possibility of this show of unity being followed up dissipated with the Russian invasion of Ukraine in February 2022. At the review conference, France, the UK and the USA reaffirmed the contents of the joint statement while condemning Russia's 'reckless nuclear actions'.[42] They also identified the principles and responsible practices that they adhered to as 'responsible custodians' of nuclear weapons.

Other issues

Not all the issues discussed over the course of the review conference found their way into the text of the draft final outcome document. As at previous review conferences, some states parties argued that nuclear-sharing arrangements—such as those whereby US nuclear weapons are deployed on the territory of its NATO allies such as Germany—run 'against the letter and the spirit of the NPT'.[43] To the surprise of some, China vociferously shared that position at the 10th review conference. It called on non-nuclear weapon states to 'stop instigating' nuclear deterrence arrangements and stated that it 'would not stand idly by' if any attempt were made to replicate nuclear sharing in the Asia-Pacific.[44]

Germany, along with a NATO representative (an observer at the conference), rejected these arguments, observing that these arrangements were 'fully consistent and compliant' with the NPT and 'seamlessly integrated' into it.[45] Separately, Lithuania condemned Belarus's public statements 'expressing its readiness to host Russian nuclear weapons' in relation to the war in Ukraine as Romania expressed concern about the 'change in [Belarus']

[41] Joint Soviet–US statement, Summit meeting, Geneva, 21 Nov. 1985; the P5 statement expanded on the Russian–US presidential joint statement on strategic stability, 16 June 2021; and the Joint Chinese–Russian statement on the 20th anniversary of the Chinese–Russian Treaty of Good Neighbourliness and Friendly Cooperation, 28 June 2021.
[42] 10th NPT review conference, 'Principles and responsible practices for nuclear weapon states', Working paper submitted by France, the United Kingdom and the United States, NPT/CONF.2020/WP.70, 29 July 2022, para. 1.
[43] E.g. 10th NPT review conference, Main Committee I, Statement by Malaysia, 4 Aug. 2022, para. 5.
[44] 10th NPT review conference, Summary record of the 4th meeting, NPT/CONF.2020/SR.4, 7 Sep. 2022, para. 10; and 10th NPT review conference, Summary record of the 7th meeting, NPT/CONF.2020/SR.7, 9 Sep. 2022, para. 80.
[45] 10th NPT review conference, NPT/CONF.2020/SR.7 (note 44), paras 55, 70.

non-nuclear status'.[46] For its part, Belarus called accusations of NPT non-compliance 'unfounded'.[47]

While China, Russia and other states called for a thorough discussion of nuclear-sharing arrangements, including ways to increase transparency around them, the draft final outcome document lacked any mention of the issue.

On other issues, the absence of text itself represented compromise among states parties. Some analysts identified red lines for nuclear weapon states that led to the removal of any mention on a moratorium on the production of fissile materials (a purported red line for China), on unconditional negative security assurances (i.e. a guarantee by a state with nuclear arms that it will never use them against a non-nuclear-armed state; a red line for the UK), and on discussions of no-first-use policies (a red line for France).[48]

The impact of the Russian invasion of Ukraine

Despite these and other issues of contention, it appeared that nearly all states parties were willing to make compromises on the final text if it meant achieving consensus on a substantive outcome. Yet, in the final plenary session, Russia observed that there was widespread dissatisfaction with the substantive content of the draft outcome document.[49] Although there was some hesitation—Austria and the Philippines referred to their disappointment with the contents of the draft, in particular on the NPT's disarmament pillar, and the New Agenda Coalition noted that it would have joined the consensus only 'reluctantly'—no other state raised objections to the text or indicated that it would have blocked consensus.[50] Others remarked that Russia alone had prevented the adoption of an outcome document. Reaching consensus had been seen as being of the utmost importance and a necessary show of support for the treaty and non-proliferation regime in the challenging security environment.

Ultimately, the lack of consensus on a substantive outcome document or recommendations seemed to have little to do with issues that have hindered past review conferences. The conference president observed that Russia raised its objections only on the final day of the conference, to text that Russia described as 'blatantly political'.[51] Zlauvinen noted that the amendments

---

[46] 10th NPT review conference, Summary record of the 6th meeting, NPT/CONF.2020/SR.6, 19 Sep. 2022, para. 88; and 10th NPT review conference, Summary record of the 2nd meeting, NPT/CONF.2020/SR.2, 7 Sep. 2022, para. 20.

[47] 10th NPT review conference, NPT/CONF.2020/SR.6 (note 46), para. 46.

[48] Jaramillo, C., 'Death by a thousand red lines: The colossal failure of the 10th NPT review conference', Ploughshares, 1 Sep. 2022.

[49] 10th NPT review conference, NPT/CONF.2020/SR.13 (note 11), para. 25.

[50] 10th NPT review conference, NPT/CONF.2020/SR.13 (note 11), paras 59, 88, 130.

[51] 10th NPT review conference, NPT/CONF.2020/SR.13 (note 11), para. 25.

that Russia suggested—in particular about the description of the situation of Ukrainian nuclear facilities under its control in relation to the Russian invasion as well as on the 1994 Budapest Memorandum on the security assurance offered to Ukraine when the latter decided to return Soviet nuclear weapons stationed on its territory and accede to the NPT as a non-nuclear weapon state—were not accepted by other states.[52]

Indeed, the Russian invasion of Ukraine in February 2022 factored heavily into the context in which the review conference took place. The USA accused Russia of undermining all three pillars of the NPT, and Germany observed the 'immediate repercussions' for the non-proliferation regime.[53] A joint statement on behalf of 55 states and the European Union condemned Russia's 'illegal war of aggression' against Ukraine and accused Russia of acting in breach of the security assurances it had offered to Ukraine in 1994.[54] It further noted that Russia had deprived Ukraine of control over its civilian nuclear facilities, thereby disrupting the state's ability to exercise its inalienable right to develop, research, produce and use nuclear energy for peaceful purposes. The statement also observed that the Russian seizure of nuclear facilities had undermined the implementation of IAEA safeguards agreements with Ukraine.

Beyond the plenary meetings, the seven pillars of nuclear safety and security—outlined in March 2022 by the IAEA director general, Rafael Grossi, in response to the situation in Ukraine's nuclear facilities—were a consistent theme of discussions at the review conference.[55] In the third week of the review conference, Russia and Ukraine traded accusations about shelling near the Zaporizhzhia Nuclear Power Plant, which resulted in Ukraine fully disconnecting two of the plant's functioning reactors from the power grid.[56]

---

[52] Zlauvinen, G., President of 10th NPT review conference, Press briefing, 26 Aug. 2022; and Memorandum on Security Assurances in Connection with Ukraine's Accession to the Treaty on the Non-Proliferation of Nuclear Weapons (Budapest Memorandum), signed and entered into force 5 Dec. 1994, *United Nations Treaty Series*, vol. 3007 (2014). On the effect of the war on nuclear facilities in Ukraine see section V of this chapter.

[53] 10th NPT review conference, NPT/CONF.2020/SR.13 (note 11), paras 95, 140.

[54] 10th NPT review conference, Statement by France on behalf of 55 states and the European Union, 26 Aug. 2022; and 1994 Budapest Memorandum (note 52).

[55] Grossi, R. M., IAEA director general, Introductory statement to the IAEA Board of Governors, 2 Mar. 2022. On the discussion at the review conference see e.g. 10th NPT review conference, 'Recognizing the IAEA's seven pillars in the context of Article IV of the Treaty on the Non-Proliferation of Nuclear Weapons', Working paper submitted by Australia, Canada, Colombia, Finland, France, Ireland, Japan, the Netherlands, Norway, Slovenia, Spain, Sweden, Switzerland and the USA, NPT/CONF.2020/WP.69, 29 July 2022. See also Fedchenko, V., 'Nuclear security during armed conflict: Lessons from Ukraine', SIPRI Research Policy Paper, Mar. 2023; Fedchenko, V. et al., 'Nuclear security in Ukraine and the Black Sea region: New threats, new risks, new consequences', SIPRI Research Policy Paper, Mar. 2023; and section V of this chapter.

[56] Balmforth, T. and Hunder, M., 'Zelenskiy says danger remains after nuclear plant resumes power supply', Reuters, 26 Aug. 2022. On the IAEA support and assistance mission to Zaporizhzhia see section V of this chapter.

Outlook

Some states parties have suggested that the work done on key issues at the 10th review conference of the Non-Proliferation Treaty could inform the work of the next review cycle.[57] For example, the elevation of gender in the discussion, including with a commitment in the draft final outcome document to 'further integrate a gender perspective in all aspects of nuclear disarmament and non-proliferation decision-making processes', provides space for potential follow-up.[58]

Moreover, there is little time to linger on the inability to reach consensus on substantive conclusions or recommendations at the 10th review conference. At the final plenary meeting the states decided to abbreviate the next review cycle from its customary five-year span to four years to compensate for the two-and-a-half-year extension of the last cycle connected to the Covid-19 pandemic, and with a view to eventually resetting the five-year cycle in 2030.[59] The 11th review conference will thus be held in 2026 and, consequently, there will be no two-year pause before the preparatory committee for the review conference meets. The first of its three sessions will take place in Vienna in 2023.

The conference president also secured agreement to establish a working group on further strengthening the NPT's review process.[60] The group is open to all interested states parties and will operate according to the rules of procedure of the 10th review conference—including agreement on substantive matters by means of consensus. Tasked to make recommendations 'on measures that would improve the effectiveness, efficiency, transparency, accountability, coordination and continuity of the review process', it will convene prior to the first meeting of the preparatory committee, in 2023, and provide recommendations to that meeting.

Nevertheless, in the aftermath of a second consecutive review conference without agreement on substantive conclusions, increasing frustration is being felt by states parties about the lack of progress being made across the three pillars and the grand bargain that together comprise the NPT. In particular, this frustration focuses on the failure to further reduce nuclear weapon inventories and the ongoing conflict involving Russia—one of the three NPT depository states—against a non-nuclear weapon state. It is clear that the NPT's review process is only one of the many contentious issues that plague the cornerstone of the international non-proliferation regime.

---

[57] 10th NPT review conference, NPT/CONF.2020/SR.13 (note 11), paras 72, 145, 173.
[58] 10th NPT review conference, NPT/CONF.2020/CRP.1/Rev.2 (note 12), para. 41.
[59] 10th NPT review conference, 'Decision on the next review cycle', NPT/CONF.2020/DEC.2, 26 Aug. 2022; and 10th NPT review conference, Final document, NPT/CONF.2020/66 (Part I), Aug. 2022, para. 23.
[60] 10th NPT review conference, NPT/CONF.2020/DEC.2 (note 59), para. c.

III. The first meeting of states parties to the Treaty on the Prohibition of Nuclear Weapons

TYTTI ERÄSTÖ

The 2017 Treaty on the Prohibition of Nuclear Weapons (TPNW) is the first multilateral treaty to comprehensively ban nuclear weapons, including their development, deployment, possession, use and threat of use.[1] Having entered into force on 22 January 2021, the treaty required the United Nations secretary-general to convene a meeting of states parties (MSP) within one year.[2] The first MSP (1MSP) was thus initially to take place in January 2022, but it was twice postponed beyond the one-year deadline due to the Covid-19 pandemic and to avoid overlap with other major meetings.[3] The meeting was eventually held on 21–23 June 2022 in Vienna.

Reflective of careful preparations and unity among TPNW states parties, 1MSP took decisions on several issues and unanimously adopted two outcome documents—a political declaration and an action plan. After a brief discussion of the lead-up to the meeting, this section reviews those two documents and other decisions of the meeting before surveying the positions on the TPNW of non-nuclear-armed states that are part of extended nuclear deterrence arrangements with the United States, sometimes called the nuclear 'umbrella'.

The lead-up to the meeting

The president-designate of the meeting was Alexander Kmentt of Austria, which had played a key role in the process leading up to the treaty negotiations in 2017. Indeed, Austria initiated the so-called 'humanitarian pledge' that paved the way for TPNW negotiations at the 2014 Conference on the Humanitarian Impact of Nuclear Weapons (HINW) in Vienna.[4] The three HINW conferences in 2013–14 built on the final consensus document of

---

[1] For a summary and other details of the TPNW, including lists of the parties and signatories, see annex A, section I, in this volume.

[2] Treaty on the Prohibition of Nuclear Weapons (note 1), Article 8. On the negotiation and entry into force see Kile, S. N., 'Treaty on the Prohibition of Nuclear Weapons', *SIPRI Yearbook 2018*, pp. 307–11; Erästö, T., 'Treaty on the Prohibition of Nuclear Weapons', *SIPRI Yearbook 2019*, 387–90; Erästö, T., Kile, S. N. and Fedchenko, V., 'Multilateral arms control, disarmament and non-proliferation treaties and initiatives', *SIPRI Yearbook 2021*, 434–43; and Erästö, T. and Fedchenko, V., 'Multilateral nuclear arms control, disarmament and non-proliferation treaties and initiatives', *SIPRI Yearbook 2022*, pp. 460–69.

[3] Kmentt, A., President-designate of TPNW 1MSP, Letter to the UN secretary-general, 10 Aug. 2021, annexed to A/75/990, 16 Aug. 2021; and United Nations, Secretary-General, Note verbale, 4 Apr. 2022. See also Erästö and Fedchenko (note 2), p. 462.

[4] Vienna Conference on the Humanitarian Impact of Nuclear Weapons, 'Humanitarian pledge', 8–9 Dec. 2014. See also e.g. Kile (note 2).

the 2010 review conference of the Non-Proliferation Treaty (NPT), which expressed 'deep concern at the catastrophic humanitarian consequences of any use of nuclear weapons'.[5] These conferences laid the foundations for the TPNW.

Austria convened a fourth HINW conference on 20 June, prior to 1MSP. This meeting included both civil society and state representatives, with a spotlight on the scientific community and survivors of nuclear weapon use and testing. While separate from 1MSP, the 2022 HINW conference provided input to the former by recalling key findings from the previous humanitarian conferences and presenting relevant new research and survivor testimonials.[6] The voices of the survivors and civil society organizations were also prominent at 1MSP, alongside several statements by countries affected by nuclear weapon testing.

By the end of 1MSP, the TPNW had been ratified by 65 states, 49 of which attended the meeting. In addition, the participants included 34 observer states, various international and non-governmental organizations, and representatives of civil society, including survivors of nuclear weapon use and testing.[7] As well as states that had signed but not yet ratified the treaty, the observers included non-signatory states, among them five states with extended nuclear deterrence arrangements with the United States.

Decisions taken at the first meeting of states parties

The treaty mandated 1MSP to set time limits related to how nuclear-armed states and states hosting nuclear weapons on their territory may join the TPNW. Article 4 states that 'each State Party that owns, possesses or controls nuclear weapons or other nuclear explosive devices shall immediately remove them from operational status, and destroy them as soon as possible but not later than a deadline to be determined by the first meeting of States Parties'.[8]

The MSP set the deadline for nuclear weapon destruction at 10 years for nuclear-armed states that join the treaty before having eliminated their nuclear arsenals. In case of 'unexpected difficulties in the disarmament process', this deadline can be extended by up to five years.[9] For states that host

---

[5] 2010 NPT review conference, Final document, vol. I, NPT/CONF.2010/50 (Vol. I), part I, para. A(v). For a summary and other details of the 1968 Treaty of the Non-Proliferation of Nuclear Weapons (NPT) see annex A, section I, in this volume.

[6] Austrian Federal Ministry for European and International Affairs (FMEIA), *The 2022 Vienna Conference on the Humanitarian Impact of Nuclear Weapons* (FMEIA: Vienna, 2022).

[7] First meeting of TPNW states parties, Report, TPNW/MSP/2022/6, 21 July 2022, paras 17–21.

[8] Treaty on the Prohibition of Nuclear Weapons (note 1), Article 4(2). The other option, provided under Article 4(1), is for a nuclear-armed state to join the treaty after the elimination of its nuclear programme.

[9] First meeting of TPNW states parties, TPNW/MSP/2022/6 (note 7), annex III, Decision 1.

the nuclear weapons of other states, the time limit for their removal was set at 90 days.[10] These decisions apparently drew on recommendations in studies published by researchers from Princeton University's Program on Science and Global Security prior to 1MSP.[11]

Although Article 4 also mandates states parties to designate a competent international authority or authorities to negotiate and verify disarmament, such designation is not required until a nuclear-armed state joins the TPNW. The states parties thus took no decision on this issue. Instead, they included relevant preparatory work as part of the action plan (see below).

In a second important set of decisions, the states parties structured intersessional work between the biennial MSPs or the sexennial review conferences in two ways. First, they appointed Ireland and Thailand as informal facilitators 'to further explore and articulate the possible areas of tangible cooperation' between the TPNW and the NPT.[12] Second, they established informal working groups related to the elimination of nuclear weapons (Article 4); victim assistance and environmental remediation (Article 6) and international cooperation and assistance (Article 7); and universalization of the treaty (Article 12).[13] During the intersessional period between 1MSP and 2MSP, Mexico and New Zealand were chosen to co-chair the group on Article 4; Kazakhstan and Kiribati to co-chair the group on articles 6 and 7, and Malaysia and South Africa to co-chair the group on Article 12. In addition, Chile was appointed as the gender focal point 'to support the implementation of the gender provisions of the Treaty and report on progress made to the second Meeting of States Parties'.[14]

1MSP also decided to establish a Scientific Advisory Group (SAG) to provide scientific and technical advice for treaty implementation.[15]

The Vienna Action Plan

The action plan adopted by 1MSP—known as the Vienna Action Plan—lists concrete steps to facilitate treaty implementation that states parties commit to take during and beyond the intersessional period between 1MSP and

---

[10] First meeting of TPNW states parties, TPNW/MSP/2022/6 (note 7).
[11] Kütt, M. and Mian, Z., 'Setting the deadline for nuclear weapon destruction under the Treaty on the Prohibition of Nuclear Weapons', *Journal for Peace and Nuclear Disarmament*, vol. 2, no. 2 (2019); and Kütt, M. and Mian, Z., 'Setting the deadline for nuclear weapon removal from host states under the Treaty on the Prohibition of Nuclear Weapons', *Journal for Peace and Nuclear Disarmament*, vol. 5, no. 1 (2022).
[12] First meeting of TPNW states parties, TPNW/MSP/2022/6 (note 7), annex III, Decision 3.
[13] First meeting of TPNW states parties, TPNW/MSP/2022/6 (note 7), annex III, Decision 4.
[14] First meeting of TPNW states parties, TPNW/MSP/2022/6 (note 7), annex III, Decision 4.
[15] First meeting of TPNW states parties, TPNW/MSP/2022/6 (note 7), annex III, Decision 2.

2MSP.[16] Like the three informal working groups, most of the 50 action points deal with TPNW articles 4, 6, 7 and 12.

As noted above, the action points relevant to Article 4 focus on preparatory work related to the designation of the competent international authority or authorities. More specifically, the Vienna Action Plan commits the states parties to undertake 'further reflection and work on developing such a mechanism', including discussions related to 'the general obligations of States Parties to the specific mandate of the international authority or authorities, and providing guidance for the designation of authorities'.[17] In addition, the states parties agreed to elaborate on the specific requirements for requests to extend the above mentioned disarmament deadlines, with input from the SAG and relevant technical agencies.[18]

The action points related to articles 6 and 7 (on victim assistance, environmental remediation, and international cooperation and assistance) include engagement with communities affected by nuclear weapon use or testing; information exchange with non-states parties that have used or tested nuclear weapons 'on their provision of assistance to affected states parties'; development of mechanisms to facilitate assistance to such states parties; and discussing 'the feasibility of . . . establishing an international trust fund for states that have been affected by the use or testing of nuclear weapons'.[19] Consideration of such a trust fund was also recommended by a working paper submitted to 1MSP by Kiribati and Kazakhstan.[20] Moreover, the Vienna Action Plan specifically tasks the affected states parties to assess the effects of nuclear weapon use or testing; to 'develop national plans for implementation of their victim assistance and environmental remediation obligations'; and to share these assessments and plans with 2MSP.[21] At the same time, others 'in a position to do so' commit themselves 'to assist those [affected] States parties with clearly demonstrated needs for external support, by contributing to the mobilization of resources and the provision of technical, material and financial assistance'.[22]

Related to Article 12, on universalization, the Vienna Action Plan commits the states parties, among other things, to urge more countries to sign and ratify the TPNW through 'ministerial or diplomatic démarches or outreach visits'; to engage in capacity building to 'clarify the steps that a prospective State party would have to undertake to implement the Treaty'; and to engage

---

[16] First meeting of TPNW states parties, TPNW/MSP/2022/6 (note 7), annex II.
[17] First meeting of TPNW states parties, TPNW/MSP/2022/6 (note 7), annex II, para. 8 and action 15.
[18] First meeting of TPNW states parties, TPNW/MSP/2022/6 (note 7), action 17.
[19] First meeting of TPNW states parties, TPNW/MSP/2022/6 (note 7), actions 19, 20, 23, 29.
[20] First meeting of TPNW states parties, 'Implementing articles 6 and 7', Working paper submitted by Kazakhstan and Kiribati, TPNW/MSP/2022/WP.5, 8 June 2022.
[21] First meeting of TPNW states parties, TPNW/MSP/2022/6 (note 7), actions 30, 31.
[22] First meeting of TPNW states parties, TPNW/MSP/2022/6 (note 7), action 32.

'with those States that for the moment remain committed to nuclear weapons and nuclear deterrence'.[23]

The declaration

The declaration of 1MSP—titled 'Our commitment to a world free of nuclear weapons'—reflects the geopolitical context marked by Russia's nuclear threats in connection with its war on Ukraine.[24] As stated in the declaration, 'we are alarmed and dismayed by threats to use nuclear weapons and increasingly strident nuclear rhetoric'.[25] Some national statements at 1MSP strongly condemned Russian nuclear threats and there was reportedly a debate behind the scenes on whether Russia should be singled out in the joint declaration.[26] However, the final declaration reflects the majority view that Russia's nuclear threats were merely one expression of the systemic problems of the international nuclear order. Thus, instead of focusing on or naming Russia, the declaration condemns 'all nuclear threats, whether they be explicit or implicit and irrespective of the circumstances', noting that

> [the use of nuclear weapons] as instruments of policy . . . highlights now more than ever the fallacy of nuclear deterrence doctrines, which are based and rely on the threat of the actual use of nuclear weapons and, hence, the risks of the destruction of countless lives, of societies, and of nations, and of inflicting global catastrophic consequences.[27]

The declaration goes on to express grave concern about the continued possession of nuclear weapons by all nine nuclear-armed states and notes that growing instability and conflict 'greatly exacerbate the risks that these weapons will be used'.[28] This contrasts starkly with, in particular, the efforts of the Western nuclear-armed states later in the year at the NPT review conference to distinguish themselves from Russia by highlighting their role as 'responsible custodians of nuclear weapons' (see section II).[29]

The declaration then argues that the TPNW is 'needed more than ever', and that states parties 'will move forward with its implementation, with the

---

[23] First meeting of TPNW states parties, TPNW/MSP/2022/6 (note 7), actions 3, 5, 15.
[24] On Russia's invasion of Ukraine see chapter 1, section V, chapter 2, section I, and chapter 12, section III, in this volume.
[25] First meeting of TPNW states parties, TPNW/MSP/2022/6 (note 7), annex I, para. 4.
[26] Davis Gibbons, R. and Herzog, S., 'The First TPNW meeting and the future of the nuclear ban treaty', *Arms Control Today*, vol. 52, no. 7 (Sep. 2022).
[27] First meeting of TPNW states parties, TPNW/MSP/2022/6 (note 7), annex I, para. 5.
[28] First meeting of TPNW states parties, TPNW/MSP/2022/6 (note 7), annex I, para. 6.
[29] 2020 NPT review conference, 'Principles and responsible practices for nuclear weapon states', Working paper submitted by France, the United Kingdom and the United States, NPT/CONF.2020/WP.70, 29 July 2022, para. 1.

aim of further stigmatizing and delegitimizing nuclear weapons and steadily building a robust global peremptory norm against them'.[30]

The positions of 'umbrella' states on the TPNW

Germany and Norway—two countries that are part of extended nuclear deterrence arrangements with the United States—had already expressed their intention to observe 1MSP in 2021.[31] To the surprise of many, three additional states with such arrangements—Australia, Belgium and the Netherlands—also announced their respective decisions to observe 1MSP shortly before the meeting.[32] The decisions of these five 'umbrella' states to observe 1MSP reflected domestic support for the TPNW. Their attendance was particularly noteworthy given the policy line of opposing the TPNW followed by the USA and the North Atlantic Treaty Organization (NATO), a position that is shared by most nuclear-armed states.[33]

In the case of Australia, this domestic support included the commitment in 2018 by the opposition Labor party to a policy of seeking TPNW membership when in government.[34] This policy was initiated by Anthony Albanese, who became prime minister in May 2022.[35] Following the change in government, Australia decided in October 2022 to abstain from voting, rather than voting against the annual UN General Assembly resolution on the TPNW.[36] This shift prompted the USA to issue a warning to its ally, arguing that the treaty 'would not allow for US extended deterrence relationships'.[37]

In contrast, Finland and Sweden—which submitted applications to join NATO in May 2022 following the renewed Russian invasion of Ukraine—voted against the UN General Assembly resolution on the TPNW for the first

---

[30] First meeting of TPNW states parties, TPNW/MSP/2022/6 (note 7), annex I, para. 8.

[31] Erästö and Fedchenko (note 2), pp. 463–64.

[32] See e.g. International Campaign to Abolish Nuclear Weapons (ICAN), 'Following parliament's vote, Netherlands will attend TPNW MSP', 18 June 2022.

[33] See e.g. North Atlantic Treaty Organization, North Atlantic Council, Statement as the Treaty on the Prohibition of Nuclear Weapons enters into force, 15 Dec. 2020; Five permanent members of the UN Security Council, Joint statement on the Treaty on the Non-Proliferation of Nuclear Weapons, 24 Oct. 2018; and United Nations, General Assembly, 'General and complete disarmament', Report of the First Committee, A/77/385, 14 Nov. 2022, para. 28. For a brief description of NATO and a list of its members (which include Belgium, Germany, the Netherlands and Norway) see annex B, section II, in this volume.

[34] International Campaign to Abolish Nuclear Weapons (ICAN) Australia, 'Australian Labor Party commits to joining nuclear ban treaty', 18 Dec. 2018. See also Australian Labor Party (ALP), *ALP National Platform* (ALP: Revesby, Mar. 2021), pp. 116–17.

[35] Albanese, A., Speech to the 48th National Conference of the Australian Labor Party, 18 Dec. 2018; and Wright, T., 'Prime Minister Albanese is a TPNW champion', International Campaign to Abolish Nuclear Weapons (ICAN) Australia, May 2021.

[36] United Nations, A/77/385 (note 33), para. 28; and UN General Assembly Resolution 77/54, 'Treaty on the Prohibition of Nuclear Weapons', adopted 7 Dec. 2022.

[37] Hurst, D., 'US warns Australia against joining treaty banning nuclear weapons', *The Guardian*, 8 Nov. 2022.

time, having previously abstained.[38] Thus, positions on the TPNW of existing and prospective US allies can be seen as an indication of domestic political shifts on the question as to whether, in the pursuit of national security, nuclear deterrence or nuclear disarmament should be prioritized.

Outlook

As noted by two observers, 'The success of the first meeting of the TPNW states-parties is difficult to deny in terms of organization and policy', even though the challenges for the treaty's core objective—nuclear disarmament— remain formidable.[39]

The main purpose of the TPNW—to strengthen the global norm against nuclear weapons and thus to generate political pressure for nuclear disarmament—might be reached even if nuclear-armed states do not join the treaty. Yet, much focus at 1MSP was directed at universalization and the provisions dealing with potential accession by a nuclear-armed state or a state hosting nuclear weapons. This work is necessary to prepare for the eventuality that a state armed with or hosting nuclear weapons will in the future decide to join the treaty. At the same time, such work and other efforts—notably those related to ensuring complementarity with the NPT— serve to counter some of the main arguments against the TPNW, which has been criticized for potentially undermining the NPT and for lacking clear verification provisions.[40]

However, perhaps the most significant short- and medium-term impact of the TPNW-implementation process launched by 1MSP will turn out to be the work to give a definite form to the treaty's provisions related to victim assistance and environmental remediation. By giving greater prominence to these issues and by mobilizing international action to address them, the TPNW is adding a new dimension to the global nuclear disarmament and non-proliferation regime. With the exception of nuclear weapon-free zone treaties—many of which include provisions banning the dumping of radioactive waste and, in the case of the Central Asian zone, a provision on the environmental rehabilitation of contaminated areas—these issues have not previously been addressed by any international legal framework.[41] The importance of articles 6 and 7 of the TPNW were also recognized by observers at 1MSP. For example, Switzerland said that turning the relevant

---

[38] United Nations, A/77/385 (note 33), para. 28; and UN General Assembly Resolution 77/54 (note 36). On the NATO applications of Finland and Sweden see chapter 1, section V, in this volume.

[39] Davis Gibbons and Herzog (note 26).

[40] E.g. First meeting of TPNW states parties, Statement by Sweden, 22 June 2022.

[41] On the 2006 Treaty of Semipalatinsk and the other nuclear weapon-free zone treaties see annex A, section II, in this volume. See also UN Office for Disarmament Affairs, 'Nuclear-weapon-free zones'; and Lovøld, M., 'Why does the Nuclear Ban Treaty matter?', International Committee of the Red Cross, 19 Jan. 2021.

obligations into action 'will need support by the widest possible group of states', suggesting that this should be a joint effort also involving states that are not party to the TPNW, as 'the humanitarian consequences should unite us all'.[42]

By the end of 2022, the number of TPNW states parties had risen to 68, in addition to which 26 states had signed but not yet ratified the treaty. The second MSP is scheduled for 27 November–1 December 2023 in New York.[43] As suggested by the Action Plan, 2MSP and the preparatory work preceding it can be expected to take forward the operationalization of the TPNW's key provisions, further establishing the treaty and increasing its impact within, and possibly also beyond, states parties.

---

[42] First meeting of TPNW states parties, 'Victim assistance and environmental remediation', Statement by Switzerland, 22 June 2022.

[43] First meeting of TPNW states parties, TPNW/MSP/2022/6 (note 7), paras 11, 23.

IV. The Joint Comprehensive Plan of Action on Iran's nuclear programme

TYTTI ERÄSTÖ

The talks with Iran that had started in Vienna in April 2021 with the aim of reviving the Joint Comprehensive Plan of Action (JCPOA) continued in 2022, without leading to a solution. They took place against the backdrop of—and were complicated by—an investigation into Iran's past nuclear activities, a government crackdown on protests in the country and its military support to Russia in the war in Ukraine.[1]

The JCPOA was concluded in 2015 by Iran on one side and, on the other, the European Union (EU) and three European states—France, Germany and the United Kingdom—and China, Russia and the United States.[2] The agreement—which was endorsed by the United Nations Security Council—sought to end a crisis that had begun in the early 2000s and escalated over a dispute over Iran's right to uranium enrichment. The JCPOA was based on a compromise whereby Iran accepted limits on and strict monitoring of its proliferation-sensitive activities in return for the lifting of international sanctions on its nuclear programme. However, in May 2018 the US administration of President Donald J. Trump ceased to implement the agreement and imposed unilateral sanctions which, despite not being accepted by other JCPOA parties, effectively constrained their ability to lift sanctions and left Iran practically cut off from the global financial system. This prompted Iran to gradually reduce its own adherence to JCPOA commitments from May 2019. After having ceased to observe all the JCPOA's key operational limits by 2020, Iran stepped up its nuclear activities by raising the level of enrichment of the isotope uranium-235 and by increasing its enrichment capacity with the instalment of advanced centrifuges.[3]

This section reviews developments related to the JCPOA and Iran's nuclear programme in 2022, including the diplomatic process aimed at restoring the agreement and reports on JCPOA implementation in Iran by the International Atomic Energy Agency (IAEA). It then describes the IAEA's investigation into Iran's past nuclear activities, which created additional challenges for diplomatic engagement.

---

[1] On Iran's involvement in the war in Ukraine see chapter 2, section I, in this volume.

[2] Joint Comprehensive Plan of Action (JCPOA), 14 July 2015, reproduced as annex A of UN Security Council Resolution 2231, 20 July 2015.

[3] On the agreement and its implementation see Erästö, T., 'The Joint Comprehensive Plan of Action on Iran's nuclear programme', *SIPRI Yearbook 2022*, pp. 449–59; and sections in the 2016–21 editions of the SIPRI Yearbook.

Diplomatic efforts to revive the JCPOA

Following seven rounds of talks to restore the JCPOA in 2021, the eighth round—which had started in late December 2021—continued in Vienna in January 2022. As before, Iran would only interact with the United States indirectly through EU mediation, which complicated the diplomatic process between the two main negotiation parties.

The first quarter of the year was marked by a heightened sense of urgency and anticipation of an agreement; for example, in February the EU high representative for foreign affairs and security policy, Josep Borrell, said that 'The moment has come to make an ultimate effort and reach a compromise', while a US spokesperson argued that Iran and the USA were 'potentially within days' of reaching an agreement 'If Iran shows seriousness'.[4] The Vienna talks temporarily seemed derailed by Russia's attempt to link restoration of the JCPOA to an exemption from the Western sanctions imposed on Russia following its February 2022 invasion of Ukraine. However, the issue was settled in March with Russia specifying that its demand related only to nuclear cooperation under the JCPOA and the USA assuring Russia that this would not be affected by US sanctions.[5] Reportedly, by mid March the negotiators had produced a 27-page draft agreement outlining the steps that Iran and the USA would need to take to return to the JCPOA and how to verify those steps.[6]

However, a final agreement remained elusive. There remained long-standing differences related to the scope of sanctions relief and Iran's demand for guarantees against a future US withdrawal from the agreement. In early March the negotiations were further complicated by Iranian demands that the USA lift its designation of the Islamic Revolutionary Guard Corps (IRGC) as a Foreign Terrorist Organization and that the IAEA drop its claims related to the investigation to its past nuclear activities (see below).[7] In the months that followed, the demand to lift the IRGC designation—which would have been politically difficult for the US administration due to bipartisan domestic opposition to such a move—seemed to have become the key obstacle to a diplomatic solution.[8] In May the EU sought to mediate on the issue, sending

---

[4] Borrell, J. (@JosepBorrellF), Twitter, 14 Feb. 2022, <https://twitter.com/josepborrellf/status/1493284524146503684>; and Price, N., Press briefing, US Department of State, 23 Feb. 2022.

[5] Slavin, B., 'Will domestic politics trump nonproliferation in stalled Iran deal?', *Arms Control Today*, vol. 52, no. 5 (June 2022); and Hickey, S. M., 'Restored Iran deal may be in reach', *Arms Control Today*, vol. 52, no. 3 (Apr. 2022).

[6] Slavin (note 5).

[7] Motamedi, M., 'Iran, IAEA hold talks as nuclear negotiations near finish line', Al Jazeera, 5 Mar. 2022. The IRGC (and its Quds Force) were designated as a Foreign Terrorist Organization by the US State Department in Apr. 2019. US Department of State, 'Designation of the Islamic Revolutionary Guard Corps', Fact sheet, 8 Apr. 2019.

[8] Ward, A. and Toosi, N., 'Biden made final decision to keep Iran's IRGC on terrorist list', Politico, 24 May 2022.

its lead negotiator, Enrique Mora, to Tehran to convey that the USA 'might be willing to discuss the IRGC sanctions issue after the deal is restored', even though it would 'not take unilateral action to lift the designation as part of the package to restore the JCPOA'.[9]

After three months of diplomatic stalemate, on 28–29 June indirect talks between Iran and the USA resumed in Doha, without results.[10] Following another meeting in Vienna on 8 August, Borrell circulated what he referred to as a 'final text' of the agreement to restore the JCPOA, appealing to Iran and the USA to respond positively.[11] The draft reportedly also included a reference to the Iranian demand related to the ongoing IAEA investigation of its past nuclear activities, saying that 'Iran will respond to the agency's inquiries with the intent of clarifying the IAEA questions, and when the IAEA is satisfied with the Iranian responses, the parties to the JCPOA will encourage the [IAEA] board of governors to close the investigation'.[12] Moreover, the draft proposed that the investigation be closed within two months.[13] While US statements suggest that the USA would have accepted the draft, Iran's additional demands in late August—which reportedly included closing the investigation even sooner and preventing any new investigations to its past nuclear activities—seemed to signal an end to the diplomatic momentum.[14] No more negotiations to restore the JCPOA were held in the remainder of the year.

In addition to the diplomatic deadlock over the terms of restoring the JCPOA, the political environment for diplomacy was also subsequently undermined by the violent crackdown on domestic protests by Iran as well as Iran's military support for Russia in the war in Ukraine.[15] The protests started in September in response to the death of Mahsa Amini, a Kurdish Iranian woman, at the hands of the Guidance Patrol (known as the 'morality police'). The harsh response by security forces had claimed hundreds of lives by the end of the year.[16] Also by the end of the year there was mounting evidence that Iran had transferred arms to Russia, notably loitering munitions,

---

[9] Davenport, K., 'EU attempts to save Iran negotiations', Arms Control Now, 20 May 2022.

[10] Middle East Monitor, 'Report: Iran–US talks in Doha reportedly end without result', 29 June 2022.

[11] Wintour, P., 'EU team submit "final text" at talks to salvage 2015 Iran nuclear deal', *The Guardian*, 8 Aug. 2022.

[12] Davenport, K., 'Iran nuclear deal negotiations reach final stage', *Arms Control Today*, vol. 52, no. 7 (Sep. 2022).

[13] Davenport, K., 'Iran nuclear talks stall again', Arms Control Now, 28 Sep. 2022.

[14] Davenport (note 13).

[15] Fassihi, F. and Engelbrecht, C., 'Tens of thousands in Iran mourn Mahsa Amini, whose death set off protests', *New York Times*, 26 Oct. 2022; and Koshiw, I., 'Drone analysis in Ukraine suggests Iran has supplied Russia since war began', *The Guardian*, 10 Nov. 2022.

[16] Hagedorn, E., '2022 in review: Iran's protests threw another wrench into JCPOA revival', Al-Monitor, 26 Dec. 2022.

that were used to attack civilian targets in Ukraine.[17] This context created new political hurdles for the JCPOA talks, which had previously been kept separate from other issues of concern. In addition to increasing opposition in the West to any engagement with the Iranian government, the latter also accused the USA of encouraging the protests.[18]

Key developments in Iran's nuclear programme relevant to the JCPOA

Despite the lack of implementation by Iran of the key provisions of the JCPOA, in 2022 the IAEA continued to report on its verification and monitoring activities in Iran 'in light of' the resolution whereby the UN Security Council had endorsed the JCPOA.[19] As noted in the reports, however, Iran's suspension in February 2021 of additional transparency measures under the JCPOA—notably the Additional Protocol to its Comprehensive Safeguards Agreement (CSA)—had 'seriously affected' the agency's monitoring and verification activities.[20] While a CSA is based on the state's declarations of its nuclear activities and materials and their verification by the IAEA, an additional protocol expands the agency's inspection authority outside the declared facilities to allow the detection of potential clandestine activities.[21] The absence of enhanced monitoring coincided with an expansion in Iranian nuclear activities, as detailed below.

End to continuous surveillance and monitoring

On 21 February 2021 Iran and the IAEA had reached a temporary understanding that allowed the agency's monitoring equipment to continue recording information at Iranian nuclear facilities, in line with the JCPOA. However, the IAEA would only gain access to the recordings in the event of a diplomatic solution that would restore the nuclear agreement. The purpose of this arrangement—and of the subsequent agreements in May, September and December 2021 to extend it—was to ensure 'continuity of knowledge' about Iran's nuclear programme.

---

[17] E.g. Kube, C. and Lee, C. E., 'Russia is providing "unprecedented" military support to Iran in exchange for drones, officials say', NBC News, 9 Dec. 2022. On Iranian arms transfers to Russia see chapter 6, section I, in this volume.

[18] Hagedorn (note 16).

[19] UN Security Council Resolution 2231 (note 2).

[20] IAEA, Board of Governors, 'Verification and monitoring in the Islamic Republic of Iran in light of United Nations Security Council Resolution 2231 (2015)', Reports by the director general, GOV/2022/4, 3 Mar. 2022; GOV/2022/24, 30 May 2022; GOV/2022/39, 7 Sep. 2022; and GOV/2022/62, 10 Nov. 2022.

[21] IAEA, 'IAEA safeguards overview: Comprehensive safeguards agreements and additional protocols'; and Protocol Additional to the Agreement between the Islamic Republic of Iran and the International Atomic Energy Agency for the Application of Safeguards in Connection with the Treaty on the Non-Proliferation of Nuclear Weapons, signed 18 Dec. 2003, no yet in force, provisionally applied from 16 Jan. 2016, IAEA INFCIRC/214/Add.1, 4 Mar. 2016.

On 8 June 2022—in response to the adoption by the IAEA Board of Governors of a resolution that censured Iran (see below)—Iran requested that the IAEA remove all surveillance and monitoring equipment related to the JCPOA. The agency did so on 9–11 June.[22] As the IAEA warned, the move would complicate potential future efforts 'to re-establish its knowledge of Iran's nuclear-related activities'.[23] If the JCPOA were to be restored, the agency 'would need to apply additional safeguards measures and Iran would need to provide comprehensive and accurate records to the Agency'. Even then, 'considerable challenges would remain to confirm the consistency of Iran's declared inventory of centrifuges and heavy water with the situation prior to 21 February 2021'.[24]

Even after 11 June, the IAEA nevertheless continued to have regular access to all key Iranian nuclear sites under the CSA, although this no longer included daily access upon its request, as mandated by the JCPOA.[25]

Enrichment activities and the enriched uranium stockpile

To prevent Iran from obtaining highly enriched uranium (HEU), the JCPOA set a limit of 3.67 per cent on the level of the isotope uranium-235 in any enriched material until 2030. During the same period, it also confined enrichment to one location, the Fuel Enrichment Plant (FEP) at Natanz, Isfahan province. Moreover, enrichment was to be done only with IR-1 centrifuges until 2025—even though the JCPOA allowed limited research and development on certain more advanced centrifuge types and, starting from 2023, their manufacturing.[26]

Iran had breached these limits since 2019.[27] Having first enriched up to 5 per cent, in 2021 it increased the level of enrichment up to 20 per cent and then to 60 per cent. While the latter is classified as HEU, it falls short of the 90 per cent threshold at which uranium is considered suitable for manufacturing a nuclear bomb.[28] In addition, from September 2019 Iran had used advanced types of centrifuge in its enrichment activities, which, in addition to the FEP, also took place at the Pilot Fuel Enrichment Plant (PFEP) at Natanz and the Fordow Fuel Enrichment Plant (FFEP), Qom province.[29]

In 2022, Iran continued to produce enriched uranium to all of the levels mentioned above, leading to a growing stockpile over 10 times larger than the

---

[22] IAEA, GOV/2022/39 (note 20), para. 7. See also 'Iran removing 27 surveillance cameras at nuclear sites: IAEA', Al Jazeera, 9 June 2022.

[23] IAEA, GOV/2022/39 (note 20), para. 8.

[24] IAEA, GOV/2022/39 (note 20), paras 62, 8.

[25] See e.g. GOV/2022/4 (note 20), para. 13, p. 4.

[26] Joint Comprehensive Plan of Action (note 2), paras 3–5, 27.

[27] Erästö, 'Implementation of the Joint Comprehensive Plan of Action', *SIPRI Yearbook 2020*, pp. 418–26.

[28] Erästö (note 3).

[29] Erästö (note 27).

JCPOA limit of 300 kilograms; by October it had reached 3673.7 kg.[30] Of particular concern was the growing stockpile of 60 per cent enriched uranium, which reached 55.6 kg in August.[31] This was well above the IAEA definition of 'significant quantity'—that is, 'The approximate amount of nuclear material for which the possibility of manufacturing a nuclear explosive device cannot be excluded'—which in the case of HEU is 25 kg of uranium-235.[32] The situation fuelled speculation among US officials that Iran could try to 'break out' by quickly enriching the 60 per cent HEU to a weapon-grade level and then transferring it elsewhere in between IAEA inspections.[33]

Such concerns were highlighted by Iran's growing enrichment capacity resulting from the instalment and operation of greater numbers of advanced centrifuges. This increase was mandated by a law passed in December 2020 by the Iranian Parliament that had, among other things, set a target of having 1000 IR-6 centrifuges installed by early 2022.[34] That target was ultimately reached in September.[35]

In January and April Iran moved the manufacturing of centrifuge components from the TESA Karaj centrifuge complex near Tehran to two new sites in Isfahan. Apart from being a response to a reported sabotage attack against the Karaj complex in June 2021, this move seemed consistent with Iranian efforts to increase its enrichment capacity.[36]

Nuclear fuel production

Iran's decisions to significantly raise enrichment levels in 2021 were partly a response to covert operations against its nuclear programme that were suspected of having been carried out by Israel.[37] However, Iran also justified the enrichment to 20 per cent in terms of a pre-existing plan to produce advanced fuel for the Tehran Research Reactor (TRR).[38] In February 2022

---

[30] IAEA, GOV/2022/4 (note 20), para. 47; IAEA, GOV/2022/24 (note 20), para. 56; IAEA, GOV/2022/39 (note 20), para. 50; and IAEA, GOV/2022/62 (note 20), para. 52.

[31] IAEA, GOV/2022/39 (note 20), para. 51.

[32] IAEA, *IAEA Safeguards Glossary*, 2022 edn, International Nuclear Verification Series no. 3 (Rev. 1) (IAEA: Vienna, 2022), p. 30. See also Goddard, B., Solodov, A. and Fedchenko, V., 'IAEA "significant quantity" values: Time for a closer look?', *Nonproliferation Review*, vol. 23, nos 5–6 (2016).

[33] Davenport, K., 'Sanctions dispute threatens Iran deal', *Arms Control Today*, vol. 52, no. 4 (May 2022).

[34] Strategic Action Law for the Lifting of Sanctions and Protection of the Interests of the Iranian People, Iranian law approved 2 Dec. 2020, English translation by National Iranian American Council, 3 Dec. 2020.

[35] Albright, D., Burkhard, S. and Faragasso, S., 'Updated highlights of comprehensive survey of Iran's advanced centrifuges', Institute for Science and International Security, 22 Sep. 2022.

[36] 'Experts reportedly see major damage in attack on Iran centrifuge plant', Times of Israel, 5 July 2021; IAEA, GOV/2022/24 (note 20), para. 5; and Murphy, F., 'Iran moves machines for making centrifuge parts to Natanz—UN nuclear watchdog', Reuters, 6 Apr. 2022.

[37] Erästö, T., 'Implementation of the Joint Comprehensive Plan of Action on Iran's nuclear programme', *SIPRI Yearbook 2021*; and Erästö (note 3).

[38] IAEA, Board of Governors, 'Verification and monitoring in the Islamic Republic of Iran in light of United Nations Resolution 2231 (2015)', Report by the director general, GOV/INF/2021/36, 6 July 2021.

Iran informed the IAEA that it would also start using 60 per cent enriched uranium to produce fuel for the TRR.[39] The process—which included the transfer of uranium hexafluoride (UF_6) to the Fuel Plate Fabrication Plant (FPFP) at Isfahan and its conversion there into triuranium octoxide (U_3O_8) powder—would be identical to one whereby Iran was producing fuel plates containing 20 per cent enriched uranium.[40] As with the earlier process, the conversion of UF_6 to powder form—which would be harder to enrich further to weapon-grade uranium—could, in principle, reduce proliferation concerns related to the HEU stockpile.[41] In practice, however, the amount that was thus converted represented only a small fraction of the overall stockpile of 60 per cent enriched uranium, which had increased to 62.3 kg by October.[42] At the same time, most of Iran's stockpile of 60 per cent enriched uranium was kept at the FPFP—a conversion facility that contained no equipment allowing further enrichment—which could also be viewed as signalling restraint.[43]

As for the stockpile of 20 per cent-enriched uranium, most was similarly stored at the FPFP. For example according to the November report, 327 kg of the total of 386.4 kg of uranium enriched up to 20 per cent was at the FPFP, whereas about 8 per cent of it was reported as being in forms other than UF_6.[44] In addition to fuel plates using U_3O_8, these other forms included a few fuel plates containing uranium silicide, which is manufactured through a different process that includes the production of uranium metal as an intermediate product. Having produced two fuel plates using uranium silicide containing 20 per cent enriched uranium in November 2021, the IAEA verified that Iran had produced three more such plates in February.[45] As with the production of fuel plates using U_3O_8, the conversion of uranium to silicide reactor fuel could be seen as reducing the proliferation risks of the UF_6 stockpile enriched to 20 per cent—even though by the end of 2022 only a small part of it had been used to manufacture silicide fuel plates.[46] At the same time, the equipment and experience gained in the production of uranium metal could be applied

---

[39] IAEA, GOV/2022/4 (note 20), paras 31, 33.

[40] IAEA, GOV/2022/4 (note 20), paras 28, 33.

[41] Davenport (note 33); and Davenport, K., 'IAEA reports signal escalating nuclear crisis with Iran', Arms Control Now, 1 June 2022.

[42] After Mar., when Iran converted about 2 kg of uranium enriched to 60% to powder form, no such conversion was reported by IAEA reports in 2022. IAEA, Board of Governors, 'Verification and monitoring in the Islamic Republic of Iran in light of United Nations Resolution 2231 (2015)', Report by the director general, GOV/INF/2022/8, 16 Mar. 2022, para. 3; and IAEA, GOV/2022/62 (note 20), para. 53.

[43] In Nov. the IAEA reported that in Oct. it had verified a total of 53 kg of uranium in the form of UF_6 enriched up to 60% at FPFP. IAEA, GOV/2022/62 (note 20), para. 35.

[44] IAEA, GOV/2022/62 (note 20), paras 35, 53.

[45] IAEA, GOV/2022/4 (note 20), paras 27, 29.

[46] Kelley, R., 'Iran is actually reducing its weapons-usable uranium inventory', IranSource, Atlantic Council, 28 Jan. 2021.

in nuclear explosives in the future—which is why the production of uranium metal had been proscribed by the JCPOA.[47]

Activities related to heavy water and reprocessing

Under the JCPOA, Iran agreed to redesign the heavy water reactor at Arak, Markazi province (renamed the Khondab Heavy Water Production Plant (HWPP) in 2018), in order to minimize the amount of plutonium in the spent nuclear fuel produced there. Iran also agreed to keep its stock of heavy water below 130 tonnes (reduced to 90 tonnes after commissioning the reactor) and not to reprocess spent fuel from any of its nuclear reactors, with an exception for producing medical and industrial radioisotopes.[48]

While Iran's reserve of heavy water had largely remained below the agreed limit until February 2021, Iran then stopped informing the IAEA about its heavy water inventory or production. Similarly, it did not allow the agency to monitor heavy water stocks or the amount of heavy water produced at the HWPP. The IAEA's monitoring equipment nevertheless remained at the facility until June 2022.[49]

As in previous years, in 2022 the IAEA reported that Iran had neither pursued the construction of the HWPP based on its original design nor carried out reprocessing-related activities at the TRR or any other declared facility.[50]

Outstanding issues under Iran's Comprehensive Safeguards Agreement

While the issue of the so-called possible military dimensions of Iran's past nuclear activities was formally closed with the adoption of the JCPOA, the IAEA reopened the investigation with new evidence apparently provided to the agency by Israel in 2018.[51] In February 2019 the IAEA conducted a visit to a warehouse that Iran had not declared to the agency—named Location 1 in previous IAEA reports but identified in May 2022 as being in the Turquzabad district of Tehran. Environmental samples taken there contained natural uranium particles, which pointed to past uranium conversion activities.[52] The IAEA subsequently requested clarification on four locations in Iran that

---

[47] Albright D. and Burkhard, S., 'Iran's recent, irreversible nuclear advances', Institute for Science and International Security, 22 Sep. 2021.
[48] JCPOA (note 2), annex I.
[49] IAEA, GOV/2022/39 (note 20), para. 7.
[50] See e.g. GOV/2022/62 (note 20), paras 12, 14.
[51] Sanger, D. E. and Specia, M., 'Israeli leader claims Iran has "secret atomic warehouse"', *New York Times*, 27 Sep. 2018.
[52] Erästö (note 27), p. 422; and IAEA, Board of Governors, 'NPT Safeguards Agreement with the Islamic Republic of Iran', Report by the director general, GOV/2021/15, 23 Feb. 2021.

it suspected of having hosted undeclared nuclear material and activities prior to 2004.[53]

In January 2022 the IAEA reported that it had no more questions on one of the four locations, which had previously been called Location 2 and which was subsequently identified as Lavisan-Shian, in north-eastern Tehran.[54] This followed an assessment that in 2003 a metal disc had undergone drilling and chemical processing at the location. Iran had not declared these activities to the IAEA, in contravention of its CSA obligations.

Questions related to the three other locations remained outstanding. On 5 March the IAEA and Iran agreed a road map to address those issues by June.[55] However, as in previous years, in 2022 the IAEA continued to find Iran's answers related to these locations to be insufficient, whereas Iran argued that it had provided the necessary clarifications to the agency and suggested that the presence of the uranium particles at the three locations was the result of third-party sabotage.[56] The IAEA's May 2022 safeguards report concluded that,

unless and until Iran provides technically credible explanations for the presence of uranium particles of anthropogenic origin at Turquzabad, Varamin [Location 3] and 'Marivan' [Location 4] and informs the Agency of the current location(s) of the nuclear material and/or of the contaminated equipment, the Agency cannot confirm the correctness and completeness of Iran's declarations under its Comprehensive Safeguards Agreement.[57]

The May safeguards report contributed to the decision by the IAEA Board of Governors to adopt a resolution that censured Iran for its 'insufficient substantive cooperation' in addressing the outstanding safeguards issues under the CSA.[58] As noted, this triggered Iran's decision to remove IAEA surveillance and monitoring equipment from its nuclear sites. When the IAEA Board adopted a similar resolution in November, Iran responded by announcing that it had started to enrich uranium to 60 per cent purity at the underground FFEP for the first time.[59]

Based on discussions they had started in September, Iran and the IAEA agreed that that the agency would 'conduct a technical visit to Tehran before

---

[53] IAEA, GOV/2021/15 (note 52).
[54] IAEA, Board of Governors, 'NPT Safeguards Agreement with the Islamic Republic of Iran', GOV/2022/5, 5 Mar. 2022, para. 7.
[55] Hickey (note 5).
[56] Davenport (note 33).
[57] IAEA, Board of Governors, 'NPT Safeguards Agreement with the Islamic Republic of Iran', Report by the director general, GOV/2022/26, 30 May 2022, para. 36.
[58] IAEA, Board of Governors, 'NPT Safeguards Agreement with the Islamic Republic of Iran', Resolution, GOV/2022/34, 8 June 2022.
[59] IAEA, Board of Governors, 'NPT Safeguards Agreement with the Islamic Republic of Iran', Resolution, GOV/2022/70, 17 Nov. 2022; and Hafezi, P. and Murphy F., 'Iran starts enriching uranium to 60% purity at Fordow plant', Reuters, 22 Nov. 2022.

the end of November 2022 . . . on matters related to the outstanding safeguards issues'.[60] The visit took place on 18 December, but no progress was reported as having resulted from it.[61]

Looking ahead

Restoration of the JCPOA would have brought apparent gains for both Iran and the United States, including the latter's long-term objective of cutting Iran's enriched uranium stocks—and thus increasing its 'break out time'. Despite this, disagreement over seemingly secondary issues once again resulted in diplomatic opportunities being missed in 2022. This led to questions about the actual degree of political commitment on both sides to reach a solution. On the Iranian side, this commitment was arguably undermined by concerns that the USA might again leave the agreement. Meanwhile, many in the USA argued that the JCPOA had lost its previous value since some of Iran's nuclear advances, such as the know-how generated by operating advanced centrifuges, were irreversible. Thus, voices on both sides questioned the long-term benefits of reviving it.

In addition, it has become increasingly difficult to isolate the nuclear issue from other political developments—such as the Russia–Ukraine War and political repression and human rights violations inside Iran—which created further obstacles for engagement between the West and Iran. Disillusionment with the JCPOA and its promise of normalization of trade with the West has already contributed to the deepening of Iran's relationship with Russia—which might in the future also involve Russian exports of advanced weapon systems to Iran.[62]

Having said this, it is hard to see any alternative that would address the key concerns of both sides as effectively as the JCPOA could. While this realization could ultimately lead to greater flexibility and new diplomatic efforts to reduce proliferation risks, the past few years have shown that the parties are also willing to live with the status quo despite the costs and risks.

---

[60] IAEA, Board of Governors, 'NPT Safeguards Agreement with the Islamic Republic of Iran', Report by the director general, GOV/2022/63, 10 Nov. 2022, para. 7.
[61] 'UN nuclear officials leave Iran after talks, result unclear', Reuters, 19 Dec. 2022.
[62] Gramer, R., 'Iran and Russia are closer than ever before', *Foreign Policy*, 5 Jan. 2023.

V. Attacks on nuclear installations in Ukraine and the response missions of the International Atomic Energy Agency

VITALY FEDCHENKO, IRYNA MAKSYMENKO AND POLINA SINOVETS

Ukraine has 15 operable nuclear reactors at four nuclear power plants (NPP), which together generate about half of its electricity. In 2022 all four NPPs, as well as other nuclear installations, were subject to military attacks, including shelling and missile strikes, while two NPPs were occupied by Russian military forces.[1] This situation presented extraordinary nuclear safety, security and safeguards challenges for the facilities' personnel, the Ukrainian authorities and the International Atomic Energy Agency (IAEA).[2]

Attacks on nuclear facilities and other installations in the nuclear fuel cycle have occurred previously, both during military conflicts and in peacetime (see box 8.1).[3] However, the attacks on nuclear installations in Ukraine are unprecedented in many respects. Never before have large, operating nuclear power plants been attacked by shelling or missile strikes by state militaries. There has been no historical precedent for the occupation by military forces and subsequent annexation of a nuclear power plant.[4] In addition, the attacks before 2022 typically aimed to avert alleged nuclear proliferation or impede illicit weapon programmes and normally involved facilities that were not subject to the IAEA's safeguards—the technical measures by which the IAEA verifies that nuclear materials and technology are used only for peaceful purposes.

This section first reviews the extraordinary challenges faced by Ukrainian nuclear installations in 2022. It then describes the response missions and other assistance that was provided by the IAEA.

Events at Ukrainian nuclear installations in 2022

Chornobyl Nuclear Power Plant and Exclusion Zone

The Chornobyl NPP (ChNPP) site contains six reactor units. Of the six, units 1–3 have been shut down, unit 4 was partially destroyed in the nuclear

---

[1] On other aspects of the war in Ukraine see chapter 1, section V, chapter 2, section I, and chapter 12, section III, in this volume.

[2] For a brief description and list of member states of the IAEA see annex B, section I, in this volume.

[3] For definitions of nuclear facility, nuclear installation and nuclear fuel cycle see IAEA, *IAEA Nuclear Safety and Security Glossary: Terminology Used in Nuclear Safety, Nuclear Security, Radiation Protection and Emergency Preparedness and Response, 2022* (interim) edn (IAEA: Vienna, 2022), pp. 135–37.

[4] On Russia's claimed annexation in 2014 of the IR-100 research reactor and subcritical uranium–water assembly located in at the Sevastopol National University of Nuclear Energy and Industry, Crimea, see Sergeyev, Yu., Permanent representative of Ukraine, Statement at the UN General Assembly meeting on the Report of the International Atomic Energy Agency, 17 Nov. 2015.

Box 8.1. Attacks on nuclear installations prior to 2022

Attacks during armed conflict

During World War II, the Allies made multiple attempts between 1942 and 1944 to destroy the Norsk Hydro heavy water-production facility in Telemark, Norway.[a]

In 1950, as part of the strategic bombing campaign during the 1950–53 Korean War, the United States Air Force destroyed the chemical complex at Hungnam, North Korea, that was reportedly processing monazite for the Soviet nuclear programme.[b] Monazite is a naturally occurring mineral containing rare earth elements, thorium and uranium.

On 30 September 1980, during the 1980–88 Iran–Iraq War, Iranian fighter-bombers attacked the Osirak research reactor that was being built in Iraq, damaging ancillary buildings but missing the reactor itself.[c]

Between 1984 and 1988 Iraq launched seven air attacks that eventually destroyed Iran's Bushehr NPP, which was in advanced stages of construction at the time.[d]

During the 1990–91 Gulf War the USA destroyed multiple Iraqi nuclear facilities, four of which contained nuclear or other radioactive material.[e] In 2000 the US government compiled a list of four nuclear facilities in Iraq that both had nuclear or other radioactive materials on site and were damaged during the Gulf War: Tuwaitha nuclear research centre, Tarmiya uranium enrichment facility, Al Qaim superphosphate fertilizer plant and Mosul feed materials-production facility.[f]

Attacks during peacetime

In 1981 an Israeli air raid destroyed the Osirak reactor in Iraq.[g]

In 1993 the USA used cruise missiles to destroy two Iraqi nuclear installations that had not been destroyed in the Gulf War.[h]

In September 2007 an Israeli air strike destroyed a suspected undeclared nuclear facility located at al-Kibar, in eastern Syria.[i]

[a] Kreps, S. E. and Fuhrmann, M., 'Attacking the atom: Does bombing nuclear facilities affect proliferation?', *Journal of Strategic Studies*, vol. 34, no. 2 (Apr. 2011), pp. 175–76.

[b] Futrell, R. F., The United States Air Force in Korea, 1950–1953 (US Air Force, Office of Air Force History: Washington, DC, 1983), pp. 186, 190.

[c] US Director of Central Intelligence, 'National intelligence daily', 1 Oct. 1980, p. 1; and 'The ghosts that hit Osirak', *The Economist*, 18 Oct. 1980, p. 54.

[d] Spector, L. S., *Nuclear Ambitions: The Spread of Nuclear Weapons 1989–1990* (Westview Press: Boulder, CA, 1990), pp. 190, 208–209.

[e] Kreps and Fuhrmann (note a), pp. 177–78.

[f] US Defense Health Agency, 'Intelligence related to possible sources of radioactive contamination during the Persian Gulf War', July 2000.

[g] Feldman, S., 'The bombing of Osiraq—Revisited', *International Security*, vol. 7, no. 2 (fall 1982), p. 114.

[h] Kreps and Fuhrmann (note a), p. 178.

[i] Kile, S. N., 'Nuclear arms control and non-proliferation', *SIPRI Yearbook 2010*, p. 393.

accident of 26 April 1986 and is currently covered by the New Safe Confinement (NSC) shelter facility, and units 5 and 6 were never operational.[5] The site also includes two spent fuel storage facilities: the wet spent fuel storage

---

[5] On the 1986 nuclear accident see Blix, H., 'The Chernobyl reactor accident: The international significance and results', *SIPRI Yearbook 1987*, 425–32.

facility ISF-1 and the dry spent fuel storage facility ISF-2, which was opened in 2021 to replace ISF-1. In addition, there are multiple radioactive waste management and disposal facilities at the ChNPP site and in the wider Chornobyl Exclusion Zone.[6]

At 6.41 a.m. CET on 24 February 2022 the State Nuclear Regulatory Inspectorate of Ukraine (SNRIU), serving in its capacity of a national competent authority under the Convention on Early Notification of a Nuclear Accident, informed the emergency response manager at the IAEA's Incident and Emergency Centre (IEC) that 'Russian troops were at the site' of the ChNPP, and that Ukraine had imposed martial law on its territory.[7] In the evening of the same day, the SNRIU reported that, as a result of a military attack, all facilities at the ChNPP site had been taken over by the Russian military.[8]

On 25 February the SNRIU reported to the IAEA that the automated radiation-measurement systems installed at the ChNPP site indicated higher than normal levels of background radiation, which was most likely caused by 'heavy military vehicles stirring up soil still contaminated from the 1986 accident'.[9] The IAEA assessed that the readings reported by the SNRIU (of up to 9.46 microsieverts per hour) did not pose any danger to the public.[10]

Normally, the Ukrainian personnel at the ChNPP would work in regularly rotating shifts. After the Russian military took control of the site, the rotation of personnel stopped, and the work shift that began on 23 February 2022 was made to keep working for several weeks, in violation of normal plant procedures and the IAEA's nuclear safety and nuclear security guidance. Rotation of the on-site personnel was only allowed to partially resume on 21 March 2022.[11]

On 31 March 2022 the Russian forces transferred control of the ChNPP to Ukrainian personnel and retreated.[12]

During the period of occupation, the ChNPP site experienced interruptions in off-site power supply and communications with the SNRIU, and the provision of radiation-monitoring data from the site to the IAEA's International Radiation Monitoring Information System (IRMIS) was cut off. These issues were remedied after the withdrawal of the Russian forces.[13]

---

[6] IAEA, 'Nuclear safety, security and safeguards in Ukraine, 24 February–28 April 2022', Summary report by the director general, 28 Apr. 2022, p. 8.

[7] IAEA, Summary report (note 6), pp. 3, 5; and Convention on Early Notification of a Nuclear Accident, opened for signature 26 Sep. 1986, entered into force 27 Oct. 1986, IAEA INFCIRC/335, 18 Nov. 1986.

[8] State Nuclear Regulatory Inspectorate of Ukraine (SNRIU), 'Про ситуацію на Чорнобильській АЕС та стан безпеки інших ядерних установках' [On the situation at the Chornobyl NPP and the safety status of other nuclear facilities], 24 Feb. 2022; and IAEA, Summary report (note 6), p. 8.

[9] IAEA, 'Update 1—IAEA director general statement on situation in Ukraine', Press release 10/2022, 25 Feb. 2022.

[10] IAEA, 'Update 1' (note 9).

[11] IAEA, 'Update 27—IAEA director general statement on situation in Ukraine', Press release 40/2022, 20 Mar. 2022.

[12] Nuclear Energy Agency (NEA), 'Ukraine: Current status of nuclear power installations', 5 Dec. 2022.

[13] IAEA, Summary report (note 6), pp. 8–12.

Zaporizhzhia Nuclear Power Plant

Zaporizhzhia NPP (ZNPP) is home to 6 of Ukraine's 15 nuclear power reactors, with an energy capacity of nearly 6 gigawatts electric (GWe).[14] It is the largest NPP in Europe.

On 1 March 2022 the Russian Permanent Mission to the IAEA stated in an official letter to the agency that Russian military forces had taken control of the territory around the ZNPP. On the same day the SNRIU requested the IAEA 'to provide immediate assistance in coordinating activities in relation to the safety of the Chornobyl NPP and other nuclear facilities'.[15]

On 4 March 2022 Ukraine informed the IAEA that the site of the ZNPP 'had been shelled overnight', but 'a fire at the site had not affected "essential" equipment'.[16] This constituted the first ever direct military attack on a large operational nuclear power plant anywhere in the world. Five hours later Ukraine reported to the IAEA that the ZNPP site was under the control of Russian military forces, but the regular staff continued to operate the plant and no release of radioactive material had taken place.[17] By 5 March only two of the ZNPP's six reactors—units 2 and 4—were producing electricity, and the remaining four were in low-power mode, under maintenance or had been shut down.[18]

From 4 March 2022 the ZNPP was operated by regular management and staff, but under the control of Russian military forces. The shelling of the site continued throughout 2022, with both Russia and Ukraine accused each other of the shelling.[19] One consequence of this, as the IAEA was repeatedly informed by the SNRIU, was that 'the personnel at the ZNPP were working under unbelievable pressure' and the 'morale and the emotional state' of staff at the ZNPP were 'very low'.[20] Another consequence was that the last operating reactor at ZNPP was shut down on 10 September 2022.[21]

Shelling of the ZNPP site and its vicinity also led to repeated damage to various power lines connected to the site. The ZNPP's connection to off-site

---

[14] Nuclear Energy Agency (note 12).

[15] IAEA, 'Update 6—IAEA director general statement on situation in Ukraine', Press release 15/2022, 2 Mar. 2022.

[16] IAEA, 'Update 10—IAEA director general statement on situation in Ukraine', Press release 19/2022, 4 Mar. 2022.

[17] IAEA, 'Update 11—IAEA director general statement on situation in Ukraine', Press release 20/2022, 4 Mar. 2022.

[18] IAEA, 'Update 12—IAEA director general statement on situation in Ukraine', Press release 21/2022, 5 Mar. 2022.

[19] Hunder, M., 'Russia and Ukraine accuse each other in shelling around Zaporizhzhia nuclear plant', Reuters, 28 Aug. 2022; and Bigg, M. M., 'Russia and Ukraine again trade blame for shelling at the Zaporizhzhia nuclear plant', *New York Times*, 20 Nov. 2022.

[20] IAEA, 'Nuclear safety, security and safeguards in Ukraine: 28 April–5 September 2022', 2nd summary report by the director general, 6 Sep. 2022, p. 14. On the increased likelihood of human error undermining the safe and secure operation of a facility when staff work under duress see Schnieder, M. et al., *World Nuclear Industry: Status Report 2022* (Mycle Schneider Consulting: Paris, Oct. 2022), pp. 257–58.

[21] IAEA, Board of Governors, 'Nuclear safety, security and safeguards in Ukraine', Report by the director general, GOV/2022/66, 10 Nov. 2022, para. 42.

power was interrupted multiple times in 2022, triggering the emergency diesel generators.[22] Off-site power lines are necessary not only for the ZNPP to provide power into the Ukrainian electricity grid, but also to provide the plant with the power required for its safety functions. Even if a nuclear power plant were to be shut down, it needs external power and water for an extended period in order to cool down the nuclear fuel in the core and in the spent fuel pools. For example, immediately after shutdown, the nuclear fuel in a reactor of the size of those installed at the ZNPP will still be producing about 200 megawatts (MW) from decay heat.[23] The loss of off-site power or the ultimate heat sink (e.g. water from a river or an ocean) can potentially lead to consequences similar to those that took place during the Fukushima Daiichi nuclear accident in 2011.[24]

On 4 October 2022 Russian President Vladimir Putin signed laws purporting to annex the Ukrainian oblasts of Donetsk, Kherson, Luhansk and Zaporizhzhia to the Russian Federation.[25] Although the annexations were widely condemned and only recognized internationally by North Korea, this led Putin to sign a further decree designating the ZNPP as Russia's 'federal property'.[26] This action was denounced by the vast majority of United Nations member states as an illegal seizure.[27]

Hostilities around the ZNPP site continued throughout 2022, leading to further damage to its infrastructure, repeated interruptions in its electricity supply, and reported psychological and physical pressure on the plant's personnel, including torture.[28]

Other nuclear facilities and installations

The other three NPPs—Khmelnytsky, Rivne and South Ukraine—remained under Ukrainian control. As a result of Russian missile strikes on 15 and

---

[22] Nuclear Energy Agency (note 12).
[23] See Schnieder et al. (note 20), p. 245.
[24] For a definition of 'ultimate heat sink' see IAEA, *Design of the Reactor Coolant System and Associated Systems for Nuclear Power Plants, Specific Safety Guide*, IAEA Safety Standards Series no. SSG-56 (IAEA: Vienna, 2020), p. 5. On the Fukushima Daiichi accident see IAEA, *The Fukushima Daiichi Accident*, Technical vol. 1/5, Description and Context of the Accident (IAEA: Vienna, Aug. 2015), pp. 2–32.
[25] 'Ukraine updates: Putin signs law "annexing" 4 regions', Deutsche Welle, 5 Oct. 2022; and Russian Federal Constitutional Laws nos 5–8 of 2022, 4 Oct. 2022, *Rossiiskaya Gazeta*, 6 Oct. 2022.
[26] Указ № 711 «Об особенностях правового регулирования в области использования атомной энергии на территории Запорожской области» [Decree no. 711 'On the specifics of legal regulation of the use of nuclear energy in the territory of Zaporizhzhia oblast'], signed 5 Oct. 2022. See also 'Putin asserts control over Ukraine nuclear plant, Kyiv disagrees', Reuters, 5 Oct. 2022; and Shin, H., 'N. Korea backs Russia's proclaimed annexations, criticises US "double standards"', Reuters, 4 Oct. 2022. Operational and personnel issues caused by the annexation are discussed below.
[27] UN General Assembly Resolution ES-11/4, 'Territorial integrity of Ukraine: Defending the principles of the Charter of the United Nation', 12 Oct. 2022.
[28] Nuclear Energy Agency (note 12); Parkinson, J. and Hinshaw, D., '"The hole": Gruesome accounts of Russian occupation emerge from Ukrainian nuclear plant', *Wall Street Journal*, 18 Nov. 2022; and Tirone, J., 'Russia's atomic grab in Ukraine corners IAEA monitors', Bloomberg, 11 Oct. 2022.

23 November 2022, they all lost connection to the Ukrainian power grid, switching to emergency diesel generator power.[29]

The Kharkiv Institute of Physics and Technology (KIPT) hosts a subcritical neutron source installation for research and production of radioisotopes.[30] Depending on the usage scenario, it has about 40 fuel assemblies each containing 41.7 grams of low-enriched uranium.[31] On 24 February the installation was shut down as a precaution in response to the beginning of hostilities.[32] On 6 March and 25 June the installation was damaged by shelling, and the external power supply was cut off due to ongoing fighting. Despite the damage, the IAEA concluded that 'measurements showed no increase in radiation and the shelling had no significant impact on safety'.[33] On 10 November an IAEA mission to KIPT found that it had been heavily damaged by shelling but concluded that there was no indication of radioactive material release or diversion of nuclear material.[34]

The State Specialized Enterprise (SSE) 'Radon' manages radioactive waste originating from medical, industrial and research facilities in Ukraine. It has five facilities for the interim storage of such waste, located in Dnipro, Kharkiv, Kyiv, Lviv and Odesa.[35] On 26 February 2022 the SNRIU reported that the Kharkiv branch had suffered some damage due to hostilities.[36] On 27 February the Kyiv branch of SSE 'Radon' sustained minor damage due to a missile strike. In both cases, no radioactive release was reported.[37]

The IAEA response and its assistance missions to Ukraine

On 2 March 2022 the IAEA Board of Governors held a meeting to discuss the 'nuclear safety, security and safeguards implications of the conflict in Ukraine as a result of the Russian Federation's military operation that began on 24 February'.[38] In his introductory remarks the IAEA director general, Rafael Mariano Grossi, summarized the Russian military's attacks on the Ukrainian

---

[29] Nuclear Energy Agency (note 12).
[30] IAEA, Summary report (note 6), p. 16.
[31] Zhong, Z. and Gohar, Y., *Passive Safety Features Evaluation of KIPT Neutron Source Facility*, ANL-16/15 (Argonne National Laboratory: Argonne, IL, June 2016), p. 2; and Konoplev, K. A. et al., 'LEU WWR-M2 fuel qualification', Paper presented at the 24th International Meeting on Reduced Enrichment for Research and Test Reactors (RERTR), San Carlos de Bariloche, 3–8 Nov. 2002.
[32] Stone, R., 'Hero city', *Science*, vol. 378, no. 6624 (9 Dec. 2022), p. 1038.
[33] IAEA, 2nd summary report (note 20), p. 32.
[34] IAEA, 'Update 125—IAEA director general statement on situation in Ukraine', Press release 186/2022, 11 Nov. 2022.
[35] IAEA, 2nd summary report (note 20), p. 32.
[36] IAEA, 'Update 2—IAEA director general statement on situation in Ukraine', Press release 11/2022, 26 Feb. 2022.
[37] IAEA, 'Update 3—IAEA director general statement on situation in Ukraine', Press release 12/2022, 27 Feb. 2022.
[38] Grossi, R. M., IAEA director general, Introductory statement to the IAEA Board of Governors, 2 Mar. 2022.

Box 8.2. IAEA General Conference resolutions and decisions on attacks against nuclear installations, 1983–2009

The General Conference is the main policymaking organ of the International Atomic Energy Agency (IAEA). Between 1983 and 2009 it issued five policy declarations concerning attacks on nuclear installations.

9 Nov. 1983	The General Conference declared that 'all armed attacks against nuclear installations devoted to peaceful purposes should be explicitly prohibited'.[a]
27 Sep. 1985	The General Conference stated that it considered 'any armed attack on and threat against nuclear facilities devoted to peaceful purposes constitutes a violation of the principles of the United Nations Charter, international law and the Statute of the Agency'.[b]
5 Oct. 1987	The General Conference authorized the IAEA director general to assist the United Nations Conference on Disarmament in development of an international convention prohibiting armed attacks on nuclear installations.[c]
21 Sep. 1990	The General Conference 'recognized' that 'attacks or threats of attack on nuclear facilities devoted to peaceful purposes could jeopardize the development of nuclear energy', and that such attacks 'on a safeguarded nuclear facility, in operation or under construction, would create a situation in which the United Nations Security Council would have to act immediately in accordance with the provisions of the United Nations Charter'.[d]
18 Sep. 2009	The General Conference adopted a decision that referenced and essentially reconfirmed the resolutions of 1985 and 1990.[e]

[a] IAEA, General Conference, 'Protection of nuclear installations devoted to peaceful purposes against armed attacks', Resolution GC(XXVII)/RES/407, 14 Oct. 1983, para. 1.

[b] IAEA, General Conference, 'Protection of nuclear installations devoted to peaceful purposes against armed attacks', Resolution GC(XXIX)/RES/444, 27 Sep. 1985, para. 2.

[c] IAEA, General Conference, 'Protection of nuclear installations against armed attacks', Resolution GC(XXXI)/RES/475, 5 Oct. 1987, para. 2. For a brief description of the Conference on Disarmament see annex B, section I, in this volume.

[d] IAEA, General Conference, 'Prohibition of all armed attacks against nuclear installations devoted to peaceful purposes whether under construction or in operation', Resolution GC(XXXIV)/RES/533, 21 Sep. 1990, paras 1, 3.

[e] IAEA, General Conference, 'Prohibition of armed attack or threat of attack against nuclear installations, during operation or under construction', Decision GC(53)/DEC/13, 18 Sep. 2009.

---

nuclear infrastructure that had been reported to date. He noted that, despite the extraordinary circumstances, the nuclear facilities continued to operate 'normally' in a technical sense, but he emphasized that 'there is nothing normal about the circumstances under which the professionals at Ukraine's four Nuclear Power Plants are managing to keep the reactors that produce half of Ukraine's electricity working'.[39]

Grossi also reminded 'all States, without exception' about an obligation that they had agreed to in 1985, 1990 and 2009 concerning armed attacks on nuclear installations (see box 8.2). This asserts that 'any armed attack on and threat against nuclear facilities devoted to peaceful purposes constitutes a

---

[39] Grossi (note 38).

violation of the principles of the United Nations Charter, international law and the Statute of the Agency'.[40]

The 'seven indispensable pillars of nuclear safety and security'

In the same remarks on 2 March 2022, Grossi put forward what later became known as the IAEA director general's 'seven indispensable pillars of nuclear safety and security' framework. These seven principles, which were derived from the existing IAEA nuclear safety standards and nuclear security guidance documents, are as follows:

1. The physical integrity of the facilities—whether it is the reactors, fuel ponds or radioactive waste stores—must be maintained.
2. All safety and security systems and equipment must be fully functional at all times.
3. The operating staff must be able to fulfil their safety and security duties and have the capacity to make decisions free of undue pressure.
4. There must be secure off-site power supply from the grid for all nuclear sites.
5. There must be uninterrupted logistical supply chains and transportation to and from the sites.
6. There must be effective on-site and off-site radiation monitoring systems and emergency preparedness and response measures.
7. There must be reliable communications with the regulator and others.[41]

The seven pillars were widely endorsed by the international community.[42]

On 26–30 September 2022, the 66th regular session of the IAEA General Conference also considered the nuclear and radiation safety, security and safeguards situation in Ukraine at length. Its general resolutions on all three of these topics discuss attacks on nuclear installations. Both the resolution on nuclear and radiation safety and the resolution on nuclear security call upon all IAEA member states 'to be mindful of the importance of nuclear safety and security regarding peaceful nuclear facilities and materials in all circumstances'.[43] The safeguards resolution urges all member states 'to refrain from

---

[40] IAEA, General Conference, 'Protection of nuclear installations devoted to peaceful purposes against armed attacks', Resolution GC(XXIX)/RES/444, 27 Sep. 1985, para. 2.

[41] Grossi (note 38).

[42] World Nuclear Association, Statement on the IAEA framework for the safety and security of Ukraine's nuclear power plants, 10 Mar. 2022; and Joint statement on the High-level Meeting on the Safety and Security of Civil Nuclear Facilities in Armed Conflicts, US Department of State, 23 Sep. 2022. See also Fedchenko, V., 'Nuclear security during armed conflict: Lessons from Ukraine', SIPRI Research Policy Paper, Mar. 2022, section IV.

[43] IAEA, General Conference, 'Nuclear and radiation safety', Resolution GC(66)/RES/6, 30 Sep. 2022, para. 36; and IAEA, General Conference, 'Nuclear security', Resolution GC(66)/RES/7, 30 Sep. 2022, para. 26.

attacks or threats of attacks on, against or in the vicinity of nuclear facilities devoted to peaceful purposes in order to ensure that the Agency is able to conduct safeguards activities in accordance with relevant safeguards agreements'.[44]

IAEA missions to Ukraine

On 3 March 2022 the IAEA Board of Governors condemned Russia's actions in Ukraine and requested that the director general and the IAEA Secretariat continue to closely monitor the situation.[45] In response to the Russian military's capture of the ZNPP and the SNRIU's request for assistance of 1 March and to the board's resolution of 3 March, Grossi announced on 4 March his intention to travel to Ukraine to 'to secure the commitment to the safety and security of all Ukraine's nuclear power plants from the parties of the conflict in the country'.[46]

The urgency of this proposed visit was emphasized by the fact that several of the seven pillars were being violated at the ChNPP and ZNPP sites and elsewhere in Ukraine. For example, shortly after the Russian military takeover of the ZNPP, the plant personnel could not fulfil their duties without the approval of the Russian commander (in violation of pillar 3), and the Russian forces cut off almost all communication with the plant (in violation of pillar 7).[47] At the ChNPP, the staff of 211 technical and security personnel were unable to rotate from the site and effectively lived there for weeks with intermittent external electrical supply and communications with their families and the national authorities. The situation at ChNPP was in violation, at a minimum, of pillars 1, 3, 4, 5 and 7.[48] Later in the year, the IAEA Board of Governors assessed that 'all of the Director General's "seven indispensable pillars for nuclear safety and security" have been compromised' at the ZNPP.[49]

As a result, Grossi led multiple missions of technical experts to Ukraine in 2022.[50] The first took place on 29–31 March to assist the South Ukraine NPP, Mykolaiv oblast, to reduce the risk of a major nuclear accident. The second mission took place on 25–28 April and comprised a high-level delegation and

---

[44] IAEA, General Conference, 'Strengthening the effectiveness and improving the efficiency of Agency safeguards', Resolution GC(66)/RES/10, 30 Sep. 2022, para. 3.
[45] IAEA, Board of Governors, 'The safety, security and safeguards implications of the situation in Ukraine', Resolution GOV/2022/17, 3 Mar. 2022, paras 1, 4.
[46] IAEA, 'IAEA director general Grossi's initiative to travel to Ukraine', Press release 21/2022, 4 Mar. 2022.
[47] IAEA, 'Update 13—IAEA director general statement on situation in Ukraine', Press release 22/2022, 6 Mar. 2022.
[48] IAEA, 'Update 20—IAEA director general statement on situation in Ukraine', Press release 32/2022, 13 Mar. 2022.
[49] IAEA, Board of Governors, 'The safety, security and safeguards implications of the situation in Ukraine', Resolution GOV/2022/58, 15 Sep. 2022, p. 1.
[50] IAEA, Board of Governors, 'Nuclear safety, security and safeguards in Ukraine', Report by the director general, GOV/2022/52, 9 Sep. 2022, paras 10–13.

technical experts to assess the safety and security at Ukrainian nuclear facilities in general, assess the situation at the ChNPP now that it had returned to Ukrainian control, and deliver radiation monitoring and personal protective equipment requested by Ukraine. The third mission was conducted at the ChNPP site and its exclusion zone from 30 May to 4 June. It assessed radiation protection, the safety of spent fuel and radioactive waste, and the nuclear security situation.

The fourth mission, the high-profile IAEA Support and Assistance Mission to Zaporizhzhya (ISAMZ), took place from 29 August to 3 September 2022 and aimed 'to help stabilize the nuclear safety and security situation at the ZNPP site'.[51] ISAMZ was agreed after several months of high-level diplomatic negotiations between the IAEA, Russia and Ukraine, with the participation of France.[52] It was led by the IAEA director general and comprised a senior delegation and a technical team. This mission stood out because it took place at an NPP operated by Ukrainian personnel under Russian military control, with ongoing hostilities in the vicinity.

In connection with the arrival of ISAMZ, the IAEA reached an agreement with Ukraine and Russia to set up a permanent presence of IAEA inspectors at the ZNPP.[53] They would stay at the station and be replaced in regular rotations. During rotations, the IAEA teams had to reach the ZNPP from the territory controlled by the Ukrainian government, because the IAEA formally recognizes the ZNPP as Ukrainian.[54] From 29 August the IAEA began to post four-person shifts of experts at ZNPP to monitor nuclear safety and the security situation, improve communication, identify priority needs for assistance, and provide technical advice.[55]

After ISAMZ, the IAEA missions to Ukraine became more routine, with the aim of assessing nuclear safety and security and providing the technical support and assistance required. In November and December 2022, the IAEA sent such missions to KIPT and SSE 'Radon' in Kharkiv, the ChNPP site, and the rest of the Ukrainian nuclear power plants.[56] On 13 December 2022 the IAEA and Ukraine agreed to also establish a 'continuous presence of nuclear safety and security experts' at the other three nuclear power plants—Khmelnytsky, Rivne and South Ukraine—as well as the ChNPP site.[57]

---

[51] IAEA, GOV/2022/52 (note 50), para. 14.
[52] 'IAEA seeks to visit Ukraine nuclear plant amid concerns', Al Jazeera, 26 Aug. 2022; and 'IAEA team "on its way" to Ukraine's Zaporizhzhia nuclear plant', Al Jazeera, 29 Aug. 2022.
[53] 'IAEA team "on its way" to Ukraine's Zaporizhzhia nuclear plant' (note 52).
[54] 'IAEA monitoring mission blocked from Zaporizhia NPP', *Nuclear Engineering International*, 23 Feb. 2023.
[55] IAEA, GOV/2022/66 (note 21), paras 9–13.
[56] IAEA, GOV/2022/66 (note 21), paras 15–16; and IAEA, 'Update 134—IAEA director general statement on situation in Ukraine', Press release 201/2022, 2 Dec. 2022.
[57] IAEA, 'Update 136—IAEA director general statement on situation in Ukraine', Press release 207/2022, 13 Dec. 2022.

The ZNPP protection zone

The IAEA has consistently called for the cessation of shelling of the ZNPP site and its vicinity to avoid further damage to the plant and to ensure the safety of the staff. The shelling and other military activities in the vicinity of the ZNPP have often resulted in the loss of electricity and water supplies to the plant, forcing the reactors to shut down.

On 6 September 2022 the IAEA director general briefed the UN Security Council about the findings and recommendations of ISAMZ and proposed the establishment of a 'nuclear safety and security protection zone' around the ZNPP site.[58] He subsequently launched a broad diplomatic effort seeking support for and implementation of such a zone, which included bilateral meetings with Ukrainian President Volodymyr Zelensky in Kyiv on 6 October and with Russian President Vladimir Putin in St Petersburg on 11 October.[59] On 2 December Grossi expressed optimism that the negotiations establishing the security zone could be concluded 'in the near future'.[60] However, it did not happen in 2022. On 4 January 2023 Petro Kotin, head of the Ukrainian nuclear utility company Energoatom, dismissed the prospects for establishing such a zone, considering it is unrealistic under current conditions.[61]

Conclusions

In 2022 a large share of Ukraine's nuclear facilities, including all of its nuclear power plants, were subject to military attacks, while two were occupied by the Russian armed forces. Nuclear facilities have been attacked elsewhere in the past in dedicated strikes, but an assault of the scale that took place in Ukraine is unique.

These attacks presented unprecedented nuclear safety, security and radiation protection challenges. In response, the IAEA put forward a conceptual framework for addressing the safety and security challenges to nuclear installations in wartime: the 'seven indispensable pillars of nuclear safety and security'. The seven pillars concept is a significant innovation that is likely to have an impact on the fields of nuclear safety, nuclear security and emergency response well after 2022. This concept can be seen as a harbinger of an adjustment of the international nuclear security framework to face a new, previously largely unaddressed, set of scenarios: operation of national nuclear security regimes during attacks and disruption caused by states,

---

[58] IAEA, GOV/2022/52 (note 50), para. 6.
[59] IAEA, GOV/2022/66 (note 21), paras 18–20; and Tirone (note 28).
[60] Tirone, J., 'Nuclear monitors near accord on Ukraine security zone at Zaporizhzhia plant', Bloomberg, 2 Dec. 2022.
[61] Tirone, J., 'Ukraine plant must be seized from Russia, nuclear chief says', Bloomberg, 4 Jan. 2023; and 'Idea of creating security zone around Zaporizhia NPP seized by Russia is unrealistic—Energoatom head', Interfax-Ukraine, 5 Jan. 2023.

rather than by non-state actors. Even during an international armed conflict, nuclear security itself is concerned with the malicious actions of individuals and non-state groups, not the actions of the armed forces of a state. However, the events of 2022 demonstrated that, in case of an international armed conflict or other such extraordinary circumstance, the nuclear security framework must continue to function, and this requires some adaptation, including through strengthening the links with the nuclear safety and emergency response frameworks.[62]

The IAEA also conducted multiple missions to Ukrainian nuclear facilities and established a permanent presence there to monitor the situation. ISAMZ is of particular significance, because it established an IAEA presence at the ZNPP—the largest nuclear power plant in Europe, controlled by Russia. The IAEA presence contributed to nuclear safety, nuclear security and the security of the nuclear facility personnel at the ZNPP.

The IAEA director general launched a broad diplomatic effort in an attempt to establish a nuclear safety and security protection zone around Ukrainian nuclear installations. That effort did not return any tangible results in 2022 and there were few signs that year that such a zone will be established in 2023. Similarly, the conflict between the de facto and de jure control over the ZNPP has only deepened since October 2022.

[62] Fedchenko (note 42).

9. Chemical, biological and health security threats

Overview

In 2022 the coronavirus causing Covid-19 remained widespread but was significantly less fatal than it was in 2020–21; in most countries, it spurred only limited changes in public behaviour. However, the origins of the pandemic continued to be a politically divisive subject and remained unresolved at the end of 2022 (see section I). In addition, an escalating global mpox outbreak was declared a public health emergency of international concern in July 2022. While the mpox outbreak was brought under control, it reinforced the lesson from the Covid-19 pandemic that the international community needs to be much better prepared for responding to future pandemics. Negotiations continued in 2022 towards a new international treaty to strengthen pandemic prevention, preparedness and response.

Russia's longstanding campaign about what it considers nefarious activities at Western 'biolabs' significantly escalated in 2022 (see section II). It led to a formal consultative meeting under Article V of the 1972 Biological and Toxin Weapons Convention (BWC) in September 2022 and to several rounds of discussions in the United Nations Security Council, culminating in an unprecedented request from Russia in October 2022 for an investigation into 'military biological activities in Ukraine'. Security Council members did not find Russia's evidence convincing and voted against Russia's proposal. However, Russia's allegations of non-compliance and its misuse of disarmament instruments for its own disinformation purposes pose significant challenges for the BWC and its credibility, and divert attention from the real work of strengthening the convention.

The principal legal instrument against biological warfare is the BWC and in 2022 Namibia became the 185th state party. A further four states have signed but not ratified the convention, and nine states have neither signed nor ratified the convention. Key biological disarmament and non-proliferation activities in 2022 were carried out in connection with the BWC preparatory committee, the First Committee of the United Nations General Assembly, and the ninth review conference (RevCon9) of the BWC (see section III).

Given the current geopolitical challenges, the longstanding BWC logjam and Russia's allegations, many political statements in the run-up to RevCon9 emphasized the need for collaboration and substantive outcomes. However, consensus again proved largely elusive. Despite agreement on an intersessional programme of work for 2023–26 and establishing a working group on strength-

SIPRI Yearbook 2023: Armaments, Disarmament and International Security
www.sipriyearbook.org

ening the BWC, the conference was unable to agree a solemn declaration, an article-by-article review, and a substantive outcome to the 2017–20 intersessional programme. Finding sufficient common ground to successfully negotiate substantive outcomes will be challenging at the 10th review conference in 2027.

As in the BWC, there were disagreements within the 1993 Chemical Weapons Convention (CWC), including continuing efforts by a handful of actors to stop, hinder, undermine and contest the authority and work of investigation teams within the Organisation for the Prohibition of Chemical Weapons (OPCW) (see section IV). The investigations into alleged chemical weapon use in Syria continued and, although no new instances of chemical weapon use were reported in 2022, the number of confirmed cases rose to 20 from a total of 71 cases investigated. None of the 20 outstanding issues related to Syria's declarations to the OPCW that were unresolved at the end of 2021 could be clarified in 2022. Hence, the OPCW continued to assess at the end of the year that Syria's declaration 'still cannot be considered accurate and complete'.

Outside of Syria, during 2022 there were also some largely inconclusive follow-up actions in relation to the poisoning of Russian citizen Alexei Navalny with a novichok nerve agent in 2020, as well as multiple but unproved allegations of illegal chemical activities during the war in Ukraine. Continuing divisions over the investigation into chemical weapon use in Syria, as well as the unresolved poisoning of Navalny and the unfolding war in Ukraine, strongly suggest that investigations will become even more contentious and complex—and important.

On 29 April 2022 the CWC celebrated the 25th anniversary of its entry into force. Future challenges include the prevention of the re-emergence of chemical weapons, a changing industry landscape, technological developments, and non-state actors harbouring an interest in chemical weapons (see section V). On a more positive note, routine and other inspections by the OPCW Technical Secretariat became more frequent in 2022, as pandemic-related restrictions eased. In addition, construction of the new Centre for Chemistry and Technology was completed in 2022 and the centre is expected to be fully operational by April 2023. Finally, the United States, the only declared possessor state party with chemical weapons yet to be destroyed, is expected to complete its remaining destruction activities according to schedule by the end of 2023.

States parties to the CWC will hold the fifth review conference of the treaty in May 2023 and in preparation for this established an open-ended working group in March 2022 that met 10 times before the end of the year. The review conference will discuss a range of important topics in particularly challenging circumstances, given the stark polarization in the OPCW's policy-making organs over compliance politics. At the same time, the review conference might set important landmarks for the way ahead.

FILIPPA LENTZOS AND UNA JAKOB

I. Health security

FILIPPA LENTZOS

Update on the Covid-19 pandemic

By the end of 2022, the World Health Organization (WHO) had received reports of over 730 million cases of Covid-19 worldwide.[1] The actual number of infections is likely to be considerably higher from undiagnosed cases and generally poor Covid-19-related data.[2] As of 31 December 2022, the WHO reported over 270 million cases in Europe, over 186 million in the Americas, over 181 million in the western Pacific, over 60 million in south-east Asia, over 23 million in the eastern Mediterranean, and nearly 10 million in Africa. The five countries with the highest cumulative number of reported cases in 2022 were, in descending order, the United States, China, India, France and Germany.[3]

During 2022 nearly 7 million deaths were recorded as caused by Covid-19, with several million likely to have gone unrecorded. The WHO reported nearly 3 million Covid-related deaths in the Americas, over 2.1 million deaths in Europe, over 800 000 deaths in south-east Asia, over 300 000 deaths each in the eastern Mediterranean and in the western Pacific, and over 175 000 deaths in Africa. The five countries with the highest cumulative number of reported deaths in 2022 were, in descending order, the USA, Brazil, India, Russia and Mexico.[4]

While for much of the pandemic the main obstacle to vaccinating the world against Covid-19 was a lack of supply, in 2022 an increasing problem facing global vaccination efforts was a lack of demand. Covax, the vaccine-sharing initiative backed in part by the WHO, saw a sharp decline in dose orders, including in countries with relatively low vaccination rates.[5] In some countries, millions of doses were thrown away unused.[6]

---

[1] World Health Organization (WHO), 'WHO coronavirus (Covid-19) dashboard', Status at 31 Dec. 2022, <https://covid19.who.int>.

[2] See e.g. Lentzos, F., 'The unfolding Covid-19 pandemic', *SIPRI Yearbook 2022*, pp. 474–76; and 'The pandemic's true death toll', *The Economist* ('excess death tracker').

[3] WHO, 'WHO coronavirus (Covid-19) dashboard' (note 1).

[4] WHO, 'WHO coronavirus (Covid-19) dashboard' (note 1).

[5] Taylor, A., 'Amid low demand, global coronavirus vaccination set to slow in 2023', *Washington Post*, 4 Jan. 2023.

[6] Ho, U., 'Binning 8.5 million Covid jabs a "shocking indictment" of vaccination campaign, says health expert', *Daily Maverick*, 14 Sep. 2022.

Studies into the origins of SARS-CoV-2

In June 2022 the WHO released the first preliminary report from the scientific advisory group for the origins of novel pathogens (SAGO).[7] The report noted that no new data had been made available to evaluate the 'lab leak' hypothesis and recommended further investigations on origins.[8] It recognized that lab leaks had happened historically with other pathogens, and that it was important to include studies to address risks of biosafety or biosecurity breaches.[9] The report provided key recommendations 'for further studies needed on humans, animals and the environment in China and around the world'. The SAGO emphasized the preliminary nature of the report, and that work was ongoing, but indicated that 'currently available epidemiological and sequencing data suggest ancestral strains to SARS-CoV-2 have a zoonotic origin'. However, the SAGO also noted that it would 'remain open to any and all scientific evidence that becomes available in the future to allow for comprehensive testing of all reasonable hypotheses'.[10]

Nevertheless, the lab leak theory continued to be a source of political tension. In response to the SAGO's preliminary report, the Chinese Ministry of Foreign Affairs reverted to its defensive narrative that the origins study must be conducted 'on the basis of science and free from political interference'.[11] It continued:

> The lab leak theory is a false claim concocted by anti-China forces for political purposes. It has nothing to do with science. The Chinese side has invited WHO experts to visit the Wuhan lab, and the joint report reached the clear conclusion that 'a laboratory origin of the pandemic was considered to be extremely unlikely'. Since the SAGO report has called for investigation into biological laboratories 'located worldwide where early Covid-19 cases have been retrospectively detected' for the next phase of study, investigation should first target highly suspicious laboratories such as those at Fort Detrick and the University of North Carolina in the US.[12]

In October 2022 a US Senate committee released its own interim report on the origins of the pandemic, which concluded that 'the Covid-19 pandemic was, more likely than not, the result of a research-related incident'.[13] It seems

---

[7] Scientific Advisory Group for the Origins of Novel Pathogens (SAGO), *Preliminary Report of the SAGO, 9 June 2022* (WHO: Geneva, 2022). For a more detailed discussion of the scientific, public, and political debates on the origins of SARS-CoV-2, see Lentzos, F., 'The unfolding Covid-19 pandemic', *SIPRI Yearbook 2021*, pp. 454–61; and Lentzos, 'The unfolding Covid-19 pandemic' (note 2), pp. 477–82.

[8] SAGO (note 7), p. 6.

[9] SAGO (note 7), p. 14.

[10] SAGO (note 7), p. 6.

[11] Chinese Ministry of Foreign Affairs, Foreign Ministry Spokesperson Zhao Lijian's regular press conference on June 10, 2022, English transcript, 10 June 2022.

[12] Chinese Ministry of Foreign Affairs (note 11).

[13] US Senate Committee on Health, Education, Labor and Pensions, Minority Oversight Staff, 'An analysis of the origins of the COVID-19 pandemic', Interim report, Oct. 2022, p. 26.

likely that politics will continue to plague further investigations into the pandemic's origins.

A pandemic treaty

The Intergovernmental Negotiating Body (INB), set up by the World Health Assembly in December 2021 to negotiate a treaty on pandemic prevention, preparedness and response, and comprised of the 194 WHO member states, held several meetings in 2022 to discuss proposals for the treaty.[14] There were also public consultations and two rounds of hearings on, respectively, which substantive elements to include in the treaty and what should be addressed at the international level to better protect against future pandemics.[15]

At its third and last meeting in 2022, at WHO headquarters in Geneva on 5–7 December, the INB agreed that its bureau would develop the 'zero draft' of a legally binding agreement in order to start negotiations at the fourth INB meeting, scheduled to start in February 2023. WHO member states called for an agreement that takes into account equity, promotes preparedness, ensures solidarity and respects sovereignty.[16]

An outbreak of mpox

On 7 May 2022 the WHO was informed of a confirmed case of mpox in an individual who had travelled from the United Kingdom to Nigeria and subsequently returned to the UK.[17] Additional lab-confirmed cases were reported from the UK, and cases began being reported to WHO from several European countries, including in Belgium, France, Germany, Italy, Netherlands, Portugal, Spain, and Sweden.[18] The clinical presentation of mpox resembles that of smallpox, but it is less contagious and causes less severe illness. There is no specific vaccine for mpox, but smallpox vaccines can provide effective protection.[19]

Speaking at the opening of the 75th World Health Assembly on 22 May 2022, the WHO director-general, referring to both the Covid-19 pandemic and the mpox outbreak, said: 'We face a formidable convergence of disease,

---

[14] WHO, Intergovernmental Negotiating Body, 'Documentation'.
[15] WHO, Intergovernmental Negotiating Body, 'Public hearings'.
[16] WHO, 'WHO member states agree to develop zero draft of legally binding pandemic accord in early 2023', WHO News, 7 Dec. 2022.
[17] WHO, 'Monkeypox: United Kingdom of Britain and Northern Ireland', Disease Outbreak News, 16 May 2022. Mpox was formerly known as 'monkeypox'. 'WHO recommends new name for monkeypox disease', WHO News, 28 Nov. 2022.
[18] WHO, 'Monkeypox: United Kingdom of Britain and Northern Ireland', Disease Outbreak News, 18 May 2022; and WHO, 'Multi-country monkeypox outbreak: Situation update', Disease Outbreak News, 10 June 2022.
[19] WHO, 'Monkeypox', Fact sheet, 19 May 2022.

drought, famine and war, fuelled by climate change, inequity and geopolitical rivalry.'[20] By early June there were confirmed cases from 28 countries in four WHO Regions where mpox is 'not usual or had not been previously reported', with clinical presentation of cases being 'variable'.[21] In July 2022, the director-general declared the escalating global mpox outbreak a public health emergency of international concern (PHEIC).[22]

While the mpox outbreak was brought under control, governments around the world are more conscious than ever of threats from infectious diseases and are investing heavily in preparedness of 'Disease X' and the next PHEIC.[23]

[20] Ghebreyesus, T. A., WHO director-general, Speech to the high-level welcome at the 75th World Health Assembly, Geneva, 22 May 2022.

[21] WHO, 'Multi-country monkeypox outbreak: Situation update' (note 18).

[22] WHO, 'WHO director-general declares the ongoing monkeypox outbreak a public health emergency of international concern', Press release, 23 July 2022.

[23] WHO, 'Prioritizing diseases for research and development in emergency contexts'.

II. Biological weapon allegations

FILIPPA LENTZOS

Russia's years-long campaign about 'biolabs' and what it considers nefarious activities significantly escalated in 2022. It led to a formal consultative meeting under Article V of the 1972 Biological and Toxin Weapons Convention (BWC) in September 2022 and to several rounds of discussions in the United Nations Security Council, culminating in an unprecedented request from Russia in October 2022 for an investigation into 'military biological activities in Ukraine'. Security Council members did not find Russia's evidence convincing and voted against Russia's proposal.

Allegations in the context of Russia's invasion of Ukraine

In advance of the Winter Olympic Games in February 2022, Chinese president Xi Jinping and Russian president Vladimir Putin, who had travelled to Beijing for the opening ceremony, held talks, after which they released an extensive and wide-ranging joint statement on their countries' friendship and international relations 'entering a new era'. A part of the joint statement covered biological security. It re-iterated claims from statements in preceding months that 'domestic and foreign bioweapons activities by the United States and its allies raise serious concerns and questions for the international community regarding their compliance with the BWC'. China and Russia shared the view that 'such activities pose a serious threat to the national security' of both countries and 'are detrimental to the security of the respective regions', and they called on the USA and its allies 'to act in an open, transparent, and responsible manner by properly reporting on their military biological activities conducted overseas and on their national territory, and by supporting the resumption of negotiations on a legally binding BWC Protocol with an effective verification mechanism'.[1]

The Russian invasion of Ukraine on 24 February 2022 was accompanied by increased political rhetoric alleging military biological activities by the USA and Ukraine. At Russia's request, the UN Security Council met on 11 March 2022 to discuss Russia's allegations of military biological activities in Ukraine.[2] Security Council members strongly rebutted the allegations, and the high representative for disarmament affairs, Izumi Nakamitsu, asserted that the UN was not aware of any biological weapons programmes.[3]

---

[1] China and Russia, Joint statement of the Russian Federation and the People's Republic of China on the international relations entering a new era and the global sustainable development, 4 Feb. 2022.

[2] Security Council Report, 'Ukraine briefing', What's in Blue, 11 Mar. 2022.

[3] United Nations, 'Security Council on Russia allegations of military biological activities in Ukraine', YouTube, 11 Mar. 2022.

The Security Council met again on 18 March 2022, to continue discussions about Russia's allegations, including on chemical weapons.[4] There were further rebuttals by Security Council members, and additional rebuttals in the UN General Assembly at meetings convened at the request of Ukraine.[5] The North Atlantic Treaty Organization (NATO) and the Group of Seven (G7) states made intelligence disclosures on the possibility of Russia using biological or chemical weapon allegations as a pretext to employ unconventional weapons in its war against Ukraine, and noted the resolve of NATO and G7 members that any such use would result in severe consequences.[6] Independent experts also rebutted the allegations, noting that Russia 'is exploiting the complex nature of biological research and biotechnology for its disinformation purposes'.[7]

Russia responded by circulating a letter on 1 April 2022, and another on 13 May 2022, to Security Council members with material claimed to relate to military biological programmes in Ukraine.[8] On 6 April 2022 Russia hosted an Arria-formula meeting of the Security Council to further push its allegations against Ukraine.[9] The Security Council met for a third time on 13 May 2022 to consider Russia's claims, which again were rebutted by several members.[10]

A formal consultative meeting

On 13 June 2022, Russia issued the USA with a diplomatic note asking it to answer 'questions' about the activities of its biological laboratories in Ukraine, which the USA stated contained no 'actual questions', only

---

[4] 'Ukraine—Security Council: Allegations on chemical weapons', United Nations, YouTube, 18 Mar. 2022.

[5] United Nations, General Assembly, 11th Emergency Special Session (Ukraine): Statement to press, 2 Mar. 2022. The emergency session was convened under Security Council Resolution 2623, 27 Feb. 2022.

[6] North Atlantic Treaty Organization (NATO), Statement by NATO heads of state and government, 24 Mar. 2022; European Council, 'G7 leaders' statement', Press release, 24 Mar. 2022; and German Federal Foreign Office, 'Statement by the G7 global partnership against the spread of weapons and materials of mass destruction on Ukraine', Press release, 29 Mar. 2022.

[7] Jakob, U. et al., 'Russian allegations of biological weapons activities in Ukraine', Peace Research Institute Frankfurt (PRIF) Blog, 22 Mar. 2022.

[8] United Nations, General Assembly and Security Council, Letter dated 1 April 2022 from the permanent representative of the Russian Federation to the United Nations addressed to the secretary-general and the president of the Security Council, A/76/785–S/2022/284, 1 Apr. 2022; and Letter dated 13 May 2022 from the permanent representative of the Russian Federation to the United Nations addressed to the secretary-general and the president of the Security Council, A/76/836–S/2022/393, 13 May 2022.

[9] United Nations, 'The situation in Ukraine: UN Security Council Arria-formula meeting organized by the Permanent Mission of the Russian Federation', UN Web TV, 6 May 2022.

[10] United Nations, 'United Nations unaware of any biological weapons programmes in Ukraine, top disarmament official affirms, as Security Council considers new claims by Russian Federation', Meetings coverage, Security Council, 9033rd meeting, SC/14890, 13 May 2022.

'assertions and mischaracterizations' of publicly available documents.[11] The USA response of 23 June was not considered 'substantive' by Russia, which on 29 June requested a formal consultative meeting (FCM) under Article V of the BWC.[12] Russia's submission to the FCM repeated the allegations against both the USA and Ukraine.[13]

In the four-decade life of the BWC there has been only one other FCM under Article V, in 1997 when Cuba alleged the USA had disseminated insects to attack its agriculture. The procedures for the FCM were developed in 1986 and 1991, and adhered to for the 2022 meeting. Dates for meetings and the agenda were agreed in July and August, with the meeting formally opened on 26 August 2022 for a brief procedural session and reconvened for four days of consultations between 5 and 9 September 2022.

The FCM was a private meeting open only to states parties and signatory states, and states parties agreed to neither prepare summary records nor make public broadcasts.[14] This makes the process opaque, but states could request that national positions and other documents be published as official working papers of the meeting. Many did so and there are over 70 working papers available, including the documentation related to Russia's allegations, the rebuttals of the USA and Ukraine, and national statements about the process and the allegations themselves.[15] Compared to the 1997 meeting which officially has only its procedural report and a follow-up letter available, the 2022 FCM was significantly more transparent.[16]

At the FCM, Russia focused on four issues: a patent issued in the USA that Russia claimed involved potential applicable usages for biological warfare; the culture collections in Ukrainian laboratories that Russia claimed were of little relevance to the predominant diseases endemic in Ukraine; a Turkish Bayraktar drone with a generating system capable of spraying more than 20 litres of aerosol; and the US funding provided to Ukraine under cooperative threat reduction programmes out of the US Defense Threat Reduction

---

[11] BWC, Formal consultative meeting of the states parties (FCM 2022), 'Response by the United States of America to the request by the Russian Federation for a consultative meeting under Article V of the Biological and Toxin Weapons Convention (BWC)', Working paper submitted by the USA, BWC/CONS/2022/WP.4, 5 Sep. 2022, para. 1.

[12] BWC, BWC/CONS/2022/WP.4 (note 11), paras 3–4.

[13] BWC, FCM 2022, 'Statement by the head of the delegation of the Russian Federation at the consultative meeting of the states parties to the Convention on the Prohibition of Biological and Toxin Weapons (BTWC) under BTWC Article V', Working paper submitted by Russia, BWC/CONS/2022/WP.6, 6 Sep. 2022.

[14] BWC, FCM 2022, Final report of the formal consultative meeting of the states parties, BWC/CONS/2022/3, 19 Sep. 2022, para. 3.

[15] See e.g. BWC, BWC/CONS/2022/WP.4 (note 11); BWC, BWC/CONS/2022/WP.6 (note 13); and other documents available at United Nations, Office of Disarmament Affairs (UNODA), 'Biological Weapons Convention—Formal consultative meeting (2022): Documents'.

[16] UNODA, 'Biological Weapons Convention—Formal consultative meeting (1997): Documents'.

Agency (DTRA) that Russia claimed violated the BWC.[17] Both the USA and Ukraine refuted the claims through statements and presentations.[18] Immediately prior to the meeting both countries, along with Armenia, Georgia, Iraq, Jordan, Liberia, the Philippines, Sierra Leone and Uganda, had issued a joint statement on the positive contribution threat reduction activity made to global health security.[19]

Up to 185 states parties to the BWC and 4 signatories could have attended the FCM. Only 90 did so: 89 states parties and Syria as a signatory. This represents less than half of the membership and suggests limited interest in dealing with, rather than simply talking about, compliance with the BWC. In total, 65 states parties, including Russia, the USA and Ukraine, expressed a view either in a national statement or in aligning with statements of others.[20]

A detailed reading of the available national or group statements, press releases and other documents indicates that responses to Russia's allegations fall into five categories. In the first category Russia stands alone and in isolation as the only state that alleges the USA and Ukraine were in non-compliance with and violation of the BWC.

Second are those states that stopped short of explicitly claiming non-compliance, but that supported Russia's use of the consultation process and indicated Russia's allegations left questions for the USA and Ukraine to answer. Of the eight states in this category (Belarus, China, Cuba, Iran, Nicaragua, Syria, Venezuela and Zimbabwe), China went further than most. Its deft use of implication rather than assertion is in substance an admonition that the USA should recognize Russia's concerns, set an example of compliance, make more comprehensive efforts to respond to the questions

---

[17] BWC, FCM 2022, 'Questions to the United States regarding compliance with the obligations under the Convention on the Prohibition of the Development, Production and Stockpiling of Bacteriological (Biological) and Toxin Weapons and on Their Destruction (BTWC), in the context of the activities of biological laboratories in the territory of Ukraine', Working paper submitted by Russia, BWC/CONS/2022/WP.2, 15 Sep. 2022, paras 1, 6, 10, 11 and 15; and 'Questions to Ukraine regarding compliance with obligations under the Convention on the Prohibition of the Development, Production and Stockpiling of Bacteriological (Biological) and Toxin Weapons and on Their Destruction (BTWC), in the context of the activities of biological laboratories', Working paper submitted by Russia, BWC/CONS/2022/WP.3, 15 Sep. 2022, paras 4, 5 and 10.

[18] See e.g. BWC, FCM 2022, 'United States technical briefing to the Article V consultative meeting under the Biological and Toxin Weapons Convention', Working paper submitted by the USA, BWC/CONS/2022/WP.38, 8 Sep. 2022; and 'Ukraine presentation, Biological and Toxin Weapons Convention Article V consultative meeting', Working paper submitted by Ukraine, BWC/CONS/2022/WP.24, 6 Sep. 2022.

[19] US Department of State, Office of the Spokesperson, 'Joint statement on the contribution of the cooperative threat reduction partnerships to global health security', Press release, 29 Aug. 2022.

[20] See e.g. BWC, FCM 2022, 'EU statement at the formal consultative meeting pursuant to Article V of states parties to the Biological and Toxin Weapons Convention', Working paper submitted by the Czech Republic on behalf of the EU and its member states, BWC/CONS/2022/WP.27, 7 Sep. 2022; and 'Joint statement of the results of the consultative meeting of the states parties to the Convention on the Prohibition of Biological and Toxin Weapons (BTWC) under BTWC Article V', Working paper submitted by the Belarus, China, Cuba, Nicaragua, Russia, Syria, Venezuela and Zimbabwe, BWC/CONS/2022/WP.63, 12 Sep. 2022.

posed and provide a clear answer to the international community. China appended to its own statement a list of questions and was at the forefront of supporting Russia's call for follow-up actions that might include lodging a non-compliance complaint with the UN Security Council under Article VI.[21]

The other states in this group were more circumspect. Russia has vigorously defended Syria in the UN Security Council and in the Organisation for the Prohibition of Chemical Weapons (OPCW; see section IV in this chapter), but Syria could only muster a tepid response about the professionalism of Russia's presentations and the technical details of the documents, before simply noting the USA and Ukraine had made no serious attempt to answer the questions.[22] Iran only supported Russia's right to request the meeting and suggested the USA should provide clarifications in a transparent manner.[23] Iran's support was so lukewarm that it did not join the other states in their joint statement declaring that questions remained unresolved and there should be some form of follow-up process.[24]

The USA and Ukraine had five times as many backers in the third category: a total of 42 states rejected the allegations. Sweden called for Russia to cease its 'unfounded allegations and stop its disinformation campaign', and Ireland urged Russia to stop misusing consultation procedures to further its efforts to undermine multilateral disarmament and non-proliferation agreements.[25] The Czech Republic spoke on behalf of all EU member states and those that aligned with the EU statement—35 states parties in total—to categorically reject the Russian claims.[26] Others, such as Norway, 'heard nothing—or read nothing—that even comes close to substantiating such allegations'.[27] The collective message of these 42 states was encapsulated by Switzerland in a polite statement that ended with a 'firm view' that Russia's allegations were not substantiated, the conclusions drawn were 'neither convincing nor

---

[21] BWC, FCM 2022, 'Remarks by HE Ambassador Li Song and questions to the United States at the formal consultative meeting of the Biological Weapons Convention', Working paper submitted by China, BWC/CONS/2022/WP.48/Rev.1, 9 Sep. 2022.

[22] BWC, FCM 2022, Working paper submitted by Syria (Arabic only), BWC/CONS/2022/WP.42, 8 Sep. 2022.

[23] BWC, FCM 2022, 'Statement by Mr. Mehdi Aliabadi, Deputy permanent representation of the Islamic Republic of Iran to the United Nations and other international organizations in Geneva before the formal consultative meeting of the states parties to the Biological Weapons Convention (BWC) pursuant to Article V', Working paper submitted by the Islamic Republic of Iran, BWC/CONS/2022/WP.65, 12 Sep. 2022, paras 3 and 7.

[24] BWC, BWC/CONS/2022/WP.63 (note 20), paras 2–3.

[25] BWC, FCM 2022, 'Swedish national statement, BWTC Article V consultative meeting', Working paper submitted by Sweden, BWC/CONS/2022/WP.43, 9 Sep. 2022, para. 5; and 'National statement of Ireland by Mr. Jamie Walsh, Deputy permanent representative of Ireland to the Conference on Disarmament', Working paper submitted by Ireland, BWC/CONS/2022/WP.33, 7 Sep. 2022, para. 9.

[26] BWC, BWC/CONS/2022/WP.27 (note 20).

[27] BWC, FCM 2022, 'National statement by Norway to the formal consultative meeting pursuant to Article V', Working paper submitted by Norway, BWC/CONS/2022/WP.55, 12 Sep. 2022, para. 4.

credible', and 'in no way' was it possible to draw the conclusion that the USA and Ukraine had violated their obligations under the BWC.[28]

The fourth category captures states that neither supported nor rejected the allegations but expressed a view in support of the BWC and the consultation mechanism under Article V. Twelve states took this approach. Some, such as South Africa and Chile, hinted at Russia's misuse of the Article V process, but most used the FCM and its challenges as a platform to reiterate their support for the BWC and biological disarmament, and their preference for a verification mechanism. These 12 states, as well as others, held that a verification procedure would resolve the issues Russia's questions purported to address.[29]

A fifth category is the 25 'silent' states that were physically present but, based on written documents, not engaged in the process. Some may have privately made their views known but chose to avoid expressing a view publicly out of realpolitik concerns. However, for the Middle East, the silence of Jordan, Kuwait, Iraq, Lebanon, Qatar, Saudi Arabia and the United Arab Emirates (UAE), was notable compared to the voices of Syria and Iran.

The meeting outcome was inconclusive (as it was in 1997). Reporting and commentary emphasized that few states sided with Russia and supported its allegations, with most concluding 35 states backed the USA in rejecting the allegations and 7 states backed Russia.[30] The 35–7 score is accurate but may mislead observers into thinking these seven other states formally backed Russia's claims of US and Ukrainian non-compliance with the BWC, when in fact Russia stood alone on this point. What support Russia did receive was limited to endorsing the consultation process under Article V of the BWC, the legitimacy of Russia's request to call such a meeting, and a view that Russia has posed some questions for the USA and Ukraine.

---

[28] BWC, FCM 2022, 'Speech by the Swiss delegation to the formal consultative meeting under Article V of the Biological Weapons Convention and the final declarations of the second and third review conferences', Working paper submitted by Switzerland, BWC/CONS/2022/WP.44, 9 Sep. 2022, para. 8.

[29] See e.g. BWC, FCM 2022, 'Statement delivered on behalf of the Republic of South Africa on the occasion of the formal consultative meeting of the states parties to the [BWC]', Working paper submitted by South Africa, BWC/CONS/2022/WP.54, 12 Sep. 2022, paras 9 and 11; and 'Declaración nacional de Chile ante la Reunión Consultiva Formal' [National declaration of Chile before the formal consultative meeting], Working paper submitted by Chile, BWC/CONS/2022/WP.60 (Spanish only), 12 Sep. 2022, paras 10–11.

[30] See e.g. Myers, S. L., 'US rebukes Russia for claims of secret bioweapons in Ukraine', *New York Times*, 13 Sep. 2022; and US Department of State, 'Conclusion of Article 5 formal consultative meeting under the Biological Weapons Convention', Press release, 13 Sep. 2022.

An unprecedented request for an investigation of non-compliance with the BWC

The UN Security Council met on 27 October 2022 at the request of Russia for a fourth briefing on 'military biological activities in Ukraine'.[31] This time was different, however. Three days earlier, Russia had filed a formal complaint in a letter circulated to Security Council members, in which Russia claimed the USA and Ukraine were in non-compliance with the BWC.[32] Russia maintained that the responses it had received at the FCM were insufficient, leading Russia to submit a draft resolution invoking Article VI of the BWC to ask the Security Council to launch an investigation.[33]

Article VI enables BWC states parties to lodge a complaint with the Security Council. The complaint must be accompanied by 'all possible evidence confirming its validity' alongside a request for the complaint and the evidence to be considered by the Security Council. If the Security Council decides to act on a complaint, it may initiate an investigation and states must cooperate with such an investigation. How the Security Council conducts its investigation is not articulated in the BWC in detail and since the procedure has never been invoked there is no precedent to fall back on.

Russia proposed a draft resolution calling for the Security Council to set up a commission of inquiry made up of the Security Council's 15 members to formally investigate the allegations. This commission would report back to the Security Council by 30 November 2022, and to BWC states parties at the ninth review conference set to begin in late November.[34]

Two things were immediately obvious. First, the evidence Russia provided in the '310-page dossier' it characterized as 'evidence' was the same as the information provided to BWC states parties at the FCM a few weeks earlier. Of the fifteen Security Council members, six had already rejected the allegations (Albania, France, Ireland, Norway, the UK and the USA), three had supported the process of consultations but not voiced any support for the actual claims Russia was making (Brazil, India and Mexico), three had been publicly silent (Ghana, Kenya and the UAE), one had offered some support to Russia (China), and one had not been present at the FCM (Gabon).

Second, to observers, Russia's commission was not a serious proposal. The draft resolution lacked any detail on how the commission would do its work, who would chair the commission, what activities it would undertake, how it would acquire and review additional information to support or question the

---

[31] United Nations, Security Council, 9171st meeting, S/PV.9171, New York, 27 Oct. 2022, p. 3.
[32] Lederer, E. M., 'Russia seeks UN probe of claims on Ukraine biological labs', AP News, 26 Oct. 2022.
[33] United Nations, S/PV.9171 (note 31), p. 5.
[34] United Nations, 'Security Council rejects text to investigate complaint concerning non-compliance of Biological Weapons Convention by Ukraine, United States', Meetings coverage, Security Council, 9180th meeting, SC/150975, 2 Nov. 2022.

evidence Russia presented, when such work could be conducted by Security Council members, and why it only had one month to complete its work and report back to the Council. As Mexico remarked at the meeting which voted on the resolution (see below), it was 'not realistic to believe that a commission can be set up as proposed and can present a report with recommendations to the Council in a period of 28 days'.[35]

At the Security Council meeting on 27 October 2022, the director and deputy high representative for disarmament affairs at the UN initially briefed the Council on the information currently available and echoed earlier statements to the Council in March and May 2022 that the UN had no knowledge of any military biological activities in Ukraine. He also stressed that the UN has neither the mandate nor the technical capacity to conduct such an investigation.[36]

Very few states explicitly supported Russia at the meeting. China, which had supported Russia's right to ask questions at the FCM, supported invoking Article VI and again called on the USA and Ukraine to respond to Russia's request. Gabon said the allegations should be taken seriously and an investigation set up. Kenya, Ghana and India remained non-committal. Brazil called for resumption of negotiations on a binding protocol on strengthening the BWC, and the UAE called for a peaceful resolution to the conflict in Ukraine, including through dialogue.[37]

Seven states (Albania, France, Ireland, Mexico, Norway, the UK and the USA) said they had listened to Russia, as provided for in BWC Article V, and studied the documents provided, but they had found no evidence to support the Russian allegations. Most of these states deplored the use of the Security Council, yet again, as a platform for disinformation and propaganda. Albania castigated the information Russia presented as evidence and said the meeting could have been called the 'Security Council briefing on nothing'.[38]

Six days later, on 2 November 2022, Russia moved its draft resolution to a vote. It lost. The summary reporting after the vote together with eight available explanations of vote, make it clear 13 states viewed the allegations as lacking evidence.[39] Only China seems to have endorsed Russia's approach. France remarked: 'Russia is isolated, more than ever, and its lies fool no one.'[40]

---

[35] United Nations, SC/150975 (note 34).

[36] United Nations, 'United Nations not aware of any biological weapons programmes in Ukraine, senior disarmament official tells Security Council', Meetings coverage, Security Council, 9171st meeting (PM), SC/15084, 27 Oct. 2022.

[37] United Nations, S/PV.9171 (note 31) pp. 9–13; and United Nations, SC/15084 (note 36).

[38] United Nations, S/PV.9171 (note 31), p. 6 (Norway), pp. 7–9 (UK, Albania, USA), p. 10 (France, Mexico), pp. 11–12 (Ireland); and United Nations, SC/15084 (note 36).

[39] United Nations, SC/150975 (note 34).

[40] De Riviere, N., Permanent representative of France to the UN Security Council, 'Ukraine: Explication de vote' [Ukraine: Explanation of vote], French Permanent Mission to the United Nations Press release, 3 Nov. 2022.

Some states were also unhappy with the procedural machinations. Norway observed that it was 'deeply problematic that the State that has lodged the complaint with the Security Council itself has "taken the pen" and submitted the resolution that addresses the complaint'.[41] Outsiders may look at the vote of two in favour and three against as a close call. The 10 abstentions, however, reveal that the non-permanent members of the Security Council abstained to protect the obligations of the BWC in substantive terms and its working methods in procedural terms.

Conclusions

Russia's non-compliance allegations and misuse of disarmament instruments in 2022 for its own disinformation purposes, did not persuade states of its perspective, but does pose significant challenges for the BWC and its credibility. And there is nothing to stop Russia submitting additional requests for further FCMs and Security Council interventions in future, needlessly wasting time and resources, and diverting attention from the real work of strengthening the convention.

---

[41] United Nations, SC/150975 (note 34).

III. Biological weapon disarmament and non-proliferation

FILIPPA LENTZOS

The principal legal instrument against biological warfare is the 1972 Convention on the Prohibition of the Development, Production and Stockpiling of Bacteriological (Biological) and Toxin Weapons and on their Destruction (Biological and Toxin Weapons Convention, BWC).[1] In 2022 Namibia deposited its instrument of accession, becoming the 185th state party.[2] A further four states have signed but not ratified the convention, and nine states have neither signed nor ratified the convention.

Key biological disarmament and non-proliferation activities in 2022 were carried out in connection with the BWC preparatory committee (PrepCom), the First Committee of the United Nations General Assembly, and the ninth review conference (RevCon9) of the BWC.

The 2022 preparatory committee

The PrepCom for RevCon9 had been opened at an initial one-day organizational meeting on 20 December 2021, which elected two vice-chairs in the absence of a clear nomination for president (which rotationally should have been from a Non-Aligned Movement (NAM) delegation).[3] The meeting had also agreed a provisional agenda and draft rules of procedure for RevCon9, for final adoption at the more substantial PrepCom on 4–11 April 2022, and had requested the Implementation Support Unit (ISU) to prepare eight background information documents.[4]

Consultations on the election of a president for RevCon9 continued into 2022. On 24 January 2022, the NAM coordinator informed states parties that the group had decided to hand over the presidency to another interested regional group.[5] The PrepCom meeting in April took note of the NAM's decision as well as its request to retain its rotational right to preside over the 10th review conference. The Western Group proceeded to nominate

---

[1] For a summary and other details of the Convention on the Prohibition of the Development, Production and Stockpiling of Bacteriological (Biological) and Toxin Weapons and on their Destruction, see annex A, section I, in this volume.

[2] United Nations, Office for Disarmament Affairs (UNODA), 'BWC News: News from 2022'.

[3] Lentzos, F., 'Biological weapon disarmament and non-proliferation', *SIPRI Yearbook 2022*, p. 491.

[4] The ISU was established within the Geneva branch of UNODA after the sixth review conference in 2006 to provide administrative support to meetings agreed by the review conference as well as comprehensive implementation and universalization of the BWC and the exchange of confidence-building measures. Lentzos, 'Biological weapon disarmament and non-proliferation' (note 3), p. 491; and BWC, Ninth review conference (RevCon9), Preparatory committee (PrepCom), 'Interim report of the preparatory committee (20 December 2021)', BWC/CONF.IX/PC/2, 21 Dec. 2022, paras 22–28.

[5] BWC, RevCon9, PrepCom, Final report, BWC/CONF.IX/PC/10, 14 Apr. 2022, para. 10; and Letters from the vice-chairpersons of the preparatory committee, BWC/CONF.IX/PC/9, 13 Apr. 2022.

Ambassador Leonardo Bencini of Italy for the role, subject to a PrepCom decision to move RevCon9 from the 8–26 August 2022 dates that had been agreed at the 2020 meeting of states parties (MSP), to later in the year.[6] The PrepCom agreed to reschedule the review conference for 28 November to 16 December 2022, and also agreed the draft provisional agenda and draft rules of procedure.[7]

The background information documents requested by the December PrepCom were circulated in advance of the resumed April session. They covered: (*a*) the history and operation of the confidence-building measures; (*b*) the overall financial status of the BWC and implications of proposals for follow-on action after the review conference; (*c*) 'additional understandings and agreements' reached by previous review conferences; (*d*) 'common understandings' reached by the MSPs from 2017 to 2020; (*e*) the status of universalization; (*f*) compliance by states parties with all their obligations under the convention; (*g*) implementation of Article VII; and (*h*) implementation of Article X. The April 2022 PrepCom requested the ISU to prepare an additional background document, on new scientific and technological developments relevant to the BWC.[8]

States parties submitted 12 working papers to the PrepCom. In the general debate, 50 groups and individual states parties, and one observer agency, made statements.[9] Ten non-governmental organizations (NGOs) delivered statements in an informal session.[10] There were eight side events, organized by states, the United Nations Office for Disarmament Affairs (UNODA) and NGOs.[11]

The PrepCom vice-chairs' summary report of the meeting statements, working papers, and discussions highlighted cooperation and assistance, national implementation, consultation and cooperation, investigation of possible breaches of the BWC, provision of assistance, the Geneva Protocol and universalization, and science and technology. Proposals for follow-on action after RevCon9 addressed the future programme of work, the ISU, financial issues and gender.[12] Reflecting on the PrepCom, the two vice-chairs noted that the committee had not only fulfilled all its procedural tasks but had also seen a 'substantive general exchange of views' that demonstrated 'a strong commitment' by all states parties to the convention.[13] Recognizing the challenging geopolitical climate, the vice-chairs emphasized that 'the

---

[6] BWC, BWC/CONF.IX/PC/10 (note 5), para. 14.
[7] BWC, BWC/CONF.IX/PC/10 (note 5), paras 29–34.
[8] BWC, BWC/CONF.IX/PC/10 (note 5), paras 35 and 36.
[9] UNODA, 'Biological Weapons Convention—Ninth preparatory committee: Statements'.
[10] UNODA, 'Biological Weapons Convention—Ninth preparatory committee: NGO statements'.
[11] UNODA, 'Biological Weapons Convention—Ninth preparatory committee: Side events'.
[12] BWC, RevCon9, PrepCom, Vice-chairs' letter to the states parties to the BWC, 29 Apr. 2022.
[13] BWC, Vice-chairs' letter to the states parties to the BWC (note 12), pp. 1 and 5.

Convention has weathered similar situations in the past and has emerged stronger'.[14]

The First Committee of the UN General Assembly

The UN General Assembly committee on disarmament and international security (First Committee) convened from 3 October to 4 November 2022. In the general debate, six groups of states and 71 individual states referred to biological weapons in their statements.[15] In the thematic cluster on other weapons of mass destruction (WMDs), a further six groups of states and 40 individual states referred to biological weapons in their statements, with disinformation in the context of Russia's war on Ukraine dominating the discussions.[16]

The annual resolution on the BWC was adopted in the First Committee without a vote, as usual, on 1 November 2022.[17] The resolution contained minor technical updates along with a new preambular paragraph on the formal consultative meeting of the BWC held in September 2022 (see section II). The new paragraph simply stated that the meeting was convened on request from Russia, that Russia presented its outstanding questions, that Ukraine and the United States responded, and that no consensus was reached on an outcome.[18]

A Russia-led resolution on the UN secretary-general's mechanism (UNSGM) for investigation of alleged use of chemical and biological weapons was overwhelmingly rejected for a third time in the First Committee.[19] There were 30 votes in favour, 65 votes against, and 77 abstentions—figures very similar to the last two rounds in 2021 and 2020.[20] Operative paragraph 3 was voted on separately and also rejected (27–63–70).[21] In its statement introducing the resolution, Russia claimed that the draft resolution was not on the UNSGM but a proposal that the secretary-general give 'willing' member

---

[14] BWC, Vice-chairs' letter to the states parties to the BWC (note 12), p. 5.

[15] Lentzos, F., 'Biological weapons', *First Committee Monitor*, vol. 20, no. 2 (8 Oct. 2022), p. 13; and Lentzos, F., 'Biological weapons', *First Committee Monitor*, vol. 20, no. 3 (15 Oct. 2022), p. 17.

[16] Lentzos, F., 'Biological weapons', *First Committee Monitor*, vol. 20, no. 4 (22 Oct. 2022), p. 20. See also section II in this chapter.

[17] Reaching Critical Will, 'Draft resolutions, voting results and explanations of vote from First Committee 2022'; and United Nations, General Assembly, First Committee, 'Convention on the Prohibition of the Development, Production and Stockpiling of Bacteriological (Biological) and Toxin Weapons and on Their Destruction', Draft resolution, A/C.1/77/L.74, 14 Oct. 2022. This became UN General Assembly Resolution 77/95, 1 Nov. 2022.

[18] UN General Assembly A/C.1/77/L.74 (note 17), p. 2.

[19] United Nations, General Assembly, First Committee, 'Secretary-general's mechanism for investigation of alleged use of chemical and biological weapons', Draft resolution, A/C.1/77/L.69, 13 Oct. 2022.

[20] Reaching Critical Will (note 17); and Lentzos, 'Biological weapon disarmament and non-proliferation' (note 3), p. 487.

[21] Reaching Critical Will (note 17).

states an opportunity to express their views on whether the UNSGM guidelines and procedures might need updating.[22] The USA, the European Union (EU), and New Zealand gave statements urging states to vote against the draft resolution. The key arguments made were that the existing guidelines and procedures already contain a provision for being updated when and if necessary; they were reviewed and updated in 2007; a list of qualified experts is maintained and relevant training courses are held on a regular basis; and the draft resolution would undermine the UNSGM's integrity, independence and impartial character.[23]

The biennial resolution on 'Measures to uphold the authority of the 1925 Geneva Protocol', which prohibits the use of chemical and biological weapons, was agreed by 182 states.[24] None voted against, but there were two abstentions, from the two states that usually abstain on this resolution (Israel and the USA).[25] The resolution renews its previous call to all states 'to observe strictly the principles and objectives of the Protocol' and to states that continue to maintain reservations to the Geneva Protocol to withdraw them.[26]

In an explanation of its vote, Russia said: 'Amid well-founded suspicions of biological weapons development, the US has defiantly refused to support the 1925 Geneva Protocol, the only arms control instrument prohibiting the use of biological weapons. This is in addition to Washington's consistent statements of reluctance to withdraw reservations reserving its ability to use the types of WMD regulated by this instrument'.[27] Russia concluded that the USA's failure to support the resolution 'is a matter of great concern to all UN member states and only confirms the need to get Ukraine and the United States to disclose their bioweapons programs as soon as possible'.[28]

The ninth review conference

In a nod to current geopolitical challenges, the years-long BWC logjam and Russia's allegations, many political statements in the run-up to RevCon9 emphasized the need for collaboration and substantive outcomes. Italy, which

---

[22] United Nations, General Assembly, First Committee, Statement by Russia on draft resolution A/C.1/77/L.69, 31 Oct. 2022.

[23] United Nations, General Assembly, First Committee, Explanation of vote on cluster 2 (Draft resolution A/C.1/77/L.69), Statement by New Zealand, Nov. 2022; and Lentzos, F., 'Biological weapons', *First Committee Monitor*, vol. 20, no. 6 (5 Nov. 2022), pp. 13–14.

[24] United Nations, General Assembly, First Committee, 'Measures to uphold the authority of the 1925 Geneva Protocol', Draft resolution, A/C.1/77/L.11, 19 Sep. 2022, formally adopted as UN General Assembly Resolution 77/50, 13 Dec. 2022. For the 1925 Geneva Protocol see annex A, section I, in this volume.

[25] Reaching Critical Will (note 17).

[26] UN General Assembly Resolution 77/50 (note 24), paras 2 and 3.

[27] United Nations, General Assembly, First Committee, Explanation of vote on cluster 2 (Draft resolution A/C.1/77/L.11), Statement by Russia, 31 Oct. 2022, p. 1.

[28] United Nations, General Assembly, Statement by Russia (note 27), p. 2.

held the review conference presidency and which was heavily impacted by Covid-19, stressed how important it was for the international community to work together to improve global biosecurity and biosafety, and urged states to end 'reciprocal recriminations' about the BWC's past and to open a 'new page' for the future of the convention.[29] Australia characterized the review conference as an 'opportunity to break the stalemate of the last two decades'; Finland emphasized the importance of adopting 'forward-looking decisions to provide a clear roadmap for the next cycle'; Burkina Faso called on states parties to show cooperation and flexibility; and Slovakia called for a constructive focus.[30]

The review conference was held in Geneva from 28 November to 16 December 2022. States parties submitted 65 working papers to the conference.[31] Under secretary-general and high representative for disarmament affairs, Izumi Nakamitsu, opened the conference on behalf of the UN secretary-general, Antonio Guterres, who addressed the conference via a video message.[32] In the general debate, 92 groups and individual states parties, and seven observer agencies, made statements.[33] In addition to a joint NGO statement, a further eight NGOs delivered statements in an informal session.[34] There were 46 side events, an exceptionally high number, organized by states, the UN, international organizations and NGOs.[35]

Unexpectedly, but with precedent outside of the BWC, Russia informed the conference of its decision to withdraw from the Eastern European Group and to 'form a new regional group under this Convention, consisting of one country—the Russian Federation'.[36] The final report of the review conference noted this decision and that the new group of one would function in accordance with the practice of the BWC 'on a non-discriminatory basis as the other regional groups'.[37] It further noted that Russia 'indicated that this withdrawal does not set a precedent, concerns only the work within the Convention and has no consequences outside of it'.[38]

---

[29] Italy, 'Other weapons of mass destruction', Statement to the First Committee, 18 Oct. 2022.
[30] Australia, Statement to the First Committee, General debate, 12 Oct. 2022, p. 4; Finland, Statement to the First Committee, General debate, 10 Oct. 2022; Burkina Faso, Statement to the First Committee, General Debate, 6 Oct. 2022, p. 5; and Slovakia, Statement to the First Committee, General debate, 7 Oct. 2022, p. 4.
[31] UNODA, 'Biological Weapons Convention—Ninth review conference: Documents', 2022.
[32] BWC, RevCon9, 'Final document of the ninth review conference', BWC/CONF.IX/9, 22 Dec. 2022, part I, paras 18, 19 and 21.
[33] BWC, BWC/CONF.IX/9 (note 32), part I, para. 36.
[34] BWC, 'Biological Weapons Convention—Ninth review conference: Statements', 2022.
[35] UNODA, 'Biological Weapons Convention—Ninth review conference', 2022.
[36] BWC, RevCon9, 'The decision of the Russian Federation to withdraw from the Eastern European Group of the Convention on the Prohibition of the Development, Production and Stockpiling of Bacteriological (Biological) and Toxin Weapons and on their Destruction (BTWC)', Working paper submitted by Russia, BWC/CONF.IX/WP.14, 2 Dec. 2022, paras 5–6.
[37] BWC, BWC/CONF.IX/9 (note 32), part I, para. 26.
[38] BWC, BWC/CONF.IX/9 (note 32), part I, para. 26; and BWC, BWC/CONF.IX/WP.14 (note 36), para. 6.

The Committee of the Whole—a committee established by the conference to facilitate discussion and negotiation, and to make recommendations for adoption by the conference in plenary meetings—convened nearly a dozen times during the conference in which it reviewed the provisions of the BWC, article by article, but it was unable to reach consensus and the final report of the review conference does not contain the traditional article-by-article review.[39] Instead, the report of the Committee of the Whole was issued as a separate document.[40]

A draft final declaration was presented at the last meeting of the review conference, but consensus again proved elusive. The final document of the ninth review conference, adopted by consensus on 16 December 2022, did not contain a final declaration and comprised two, rather than the usual three, parts: I Organization and work of the conference, and II Decisions and recommendations.[41]

There was no substantive outcome of the 2017–20 intersessional programme. The final report simply noted that the conference's consideration of proposals to reflect the deliberations on steps to further strengthen treaty implementation was 'inconclusive', and that the conference 'regrets that no consensus was reached'.[42]

The most successful outcome of the review conference was agreement on an intersessional programme of work for 2023–26. The conference decided that three-day MSPs will be held annually, with the first scheduled for 11–13 December 2023. In addition, the conference established a working group on the strengthening of the convention, open to all states parties and to conduct its work by consensus.[43] The aim of the working group is 'to identify, examine and develop specific and effective measures, including possible legally-binding measures, and to make recommendations to strengthen and institutionalise the Convention in all its aspects, to be submitted to States Parties for consideration and any further action'.[44] More specifically, the conference allocated 15 days every year from 2023 to 2026 for its substantive meetings to address measures on: (*a*) international cooperation and assistance under Article X of the BWC; (*b*) scientific and technological developments relevant to the BWC; (*c*) confidence-building and transparency; (*d*) compliance and verification; (*e*) national implementation of the

---

[39] For the article-by-article review see e.g. BWC, RevCon9, 'Proposals made to the Committee of the Whole (as at 15.00, 3 December 2022)', Submitted by the Chair of the Committee of the Whole, BWC/CONF.IX/COW/INF.1.

[40] BWC, RevCon9, 'Combined proposals made to the Committee of the Whole', Submitted by the Chair of the Committee of the Whole BWC/CONF.IX/COW/INF.2, 8 Dec. 2022 and 'Addendum', BWC/CONF.IX/COW/INF.2/Add.1, 8 Dec. 2022.

[41] BWC, BWC/CONF.IX/9 (note 32), part I, para. 42.

[42] BWC, BWC/CONF.IX/9 (note 32), part II, paras 1–3.

[43] BWC, BWC/CONF.IX/9 (note 32), part II, paras 8 and 11.

[44] BWC, BWC/CONF.IX/9 (note 32), part II, para. 8.

convention; (f) assistance, response and preparedness under Article VII; and (g) organizational, institutional and financial arrangements.[45]

Finally, the conference decided to renew the mandate of the ISU from 2023 to 2027, as well as to add one new position, bringing full-time staff numbers up from three to four.[46]

Commentaries on RevCon9 spoke of a 'modest' success.[47] In a post-conference interview, the conference president, Ambassador Leonardo Bencini of Italy, said the conference 'succeeded in breaking the deadlock and set out a very good plan of action'.[48] While establishing a working group, and just agreeing to keep talking, may seem like a minimal accomplishment, Bencini indicated it was 'as far as we could go'.[49] And it matters, he said, because 'we don't want fragmentation of the way in which the international community deals with nonproliferation of weapons of mass destruction. It is absolutely vital that we have a forum where all countries meet and discuss and try to find shared solutions'.[50] A spokesperson for the UN secretary-general characterized the outcome as 'a glimmer of hope in an overall bleak international security environment'.[51] Long-standing BWC commentator Richard Guthrie noted that the loss of the Solemn Declaration as the overarching political statement from the review conference was a significant loss, 'perhaps more important than the loss of the article-by-article review'.[52] But the establishment of the working group, 'primed to discuss possible compliance activities that could be agreed for the BWC', was 'a significant step forward'.[53]

Conclusions and outlook

Given current geopolitical tensions, there is a risk that the BWC logjam will persist and that the intersessional programme will again end up with no substantive outcomes at the 10th review conference. There are certainly no guarantees of agreement on substantive issues in future, but, for now at least, a process for continued dialogue under the convention has been preserved.[54]

---

[45] BWC, BWC/CONF.IX/9 (note 32), part II, paras 8 and 12.
[46] BWC, BWC/CONF.IX/9 (note 32), part II, paras 24–25.
[47] See e.g. Kirby, J., 'The treaties that make the world safer are struggling', Vox, 5 Jan. 2023.
[48] 'Assessing the ninth BWC review conference: An interview with conference president Leonardo Bencini', Arms Control Today, vol. 53, no. 1 (Jan./Feb. 2023), p. 18.
[49] 'Assessing the ninth BWC review conference' (note 48), p. 19.
[50] 'Assessing the ninth BWC review conference' (note 48), p. 18.
[51] United Nations, Secretary-General, Statement attributable to the spokesperson for the secretary-general on the ninth review conference of the Biological Weapons Convention, 16 Dec. 2022.
[52] Guthrie, R., 'The final document of the review conference and some reflections', Bioweapons Prevention Project, RevCon Report no. 17, 17 Jan. 2023, p. 2.
[53] Guthrie (note 52), p. 2.
[54] 'Assessing the ninth BWC review conference' (note 48), p. 19.

IV. Allegations of and reactions to chemical weapon use

UNA JAKOB*

This section discusses the ongoing investigations of previous allegations of chemical weapon use in Syria (2013–18) and follow-up actions in relation to the poisoning of Russian citizen Alexei Navalny with a novichok nerve agent in 2020, as well as multiple but unsubstantiated allegations of illegal chemical activities during the war in Ukraine in 2022.[1]

Chemical weapon disarmament and investigations in Syria

The Organisation for the Prohibition of Chemical Weapons (OPCW) continued to investigate incidents of alleged chemical weapon use in Syria and to clarify concerns that Syria might not have fully disclosed its past and present chemical weapon activities. All declared Syrian chemical weapon facilities and stockpiles were destroyed under OPCW verification. However, several OPCW verification activities have indicated that the initial declarations as submitted by Syria were incomplete and inaccurate. Moreover, chemical weapon attacks occurred even though the chemical weapon programme was supposed to be terminated upon Syria's accession to the Chemical Weapons Convention (CWC) in 2013.[2] Activities of the OPCW to address the chemical weapon issue in Syria include those of the Fact-Finding Mission (FFM), the Declaration Assessment Team (DAT) and the Investigation and Identification Team (IIT), as well as inspections at sites identified as relevant by earlier OPCW and United Nations investigations (table 9.1).[3] The activities are supported by the Trust Fund for Syria Missions, established in November 2015, which had received a total of € 37.7 million from 22 CWC states parties and the European Union (EU) as of December 2022.[4]

Syria regularly submitted its monthly reports on the destruction of its chemical weapon programme to the OPCW Technical Secretariat in 2022 but has otherwise cooperated with the secretariat and its dedicated bodies in a very limited way or not at all, including by denying inspectors access to

---

[1] See also Jakob, U., 'Allegations of chemical weapons use in Syria', *SIPRI Yearbook 2022*, pp. 496–503.

[2] For a summary and other details of the Chemical Weapons Convention (CWC) see annex A, section I, in this volume. For an update on the CWC see section V in this chapter.

[3] See e.g. Arms Control Association, 'Timeline of Syrian chemical weapons activity, 2012–2022', Fact Sheets & Briefs, last reviewed May 2021; and Organisation for the Prohibition of Chemical Weapons (OPCW), Executive Council, 'Progress in the elimination of the Syrian chemical weapons programme', Report by the director-general, EC-102/DG.3, 23 Dec. 2022.

[4] OPCW, EC-102/DG.3 (note 3), para. 39.

* The author would like to acknowledge the valuable research assistance of Henrike Buch for this section.

Table 9.1. Overview of ad hoc mechanisms of the Organisation for the Prohibition of Chemical Weapons to address the issue of chemical weapons in Syria

Mechanism	Duration	Mandate	Source
Declaration Assessment Team (DAT)	Since 2014	Resolve identified gaps and inconsistencies in Syria's declarations	Established by OPCW director-general
Fact-Finding Mission (FFM)	Since 2014	Establish facts surrounding alleged chemical weapon use in Syria	Established by OPCW director-general, endorsed by OPCW Executive Council and UN Security Council[a]
OPCW–UN Joint Investigative Mechanism (JIM)	2015–17	Identify perpetrators of chemical weapon attacks established by the FFM	UN Security Council Resolution 2235[b]
Investigation and Identification Team (IIT)	Since 2018	Identify those involved in cases of chemical weapon use established by the FFM but not investigated by the JIM	Decision by OPCW Conference of the States Parties[c]

OPCW = Organisation for the Prohibition of Chemical Weapons; UN = United Nations.

[a] OPCW, Executive Council, 'Reports of the OPCW Fact-Finding Mission in Syria', Decision, EC-M-48/DEC.1(2015), 4 Feb. 2015; and UN Security Council Resolution 2209, 6 Mar. 2015.

[b] UN Security Council Resolution 2235, 7 Aug. 2015.

[c] OPCW, Conference of the States Parties, 'Addressing the threat from chemicals weapons use', Decision, C-SS-4/DEC.3, 27 June 2018.

Sources: OPCW, 'Syria and the OPCW'; and Jakob, U., 'Allegations of chemical weapons use in Syria', *SIPRI Yearbook 2022*, p. 498, table 12.1.

relevant sites and by not providing information as requested.[5] The Syrian government has submitted a document to the Technical Secretariat that, according to the title given in the director-general's November 2022 report, outlines Syria's perspective on its cooperation with the OPCW.[6]

Ongoing work of the FFM

During 2022, the FFM continued to investigate cases of alleged chemical weapon use in Syria. In fulfilling its mandate to determine 'whether toxic chemical have been used as weapons in the Syrian Arab Republic', as of 31 December 2022 the FFM had in total deployed to Syria 112 times, had interviewed more than 600 people and had collected more than 450 samples. Its 19 reports to date cover 71 instances of alleged chemical weapon use, and

---

[5] See the director-general's regular reports to the OPCW Executive Council on 'Progress in the elimination of the Syrian chemical weapons programme', available at OPCW, 'Documents: Executive Council'.

[6] OPCW, Executive Council, 'Progress in the elimination of the Syrian chemical weapons programme', Report by the director-general, EC-102/DG.2, 24 Nov. 2022, para. 17.

the FFM confirmed such use in 20 cases. Chlorine was used as a weapon in 14 cases, sarin in 3 cases and sulfur mustard in 3 cases.[7]

In January 2022, the FFM published two reports. The first covered two incidents that occurred in Marea on 1 and 3 September 2015. Regarding the incident on 1 September 2015, the FFM concluded that there are reasonable grounds to believe that sulfur mustard was used as a weapon.[8] For the incident on 3 September 2015, the FFM could reach no conclusion as casualties were not available for interviews.[9] In the second report the FFM concluded that there were reasonable grounds to believe that chlorine was used as a weapon in Kafr Zeita on 1 October 2016.[10]

Russia and Syria, while condemning chemical weapon attacks in principle, rejected the findings of the FFM reports and accused the FFM of having conducted its work in an unprofessional manner, including by not respecting established investigation and chain of custody protocols and moving outside the scope of the CWC.[11] Western and other countries condemned the attacks and expressed their confidence in and support for the work of the Technical Secretariat in investigating chemical weapon attacks in Syria; they also called on Syria to cooperate with the OPCW and fully comply with the CWC.[12] Some other states parties from other OPCW regional groups also spoke out against chemical weapon use in general terms, but did not explicitly address the cases at hand.[13]

---

[7] OPCW, 'Fact-Finding Mission'.

[8] OPCW, Technical Secretariat, Report of the OPCW Fact-Finding Mission in Syria regarding the incidents of the alleged use of chemicals as a weapon in Marea, Syrian Arab Republic, on 1 and 3 September 2015, S/2017/2022, 24 Jan. 2022, paras 1.14 and 8.10.

[9] OPCW, S/2017/2022 (note 8), paras 1.15 and 8.11.

[10] OPCW, Technical Secretariat, Report of the OPCW Fact-Finding Mission in Syria regarding the incident of the alleged use of chemicals as a weapon in Kafr Zeita, Syrian Arab Republic, 1 October 2016, S/2020/2022, 31 Jan. 2022, paras 1.11 and 8.15.

[11] Syria, Statement by HE Ambassador Milad Atieh, Permanent representative of the Syrian Arab Republic to the OPCW at the 99th session of the Executive Council under agenda item 7(c), EC-99/NAT.78, 8 Mar. 2022, pp. 4–6; and Russia, Statement by HE Ambassador A.V. Shulgin, Permanent representative of the Russian Federation to the OPCW at the 99th session of the Executive Council under agenda item 7(e), EC-99/NAT.51, 8 Mar. 2022.

[12] See e.g. Ireland, Statement by HE Ambassador Brendan Rogers, Permanent representative of Ireland to the OPCW at the 99th session of the Executive Council, EC-99/NAT.49, 8 Mar. 2022, p. 2; Japan, Statement by HE Ambassador Hidehisa Horinouchi, Permanent representative of Japan to the OPCW at the 99th session of the Executive Council, EC-99/NAT.35, 8 Mar. 2022, p. 2; United States, Statement by HE Ambassador Joseph Manso, Permanent representative of the United States of America to the OPCW at the 99th session of the Executive Council, EC-99/NAT.12, 8 Mar. 2022, p. 2; Argentina, Statement by the delegation of the Argentine Republic to the OPCW at the 27th session of the conference of the states parties, C-27/NAT.72, 28 Nov. 2022, p. 1; and France, Joint statement at the 27th session of the conference of the states parties under agenda item 9(d), 30 Nov. 2022.

[13] See e.g. South Africa, Statement on behalf of the Group of African states parties to the Chemical Weapons Convention, delivered by HE Ambassador Vusimuzi Philemon Madonsela, Permanent representative of the Republic of South Africa to the OPCW at the 99th session of the Executive Council, EC-99/NAT.69, 8 Mar. 2022, p. 3. See also Azerbaijan, Statement on behalf of the member states of the Non-Aligned Movement that are states parties to the Chemical Weapons Convention and China, delivered by HE Ambassador Fikrat Akhundov, Permanent representative of the Republic of

A further FFM deployment to Syria had been planned from 22 January to 4 February 2022 but had to be postponed due to Covid-19-related events.[14] The FFM deployed to Syria again between 6 and 12 November 2022 'to conduct interviews with witnesses regarding several of the incidents under review'.[15]

Clarification of Syria's declarations and of subsequent inspection findings

Through the DAT, the Technical Secretariat continued its work to clarify all outstanding issues regarding the initial and subsequent declarations submitted by Syria.[16] By the end of 2022 the DAT had visited Syria 25 times, holding over 150 technical meetings, carrying out more than 70 interviews with people who were involved in the Syrian chemical weapon programme, visiting chemical weapon sites and facilities over 40 times, and collecting more than 16 samples.[17]

However, the DAT's work was still hampered by Syria's refusal to fully cooperate with the OPCW in this respect.[18] At the end of 2022 Syria had not provided any new information or additional declarations, consultations in Syria had still not taken place, and consequently none of the 20 outstanding issues that were unresolved at the end of 2021 could be clarified.[19] Hence, the Technical Secretariat continued to assess that 'the declaration submitted by the Syrian Arab Republic still cannot be considered accurate and complete'.[20]

The 25th round of DAT consultations, which had been on hold since April 2021, could still not be carried out in 2022.[21] The Technical Secretariat submitted several proposals throughout the year to enable at least some limited activities under the mandate of the DAT to take place. Consultations in Syria were initially planned for April 2022 but the Syrian government denied an entry visa for the lead technical expert on the team.[22] In the course of 2022,

---

Azerbaijan to the OPCW at the 99th session of the Executive Council, EC-99/NAT.31, 8 Mar. 2022, p. 3; and India, Statement by the delegation of the Republic of India to the OPCW at the 99th session of the Executive Council, EC-99/NAT.66, 8 Mar. 2022, p. 2. For a more critical non-Western stance regarding the Syrian policy see e.g. Mexico, Statement by HE Ambassador José Antonio Zabalgoitia, Permanent representative of the United Mexican States to the OPCW at the 99th session of the Executive Council, EC-99/NAT.55, 8 Mar. 2022, p. 2.

[14] OPCW, Executive Council, 'Progress in the elimination of the Syrian chemical weapons programme', Report by the director-general, EC-99/DG.13, 24 Feb. 2022, para. 29.

[15] OPCW, EC-102/DG.2 (note 6), para. 28.

[16] OPCW, EC-102/DG.3 (note 3), para. 10.

[17] OPCW, 'Declaration Assessment Team', Status as at 23 Feb. 2023.

[18] See e.g. OPCW, EC-102/DG.3 (note 3).

[19] See Jakob, 'Allegations of chemical weapons use in Syria' (note 1), pp. 498–99.

[20] OPCW, EC-102/DG.3 (note 3), para. 18.

[21] OPCW, EC-102/DG.3 (note 3), para. 11.

[22] OPCW, Executive Council, 'Progress in the elimination of the Syrian chemical weapons programme', Report by the director-general, EC-100/DG.14, 23 June 2022, para. 12. For Syria's perspective see Syria, Statement by HE Ambassador Milad Atieh, Permanent representative of the Syrian Arab Republic to the OPCW at the 99th session of the Executive Council under agenda item 7(c), EC-99/NAT.78, 8 Mar. 2022, pp. 2–4.

the Secretariat changed its approach and proposed to continue the work through a written exchange instead of consultations on the ground, even though it assessed that the results of such an approach would not be comparable to those reached through consultations.[23] The Secretariat invited Syria to submit all of the declarations and documents, including on previously undeclared activities, which the DAT had already requested from Syria but had not received to date.[24] In addition to the written exchange, the Secretariat proposed to hold a limited round of consultations in Beirut, Lebanon. Syria agreed to this procedure but continued to insist that one particular DAT member would have to be excluded from the consultations; later it requested that the Technical Secretariat cover the costs arising from these consultations for the Syrian delegation. The Technical Secretariat refused both requests as they were incompatible with the legal framework within which the DAT operates.[25] In a further effort to make progress, the Secretariat then proposed on 8 December 2022 to send a reduced team to conduct limited in-country activities in Syria in January 2023. Syria welcomed the proposal and 'requested supplementary information in order to make the necessary arrangements'.[26]

In June 2022 the Technical Secretariat provided Syria with its final report of the 2021 inspections of the Barzah and Jamrayah facilities at the Syrian Scientific Research Centre.[27] In September 2022, the Secretariat conducted the ninth round of inspections at these facilities, as mandated by an OPCW Executive Council decision in 2016 in response to earlier findings by the JIM.[28] Another round of inspections had been envisaged for December 2022 but had to be postponed for 'operational reasons' until 2023.[29]

In December 2022 the Technical Secretariat reported that despite its requests it had still not received information that would allow it to clarify either of two other outstanding issues—a chemical listed in Schedule 2.B.04 that OPCW inspectors detected at the Barzah facility in November 2018 during the third round of inspections, and two chlorine cylinders related to the April 2018 chemical attack in Douma that Syria had reported to the OPCW as destroyed in July 2021.[30] On the latter issue, the cylinders were stored and inspected by the Technical Secretariat in November 2020 at a location a considerable distance from the site of the reported July 2021 attack. The Secre-

---

[23] OPCW, EC-100/DG.14 (note 22), para. 13.
[24] See e.g. OPCW, Technical Secretariat, 'Progress in the elimination of the Syrian chemical weapons programme', Report by the director-general, EC-101/DG.4, 24 Aug. 2022, para. 14.
[25] See e.g. OPCW, EC-101/DG.4 (note 24), para. 11.
[26] OPCW, EC-102/DG.3 (note 3), paras 15–16.
[27] OPCW, Technical Secretariat, 'Progress in the elimination of the Syrian chemical weapons programme', Report by the director-general, EC-101/DG.22, 23 Sep. 2022, para. 17.
[28] OPCW, EC-101/DG.22 (note 27), para. 17.
[29] OPCW, EC-102/DG.2 (note 6), para. 21.
[30] OPCW, EC-102/DG.3 (note 3), para. 21.

tariat had requested clarification from Syria on the 'unauthorized movement' of the cylinders from the inspected site to the site of the attack.[31]

The work of the IIT and efforts to restore Syrian compliance

The IIT also continued its investigations in 2022. Established by the conference of the states parties (CSP) in June 2018 as part of the OPCW Technical Secretariat under the director-general's authority, the team is tasked with identifying the perpetrators of those chemical attacks in Syria which the FFM has confirmed and which were not investigated by the JIM.[32] By end of December 2022, the IIT had deployed to Syria 16 times.[33] Prior to 2022, the IIT had identified the Syrian Armed Forces as perpetrators in three attacks in Ltamenah in March 2017 and one in Saraqib in February 2018.[34]

In the course of 2022, the IIT continued to investigate a chemical attack that took place in Douma on 7 April 2018 and for which the FFM in 2019 established chlorine use, and concluded that there were reasonable grounds to believe that the Syrian Armed Forces used chlorine as a weapon in that attack.[35] This conclusion ties in with the earlier FFM findings on Douma which upon their release were highly contested, including by Syria and Russia who put forward alternative scenarios to explain the incident.[36] The IIT investigated these alternative scenarios in detail but could not corroborate any of them.[37] As in its previous reports, the IIT stated that it applied established standards of international fact-finding, and the 'reasonable grounds' standard used for the Douma findings represents a level of confidence that would allow the opening of a judicial investigation.[38] As in previous IIT investigations, the team members were not able to visit the site of the investi-

---

[31] OPCW, Executive Council, 'Progress in the elimination of the Syrian chemical weapons programme', Report by the director-general, EC-101/DG.2, 22 July 2022, para. 23; and OPCW, EC-102/DG.3 (note 3), para. 23.

[32] OPCW, 'Investigation and Identification Team (IIT)'; and OPCW, Conference of the States Parties, 'Addressing the threat from chemical weapons use', Decision, C-SS-4/DEC.3, 27 June 2018, para. 10.

[33] OPCW, 'Investigation and Identification Team (IIT)' (note 32).

[34] OPCW, Technical Secretariat, 'First report by the OPCW Investigation and Identification Team pursuant to paragraph 10 of Decision C-SS-4/DEC.3 "Addressing the threat form chemical weapons use", Ltamenah (Syrian Arab Republic), 24, 25, and 30 March 2017', S/1867/2020, 8 Apr. 2020; and OPCW, Technical Secretariat, 'Second report by the OPCW Investigation and Identification Team pursuant to paragraph 10 of Decision C-SS-4/DEC.3 "Addressing the threat from chemical weapons use", Saraqib (Syrian Arab Republic), 4 February 2018', S/1943/2021, 12 Apr. 2021.

[35] OPCW, Technical Secretariat, 'Report of the Fact-Finding Mission regarding the incident of alleged use of toxic chemicals as a weapon in Douma, Syrian Arab Republic, on 7 April 2018', S/1731/2019, 1 Mar. 2019; and OPCW, Technical Secretariat, 'Third report by the OPCW Investigation and Identification Team pursuant to paragraph 10 of Decision C-SS-4/DEC.3 "Addressing the threat from chemical weapons use", Douma (Syrian Arab Republic)–7 April 2018', S/2125/2023, 27 Jan. 2023, Executive summary para. 6.

[36] On the Douma attack see McLeish, C., 'Allegations of use of chemical weapons in Syria', *SIPRI Yearbook 2019*, pp. 400–404.

[37] OPCW, S/2125/2023 (note 35), Executive summary para. 6.

[38] OPCW, S/2125/2023 (note 35), para. 3.3.

gated attack because Syria did not grant them access despite its obligation to cooperate with the OPCW.[39]

The Syrian government continues to deny its use of chemical weapons and has repeatedly stated that 'it categorically rejects the use of chemical weapons by anyone, anywhere, and under any circumstances . . .'.[40] Syria justifies its refusal to cooperate with the IIT by claiming, along with Russia and Iran, that the IIT and its mandate go beyond the scope of the CWC.[41] Other states have repeatedly emphasized Syria's obligation to fully cooperate with any OPCW investigation, or expressed their confidence in and full support for the work of the Technical Secretariat.[42] In their criticism of the IIT, Syria and Russia also objected to the transfer of information gathered in the course of the IIT investigations to other investigation bodies, in particular the UN International, Impartial and Independent Mechanism (IIIM), claiming this would be a violation of Article VIII, paragraph 34 of the CWC.[43] As part of its activities and in accordance with its mandate, the IIT prepares and preserves the evidence that it has collected in a way that makes it usable by other UN entities in potential future investigations or trials related to international law violations in Syria.[44]

In response to the concerns about Syria's non-compliance with the CWC, in 2020 the Executive Council requested Syria, under Article VIII, paragraph 36 of the CWC, to declare its facilities related to confirmed chemical weapon attacks and all remaining chemical weapon stockpiles, and to resolve all outstanding issues regarding its initial chemical weapon–related declarations, within 90 days of Decision EC-94/DEC.2.[45] Since this deadline passed without Syria having responded to any of these requirements, states parties invoked the compliance provision in Article XII and, by majority

---

[39] OPCW, S/2125/2023 (note 35), Executive summary para. 7.

[40] See e.g. Syria, Statement by HE Ambassador Milad Atieh, Permanent representative of the Syrian Arab Republic to the OPCW at the 100th session of the Executive Council under agenda item 6(f), EC-100/NAT.70, 5 July 2022, p. 1.

[41] See e.g. Syria, Statement by HE Ambassador Milad Atieh, Permanent representative of the Syrian Arab Republic to the OPCW at the 100th session of the Executive Council under agenda item 9, EC-100/NAT.65, 6 July 2022, p. 2; Syria, EC-100/NAT.70 (note 40), p. 2; Iran, Statement by HE Ambassador Alireza Kazemi Abadi, Permanent representative of the Islamic Republic of Iran to the OPCW at the 101st session of the Executive Council under agenda item 6(g), EC-101/NAT.23, 4 Oct. 2022, p. 1; and Russia, Statement by HE Ambassador A. V. Shulgin, Permanent representative of the Russian Federation to the OPCW at the 100th session of the Executive Council under agenda item 9, EC-100/NAT.73, 6 July 2022, p. 1.

[42] See e.g. Sweden, Statement by HE Ambassador Johannes Oljelund, Permanent representative of the Kingdom of Sweden to the OPCW at the 99th session of the Executive Council, EC-99/NAT.18, 8 Mar. 2022, p. 2; and Türkiye, Statement by HE Ambassador Şaban Dişli, Permanent representative of the Republic of Turkey to the OPCW at the 99th session of the Executive Council, EC-99/NAT.67, 8 Mar. 2022, p. 2.

[43] See e.g. Russia, EC-100/NAT.73 (note 41), p. 1.

[44] OPCW, S/2125/2023 (note 35), para. 2.4, Executive summary para. 8.

[45] OPCW, Executive Council, 'Addressing the possession and use of chemical weapons by the Syrian Arab Republic', Decision, EC-94/DEC.2, 9 July 2020, p. 4.

vote, in 2021 decided to suspend several of Syria's rights and privileges as an OPCW member.[46] Since Syria had not fulfilled any of the requirements by the end of 2022, the suspension of these rights and privileges remained in place.

At the March 2022 meeting of the Executive Council, Iran and Russia criticized this approach once more, with Iran deeming the decision to suspend Syria's rights and privileges as 'unfair and unacceptable'.[47] China also stated in its general statement that it viewed the establishment of the IIT as going beyond the scope of the CWC.[48] At the November 2022 CSP, other states—including in a statement by France on behalf of 57 states parties—reaffirmed their support for the OPCW and confidence in the findings of its investigations and called on Syria to restore its compliance with the CWC.[49] The EU considered the suspension of the voting rights and privileges 'an appropriate response' and announced the addition of two Syrian businesspersons and their company to the EU sanctions list.[50]

Aftermath of the poisoning of Alexei Navalny

In August 2020, the Russian citizen Alexei Navalny was poisoned with a nerve agent from the novichok family on a domestic flight in Russia.[51] He was subsequently transferred to Berlin, Germany, for medical treatment.[52] The use of a novichok agent was first identified by a German laboratory and later independently confirmed by two other OPCW-accredited labs located in Switzerland and Sweden and by the OPCW laboratory. Germany requested

---

[46] OPCW, Conference of the States Parties, 'Addressing the possession and use of chemical weapons by the Syrian Arab Republic', Decision, C-25/DEC.9, 21 Apr. 2021. See Jakob, 'Allegations of chemical weapons use in Syria' (note 1), pp. 502–503.

[47] Iran, Statement by HE Ambassador Alireza Kazemi Abadi, Permanent representative of the Islamic Republic of Iran to the OPCW at the 99th session of the Executive Council under agenda item 7(e), EC-99/NAT.23, 8 Mar. 2022; Russia, EC-99/NAT.51 (note 11); and Syria, Statement by Ambassador Milad Atieh, Permanent representative of the Syrian Arab Republic to the OPCW for the 99th session of the Executive Council under agenda item 7(e), EC-99/NAT.77, 8 Mar. 2022.

[48] China, Statement by HE Ambassador Tan Jian, Permanent representative of the People's Republic of China to the OPCW at the 99th session of the Executive Council, EC-99/NAT.47, 8 Mar. 2022, p. 2.

[49] See e.g. New Zealand, Statement by HE Ambassador Susannah Gordon, Permanent representative of New Zealand to the OPCW at the 27th session of the conference of the states parties, C-27/NAT.7, 28 Nov. 2022, p. 2; Spain, Statement by the delegation of the Kingdom of Spain to the OPCW at the 27th session of the conference of the states parties, C-27/NAT.58, 28 Nov. 2022, p. 2; Slovakia, Statement by HE Ambassador Juraj Machác, Permanent representative of the Slovak Republic to the OPCW at the 27th session of the conference of the states parties, C-27/NAT.4, 28 Nov. 2022, p. 2; and France, Joint statement at the 27th session of the conference of the states parties under agenda item 9(d), 30 Nov. 2022.

[50] European Union, Statement on behalf of the European Union delivered by HE Ambassador Markus Leinonen, European External Action Service, at the 27th session of the conference of the states parties under agenda item 9(d), C-27/NAT.39, 29 Nov. 2022.

[51] See also Jakob, U., 'Chemical arms control and disarmament', *SIPRI Yearbook 2022*, pp. 504–505; and McLeish, C., 'Use of novichok agents', *SIPRI Yearbook 2021*, pp. 489–93.

[52] A detailed account of the case of Alexei Navalny can be found in Council of Europe, Parliamentary Committee on Legal Affairs and Human Rights, 'Poisoning of Alexei Navalny', Report, Doc. no. 15434, 10 Jan. 2022. See also McLeish, 'Use of novichok agents' (note 51), pp. 489–93.

and received a technical assistance visit (TAV) from the OPCW which confirmed its initial analysis. Western countries accused the Russian government of being involved in this incident, which Russia continues to deny.[53]

France, Germany, Sweden and the United Kingdom, supported by a group of other countries, have engaged in an exchange with Russia of requests for clarification in accordance with Article IX of the CWC.[54] The exchange continued into early 2022 but neither side has so far expressed satisfaction with the replies received. Russia has continued to insist that it required the information requested from, but not provided by, the OPCW Technical Secretariat and Germany, France, Sweden and the UK, for it to open a domestic criminal investigation into the incident, and that it had in turn provided 'every detail of the steps taken . . . to explain all of the circumstances' of Navalny's case.[55] Germany, France, Sweden and others, however, repeatedly stated that the information requested by Russia was either irrelevant or could not be provided due to data protection and other regulations, and that Russia had still not addressed the requests it had received from a group of 45 countries.[56] They also continued to call on Russia to open an investigation into the Navalny case.[57]

In a similar vein, on 26 January 2022 the Parliamentary Assembly of the Council of Europe issued a resolution on the 'Poisoning of Alexei Navalny' in which it called on Russia to, among other things, fulfil its obligations under the CWC, including by 'investigating the alleged development, production, stockpiling and use of a chemical weapon on Russian territory', and to agree to a TAV from the OPCW 'on the standard conditions that guarantee the independence of its technical secretariat . . . at the very earliest opportunity'.[58]

---

[53] Jakob, 'Chemical arms control and disarmament' (note 51), p. 505.

[54] See Jakob, 'Chemical arms control and disarmament' (note 51), p. 506.

[55] Russia, Statement by HE Ambassador A.V. Shulgin, Permanent representative of the Russian Federation to the OPCW at the 99th session of the Executive Council in exercise of the right of reply to the statements of Ukraine and a number of other countries, EC-99/NAT.50, 8 Mar. 2022, p. 2; see also Russia, 'Request for circulation of a document at the 99th session of the Executive Council, EC-99/NAT.2, 15 Nov. 2021.

[56] See e.g. Germany, Statement by HE Ambassador Thomas Schieb, Permanent representative of the Federal Republic of Germany to the OPCW at the 101st session of the Executive Council, EC-101/NAT.15, 4 Oct. 2022, pp. 1–2; and Sweden, Statement by HE Ambassador Johannes Oljelund, Permanent representative of the Kingdom of Sweden to the OPCW at the 100th session of the Executive Council, EC-100/NAT.23, 5 July 2022, p. 2. See also Jakob, 'Chemical arms control and disarmament' (note 51), p. 506.

[57] See e.g. France, Statement by HE Ambassador Francois Alabrune, Permanent representative of the French Republic to the OPCW at the 27th session of the conference of the states parties, C-27/NAT.60, 28 Nov. 2022, p. 2; Germany, National Statement delivered by Ambassador Thomas Schieb, Permanent representative of the Federal Republic of Germany to the OPCW at the 27th session of the conference of the states parties, Nov. 2022, p. 2; and Germany, Joint statement on behalf of forty-nine member states of the OPCW delivered by the delegation of the Federal Republic of Germany to the OPCW at the 99th session of the Executive Council under agenda item 7(e), EC-99/NAT.36, 8 Mar. 2022.

[58] Council of Europe Parliamentary Assembly, 'Poisoning of Alexei Navalny', Resolution 2423 (2022).

In October 2022, the EU extended its existing sanctions pertaining to the proliferation and use of chemical weapons for another year, including sanctions against six Russian government officials allegedly involved in the preparation or execution of the attack on Navalny, and for similar reasons added another eight persons to its sanctions list on 14 November 2022.[59]

Regarding the TAV which Russia had requested from the Technical Secretariat shortly after the Navalny incident but later made conditional on procedures that do not correspond to standard OPCW procedures, the director-general reported to the Executive Council in March 2022 that the Technical Secretariat could not deploy a TAV to Russia while 'that country continues to request that the TAV be conducted in contravention of some of the basic rules and applicable procedures for these activities, such as guaranteeing the independence of the TAV team'.[60]

Allegations of illegal chemical activities in Ukraine

Shortly after Russia's invasion of Ukraine on 24 February 2022, Ukraine voiced concerns to the OPCW that Russia may be preparing 'provocations' by blowing up chemical facilities in the Donetsk region.[61] Referring directly to the Ukrainian concerns, France on behalf of the 27 EU member states on 3 March 2022 condemned both the war and possible chemical 'false flag' provocations, a position which many states parties and the EU repeated multiple times throughout 2022.[62] On 10 March, Russia conveyed the first of 39 communications to the OPCW (in the form of notes verbales) in which it accused Ukrainian groups, supported by the United States, of preparing

[59] Council of the European Union, 'Chemical weapons: EU sanctions renewed for a further year', Press release, 13 Oct. 2022; European Union, Statement on behalf of the European Union, delivered by Ambassador Markus Leinonen, European External Action Service, at the 27th session of the conference of the states parties under agenda item 9(d), C-27/NAT.40, 29 Nov. 2022, p. 2; and Council of the European Union, Council Implementing Regulation (EU) 2022/2228 of 14 November 2022 implementing Regulation (EU) No 2018/1542 concerning restrictive measures against the proliferation and use of chemical weapons, *Official Journal of the European Union*, L293, pp. 1–8, paras 4–5 and Annex.

[60] OPCW, Executive Council, Opening statement by the director-general to the Executive Council at its 99th session, EC-99/DG.17, 8 Mar. 2022, para. 36.

[61] Ukraine, Note verbale no. 61219/30-196/50-3, 27 Feb. 2022. This note verbale and all others quoted in this section are contained in the 'Compendium of correspondence shared by states parties on Ukraine', compiled by the OPCW. See OPCW, 'Ukraine'.

[62] France, Note verbale no. 2022-0106026, 3 Mar. 2022. See e.g. Germany (on behalf of 53 states parties), Statement by HE Ambassador Gudrun Lingner, Permanent representative of the Federal Republic of Germany to the OPCW at the 100th session of the Executive Council, EC-100/NAT.51, 5 July 2022; Australia (on behalf of Canada, New Zealand and Australia), Statement by HE Ambassador Matthew Neuhaus, Permanent representative of Australia to the OPCW at the 99th session of the Executive Council under agenda item 7(e), EC-99/NAT.28, 8 Mar. 2022; Mexico, Statement by HE Ambassador José Antonio Zabalgoitia, Permanent representative of the United Mexican States to the OPCW at the 99th session of the Executive Council under agenda item 7(e), WC-99/NAT.64, 8 Mar. 2022; and European Union, C-27/NAT.40 (note 59).

chemical 'provocations'.[63] This exchange of notes verbales marked the start of a series of diplomatic communications through the OPCW primarily between Russia and Ukraine accusing each other of disinformation about planned or actual intentional release of toxic substances. The Technical Secretariat compiled all notes verbales that it received in this context in a compendium of correspondence, which is publicly available on the OPCW website.[64] In August 2022, when the last entry was added to the compendium, the document comprised 121 pages.

Most of the Russian allegations concerned the claim that Ukrainian troops or fighters could be planning, preparing, provoking or carrying out deliberate detonations at chemical facilities or depots, or of vehicles loaded with chemicals, with the intention to blame such incidents on Russia or to secure more Western military assistance.[65] In one note, Russia accused the OPCW of being complicit in the 'false flag' strategy of Ukraine targeted against Russia, which prompted the Technical Secretariat to emphasize in its reply the impartial character of its work.[66] Russia subsequently backtracked from its direct accusation against the Technical Secretariat.[67]

In addition to condemning the Russian actions in Ukraine and warning against the use of chemical weapons, the USA explicitly accused Russia of maintaining a chemical weapon programme in violation of its obligations under the CWC and rejected the Russian claims that the USA was supporting Ukrainian chemical 'provocations'.[68] The UK also rejected such allegations and cited Russian disinformation in relation to Syria's chemical weapons and the Novichok poisonings.[69] Russia in turn dismissed the UK accusations as part of a UK and Ukrainian disinformation campaign.[70]

Through its notes verbales, Ukraine repeatedly warned of imminent Russian chemical attacks, denied that it had the means or intention to carry out chemical attacks itself (and countered Russian allegations regarding specific locations or planned incidents), and cautioned against Russian disinformation.[71] Later in the process, Ukraine reported on Russian attacks on civilian chemical infrastructure in Ukraine that released chemicals such as

[63] Russia, Note verbale no. 01/22, 10 Mar. 2022.
[64] 'Compendium of correspondence shared by states parties on Ukraine' (note 61).
[65] For Russian notes verbales on the intention to blame, see e.g. no. 5, 10 Mar. 2022; no. 17, 7 May 2022; no. 19, 18 May 2022; no. 23, 30 May 2022; no. 28, 6 June 2022; and no. 39, 12 Aug. 2022. For an example claiming the intention to secure military assistance, see Russia, Note verbale no. 18, 12 May 2022.
[66] Russia, Note verbale no. 29, 9 June 2022; and OPCW, Note verbale no. NV/ODG-290/22, 10 June 2022.
[67] Russia, Note verbale no. 30, 14 June 2022.
[68] United States, Note verbale no. 01/22, 11 Mar. 2022.
[69] United Kingdom, Note verbale no. 63/2022, 1 June 2022.
[70] Russia, Note verbale no. 27, 6 June 2022.
[71] Ukraine, Note verbale no. 61219/35-196/50-18783, 11 Mar. 2022; Ukraine, Note verbale no. 61219/35-196/50-28451, 25 Apr. 2022; and Ukraine, Note verbale no. 61219/35-196/50-34885, 24 May 2022.

ammonia and nitric acid, and accused Russia of having used toxic substances in Mariupol, among other places.[72]

In many of the notes, Russia seemed to use 'chemical attacks', 'chemical provocations', 'intentional release of toxic substances' and 'chemical weapon use' as interchangeable terms. Since the definition of chemical weapons is based on the general purpose criterion and not dependent on specific chemical substances or means of dissemination, the intentional release of toxic chemicals could fall within the purview of the OPCW, depending on the exact circumstances. No formal CWC procedures related to alleged chemical weapon use or other treaty violations have been invoked so far with respect to the situation in Ukraine. Ukraine did, however, request bilateral assistance from CWC states parties under Article X for protection against possible chemical weapon attacks.[73] It also requested, and received, assistance from the Technical Secretariat.[74]

The Technical Secretariat published a statement expressing concern at the reports of chemical weapon use in Mariupol. The statement also reiterated the comprehensive nature of the chemical weapon prohibition and emphasized that the Secretariat 'has also uninterruptedly been monitoring the situation around declared chemical industrial sites in Ukraine', and reaffirmed its readiness to provide assistance to states parties in case of the use or threat of use of chemical weapons.[75]

---

[72] See e.g. Ukraine notes verbales no. 61219/35-196/50-21493, 22 Mar. 2022; no. 61219/35-196/50-24179, 7 Apr. 2022; no. 61219/35-196/50-25231, 12 Apr. 2022; no. 61219/35-196/50-31834, 11 May 2022; no. 61219/35-196/50-36735, 30 May 2022; no. 61219/35-196/50-37431, 31 May; and no. 61219/35-196/50-55446, 28 July 2022.

[73] Ukraine, Note verbale no. 61219/35-196/50-20231, 18 Mar. 2022.

[74] OPCW, Executive Council, Opening statement by the director-general to the Executive Council at its 101st session, EC-101/DG.28, 4 Oct. 2022, para. 5.

[75] OPCW, Statement on Ukraine from the OPCW spokesperson', OPCW News, 12 Apr. 2022.

V. Chemical weapon control and disarmament

UNA JAKOB*

The Chemical Weapons Convention (CWC) contains a comprehensive and unequivocal prohibition of chemical weapons and chemical warfare. There was no change to states parties to the CWC during 2022: as of December 2022, there were still 193 states parties and 4 states not party to the CWC, including Israel, which has signed but not ratified it, and Egypt, North Korea and South Sudan, which have neither signed nor ratified or acceded to the CWC.[1]

On 29 April 2022 the CWC celebrated the 25th anniversary of its entry into force. In a speech, the director-general of the Organisation for the Prohibition of Chemical Weapons (OPCW, the implementing body for the CWC), Fernando Arias, emphasized both the achievements of the CWC to date and the challenges it is facing. These challenges included, among others, the risk of chemical weapons proliferation and use, a changing industry landscape, technological developments, and non-state actors harbouring an interest in chemical weapons.[2] The OPCW held its official commemorative event on 20 May 2022 at its headquarters in The Hague. During two panel discussions, diplomats, OPCW representatives and external experts addressed opportunities for strengthening the implementation of the CWC, threats from chemical terrorism, and raising awareness of the CWC and OPCW, particularly among the younger generation.[3]

This section provides an update on other developments in relation to the CWC and OPCW during 2022.

Chemical weapon destruction

By the end of 2022, more than 99 per cent of all declared chemical weapon stockpiles worldwide had been destroyed under OPCW verification.[4] Destruction is ongoing in the United States as well as in relation to chemical weapons abandoned in China by Japan. All three states submitted progress reports on the destruction and removal processes to the OPCW Executive Council.[5] The process of the removal and destruction of abandoned chemical

---

[1] For a summary and other details of the Chemical Weapons Convention see annex A, section I, in this volume.

[2] OPCW, Director-General, 'Achievements of the Chemical Weapons Convention and future challenges', Speech at the launch of the Competence Network CBWNet, 29 Apr. 2022, Berlin.

[3] OPCW, 'OPCW @ 25: Seminar focusses on achievements, future challenges and opportunities', OPCW News, 20 May 2022.

[4] OPCW, 'Destruction progress: As of 31 December 2022', OPCW by the numbers.

[5] OPCW, Executive Council, Report of the 101st session of the Executive Council, EC-101/5, 7 Oct. 2022, paras 6.8–6.9. The respective documents are listed in the report as EC-101/NAT.1 (USA), EC-101/NAT.2 (China), and EC-101/NAT.3 (Japan) but are not publicly available.

* The author would like to acknowledge the valuable research assistance of Henrike Buch for this section.

weapons in China was hampered by the Covid-19 pandemic, but China and Japan resumed their activities in 2022 and jointly submitted a destruction plan for future activities to the Executive Council.[6] The USA reported that as of September 2022, over 98.27 per cent of its declared stockpile had been eliminated and that the destruction of the remaining stocks was expected to be completed according to schedule by the end of 2023.[7]

Developments in the OPCW

International cooperation and assistance

The Technical Secretariat reported on a range of cooperation and assistance activities carried out during 2022, including in the 'three focus areas of integrated chemical management, enhancement of laboratory capabilities, and chemical knowledge promotion and exchange'.[8] The area of chemical management encompassed a wide range of issues related to capacity building in chemical safety and security.[9] Activities to enhance laboratory capacities included 'a range of general analytical chemistry courses . . ., the Laboratory Twinning and Assistance Programme, proficiency testing training, customs laboratory training, and the Equipment Exchange Programme'.[10] In the area of chemical knowledge promotion and exchange, the Secretariat continued its work through its standing programmes on support for conferences and research projects as well as a fellowship programme, and awareness-raising activities.[11]

The end of 2022 saw the conclusion of the fifth phase of the Africa Programme of the OPCW.[12] This programme is tailored to the particular needs of African countries in promoting the peaceful use of chemistry and enhancing chemical safety and security.[13] Like many other areas, the implementation of the programme was still impacted by the Covid-19 pandemic in 2022. The Secretariat had to adapt its activities accordingly before it could return to a more regular course of action later in the year. One major innovation was the establishment of the OPCW Africa Network and the launch of an annual OPCW Africa Bulletin.[14] In March 2022 the Technical Secretariat started

---

[6] OPCW, EC-101/5 (note 5), paras 6.9, 6.13, 6.14.

[7] United States, Statement by HE Ambassador Joseph Manso, Permanent representative of the United States of America to the OPCW at the 101st session of the Executive Council, 29 Sep. 2022, p. 1.

[8] OPCW, Executive Council, 'Progress made and review of the status of implementation of Article XI of the Chemical Weapons Convention', Report by the director-general, EC-101/DG.9, 31 Aug. 2022, para. 2.

[9] OPCW, EC-101/DG.9 (note 8), paras 20–40.

[10] OPCW, EC-101/DG.9 (note 8), para. 41; see also paras 42–61 for details of the activities.

[11] OPCW, EC-101/DG.9 (note 8), para. 62; see also paras 63–71 for details of the programmes.

[12] For details see OPCW, Executive Council, 'The Programme to Strengthen Cooperation with Africa on the Chemical Weapons Convention', Note by the director-general, EC-101/DG.12, 7 Sep. 2022.

[13] OPCW, 'Capacity building: Africa Programme'.

[14] OPCW, EC-101/DG.12 (note 12), para. 41.

preparing for the sixth phase of the programme, intended to cover the period 2023–25.[15] Several states parties from the African Group commented positively on the programme and its previous implementation, encouraged its continuation, and called for it to be funded from the regular budget instead of from voluntary contributions.[16]

Organizational matters

At the 101st session of the Executive Council in October 2022, states parties discussed and agreed several administrative and governance issues, including a revised programme and budget for 2023. Budgetary issues have been subject to a vote ever since the Investigation and Identification Team (IIT) was established in 2018 and included in the budget of the Technical Secretariat, since not all states parties accept the addition of the IIT as legitimate (see section IV in this chapter). Of the 41 members of the Executive Council, 35 voted in favour of the budget decision, China and Russia voted against it, and Pakistan and Sudan abstained.[17] The conference of the states parties (CSP) likewise adopted the revised programme and budget for 2023 by majority vote—with 99 votes in favour, 7 against and 15 abstentions—on 29 November 2023.[18]

Another key decision, adopted by consensus on 28 November 2022, provides for the continued option to rehire individuals who had previously been employed as OPCW inspectors under certain conditions.[19] This topic is related to the broader question of the OPCW's tenure policy. Due to a combination of different factors, including an increased turnover rate during the pandemic and scheduled separations, the turnover rate is expected to be significantly higher in the coming years than initially envisaged. To maintain the necessary capabilities within the Technical Secretariat, the tenure policy will have to be addressed including and beyond the question of the rehiring

---

[15] OPCW, EC-101/DG.12 (note 12), paras 24 and 26.

[16] See e.g. Kenya, Statement by Ambassador Judith Sijeny of the permanent representation of the Republic of Kenya to the OPCW at the 100th session of the Executive Council, EC-100/NAT.25, 5 July 2022; Ghana, Statement by HE Ambassador Francis Danti Kotia, Permanent representative of the Republic of Ghana to the OPCW at the 99th session of the Executive Council, EC-99/NAT.20, 8 Mar. 2022; and Senegal, Statement by HE Ambassador Momar Gueye, Permanent representative of the Republic of Senegal to the OPCW at the 99th session of the Executive Council, EC-99/NAT.80, 8 Mar. 2022.

[17] OPCW, Executive Council, 'Draft revised programme and budget of the OPCW for 2023', Decision, EC-101/DEC.6, 5 Oct. 2022; and OPCW, EC-101/5 (note 5), para. 10.21.

[18] OPCW, Conference of the States Parties, 'Revised programme and budget of the OPCW for 2023', Decision, C-27/DEC.11, 29 Nov. 2022; and OPCW, Conference of the States Parties, Report of the 27th session of the conference of the states parties, C-27/5, 1 Dec. 2022, para. 13.5.

[19] OPCW, Conference of the States Parties, 'Rehiring of inspectors', Decision, C-27/DEC.9, 28 Nov. 2022; OPCW, C-27/5 (note 18), para. 17.8; and OPCW, Executive Council, 'Rehiring of inspectors', Decision, EC-DEC.5, 5 Oct. 2022.

of inspectors. States parties are expected to discuss this topic during the fifth review conference (RevCon5).[20]

The new OPCW Centre for Chemistry and Technology

The construction of a new OPCW Centre for Chemistry and Technology (ChemTech Centre) was initiated in 2017 to upgrade and expand the capabilities of the previous OPCW Laboratory and Equipment Store. The new centre is intended to fulfil a range of purposes, including enabling research to strengthen verification, enhancing the OPCW's analytical capabilities, acting as a 'knowledge repository', and providing capabilities for capacity building, training and education, among other things.[21]

According to the director-general the construction of the ChemTech Centre was on schedule, both in terms of timing and expenditures, despite the pandemic and rising costs.[22] Construction was completed at the end of 2022 and the project entered a training and testing phase to prepare for the final transition from the old facility in Rijswijk to the new centre in early January 2023.[23] The OPCW expects the ChemTech Centre to be fully operational by April 2023, and has planned a high-level inauguration ceremony for 12 May 2023.[24]

The project is being funded by voluntary contributions to the ChemTech Centre Trust Fund received from 54 countries, the European Union (EU), six non-governmental entities and from 'personal contributions'; as of October 2022, all of these contributions totalled approximately €34.32 million.[25]

Impact of the Covid-19 pandemic and the Executive Council Business Continuity Initiative

During 2022, the OPCW returned to more regular proceedings after the pandemic had disrupted many of its activities.[26] In particular, inspections and cooperation activities resumed in higher frequency, and meetings were held in-person again.[27] The number of scheduled industry inspections was reduced from 241 in previous years to 180 inspections in 2022. While ongoing pandemic-related restrictions meant the Technical Secretariat was still

---

[20] See e.g. OPCW, Conference of the States Parties, Opening statement by the director-general to the conference of the states parties at its twenty-seventh session, C-27/DG.16, 28 Nov. 2022, para. 21.

[21] OPCW, 'Centre for Chemistry and Technology Project'.

[22] OPCW, Technical Secretariat, 'Progress in the project to upgrade the OPCW Laboratory and Equipment Store to a Centre for Chemistry and Technology', S/2112/2022, 17 Nov. 2022, p. 6.

[23] OPCW, Technical Secretariat, 'Centre for Chemistry and Technology: Inauguration ceremony 12 May 2023', S/2119/2022, 14 Dec. 2022; and OPCW, S/2112/2022 (note 22), pp. 2–3.

[24] OPCW, S/2119/2022 (note 23).

[25] OPCW, 'Centre for Chemistry and Technology Project' (note 21).

[26] McLeish, C., 'Chemical weapons: Arms control and disarmament', *SIPRI Yearbook 2021*, p. 495; and Jakob, U., 'Allegations of chemical weapons use in Syria', *SIPRI Yearbook 2022*, p. 507.

[27] See e.g. OPCW, Executive Council, Opening statement by the director-general to the Executive Council at its 101st session, EC-101/DG.28, 4 Oct. 2022, para. 46.

unable to carry out all scheduled inspections, it expected to complete 90 per cent of them by the end of 2022—a significantly higher number than the one-third that were achieved under pandemic conditions.[28]

Supported by a group of like-minded states, Germany continued to pursue the Executive Council Business Continuity Initiative, which 'aims at defining procedures that allow the Council to convene when in-person meetings are not possible, using virtual meeting technology'.[29] Germany reported that there was very wide cross-regional support for the initiative. However, by the end of 2022 there was no consensus and consultations will continue with the aim of tabling a revised draft decision at the 102nd session of the Executive Council in 2023.[30]

Security challenges for the OPCW

The OPCW has been faced with challenges in terms of both physical and cybersecurity threats. In December 2021, about 40 protesters stormed the OPCW building during a violent demonstration.[31] In the wake of this incident, the Technical Secretariat initiated upgrades of the physical security measures at OPCW headquarters. By the end of 2022, completed measures included enhanced access controls and reinforcement of the perimeter fence, gates and entrance area, with a few additional measures still under construction. The Netherlands as host country has been providing additional security support such as enhanced police protection.[32]

The OPCW has also faced increasing numbers of cyber attacks, including phishing, malware and network perimeter attacks. As the director-general reported to the CSP in November 2022, approximately 30 000 attacks against the OPCW's internet-based services had been registered in the four months preceding the conference. Consequently, the Technical Secretariat installed additional cybersecurity measures, largely funded by voluntary contributions from states parties.[33]

Scientific Advisory Board of the OPCW

The Scientific Advisory Board (SAB) held three meetings during 2022. While the first meeting in March still had to be held virtually due to the ongoing

---

[28] OPCW, C-27/DG.16 (note 20), para. 39.
[29] Germany, Statement by HE Ambassador Gudrun Lingner, Permanent representative of the Federal Republic of Germany to the OPCW at the 99th session of the Executive Council, EC-99/NAT.13, 8 Mar. 2022, p. 3. For an earlier version of a draft decision and an explanatory memorandum see also Germany, Verbal Note no. 33/2021, CW 370.45/7-DEU, 28 Sep. 2021.
[30] Germany, Statement by HE Ambassador Thomas Schieb, Permanent representative of the Federal Republic of Germany to the OPCW at the 101st session of the Executive Council, EC-101/NAT.15, 4 Oct. 2022, p. 3.
[31] OPCW, Executive Council, Opening statement by the director-general to the Executive Council at its 99th session, EC-99/DG.17, 8 Mar. 2022, para. 13.
[32] OPCW, EC-101/DG.28 (note 27), paras 14–18.
[33] OPCW, C-27/DG.16 (note 20), para. 15.

Covid-19 pandemic, the June and September meetings were in-person meetings.[34] The SAB heard several presentations from external experts on technical matters and research projects of relevance to the CWC. These included the chemical attribution signatures of VX nerve agents; risks arising from additive manufacturing in the context of chemical weapon proliferation; the neutralization and detection of organophosphates, forensic signature(s) of the nerve agent precursor DMPADC; insects as environmental samplers; and a method for the attribution of sulfur mustard.[35] Other important topics included discussions on possible activities that could be hosted at the new ChemTech Centre, continued consideration of central nervous system–acting chemicals, and the preparation of the SAB report for RevCon5.[36] This report, published in February 2023, contains a summary of relevant scientific and technological developments in chemistry and other relevant scientific fields such as artificial intelligence (AI), additive manufacturing and biotechnology, and it provides a number of recommendations to the OPCW that are designed to help it keep up with current and potential challenges.[37]

In addition to its regular sessions, the SAB held two thematic workshops in June 2022, one in partnership with the International Union of Pure and Applied Chemistry (IUPAC) on AI-assisted chemistry, and one together with industry partners on emerging scientific trends and directions in the chemical industry.[38]

The SAB's temporary working group (TWG) on the analysis of biotoxins, established in 2021, held three meetings in 2022, in March (virtually), June and October 2022. The TWG discussed a range of topics related to identification and analysis of biological toxins with external experts and internally in five TWG subgroups. The subgroups covered, among other things, the underlying and the technical requirements for the analysis of biotoxins and for investigations of their use as weapons; the most relevant biotoxins as well as compounds of biological origin other than toxins that could also be relevant in a CWC context; analytical standards and requirement of other investigative authorities, including the UN secretary-general's mechanism for

---

[34] OPCW, Scientific Advisory Board, Report of the Scientific Advisory Board at its 34th session, SAB-34/1, 17 Mar. 2022, p. 1; Report of the Scientific Advisory Board at its 35th session, SAB-35/1, 16 June 2022, p. 1; and Report of the Scientific Advisory Board at its 36th session, SAB-36/1, 29 Sep. 2022, p. 1.

[35] OPCW, SAB-34/1 (note 34), p. 2. DMPADC stands for N,N-dimethylphosphoramidic dichloride, which is a precursor for the nerve agent Tabun (para 10.1).

[36] OPCW, SAB-34/1 (note 34); SAB-35/1 (note 34); and OPCW, SAB-36/1 (note 34), p. 1. On central nervous system–acting chemicals see OPCW, 'Understanding regarding the aerosolised use of central nervous system-acting chemicals for law enforcement purposes', C-26/DEC.10, 1 Dec. 2021.

[37] OPCW, Review Conference, Report of the Scientific Advisory Board on developments in Science and Technology to the fifth special session of the conference of the states parties to review the operation of the Chemical Weapons Convention, Report by the director-general, RC-5/DG.1, 22 Feb. 2023.

[38] OPCW, Executive Council, 'Response to the report of the 35th session of the Scientific Advisory Board', Note by the director-general, EC-101/DG.21, 19 Sep. 2022, para. 19.

investigation of alleged use of chemical and biological weapons (UNSGM); possibilities for harmonization of laboratory capabilities for the analysis of biotoxins; and measures to facilitate cooperation between the OPCW and other relevant organizations. The TWG is expected to complete its work and present its final report in 2023.[39]

OPCW Advisory Board on Outreach and Education

The Advisory Board on Outreach and Education (ABEO) met twice in 2022, virtually in February and in person in July.[40] The focus of the board's work in 2022 was on e-learning as well as outreach and the dissemination of information about the OPCW and the CWC, including a 'contact pack' for universities.[41] The ABEO also discussed its potential role in raising awareness of job opportunities at the OPCW to enhance geographical and gender balance within the Technical Secretariat.[42]

Open-ended working group on terrorism

The open-ended working group on terrorism (OEWG-T), initiated in 2001, continues to serve as 'the primary platform for States Parties to exchange views on chemical terrorism'.[43] In 2022, it met three times: in February, March and September. The participants of the OEWG-T heard briefings from the Technical Secretariat on OPCW activities related to chemical terrorism as well as presentations on EU and Association of Southeast Asian Nations (ASEAN) approaches to the topic. Topics discussed included measures related to national implementation of the CWC and to awareness-raising, and the sharing of experiences and best practices. In preparation for RevCon5, the group discussed possible contributions to the preparatory process.[44]

The work of the OEWG-T in 2022 coincided with investigations carried out by the UN Investigative Team to Promote Accountability for Crimes Committed by Da'esh/Islamic State in Iraq and the Levant (UNITAD). These

---

[39] OPCW, SAB-36/1 (note 34), para. 9; 'Summary of the fifth meeting of the Scientific Advisory Board's temporary working group on the analysis of biotoxins', SAB-36/WP.2, 17 Nov. 2022; and 'Summary of the fourth meeting of the Scientific Advisory Board's temporary working group on the analysis of biotoxins', SAB-36/WP.1, 29 July 2022.

[40] OPCW, Advisory Board on Outreach and Education, Report of the 13th session of the Advisory Board on Education and Outreach', ABEO-13/1, 21 July 2022; and Report of the 12th session of the Advisory Board on Education and Outreach', ABEO-12/1, 10 Feb. 2022.

[41] OPCW, ABEO-12/1 (note 40), para. 11.

[42] OPCW, ABEO-12/1 (note 40), para. 13.

[43] OPCW, Executive Council, Report by HE Ambassador Vusimuzi Philemon Madonsela, chairperson of the open-ended working group on terrorism to the Executive Council at its 99th session, EC-99/WP.3, 9 Mar. 2022, para. 2.

[44] OPCW, EC-99/WP.3 (note 43); Report by HE Ambassador Vusimuzi Philemon Madonsela, chairperson of the open-ended working group on terrorism to the Executive Council at its 100th session, EC-100/WP.3, 6 July 2022; and Report by HE Ambassador Vusimuzi Philemon Madonsela, chairperson of the open-ended working group on terrorism to the Executive Council at its 101st session, EC-101/WP.2, 5 Oct. 2022.

investigations revealed more detailed insights into ISIL's chemical and biological weapon capabilities and found that ISIL had established a 'centre of operations to produce chemical weapons', including sulfur mustard, ricin and chlorine, at the University of Mossul, Iraq.[45]

Preparations for the fifth CWC review conference

From 15 to 19 May 2023, the states parties to the CWC will hold the fifth review conference of the treaty. To prepare for this conference, the Executive Council in March 2022 established the open-ended working group of the fifth review conference (OEWG-RC). The objective of the OEWG-RC is to structure the preparatory process and in cooperation with the Technical Secretariat carry out substantive preparations for RevCon5. The group is led by a bureau of representatives from all regional groups and chaired by Ambassador Lauri Kuusing of Estonia.[46]

The OEWG-RC held its first meeting on 7 June 2022 and subsequently held nine more meetings before the end of 2022. This meeting cycle represented the first work phase and covered the review part of the preparations. The meetings were held in hybrid format to facilitate participation by national authorities and other delegates or experts. In identifying the issues that should be addressed in the preparatory process and at the review conference, the OEWG-RC followed a thematic approach and elicited input from states parties through consultations and a survey regarding their views on past achievements, possible recommendations from RevCon5 and priority areas for the future.[47] The OEWG-RC heard various presentations from the Technical Secretariat (see below) as well as from the SAB and the ABEO, and it also interacted with industry representatives and received submissions on key issues from civil society actors.[48] The second work phase starting from January 2023 will see more substantive work through a 'draft provisional text' prepared by the chair of the OEWG-RC and based on discussions of the OEWG-RC, proposals and papers submitted by states parties, the results of the survey, and presentations and papers presented by the Secretariat.[49]

The programme of work for RevCon5 had not been finalized by the end of 2022, but the OEWG-RC chair's report contained indications as to which

---

[45] United Nations, Security Council, Eighth report of the special adviser and head of the United Nations Investigative Team to Promote Accountability for Crimes Committed by Da'esh/Islamic State in Iraq and the Levant, S/2022/434, 26 May 2022, paras 10–14.

[46] OPCW, Conference of the States Parties, Report by HE Ambassador Lauri Kuusing of Estonia, Chairperson of the open-ended working group for the preparation of the fifth review conference to the conference of the states parties at its twenty-seventh session, C-27/WP.1, 30 Nov. 2022, p. 1.

[47] OPCW, C-27/WP.1 (note 46).

[48] OPCW, Conference of the States Parties, 'Engaging the chemical industry associations', Note by the director-general, C-27/DG.14, 20 Oct. 2022, para. 25.

[49] OPCW, C-27/WP.1 (note 46), p. 3.

topics would figure prominently, stemming from the purpose of the review conference itself as well as from the discussions within the OPCW organs over the past few years. The Technical Secretariat's presentations at the 10 meetings 'focused on key achievements since the fourth review conference and provided food for thought regarding future challenges and priorities' for RevCon5, covering the following key themes: 'verification-related issues'; 'non-routine missions'; 'international cooperation and assistance'; 'engagement with external stakeholders'; 'contribution of the OPCW to the global counterterrorism efforts'; and 'organisational governance'.[50] One prominent example in the latter category is the question of the OPCW's tenure policy and the rehiring of inspectors.[51] Given the current situation and known challenges, discussion at RevCon5 on the other themes would likely include key issues such as the transition to the post-destruction phase and the prevention of the re-emergence of chemical weapons, adaptations to the changing chemical industry landscape, and the reactions to Syria's chemical weapon use. Conference deliberations will also likely cover the report of the SAB and its implications, the new ChemTech Centre, and the issue of gender and chemical weapons.[52]

Outlook

In 2023, 30 years after the CWC was opened for signature in Paris, the convention and the OPCW will reach several important milestones. The new ChemTech Centre, which will become operational and be formally inaugurated by May 2023, is expected to provide new and enhanced capacities and possibilities for analytics, international cooperation and outreach activities. The USA is expected to destroy the last of its remaining chemical weapon stocks by the end of 2023, thereby completing the destruction of all declared chemical weapon stockpiles worldwide. Last but not least, RevCon5 will discuss a range of important topics in particularly challenging circumstances, given the stark polarization in the OPCW's policy-making organs over compliance politics. At the same time, the review conference might set important landmarks for the way ahead.

[50] OPCW, C-27/WP.1 (note 46), p. 2.
[51] OPCW, C-27/DEC.9 (note 19), p. 2.
[52] See also Ghionis, A., Kelle, A. and Garzón Maceda, M., 'Preparing for success at the fifth review conference of the Chemical Weapons Convention: A guide to the issues' (United Nations Institute for Disarmament Research: Geneva, 2023), pp. 23–28.

10. Conventional arms control and regulation of new weapon technologies

Overview

Europe is the only region that has created an integrated conventional arms control architecture. However, geopolitical divisions between Russia and most of the rest of the Europe over the past two decades have resulted in its erosion to the point of collapse or irrelevance—part of a wider crisis in arms control. While the Vienna Document made it possible to draw critical attention to Russia's military build-up on its border with Ukraine, for example, it could not reverse the escalation or prevent the full-scale Russian invasion in February 2022 (see section I). The existing conventional arms control instruments also appear to have little relevance to conflict management in other long-standing, simmering conflicts in Europe, and rebuilding a new order containing supporting elements of arms control will be extremely difficult.

Many of the contemporary debates on conventional arms control are shaped by the concept of 'humanitarian disarmament' (see section II). The need for strong and effective humanitarian disarmament law has been underscored by Russia's invasion of Ukraine and the use there of cluster munitions, anti-personnel mines (APMs) and explosive weapons in populated areas (EWIPA), especially those with wide-area effects. These attacks have resulted in large numbers of civilian casualties, but they have also generated strong international condemnation precisely because they involved weapons banned or restricted under humanitarian disarmament treaties and norms. The main multilateral treaty for regulating inhumane weapons is the 1981 Certain Conventional Weapons (CCW) Convention, alongside the 1997 Anti-Personnel Mine Convention and the 2008 Convention on Cluster Munitions. Because the CCW regime operates by consensus, a small number of states that have chosen to retain, develop or use weapons seen as inhumane by others have repeatedly vetoed or stalled progress on strengthening the CCW Convention.

Nonetheless, there were four positive developments in 2022. First, after many years of failing to make progress in addressing the humanitarian harm of EWIPA within the CCW framework, a separate process led by Ireland resulted in the adoption in November 2022 of a political declaration on this issue by 83 states. Second, new standards were set regarding the environment and armed conflict when the United Nations General Assembly adopted by consensus the Principles on the Protection of the Environment in Relation to Armed Conflicts in December 2022. Third, in June 2022 the United States announced a new policy on APMs, effectively banning their transfer, development,

SIPRI Yearbook 2023: Armaments, Disarmament and International Security
www.sipriyearbook.org

production or acquisition—the fifth change in US policy on this issue in as many administrations, dating back to the 1990s. Finally, in the context of the UN Programme of Action (POA) on small arms and light weapons (SALW), states agreed to consider discussing the impact of technological developments on SALW manufacturing and continued to acknowledge the gender-related impact of illicit SALW. Outside the POA process, states also started working on the development of a new global framework for ammunition management.

One of the most prominent efforts within the CCW regime has been to consider the regulation of autonomous weapon systems (AWS; see section III). Since 2017 a group of governmental experts has been leading these efforts. States have expressed different views on whether the adoption of a new regulation is warranted. During the discussions in 2022, most states agreed that the 'normative and operational framework' governing AWS needed to be developed further and that one possible way to proceed was through a two-tiered approach: prohibiting certain AWS, while placing specific limits and requirements on the development and use of all other AWS. However, a handful of states continued to oppose even this approach, reigniting the question of whether CCW is the appropriate forum to address the issue of AWS.

Beyond arms control, international security can also be improved by states acting to build mutual confidence through transparency about their armaments. This can be by sharing information on arms procurement or military expenditure (see section IV). However, the existing instruments within the UN and the Organization for Security and Co-operation in Europe are in urgent need of revitalization, as participation in 2022 continued to be low—despite a notable increase in participation in the UN Register of Conventional Arms—and parts of the submissions were incomplete.

The Hague Code of Conduct against Ballistic Missile Proliferation (HCOC) is a multilateral transparency and confidence-building measure covering ballistic missile and space-launch vehicle programmes, policies and activities (see section V). The HCOC's annual regular meeting in 2022 failed to agree on a public statement over disagreements linked to Russia's invasion of Ukraine, but the exchange of pre-launch notifications continued and the HCOC continued to receive significant political support through a biannual UN General Assembly resolution. The effectiveness of the HCOC in curbing ballistic missile proliferation is difficult to discern, but the focus on restraining the development and proliferation of ballistic missiles capable of delivering weapons of mass destruction appears increasingly out of step with technological developments and broader missile proliferation trends.

IAN DAVIS

I. The Russia–Ukraine War and conventional arms control in Europe

IAN DAVIS

Europe is the only region that has created an integrated conventional arms control architecture (see box 10.1). However, the deep-rooted and growing geopolitical divisions between the Russian Federation and most of the rest of Europe over the past two decades has resulted in this architecture being eroded to the point of collapse or irrelevance—part of a wider crisis in arms control.[1] The effect of previously agreed operational constraints and limitations on conventional force structures has also been diminished by the broader trend of rapid technological modernization.[2] Moreover, as the Russia–Ukraine crisis deepened at the end of 2021, the pillars of the arms control architecture were suffering from a spate of major violations, suspensions and withdrawals.

Russia suspended its participation in the 1990 Treaty on Conventional Armed Forces in Europe (CFE Treaty) in 2007 and 'halted' compliance entirely in 2015, although it never formally withdrew. To justify these steps, it cited plans by the United States to put bases in Bulgaria and Romania as a breach.[3] The Vienna Document 2011 on Confidence- and Security-Building Measures (CSBMs) should be reissued every five years by the states participating in the Organization for Security and Co-operation in Europe (OSCE).[4] Yet it has not been updated since 2011. Four changes have been agreed—including on prior notification of sub-threshold major military activities and on the lengths of air base visits—and are currently being implemented as part of the broader Vienna Document Plus, but they are not yet an official part of the Vienna Document.[5] Other modernization proposals are pending as they have not yet found consensus among the participating states and are not part of the Vienna Document Plus. The roots of the absence of consensus are that Russia conditioned modernization of the Vienna Document on changes in

---

[1] See e.g. Graef, A., 'Beyond stability: The politics of conventional arms control in Europe', *Zeitschrift für Friedens- und Konfliktforschung*, vol. 10, no. 2 (Oct. 2021); and Anthony, I., 'A relaunch of conventional arms control in Europe?', *SIPRI Yearbook 2017*, pp. 575–79. On the wider crisis in arms control see Wisotzki, S. and Kühn, U., 'Crisis in arms control: An introduction', *Zeitschrift für Friedens- und Konfliktforschung*, vol. 10, no. 2 (Oct. 2021).

[2] Nelson, A. J., 'How emerging technology is breaking arms control', Lawfare, 24 Apr. 2022; and Roulo, C., 'Low-cost tech shaping modern battlefield, Socom commander says', US Army, 27 July 2022.

[3] Low, C., 'Russia treaty freeze a warning to NATO', Reuters, 11 Dec. 2007; and Nuclear Threat Initiative, 'Treaty on Conventional Armed Forces in Europe (CFE)'.

[4] For a brief description of the OSCE and list of its participating states see annex B, section II, in this volume.

[5] OSCE, Forum for Security Co-operation, 'On prior notification of major military activities', Vienna Document Plus Decision no. 9/12, FSC.DEC/9/12, 17 Oct. 2012; and OSCE, Forum for Security Co-operation, 'Duration of visits to air bases', Vienna Document Plus Decision no. 4/13, FSC.DEC/4/13, 17 July 2013. See also US Department of State, 'Overview of Vienna Document 2011'.

> **Box 10.1.** The European conventional arms control architecture
>
> The architecture of European conventional arms control has three pillars:
>
> **Treaty restrictions on conventional armed forces.** These restrictions are contained in two treaties. The 1990 Treaty on Conventional Armed Forces in Europe (CFE Treaty) set legally binding limits on five categories of equipment: battle tanks, artillery, armoured combat vehicles, combat aircraft and combat helicopters. The 1992 Concluding Act of the Negotiation on Personnel Strength of Conventional Armed Forces in Europe (CFE-1A) set politically binding ceilings on military personnel numbers in Europe.
>
> **Binding and verifiable confidence- and security-building measures (CSBMs).** These were originally established by the 1990 Vienna Document on CSBMs of the Organization for Security and Co-operation in Europe (OSCE). It has been periodically revised and reissued, most recently in 2011.
>
> **A legally binding commitment to facilitate overflights of sovereign territory.** This commitment to enhance transparency is set out in the 1992 Treaty on Open Skies.
>
> *Sources*: For summaries and other details of the CFE Treaty, CFE-1A, the Vienna Document and the Open Skies Treaty see annex A, section II, in this volume.

behaviour by the North Atlantic Treaty Organization (NATO), while NATO member states accused Russia of non-compliance with the agreement and of exploiting its loopholes.[6] Finally, the 1992 Treaty on Open Skies is at risk of failure following the withdrawal of both the USA and Russia in 2020–21.[7]

The lessons from the Georgian–Russian War in 2008, the Second Nagorno-Karabakh War in 2020, Russia's illegal annexation of Crimea in 2014 and the subsequent war in eastern Ukraine show that this depleted conventional arms control architecture is unable to prevent armed conflict. When one or several parties have deliberately sought war, 'they tend to undertake measures to dilute compliance, to diminish transparency and to conceal intent through disinformation'.[8] At best, the architecture can serve as an early-warning mechanism. Indeed, this proved to be the case with the full-scale Russian invasion of Ukraine in February 2022: the last pillar standing, the Vienna Document, made it possible to draw critical attention to Russia's military build-up, but not reverse it or prevent the attack.

This section reviews the functioning of the conventional arms control regime in Europe in the lead-up to Russia's full-scale invasion of Ukraine in February 2022. It highlights where the Vienna Document was invoked,

---

[6] See e.g. 'Александр Грушко: не уверены, что НАТО воздержится от провокаций во время парада Победы' [Alexander Grushko: Not sure that NATO will refrain from provocations during the victory parade], TASS, 6 June 2020; and NATO, 'Press point by the NATO Secretary General Jens Stoltenberg following the meeting of the NATO–Russia Council', 2 Nov. 2017.

[7] Davis, I., 'The withdrawal of the United States from the Treaty on Open Skies', *SIPRI Yearbook 2021*; and Graef, A., 'The withdrawal of Russia from the Treaty on Open Skies', *SIPRI Yearbook 2022*, pp. 545–50.

[8] Engvall, J., 'Military confidence-building in crises: Lessons from Georgia and Ukraine', *Defence Studies*, vol. 20, no. 3 (2020).

where it functioned as intended and where it did not. It concludes with an assessment of the outlook for conventional arms control in Europe.

Prelude to the Russian invasion

The Vienna Document contributes to European security by enhancing military transparency among the 57 OSCE participating states. Its major provisions are on exchanges of military information and details of defence policy and expenditure and on enabling inspection and observation of certain military activities (that exceed 13 000 troops, 300 tanks, 500 armoured combat vehicles (ACVs) or 250 pieces of artillery). It also contains rules on prior notification of exercises and new deployments (of over 9000 troops, 250 tanks, 500 ACVs or 250 pieces of artillery).[9] NATO member states have argued in recent years that Russia was frequently circumventing the thresholds by reconfiguring large exercises into smaller components, classed as a mix of regular and snap exercises, each under the 13 000-troop limit—thereby avoiding observation. NATO has also complained about Russia's failure to be more transparent and to provide reassurance to others of its intentions.[10] For its part, Russia has regularly complained about NATO capabilities and military exercises near its borders and has consistently highlighted its own set of concerns about the Vienna Document's deficiencies.[11] This dynamic of mistrust was clearly in evidence as Russia built up forces near Ukraine in 2021.

In April 2021 Ukraine invoked the Vienna Document and formally requested a joint meeting of the OSCE's two main decision-making bodies, the Permanent Council and the Forum for Security Co-operation (FSC), to try to get an explanation for Russia's military activities near the Ukrainian border and in Crimea.[12] Russia reportedly did not attend the meeting.[13] It did, however, agree to an inspection by Switzerland under the Vienna Document framework in May 2021, which was conducted in Voronezh and Belgorod oblasts to determine the scope of Russia's military activity.[14] The outcome of

---

[9] As noted in section IV, Russia and Ukraine both, perhaps surprisingly, reported in 2022 on their arms imports and exports for 2021.

[10] Graef, A., 'Getting deterrence right on NATO's eastern flank', *Berlin Policy Journal*, 25 July 2019; and Emmott, R., 'NATO calls on Russia to be transparent with military exercises', Reuters, 3 Sep. 2021.

[11] Schmitt, O., 'The Vienna Document and the Russian challenge to the European security architecture', eds B. Heuser, T. Heier and G. Lasconjarias, *Military Exercises: Political Messaging and Strategic Impact*, Forum Paper 26 (NATO Defence College: Rome, Apr. 2018), pp. 278–79.

[12] US Mission to the OSCE, 'Meeting requested by Ukraine under Vienna Document Chapter III regarding unusual Russian military activity', 10 Apr. 2021. See also Bush, N., Head of British delegation to the OSCE, 'OSCE joint FSC–PC meeting under Vienna Document Chapter 3: UK statement', British Foreign, Commonwealth and Development Office, 14 Apr. 2021.

[13] Axelrod, T., 'Western countries knock Russia for not attending talks on Ukraine', *The Hill*, 10 Apr. 2021.

[14] 'Swiss specialists to inspect specified area in Russia under 2011 Vienna Document', TASS, 19 May 2021.

the inspection was not disclosed and the inspection report remains classified (i.e. restricted to OSCE participating states).

The final build-up

In November 2021 Russia once again deployed thousands of troops near its border with Ukraine, having only partially pulled back its forces from the April build-up.[15] Russian officials continued to deny that its troops posed any threat to Ukraine, but the situation remained clouded by a lack of Russian transparency and conflicting assessments of the crisis.

On 29 December 2021, during their bilateral meeting in St Petersburg, Russian President Vladimir Putin and Belarusian President Alexander Lukashenko agreed to hold a joint military exercise in February or March 2022.[16] This joint Russia–Belarus military exercise, Allied Resolve ('Soyuznaya reshimost'), took place on 10–20 February 2022 in Belarus.[17] An OSCE inspection requested by Latvia in line with Chapter IX (on compliance and verification) of the Vienna Document was scheduled to take place in January in specified areas in Russia's Bryansk and Smolensk oblasts. However, the request was declined by Russia, which reportedly cited Covid-19 concerns.[18]

On 8 February 2022 French President Emmanuel Macron held talks in Moscow with President Putin as part of his ongoing strategic dialogue discussions with Russia that were first initiated in 2019. Macron said that Putin gave him personal assurances that Russia would not worsen the crisis.[19] A day later, Estonia, Latvia and Lithuania invoked Chapter III of the Vienna Document (on risk reduction) to request a detailed explanation of the imminent exercise from Belarus.[20] The Belarusian official response—echoed by the Russian ambassador to Belarus—was that the size of the exercise was under

---

[15] Davis, I., 'Armed conflict in Ukraine and the risk of spillover to a major interstate war', *SIPRI Yearbook 2022*, pp. 153–54; and Kramer, A. E. and Troianovski, A., 'Russia orders partial pullback from Ukraine border region', *New York Times*, 22 Apr. 2021.

[16] 'Путин анонсировал российско-белорусские военные учения в 2022 году' [Putin announces Russian–Belarusian military exercises in 2022], *Izvestia*, 29 Dec. 2021.

[17] 'Satellite images show troop deployment to Belarus border with Ukraine ahead of Russian drills', Reuters, 6 Feb. 2022.

[18] Latvian Ministry of Defence, 'Russia's Defence Ministry declines Latvian OSCE inspection and publishes false statements about arrival of Latvian inspectors to its neighbouring country', 25 Jan. 2022.

[19] Faure, J., 'Macron's dialogue with Russia: A French attempt to fix the European security architecture', Russia Matters, Harvard Kennedy School, Belfer Center for Science and International Affairs, 12 May 2021; and Harding, L. et al., 'Macron claims Putin gave him personal assurances on Ukraine', *The Guardian*, 8 Feb. 2022.

[20] Sprenger, S., 'Baltic nations launch OSCE appeal over Russia–Belarus drill', *Defense News*, 9 Feb. 2022.

the reporting threshold.[21] Although Estonian officials described the Belarusian response as 'insufficient', on 14 February Belarus and Ukraine agreed some limited confidence-building and transparency measures, including mutual observation visits to their respective military exercises.[22]

On 11 February 2022 Ukraine also invoked Chapter III of the Vienna Document to request Russia to provide 'detailed explanations on military activities in the areas adjacent to the territory of Ukraine and in the temporarily occupied Crimea'.[23] After Russia failed to respond by the required 48-hour deadline, on 13 February Ukraine requested an emergency meeting of OSCE participant states.[24] An OSCE consultation meeting was held two days later, but Russia's representative failed to attend.[25]

The emergency OSCE meeting took place on 18 February in the format of a joint session of the FSC and the Permanent Council. Again, Russia did not attend.[26] By mid February 2022 Russia had roughly 190 000 troops massed around Ukraine in Belarus, Russia and Crimea, and on 24 February these forces attacked Ukraine from the north, east and south.[27]

The outlook for European conventional arms control

Even before Russia attacked neighbouring Ukraine on 24 February 2022, it was generally agreed that the available instruments of European conventional arms control were proving insufficient and were no longer relevant.[28] Concepts of military advantage and deterrence were once again the central driving motivations of most of the key parties involved. The conflict has resulted in the heaviest fighting on the continent since at least the Balkan

---

[21] 'Russian ambassador: Allied Resolve exercise does not exceed Vienna Document limit', BelTA, 9 Feb. 2022; and Babinich, A., 'Российские войска прибывают в Беларусь—Сколько, с чем и зачем?' [Russian troops arrive in Belarus—How many, with what and why?], Reformation, 25 Jan. 2022.

[22] 'Belarus military exercises OSCE rules clarification requested for Monday', ERR News, 14 Feb. 2022; Ukrainian Ministry of Defence, 'Олексій Резніков провів телефонну розмову з Міністром оборони Республіки Білорусь Віктором Хреніним' [Oleksiy Reznikov held a telephone conversation with the Minister of Defence of the Republic of Belarus Viktor Khrenin], 14 Feb. 2022; and Ukrainian Ministry of Defence, Speech of Minister of Defence of Ukraine Oleksii Reznikov during the hour of questions to the government', 18 Feb. 2022.

[23] Sprenger, S., 'Ukraine joins Baltic nations in OSCE query of Russian troop movements', *Defense News*, 11 Feb. 2022; and 'Ukraine asks Russia to provide clarifications on military activities in regions adjacent to Ukrainian territory', Interfax-Ukraine, 11 Feb. 2022.

[24] 'Ukraine requests OSCE meeting over Russia's military build-up', Ukrinform, 13 Feb. 2022.

[25] 'Russia skips OSCE meeting on Ukraine crisis', WION, 16 Feb. 2022; 'Ukraine's request for consultations under Vienna Document groundless—Russia', TASS, 15 Feb. 2022; and US Mission to the OSCE, 'US statement for the meeting under Vienna Document Chapter III 16.2', 15 Feb. 2022.

[26] OSCE, Permanent Council and Forum for Security Co-operation, 85th (special) joint meeting, FSC-PC.JOUR/72, 18 Feb. 2022; and US Mission to the OSCE, 'US statement for the Vienna Document joint PC–FSC Chapter III meeting', 18 Feb. 2022.

[27] Wintour, P., 'Russia has amassed up to 190,000 troops on Ukraine borders, US warns', *The Guardian*, 18 Feb. 2022. On the progress of the war during 2022 see chapter 1, section V, and chapter 2, section I, in this volume.

[28] E.g. Graef (note 1); and Wisotzki and Kühn (note 1).

wars of the 1990s, but probably since World War II, and included the spectre of nuclear weapon use.[29] Although Western states have not been directly involved in the fighting, they have provided military support (intelligence, training and weapon supplies) to Ukraine, imposed wide-ranging economic sanctions on Russia and issued their own (mainly non-nuclear) deterrent threats.[30] Moreover, NATO is on the brink of a further enlargement, with Finland and Sweden applying to join in May 2022 and invited to do so at NATO's summit in Madrid in June.[31]

The existing conventional arms control instruments also appear to have little relevance to conflict management in other long-standing simmering or frozen conflicts in Europe, especially those in the post-Soviet space and the Western Balkans.[32] With the war in Ukraine ongoing, and European states currently unwilling to agree to new arms control regulations and transparency measures, the future contours of a new European security architecture are hard to foresee. However, experts and analysts are already producing suggestions for how the states of the region might limit deployments and force sizes in the context of the changed security environment.[33]

Rebuilding a new order containing supporting elements of arms control will be extremely difficult. There were no new formal initiatives taken during 2022 and there is no prospect of dialogue on conventional arms control and CSBMs being relaunched in the OSCE any time soon. However, the progression of the war in Ukraine has shown that the equipment categories subject to CFE limits remain important. In the longer-term, European states—including both Ukraine and Russia—might see an interest in some bilateral or regional mutual military limitations that could also include new types of weapon and new technologies (such as armed uncrewed aerial vehicles).

---

[29] Picheta, R. and Mullery, W., '6 months of war in Ukraine: These numbers tell the story of Russia's invasion', CNN, 24 Aug. 2022; and Diaz-Maurin, F., '"Not a bluff": Losing ground in Ukraine, Putin raises nuclear threats', *Bulletin of the Atomic Scientists*, 21 Sep. 2022.

[30] Forum on the Arms Trade, 'Arms transfers to Ukraine', accessed 16 Dec. 2022; US Department of State, Bureau of Political-Military Affairs, 'US security cooperation with Ukraine', Fact sheet, 25 Jan. 2023; Kiel Institute for the World Economy, 'Ukraine support tracker', accessed 16 Dec. 2022; Schwatz, F., Foy, H. and Seddon, M., 'Kyiv's Western allies boost nuclear deterrence after Putin's threats', *Financial Times*, 25 Sep. 2022; and Bown, C. P., 'Russia's war on Ukraine: A sanctions timeline', Peterson Institute for International Economics, 10 Jan. 2023. On arms transfers to Ukraine see also chapter 6, sections 1 and 2, and chapter 12, section II, in this volume.

[31] NATO, North Atlantic Council, 'Madrid summit declaration', 29 June 2022; and Brooke-Holland, L., *NATO Enlargement: Sweden and Finland*, Research Briefing no. 09574 (British House of Commons Library: London, 15 July 2022).

[32] On frozen conflicts see Klosek, K. C. et al., 'Frozen conflicts in world politics: A new dataset', *Journal of Peace Research*, vol. 58, no. 4 (2021).

[33] See e.g. Rosa Hernández, G. I. and Oliker, O., *The Art of the Possible: Minimizing Risks as a New European Security Order Takes Shape* (Foreign Policy Research Institute: Philadelphia, PA, Nov. 2022); Jones, P., 'Ukraine settlement options: Disengagement of forces and confidence and security building measures', University of Cambridge, Lauterpacht Centre for International Law, May 2022; and International Crisis Group, 'Seven priorities for preserving the OSCE in a time of war', Crisis Group Special Briefing no. 9, 29 Nov. 2022.

Similarly, the Vienna Document could provide a framework for further bilateral or regional risk-reduction measures, including lower thresholds for notification and observation of military activities, limits on snap exercises and the deployment of forces close to borders, and new arrangements in the maritime domain, which has largely remained unconstrained.[34]

[34] On maritime security see Anthony, I., Su, F. and Saalman, L., 'Naval incident management in Europe, East Asia and South East Asia', SIPRI Insights on Peace and Security no. 2023/03, Mar. 2023.

II. Multilateral regulation of inhumane weapons and other conventional weapons of humanitarian concern

IAN DAVIS AND GIOVANNA MALETTA

Many of the contemporary debates on conventional arms control are shaped by the concept of 'humanitarian disarmament', which prioritizes the protection, security and well-being of people as opposed to states. This approach strives to increase the protection of civilians and combatants by banning certain types of weapon or restricting their use.[1] Victim assistance has become a core element of the humanitarian disarmament agenda.[2]

One of the main multilateral treaties designed for regulating weapons that are considered to cause unnecessary or unjustifiable suffering to combatants or to affect civilians indiscriminately is the 1981 Certain Conventional Weapons Convention (CCW Convention) and its five protocols. Its scope extends to landmines, incendiary weapons and explosive remnants of war (ERW), among other weapon types. Since the CCW Convention is an umbrella treaty, agreements on additional weapon types can be regulated through the adoption of new protocols. In recent decades, however, there have been increasing tensions between the prioritization of humanitarian demands and the perceived military needs of certain states. This led in the 1990s and 2000s to smaller groups of states agreeing to ban anti-personnel mines and cluster munitions through treaties outside the CCW framework: the 1997 Anti-Personnel Mine (APM) Convention and the 2008 Convention on Cluster Munitions (CCM).

The alleged use of cluster munitions, incendiary weapons and unguided missiles on residential areas during the war in Ukraine in 2022 has exacerbated these tensions (see also section I). Because the CCW regime operates by consensus, a small number of states that have chosen to retain, develop or use weapons seen as inhumane by others have simply vetoed or stalled progress on strengthening that treaty.[3]

---

[1] See the discussions on humanitarian disarmament in Anthony, I., 'International humanitarian law: ICRC guidance and its application in urban warfare', *SIPRI Yearbook 2017*, pp. 545–53; and Davis, I. and Verbruggen, M., 'The Convention on Certain Conventional Weapons', *SIPRI Yearbook 2018*, p. 381. See also International Committee of the Red Cross (ICRC), 'International humanitarian law and the challenges of contemporary armed conflicts: Recommitting to protection in armed conflict on the 70th anniversary of the Geneva Conventions', *International Review of the Red Cross*, vol. 101, no. 911 (Aug. 2019).

[2] Docherty, B. and Sanders-Zakre, A., 'The origins and influence of victim assistance: Contributions of the Mine Ban Treaty, Convention on the Rights of Persons with Disabilities and Convention on Cluster Munitions', *International Review of the Red Cross*, vol. 105, no. 922 (Apr. 2023).

[3] See e.g. the discussion on the 2016 CCW review conference in Davis, I. et al., 'Humanitarian arms control regimes: Key developments in 2016', *SIPRI Yearbook 2017*, pp. 554–61; and on developments since then in the 2018–22 editions of the SIPRI Yearbook.

Table 10.1. Meetings of the Certain Conventional Weapons Convention in 2022

Dates	Meeting
7–11 March	Group of governmental experts on lethal autonomous weapon systems
20 July	Amended Protocol II group of experts
22 July	Protocol V meeting of experts
25–29 July	Group of governmental experts on lethal autonomous weapon systems
14 November	16th annual conference of the parties to Protocol V
15 November	24th annual conference of the parties to Amended Protocol II
16–18 November	Meeting of the high contracting parties

Note: All meetings took place in Geneva.

As of 31 December 2022, 126 states were party to the CCW Convention and at least two of its five protocols; Malawi joined on 23 September 2022 and was the only new state party to do so during the year.[4] In 2022 the parties held a total of seven CCW-related meetings (see table 10.1). The annual meeting of high contracting parties in November 2022 once again demonstrated the weaknesses in the consensus process, with no substantive progress and a single delegation—the Russian Federation—overriding the interests and priorities of most states parties, despite the urgency around many issues on its agenda.[5]

The main consequence of a handful of states obstructing advances in most of the CCW agenda has been a perpetual stalemate in the regime in recent years. This, in turn, has led to regulatory progress in some areas being sought outside the CCW process. As was the case on landmines and cluster munitions, this is being done by groups of small and middle-power states supported by civil society networks. Most notably in 2022, an Ireland-led process to address the use of explosive weapons in populated areas (EWIPA) resulted in the adoption of a new political declaration on the issue.

Other categories of conventional weapon that raise humanitarian concerns are dealt with by other legal and political processes. For example, small arms and light weapons (SALW) are regulated by a series of regional and subregional treaties and by two politically binding agreements: the 2001 United Nations Programme of Action on SALW (POA) and the 2005 International Tracing Instrument (ITI).[6] They also fall within the scope of the 2013 Arms Trade Treaty (ATT). There have been calls for further and tighter regulation of SALW, especially regarding ammunition.

---

[4] For a summary and other details of the Convention on Prohibitions or Restrictions on the Use of Certain Conventional Weapons which may be Deemed to be Excessively Injurious or to have Indiscriminate Effects (CCW Convention), including lists of the states parties that have ratified the original, amended and additional protocols, see annex A, section I, in this volume.

[5] Acheson, R., 'Procedural tyranny continues at the CCW', *CCW Report*, vol. 10, no. 11 (22 Nov. 2022). For documents and statements of the 2022 meeting of high contracting parties see UN Office for Disarmament Affairs (UNODA), 'Convention on Certain Conventional Weapons—Meeting of high contracting parties', UNODA Meetings Place, 2022.

[6] On the regional and subregional treaties regulating SALW see annex A, section II, in this volume.

Similarly, armed uncrewed aerial vehicles (UAVs), including loitering munitions, have been addressed to some extent in the UN General Assembly, the Missile Technology Control Regime (MTCR) and the ATT.[7] However, there is no dedicated multilateral process on the regulation of armed UAVs, and both Russia and Ukraine were able to import and use thousands of loitering munitions in their war in 2022.[8]

This section reviews the key developments and treaty negotiations that took place in 2022 in relation to weapons deemed to be inhumane and weapons that raise humanitarian concerns. It first looks, in turn, at weapon types addressed principally within the CCW regime and parallel frameworks (the CCM and APM Convention): incendiary weapons, EWIPA, cluster munitions, landmines, improvised explosive devices (IEDs) and ERW. The challenges posed by autonomous weapon systems and the prominent intergovernmental efforts within the CCW regime to address them are discussed in section III. This section concludes by looking at developments related to SALW and conventional ammunition.

Incendiary weapons

Incendiary weapons produce heat and fire through the chemical reaction of a flammable substance. They cause extremely painful burn injuries that are difficult to treat and start fires that can destroy civilian infrastructure. Protocol III to the CCW Convention regulates the use of incendiary weapons, but critics argue that it is being undermined by two loopholes.[9] First, it prohibits the use of air-dropped incendiary weapons in civilian areas but permits the use of ground-launched versions under certain circumstances. Second, it does not encompass white phosphorus or other munitions that are 'primarily designed' to create smokescreens or to signal troops, yet still produce the same incendiary effects. Protocol III has been accepted by 115 of the CCW states parties.

In 2022 there were allegations that incendiary weapons were being repeatedly used in the Russia–Ukraine War, despite both sides being party

---

[7] On the shortfalls in regulatory policy development in this area see Davis, I. and Maletta, G., 'Multilateral regulation of inhumane weapons and other conventional weapons of humanitarian concern', *SIPRI Yearbook 2022*, pp. 526–28. On developments in the MTCR see chapter 12, section IV, in this volume.

[8] Albon, C., 'US army seeks defense against "kamikaze" drone threat seen in Ukraine', *Defense News*, 12 Oct. 2022; and 'How are "kamikaze" drones being used by Russia and Ukraine?', BBC News, 3 Jan. 2023; and Yousif, E., 'Drone warfare in Ukraine: Understanding the landscape', Stimson Center, 30 June 2022. On international transfers of UAVs to the conflict parties see chapter 6, section I, in this volume.

[9] Human Rights Watch (HRW) and International Human Rights Clinic, *'They Burn Through Everything': The Human Cost of Incendiary Weapons and the Limits of International Law* (HRW: New York, Nov. 2020), pp. 38–39.

to Protocol III.[10] Human Rights Watch (HRW) reviewed visual evidence showing at least 37 attacks using surface-fired incendiary weapons and positively identified remnants of unguided, ground-launched 9M22S Grad incendiary rockets at some of the affected locations. However, HRW was unable to attribute responsibility for these attacks, as both Russia and Ukraine possess this type of incendiary weapon.[11] This type was previously used in eastern Ukraine in 2014, although attribution could not be verified, and in Syria in 2013–19 by the Russian–Syrian military alliance.

In recent years over 20 states along with the European Union (EU), the International Committee of the Red Cross (ICRC) and many non-governmental organizations (NGOs) have raised concerns about incendiary weapons. However, a widely supported proposal by Ireland at the sixth CCW review conference, in 2021, to hold informal consultations on Protocol III in 2022 was blocked by Cuba and Russia.[12]

At the meeting of parties of the CCW in November 2022, Austria, Ireland, Mexico, New Zealand, Norway and Switzerland jointly expressed concern about the misuse of the consensus rule, saying that its purpose should be 'to protect vital national interests, not to veto discussions in a multilateral forum'.[13] They also called for a decision in the final report to request the incoming president of the CCW meeting of parties to conduct informal consultations on the implementation and universalization of Protocol III, and report the findings to the 2023 meeting. This proposal was additionally supported by Belgium, Germany and Panama. However, Russia successfully blocked the inclusion of any language on incendiary weapons in the final report of the 2022 meeting.[14]

Explosive weapons in populated areas

The use of EWIPA—and especially the use of explosive weapons with a large destructive radius, an inaccurate delivery system or the capacity to deliver multiple munitions over a wide area—has frequently led to situations in armed conflict, including in such places as Ethiopia, Syria, Ukraine and Yemen, where around 90 per cent of casualties in populated areas are civilian

---

[10] See e.g. 'Burning munitions cascade down on Ukrainian steel plant, video shows', Reuters, 15 May 2022; and Ott, H., 'What is white phosphorous, and what does it mean that Russia may be using it in Ukraine?', CBS News, 25 Mar. 2022.

[11] United Nations, General Assembly, First Committee, Joint civil society statement on incendiary weapons, Human Rights Watch, 18 Oct. 2022.

[12] Davis and Maletta (note 7), pp. 517–18.

[13] CCW Convention, Meeting of the high contracting parties, 'Working paper on incendiary weapons', Submitted by Austria, Ireland, Mexico, New Zealand, Norway and Switzerland, CCW/MSP/2022/WP.3, 18 Nov. 2022.

[14] Acheson, R. and Varella, L., 'Consideration of the draft final report', *CCW Report*, vol. 10, no. 11 (22 Nov. 2022); and CCW Convention, Meeting of the high contracting parties, Final report, Advanced version, CCW/MSP/2022/7, 24 Nov. 2022.

rather than combatants.[15] A study by Action on Armed Violence (AOAV), an independent weapon-related research and advocacy organization, recorded 357 370 casualties (155 118 people killed and 202 252 injured) from explosive weapons in the decade 2011–20, 73 per cent of whom were civilians.[16] Of the recorded incidents, 60 per cent took place in populated areas. The use of EWIPA also has reverberating effects, with impacts on water, sanitation, ecosystems, healthcare, education and psychological well-being.[17]

Use of EWIPA in the Russia–Ukraine War

The use of EWIPA in the Russia–Ukraine War has resulted in widespread death, injuries and destruction. According to AOAV, the number of civilian casualties from explosive violence since the invasion on 24 February 2022 had reached 10 680 by 13 January 2023, including 3813 killed and 6867 injured. Of the civilian casualties, 94 per cent (10 055) occurred in populated areas.[18] Based on its investigations of the events in Kyiv, Chernihiv, Kharkiv and Sumy oblasts in late February and March 2022, the report of the Independent International Commission of Inquiry on Ukraine found the 'relentless use' of explosive weapons with wide-area effects in populated areas that were under attack by Russian armed forces.[19] The commission documented indiscriminate attacks using cluster munitions (see below), unguided rockets and air strikes. Residential buildings, schools and hospitals, among other parts of the civilian infrastructure, were damaged or destroyed.[20]

Agreement of the Political Declaration on the use of EWIPA

In June 2022 negotiations were concluded on the Political Declaration on Strengthening the Protection of Civilians from the Humanitarian Consequences Arising from the Use of Explosive Weapons in Populated

---

[15] Action on Armed Violence (AOAV), *Explosive Violence Monitor 2021* (AOAV: London, 2022), p. 3. See also ICRC, *Explosive Weapons with Wide Area Effects: A Deadly Choice in Populated Areas* (ICRC: Geneva, Jan. 2022); and International Network on Explosive Weapons (INEW), 'Protecting civilians from the use of explosive weapons in populated areas', May 2020.

[16] The study was based on the monitoring of 29 000 incidents in 123 countries recorded by English-language media. AOAV, *A Decade of Explosive Violence Harm* (AOAV: London, May 2021), p. 9.

[17] For a detailed taxonomy of these effects see Baldo, A. M. and Batault, F., *Second Menu of Indicators to Measure the Reverberating Effects on Civilians from the Use of Explosive Weapons in Populated Areas* (UNIDIR: Geneva, Feb. 2022). See also UN Children's Fund (UNICEF), *Water Under Fire*, vol. 3, *Attacks on Water and Sanitation Services in Armed Conflict and the Impacts on Children* (UNICEF: New York, 2021).

[18] AOAV, 'Ukraine: AOAV explosive violence data on harm to civilians', 13 Jan. 2023.

[19] United Nations, General Assembly, Report of the Independent International Commission of Inquiry on Ukraine, A/77/533, 18 Oct. 2022, p. 2. The commission of inquiry was established by UN Human Rights Council Resolution 49/1, 'Situation of human rights in Ukraine stemming from the Russian aggression', 4 Mar. 2022. It was requested to undertake the inquiry by UN Human Rights Council Resolution S-34/1, 'The deteriorating human rights situation in Ukraine stemming from the Russian aggression', 12 May 2022.

[20] United Nations, A/77/533 (note 19), pp. 8–9. Also see PAX, 'Impact on healthcare from bombing and shelling in Ukraine', 31 Mar. 2022.

Areas.[21] The political declaration, while falling short of a legally binding commitment, is the first formal international recognition that the use of EWIPA has severe humanitarian consequences that need to be urgently addressed. It promotes stronger standards for the protection of civilians and commits states that sign the declaration to implement these standards through changes to their national policy and practice. The declaration can also provide a basis for stigmatizing harmful actions, such as use of explosive weapons with wide-area effects in populated areas.

The International Network on Explosive Weapons (INEW), a coalition of NGOs, was the first to articulate EWIPA as an issue that demanded attention in the early 2010s.[22] This led to calls from an increasing number of states, successive UN secretary-generals, international bodies and other NGOs for measures to provide better protection for civilians and to prevent harm from EWIPA.[23] After many years of failing to make progress within the CCW framework, and as a result of this increasing international political pressure, a separate consultation process led by Ireland gathered momentum from late 2019, but stalled somewhat due to the Covid-19 pandemic in 2020–21.[24]

On 6–8 April 2022 over 65 states (with 200 delegates), international organizations and civil society groups resumed face-to-face dialogue on the issue at the United Nations in Geneva.[25] This fourth round of consultations considered the third draft of the declaration and brought the process close to completion.[26] On 17 June 2022 the same parties met again in Geneva, where the final text of the political declaration was presented by Ireland, and

---

[21] Political Declaration on Strengthening the Protection of Civilians from the Humanitarian Consequences Arising from the Use of Explosive Weapons in Populated Areas, Irish Department of Foreign Affairs, 17 June 2022.

[22] See e.g. INEW, *Stop Bombing Civilians: An Advocacy Guide on Explosive Weapons in Populated Areas* (INEW: London, [Sep. 2012]).

[23] See e.g. Austrian Federal Ministry for Europe, Integration and Foreign Affairs, 'Vienna Conference on Protecting Civilians in Urban Warfare: Summary of the conference', Vienna, 1–2 Oct. 2019; and United Nations, 'Joint appeal by the UN secretary-general and the president of the International Committee of the Red Cross on the use of explosive weapons in cities', Press release SG/2251, 18 Sep. 2019. For a list of 112 states and territories and 9 state groupings that have publicly acknowledged the harm caused by EWIPA in statements see INEW, 'Political response'.

[24] Irish Department of Foreign Affairs, 'Protecting civilians in urban warfare'. For developments in 2019–21 see Davis, I., 'Global instruments for conventional arms control', *SIPRI Yearbook 2020*, pp. 496–99; Davis, I., 'Global and regional instruments for conventional arms control', *SIPRI Yearbook 2021*, pp. 508–10; and Davis and Maletta (note 7), pp. 518–20.

[25] INEW, 'States near agreement committing to reduce civilian harm from use of explosive weapons in towns and cities', Press release, 8 Apr. 2022.

[26] Draft Political Declaration on Strengthening the Protection of Civilians from the Humanitarian Consequences Arising from the Use of Explosive Weapons in Populated Areas, Rev. 2, Irish Department of Foreign Affairs, circulated 3 Mar. 2022. For an outline of the key discussions see Acheson, R., 'The political declaration on explosive weapon use must protect civilians, not militaries', Reaching Critical Will, 14 Apr. 2022.

subsequently agreed without changes.[27] At the signing conference in Dublin on 18 November 2022, 83 states formally adopted the declaration.[28]

Several states and civil society organizations accepted that the declaration—particularly its key commitment in paragraph 3.3—fell short of expectations for a clear and explicit commitment to avoid the use of EWIPA when they have wide-area effects.[29] However, it was widely agreed that implementation of the declaration at the national level provides a means through which to promote changes in state policy and practice. In this regard, the adoption of the political declaration should be seen as the first step towards establishing an effective norm against EWIPA.

The environment and armed conflict

New standards were also set during 2022 regarding the environment and armed conflict. On 7 December 2022 the UN General Assembly adopted by consensus the Principles on the Protection of the Environment in Relation to Armed Conflicts.[30] The principles had been drafted by the International Law Commission in a 10-year process.[31]

These 27 non-binding principles call for designated protection zones, the explicit application of existing international humanitarian law to the environment, and rules to protect the environment during times of occupation.[32] The principles apply throughout the cycle of armed conflicts and establish a minimum standard of environmental conduct for militaries, as well as for a range of non-state actors. As with the Political Declaration on EWIPA, these principles will require further promotion and implementation by supportive states and civil society.

Cluster munitions

Cluster munitions are air-dropped or ground-launched weapons that release smaller submunitions intended to kill enemy personnel or destroy vehicles. There are three main criticisms of cluster munitions: they disperse large

---

[27] Varella, L., 'States agree to final text of political declaration on the use of explosive weapons', Reaching Critical Will, 22 June 2022.

[28] Explosive Weapons in Populated Areas, Dublin Conference 2022, 'List of endorsing states', 18 Nov. 2022.

[29] See e.g. International Network on Explosive Weapons (INEW), 'States agree final text of political declaration on the use of explosive weapons', 17 June 2022; Varella (note 27); and Bagshaw, S., 'Implementing the political declaration on the use of explosive weapons in populated areas: Key areas and implementing action', Policy briefing, Article 36, Nov. 2022.

[30] UN General Assembly Resolution 77/104, 'Protection of the environment in relation to armed conflicts', 7 Dec. 2022. See also Conflict and Environment Observatory, 'States adopt new legal framework on the environmental impact of war', 8 Dec. 2022.

[31] United Nations, General Assembly, Report of the 73th session of the International Law Commission, A/77/10, 2022, paras 45–58.

[32] UN General Assembly Resolution 77/104 (note 30), annex.

numbers of submunitions imprecisely over an extended area; they are difficult to detect; and they frequently fail to detonate, thereby leaving unexploded submunitions that can remain explosive hazards for many decades.[33]

The humanitarian consequences of cluster munitions and the harm to civilians that they cause are addressed by the 2008 Convention on Cluster Munitions.[34] The CCM establishes an unconditional prohibition on cluster munitions. It also requires its states parties to destroy their stockpiles within 8 years of entry into force of the convention (Article 3), clear areas contaminated by cluster munition remnants within 10 years (Article 4) and provide assistance for victims of such weapons (Article 5). As of 31 December 2022, the CCM had 110 parties and 13 signatory states, among which are former major producers and users of cluster munitions as well as affected states. In December 2022, 144 states voted to adopt the eighth UN General Assembly resolution supporting the CCM, with 1 vote against (Russia).[35]

Use and production: Cluster munition attacks in Ukraine

No CCM state party has used cluster munitions since the convention was adopted, and most of the states still outside the convention abide de facto by the ban on the use and production of these weapons. Since the CCM entered into force in August 2010, cluster munitions have been used in eight non-signatory states: Azerbaijan in 2020; Cambodia in 2011; Libya in 2011, 2015 and 2019; South Sudan in 2014; Sudan in 2012–15; Syria in 2012–21; Ukraine in 2014–15 and 2022; and Yemen in 2015–17.[36]

Ukraine was the only country in the world where cluster munitions were used in 2022. The extensive use of cluster munitions by Russia in its invasion of Ukraine has been documented by NGOs and the Independent International Commission of Inquiry on Ukraine. HRW, for example, reported that Russian armed forces used at least six types of cluster munition in hundreds of attacks in at least eight of Ukraine's oblasts between 24 February and 10 May 2022, while the commission documented indiscriminate attacks with the use of cluster munitions on Chernihiv city on 17 March 2022.[37] Hundreds of civilians were killed and injured in these cluster munition attacks: preliminary data indicates at least 689 civilian casualties in the

---

[33] Feickert, A. and Kerr, P. K., *Cluster Munitions: Background and Issues for Congress*, Congressional Research Service (CRS) Report for Congress RS22907 (US Congress, CRS: Washington, DC, 9 Mar. 2022).

[34] For a summary and other details of the CCM see annex A, section I, in this volume.

[35] UN General Assembly Resolution 77/79, 'Implementation of the Convention on Cluster Munitions', 7 Dec. 2022.

[36] Cluster Munition Coalition (CMC), *Cluster Munition Monitor 2022* (International Campaign to Ban Landmines–CMC: Geneva, Aug. 2022), p. 14. *Cluster Munition Monitor 2022* focuses on the calendar year 2021 with information included up to Aug. 2022 where possible.

[37] HRW, *Intense and Lasting Harm: Cluster Munition Attacks in Ukraine* (HRW: New York, May 2022); and United Nations, A/77/533 (note 19), p. 9. See also Amnesty International, 'Ukraine: Cluster munitions kill child and two other civilians taking shelter at preschool', 27 Feb. 2022.

first half of 2022.[38] The International Criminal Court's investigation into allegations of Russian war crimes in Ukraine may also examine allegations of indiscriminate use of cluster munitions.[39] There are also allegations that Ukraine used cluster munitions at least three times in 2022.[40] Neither Russia nor Ukraine is party to the CCM.

The cluster munition attacks in Ukraine were condemned by the UN high commissioner for human rights, UN special rapporteurs, experts and the non-governmental Cluster Munition Coalition, the EU and its member states, at least 21 other states, and the secretary-general of the North Atlantic Treaty Organization (NATO).[41] The NATO secretary-general, Jens Stoltenberg, for example, called Russia's use of cluster munitions in Ukraine 'inhumane' and 'in violation' of international law.[42]

Although the United States also expressed concern at Russia's use of cluster munitions, it has remained unwilling to join the CCM.[43] On 22 April 2022, in a letter to the US president, 27 members of the US Congress called cluster munitions 'barbaric and indiscriminate weapons' and said that they 'strongly believe the credible allegations of Russian use of cluster munitions necessitate a change to the administration's cluster munitions policy'.[44] However, the US military has strenuously resisted efforts to fully curtail the availability of cluster munitions and US policy seems unlikely to change any time soon.[45]

The Cluster Munition Coalition lists 16 states as producers of cluster munitions: Brazil, China, Egypt, Greece, India, Iran, Israel, North Korea, South Korea, Pakistan, Poland, Romania, Russia, Singapore, Türkiye and the USA.[46] None of them is party to the CCM. Russia has continued to

---

[38] Cluster Munition Coalition (note 36), p. 37.

[39] Khan, K. A. A., ICC Prosecutor, 'I have decided to proceed with opening an investigation', Statement on the situation in Ukraine, International Criminal Court (ICC), 28 Feb. 2022.

[40] Cluster Munition Coalition (note 36), p. 15; and Gibbons-Neff, T. and Ismay, J., 'To push back Russians, Ukrainians hit a village with cluster munitions', *New York Times*, 18 Apr. 2022.

[41] E.g. M. Bachelet, UN High Commissioner for Human Rights, Statement on Ukraine, UN Human Rights Council, 30 Mar. 2022. States have condemned the use of cluster munition in Ukraine in national or joint statements at UN bodies including the Human Rights Council, the General Assembly and the Security Council. See Human Rights Watch (note 37), pp. 18–19.

[42] NATO, 'Press conference by NATO Secretary General Jens Stoltenberg following the extraordinary meeting of NATO ministers of foreign affairs', 4 Mar. 2022. Of NATO's 30 member states, 23 have ratified the CCM, the 7 exceptions being Estonia, Greece, Latvia, Poland, Romania, Türkiye and the USA.

[43] Crocker, S., US Permanent Representative to the UN and Other International Organizations in Geneva, Statement at the Human Rights Council urgent debate on the human rights situation in Ukraine, 3 Mar. 2022.

[44] Keating, W. R., Chair of the US House of Representatives Committee on Foreign Affairs Subcommittee on Europe, Energy the Environment and Cyber, and 26 others, Letter to President Joe Biden, 22 Apr. 2022.

[45] Feickert, A. and Kerr, P. K., *Cluster Munitions: Background and Issues for Congress*, CRS Report for Congress RS22907 (US Congress, CRS: Washington, DC, 9 Mar. 2022); and Pomper, S., 'US policy on cluster munitions and Russia's war in Ukraine', Just Security, 4 May 2022.

[46] Cluster Munition Coalition (note 36), pp. 17–18.

produce new cluster munitions and its armed forces used at least two newly developed types in Ukraine in 2022.[47] A lack of transparency means that it is unclear whether any of the other 15 listed states were actively producing such munitions in 2021–22.

Cluster munition clearance and stockpile destruction

Stockpile destruction is one of the CCM's major successes: 38 of the 42 states parties that had declared possession of cluster munitions have completed the destruction of their stockpiles. This destruction of 1.5 million stockpiled cluster munitions containing 178 million submunitions represents the destruction of 99 per cent of all the cluster munitions and submunitions declared as stockpiled under the CCM. Four states parties—Bulgaria, Peru, Slovakia and South Africa—have cluster munition stocks still to destroy.[48]

The quantity of cluster munitions currently stockpiled by non-CCM signatories is unknown. Similarly, it is not possible to provide an accurate estimate of the total size of the area contaminated by cluster munition remnants, but at least 26 UN member states and 3 other states or areas remain contaminated by cluster munitions.[49] These include 10 CCM states parties (Afghanistan, Bosnia and Herzegovina, Chad, Chile, Germany, Iraq, Laos, Lebanon, Mauritania, and Somalia) and two signatory states (Angola and the Democratic Republic of the Congo, DRC). In addition, there are remnants in 14 non-signatory UN member states (Armenia, Azerbaijan, Cambodia, Georgia, Iran, Libya, Serbia, South Sudan, Sudan, Syria, Tajikistan, Ukraine, Viet Nam and Yemen) and 3 other states or areas (Kosovo, Nagorno-Karabakh and Western Sahara). Over the past decade, six CCM states parties (the Republic of the Congo, Croatia, Grenada, Montenegro, Mozambique and Norway) have completed clearance of areas contaminated by cluster munition remnants.[50]

The 10th meeting of states parties

The 10th meeting of states parties to the CCM, held in Geneva on 30 August– 2 September 2022, was the first formal meeting of the convention after the adoption of the Lausanne Action Plan at the second CCM review conference, in 2021. The Action Plan is a five-year (2021–26) road map for the states parties to progress towards the full universalization and implementation of the CCM.[51]

The meeting expressed 'grave concern' over the use of cluster munitions in Ukraine, but welcomed the continued progress in stockpile destruction,

---

[47] Cluster Munition Coalition (note 36), p. 17.
[48] Cluster Munition Coalition (note 36), pp. 22–25.
[49] Cluster Munition Coalition (note 36), pp. 39–47.
[50] Cluster Munition Coalition (note 36), pp. 39–40.
[51] Convention on Cluster Munitions (CCM), *Lausanne Action Plan* (CCM Implementation Support Unit: Geneva, Sep. 2021). Also see Davis and Maletta (note 7), pp. 522–23.

including the confirmation by Guinea-Bissau that it did not have any cluster munitions in its armouries.[52] The meeting also granted Bulgaria an extension of its deadline for the destruction of its cluster munition stockpile, as well as extensions to Bosnia and Herzegovina, Chad and Chile for completing the clearance and destruction of cluster munition remnants.[53]

Landmines, improvised explosive devices and explosive remnants of war

Anti-personnel mines are mines that detonate on human contact—that is, they are victim activated—and therefore encompass improvised explosive devices that act as anti-personnel mines, also known as 'improvised mines'.[54] They are prohibited under the 1997 APM Convention.[55] As of 31 December 2022 there were 164 states parties to the APM Convention; no new accession to the convention has taken place since 2017. Amended Protocol II of the CCW Convention, with 106 states parties, also regulates (but does not entirely ban) landmines—including APMs and anti-vehicle mines, known as mines other than APMs (MOTAPMs)—as well as booby-traps and IEDs. A dedicated group of experts under this protocol has been working on these devices since 2009. Explosive remnants of war—including landmines, unexploded ordnance and abandoned explosive ordnance—are regulated by CCW Protocol V, which has 97 states parties. IEDs are also discussed in the First Committee of the UN General Assembly, including through the submission of resolutions.

Use and production of APMs in 2021–22

In 2021, the most recent year for which comparative data is available, over 5500 people were killed or injured by APMs in 50 countries and areas—the sixth successive year of high casualties. Of the casualties whose status was known, 76 per cent were civilians. The two states with the most casualties in 2021 were Syria (1227) and Afghanistan (1074).[56]

The deployment of new APMs by states is now extremely rare. According to the International Campaign to Ban Landmines (ICBL), only two states—Myanmar and Russia (neither a party to the APM Convention)—used APMs in the period mid 2021 to October 2022. Myanmar had been deploying them

---

[52] Convention on Cluster Munitions, 10th meeting of states parties, Final report, CCM/MSP/2022/12, 19 Sep. 2022, paras 21, 26.

[53] Convention on Cluster Munitions, CCM/MSP/2022/12 (note 52), paras 27–43.

[54] Seddon, B. and Malaret Baldo, A., *Counter-IED: Capability Maturity Model & Self-assessment Tool* (UN Institute for Disarmament Research: Geneva, 2020).

[55] For a summary and other details of the Convention on the Prohibition of the Use, Stockpiling, Production and Transfer of Anti-Personnel Mines and on their Destruction (APM Convention) see annex A, section I, in this volume.

[56] International Campaign to Ban Landmines (ICBL), *Landmine Monitor 2022* (ICBL–Cluster Munition Coalition: Geneva, Nov. 2022), pp. 48–54. *Landmine Monitor 2022* focuses on the calendar year 2021 with information included up to Oct. 2022 where possible.

for the previous 20 years. Russia has used at least seven types of APM in multiple areas across Ukraine since it invaded the country on 24 February 2022. It is unprecedented for a country that is not a party to the treaty to have used APMs on the territory of a state party such as Ukraine.[57] In a potential violation of Ukraine's own treaty commitments not to use the weapons, HRW alleged in early 2023 that Ukrainian forces had also fired 'thousands' of APMs into Russian-occupied territory 'in and around' the eastern Ukrainian city of Izyum while it was occupied by Russian forces in April to September 2022.[58] The Ukrainian Ministry of Foreign Affairs said in a statement that it 'took note' of the report, which it said would be 'duly studied by the competent authorities of Ukraine'.[59] Post-war clearance of APMs in Ukraine is expected to take at least a decade.[60]

New information in 2022 linked the Wagner Group, a Russian private military and security company, to the use of APMs in Libya in 2019–20 that killed at least three Libyan deminers.[61] More than 50 states have produced APMs in the past, but the ICBL identifies only 11 as possible current producers (1 fewer than in 2021 following a change in US policy; see below), and only 5 as the most likely to be active producers: India, Iran, Myanmar, Pakistan and Russia.[62]

While there is a de facto moratorium on the production and use of APMs among most states in the world, the use of these weapons, including victim-activated IEDs, by non-state armed groups in conflicts is a growing problem.[63] APMs were used by such groups in at least five states between mid 2021 and October 2022: the Central African Republic, Colombia, the DRC, India and Myanmar.[64]

At its meeting in July 2022, the group of experts of Amended Protocol II continued its discussion of IEDs. Its focus remained on voluntary exchange of information on national and multilateral measures and on best practices

---

[57] ICBL (note 56), pp. 2, 8–16. See also HRW, 'Background briefing on landmine use in Ukraine', June 2022.

[58] HRW, 'Ukraine: Banned landmines harm civilians', 31 Jan. 2023.

[59] Ukrainian Ministry of Foreign Affairs, 'Коментар МЗС України щодо Звіту організації Human Rights Watch' [Commentary of the MFA of Ukraine on the report of the Human Rights Watch organization], 31 Jan. 2023 (author translation).

[60] Tondo, L. and Koshiw, I., '"The Russians mined everything": Why making Kherson safe could take years', *The Guardian*, 16 Nov. 2022.

[61] HRW, 'Libya: Russia's Wagner Group set landmines near Tripoli', 31 May 2022. On the Wagner Group, and private military and security companies more generally, see chapter 4, in this volume.

[62] ICBL (note 56), p. 22. The other 6 listed producers are China, Cuba, North Korea, South Korea, Singapore and Viet Nam.

[63] E.g. Luke, D., *Old Issues, New Threats: Mine Action and IEDs in Urban Environments* (LSE Ideas: London, Feb. 2020).

[64] ICBL (note 56), pp. 2, 16–19.

regarding identification, humanitarian clearance and civilian protection from IEDs.[65]

Revised policy on APMs announced by the United States

On 21 June 2022 the United States announced a new policy on APMs, effectively banning their transfer, development, production or acquisition. It also states that the USA will 'Not assist, encourage, or induce anyone, outside of the context of the Korean Peninsula, to engage in any activity that would be prohibited by the [APM] Convention'.[66] The so-called Korean exception allows the USA to use and stockpile APMs for the defence of South Korea.[67] The USA has a stockpile of approximately 3 million APMs.[68]

The announcement came after a comprehensive review that began in April 2021 and essentially reversed the APM policy adopted in January 2020 by the previous administration. This was the fifth change in US policy in as many administrations, dating back to the 1990s. Meanwhile, the country last used APMs in 1991 (except for one use in Afghanistan in 2002) and has not exported them since 1992 or produced them since 1997.[69]

APM clearance and stockpile destruction

An estimated 132 square kilometres of land were cleared of APMs in 2021 (compared to 146 km^2 in 2020 and 156 km^2 in 2019) and nearly 118 000 APMs were destroyed (compared to 135 000 in 2020 and 122 000 in 2019).[70] Cambodia cleared the most land during 2021 (43.7 km^2), followed by Croatia (34.5 km^2). Sri Lanka cleared and destroyed the most landmines in 2021, with 26 804 cleared from 4.1 km^2 of land. The 60 states and other areas that are known to have mine contamination include 33 states parties to the APM Convention. Among them are some of the most mine-affected states in the world: Afghanistan, Bosnia and Herzegovina, Cambodia, Croatia, Ethiopia, Iraq, Türkiye, Ukraine and Yemen.[71]

Collectively, states parties have destroyed more than 55 million stockpiled APMs since the convention entered into force. Only two states parties have remaining stockpile-destruction obligations—Greece (0.3 million) and

---

[65] Amended Protocol II to the CCW Convention, 24th annual conference, 'Report on improvised explosive devices', CCW/AP.II/CONF.24/2, 14 Sep. 2022.

[66] White House, 'Changes to US anti-personnel landmine policy', Fact sheet, 21 June 2022. See also Stohl, R., 'Biden administration announces new APL landmines policy', Stimson Center, 24 June 2022.

[67] Troxell, J. F., 'Landmines: Why the Korea exception should be the rule', *Parameters*, vol. 30, no. 1 (2000).

[68] US Department of State, 'Briefing on the United States' updated anti-personnel landmine policy', 21 June 2022.

[69] On the political and norm-setting nature of the change see Human Rights Watch, 'Landmines: US moves closer towards global ban', 21 June 2021; and 'New US anti-personnel landmine policy adopted', *American Journal of International Law*, vol. 116, no. 4 (Oct. 2022).

[70] ICBL (note 56), pp. 54–59.

[71] ICBL (note 56), pp. 34–48.

Ukraine (3.3 million)—and both are in violation of the treaty for missing their destruction deadlines. The total remaining global stockpile of APMs held by non-states parties is estimated to be fewer than 50 million, down from about 160 million in 1999. With the exception of Ukraine, the largest stockpilers are non-signatories: Russia (26.5 million), Pakistan (6 million), India (4–5 million), China (5 million), Ukraine (3.3 million) and the USA (3 million).[72] At the 20th meeting of the states parties to the APM Convention, which took place on 21–25 November 2022 in Geneva, eight states were granted extensions to their mine-clearance obligations under Article 5: Afghanistan (until 2025), Argentina (2026), Ecuador (2025), Guinea-Bissau (2024), Serbia (2024), Sudan (2027), Thailand (2026) and Yemen (2028).[73]

The situation in Afghanistan

The impact of the end of the 2001–21 Afghanistan War on the APM situation in the country has been mixed. First, no new deployments of APMs were reported in Afghanistan in 2021–22 for the first time since 2007, although the legacy of past use means that future casualty rates are likely to remain high.[74]

Second, mine clearance and other mitigation activities are being severely constrained by the freeze by Western governments on the provision of development assistance to the Taliban-led government. For example, the Afghan government agency that oversees mine clearance reportedly lost about US$3 million funding and laid off about 120 staff in April 2022.[75] Even before the Taliban takeover in August 2021, funding for mine action in Afghanistan had been decreasing steadily, falling from $113 million in 2011 to $32 million by 2020.[76]

Third, as noted above, the current Afghan government has continued to actively engage with the APM Convention, having requested and received permission to extend its clearance deadline for two years until March 2025. Meeting that deadline will, however, require the restoration of international funding.

---

[72] ICBL (note 56), pp. 2, 24–26.

[73] On the proceedings, documents and statements by states parties see APM Convention, '20th meeting of the states parties (20MSP)', 21–25 Nov. 2022. For details of each of the extension requests, additional information submitted by the state party, analysis and decisions see APM Convention, 20th meeting of the states parties, Draft final report, APLC/MSP.20/2022/CRP.1, 25 Nov. 2022, sections A–G.

[74] ICBL (note 56), p. 16.

[75] Greenfield, C. and Yawar, M. Y., 'How isolating the Afghan Taliban could mean more young landmine victims', Reuters, 7 July 2022.

[76] Gupta, K., 'In Afghanistan, landmines are making peace deadly', World Politics Review, 10 May 2022.

Small arms and light weapons

The 2001 UN Programme of Action to Prevent, Combat and Eradicate the Illicit Trade in Small Arms and Light Weapons in All its Aspects and the 2005 International Instrument to Enable States to Identify and Trace, in a Timely and Reliable Manner, Illicit Small Arms and Light Weapons are politically binding agreements that were negotiated on the basis of consensus under the auspices of the First Committee of the UN General Assembly.[77] These instruments outline steps that states should take at the international, regional and national levels to counter the illicit trade in and diversion of SALW. The UN Office for Disarmament Affairs (UNODA) administers the two instruments, and states voluntarily submit a report every two years that outlines how they implement both the POA and the ITI.[78] In addition, states meet at a biennial meeting of states (BMS) to 'consider' the implementation of both instruments and at a review conference every six years that allows for a more in-depth assessment of the progress made on implementation.

From 27 June to 1 July 2022, states gathered in New York for the eighth BMS. Exceptionally, BMS8 took place just one year after BMS7, which had been postponed because of the Covid-19 pandemic. The meeting was held in a fully in-person format that, in contrast to BMS7, allowed the physical participation of both state delegates and representatives of civil society.[79] The meeting was initially chaired by Ambassador Enrique Manalo of the Philippines. However, on the second day of the meeting it was announced that he was to be appointed as secretary of foreign affairs of the Philippines. As a result, the rest of the process was managed by the vice-chairs.[80]

Contentious issues at BMS8

At BMS8 states were able to adopt an outcome document by consensus although discussions showed that several issues remained contentious. These included in particular the expansion of the scope of the POA to include ammunition, the explicit recognition of synergies between the POA and other relevant international instruments, and the inclusion of gender-related language in the outcome document.

EU member states and a number of states from Africa, Latin America and the Caribbean, among others, continued to advocate in favour of including

---

[77] United Nations, General Assembly, Programme of Action to Prevent, Combat and Eradicate the Illicit Trade in Small Arms and Light Weapons in All its Aspects (POA), pp. 7–17 of A/CONF.192/15, 20 July 2001; and United Nations, General Assembly, International Instrument to Enable States to Identify and Trace, in a Timely and Reliable Manner, Illicit Small Arms and Light Weapons (International Tracing Instrument, ITI), Decision 60/519, 8 Dec. 2005.

[78] UNODA, 'Programme of action on small arms and light weapons: National reports'.

[79] Davis and Maletta (note 7), p. 529.

[80] International Action Network on Small Arms (IANSA), 'BMS8 daily briefing day 2', 28 June 2022.

ammunition within the scope of the POA.[81] They faced opposition from, among others, the Arab Group of states, the United States and Russia, which argued against the consideration of issues on which there is no consensus within the POA. Some of these states argued that the topic could be discussed in other forums that they deemed to be more appropriate, including the open-ended working group (OEWG) on ammunition established by the UN General Assembly in 2021 (see below).[82] As a result, the outcome document simply 'took note' of the establishment of the OEWG. There was no meaningful development regarding the possibility of expanding the scope of the POA to ammunition.[83]

The recognition of synergies between the POA and the Arms Trade Treaty (ATT) continued to be firmly opposed by states that are not party to the ATT, such as Algeria, Cuba, Iran, Iraq and Venezuela.[84] Discussions at BMS8 did not register any progress in this specific area, but the outcome document still retained references to the linkages between the implementation of the POA and other relevant documents such as the 2030 Agenda for Sustainable Development and the Women and Peace and Security Agenda.[85]

Gender-related language in the outcome document referred, among other things, to the importance of women's participation in SALW-related decision-making processes and the role of illicit SALW in facilitating gender-based violence. Again, during relevant discussions at BMS8, some states raised concerns about discussing issues on which there is no clear consensus or that are 'unclear' in the context of the POA, which was interpreted as also referring to gender-related issues.[86] Gender-related language was eventually included; although in the closing statements that followed the adoption of the outcome document, Iran and Russia expressed their dissatisfaction with the decision to do so.[87]

Progress achieved at BMS8

The states at BMS8 still managed to achieve some limited progresses in expanding the scope of international cooperation and assistance and in

---

[81] European External Action Service, EU statement on the consideration of the implementation of the Programme of Action, Eighth POA Biennial meeting of states, 27 June 2022; IANSA, 'BMS8 daily briefing day 1', 27 June 2022; IANSA, 'BMS8 daily briefing day 4', 30 June 2022; and Control Arms, 'The eighth biennial meeting of states on the PoA', 27 July 2022.

[82] IANSA, 'BMS8 daily briefing day 1' (note 81); and IANSA, 'BMS8 daily briefing day 4' (note 81).

[83] Eighth POA biennial meeting of states, Report, A/CONF.192/BMS/2022/1, 12 July 2022, annex, para. 19.

[84] IANSA, 'BMS8 daily briefing day 1' (note 81).

[85] Eighth POA biennial meeting of states, A/CONF.192/BMS/2022/1 (note 83), annex, paras 9, 50, 51, 53, 54. See also UN General Assembly Resolution 70/1, 'Transforming our world: The 2030 Agenda for Sustainable Development', 5 Sep. 2015; and on the Women and Peace and Security Agenda see UN Women, 'Peace and Security'.

[86] IANSA, 'BMS8 daily briefing day 1' (note 81).

[87] Eighth POA biennial meeting of states, A/CONF.192/BMS/2022/1 (note 83), annex, paras 10, 74–79, IANSA, 'BMS8 daily briefing day 5', 1 July 2022.

addressing new developments in SALW manufacturing. Specifically, they decided to establish a fellowship training programme to strengthen expertise relevant to the implementation of the POA and the ITI, especially in countries in the Global South.[88]

Further—and following up on the outcome of BMS7 and a proposal tabled by Belgium at BMS8—states also agreed to discuss at the fourth review conference (scheduled for 2024) the establishment of an open-ended technical expert group on how to strengthen implementation of the POA and the ITI in the light of technological developments in SALW manufacturing.[89] Exchanges during BMS8 on this topic raised some concerns that these discussions could add pressure on states with limited financial and technical resources for POA implementation, as well as questions as to whether such technical issues should be discussed in a diplomatic forum.[90] States eventually agreed to include several references in the outcome document to the challenges and opportunities that technological advancements pose to SALW controls.

Overall, at BMS8 states took some limited steps to advance implementation of the POA and the ITI. The main challenge that states face in the run-up to the 2024 review conference will be to make all the necessary arrangements and preparations to facilitate constructive discussions around the establishment of the expert group on developments in SALW manufacturing. Other challenges—including the resistance to bringing ammunition within the scope of the POA and establishing linkages with the ATT—are likely to remain, especially as discussions are expected to become increasingly politicized in an international environment characterized by geopolitical competition. In the long run, these disagreements risk limiting the ability of the POA to promote a comprehensive approach to addressing diversion of and trafficking in SALW.[91] For this reason, like-minded states may be more likely to achieve progress in advancing some of these issues in other forums, as is currently being done in the case of ammunition.

The open-ended working group on conventional ammunition

On 24 December 2021 the UN General Assembly established an open-ended working group 'to elaborate a set of political commitments as a new global framework' to 'address existing gaps in through-life ammunition

---

[88] Eighth POA biennial meeting of states, A/CONF.192/BMS/2022/1 (note 83), annex, para. 83.
[89] Eighth POA biennial meeting of states, A/CONF.192/BMS/2022/1 (note 83), annex, paras 13, 67–75; and Eighth POA biennial meeting of states, 'Recent developments in the production, technology and design of small arms and light weapons (SALW)', Working paper submitted by Belgium, 27 June–1 July 2022. On relevant discussions at BMS7 see Davis and Maletta (note 7), pp. 528–31.
[90] IANSA, 'BMS8 daily briefing day 2' (note 80).
[91] Control Arms (note 81).

management'.[92] This followed the recommendations included in the final report of the group of governmental experts (GGE) that the General Assembly had established in 2020 to consider problems arising from the accumulation of surplus conventional ammunition stockpiles.[93] The GGE's report highlighted the need to adopt a more comprehensive approach to ammunition management in order to ensure the safety and security of stockpiles. It also identified a regulatory gap in this regard that the General Assembly mandated the OEWG to fill. The OEWG is to submit its recommendation on the establishment of such a regulatory framework in 2023, after three substantive sessions and a series of informal consultations.[94]

The first two substantive sessions of the OEWG took place in May and August 2022, in New York and Geneva respectively, under the chairmanship of Ambassador Albrecht von Wittke of Germany. Unlike the GGE, the sessions of the OEWG were open to participation by representatives of all UN member states, and they were also open to NGO representatives.[95] During the first substantive session, delegations had the opportunity to start exchanging views on national and regional approaches to ammunition management and the recommendations of the GGE.[96] The OEWG received briefings from representatives of expert organizations—including the UN Mine Action Service (UNMAS) and Conflict Armament Research, an NGO, among others—and heard statements from other international and regional organizations and NGOs.[97]

These discussions informed the development of a document outlining draft elements of a new global ammunition framework that the chair shared with delegations ahead of the second substantive session of the OEWG.[98] Following inputs received by the chair during and after this session, in November 2022 the chair prepared a 'zero draft' of the global framework that the OEWG was mandated to develop. The draft is to be discussed in the intersessional period leading to the third substantive session in February 2023.[99]

---

[92] UN General Assembly Resolution 76/233, 'Problems arising from the accumulation of conventional ammunition stockpiles in surplus', 30 Dec. 2021, para. 17.

[93] United Nations, General Assembly, Report of the group of governmental experts established pursuant to General Assembly Resolution 72/55 on problems arising from the accumulation of conventional ammunition stockpiles in surplus, A/76/324, 14 Sep. 2021.

[94] UN General Assembly Resolution 76/233 (note 92), paras 9–20.

[95] UNODA, 'Aide memoire for non-governmental organizations', 11 May 2022; and UNODA, 'Aide memoire for non-governmental organizations', 1 Aug. 2022.

[96] UNODA, 'OEWG on conventional ammunition holds its first substantive session', *Saving Lives Information Bulletin*, no. 8 (June 2022).

[97] UNODA (note 96).

[98] von Wittke, A., 'Chair's main takeaways from the United Nations open-ended working group on conventional ammunition first substantive session, 23–27 May 2022', 27 May 2022; and von Wittke, A., Letter from the chair, 1 Aug. 2022.

[99] von Wittke, A., Letter from the chair, 26 Aug. 2022; and von Wittke, A., Letter from the chair, 3 Nov. 2022.

Conclusions

The need for strong and effective humanitarian disarmament law has been underscored by Russia's invasion of Ukraine and the use there of cluster munitions, APMs and explosive weapons with wide-area effects in populated areas. These attacks have resulted in large numbers of civilian casualties, but they have also generated weighty international condemnation precisely because they involved weapons banned or restricted under humanitarian disarmament treaties and norms. Global norms on civilian protection undoubtedly contribute to minimizing civilian suffering, but more needs to be done to prevent and redress arms-related human and environmental harm in Ukraine and in other armed conflicts around the world.

Regrettably, humanitarian disarmament continued to register minimal progress in 2022. States adopted important new standards and commitments on the use of EWIPA and on the environment and armed conflict. They also agreed to discuss the impact of technological developments on SALW manufacturing and continued to acknowledge the gender-related impact of illicit SALW. But these standards and commitments will only be as effective as their interpretation and implementation. Generally, more comprehensive and inclusive approaches to humanitarian disarmament continue to be resisted by a vocal minority of states. Since it is unlikely that these divergent views will be reconciled in the foreseeable future, those seeking more ambitious results may well continue to pursue them outside the CCW, POA and ITI frameworks.

III. Intergovernmental efforts to address the challenges posed by autonomous weapon systems

VINCENT BOULANIN

An intergovernmental debate on emerging technologies in the area of autonomous weapon systems (AWS) started in 2013 under the auspices of the 1981 Convention on Certain Conventional Weapons (CCW Convention).[1] The debate, which has been led since 2017 by a group of governmental experts (GGE), focuses on the humanitarian and security challenges posed by the development and use of AWS.[2] From the start, the underlying policy question has been whether such challenges warrant the adoption of a new, legally binding regulation, such as a new protocol to the CCW Convention.[3] Despite nearly a decade of expert discussions, states continued to express different views on that question in 2022.

Nonetheless, the deliberations of the 2022 GGE showed that the gap between states' positions has narrowed. Most states could agree that the normative and operational framework governing AWS needs to be developed further and that one possible way to proceed is through a two-tiered approach.[4] Such an approach would, on the one hand, prohibit certain AWS and, on the other hand, place specific limits and requirements on the development and use of all other AWS. However, a handful of states oppose this approach, and so the convergence in positions was not reflected in the

---

[1] On earlier discussions on the regulation of AWS see Anthony, I. and Holland, C., 'The governance of autonomous weapon systems', *SIPRI Yearbook 2014*, pp. 423–31; Davis, I. et al., 'Humanitarian arms control regimes: Key development in 2016', *SIPRI Yearbook 2017*, pp. 559–61; Davis, I. and Verbruggen, M., 'The Convention on Certain Conventional Weapons', *SIPRI Yearbook 2018*, pp. 383–86; Boulanin, V., Davis, I. and Verbruggen, M., 'The Convention on Certain Conventional Weapons and lethal autonomous weapon systems', *SIPRI Yearbook 2019*, pp. 449–61; Peldán Carlsson, M. and Boulanin, V., 'The group of governmental experts on lethal autonomous weapon systems', *SIPRI Yearbook 2020*, pp. 502–12; Bruun, L., 'The group of governmental experts on lethal autonomous weapon systems', *SIPRI Yearbook 2021*, pp. 518–24; and Bruun, L., 'Intergovernmental efforts to address the challenges posed by autonomous weapon systems', *SIPRI Yearbook 2022*, pp. 532–44.

[2] On the GGE see UN Office for Disarmament Affairs, 'Background on LAWS in the CCW'. Although the GGE is mandated to address emerging technologies in the area of lethal autonomous weapon systems (LAWS), the term AWS is preferable because the concept of 'lethality' pertains to how the weapon system is used and its effects rather than the way it is designed. Moreover, AWS are capable of causing harm in the form of material damage or injury, irrespective of whether death was the intended or actual result.

[3] For a summary and other details of the Convention on Prohibitions or Restrictions on the Use of Certain Conventional Weapons which may be Deemed to be Excessively Injurious or to have Indiscriminate Effects (CCW Convention) and its protocols see annex A, section I, in this volume. On developments in 2022 see section II in this chapter.

[4] Acheson, R., 'Denial cannot stop the reality of momentum', *CCW Report*, vol. 10, no. 9 (28 July 2022).

report that the GGE presented to the annual meeting of parties to the CCW Convention in November 2022.[5]

Many states and observers considered the opposition from those states—especially the Russian Federation—as the product of a systematic and politically motivated reluctance to use the CCW regime to achieve any substantive outcome on AWS.[6] In their view, the likelihood that such reluctance will persist reignited the question of whether the CCW Convention was the appropriate forum to address the issue of AWS.

This section takes stock of the developments in 2022 in greater detail. After assessing the impact of the war in Ukraine on the GGE process, it gives an overview of the proposals discussed by the 2022 GGE followed by an overview of the outcome and the way ahead.

The impact of the Russia–Ukraine War on an already weakened GGE process

The prospects of the GGE achieving a significant outcome in 2022 were deemed to be low from the start. Many of the diplomats involved were disillusioned by the (lack of) outcome of the review conference of the CCW Convention in December 2021.[7] Many delegations had considered that conference to be a critical juncture, a stocktaking event that would allow the convention's states parties to consolidate the progress made over the years and show the world that the CCW framework was not just a talking shop.

The ambition was that the review conference would adopt a new and meaningful political commitment for the regulation of AWS. However, despite the efforts by many delegations to propose language that could accommodate the wide spectrum of views, the 2021 GGE had failed to adopt a substantive report by consensus.[8] Much of that failure could be attributed to the opposition of Russia and a handful of other delegations (India and Cuba in particular) to most of the elements contained in the draft text. The chair of the GGE, Ambassador Marc Pecsteen de Buytswerve of Belgium, had no choice but to turn the draft report into a chair's summary under his sole responsibility.[9] Consequently, the 2021 review conference had little of substance to build on, except a proposal for a new GGE mandate. For the

---

[5] CCW Convention, Group of governmental experts on emerging technologies in the area of lethal autonomous weapons systems, Report of the 2022 session, CCW/GGE.1/2022/2, 31 Aug. 2022.

[6] Acheson, R., 'Road to nowhere', *CCW Report*, vol. 10, no. 10 (29 July 2022).

[7] Chilean diplomat, Interview with author, 26 July 2022; and Sixth CCW review conference, Final document, CCW/CONF.VI/11, 22 Apr. 2022, part II. See also Bruun, *SIPRI Yearbook 2022* (note 1).

[8] Acheson, R., '"Our position has not changed"', *CCW Report*, vol. 9, no. 13 (17 Dec. 2021); and Bruun, *SIPRI Yearbook 2022* (note 1).

[9] CCW Convention, Group of governmental experts on emerging technologies in the area of lethal autonomous weapons systems, Report of the 2021 session, CCW/GGE.1/2021/3, 22 Feb. 2022, annex III.

most part, this had been pre-negotiated informally behind closed doors and in substance mainly rolled over the previous mandate with some minor adjustments. The states parties eventually adopted that proposal.[10] For many, if not most, delegations, this outcome was a major disappointment. Some states issued a joint statement that condemned Russia, without naming it, for abusing the consensus-based decision-making practice of the CCW regime.[11]

In such a context, the war in Ukraine could only reinforce the apparent political deadlock of the CCW process on AWS. The first GGE session of 2022 took place on 7–11 March, only a few weeks after Russia's invasion of Ukraine. On the first day, most delegations condemned Russia's behaviour in their statements.[12] The Russian delegation responded robustly to such statements. It also called for the meeting to be postponed, invoking a battery of arguments, including that it had been discriminated against, as some of its experts had been unable to fly directly from Moscow to Geneva due to Western sanctions. Two days into the five-day meeting, the delegations were still discussing whether and how the GGE's deliberations could take place. Eventually, the chair—Ambassador Flávio Soaeres Damico of Brazil—decided to turn the GGE session into an informal meeting. Since informal meetings are not governed by the normal rules and procedures, this allowed for some substantive exchanges on a series of written proposals that had been submitted by different groups of states (see table 10.2).[13] As a sign of opposition, the Russian delegation remained generally silent and engaged only to respond to statements related to Ukraine.

The second session, which took place 25–29 July, started on a somewhat better basis as it was held in a formal format and was centred around a draft text tabled by the chair of the GGE. This captured the commonalities between the different proposals and suggested possible conclusions and recommendations for the GGE. Nonetheless, the deliberation remained highly politicized. Russia, this time represented by a full delegation, seized many opportunities to hamper substantive exchanges with comments on formalities and rules of procedure, which often related to the participation of civil society. While these comments were sometimes echoed by Cuba and India, in general most delegations refuted them. Nonetheless, these interventions succeeded in significantly reducing the time available for detailed exchanges, notably on the draft proposals that had been tabled by

---

[10] Sixth CCW review conference, CCW/CONF.VI/11 (note 7), decision 1, para. 38.

[11] Sixth CCW review conference, Joint statement by Austria, Belgium, Brazil, Chile, Finland, Germany, Ireland, Italy, Luxembourg, Mexico, the Netherlands, New Zealand, Norway, South Africa, Sweden and Switzerland, 17 Dec. 2021.

[12] CCW Convention, Group of governmental experts on emerging technologies in the area of lethal autonomous weapons systems, 2022 session, 1st meeting, 7 Mar. 2022, UN Web TV.

[13] The rules are contained in fifth CCW review conference, Draft rules of procedure, CCW/CONF.V/4, 28 Sep. 2016.

Table 10.2. Written proposals presented by states to the 2022 Group of Governmental Experts on Emerging Technologies in the Area of Lethal Autonomous Weapons Systems

	Document	Submitted by
1.	'Group of governmental experts (GGE) document on the application of international humanitarian law to emerging technologies in the area of lethal autonomous weapons systems (LAWS)', CCW/GGE.1/2022/WP.1, 8 Aug. 2022	United Kingdom
2.	'Principles and good practices on emerging technologies in the area of lethal autonomous weapons systems', CCW/GGE.1/2022/WP.2, 8 Aug. 2022	Australia, Canada, Japan, South Korea, United Kingdom, United States
3.	'Roadmap towards new protocol on autonomous weapons systems', CCW/GGE.1/2022/WP.3, 8 Aug. 2022	Argentina, Costa Rica, Guatemala, Kazakhstan, Nigeria, Palestine, Panama, Philippines, Sierra Leone, Uruguay
4.	Working paper on the future working of the group, CCW/GGE.1/2022/WP.4, 8 Aug. 2022	Argentina, Austria, Belgium, Chile, Costa Rica, Ecuador, Guatemala, Ireland, Kazakhstan, Liechtenstein, Luxembourg, Malta, Mexico, New Zealand, Nigeria, Palestine, Panama, Peru, Philippines, Sierra Leone, Sri Lanka, Switzerland, Uruguay
5.	'Elements for a legally binding instrument to address the challenges posed by autonomy in weapon systems', CCW/GGE.1/2022/WP.5, 8 Aug. 2022	Chile, Mexico
6.	Working paper on LAWS, CCW/GGE.1/2022/WP.6, 9 Aug. 2022	China
7.	Working paper, CCW/GGE.1/2022/WP.7, 9 Aug. 2022	Finland, France, Germany, Netherlands, Norway, Spain, Sweden
8.	'Draft Protocol VI', CCW/GGE.1/2022/WP.8, 9 Aug. 2022	Argentina, Costa Rica, Ecuador, El Salvador, Guatemala, Kazakhstan, Nigeria, Panama, Philippines, Sierra Leone, Uruguay
9.	'Application of international law to lethal autonomous weapons systems (LAWS)', CCW/GGE.1/2022/WP.9, 9 Aug. 2022	Russia
10.	Working paper submitted on behalf of the Non-Aligned Movement (NAM) and Other States Parties, CCW/GGE.1/2022/WP.10, 9 Aug. 2022	Venezuela, NAM

states, and they eventually undermined the adoption of substantive conclusions and recommendations.

Overview of the proposals discussed by the 2022 group of governmental experts

The 2022 GGE was mandated to 'consider proposals and elaborate, by consensus, possible measures . . . and other options related to the normative and operational framework on emerging technologies'.[14] At the invitation of the chair, several states submitted written proposals for the GGE's consideration. Most were submitted by coalitions of like-minded states, rather than individual states.

These proposals generally reflect the pre-existing spectrum of views that had developed over the years on how AWS should be regulated. They fall into two distinct groups. One group is based on the premise that international humanitarian law (IHL) is sufficient to regulate the development and use of AWS; these proposals consequently focus on voluntary measures to support compliance with IHL (i.e. the British proposal (numbered 1 in table 10.2), the United States-led joint proposal (2) and the Russian proposal (9)). The other group starts from the premise that IHL is insufficient and that new limits and requirements on the development and use of AWS are needed. In that second group, some proposals expressly call for the introduction of a legally binding instrument (i.e. Chile and Mexico's proposal (5); the road map (3), working paper (4) and draft protocol (8) submitted by Argentina and various other states; and the working paper (10) submitted on behalf of the Non-Aligned Movement). Others limit themselves to articulating the need to move forward with a two-tiered approach that would prohibit certain AWS and regulate the lawful use of all other AWS (i.e. China's working paper (6) and the working paper (7) submitted by Finland and others).

While the proposals arrive at different conclusions in terms of the policy measures that the GGE should recommend, they converge on some points of substance. Foremost, they take IHL as the fundamental baseline to gauge the acceptability of AWS. Any AWS that cannot be used in compliance with IHL is de facto prohibited. They also all stress that human decision-making, as well as being essential for IHL compliance, is also needed to ensure accountability in the use of AWS. These points about compliance with IHL and the centrality of human responsibility have, to a large extent, already been captured in the previous work of the GGE, not least the 11 guiding

---

[14] Sixth CCW review conference, CCW/CONF.VI/11 (note 7), decision 1, para. 38.

principles adopted in 2019.[15] However, the written proposals demonstrated a willingness on the part of states to elaborate on what such points would entail. For example, the proposals typically attempt to provide greater clarity on the types of design feature and forms of human–machine interaction that would make the development and use of AWS lawful (or unlawful) and also acceptable (or unacceptable) from an ethical or security perspective.[16]

The proposals, as well as the exchanges around their content, also showed that there was an emerging consensus that a two-tiered approach could be a valuable vehicle to discuss the further regulation of AWS. Even states that submitted proposals on good practices and IHL compliance (i.e. the states behind proposals 1 and 2, notably the USA) acknowledged in their statements that their proposals and the two-tiered approach were not necessarily mutually exclusive.[17]

The question of how the two-tiered approach should be enacted remained unresolved. States continued to take different points of departure to define the contours of a potential prohibition on certain AWS and identify the elements of responsible development and use of other AWS. For some, the goal is to rearticulate or clarify the limits and requirements that already exist in IHL and that have already been agreed upon by the GGE through the 2019 guiding principles. For others, the goal is not just to clarify IHL but to go further by addressing concerns related to human rights and ethical considerations. The latter consequently suggest prohibiting specific use cases (e.g. prohibiting anti-personnel AWS is recommend by the International Committee of the Red Cross and also states such as Argentina and Palestine) and requiring specific human control over the use of force (e.g. Chile and Mexico recommend allowing for constant human supervision).[18]

The legal form that a potential two-tiered regulation should take also remains contested. The group of states behind the US-led joint proposal (proposal 2) continued to argue that it was premature to state that the two-tiered approach should be enacted in a legally binding instrument, since 'form should follow function' as the head of the US delegation stated multiple

---

[15] CCW Convention, Group of governmental experts on emerging technologies in the area of lethal autonomous weapons systems, Report of the 2019 session, CCW/GGE.1/2019/3, 25 Sep. 2019, annex IV. On the adoption of the guiding principles see Peldán Carlsson and Boulanin (note 1).

[16] Anand, A. and Puscas, I., *Proposals Related to Emerging Technologies in the Area of Lethal Autonomous Weapons Systems: A Resource Paper* (UNIDIR: Geneva, 2022).

[17] CCW Convention, Group of governmental experts on emerging technologies in the area of lethal autonomous weapons systems, 2022 session, 2nd meeting, 26 July 2022, UN Web TV, 0:47:00–0:53:00.

[18] International Committee of the Red Cross (ICRC), 'ICRC position on autonomous weapon systems', 12 May 2021; CCW Convention, Group of governmental experts on emerging technologies in the area of lethal autonomous weapons systems, Written contribution for the chair, Submitted by Argentina, Costa Rica, Ecuador, El Salvador, Panama, Palestine, Peru, the Philippines, Sierra Leone and Uruguay, Sep. 2021; and CCW Convention, Group of governmental experts on emerging technologies in the area of lethal autonomous weapons systems, 'Elements for a legally binding instrument to address the challenges posed by autonomy in weapon systems', Working paper submitted by Chile and Mexico, CCW/GGE.1/2022/WP.5, 8 Aug. 2022.

times.[19] In their view, the GGE should first agree on an understanding of the limits and requirements that it deems to be needed for the responsible development and use of AWS. In contrast, states that called for a legally binding instrument stressed that one of the functions of the CCW Convention is to continue the codification of IHL, and that the GGE should aim for legally binding rules.

The outcome and way ahead

In his drafts of the GGE report, the chair tried to integrate the different views on the text that he had presented at the second session of the GGE. His first draft report included language that tried to capture the convergence between states on possible limits on and requirements for the design and use of AWS.[20] It also included language that tried to provide clarification on what compliance with international humanitarian law requires in terms of human involvement in the use of AWS (e.g. in the form of human control or human judgement).[21] Similarly, it sought to address concerns around accountability by covering the responsibility of the state for internationally wrongful acts.[22]

These proposals were the focus of intense, yet generally constructive, discussions between delegations. In their intervention, many welcomed the efforts of the chair and some delegations to find compromise language that could accommodate the spectrum of views. Russia, Cuba and, to some extent, India remained critical of most aspects of the text. They spent a significant portion of their statements questioning formalities.[23]

The GGE eventually succeeded in adopting a report but at the cost of substantive conclusions.[24] Most of the language from the original draft had been edited out. The GGE could only find consensus on the recommendation that consideration of the different proposals should 'intensify' in 2023.[25]

The fact that in 2022 the GGE was once again unable to capture in writing the progress made on substance and could not agree on a more ambitious mandate reignited the question of whether it is still the appropriate forum to address the challenges posed by AWS.[26]

[19] CCW Convention, Group of governmental experts on emerging technologies in the area of lethal autonomous weapons systems, 2022 session, 28 July 2022, UN Web TV.
[20] CCW Convention, Group of governmental experts on emerging technologies in the area of lethal autonomous weapons systems, Draft report of the 2022 session, CCW/GGE.1/2022/CRP.1, 29 July 2022, paras 17–18.
[21] CCW Convention, CCW/GGE.1/2022/CRP.1 (note 20), para. 19.
[22] CCW Convention, CCW/GGE.1/2022/CRP.1 (note 20), para. 20.
[23] Acheson (note 4).
[24] CCW Convention, Group of governmental experts on emerging technologies in the area of lethal autonomous weapons system, Report of the 2022 session, CCW/GGE.1/2022/CRP.1/Rev 1, 29 July 2022.
[25] CCW Convention, CCW/GGE.1/2022/2 (note 5), para. 20(a).
[26] Acheson (note 6).

For representatives of the campaigning group Stop Killer Robots and several countries in favour of a ban on AWS, including Chile and Mexico, there is little doubt that the CCW process has reached a dead end and that an effective ban on AWS will have to be developed elsewhere.[27] For them, the consensus-based decision-making practice of the CCW regime will prevent a substantive political outcome being reached in the current geopolitical situation.

While many states—in particular, major military powers such as the France, India and the United States—continued to maintain that the CCW Convention is the most appropriate forum to discuss the issue, there were two important developments outside the CCW.[28] In October 2022 the UN Human Rights Council adopted a resolution on the 'Human rights implications of new and emerging technologies', while Austria delivered a joint statement on AWS on behalf of 70 states at a meeting of the UN General Assembly's First Committee (on disarmament and international security).[29] The joint statement attracted particular attention, not least because it received the support of states that have historically opposed the introduction of new legally binding rules on AWS, such as the USA. Although the statement makes clear that the immediate intent was not to start a process outside the CCW framework, it showed that there is a willingness even on the part of major military powers to move forward with the development of specific norms on AWS. This is an important prerequisite for the emergence of a new formalized intergovernmental process outside the CCW regime.

[27] Noor, O., 'Russia leads an assault on progress at UN discussions, the CCW has failed', Stop Killer Robots, 4 Aug. 2022; and Acheson (note 6).
[28] Nadibaidze, A., 'Regulation and prohibition of autonomous weapon systems: A future outside the CCW?', AutoNorms, 3 Nov. 2022.
[29] United Nations, Human Right Council, 'Human rights implications of new and emerging technologies in the military domain', Resolution 51/22, 7 Oct. 2022; and United Nations, General Assembly, First Committee, 'Joint statement on lethal autonomous weapon systems', Delivered by Austria, 21 Oct. 2022.

IV. International transparency in arms procurement and military expenditure as confidence-building measures

PIETER D. WEZEMAN AND SIEMON T. WEZEMAN

In order to support arms control and build confidence between states, global and regional multilateral organizations have established transparency instruments on arms procurement and military spending. At the global level, two such instruments within the United Nations are the UN Register of Conventional Arms (UNROCA) and the UN Report on Military Expenditures (UNMILEX). Among regional organizations, only the Organization for Security and Co-operation in Europe (OSCE) has visibly active transparency instruments.

This section assesses developments in 2022 regarding the multilateral instruments to which states report, as a confidence-building measure (CBM), on aspects of arms procurement and military spending. It looks in turn at UNROCA, UNMILEX and regional transparency mechanisms. It focuses on reports on arms transfers, arms holdings and military spending submitted by states by 31 December 2022, which mainly provide data for 2021.

There are other transparency mechanisms that may also help to build confidence between states. These include reporting on arms exports within the framework of arms trade regulations such as the 2013 Arms Trade Treaty (ATT) and the European Union (EU) report on arms exports. They also include public transparency measures, such as national arms export reports and military expenditure transparency at the national level. However, building confidence between states is not their primary function and so they are discussed elsewhere.[1]

The United Nations Register of Conventional Arms

UNROCA was established in 1991 by the UN General Assembly. Its main aims are to enhance confidence between states, 'prevent the excessive and destabilizing accumulation of arms', 'encourage restraint' in the transfer and production of arms, and 'contribute to preventive diplomacy'.[2] While UNROCA's objectives relate to armament developments in general, including

---

[1] On multilateral reporting on arms exports under the ATT see chapter 12, section I, in this volume. On the EU report see chapter 12, section V, in this volume. On national reports on arms exports see SIPRI, 'National reports on arms exports'.

[2] UN General Assembly Resolution 46/36L, 'Transparency in armaments', 6 Dec. 1991, para. 2; and UN Office for Disarmament Affairs (UNODA), 'UN Register of Conventional Arms'. On the development of UNROCA see United Nations, General Assembly, Report on the continuing operation of the United Nations Register of Conventional Arms and its further development, A/77/126, 30 June 2022, paras 5–9.

current holdings and domestic procurement, its focus in terms of reporting is on arms transfers between states.

UN member states are requested to report annually, in a standardized format and on a voluntary basis, information on their exports and imports in the previous year of seven categories of major arms that are deemed to be 'indispensable to offensive operations'.[3] These categories are battle tanks, armoured combat vehicles, large-calibre artillery systems, combat aircraft, attack helicopters, warships, and missiles and missile launchers. Since 2003, states have also been able to provide information on transfers of an eighth category: small arms and light weapons (SALW). The inclusion of SALW was largely related to efforts to prevent the illicit trade in these weapons (see section II), and not to UNROCA's function as a CBM between states.[4]

In addition, 'states in a position to do so' are invited (indicating a lower level of commitment) to provide information on their holdings of major arms and procurement of such arms through national production.[5]

Participation

The number of states submitting reports to UNROCA increased in 2022 to 56 from an all-time low of 41 in 2021.[6] In most years of the 1990s, over 90 states reported to UNROCA and in the early 2000s over 110 states did so. Participation in 2022 exceeded 50 for the first time since 2014. Of the 56 states that reported for 2021, 34 are in Europe, 10 in Asia and Oceania, 5 in Africa, 5 in the Americas and 2 in the Middle East.

Most of the states identified by SIPRI as large exporters of major arms in 2018–22 have been regular participants in UNROCA.[7] In 2022 the United States (by far the world's largest exporter of major arms) was the only exporter among the 10 largest exporters in 2018–22 that did not report for 2021. However, the USA belatedly submitted a report for 2020. The lack

---

[3] United Nations, General Assembly, Report on the continuing operation of the United Nations Register of Conventional Arms and its further development, A/71/259, 29 July 2016, para. 61(g).

[4] See e.g. United Nations, General Assembly, Report on the continuing operation of the United Nations Register of Conventional Arms and its further development, A/58/274, 13 July 2003, paras 92–108.

[5] UN General Assembly Resolution 74/53, 'Transparency in armaments', 12 Dec. 2019.

[6] UNROCA submissions are made public in annual reports by the UN secretary-general, the latest (covering most submissions on 2021 made in 2022) being United Nations, General Assembly, 'United Nations Register of Conventional Arms', Report of the secretary-general, A/77/165, 14 July 2022. Earlier annual reports are available from UN Office for Disarmament Affairs (note 2). Most of those submissions as well as submissions that have been received after the compilation of the annual reports can also be found in the online UNROCA database. As neither source is complete, all numbers given here are based on an aggregation of reports in both sources and on communications with UNODA. Figures are according to the public records available on 31 Dec. 2022. The total of 41 includes 2 belated reports for 2020 submitted in 2022.

[7] On the largest exporters of major arms in 2018–22 see chapter 6, section II, in this volume.

of reporting for 2021 was due to staffing problems, and in early 2023 it was expected that the US report would be submitted belatedly.[8]

Four of the 10 largest arms importers in the period 2018–22 did not report to UNROCA for reporting year 2021: Saudi Arabia, Qatar, Egypt and Pakistan.[9] Saudi Arabia has never reported, Egypt has reported only once (in 1992) and Qatar only three times. Pakistan has not reported since 2015.

Several states involved in armed conflict reported to UNROCA. Russia, which had reported for all years since 1992, and Ukraine, which had reported for most years since 1992, submitted UNROCA reports in mid 2022 on arms exports and imports in 2021, despite the ongoing war between the two countries.[10] Israel and Türkiye, which had reported for most years since 1992, also did so in 2022.[11]

A significant reason for the above-noted increase in submissions to UNROCA appears to have been that, starting in 2022, an ATT state party has the option—with a straightforward tick of a box—to authorize the ATT Secretariat to submit its report under the ATT to UNROCA.[12] The annual reporting on arms exports and imports required by the ATT involves reporting templates similar to those used for reporting on arms transfers to UNROCA. In addition, the ATT follows the UNROCA definitions of major arms. Of the 110 states parties to the ATT that were required to submit a report covering 2021, 68 had done so by 31 December 2022—slightly more than the number that had reported to UNROCA.[13]

The level of reporting on military holdings and arms procurement through national production was even lower than on arms transfers. While all 56 reports for 2021 included information on arms transfers, only 18 reported on military holdings and as few as 4 included information on procurement from national production. Major military powers such as China, India and Russia submitted data for 2021 on arms transfers but did not provide data on holdings or arms procurement through national production. In contrast, France, Germany, Japan and the United Kingdom did include such data in their submissions for 2021, and the USA did so in its belated submission covering 2020. However, their reports varied widely in the level of detail included.

---

[8] Official, US Department of State, Communication with author, 10 Jan. 2023.
[9] On the largest importers of major arms in 2018–22 see chapter 6, section III, in this volume.
[10] On the Russia–Ukraine War see chapter 1, section V, and chapter 2, section I, in this volume.
[11] On the conflicts involving Israel and Türkiye see chapter 2, section I, in this volume.
[12] Holtom, P. and Mensah, A. E. E., 'The end of transparency in international arms transfers?', UN Institute for Disarmament Research (UNIDIR), 14 Sep. 2022.
[13] On ATT reporting see chapter 12, section I, in this volume.

Transparency versus data inaccuracies

As in previous years, several submissions to UNROCA included significant information on arms transfers or details of such arms transfers that had not been available in the public domain before. These reports are therefore likely to have contributed to increased transparency between states. For example, China reported on the export of armoured vehicles to several states in Africa, including details such as the numbers of vehicles that had not been reported in other open sources. Similarly, Türkiye reported details that were not previously publicly available on transfers of armoured vehicles to Rwanda and the United Arab Emirates.

However, comparison of UNROCA submissions and the SIPRI Arms Transfers Database shows that there were again significant omissions in some of the reports that were submitted in 2022.[14] For example the USA is estimated to have delivered 50 F-35 combat aircraft to a total of nine states in 2020, whereas no such transfer is included in the belated USA UNROCA report for 2020. For 2021, the Republic of Korea (South Korea) reported the delivery of a second-hand corvette to Peru but omitted the delivery of a frigate to the Philippines, while Italy omitted the delivery of five F-35 combat aircraft from the Italian F-35 production line to the Netherlands and two other combat aircraft to Kuwait. The UK omitted the import of four anti-submarine warfare aircraft and three combat aircraft in 2021, although it reported most of these aircraft in its UNROCA submission on holdings.

In other cases, states submitted premature or seemingly exaggerated information, information with no relevance for understanding developments in armaments, or reports that lacked descriptions of the equipment beyond the general category. The submission of such information is confusing and hampers the assessment of the potential impact on peace and security of reported transfers. Italy reported the actual transfer in 2021 of 11 448 armoured combat vehicles to the USA and 918 armoured combat vehicles to the Netherlands, without adding details on the models involved. While the latter probably refers to a contract for export of light armoured vehicles to the Netherlands with planned deliveries in 2023–26, it is not clear to what the former transfer refers and the number involved has no relation to any actual US import of armoured vehicles in 2021 or planned imports in coming years. The UK continued to report exports of armoured vehicles to museums, including a replica of an early 1940s German Tiger tank, but omitted detailed descriptions of over 600 missiles that it reported as exported in 2021. Omitting or partially omitting descriptions of the weapon models is common. For example, the USA included in its report for 2020 full

---

[14] SIPRI Arms Transfers Database, Mar. 2023. See also Wezeman, P. D. and Wezeman, S. T., 'International transparency in arms procurement and military expenditure as confidence-building measures', *SIPRI Yearbook 2022*, pp. 551–57.

designations of equipment for some entries in its submission, more generic descriptions in other entries and, in a few cases, no description at all. Submissions for 2021 by, for example, China and Russia do not include any details on designations.

Conclusions of the group of governmental experts on UNROCA

UNROCA has been regularly reviewed by groups of governmental experts (GGEs) with the goal of increasing the register's relevance and achieving universal participation. Compared to the rather revolutionary decision to establish UNROCA and the discussions that led up to it, the GGEs have been generally unsuccessful in further developing UNROCA since the inclusion of SALW in the registry in 2003. While many ideas for increasing the relevance of UNROCA have been discussed by the GGEs since 1992, including expanding the scope to more weapon types or weapon categories or beyond transfers between states, few have become formal recommendations from the GGEs, and even those were not all adopted by the General Assembly.[15]

In 2022 a new GGE—the 10th since UNROCA became operational in 1992—again discussed many of the issues from earlier GGEs as well as some new ones. These included the key problems of low participation, the lack of further development of the instrument's scope and the lack of use of the data in the UN system. However, the GGE once more ended with recommendations for only marginal changes to the description of UNROCA categories.[16] Notably, and similar to earlier GGEs, the main issue for the 10th GGE was low participation in UNROCA, while at the same time it included representatives from several states that have reported to UNROCA rarely or irregularly.

The United Nations Report on Military Expenditures

In 1980 the UN General Assembly agreed to establish an annual report in which all UN member states could voluntarily provide data on their military expenditure in the previous year.[17] The report, which has been known as the UN Report on Military Expenditures since 2012, aims to enhance

---

[15] For an overview of the work, recommendations and adopted recommendations of the GGEs until 2019 see UN Secretariat, 'The UN Register of Conventional Arms (UNROCA): Developments, trends, challenges and opportunities', Background paper, [16 Feb. 2022].

[16] United Nations, A/77/126 (note 3); and UN Office for Disarmament Affairs, '2022 GGE on UN Register on Conventional Arms concludes work with forward-looking recommendations to promote participation, relevance, and continuing operation of the Register', 12 July 2022.

[17] UN General Assembly Resolution 35/142 B, 'Reduction of military budgets', 12 Dec. 1980; and United Nations, General Assembly, Report of the group of governmental experts to review the operation and further development of the United Nations Report on Military Expenditures, A/72/293, 4 Aug. 2017, paras 2–5. For a detailed description of the history of the instrument see Spies, M., *United Nations Efforts to Reduce Military Expenditures: A Historical Overview*, UN Office for Disarmament Affairs (UNODA) Occasional Papers no. 33 (United Nations: New York, Oct. 2019).

transparency in military matters, increase predictability of military activities, reduce the risk of military conflict and raise public awareness of disarmament matters.[18]

The highest rate of participation in UNMILEX was reporting for 2001, when 81 states participated.[19] Of the 193 UN member states, 43 submitted information on their military spending in 2020, while by 31 December 2022 only 36 had done so for 2021.[20] Of these 36 states, 26 are in Europe, 6 in the Americas, 2 in Asia and Oceania, 2 in the Middle East and none in Africa. Of the 15 states that SIPRI identified as having the highest military spending levels in 2021, 8 did not report to UNMILEX for 2021: the USA, China, the UK, Russia, Saudi Arabia, South Korea, Canada and Spain (in order of spending levels). The most significant omission was the USA, which most recently reported for 2015. At the same time, in 2022 China restarted reporting, with a belated submission for 2020, after not having reported for 2018 and 2019.

Based on SIPRI military expenditure figures, the 36 states that had reported for 2021 by end-2022 accounted for 20 per cent of total world spending in 2021.[21] In contrast to the low level of reporting to UNMILEX, almost all states provide information on their military spending at a national level. Of the 168 states for which SIPRI attempted to estimate military expenditure in 2022, 148 published their military budgets in official sources. To promote participation in UNMILEX, in 2022 SIPRI prepared a practical guide for states that want to use such public government documents to prepare their submissions for UNMILEX in a straightforward and efficient manner.[22]

Regional transparency mechanisms

In 2022 the only visibly active regional efforts that aim at multilateral transparency in armaments were the information exchanges between the OSCE's 57 participating states across North America, Europe and Central and Northern Asia. The OSCE aims to 'contribute to reducing the dangers . . . of

---

[18] United Nations, A/72/293 (note 17), para. 3.

[19] United Nations, General Assembly, Report of the group of governmental experts on the operation and further development of the United Nations Standardized Instrument for Reporting Military Expenditures, A/66/89, 14 June 2011, p. 26.

[20] United Nations, General Assembly, 'Objective information on military matters, including transparency of military expenditures', Report of the secretary-general, A/76/129, 9 July 2021; United Nations, General Assembly, 'Objective information on military matters, including transparency of military expenditures', Report of the secretary-general, A/77/159, 13 July 2022; and UN Office for Disarmament Affairs (UNODA), 'Military expenditures'. As none of these sources is complete, all numbers given here are based on an aggregation the sources. Figures are according to the public records available on 31 Dec. 2022.

[21] SIPRI Military Expenditure Database, Apr. 2023.

[22] Wezeman, P. D. et al., 'A practical guide to state participation in the UN Report on Military Expenditures', SIPRI Good Practice Guide, Sep. 2022.

misunderstanding or miscalculation of military activities which could give rise to apprehension'.[23]

The Vienna Document 2011 on Confidence- and Security-Building Measures requires the OSCE states to participate in an annual exchange of information on their military holdings and procurement of major arms.[24] This information is not made public. Only five OSCE participating states reported on their national military holdings while there were no reports on procurement through national production.[25] In addition, OSCE participating states have agreed to share information on imports and exports of major arms based on the categories and format of UNROCA.[26] Since 2017 these submissions have been publicly available on the OSCE website.[27] In 2022, 45 of the 57 states reported to the OSCE on their arms transfers in 2021, the same number as in 2021. The most notable omission in 2022 was the USA.

Concerning military expenditure, the OSCE CBMs include a requirement for participating states to annually exchange information on military budgets. This information is not made publicly available.[28] Of the 57 OSCE participating states, 39 reported for 2021, 47 reported for 2020 and 49 reported for 2019.[29]

In the Americas, the 17 states parties of the Inter-American Convention on Transparency in Conventional Weapons Acquisition (Convención Interamericana sobre Transparencia en las Adquisiciones de Armas Convencionales, CITAAC) are required to submit annual reports to the Organization of American States (OAS) on arms transfers.[30] However, since 2015 there is only one public record of a state (Chile in 2021) having submitted information under the convention.[31] For only the second time since CITAAC entered into force in 2002, a conference of the states parties to the convention took place on 19 April 2022. Among other things, the conference formally established a CITAAC Technical Secretariat and Consultative Committee to

---

[23] Conference on Security and Co-operation in Europe, Final act, Helsinki, 1 Aug. 1975, p. 10. For a brief description and list of states participating in the OSCE see annex B, section II, in this volume. On the activities of the OSCE in relation to the Russia–Ukraine War in 2022 see section I of this chapter.

[24] Vienna Document 2011, para. 11 and annex III. For a summary and other details of the Vienna Document 2011 see annex A, section II, in this volume. See also section I of this chapter; and OSCE, 'Ensuring military transparency—The Vienna Document'.

[25] Official, OSCE, Communication with author, 10 Feb. 2023.

[26] OSCE, Forum for Security Co-operation, Decision no. 13/97, 16 July 1997; OSCE, Forum for Security Co-operation, Decision no. 8/98, 4 Nov. 1998; and OSCE, Forum for Security Co-operation, 'Updating the reporting categories of weapon and equipment systems subject to the information exchange on conventional arms transfers', Decision no. 8/08, 16 July 2008.

[27] OSCE, 'Information Exchange on Conventional Arms Transfer'.

[28] Vienna Document 2011 (note 24), paras 15.3–15.4.

[29] Official, OSCE (note 25).

[30] For a summary and other details of the convention see annex A, section II, in this volume.

[31] United Nations, General Assembly, 'United Nations Register of Conventional Arms', Report of the secretary-general, A/76/130, 19 July 2021, pp. 19–20. For the reports submitted up to 2015 see Organization of American States, Committee on Hemispheric Security, 'Inter-American Convention on Transparency in Conventional Weapon Acquisition (CITAAC)'.

support implementation and encourage submission of annual reports.[32] The committee will meet for the first time in 2023.[33]

Conclusions

A noteworthy positive development in 2022 was the increase in participation in UNROCA, mainly due to a simplified process of submitting the same reports to both the ATT and UNROCA. Furthermore, reporting by the two countries with the largest militaries improved: China again reported on time to UNROCA and restarted reporting to UNMILEX and the USA reported belatedly to UNROCA.

However, fewer than one-third of UN member states participated in UNROCA and fewer than one-quarter in UNMILEX in 2022. In several submissions there were obvious major gaps in the reporting and the USA did not report on military expenditure even though it is by far the largest military spender in the world. While concerns related to global armament trends were on the increase in 2022, the data shared in the transparency instruments still lacked in comprehensiveness and detail and continued to suffer from major and glaring omissions. Together, these gaps continued to undermine the usefulness of these instruments as CBMs and as indicators of key global trends in military matters.

At the regional level, the information-sharing within the OSCE continued to have a high level of participation, despite the war in Ukraine and the high tensions between Russia and many other OSCE states. After years of being virtually dormant, in 2022 initial steps were made to revitalize CITAAC.

---

[32] OAS Department of Public Security (@OEA_Seguridad), Twitter, 19 Apr. 2022, <https://twitter.com/OEA_Seguridad/status/1516491119034519552>; and CITAAC, Conference of the States Parties, Recommendations, CITAAC/CEP-II/doc.8/22 rev.2, 19 Apr. 2022.

[33] OAS General Assembly Resolution 2986, 'Advancing hemispheric security: A multidimensional approach', 6 Oct. 2022, para. 72.

V. The Hague Code of Conduct against Ballistic Missile Proliferation

KOLJA BROCKMANN AND LAURIANE HÉAU

The Hague Code of Conduct against Ballistic Missile Proliferation (HCOC) is a multilateral transparency and confidence-building measure covering ballistic missile and space-launch vehicle programmes, policies and activities.[1] By subscribing to the HCOC, states commit to curbing the proliferation of ballistic missile systems capable of delivering weapons of mass destruction (WMD) and to exercising 'maximum possible restraint' in the development, testing and deployment of ballistic missiles.[2] The HCOC was developed from discussions within the framework of the Missile Technology Control Regime (MTCR) in 2002, but created as an independent politically binding instrument that is complementary to the MTCR.[3] The HCOC is open for subscription by all states and the number of subscribing states has increased from 93 at its inception to 143 today. Since Somalia joined in February 2020, no additional states have subscribed to the HCOC.[4] Subscribing states commit to several transparency measures, including providing non-public annual declarations on their national ballistic missile and space-launch vehicle programmes and policies, which is done through a restricted website managed by Austria in its role as the HCOC Immediate Central Contact (Executive Secretariat).[5] Via this website, they also exchange pre-launch notifications on launches and test flights of ballistic missiles and space-launch vehicles.[6] However, the HCOC does not include a verification mechanism for subscribing states' declarations and notifications.

Current trends in ballistic missile proliferation

In 2022 at least 27 states possessed ballistic missiles—including all the nuclear weapon possessor states—compared to 34 when the HCOC was created in 2002. However, during the same time period, the number of different types of ballistic missile deployed has increased significantly. This reflects both the

---

[1] Hague Code of Conduct (HCOC), 'The Hague Code of Conduct against Ballistic Missile Proliferation (HCOC)', accessed 22 Feb. 2023.

[2] HCOC, 'Text of the HCOC', accessed 22 Feb. 2023.

[3] Van Diepen, V. H., 'Origins and development of the Hague Code of Conduct', HCOC Research Paper no. 11, Oct. 2022; and Brockmann, K., 'Controlling ballistic missile proliferation: Assessing complementarity between the HCOC, MTCR and UNSCR 1540', HCOC Research Paper no. 7, June 2020.

[4] HCOC, 'List of HCOC subscribing states', accessed 22 Feb. 2023. For a list of subscribing states, also see annex B, section II, in this volume.

[5] HCOC (note 1).

[6] HCOC, 'How to join HCOC', accessed 22 Feb. 2023.

phasing out of old Soviet-era ballistic missiles by many states and the vertical proliferation of ballistic missiles among a small number of states with significant ballistic missile programmes. In contrast, the number of states possessing cruise missiles—which are outside the scope of the HCOC—has increased sharply since the creation of the HCOC, from 3 in 2002 to at least 25 in 2022.[7] Proliferation concerns about ballistic missiles remain, especially linked to regional dynamics in the Middle East, Europe and East Asia, and regarding non-state actors.[8] To circumvent scrutiny or export control mechanisms, an increasing number of states and a few non-state actors have become missile producers. The emergence of new missile technologies, including hypersonic boost-glide vehicles, also pose new challenges in the fight against missile proliferation.[9]

The 21st annual regular meeting

The 21st annual regular meeting (ARM) of the HCOC took place in Vienna on 30–31 May 2022. At the meeting, Nigeria assumed the chair for the 2022–23 period.[10] The significant number of missile tests conducted by North Korea in violation of United Nations Security Council resolutions was identified as a particular source of concern for subscribing states.[11] Several states continued to argue for the expansion of the scope of the HCOC to include cruise missiles and to develop definitions of the types of activity that require the issuing of pre-launch notifications, but no agreement was reached.

Like many other multilateral arms control instruments, the meeting was impacted by Russia's invasion of Ukraine in February 2022. Specifically, Western states denounced Russia's actions while Russia levelled accusations against Ukraine, leading to walkouts from the meeting.[12] The meeting ended prematurely on 30 May due to insurmountable differences over the inclusion

---

[7] Wright, T., 'Evolution and relevance of the Hague Code of Conduct today', Presentation delivered at the conference 'Marking 20 Years of HCOC', 1 June 2022, Vienna, Austria.

[8] Iran Project (IP) and the European Leadership Network (ELN), *Ballistic Missiles and Middle East Security: An Alternative Approach* (IP/ELN: Jan. 2022); and Héau, L. and Maitre, E., 'The Hague Code of Conduct and Southeast Asian states', HCOC Issue Brief, Oct. 2021.

[9] Borrie, J., Dowler, A. and Podvig, P., *Hypersonic Weapons: A Challenge and Opportunity for Strategic Arms Control* (UNIDIR/UNODA: New York, Feb. 2019); and Brockmann, K. and Stefanovich, D., *Hypersonic Boost-glide Systems and Hypersonic Cruise Missiles: Challenges for the Missile Technology Control Regime* (SIPRI: Stockholm, Apr. 2022).

[10] Foundation for Strategic Research (FRS), 'Nigeria is the new HCOC chair for 2022–2023', 30–31 May 2023.

[11] Delegation of the European Union to the International Organisations in Vienna, EU statement at the 21st Annual Regular Meeting of the Hague Code of Conduct against Ballistic Missile Proliferation (HCOC) as delivered on 30 May 2022, 30 May 2022; and Japanese Ministry of Foreign Affairs, Statement by Japan at the 21st Regular Meeting of the Hague Code of Conduct against Ballistic Missile Proliferation, 30 May 2022.

[12] Delegation of the European Union to the International Organisations in Vienna (@euunvie), Twitter, 30 May 2022, <https://twitter.com/euunvie/status/1531276632853471234>.

of references to Russia's invasion of Ukraine in the customary public statement. Despite the ongoing conflict, the HCOC's transparency and confidence-building measures remained operational, including for missile test launches.[13]

Outreach activities

In 2022, subscribing states continued to focus their efforts on the universalization of the HCOC by conducting a range of outreach activities targeting non-subscribing states. Argentina, as HCOC chair in 2021–22, participated in the 28th Asian Export Control Seminar on 15–17 February 2022 and presented on the HCOC and the latest efforts to strengthen the code under its chairpersonship. On 16–17 March 2022, Japan and France co-organized a session on strengthening the activities of the HCOC as part of the 17th Asia Senior-Level Talks on Non-Proliferation.[14] In addition, subscribing states, the European Union (EU) and the Foundation for Strategic Research (FRS), as part of its EU-funded project supporting the HCOC, organized an outreach event to mark the 20-year anniversary of the HCOC; and the FRS organized an outreach seminar with member states of the Association of Southeast Asian Nations and an expert mission to the United Arab Emirates.[15] France, in cooperation with the FRS, organized a visit to the Guiana Space Centre in Kourou, French Guiana, on 13–16 December, inviting international observers to the spaceport. France stressed that the visit also served as a transparency measure, as provided for in the HCOC, and involved both subscribing and non-subscribing states.[16]

United Nations General Assembly resolutions in support of the HCOC

Subscribing states have submitted biannual resolutions to the UN General Assembly since 2004, both to garner support for the HCOC and to demonstrate the legitimacy of the instrument. The voting record for the resolutions provides a helpful indicator of the success of the HCOC. It also shows trends in political support for missile non-proliferation and for restraint and transparency in activities related to missiles and space-launch

---

[13] United States Air Force Space Operations Command, 'Unarmed Minuteman III test launch to showcase readiness of US nuclear force's safe, effective deterrent', 15 Aug. 2022.

[14] Japanese Ministry of Foreign Affairs, 'The 17th Asia Senior-Level Talks on Non-Proliferation (ASTOP)', Press release, 18 Mar. 2022.

[15] See e.g. Foundation for Strategic Research (FRS), '20th anniversary of the HCOC', 1 June 2022; FRS, 'Marking 20 years of the Hague Code of Conduct: FRS side-event in the margins of the UNGA First Committee', 11 Oct. 2022; FRS, 'Virtual seminar dedicated to ASEAN countries', 5–6 Apr. 2022; and FRS, 'Ballistic missile proliferation in the Middle East: What role for CBMs such as the HCOC?', 17 May 2022.

[16] French Ministry for Europe and Foreign Affairs, Directorate for Strategic Affairs, Security and Disarmament (@francediplo_ASD), Twitter, 15 Dec. 2022, <https://twitter.com/francediplo_ASD/status/1603282402742345731>; and FRS, 'Visit of the Guyanese Space Centre (CSG)', 13–16 Dec. 2022.

Table 10.3. The voting record for United Nations General Assembly resolutions in support of the Hague Code of Conduct against Ballistic Missile Proliferation

	Date adopted	Number of states		
		In favour	Against	Abstentions
Resolution 77/58	7 Dec. 2022	167	2	9
Resolution 75/60	7 Dec. 2020	176	1	10
Resolution 73/49	5 Dec. 2018	171	1	12
Resolution 71/33	5 Dec. 2016	166	1	16
Resolution 69/44	2 Dec. 2014	162	1	17
Resolution 67/42	3 Dec. 2012	162	1	20
Resolution 65/73	8 Dec. 2010	162	1	17
Resolution 63/64	2 Dec. 2008	159	1	18
Resolution 60/62	8 Dec. 2005	158	1	11
Resolution 59/91	3 Dec. 2004	161	2	15

Sources: Foundation for Strategic Research (FRS), 'UNGA resolutions', accessed 22 Feb. 2023; and United Nations Digital Library, 'Voting data', accessed 22 Feb. 2023.

vehicles (see table 10.3). On 11 October 2022, Nigeria submitted the biannual resolution to the First Committee of the UN General Assembly.[17] Identical in content to the previous resolution, it was adopted as Resolution 77/58 on 7 December 2022 with 167 votes in favour, 2 against (Iran, Central African Republic) and 9 abstentions. The lower number of votes in favour can largely be attributed to a lower number of states voting on the resolution. The Central African Republic was the first subscribing state to vote against the biannual resolution. Madagascar switched from abstaining to voting in favour of the resolution, bringing the number of states abstaining to a record low.[18]

Conclusions

The effectiveness of the HCOC over 20 years in curbing ballistic missile proliferation is difficult to discern. The rate of submission of annual declarations and pre-launch notifications is not public, and the number of ballistic missile possessor states does not in itself provide an adequate metric of success. The rate of support for the biannual UN General Assembly resolution on the HCOC is one limited indicator of the code's political support (including beyond HCOC subscribing states), as is the continuation of the transparency and confidence-building measures despite the war in Ukraine. However, the HCOC's focus on restraining the development and proliferation of ballistic missiles capable of delivering WMD appears increasingly out of step with technological developments and broader missile proliferation trends.

[17] United Nations, General Assembly, 'General and complete disarmament: The Hague Code of Conduct against Ballistic Missile Proliferation', 77th session, First Committee, Agenda item 99 (z), A/C.1/77/L.29, 11 Oct. 2022.

[18] United Nations Digital Library, 'The Hague Code of Conduct against Ballistic Missile Proliferation: Resolution / adopted by the General Assembly', A/77/385, 7 Dec. 2022.

11. Space and cyberspace

Overview

The space and cyberspace domains featured prominently in the war in Ukraine in 2022, illustrating their overlap: the space–cyber nexus. There are three aspects to this overlap (see section I). First, there is scope for cyberattacks to be directed against space systems, in particular the digital components on which they rely to transmit data. Second, the two domains share similar challenges with respect to international governance due to the difficulties in attributing the source of attacks and in establishing state accountability. Third, international law, including international humanitarian law, applies to both the space and cyberspace domains, yet because their systems are often dual-use—serving both civilian and military functions—and used by multiple states, there are questions regarding lawful targeting of such systems.

The war in Ukraine demonstrated the growing significance and confluence of these two domains, where space systems and a range of other critical infrastructure were the target of persistent cyberattacks (see section II). These included a cyberattack on the ground terminals of a commercial satellite communications company, which had ripple effects across Europe. Cyberattacks were also directed against key Ukrainian governmental departments, such as its defence ministry and armed forces. Cyberattacks further targeted organizations in the information technology, agricultural and financial sectors, and disrupted Ukrainian telecommunications networks and power facilities.

These attacks at the nexus of the space and cyber domains disrupt or deny essential services, either temporarily or permanently. Because the attacks are difficult to attribute, discussions in multilateral forums about the governance of space and of cyberspace have highlighted the need for further measures to clarify state accountability and prevent or mitigate impacts on civilians.

In terms of space governance, a small but significant step towards new measures was the successful adoption of a resolution banning destructive, debris-generating, direct-ascent anti-satellite (DA-ASAT) missile tests by a majority of states at the United Nations General Assembly (see section III). Destructive DA-ASAT tests were among the threats to space systems discussed at the UN open-ended working group (OEWG) on reducing space threats, which convened under Resolution 76/231 for its first and second sessions in 2022.

In terms of cyber governance, the OEWG on 'security of and in the use of information and communications technology 2021–2025' continued its work in the face of the challenging geopolitical environment (see section IV). The First Committee of the General Assembly welcomed a proposal for a programme of action (POA) to continue as a permanent, inclusive, action-oriented mechanism after the conclusion of the current OEWG. Nevertheless, this proposal remains contentious, as does participation in these UN meetings by the private sector and non-governmental organizations. Further, the ongoing cyberattacks on civilian critical infrastructure—allegedly conducted by both Russian and Ukrainian state and non-state actors before and during the Ukraine conflict—demonstrate the difficulty in enforcing the voluntary norms formulated during the ongoing UN process.

The activities and mechanisms required to enforce cyberspace norms are far from dormant, however. Cyber capacity-building and confidence-building measures have been developed under the second OEWG, including the development of a points of contact directory. In addition, international policing collaboration in apprehending cybercriminals has been evolving, not only with Ukraine but even between Russia and the United States. The 2022 international summit of the Counter Ransomware Initiative provided an action plan against ransomware, which is being leveraged for cyberwarfare as well as cybercrime aims. Cooperation with industry has also been expanding, as with a request by the US government for Microsoft to provide the code of FoxBlade malware to European countries to help them combat cyberattacks.

Government collaboration with the private sector in cyberspace mirrors the space domain, where commercial actors are increasingly engaged to support military services. In particular, Russian statements regarding the potential targeting of commercial space assets that support Ukrainian military services imply potential escalation and impacts on governance. However, some states' objections to the involvement of non-governmental organizations and the private sector in UN processes governing space and cyberspace pose longer-term challenges for engaging both governmental and non-governmental stakeholders in the creation of norms and their enforcement.

NIVEDITA RAJU AND LORA SAALMAN

I. The space–cyber nexus

NIVEDITA RAJU AND LORA SAALMAN

There is a distinct overlap between the domains of space and cyberspace. For example, space assets rely on cyber components for the transmission and storage of data, making them vulnerable to cyberattack or harmful interference.[1] Equally, cyber assets rely on satellite and communications networks that are vulnerable to physical attacks.[2]

The term 'counterspace' is broadly used to refer to capabilities or techniques used to disrupt or damage another entity's space object (belonging to either a state or non-state actor), with the objective of gaining superiority over an adversary. It can refer to both kinetic and non-kinetic attacks against space systems. Kinetic attacks rely on physical destruction of the target using, for example, direct-ascent or co-orbital anti-satellite (ASAT) weapons. Non-kinetic attacks may or may not cause physical damage to the system; for example using lasers to blind the optical sensors of a satellite, cyberattacks against satellites, or electronic attacks targeting the electromagnetic spectrum (e.g. jamming satellite signals).[3]

A cyberattack is an action designed to target a computer or any element of a computerized information system—such as the digital components of a space system—to change, destroy or steal data, as well as to exploit or harm a network.[4] Cyberattacks are related to, but distinct from, a cyber intrusion, which causes digital systems to enter an insecure state.[5] An intrusion often serves as the preliminary preparation and penetration required to carry out a cyberattack. Among the malware used to carry out the cyberattacks featured in this chapter are backdoors, ransomware, trojans and wipers (see box 11.1 and the examples in sections II–IV).

There are two further aspects of the overlap between the space and cyberspace domains: the difficulty of applying international law and the challenges with respect to international governance.

---

[1] Weeden, B. and Sampson, V. (eds), *Global Counterspace Capabilities: An Open Source Assessment* (Secure World Foundation: Broomfield, CO, Apr. 2022).

[2] See e.g. United Nations, General Assembly, Open-ended working group (OEWG) on reducing space threats, 2nd session, Statement by Russia, 12 Sep. 2022, p. 2.

[3] On electronic warfare see also Raju, N., 'A proposal for a ban on destructive anti-satellite testing: A role for the EU?', EU Non-Proliferation and Disarmament Papers no. 74, EU Non-proliferation and Disarmament Consortium, Apr. 2021, p. 2.

[4] Computer Security Research Center, 'Cyber attack', US National Institute of Standards and Technology, Information Technology Laboratory.

[5] National Initiative for Cybersecurity Careers and Studies, 'Cyber intrusions', US Cybersecurity and Infrastructure Security Agency, 17 Sep. 2018.

> **Box 11.1.** Some types of malware used in cyberattacks
>
> **Backdoor**
>
> A backdoor allows access to a computer system or encrypted data through bypassing the system's security mechanisms.
>
> **Ransomware**
>
> Ransomware threatens to publish the victim's data or permanently block access to it unless a ransom is paid.
>
> **Trojan**
>
> A trojan downloads malware disguised as a legitimate programme onto a computer.
>
> **Wiper**
>
> A wiper erases user data and partition information from attached drives, making the system inoperable and unrecoverable.
>
> *Source*: Baker, K., 'The 12 most common types of malware', Crowdstrike, 28 Feb. 2023.

Among the challenges when it comes to international governance is attribution of offensive cyber activities under international law.[6] It can be difficult to identify and verify the source of an attack, potentially allowing states to avoid accountability. The Viasat cyberattack in February 2022 (see section II) illustrates further hurdles to regulation in that most space systems serve both civilian and military functions (i.e. they are dual-use) and they frequently have users in multiple states that may not be involved in a conflict. These factors raise questions as to when and how these systems can be lawfully targeted during armed conflict in a way that conforms to the strict requirements of international humanitarian law.

Under international humanitarian law, civilian objects—such as satellites providing civilians with essential services—cannot be targeted.[7] If the space system is dual-use—for example, it provides communications services to both the armed forces of the state and civilians—then it may only be lawfully targeted if it qualifies as a military objective by its nature, location, purpose or use.[8] Furthermore, indiscriminate attacks—including attacks which may cause 'incidental loss of civilian life, injury to civilians, damage to civilian objects, or a combination thereof, which would be excessive in relation to the concrete and direct military advantage anticipated'— are prohibited.[9] Legality is even more complex when a state targets space systems that also have an impact on third-party states that are not involved in the conflict. In certain

---

[6] Kastelic, A., *Non-escalatory Attribution of International Cyber Incidents: Facts, International Law and Politics* (UNIDIR: Geneva, Jan. 2022).

[7] Protocol Additional to the 1949 Geneva Conventions, and Relating to the Protection of Victims of International Armed Conflicts (Additional Protocol I, AP I), Article 48. For a summary and other details of the protocol see annex A, section I, in this volume.

[8] Additional Protocol I (note 7), Article 52.

[9] Additional Protocol I (note 7), Article 51.

situations, the rules governing neutrality may apply. For example, in a potential armed conflict between two states, a third state that seeks to be neutral must practice 'impartiality' by treating both belligerent states equally.[10] This can be complicated in the space domain because satellites are owned and operated not only by states but also by private entities, indicating scenarios in which the 'neutral' status of a state may be called into question.[11]

Since 2004 the United Nations has worked through its groups of governmental experts (GGEs) and open-ended working groups (OEWGs) to develop principles for responsible state behaviour in cyberspace and on information and communications technology (ICT) in the context of international security (see section IV). Their work is reflected in regular reports through which UN member states have developed and adopted a set of voluntary norms that describe what states should and should not be doing in cyberspace. Some of the norms are actions that states want to encourage, while others involve actions that states should avoid, such as knowingly allowing their territory to be used to conduct cyberattacks or attacks targeting civilian critical infrastructure.

The UN has also established GGEs and, more recently, an OEWG on space security governance. Threats arising at the space–cyber nexus were the subject of discussion at the September 2022 meeting of the OEWG, which focuses on developing norms, rules and principles of responsible behaviour to reduce threats to space systems (see section III). Many exchanges at this OEWG referred to the parallel forums for cyber governance, which some suggested could inform future approaches to the governance of cyberattacks on space systems, while others expressed concern regarding overlaps in the subject matter being discussed in parallel processes.[12] There are differences in the governance of both domains—notably that, unlike cyber, the space domain has been governed by legally binding treaties for decades. However, the attacks in Ukraine (see section II) highlight the need to ensure that ongoing multilateral processes on space and cyberspace governance are consistent and informed by each other's work. This can in turn ensure that any norms, rules or principles proposed in these processes are reinforced. Indeed, in the OEWG session the German delegation pointed to their national submission

---

[10] Koplow, D. A., 'Reverse distinction: A US violation of the law of armed conflict in space', *Harvard National Security Journal*, vol. 13 (2022), pp. 100–102.

[11] Koplow (note 10), p. 102.

[12] For comments on the scope for consistency between space and cyber processes see e.g. the German delegation's comments in the general exchange between member states at the 10th meeting, 2nd session of the UN OEWG on reducing space threats, 16 Sep. 2022, UN Web TV, 01:04:47–1:07:00. For concerns about overlap see e.g. the Russian delegation's comments in the same forum at 00:26:08–28:08.

to the UN secretary-general in 2021 regarding responsible behaviours in outer space, which was informed by work in the cyber process.[13]

Diverse activities have also been carried out by the private sector in coordination with governments in both space and cyberspace. For example, the US government requested that Microsoft share with European states details of the malware FoxBlade that Microsoft discovered in Ukraine.[14] In addition, Mykhailo Fedorov, a Ukrainian vice-prime minister, requested SpaceX to provide Ukraine with access to its Starlink satellite internet service and asked cryptocurrency exchanges and even the Internet Corporation for Assigned Names and Numbers (ICANN) to implement sanctions against Russia.[15] Such cooperation between government and industry provides scope for exploring how to effectively advance governance for both space and cyberspace in a manner that accounts for the nexus between the two domains. However, some of this cooperation, particularly in relation to offensive cyber operations, is likely to add to the regulatory complexity. These issues are explored in the following sections.

---

[13] See the German delegation's comments (note 12); and United Nations, General Assembly, 'German national contribution to the secretary general in reference to the Resolution 75/36 on norms, rules and principles of responsible behaviours in outer space', Submission by Germany, Apr. 2021.

[14] Sanger, D. E, Barnes, J. E. and Conger, K., 'As tanks rolled into Ukraine, so did malware. Then Microsoft entered the war', *New York Times*, 28 Feb. 2022.

[15] Brodkin, J., 'Ukraine asks Musk for Starlink terminals as Russian invasion disrupts broadband', Ars Technica, 28 Feb. 2022; and Fedorov, M., Letter to the Internet Corporation for Assigned Names and Numbers (ICANN), 28 Feb. 2022.

II. Space attacks and cyberattacks in Ukraine

NIVEDITA RAJU AND LORA SAALMAN

Ukraine became the front line of a range of attacks against space systems and cyberattacks, following the Russian invasion in February 2022. Space systems were the targets of both electronic attacks and cyberattacks.[1] One such cyberattack had significant impact as tens of thousands of internet customers across Europe, including emergency services in France and wind turbines in Germany, were unable to communicate. It was reported that 'more than 40 per cent of the destructive cyberattacks [involving Ukraine] were aimed at organizations in critical infrastructure sectors that could have negative second-order effects on the government, military, economy, and people'.[2] With some of the attacks blurring the line between cybercrime and cyberwarfare and impacting both military and civilian sectors across state borders, the war in Ukraine underscores the issues that must be addressed by international space and cyber governance.[3]

This section reviews attacks on space assets and cyberattacks that targeted Ukraine in 2022. It looks at cyberattacks on, in turn, space assets, government and finance institutions, telecommunications networks and power facilities.[4]

Cyberattacks on space assets

Coinciding with the early hours of the invasion of Ukraine on 24 February 2022, a cyberattack targeted a single consumer-oriented partition of the KA-SAT satellite broadband network, which is operated by Skylogic, a subsidiary of French satellite operator Eutelsat, on behalf of the US satellite communications company Viasat.[5] During the distributed-denial-of-service (DDoS) attack, high volumes of focused, malicious traffic were detected emanating from several modems and other customer equipment physically located within Ukraine.

---

[1] On electronic attacks (e.g. signals jamming of space assets), which are not discussed here, see e.g. EU Aviation Safety Agency (EASA), 'Global navigation satellite system outage leading to navigation/surveillance degradation', Safety Information Bulletin no 2022-02R1, 17 Mar. 2022; and Nilsen, T., 'More Russian GPS jamming than ever across border to Norway', *Barents Observer*, 9 July 2022.

[2] Microsoft, Digital Security Unit, 'Special report: Ukraine—An overview of Russia's cyberattack activity in Ukraine', 27 Apr. 2022, p. 4.

[3] While there is no universally accepted definition of cyberwarfare or cybercrime, the United Nations Office on Drugs and Crime (UNODC) defines cyberwarfare as 'cyber acts that compromise and disrupt critical infrastructure systems, which amount to an armed attack' and cybercrime as an 'act that violates the law, which is perpetrated using information and communication technology (ICT) to either target networks, systems, data, websites and/or technology or facilitate a crime'. UNODC, 'Cyberwarfare'; and UNODC, 'Cybercrime in brief'.

[4] On other aspects of the war in Ukraine see chapter 1, section V, chapter 2, section I, chapter 5, section I, chapter 8, section V, chapter 10, section I, and chapter 12, section III, in this volume.

[5] Viasat, 'KA-SAT network cyber attack overview', 30 Mar. 2022.

The impact across Europe was significant. While this cyberattack was almost certainly designed to disrupt the Ukrainian military's satellite communications, it also caused far-reaching civilian disruptions. Viasat reported that the cyberattack had an impact on 'several thousand customers located in Ukraine and tens of thousands of other fixed broadband customers across Europe'.[6] It disrupted emergency services in France and interrupted remote monitoring and control of 5800 wind turbines in Germany.[7] Victor Zhora, deputy head of the Ukrainian State Service of Special Communications and Information Protection (SSSCIP), confirmed that the attack targeted Ukraine's satellite communications and suggested that it 'partially succeeded'.[8] While Russia did not claim responsibility for the attack, several states, including member states of the European Union (EU), the United Kingdom and the United States, attributed the attack to Russia.[9]

The vectors of the cyberattack remain in dispute. Viasat contends that the malware executed 'legitimate, targeted management commands' and 'overwrote key data in flash memory on the modems, rendering the modems unable to access the network, but not permanently unusable'.[10] In contrast, Sentinel Lab researchers suggest that the cyberattack used the KA-SAT management mechanism in a supply chain attack to push the AcidRain wiper, which is designed to overwrite key data in a modem's flash memory, rendering it inoperable.[11] They noted AcidRain wiper's developmental similarities to VPNFilter malware, which was previously attributed to Russia's Sofacy Group—also known as Advanced Persistent Threat (APT) 28, Sandworm (see below), Strontium, X-Agent, Pawn Storm, Fancy Bear and Sednit.[12] Their findings suggest that, rather than the attacks temporarily disabling these systems (as Viasat suggested), they were destructive and likely to have Russian sources.

---

[6] Viasat (note 5).

[7] French National Assembly, National Defence and Armed Forces Committee, 'Compte rendu: Audition, à huis clos, de M. Stéphane Bouillon, Secrétaire général de la défense et de la sécurité nationale' [Report: Closed doors hearing of Mr Stéphane Bouillon, secretary-general for defence and national security], Report no. 5, Extraordinary session of 2021–22, 13 July 2022; and Enercon, 'Over 95 per cent of WECs back online following disruption to satellite communication', 19 Apr. 2022.

[8] Victor Zhora (@VZhora), Twitter, 10 May 2022, <https://twitter.com/VZhora/status/1524080689452359680>.

[9] Council of the European Union, 'Russian cyber operations against Ukraine: Declaration by the High Representative on behalf of the European Union', Press release, 10 May 2022; British Foreign, Commonwealth and Development Office, 'Russia behind cyberattack with Europe-wide impact an hour before Ukraine invasion', Press release, 10 May 2022; and Blinken, A. J., US secretary of state, 'Attribution of Russia's malicious cyber activity against Ukraine', Press statement, US Department of State, 10 May 2022.

[10] Viasat (note 5).

[11] Guerrero-Saade, J. A. and van Amerongen, M., 'AcidRain—A modem wiper rains down on Europe', Sentinel Labs, 31 May 2022.

[12] US Department of Justice, 'Justice Department announces actions to disrupt Advanced Persistent Threat 28 botnet of infected routers and network storage devices', 23 May 2018. On other activities connected with Strontium see section IV in this chapter.

Cyberattacks on government and industry

Even prior to Russia's invasion of Ukraine, in January 2022 Microsoft identified a destructive malware operation, known as WhisperGate, aimed at multiple organizations in Ukraine.[13] These wiper attacks masqueraded as ransomware, threatening to encrypt the master boot record (MBR)—the first sector on a hard drive containing code necessary to start the operating system—unless a ransom were paid. However, multiple forensic laboratories determined that the intended aim was to destroy the MBR.[14] By 15 February, while Russian troops were massing at the Ukrainian border, DDoS attacks affected the Ukrainian Ministry of Defence and armed forces, with further DDoS attacks targeting the websites of two banks, Privatbank and Oschadbank.[15]

Several hours before the launch of the invasion on 24 February, offensive and destructive cyberattacks were directed against Ukraine's digital infrastructure. Notable among these was FoxBlade—also known as Hermetic Wiper and with alleged links to Russian military intelligence (see below)—which, like the WhisperGate wiper, served as decoy ransomware.[16] It destroyed systems and information across more than 12 organizations in the governmental, ICT, energy, agricultural and financial sectors in Ukraine, and also appeared in Latvia and Lithuania.[17]

The vectors of cyber intrusion and attack expanded even further in March 2022, when an open-source backdoor named GoMet affected a large software-development company whose software is used in various Ukrainian state organizations.[18] This suggests a supply chain attack in which systems are compromised through a third-party service provider.

By August 2022, cyber intrusions shifted again, towards data exfiltration. Ukrainian government agencies were infected by a phishing campaign—a form of 'social engineering' in which the targets are deceived into revealing sensitive information or installing malware—allegedly conducted through

---

[13] 'Destructive malware targeting Ukrainian organizations', Microsoft Security Blog, 15 Jan. 2022.
[14] Mandiant, 'Evacuation and humanitarian documents used to spear phish Ukrainian entities', 20 July 2022; and Microsoft, 'Special report' (note 2).
[15] Ukrainian State Service of Special Communications and Information Protection (SSSCIP), 'Cyberattacks on the sites of military structures and state banks', 15 Feb. 2022.
[16] Constantinescu, V., 'New FoxBlade malware hit Ukraine hours before invasion, Microsoft says', BitDefender Blog, 1 Mar. 2022; Microsoft Security Intelligence, 'DoS:Win32/FoxBlade.A!dha', 23 Feb. 2022; and Guerrero-Saade, J. A., 'HermeticWiper—New destructive malware used in cyber attacks on Ukraine', Sentinel Labs, 23 Feb. 2022.
[17] Microsoft, 'Special report' (note 2); and Uchill, J., 'Ransomware may have been a decoy to launch new wiper malware seen in Ukraine cyberattacks', SC Media, 24 Feb. 2022.
[18] Schultz, J., 'Attackers target Ukraine using GoMet backdoor', Talos Threat Spotlight Blog, 21 July 2022.

Gamaredon (also known as Actinium), an APT linked to the Russian Federal Security Service (Federal'naya Sluzhba Bezopasnosti, FSB).[19]

In October 2022, Prestige ransomware targeted organizations in the transportation and logistics industries in both Ukraine and Poland.[20] This laid the foundations for these key economic sectors to be degraded by the Iridium group, which is allegedly connected to the Sandworm hacking unit (Unit 74455) of Russia's military intelligence agency, the Main Directorate of the General Staff of the Armed Forces (Glavnoe Razvedyvatel'noe Upravlenie, GRU).[21] This unit is also thought to be linked to the deployment of the wipers FoxBlade, CaddyWiper and Industroyer2 in Ukraine.[22]

Cyberattacks on telecommunications

From February 2022 Kyivstar, a Ukrainian ICT operator which provides mobile service to almost 26 million people, highlighted its fight against a barrage of cyberattacks and physical attacks (including missile strikes) that destroyed almost 10 per cent of its base stations.[23] Notably, this combination of attacks coincided with Russian efforts to divert internet traffic in occupied parts of Ukraine through its own networks.[24] This meant that Russian authorities could monitor, exfiltrate and manipulate data in Ukraine.[25] Kyivstar alleged that phishing attacks tripled, combined with a doubling of DDoS attacks aimed at overwhelming company websites with online traffic, attempted exfiltration of data on phone calls and cyber intrusions into third parties to gain access to Kyivstar networks.[26]

By March 2022 cyberattacks on telecommunications firms again grew in scope as Ukrtelecom, an internet service provider, was the target of a 'massive cyberattack'.[27] Connectivity collapsed to 13 per cent of pre-conflict levels. While Ukrtelecom resumed some service on the day of the attack, it emphasized that, 'to continue providing services to Ukraine's Armed Forces and other military formations as well as to the customers', it had limited

---

[19] Malhotra, A. and Venere, G., 'Gamaredon APT targets Ukrainian government agencies in new campaign', Talos Threat Spotlight Blog, 15 Sep. 2022; and Mandiant (note 14).

[20] Microsoft, 'New "Prestige" ransomware impacts organizations in Ukraine and Poland', 14 Oct. 2022.

[21] Microsoft, 'Special report' (note 2).

[22] On Sandworm see e.g. Holt, R., 'Sandworm: A tale of disruption told anew', WeLiveSecurity by ESET, 21 Mar. 2022; and US Cybersecurity and Infrastructure Security Agency, 'New Sandworm malware Cyclops Blink replaces VPNFilter', Alert no. AA22-054A, 23 Feb. 2022.

[23] Satariano, A., 'How Russia took over Ukraine's internet in occupied territories', New York Times, 9 Aug. 2022; and Bergengruen, V., 'The battle for control over Ukraine's internet', Time, 18 Aug. 2022.

[24] On the alleged coordination between cyberattacks and physical attacks see Khmelova, I., Cyber, Artillery, Propaganda: Comprehensive Analysis of Russian Warfare Dimensions (SSSCIP: Kyiv, 2022).

[25] Satariano (note 23).

[26] Miller, M., 'Ukraine's largest telecom stands against Russian cyberattacks', Politico, 7 Sep. 2022.

[27] Condon, S., '"Massive cyberattack" against Ukrainian ISP has been neutralized, Ukraine says', ZDNet, 28 Mar. 2022.

services to the 'majority of private users and business-clients', indicating the toll on civilian users.[28] In this ongoing compromise of telecommunications firms, in June 2022 the SSSCIP's Computer Emergency Response Team of Ukraine (CERT-UA) warned of emails containing a document file that would load a DarkCrystal remote-access trojan that again targeted Ukrainian telecommunications operators and service providers.[29]

Cyberattacks on power facilities

In April 2022 CERT-UA worked with ESET, a Slovakia-based international cybersecurity company, to analyse an intended cyberattack against Ukrainian high-voltage electrical substations that some have attributed to Sandworm.[30] The cyber intrusion, which occurred in February with an intended deployment date in April, employed malware against industrial control systems (ICSs), which monitor, control and regulate automated processes of industrial systems. Forensics revealed this malware—named Industroyer2—to be an updated version of the Industroyer malware used in 2016 to sever power supplies in Ukraine, also allegedly linked to Sandworm.[31] The Industroyer2 cyberattack allegedly used other destructive malware, including CaddyWiper, OrcShred, SoloShred and AwfulShred. While this particular cyberattack failed, it suggested the potential for similar future attacks on critical infrastructure and power supply.

Farid Safarov, a Ukrainian deputy minister of energy, attributed the attempted cyberattack to Russia, alleging that it sought to prevent Ukraine connecting to the 'Pan European electrical grid'.[32] Pointing to the humanitarian costs of such an outage, Zhora of the SSSCIP emphasized that the attack was intended to harm civilian targets: 'It was supposed to start working in a way to cause electricity outages [in] a number of areas in Ukraine that [would] deprive the civil population of electricity and I stress the point that this civil infrastructure was targeted to disrupt electricity supply.'[33] Further, in the weeks that followed, Russian hackers allegedly broke into a Ukrainian power company and temporarily shut down nine electricity substations,

[28] Condon (note 27).
[29] SSSCIP, 'Hackers attack Ukrainian telecom operators and service providers', 25 June 2022.
[30] ESET Research, 'Industroyer2: Industroyer reloaded', WeLiveSecurity by ESET, 12 Apr. 2022.
[31] US Department of Justice, Office of Public Affairs, 'Six Russian GRU officers charged in connection with worldwide deployment of destructive malware and other disruptive actions in cyberspace', Press release, 19 Oct. 2020.
[32] Uchill, J., '"The criminals are guided by the Russian Federation": Ukraine responds to Industroyer2', SC Media, 12 Apr. 2022. See also Blaustein, A., 'How Ukraine unplugged from Russia and joined Europe's power grid with unprecedented speed', *Scientific American*, 23 Mar. 2022.
[33] Uchill, '"The criminals are guided by the Russian Federation"' (note 32).

according to a non-public document reportedly shared with *MIT Technology Review*.[34]

Conclusions

The sustained attacks on ICT systems and critical infrastructure in Ukraine—which also affected users across Europe—highlight both the cyber and physical costs of such attacks on the civilian population, possibly in breach of international humanitarian law. Further, the confluence of these various cyber intrusions and attacks demonstrate that destructive impacts crossed national and industry borders, military and civilian sectors, and—in the form of wipers masquerading as ransomware—technological boundaries. Such attacks also evidence the convergence of cybercrime tactics and cyberwarfare aims. These trends indicate an urgent need to advance governance in both the space and cyber domains, discussed in sections III and IV, respectively.

---

[34] O'Neill, P. H., 'Russian hackers tried to bring down Ukraine's power grid to help the invasion', *MIT Technology Review*, 12 Apr. 2022.

III. Developments in space governance and the impact of the war in Ukraine

NIVEDITA RAJU

The open-ended working group (OEWG) on reducing space threats through norms, rules and principles of responsible behaviours, which was established by the United Nations General Assembly in 2021, convened twice in 2022. While political circumstances following the invasion of Ukraine suggested that the talks would be challenging, states nonetheless met and exchanged views on the existing international framework governing space activities, and current and future threats to space systems. Examples of such threats in 2022 were a cyberattack on a communications satellite and jamming of the signals of navigation and communication satellites, including satellites owned by private entities (see section II).[1] Discussions at the OEWG referred to these incidents to acknowledge that non-kinetic threats to space systems are significant. Several stakeholders at the OEWG also noted the increase in the number of destructive direct-ascent anti-satellite (DA-ASAT) tests, the most recent being a test by Russia in 2021. The pledge by the United States not to conduct such tests encouraged several states to follow suit and fuelled momentum towards a US-led UN General Assembly resolution.

This section first reviews the sessions of the OEWG in 2022 and then presents an overview of state deliberations regarding the banning of destructive DA-ASAT tests. Finally, in light of the role of non-state actors in the war in Ukraine, the section looks at how governments cooperate with private companies in space, and the implications for space governance.

The open-ended working group on reducing space threats

Multilateral engagement in space governance took a tentative step forward in 2022. In 2020 the UN General Assembly had adopted a resolution on reducing space threats norms, rules and principles of responsible behaviours in outer space, proposed by the United Kingdom.[2] In a subsequent resolution in 2021, the General Assembly decided to convene an OEWG on this topic.[3] In line with that resolution, the group was set to meet for two sessions in each of 2022 and 2023. The first 2022 session was delayed due to procedural objections raised by the Russian delegation regarding sufficient time allotted for preparation and questions raised by Russia and Cuba regarding

---

[1] Zarkan, L. C., 'Commercial space operators on the digital battlefield', Centre for International Governance Innovation (CIGI) Essays on Cybersecurity and Outer Space, 29 Jan. 2023.
[2] UN General Assembly Resolution 75/36, 7 Dec. 2020.
[3] UN General Assembly Resolution 76/231, 24 Dec. 2021. See also Raju, N., 'Developments in space security', *SIPRI Yearbook 2022*, pp. 578–79.

participation of non-state actors.[4] As the first session was initially scheduled for 14 February, it is notable that Russia's objections were raised shortly before its invasion of Ukraine.[5]

While the timing indicated that progress on substance would be difficult, the OEWG thereafter convened twice in 2022 for substantive sessions, in May and September. Both sessions saw strong engagement that was not limited to traditional 'space powers', but also significant regional participation, including states from the Asia-Pacific and Latin American regions. The latter included initiatives to advance legal interpretation of 'due regard' under the Outer Space Treaty in line with 'responsible behaviour', submitted by the Philippines.[6] Furthermore, despite initial procedural objections by some states, the inclusivity of this process was also reflected in the approval granted for civil society and non-governmental organizations (NGOs) to participate in these sessions. This was a positive development, given that participation of non-state actors in UN processes can be contentious (see section IV).

Discussions at the OEWG's first session, in May, were constructive as they focused on applicable laws and gaps in the current space governance framework. The OEWG sought primarily to establish that voluntary measures such as norms, rules and principles of responsible behaviour are not contradictory to, but rather support, the development of legally binding measures. China and Russia advocated for the use of their jointly proposed Draft Treaty on the Prevention of the Placement of Weapons in Outer Space and of the Threat or Use of Force against Outer Space Objects as a basis for new legal measures on space governance. They argued that the proposed treaty aligned more clearly with the objectives of the Conference on Disarmament regarding the prevention of an arms race in outer space (PAROS).[7]

The September session, which focused on current and future threats to space systems, proved more challenging due to the subjectivity of threat perceptions and sensitivities surrounding the discussion of the capabilities of various states. Russia indicated that it would initiate a new UN group of governmental experts (GGE) on PAROS and on the prevention of placement

---

[4] UN General Assembly Resolution 76/231 (note 3), para. 6; and Hitchens, T., 'No love from Russia for UN military space norms meeting', Breaking Defense, 9 Feb. 2022.

[5] On the war in Ukraine see chapter 1, section V, chapter 2, section I, chapter 5, section I, chapter 8, section V, chapter 10, section I, and chapter 12, section III, in this volume.

[6] United Nations, General Assembly, Open-ended working group (OEWG) on reducing space threats, 'The duty of "due regard" as a foundational principle of responsible behavior in space', Working paper submitted by the Philippines, A/AC.294/2022/WP.12, 11 May 2022.

[7] Conference on Disarmament, 'Draft Treaty on the Prevention of the Placement of Weapons in Outer Space, the Threat or Use of Force against Outer Space Objects', Submitted by China and Russia, CD/1985, 12 June 2014; and UN General Assembly Resolution 76/23, 6 Dec. 2021. For a brief description and list of members of the Conference on Disarmament see annex B, section I, in this volume.

of weapons in outer space.[8] The GGE, established through a UN General Assembly resolution, would continue the work of the previous GGE on PAROS, which concluded in 2019, and would commence work in 2023.[9] The third and fourth substantive sessions of the OEWG, scheduled for January–February and August 2023, will determine the outcome and future of the working group, before the first session of the GGE is convened.

Banning destructive anti-satellite tests

The most recent destructive DA-ASAT test was conducted by Russia in November 2021 against one of its own space objects, generating a significant amount of space debris.[10] By 2022, while much of the debris had reportedly left orbit, hundreds of catalogued fragments remained there.[11] Since space debris poses an indiscriminate threat to all states conducting space activities, including the state responsible for the test, many delegates at the OEWG sessions raised this as a recurring issue.

In the week preceding the first session of the OEWG, the USA referred to Russia's destructive DA-ASAT test in 2021 and committed to not conducting such tests.[12] The US commitment was welcomed by many in the international community, as stakeholders have strongly recommended such tests be banned in the interest of safer, more secure and sustainable space activities.[13] Following the US commitment, Canada made its own pledge at the first session of the OEWG.[14]

Banning destructive DA-ASAT tests was referred to throughout the OEWG session as 'low-hanging fruit', being an issue that was possibly less controversial. This is because such a ban would be limited in scope, prohibiting only destructive tests against an object (excluding simulated tests or fly-bys), and would exclude development or, indeed, use of the same technology. However, the US commitment was not welcomed by all. Some states labelled

---

[8] United Nations, General Assembly, OEWG on reducing space threats, 2nd session, Statement by Russia, 12 Sep. 2022.

[9] UN General Assembly Resolution 77/250, 30 Dec. 2022. On the earlier GGE see Porras, D., 'Creeping towards an arms race in outer space', *SIPRI Yearbook 2020*, pp. 517–18.

[10] Raju, 'Developments in space security' (note 3), pp. 574–75; and Raju, N., 'Russia's anti-satellite test should lead to a multilateral ban', SIPRI Commentary, 7 Dec. 2021.

[11] Foust, J., 'Majority of tracked Russian ASAT debris has deorbited', SpaceNews, 29 Sep. 2022; and Foust, J., 'Starlink satellites encounter Russian ASAT debris squalls', SpaceNews, 9 Aug. 2022.

[12] White House, 'Remarks by Vice President Harris on the ongoing work to establish norms in space', 18 Apr. 2022.

[13] Ortega, A. A. and Zarkan, L. C., 'The road to a moratorium on kinetic ASAT testing is paved with good intentions, but is it feasible?', Fondation pour la recherche stratégique (FRS) Note no. 22/22, May 2022; Raju, 'Russia's anti-satellite test should lead to a multilateral ban' (note 10); and Byers, M. et al., 'Kinetic ASAT test ban treaty', Open letter to Volkan Bozkır, President of the UN General Assembly, Outer Space Institute, 2 Sep. 2021.

[14] United Nations, General Assembly, OEWG on reducing space threats, 1st session, Statement by Canada, 9 May 2022.

it 'hypocritical' considering that the USA had conducted ASAT tests in the past, including as recently as 2008.[15] Others suggested that the scope of the proposed ban was insufficient as it did not cover the development or deployment of DA-ASAT weapons, or other means of threatening or disrupting space systems.[16]

Other states subsequently made similar pledges, including Australia, France, Germany, Japan, South Korea, New Zealand, Switzerland and the UK. Based on this growing momentum, the USA proposed a resolution in the UN General Assembly calling on states to commit to not conducting destructive DA-ASAT tests.[17] While 155 states voted in favour, 9 voted against (including China and Russia) and 9 abstained (including India).[18] Notably, China, India, Russia and the USA are the only four states to have conducted destructive DA-ASAT tests. This voting pattern therefore indicates a difficult path ahead for consensus-based decision-making on space security governance, even for issues that some considered uncontroversial.

Cooperation between governments and companies

The role in space activities of non-state actors, particularly companies, has rapidly increased with the commercialization of the space domain. This trend was highlighted by dramatic developments in 2022. In February, in the wake of Russia's invasion of Ukraine, Mykhailo Fedorov, a Ukrainian vice prime minister and minister of digital transformation, made a series of appeals to private-sector entities. These included a request that SpaceX send user terminals for its Starlink satellite internet service to Ukraine, to which the company's chief executive officer (CEO), Elon Musk, responded positively.[19] This cooperation between SpaceX and the Ukrainian government had reportedly been planned for weeks prior to the public exchange on Twitter.[20]

Because Starlink was now being used by Ukrainian military forces, an official of the Russian Ministry of Foreign Affairs stated in October 2022 that 'quasi-civilian infrastructure' might be targeted for a retaliation strike.[21] It is

[15] United Nations, General Assembly, OEWG on reducing space threats, 2nd session, 'Responsible behavior as an elusive and diversionary concept for Prevention of an Arms Race in Outer Space (PAROS)', Working paper submitted by Iran, A/AC.294/2022/WP.22, 21 Sep. 2022, p. 5.

[16] United Nations, General Assembly, OEWG on reducing space threats, 1st session, General remarks by China, 9 May 2022, p. 4.

[17] UN General Assembly Resolution 77/41, 7 Dec. 2022.

[18] United Nations, Digital Library, 'Destructive direct-ascent anti-satellite missile testing: Resolution adopted by the General Assembly', 7 Dec. 2022.

[19] Mykhailo Fedorov (@FedorovMykhailo), Twitter, 26 Feb. 2022, <https://twitter.com/FedorovMykhailo/status/1497543633293266944>; Elon Musk (@elonmusk), Twitter, 26 Feb. 2022, <https://twitter.com/elonmusk/status/1497701484003213317>; and Brodkin, J., 'Ukraine asks Musk for Starlink terminals as Russian invasion disrupts broadband', Ars Technica, 28 Feb. 2022.

[20] Foust, J., 'SpaceX worked for weeks to begin Starlink service in Ukraine', SpaceNews, 8 Mar. 2022.

[21] United Nations, General Assembly, OEWG on reducing space threats, Statement by Russia (note 8), p. 2.

unclear whether this statement was solely intended as a general warning to US-based companies assisting the Ukrainian military, such as SpaceX, or if it also signalled an immediate willingness to carry out such an attack. In the latter case, Russian DA-ASAT attacks would be impractical and expensive against Starlink in particular, because the attack would require destruction of multiple space objects with multiple missiles. Furthermore, such action would not only be considered escalatory, but would constitute a use of force against another state's space object and potentially spark conflict in space with a broad impact, particularly on civilians. In any event, the statement highlighted the potential scope for future escalation with respect to space systems in the conflict in Ukraine. Indeed, some have noted that even cyberattacks that begin in space can be escalatory and could lead to conflict on earth (see section IV).[22]

The 1967 Outer Space Treaty establishes that international law applies to outer space.[23] This includes provisions under international humanitarian law (IHL), as has been reaffirmed by several states.[24] However, at the second session of the OEWG on reducing space threats in September 2022, the Russian delegation argued that it is 'unreasonable and inappropriate' to discuss IHL in the OEWG.[25] Russia submitted this argument on the basis that discussing specifics of IHL is problematic because it raises 'admissibility of an armed conflict in outer space'.[26] Other states have adopted similar views and also argued against consideration of IHL issues in such talks.[27] While IHL applies to the space domain, these exchanges highlight the sensitivities surrounding discussion of the topic in the OEWG and similar forums.

Conclusions

The war in Ukraine has witnessed cyberattacks, as well as the threat of kinetic attacks, against space systems. These reveal the critical role played by space technologies and the need for further governance measures. In the light of continuing hostilities in Ukraine and differing views on priorities for space

---

[22] West, J., 'Where outer space meets cyberspace: A human-centric look at space security', CIGI Essays on Cybersecurity and Outer Space, 29 Jan. 2023.

[23] Treaty on Principles Governing the Activities of States in the Exploration and Use of Outer Space, including the Moon and Other Celestial Bodies (Outer Space Treaty), Article III. For a summary and other details of the Outer Space Treaty see annex A, section I, in this volume.

[24] See e.g. United Nations, General Assembly, OEWG on reducing space threats, 1st session, Submission by the EU, A/AC.294/2022/WP.5, 5 May 2022, p. 1.

[25] United Nations, General Assembly, OEWG on reducing space threats, 2nd session, Statement by Russia, 12 Sep. 2022, pp. 4–5.

[26] United Nations, General Assembly, OEWG on reducing space threats, 'On counterproductive nature of consideration of the applicability of international humanitarian law (IHL) to outer space activities', Working paper submitted by Russia, A/AC.294/2023/WP.11, 30 Jan. 2023, p. 1.

[27] See e.g. objections to discussion of IHL by the Cuban delegation in the general exchange between member states at the 10th meeting, 2nd session of the UN OEWG on reducing space threats, 16 Sep. 2022, UN Web TV, 00:54:54–56:50.

governance, achieving consensus on future measures through multilateral deliberations will be challenging. The procedural objections raised by some regarding the extent of non-governmental stakeholders' participation in the OEWG on reducing space threats also highlights the difficulties of ensuring the inclusivity of these processes. However, as evidenced by the UN General Assembly resolution on banning destructive DA-ASAT tests, there is still scope for progress, albeit in small steps.

IV. Developments in governance of cyberspace and the impact of the war in Ukraine

LORA SAALMAN

Cyber governance is understood to mean the legal and normative framework that regulates activities in cyberspace. The norms that have been developed in the long-running United Nations process on cyber governance were severely challenged in 2022 by the war in Ukraine. These norms were violated both prior to and during the conflict, including the alleged use of both Ukrainian and Russian territory with government knowledge and support for wrongful acts using information and communications technology (ICT).[1] Cyberattacks and cyber intrusions by both sides damaged critical civilian infrastructure and harmed information systems (see section II).

Nevertheless, there was international cooperation in prosecuting criminal use of ICT. Notably, intergovernmental cooperation was not just between Ukraine and the United States, or Ukraine and the European Union (EU), but even between Russia and the USA. In addition, cooperation between governments and industry included the provision by a range of companies of computing hardware and software services. However, this engagement with companies did not translate to the UN cyber governance process, where there were efforts to block accreditation of private-sector and non-governmental organizations (NGOs).

This section first reviews developments in UN cyber governance in 2022. It then looks at two sets of international cooperation: between Russian and US law enforcement agencies on ICT-related crimes; and between Ukraine and state and non-state actors on cyber resilience, cyber governance and even alleged cyberattacks. The section concludes by briefly assessing the prospects for achieving consensus in the governance of cyberspace.

The second United Nations open-ended working group on ICT security

The current UN process on cyber governance started with a series of groups of governmental experts (GGEs) established by the General Assembly from 2004. The process bifurcated in 2019, with a US-sponsored GGE—with a limited membership—on 'advancing responsible state behaviour in cyberspace in the context of international security' meeting in parallel with a Russian-sponsored open-ended working group (OEWG)—open to all UN member states—on 'developments in the field of information and telecommunications in the context of international security' (OEWG I). A second

---

[1] Przetacznik, J. and Tarpova, S., 'Russia's war on Ukraine: Timeline of cyberattacks', European Parliamentary Research Service, June 2022.

OEWG, on 'security of and in the use of information and communications technology 2021–2025' (OEWG II) held its first meeting in 2021.[2]

UN General Assembly reports issued in 2022 indicate that there was a concerted effort to keep channels of engagement open in the context of the war in Ukraine and in the face of 'a challenging geopolitical environment'.[3] This allowed states to address ongoing concerns over the development of ICT capabilities for military purposes; the malicious use of ICT by state and non-state actors; and harmful ICT activity against critical infrastructure that provides essential services to the public, thereby compromising the availability and integrity of internet services and health care.[4] Accordingly, the UN reports included a variety of proposals for both capacity building and confidence building, such as a directory of points of contact on ICT security who 'could be reached in times of urgency'.[5]

The UN General Assembly also adopted a resolution on initiating steps leading to an agreed programme of action (POA) 'to advance responsible State behaviour in the use of information and communications technologies in the context of international security'.[6] However, the proposal of a POA remained contentious due to concerns that it might establish a body parallel to OEWG II.[7] If the General Assembly is able to adopt a POA as a permanent, inclusive, action-oriented mechanism after the conclusion of OEWG II in 2025, this will at a minimum maintain UN channels of engagement. However, NGO participation is likely to face increasing obstacles (see discussion of Ukraine and the private sector below).

Despite these signs of progress, the widespread cyberattacks on civilian critical infrastructure both preceding and during the Russian invasion of Ukraine—and allegedly carried out by state and non-state actors on both sides—showed that challenges to enforcing international law in cyberspace

---

[2] UN General Assembly Resolution 75/240, 31 Dec. 2020. On the GGE and OEWG processes see Pytlak, A., 'Cyberspace and the malicious use of information and communications technology', *SIPRI Yearbook 2022*, pp. 558–71; and UN Office for Disarmament Affairs (UNODA), 'Developments in the field of information and telecommunications in the context of international security'.

[3] United Nations, General Assembly, OEWG on security of and in the use of ICT 2021–25, 3rd substantive session, Draft annual progress report, A/AC.292/2022/CRP.1, 28 July 2022, para. 1.

[4] United Nations, General Assembly, 'Developments in the field of information and telecommunications in the context of international security', Report of the First Committee, A/77/380, 14 Nov. 2022; UN General Assembly Resolution 77/37, 7 Dec. 2022; and United Nations, General Assembly, OEWG on security of and in the use of ICT 2021–25, 'Developments in the field of information and telecommunications in the context of international security', Note by the secretary-general, A/77/275, 8 Aug. 2022.

[5] United Nations, A/AC.292/2022/CRP.1 (note 3), para. 16(b).

[6] UN General Assembly Resolution 77/37 (note 4).

[7] Meyer, P., 'Cyber security at the UN General Assembly First Committee—Déjà vu all over again', ICT for Peace Foundation, 11 Nov. 2022.

remained. This was reaffirmed by OEWG I in its final report in 2021.[8] In fact, cyberattacks that targeted government, finance, telecommunications and power facilities (see section II) indicated that both Russian and Ukrainian state and non-state actors violated the norms identified by the GGEs and OEWGs on ICT.[9] These violations included government knowledge of its territory being used for intentionally wrongful acts using ICT; intentional damage to or impairment of critical infrastructure; and harming of information systems that provide services to the public.

While such violations highlighted the growing need for strengthened cyber governance, they also revealed the complexity of enforcing it. These difficulties are compounded by the persistent challenge of attribution that is exacerbated by the involvement of both state and non-state actors in the Ukraine conflict and the dual-use nature of cyberspace for civilian and military aims, combined with the voluntary nature of the norms process.

International cooperation with Russia

In the conflict between Russia and Ukraine, other European states and the USA have predominantly supported Ukraine and sought to apply diplomatic pressure to Russia. However, in cooperation with other governments, Russia made some notable efforts in 2022 to implement the cyberspace norms of the GGEs and OEWGs, particularly in terms of information exchange to assist in prosecuting criminal use of ICTs.

In January 2022, just prior to the invasion of Ukraine, the Russian Federal Security Service (Federal'naya Sluzhba Bezopasnosti, FSB) and law enforcement agencies cooperated with US counterparts to arrest four members, including the alleged leader, of the Infraud Organization hacker group (also known as Unicc, Faaxxx and Faxtrod), which had caused losses estimated at US$560 million in its seven years of activity.[10] Earlier that month, the FSB—in response to US requests—conducted raids and arrested 14 alleged members of the DarkSide and REvil ransomware groups. These included a hacker who US officials said executed a cyberattack on Colonial Pipeline, the largest US pipeline system for refined oil products.[11]

---

[8] United Nations, General Assembly, OEWG on developments in the field of ICT in the context of international security, Final substantive report, A/75/816, 18 Mar. 2021, paras 34–40, and annex II, para. 18. See also United Nations, General Assembly, GGE on advancing responsible state behaviour in cyberspace in the context of international security, Report, A/76/135, 14 July 2021, para. 71(f).

[9] United Nations, A/77/380 (note 4); UN General Assembly Resolution 77/37 (note 4); and United Nations, A/77/275 (note 4).

[10] Ilascu, I., 'Russia arrests leader of "Infraud Organization" hacker group', Bleeping Computer, 25 Jan. 2022.

[11] Burgess, M., 'Russia takes down REvil hackers as Ukraine tensions mount', Wired, 14 Jan. 2022; and Dixon, R. and Nakashima, E., 'Russia arrests 14 alleged members of REvil ransomware gang, including hacker US says conducted Colonial Pipeline attack', Washington Post, 14 Jan. 2022.

Some have tied these actions to efforts by Russia to mitigate the severity of the US response to its intended invasion of Ukraine.[12] They nevertheless indicate Russia's willingness to cooperate on some key norms in cyberspace, even with countries with which it has adversarial relations.

International cooperation with Ukraine

Support for Ukraine from other governments

During 2022, Ukraine worked in close consultation with other governments in terms of both cyber resilience and cyber governance.

In February 2022 US Secretary of State Anthony J. Blinken issued a statement denouncing cyberattacks against Ukraine and pledging enhanced support for 'Ukraine's digital connectivity, including by providing satellite phones and data terminals to Ukrainian government officials, essential service providers, and critical infrastructure operators'.[13] Further, in May 2022 the head of US Cyber Command, General Paul Nakasone, declared that his agency had deployed a 'hunt forward' team to help Ukraine shore up its cyber defences against active threats.[14] In fact, in June 2022 Nakasone confirmed that the USA had undertaken offensive cyber operations in support of Ukraine, saying that they had 'conducted a series of operations across the full spectrum: offensive, defensive, [and] information operations'.[15] A month later, the USA disclosed evidence of 20 possible intrusions into Ukrainian systems that it had uncovered.[16]

The EU also made cyber commitments to Ukraine. In March 2022 the Estonian e-Governance Academy began implementation of a 12-month, €10 million EU project to strengthen cybersecurity and to keep public services available in Ukraine.[17] The project focused on three main areas: (*a*) the security of the Ukrainian government's Trembita secure data-exchange platform and the management of public registries, including identifying and neutralizing possible cyberthreats; (*b*) protection of critical infrastructure and public data, including the replacement of destroyed equipment; and (*c*) provision of security tools to enable operational staff to maintain and service critical public infrastructure. In December 2022 the EU also unveiled a

---

[12] Dixon and Nakashima (note 11).

[13] Blinken, A. J., US secretary of state, 'Attribution of Russia's malicious cyber activity against Ukraine', Press statement, US Department of State, 10 May 2022.

[14] Kagubare, I., 'Top US cyber officials warn against underestimating Russia's cyber capability', *The Hill*, 4 May 2022.

[15] Kagubare, I., 'Cyber Command chief confirms US took part in offensive cyber operations', *The Hill*, 1 June 2022.

[16] Cyber National Mission Force Public Affairs, 'Cyber National Mission Force discloses IOCs from Ukrainian networks', US Cyber Command, 20 July 2022.

[17] EU4Digital, 'EU supports cybersecurity in Ukraine with over €10 million', 21 Oct. 2022.

cyber laboratory in Kyiv to develop Ukraine's cyber defence capacities.[18] This was paid for from a €31 million fund to support the Ukrainian armed forces agreed in December 2021 under the EU's European Peace Facility.

More broadly, the 2022 international summit of the Counter Ransomware Initiative was held in October and November in Washington, DC, at which 37 country participants were in attendance, including Ukraine but not Russia.[19] The outcome of the summit was an action plan for states to cooperate on holding ransomware actors accountable for their crimes and not providing them safe haven; disrupting and bringing to justice ransomware actors and their enablers; and information sharing and securing of national cyber infrastructure against ransomware attacks. While not directed at Ukraine, the plan has implications for its combat of 'decoy ransomware' (the use of wipers masquerading as ransomware; see section II) for cyberwarfare aims.

Support for Ukraine from the private sector

The private sector was extremely active in both cyber resilience and cyber governance efforts related to Ukraine in 2022.

Immediately after the invasion, Amazon Web Services (AWS), a US cloud computing company, began to provide Snowball devices to Ukrainian ministries, schools and dozens of other private sector companies.[20] This ruggedized computing and storage hardware helped to transfer data from local servers in Ukraine to the cloud—by June 2022 over 10 petabytes had migrated to more secure, remote storage. Cisco Talos Intelligence Group, a US cybersecurity company, also worked closely with the Ukrainian State Service of Special Communications and Information Protection (SSSCIP), the Cyberpolice Department of the National Police and the National Cybersecurity Coordination Centre (NCCC) to help them respond to cyberattacks.[21] Other vendors, including Bitdefender, Cloudflare, ESET, Google and Sophos, reportedly provided additional or free security services, mechanisms for rapid sharing of intelligence, and encryption key relocation services in Ukraine.[22]

Further, in February 2022 Microsoft issued a statement of support for Ukraine in four areas: 'protecting Ukraine from cyberattacks; protection from state-sponsored disinformation campaigns; support for humanitarian

---

[18] European External Action Service (EEAS), 'Ukraine: EU sets up a cyber lab for the Ukrainian armed forces', 2 Dec. 2022.

[19] European Commission, 'International Counter Ransomware Initiative: Strengthening cybersecurity cooperation & actions', 3 Nov. 2022.

[20] Amazon Web Services, 'Amazon's assistance in Ukraine', 1 Dec. 2022; and Amazon Web Services, 'Safeguarding Ukraine's data to preserve its present and build its future', 9 June 2022.

[21] Biasini, N. et al., 'Ukraine campaign delivers defacement and wipers, in continued escalation', Talos in the Headlines Blog, 21 Jan. 2022.

[22] Beecroft, N., 'Evaluating the international support to Ukrainian cyber defense', Carnegie Endowment for International Peace, 3 Nov. 2022.

assistance; and the protection of [Microsoft's] employees' in Ukraine, Russia and 'the broader region'.[23] While noting that Microsoft is 'a company and not a government or a country', this statement emphasized an unprecedented level of close consultation with the Ukrainian government, the EU, European states, the US government, the North Atlantic Treaty Organization (NATO) and the UN. In fact, the US deputy national security adviser for cyber and emerging technologies, Anne Neuberger, reportedly asked if Microsoft would consider sharing details of the FoxBlade code with Estonia, Latvia, Lithuania, Poland and other European states (see section II), to address US concerns that the malware would spread beyond Ukraine's borders and cripple NATO or West and Central European banks.[24] Microsoft's support for Ukraine became even more direct in April 2022, when it obtained a court order authorizing it to take control of seven internet domains belonging to the Russian hacking group Strontium (also known by other names, such as Sandworm; see section II), which the group had allegedly used to conduct cyberattacks against media organizations, government institutions and think tanks in Ukraine, the USA and the EU.[25]

In February 2022, in addition to asking for Starlink satellite internet terminals (see section III), Mykhailo Fedorov, a Ukrainian vice-prime minister and minister of digital transformation, appealed to 'all major crypto exchanges to block addresses of Russian users' in order to freeze ordinary users, not just Russian and Belarusian politicians.[26] In response, Binance, a cryptocurrency exchange, said that it would block 'accounts of those on the sanctions list' but would not extend this to ordinary users.[27] Dmarket, a non-fungible token (NFT) platform originating from Ukraine, took a more comprehensive approach by cutting 'all relationships with Russia and Belarus', prohibiting sign-ups and freezing the assets of previously registered users in these countries.[28] In March 2022 Fedorov requested that two US computer software companies—Oracle and SAP—end their business relationships in Russia, to which the companies reportedly agreed.[29]

[23] Smith, B., 'Digital technology and the war in Ukraine', Microsoft on the Issues Blog, 28 Feb. 2022.
[24] Sanger, D. E., Barnes, J. E. and Conger, K., 'As tanks rolled into Ukraine, so did malware. Then Microsoft entered the war', *New York Times*, 28 Feb. 2022.
[25] Burt, T., 'Disrupting cyberattacks targeting Ukraine', Microsoft on the Issues Blog, 7 Apr. 2022; and Microsoft, Digital Security Unit, 'An overview of Russia's cyberattack activity in Ukraine', 27 Apr. 2022.
[26] Mykhailo Fedorov (@FedorovMykhailo), Twitter, 27 Feb. 2022, <https://twitter.com/FedorovMykhailo/status/1497922588491792386>. See also Osborne, C., 'Ukraine asks cryptocurrency firms to block Russian users', ZDNET, 1 Mar. 2022.
[27] Wilson, T., 'Crypto exchange Binance blocks Russian users targeted by sanctions', Reuters, 28 Feb. 2022.
[28] Osborne, 'Ukraine asks cryptocurrency firms to block Russian users' (note 26).
[29] Osborne, C., 'Ukraine calls for corporate support as Oracle suspends Russian operations', ZDNET, 2 Mar. 2022.

Not all cases of industry cooperation with Ukraine, however, have resulted in Russian cyber-related interests being successfully isolated. In part, this has been complicated by alleged Russian false flag operations.[30] To circumvent cyberspace-related restrictions, Russia created its own transport layer security (TLS) certificate authority—a trusted entity that issues digital certificates to authenticate content sent from web servers.[31] This solved website access problems following sanctions that prevented certificate renewals and caused browsers to block access to sites with expired certificates. Moreover, not all cyberspace entities have complied with sanction requests from Ukraine. In March 2022, the Internet Corporation for Assigned Names and Numbers (ICANN) responded to a request from Fedorov, stating:

> Within our mission, we maintain neutrality and act in support of the global Internet. Our mission does not extend to taking punitive actions, issuing sanctions, or restricting access against segments of the Internet—regardless of the provocations.... To make unilateral changes would erode trust in the multistakeholder model and the policies designed to sustain global Internet interoperability.[32]

Whether successful or not, such appeals from governments to the private sector have contributed to objections from Russia and China as to the participation of non-governmental stakeholders in OEWG meetings. In 2022, for example, Russia blocked the accreditation of 27 NGOs, including the Cybersecurity Tech Accord, which represents 150 technology companies, from OEWG II meetings.[33]

Challenges to cyber governance from state–non-state cooperation

Some forms of cooperation are potentially more problematic in terms of their impact on cyber governance. In February 2022, for example, Fedorov issued a call for the formation of an Information Technology Army of Ukraine (IT Army)—a crowdsourced community of hackers, including the Anonymous hacker group.[34] Officials from the Ukrainian Ministry of Defence also reportedly approached Yegor Aushev, a Ukrainian businessman and cybersecurity expert, to help organize this unit of hackers via a Telegram channel

---

[30] Biasini et al. (note 21).
[31] Toulas, B., 'Russia creates its own TLS certificate authority to bypass sanctions', Bleeping Computer, 10 Mar. 2022.
[32] Internet Corporation for Assigned Names and Numbers (ICANN), Letter from Göran Marby to Mykhailo Fedorov, 2 Mar. 2022.
[33] Cybersecurity Tech Accord, 'Industry perspective rejected: Cybersecurity Tech Accord releases joint statement on veto by UN cyber working group', 21 July 2022; and Hurel, L. M., 'The rocky road to cyber norms at the United Nations', Council on Foreign Relations, 6 Sep. 2022.
[34] Brewster, T., '"If Kyiv falls, we keep hacking Putin": On the cyber front line in Ukraine', *Forbes*, 25 Feb. 2022; and Miller, M., 'Ukraine's largest telecom stands against Russian cyberattacks', Politico, 7 Sep. 2022.

listing new Russian targets for volunteers to attack.[35] The head of the Ukrainian mobile operator Kyivstar stressed that Ukraine's IT Army has been essential to the company's defence, while the deputy head of the SSSCIP, Victor Zhora, expressed gratitude for its assistance but stressed that the IT Army had no government connection.[36]

This nexus of state and non-state actors has complicated already contentious UN norm-building efforts, particularly when it comes to cyberattacks on civilian critical infrastructure. According to the Ukrainian Ministry of Digital Transformation—the ministry headed by Fedorov—by late February 2022 the IT Army had conducted offensive cyber operations against the Russian public services portal; financial targets including the Moscow Stock Exchange, Sberbank, the BestChange cryptoexchange and the Belarusian National Bank; the websites of the FSB, Roskomnadzor (the media regulation agency), the president, the government and the parliament; and media organizations including TASS, *Kommersant* and Fontanka.[37] The targets cited for potential cyberattack by the IT Army also included railways and the power grid, while an Anonymous-affiliated hacking group called NB65 made disputed claims to have 'shut down the control center' of Russia's Roscosmos space agency.[38]

Whether or not these incidents are regarded as a legitimate response to Russia's aggression, Ukraine's promotion of non-state and state cyberattacks on civilian critical infrastructure inside Russia suggests a longer-term challenge for cyber governance.[39]

Conclusions

The war in Ukraine has witnessed numerous cyberattacks against both civilian and military critical infrastructure, including government and finance institutions, telecommunications networks and power facilities. These ongoing cyberattacks highlight the difficulties in enforcing cyber norms and enhancing cyber governance.

In the light of continuing hostilities in Ukraine and differing views on priorities for cyber governance, it will be difficult to achieve consensus on future

---

[35] Reuters, 'Ukrainian cyber resistance group targets Russian power grid, railways', Gadgets360, 2 Mar. 2022.

[36] Miller (note 34).

[37] Ukrainian Ministry of Digital Transformation, 'IT army blocks Russian sites in a few minutes—The main victories of Ukraine on the cyber front', Ukrainian Government Portal, 28 Feb. 2022.

[38] Schectman, J., Bing, C. and Pearson, J., 'Ukrainian cyber resistance group targets Russian power grid, railways', Reuters, 1 Mar. 2022; and Browne, E., 'Roscosmos head rejects Anonymous claim that Russian satellites were hacked', *Newsweek*, 2 Mar. 2022. See also Council on Foreign Relations, 'Ukrainian IT Army'.

[39] For more on these dynamics see Väljataga, A., 'Cyber vigilantism in support of Ukraine: A legal analysis', NATO Cooperative Cyber Defence Centre of Excellence, Mar. 2022.

measures through multilateral deliberations. There remains potential for a future programme of action on cyberspace after the conclusion of OEWG II in 2025, but this proposed mechanism remains contentious. Debates over private sector and NGO involvement in UN processes also highlight the longer-term challenges in engaging both both governmental and non-governmental stakeholders in norm building and in enforcement.

Nevertheless, there are points of intersection, such as Russia's engagement in bilateral efforts to address cybercrime and the Counter Ransomware Initiative's action plan to combat ransomware, which may have implications for addressing evolving trends in cyberwarfare. However, the crossover between cybercrime tactics and cyberwarfare aims, combined with state engagement of non-state actors in conducting cyberattacks, means that there is greater work to be done on incorporating these points of intersection into cyber governance processes.

12. Dual-use and arms trade controls

Overview

During 2022 a range of global, multilateral and regional efforts sought to strengthen controls on the trade in military items and in dual-use items relevant for conventional, chemical, biological and nuclear weapons and their delivery systems. Membership of the different international and multilateral instruments that seek to establish and promote agreed standards for the trade in arms and dual-use items remained unchanged. However, Russia's invasion of Ukraine in February 2022 significantly disrupted or affected states' efforts in the field of coordinated export measures. Export controls were a key tool through which states in the West sought to limit the capacities of Russia's military and to influence both Russian and Belarusian decision-making. The international tensions arising from the invasion also significantly affected the functioning of the systems of multilateral export controls. The extent to which key aspects of the existing architecture can survive the current crisis remains an open question which will be largely determined by the course of the conflict and the ways in which states continue to use export controls to respond to Russia's actions.

The eighth conference of states parties (CSP8) to the Arms Trade Treaty (ATT) took place from 22 to 26 August 2022 under the presidency of Ambassador Thomas Göbel of Germany, with post-shipment controls as the main thematic focuses of the CSP8 cycle (section I). At CSP8 the Diversion Information Exchange Forum was convened for the first time. As in previous years, levels of reporting declined. There were also ongoing challenges created by, and disagreements about how to respond to, the failure of many states to provide the funds needed to support the ATT Secretariat and the annual cycle of conferences and preparatory meetings. Despite the steady but slow growth in the number of states parties, significant gaps in membership remain, particularly among states in Asia and the Middle East.

During 2022, 14 United Nations embargoes, 22 European Union (EU) embargoes and 1 League of Arab States embargo were in force (section II). A partial UN arms embargo imposed on Haiti, initially proposed by China, was the only new multilateral arms embargo in 2022 and the first new UN arms embargo since the embargo on South Sudan in 2018. The level of international consensus around decisions to lift or extend UN arms embargoes deteriorated in 2022, with disagreements between, on the one hand, China, Russia and several like-minded African states, and mainly Western powers on the other. This was evident in discussions about extending the systems of notification and authorization for transfers to governmental forces that are attached to the UN arms embargoes on the Central African Republic, the Democratic Republic of

SIPRI Yearbook 2023: Armaments, Disarmament and International Security
www.sipriyearbook.org

the Congo, Somalia, South Sudan and Sudan (Darfur). Western states argued in favour of their maintenance while those opposed argued that they impacted these states' ability to improve their security forces.

Together with the United States and 10 like-minded states, the EU put in place a set of security-focused trade restrictions on Russia and Belarus—implemented via member states' domestic export control systems—that were the most significant and wide-ranging ever imposed on a major industrialized state in the post–cold war period (section III). The restrictions clearly disrupted the flow of parts and components to Russia's defence industry, including many that were not previously captured by export control measures and which the Russian defence industry is unable to procure domestically. Nonetheless, there were indications that Russia continued to acquire many of these items in states that are not part of the group that adopted these controls, raising questions about the effectiveness of these measures.

The increased geopolitical tensions precipitated by Russia's invasion of Ukraine significantly affected the work of the four multilateral export control regimes—the Australia Group (on chemical and biological weapons), the Missile Technology Control Regime (MTCR), the Nuclear Suppliers Group (NSG), and the Wassenaar Arrangement on Export Controls for Conventional Arms and Dual-use Goods and Technologies (WA)—but the nature and extent of the disruption varied (section IV). Despite these challenges, the regimes all returned to holding in-person plenary meetings, exchanged experiences and good practices, adopted small numbers of changes to their respective control lists and continued their technical deliberations—including on various emerging technologies. Some, mainly US-based, experts questioned the effectiveness of the multilateral export control regimes during the current crisis and reiterated longstanding calls for potential reforms or new mechanisms.

To implement these four regimes in its single market, the EU has established a common legal basis for controls on the export, brokering, transit and transshipment of dual-use items, software and technology and some military items (section V). The EU is the only regional organization to have developed such a framework. During 2022 the EU took steps to implement a new version of the dual-use regulation which entered into force in 2021. However, the adoption of guidelines required by the new regulation was delayed. The EU and its member states also reported on steps taken to implement the foreign direct investment screening regulation, including its implementation vis-à-vis Russian and Belarussian transactions, and continued to expand its coordination with the USA on export control issues, particularly via the work of the Trade and Technology Council established in 2021. The EU also began work on a review of the common position and discussed how exports of military materiel funded by the European Peace Facility will be managed.

MARK BROMLEY

I. The Arms Trade Treaty

GIOVANNA MALETTA AND LAURIANE HÉAU

Introduction

The 2013 Arms Trade Treaty (ATT) is the first legally binding international agreement to establish standards for regulating the international trade in conventional arms and preventing their illicit transfers.[1] As of 31 December 2022, 113 states were party to the ATT and 28 had signed but not yet ratified it. Three states—Andorra, Gabon and the Philippines—became parties to the treaty in 2022.[2]

Following the disruptions created by the Covid-19 pandemic in 2020 and 2021, the regular ATT meetings cycle, including the conference of states parties (CSP), resumed in 2022. The Working Group on Effective Treaty Implementation (WGETI), the Working Group on Transparency and Reporting (WGTR) and the Working Group on Treaty Universalization (WGTU) held two sets of preparatory meetings in a hybrid format.

The eighth CSP (CSP8) took place from 22 to 26 August 2022 under the presidency of Germany, whose main thematic focus was post-shipment controls. Germany previously indicated that universalization and 'stocktaking with regard to achievements and shortcomings in implementation of the ATT' would also be part of the presidency's themes.[3] CSP8 was conducted in-person although its proceedings were live-streamed from Geneva, enabling virtual attendance but not active participation—unlike the hybrid format adopted for the preparatory meetings. At CSP8 the Diversion Information Exchange Forum (DIEF) was convened for the first time. In attendance at CSP8 were 108 states and representatives from 49 non-state organizations (regional and international organizations, non-governmental organizations (NGOs), research institutes, industry associations and national implementing agencies).[4]

---

[1] For a summary and other details of the Arms Trade Treaty see annex A, section I, in this volume. The 2001 UN Firearms Protocol is also legally binding but only covers controls on the trade in firearms. UN General Assembly Resolution 55/255, Protocol against the Illicit Manufacturing of and Trafficking in Firearms, their Parts and Components and Ammunition, supplementing the UN Convention against Transnational Organized Crime (UN Firearms Protocol), adopted 31 May 2001, entered into force 3 July 2005.

[2] Arms Trade Treaty, 'Treaty status', accessed on 9 Jan. 2023; and Arms Trade Treaty, 'States parties to the ATT (in order of deposit of instrument of ratification, approval, acceptance, or accession)', 2 Dec. 2022.

[3] Arms Trade Treaty, CSP8, 'Final report', ATT/CSP8/2022/SEC/739/Conf.FinRep.Rev 2, 26 Aug. 2022, para. 21; and Maletta, G. and Varisco, A. E., 'The Arms Trade Treaty', *SIPRI Yearbook 2022*, p. 584.

[4] CSP8 was attended by 87 states parties, 20 signatory states and 1 observer state. Non-state actors included 10 observer organizations (including the European Union) and 40 civil society organizations. Arms Trade Treaty, ATT/CSP8/2022/SEC/739/Conf.FinRep.Rev 2 (note 3), paras 3, 7 and 10–15.

The Russian invasion of Ukraine in February 2022 impacted ATT discussions during both the second preparatory meetings and at CSP8, with some states stressing that arms transfers to Russia would violate the provisions of the ATT and calling for such transfers to be halted (see below). The conference determined that South Korea will preside over the ninth CSP (CSP9) in August 2023 in Geneva, with a thematic focus on the role of industry in responsible international transfers of conventional arms.[5]

This section provides an overview of key ATT-related developments during 2022 and at CSP8. First, it focuses on issues related to treaty implementation, particularly the thematic discussion on post-shipment controls. It then looks at the status of ATT transparency and reporting, followed by the status of universalization and developments regarding the provision of international assistance. Finally, it analyses issues related to the financial health and functioning of the treaty and concludes with a summary of the main achievements and shortcomings of CSP8.

Treaty implementation

Addressing diversion through 'post-shipment controls and coordination'

The German presidency's approach towards the theme of post-shipment controls evolved throughout the CSP8 cycle. Initially seen as a tool for exporting states, such controls were eventually presented as one of the collaborative measures that exporting and importing states could use to prevent arms diversion, which is one of the stated objectives of the ATT.[6]

The ATT has addressed post-shipment controls regularly since the fourth CSP, including at side-events organized by Germany and Switzerland and through exchanges in the framework of the WGETI sub-working group on Article 11.[7] In 2021, Canada also sent a questionnaire to ATT states parties to collect information on best practices in post-shipment controls, although the results were not made public.[8] In the run-up to CSP8, Germany organized two side events to facilitate discussions on the topic. The first took place in

---

[5] Arms Trade Treaty, 'President'; Arms Trade Treaty, ATT/CSP8/2022/SEC/739/Conf.FinRep.Rev 2 (note 3), para. 39; and Control Arms, '8th conference of states parties to the Arms Trade Treaty: Daily summary analysis report—26 August 2022', 26 Aug. 2022, p. 5.

[6] Arms Trade Treaty, CSP8 president, 'Post-shipment controls and coordination: Effective export verification and good-faith cooperation between exporters and importers—status quo and guidance ("Toolbox")', Working paper, ATT/CSP8/2022/PRES/732/Conf.PostShip, 22 July 2022.

[7] See e.g. Arms Trade Treaty, 'CSP4 schedule of side events'; ATT Working Group on Effective Treaty Implementation (WGETI), 'Possible measures to prevent and address diversion', July 2018; 'Post-shipment verifications: A new instrument of arms export controls', Side-event hosted by the governments of Germany and Switzerland at the fifth CSP, 28 Aug. 2019; and Control Arms, 'ATT working group and information preparatory meetings for the seventh conference of states parties to the Arms Trade Treaty', Summary Analysis Report, 26 Apr. 2021.

[8] Gallagher, K., 'The ATT in 2022: Focus on post-shipment controls', *Ploughshares Monitor*, vol. 43, no. 2 (6 June 2022).

February 2022 during the first CSP8 working group and informal preparatory meetings and was open only to ATT states parties.[9] The second event, open to all ATT stakeholders, including civil society and industry, was organized in April 2022 during the second round of CSP8 preparatory meetings.[10] These discussions informed the drafting of a working paper on post-shipment controls and coordination that Germany presented at CSP8, which explains that, in line with German practice, the term 'post-shipment controls' would be 'primarily used' in the document to refer to the 'physical on-site inspection of items by the exporting state after they have been delivered to the final end-user'.[11] The paper outlines the legal and operational challenges which can arise in adopting and carrying out these inspections and serves as a 'toolbox' to address such difficulties. At the same time, the paper also acknowledges the existence of different forms of 'post-shipment control' measures and refers to the opportunity to frame this activity as a way to promote post-delivery coordination between importing and exporting states.[12]

While CSP8 welcomed the discussion on post-shipment controls, the language agreed by states parties in the final report was more limited than the set of draft recommendations put forward by Germany. States parties agreed 'to continue discussing approaches and understandings' of post-shipment controls, and to 'share their experiences' regarding the implementation of this policy tool, but dropped references to defining a 'common understanding' and a 'common approach' to post-shipment controls, while adding a reference to avoiding 'setting additional burdens beyond the obligations of the Treaty'.[13] Several states parties expressed an interest in pursuing discussions on post-shipment controls beyond CSP8, and 'post-delivery cooperation' will continue to be explored by the WGETI sub-working group on Article 11 during CSP9.[14]

Developments in the Working Group on Effective Treaty Implementation

The WGETI is currently divided into three sub-working groups covering specific areas of ATT implementation, namely Article 6 ('Prohibitions') and Article 7 ('Export and Export Assessment'), Article 9 ('Transit or Trans-shipment'), and Article 11 ('Diversion').

The sub-working group on articles 6 and 7 continued to focus on the development of a voluntary guide to assist states parties in implementing

---

[9] German Federal Foreign Office, 'Thematic debate on "post shipment control" (to start at PrepMeet 1)', Concept Paper, 2022.
[10] Arms Trade Treaty, 'Working group meetings and 2nd CSP8 informal preparatory meeting'.
[11] Arms Trade Treaty, ATT/CSP8/2022/PRES/732/Conf.PostShip (note 6), p. 4.
[12] Arms Trade Treaty, ATT/CSP8/2022/PRES/732/Conf.PostShip (note 6), p. 4.
[13] Arms Trade Treaty, ATT/CSP8/2022/SEC/739/Conf.FinRep.Rev 2 (note 3), para. 21; and Arms Trade Treaty, CSP8, 'Draft final report', ATT/CSP8/2022/SEC/739/Conf.FinRep, 26 Aug. 2022, para. 21.
[14] Control Arms, '8th conference of states parties to the Arms Trade Treaty: Daily summary analysis report—26 August 2022' (note 5), pp. 2–5.

these articles, and discussing and completing the draft of chapter 1 ('Key concepts') during the CSP8 preparatory process.[15] In response to concerns raised by some states and NGOs, the facilitator of the sub-working group stressed that the aim of this exercise was not to reinterpret concepts of international law, but to ensure that definitions agreed under international law are made available in the voluntary guide.[16] CSP8 noted the completion of chapter 1, 'as a living document of a voluntary nature' that the WGETI would update 'as appropriate'.[17] The facilitator of the sub-working group will begin work on chapter 2 ('Prohibitions') of the voluntary guide, to be presented during the first meeting of the CSP9 cycle in 2023.[18] Once all chapters of the guide are final, the group will submit the document to the CSP for endorsement.[19]

The sub-working group on Article 9 focused on measures to regulate the transit and trans-shipment of arms by land, air and sea, as well as the role of the private sector. The facilitator will begin work on draft elements for a possible voluntary guide on the implementation of Article 9 to be presented in the first meeting of the sub-working group in the CSP9 cycle in 2023.[20]

The sub-working group on Article 11 held discussions on diversion prevention both during and after arms deliveries, and submitted a draft background paper on the role of transit and trans-shipment states in preventing diversion.[21] The sub-working group also addressed post-delivery cooperation, holding exchanges on the role of importing states in preventing diversion, and the role of the private sector and civil society in mitigating it.[22] The sub-working group on Article 11 reached the end of its multi-year workplan, but CSP8 agreed to extend its mandate for one more year to focus on post-delivery cooperation, notably to continue the work undertaken by the CSP8 presidency.[23]

More substantial exchanges on treaty implementation emerged during the general debate in connection with concerns raised regarding the Russian invasion of Ukraine. Some statements called for states parties to refrain from exporting weapons to Russia, arguing that such actions would constitute a

---

[15] Arms Trade Treaty, CSP8, WGETI, 'Chair's draft report to CSP8', ATT/CSP8.WGETI/2022/CHAIR/733/Conf.Rep, 22 July 2022, para. 37(a).
[16] ATT Secretariat, 'ATT working groups' and 1st CSP8 informal preparatory meetings, Day 1, English', YouTube, 15 Feb. 2022.
[17] Arms Trade Treaty, ATT/CSP8/2022/SEC/739/Conf.FinRep.Rev 2 (note 3), para. 23.
[18] Arms Trade Treaty, ATT/CSP8.WGETI/2022/CHAIR/733/Conf.Rep (note 15), para. 24.
[19] Arms Trade Treaty, ATT/CSP8/2022/SEC/739/Conf.FinRep.Rev 2 (note 3), para. 23.
[20] Arms Trade Treaty, ATT/CSP8.WGETI/2022/CHAIR/733/Conf.Rep (note 15), p. 5; and Arms Trade Treaty, ATT/CSP8/2022/SEC/739/Conf.FinRep.Rev 2 (note 3), para. 25.
[21] Arms Trade Treaty, ATT/CSP8.WGETI/2022/CHAIR/733/Conf.Rep (note 15), para. 13.
[22] Arms Trade Treaty, ATT/CSP8.WGETI/2022/CHAIR/733/Conf.Rep (note 15), p. 6.
[23] Arms Trade Treaty, ATT/CSP8/2022/SEC/739/Conf.FinRep.Rev 2 (note 3), para. 26.

violation of the principles and provisions of the treaty.[24] This was only the second time that such calls had been made during an official ATT meeting, the other time being at the third CSP in relation to arms transfers to Venezuela.[25] Conversely, some states recognized the legitimacy of arms transfers towards Ukraine under the ATT. This was justified as being both in line with the right of Ukraine to acquire weapons in the exercise of its right to self-defence, as also recognized by the ATT, and in compliance with articles 6 and 7.[26] China, in contrast, stressed the 'irresponsible and escalatory nature of arms transfers to conflict zones'.[27]

The Diversion Information Exchange Forum

The DIEF is a subsidiary body established by the sixth CSP (CSP6) in 2020 to enable 'informal voluntary exchanges' concerning cases of detected or suspected diversion.[28] However, the ongoing Covid-19 pandemic prevented the DIEF from convening until 2022, when it held its first meeting during CSP8, chaired by Alejandro Alba Fernández of Mexico. To enable discussions on a particularly sensitive topic, DIEF meetings are convened in a closed format—that is, they are only open to states parties and signatory states.[29] The oral report from the DIEF chair to CSP8 indicated that at the inaugural DIEF meeting, four states parties gave presentations, which covered suspected and detected cases of diversion, and bilateral cooperation to address illicit arms trafficking.[30] Two DIEF meetings are scheduled to take place during the CSP9 meetings cycle in May and August 2023.[31] A review regarding the usefulness

---

[24] See e.g. Arms Trade Treaty, CSP8, European Union, 'EU general statement', Aug. 2022, pp. 2–3; Italy, 'General statement', 22 Aug. 2022, p. 2; United Kingdom, 'General debate statement: Agenda item 5', Aug. 2022, p. 1; Netherlands, 'Statement of the Netherlands', 23 Aug. 2022, p. 3; and Control Arms, 'General statement', 23 Aug. 2022, p. 2. See also Control Arms, '8th conference of states parties to the Arms Trade Treaty: Daily summary analysis report—22 August 2022', 22 Aug. 2022, p. 4; and Control Arms, '8th conference of states parties to the Arms Trade Treaty: Daily summary analysis report—23 August 2022', 23 Aug. 2022, p. 5.

[25] See Varisco, A. E., Maletta, G. and Robin, L., *Taking Stock of the Arms Trade Treaty: Achievements, Challenges and Ways Forward* (SIPRI: Stockholm, Dec. 2021), pp. 18–19.

[26] Control Arms, '8th conference of states parties to the Arms Trade Treaty: Daily summary analysis report—23 August 2022' (note 24), p. 1; and Arms Trade Treaty, CSP8, Austria, 'Statement by Austria/General debate', 22 Aug. 2022.

[27] Control Arms, '8th conference of states parties to the Arms Trade Treaty: Daily summary analysis report—23 August 2022' (note 24), p. 1.

[28] Arms Trade Treaty, Diversion Information Exchange Forum, 'Terms of reference', Aug. 2020, p. 2, para. 1.

[29] States can propose to invite non-state experts with specific expertise in investigating, establishing. identifying or addressing cases of diversion to take part in a presentation on a concrete diversion case and the subsequent debate on that case.

[30] Control Arms, '8th conference of states parties to the Arms Trade Treaty: Daily summary analysis report—25 August 2022', 25 Aug. 2022, p. 1.

[31] Control Arms, 'ATT Working Group Meetings and 1st CSP9 Informal Preparatory Meeting: Summary analysis report', 14–17 Feb. 2023, p. 19.

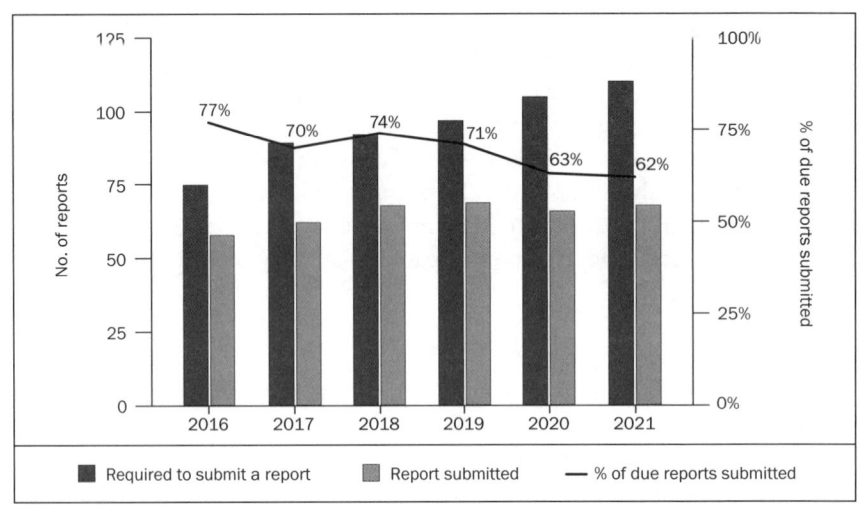

Figure 12.1. Number of Arms Trade Treaty states parties submitting annual reports, 2016–21

Source: ATT Secretariat, 'Annual reports', Status at 10 Jan. 2023.

of the DIEF is scheduled to take place 'at the first CSP following two cycles of DIEF meetings'.[32]

Transparency and reporting

Article 13(1) of the ATT requires states parties to provide an initial report to the ATT Secretariat of 'measures undertaken in order to implement' the treaty within one year after entry into force at the national level. According to the same provision, states are also required to report when appropriate 'on any new measures undertaken in order to implement' the treaty. No new state party was due to submit an initial report to the secretariat in 2022 and no new reports were submitted. One state, Romania, provided an updated initial report, making use of the template endorsed in 2021 at the seventh CSP (CSP7).[33] As a result, as of 31 December 2022, the number of states parties that have failed to submit their initial report when due remained unchanged (24 out of 110, 22 per cent).[34] States can choose to make their initial reports available only to other states parties. The total number of restricted access

---

[32] Arms Trade Treaty, CSP7, 'Final report', ATT/CSP7/2021/SEC/681/Conf.Fin.Rep.Rev1, 2 Sep. 2021, para. 27; see Maletta and Varisco (note 3), p. 587.

[33] Romanian government, 'Initial report on measures undertaken to implement the Arms Trade Treaty, in accordance with its article 13(1)', Update, 7 Feb. 2022.

[34] ATT Secretariat, 'Initial reports', Status at 28 Apr. 2022.

initial reports stands at 21 (24 per cent of the 86 initial reports submitted).[35] The recent trend has been to increasingly restrict access to initial reports, with 9 of the 13 initial reports submitted since 2018 not made public.[36]

Under Article 13(3) of the ATT, states parties are also required to submit an annual report to the secretariat on 'authorized or actual exports and imports of conventional arms'. Out of the 110 states required to submit an annual report covering 2021, 68 (62 per cent) had done so by 31 December 2022.[37] While the overall number of reports is consistent with previous years, the percentage of states parties making submissions is falling (figure 12.1). Moreover, the rate of annual reports submitted on time (i.e. by 31 May 2022) fell from 75 per cent in 2021 to 71 per cent in 2022. Several states also chose to aggregate data or leave certain sections blank, which limited the comprehensiveness of their reports.[38] About half (33) of the states that submitted a report have done so by using the reporting template endorsed by CSP7 in 2021.[39] China submitted its first annual report in 2022, in accordance with its treaty obligations, but did not make the report publicly available. Six other states—Botswana, Côte d'Ivoire, Guatemala, Iceland, Niger, and the Seychelles—started submitting annual reports for the first time after one or more years of non-compliance.[40] In 2022, Côte d'Ivoire also submitted all of its required reports from previous years, going back to 2016.[41] However, with the exception of Iceland, all of these states chose to make their reports available only to other states parties.

Of the 110 annual reports due for 2021, 64 reports were either not submitted (42) or not made public (22).[42] However, four states parties (Albania, Burkina Faso, Maldives and Malta) made their annual report publicly available after sending restricted-access reports in the past. As in previous years, the list of states parties that submitted a restricted-access annual report for 2021 includes countries (e.g. China, Greece, Latvia and Lithuania) that made their submission public in the context of other reporting instruments that have a similar scope, such as the United Nations Register of Conventional Arms (UNROCA).[43] On a positive note, for the first time in 2022, ATT states parties

---

[35] ATT Secretariat, 'Initial reports' (note 34). In 2022, Grenada decided to change the access to its initial report from public to restricted. Countries that had already restricted access to their initial reports include Benin, Botswana, Burkina Faso, Cameroon, Chile, China, Cyprus, Greece, Guatemala, Honduras, Kazakhstan, Madagascar, Maldives, Malta, Mauritius, Nigeria, Saint Vincent and the Grenadines, Senegal, Palestine and Tuvalu.
[36] Maletta and Varisco (note 3), p. 589.
[37] ATT Secretariat, 'Annual reports', Status at 10 Jan. 2023.
[38] Stohl, R. and Fletcher, R., 'Mixed reviews: Positive developments and negative trends in 2021 ATT annual reports', Stimson Center, Oct. 2022, p. 20.
[39] '1st meeting, Working Group on Transparency and Reporting (WGTR)—Arms Trade Treaty', UN Web TV, 14 Feb. 2023, c. 00:22:12 to 00:41:10.
[40] ATT Secretariat, 'Annual reports' (note 37).
[41] Stohl and Fletcher (note 38), p. 5.
[42] ATT Secretariat, 'Annual reports' (note 37).
[43] United Nations Register of Conventional Arms (UNROCA), 'National reports', 2022. On reporting within UNROCA see chapter 10, section IV, in this volume.

Table 12.1. Arms Trade Treaty numbers of ratifications, accessions and signatories, by region, December 2022

Region	States	States parties	Signatories	Other non-parties
Africa	53	29	11	13
Americas	35	27	3[a]	5
Asia	29	7	6	16
Europe	48[b]	42	1	5[b]
Middle East	16[c]	2[c]	4	10
Oceania	16[d]	6[e]	3	7[f]
Total	**197**	**113**	**28**	**56**

Notes: The treaty was open for signature until it entered into force in Dec. 2014. Existing signatories may accept, approve or ratify the treaty in order to become a state party. A non-signatory state must now directly accede to the treaty in order to become a state party.

[a] This figure includes the United States. On 18 July 2019, the USA announced its intention not to become a state party to the treaty.
[b] This figure includes the Holy See.
[c] This figure includes Palestine.
[d] This figure includes Niue and the Cook Islands.
[e] This figure includes Niue.
[f] This figure includes the Cook Islands.

Source: United Nations, UN Treaty Collection, Status of Treaties, Status at 31 Dec. 2022.

could check a box in their ATT annual report to allow its use as the basis for their UNROCA submission, and at least 23 states parties did so.[44]

The CSP8 final report highlighted 'concern for the low rate of compliance with the reporting obligations'.[45] During the CSP8 meetings cycle, the WGTR examined the status of and challenges to effective reporting, including the quality of the data reported, and revised the 'FAQ'-type guidance document on the annual reporting obligation.[46] The CSP8 endorsed the revised document and mandated the WGTR co-chairs to 'continue to focus on enhancing compliance with the reporting requirements' as well as to discuss 'mechanisms, processes or formats that facilitate information exchange and topics related to the IT platform' during the CSP9 cycle.[47] The IT platform—developed and managed by the ATT Secretariat—enables states parties to exchange information and submit their reports online, but it remains under-used (e.g. only 10 states used the online reporting tool for their 2021 reports).[48] The CSP8 reporting mandate contained fewer specific tasks

---

[44] ATT Secretariat, 'Annual reports' (note 37). See also Holtom, P. and Mensah, A. E. E., 'The end of transparency in international arms?', UNIDIR Comment, 14 Sep. 2022.
[45] Arms Trade Treaty, ATT/CSP8/2022/SEC/739/Conf.FinRep.Rev 2 (note 3), pp. 6–7.
[46] Arms Trade Treaty, CSP8, Working Group on Transparency and Reporting (WGTR), 'Co-chairs' draft report to CSP8', ATT/CSP8.WGTR/2022/CHAIR/734/Conf.Rep, 22 July 2022, pp. 2–4.
[47] Arms Trade Treaty, ATT/CSP8/2022/SEC/739/Conf.FinRep.Rev 2 (note 3), para. 27; and WGTR (note 46), p. 5.
[48] Arms Trade Treaty, CSP8, WGTR (note 46), p. 4; and '1st meeting, Working Group on Transparency and Reporting—Arms Trade Treaty' (note 39), c. 00:22:12 to 00:41:10.

Treaty universalization and international assistance

Status of treaty universalization

In 2022, three new states (Andorra, Gabon and the Philippines) joined or ratified the ATT, bringing the overall number of states parties to 113 (table 12.1).[49] The level of participation in the ATT by states in the Asia-Pacific and Middle East regions continues to be comparatively low.[50]

During the CSP8 cycle the co-chairs of the WGTU pursued efforts to promote the treaty's universalization. These included activities targeting the Asia-Pacific region, diplomatic initiatives ('demarches') to specific countries supported by the European Union (EU), and bilateral engagements with states that were considered to be close to joining the treaty.[51] The WGTU co-chairs also reflected on the role of the working group and prepared a draft paper containing elements on how to improve its functioning.[52] The paper seeks to promote a longer-term approach in the work of the WGTU—in line with the extended timelines of ratification and accession processes—as well as to improve coordination among different efforts in support of ATT universalization. The CSP8 adopted the paper and mandated the WGTU to develop the recommended measures into a proposal to be presented at CSP9.[53]

International assistance

In 2022, of 16 applications received, 6 assistance projects were selected for funding under the ATT Voluntary Trust Fund (VTF), bringing the total number of VTF projects funded to 69.[54] This was the lowest number of projects selected in a VTF cycle since the fund was established in 2016.[55] To date, the VTF has received over US$11 million in voluntary contributions from 28 states, of which $6.2 million were either spent or committed up to August

---

[49] Arms Trade Treaty, 'Treaty status' (note 2).

[50] Dladla, D., 'Arms Trade Treaty: Status of participation', Presentation at the Arms Trade Treaty, CSP8, Geneva, 23 Aug. 2022; and Control Arms, '8th conference of states parties to the Arms Trade Treaty: Daily summary analysis report—23 August 2022' (note 24), p. 4.

[51] Arms Trade Treaty, CSP8, Working Group on Universalization (WGTU), 'Co-Chairs draft report to CSP8', ATT/CSP8.WGTU/2022/CHAIR/735/Conf.Rep, 22 July 2022.

[52] Arms Trade Treaty, ATT/CSP8.WGTU/2022/CHAIR/735/Conf.Rep (note 51), pp. 5–6.

[53] Arms Trade Treaty, ATT/CSP8/2022/SEC/739/Conf.FinRep.Rev 2 (note 3), para. 22(a).

[54] Since the first VTF funding cycle was launched a total of 74 project applications were initially approved for funding, including 5 later withdrawn and 1 discontinued. ATT Secretariat, 'Report on the work of the ATT Voluntary Trust Fund (VTF) for the period August 2021 to August 2022', ATT/VTF/2022/CHAIR/736/Conf.Rep, 2022.

[55] ATT Secretariat, ATT/VTF/2022/CHAIR/736/Conf.Rep (note 54).

2022.[56] During 2022, the ATT Secretariat also started the Covid-19 delayed evaluation of VTF projects concluded in 2017, and will report on the outcome of this exercise at CSP9.[57]

EU support for ATT implementation included activities undertaken by the ATT Secretariat as part of an EU-funded project launched in 2021.[58] In 2022, these activities included two briefings, a train-the-trainer workshop, the development of a guidance document for the ATT national points of contact and an ATT training manual.[59]

The EU also launched the third phase of the EU ATT Outreach Project.[60]

The contentious issue of whether compliance with financial obligations under the ATT should be a criterion for selection of VTF projects took centre stage during CSP8, highlighting traditional UN regional divisions. Past conferences (particularly the fifth and sixth CSPs) had discussed the proposed financial obligations–assistance linkage, which primarily Western states support as an incentive for states in arrears to pay their financial contributions. However, the states—particularly from Africa and Latin America and the Caribbean—that are most in need of international assistance and those struggling with financial obligations have always strongly opposed this position.[61] At CSP8, states' divergent views on the issue resurfaced and required additional discussions to find consensus on relevant language in the final report. Some states (e.g. Canada, the Netherlands and the United Kingdom) advanced proposals to make compliance with financial obligations part of the VTF selection criteria, while the German presidency proposed deferring discussions to CSP9. All these proposals were rejected.[62] As a result, the CSP8 final report confirmed that the work of the VTF Selection Committee 'will continue to be guided by the VTF Terms of Reference' and did not exclude states in arrears with their financial contributions from being beneficiaries of VTF projects.[63]

---

[56] ATT Secretariat, ATT/VTF/2022/CHAIR/736/Conf.Rep (note 54), p. 9; and Dladla, D., 'Arms Trade Treaty: Status of VTF finances', Presentation at the Arms Trade Treaty, CSP8, Geneva, 25 Aug. 2022.

[57] ATT Secretariat, ATT/VTF/2022/CHAIR/736/Conf.Rep (note 54), para. 27.

[58] Maletta and Varisco (note 3), p. 592.

[59] ATT Secretariat, 'Report on the ATT Secretariat's work for the period 2021/2022', ATT/CSP8/2022/SEC/729/Conf.SecRep, 22 July 2022, pp. 6–7. For the workshop see 'Key activities', UNIDIR Update, Jan. 2023.

[60] Control Arms, '8th conference of states parties to the Arms Trade Treaty: Daily summary analysis report—24 August 2022', 24 Aug. 2022, p. 4; and Council of the European Union, Council Decision (CFSP) 2021/2309 of 22 December 2021 on Union outreach activities in support of the implementation of the Arms Trade Treaty, *Official Journal of the European Union*, L461, 22 Dec. 2022.

[61] See Varisco, A. E., Maletta, G. and Robin, L., 'The Arms Trade Treaty', *SIPRI Yearbook 2021*, pp. 562–63; and Maletta, G. and Bromley, M., 'The Arms Trade Treaty', *SIPRI Yearbook 2020*, pp. 529–31.

[62] Control Arms, '8th conference of states parties to the Arms Trade Treaty: Daily summary analysis report—25 August 2022' (note 30).

[63] Arms Trade Treaty, ATT/CSP8/2022/SEC/739/Conf.FinRep.Rev 2 (note 3), para. 31.

The financial situation of the ATT

In 2022, the financial situation of the ATT continued to deteriorate. The financial rules of the ATT require all states parties and signatories, as well as states attending conferences as observers, to make financial contributions to cover the costs of organizing relevant meetings and the work of the ATT Secretariat. However, as at 31 October 2022, 58 out of the 155 states that have been obliged to make contributions since 2015 had failed to do so, creating an accumulated deficit of $512 559.[64] The head of the ATT Secretariat outlined the detrimental impact this budget deficit is likely to have and also noted that no state had made use of the procedures agreed at CSP7 to assist states in arrears. Finally, he reminded states that they can also voluntarily contribute to an ATT reserve fund to which Germany had already pledged €50 000.[65] One proposal was to cut costs by reducing the number of preparatory meetings, and CSP8 mandated the Management Committee to explore this possibility and submit a proposal to CSP9.[66]

Conclusions

Key developments within the ATT in 2022 and at CSP8 highlight long-standing challenges of improving transparency through reporting on arms transfers, expanding ATT membership and ensuring the financial stability of the treaty. Discussions at CSP8 also highlighted the presence of different views among states parties regarding some aspects of ATT implementation. The main topic of contention proved to be whether to make compliance with financial obligations one of the selection criteria for VTF projects. Financial-related issues continued to absorb a large amount of time and to generate the most heated discussions, while, in comparison, limited attention was given to addressing cases where states parties' arms transfers appeared to violate core provisions of the ATT, particularly its prohibition and risk assessment criteria.[67]

However, some substantial discussions at CSP8 did take place in relation to arms transfers in the war in Ukraine. A series of statements called on states parties to refrain from exporting weapons to Russia, in response to its invasion of Ukraine, and stressed that such transfers would violate the prin-

---

[64] ATT Secretariat, 'Status of contributions to ATT budgets', Status at 31 Oct. 2022.
[65] Dladla, D., 'Arms Trade Treaty: Status of ATT finances', Presentation at the Arms Trade Treaty, CSP8, Geneva, 25 Aug. 2022.
[66] Control Arms, '8th conference of states parties to the Arms Trade Treaty: Daily summary analysis report—26 August 2022' (note 5); and Arms Trade Treaty, ATT/CSP8/2022/SEC/739/Conf.FinRep. Rev 2 (note 3), para. 36.
[67] See e.g. Republic of Panama, Permanent Mission to the United Nations, 'Punto de la agenda 10—Asistencia internacional' [Agenda item 10–International assistance], Statement by G. Rodríguez to the Arms Trade Treaty, CSP8, 25 Aug. 2022. See also Maletta and Bromley (note 61), p. 562.

ciples and provisions of the treaty. NGO representatives noted these calls positively, and also called for states parties to provide details on their arms transfer decisions concerning other conflict-affected recipients.[68]

Further exchanges between states parties took place during CSP8 on post-shipment controls, and again, there were significantly differing views on the topic. This led to weaker language in the final report and no concrete recommendations beyond calling for more discussions on the issue. Future meetings of the DIEF, which became fully operational during CSP8, offer the opportunity for more substantial exchanges among states on how different types of post-shipment control measures can be used to prevent or mitigate the risk of diversion.

[68] See e.g. Arms Trade Treaty, CSP8, Control Arms, 'General statement' (note 24), p. 2.

II. Multilateral arms embargoes

PIETER D. WEZEMAN

Arms embargoes are restrictions on transfers of arms and related services and, in certain cases, dual-use items. This section discusses developments in multilateral arms embargoes, that is, those imposed by the United Nations, European Union (EU) and other multilateral bodies. The UN Security Council uses its powers under Chapter VII of the UN Charter to impose arms embargoes that are binding for all UN member states and which form part of what the UN generally refers to as 'sanctions measures'.[1] During 2022, 14 UN arms embargoes were in force (see table 12.2, end of section). The EU imposes arms embargoes under its Common Foreign and Security Policy (CFSP) that are binding for EU member states and which form part of what the EU generally refers to as 'restrictive measures'.[2] During 2022, 22 EU arms embargoes were in force, of which 11 matched the coverage of a UN arms embargo; 3 (Iran, South Sudan and Sudan) were broader in duration, geographical scope or the types of arms covered; while 8 had no UN counterpart. The Arab League had one arms embargo in place (on Syria) that also had no UN counterpart. In addition, one voluntary multilateral embargo imposed by the Conference on Security and Co-operation in Europe (CSCE, now renamed the Organization for Security and Co-operation in Europe, OSCE) was in force for arms deliveries to forces engaged in combat in the Nagorno-Karabakh area.[3]

One new multilateral arms embargo was imposed in 2022, a UN partial arms embargo on Haiti. This was the first new UN arms embargo since measures were imposed on South Sudan in 2018.

Multilateral arms embargoes vary in their terms. Most cover arms, military materiel and related services. Some UN and EU arms embargoes also cover certain exports or imports of dual-use items that can be used both for civilian purposes and to produce, maintain or operate conventional, biological, chemical or nuclear weapons.[4] Certain EU arms embargoes also cover equipment that might be used for internal repression or certain types of communication surveillance equipment. Multilateral arms embargoes also

---

[1] United Nations, Security Council, 'Sanctions'.
[2] European Council, 'Sanctions: How and when the EU adopts restrictive measures'.
[3] Conference on Security and Co-operation in Europe, Committee of Senior Officials, Statement, Annex 1 to Journal no. 2 of the seventh meeting of the Committee, Prague, 27–28 Feb. 1992.
[4] The UN and EU embargoes on Iran and North Korea apply to dual-use items on the control lists of the Nuclear Suppliers Group (NSG) and the Missile Technology Control Regime (MTCR). The UN and EU embargoes on Somalia apply to certain dual-use items on the control lists of the Wassenaar Arrangement that can be used to produce, maintain and operate improvised explosive devices. The EU embargo on Russia applies to transfers to military end-users of all items on the EU's dual-use list. For details of the NSG, MTCR and the Wassenaar Arrangement, see annex B, section III, in this volume.

vary in the types of restrictions imposed and recipients targeted. Some place a ban on all transfers to the state in question, while others ban transfers to a non-state actor or group of non-state actors. Some embargoes are 'partial', in that they allow transfers to the state in question provided the supplier or recipient state has received permission from, or notified, the relevant UN sanctions committee or the UN Security Council.

This section reviews significant developments and implementation issues in UN arms embargoes in 2022. In particular, the section highlights cases where new embargoes or amendments to embargoes were implemented or debated. It also gives examples of actual or alleged embargo violations as reported in UN investigations or discussed in the UN Security Council.[5] Unlike the UN, neither the EU, the Arab League nor the OSCE has systematic mechanisms in place for monitoring compliance with their arms embargoes. There were no significant developments in Arab League and OSCE arms embargoes in 2022. The main development in EU arms embargoes was the significant expansion in the scope of its arms embargoes on Belarus and Russia in response to Russia's invasion of Ukraine in February 2022. These measures—which were taken in coordination with the United States and a coalition of ten other like-minded states—are discussed in section III of this chapter.

United Nations arms embargoes: Developments and implementation issues

During 2022 the UN introduced one new arms embargo, but made few significant amendments to existing embargoes. This subsection provides a concise overview of the most notable developments in UN arms embargoes in 2022 in relation to the Central African Republic (CAR), Democratic Republic of Congo (DRC), Haiti, Iran, Libya, South Sudan and Sudan. It also highlights notable violations and alleged violations of UN arms embargoes in 2022, primarily based on reports by UN panels and groups of experts that monitor them.

Disagreement on UN sanctions that restrict arms supplies to governments

The UN arms embargoes on CAR, the DRC, Somalia, South Sudan and Sudan (Darfur) are all 'partial' in that they ban any arms transfers to non-state armed groups while maintaining systems of permission or notification for supplies of arms to the government forces of these states. In 2022 disagreement within the UN Security Council about these systems of permission or notification

---

[5] See e.g. Varisco, A. E., Wezeman, P. D. and Kuimova, A., *Illicit Small Arms and Light Weapons in Sub-Saharan Africa: Using UN Reports on Arms Embargoes to Identify Sources, Challenges and Policy Measures* (SIPRI: Stockholm, Dec. 2022).

increased. A majority of Security Council members were in favour of keeping them in place in some form, while in each case several states argued for lifting them and abstained from the votes on resolutions calling for their extension.

The systems of permission or notification attached to the UN arms embargo on CAR have been gradually eased in recent years. From 2019 delivery of most types of small arms and light weapons (SALW) was allowed if the government provided advance notification to the relevant UN sanctions committee, while other arms could be supplied after advance approval from the sanctions committee. In 2020 and 2021 the UN further expanded the category of weapons for which only advance notification was required, but in 2022 fully dropped the requirement for advance approval, leaving only a requirement for advance notification of any arms supplies.[6]

In 2021 for the first time one of the five permanent members, China, abstained from the vote on extending the embargo on CAR.[7] In 2022 five countries (China, Gabon, Ghana, Kenya and Russia) abstained from the vote for the resolution on amending and extending the embargo, stressing that the resolution did not include a full lifting of the restrictions on arms supplies to the government of CAR, as called for by the African Union, the Economic Community of Central African States and the International Conference on the Great Lakes Region.[8] Russia argued that opposition to the views of Africans on the full lifting of sanctions had 'become a trend', pointing at similar discussions in the Security Council about lifting restrictions on arms supplies to South Sudan and the DRC, and claimed that Western states in particular have a desire to maintain 'political influence' by 'using Security Council sanctions mechanisms . . . for their own opportunistic purposes'.[9]

The UN arms embargo on South Sudan allows arms supplies to government forces if they are approved in advance by the UN sanctions committee. When the embargo was imposed in 2018 and extended in 2019 and 2020, China, Russia and several elected member states abstained from the vote, arguing that the sanctions did not take into account progress in the South Sudan peace process. In 2021 China and Russia voted in favour of an extension, but remained sceptical about the restrictions and controls on arms supplies to the government.[10] In 2022 China and Russia again abstained, together with Gabon, India and Kenya, in the vote to extend the restrictions by another year. All five states mentioned the positive developments towards peace in South Sudan and the need for its government to be able to acquire military equipment as key reasons for abstaining. Russia argued that the current

---

[6] UN Security Council Resolution 2536, 28 July 2020; UN Security Council Resolution 2588, 29 July 2021; and UN Security Council Resolution 2648, 29 July 2022.
[7] Bromley, M. and Wezeman, P. D., 'Multilateral arms embargoes', *SIPRI Yearbook 2022*, pp. 600–601.
[8] United Nations, Security Council, 9105th meeting, S/PV.9105, 29 July 2022, pp. 4–8.
[9] United Nations, Security Council, S/PV.9105 (note 8), 29 July 2022, p. 6.
[10] Bromley and Wezeman (note 7), pp. 605–606.

UN sanctions no longer corresponded to the situation on the ground and hindered the government's state-building efforts and formation of security forces. China also argued that the sanctions restricted South Sudan from building up its security capacity. China, Gabon, Kenya and Russia each also referred to the call by the Intergovernmental Authority on Development and the African Union to lift the arms embargo as a reason for abstaining.[11]

In 2022 China, Gabon, Ghana and Russia abstained from a vote on a resolution that included extending arms procurement notification requirements for the supply to the government of Somalia of certain weapons categories and advance approval requirements for others. In doing so, they cited similar reasons to those that underpinned their opposition to elements of the resolutions on CAR and South Sudan.[12] China, Gabon, Ghana, Kenya and Russia also abstained from a vote on a resolution that included extending arms procurement notification requirements for the government of the DRC.[13]

There was also disagreement in 2022 about the open-ended UN arms embargo on Sudan, under which military supplies by the government of Sudan into the Darfur region require prior approval from the UN sanctions committee. The Security Council stated its intention to agree by 31 August 2022 on a set of 'benchmarks to assess the measures on Darfur', which Sudan would need to achieve to have those measures adjusted.[14] In this context China argued that the ability of Sudanese authorities to improve the capacities of its security forces in Darfur urgently needed strengthening, as they had been 'negatively impacted by the arms embargo'. Russia stated that the Sudanese sanctions regime no longer corresponded with the situation in Darfur, and that several Security Council members had prevented an agreement on benchmarks in 2021.[15] However, ongoing disagreement between members meant the Security Council did not meet the 31 August deadline for setting the benchmarks.[16]

Haiti

In response to months of violence and lawlessness in Haiti that fuelled a major humanitarian crisis, in October 2022 the UN Security Council unanimously voted for a resolution that included an arms embargo, for an initial period of one year, on individuals and entities in Haiti designated by the sanctions committee.[17] China had led calls for the adoption of an arms embargo in July, as part of a broader package of proposed measures that also included sending

---

[11] United Nations, Security Council, 9045th meeting, S/PV.9045, 26 May 2022, pp. 3–5.
[12] United Nations, Security Council, 9196th meeting, S/PV.9196, 17 Nov. 2022, pp. 2–4, 6.
[13] United Nations, Security Council, 9084th meeting, S/PV.9084, 30 June 2022, p. 2.
[14] UN Security Council Resolution 2620 (2022), 15 Feb. 2022, para. 5.
[15] United Nations, Security Council, 8964th meeting, S/PV.8964, 15 Feb. 2022, pp. 2–3.
[16] Security Council Report, 'Sudan: Briefing and consultations', What's in Blue Insight, 12 Sep. 2022.
[17] UN Security Council Resolution 2653, 21 Oct. 2022.

a regional police force to Haiti.[18] China stressed that it had 'always called for caution in the use of UN sanctions, regardless of the circumstances', but that considering the urgency of the situation in Haiti, it had been 'the first in the Council to propose targeted sanctions against Haitian criminal gangs'.[19] At that time, in July, other states were not convinced that an arms embargo on Haiti was either enforceable or meaningful.[20] By October other states had altered their position, and the USA and Mexico included the arms embargo in the draft resolution they tabled, which the Council adopted unanimously as Resolution 2653.[21] However, the embargo remained very limited in scope as the list of sanctioned entities and individuals included in it contained only a single person, a leader of a major criminal gang in Haiti.[22]

Iran

In accordance with the terms of the UN's 2015 Joint Comprehensive Programme of Action (JCPOA), the transfer to and from Iran of missiles and uncrewed aerial vehicles (UAVs) with a range of 300 km or more, and of items and technology that could contribute to the development of nuclear weapon delivery systems, is only allowed after prior approval from the Security Council.[23] This embargo, as agreed in Resolution 2231, is scheduled to expire on 18 October 2023.

In September and October 2022 the scope of these UN restrictions was the subject of dispute between Ukraine, France, Germany, the UK and the USA on the one hand, and Russia and Iran on the other. The first group argued that the transfer of UAVs by Iran to Russia in 2022, without the required approval, was in violation of the restrictions, and called for the UN Secretariat team responsible for monitoring the implementation of Resolution 2231 to inspect the transfer of UAVs in the light of the prohibitions.[24] Russia and Iran argued that the UN Secretariat had no mandate for any such inspection.[25] In addition, Iran argued that Resolution 2231 only restricted a state's transfer of goods and technology that the state determined could contribute to the development of nuclear weapon delivery systems, and that Iran, as the relevant state in the

---

[18] Nichols, M., 'China pushes for UN arms embargo on Haiti criminal gangs', Reuters, 15 July 2023; and News Wires, 'China pushes UN to ban small arms to Haiti amidst gang violence, diplomats', France 24, 15 July 2022.

[19] United Nations, Security Council, 9159th meeting, S/PV.9159, 21 Oct. 2022, p. 3. See also previous arms embargo sections in SIPRI Yearbooks on China's position on UN sanctions.

[20] News Wires (note 18).

[21] United Nations, Security Council, S/PV.9159 (note 19), p. 2; and UN Security Council Resolution 2653, 21 Oct. 2022.

[22] UN Security Council Resolution 2653 (note 21), Annex.

[23] UN Security Council Resolution 2231, 20 July 2015, Annex B para. 4. On efforts to renew the JCPOA in 2022, see chapter 8, section IV, in this volume.

[24] United Nations, Security Council, 'Implementation of Security Council Resolution 2231 (2015)', 14th Report of the secretary-general, S/2022/912, 12 Dec. 2022, para. 19.

[25] United Nations, Security Council, 'Fourteenth six-month report of the Facilitator on the implementation of Security Council Resolution 2231 (2015)', S/2022/937, 12 Dec. 2022, paras 20–29.

context of the export of the UAVs, had never produced or supplied goods and technology that met this definition.[26] By the end of 2022 the UN Secretariat was still examining the issue.

The UN Secretariat also investigated other allegations of Iran violating the UN embargo on exports of missiles and long-range UAVs. It continued its investigations of the debris of ballistic missiles, cruise missiles and UAVs that had been used in attacks on Saudi Arabia and United Arab Emirates (UAE) territory and which were alleged to have been transferred by Iran to Houthi forces in Yemen in violation of the UN restrictions. The UN Secretariat investigated cruise missile parts that the British navy had seized in early 2022 from two ships in international waters south of Iran and that showed similarities with the missile debris found in Saudi Arabia and the UAE.[27] The investigations did not lead to any firm conclusions in 2022.

Libya

The UN arms embargo on Libya bans arms transfers and technical assistance related to military activities to non-state armed groups, but permits deliveries to the internationally recognized Government of National Accord— which was incorporated into the Government of National Unity (GNU) in 2021—provided that the transfers have been approved in advance by the UN sanctions committee for Libya. However, the panel of experts on Libya concluded in its May 2022 report that the arms embargo remained ineffective. It mentioned especially that Russia and the UAE were supplying arms to one party on the conflict in Libya (the Haftar Affiliated Forces) while Türkiye was supplying arms to another party (the GNU Affiliated Forces). However, the number of identified violations was much lower than during 2019 and 2020, and the number of suspicious flights into Libya was significantly lower.[28]

Conclusions

In 2022 there were several major divisions between UN member states about UN arms embargoes (reversing the greater degree of consensus that had prevailed in 2021). Significant disagreement occurred within the UN Security Council about existing arms embargoes. Russia and the West disagreed on the scope of the remaining arms-related UN sanctions on Iran, especially about whether it allowed Iran to export UAVs. There was also increasing disagreement—with Russia, China and several African states on one side, and

---

[26] United Nations, Security Council, Letter dated 24 October 2022 from the permanent representative of the Islamic Republic of Iran to the United Nations addressed to the secretary-general and the president of the Security Council, S/2022/794, 24 Oct. 2022, p. 2.

[27] United Nations, Security Council, S/2022/912 (note 24), para. 19.

[28] United Nations, Security Council, Report of the panel of experts established pursuant to Resolution 1973 (2011) concerning Libya, S/2022/427, 27 May 2022, p. 2 and para. 87.

the other Security Council members on the other—over the use of restrictions and controls on arms procurement by government forces in CAR, the DRC, Somalia, South Sudan and Sudan.

Compliance with UN arms embargoes was mixed in 2021. As in previous years there were reports of significant violations of the UN arms embargo on Libya, including by Russia. The agreement to impose an arms embargo on Haiti was notable, given that China was its leading proponent, in contrast with China's previous careful approach to supporting such embargoes. However, the relevance of the embargo is limited as it is aimed solely at stopping arms transfers to criminal gangs, which states can in any case be expected to prevent. As such the embargo is arguably merely a formal statement with little actual effect.

Table 12.2. Multilateral arms embargoes in force during 2022

Target (entities or territory covered)[a]	Date embargo first imposed (duration type)	Materiel covered[a]	Key developments, 2022
United Nations arms embargoes			
Afghanistan (Taliban: NGF)	16 Jan. 2002 (OE)	Arms and related materiel and services	
Central African Republic (government: PT; NGF)	5 Dec. 2013 (TL)	Arms and military materiel (small arms exempted for government)	Extended until 31 July 2023
Democratic Republic of the Congo (government: PT; NGF)	28 July 2003 (TL)	Arms and military materiel	Extended until 1 July 2023; requirement to notify supplies of major arms to government lifted June 2022; requirement to notify supplies of other arms to government lifted Dec. 2022
Haiti (NGF)	21 Oct. 2022 (TL)	Arms and military materiel	
Iran (whole country: PT)	23 Dec. 2006 (TL)	Items related to nuclear weapon delivery systems; Items used in the nuclear fuel cycle	
Iraq (NGF)	6 Aug. 1990 (OE)	Arms and military materiel	
ISIL (Da'esh), al-Qaeda and associated individuals and entities (NGF)	16 Jan. 2002 (OE)	Arms and military materiel	
Korea, North (whole country)	15 July 2006 (OE)	Arms and military materiel; Items relevant to nuclear, ballistic missiles and other weapons of mass destruction related programmes	
Lebanon (NGF)	11 Aug. 2006 (OE)	Arms and military materiel	
Libya (government: PT; NGF)	26 Feb. 2011 (OE)	Arms and military materiel	
Somalia (government: PT; NGF)	23 Jan. 1992 (TL)	Arms and military materiel; Components for improvised explosive devices	Extended until 17 Nov. 2023

Target (entities or territory covered)[a]	Date embargo first imposed (duration type)	Materiel covered[a]	Key developments, 2022
South Sudan (government: PT; NGF)	13 July 2018 (TL)	Arms and military materiel	Extended until 31 May 2023
Sudan (Darfur: PT)	30 July 2004 (OE)	Arms and military materiel	
Yemen (NGF)	14 Apr. 2015 (OE)	Arms and military materiel	

European Union arms embargoes without UN counterpart or with broader scope than UN embargoes on the same target

Target	Date	Materiel covered	Key developments, 2022
Belarus (whole country)	20 June 2011 (TL)	Arms and military materiel; Dual-use materiel; Communication surveillance equipment	Coverage expanded to include exports of all dual-use materiel to all end-users and end-uses; Extended until 28 Feb. 2023
China[b] (whole country)	27 June 1989 (OE)	Arms	
Egypt[b] (whole country)	21 Aug. 2013 (OE)	Equipment which might be used for internal repression	
Iran (whole country)	27 Feb. 2007 (TL)	Arms and military materiel; Equipment which might be used for internal repression; Communication surveillance equipment	Extended until 13 April 2023
Myanmar (whole country)	29 July 1991 (TL)	Arms and military materiel; Communication surveillance equipment	Extended until 30 April 2023
Russia (whole country)	31 July 2014 (TL)	Arms and military materiel; Dual-use materiel	Coverage expanded to include exports of all dual-use materiel to all end-users and end-uses; Extended until 31 Jan. 2023.
South Sudan (whole country)	18 July 2011 (OE)	Arms and military materiel	
Sudan (whole country)	15 Mar. 1994 (OE)	Arms and military materiel	
Syria (whole country)	9 May 2011 (OE)	Equipment which might be used for internal repression; Communication surveillance equipment	

Target (entities or territory covered)[a]	Date embargo first imposed (duration type)	Materiel covered[a]	Key developments, 2022
Venezuela (whole country)	13 Nov. 2017 (TL)	Arms and equipment which might be used for internal repression; Communication surveillance equipment	Extended until 14 Nov. 2023
Zimbabwe (whole country)	18 Feb. 2002 (TL)	Arms and military materiel	Extended until 20 Feb. 2023
League of Arab States arms embargoes			
Syria (whole country)	3 Dec. 2011 (OE)	Arms	

ISIL = Islamic State in Iraq and the Levant; NGF = non-governmental forces; OE = open-ended; PT = partial, i.e. embargo allows transfers to the state in question provided the supplier or recipient state has received permission from, or notified, the relevant United Nations sanctions committee or the UN Security Council; TL = time-limited.

[a] The target, entities and territory, and materiel covered may have changed since the first imposition of the embargo. The target, entities and material stated in this table are as at the end of 2022.

[b] The EU embargoes on China and Egypt are political declarations whereas the other embargoes are legal acts imposed by EU Council decisions and EU Council Regulations.

Sources: UN Security Council, 'Sanctions'; and Council of the EU, 'EU Sanctions Map'. The SIPRI Arms Embargo Archive provides a detailed overview of most multilateral arms embargoes that have been in force since 1950 along with the principal instruments establishing or amending the embargoes.

III. The role and impact of multilateral trade restrictions on Russia and Belarus

MARK BROMLEY*

Russia's invasion of Ukraine in February 2022 galvanized the European Union (EU), the United States and several other Western-aligned countries to apply a series of sanctions against both Russia and Belarus.[1] These measures included sectoral sanctions, banking restrictions, road and maritime transport bans, travel bans and asset freezes. While the sanctions lists do not always overlap, by the end of December 2022, the USA, the EU and the United Kingdom had each added approximately 1500 new Russia-related individuals and entities to their respective consolidated lists of sanctioned persons.[2] Within the EU's nine sanctions packages, for example, this represented an approximate doubling of its entire sanctions portfolio across the dozens of sanctions regimes it implements.

In addition to economic and financial sanctions, the EU, the USA and their allies also either adopted wide-ranging arms embargoes on Russia and Belarus or expanded their existing measures. The 27 EU member states, the USA and 10 other states committed to adopting trade restrictions on Russia and Belarus that were 'substantially similar', creating a coalition of 38 states that progressively enacted a set of aligned and expanding export control measures during 2022.[3] These controls, covering both military items and a broad range of dual-use items, were imposed by 15 of the 20 largest exporters of goods to Russia in 2021, the exceptions being (in order of size) China, Türkiye, Belarus, India and Brazil.[4] These measures together represent one of the most comprehensive sets of trade restrictions ever imposed on an industrialized state by its major trading partners. They were imposed more quickly and are broader in coverage than the arms embargoes previously imposed by the United Nations and the EU on Iran, North Korea and Libya.[5] The scope of these measures and the speed of their adoption served to

---

[1] 'What are the sanctions on Russia and are they hurting?', BBC News, 30 Sep. 2022.
[2] US Department of State, Office of the Spokesperson, 'The impact of sanctions and export controls on the Russian Federation', Fact Sheet, 20 Oct. 2022; European Council, 'EU restrictive measures against Russia over Ukraine (since 2014)'; Neate, R., 'UK sanctions now cover £18bn of Russian-owned assets', *The Guardian*, 10 Nov. 2022; and British Foreign, Commonwealth and Development Office, 'UK sanctions following Russia's invasion of Ukraine', 13 May 2022 (updated 8 Feb. 2023).
[3] These 10 additional states are Australia, Canada, Iceland, Japan, Republic of Korea, Liechtenstein, New Zealand, Norway, Switzerland and the UK.
[4] United Nations, Statistics Division, UN Comtrade Database. Ukraine was one the 20 largest exporters to Russia in 2021 and has not joined the coalition of states imposing restrictions. However, all trade with Russia came to a halt with the invasion and Ukraine imposed a full trade embargo with Russia in Apr. 2022. 'Ukraine imposes full trade embargo against Russia', LB.ua, 9 Apr. 2022.
[5] For a historical overview of sanctions on Iran, see Anthony, I., Bromley, M. and Wezeman, P., 'The role and impact of sanctions on Iran', *SIPRI Yearbook 2016*, pp. 87–114.

* SIPRI intern Louison Ferant conducted background research for this section.

accelerate debates—particularly in the USA—about the value and potential of establishing a new multilateral export control regime that would replace or supplement the existing regimes in which Russia participates and that would be partly aimed at restricting exports of technology to Russia (see section IV in this chapter).

This section outlines the trade restrictions that the EU, the USA and others have imposed; highlights the enforcement and compliance challenges that these restrictions have generated; and reviews assessments of their impact on Russia.

EU trade restrictions

Following Russia's annexation of Crimea in 2014 the EU imposed a ban on exports of military items to Russia as well as restrictions on exports of dual-use items.[6] In response to the deteriorating human rights, democracy and rule-of-law conditions in Belarus, in 2011 the EU imposed a ban on exports of military items and equipment used for internal repression, and in 2021 imposed restrictions on exports of dual-use items and telecommunications equipment.[7] These pre-2022 restrictions on exports to Belarus and Russia contained several exemptions that allowed certain exports to continue and new licences to be issued. For example, the restrictions on exports of dual-use items only covered transfers 'for military use . . . or for any military end-user' in Russia or Belarus.[8] In addition, under a set of so-called grandfather clauses, new licences could be issued for exports of dual-use items and military items to Russia and dual-use items to Belarus if they concerned transfers covered by contracts signed before the embargoes were imposed. This meant that certain EU member states continued to grant licences for exports of military items to Russia after the imposition of the 2014 sanctions measures. For example, from 2015 onwards France continued to issue licences for the export of thermal imaging cameras that were integrated into Russian-made tanks, as

---

[6] European Council, Council Decision 2014/512/CFSP of 31 July 2014 concerning restrictive measures in view of Russia's actions destabilising the situation in Ukraine, *Official Journal of the European Union*, L229, 31 July 2014.

[7] European Council, Council Decision 2011/357/CFSP of 20 June 2011 amending Decision 2010/639/CFSP concerning restrictive measures against certain officials of Belarus, *Official Journal of the European Union*, L161, 21 June 2011; and European Council, Council Decision (CFSP) 2021/1031 of 24 June 2021 amending Council Decision 2012/642/CFSP concerning restrictive measures in view of the situation in Belarus, *Official Journal of the European Union*, L224, 24 June 2021.

[8] European Council, Council Decision 2014/512/CFSP of 31 July 2014 concerning restrictive measures in view of Russia's actions destabilising the situation in Ukraine (note 6); and European Council, Council Decision (CFSP) 2021/1031 of 24 June 2021 amending Council Decision 2012/642/CFSP concerning restrictive measures in view of the situation in Belarus (note 7).

well as navigation systems and infrared detectors that were integrated into Russian-made combat aircraft and attack helicopters.[9]

Between Russia's invasion of Ukraine in February 2022 and 31 December 2022, the EU adopted a series of nine sanctions packages.[10] These sanctions packages have progressively expanded the existing trade restrictions on Russia and Belarus. Under measures adopted in February and March 2022, the restrictions on exports of dual-use items were extended to all end-users in Russia and Belarus, regardless of whether they were for military end-use or for a military end-user.[11] The coverage of the trade restrictions has also progressively broadened beyond the list of controlled items covered by the EU military list and EU dual-use list. On 9 March 2022 the EU banned transfers of 'maritime navigation goods and technology' to Russia and on 8 April 2022 it banned transfers of 'goods which could contribute in particular to the enhancement of Russia's industrial capacities'.[12] The EU also began the process of establishing a control list for these items.

The list of items that these additional controls cover is laid out in Annex VII of the relevant EU regulation and includes 'cutting-edge technology (e.g. quantum computers and advanced semiconductors, high-end electronics and software'; 'certain types of machinery and transportation equipment'; 'aviation and space industry goods and technology (e.g. aircraft, aircraft engines, spare parts or any kind of equipment for planes and helicopters, jet fuel)'; and 'maritime navigation goods and radio communication technology'.[13] The range of items captured is broader than Western states imposed on the Soviet Union during the cold war.[14] Many of the items are not included in any existing export control regime or national export control lists. This has created implementation challenges for the companies prod-

---

[9] Guckert, E. et al., 'War in Ukraine: How France delivered weapons to Russia until 2020', *Disclose*, 14 Mar. 2022.

[10] See European Council, 'Timeline: EU restrictive measures against Russia over Ukraine'.

[11] European Council, Council Decision (CFSP) 2022/327 of 25 February 2022 amending Decision 2014/512/CFSP concerning restrictive measures in view of Russia's actions destabilising the situation in Ukraine, *Official Journal of the European Union*, L48, 15 Feb. 2022; and European Council, Council Decision (CFSP) 2022/399 of 9 March 2022 amending Decision 2012/642/CFSP concerning restrictive measures in view of the situation in Belarus and the involvement of Belarus in the Russian aggression against Ukraine, *Official Journal of the European Union*, L82, 9 Mar. 2022.

[12] European Council, Council Decision (CFSP) 2022/395 of 9 March 2022 amending Decision 2014/512/CFSP concerning restrictive measures in view of Russia's actions destabilising the situation in Ukraine, *Official Journal of the European Union*, L81, 9 Mar. 2022; and European Council, Council Decision (CFSP) 2022/578 of 8 April 2022 amending Decision 2014/512/CFSP concerning restrictive measures in view of Russia's actions destabilising the situation in Ukraine, *Official Journal of the European Union*, L111, 8 Apr. 2022.

[13] European Council, 'EU sanctions against Russia explained', 18 Jan. 2023 (emphasis omitted).

[14] The Coordinating Committee for Multilateral Export Controls (COCOM) was the main means through which Western states imposed restrictions on transfers of both military equipment and dual-use items to the eastern bloc during the cold war. See Mastanduno, M., *Economic Containment: CoCom and the Politics of East–West Trade* (Cornell University Press: Ithaca, NY, 1992).

ucing and exporting these items and enforcement challenges for the national authorities charged with ensuring that the sanctions are applied.[15]

The EU sanctions have also progressively removed the set of 'grandfather clauses' that applied to the Russia and Belarus sanctions prior to February 2022. The grandfather clause that allowed licences to be issued for exports of dual-use items to Russia and Belarus was removed on 25 February (new licences could be issued but only until 1 May 2022) and the grandfather clause that allowed licences to be issued for exports of military items to Russia was removed on 8 April. Several states have gone further than what is specifically required under the EU sanctions measures. For example, on 24 February all three regions of Belgium (Brussels, Flanders and Wallonia) suspended all licences for the export of dual-use items to Russia and Belarus, and Finland, Italy, Luxembourg and the Netherlands had all done so by 11 March.[16] The EU restrictive measures prohibit exports of dual-use items except in certain limited cases but do not require member states to suspend licences issued before the they came into force.[17]

US trade restrictions

Since they are imposed via the US government's system of strategic trade controls, the US sanctions on Russia and Belarus carry additional extraterritorial controls. This means that any item produced outside the USA using US-origin dual-use items are also banned from being supplied to Russia and Belarus.[18] These types of controls—according to which the USA asserts that companies based outside its territory are subject to its laws—are unique to the USA and have often been a source of tension with other states, including EU member states. In an unprecedented move the USA has exempted the 37 states that have adopted the set of trade restrictions on Russia and Belarus from the new requirements.[19]

---

[15] See Sidley Austin LLP, 'One year of Russia restrictions: Six key trends and lessons for trade compliance', Sidley Updates: Global Arbitration, Trade and Advocacy, 22 Feb. 2023.

[16] Bovy, G., Van Reet, L. and Vynckier, J., 'Belgium: Flanders, Brussels and Wallonia suspend export licenses to Russia', *Sanctions & Export Controls Update*, 24 Feb. 2022; 'Russia's invasion of Ukraine', Loyens & Loeff Blog, 11 Mar. 2023; Finnish Ministry for Foreign Affairs, 'Authorisations to export dual-use items to Russia revoked', Export Control News, 1 Mar. 2022; and Belfiori, O., Rossetti, D. and Tona, M., 'Global sanctions alert: Italy', Lexology, 11 Mar. 2022.

[17] See European Commission, 'Consolidated FAQs on the implementation of Council Regulation no. 833/2014; and Council Regulation no. 269/2014', 22 June 2022 (Update of 3 Mar. 2023), p. 133.

[18] Contini, K. B., Test, L. S. and Howard, C., 'BIS expands sanctions against Russia and Belarus and adds four countries to global export controls coalition', *Sanctions & Export Controls Update*, 12 Apr. 2022.

[19] Contini, Test and Howard (note 18).

Impact of the trade restrictions

Following Russia's invasion of Crimea in 2014 and the subsequent EU and US imposition of sanctions, Russia announced plans to increase the level of self-sufficiency in the Russian defence industry and reduce its reliance on foreign-made components. In May 2014 President Vladimir Putin declared: 'We need to do our utmost for anything used in our defence sector to be produced on our territory, so that we are not dependent on anyone'.[20] Despite these stated ambitions, a series of investigations during 2022 revealed that Russian military equipment deployed in Ukraine relied heavily on parts and components manufactured abroad. For example, Conflict Armament Research investigations identified '144 non-Russian manufacturers of more than 650 unique component models in Russian materiel used in the war on Ukraine'.[21]

Many of these parts and components were not covered by the trade restrictions in place at the time that the shipments occurred. However, the expanding set of measures that have been adopted by the coalition of 38 states mean that many have become subject to export control measures during 2022. For example, commenting on reports concerning the supply of Swiss components used in Russian missiles, a spokesman for the Swiss export licensing authority noted that in February 2022 the items were not classed as controlled dual-use items.[22] However, the spokesman noted that 'since the comprehensive goods sanctions against Russia came into force on March 4, 2022, such goods have been banned for delivery and sale to Russia'.[23]

Investigations by the Royal United Services Institute and by Reuters also highlighted cases of transfers that would have potentially breached export control restrictions in place at the time.[24] This supported previous reports noting that since 2014 Russia had been engaged in longstanding and widespread efforts to bypass the trade restrictions imposed by the EU and the USA and to obtain controlled technology.[25] Reports have also pointed to Russia's continued ability to access Western-produced parts and components, even after the imposition of the expanded sanctions measures, via a range of distributors based in countries not part of the coalition of 38 states. For example, a report in December 2022 highlighted transfers of US-made

---

[20] 'UPDATE 1: Putin wants Russian defence industry to be self-sufficient', Reuters, 14 May 2014.

[21] Conflict Armament Research, 'Component commonalities in advanced Russian weapon systems', Sep. 2022.

[22] Dahm, V. P., 'Putin hortet haufenweise Schweizer Hightech-Bauteile für seine Waffen [Putin hoards heaps of Swiss high-tech components for his weapons]', Blue News, 16 Aug. 2022.

[23] Dahm (note 22).

[24] See Byrne, J. et al., *Silicon Lifeline: Western Electronics at the Heart of Russia's War Machine* (Royal United Services Institute: London, 8 Aug. 2022); and Grey, S., Tamman, M. and Zholobova, M., 'Exclusive: The global supply trail that leads to Russia's killer drones', Reuters, 15 Dec. 2022.

[25] See Rettman, A., 'EU arms firms trying to flout Belarus and Russia ban', EUobserver, 6 Oct. 2021.

components from a Hong Kong–based company to a firm in St Petersburg with close ties to a key manufacturer of drones used by the Russian military.[26] Analysis of Iranian-made drones used by Russia in Ukraine has also demonstrated that Iran has utilized a wide range of both controlled and non-controlled dual-use items produced in the USA and other Western states that strictly control exports of such goods to Iran.[27]

Conclusions

The trade restrictions imposed by the USA, the EU and 10 other like-minded states on Russia and Belarus represent one of the most comprehensive sets of trade restrictions imposed in the post–cold war period on a major trade partner. These restrictions went well beyond the scope of the military and dual-use items covered by the control lists of the multilateral export control regimes. In particular, the restrictions on exports to Russia were expanded to cover items that might be of relevance for both the development and use of weapon systems but also for Russia's industrial capabilities more broadly. As such, the restrictions indicate a willingness on the part of the EU, the USA and their allies to use export controls as tools of economic warfare. The restrictions have also highlighted the ability of coalitions of states to work outside the frameworks of both the UN and the existing multilateral export control regimes when developing and applying coordinated export control measures.

[26] Grey, Tamman and Zholobova (note 24).
[27] Albright, D., Burkhard, S. and Faragasso, S., 'Iranian drones in Ukraine contain Western brand components', Institute for Science and International Security Report, 31 Oct. 2022.

IV. The multilateral export control regimes

KOLJA BROCKMANN

The Australia Group (AG), the Missile Technology Control Regime (MTCR), the Nuclear Suppliers Group (NSG) and the Wassenaar Arrangement on Export Controls for Conventional Arms and Dual-use Goods and Technologies (Wassenaar Arrangement, WA) are the four main multilateral export control regimes.[1] The regimes are informal groups of participating states which agree on guidelines for the implementation of export controls on goods and technologies in the areas of chemical and biological weapons, missiles and other weapon of mass destruction (WMD) delivery systems, nuclear fuel cycle technologies and nuclear weapons, and conventional arms and dual-use goods and technologies (table 12.3). Within each regime the participating states coordinate trade controls and related policies, share good practices on their implementation, and exchange information on proliferation cases, illicit acquisition attempts and licence denials, and in some cases licences granted.

The participating states continuously update the regimes' control lists and discuss relevant technological developments. The regimes create important forums for exchanges among national policy and licensing officials, technical experts, and enforcement and intelligence officers. Notably, the participating states take all decisions in the regimes by consensus, and the resulting guidelines, control lists and good practice documents are politically rather than legally binding. Each participating state implements regime-prescribed trade controls and policies through national laws and their respective national export control systems—as do an increasing number of non-participating states.

While the Covid-19 pandemic continued in 2022, all multilateral export control regimes were able to return to in-person plenary meetings. However, rather than all regimes being able to resume normal operations, Russia's invasion of Ukraine in February 2022 severely impacted the MTCR, NSG and WA, where both Russia and Ukraine are members. As was the case with other multilateral bodies whose members included Russia and Western powers, accusations connected to the conflict were exchanged. The invasion also sparked debates about the long-term viability of both the regimes and Russia's continued membership. The AG is the only regime in which Russia is not a member, and it adopted language strongly condemning Russia's actions. An additional layer of complexity arose when the United States, the European Union (EU) and other like-minded states supporting Ukraine

---

[1] For brief descriptions and lists of the participating states in each of these regimes see annex B, section III, in this volume.

Table 12.3. The four multilateral export control regimes

Regime (year established)	Scope	No. of participants[a]	2022 plenary chair	2022 plenary
Australia Group (1985)	Equipment, materials, technology and software that could contribute to chemical and biological weapon activities	43	Australia	Paris, 4–8 July 2022
Missile Technology Control Regime (1987)	Unmanned aerial vehicles capable of delivering weapons of mass destruction	35	Switzerland	Montreux, 17–21 Oct. 2022
Nuclear Suppliers Group (1974)	Nuclear and nuclear-related materials, software and technology	48[b]	Poland[c]	Warsaw, 20–24 June 2022
Wassenaar Arrangement (1996)	Conventional arms and dual-use items and technologies	42	Ireland	Vienna, 30 Nov.– 1 Dec. 2022

[a] Participant numbers are as of 31 December 2022. For lists of participants see annex B, section III, in this volume.

[b] In addition, the European Union and the chair of the Zangger Committee are permanent observers of the Nuclear Suppliers Group (NSG).

[c] The NSG changed its procedures so that participating states host a plenary at the end of their period as chair. At the 2022 NSG plenary, Poland handed the chair over to Argentina for the 2022–23 period.

Sources: Australia Group; Missile Technology Control Regime; Nuclear Suppliers Group; and Wassenaar Arrangement on Export Controls for Conventional Arms and Dual-use Goods and Technologies.

adopted a series of trade restrictions against Russia which used the control lists of the regimes as part of the basis for the lists of restricted dual-use goods and technologies (see section III in this chapter).

The Australia Group

The AG provides a forum for participating states to coordinate and harmonize export controls on chemical and biological weapons and related dual-use goods and technologies. The AG participating states seek to reduce the risk of contributing to the proliferation of chemical and biological weapons.[2] An initiative by Australia in 1985 led to the creation of the AG. A United Nations investigation had found that chemical weapons used in the 1980–88 Iran–Iraq War had been produced using precursor chemicals, equipment and materials procured from several Western states.[3] This created significant momentum

---

[2] Australia Group, 'The Australia Group: An introduction'; and Australia Group, 'Objectives of the Group'.

[3] Australia Group, 'The origins of the Australia Group'.

for strengthening trade control measures for the non-proliferation of chemical weapons. While the initial focus of the AG was on chemical weapons and precursors, its coverage has since significantly expanded to include biological weapons and a wider range of equipment, materials and technology relevant to the development, production and use of chemical and biological weapons.[4] The AG is permanently chaired by Australia, which also runs an informal secretariat situated within the Australian Department of Foreign Affairs and Trade.

The AG has 43 participants, including the EU which is a member with full voting rights. While the number of participants has increased from 18 in 1985, membership growth has largely stagnated since the 2010s. The only new participating states in the last 10 years were Mexico (2013) and India (2018).[5] The AG encourages states not participating in the regime to become AG adherents by notifying the chair of their 'political commitment to adhere' to the guidelines and common control lists. It offers adherents access to additional information and assistance from AG participating states. Kazakhstan is the only state that has submitted the required notification, but in 2022 Chile announced its intention to become an adherent.[6]

On 4–8 July 2022, in Paris, the AG held its first in-person annual plenary meeting since 2019, at which it continued discussing technical issues. The licensing and enforcement experts meeting (LEEM) discussed good practices in preventing the proliferation of dual-use items, with a particular focus on preventing unauthorized intangible technology transfers (ITT) and informing industry and academia about ITT risks. Technical experts discussed emerging technologies, including synthetic biology and novel delivery systems.[7] The participants added new items to, and removed items from, the AG's control lists, with changes including adjustments to certain pathogens according to their taxonomy, addition of four marine toxins, and the deletion of cholera toxin from the lists.[8] The AG also continued its practice of inviting several guest speakers to address the plenary, including on dual-use risks of drug discovery using artificial intelligence and the use of blockchain technology to track and trace dual-use chemicals.[9]

The Australia Group chair and head of secretariat resumed outreach efforts, in particular by way of participation in international meetings, including the Asian Export Control Seminar on 15–17 February and the European Union

---

[4] Australia Group, 'The origins of the Australia Group' (note 3).
[5] Australia Group, 'Australia Group participants'.
[6] Australia Group, 'Australia Group adherents'; and Australia Group, Statement by the chair of the 2022 Australia Group Plenary, 8 July 2022, para. 23.
[7] Australia Group, Statement by the chair of the 2022 Australia Group Plenary (note 6), paras 15–17.
[8] Australia Group, 'Australia Group Common Control Lists'.
[9] For the work the subject of these presentations see, respectively, Urbina, F. et al., 'Dual use of artificial-intelligence-powered drug discovery', *Nature Machine Intelligence*, no. 4 (Mar. 2022); and Stimson Center, 'MATCH prototype'.

Partner-to-Partner (EUP2P) programmes' third dialogue on export control governance in October 2022.[10]

The Missile Technology Control Regime

The MTCR seeks to prevent the proliferation of missiles and other uncrewed delivery systems capable of delivering chemical, biological or nuclear (CBN) weapons. It was created in 1987 by the Group of Seven (G7) largest industrialized states with the objective of contributing to preventing the proliferation of nuclear weapons by creating harmonized export controls on goods and technologies related to missiles capable of carrying such weapons.[11] Since then, the scope of the MTCR has expanded to include ballistic and cruise missiles, and all uncrewed aerial vehicles (UAVs) capable of delivering CBN weapons.[12] Category I of the MTCR control list covers missiles and UAVs 'capable of delivering a payload of at least 500 kg to a range of at least 300 km', or destined to be used to deliver CBN weapons. The MTCR participating states—referred to as 'the partners'—should exercise an 'unconditional strong presumption of denial' for transfers of items covered by Category I and should only diverge from this on 'rare occasions'.[13] Category II covers missiles and UAVs with a maximum range of at least 300 km and a wide range of less-sensitive and dual-use goods, materials and technologies for missile, UAV and space-launch applications.[14] Transfers of these items are subject to case-by-case licensing decisions by partner governments and to a strong presumption of denial if they are 'intended for use in WMD delivery'.[15]

The membership of the MTCR has grown from 7 to 35 participating states, but has not increased since the 2016 admission of India. Several applications are pending.[16] In 2014 the MTCR introduced a formalized system for non-partner states to be recognized as 'adherents' to the MTCR guidelines and control lists. The MTCR encourages all states to submit declarations of adherence to the MTCR point of contact, run by France. The regime also provides incentives for becoming an adherent, including invitations to technical outreach meetings, briefings on control list changes, meetings with the MTCR chair and access to some presentations from the MTCR LEEM.[17]

---

[10] Government of Japan, The 28th Asian Export Control Seminar; and the author participated as a keynote speaker in the EUP2P Third Dialogue on Export Control Governance in Brussels on 25–26 Oct. 2022.
[11] Missile Technology Control Regime, 'Frequently asked questions (FAQs)'. The G7 states are Canada, France, Germany, Italy, Japan, the United Kingdom and the United States.
[12] Missile Technology Control Regime, 'Frequently asked questions (FAQs)' (note 11).
[13] Missile Technology Control Regime, 'Frequently asked questions (FAQs)' (note 11).
[14] Missile Technology Control Regime, 'MTCR Guidelines and the Equipment, Software and Technology Annex'.
[15] Missile Technology Control Regime, 'Frequently asked questions (FAQs)' (note 11).
[16] Missile Technology Control Regime, 'Partners'.
[17] Missile Technology Control Regime, 'Adherence policy'.

However, since the creation of the adherent status, only three states have unilaterally declared their adherence: Estonia, Kazakhstan and Latvia.

The 2022 plenary of the MTCR took place according to the normal schedule, and with full participation from all partners, on 17–21 October 2022 in Montreux, hosted by Switzerland. The work of the MTCR was particularly affected by Russia's actions in Ukraine since Russia held the annually rotating chair when it began its invasion in February 2022. Most partners, including the chairs and co-chairs of the regime sub-groups, ceased their collaboration with the Russian chair, for example on outreach activities. Nevertheless, exchanges among the experts continued on the technical level both intersessionally and at the plenary where Switzerland assumed the role as chair for the 2022–23 period.

One topic of particular focus at the plenary was NewSpace and the missile non-proliferation and export control challenges associated with the commercial space industry.[18] The technical experts meeting (TEM), the LEEM and the information exchange meeting (IEM) discussed the topic in a joint meeting and SIPRI presented relevant research during a side-event co-organized with Switzerland and Germany.[19] The partners agreed on a small number of editorial changes and clarifications for items in the Equipment, Software and Technology Annex.[20] However, the partners failed to agree on a public statement. Instead, the Swiss chair first issued a short statement to mark the occasion of the 35th anniversary of the MTCR, and later, in December, the chair's report on the plenary.[21]

The Russian chair conducted a series of official MTCR outreach missions during 2022, even after Russia's invasion of Ukraine—albeit largely without the participation of sub-group chairs and very limited participation from Western MTCR partners. The Russian chair conducted outreach visits to Belarus on 2–3 March, the United Arab Emirates on 24 May, Viet Nam on 26–27 May, Mexico on 24 August and Pakistan in September 2022.[22] The MTCR chair and sub-group chairs also participated in conferences, workshops and other activities upon invitation by international organizations, states and think

---

[18] See e.g. Brockmann, K. and Raju, N., *NewSpace and the Commercialization of the Space Industry: Challenges for the Missile Technology Control Regime* (SIPRI: Stockholm, Oct. 2022).
[19] Missile Technology Control Regime, Report by the MTCR chair: Plenary meeting in Montreux, Switzerland, October 2022, 21 Dec. 2022.
[20] Missile Technology Control Regime, 'Equipment, Software and Technology Annex' [Current version, showing changes from previous version], 21 Oct. 2022.
[21] Missile Technology Control Regime, Message on the occasion of the 35th anniversary of the MTCR, 8 Nov. 2022 (Updated on 21 Dec. 2022); and Missile Technology Control Regime, Report by the MTCR Chair: Plenary meeting in Montreux, Switzerland, October 2022 (note 19).
[22] MTCR (@MTCR_Chair), Twitter, 3 Mar. 2022, <https://twitter.com/MTCR_Chair/status/1499449199422849037>; MTCR (@MTCR_Chair), Twitter, 30 May 2022, <https://twitter.com/MTCR_Chair/status/1531167003150540800>; MTCR (@MTCR_Chair), Twitter, 1 Sep. 2022, <https://twitter.com/MTCR_Chair/status/1565218373163704325>; and MTCR (@MTCR_Chair), Twitter, 8 Sep. 2022, <https://twitter.com/MTCR_Chair/status/1567733418615619586>.

tanks as part of their outreach work. The Russian chair also participated in a workshop organized by the International Institute for Strategic Studies in Berlin in early February—prior to the invasion.[23]

The Nuclear Suppliers Group

The NSG seeks to contribute to the non-proliferation of nuclear weapons by implementing guidelines for export controls on transfers of nuclear and nuclear-related material, equipment, software and technology. It was established as the 'London Club' of seven major nuclear supplier states in reaction to India's first nuclear test in 1974, the first explosion of a nuclear weapon by a state not recognized as a nuclear-weapon state by the Treaty on the Non-proliferation of Nuclear Weapons (NPT).[24] Initially, the NSG participants created a set of guidelines incorporating a list of items triggering International Atomic Energy Agency safeguards with a slightly different scope than the list previously created by the Zangger Committee. Between 1978 and 1991, the NSG was largely inactive. However, following recommendations adopted at the 1990 NPT review conference, the 1992 NSG plenary established guidelines for transfers of nuclear-related dual-use equipment, material and technology, an information exchange, an exchange of denial notifications, and a requirement for a full-scale safeguards agreement to trigger list item recipients.[25] The NSG currently has 48 participating governments and the European Commission and the chair of the Zangger Committee have permanent observer status. No state has joined the group since 2013.[26]

In 2022 the NSG held its annual plenary in Warsaw on 20–24 June, hosted by the outgoing Polish chair. The plenary marked the 30th anniversary of the first regular plenary meeting of the NSG, also held in Warsaw in 1992. As with the other regimes where Russia and Ukraine are participating governments, the NSG plenary could not find consensus on a public statement to be adopted. However, despite the inability to agree on a consensus statement, the participating governments completed the three-yearly fundamental review of Information Circular 539 on the NSG's guidelines, origins, structure and role, adding to the record decisions on an explanatory video about the NSG and on the new timing of NSG plenaries at the end of a chair's term.[27]

---

[23] MTCR (@MTCR_Chair), Twitter, 22 Feb. 2022, <https://twitter.com/MTCR_Chair/status/1496077979151220738>.

[24] Nuclear Suppliers Group, 'About the NSG'.

[25] International Atomic Energy Agency, Communication received from the Permanent Mission of the Argentine Republic to the International Atomic Energy Agency on behalf of the participating governments of the Nuclear Suppliers Group, Information Circular 539 (revised), INFCIRC/539/Rev.8, 28 July 2022.

[26] Nuclear Suppliers Group, 'Participants'.

[27] International Atomic Energy Agency, INFCIRC/539/Rev.8 (note 25), paras 34–35.

The participating governments also agreed on two small technical changes to the control list in the annex to NSG Guidelines Part 2, aligning the coverage of flow-forming machines that can be used to produce gas centrifuge rotors and the dimensions of such rotors with the controlled parameters of gas centrifuges.[28] The incoming Argentinian chair outlined the objectives for the 2022–23 period as continuing 'the valuable technical work of the NSG in the spirit of a constructive multilateral approach' and a specific interest in 'transit and transshipment issues'.[29] The Argentinian chair, together with Denmark and the UK, organized a side event at the 10th review conference of the Treaty on the Non-proliferation of Nuclear Weapons (see chapter 8 section II) on 18 August 2022, highlighting the important linkage between the two instruments.[30]

The Wassenaar Arrangement

The Wassenaar Arrangement is the main multilateral export control regime concerned with conventional weapons and a wide range of dual-use goods and technologies. It was created in 1996 as the successor to the cold war–era Coordinating Committee for Multilateral Export Controls (COCOM) through which Western states imposed restrictions on transfers of military equipment and dual-use items to the Eastern bloc. The creation of the WA marked a move away from the COCOM's approach of using export controls to target a specific group of adversarial states. Rather, the WA participating states aim to prevent transfers that contribute to 'destabilising accumulations' of conventional weapons and dual-use goods and technologies that could threaten international and regional security and stability. The scope of the WA was later expanded to preventing transfers to terrorists. Through the WA the participating states also aim to promote 'transparency and greater responsibility' in the transfers of conventional arms and dual-use goods and technologies. As of the end of 2022, 42 states were participating in the WA, which has not expanded since the admission of India in 2017.[31]

The WA returned to convening a regular annual plenary in 2022, which took place on 30 November and 1 December in Vienna. The work of the WA was also affected by Russia's invasion of Ukraine. However, because the WA issues a 'chair's statement' rather than a consensus statement at the end of its regular annual plenary, in contrast to the MTCR and the NSG, it was able to

---

[28] International Atomic Energy Agency, Communication received from the Permanent Mission of the Argentine Republic to the International Atomic Energy Agency regarding certain member states' guidelines for transfers of nuclear-related dual-use equipment, materials, software and related technology, Information Circular 245 (revised), INFCIRC/254/Rev.12/Part 2a, 29 July 2022.
[29] Nuclear Suppliers Group, 'Chair's corner'.
[30] United Nations, 'Tenth Non-Proliferation of Nuclear Weapons (NPT) review conference side events organized by states parties'.
[31] Wassenaar Arrangement, 'About us', Updated 17 Dec. 2020.

report on its plenary using the usual channel. Notably, according to the WA secretariat, the WA managed to continue technical discussions during the Covid-19 pandemic during 2020–21, both in person and via videoconferences, and continues to be committed to its core technical work despite the current geopolitical situation.[32]

WA participating states submitted 105 national proposals as part of the 2022 review of the WA control lists. The WA agreed on a series of changes to its dual-use goods and technologies and munitions list, including updates on existing controls of high-performance digital computers, certain types of lasers, submunitions and grenades, aircraft ground equipment, navigational satellite jamming equipment and inertial measurement equipment.[33] New entries were created for certain permanent magnet electric propulsion motors for submarine propulsion, including rim-driven motors, and for supersonic flight technology. The WA also removed the validity notes from previously created entries for sub-orbital craft, lawful interception technology and digital investigation tools.[34] The WA continues to discuss several proposals for possible future controls on emerging technologies, including quantum technologies, additive manufacturing, communications interception and UAV jamming, and will likely require more time to reach consensus irrespective of the geopolitical situation.[35] The WA also continued the process of updating its best practice materials, publishing new versions of the best practices for exercising extreme vigilance regarding Very Sensitive List items and its consolidated indicative list of end-user assurances commonly used.[36]

At the end of 2022, Ireland handed over the plenary chair to India, marking the first time India has assumed the chair of one of the regimes. Argentina and Mexico assumed the respective chairs of the general working group and the expert group, and Switzerland continued to chair the LEEM. In addition, the WA participating states appointed Ambassador György Molnár of Hungary to succeed Ambassador Philip Griffiths of New Zealand as Head of Secretariat of the WA from January 2023.[37]

In September 2022, the WA chair and secretariat briefed the UN disarmament fellows during their visit to the WA, and in November the secretariat briefed the participants in the Scholarship for Peace and Security

---

[32] Fleuriot, V., Presentation delivered at the EUP2P Third Dialogue on Export Control Governance, Brussels, 25 Oct. 2022.
[33] Fleuriot (note 32).
[34] Wassenaar Arrangement, Statement issued by the plenary chair, Vienna, 1 Dec. 2022.
[35] Wassenaar Arrangement, Secretariat, Presentation delivered during the EUP2P Third Dialogue on Export Control Governance, Brussels, 25 Oct. 2022.
[36] Wassenaar Arrangement, 'Extreme vigilance: Sub-set of tier 2 (VSL) items "best practices"', 1 Dec. 2022; and Wassenaar Arrangement, 'End-user assurances commonly used: Consolidated indicative list', 1 Dec. 2022.
[37] Wassenaar Arrangement, Statement issued by the plenary chair (note 34), p. 2.

programme.[38] The WA reported that it had continued expert-level informal technical contacts with the MTCR and the NSG on issues of common interest.[39]

Conclusions

The impact of the global Covid-19 pandemic on the operation of the multilateral export control regimes progressively subsided in 2022, enabling all regimes to return to in-person plenary meetings at the usual time. However, Russia's invasion of Ukraine further disrupted the fragile political agreement in the regimes and in many cases prevented consensus statements being issued. Limited progress on control list updates were nevertheless made by all regimes, with participating states stressing the importance of the regimes' technical work. Regime membership continues to stagnate and interest in the regime adherence procedures continues to be low, with the notable exception of Chile's move to declare adherence to the AG.

Criticism continues to be levelled against the regimes by commentators, particularly from the United States, claiming that they are outdated and failing to deliver results, particularly when it comes to keeping pace with developments in the field of emerging technologies.[40] Russia's invasion of Ukraine and the speed and breadth of the trade restrictions imposed by Western states were also highlighted as legitimizing calls for the regimes to be replaced or supplemented by other arrangements.[41] However, these criticisms often mix objectives linked to geopolitical competition and national security with the non-proliferation and international stability objectives of the regimes. All regimes actively work to address relevant emerging technologies, albeit at a slow pace—due not only to lack of agreement, but also the inherent difficulty of creating adequate list-based controls for emerging technologies where the listings do not become obsolete quickly. The standoff between Russia and other participating states will make the work of the regimes more challenging but have clearly not—to date—made their work impossible or prevented additions and changes to the control lists. Whether this continues to be the case will depend both on the course of the conflict and the wider development of multilateral cooperation on non-proliferation and arms control.

---

[38] Wassenaar Arrangement, 'Outreach', Updated 1 Dec. 2022.
[39] Wassenaar Arrangement, Statement issued by the plenary chair (note 34), p. 2.
[40] See e.g. Shivakumar, S., Wessner, C. and Uno, H., 'Toward a new multilateral export control regime', Center for Strategic and International Studies (CSIS), 10 Jan. 2023.
[41] Wolf, K. and Weinstein, E. S., 'COCOM's daughter?', *WorldECR*, no. 109 (May 2022); and Lewis, J. A., 'Notes on creating an export control regime', CSIS, 15 Dec. 2022.

V. Developments in the European Union's dual-use and arms trade controls

KOLJA BROCKMANN, MARK BROMLEY AND GIOVANNA MALETTA

The European Union (EU) is currently the only regional organization with a common legal framework for controls on the export, brokering, transit and trans-shipment of dual-use items and also, to a certain extent, military items. The key elements of this legal framework are the EU's arms embargoes (addressed in section II of this chapter), the dual-use regulation, foreign and direct investment (FDI) screening regulation, the common position on arms exports, the directive on intra-Community transfers, and the anti-torture regulation. During 2022 the EU took steps to implement a new version of the dual-use regulation which was adopted in 2021. The EU and its member states also reported on steps taken to implement the FDI screening regulation, which entered into force in 2020, and continued to expand its coordination with the United States on export control issues, particularly via the work of the Trade and Technology Council (TTC). The EU also began work on a review of the common position. No major developments took place in the directive on intra-Community transfers or the anti-torture regulation. In a set of parallel developments the EU also discussed how exports of military materiel funded by the European Peace Facility (EPF) will be managed and the steps that will be taken at the EU and member state level to prevent the diversion of supplied weapons.

The EU dual-use regulation

The EU dual-use regulation covers controls on the export, re-export, brokering and transit of dual-use goods, software and technology. The regulation is directly applicable law in EU member states but is implemented and enforced via their national control systems. The regulation was recast as Regulation (EU) 2021/821, which was adopted by the European Parliament in May 2021 and entered into force on 9 September 2021.[1] Regulation (EU) 2021/821 introduces several new elements and consultation procedures.

---

[1] Regulation (EU) 2021/821 of the European Parliament and of the Council of 20 May 2021 setting up a Union regime for the control of exports, brokering, technical assistance, transit and transfer of dual-use items (recast), *Official Journal of the European Union*, L206, 11 June 2021. For a detailed overview of the content of the new regulation, see Bromley, M., Brockmann, K. and Maletta, G., 'Developments in the European Union's dual-use and arms trade controls', *SIPRI Yearbook 2021*, pp. 587–96; Bromley, M., Brockmann, K. and Maletta, G., 'Developments in the European Union's dual-use and arms trade controls', *SIPRI Yearbook 2022*, pp. 620–24; and Bromley, M. and Brockmann, K., 'Implementing the 2021 recast of the EU dual-use regulation: Challenges and opportunities', Non-proliferation and Disarmament Paper no. 77, EU Non-proliferation and Disarmament Consortium, Sep. 2021.

During 2022 the EU took steps to develop guidelines to clarify how these new elements would work.

One of the most significant changes introduced by Regulation (EU) 2021/821 is a new catch-all control for non-listed cybersurveillance items. The regulation commits the Commission and the Council to producing guidelines to help exporters comply with the due-diligence requirements created by the catch-all. The initial aim had been to publish these guidelines by September 2022 following a period of stakeholder review.[2] During 2022 work continued in the surveillance technology experts group (STEG)—a subsidiary body of the EU Dual-Use Coordination Group—on developing these guidelines. However, as of 31 December 2022 no document had been sent out for review. Work was delayed following Russia's invasion of Ukraine and the reallocation of both European Commission and EU member state resources to the development and implementation of the related sanctions measures (see section III in this chapter).[3]

Regulation (EU) 2021/821 also creates new obligations for public reporting on exports of dual-use items, particularly with regard to cybersurveillance items. Here, the EU commits itself to publishing annual data on licence applications by item, origin and destination.[4] The recast tasks the Commission and the Council with developing guidelines to clarify which data will be collected and published.[5] Work on these guidelines began in 2022 in a new technical experts group on data collection and transparency (TEG-Transparency), a subsidiary body of the EU Dual-Use Coordination Group. 2022 also saw the first meetings of some of the new subsidiary bodies established by the regulation. This included a new Enforcement Coordination Mechanism (ECM), which is aimed at bringing together member states' licensing authorities and enforcement agencies to exchange information on 'the detection and prosecution of unauthorised exports of dual-use items' and develop 'best practices among licensing and enforcement authorities in the EU'.[6]

The EU foreign direct investment screening regulation

The EU's 2019 FDI screening regulation seeks to enable the EU and EU member states to identify and respond to cases where FDI might allow foreign companies and governments to own and control critical infrastructure,

---

[2] Farcas-Hutchinson, C., 'Export control of cyber-surveillance items in the EU', Presentation at the 2021 Export Control Forum, Brussels, 8 Dec. 2021.

[3] Communication with EU member state official, 9 Feb. 2023.

[4] Regulation 2021/821 (note 1), Article 26(2).

[5] Regulation 2021/821 (note 1), Article 26(2).

[6] Regulation 2021/821 (note 1), Article 25(2); and European Commission, 'Report for the Commission to the European Parliament and the Council on the implementation of Regulation (EU) 2021/821 setting up a Union regime for the control of exports, brokering, technical assistance, transit and transfer of dual-use items', COM(2021) 716 final, 1 Sep. 2022.

or to gain access to knowledge and technology which may or may not be subject to export controls but which could benefit their defence and security capabilities. The screening regulation does not require EU member states without a screening mechanism in place to establish one. However, the regulation creates obligations for member states to share information about FDI cases that are being screened, while creating a mechanism for other EU member states to provide comments and for the Commission to issue non-binding opinions on certain cases.[7] The FDI screening regulation is not framed as targeting any particular non-EU state. However, it was developed against a background of heightened concern about Chinese investments, while Russia's invasion of Ukraine in February 2022 led to an increased focus on investments from Russia and Belarus.

On 1 September 2022 the Commission published its second annual report on the implementation of the FDI screening regulation, covering the year 2021. The first annual report had already covered the first half of 2021.[8] However, to move to an annual reporting cycle, the information and data provided in the second report overlaps with that provided in the first. The second report was again published together with the Commission's annual report on the implementation of the dual-use regulation, continuing to stress the two instruments' shared focus.[9]

The second annual report noted that by the end of 2021, 18 EU member states had FDI screening mechanisms in place, while 7 were in the process of 'a consultative or legislative process expected to result in the adoption of a new mechanism'.[10] Only two member states (Bulgaria and Cyprus) neither had a mechanism in place nor were in the process of developing one. During 2021, three member states adopted new screening regulations while six updated existing mechanisms.[11] In April 2022 the Commission issued guidance for the member states concerning FDI from Russia and Belarus in the context of the sanctions measures adopted in response to Russia's invasion of Ukraine.

[7] Regulation (EU) 2019/452 of the European Parliament and of the Council of 19 March 2019 establishing a framework for the screening of foreign direct investments into the Union, *Official Journal of the European Union*, L79 I, 21 Mar. 2019, Preamble para. 19.
[8] European Commission, 'First annual report on the screening of foreign direct investments into the Union', Report to the European Parliament and the Council, COM(2021) 714 final, 23 Nov. 2021.
[9] European Commission, 'Report from the Commission to the European Parliament and the Council on the implementation of Regulation (EU) 2021/821 setting up a Union regime for the control of exports, brokering, technical assistance, transit and transfer of dual-use items', COM(2022) 434 final, 2 Sep. 2022.
[10] European Commission, 'Second annual report on the screening of foreign direct investments into the Union', Report to the European Parliament and the Council, COM(2022) 433 final, 1 Sep. 2022, p. 9.
[11] European Commission, COM(2022) 433 final (note 10), pp. 8–9.

As part of the guidance, the Commission again called on all member states to set up adequate FDI screening mechanisms.[12]

The second annual report noted that in 2021, member states reported 1563 requests for authorization and ex-officio cases, 29 per cent of which were formally screened, marking a considerable increase over the 2020 screening rate of 20 per cent.[13] During 2021, member states notified the Commission of 414 transactions with the information and communications technology (36 per cent) and manufacturing (25 per cent) sectors accounting for the largest shares of notified transactions. Over 85 per cent of the cases submitted came from only five member states: Austria, France, Germany, Italy and Spain.[14] Investors from Russia (<1.5 per cent) and Belarus (0.2 per cent) only accounted for a very small share of notified transactions. The largest share of countries of origin of investors in notified cases came, in decreasing order, from the USA, the United Kingdom, China, Cayman Islands and Canada.[15] The Commission closed 86 per cent of notified cases after an initial review phase, while 11 per cent proceeded to the second review phase with the Commission requesting additional information from the member state. The remaining 3 per cent of notified cases were still ongoing at the cut-off time of the report. In less than 3 per cent of notified cases the Commission issued an opinion, which may include sharing relevant information with the screening member state and suggesting mitigating measures to address identified risks.[16] National authorities blocked transactions in only 1 per cent of decided cases, and 3 per cent were withdrawn by the applicants.[17] The second report largely confirmed the same trends outlined in the first report, including 'the trend toward more diversification of screening among member states'—the share of screenings conducted by only four member states dropped from 86.5 per cent in the first report to 70 per cent.[18]

To improve consistency and completeness of notifications, the Commission updated the notification form for investors and its frequently asked questions document.[19] The Organisation for Economic Co-operation and Development (OECD) published findings from an EU-funded study in 2021–22 that assessed

---

[12] European Commission, 'Guidance to the Member States concerning foreign direct investment from Russia and Belarus in view of the military aggression against Ukraine and the restrictive measures laid down in recent Council Regulations on sanctions', *Official Journal of the European Union*, C 151 I, 6 Apr. 2022, pp. 2–3.
[13] European Commission, COM(2022) 433 final (note 10), p. 11.
[14] European Commission, COM(2022) 433 final (note 10), p. 14.
[15] European Commission, COM(2022) 433 final (note 10), p. 18.
[16] European Commission, COM(2022) 433 final (note 10), pp. 14–16, 19.
[17] European Commission, COM(2022) 433 final (note 10), p. 12.
[18] European Commission, COM(2022) 433 final (note 10), p. 19.
[19] European Commission, 'Request for information from the investor for the purposes of notifications pursuant to Article 6 of Regulation (EU) 2019/452', Apr. 2021; and European Commission, 'Frequently asked questions on Regulation (EU) 2019/452 establishing a framework for the screening of foreign direct investments into the Union', June 2019, Update of 22 June 2021.

the EU's FDI screening regulation and ways to improve its effectiveness and efficiency. The study identified a list of issues to be addressed, including a lack of screening mechanism in some member states, gaps in coverage in others, lack of prioritization, resources, competencies and accountability, short timelines, inefficiencies in information exchange and issues with screening multi-jurisdictional transactions.[20] While the context of Russia's invasion of Ukraine and the continuing geopolitics and competition with China have brought additional attention to the EU's FDI screening framework, most member states are still setting up or updating their systems. The EU will likely continue to work on revisions to the screening regulation and improvements to its implementation.

European and United States cooperation on export controls

Cooperation between the USA and the EU in the field of export controls continued to deepen in 2022. The most visible manifestation of this cooperation was the adoption of aligned trade restrictions on Russia and Belarus in response to Russia's invasion of Ukraine (see section III in this chapter). The USA and the EU also conducted regular meetings of the Trade and Technology Council (TTC), whose ten working groups on a wide range of trade and technology topics include two on the 'misuse of technology threatening security and human rights' and export controls.[21] The imposition of trade restrictions on Russia and Belarus became one of the main focuses for the work of the TTC in 2022 and the body became a key means for the EU and the USA to exchange information on their implementation. At the TTC's second ministerial meeting, held in Paris in May 2022, the EU and the USA agreed to expand the work on sanctions measures by focusing on exports of 'critical' US and EU technology, 'with an initial focus on Russia and other potential sanctions evaders'.[22] At the third ministerial meeting, held in December 2022 in College Park, Maryland, the EU and the USA also agreed to 'further cooperate' on export controls on advanced technologies against Russia, 'particularly with respect to information sharing'.[23] More broadly, the TTC discussed ways in which the EU and the USA could coordinate in the

---

[20] Organisation for Economic Co-operation and Development (OECD) Secretariat, Directorate for Financial and Enterprise Affairs, Investment Division, *Framework for Screening Foreign Direct Investment into the EU: Assessing Effectiveness and Efficiency* (OECD: Paris, 2022), chapter 2.

[21] European Commission, 'EU–US launch Trade and Technology Council to lead values-based global digital transformation', Press release, IP/2021/2990, 15 June 2021.

[22] White House, 'US–EU Trade and Technology Council establishes economic and technology policies & initiatives', Fact Sheet, 16 May 2022.

[23] European Commission, 'EU–US Trade and Technology Council addresses common challenges and responds to global crises', Press release, IP/22/7433, 5 Dec. 2022.

provision of outreach and assistance efforts, expand information sharing on export licence denials, and collaborate on enforcement measures.[24]

The EU common position on arms exports

The EU common position on arms exports (common position) covers controls on the export, transit, trans-shipment and brokering of military equipment and technology.[25] Discussions among EU member states on issues related to the implementation of the common position occur at a regular basis at the Council Working Party on Conventional Arms Exports (COARM), chaired by the European External Action Service (EEAS).

In 2022, COARM continued to work towards the implementation of the 2019 Council conclusions that were agreed as the outcome of the last review of the common position.[26] The conclusions highlighted the need to improve the level of transparency in arms exports. However, the 24th EU annual report on arms exports—which provides disaggregated data on the financial value and number of member states' export licences, the value of their actual exports, and aggregated data on licence denials in 2021—was only published in December 2022.[27] This represented a negative development in comparison with the progress in timeliness achieved in the previous two years, as the 22nd and the 23rd annual reports were published in November 2020 and September 2021, respectively.[28] Further, the annual report showed, once again, that not all EU member states were able to make a complete submission, with several still unable to deliver disaggregated data on actual exports (table 12.4).[29]

The main development in the implementation of the 2019 Council conclusions was the launch in 2022 of a closed database for licensing officers from EU member states. The platform allows users to access relevant and open-source information on potential countries of destination of mili-

---

[24] European Commission, 'EU–US joint statement of the Trade and Technology Council', Statement 22/7516, 5 Dec. 2022.

[25] Council Common Position 2008/944/CFSP of 8 December 2008 defining common rules governing control of exports of military technology and equipment, *Official Journal of the European Union*, L335, 8 Dec. 2008.

[26] Council of the European Union, 'Council conclusions on the review of Council Common Position 2008/944/CFSP of 8 December 2008 on the control of arms exports', 12195/19, 16 Sep. 2019.

[27] European External Action Service (EEAS), '24th annual report on arms exports (for 2021) launched: EU is a transparent and responsible trader in arms', 19 Dec. 2022; and Council of the European Union, 'Twenty-fourth annual report according to Article 8(2) of Council Common Position 2008/944/CFSP defining common rules governing the control of exports of military technology and equipment', *Official Journal of the European Union*, C59, 16 Feb. 2023 (published on 19 Dec. 2022 as Council document 16164/22).

[28] Bromley, Brockmann and Maletta, *SIPRI Yearbook 2022* (note 1), p. 629.

[29] In particular, according to the EU annual report, 'Belgium, Cyprus, Germany, Greece and Latvia do not provide these data'. Council of the European Union, 16164/22 (note 27), p. 9.

Table 12.4. Submissions of information to the European Union annual report on arms exports, 2011–21

Annual report	Year covered	No. of states obliged to make submissions	No. of states making submissions	No. of states making full submissions[a]	Proportion of states making full submissions (%)
24th	2021	27	27	22	82
23rd	2020	27[b]	27	23	85
22nd	2019	28	28	21	75
21st	2018	28	28	21	75
20th	2017	28	27[c]	19	68
19th	2016	28	27[c]	19	68
18th	2015	28	27[c]	19	68
17th	2014	28	28	21	75
16th	2013	28	27[c]	21	75
15th	2012	27[d]	27	20	74
14th	2011	27	27	18	67

[a] A 'full submission' is taken to be data on the financial value of both arms export licences issued and actual exports, broken down by both destination and European Union (EU) military list category.

[b] The United Kingdom officially left the EU on 31 January 2020 and was not obliged to submit data for 2020.

[c] Greece did not submit data to the 16th, 18th, 19th and 20th reports.

[d] Croatia joined the EU in 2013 and was not obliged to submit data for 2012. It submitted data for the first time to the 16th report.

Sources: Council of the European Union, 'Twenty-fourth annual report according to Article 8(2) of Council Common Position 2008/944/CFSP defining common rules governing the control of exports of military technology and equipment', *Official Journal of the European Union*, C59, 16 Feb. 2023.

tary materiel and is meant to enhance convergence in the way arms export decisions are taken across the EU.[30]

In 2022 COARM also started preparations for the next review of the common position, scheduled to be completed in 2024.[31] As part of this process, three focus groups will look specifically at issues related to harmonization (under the lead of Germany and Sweden), enforcement (under the lead of Italy and Czechia) and commonly produced military equipment (under the lead of France and the Netherlands).[32] Further, COARM will also continue discussing the export control implications of initiatives and developments in the field of EU defence and security policy, including those related to the implementation of the EPF.[33]

---

[30] Council of the European Union, 16164/22 (note 27), p. 2.

[31] Council of the European Union, 16164/22 (note 27), p. 5.

[32] Romestan, D., 'Aux armes, citoyens?' [To arms, citizens?], *WorldECR*, no. 114 (Nov. 2022); Saferworld, 'European Arms Export Control in a changing European defence landscape', Aug. 2022, p. 6; and EU official, email exchange with authors, 27 Feb. 2023.

[33] Council of the European Union, 16164/22 (note 27), p. 5.

Arms transfers to Ukraine through the European Peace Facility

The EPF, an off-budget mechanism established in March 2021, provides funding for EU external actions in the field of crisis management and conflict prevention that have military and defence implications. These actions can encompass assistance measures to strengthen the military and defence capacities of third states, including through the supply of lethal military materiel (i.e. weapons).[34]

In February 2022, one of the measures that the EU adopted in response to the Russian invasion of Ukraine was to use the EPF to fund the transfer of military materiel to Ukrainian armed forces, including weapon systems.[35] This marks the first time that the EU has used this mechanism to fund the supply of lethal military equipment and the first time that arms transfers have been funded through resources pooled and managed at the EU level. At the end of 2022, EPF assistance measures providing military assistance to Ukraine were worth more than €3 billion, most of which was allocated to fund the supply of lethal military equipment by EU member states.[36] Additional EPF resources (€16 million) were allocated to fund the supply of weapons and ammunition, among others things, to Kyiv as part of the work of the EU Military Assistance Mission in support of Ukraine.[37]

In this context, the EPF has been used to partially reimburse EU member states for the weapons that they have been delivering to Ukraine since the beginning of the conflict.[38] These requests are coordinated through a clearing house mechanism set up by the EU military staff which also allows for the matching of Ukraine's requests for equipment with what EU member states—and other like-minded states—can provide.[39]

However, to the extent the EU, through the EEAS, is responsible for the implementation of EPF assistance measures, the establishment of this mechanism has assigned an unprecedented role to the Union in the implementation of arms export controls in both the pre- and post-licensing

---

[34] Council Decision 2021/509 of 22 March 2021 establishing a European Peace Facility, and repealing Decision (CFSP) 2015/528, *Official Journal of the European Union*, L102/14, 24 Mar. 2021; and Maletta, G. and Héau, L., *Funding Arms Transfers Through the European Peace Facility: Preventing Risks of Diversion and Misuse* (SIPRI: Stockholm, June 2022).

[35] Council Decision (CFSP) 2022/338 of 28 February 2022 on an assistance measure under the European Peace Facility for the supply to the Ukrainian armed forces of military equipment, and platforms, designed to deliver lethal force, *Official Journal of the European Union*, L60, 28 Feb. 2022; and EEAS, 'EU adopts new set of measures to respond to Russia's military aggression against Ukraine', Press release, 28 Feb. 2022.

[36] Bilquin, B., 'European Peace Facility: Ukraine and beyond', European Parliament Think Tank, 18 Nov. 2022.

[37] Council of the European Union, 'Ukraine: EU launches Military Assistance Mission', Press release 953/22, 15 Nov. 2022.

[38] Brzozowski, A., 'EU arms fund faces reimbursement issues amid increased Ukrainian needs', EURACTIV, 14. Oct. 2022.

[39] Maletta and Héau (note 34), p. 6; and Bilquin (note 36).

phase, a process that the provision of military assistance to Ukraine has accelerated. In this context, the EU completed assessments of the risk and impact of such assistance and conducted at least one post-shipment on-site verification visit of the materiel delivered in Ukraine. This raises questions on how to coordinate these EU-level efforts with those at member-state level to avoid duplication, with a view to creating a harmonized approach and making best use of the resources available at both levels.[40]

Conclusions

Discussions and processes concerning the content and implementation of the EU's system of dual-use and arms trade controls were dominated in 2022 by the repercussions of Russia's invasion of Ukraine and the adoption of comprehensive and wide-ranging trade restrictions on Belarus and Ukraine. Formulating and applying these controls occupied a significant amount of the working time of export control staff at both the EU and member-state levels during 2022. This diversion of resources may account for some of the delays seen in the adoption of the required measures associated with implementing the recast of the dual-use regulation. At the same time, the trade restrictions on Russia and Belarus demonstrated the relevance of the recast dual-use regulation, as well as other mechanisms and processes that the EU has developed in recent years for coordinating export control measures internally and in cooperation with the USA. These included the newly created ECM, the TTC, and the FDI screening mechanism, all of which were used to either coordinate or enforce new trade control measures on Russia and Belarus. The EU's response to Russia's invasion of Ukraine also saw it use the newly created EPF to fund significant quantities of arms transfers to Ukraine. This represents a significant departure for the EU and creates challenges concerning both preventing diversion and ensuring the effective coordination of EU and member states' resources and expertise.

---

[40] European Parliament, 'The war in Ukraine: Implications for arms export policies at the EU level', Hearing of the Subcommittee on Security and Defence of the European Parliament, 29 Nov. 2022.

Annexes

Annex A. Arms control and disarmament agreements

Annex B. International security cooperation bodies

Annex C. Chronology 2022

Annex A. Arms control and disarmament agreements

This annex lists multi- and bilateral treaties, conventions, protocols and agreements relating to arms control and disarmament. Unless otherwise stated, the status of agreements and of their parties and signatories is as of 1 January 2023. On the international security cooperation bodies mentioned here, see annex B.

Notes

1. The agreements are divided into universal treaties (i.e. multilateral treaties open to all states, in section I), regional treaties (i.e. multilateral treaties open to states of a particular region, in section II) and bilateral treaties (in section III). Within each section, the agreements are listed in the order of the date on which they were adopted, signed or opened for signature (multilateral agreements) or signed (bilateral agreements). The date on which they entered into force and the depositary for multilateral treaties are also given.

2. The main source of information is the lists of signatories and parties provided by the depositaries of the treaties. In lists of parties and signatories, states whose name appears in italics ratified, acceded or succeeded to, or signed the agreement during 2022.

3. States and organizations listed as parties had ratified, acceded to or succeeded to the agreements by 1 January 2023. Since many agreements delay the entry into force for a state for a certain period after ratification or accession, when that occurred late in 2022 the agreement may not have fully entered into force for that state by 1 January 2023.

4. Former non-self-governing territories, upon attaining statehood, sometimes make general statements of continuity to all agreements concluded by the former governing power. This annex lists as parties only those new states that have made an uncontested declaration on continuity or have notified the depositary of their succession. The Russian Federation continues the international obligations of the Soviet Union.

5. Unless stated otherwise, the multilateral agreements listed in this annex are open to all states, to all states in the respective zone or region, or to all members of a certain international organization for signature, ratification, accession or succession. Not all the signatories and parties are United Nations members. Taiwan, while not recognized as a sovereign state by many countries, is listed as a party to the agreements that it has ratified.

6. Where possible, the location (in a printed publication or online) of an accurate copy of the treaty text is given. This may be provided by a treaty depositary, an agency or secretariat connected with the treaty, or in the *United Nations Treaty Series* (available online at <https://treaties.un.org/>).

SIPRI Yearbook 2023: Armaments, Disarmament and International Security
www.sipriyearbook.org

I. Universal treaties

Convention for the Supervision of the International Trade in Arms and Ammunition and in Implements of War

Signed at Geneva on 17 June 1925; never entered into force; depositary French government

The convention would have created a system for supervision and transparency in the international arms trade. It would also have banned the import or export of weapons otherwise prohibited by international law. It was to have entered into force after ratification by 14 states, but it never did so since many states conditioned their ratification on ratification by others.

Ratifications deposited (16): Australia*, Canada, China, Denmark*, Egypt, France*, Iraq, Latvia*, Liberia, Netherlands, Poland*, Spain, Sweden*, UK*, USA, Venezuela

Signed but never ratified (22): Austria, Belgium, Brazil, Bulgaria, Chile, Czechoslovakia, El Salvador, Estonia*, Ethiopia, Finland*, Germany, Hungary, India, Italy, Japan, Luxembourg, Norway, Romania*, Switzerland, Thailand, Uruguay, Yugoslavia

* With reservation and/or declaration.

Convention text: League of Nations, *Conference for the Supervision of the International Trade in Arms and Ammunition and in Implements of War* (League of Nations: Geneva, 20 July 1925), <https://archives.ungeneva.org/kqhq-4p3a-ksmf>

Protocol for the Prohibition of the Use in War of Asphyxiating, Poisonous or Other Gases, and of Bacteriological Methods of Warfare (1925 Geneva Protocol)

Signed at Geneva on 17 June 1925; entered into force on 8 February 1928; depositary French government

The protocol prohibits the use in war of asphyxiating, poisonous or other gases and of bacteriological methods of warfare. The protocol remains a fundamental basis of the international prohibition against chemical and biological warfare, and its principles, objectives and obligations are explicitly supported by the 1972 Biological and Toxin Weapons Convention and the 1993 Chemical Weapons Convention.

Parties (147): Afghanistan, Albania, Algeria, Angola, Antigua and Barbuda, Argentina, Armenia, Australia, Austria, Bahrain, Bangladesh, Barbados, Belgium, Benin, Bhutan, Bolivia, Brazil, Bulgaria, Burkina Faso, Cabo Verde, Cambodia, Cameroon, Canada, Central African Republic, Chile, China, Colombia, Costa Rica, Côte d'Ivoire, Croatia, Cuba, Cyprus, Czechia, Denmark, Dominican Republic, Ecuador, Egypt, El Salvador, Equatorial Guinea, Estonia, Eswatini, Ethiopia, Fiji, Finland, France, Gambia, Germany, Ghana, Greece, Grenada, Guatemala, Guinea-Bissau, Holy See, Hungary, Iceland, India, Indonesia, Iran, Iraq, Ireland, Israel, Italy, Jamaica, Japan, Jordan, Kazakhstan, Kenya, Korea (North), Korea (South), Kuwait, Kyrgyzstan, Laos, Latvia, Lebanon, Lesotho, Liberia, Libya, Liechtenstein, Lithuania, Luxembourg, Madagascar, Malawi, Malaysia, Maldives, Malta, Mauritius, Mexico, Moldova, Monaco, Mongolia, Morocco, Nepal, Netherlands, New Zealand, Nicaragua, Niger, Nigeria, North Macedonia, Norway, Pakistan, Palestine, Panama, Papua New

Guinea, Paraguay, Peru, Philippines, Poland, Portugal, Qatar, Romania, Russia, Rwanda, Saint Kitts and Nevis, Saint Lucia, Saint Vincent and the Grenadines, Saudi Arabia, Senegal, Serbia, Sierra Leone, Slovakia, Slovenia, Solomon Islands, South Africa, Spain, Sri Lanka, Sudan, Sweden, Switzerland, Syria, Taiwan, Tajikistan, Tanzania, Thailand, Togo, Tonga, Trinidad and Tobago, Tunisia, Türkiye, Uganda, UK, Ukraine, Uruguay, Uzbekistan, USA, Venezuela, Viet Nam, Yemen

Notes: On joining the protocol, some states entered reservations which upheld their right to employ chemical or biological weapons against non-parties to the protocol, against coalitions which included non-parties or in response to the use of these weapons by a violating party. Many of these states have withdrawn these reservations, particularly after the conclusion of the 1972 Biological and Toxin Weapons Convention and the 1993 Chemical Weapons Convention since the reservations are incompatible with their obligation under the conventions.

In addition to these, 'explicit', reservations, a number of states that made a declaration of succession to the protocol on gaining independence inherited 'implicit' reservations from their respective predecessor states. For example, these implicit reservations apply to the states that gained independence from France and the UK before the latter states withdrew or amended their reservations. States that acceded (rather than succeeded) to the protocol did not inherit reservations in this way.

Protocol text: League of Nations, *Treaty Series*, vol. 94 (1929), <https://treaties.un.org/doc/Publication/UNTS/LON/Volume 94/v94.pdf>

Convention on the Prevention and Punishment of the Crime of Genocide (Genocide Convention)

Opened for signature at Paris on 9 December 1948; entered into force on 12 January 1951; depositary UN secretary-general

Under the convention any commission of acts intended to destroy, in whole or in part, a national, ethnic, racial or religious group as such is declared to be a crime punishable under international law.

Parties (153): Afghanistan, Albania*, Algeria*, Andorra, Antigua and Barbuda, Argentina*, Armenia, Australia, Austria, Azerbaijan, Bahamas, Bahrain*, Bangladesh*, Barbados, Belarus*, Belgium, Belize, Benin, Bolivia, Bosnia and Herzegovina, Brazil, Bulgaria*, Burkina Faso, Burundi, Cabo Verde, Cambodia, Canada, Chile, China*, Colombia, Comoros, Congo (Democratic Republic of the), Costa Rica, Côte d'Ivoire, Croatia, Cuba, Cyprus, Czechia, Denmark, Dominica, Ecuador, Egypt, El Salvador, Estonia, Ethiopia, Fiji, Finland, France, Gabon, Gambia, Georgia, Germany, Ghana, Greece, Guatemala, Guinea, Guinea-Bissau, Haiti, Honduras, Hungary*, Iceland, India*, Iran, Iraq, Ireland, Israel, Italy, Jamaica, Jordan, Kazakhstan, Korea (North), Korea (South), Kuwait, Kyrgyzstan, Laos, Latvia, Lebanon, Lesotho, Liberia, Libya, Liechtenstein, Lithuania, Luxembourg, Malawi, Malaysia*, Maldives, Mali, Malta, Mauritius, Mexico, Moldova, Monaco, Mongolia*, Montenegro*, Morocco*, Mozambique, Myanmar*, Namibia, Nepal, Netherlands, New Zealand, Nicaragua, Nigeria, North Macedonia, Norway, Pakistan, Palestine, Panama, Papua New Guinea, Paraguay, Peru, Philippines*, Poland*, Portugal, Romania*, Russia*, Rwanda, Saint Vincent and the Grenadines, San Marino, Saudi Arabia, Senegal, Serbia*, Seychelles, Singapore*, Slovakia, Slovenia, South Africa, Spain, Sri Lanka, Sudan, Sweden, Switzerland, Syria, Tajikistan, Tanzania, Togo, Tonga, Trinidad and Tobago, Tunisia, Türkiye, Turkmenistan, Uganda, UK, Ukraine*, United Arab Emirates*, Uruguay, USA*, Uzbekistan, Venezuela*, Viet Nam*, Yemen*, *Zambia*, Zimbabwe

* With reservation and/or declaration.

Signed but not ratified (1): Dominican Republic

Convention text: United Nations Treaty Collection, <https://treaties.un.org/doc/Treaties/1951/01/19510112 08-12 PM/Ch_IV_1p.pdf>

Geneva Convention (IV) Relative to the Protection of Civilian Persons in Time of War

Opened for signature at Geneva on 12 August 1949; entered into force on 21 October 1950; depositary Swiss Federal Council

The Geneva Convention (IV) establishes rules for the protection of civilians in areas covered by war and in occupied territories. Three other conventions were formulated at the same time, at a diplomatic conference held from 21 April to 12 August 1949: Convention (I) for the Amelioration of the Condition of the Wounded and Sick in Armed Forces in the Field; Convention (II) for the Amelioration of the Condition of the Wounded, Sick and Shipwrecked Members of Armed Forces at Sea; and Convention (III) Relative to the Treatment of Prisoners of War.

A party may withdraw from the convention, having given one year's notice. But if the party is involved in an armed conflict at that time, the withdrawal will not take effect until peace has been concluded and that party's obligations under the convention fulfilled.

Parties (196): Afghanistan, Albania*, Algeria, Andorra, Angola*, Antigua and Barbuda, Argentina, Armenia, Australia*, Austria, Azerbaijan, Bahamas, Bahrain, Bangladesh*, Barbados*, Belarus, Belgium, Belize, Benin, Bhutan, Bolivia, Bosnia and Herzegovina, Botswana, Brazil, Brunei Darussalam, Bulgaria, Burkina Faso, Burundi, Cabo Verde, Cambodia, Cameroon, Canada, Central African Republic, Chad, Chile, China*, Colombia, Comoros, Congo (Democratic Republic of the), Congo (Republic of the), Cook Islands, Costa Rica, Côte d'Ivoire, Croatia, Cuba, Cyprus, Czechia*, Denmark, Djibouti, Dominica, Dominican Republic, Ecuador, Egypt, El Salvador, Equatorial Guinea, Estonia, Eritrea, Eswatini, Ethiopia, Fiji, Finland, France, Gabon, Gambia, Georgia, Germany*, Ghana, Greece, Grenada, Guatemala, Guinea, Guinea-Bissau*, Guyana, Haiti, Holy See, Honduras, Hungary, Iceland, India, Indonesia, Iran*, Iraq, Ireland, Israel*, Italy, Jamaica, Japan, Jordan, Kazakhstan, Kenya, Kiribati, Korea (North)*, Korea (South)*, Kuwait*, Kyrgyzstan, Laos, Latvia, Lebanon, Lesotho, Liberia, Libya, Liechtenstein, Lithuania, Luxembourg, Madagascar, Malawi, Malaysia, Maldives, Mali, Malta, Marshall Islands, Mauritania, Mauritius, Mexico, Micronesia, Moldova, Monaco, Mongolia, Montenegro, Morocco, Mozambique, Myanmar, Namibia, Nauru, Nepal, Netherlands, New Zealand*, Nicaragua, Niger, Nigeria, North Macedonia*, Norway, Oman, Pakistan*, Palau, Palestine, Panama, Papua New Guinea, Paraguay, Peru, Philippines, Poland, Portugal*, Qatar, Romania, Russia*, Rwanda, Saint Kitts and Nevis, Saint Lucia, Saint Vincent and the Grenadines, Samoa, San Marino, Sao Tome and Principe, Saudi Arabia, Senegal, Serbia, Seychelles, Sierra Leone, Singapore, Slovakia, Slovenia, Solomon Islands, Somalia, South Africa, South Sudan, Spain, Sri Lanka, Sudan, Suriname*, Sweden, Switzerland, Syria, Tajikistan, Tanzania, Thailand, Timor-Leste, Togo, Tonga, Trinidad and Tobago, Tunisia, Türkiye, Turkmenistan, Tuvalu, Uganda, UK*, Ukraine*, United Arab Emirates, Uruguay*, USA*, Uzbekistan, Vanuatu, Venezuela, Viet Nam*, Yemen*, Zambia, Zimbabwe

* With reservation and/or declaration.

Convention text: Swiss Federal Department of Foreign Affairs, <https://www.fdfa.admin.ch/dam/eda/fr/documents/aussenpolitik/voelkerrecht/geneve/070116-conv4_e.pdf>

Protocol I Additional to the 1949 Geneva Conventions, and Relating to the Protection of Victims of International Armed Conflicts

Protocol II Additional to the 1949 Geneva Conventions, and Relating to the Protection of Victims of Non-International Armed Conflicts

Opened for signature at Bern on 12 December 1977; entered into force on 7 December 1978; depositary Swiss Federal Council

The protocols confirm that parties engaged in an armed conflict do not have an unlimited right to choose methods or means of warfare and that the use of weapons or means of warfare that cause superfluous injury or unnecessary suffering is prohibited.

Article 36 of Protocol I requires a state party, when developing or acquiring a new weapon, to determine whether its use could be prohibited by international law.

Parties to Protocol I (174) and Protocol II (169): Afghanistan, Albania, Algeria*, Angola*, Antigua and Barbuda, Argentina*, Armenia, Australia*, Austria*, Bahamas, Bahrain, Bangladesh, Barbados, Belarus*, Belgium*, Belize, Benin, Bolivia*, Bosnia and Herzegovina*, Botswana, Brazil*, Brunei Darussalam, Bulgaria*, Burkina Faso*, Burundi, Cabo Verde*, Cambodia, Cameroon, Canada*, Central African Republic, Chad, Chile*, China*, Colombia*, Comoros, Congo (Democratic Republic of the)*, Congo (Republic of the), Cook Islands*, Costa Rica*, Côte d'Ivoire, Croatia*, Cuba, Cyprus*, Czechia*, Denmark*, Djibouti, Dominica, Dominican Republic, Ecuador, Egypt*, El Salvador, Equatorial Guinea, Estonia*, Eswatini, Ethiopia, Fiji, Finland*, France*, Gabon, Gambia, Georgia, Germany*, Ghana, Greece*, Grenada, Guatemala, Guinea*, Guinea-Bissau, Guyana, Haiti, Holy See*, Honduras, Hungary*, Iceland*, Iraq[1], Ireland*, Italy*, Jamaica, Japan*, Jordan, Kazakhstan, Kenya, Korea (North)[1], Korea (South)*, Kuwait*, Kyrgyzstan, Laos*, Latvia, Lebanon, Lesotho*, Liberia, Libya, Liechtenstein*, Lithuania*, Luxembourg*, Madagascar*, Malawi*, Maldives, Mali*, Malta*, Mauritania, Mauritius*, Mexico[1], Micronesia, Moldova, Monaco*, Mongolia*, Montenegro*, Morocco, Mozambique, Namibia*, Nauru, Netherlands*, New Zealand*, Nicaragua, Niger, Nigeria, North Macedonia*, Norway*, Oman*, Palau, Palestine, Panama*, Paraguay*, Peru, Philippines*, Poland*, Portugal*, Qatar*, Romania*, Russia*, Rwanda*, Saint Kitts and Nevis*, Saint Lucia, Saint Vincent and the Grenadines*, Samoa, San Marino, Sao Tome and Principe, Saudi Arabia*, Senegal, Serbia*, Seychelles*, Sierra Leone, Slovakia*, Slovenia*, Solomon Islands, South Africa, South Sudan, Spain*, Sudan, Suriname, Sweden*, Switzerland*, Syria*[1], Tajikistan*, Tanzania, Timor-Leste, Togo*, Tonga*, Trinidad and Tobago*, Tunisia, Turkmenistan, Uganda, UK*, Ukraine*, United Arab Emirates*, Uruguay*, Uzbekistan, Vanuatu, Venezuela, Viet Nam[1], Yemen, Zambia, Zimbabwe

* With reservation and/or declaration.
[1] Party only to Protocol I.

Signed but not ratified Protocols I and II (3): Iran, Pakistan, USA

Protocol I text: Swiss Federal Department of Foreign Affairs, <https://www.fdfa.admin.ch/dam/eda/fr/documents/aussenpolitik/voelkerrecht/geneve/77prot1_en.pdf>

Protocol II text: Swiss Federal Department of Foreign Affairs, <https://www.fdfa.admin.ch/dam/eda/fr/documents/aussenpolitik/voelkerrecht/geneve77/prot2_en.pdf>

Antarctic Treaty

Signed by the 12 original parties at Washington, DC, on 1 December 1959; entered into force on 23 June 1961; depositary US government

The treaty declares the Antarctic an area to be used exclusively for peaceful purposes. It prohibits any measure of a military nature in the Antarctic, such as the establishment of military bases and fortifications and the carrying out of military manoeuvres or the testing of any type of weapon. The treaty bans any nuclear explosion as well as the disposal of radioactive waste material in Antarctica.

States that demonstrate their interest in Antarctica by conducting substantial scientific research activity there, such as the establishment of a scientific station or the dispatch of a scientific expedition, are entitled to become consultative parties. The consultative parties meet each year in an Antarctic Treaty Consultative Meeting. Consultative parties have a right to inspect any station or installation in Antarctica to ensure compliance with the treaty's provisions. A secretariat, based in Buenos Aires, was established in 2001.

Parties (55): Argentina*, Australia*, Austria, Belarus, Belgium*, Brazil*, Bulgaria*, Canada, Chile*, China*, Colombia, *Costa Rica*, Cuba, Czechia*, Denmark, Ecuador*, Estonia, Finland*, France*, Germany*, Greece, Guatemala, Hungary, Iceland, India*, Italy*, Japan*, Kazakhstan, Korea (North), Korea (South)*, Malaysia, Monaco, Mongolia, Netherlands*, New Zealand*, Norway*, Pakistan, Papua New Guinea, Peru*, Poland*, Portugal, Romania, Russia*, Slovakia, Slovenia, South Africa*, Spain*, Sweden*, Switzerland, Türkiye, UK*, Ukraine*, Uruguay*, USA*, Venezuela

* Consultative party (29) under Article IX of the treaty.

Note: In addition to the 55 states parties as of 1 Jan. 2023, San Marino acceded to the treaty on 14 Feb. 2023.

Treaty text: Secretariat of the Antarctic Treaty, <https://www.ats.aq/documents/ats/treaty_original.pdf>

> The Protocol on Environmental Protection (**1991 Madrid Protocol**) was opened for signature on 4 October 1991 and entered into force on 14 January 1998. It designated Antarctica as a natural reserve, devoted to peace and science.
>
> *Protocol text*: Secretariat of the Antarctic Treaty, <https://www.ats.aq/documents/recatt/Att006_e.pdf>

Treaty Banning Nuclear Weapon Tests in the Atmosphere, in Outer Space and Under Water (Partial Test-Ban Treaty, PTBT)

Signed by three original parties at Moscow on 5 August 1963 and opened for signature by other states at London, Moscow and Washington, DC, on 8 August 1963; entered into force on 10 October 1963; depositaries British, Russian and US governments

The treaty prohibits the carrying out of any nuclear weapon test explosion or any other nuclear explosion (*a*) in the atmosphere, beyond its limits, including outer space, or under water, including territorial waters or high seas; and (*b*) in any other environment if such explosion causes radioactive debris to be present outside the territorial limits of the state under whose jurisdiction or control the explosion is conducted.

A party may withdraw from the treaty, having given three months' notice, if it decides that its supreme interests have been jeopardized by extraordinary events related to the treaty's subject matter.

Parties (126): Afghanistan, Antigua and Barbuda, Argentina, Armenia, Australia, Austria, Bahamas, Bangladesh, Belarus, Belgium, Benin, Bhutan, Bolivia, Bosnia and Herzegovina, Botswana, Brazil, Bulgaria, Cabo Verde, Canada, Central African Republic, Chad, Chile, Colombia, Congo (Democratic Republic of the), Costa Rica, Côte d'Ivoire, Croatia, Cyprus, Czechia, Denmark, Dominican Republic, Ecuador, Egypt, El Salvador, Equatorial Guinea, Eswatini, Fiji, Finland, Gabon, Gambia, Germany, Ghana, Greece, Guatemala, Guinea-Bissau, Honduras, Hungary, Iceland, India, Indonesia, Iran, Iraq, Ireland, Israel, Italy, Jamaica, Japan, Jordan, Kenya, Korea (South), Kuwait, Laos, Lebanon, Liberia, Libya, Luxembourg, Madagascar, Malawi, Malaysia, Malta, Mauritania, Mauritius, Mexico, Mongolia, Montenegro, Morocco, Myanmar, Nepal, Netherlands, New Zealand, Nicaragua, Niger, Nigeria, Norway, Pakistan, Panama, Papua New Guinea, Peru, Philippines, Poland, Romania, Russia, Rwanda, Samoa, San Marino, Senegal, Serbia, Seychelles, Sierra Leone, Singapore, Slovakia, Slovenia, South Africa, Spain, Sri Lanka, Sudan, Suriname, Sweden, Switzerland, Syria, Taiwan, Tanzania, Thailand, Togo, Tonga, Trinidad and Tobago, Tunisia, Türkiye, Uganda, UK, Ukraine, Uruguay, USA, Venezuela, Yemen, Zambia

Signed but not ratified (10): Algeria, Burkina Faso, Burundi, Cameroon, Ethiopia, Haiti, Mali, Paraguay, Portugal, Somalia

Treaty text: Russian Ministry of Foreign Affairs, <https://mddoc.mid.ru/api/ia/download/?uuid=561590f5-ed1a-4e2a-a04e-f715bccb16ad>

Treaty on Principles Governing the Activities of States in the Exploration and Use of Outer Space, Including the Moon and Other Celestial Bodies (Outer Space Treaty)

Opened for signature at London, Moscow and Washington, DC, on 27 January 1967; entered into force on 10 October 1967; depositaries British, Russian and US governments

The treaty prohibits the placing into orbit around the earth of any object carrying nuclear weapons or any other kind of weapon of mass destruction, the installation of such weapons on celestial bodies, or the stationing of them in outer space in any other manner. The establishment of military bases, installations and fortifications, the testing of any type of weapon and the conducting of military manoeuvres on celestial bodies are also forbidden.

A party may withdraw from the treaty having given one year's notice.

Parties (113): Afghanistan, Algeria, Antigua and Barbuda, Argentina, Armenia, Australia, Austria, Azerbaijan, Bahamas, Bahrain, Bangladesh, Barbados, Belarus, Belgium, Benin, Bosnia and Herzegovina, Brazil, Bulgaria, Burkina Faso, Canada, Chile, China, Cuba, Cyprus, Czechia, Denmark, Dominican Republic, Ecuador, Egypt, El Salvador, Equatorial Guinea, Estonia, Fiji, Finland, France, Germany, Greece, Guinea-Bissau, Hungary, Iceland, India, Indonesia, Iraq, Ireland, Israel, Italy, Jamaica, Japan, Kazakhstan, Kenya, Korea (North), Korea (South), Kuwait, Laos, Lebanon, Libya, Lithuania, Luxembourg, Madagascar, Mali, Malta, Mauritius, Mexico, Mongolia, Morocco, Myanmar, Nepal, Netherlands, New Zealand,

Nicaragua, Niger, Nigeria, Norway, *Oman*, Pakistan, Papua New Guinea, Paraguay, Peru, Poland, Portugal, Qatar, Romania, Russia, Saint Vincent and the Grenadines, San Marino, Saudi Arabia, Seychelles, Sierra Leone, Singapore, Slovakia, Slovenia, South Africa, Spain, Sri Lanka, Sweden, Switzerland, Syria, Taiwan, Thailand, Togo, Tonga, Tunisia, Türkiye, Uganda, UK, Ukraine, United Arab Emirates, Uruguay, USA, Venezuela, Viet Nam, Yemen, Zambia

Signed but not ratified (23): Bolivia, Botswana, Burundi, Cameroon, Central African Republic, Colombia, Congo (Democratic Republic of the), Ethiopia, Gambia, Ghana, Guyana, Haiti, Holy See, Honduras, Iran, Jordan, Lesotho, Malaysia, Panama, Philippines, Rwanda, Somalia, Trinidad and Tobago

Note: In addition to the 113 states parties as of 1 Jan. 2023, Croatia acceded to the treaty on 10 Mar. 2023.

Treaty text: British Foreign and Commonwealth Office, Treaty Series no. 10 (1968), <https://assets.publishing.service.gov.uk/government/uploads/system/uploads/attachment_data/file/270006/Treaty_Principles_Activities_Outer_Space.pdf>

Treaty on the Non-Proliferation of Nuclear Weapons (Non-Proliferation Treaty, NPT)

Opened for signature at London, Moscow and Washington, DC, on 1 July 1968; entered into force on 5 March 1970; depositaries British, Russian and US governments

The treaty defines a nuclear weapon state to be a state that manufactured and exploded a nuclear weapon or other nuclear explosive device prior to 1 January 1967. According to this definition, there are five nuclear weapon states: China, France, Russia, the United Kingdom and the United States. All other states are defined as non-nuclear weapon states.

The treaty prohibits the nuclear weapon states from transferring nuclear weapons or other nuclear explosive devices or control over them to any recipient and prohibits them from assisting, encouraging or inducing any non-nuclear weapon state to manufacture or otherwise acquire such a weapon or device. It also prohibits non-nuclear weapon states parties from receiving nuclear weapons or other nuclear explosive devices from any source, from manufacturing them, or from acquiring them in any other way.

The parties undertake to facilitate the exchange of equipment, materials, and scientific and technological information for the peaceful uses of nuclear energy and to ensure that potential benefits from peaceful applications of nuclear explosions will be made available to non-nuclear weapon states party to the treaty. They also undertake to pursue negotiations in good faith on effective measures relating to cessation of the nuclear arms race at an early date and to nuclear disarmament, and on a treaty on general and complete disarmament.

Non-nuclear weapon states parties undertake to conclude safeguard agreements with the International Atomic Energy Agency (IAEA) with a view to preventing diversion of nuclear energy from peaceful uses to nuclear weapons or other nuclear explosive devices. A Model Protocol Additional to the Safeguards Agreements, strengthening the measures, was approved in 1997; additional safeguards protocols are signed by states individually with the IAEA.

The parties meet in a Review Conference every five years (most recently in 2022), preceded by three annual sessions of a preparatory committee. A Review and Extension Conference, convened in 1995 in accordance with the treaty, decided that the treaty should remain in force indefinitely. A party may withdraw from the treaty, having given three months' notice, if it decides that its supreme interests have been jeopardized by extraordinary events related to the treaty's subject matter.

Parties (192): Afghanistan*, Albania*, Algeria*, Andorra*, Angola*, Antigua and Barbuda*, Argentina*, Armenia*, Australia*, Austria*, Azerbaijan*, Bahamas*, Bahrain*, Bangladesh*, Barbados*, Belarus*, Belgium*, Belize*, Benin*, Bhutan*, Bolivia*, Bosnia and Herzegovina*, Botswana*, Brazil*, Brunei Darussalam*, Bulgaria*, Burkina Faso*, Burundi*, Cabo Verde*, Cambodia*, Cameroon*, Canada*, Central African Republic*, Chad*, Chile*, China*[†], Colombia*, Comoros*, Congo (Democratic Republic of the)*, Congo (Republic of the)*, Costa Rica*, Côte d'Ivoire*, Croatia*, Cuba*, Cyprus*, Czechia*, Denmark*, Djibouti*, Dominica*, Dominican Republic*, Ecuador*, Egypt*, El Salvador*, Equatorial Guinea, Eritrea*, Estonia*, Eswatini*, Ethiopia*, Fiji*, Finland*, France*[†], Gabon*, Gambia*, Georgia*, Germany*, Ghana*, Greece*, Grenada*, Guatemala*, Guinea, Guinea-Bissau*, Guyana*, Haiti*, Holy See*, Honduras*, Hungary*, Iceland*, Indonesia*, Iran*, Iraq*, Ireland*, Italy*, Jamaica*, Japan*, Jordan*, Kazakhstan*, Kenya*, Kiribati*, Korea (South)*, Korea (North)[‡], Kuwait*, Kyrgyzstan*, Laos*, Latvia*, Lebanon*, Lesotho*, Liberia*, Libya*, Liechtenstein*, Lithuania*, Luxembourg*, Madagascar*, Malawi*, Malaysia*, Maldives*, Mali*, Malta*, Marshall Islands*, Mauritania*, Mauritius*, Mexico*, Micronesia*, Moldova*, Monaco*, Mongolia*, Montenegro*, Morocco*, Mozambique*, Myanmar*, Namibia*, Nauru*, Nepal*, Netherlands*, New Zealand*, Nicaragua*, Niger*, Nigeria*, North Macedonia*, Norway*, Oman*, Palau*, Palestine*, Panama*, Papua New Guinea*, Paraguay*, Peru*, Philippines*, Poland*, Portugal*, Qatar*, Romania*, Russia*[†], Rwanda*, Saint Kitts and Nevis*, Saint Lucia*, Saint Vincent and the Grenadines*, Samoa*, San Marino*, Sao Tome and Principe, Saudi Arabia*, Senegal*, Serbia*, Seychelles*, Sierra Leone*, Singapore*, Slovakia*, Slovenia*, Solomon Islands*, Somalia, South Africa*, Spain*, Sri Lanka*, Sudan*, Suriname*, Sweden*, Switzerland*, Syria*, Taiwan*, Tajikistan*, Tanzania*, Thailand*, Timor-Leste, Togo*, Tonga*, Trinidad and Tobago*, Tunisia*, Türkiye*, Turkmenistan*, Tuvalu*, Uganda*, UK*[†], Ukraine*, United Arab Emirates*, Uruguay*, USA*[†], Uzbekistan*, Vanuatu*, Venezuela*, Viet Nam*, Yemen*, Zambia*, Zimbabwe*

[*] Party (186) with safeguards agreements in force with the IAEA, as required by the treaty, or concluded by a nuclear weapon state on a voluntary basis. In addition to these 186 states, as of 1 Jan. 2023 Guinea and Timor-Leste had each signed a safeguards agreement that had not yet entered into force.

[†] Nuclear weapon state as defined by the treaty.

[‡] On 12 Mar. 1993 North Korea announced its withdrawal from the NPT with effect from 12 June 1993. It decided to 'suspend' the withdrawal on 11 June. On 10 Jan. 2003 North Korea announced its 'immediate' withdrawal from the NPT. A safeguards agreement was in force at that time. The current status of North Korea is disputed by the other parties.

Treaty text: International Atomic Energy Agency, INFCIRC/140, 22 Apr. 1970, <https://www.iaea.org/sites/default/files/publications/documents/infcircs/1970/infcirc140.pdf>

Additional safeguards protocols in force (141): Afghanistan, Albania, Andorra, Angola, Antigua and Barbuda, Armenia, Australia, Austria, Azerbaijan, Bahrain, Bangladesh, Belgium, Benin, Bosnia and Herzegovina, Botswana, Bulgaria, Burkina Faso, Burundi, *Cabo Verde*, Cambodia, Cameroon, Canada, Central African Republic, Chad, Chile, China, Colombia, Comoros, Congo (Democratic Republic of the), Congo (Republic of), Costa Rica, Côte d'Ivoire, Croatia, Cuba, Cyprus, Czechia, Denmark[1], Djibouti, Dominican Republic, Ecuador, El Salvador, Eritrea, Estonia, Eswatini, Ethiopia, Euratom, Fiji, Finland, France, Gabon, Gambia, Georgia, Germany, Ghana, Greece, Guatemala, *Guinea-Bissau*, Haiti, Holy See, Honduras, Hungary,

Iceland, India, Indonesia, Iraq, Ireland, Italy, Jamaica, Japan, Jordan, Kazakhstan, Kenya, Korea (South), Kuwait, Kyrgyzstan, Latvia, Lesotho, Liberia, Libya, Liechtenstein, Lithuania, Luxembourg, Madagascar, Malawi, Mali, Malta, Marshall Islands, Mauritania, Mauritius, Mexico, Moldova, Monaco, Mongolia, Montenegro, Morocco, Mozambique, Namibia, Netherlands, New Zealand, Nicaragua, Niger, Nigeria, North Macedonia, Norway, Palau, Panama, Paraguay, Peru, Philippines, Poland, Portugal, Romania, Russia, Rwanda, Saint Kitts and Nevis, Senegal, Serbia, Seychelles, Singapore, Slovakia, Slovenia, South Africa, Spain, Sweden, Switzerland, Tajikistan, Tanzania, Thailand, Togo, Türkiye, Turkmenistan, Uganda, UK, Ukraine, United Arab Emirates, Uruguay, USA, Uzbekistan, Vanuatu, Viet Nam, Zimbabwe

[1] A separate additional protocol is also in force for the Danish territory of Greenland.

Note: Taiwan has agreed to apply the measures contained in the Model Additional Protocol.

Additional safeguards protocols signed but not yet in force (13): Algeria, Belarus, Bolivia, Guinea, Iran*, Kiribati, Laos, Malaysia, Myanmar, Sierra Leone, Timor-Leste, Tunisia, Zambia

* Iran notified the IAEA that as of 16 Jan. 2016 it would provisionally apply the Additional Protocol that it signed in 2003 but has not yet ratified. It has not been applied since 23 Feb. 2021.

Model Additional Safeguards Protocol text: International Atomic Energy Agency, INFCIRC/540 (corrected), Sep. 1997, <https://www.iaea.org/sites/default/files/infcirc540c.pdf>

Treaty on the Prohibition of the Emplacement of Nuclear Weapons and other Weapons of Mass Destruction on the Seabed and the Ocean Floor and in the Subsoil thereof (Seabed Treaty)

Opened for signature at London, Moscow and Washington, DC, on 11 February 1971; entered into force on 18 May 1972; depositaries British, Russian and US governments

The treaty prohibits implanting or emplacing on the seabed and the ocean floor and in the subsoil thereof beyond the outer limit of a 12-nautical mile (22-kilometre) seabed zone any nuclear weapon or any other type of weapon of mass destruction as well as structures, launching installations or any other facilities specifically designed for storing, testing or using such weapons.

The parties met in a Review Conference in 1977, 1983 and 1989. A fourth Review Conference can be convened at the request of 10 states parties. A party may withdraw from the treaty, having given three months' notice, if it decides that its supreme interests have been jeopardized by extraordinary events related to the treaty's subject matter.

Parties (95): Afghanistan, Algeria, Antigua and Barbuda, Argentina, Australia, Austria, Bahamas, Belarus, Belgium, Benin, Bosnia and Herzegovina, Botswana, Brazil*, Bulgaria, Canada*, Cabo Verde, Central African Republic, China, Congo (Republic of the), Côte d'Ivoire, Cuba, Cyprus, Czechia, Denmark, Dominican Republic, Eswatini, Ethiopia, Finland, Germany, Ghana, Greece, Guatemala, Guinea-Bissau, Hungary, Iceland, India*, Iran, Iraq, Ireland, Italy*, Jamaica, Japan, Jordan, Korea (South), Laos, Latvia, Lesotho, Libya, Liechtenstein, Luxembourg, Malaysia, Malta, Mauritius, Mexico*, Mongolia, Montenegro, Morocco, Nepal, Netherlands, New Zealand, Nicaragua, Niger, Norway, Panama, Philippines, Poland, Portugal, Qatar, Romania, Russia, Rwanda, Saint Kitts and Nevis, Saint Vincent and the Grenadines, Sao Tome and Principe, Saudi Arabia, Serbia*, Seychelles, Singapore, Slovakia, Slovenia, Solomon Islands, South Africa, Spain, Sweden, Switzerland, Taiwan, Togo, Tunisia, Türkiye*, UK, Ukraine, USA, Viet Nam*, Yemen, Zambia

* With reservation and/or declaration.

Signed but not ratified (21): Bolivia, Burundi, Cambodia, Cameroon, Colombia, Costa Rica, Equatorial Guinea, Gambia, Guinea, Honduras, Lebanon, Liberia, Madagascar, Mali, Myanmar, Paraguay, Senegal, Sierra Leone, Sudan, Tanzania, Uruguay

Treaty text: British Foreign and Commonwealth Office, Treaty Series no. 13 (1973), <https://assets.publishing.service.gov.uk/government/uploads/system/uploads/attachment_data/file/269694/Treaty_Prohib_Nuclear_Sea-Bed.pdf>

Convention on the Prohibition of the Development, Production and Stockpiling of Bacteriological (Biological) and Toxin Weapons and on their Destruction (Biological and Toxin Weapons Convention, BWC)

Opened for signature at London, Moscow and Washington, DC, on 10 April 1972; entered into force on 26 March 1975; depositaries British, Russian and US governments

The convention prohibits the development, production, stockpiling or acquisition by other means or retention of microbial or other biological agents or toxins (whatever their origin or method of production) of types and in quantities that have no justification of prophylactic, protective or other peaceful purposes. It also prohibits weapons, equipment or means of delivery designed to use such agents or toxins for hostile purposes or in armed conflict. The destruction of the agents, toxins, weapons, equipment and means of delivery in the possession of the parties, or their diversion to peaceful purposes, should be completed not later than nine months after the entry into force of the convention for each country.

The parties meet in a Review Conference every five years (most recently in 2022) and, in intervening years, in an annual Meeting of States Parties, which is preceded by Meetings of Experts on various topics. A three-person Implementation Support Unit (ISU), based in Geneva, was established in 2007 to support the parties in implementing the treaty, including facilitating the collection and distribution of annual confidence-building measures and supporting their efforts to achieve universal membership.

A party may withdraw from the convention, having given three months' notice, if it decides that its supreme interests have been jeopardized by extraordinary events related to the treaty's subject matter.

Parties (185): Afghanistan, Albania, Algeria, Andorra, Angola, Antigua and Barbuda, Argentina, Armenia, Australia, Austria*, Azerbaijan, Bahamas, Bahrain*, Bangladesh, Barbados, Belarus, Belgium, Belize, Benin, Bhutan, Bolivia, Bosnia and Herzegovina, Botswana, Brazil, Brunei Darussalam, Bulgaria, Burkina Faso, Burundi, Cabo Verde, Cambodia, Cameroon, Canada, Central African Republic, Chile, China*, Colombia, Congo (Democratic Republic of the), Congo (Republic of the), Cook Islands, Costa Rica, Côte d'Ivoire, Croatia, Cuba, Cyprus, Czechia*, Denmark, Dominica, Dominican Republic, Ecuador, El Salvador, Equatorial Guinea, Estonia, Eswatini, Ethiopia, Fiji, Finland, France, Gabon, Gambia, Georgia, Germany, Ghana, Greece, Grenada, Guatemala, Guinea, Guinea-Bissau, Guyana, Holy See, Honduras, Hungary, Iceland, India*, Indonesia, Iran, Iraq, Ireland*, Italy, Jamaica, Japan, Jordan, Kazakhstan, Kenya, Korea (North), Korea (South)*, Kuwait*, Kyrgyzstan, Laos, Latvia, Lebanon, Lesotho, Liberia, Libya, Liechtenstein, Lithuania, Luxembourg, Madagascar, Malawi, Malaysia*, Maldives, Mali, Malta, Marshall Islands, Mauritania, Mauritius, Mexico*, Moldova, Monaco, Mongolia, Montenegro, Morocco, Mozambique, Myanmar, *Namibia*, Nauru, Nepal,

Netherlands, New Zealand, Nicaragua, Niger, Nigeria, Niue, North Macedonia, Norway, Oman, Pakistan, Palau, Palestine, Panama, Papua New Guinea, Paraguay, Peru, Philippines, Poland, Portugal, Qatar, Romania, Russia, Rwanda, Saint Kitts and Nevis, Saint Lucia, Saint Vincent and the Grenadines, Samoa, San Marino, Sao Tome and Principe, Saudi Arabia, Senegal, Serbia, Seychelles, Sierra Leone, Singapore, Slovakia*, Slovenia, Solomon Islands, South Africa, Spain, Sri Lanka, Sudan, Suriname, Sweden, Switzerland*, Taiwan, Tajikistan, Tanzania, Thailand, Timor-Leste, Togo, Tonga, Trinidad and Tobago, Tunisia, Türkiye, Turkmenistan, Uganda, UK*, Ukraine, United Arab Emirates, Uruguay, USA, Uzbekistan, Vanuatu, Venezuela, Viet Nam, Yemen, Zambia, Zimbabwe

* With reservation and/or declaration.

Signed but not ratified (4): Egypt, Haiti, Somalia, Syria

Note: In addition to the 185 states parties as of 1 Jan. 2023, South Sudan acceded to the convention on 15 Feb. 2023.

Treaty text: British Foreign and Commonwealth Office, Treaty Series no. 11 (1976), <https://assets.publishing.service.gov.uk/government/uploads/system/uploads/attachment_data/file/269698/Convention_Prohibition_Stock_Bacterio.pdf>

Convention on the Prohibition of Military or Any Other Hostile Use of Environmental Modification Techniques (Enmod Convention)

Opened for signature at Geneva on 18 May 1977; entered into force on 5 October 1978; depositary UN secretary-general

The convention prohibits military or any other hostile use of environmental modification techniques that have widespread, long-lasting or severe effects as the means of destruction, damage or injury to states parties. The term 'environmental modification techniques' refers to any technique for changing—through the deliberate manipulation of natural processes—the dynamics, composition or structure of the earth, including its biota, lithosphere, hydrosphere and atmosphere, or of outer space. Understandings reached during the negotiations, but not written into the convention, define the terms 'widespread', 'long-lasting' and 'severe'.

The parties met in a Review Conference in 1984 and 1992. A third Review Conference can be convened at the request of a majority of the states parties.

Parties (78): Afghanistan, Algeria, Antigua and Barbuda, Argentina*, Armenia, Australia, Austria*, Bangladesh, Belarus, Belgium, Benin, Brazil, Bulgaria, Cabo Verde, Cameroon, Canada, Chile, China, Costa Rica, Cuba, Cyprus, Czechia, Denmark, Dominica, Egypt, Estonia, Finland, Germany, Ghana, Greece, Guatemala*, Honduras, Hungary, India, Ireland, Italy, Japan, Kazakhstan, Korea (North), Korea (South)*, Kuwait*, Kyrgyzstan, Lithuania, Laos, Malawi, Mauritius, Mongolia, Netherlands*, New Zealand*, Nicaragua, Niger, Norway, Pakistan, Palestine, Panama, Papua New Guinea, Poland, Romania, Russia, Saint Lucia, Saint Vincent and the Grenadines, Sao Tome and Principe, Slovakia, Slovenia, Solomon Islands, Spain, Sri Lanka, Sweden, Switzerland*, Tajikistan, Tunisia, UK, Ukraine, Uruguay, USA, Uzbekistan, Viet Nam, Yemen

* With reservation and/or declaration.

Signed but not ratified (16): Bolivia, Congo (Democratic Republic of the), Ethiopia, Holy See, Iceland, Iran, Iraq, Lebanon, Liberia, Luxembourg, Morocco, Portugal, Sierra Leone, Syria, Türkiye, Uganda

Convention text: United Nations Treaty Collection, <https://treaties.un.org/doc/Treaties/1978/10/19781005 00-39 AM/Ch_XXVI_01p.pdf>

Convention on the Physical Protection of Nuclear Material and Nuclear Facilities

Original convention opened for signature at New York and Vienna on 3 March 1980; entered into force on 8 February 1987; amendments adopted on 8 July 2005; amended convention entered into force for its ratifying states on 8 May 2016; depositary IAEA director general

The original convention—named the **Convention on the Physical Protection of Nuclear Material**—obligates its parties to protect nuclear material for peaceful purposes while in international transport.

The convention as amended and renamed also obligates its parties to protect nuclear facilities and material used for peaceful purposes while in storage.

The parties to the original convention met in a Review Conference in 1992. The parties to the amended convention met in a Review Conference in 2022 and are scheduled to meet again in 2027. A party may withdraw from the convention, having given 180 days' notice.

Parties to the original convention (164): Afghanistan, Albania, Algeria*, Andorra, Angola, Antigua and Barbuda, Argentina*, Armenia, Australia*, Austria*, Azerbaijan*, Bahamas*, Bahrain*, Bangladesh, Belarus*, Belgium*, Benin, Bolivia, Bosnia and Herzegovina, Botswana, Brazil, Bulgaria, Burkina Faso, Cabo Verde, Cambodia, Cameroon, Canada*, Central African Republic, Chad, Chile, China*, Colombia, Comoros, Congo (Democratic Republic of the), Congo (Republic of the), Costa Rica, Côte d'Ivoire, Croatia, Cuba*, Cyprus*, Czechia, Denmark, Djibouti, Dominica, Dominican Republic, Ecuador, El Salvador*, Equatorial Guinea, Eritrea*, Estonia, Eswatini, Euratom*, Fiji, Finland*, France*, Gabon, Georgia, Germany*, Ghana, Greece*, Grenada, Guatemala*, Guinea, Guinea-Bissau, Guyana, Honduras, Hungary, Iceland, India*, Indonesia*, Iraq, Ireland*, Israel*, Italy*, Jamaica, Japan, Jordan*, Kazakhstan, Kenya, Korea (South)*, Kuwait*, Kyrgyzstan, Laos*, Latvia, Lebanon, Lesotho, Libya, Liechtenstein, Lithuania, Luxembourg*, Madagascar, Malawi, Mali, Malta, Marshall Islands, Mauritania, Mexico, Moldova, Monaco, Mongolia, Montenegro, Morocco, Mozambique*, Myanmar*, Namibia, Nauru, Netherlands*, New Zealand, Nicaragua, Niger, Nigeria, Niue, North Macedonia, Norway*, Oman*, Pakistan*, Palau, Palestine, Panama, Paraguay, Peru*, Philippines, Poland, Portugal*, Qatar*, Romania*, Russia, Rwanda, Saint Kitts and Nevis, Saint Lucia*, San Marino, Saudi Arabia*, Senegal, Serbia, Seychelles, Singapore*, Slovakia, Slovenia, South Africa*, Spain*, Sudan, Sweden*, Switzerland*, Syria*, Tajikistan, Tanzania, Thailand, Togo, Tonga, Trinidad and Tobago, Tunisia, Türkiye*, Turkmenistan, Uganda, UK*, Ukraine, United Arab Emirates, Uruguay, USA*, Uzbekistan, Viet Nam*, Yemen, Zambia, Zimbabwe

* With reservation and/or declaration.

Signed but not ratified (1): Haiti

Convention text: International Atomic Energy Agency, INFCIRC/274, Nov. 1979, <https://www.iaea.org/sites/default/files/infcirc274.pdf>

Parties to the amended convention (131): Albania, Algeria, Angola, Antigua and Barbuda, Argentina, Armenia*, Australia, Austria, Azerbaijan*, Bahrain, Bangladesh, Belgium*, Benin, Bolivia, Bosnia and Herzegovina, Botswana, *Brazil*, Bulgaria, Burkina Faso, Cameroon, Canada*, Chad, Chile, China*, Colombia, Comoros, Costa Rica, Côte d'Ivoire, Croatia, Cuba, Cyprus, Czechia, Denmark, Djibouti, Dominican Republic, Ecuador, El Salvador, Eritrea, Estonia, Eswatini, Euratom*, Fiji, Finland, France, Gabon, Georgia, Germany, Ghana, Greece, Hungary, Iceland, India, Indonesia, Ireland, Israel*, Italy, Jamaica, Japan, Jordan, Kazakhstan, Kenya, Korea (South), Kuwait, Kyrgyzstan, Latvia, Lesotho, Libya,

Liechtenstein, Lithuania, Luxembourg, Madagascar, *Malawi*, Mali, Malta, Marshall Islands, Mauritania, Mexico, Moldova, Monaco, Montenegro, Morocco, *Mozambique*, Myanmar*, Namibia, Nauru, Netherlands, New Zealand, Nicaragua, Niger, Nigeria, North Macedonia, Norway, *Oman*, Pakistan*, Palestine, Panama, Paraguay, Peru, Philippines, Poland, Portugal, Qatar, Romania, Russia, Rwanda, Saint Kitts and Nevis, Saint Lucia, San Marino, Saudi Arabia, Senegal, Serbia, Seychelles, Singapore*, Slovakia, Slovenia, Spain, Sweden, Switzerland, Syria*, Tajikistan, Thailand, Tunisia, Türkiye*, Turkmenistan, UK, Ukraine, United Arab Emirates, Uruguay, USA*, Uzbekistan, Viet Nam

* With reservation and/or declaration.

Note: In addition to the 131 states parties as of 1 Jan. 2023, Laos ratified the amended convention on 12 Apr. 2023.

Amendment text and consolidated text of amended convention: International Atomic Energy Agency, INFCIRC/274/Rev.1/Mod.1 (Corrected), 18 Oct. 2021, <https://www.iaea.org/sites/default/files/publications/documents/infcircs/1979/infcirc274r1m1c.pdf>

Convention on Prohibitions or Restrictions on the Use of Certain Conventional Weapons which may be Deemed to be Excessively Injurious or to have Indiscriminate Effects (CCW Convention, or 'Inhumane Weapons' Convention)

Opened for signature with protocols I, II and III at New York on 10 April 1981; entered into force on 2 December 1983; depositary UN secretary-general

The convention is an umbrella treaty, under which specific agreements can be concluded in the form of protocols. In order to become a party to the convention a state must ratify at least two of the protocols.

The amendment to Article I of the original convention was opened for signature at Geneva on 21 November 2001. It expands the scope of application to non-international armed conflicts. The amended convention entered into force on 18 May 2004.

Protocol I prohibits the use of weapons intended to injure using fragments that are not detectable in the human body by X-rays.

Protocol II prohibits or restricts the use of mines, booby-traps and other devices. *Amended Protocol II*, which entered into force on 3 December 1998, reinforces the constraints regarding anti-personnel mines.

Protocol III restricts the use of incendiary weapons.

Protocol IV, which entered into force on 30 July 1998, prohibits the employment of laser weapons specifically designed to cause permanent blindness to unenhanced vision.

Protocol V, which entered into force on 12 November 2006, recognizes the need for measures of a generic nature to minimize the risks and effects of explosive remnants of war.

The parties to the convention meet in a Review Conference every five years (most recently in 2021) and, in intervening years, in an annual Meeting of the High Contracting Parties. The parties to Amended Protocol II and Protocol V meet in separate annual conferences. These meetings also consider the work of the groups of governmental experts, convened since 2001 in various formats, the Amended Protocol II Group of Experts and the Protocol V Meeting of Experts.

A party may withdraw from the convention and its protocols, having given one year's notice. But if the party is involved in an armed conflict or occupation at that time, the withdrawal will not take effect until the conflict or occupation has ended and that party's obligations fulfilled.

Parties to the original convention (126) and protocols I (119), II (96) and III (115): Afghanistan[2], Albania, Algeria[2], Antigua and Barbuda[2], Argentina*, Australia, Austria, Bahrain[5], Bangladesh, Belarus, Belgium, Benin[2], Bolivia, Bosnia and Herzegovina, Brazil, Bulgaria, Burkina Faso, Burundi[4], Cabo Verde, Cambodia, Cameroon[6], Canada*, Chile[2], China*, Colombia, Costa Rica, Côte d'Ivoire[4], Croatia, Cuba, Cyprus*, Czechia, Denmark, Djibouti, Dominican Republic[6], Ecuador, El Salvador, Estonia[2], Finland, France*, Gabon[2], Georgia, Germany, Greece, Grenada[2], Guatemala, Guinea-Bissau, Holy See*, Honduras, Hungary, Iceland, India, Iraq, Ireland, Israel*[1], Italy*, Jamaica[2], Japan, Jordan[2], Kazakhstan[2], Korea (South)[3], Kuwait[2], Laos, Latvia, Lebanon[2], Lesotho, Liberia, Liechtenstein, Lithuania[2], Luxembourg, Madagascar, *Malawi*[1], Maldives[2], Mali, Malta, Mauritius, Mexico, Moldova, Monaco[3], Mongolia, Montenegro, Morocco[4], Nauru, Netherlands*, New Zealand, Nicaragua[2], Niger, North Macedonia, Norway, Pakistan, Palestine[2], Panama, Paraguay, Peru[2], Philippines, Poland, Portugal, Qatar[2], Romania*, Russia, Saint Vincent and the Grenadines[2], Saudi Arabia[2], Senegal[5], Serbia, Seychelles, Sierra Leone[2], Slovakia, Slovenia, South Africa, Spain, Sri Lanka, Sweden, Switzerland, Tajikistan, Togo, Tunisia, Türkiye*[3], Turkmenistan[1], Uganda, UK*, Ukraine, United Arab Emirates[2], Uruguay, USA*, Uzbekistan, Venezuela, Zambia

* With reservation and/or declaration.
[1] Party only to 1981 protocols I and II.
[2] Party only to 1981 protocols I and III.
[3] Party only to 1981 Protocol I.
[4] Party only to 1981 Protocol II.
[5] Party only to 1981 Protocol III.
[6] Party to none of the original protocols.

Signed but not ratified the original convention and protocols (4): Egypt, Nigeria, Sudan, Viet Nam

Parties to the amended convention (88): Afghanistan, Algeria, Albania, Argentina, Australia, Austria, Bangladesh, Belarus, Belgium, Benin, Bosnia and Herzegovina, Brazil, Bulgaria, Burkina Faso, Canada, Chile, China, Colombia, Costa Rica, Croatia, Cuba, Czechia, Denmark, Dominican Republic, Ecuador, El Salvador, Estonia, Finland, France, Georgia, Germany, Greece, Grenada, Guatemala, Guinea-Bissau, Holy See*, Hungary, Iceland, India, Iraq, Ireland, Italy, Jamaica, Japan, Korea (South), Kuwait, Latvia, Lebanon, Lesotho, Liberia, Liechtenstein, Lithuania, Luxembourg, *Malawi*, Malta, Mexico*, Moldova, Montenegro, Netherlands, New Zealand, Nicaragua, Niger, North Macedonia, Norway, Panama, Paraguay, Peru, *Philippines*, Poland, Portugal, Romania, Russia, Serbia, Sierra Leone, Slovakia, Slovenia, South Africa, Spain, Sri Lanka, Sweden, Switzerland, Tunisia, Türkiye, UK, Ukraine, Uruguay, USA, Zambia

* With reservation and/or declaration.

Parties to Amended Protocol II (106): Afghanistan, Albania, Argentina, Australia, Austria*, Bangladesh, Belarus*, Belgium*, Benin, Bolivia, Bosnia and Herzegovina, Brazil, Bulgaria, Burkina Faso, Cabo Verde, Cambodia, Cameroon, Canada*, Chile, China*, Colombia, Costa Rica, Croatia, Cyprus, Czechia, Denmark*, Dominican Republic, Ecuador, El Salvador, Estonia, Finland*, France*, Gabon, Georgia, Germany*, Greece*, Grenada, Guatemala, Guinea-Bissau, Holy See, Honduras, Hungary*, Iceland, India, Iraq, Ireland*, Israel*, Italy*, Jamaica, Japan, Jordan, Korea (South)*, Kuwait, Latvia, Lebanon, Liberia, Liechtenstein*, Lithuania, Luxembourg, Madagascar, Maldives, Mali, Malta, Mauritius, Moldova, Monaco, Montenegro, Morocco, Nauru, Netherlands*, New Zealand, Nicaragua, Niger, North Macedonia, Norway, Pakistan*, Panama, Paraguay, Peru, Philippines, Poland, Portugal,

Romania, Russia*, Saint Vincent and the Grenadines, Senegal, Serbia, Seychelles, Sierra Leone, Slovakia, Slovenia, South Africa*, Spain, Sri Lanka, Sweden*, Switzerland*, Tajikistan, Tunisia, Türkiye, Turkmenistan, UK*, Ukraine*, Uruguay, USA*, Venezuela, Zambia

* With reservation and/or declaration

Parties to Protocol IV (109): Afghanistan, Algeria, Albania, Antigua and Barbuda, Argentina, Australia*, Austria*, Bahrain, Bangladesh, Belarus, Belgium*, Benin, Bolivia, Bosnia and Herzegovina, Brazil, Bulgaria, Burkina Faso, Cabo Verde, Cambodia, Cameroon, Canada*, Chile, China, Colombia, Costa Rica, Croatia, Cuba, Cyprus, Czechia, Denmark, Dominican Republic, Ecuador, El Salvador, Estonia, Finland, France, Gabon, Georgia, Germany*, Greece*, Grenada, Guatemala, Guinea-Bissau, Holy See, Honduras, Hungary, Iceland, India, Iraq, Ireland*, Israel*, Italy*, Jamaica, Japan, Kazakhstan, Kuwait, Latvia, Lesotho, Liberia, Liechtenstein*, Lithuania, Luxembourg, Madagascar, Maldives, Mali, Malta, Mauritius, Mexico, Moldova, Mongolia, Montenegro, Morocco, Nauru, Netherlands*, New Zealand, Nicaragua, Niger, North Macedonia, Norway, Pakistan, Panama, Paraguay, Peru, Philippines, Poland*, Portugal, Qatar, Romania, Russia, Saint Vincent and the Grenadines, Saudi Arabia, Serbia, Seychelles, Sierra Leone, Slovakia, Slovenia, South Africa*, Spain, Sri Lanka, Sweden*, Switzerland*, Tajikistan, Tunisia, Türkiye, UK*, Ukraine, Uruguay, USA*, Uzbekistan

* With reservation and/or declaration.

Parties to Protocol V (97): Afghanistan, Albania, Argentina*, Australia, Austria, Bahrain, Bangladesh, Belarus, Belgium, Benin, Bosnia and Herzegovina, Brazil, Bulgaria, Burkina Faso, Burundi, Cameroon, Canada, Chile, China, Costa Rica, Côte d'Ivoire, Croatia, Cuba, Cyprus, Czechia, Denmark, Dominican Republic, Ecuador, El Salvador, Estonia, Finland, France, Gabon, Georgia, Germany, Greece, Grenada, Guatemala, Guinea-Bissau, Holy See*, Honduras, Hungary, Iceland, India, Iraq, Ireland, Italy, Jamaica, Korea (South), Kuwait, Laos, Latvia, Lesotho, Liberia, Liechtenstein, Lithuania, Luxembourg, Madagascar, Mali, Malta, Mauritius, Moldova, Montenegro, Netherlands, New Zealand, Nicaragua, North Macedonia, Norway, Pakistan, Palestine, Panama, Paraguay, Peru, *Philippines*, Poland, Portugal, Qatar, Romania, Russia, Saint Vincent and the Grenadines, Saudi Arabia, Senegal, Sierra Leone, Slovakia, Slovenia, South Africa, Spain, Sweden, Switzerland, Tajikistan, Tunisia, Turkmenistan, Ukraine, United Arab Emirates, Uruguay, USA*, Zambia

* With reservation and/or declaration.

Original convention and protocol text: United Nations Treaty Collection, <https://treaties.un.org/doc/Treaties/1983/12/19831202 01-19 AM/XXVI-2-revised.pdf>

Convention amendment text: United Nations Treaty Collection, <https://treaties.un.org/doc/Treaties/2001/12/20011221 01-23 AM/Ch_XXVI_02_cp.pdf>

Amended Protocol II text: United Nations Treaty Collection, <https://treaties.un.org/doc/Treaties/1996/05/19960503 01-38 AM/Ch_XXVI_02_bp.pdf>

Protocol IV text: United Nations Treaty Collection, <https://treaties.un.org/doc/Treaties/1995/10/19951013 01-30 AM/Ch_XXVI_02_ap.pdf>

Protocol V text: United Nations Treaty Collection, <https://treaties.un.org/doc/Treaties/2003/11/20031128 01-19 AM/Ch_XXVI_02_dp.pdf>

Convention on the Prohibition of the Development, Production, Stockpiling and Use of Chemical Weapons and on their Destruction (Chemical Weapons Convention, CWC)

Opened for signature at Paris on 13 January 1993; entered into force on 29 April 1997; depositary UN secretary-general

The convention prohibits the development, production, acquisition, transfer, stockpiling and use of chemical weapons. The CWC regime consists of four pillars: disarmament, non-proliferation, assistance and protection against chemical weapons, and international cooperation on the peaceful uses of chemistry. The convention established the Organisation for the Prohibition of Chemical Weapons (OPCW) as its implementing body.

Each party undertook to destroy its chemical weapon stockpiles by 29 April 2012. Of the seven parties that had declared stocks of chemical weapons by that date, three had destroyed them (Albania, India and South Korea). Libya and Russia completed the destruction of their stockpiles in 2017 and Iraq did so in 2018, while the USA continues to destroy its stocks. The stockpile of chemical weapons that Syria declared when it acceded to the CWC in 2013 was destroyed in 2016, although gaps, inconsistencies and discrepancies in the 2013 declaration continue to be investigated. Old and abandoned chemical weapons will continue to be destroyed as they are uncovered from, for example, former battlefields.

The parties meet in a Review Conference every five years (the fifth being held in 2023) and in an annual Conference of the States Parties. A party may withdraw from the convention, having given 90 days' notice, if it decides that its supreme interests have been jeopardized by extraordinary events related to the treaty's subject matter.

Parties (193): Afghanistan, Albania, Algeria, Andorra, Angola, Antigua and Barbuda, Argentina, Armenia, Australia, Austria*, Azerbaijan, Bahamas, Bahrain, Bangladesh, Barbados, Belarus, Belgium*, Belize, Benin, Bhutan, Bolivia, Bosnia and Herzegovina, Botswana, Brazil, Brunei Darussalam, Bulgaria, Burkina Faso, Burundi, Cabo Verde, Cambodia, Cameroon, Canada, Central African Republic, Chad, Chile, China*, Colombia, Comoros, Congo (Democratic Republic of the), Congo (Republic of the), Cook Islands, Costa Rica, Côte d'Ivoire, Croatia, Cuba*, Cyprus, Czechia, Denmark*, Djibouti, Dominica, Dominican Republic, Ecuador, El Salvador, Equatorial Guinea, Eritrea, Estonia, Eswatini, Ethiopia, Fiji, Finland, France*, Gabon, Gambia, Georgia, Germany*, Ghana, Greece*, Grenada, Guatemala, Guinea, Guinea-Bissau, Guyana, Haiti, Holy See*, Honduras, Hungary, Iceland, India, Indonesia, Iran*, Iraq, Ireland*, Italy*, Jamaica, Japan, Jordan, Kazakhstan, Kenya, Kiribati, Korea (South), Kuwait, Kyrgyzstan, Laos, Latvia, Lebanon, Lesotho, Liberia, Libya, Liechtenstein, Lithuania, Luxembourg*, Madagascar, Malawi, Malaysia, Maldives, Mali, Malta, Marshall Islands, Mauritania, Mauritius, Mexico, Micronesia, Moldova, Monaco, Mongolia, Montenegro, Morocco, Mozambique, Myanmar, Namibia, Nauru, Nepal, Netherlands*, New Zealand, Nicaragua, Niger, Nigeria, Niue, North Macedonia, Norway, Oman, Pakistan*, Palau, Palestine, Panama, Papua New Guinea, Paraguay, Peru, Philippines, Poland, Portugal*, Qatar, Romania, Russia, Rwanda, Saint Kitts and Nevis, Saint Lucia, Saint Vincent and the Grenadines, Samoa, San Marino, Sao Tome and Principe, Saudi Arabia, Senegal, Serbia, Seychelles, Sierra Leone, Singapore, Slovakia, Slovenia, Solomon Islands, Somalia, South Africa, Spain*, Sri Lanka, Sudan*, Suriname, Sweden, Switzerland, Syria*, Tajikistan, Tanzania, Thailand, Timor-Leste, Togo, Tonga, Trinidad and Tobago, Tunisia, Türkiye, Turkmenistan, Tuvalu, Uganda, UK*, Ukraine, United Arab Emirates, Uruguay, USA*, Uzbekistan, Vanuatu, Venezuela, Viet Nam, Yemen, Zambia, Zimbabwe

* With reservation and/or declaration.

Signed but not ratified (1): Israel

Convention text: United Nations Treaty Collection, <https://treaties.un.org/doc/Treaties/1997/04/19970429 07-52 PM/CTC-XXVI_03_ocred.pdf>

Comprehensive Nuclear-Test-Ban Treaty (CTBT)

Opened for signature at New York on 24 September 1996; not in force; depositary UN secretary-general

The treaty would prohibit the carrying out of any nuclear weapon test explosion or any other nuclear explosion and urges each party to prevent any such nuclear explosion at any place under its jurisdiction or control and refrain from causing, encouraging or in any way participating in the carrying out of any nuclear weapon test explosion or any other nuclear explosion.

The verification regime established by the treaty will consist of an International Monitoring System (IMS) to detect signs of nuclear explosions, an International Data Centre to collect and distribute data from the IMS, and the right to on-site inspection to determine whether an explosion has taken place. Work under the treaty will be implemented by the Comprehensive Nuclear-Test-Ban Treaty Organization (CTBTO).

The treaty will enter into force 180 days after the date that all of the 44 states listed in an annex to the treaty have deposited their instruments of ratification. All 44 states possess nuclear power reactors or nuclear research reactors. Pending entry into force, a Preparatory Commission is preparing for the treaty's implementation and the establishment of the CTBTO and the IMS.

Once the treaty enters into force, it will be governed by an annual Conference of the States Parties and a 10-yearly Review Conference. Pending entry into force, the states signatories meet twice a year in plenary sessions and in working groups on budgetary and administrative matters and on implementation issues. Every two years, the UN secretary-general convenes a meeting of the ratifying states under Article XIV of the treaty to promote entry into force.

After entry into force, a party will be able to withdraw from the treaty, having given six months' notice, if it decides that its supreme interests have been jeopardized by extraordinary events related to the treaty's subject matter.

States whose ratification is required for entry into force (44): Algeria, Argentina, Australia, Austria, Bangladesh, Belgium, Brazil, Bulgaria, Canada, Chile, China*, Colombia, Congo (Democratic Republic of the), Egypt*, Finland, France, Germany, Hungary, India*, Indonesia, Iran*, Israel*, Italy, Japan, Korea (North)*, Korea (South), Mexico, Netherlands, Norway, Pakistan*, Peru, Poland, Romania, Russia, Slovakia, South Africa, Spain, Sweden, Switzerland, Türkiye, UK, Ukraine, USA*, Viet Nam

* Has not ratified the treaty.

Ratifications deposited (176): Afghanistan, Albania, Algeria, Andorra, Angola, Antigua and Barbuda, Argentina, Armenia, Australia, Austria, Azerbaijan, Bahamas, Bahrain, Bangladesh, Barbados, Belarus, Belgium, Belize, Benin, Bolivia, Bosnia and Herzegovina, Botswana, Brazil, Brunei Darussalam, Bulgaria, Burkina Faso, Burundi, Cabo Verde, Cambodia, Cameroon, Canada, Central African Republic, Chad, Chile, Colombia, Comoros, Congo

(Democratic Republic of the), Cook Islands, Costa Rica, Côte d'Ivoire, Congo (Republic of the), Croatia, Cuba, Cyprus, Czechia, Denmark, Djibouti, *Dominica*, Dominican Republic, Ecuador, El Salvador, *Equatorial Guinea*, Eritrea, Estonia, Eswatini, Ethiopia, Fiji, Finland, France, Gabon, *Gambia*, Georgia, Germany, Ghana, Greece, Grenada, Guatemala, Guinea, Guinea-Bissau, Guyana, Haiti, Holy See, Honduras, Hungary, Iceland, Indonesia, Iraq, Ireland, Italy, Jamaica, Japan, Jordan, Kazakhstan, Kenya, Kiribati, Korea (South), Kuwait, Kyrgyzstan, Laos, Latvia, Lebanon, Lesotho, Liberia, Libya, Liechtenstein, Lithuania, Luxembourg, Madagascar, Malawi, Malaysia, Maldives, Mali, Malta, Marshall Islands, Mauritania, Mexico, Micronesia, Moldova, Monaco, Mongolia, Montenegro, Morocco, Mozambique, Myanmar, Namibia, Nauru, Netherlands, New Zealand, Nicaragua, Niger, Nigeria, Niue, North Macedonia, Norway, Oman, Palau, Panama, Paraguay, Peru, Philippines, Poland, Portugal, Qatar, Romania, Russia, Rwanda, Saint Kitts and Nevis, Saint Lucia, Saint Vincent and the Grenadines, Samoa, San Marino, *Sao Tome and Principe*, Senegal, Serbia, Seychelles, Sierra Leone, Singapore, Slovakia, Slovenia, South Africa, Spain, Sudan, Suriname, Sweden, Switzerland, Tajikistan, Tanzania, Thailand, *Timor-Leste*, Togo, Trinidad and Tobago, Tunisia, Türkiye, Turkmenistan, *Tuvalu*, Uganda, UK, Ukraine, United Arab Emirates, Uruguay, Uzbekistan, Vanuatu, Venezuela, Viet Nam, Zambia, Zimbabwe

Signed but not ratified (10): China, Egypt, Iran, Israel, Nepal, Papua New Guinea, Solomon Islands, Sri Lanka, USA, Yemen

Note: In addition to the 176 states that had ratified the treaty as of 1 Jan. 2023, Solomon Islands ratified it on 20 Jan. 2023.

Treaty text: United Nations Treaty Collection, <https://treaties.un.org/doc/Treaties/1997/09/19970910 07-37 AM/Ch_XXVI_04p.pdf>

Convention on the Prohibition of the Use, Stockpiling, Production and Transfer of Anti-Personnel Mines and on their Destruction (APM Convention)

Opened for signature at Ottawa on 3–4 December 1997 and at New York on 5 December 1997; entered into force on 1 March 1999; depositary UN secretary-general

The convention prohibits anti-personnel mines (APMs), which are defined as mines designed to be exploded by the presence, proximity or contact of a person and which will incapacitate, injure or kill one or more persons.

Each party undertakes to destroy all of its stockpiled APMs as soon as possible but not later than four years after the entry into force of the convention for that state party. Each party also undertakes to destroy all APMs in mined areas under its jurisdiction or control not later than 10 years after the entry into force of the convention for that state party. Of the 164 parties, 162 no longer had stockpiles of APMs and 30 of the 63 parties that reported areas containing APMs had cleared them by 1 January 2023. A three-person ISU, based in Geneva, provides advice and technical support on implementing the convention to the states parties.

The parties meet in a Review Conference every five years (most recently in 2019), in an annual Meeting of the States Parties in intervening years and in annual intersessional meetings. A party may withdraw from the convention, having given six months' notice. But if the party is involved in an armed conflict at that time, the withdrawal will not take effect until that conflict has ended.

Parties (164): Afghanistan[‡], Albania, Algeria, Andorra, Angola[‡], Antigua and Barbuda, Argentina[*‡], Australia[*], Austria, Bahamas, Bangladesh, Barbados, Belarus, Belgium, Belize,

Benin, Bhutan, Bolivia, Bosnia and Herzegovina‡, Botswana, Brazil, Brunei Darussalam, Bulgaria, Burkina Faso, Burundi, Cabo Verde, Cambodia‡, Cameroon, Canada*, Central African Republic, Chad‡, Chile*, Colombia‡, Comoros, Congo (Democratic Republic of the)‡, Congo (Republic of the), Cook Islands, Costa Rica, Côte d'Ivoire, Croatia‡, Cyprus‡, Czechia*, Denmark, Djibouti, Dominica, Dominican Republic, Ecuador‡, El Salvador, Equatorial Guinea, Eritrea‡, Estonia, Eswatini, Ethiopia‡, Fiji, Finland, France, Gabon, Gambia, Germany, Ghana, Greece*†, Grenada, Guatemala, Guinea, Guinea-Bissau, Guyana, Haiti, Holy See, Honduras, Hungary, Iceland, Indonesia, Iraq‡, Ireland, Italy, Jamaica, Japan, Jordan, Kenya, Kiribati, Kuwait, Latvia, Lesotho, Liberia, Liechtenstein, Lithuania*, Luxembourg, Madagascar, Malawi, Malaysia, Maldives, Mali, Malta, Mauritania‡, Mauritius, Mexico, Moldova, Monaco, Montenegro*, Mozambique, Namibia, Nauru, Netherlands, New Zealand, Nicaragua, Niger‡, Nigeria‡, Niue, North Macedonia, Norway, Oman‡, Palau, Palestine‡, Panama, Papua New Guinea, Paraguay, Peru‡, Philippines, Poland*, Portugal, Qatar, Romania, Rwanda, Saint Kitts and Nevis, Saint Lucia, Saint Vincent and the Grenadines, Samoa, San Marino, Sao Tome and Principe, Senegal‡, Serbia*‡, Seychelles, Sierra Leone, Slovakia, Slovenia, Solomon Islands, Somalia‡, South Africa, South Sudan‡, Spain, Sri Lanka†‡, Sudan‡, Suriname, Sweden, Switzerland, Tajikistan‡, Tanzania, Thailand‡, Timor-Leste, Togo, Trinidad and Tobago, Tunisia, Türkiye‡, Turkmenistan, Tuvalu, Uganda, UK*, Ukraine†‡, Uruguay, Vanuatu, Venezuela, Yemen‡, Zambia, Zimbabwe‡

* With reservation and/or declaration.
† Party with remaining APM stockpile.
‡ Party with areas containing uncleared APMs.

Signed but not ratified (1): Marshall Islands

Convention text: United Nations Treaty Collection, <https://treaties.un.org/doc/Treaties/1997/09/19970918 07-53 AM/Ch_XXVI_05p.pdf>

Rome Statute of the International Criminal Court

Opened for signature at Rome on 17 July 1998 and at New York on 18 October 1998; entered into force on 1 July 2002; depositary UN secretary-general

The Rome Statute established the International Criminal Court (ICC), a permanent international court dealing with accusations of genocide, crimes against humanity, war crimes and the crime of aggression. The ICC can investigate and prosecute an alleged crime that takes place on the territory of a state party, is committed by a state party or is referred to it by the UN Security Council. The ICC may only prosecute a crime if the domestic courts are unwilling or unable to do so.

The *Amendment to Article 8 adopted on 10 June 2010* makes it a war crime to use chemical weapons and expanding bullets in non-international conflicts. A series of *Amendments to Article 8 adopted on 14 December 2017* make it a war crime to use weapons which use microbial or other biological agents, or toxins; weapons the primary effect of which is to injure by fragments undetectable by X-rays in the human body; and blinding laser weapons. The *Amendment to Article 8 adopted on 6 December 2019* makes intentional use of starvation of civilians a war crime. Amendments to Article 8 enter into force for the parties that have accepted them one year after that acceptance.

Amendments adopted on 11 June 2010 define the crime of aggression. The ICC's jurisdiction over the crime of aggression was activated on 17 July 2018. From that date, the ICC may investigate an apparent act of aggression committed by a state that is party to the statute (and that has not opted out of jurisdiction over the crime of aggression) on the territory of another party; such acts on or by any state (regardless of whether it is a party to the statute) may also be referred to the ICC by the UN Security Council.

The parties meet annually in the Assembly of States Parties. A state may withdraw from the statute and the ICC by giving 12 months' notice. Burundi withdrew from the statute and the ICC on 27 October 2017 and the Philippines on 17 March 2019.

Parties to the Rome Statute (123): Afghanistan, Albania, Andorra, Antigua and Barbuda, Argentina*, Australia*, Austria, Bangladesh, Barbados, Belgium, Belize, Benin, Bolivia, Bosnia and Herzegovina, Botswana, Brazil, Bulgaria, Burkina Faso, Cabo Verde, Cambodia, Canada, Central African Republic, Chad, Chile, Colombia*, Comoros, Congo (Democratic Republic of the), Congo (Republic of the), Cook Islands, Costa Rica, Côte d'Ivoire, Croatia, Cyprus, Czechia, Denmark, Djibouti, Dominica, Dominican Republic, Ecuador, El Salvador, Estonia, Fiji, Finland, France*, Gabon, Gambia, Georgia, Germany, Ghana, Greece, Grenada, Guatemala, Guinea, Guyana, Honduras, Hungary, Iceland, Ireland, Italy, Japan, Jordan*, Kenya, Kiribati, Korea (South), Latvia, Lesotho, Liberia, Liechtenstein, Lithuania, Luxembourg, Madagascar, Malawi, Maldives, Mali, Malta*, Marshall Islands, Mauritius, Mexico, Moldova, Mongolia, Montenegro, Namibia, Nauru, Netherlands, New Zealand*, Niger, Nigeria, North Macedonia, Norway, Palestine, Panama, Paraguay, Peru, Poland, Portugal*, Romania, Saint Kitts and Nevis, Saint Lucia, Saint Vincent and the Grenadines, Samoa, San Marino, Senegal, Serbia, Seychelles, Sierra Leone, Slovakia, Slovenia, South Africa, Spain, Suriname, Sweden*, Switzerland, Tajikistan, Tanzania, Timor-Leste, Trinidad and Tobago, Tunisia, Uganda, UK*, Uruguay, Vanuatu, Venezuela, Zambia

* With reservation and/or declaration.

Signed but not ratified (31): Algeria, Angola, Armenia, Bahamas, Bahrain, Cameroon, Egypt, Eritrea, Guinea-Bissau, Haiti, Iran, Israel*, Jamaica, Kuwait, Kyrgyzstan, Monaco, Morocco, Mozambique, Oman, Russia*, Sao Tome and Principe, Solomon Islands, Sudan*, Syria, Thailand, Ukraine†, United Arab Emirates, USA*, Uzbekistan, Yemen, Zimbabwe

* These states have declared that they no longer intend to become parties to the statute.

† Although Ukraine is not a party to the statute, it has accepted the jurisdiction of the ICC with respect to alleged crimes committed on its territory since 21 Nov. 2013. This jurisdiction extends to action committed by citizens of non-parties to the statute on Ukrainian territory but, since Ukraine itself is not a party, not the crime of aggression without a referral from the UN Security Council.

Parties to the Amendment to Article 8 of 10 June 2010 (44): Andorra, Argentina, Austria, Belgium, Botswana, Chile, Costa Rica, Croatia, Cyprus, Czechia, El Salvador, Estonia, Finland, Georgia, Germany, Guyana, *Italy*, Latvia, Liechtenstein, Lithuania, Luxembourg, Malta, Mauritius, Mongolia, Netherlands, New Zealand, North Macedonia, Norway, Palestine, Panama, Paraguay, *Peru*, Poland, Portugal, *Romania*, Samoa, San Marino, Slovakia, Slovenia, Spain, *Sweden*, Switzerland, Trinidad and Tobago, Uruguay

Note: In addition to the 44 states that were party to the amendment as of 1 Jan. 2023, Mexico accepted it on 20 Jan. 2023.

Parties to the Amendments of 11 June 2010 defining the crime of aggression (44): Andorra, Argentina, Austria, Belgium, Bolivia, Botswana, Chile, Costa Rica, Croatia, Cyprus, Czechia, Ecuador, El Salvador, Estonia, Finland, Georgia, Germany, Guyana, Iceland, Ireland, *Italy*, Latvia, Liechtenstein, Lithuania, Luxembourg, Malta, Mongolia, Netherlands, North Macedonia, Palestine, Panama, Paraguay, *Peru*, Poland, Portugal, Samoa, San Marino, Slovakia, Slovenia, Spain, *Sweden*, Switzerland, Trinidad and Tobago, Uruguay

Note: In addition to the 44 states that were party to the amendment as of 1 Jan. 2023, Niger ratified it on 14 Apr. 2023.

Parties to the Amendment to Article 8 of 14 December 2017 on weapons which use microbial or other biological agents, or toxins (13): Croatia, Czechia, Latvia, *Liechtenstein*, Luxembourg, Netherlands, New Zealand, Norway, *Romania*, Slovakia, *Slovenia*, Sweden, Switzerland

Note: In addition to the 13 states that were party to the amendment as of 1 Jan. 2023, Mexico accepted it on 20 Jan. 2023 and Uruguay ratified it on 21 Mar.

Parties to the Amendment to Article 8 of 14 December 2017 on weapons the primary effect of which is to injure by fragments undetectable by X-rays in the human body (11): Croatia, Czechia, Latvia, Luxembourg, Netherlands, New Zealand, Norway, *Romania*, Slovakia, *Slovenia*, Switzerland

Note: In addition to the 11 states that were party to the amendment as of 1 Jan. 2023, Mexico accepted it on 20 Jan. 2023 and Uruguay ratified it on 21 Mar.

Parties to the Amendment to Article 8 of 14 December 2017 on blinding laser weapons (11): Croatia, Czechia, Latvia, Luxembourg, Netherlands, New Zealand, Norway, *Romania*, Slovakia, *Slovenia*, Switzerland

Note: In addition to the 11 states that were party to the amendment as of 1 Jan. 2023, Mexico accepted it on 20 Jan. 2023 and Uruguay ratified it on 21 Mar.

Parties to the Amendment to Article 8 of 6 December 2019 on intentional starvation of civilians (11): Andorra, Croatia, *Liechtenstein*, Luxembourg, Netherlands, New Zealand, Norway, Portugal, *Romania*, Slovenia, Switzerland

Note: In addition to the 11 states that were party to the amendment as of 1 Jan. 2023, Uruguay ratified it on 21 Mar. 2023.

Statute text: United Nations Treaty Collection, <https://treaties.un.org/doc/Treaties/1998/07/19980717 06-33 PM/Ch_XVIII_10p.pdf>

Text of the Amendment to Article 8 of 10 June 2010: United Nations Treaty Collection, <https://treaties.un.org/doc/Treaties/2010/10/20101011 05-46 PM/CN.533.2010.pdf>

Text of the Amendments of 11 June 2010 defining the crime of aggression: United Nations Treaty Collection, <https://treaties.un.org/doc/Treaties/2010/06/20100611 05-56 PM/CN.651.2010.pdf>

Text of the Amendment to Article 8 of 14 December 2017 on weapons which use microbial or other biological agents or toxins: United Nations Treaty Collection, <https://treaties.un.org/doc/Publication/CN/2018/CN.116.2018-Eng.pdf>

Text of the Amendment to Article 8 of 14 December 2017 on weapons the primary effect of which is to injure by fragments undetectable by X-rays in the human body: United Nations Treaty Collection, <https://treaties.un.org/doc/Publication/CN/2018/CN.125.2018-Eng.pdf>

Text of the Amendment to Article 8 of 14 December 2017 on blinding laser weapons: United Nations Treaty Collection, <https://treaties.un.org/doc/Publication/CN/2018/CN.126.2018-Eng.pdf>

Text of the Amendment to Article 8 of 6 December 2019 on intentional starvation of civilians: United Nations Treaty Collection, <https://treaties.un.org/doc/Publication/CN/2020/CN.394.2020-Eng.pdf>

Convention on Cluster Munitions

Opened for signature at Oslo on 3 December 2008; entered into force on 1 August 2010; depositary UN secretary-general

The convention's objectives are to prohibit the use, production, transfer and stockpiling of cluster munitions that cause unacceptable harm to civilians. It also establishes a framework for cooperation and assistance to ensure adequate provision of care and rehabilitation for victims, clearance of contaminated areas, risk-reduction education and destruction of stockpiles. The convention does not apply to mines.

Each party undertakes to destroy all of its stockpiled cluster munitions as soon as possible but not later than eight years after the entry into force of the convention for that state party. The first deadlines for stockpile destruction were in 2018. As of 1 January 2023, four states had outstanding stockpile-destruction obligations. Each party also undertakes to clear and destroy all cluster munitions in contaminated areas under its jurisdiction or control not later than 10 years after the entry into force of the convention for that state party. The first deadlines for clearance were in 2020. As of 1 January 2023, 10 states had outstanding clearance obligations.

A three-person ISU, based in Geneva, was established in 2015 to, among other things, provide advice and technical support to the parties.

The parties meet in a Review Conference every five years (most recently in 2020), in an annual Meeting of States Parties in intervening years and, if the parties so decide, in an annual intersessional meeting. A party may withdraw from the convention, having given six months' notice. But if the party is involved in an armed conflict at that time, the withdrawal will not take effect until that conflict has ended.

Parties (110): Afghanistan, Albania, Andorra, Antigua and Barbuda, Australia, Austria, Belgium, Belize, Benin, Bolivia, Bosnia and Herzegovina, Botswana, Bulgaria, Burkina Faso, Burundi, Cabo Verde, Cameroon, Canada, Chad, Chile, Colombia*, Comoros, Congo (Republic of the), Cook Islands, Costa Rica, Côte d'Ivoire, Croatia, Cuba, Czechia, Denmark, Dominican Republic, Ecuador, El Salvador*, Eswatini, Fiji, France, Gambia, Germany, Ghana, Grenada, Guatemala, Guinea, Guinea-Bissau, Guyana, Holy See*, Honduras, Hungary, Iceland, Iraq, Ireland, Italy, Japan, Laos, Lebanon, Lesotho, Liechtenstein, Lithuania, Luxembourg, Madagascar, Malawi, Maldives, Mali, Malta, Mauritania, Mauritius, Mexico, Moldova, Monaco, Montenegro, Mozambique, Namibia, Nauru, Netherlands, New Zealand, Nicaragua, Niger, Niue, North Macedonia, Norway, Palestine, Palau, Panama, Paraguay, Peru, Philippines, Portugal, Rwanda, Saint Kitts and Nevis, Saint Lucia, Saint Vincent and the Grenadines, Samoa, San Marino, Sao Tome and Principe, Senegal, Seychelles, Sierra Leone, Slovakia, Slovenia, Somalia, South Africa, Spain, Sri Lanka, Sweden, Switzerland, Togo, Trinidad and Tobago, Tunisia, UK, Uruguay, Zambia

* With reservation and/or declaration.

Signed but not ratified (13): Angola, Central African Republic, Congo (Democratic Republic of the), Cyprus, Djibouti, Haiti, Indonesia, Jamaica, Kenya, Liberia, Nigeria, Tanzania, Uganda

Note: In addition to the 110 states parties as of 1 Jan. 2023, Nigeria ratified the convention on 28 Feb. 2023.

Convention text: United Nations Treaty Collection, <https://treaties.un.org/doc/Publication/CTC/26-6.pdf>

Arms Trade Treaty (ATT)

Opened for signature at New York on 3 June 2013; entered into force on 24 December 2014; depositary UN secretary-general

The object of the treaty is to establish the highest possible common international standards for regulating the international trade in conventional arms; and to prevent and eradicate the illicit trade in conventional arms and prevent their diversion.

Among other things, the treaty prohibits a state party from authorizing a transfer of arms if they are to be used in the commission of genocide, crimes against humanity or war crimes. The treaty also requires the exporting state to assess the potential for any arms proposed for export to undermine peace and security or be used to commit serious violations of international humanitarian law or international human rights law. This assessment must take into account the risk of the arms being used to commit or facilitate serious acts of gender-based violence or serious acts of violence against women and children.

Each party must submit an annual report on its authorized or actual exports and imports of conventional arms.

The treaty established the ATT Secretariat, based in Geneva, to support the parties in its implementation. Among other tasks, it collects the annual reports submitted by each party.

The parties meet in an annual Conference of States Parties, which has established working groups (on effective treaty implementation, on transparency and reporting, and on treaty universalization) that meet more frequently. A party may withdraw from the treaty, having given 90 days' notice.

Parties (113): Afghanistan, Albania, *Andorra*, Antigua and Barbuda, Argentina, Australia, Austria, Bahamas, Barbados, Belgium, Belize, Benin, Bosnia and Herzegovina, Botswana, Brazil, Bulgaria, Burkina Faso, Cabo Verde, Cameroon, Canada, Central African Republic, Chad, Chile, China, Costa Rica, Côte d'Ivoire, Croatia, Cyprus, Czechia, Denmark, Dominica, Dominican Republic, El Salvador, Estonia, Finland, France, *Gabon*, Georgia, Germany, Ghana, Greece, Grenada, Guatemala, Guinea, Guinea-Bissau, Guyana, Honduras, Hungary, Iceland, Ireland, Italy, Jamaica, Japan, Kazakhstan*, Korea (South), Latvia, Lebanon, Lesotho, Liberia, Liechtenstein*, Lithuania, Luxembourg, Madagascar, Maldives, Mali, Malta, Mauritania, Mauritius, Mexico, Moldova, Monaco, Montenegro, Mozambique, Namibia, Netherlands, New Zealand*, Niger, Nigeria, Niue, North Macedonia, Norway, Palau, Palestine, Panama, Paraguay, Peru, *Philippines*, Poland, Portugal, Romania, Saint Kitts and Nevis, Saint Lucia, Saint Vincent and the Grenadines, Samoa, San Marino, Sao Tome and Principe, Senegal, Serbia, Seychelles, Sierra Leone, Slovakia, Slovenia, South Africa, Spain, Suriname, Sweden, Switzerland*, Togo, Trinidad and Tobago, Tuvalu, UK, Uruguay, Zambia

* With reservation and/or declaration.

Signed but not ratified (28): Angola, Bahrain, Bangladesh, Burundi, Cambodia, Colombia, Comoros, Congo (Republic of the), Djibouti, Eswatini, Haiti, Israel, Kiribati, Libya, Malawi, Malaysia, Mongolia, Nauru, Rwanda, Singapore, Tanzania, Thailand, Türkiye, Ukraine, United Arab Emirates, USA*, Vanuatu, Zimbabwe

* This state has declared that it no longer intends to become a party to the treaty.

Treaty text: United Nations Treaty Collection, <https://treaties.un.org/doc/Treaties/2013/04/20130410 12-01 PM/Ch_XXVI_08.pdf>

Treaty on the Prohibition of Nuclear Weapons (TPNW)

Opened for signature at New York on 20 September 2017; entered in force on 22 January 2021; depositary UN secretary-general

In its preamble, the treaty cites the catastrophic humanitarian and environmental consequences of the use of nuclear weapons and invokes the principles of international humanitarian law and the rules of international law applicable in armed conflict. The treaty prohibits parties from developing, testing, producing, manufacturing, acquiring, possessing or stockpiling nuclear weapons or other nuclear explosive devices. Parties are prohibited from using or threatening to use nuclear weapons and other nuclear explosive devices. Finally, parties cannot allow the stationing, installation or deployment of nuclear weapons and other nuclear explosive devices in their territory.

The treaty outlines procedures for eliminating the nuclear weapons of any party that owned, possessed or controlled them after 7 July 2017, to be supervised by a 'competent international authority or authorities' to be designated by the states parties. Each party is required to maintain its existing safeguards agreements with the IAEA and must, at a minimum, conclude and bring into force a comprehensive safeguards agreement with the agency. The treaty also contains provisions on assisting the victims of the testing or use of nuclear weapons and taking necessary and appropriate measures for the environmental remediation of contaminated areas.

The parties meet in an annual Meeting of States Parties and, every six years, in a Review Conference (with the first scheduled for 2026). A Scientific Advisory Group will report to the Meeting of States Parties.

Membership of the treaty does not prejudice a party's other, compatible international obligations (such as the NPT and the CTBT). A party may withdraw from the treaty, having given 12 months' notice, if it decides that its supreme interests have been jeopardized by extraordinary events related to the treaty's subject matter. But if the party is involved in an armed conflict at that time, the withdrawal will not take effect until it is no longer party to an armed conflict.

Ratifications deposited (68): Antigua and Barbuda, Austria, Bangladesh, Belize, Benin, Bolivia, Botswana, *Cabo Verde*, Cambodia, Chile, Comoros, *Congo (Democratic Republic of the)*, *Congo (Republic of the)*, Cook Islands*, Costa Rica, *Côte d'Ivoire*, Cuba*, Dominica, *Dominican Republic*, Ecuador, El Salvador, Fiji, Gambia, *Grenada*, *Guatemala*, Guinea-Bissau, Guyana, Holy See, Honduras, Ireland, Jamaica, Kazakhstan, Kiribati, Laos, Lesotho, *Malawi*, Malaysia, Maldives, Malta, Mexico, Mongolia, Namibia, Nauru, New Zealand, Nicaragua, Nigeria, Niue, Palau, Palestine, Panama, Paraguay, Peru, Philippines, Saint Kitts and Nevis, Saint Lucia, Saint Vincent and the Grenadines, Samoa, San Marino, Seychelles, South Africa, Thailand, *Timor-Leste*, Trinidad and Tobago, Tuvalu, Uruguay, Vanuatu, Venezuela, Viet Nam

* With reservation and/or declaration.

Signed but not ratified (26): Algeria, Angola, *Barbados*, Brazil, Brunei Darussalam, *Burkina Faso*, Central African Republic, Colombia, *Equatorial Guinea*, Ghana, *Haiti*, Indonesia, Libya, Liechtenstein, Madagascar, Mozambique, Myanmar, Nepal, Niger, Sao Tome and Principe, *Sierra Leone*, Sudan, Tanzania, Togo, Zambia, Zimbabwe

Note: In addition to the 26 states that had signed by not yet ratified the treaty as of 1 Jan. 2023, Djibouti signed it on 9 Jan. 2023.

Treaty text: United Nations Treaty Collection, <https://treaties.un.org/doc/Treaties/2017/07/20170707 03-42 PM/Ch_XXVI_9.pdf>

II. Regional treaties

Treaty for the Prohibition of Nuclear Weapons in Latin America and the Caribbean (Treaty of Tlatelolco)

Original treaty opened for signature at Mexico City on 14 February 1967; entered into force on 22 April 1968; treaty amended in 1990, 1991 and 1992; depositary Mexican government

The treaty prohibits the testing, use, manufacture, production or acquisition by any means, as well as the receipt, storage, installation, deployment and any form of possession of any nuclear weapons by any country of Latin America and the Caribbean and in the surrounding seas.

The parties should conclude agreements individually with the IAEA for the application of safeguards to their nuclear activities. The IAEA has the exclusive power to carry out special inspections. The treaty also established the Agency for the Prohibition of Nuclear Weapons in Latin America and the Caribbean (Organismo para la Proscripción de las Armas Nucleares en la América Latina y el Caribe, OPANAL) to ensure compliance with the treaty.

The treaty is open for signature by all the independent states of Latin America and the Caribbean. A party may withdraw from the treaty, having given three months' notice, if it decides that its supreme interests or the peace and security of another party or parties have been jeopardized by new circumstances related to the treaty's content.

Under *Additional Protocol I* the states with territories within the zone—France, the Netherlands, the UK and the USA—undertake to apply the statute of military denuclearization to these territories.

Under *Additional Protocol II* the recognized nuclear weapon states—China, France, Russia, the UK and the USA—undertake to respect the military denuclearization of Latin America and the Caribbean and not to contribute to acts involving a violation of the treaty, nor to use or threaten to use nuclear weapons against the parties to the treaty.

Parties to the original treaty (33): Antigua and Barbuda[1], Argentina[1], Bahamas, Barbados[1], Belize[2], Bolivia[1], Brazil[1], Chile[1], Colombia[1], Costa Rica[1], Cuba, Dominica, Dominican Republic[3], Ecuador[1], El Salvador[1], Grenada[1], Guatemala[1], Guyana[3], Haiti, Honduras[1], Jamaica[1], Mexico[1], Nicaragua[1], Panama[1], Paraguay[1], Peru[1], Saint Kitts and Nevis[1], Saint Lucia[1], Saint Vincent and the Grenadines[4], Suriname[1], Trinidad and Tobago[1], Uruguay[1], Venezuela[1]

[1] Has ratified the amendments of 1990, 1991 and 1992.
[2] Has ratified the amendments of 1990 and 1992 only.
[3] Has ratified the amendment of 1992 only.
[4] Has ratified the amendments of 1991 and 1992 only.

Parties to Additional Protocol I (4): France*, Netherlands*, UK*, USA*

Parties to Additional Protocol II (5): China*, France*, Russia*, UK*, USA*

* With reservation and/or declaration.

Original treaty text: United Nations Treaty Series, vol. 634 (1968), <https://treaties.un.org/doc/Publication/UNTS/Volume 634/v634.pdf>

Amended treaty text: Agency for the Prohibition of Nuclear Weapons in Latin America and the Caribbean, Inf.11/2018, 5 June 2018, <https://www.opanal.org/wp-content/uploads/2019/10/Inf_11_2018_Treaty_Tlatelolco.pdf>

South Pacific Nuclear Free Zone Treaty (Treaty of Rarotonga)

Opened for signature at Rarotonga on 6 August 1985; entered into force on 11 December 1986; depositary secretary general of the Pacific Islands Forum Secretariat

The South Pacific Nuclear Free Zone is defined as the area between the zone of application of the Treaty of Tlatelolco in the east and the west coast of Australia and the western border of Papua New Guinea and between the zone of application of the Antarctic Treaty in the south and, approximately, the equator in the north.

The treaty prohibits the manufacture or acquisition of any nuclear explosive device, as well as possession or control over any such device by the parties anywhere inside or outside the zone. The parties also undertake not to supply nuclear material or equipment, unless subject to IAEA safeguards; to prevent the stationing or testing of any nuclear explosive device in their territories; and not to dump, and to prevent the dumping of, radioactive waste and other radioactive matter at sea anywhere within the zone. Each party remains free to allow visits, as well as transit, by foreign ships and aircraft.

The treaty is open for signature by the members of the Pacific Islands Forum. The parties can review the operation of the treaty in a meeting of the Consultative Committee convened at the request of any party. The first such meeting was held in 2021. If any party violates an essential provision or the spirit of the treaty, every other party may withdraw from the treaty, having given 12 months' notice.

Under *Protocol 1* France, the UK and the USA undertake to apply the treaty prohibitions relating to the manufacture, stationing and testing of nuclear explosive devices in the territories situated within the zone for which they are internationally responsible.

Under *Protocol 2* China, France, Russia, the UK and the USA undertake not to use or threaten to use a nuclear explosive device against the parties to the treaty or against any territory within the zone for which a party to Protocol 1 is internationally responsible.

Under *Protocol 3* China, France, Russia, the UK and the USA undertake not to test any nuclear explosive device anywhere within the zone.

Parties (13): Australia, Cook Islands, Fiji, Kiribati, Nauru, New Zealand, Niue, Papua New Guinea, Samoa, Solomon Islands, Tonga, Tuvalu, Vanuatu

Parties to Protocol 1 (2): France*, UK*; *signed but not ratified (1)*: USA

Parties to Protocol 2 (4): China*, France*, Russia*, UK*; *signed but not ratified (1)*: USA

Parties to Protocol 3 (4): China*, France*, Russia*, UK*; *signed but not ratified (1)*: USA

* With reservation and/or declaration.

Treaty text: Pacific Islands Forum Secretariat, <https://www.forumsec.org/wp-content/uploads/2018/02/South-Pacific-Nuclear-Zone-Treaty-Raratonga-Treaty-1.pdf>

Protocol texts: Pacific Islands Forum Secretariat, <https://www.forumsec.org/wp-content/uploads/2018/02/South-Pacific-Nuclear-Zone-Treaty-Protocols-1.pdf>

Treaty on Conventional Armed Forces in Europe (CFE Treaty)

Original treaty signed by the 16 member states of the North Atlantic Treaty Organization (NATO) and the 6 member states of the Warsaw Treaty Organization (WTO) at Paris on 19 November 1990; entered into force on 9 November 1992; depositary Dutch government

The treaty sets ceilings on five categories of treaty-limited equipment (TLE)—battle tanks, armoured combat vehicles, artillery of at least 100-mm calibre, combat aircraft and attack helicopters—in an area stretching from the Atlantic Ocean to the Ural Mountains (the Atlantic-to-the-Urals, ATTU). The treaty established the Joint Consultative Group (JCG) to promote its objectives and implementation.

The treaty was negotiated by the member states of the WTO and NATO within the framework of the Conference on Security and Co-operation in Europe (from 1995 the Organization for Security and Co-operation in Europe, OSCE).

The **1992 Tashkent Agreement**, adopted by the former Soviet republics with territories within the ATTU area of application (with the exception of Estonia, Latvia and Lithuania) and the **1992 Oslo Document** (Final Document of the Extraordinary Conference of the States Parties to the CFE Treaty) introduced modifications to the treaty required because of the emergence of new states after the break-up of the Soviet Union.

A party may withdraw from the treaty, having given 150 days' notice, if it decides that its supreme interests have been jeopardized by extraordinary events related to the treaty's subject matter.

Parties (30): Armenia, Azerbaijan, Belarus, Belgium[2], Bulgaria[2], Canada[2], Czechia[2], Denmark[2], France, Georgia, Germany[2], Greece, Hungary[2], Iceland[2], Italy[2], Kazakhstan, Luxembourg[2], Moldova[2], Netherlands[2], Norway, Poland, Portugal[2], Romania, Russia[1], Slovakia[2], Spain, Türkiye[2], UK[2], Ukraine, USA[2]

[1] On 14 July 2007 Russia declared its intention to suspend its participation in the CFE Treaty and associated documents and agreements, which took effect on 12 Dec. 2007. In Mar. 2015 Russia announced that it had decided to completely halt its participation in the treaty, including the JCG.

[2] In Nov.–Dec. 2011 these countries notified the depositary or the JCG that they would cease to perform their obligations under the treaty with regard to Russia.

The parties meet in a Review Conference every five years (most recently in 2021). The first Review Conference adopted the **1996 Flank Document**, which reorganized the flank areas geographically and numerically, allowing Russia and Ukraine to deploy TLE in a less constraining manner.

Original (1990) treaty text: Dutch Ministry of Foreign Affairs, <https://repository.overheid.nl/frbr/vd/004285/1/pdf/004285_Gewaarmerkt_0.pdf>

Consolidated (1993) treaty text: Dutch Ministry of Foreign Affairs, <https://wetten.overheid.nl/BWBV0002009/>

Flank Document text: Organization for Security and Co-operation in Europe, <https://www.osce.org/library/14099?download=true>, annex A

Concluding Act of the Negotiation on Personnel Strength of Conventional Armed Forces in Europe (CFE-1A Agreement)

Signed by the parties to the CFE Treaty at Helsinki on 10 July 1992; entered into force simultaneously with the CFE Treaty; depositary Dutch government

This politically binding agreement sets ceilings on the number of personnel of the conventional land-based armed forces of the parties within the ATTU area.

Agreement text: Organization for Security and Co-operation in Europe, <https://www.osce.org/library/14093?download=true>

Agreement on Adaptation of the Treaty on Conventional Armed Forces in Europe

Signed by the parties to the CFE Treaty at Istanbul on 19 November 1999; not in force; depositary Dutch government

With the dissolution of the WTO and the accession of some former members to NATO, this agreement would have replaced the CFE Treaty's bloc-to-bloc military balance with a regional balance, established individual state limits on TLE holdings, and provided for a new structure of limitations and new military flexibility mechanisms, flank sub-limits and enhanced transparency. It would have opened the CFE regime to all other European states. It would have entered into force when ratified by all of the signatories.

The **1999 Final Act of the Conference of the CFE States Parties**, with annexes, contains politically binding arrangements with regard to Georgia, Moldova and Central Europe and to withdrawals of armed forces from foreign territories (known as the Istanbul commitments). Many signatories of the Agreement on Adaptation made their ratification contingent on the implementation of these political commitments.

Ratifications deposited (3): Belarus, Kazakhstan, Russia*[1]

* With reservation and/or declaration.

Signed but not ratified (27): Armenia, Azerbaijan, Belgium, Bulgaria, Canada, Czechia, Denmark, France, Germany, Georgia, Greece, Hungary, Iceland, Italy, Luxembourg, Moldavia, Netherlands, Norway, Poland, Portugal, Romania, Slovakia, Spain, Türkiye, Ukraine[2], UK, USA

[1] On 14 July 2007 Russia declared its intention to suspend its participation in the CFE Treaty and associated documents and agreements, which took effect on 12 Dec. 2007. In Mar. 2015 Russia announced that it had decided to completely halt its participation in the treaty, including the JCG.

[2] Ukraine ratified the Agreement on Adaptation on 21 Sep. 2000 but did not deposit its instrument with the depositary.

Agreement text: Dutch Ministry of Foreign Affairs, <https://repository.overheid.nl/frbr/vd/009241/1/pdf/009241_Gewaarmerkt_0.pdf>

Treaty text as amended by 1999 agreement: SIPRI Yearbook 2000, <https://www.sipri.org/sites/default/files/SIPRI Yearbook 2000.pdf>, appendix 10B

Final Act text: Organization for Security and Co-operation in Europe, <https://www.osce.org/library/14114?download=true>

Treaty on Open Skies

Opened for signature at Helsinki on 24 March 1992; entered into force on 1 January 2002; depositaries Canadian and Hungarian governments

The treaty obligates the parties to submit their territories to short-notice unarmed surveillance flights. The area of application initially stretched from Vancouver, Canada, eastward to Vladivostok, Russia. The treaty established the Open Skies Consultative Commission (OSCC) to monitor implementation.

The treaty was negotiated between the member states of the WTO and NATO. Since 1 July 2002 any state can apply to accede to the treaty. The parties meet in a Review Conference every five years (most recently in 2020). A party may withdraw from the treaty, having given six months' notice. The USA withdrew from the treaty on 22 November 2020 and Russia withdrew on 18 December 2021.

Parties (32): Belarus, Belgium, Bosnia and Herzegovina, Bulgaria, Canada*, Croatia, Czechia, Denmark, Estonia, Finland, France, Georgia, Germany, Greece, Hungary, Iceland, Italy, Latvia, Lithuania, Luxembourg, Netherlands, Norway, Poland, Portugal, Romania, Slovakia, Slovenia, Spain*, Sweden*, Türkiye, UK, Ukraine

* With reservation and/or declaration.

Signed but not ratified (1): Kyrgyzstan

Treaty text: Canada Treaty Information, <https://www.treaty-accord.gc.ca/text-texte.aspx?id=102747>

Treaty on the Southeast Asia Nuclear Weapon-Free Zone (Treaty of Bangkok)

Signed by the 10 member states of the Association of Southeast Asian Nations (ASEAN) at Bangkok on 15 December 1995; entered into force on 27 March 1997; depositary Thai government

The South East Asia Nuclear Weapon-Free Zone includes the territories, the continental shelves and the exclusive economic zones (EEZs) of the states parties. The treaty prohibits the development, manufacture, acquisition or testing of nuclear weapons inside or outside the zone as well as the stationing and transport of nuclear weapons in or through the zone. Each state party may decide for itself whether to allow visits and transit by foreign ships and aircraft. The parties undertake not to dump at sea or discharge into the atmosphere anywhere within the zone any radioactive material or waste or dispose of radioactive material on land. The parties should conclude an agreement with the IAEA for the application of full-scope safeguards to their peaceful nuclear activities.

The treaty established the Commission for the Southeast Asia Nuclear Weapon-Free Zone to oversee implementation. The parties met in 2007 to review the treaty and may do so again whenever there is consensus among them. The treaty is open for accession by all states of South East Asia. If any party breaches an essential provision of the treaty, every other party may withdraw from the treaty.

Under a *Protocol* to the treaty, China, France, Russia, the UK and the USA are to undertake not to use or threaten to use nuclear weapons against any state party to the treaty. They should further undertake not to use nuclear weapons within the zone. The protocol will enter into force for each state party on the date of its deposit of the instrument of ratification. None of these states has signed the protocol since they object, among other things, to the inclusion of continental shelves and EEZs in the zone.

Parties (10): Brunei Darussalam, Cambodia, Indonesia, Laos, Malaysia, Myanmar, Philippines, Singapore, Thailand, Viet Nam

Protocol (0): no signatures, no parties

Treaty text: ASEAN Secretariat, <https://asean.org/treaty-on-the-southeast-asia-nuclear-weapon-free-zone/>

Protocol text: ASEAN Secretariat, <https://asean.org/protocol-to-the-treaty-on-the-south east-asia-nuclear-weapon-free-zone/>

African Nuclear-Weapon-Free Zone Treaty (Treaty of Pelindaba)

Opened for signature at Cairo on 11 April 1996; entered into force on 15 July 2009; depositary secretary-general of the African Union

The African Nuclear Weapon-Free Zone includes the territory of the continent of Africa, island states members of the African Union (AU) and all islands considered by the AU to be part of Africa.

The treaty prohibits the research, development, manufacture and acquisition of nuclear explosive devices and the testing or stationing of any nuclear explosive device in the zone. Each party remains free to allow visits and transit by foreign ships and aircraft. The treaty also prohibits any attack against nuclear installations in the zone. The parties undertake not to dump or permit the dumping of radioactive waste and other radioactive matter anywhere within the zone. Each party should individually conclude an agreement with the IAEA for the application of comprehensive safeguards to their peaceful nuclear activities. The treaty also established the African Commission on Nuclear Energy (AFCONE) to ensure compliance with the treaty.

The parties meet every two years in a Conference of States Parties. The treaty is open for accession by all the states of Africa. A party may withdraw from the treaty, having given 12 months' notice, if it decides that its supreme interests have been jeopardized by extraordinary events related to the treaty's subject matter.

Under *Protocol* I China, France, Russia, the UK and the USA undertake not to use or threaten to use a nuclear explosive device against the parties to the treaty.

Under *Protocol II* China, France, Russia, the UK and the USA undertake not to test nuclear explosive devices within the zone.

Under *Protocol III* France and Spain are to undertake to observe certain provisions of the treaty with respect to the territories within the zone for which they are internationally responsible.

Parties (44): Algeria, Angola, Benin, Botswana, Burkina Faso, Burundi, Cabo Verde, Cameroon, Chad, Comoros, *Congo (Democratic Republic of the)*, Congo (Republic of the), Côte d'Ivoire, Equatorial Guinea, Eswatini, Ethiopia, Gabon, Gambia, Ghana, Guinea, Guinea-Bissau, Kenya, Lesotho, Libya, Madagascar, Malawi, Mali, Mauritania, Mauritius, *Morocco*, Mozambique, Namibia, Niger, Nigeria, Rwanda, Sahrawi Arab Democratic Republic (Western Sahara), Seychelles, Senegal, South Africa, Tanzania, Togo, Tunisia, Zambia, Zimbabwe

Signed but not ratified (10): Central African Republic, Djibouti, Egypt, Eritrea, Liberia, Sao Tome and Principe, Sierra Leone, Somalia, Sudan, Uganda

Parties to Protocol I (4): China, France*, Russia*, UK*; *signed but not ratified (1)*: USA*

Parties to Protocol II (4): China, France*, Russia*, UK*; *signed but not ratified (1)*: USA*

Parties to Protocol III (1): France*

* With reservation and/or declaration.

Treaty text: African Union, <https://au.int/sites/default/files/treaties/37288-treaty-0018_-_the_african_nuclear-weapon-free_zone_treaty_the_treaty_of_pelindaba_e.pdf>

Agreement on Sub-Regional Arms Control (Florence Agreement)

Adopted by the 5 original parties at Florence and entered into force on 14 June 1996

The agreement was negotiated under the auspices of the OSCE in accordance with the mandate in Article IV of Annex 1-B of the 1995 General Framework Agreement for Peace in Bosnia and Herzegovina (Dayton Agreement). It sets numerical ceilings on armaments of the former warring parties. Five categories of heavy conventional weapons are included: battle tanks, armoured combat vehicles, heavy artillery (75 mm and above), combat aircraft and attack helicopters. The limits were reached by 31 October 1997; by that date 6580 weapon items, or 46 per cent of pre-June 1996 holdings, had been destroyed. By 2021 a total of 10 292 items had been destroyed voluntarily.

The implementation of the agreement was monitored and assisted by the OSCE's Personal Representative of the Chairman-in-Office and the Contact Group (France, Germany, Italy, Russia, the UK and the USA) and supported by other OSCE states. Under a two-phase action plan agreed in November 2009, responsibility for the implementation of the agreement and mutual inspection was transferred to the parties on 5 December 2014, following the signing of a new set of amendments to the agreement. The Sub-Regional Consultative Commission (SRCC) monitors implementation.

Parties (4): Bosnia and Herzegovina, Croatia, Montenegro, Serbia

Agreement text: RACVIAC–Centre for Security Cooperation, <https://web.archive.org/web/20170405151539/www.racviac.org/downloads/treaties_agreements/aIV.pdf>

Inter-American Convention Against the Illicit Manufacturing of and Trafficking in Firearms, Ammunition, Explosives, and Other Related Materials (CIFTA)

Opened for signature by the member states of the Organization of American States (OAS) at Washington, DC, on 14 November 1997; entered into force on 1 July 1998; depositary General Secretariat of the OAS

The purpose of the convention is to prevent, combat and eradicate the illicit manufacturing of and the trafficking in firearms, ammunition, explosives and other related materials; and to promote and facilitate cooperation and the exchange of information and experience among the parties.

The convention established a Consultative Committee, which meets annually. A Conference of States Parties meets every three–five years (most recently in 2021). A party may withdraw from the convention, having given six months' notice.

Parties (31): Antigua and Barbuda, Argentina*, Bahamas, Barbados, Belize, Bolivia, Brazil, Chile, Colombia, Costa Rica, Dominica, Dominican Republic, Ecuador, El Salvador, Grenada, Guatemala, Guyana, Haiti, Honduras, Mexico, Nicaragua, Panama, Paraguay, Peru, Saint Kitts and Nevis, Saint Lucia, Saint Vincent and the Grenadines, Suriname, Trinidad and Tobago, Uruguay, Venezuela

* With reservation.

Signed but not ratified (3): Canada, Jamaica, USA

Convention text: OAS, <https://www.oas.org/en/sla/dil/inter_american_treaties_A-63_illicit_manufacturing_trafficking_firearms_ammunition_explosives.asp>

Inter-American Convention on Transparency in Conventional Weapons Acquisitions

Opened for signature by the member states of the OAS at Guatemala City on 7 June 1999; entered into force on 21 November 2002; depositary General Secretariat of the OAS

The objective of the convention is to contribute more fully to regional openness and transparency in the acquisition of conventional weapons by exchanging information regarding such acquisitions, for the purpose of promoting confidence among states in the Americas.

A Conference of the States Parties met in 2009 and 2022, and a Consultative Committee is to meet for the first time in 2023. A party may withdraw from the convention, having given 12 months' notice.

Parties (17): Argentina, Barbados, Brazil, Canada, Chile, Costa Rica, Dominican Republic, Ecuador, El Salvador, Guatemala, Mexico, Nicaragua, Panama, Paraguay, Peru, Uruguay, Venezuela

Signed but not ratified (6): Bolivia, Colombia, Dominica, Haiti, Honduras, USA

Convention text: OAS, <https://www.oas.org/en/sla/dil/inter_american_treaties_A-64_transparency_conventional_weapons_acquisitions.asp>

Protocol on the Control of Firearms, Ammunition and other related Materials in the Southern African Development Community (SADC) Region

Opened for signature by the members states of SADC at Blantyre on 14 August 2001; entered into force on 8 November 2004; depositary SADC Executive Secretary

The objectives of the protocol include the prevention, combating and eradication of the illicit manufacturing of firearms, ammunition and other related materials, and the prevention of their excessive and destabilizing accumulation, trafficking, possession and use in the region. A party may withdraw from the protocol, having given 12 months' notice.

An agreement amending the protocol was approved by the 40th ordinary SADC summit on 17 August 2020. The agreement broadens the scope of the protocol to include other conventional weapons, aligns it with the ATT and other international and regional conventions, and incorporates contemporary best practices and standards on corruption, tracing and cooperation. It will enter into force once ratified by seven states.

Parties to the original protocol (11): Botswana, Eswatini, Lesotho, Malawi, Mauritius, Mozambique, Namibia, South Africa, Tanzania, Zambia, Zimbabwe

Signed but not ratified (2*): Congo (Democratic Republic of the), Seychelles[†]

   * Three member states of SADC—Angola, the Comoros and Madagascar—have neither signed nor ratified the original protocol.
   [†] Seychelles signed the protocol in 2001 but did not ratify it before withdrawing from SADC in 2004. It rejoined SADC in 2008.

Original protocol text: SADC, <https://www.sadc.int/sites/default/files/2021-08/Protocol_on_the_Control_of_Firearms_Ammunition2001.pdf>

Nairobi Protocol for the Prevention, Control and Reduction of Small Arms and Light Weapons in the Great Lakes Region and the Horn of Africa

Signed by the 10 member states of the Nairobi Secretariat on Small Arms and Light Weapons and the Seychelles at Nairobi on 21 April 2004; entered into force on 5 May 2006; depositary Regional Centre on Small Arms in the Great Lakes Region, the Horn of Africa and Bordering States (RECSA)

The objectives of the protocol include the prevention, combating and eradication of the illicit manufacture of, trafficking in, possession and use of small arms and light weapons (SALW) in the subregion. Its implementation is overseen by RECSA.

Parties (12): Burundi, Central African Republic, Congo (Democratic Republic of the), Congo (Republic of the), Djibouti, Eritrea, Ethiopia, Kenya, Rwanda, South Sudan, Sudan, Uganda

Signed but not ratified (3*): Seychelles, Somalia, Tanzania

   * The accuracy of this list is uncertain. Some or all of these 3 states may have ratified the treaty. They all participate in the implementation activities of RECSA.

Protocol text: RECSA, <https://recsasec.org/uploads/documents/73703297.pdf>

ECOWAS Convention on Small Arms and Light Weapons, their Ammunition and Other Related Materials

Adopted by the 15 member states of the Economic Community of West African States (ECOWAS) at Abuja, on 14 June 2006; entered into force on 29 September 2009; depositary president of the ECOWAS Commission

The convention obligates the parties to prevent and combat the excessive and destabilizing accumulation of SALW in the ECOWAS member states. The convention bans the transfer of SALW into, through or from the territories of the parties. The ECOWAS member states may, by consensus, grant a party an exemption for national defence and security needs or for use in multilateral peace operations. Possession of light weapons by civilians is banned and their possession of small arms must be regulated. Each party must also control the manufacture of SALW, establish registers of SALW and establish a national commission to implement the convention.

A party may withdraw from the treaty, having given 12 months' notice, if it decides that its supreme interests have been jeopardized by extraordinary events related to the treaty's subject matter.

Parties (14): Benin, Burkina Faso, Cabo Verde, Côte d'Ivoire, Ghana, Guinea, Guinea-Bissau, Liberia, Mali, Niger, Nigeria, Senegal, Sierra Leone, Togo

Signed but not ratified (1): Gambia

Convention text: ECOWAS Commission, <https://web.archive.org/web/20180127191610/documentation.ecowas.int/download/en/legal_documents/protocols/Convention on Small Arms and Light Weapons, their Ammunitions and other Related Matters.pdf>

Treaty on a Nuclear-Weapon-Free Zone in Central Asia (Treaty of Semipalatinsk)

Signed by the 5 Central Asian states at Semipalatinsk on 8 September 2006; entered into force on 21 March 2009; depositary Kyrgyz government

The Central Asian Nuclear Weapon-Free Zone is defined as the territories of Kazakhstan, Kyrgyzstan, Tajikistan, Turkmenistan, Uzbekistan. The treaty obligates the parties not to conduct research on, develop, manufacture, stockpile or otherwise acquire, possess or have control over nuclear weapons or any other nuclear explosive device by any means anywhere.

The parties hold annual Consultative Meetings. A party may withdraw from the treaty, having given 12 months' notice, if it decides that its supreme interests have been jeopardized by extraordinary events related to the treaty's subject matter.

Under a *Protocol* China, France, Russia, the UK and the USA undertake not to use or threaten to use a nuclear explosive device against the parties to the treaty.

Parties (5): Kazakhstan, Kyrgyzstan, Tajikistan, Turkmenistan, Uzbekistan

Parties to the protocol (4): China, France*, Russia, UK*; *signed but not ratified (1)*: USA

* With reservations and/or declaration.

Treaty and protocol text: United Nations Treaty Series, vol. 2970 (2014), <https://treaties.un.org/doc/Publication/UNTS/Volume 2970/Part/volume-2970-I-51633.pdf>

Central African Convention for the Control of Small Arms and Light Weapons, Their Ammunition and All Parts and Components That Can Be Used for Their Manufacture, Repair and Assembly (Kinshasa Convention)

Opened for signature by the 10 member states of the Communauté économique d'États de l'Afrique Centrale (CEEAC, Economic Community of Central African States) and Rwanda at Brazzaville on 19 November 2010; entered into force on 8 March 2017; depositary UN secretary-general

The objectives of the convention are to prevent, combat and eradicate illicit trade and trafficking in SALW in Central Africa (defined to be the territory of the members of CEEAC and Rwanda); to strengthen the control in the region of the manufacture, trade, transfer and use of SALW; to combat armed violence and ease the human suffering in the region caused by SALW; and to foster cooperation and confidence among the states parties.

The parties met in the first Conference of States Parties in 2018 and were scheduled to reconvene every two years and to meet in the first Review Conference in 2022. A party may withdraw from the treaty, having given 12 months' notice.

Parties (8): Angola, Cameroon, Central African Republic, Chad, Congo (Republic of the), Equatorial Guinea, Gabon, Sao Tome and Principe

Signed but not ratified (3): Burundi, Congo (Democratic Republic of the), Rwanda

Treaty text: United Nations Treaty Collection, <https://treaties.un.org/doc/Treaties/2010/04/20100430 01-12 PM/Ch_xxvi-7.pdf>

Vienna Document 2011 on Confidence- and Security-Building Measures

Adopted by the participating states of the Organization for Security and Co-operation in Europe at Vienna on 30 November 2011; entered into force on 1 December 2011

The Vienna Document 2011 builds on the 1986 Stockholm Document on Confidence- and Security-Building Measures (CSBMs) and Disarmament in Europe and previous Vienna Documents (1990, 1992, 1994 and 1999). The Vienna Document 1990 provided for annual exchanges of military information and military budgets, risk-reduction procedures, a communication network and an annual CSBM implementation assessment. The Vienna Document 1992 and the Vienna Document 1994 extended the area of application and introduced new mechanisms and parameters for military activities, defence planning and military contacts. The Vienna Document 1999 introduced regional measures aimed at increasing transparency and confidence in a bilateral, multilateral and regional context and some improvements, in particular regarding the constraining measures.

The Vienna Document 2011 incorporates revisions on such matters as the timing of verification activities and demonstrations of new types of weapon and equipment system. It also establishes a procedure for updating the Vienna Document every five years. However, no updates were agreed in 2016 and 2021, and the process of modernizing or adapting the document remains frozen. Changes agreed since 2011 are implemented as part of the broader Vienna Document Plus, but they are not yet an official part of the Vienna Document.

The participating states discuss implementation of the Vienna Document in the OSCE's Forum for Security Co-operation (FSC).

Participating states of the OSCE (57): See annex B

Document text: Organization for Security and Co-operation in Europe, <https://www.osce.org/files/f/documents/a/4/86597.pdf>

III. Bilateral treaties

Treaty on the Limitation of Anti-Ballistic Missile Systems (ABM Treaty)

Signed by the USA and the USSR at Moscow on 26 May 1972; entered into force on 3 October 1972; not in force from 13 June 2002

The parties—Russia and the USA—undertook not to build nationwide defences against ballistic missile attack and to limit the development and deployment of permitted strategic missile defences. The treaty prohibited the parties from giving air defence missiles, radars or launchers the technical ability to counter strategic ballistic missiles and from testing them in a strategic ABM mode. It also established a standing consultative commission to promote its objectives and implementation. The **1974 Protocol** to the ABM Treaty introduced further numerical restrictions on permitted ballistic missile defences.

In 1997 Belarus, Kazakhstan, Russia, Ukraine and the USA signed a memorandum of understanding that would have made Belarus, Kazakhstan and Ukraine parties to the treaty along with Russia as successor states of the USSR and a set of agreed statements that would specify the demarcation line between strategic missile defences (which are not permitted under the treaty) and non-strategic or theatre missile defences (which are permitted under the treaty). The 1997 agreements were ratified by Russia in April 2000, but the USA did not ratify them and they did not enter into force.

On 13 December 2001 the USA notified Russia that it had decided to withdraw from the treaty, citing the ballistic missile threat to its territory from other states; the withdrawal came into effect six months later, on 13 June 2002.

Treaty text: United Nations Treaty Series, vol. 944 (1974), <https://treaties.un.org/doc/Publication/UNTS/Volume 944/v944.pdf>

Protocol text: US Department of State, <https://2009-2017.state.gov/t/avc/trty/101888.htm#protocolabm>

Treaty on the Limitation of Underground Nuclear Weapon Tests (Threshold Test-Ban Treaty, TTBT)

Signed by the USA and the USSR at Moscow on 3 July 1974; entered into force on 11 December 1990

The parties—Russia and the USA—undertake not to carry out any underground nuclear weapon test having a yield exceeding 150 kilotons. The 1974 verification protocol was replaced in 1990 with a new protocol.

Either party may withdraw from the treaty, having given the other 12 months' notice, if it decides that its supreme interests have been jeopardized by extraordinary events related to the treaty's subject matter.

Treaty and protocol texts: United Nations Treaty Series, vol. 1714 (1993), <https://treaties.un.org/doc/Publication/UNTS/Volume 1714/v1714.pdf>

Treaty on Underground Nuclear Explosions for Peaceful Purposes (Peaceful Nuclear Explosions Treaty, PNET)

Signed by the USA and the USSR at Moscow and Washington, DC, on 28 May 1976; entered into force simultaneously with the TTBT, on 11 December 1990

The parties—Russia and the USA—undertake not to carry out any individual underground nuclear explosion for peaceful purposes having a yield exceeding 15 kilotons or any group explosion having an aggregate yield exceeding 150 kilotons; and not to carry out any group explosion having an aggregate yield exceeding 1500 kilotons unless the individual explosions in the group could be identified and measured by agreed verification procedures. The treaty established a joint consultative commission to promote its objectives and implementation. The 1976 verification protocol was replaced in 1990 with a new protocol.

The treaty cannot be terminated while the TTBT is in force. If the TTBT is terminated, then either party may withdraw from this treaty at any time.

Treaty and protocol texts: United Nations Treaty Series, vol. 1714 (1993), <https://treaties.un.org/doc/Publication/UNTS/Volume 1714/v1714.pdf>

Treaty on the Elimination of Intermediate-range and Shorter-range Missiles (INF Treaty)

Signed by the USA and the USSR at Washington, DC, on 8 December 1987; entered into force on 1 June 1988; not in force from 2 August 2019

The treaty obligated the original parties—the USA and the USSR—to destroy all ground-launched ballistic and cruise missiles with a range of 500–5500 kilometres (intermediate-range, 1000–5500 km; and shorter-range, 500–1000 km) and their launchers by 1 June 1991. The treaty established a Special Verification Commission (SVC) to promote its objectives and implementation.

A total of 2692 missiles were eliminated by May 1991. For 10 years after 1 June 1991 on-site inspections were conducted to verify compliance. The use of surveillance satellites for data collection continued after the end of on-site inspections on 31 May 2001.

In 1994 treaty membership was expanded to include Belarus, Kazakhstan and Ukraine in addition to Russia and the USA.

On 2 February 2019 the USA notified the other parties that it would withdraw from the treaty in six months, citing the alleged deployment by Russia of a missile in breach of the treaty's limits. The USA and then Russia also suspended their obligations under the treaty. The withdrawal came into effect on 2 August 2019.

Treaty text: United Nations Treaty Series, vol. 1657 (1991), <https://treaties.un.org/doc/Publication/UNTS/Volume 1657/v1657.pdf>

Treaty on the Reduction and Limitation of Strategic Offensive Arms (START I)

Signed by the USA and the USSR at Moscow on 31 July 1991; entered into force on 5 December 1994; expired on 5 December 2009

The treaty obligated the original parties—the USA and the USSR—to make phased reductions in their offensive strategic nuclear forces over a seven-year period. It set numerical limits on deployed strategic nuclear delivery vehicles—intercontinental ballistic missiles (ICBMs), submarine-launched ballistic missiles (SLBMs) and heavy bombers—and the nuclear warheads they carry.

In the Protocol to Facilitate the Implementation of START (**1992 Lisbon Protocol**), which entered into force on 5 December 1994, Belarus, Kazakhstan and Ukraine also assumed the obligations of the former USSR under the treaty alongside Russia.

Treaty and protocol texts: US Department of State, <https://2009-2017.state.gov/t/avc/trty/146007.htm>

Treaty on Further Reduction and Limitation of Strategic Offensive Arms (START II)

Signed by Russia and the USA at Moscow on 3 January 1993; not in force

The treaty would have obligated the parties to eliminate their ICBMs with multiple independently targeted re-entry vehicles (MIRVs) and reduce the number of their deployed strategic nuclear warheads to no more than 3000–3500 each (of which no more than 1750 were to be deployed on SLBMs) by 1 January 2003. On 26 September 1997 the two parties signed a *Protocol* to the treaty providing for the extension until the end of 2007 of the period of implementation of the treaty.

The two signatories ratified the treaty but never exchanged the instruments of ratification. The treaty thus never entered into force. On 14 June 2002, as a response to the taking effect on 13 June of the USA's withdrawal from the ABM Treaty, Russia declared that it would no longer be bound by START II.

Treaty and protocol texts: US Department of State, <https://2009-2017.state.gov/t/avc/trty/102887.htm>

Treaty on Strategic Offensive Reductions (SORT, Moscow Treaty)

Signed by Russia and the USA at Moscow on 24 May 2002; entered into force on 1 June 2003; not in force from 5 February 2011

The treaty obligated the parties to reduce the number of their operationally deployed strategic nuclear warheads so that the aggregate numbers did not exceed 1700–2200 for each party by 31 December 2012. The treaty was superseded by New START on 5 February 2011.

Treaty text: United Nations Treaty Series, vol. 2350 (2005), <https://treaties.un.org/doc/Publication/UNTS/Volume 2350/v2350.pdf>

Treaty on Measures for the Further Reduction and Limitation of Strategic Offensive Arms (New START, Prague Treaty)

Signed by Russia and the USA at Prague on 8 April 2010; entered into force on 5 February 2011

The treaty obligates the parties—Russia and the USA—to each reduce their number of (*a*) deployed ICBMs, SLBMs and heavy bombers to 700; (*b*) warheads on deployed ICBMs and SLBMs and warheads counted for deployed heavy bombers to 1550; and (*c*) deployed and non-deployed ICBM launchers, SLBM launchers and heavy bombers to 800. The reductions were achieved by 5 February 2018, as required by the treaty.

The treaty established a Bilateral Consultative Commission (BCC) to resolve questions about compliance and other implementation issues. A *Protocol* to the treaty contains verifications mechanisms.

The treaty followed on from START I and superseded SORT. After being in force for an initial period of 10 years, the treaty was extended on 3 February 2021 for a further period of 5 years, until 5 February 2026. It cannot be extended further but may be superseded by a subsequent agreement. Either party may also withdraw from the treaty, having given the other three months' notice, if it decides that its supreme interests have been jeopardized by extraordinary events related to the treaty's subject matter.

Note: On 28 Feb. 2023 Russia adopted a law that 'suspended' the treaty. It did not withdraw from the treaty and stated that it would continue to observe the numerical limits on its nuclear forces.

Treaty and protocol texts: US Department of State, <https://2009-2017.state.gov/t/avc/newstart/c44126.htm>

Annex B. International security cooperation bodies

This annex describes the main international organizations, intergovernmental bodies, treaty-implementing bodies and transfer control regimes whose aims include the promotion of security, stability, peace or arms control and lists their members or participants as of 1 January 2023. The bodies are divided into three categories: those with a global focus or membership (section I), those with a regional focus or membership (section II) and those that aim to control strategic trade (section III).

The member states of the United Nations and organs within the UN system are listed first, followed by all other bodies in alphabetical order. Not all members or participants of these bodies are UN member states. States that joined or first participated in the body during 2022 are shown in italics. The address of an internet site with information about each organization is provided where available. On the arms control and disarmament agreements mentioned here, see annex A.

I. Bodies with a global focus or membership

United Nations (UN)

The UN, the world intergovernmental organization, was founded in 1945 through the adoption of its Charter. Its headquarters are in New York, United States. The six principal UN organs are the General Assembly, the Security Council, the Economic and Social Council (ECOSOC), the Trusteeship Council (which suspended operation in 1994), the International Court of Justice (ICJ) and the Secretariat.

The General Assembly has six main committees. The First Committee (Disarmament and International Security Committee) deals with disarmament and related international security questions. The Fourth Committee (Special Political and Decolonization Committee) deals with a variety of subjects including decolonization, Palestinian refugees and human rights, peacekeeping, mine action, outer space, public information, atomic radiation and the University for Peace.

The UN Office for Disarmament Affairs (UNODA), an office of the UN Secretariat, promotes disarmament of nuclear, biological, chemical and conventional weapons. The UN also has a large number of specialized agencies and other autonomous bodies.

UN member states (193) and year of membership

Afghanistan, 1946
Albania, 1955
Algeria, 1962
Andorra, 1993
Angola, 1976
Antigua and Barbuda, 1981
Argentina, 1945
Armenia, 1992
Australia, 1945
Austria, 1955
Azerbaijan, 1992
Bahamas, 1973
Bahrain, 1971
Bangladesh, 1974
Barbados, 1966
Belarus, 1945
Belgium, 1945
Belize, 1981
Benin, 1960
Bhutan, 1971
Bolivia, 1945
Bosnia and Herzegovina, 1992
Botswana, 1966
Brazil, 1945
Brunei Darussalam, 1984
Bulgaria, 1955
Burkina Faso, 1960
Burundi, 1962
Cabo Verde, 1975
Cambodia, 1955
Cameroon, 1960
Canada, 1945
Central African Republic, 1960
Chad, 1960
Chile, 1945
China, 1945
Colombia, 1945
Comoros, 1975
Congo, Democratic Republic of the, 1960
Congo, Republic of the, 1960
Costa Rica, 1945
Côte d'Ivoire, 1960
Croatia, 1992
Cuba, 1945
Cyprus, 1960
Czechia, 1993
Denmark, 1945
Djibouti, 1977
Dominica, 1978
Dominican Republic, 1945

Ecuador, 1945
Egypt, 1945
El Salvador, 1945
Equatorial Guinea, 1968
Eritrea, 1993
Estonia, 1991
Eswatini, 1968
Ethiopia, 1945
Fiji, 1970
Finland, 1955
France, 1945
Gabon, 1960
Gambia, 1965
Georgia, 1992
Germany, 1973
Ghana, 1957
Greece, 1945
Grenada, 1974
Guatemala, 1945
Guinea, 1958
Guinea-Bissau, 1974
Guyana, 1966
Haiti, 1945
Honduras, 1945
Hungary, 1955
Iceland, 1946
India, 1945
Indonesia, 1950
Iran, 1945
Iraq, 1945
Ireland, 1955
Israel, 1949
Italy, 1955
Jamaica, 1962
Japan, 1956
Jordan, 1955
Kazakhstan, 1992
Kenya, 1963
Kiribati, 1999
Korea, Democratic People's Republic of (North Korea), 1991
Korea, Republic of (South Korea), 1991
Kuwait, 1963
Kyrgyzstan, 1992
Laos, 1955
Latvia, 1991
Lebanon, 1945
Lesotho, 1966
Liberia, 1945
Libya, 1955

Liechtenstein, 1990
Lithuania, 1991
Luxembourg, 1945
Madagascar, 1960
Malawi, 1964
Malaysia, 1957
Maldives, 1965
Mali, 1960
Malta, 1964
Marshall Islands, 1991
Mauritania, 1961
Mauritius, 1968
Mexico, 1945
Micronesia, 1991
Moldova, 1992
Monaco, 1993
Mongolia, 1961
Montenegro, 2006
Morocco, 1956
Mozambique, 1975
Myanmar, 1948
Namibia, 1990
Nauru, 1999
Nepal, 1955
Netherlands, 1945
New Zealand, 1945
Nicaragua, 1945
Niger, 1960
Nigeria, 1960
North Macedonia, 1993
Norway, 1945
Oman, 1971
Pakistan, 1947
Palau, 1994
Panama, 1945
Papua New Guinea, 1975
Paraguay, 1945
Peru, 1945
Philippines, 1945
Poland, 1945
Portugal, 1955
Qatar, 1971
Romania, 1955
Russia, 1945
Rwanda, 1962
Saint Kitts and Nevis, 1983
Saint Lucia, 1979
Saint Vincent and the Grenadines, 1980
Samoa, 1976
San Marino, 1992
Sao Tome and Principe, 1975

Saudi Arabia, 1945	Suriname, 1975	Uganda, 1962
Senegal, 1960	Sweden, 1946	UK, 1945
Serbia, 2000	Switzerland, 2002	Ukraine, 1945
Seychelles, 1976	Syria, 1945	United Arab Emirates, 1971
Sierra Leone, 1961	Tajikistan, 1992	Uruguay, 1945
Singapore, 1965	Tanzania, 1961	USA, 1945
Slovakia, 1993	Thailand, 1946	Uzbekistan, 1992
Slovenia, 1992	Timor-Leste, 2002	Vanuatu, 1981
Solomon Islands, 1978	Togo, 1960	Venezuela, 1945
Somalia, 1960	Tonga, 1999	Viet Nam, 1977
South Africa, 1945	Trinidad and Tobago, 1962	Yemen, 1947
South Sudan, 2011	Tunisia, 1956	Zambia, 1964
Spain, 1955	Türkiye, 1945	Zimbabwe, 1980
Sri Lanka, 1955	Turkmenistan, 1992	
Sudan, 1956	Tuvalu, 2000	

Non-member observer states (2): Holy See, Palestine

Website: <https://www.un.org/>

UN Security Council

The Security Council has responsibility for the maintenance of international peace and security. All UN members states must comply with its decisions. It has 5 permanent members, which can each exercise a veto on the Council's decisions, and 10 non-permanent members elected by the UN General Assembly for two-year terms.

Permanent members (the P5): China, France, Russia, UK, USA

Non-permanent members (10): Albania*, Brazil*, *Ecuador*†, Gabon*, Ghana*, *Japan*†, *Malta*†, *Mozambique*†, *Switzerland*†, United Arab Emirates*

* Member in 2022–23.
† Member in 2023–24.

Website: <https://www.un.org/securitycouncil/>

Conference on Disarmament (CD)

The CD is intended to be the single multilateral arms control and disarmament negotiating forum of the international community. It has been enlarged and renamed several times since 1960. It is not a UN body but reports to the UN General Assembly. It is based in Geneva, Switzerland.

Members (65): Algeria, Argentina, Australia, Austria, Bangladesh, Belarus, Belgium, Brazil, Bulgaria, Cameroon, Canada, Chile, China, Colombia, Congo (Democratic Republic of the), Cuba, Ecuador, Egypt, Ethiopia, Finland, France, Germany, Hungary, India, Indonesia, Iran, Iraq, Ireland, Israel, Italy, Japan, Kazakhstan, Kenya, Korea (North), Korea (South), Malaysia, Mexico, Mongolia, Morocco, Myanmar, Netherlands, New Zealand, Nigeria, Norway, Pakistan, Peru, Poland, Romania, Russia, Senegal, Slovakia, South Africa, Spain, Sri Lanka, Sweden, Switzerland, Syria, Tunisia, Türkiye, UK, Ukraine, USA, Venezuela, Viet Nam, Zimbabwe

Website: <https://www.un.org/disarmament/conference-on-disarmament/>

UN Disarmament Commission (UNDC)

The UNDC in its original form was established in 1952. It was re-established in 1978 after the Conference on Disarmament was established in its current form (see above). It meets for three weeks each year in New York to consider a small number of disarmament issues—currently two substantive items per session—and formulate consensus principles, guidelines and recommendations. It has generally been unable to reach agreement on any such outcome since 2000, but in 2017 adopted consensus recommendations on 'Practical confidence-building measures in the field of conventional weapons'.

Members (193): The UN member states

Website: <https://www.un.org/disarmament/institutions/disarmament-commission/>

UN Peacebuilding Commission (PBC)

The PBC was established in 2005 by the General Assembly and the Security Council to advise them on post-conflict peacebuilding and recovery, to marshal resources and to propose integrated strategies.

The General Assembly, the Security Council and ECOSOC each elect seven members of the PBC for two-year terms; the remaining members are the top five providers of military personnel and civilian police to UN missions and the top five contributors of funds to the UN. Additional states and organizations participate in country-specific meetings on countries on the PBC agenda.

Members (31): Bangladesh**[||], Brazil**[§], Bulgaria*[†], Canada**[#], China*[‡], *Croatia***[§], *Denmark***[§], Dominican Republic*[†], *Ecuador**[‡], Egypt**[†], Ethiopia**[||], France*[‡], Germany**[#], India**[||], *Italy***[§], Japan**[#], Kenya**[†], Korea (South)**[§], *Mozambique**[‡], Nepal**[||], Nigeria*[§], *Norway***[#], *Peru***[§], Qatar**[†], Russia*[‡], Rwanda**[||], *Saint Vincent and the Grenadines***[†], South Africa**[†], Sweden**[#], UK*[‡], USA*[‡]

 * Member until 31 Dec. 2023.
 ** Member until 31 Dec. 2024.
 [†] Elected by the General Assembly.
 [‡] Elected by the Security Council.
 [§] Elected by ECOSOC.
 [||] Top 5 contributor of personnel.
 [#] Top 5 contributor of funds.

Website: <https://www.un.org/peacebuilding/commission/>

International Atomic Energy Agency (IAEA)

The IAEA is an intergovernmental organization within the UN system. It is mandated by its Statute, which entered into force in 1957, to promote the peaceful uses of atomic energy and ensure that nuclear activities are not used to further any military purpose. Under the 1968 Non-Proliferation Treaty and the nuclear weapon-free zone treaties, non-nuclear weapon states must accept IAEA nuclear safeguards to demonstrate the fulfilment of their obligation not to manufacture nuclear weapons. Its headquarters are in Vienna, Austria.

Members (175): Afghanistan, Albania, Algeria, Angola, Antigua and Barbuda, Argentina, Armenia, Australia, Austria, Azerbaijan, Bahamas, Bahrain, Bangladesh, Barbados, Belarus, Belgium, Belize, Benin, Bolivia, Bosnia and Herzegovina, Botswana, Brazil, Brunei Darussalam, Bulgaria, Burkina Faso, Burundi, Cambodia, Cameroon, Canada, Central African Republic, Chad, Chile, China, Colombia, Comoros, Congo (Democratic Republic of the), Congo (Republic of the), Costa Rica, Côte d'Ivoire, Croatia, Cuba, Cyprus, Czechia, Denmark, Djibouti, Dominica, Dominican Republic, Ecuador, Egypt, El Salvador, Eritrea, Estonia, Eswatini, Ethiopia, Fiji, Finland, France, Gabon, Georgia, Germany, Ghana, Greece, Grenada, Guatemala, Guyana, Haiti, Holy See, Honduras, Hungary, Iceland, India, Indonesia, Iran, Iraq, Ireland, Israel, Italy, Jamaica, Japan, Jordan, Kazakhstan, Kenya, Korea (South), Kuwait, Kyrgyzstan, Laos, Latvia, Lebanon, Lesotho, Liberia, Libya, Liechtenstein, Lithuania, Luxembourg, Madagascar, Malawi, Malaysia, Mali, Malta, Marshall Islands, Mauritania, Mauritius, Mexico, Moldova, Monaco, Mongolia, Montenegro, Morocco, Mozambique, Myanmar, Namibia, Nepal, Netherlands, New Zealand, Nicaragua, Niger, Nigeria, North Macedonia, Norway, Oman, Pakistan, Palau, Panama, Papua New Guinea, Paraguay, Peru, Philippines, Poland, Portugal, Qatar, Rwanda, Romania, Russia, *Saint Kitts and Nevis*, Saint Lucia, Saint Vincent and the Grenadines, Samoa, San Marino, Saudi Arabia, Senegal, Serbia, Seychelles, Sierra Leone, Singapore, Slovakia, Slovenia, South Africa, Spain, Sri Lanka, Sudan, Sweden, Switzerland, Syria, Tajikistan, Tanzania, Thailand, Togo, *Tonga*, Trinidad and Tobago, Tunisia, Türkiye, Turkmenistan, Uganda, UK, Ukraine, United Arab Emirates, Uruguay, USA, Uzbekistan, Vanuatu, Venezuela, Viet Nam, Yemen, Zambia, Zimbabwe

Notes: North Korea was a member of the IAEA until June 1994. In addition to the 175 members as of 1 Jan. 2023, the Gambia became a member on 3 Jan. 2023. The IAEA General Conference had also approved the membership of Cabo Verde and Guinea; each will take effect once the state deposits the necessary legal instruments with the IAEA.

Website: <https://www.iaea.org/>

International Court of Justice (ICJ)

The ICJ was established in 1945 by the UN Charter and is the principal judicial organ of the UN. The court's role is to settle legal disputes submitted to it by states and to give advisory opinions on legal questions referred to it by authorized UN organs and specialized agencies. The court is composed of 15 judges, who are elected for terms of office of nine years by the UN General Assembly and the Security Council. Its seat is at The Hague, the Netherlands.

Website: <https://www.icj-cij.org/>

Bilateral Consultative Commission (BCC)

The BCC is a forum established under the 2010 Russian–US Treaty on Measures for the Further Reduction and Limitation of Strategic Offensive Arms (New START, Prague Treaty) to discuss issues related to the treaty's implementation. It replaced the joint compliance and inspection commission (JCIC) of the 1991 START treaty. The BCC is required to meet at least twice each year in Geneva, Switzerland, unless the parties agree otherwise. Its work is confidential.

Note: On 28 Feb. 2023 Russia adopted a law that 'suspended' New START, including participation in the BCC.

Website: US Department of Defense, Office of the Assistant Secretary of Defense for Acquisition, <https://www.acq.osd.mil/asda/ssipm/sdc/tc/nst/index.html>

Commonwealth of Nations

Established in its current form in 1949, the Commonwealth is an organization of developed and developing countries whose aim is to advance democracy, human rights, and sustainable economic and social development within its member states and beyond. It adopted a charter reaffirming its core values and principles in 2012. The members' leaders meet in the biennial Commonwealth Heads of Government Meetings (CHOGMs). Its secretariat is in London, UK.

Members (56): Antigua and Barbuda, Australia, Bahamas, Bangladesh, Barbados, Belize, Botswana, Brunei Darussalam, Cameroon, Canada, Cyprus, Dominica, Eswatini, Fiji, *Gabon*, Gambia, Ghana, Grenada, Guyana, India, Jamaica, Kenya, Kiribati, Lesotho, Malawi, Malaysia, Maldives, Malta, Mauritius, Mozambique, Namibia, Nauru, New Zealand, Nigeria, Pakistan, Papua New Guinea, Rwanda[†], Saint Kitts and Nevis, Saint Lucia, Saint Vincent and the Grenadines, Samoa, Seychelles, Sierra Leone, Singapore, Solomon Islands, South Africa, Sri Lanka, Tanzania, *Togo*, Tonga, Trinidad and Tobago, Tuvalu, Uganda, UK[*], Vanuatu, Zambia

[*] CHOGM host in 2018 and Chair-in-Office in 2018–22.
[†] CHOGM host in 2022 and Chair-in-Office in 2022–24.

Note: Zimbabwe (which withdrew in 2013) applied to rejoin the Commonwealth in May 2018.

Website: <https://www.thecommonwealth.org/>

Comprehensive Nuclear-Test-Ban Treaty Organization (CTBTO)

The CTBTO will become operational when the 1996 Comprehensive Nuclear-Test-Ban Treaty (CTBT) has entered into force. It will resolve questions of compliance with the treaty and act as a forum for consultation and cooperation among the states parties. A Preparatory Commission and provisional Technical Secretariat are preparing for the work of the CTBTO, in particular by establishing the International Monitoring System, consisting of seismic, hydro-acoustic, infrasound and radionuclide stations from which data is transmitted to the CTBTO International Data Centre. Their headquarters are in Vienna, Austria.

Signatories to the CTBT (186): See annex A

Website: <https://www.ctbto.org/>

Financial Action Task Force (FATF)

The FATF is an intergovernmental policymaking body whose purpose is to establish international standards and develop and promote policies at both national and international levels. It was established in 1989 by the Group of Seven (G7), initially to examine and develop measures to combat money laundering; its mandate was expanded in 2001 to incorporate efforts to combat terrorist financing and again in 2008 to include the financing of weapon of mass destruction (WMD) proliferation efforts. It published revised recommendations in 2012, which are updated regularly. Its secretariat is in Paris, France.

Members (39): Argentina, Australia, Austria, Belgium, Brazil, Canada, China, Denmark, European Commission, Finland, France, Germany, Greece, Gulf Cooperation Council, Hong Kong (China), Iceland, India, Ireland, Israel, Italy, Japan, Korea (South), Luxembourg, Malaysia, Mexico, Netherlands, New Zealand, Norway, Portugal, Russia*, Saudi Arabia, Singapore, South Africa, Spain, Sweden, Switzerland, Türkiye, UK, USA

* FATF suspended the membership of Russia on 24 Feb. 2023.

Website: <https://www.fatf-gafi.org/>

Global Initiative to Combat Nuclear Terrorism (GICNT)

The GICNT was established in 2006 as a voluntary international partnership of states and international organizations that are committed to strengthening global capacity to prevent, detect and respond to nuclear terrorism. The GICNT works towards this goal by conducting multilateral activities that strengthen the plans, policies, procedures and interoperability of its partner. The partners meet at biennial plenaries. Russia and the USA act as co-chairs and Morocco leads the implementation and assessment group.

In 2022 the GICNT paused all official meetings and working groups until further notice.

Partners (89): Afghanistan, Albania, Algeria, Argentina, Armenia, Australia, Austria, Azerbaijan, Bahrain, Belarus, Belgium, Bosnia and Herzegovina, Bulgaria, Cabo Verde, Cambodia, Canada, Chile, China, Côte d'Ivoire, Croatia, Cyprus, Czechia, Denmark, Estonia, Finland, France, Georgia, Germany, Greece, Hungary, Iceland, India, Iraq, Ireland, Israel, Italy, Japan, Jordan, Kazakhstan, Korea (South), Kyrgyzstan, Latvia, Libya, Lithuania, Luxembourg, Madagascar, Malaysia, Malta, Mauritius, Mexico, Moldova, Montenegro, Morocco, Nepal, Netherlands, New Zealand, Nigeria, North Macedonia, Norway, Pakistan, Palau, Panama, Paraguay, Philippines, Poland, Portugal, Romania, Russia, Saudi Arabia, Serbia, Seychelles, Singapore, Slovakia, Slovenia, Spain, Sri Lanka, Sweden, Switzerland, Tajikistan, Thailand, Türkiye, Turkmenistan, UK, Ukraine, United Arab Emirates, USA, Uzbekistan, Viet Nam, Zambia

Official observers (6): European Union, International Atomic Energy Agency, International Criminal Police Organization (INTERPOL), UN Interregional Crime and Justice Research Institute, UN Office of Counter-Terrorism, UN Office on Drugs and Crime

Website: <https://gicnt.org/>

Group of Seven (G7)

The G7 is a group of leading industrialized countries that have met informally, at the level of head of state or government, since the 1970s. The presidents of the European Council and the European Commission represent the European Union at summits.

Between 1997 and 2013 the G7 members and Russia met together as the Group of Eight (G8). Following Russia's annexation of Crimea, the G7 states decided in March 2014 to meet without Russia until further notice.

Members (7): Canada, France, Germany‡, Italy‡, Japan†, UK, USA

* G7 presidency and summit host in 2022.
† G7 presidency and summit host in 2023.
‡ G7 presidency and summit host in 2024.

Website: <https://www.international.gc.ca/world-monde/international_relations-relations_internationales/g7/index.aspx>

Global Partnership against the Spread of Weapons and Materials of Mass Destruction

The Global Partnership was launched in 2002 by the G8 to address non-proliferation, disarmament, counterterrorism and nuclear safety issues. The members meet twice each year, hosted by the state holding the G7 presidency, with the main goal of launching specific projects to tackle the abuse of weapons and materials of mass destruction and reduce chemical, biological, radioactive and nuclear risks. The Global Partnership was extended for an unspecified period in May 2011.

Partners (31): Australia, Belgium, Canada, Chile, Czechia, Denmark, European Union, Finland, France, Georgia, Germany, Hungary, Ireland, Italy, Japan, Jordan, Kazakhstan, Korea (South), Mexico, Netherlands, New Zealand, Norway, Philippines, Poland, Portugal, Spain, Sweden, Switzerland, UK, Ukraine, USA

Note: Russia was a founding partner of the Global Partnership, but it ceased to be a partner following its exclusion from the G8.

Website: <https://www.gpwmd.com/>

International Criminal Court (ICC)

The ICC is a permanent international court dealing with the crime of genocide, crimes against humanity, war crimes and the crime of aggression. Its seat is at The Hague, the Netherlands, and it has field offices in the Central African Republic, Côte d'Ivoire, the Democratic Republic of the Congo, Georgia, Mali and Uganda. The court has 18 judges and an independent prosecutor, elected by the Assembly of States Parties for nine-year terms.

The court's powers and jurisdiction are defined by the 1998 Rome Statute and its amendments. While the ICC is independent of the UN, the Rome Statute grants the UN Security Council certain powers of referral and deferral.

Parties to the Rome Statute (123) and its amendments: See annex A

Website: <https://www.icc-cpi.int/>

Non-Aligned Movement (NAM)

NAM was established in 1961 as a forum for non-aligned states to consult on political, economic and arms control issues and coordinate their positions in the UN.

Members (120): Afghanistan, Algeria, Angola, Antigua and Barbuda, Azerbaijan*, Bahamas, Bahrain, Bangladesh, Barbados, Belarus, Belize, Benin, Bhutan, Bolivia, Botswana, Brunei Darussalam, Burkina Faso, Burundi, Cabo Verde, Cambodia, Cameroon, Central African Republic, Chad, Chile, Colombia, Comoros, Congo (Democratic Republic of the), Congo

(Republic of the), Côte d'Ivoire, Cuba, Djibouti, Dominica, Dominican Republic, Ecuador, Egypt, Equatorial Guinea, Eritrea, Eswatini, Ethiopia, Fiji, Gabon, Gambia, Ghana, Grenada, Guatemala, Guinea, Guinea-Bissau, Guyana, Haiti, Honduras, India, Indonesia, Iran, Iraq, Jamaica, Jordan, Kenya, Korea (North), Kuwait, Laos, Lebanon, Lesotho, Liberia, Libya, Madagascar, Malawi, Malaysia, Maldives, Mali, Mauritania, Mauritius, Mongolia, Morocco, Mozambique, Myanmar, Namibia, Nepal, Nicaragua, Niger, Nigeria, Oman, Pakistan, Palestine Liberation Organization, Panama, Papua New Guinea, Peru, Philippines, Qatar, Rwanda, Saint Kitts and Nevis, Saint Lucia, Saint Vincent and the Grenadines, Sao Tome and Principe, Saudi Arabia, Senegal, Seychelles, Sierra Leone, Singapore, Somalia, South Africa, Sri Lanka, Sudan, Suriname, Syria, Tanzania, Thailand, Timor-Leste, Togo, Trinidad and Tobago, Tunisia, Turkmenistan, Uganda[†], United Arab Emirates, Uzbekistan, Vanuatu, Venezuela, Viet Nam, Yemen, Zambia, Zimbabwe

* NAM chair in 2019–23 and summit host in 2019.
† NAM chair from 2023 and summit host in 2023.

Note: A 60th anniversary commemorative summit was held in Serbia in 2021.

Website: <https://www.namazerbaijan.org/>

Organisation for Economic Co-operation and Development (OECD)

Established in 1961, the OECD's objectives are to promote economic and social welfare by coordinating policies among the member states. Its headquarters are in Paris, France.

Members (38): Australia, Austria, Belgium, Canada, Chile, Colombia, Costa Rica, Czechia, Denmark, Estonia, Finland, France, Germany, Greece, Hungary, Iceland, Ireland, Israel, Italy, Japan, Korea (South), Latvia, Lithuania, Luxembourg, Mexico, Netherlands, New Zealand, Norway, Poland, Portugal, Slovakia, Slovenia, Spain, Sweden, Switzerland, Türkiye, UK, USA

Website: <https://www.oecd.org/>

Organisation for the Prohibition of Chemical Weapons (OPCW)

The OPCW implements the 1993 Chemical Weapons Convention (CWC). Among other things, it oversees the destruction of chemical weapon stockpiles and associated infrastructure, implements a verification regime to ensure that such weapons do not re-emerge, provides assistance and protection to states parties threatened by such weapons, and facilitates and engages in international cooperation to strengthen treaty compliance and to promote the peaceful uses of chemistry. In addition to the responsibility to investigate alleged use of chemical weapons, in 2018 the OPCW gained the power to attribute responsibility for any chemical weapon use on the territory of a member state if requested to do so by that state.

The work of the OPCW and its Technical Secretariat is overseen by the Executive Council, whose 41 members are elected for two-year terms by the Conference of States Parties. The director-general of the OPCW is advised by a Scientific Advisory Board (SAB). The organization is based in The Hague, the Netherlands.

Parties to the Chemical Weapons Convention (193): See annex A

Website: <https://www.opcw.org/>

Organisation of Islamic Cooperation (OIC)

The OIC (formerly the Organization of the Islamic Conference) was established in 1969 by Islamic states to promote cooperation among the members and to support peace, security, and the struggle of the people of Palestine and all Muslim people. Among its organs are the Independent Permanent Human Rights Commission (IPHRC) and the Islamic Development Bank (IDB). Its members meet in the Islamic Summit every three years. Its secretariat is in Jeddah, Saudi Arabia.

Members (57): Afghanistan, Albania, Algeria, Azerbaijan, Bahrain, Bangladesh, Benin, Brunei Darussalam, Burkina Faso, Cameroon, Chad, Comoros, Côte d'Ivoire, Djibouti, Egypt, Gabon, Gambia, Guinea, Guinea-Bissau, Guyana, Indonesia, Iran, Iraq, Jordan, Kazakhstan, Kuwait, Kyrgyzstan, Lebanon, Libya, Malaysia, Maldives, Mali, Mauritania, Morocco, Mozambique, Niger, Nigeria, Oman, Pakistan, Palestine, Qatar, Saudi Arabia, Senegal, Sierra Leone, Somalia, Sudan, Suriname, Syria, Tajikistan, Togo, Tunisia, Türkiye, Turkmenistan, Uganda, United Arab Emirates, Uzbekistan, Yemen

Website: <https://www.oic-oci.org/>

II. Bodies with a regional focus or membership

African Commission on Nuclear Energy (AFCONE)

AFCONE was established by the 1996 African Nuclear-Weapon-Free Zone Treaty (Treaty of Pelindaba) to ensure compliance with the treaty and to advance the peaceful application of nuclear science and technology in Africa. Its seat is in Pretoria, South Africa.

Parties to the Treaty of Pelindaba (44): See annex A

Website: <https://www.afcone.org/>

African Union (AU)

The AU was formally established in 2001 and launched in 2002. It replaced the Organization for African Unity (OAU), which had been established in 1963. Membership is open to all African states. The AU promotes unity, security and conflict resolution, democracy, human rights, and political, social and economic integration in Africa. Its main organs include the Assembly of Heads of State and Government (the supreme body), the Executive Council (made up of designated national ministers), the AU Commission (the secretariat), the Pan-African Parliament, and the Peace and Security Council. The AU's headquarters are in Addis Ababa, Ethiopia.

Members (55): Algeria, Angola, Benin, Botswana, Burkina Faso*, Burundi, Cabo Verde, Cameroon, Central African Republic, Chad, Comoros, Congo (Democratic Republic of the), Congo (Republic of the), Côte d'Ivoire, Djibouti, Egypt, Equatorial Guinea, Eritrea, Eswatini, Ethiopia, Gabon, Gambia, Ghana, Guinea[†], Guinea-Bissau, Kenya, Lesotho, Liberia, Libya, Madagascar, Malawi, Mali[‡], Mauritania, Mauritius, Morocco, Mozambique, Namibia, Niger, Nigeria, Rwanda, Sahrawi Arab Democratic Republic (Western Sahara), Sao Tome and Principe, Senegal, Seychelles, Sierra Leone, Somalia, South Africa, South Sudan, Sudan[§], Tanzania, Togo, Tunisia, Uganda, Zambia, Zimbabwe

* Burkina Faso was suspended from the AU on 31 Jan. 2022 following the military coup of 24 Jan. 2022.
† Guinea was suspended from the AU on 10 Sep. 2021 following the military coup of 5 Sep.
‡ Mali was suspended from the AU on 1 June 2021 following the military coup of 24 May. It had previously been suspended on 19 Aug. 2020 following the military coup of 18 Aug. That suspension was lifted on 9 Oct. 2020 after agreement on an 18-month transition to a civilian-led government.
§ Sudan was suspended from the AU on 26 Oct. 2021 following the military coup on the previous day. It had previously been suspended between 6 June and 6 Sep. 2019.

Website: <https://www.au.int/>

Peace and Security Council (PSC)

The PSC is the AU's standing decision-making organ for the prevention, management and resolution of conflicts. Its 15 members are elected by the Executive Council subject to endorsement by the Assembly. It is the main pillar of the African Peace and Security Architecture (APSA).

Members for a 3-year term 1 Apr. 2022–31 Mar. 2025 (5): Cameroon, Djibouti, Morocco, Namibia, Nigeria

Members for a 2-year term 1 Apr. 2022–31 Mar. 2024 (10): Burundi, Congo (Republic of the), Gambia, Ghana, Senegal, South Africa, Uganda, Tanzania, Tunisia, Zimbabwe

Website: <https://www.peaceau.org/>

Asia-Pacific Economic Cooperation (APEC)

APEC was established in 1989 as a regional economic forum to enhance open trade and economic prosperity in the Asia-Pacific region. Since 2001 the forum has been engaged in helping to protect the economies in the region from terrorism. A task force established in 2003 became the Counter-Terrorism Working Group in 2013. The APEC Secretariat is based in Singapore.

Member economies (21): Australia, Brunei Darussalam, Canada, Chile, China, Hong Kong, Indonesia, Japan, Korea (South), Malaysia, Mexico, New Zealand, Papua New Guinea, Peru‡, Philippines, Russia, Singapore, Taiwan, Thailand*, USA†, Viet Nam

* Host of APEC Economic Leaders' Meeting in 2022.
† Host of APEC Economic Leaders' Meeting in 2023.
‡ Host of APEC Economic Leaders' Meeting in 2024.

Website: <https://www.apec.org/>

Association of Southeast Asian Nations (ASEAN)

ASEAN was established in 1967 to promote economic, social and cultural development as well as regional peace and security in South East Asia. Development of the ASEAN Political–Security Community is one of the three pillars (along with the Economic and Sociocultural communities) of the ASEAN Community, which was launched in 2015 as a framework for further integration. The ASEAN Secretariat is in Jakarta, Indonesia.

Members (10): Brunei Darussalam, Cambodia*, Indonesia†, Laos‡, Malaysia, Myanmar, Philippines, Singapore, Thailand, Viet Nam

* ASEAN chair and summit host in 2022.
† ASEAN chair and summit host in 2023.
‡ ASEAN chair and summit host in 2024.

Website: <https://www.asean.org/>

ASEAN Regional Forum (ARF)

The ARF was established in 1994 to foster constructive dialogue and consultation on political and security issues and to contribute to confidence-building and preventive diplomacy in the Asia-Pacific region.

Participants (27): The ASEAN member states and Australia, Bangladesh, Canada, China, European Union, India, Japan, Korea (North), Korea (South), Mongolia, New Zealand, Pakistan, Papua New Guinea, Russia, Sri Lanka, Timor-Leste, USA

Website: <https://aseanregionalforum.asean.org/>

ASEAN Plus Three (APT)

The APT cooperation began in 1997, in the wake of the Asian financial crisis, and was institutionalized in 1999. It aims to foster economic, political and security cooperation and financial stability among its participants.

Participants (13): The ASEAN member states and China, Japan, Korea (South)

Website: <https://aseanplusthree.asean.org/>

East Asia Summit (EAS)

The East Asia Summit started in 2005 as a regional forum for dialogue on strategic, political and economic issues with the aim of promoting peace, stability and economic prosperity in East Asia. The annual meetings are held in connection with the ASEAN summits.

Participants (18): The ASEAN member states and Australia, China, India, Japan, Korea (South), New Zealand, Russia, USA

Website: <https://eastasiasummit.asean.org/>

Collective Security Treaty Organization (CSTO)

The CSTO was formally established in 2002–2003 by six signatories of the 1992 Collective Security Treaty. It aims to promote military and political cooperation among its members. Under Article 4 of the 1992 treaty, aggression against one member state is considered to be aggression against them all. An objective of the CSTO is to provide a more efficient response to strategic problems such as terrorism and narcotics trafficking. Its seat is in Moscow, Russia.

Members (6): Armenia, Belarus, Kazakhstan, Kyrgyzstan, Russia, Tajikistan

Website: <https://odkb-csto.org/>

Commonwealth of Independent States (CIS)

The CIS was established in 1991 as a framework for multilateral cooperation among former republics of the Soviet Union. The institutions of the CIS were established by the 1993 Charter. Their headquarters are in Minsk, Belarus.

The Council of Defence Ministers coordinates military cooperation among the members. It controls the Joint CIS Air Defence System (which covers the 6 members of the CSTO).

Members (10): Armenia, Azerbaijan, Belarus, Kazakhstan, Kyrgyzstan, Moldova*, Russia, Tajikistan, Turkmenistan†, Uzbekistan

* Moldova announced in Nov. 2022 that it had suspended its participation in CIS meetings.

† Turkmenistan has not ratified the 1993 CIS Charter but since 26 Aug. 2005 has participated in CIS activities as an associate member.

Note: Although Ukraine did not ratify the CIS Charter, it was an unofficial associate member from 1993. Ukraine decided to end its participation in CIS institutions in May 2018; it completed the process of withdrawing from the CIS coordination bodies in Feb. 2019. It continues to withdraw from CIS agreements.

Website: <https://www.cis.minsk.by/>

Communauté économique des États de l'Afrique Centrale (CEEAC, Economic Community of Central African States, ECCAS)

CEEAC was established in 1983 to promote political dialogue, create a customs union and establish common policies in Central Africa. It also coordinates activities under the 2010 Central African Convention for the Control of Small Arms and Light Weapons, Their Ammunition and All Parts and Components That Can Be Used for Their Manufacture, Repair and Assembly (Kinshasa Convention). Its secretariat is in Libreville, Gabon.

The **Council for Peace and Security in Central Africa (Conseil de paix et de sécurité de l'Afrique Centrale, COPAX)** is a mechanism for promoting joint political and military strategies for conflict prevention, management and resolution in Central Africa.

Members (11): Angola, Burundi, Cameroon, Central African Republic, Chad, Congo (Democratic Republic of the), Congo (Republic of the), Equatorial Guinea, Gabon, Rwanda, Sao Tome and Principe

Website: <https://ceeac-eccas.org/>

Conference on Interaction and Confidence-building Measures in Asia (CICA)

Initiated in 1992, CICA was formally established in 1999 as a forum to enhance security cooperation and confidence-building measures among the member states. It also promotes economic, social and cultural cooperation. Its secretariat is in Astana, Kazakhstan.

Members (28): Afghanistan, Azerbaijan, Bahrain, Bangladesh, Cambodia, China, Egypt, India, Iran, Iraq, Israel, Jordan, Kazakhstan*, Korea (South), *Kuwait*, Kyrgyzstan, Mongolia, Pakistan, Palestine, Qatar, Russia, Sri Lanka, Tajikistan, Thailand, Türkiye, United Arab Emirates, Uzbekistan, Viet Nam

* Chair in 2020–22 and 2022–24.

Website: <https://www.s-cica.org/>

Council of Europe (COE)

The Council was established in 1949. Membership is open to all European states that accept the principle of the rule of law and guarantee their citizens' human rights and fundamental freedoms. Its seat is in Strasbourg, France. Among its organs are the Committee of Ministers, the Parliamentary Assembly, the European Court of Human Rights and the Council of Europe Development Bank.

Members (46): Albania, Andorra, Armenia, Austria, Azerbaijan, Belgium, Bosnia and Herzegovina, Bulgaria, Croatia, Cyprus, Czechia, Denmark, Estonia, Finland, France, Georgia, Germany, Greece, Hungary, Iceland, Ireland, Italy, Latvia, Liechtenstein, Lithuania, Luxembourg, Malta, Moldova, Monaco, Montenegro, Netherlands, North Macedonia, Norway, Poland, Portugal, Romania, San Marino, Serbia, Slovakia, Slovenia, Spain, Sweden, Switzerland, Türkiye, UK, Ukraine

Note: Following Russia's invasion of Ukraine on 24 Feb. 2022, the Committee of Ministers suspended Russia from its rights of representation in the Committee of Ministers and the Parliamentary Assembly on 25 Feb. On 15 Mar. Russia formally notified the COE that it would withdraw, with effect from 31 Dec. 2022. On 16 Mar. the Committee of Ministers expelled Russia with immediate effect.

Website: <https://www.coe.int/>

Council of the Baltic Sea States (CBSS)

The CBSS was established in 1992 as a regional intergovernmental organization for cooperation among the states of the Baltic Sea region. Its secretariat is in Stockholm, Sweden.

Members (11): Denmark, Estonia, European Union, Finland, Germany, Iceland, Latvia, Lithuania, Norway, Poland, Sweden

Note: Following Russia's invasion of Ukraine on 24 Feb. 2022, Russia was suspended from the CBSS on 3 Mar. It withdrew from the CBSS on 17 May 2022.

Website: <https://www.cbss.org/>

Economic Community of West African States (ECOWAS)

ECOWAS was established in 1975 to promote trade and cooperation and contribute to development in West Africa. In 1981 it adopted the Protocol on Mutual Assistance in Defence Matters. Its Commission, Court of Justice and Parliament are based in Abuja, Nigeria.

Members (15): Benin, Burkina Faso*, Cabo Verde, Côte d'Ivoire, Gambia, Ghana, Guinea[†], Guinea-Bissau, Liberia, Mali[‡], Niger, Nigeria, Senegal, Sierra Leone, Togo

* Burkina Faso was suspended from ECOWAS on 28 Jan. 2022 following the military coup of 24 Jan. 2022.

[†] Guinea was suspended from ECOWAS on 8 Sep. 2021 following the military coup of 5 Sep.

[‡] Mali was suspended from ECOWAS on 30 May 2021 following the military coup of 24 May. It had previously been suspended on 20 Aug. 2020 following the military coup of 18 Aug. That suspension was lifted on 6 Oct. 2020 after agreement on an 18-month transition to a civilian-led government.

Note: In June 2017 ECOWAS agreed in principle to admit Morocco as its 16th member.

Website: <https://www.ecowas.int/>

European Union (EU)

The EU is an organization of European states that cooperate in a wide field, including a single market with free movement of people, goods, services and capital, a common currency (the euro) for some members, and a Common Foreign and Security Policy (CFSP), including a Common Security and Defence Policy (CSDP). The EU's main bodies are the European Council, the Council of the European Union (also known as the Council of Ministers or the Council), the European Commission (the executive), the European Parliament and the European Court of Justice.

The CFSP and CSDP are coordinated by the High Representative of the Union for Foreign Affairs and Security Policy, assisted by the European External Action Service (EEAS) and the EU Military Staff.

The principal seat of the EU is in Brussels, Belgium.

Members (27): Austria, Belgium, Bulgaria, Croatia, Cyprus, Czechia, Denmark, Estonia, Finland, France, Germany, Greece, Hungary, Ireland, Italy, Latvia, Lithuania, Luxembourg, Malta, Netherlands, Poland, Portugal, Romania, Slovakia, Slovenia, Spain, Sweden

Website: <https://europa.eu/>

European Atomic Energy Community (Euratom, or EAEC)

Euratom was created by the 1957 Treaty Establishing the European Atomic Energy Community (Euratom Treaty) to promote the development of nuclear energy for peaceful purposes and to administer (in cooperation with the IAEA) the multinational regional safeguards system covering the EU member states. The Euratom Supply Agency, located in Luxembourg, has the task of ensuring a regular and equitable supply of ores, source materials and special fissile materials to EU member states.

Members (27): The EU member states

Website: <https://euratom-supply.ec.europa.eu/>

European Defence Agency (EDA)

The EDA is an agency of the EU, under the direction of the Council. It was established in 2004 to help develop European defence capabilities, to promote European armaments cooperation and to work for a strong European defence technological and industrial base. The EDA's decision-making body is the Steering Board, composed of the defence ministers of the participating member states and the EU's High Representative for Foreign Affairs and Security Policy (as head of the agency). The EDA is located in Brussels, Belgium.

Participating member states (26): The EU member states other than Denmark*

* Following a referendum on 1 June 2022, Denmark ended its 30-year opt-out from EU cooperation on security and defence on 1 July 2022. This allowed Denmark to join the EDA, which it did on 23 Mar. 2023.

Note: The EDA has signed administrative arrangements with Norway (2006),

Switzerland (2012), Serbia (2013), Ukraine (2015) and the USA (2023) that enable these states to participate in its projects and programmes.

Website: <https://eda.europa.eu/>

Permanent Structured Cooperation (PESCO)

The Council of the EU established PESCO in 2017 as a framework to deepen security and defence cooperation between EU member states. Through joint projects, it aims to increase the military capabilities available to EU member states. The EDA and the EEAS jointly act as the PESCO secretariat.

Participating member states (25): The EU member states other than Denmark* and Malta

   * Following a referendum on 1 June 2022, Denmark ended its 30-year opt-out from EU cooperation on security and defence on 1 July 2022. This will allow Denmark to apply to participate in PESCO.

Website: <https://pesco.europa.eu/>

G5 Sahel

The G5 Sahel was established in 2014 with the aim of guaranteeing conditions for development and security in its members. Its Defence and Security Committee brings together the chiefs of general staff of the armed forces and other security officials of each member. The G5 Sahel Joint Force was established in 2017 to respond to the expansion of armed and violent extremist groups and to the deteriorating security situation in the region. The G5 Sahel's headquarters and its Defence College are in Nouakchott, Mauritania.

Members (4): Burkina Faso, Chad, Mauritania, Niger

   Note: Mali withdrew from the G5 Sahel on 15 May 2022.

Website: <https://www.g5sahel.org>

Gulf Cooperation Council (GCC)

Formally called the Cooperation Council for the Arab States of the Gulf, the GCC was created in 1981 to promote regional integration in such areas as economy, finance, trade, administration and legislation and to foster scientific and technical progress. The members also cooperate in areas of foreign policy and military and security matters. The Supreme Council (consisting of the head of each member state) is the highest GCC authority. The GCC's headquarters are in Riyadh, Saudi Arabia.

Members (6): Bahrain, Kuwait, Oman, Qatar, Saudi Arabia, United Arab Emirates

Website: <https://www.gcc-sg.org/>

Intergovernmental Authority on Development (IGAD)

IGAD was established in 1996 to expand regional cooperation and promote peace and stability in the Horn of Africa. It superseded the Intergovernmental Authority on Drought and Development (IGADD), which was established in 1986. Its specialized institutions include the Conflict Early Warning and Response Mechanism (CEWARN) and the Centre of Excellence for Preventing and Countering Violent Extremism (ICEPCVE). Its secretariat is in Djibouti.

Members (8): Djibouti, Eritrea, Ethiopia, Kenya, Somalia, South Sudan*, Sudan, Uganda

* IGAD suspended South Sudan in Dec. 2021 due to non-payment of fees but continues its work there.

Website: <https://www.igad.int/>

International Conference on the Great Lakes Region (ICGLR)

The ICGLR, which was initiated in 2004, works to promote peace and security, political and social stability, and growth and development in the Great Lakes region. In 2006 the member states adopted the Pact on Security, Stability and Development in the Great Lakes Region, which entered into force in 2008. Its executive secretariat is in Bujumbura, Burundi.

The ICGLR Joint Intelligence Fusion Centre (JIFC) and the Expanded Joint Verification Mechanism (EJVM) were launched in 2012 in Goma, Democratic Republic of the Congo. The JIFC collects, analyses and disseminates information on armed groups in the region and recommends action to member states. The EJVM monitors and investigates security incidents.

Members (12): Angola, Burundi, Central African Republic, Congo (Republic of the), Congo (Democratic Republic of the), Kenya, Rwanda, South Sudan, Sudan, Tanzania, Uganda, Zambia

Website: <https://www.icglr.org/>

League of Arab States

The Arab League was established in 1945 to form closer union among Arab states and foster political and economic cooperation. An agreement for collective defence and economic cooperation among the members was signed in 1950. In 2015 the Arab League agreed to create a joint Arab military force for regional peacekeeping, but no progress in its establishment has been subsequently made. The general secretariat of the Arab League is in Cairo, Egypt

Members (22): Algeria, Bahrain, Comoros, Djibouti, Egypt, Iraq, Jordan, Kuwait, Lebanon, Libya, Mauritania, Morocco, Oman, Palestine, Qatar, Saudi Arabia, Somalia, Sudan, Syria*, Tunisia, United Arab Emirates, Yemen

* Syria was suspended from the organization on 16 Nov. 2011.

Website: <http://www.leagueofarabstates.net/>

North Atlantic Treaty Organization (NATO)

NATO was established in 1949 by the North Atlantic Treaty (Washington Treaty) as a Western military alliance. Article 5 of the treaty defines the members' commitment to respond to an armed attack against any party to the treaty. Its headquarters are in Brussels, Belgium.

Members (30): Albania, Belgium, Bulgaria, Canada, Croatia, Czechia, Denmark, Estonia, France, Germany, Greece, Hungary, Iceland, Italy, Latvia, Lithuania, Luxembourg, Montenegro, Netherlands, Norway, North Macedonia, Poland, Portugal, Romania, Slovakia, Slovenia, Spain, Türkiye, UK, USA

Note: In addition to the 30 members as of 1 Jan. 2023, Finland became a member on 4 Apr. 2023. On 5 July 2022 NATO members also signed a protocol to the North Atlantic Treaty on the accession of Sweden. It will become a member once the protocol has been ratified by all members states and it has deposited its instruments of accession.

Website: <https://www.nato.int/>

Euro-Atlantic Partnership Council (EAPC)

The EAPC brings together NATO and its Partnership for Peace (PFP) partners for dialogue and consultation. It is the overall political framework for the bilateral PFP programme.

Members (50): The NATO member states and Armenia, Austria, Azerbaijan, Belarus*, Bosnia and Herzegovina, Finland, Georgia, Ireland, Kazakhstan, Kyrgyzstan, Malta, Moldova, Russia†, Serbia, Sweden, Switzerland, Tajikistan, Turkmenistan, Ukraine, Uzbekistan

   * NATO suspended all practical cooperation with Belarus in Nov. 2021 while continuing necessary dialogue.
   † NATO suspended all practical cooperation with Russia in Apr. 2014 while continuing necessary dialogue.

Website: <https://www.nato.int/cps/en/natohq/topics_49276.htm>

Istanbul Cooperation Initiative (ICI)

The ICI was established in 2004 to contribute to long-term global and regional security by offering practical bilateral security cooperation with NATO to countries of the broader Middle East region.

Participants (34): The NATO member states and Bahrain, Kuwait, Qatar, United Arab Emirates

Note: In addition to the 34 participating states, Oman and Saudi Arabia participate in selected activities within the ICI framework.

Website: <https://www.nato.int/cps/en/natohq/topics_52956.htm>

Mediterranean Dialogue

NATO's Mediterranean Dialogue was established in 1994 as a forum for political dialogue and practical cooperation between NATO and countries of the Mediterranean and North Africa. It reflects NATO's view that security in Europe is closely linked to security and stability in the Mediterranean.

Participants (37): The NATO member states and Algeria, Egypt, Israel, Jordan, Mauritania, Morocco, Tunisia

Website: <https://www.nato.int/cps/en/natohq/topics_52927.htm>

NATO–Georgia Commission (NGC)

The NGC was established in September 2008 to serve as a forum for political consultations and practical cooperation to help Georgia achieve its goal of joining NATO.

Participants (31): The NATO member states and Georgia

Website: <https://www.nato.int/cps/en/natohq/topics_52131.htm>

NATO–Russia Council (NRC)

The NRC was established in 2002 as a mechanism for consultation, consensus building, cooperation, and joint decisions and action on security issues. It focuses on areas of mutual interest identified in the 1997 NATO–Russia Founding Act on Mutual Relations, Cooperation and Security and new areas, such as terrorism, crisis management and non-proliferation.

Participants (31): The NATO member states and Russia

Note: In Apr. 2014, following Russian military intervention in Ukraine, NATO suspended all practical cooperation with Russia, although political dialogue in the NRC continues at the ambassadorial level or above.

Website: <https://www.nato.int/nrc-website/>

NATO–Ukraine Commission (NUC)

The NUC was established in 1997 for consultations on political and security issues, conflict prevention and resolution, non-proliferation, transfers of arms and technology, and other subjects of common concern.

Participants (31): The NATO member states and Ukraine

Website: <https://www.nato.int/cps/en/natohq/topics_50319.htm>

Organisation Conjointe de Coopération en matière d'Armement (OCCAR, Organisation for Joint Armament Cooperation)

OCCAR was established in 1996, with legal status since 2001, to provide more effective and efficient arrangements for the management of specific collaborative armament programmes. Its headquarters are in Bonn, Germany.

Members (6): Belgium, France, Germany, Italy, Spain, UK

Participants (8): Finland, Lithuania, Luxembourg, Netherlands, Poland, *Slovenia*, Sweden, Türkiye

Website: <https://www.occar.int/>

Organismo para la Proscripción de las Armas Nucleares en la América Latina y el Caribe (OPANAL, Agency for the Prohibition of Nuclear Weapons in Latin America and the Caribbean)

OPANAL was established by the 1967 Treaty of Tlatelolco to resolve, together with the IAEA, questions of compliance with the treaty. The organization is governed by a General Conference of its members, which meets every two years, and by a five-member Council. Its seat is in Mexico City, Mexico.

Parties to the Treaty of Tlatelolco (33): See annex A

Website: <https://www.opanal.org/>

Organization for Democracy and Economic Development–GUAM

GUAM is a group of four states, established to promote stability and strengthen security, whose history goes back to 1997. The organization was established in 2006. The members cooperate to promote social and economic development and trade in eight working groups. Its secretariat is in Kyiv, Ukraine.

Members (4): Azerbaijan, Georgia, Moldova, Ukraine

Website: <https://guam-organization.org/>

Organization for Security and Co-operation in Europe (OSCE)

The Conference on Security and Co-operation in Europe (CSCE), which had been initiated in 1973, was renamed the OSCE in 1995. It is intended to be the primary instrument of comprehensive and cooperative security for early warning, conflict prevention, crisis management and post-conflict rehabilitation in its area. Its headquarters are in Vienna, Austria, and its other institutions are based elsewhere in Europe.

The OSCE Troika consists of representatives of the states holding the chair in the current year, the previous year and the succeeding year. The Forum for Security Cooperation (FSC) deals with arms control and confidence- and security-building measures.

Participants (57): Albania, Andorra, Armenia, Austria, Azerbaijan, Belarus, Belgium, Bosnia and Herzegovina, Bulgaria, Canada, Croatia, Cyprus, Czechia, Denmark, Estonia, Finland[‡], France, Georgia, Germany, Greece, Holy See, Hungary, Iceland, Ireland, Italy, Kazakhstan, Kyrgyzstan, Latvia, Liechtenstein, Lithuania, Luxembourg, Malta, Moldova, Monaco, Mongolia, Montenegro, Netherlands, North Macedonia[†], Norway, Poland[*], Portugal, Romania, Russia, San Marino, Serbia, Slovakia, Slovenia, Spain, Sweden, Switzerland, Tajikistan, Türkiye, Turkmenistan, UK, Ukraine, USA, Uzbekistan

[*] Chair in 2022.
[†] Chair in 2023.
[‡] Chair in 2025.

Note: The OSCE Ministerial Council failed to appoint a chair for 2024 at its meetings in Dec. 2021 and Dec. 2022.

Website: <https://www.osce.org/>

Joint Consultative Group (JCG)

The JCG is an OSCE-related body established by the 1990 Treaty on Conventional Armed Forces in Europe (CFE Treaty) to promote the objectives and implementation of the treaty by reconciling ambiguities of interpretation and implementation. Its seat is in Vienna, Austria.

Parties to the CFE Treaty (30): See annex A

Note: In 2007 Russia suspended its participation in the CFE Treaty, and in Mar. 2015 it announced that it had decided to completely halt its participation in the treaty, including the JCG.

Website: <https://www.osce.org/jcg/>

Minsk Group

The Minsk Group supports the Minsk Process, an ongoing forum for negotiations on a peaceful settlement of the conflict in Nagorno-Karabakh.

Members (13): Armenia, Azerbaijan, Belarus, Finland, France*, Germany, Italy, Russia*, Sweden, Türkiye, USA*, OSCE Troika (North Macedonia and Poland)

* The representatives of these 3 states co-chair the group.

Website: <https://www.osce.org/mg/>

Open Skies Consultative Commission (OSCC)

The OSCC was established by the 1992 Treaty on Open Skies to resolve questions of compliance with the treaty. Each year it reviews the parties' surveillance flight quotas.

Parties to the Open Skies Treaty (32): See annex A

Note: The USA withdrew from the treaty and the OSCC on 22 Nov. 2020 and Russia withdrew on 18 Dec. 2021.

Website: <https://www.osce.org/oscc/>

Organization of American States (OAS)

The OAS, which adopted its charter in 1948, has the objective of strengthening peace and security in the western hemisphere. Its activities are based on the four pillars of democracy, human rights, security and development. Its general secretariat is in Washington, DC, USA.

Members (35): Antigua and Barbuda, Argentina, Bahamas, Barbados, Belize, Bolivia, Brazil, Canada, Chile, Colombia, Costa Rica, Cuba*, Dominica, Dominican Republic, Ecuador, El Salvador, Grenada, Guatemala, Guyana, Haiti, Honduras, Jamaica, Mexico, Nicaragua†, Panama, Paraguay, Peru, Saint Kitts and Nevis, Saint Lucia, Saint Vincent and the Grenadines, Suriname, Trinidad and Tobago, Uruguay, USA, Venezuela‡

* By a resolution of 3 June 2009, the 1962 resolution that excluded Cuba from the OAS ceased to have effect; according to the 2009 resolution, Cuba's participation in the organization 'will be the result of a process of dialogue'. Cuba has declined to participate in OAS activities.

† On 19 Nov. 2021 Nicaragua initiated the 2-year process of withdrawal from the OAS. In Apr. 2022 Nicaragua withdrew its representative from the OAS and closed the OAS office in Managua.

‡ On 27 Apr. 2017 the Venezuelan government initiated the 2-year process of withdrawal from the OAS. On 8 Feb. 2019, following disputed presidential elections, the opposition-appointed interim president annulled the withdrawal and on 9 Apr. the OAS accepted the nomination of a representative by the interim president. The Venezuelan government continued the withdrawal process and on 27 Apr. 2019 announced its completion. On 5 Jan. 2023 the opposition's parallel administration was dissolved and the post of OAS representative became vacant.

Website: <https://www.oas.org/>

Inter-American Defense Board (IADB)

The IADB advises the OAS and its member states on military and defence matters. It was established in 1942 and has been an OAS entity since 2006.

Members (29): Antigua and Barbuda, Argentina, Barbados, Belize, Bolivia, Brazil, Canada, Chile, Colombia, Dominican Republic, Ecuador, El Salvador, Grenada, Guatemala, Guyana, Haiti, Honduras, Jamaica, Mexico, Nicaragua, Panama, Paraguay, Peru, Saint Kitts and Nevis, Suriname, Trinidad and Tobago, Uruguay, USA, Venezuela

Website: <https://www.jid.org/>

Organization of the Black Sea Economic Cooperation (BSEC)

The BSEC initiative was established in 1992 and became a full regional economic organization when its charter entered into force in 1999. Its aims are to ensure peace, stability and prosperity and to promote and develop economic cooperation and progress in the Black Sea region. Its permanent secretariat is in Istanbul, Türkiye.

Members (13): Albania, Armenia, Azerbaijan, Bulgaria, Georgia, Greece, Moldova, North Macedonia, Romania, Russia, Serbia, Türkiye, Ukraine

Website: <http://www.bsec-organization.org/>

Pacific Islands Forum

The forum, which was founded in 1971 as the South Pacific Forum, aims to enhance cooperation in sustainable development, economic growth, governance and security. It also monitors implementation of the 1985 South Pacific Nuclear Free Zone Treaty (Treaty of Rarotonga). Its secretariat is in Suva, Fiji.

Members (17): Australia, Cook Islands, Fiji, French Polynesia, Marshall Islands, Micronesia, Nauru, New Caledonia, New Zealand, Niue, Palau, Papua New Guinea, Samoa, Solomon Islands, Tonga, Tuvalu, Vanuatu

Note: Following a dispute over the appointment of a new secretary-general, in Feb. 2021 Kiribati, Marshall Islands, Micronesia, Nauru and Palau agreed to initiate the formal process of leaving the forum. In Feb. 2022 the 5 states 'temporarily rescinded' their withdrawal after a compromise was agreed. Following adjustment to the compromise, Kiribati withdrew from the forum on 9 July 2022 'with immediate effect'. On 30 Jan. 2023 it announced its intention to re-join.

Website: <https://www.forumsec.org/>

Regional Centre on Small Arms in the Great Lakes Region, the Horn of Africa and Bordering States (RECSA)

The Nairobi Secretariat on Small Arms and Light Weapons was established to coordinate implementation of the 2000 Nairobi Declaration on the Problem of Illicit Small Arms and Light Weapons in the Great Lakes Region and the Horn of Africa. It was transformed into RECSA in 2005 to oversee the implementation of the 2004 Nairobi Protocol for the Prevention, Control and Reduction of Small Arms and Light Weapons. It is based in Nairobi, Kenya.

Members (15): Burundi, Djibouti, Central African Republic, Congo (Democratic Republic of the), Congo (Republic of the), Eritrea, Ethiopia, Kenya, Rwanda, Seychelles, Somalia, South Sudan, Sudan, Tanzania, Uganda

Website: <https://www.recsasec.org/>

Regional Cooperation Council

The RCC was launched in 2008 as the successor of the Stability Pact for South Eastern Europe that was initiated by the European Union at the 1999 Conference on South Eastern Europe. It promotes mutual cooperation and European and Euro-Atlantic integration of states in South Eastern Europe in order to inspire development in the region for the benefit of its people. It focuses on six areas: economic and social development, energy and infrastructure, justice and home affairs, security cooperation, building human capital, and parliamentary cooperation. Its secretariat is in Sarajevo, Bosnia and Herzegovina, and it has a liaison office in Brussels, Belgium.

Participants (46): Albania, Austria, Bosnia and Herzegovina, Bulgaria, Canada, Council of Europe, Council of Europe Development Bank, Croatia, Czechia, Denmark, European Bank for Reconstruction and Development, European Investment Bank, European Union, Germany, Finland, France, Greece, Hungary, International Organization for Migration, Ireland, Italy, Kosovo, Latvia, Moldova, Montenegro, North Atlantic Treaty Organization, North Macedonia, Norway, Organisation for Economic Co-operation and Development, Organization for Security and Cooperation in Europe, Poland, Romania, Serbia, Slovakia, Slovenia, South East European Cooperative Initiative, Spain, Sweden, Switzerland, Türkiye, UK, United Nations, UN Economic Commission for Europe, UN Development Programme, USA, World Bank

Website: <https://www.rcc.int/>

Shanghai Cooperation Organisation (SCO)

The SCO's predecessor group, the Shanghai Five, was founded in 1996; it was renamed the SCO in 2001 and opened for membership of all states that support its aims. The member states cooperate on confidence-building measures and regional security and in the economic sphere. Its secretariat is in Beijing, China. The SCO Regional Anti-Terrorist Structure (RATS) is based in Tashkent, Uzbekistan.

Members (8): China, India, Kazakhstan, Kyrgyzstan, Pakistan, Russia, Tajikistan, Uzbekistan

Note: The process to admit Iran as a member of the SCO was initiated on 17 Sep. 2021. It is likely to conclude in 2023 once all agreements are ratified. The process to admit Belarus as a member was initiated on 16 Sep. 2022.

Website: <http://www.sectsco.org/>

Sistema de la Integración Centroamericana (SICA, Central American Integration System)

SICA was launched in 1993 on the basis of the 1991 Tegucigalpa Protocol. Its objective is the integration of Central America to constitute a region of peace, freedom, democracy and development, based on respect for and protection and promotion of human rights. The SICA headquarters are in San Salvador, El Salvador.

The **Comisión de Seguridad de Centroamérica (CSC, Central American Security Commission)** was established by the 1995 Framework Treaty on Democratic Security in Central America. Its objectives include following up on proposals on regional security, based on a reasonable balance of forces, strengthening civilian power, and eradicating violence, corruption, terrorism, drug trafficking and arms trafficking.

Members (8): Belize, Costa Rica, Dominican Republic, El Salvador, Guatemala, Honduras, Nicaragua, Panama

Website: <https://www.sica.int/>

Southern African Development Community (SADC)

SADC was established in 1992 to promote regional economic development and the fundamental principles of sovereignty, peace and security, human rights and democracy. It superseded the Southern African Development Coordination Conference (SADCC), established in 1980. Its secretariat is in Gaborone, Botswana.

The **SADC Organ on Politics, Defence and Security Cooperation (OPDS)** is mandated to promote peace and security in the region.

Members (16): Angola, Botswana, Comoros, Congo (Democratic Republic of the), Eswatini, Lesotho, Madagascar, Malawi, Mauritius, Mozambique, Namibia, Seychelles, South Africa, Tanzania, Zambia, Zimbabwe

Website: <https://www.sadc.int/>

Sub-Regional Consultative Commission (SRCC)

The SRCC meets regularly to monitor implementation of the 1996 Agreement on Sub-Regional Arms Control (Florence Agreement) in the former Yugoslavia. Representatives of the Contact Group consisting of France, Italy, Germany, Russia, the UK and the USA also take part in these sessions.

Parties to the Agreement on Sub-Regional Arms Control (4): See annex A

Unión de Naciones Suramericanas (UNASUR, Union of South American Nations)

UNASUR is an intergovernmental organization with the aim of strengthening regional integration, political dialogue, economic development and coordination in defence matters among its member states. Its 2008 Constitutive Treaty entered into force on 11 March 2011 and it was intended to gradually replace the Andean Community and the Mercado Común del Sur (MERCOSUR, Southern Common Market). Its headquarters were in Quito, Ecuador.

The **Consejo de Defensa Suramericano (CDS, South American Defence Council)** met for the first time in March 2009. Its objectives are to consolidate South America as a zone of peace and to create a regional identity and strengthen regional cooperation in defence issues.

Members (5): Bolivia, Guyana, Peru, Suriname, Venezuela

Notes: Argentina, Brazil, Chile, Colombia, Ecuador, Paraguay and Uruguay withdrew from UNASUR during 2019–20. Peru suspended its participation in Apr. 2018. Bolivia suspended its participation in Nov. 2019 but resumed again in Nov. 2020.

At a summit in Santiago, Chile, on 22 Mar. 2019, Argentina, Brazil, Chile, Colombia, Ecuador, Guyana, Paraguay and Peru launched a process to form a new regional group, known as the Forum for the Progress of South America (Foro para el Progreso de América del Sur, PROSUR). Suriname joined the process on 28 Jan. 2022. Chile suspended its involvement on 3 Apr. 2022.

In Apr. 2023 Argentina and Brazil announced that they were to rejoin UNASUR.

Website: <http://www.unasursg.org/>

III. Strategic trade control regimes

Australia Group

The Australia Group is an informal group of states and the European Commission formed in 1985. It meets annually to exchange views and best practices on strategic trade controls in order to ensure that dual-use material, technology and equipment are not used to support chemical and biological warfare activity or weapon programmes.

Participants (43): Argentina, Australia*, Austria, Belgium, Bulgaria, Canada, Croatia, Cyprus, Czechia, Denmark, Estonia, European Commission, Finland, France, Germany, Greece, Hungary, Iceland, India, Ireland, Italy, Japan, Korea (South), Latvia, Lithuania, Luxembourg, Malta, Mexico, Netherlands, New Zealand, Norway, Poland, Portugal, Romania, Slovakia, Slovenia, Spain, Sweden, Switzerland, Türkiye, UK, Ukraine, USA

* Permanent chair.

Website: <https://www.australiagroup.net/>

European Union–United States Trade and Technology Council (TTC)

The TTC was established in June 2021 as a forum for the European Union and the USA to coordinate approaches to key global trade, economic and technology issues. Among its goals are ensuring that trade policies and the deployment of emerging technologies are informed by national security priorities; and countering the influence of authoritarian states in cyberspace and emerging technology. The TCC is co-chaired by three US cabinet secretaries and two vice-presidents of the European Commission, who meet biannually, while 10 working groups focus on specific policy areas.

Participants (2): European Union, USA

Website: <https://www.trade.gov/useuttc>

Hague Code of Conduct against Ballistic Missile Proliferation (HCOC)

The principle of the 2002 HCOC is the need to curb the proliferation of ballistic missile systems capable of delivering WMD. Subscribing states commit to exercise restraint in the development, testing and deployment of such missiles, to issue pre-launch notifications and to provide annual declarations on their policies concerning ballistic missiles and space-launch vehicles. The Ministry for Foreign Affairs of Austria acts as the HCOC Secretariat.

Subscribing states (143): Afghanistan, Albania, Andorra, Antigua and Barbuda, Argentina*, Armenia, Australia, Austria, Azerbaijan, Belarus, Belgium, Benin, Bosnia and Herzegovina, Bulgaria, Burkina Faso, Burundi, Cabo Verde, Cambodia, Cameroon, Canada, Central African Republic, Chad, Chile, Colombia, Comoros, Congo (Republic of the), Cook Islands, Costa Rica, Croatia, Cyprus, Czechia, Denmark, Dominica, Dominican Republic, Ecuador, El Salvador, Equatorial Guinea, Eritrea, Estonia, Ethiopia, Fiji, Finland, France, Gabon, Gambia, Georgia, Germany, Ghana, Greece, Guatemala, Guinea, Guinea-Bissau, Guyana, Haiti, Holy See, Honduras, Hungary, Iceland, India, Iraq, Ireland, Italy, Japan, Jordan, Kazakhstan, Kenya, Kiribati, Korea (South), Latvia, Lesotho, Liberia, Libya, Liechtenstein, Lithuania, Luxembourg, Madagascar, Malawi, Maldives, Mali, Malta, Marshall Islands, Mauritania, Micronesia, Moldova, Monaco, Mongolia, Montenegro, Morocco, Mozambique, Netherlands, New Zealand, Nicaragua, Niger, Nigeria†, North Macedonia, Norway, Palau, Panama, Papua New Guinea, Paraguay, Peru, Philippines, Poland, Portugal, Romania, Russia, Rwanda, Saint Kitts and Nevis, Saint Vincent and the Grenadines, Samoa, San Marino, Senegal, Serbia, Seychelles, Sierra Leone, Singapore, Slovakia, Slovenia, Somalia, South Africa, Spain, Sudan, Suriname, Sweden, Switzerland, Tajikistan, Tanzania, Timor-Leste, Togo, Tonga, Tunisia, Türkiye, Turkmenistan, Tuvalu, Uganda, UK, Ukraine, Uruguay, USA, Uzbekistan, Vanuatu, Venezuela, Zambia

* Chair in 2021/22.
† Chair in 2022/23.

Website: <https://www.hcoc.at/>

Missile Technology Control Regime (MTCR)

The MTCR, established in 1987, is an informal group of countries that seeks to coordinate national export licensing efforts aimed at preventing the proliferation of missiles and other delivery systems capable of delivering WMD. The partner countries apply the Guidelines for Sensitive Missile-relevant Transfers. The MTCR has no secretariat. A point of contact based in the Ministry for Foreign Affairs of France distributes the regime's working papers and hosts regular policy and information-exchange meetings.

Partners (35): Argentina, Australia, Austria, Belgium, Brazil‡, Bulgaria, Canada, Czechia, Denmark, Finland, France, Germany, Greece, Hungary, Iceland, India, Ireland, Italy, Japan, Korea (South), Luxembourg, Netherlands, New Zealand, Norway, Poland, Portugal, Russia*, South Africa, Spain, Sweden, Switzerland†, Türkiye, UK, Ukraine, USA

* Chair in 2021/22.
† Chair in 2022/23.
‡ Chair in 2023/24.

Website: <https://www.mtcr.info/>

Nuclear Suppliers Group (NSG)

The NSG, formerly also known as the London Club, was established in 1975. It coordinates national transfer controls on nuclear materials according to its Guidelines for Nuclear Transfers (London Guidelines, first agreed in 1978), which contain a 'trigger list' of materials that should trigger IAEA safeguards when they are to be exported for peaceful purposes to any non-nuclear weapon state, and the Guidelines for Transfers of Nuclear-related Dual-use Equipment, Materials, Software and Related Technology (Warsaw Guidelines). The NSG Guidelines are implemented by each participating state in accordance with its national laws and practices. The NSG has no secretariat. The Permanent Mission of Japan to the IAEA in Vienna acts as a point of contact and carries out practical support functions.

Participants (48): Argentina†, Australia, Austria, Belarus, Belgium, Brazil, Bulgaria, Canada, China, Croatia, Cyprus, Czechia, Denmark, Estonia, Finland, France, Germany, Greece, Hungary, Iceland, Ireland, Italy, Japan, Kazakhstan, Korea (South), Latvia, Lithuania, Luxembourg, Malta, Mexico, Netherlands, New Zealand, Norway, Poland*, Portugal, Romania, Russia, Serbia, Slovakia, Slovenia, South Africa, Spain, Sweden, Switzerland, Türkiye, UK, Ukraine, USA

* Chair in 2021/22.
† Chair in 2022/23.

Note: In addition, the European Union and the chair of the Zangger Committee are permanent observers.

Website: <https://www.nuclearsuppliersgroup.org/>

Proliferation Security Initiative (PSI)

Based on a US initiative announced in 2003, the PSI is a multilateral forum focusing on law enforcement cooperation for the interdiction and seizure of illegal WMD, missile technologies and related materials when in transit on land, in the air or at sea. The PSI Statement of Interdiction Principles was issued in 2003. The PSI has no secretariat, but its activities are coordinated by a 21-member Operational Experts Group.

Participants (107): Afghanistan, Albania, Andorra, Angola, Antigua and Barbuda, Argentina*, Armenia, Australia*†, Austria, Azerbaijan, Bahamas, Bahrain, Belarus, Belgium, Belize, Bosnia and Herzegovina, Brunei Darussalam, Bulgaria, Cambodia, Canada*, Chile, Colombia, Croatia†, Cyprus, Czechia†, Denmark*, Djibouti†, Dominica, Dominican Republic, El Salvador, Estonia, Fiji, Finland, France*†, Georgia, Germany*†, Greece*, Holy See, Honduras, Hungary, Iceland, Iraq, Ireland, Israel, Italy*†, Japan*†, Jordan, Kazakhstan, Korea (South)*†, Kyrgyzstan, Kuwait, Latvia, Liberia, Libya, Liechtenstein, Lithuania†, Luxembourg, Malaysia, Malta, Marshall Islands, Micronesia, Moldova, Mongolia, Montenegro, Morocco, Netherlands*†, New Zealand*†, North Macedonia, Norway*†, Oman, Palau, Panama, Papua New Guinea, Paraguay, Philippines, Poland*†, Portugal*†, Qatar†,

Romania, Russia*, Saint Lucia, Saint Vincent and the Grenadines, Samoa, San Marino, Saudi Arabia, Serbia, Singapore*†, Slovakia, Slovenia†, Spain*†, Sri Lanka, Sweden, Switzerland, Tajikistan, Thailand, Trinidad and Tobago, Tunisia, Türkiye*†, Turkmenistan, UK*†, Ukraine†, United Arab Emirates†, USA*†, Uzbekistan, Vanuatu, Viet Nam, Yemen

* Member of the Operational Experts Group.
† PSI exercise host, 2003–22.

Website: <https://www.psi-online.info>

Wassenaar Arrangement on Export Controls for Conventional Arms and Dual-Use Goods and Technologies

The Wassenaar Arrangement was formally established in 1996 as the successor to the cold war-era Coordinating Committee for Multilateral Export Controls (COCOM). It aims to promote transparency and responsibility in the transfers of conventional weapons and dual-use goods and technologies. Participating states seek to prevent transfers of armaments and sensitive dual-use goods and technologies that contribute to destabilizing accumulations of weapons, as well as transfers to terrorists. Its secretariat is located in Vienna, Austria.

Participants (42): Argentina, Australia, Austria, Belgium, Bulgaria, Canada, Croatia, Czechia, Denmark, Estonia, Finland, France, Germany, Greece, Hungary, India†, Ireland*, Italy, Japan, Korea (South), Latvia, Lithuania, Luxembourg, Malta, Mexico, Netherlands, New Zealand, Norway, Poland, Portugal, Romania, Russia, Slovakia, Slovenia, South Africa, Spain, Sweden, Switzerland, Türkiye, UK, Ukraine, USA

* Chair in 2022.
† Chair in 2023.

Website: <https://www.wassenaar.org/>

Zangger Committee

Established in 1971–74, the Zangger Committee (also called the Nuclear Exporters Committee) is an informal group of nuclear supplier countries that coordinate transfer controls on nuclear materials. It maintains a trigger list of items which, when exported, must be subject to IAEA safeguards. It complements the work of the Nuclear Suppliers Group.

Members (39): Argentina, Australia, Austria, Belarus, Belgium, Bulgaria, Canada, China, Croatia, Czechia, Denmark, Finland, France, Germany, Greece, Hungary, Ireland, Italy, Japan, Kazakhstan, Korea (South), Luxembourg, Netherlands, New Zealand, Norway, Poland, Portugal, Romania, Russia, Slovakia, Slovenia, South Africa, Spain, Sweden, Switzerland, Türkiye, UK, Ukraine, USA

Website: <http://www.zanggercommittee.org/>

Annex C. Chronology 2022

This chronology lists the significant events in 2022 related to armaments, disarmament and international security. Keywords are indicated in the right-hand column.

January

3 Jan.	The five permanent members of the United Nations Security Council (P5) issue a joint statement on the need to prevent nuclear war.	Nuclear arms control; P5
6–19 Jan.	The Collective Security Treaty Organization (CSTO) deploys its first multilateral peace operation, the CTSO Collective Peacekeeping Forces to Kazakhstan, when violent protests spark a domestic crisis in Kazakhstan.	CSTO; Kazakhstan; peace operation
9 Jan.	At least 200 people are killed and 10 000 displaced by armed gangs in the north-western Nigerian state of Zamfara, after military raids on their camps, amid a continuing struggle for order in the region.	Nigeria
10 Jan.	The United States reports 1.34 million new Covid-19 infections, a global record, with the Omicron variant accounting for an estimated 95 per cent of cases.	Covid-19; USA
10 Jan.	An extraordinary meeting of the Strategic Stability Dialogue is held between US and Russian delegations in Geneva. The two sides exchange security concerns but differences on several key issues are intractable.	nuclear arms control; Russia; USA
13 Jan.	Australia equals the hottest temperature on record of 50.7°C in Onslow, Western Australia.	Australia; climate change
17 Jan.–2 Feb.	The United Arab Emirates (UAE) is hit by several uncrewed aerial vehicle (UAV, drone) and missile attacks amid an escalation of the conflict in Yemen.	UAE; Yemen
21 Jan.	A detention centre in Sa'dah, Yemen, held by rebel Houthis is attacked, killing more than 70 people. The Saudi Arabian-led coalition fighting Houthi forces in the country denies it carried out the air strike.	Yemen
24 Jan.	The military in Burkina Faso seizes power and overthrows President Roch Marc Christian Kaboré in a coup.	Burkina Faso; coup
30 Jan.	Kurdish-led militia and US forces regain control of Sinaa prison in Hasaka, Syria, after a week-long assault by Islamic State forces, with the loss of 500 lives.	Islamic State; Syria; USA

February

1 Feb.	An attack by armed militants on the Plaine Savo camp for displaced persons in eastern Democratic Republic of the Congo (DRC) kills 60 people.	DRC

SIPRI Yearbook 2023: Armaments, Disarmament and International Security
www.sipriyearbook.org

3 Feb.	An operation by US forces in north-western Syria results in the death of Islamic State leader Abu Ibrahim al-Hashimi al-Qurayshi.	Islamic State; Syria; USA
3 Feb.	The Economic Community of West African States (ECOWAS) Guinea Bissau Stabilisation Support Mission is established following a coup attempt against Guinea-Bissau President Umaro Sissoco Embaló. The peace operation starts deployment in Apr. 2022.	ECOWAS; Guinea-Bissau; peace operation
4 Feb.	In a joint statement, Russian President Vladimir Putin and Chinese President Xi Jinping avow that their partnership has no limits, with no areas where cooperation is off the table.	China; Russia
8 Feb.	The UN World Food Programme (WFP) warns that 13 million people in the Horn of Africa are facing a humanitarian crisis, amid a drought where the rainy season has failed three years in a row.	climate change; Horn of Africa
12 Feb.	Operation Barkhane, the French-led counterterrorist force in the Sahel region, kills 40 suspected militants in air strikes in Burkina Faso. The militants are said to be linked to earlier attacks by non-state armed groups in neighbouring Benin.	Benin; Burkina Faso; France; Operation Barkhane
14 Feb.	Climate scientists declare the megadrought affecting the south-west USA as the worst for 1200 years.	climate change; USA
21 Feb.	Australia's international border reopens to tourists who have been vaccinated against Covid-19 after being closed for 704 days—nearly two years.	Australia; Covid-19
21 Feb.	President Putin recognizes Russian-backed separatists in two Ukrainian regions, Donetsk and Luhansk, ordering in troops for so-called peacekeeping functions.	Russia; Ukraine
22 Feb.	US President Joe Biden announces new sanctions against Russia, saying its latest moves in Ukraine amount to the start of a Russian invasion.	Russia; Ukraine; USA
24 Feb.	Russia launches a full-scale invasion of Ukraine, which it describes as a special military operation for the 'demilitarization and denazification of Ukraine'. Western states condemn the invasion and rally behind Ukraine.	Russia–Ukraine War
24 Feb.	A cyberattack targets Viasat, a satellite communications company, impacting users in Ukraine and other parts of Europe.	cyber; Russia–Ukraine War; space
27 Feb.	Several countries sanction Russia for its invasion of Ukraine, the European Union (EU) closes its airspace to Russian aeroplanes and Russian banks are excluded from the worldwide Swift payment system. Europe faces a major humanitarian crisis with 18 million Ukrainians displaced and 4 million refugees fleeing the country.	refugees; Russia–Ukraine War; sanctions
28 Feb.	A report by the UN Intergovernmental Panel on Climate Change (IPCC) warns climate change is outpacing human efforts to adapt. If the world's average temperatures rise by 1.5°C—the goal of the 2015 Paris Agreement on climate change—it estimates up to 14 per cent of land species face a very high risk of extinction.	climate change; IPCC

March

1 Mar.	Russia and the USA establish a military-to-military deconfliction line to reduce the risks of miscalculation amid the war in Ukraine.	Russia; USA
2 Mar.	UN states agree to create a legally binding plastic pollution treaty (to be completed in 2024) after talks in Nairobi, Kenya.	plastic pollution treaty; UN
2 Mar.	Rafael Mariano Grossi, the director general of the International Atomic Energy Agency (IAEA), sets out seven pillars of nuclear safety and security in the light of growing concerns about Russian military attacks on Ukrainian nuclear infrastructure.	IAEA; nuclear safety; Russia–Ukraine War
3 Mar.	Russian forces seize the Zaporizhzhia Nuclear Power Plant in Ukraine—the largest in Europe.	nuclear risk; Russia–Ukraine War; nuclear risk
4 Mar.	A bomb attack by Islamic State–Khorasan Province on a Shia mosque in the Pakistani city of Peshawar kills at least 63 people and injures 196.	Islamic State–Khorasan Province; Pakistan
7–10 Mar.	The World Health Organization (WHO) estimates that the global death toll from Covid-19 has surpassed 6 million A study by Washington University on 10 Mar. estimates the global death toll from Covid-19 at 18.2 million.	Covid-19
9 Mar.	India accidentally launches a conventional BrahMos cruise missile into Pakistani territory during a 'routine maintenance and inspection' exercise.	India; Pakistan
14 Mar.	Civilians can leave the heavily bombed Ukrainian city of Mariupol for the first time, amid a death toll of 2500 and a humanitarian crisis in the city.	Russia–Ukraine War
24 Mar.	North Korea test launches what it claims to be an intercontinental ballistic missile test, ending a self-imposed moratorium on that type of delivery system.	missile proliferation; North Korea
24 Mar.	The Ethiopian government and the Tigray People's Liberation Front (TPLF) agree to a humanitarian ceasefire in the war that broke out in the Tigray region of northern Ethiopia in Nov. 2020.	ceasefire; Ethiopia; TPLF
27 Mar.	El Salvador declares a state of emergency and launches an anti-gang crackdown that raises concerns about government repression.	El Salvador
27–31 Mar.	Malian armed forces and mercenaries from the Russian Wagner Group allegedly kill up to 300 civilians in the central Malian town of Moura.	Mali; Wagner Group
29 Mar.	In a major victory for Ukraine, Russia announces it is withdrawing its forces from around Ukraine's capital, Kyiv.	Russia–Ukraine War
29 Mar.	A helicopter of the UN Organization Stabilization Mission in the DRC (MONUSCO) crashes in eastern DRC, killing eight peacekeepers.	DRC; peace operation

31 Mar.	The Organization for Security and Co-operation in Europe (OSCE) Special Monitoring Mission in Ukraine officially closes, following Russia's refusal to join the consensus to extend its mandate for another year.	OSCE; peace operation; Ukraine

April

1 Apr.	The African Union Transition Mission in Somalia (ATMIS) replaces the African Union Mission in Somalia (AMISOM), with a mandate to support the national government in the fight against al-Shabab, develop national capacity and support peace and reconciliation in the country.	peace operations; Somalia
2 Apr.	Ukraine liberates the entire Kyiv region from retreating Russian forces.	Russia–Ukraine War
2 Apr.	A UN-mediated ceasefire is agreed between the Houthis and the internationally recognized Yemeni government. It includes a halt to all offensive military operations inside and outside Yemen.	ceasefire; UN; Yemen
4 Apr.	The Ukrainian government begins a war crimes investigation after 410 civilians are found dead following the withdrawal of Russian forces from around the Kyiv region.	Russia–Ukraine War; war crimes
13–18 Apr.	At least 448 people are killed after heavy rains and flooding in KwaZulu-Natal province, in what is described as one of the worst storms in South Africa's history. President Cyril Ramaphosa declares a national state of disaster on 18 Apr.	climate change; South Africa
14 Apr.	The cruiser *Moskva*, the flagship of Russia's Black Sea Fleet and part of its weeks-long offensive in southern and central Ukraine, sinks amid conflicting accounts.	Russia–Ukraine War
24 Apr.	Violent clashes between Arab nomads and members of the Masalit community in Sudan's West Darfur state result in the deaths of at least 168 people.	Sudan
26 Apr.	The USA announces the formation of the Ukraine Defense Contact Group (Ramstein Group), with more than 40 member states, to coordinate Western military and humanitarian assistance to Ukraine.	Russia–Ukraine War
26 Apr.	The World Bank warns the war in Ukraine will cause the largest commodity shock since the 1970s, with large economic and humanitarian effects.	Russia–Ukraine War; World Bank
28 Apr.	Russian missiles strike Kyiv during a visit by UN Secretary-General António Guterres.	Russia–Ukraine War
29 Apr.	The Chemical Weapons Convention (CWC) celebrates the 25th anniversary of its entry into force.	CWC

May

5 May	A WHO report of excess deaths worldwide says 15 million more people have died than normal, far above the official Covid-19 death toll of 6 million.	Covid-19; WHO
11 May	Costa Rica declares a state of emergency after a ransomware attack infiltrates and cripples several government agencies.	Costa Rica; cyberattack
14 May	The USA records 1 million Covid-19 deaths.	Covid-19; USA

15 May	Mali announces its withdrawal from the G5 Sahel and its Joint Force.	G5 Sahel; Mali
15–16 May	Finland says it intends to apply to join the North Atlantic Treaty Organization (NATO) following the Russian invasion of Ukraine, ending decades of military non-alignment. A day later, Sweden also announces its intention to join after 200 years of military non-alignment.	Finland; NATO; Sweden
16 May	Ukraine evacuates the last of its forces from the Azovstal steelworks in Mariupol, which had become a symbol of Ukrainian resistance.	Russia–Ukraine War
16 May	US President Biden approves the redeployment of several hundred US ground troops to Somalia, reversing a decision by President Donald J. Trump.	Somalia; USA
23 May	The USA, together with 13 other founding member states (including India, Japan and South Korea), launches the Indo-Pacific Economic Framework (IPEF)—an economic alliance of Asia-Pacific states to counter Chinese influence.	IPEF; USA

June

5 June	An attack on a church in the city of Owo in Ondo State, Nigeria, kills at least 40 people. Islamic State–West Africa Province is suspected of carrying out the attack.	Islamic State–West Africa Province; Nigeria
14 June–30 Sep.	During its monsoon season, Pakistan experiences a series of deadly floods that claim 1739 lives.	climate change; Pakistan
18 June	Ethnic violence in western Ethiopia leaves a reported 250 people dead, killed by Oromo rebels amid worsening ethnic conflict in the country.	Ethiopia
20 June	In the face of the deteriorating situation in eastern DRC, the East African Community (EAC) establishes its first peace operation: the EAC Regional Force in the DRC.	DRC; peace operation
21 June	The USA announces a new policy on anti-personnel mines (APMs), effectively banning their transfer, development, production or acquisition—the fifth change in US policy on this issue in as many administrations, dating back to the 1990s.	APMs; USA
21–23 June	The first meeting of states parties to the 2017 Treaty on the Prohibition of Nuclear Weapons (TPNW) reaches agreement on several key issues. As well as establishing a scientific advisory group, the parties unanimously adopt two outcome documents.	TPNW
25 June	Russia announces it will provide Belarus with nuclear-capable Iskander-M missiles and is willing to upgrade the country's combat aircraft to allow them to carry tactical nuclear weapons.	Belarus; nuclear weapons; Russia
25 June	The eastern Ukrainian city of Severodonetsk falls to Russian forces after weeks of fighting in the area.	Russia–Ukraine War
27–30 June	NATO's Madrid Summit agrees a new strategic concept, strengthened deterrence and defence, more support for Ukraine and membership invitations for Finland and Sweden.	NATO

27 June–1 July	At the eighth biennial meeting of states parties to the UN Programme of Action to Prevent, Combat and Eradicate the Illicit Trade in Small Arms and Light Weapons in All its Aspects (POA), states agree to consider the impact of technological developments on manufacturing of small arms and light weapons (SALW) and acknowledge the gender-related impact of illicit SALW.	POA; SALW
28–29 June	Indirect talks between Iran and the USA to restore the 2015 Joint Comprehensive Plan of Action (JCPOA) resume in Doha, Qatar, without results.	Iran; JCPOA; USA
30 June	The International Monitoring Team (IMT) in Mindanao, the Philippines, ends after almost two decades of monitoring activities.	peace operation; Philippines
30 June	The French-led European multinational Task Force Takuba officially ceases operating in Mali, ending a year-long counterterrorism effort in the country that soured after military coups in 2020 and 2021.	France; Mali; Task Force Takuba

July

8–17 July	Ten days of gang violence in Port-au-Prince, Haiti, result in 208 people being killed and a further 254 injured with gunshot wounds.	Haiti
9 July	A Russian air strike on a residential building in Chasiv Yar, eastern Ukraine, kills at least 47 people.	Russia–Ukraine War
14 July	A temperature of 47°C is recorded in Pinhão, Portugal—the highest in a series of persistent summer heatwaves affecting much of Europe. From June to Aug., the heatwaves cause wildfires and evacuations across mainland Europe, and over 20 000 heat-related deaths, making it the deadliest meteorological event in 2022.	climate change; Europe
22 July	In a deal brokered by the UN and Türkiye, Russia and Ukraine sign the Black Sea Grain Initiative to resume exports of Ukrainian grain through the Black Sea. Ukraine is one of the world's biggest wheat exporters, and the blockade pushed up global food prices.	food security; Russia–Ukraine War

August

1 Aug.	The first grain ship leaves the Ukrainian port of Odesa as part of the deal brokered by the UN and Türkiye in July.	food security; Russia–Ukraine War
1–26 Aug.	The 10th review conference of the 1968 Treaty on the Non-Proliferation of Nuclear Weapons (NPT) fails to reach consensus on the contents of a substantive final outcome document.	NPT
3 Aug.	Nancy Pelosi, the Speaker of the US House of Representatives visits Taiwan—the first US speaker to do so in 25 years—prompting condemnation from China.	China; Taiwan; USA
4 Aug.	All signatories to the 2018 Revitalised Agreement on the Resolution of the Conflict in the Republic of South Sudan agree to a road map extending the transitional period by 24 months to enable the implementation of its key outstanding tasks.	South Sudan

7 Aug.	A ceasefire comes into effect in Gaza after 43 people were killed in three days of violence between the Israeli military and the Palestinian Islamic Jihad.	Israel; Palestine
8 Aug.	Russia informs the USA that, in response to sanctions linked to the war in Ukraine, it will not resume inspections under the New START nuclear arms control treaty.	New START; Russia; USA
17 Aug.	China issues its highest red alert heat warning for at least 138 cities and counties amid the country's longest heatwave since records began (64 days).	climate change; China
19 Aug.	A 30-hour hotel siege by al-Shabab militants begins in Mogadishu, Somalia, resulting in 21 dead and 117 injured.	al-Shabab; Somalia
20 Aug.	The WFP warns that 22 million people are now at risk of starvation in the Horn of Africa, up 9 million since February, after the worst drought in 40 years.	climate change; food security; Horn of Africa
24 Aug.	Fighting erupts in northern Ethiopia between government and Tigrayan forces, breaking a five-month humanitarian truce.	Ethiopia
28 Aug.	Pakistan appeals for international aid as the death toll from monsoon rain and floods rises to over 1000 people.	climate change; Pakistan
29 Aug.	Violence in the Iraqi capital Baghdad results in 30 people being killed and 700 injured after Shia leader Muqtada al-Sadr announces he is withdrawing from politics.	Iraq
29 Aug.–3 Sep.	After several months of diplomacy between the IAEA, Russia and Ukraine, the IAEA Support and Assistance Mission to Zaporizhzhya takes place to help stabilize the nuclear safety and security situation at the Zaporizhzhia Nuclear Power Plant. It is the fourth mission of IAEA technical experts to Ukrainian nuclear sites during 2022.	IAEA; nuclear safety; Russia–Ukraine War
30 Aug.–10 Sep.	The 10th meeting of states parties to the Convention on Cluster Munitions expresses grave concern over the use of cluster munitions in Ukraine.	cluster munitions; Russia–Ukraine War
31 Aug.	The UN High Commissioner for Human Rights releases a report accusing China of serious human rights abuses against Uighurs in its western Xinjiang region.	China; human rights; UN

September

2 Sep.	Russian state-controlled energy company Gazprom indefinitely suspends supplies of natural gas to Europe via the Nord Stream 1 pipeline, amid accusations of weaponizing its energy supplies.	energy security; Russia–Ukraine War
8 Sep.	The North Korean Parliament adopts a new nuclear doctrine for the country that specifies updated principles and conditions for the use of nuclear weapons.	North Korea; nuclear weapons
10 Sep.	UN Secretary-General António Guterres calls for international support for flood-ravaged Pakistan, where 33 million people are displaced and damage is estimated at $30 billion.	climate change; Pakistan

12 Sep.	An outbreak of fighting on the border between Armenia and Azerbaijan kills about 100 soldiers.	Armenia; Azerbaijan
14–21 Sep.	Border clashes between Kyrgyz and Tajik forces result in at least 100 deaths, including 37 civilians.	Kyrgyzstan; Tajikistan
14 Sep.	The head of the WHO, Tedros Adhanom Ghebreyesus, says the end of the Covid-19 pandemic is in sight. The health crisis has killed over 6 million people since early 2020.	Covid-19; WHO
15 Sep.	Ukrainian authorities reveal the discovery of a mass grave with 450 bodies near Izyum, some showing evidence of torture, after the withdrawal of Russian forces.	Russia–Ukraine War; war crimes
16 Sep.	Mahsa Amini dies in the custody of Iran's Guidance Patrol (morality police), sparking widespread protests throughout the country against the mistreatment of women. By the end of 2022, Iranian security forces had killed as many as 450 protestors.	Iran; women's rights
21 Sep.	President Putin announces a partial mobilization of the Russian population, drafting between 300 000 and 1.2 million men to fight against Ukraine, prompting demonstrations around the country.	Russia–Ukraine War
26 Sep.	Two Nord Stream pipelines delivering Russian gas to Europe are sabotaged by explosions in Swedish and Danish waters. The identities of the perpetrators and the motives behind the sabotage are unknown.	energy security; Russia–Ukraine War;
30 Sep.	President Putin announces Russia's illegal annexation of four Ukrainian provinces, Donetsk, Kherson, Luhansk and Zaporizhzhia, despite Russia occupying only part of each region.	Russia–Ukraine War
30 Sep.	A coup in Burkina Faso removes interim President Paul-Henri Sandaogo Damiba over his alleged inability to deal with the country's Islamist insurgency. Damiba had come to power in a coup just eight months earlier.	Burkina Faso; coup

October

1 Oct.	Ukrainian forces make Russian forces retreat from the town of Lyman in Donetsk, barely a day after President Putin announced Russia's illegal annexation of Donetsk.	Russia–Ukraine War
2 Oct.	The UN-mediated truce in Yemen ends as the warring sides reject a proposal presented by UN Special Envoy for Yemen Hans Grundberg to extend and expand the Apr. agreement.	Yemen
8 Oct.	The Kerch bridge, built by Russia to link Crimea to Russia and a symbol of Russia's illegal occupation of Ukraine, is partly damaged in a sabotage attack.	Russia–Ukraine War
12 Oct.	The UN General Assembly passes a resolution condemning Russia's attempted annexation of Ukrainian territory.	Russia–Ukraine War; UN General Assembly
16 Oct.	Flooding in Nigeria that began in early summer is the worst seasonal flooding in a decade, resulting in over 600 deaths and more than 1.3 million displaced people.	climate change; Nigeria

21 Oct.	A partial UN arms embargo is imposed on Haiti. Initially proposed by China in July, it is the only new multilateral arms embargo in 2022 and the first new UN arms embargo since 2018.	arms embargo; Haiti; UN
27 Oct.	The USA publishes an unclassified version of its Nuclear Posture Review (NPR) as part of its 2022 National Defense Strategy. The NPR establishes US nuclear policy, strategy, capabilities and force posture for the next 5–10 years. The NPR supports retention of a triad and continued investments in most existing major US nuclear modernization programmes.	nuclear weapons; USA
29 Oct.	Twin car bombs planted by al-Shabab militants in Mogadishu, Somalia, kill at least 120 people.	al-Shabab; Somalia
November		
2 Nov.	North Korea test launches at least 23 ballistic missiles, the highest number ever launched by the country in a single day.	ballistic missiles; North Korea;
2 Nov.	The Ethiopian government and Tigrayan leaders sign a peace deal that ends a two-year long civil war which displaced more than 5.1 million people.	Ethiopia; peace agreement; Tigray
9 Nov.	Russia announces a retreat from the strategically important city of Kherson in southern Ukraine, eight months after capturing the area, in one of the most significant reversals of the Russian war effort.	Russia–Ukraine War
9 Nov.	France formally announces the end of Operation Barkhane, a counterterrorist operation in the Sahel region that started in August 2014. France had begun withdrawing its troops from Mali on 17 Feb. 2022 and had fully withdrawn its forces from the country on 15 Aug. 2022.	France; Mali; Operation Barkhane; Sahel
15 Nov.	At the Group of Twenty (G20) meeting in Indonesia, Ukrainian President Volodymyr Zelensky proposes a 10-point peace plan to end the war in his country.	Russia–Ukraine War
15 Nov.	During a meeting on the sidelines of the G20 summit, Chinese President Xi and US President Biden agree to work to reduce mutual tensions and pledge cooperation in areas such as climate change and public health.	China; G20; USA
15 Nov.	The UN reports that the global population has reached 8 billion, just 11 years after passing 7 billion, although the rate of growth is now slowing down (expected to reach 9 billion by about 2037).	global population
18 Nov.	After many years of failing to make progress in addressing the humanitarian harm of explosive weapons in populated areas (EWIPA), a process led by Ireland results in the adoption of a political declaration on this issue by 83 states.	EWIPA
20 Nov.	The 27th Conference of Parties (COP27) of the UN Framework Convention on Climate Change (UNFCCC) at Sharm el-Sheikh, Egypt, ends with a loss and damage agreement that commits wealthy countries to compensate poor countries harmed by climate change.	climate change; COP27; UNFCCC

28 Nov.–16 Dec.	The ninth review conference of the 1972 Biological and Toxins Weapons Convention (BWC) agrees an intersessional programme of work for 2023–26 and establishes a working group on strengthening the BWC.	BWC

December

1–2 Dec.	For the first time, the annual OSCE Ministerial Council meeting fails to adopt any decisions, including a budget. Fallout from the Russia–Ukraine War is blamed.	OSCE; Russia–Ukraine War
5 Dec.	At least two of Russia's strategic bombers are damaged by a Ukrainian air strike on Engels airbase in Saratov Oblast, Russia.	Russia–Ukraine War
5 Dec.	Iran closes its morality police in a concession to three months of nationwide protests, but the police force seems likely to continue in a different form.	Iran
5 Dec.	The Sudanese military conclude a framework agreement with dozens of civilian leaders in which the generals promise to relinquish much of their political power.	Sudan
7 Dec.	After widespread public protests China announces a major loosening of Covid-19 restrictions, allowing home quarantine and scrapping Covid-tracking QR codes, and effectively ending its zero-Covid policy.	China; Covid-19
7 Dec.	The UN General Assembly adopts by consensus the Principles on the Protection of the Environment in Relation to Armed Conflicts, which call for designated protection zones, the application of international humanitarian law to the environment and rules to protect the environment during times of occupation.	environment and armed conflict; UN General Assembly
13 Dec.	The IAEA and Ukraine agree to establish a continuous presence at Ukraine's four nuclear power plants, with teams of nuclear safety and security experts.	IAEA; nuclear safety; Ukraine
16 Dec.	Japan announces its biggest military build-up since World War II, amid concerns over China and North Korea.	Japan; military spending
19 Dec.	The 15th Conference of Parties (COP15) of the UN Convention on Biological Diversity (CBD) successfully adopts a new framework for action to halt biodiversity loss.	CBD; COP15
20 Dec.	The Taliban-led government suspend university education for female students in Afghanistan as part of a wider crackdown on women's rights in the country.	Afghanistan; women's rights
26 Dec.	Taiwan reports 71 Chinese Air Force aircraft, including combat aircraft and drones, entering its air defence identification zone, in the largest reported incursion to date.	China; Taiwan
29 Dec.	The African Union Monitoring, Verification and Compliance Mission is launched in Mekele, the Tigray region of Ethiopia.	Ethiopia; peace operation

About the authors

Ana Carolina de Oliveira Assis (Brazil) is a Guest Researcher in the SIPRI Military Expenditure and Arms Production Programme. Her research interests are the drivers of military equipment spending, the arms industry, military expenditure and naval weapons procurement.

Dr Lucie Béraud-Sudreau (France) is the Director of the SIPRI Military Expenditure and Arms Production Programme, where her work focuses on the dynamics and implications of global military spending, arms production and transfers. Previously, she was a Research Fellow for Defence Economics and Procurements at the International Institute for Strategic Studies (IISS).

Dr Vincent Boulanin (France/Sweden) is the Director of the SIPRI Governance of Artificial Intelligence Programme. His work focuses on issues related to the development, use and control of autonomy in weapon systems and military applications of artificial intelligence. He regularly presents his work to and engages with governments, United Nations bodies, international organizations and the media.

Kolja Brockmann (Germany) is a Senior Researcher in the SIPRI Dual-use and Arms Trade Control Programme. He conducts research in the fields of export control, non-proliferation and technology governance. He focuses on the multilateral export control regimes, controls on emerging technologies, particularly additive manufacturing, and missile and space launch technology.

Mark Bromley (United Kingdom/Sweden) is a Senior Researcher in the SIPRI Dual-use and Arms Trade Control Programme, where his work focuses on national, regional and international efforts to regulate the international trade in conventional arms and dual-use items. Previously, he was a Policy Analyst for the British American Security Information Council (BASIC).

Dr Marina Caparini (Canada) is a Senior Researcher at the United Nations University Centre for Policy Research (UNU-CPR) and former Director of the SIPRI Governance and Society Programme. Her current research focuses on multilateral responses to transnational organized crime, and Chinese and Russian private military and security companies in Africa.

Anastasia Cucino (Italy) was an intern in the SIPRI Military Expenditure and Arms Production Programme. She assisted the team with collecting and analysing data for projects relating to military spending and the arms industry, including SIPRI's Top 100 Arms-producing and Military Services Companies and SIPRI's Military Expenditure Database.

Dr Ian Davis (United Kingdom) is the Executive Editor of the SIPRI Yearbook and an Associate Senior Fellow within Conflict and Peace at SIPRI. In 2014–16 he was the Director of SIPRI's Editorial and Publications Department.

Dr Tytti Erästö (Finland) is a Senior Researcher in the SIPRI Weapons of Mass Destruction Programme. Her research interests include the role of 'nuclear umbrella states' in the global nuclear order, arms control and strategic stability dynamics among China, Russia and the USA, the Iran nuclear deal and the global disarmament and non-proliferation regime more generally.

Vitaly Fedchenko (Russia) is a Senior Researcher in the SIPRI Weapons of Mass Destruction Programme, where he is responsible for nuclear security issues and the political, technological and educational dimensions of nuclear arms control and non-proliferation. He is the author or co-author of multiple publications on nuclear forensics, nuclear security and nuclear non-proliferation, including *The New Nuclear Forensics* (Oxford University Press, 2015).

Richard Gowan (United Kingdom) is the United Nations Director for the International Crisis Group. He is also an Associate Senior Policy Fellow at the European Council on Foreign Relations.

Lauriane Héau (France) is a Research Assistant in the SIPRI Dual-use and Arms Trade Control Programme. She undertakes research focused on dual-use export controls in the Middle East, risks of diversion and misuse following arms exports, and developments within the multilateral export control regimes. She also follows cooperation and assistance activities linked to the Arms Trade Treaty.

Dr Una Jakob (Germany) is a Senior Researcher in the International Security research department and Head of the Research Group on Biological and Chemical Weapons Control at the Peace Research Institute Frankfurt (PRIF). Her research interests include the disarmament and non-proliferation of chemical and biological weapons.

Matt Korda (Canada) is an Associate Researcher with the SIPRI Nuclear Disarmament, Arms Control and Non-proliferation Programme, and a Senior Research Associate and Project Manager with the Nuclear Information Project at the Federation of American Scientists (FAS).

Hans M. Kristensen (Denmark) is the Director of the Nuclear Information Project at the Federation of American Scientists (FAS) in Washington, DC, and a SIPRI Associate Senior Fellow.

Dr Moritz Kütt (Germany) is a Senior Researcher at the Institute for Peace Research and Security Policy at the University of Hamburg and a Visiting Research Fellow with Princeton University's Program on Science and Global Security. With his research, he aims to provide the technical basis for nuclear disarmament.

Dr Filippa Lentzos (Norway) is a Reader (Associate Professor) in Science & International Security at King's College London, where she is jointly appointed in the Department of War Studies and the Department of Global Health & Social Medicine.

Xiao Liang (China) is a Research Assistant in the SIPRI Military Expenditure and Arms Production Programme. He collects and analyses data on military spending and the arms industry. His research areas cover the opportunity costs and reduction of military spending, the relationship between military aid and development assistance, and regional trends in the Asia-Pacific.

Madison Lipson (United States) was an intern in the SIPRI Military Expenditure and Arms Production Programme. She assisted the team with collecting data for projects relating to the defence sector and space, and for SIPRI's Top 100 Arms-producing and Military Services Companies.

Dr Diego Lopes da Silva (Brazil) is a Senior Researcher in the SIPRI Military Expenditure and Arms Production Programme. He holds a PhD in peace, defence and international security studies from São Paulo State University. His research focuses on the interplay between political institutions and military spending.

Dr Sorcha MacLeod (United Kingdom) is an Associate Professor in the Faculty of Law at the University of Copenhagen, specializing in human rights and international humanitarian law issues around private military and security companies and mercenaries. She is also an independent human rights expert in the United Nations Working Group on the Use of Mercenaries.

Dr Iryna Maksymenko (Ukraine) is a Senior Researcher at the Odesa Center for Nonproliferation (OdCNP), and an Associate Professor in the Department of International Relations at Odesa I.I. Mechnikov National University. Her research focuses on European security and stability, and Ukraine and regional security, in particular the Black Sea and Eastern Europe.

Giovanna Maletta (Italy) is a Senior Researcher and Acting Director in the SIPRI Dual-use and Arms Trade Control Programme. Her research covers issues related to the implementation of international and regional instruments in the field of arms export controls, with a particular focus on the Arms Trade Treaty and the European Union and its member states.

Dr Zia Mian (United States) is the Co-Director of the Program on Science and Global Security at Princeton University's School of Public and International Affairs. A physicist, his work focuses on nuclear weapon non-proliferation, arms control and disarmament, and nuclear energy issues.

Dr Claudia Pfeifer Cruz (Brazil) is a Researcher in the SIPRI Peace Operations and Conflict Management Programme. Her research focuses on data and trends in peace operations, and the role of human rights in peace operations—particularly United Nations peace operations. She also maintains SIPRI's database on multilateral peace operations.

Dr Pavel Podvig (Russia) is a Researcher in the Program on Science and Global Security at Princeton University and a Senior Researcher at the United Nations Institute for Disarmament Research (UNIDIR).

Nivedita Raju (India) is a Researcher in the SIPRI Weapons of Mass Destruction Programme. Her research focus is space security. On behalf of SIPRI, she also coordinates research activities in the EU Non-Proliferation and Disarmament Consortium. She was previously a Research Fellow at Open Lunar Foundation and a Research Assistant at McGill University's Institute of Air and Space Law.

Dr Lora Saalman (United States) is a Senior Researcher within SIPRI's Armament and Disarmament, and Conflict, Peace and Security research areas. She also serves as a Member of the Committee on International Security and Arms Control (CISAC) and as an Adjunct Senior Fellow at the East–West Center.

Lorenzo Scarazzato (Italy) is a Research Assistant in the SIPRI Military Expenditure and Arms Production Programme. His research is mostly focused on the European arms industry. He collects and analyses data to support SIPRI publications and externally funded projects.

Dr Polina Sinovets (Ukraine) is the Head of the Odesa Center for Nonproliferation (OdCNP) at Odesa I.I. Mechnikov National University (ONU). She also works as an Associate Professor in the Faculty of International Relations, Political Science and Sociology at ONU. Her subject expertise is nuclear deterrence and arms control, states' nuclear policy, and nuclear security.

Timo Smit (Netherlands/Sweden) is a Senior Researcher in the SIPRI Peace Operations and Conflict Management Programme. He contributes to the maintenance of the SIPRI Database on Multilateral Peace Operations and conducts research on trends in peace operations and crisis management missions, in particular those conducted in the framework of the European Union's Common Security and Defence Policy (CSDP).

Dan Smith (Sweden/United Kingdom) is the Director of SIPRI. He has a long record of research and publication on a wide range of conflict and peace issues. His current work focuses on the relationship between ecological disruption and insecurity, on peace and security issues in the Middle East and North East Asia, and on global conflict trends.

Dr Ori Swed (Israel) is an Assistant Professor in the Sociology Department at Texas Tech University. He is also the Director of the Peace, War, & Social Conflict Laboratory, where he leads multiple research projects on new technologies and emerging security threats. His research focuses on the role of violent non-state actors in contemporary conflict settings, among them private military and security contractors and mercenaries.

Dr Nan Tian (South Africa) is a Senior Researcher in the SIPRI Military Expenditure and Arms Production Programme, where he leads the Military Expenditure Project. His research interests focus on the causes and impact of military expenditure and civil conflict, and the issues relating to transparency and accountability in military budgeting, spending and procurement.

Sanem Topal (Türkiye) was an EU Non-Proliferation and Disarmament Consortium intern in the SIPRI Military Expenditure and Arms Production Programme. Her work focused on collecting data for projects relating to the defence sector, such as military spending and SIPRI's Top 100 Arms-producing and Military Services Companies. She is a master's student of international relations at Bilkent University in Ankara.

Dr Wilfred Wan (United States) is the Director of the SIPRI Weapons of Mass Destruction Programme. His recent research focuses on nuclear weapon risk reduction, nuclear disarmament verification, and other issues related to arms control and disarmament. He is the author of *Regional Pathways to Nuclear Nonproliferation* (University of Georgia Press, 2018).

Pieter D. Wezeman (Netherlands/Sweden) is a Senior Researcher in the SIPRI Arms Transfers Programme. His recent research has focused on global trends in arms transfers, arms industry, small arms proliferation in Africa, transparency in armaments and multilateral arms embargoes.

Siemon T. Wezeman (Netherlands) is a Senior Researcher in the SIPRI Arms Transfers Programme. His areas of research include the monitoring of arms transfers and the use of weapons in conflicts, transparency in arms transfers, and the development of conventional military technologies and doctrines.

Index

3e Global 123
2030 Agenda for Sustainable Development 459

ABM Treaty (Anti-Ballistic Missile Systems Treaty, 1972) 597
Academi 129
AcidRain 490
Actinium 492
Action on Armed Violence (AOAV) 448
Advance Persistent Threat (APT) 490
Advanced Electronics Company (AEC) 204
Advent International 198
AECOM 196
Aegis Defence Services 123, 129
Afghanistan:
　arms embargo 532
　cluster munitions 453
　conflict 33, 37
　conflict fatalities 36, 37
　landmines 455, 457–58
　military expenditure 185
　peace process 57
　PMSCs in 105, 107, 108, 115–16, 120, 122, 123, 127, 129
　RSM 94, 95
　UNAMA 54, 102
　UNSC and 29–30
　women's rights 37, 638
Africa:
　arms imports 209, 233–38
　　conflicts and 216–17
　　table 236
　ATT states parties 520
　chemical weapons: Africa Programme 426–27
　conflicts 29, 47–52, 65–67, 216–17
　　fatalities 48
　counterterrorism 106
　coups d'état 51–52, 56
　Covid-19 pandemic 393
　military expenditure 158, 166, 167
　　2013–22 table 170
　　2022 172–75
　　burden 171
　Pelindaba Treaty (1996) 591–92, 610
　PMSCs in 106, 107, 126–42
　see also individual countries

African Commission on Nuclear Energy (AFCONE) 610
African Union (AU) 610–11
　arms embargoes and 527, 528
　arms imports 233
　CAR and 527
　conflict management 56
　Ethiopian peace process 51, 69
　Peace and Security Council 78, 92–93, 611
　peace operations 92–93
　　AMISOM 72–73, 78, 100, 632
　　ATMIS 69, 72–74, 78, 81, 82, 92, 100, 102, 217, 632
　　Libya 92, 102
　　MCVM in Ethiopia 69, 76, 92, 102, 638
　　MISAC 92, 93, 102
　　MISAHEL 92, 102
　　MOUACA 92–93, 102
　　table 102
　Somalia and 50
　South Sudan and 528
　Sudan peace process 59
Ahmed, Abiy 60
Airbus 200, 201, 204
Akufo-Addo, President Nana Addo Dankwa 137
Albanese, Anthony 365
Albania:
　arms imports 230
　ATT reporting 519
　biological weapons and 104, 403
　OSCE Presence 103
Algeria:
　arms imports 233, 236–37
　military expenditure 167, 172–73
　SALW and 459
Almaz-Antey 202, 206
Amazon Web Services 505
Amentum 129, 196, 198
Americas:
　arms imports 209, 236, 238–39
　arms industry 195–98
　arms transfers 217–18
　　transparency 477–78
　ATT states parties 520
　CITAAC 477–78, 593
　conflicts 35–36, 63
　　fatalities 34

Covid-19 pandemic 393
military expenditure 158, 159, 166, 167
   2013–22 table 170
   2022 175–81
   burden 171
OAS *see* **Organization of American States**
see also individual countries
Amini, Mahsa 370, 636
AMISOM (African Union Mission in Somalia) 72–73, 78, 100, 632
ammunition: control 459, 460–62
Andorra: ATT state party 513, 521
Andrzejcak, Raimund 160–61
Angola:
   arms imports 237
   cluster munitions 453
   conflict fatalities 48
Antarctic Treaty (1959) 566
anti-personnel mines *see* **landmines**
Anti-Personnel Mines Convention (APM Convention, 1997) 444, 454, 457, 458, 579–80
APEC (Asia-Pacific Economic Cooperation) 611
APMs *see* **landmines**
Arab League 525, 526, 534, 617
Argentina:
   HCOC and 481
   HEU 334
   landmines 457
   military expenditure 181
ARGUS 117
Arias, Fernando 425
armed conflicts:
   2022 table 61–68
   Africa 29, 47–52, 65–67
   Americas 34, 35–36, 63
   arms transfers and 208, 216–23
   Asia 36, 37–41, 63–64
   casualties 29, 61, 62
      Africa 48
      Americas 34
      Europe 43
      Middle East 46
      statistics 32–33
   categories 31, 61
   conflict management 52–60
   economic shocks 33–34
   environmental protection 435, 450, 638
   Europe 41–45
   global trends 30–35
   international conflict management 53–60

Middle East 45–47, 64–65
   numbers 29, 61
   political instability and 34–35
   regional trends 35–52
   trends 3, 8, 29–39
   see also specific countries
Armenia:
   biosecurity and 400
   cluster munitions 453
   conflict fatalities 44
   EUMCAP 94
   see also **Nagorno-Karabakh conflict**
Armor Group 123
arms control:
   conventional arms *see* **conventional arms control**
   treaties 561–600
      bilateral treaties 597–600
      regional treaties 586–97
      universal treaties 562–86
   see also **arms trade control**, **nuclear weapons** and specific treaties and weapons
arms embargoes:
   2022 table 532–34
   categories of weapon 525–27
   European Union 525
      Russia and Belarus 526, 533
      table 533–34
   monitoring 526
   overview 511–12
   survey 525–34
   United Nations
      categories of weapon 526–27
      compliance 531
      disagreements 526–28
      Haiti 525, 528–29, 532, 636
      Iran 529–30, 532
      Libya 530, 532
      numbers 525
      powers 525
      survey 526–33
arms industry:
   2012–21 trends 196
   Americas 195–98
   Asia and Oceania 198–200
   Covid-19 and 204–205
   Europe 200–201
   increased sales 158, 195
   Middle East 202–203
   private equity firms 198
   survey 195–206
   Ukraine war and 201, 205–206
   see also individual countries

arms trade control:
1925 Convention 562
ATT *see* **Arms Trade Treaty**
control regimes 512
dual-use items *see* **dual-use goods**
embargoes *see* **arms embargoes**
EU *see* **European Union**
FDI screening 551–54
multilateral export control regimes 541–49, 625–28
  see also specific regimes
overview 511–12
reporting 511
sanctions *see* **trade sanctions**
Ukraine war and 511
Arms Trade Treaty (ATT, 2013) 584
2022 developments 513–24
assessment 523–24
CSP8 511, 513–18, 520–24
Diversion Information Exchange Forum 511, 513, 517–18
diversion prevention 511, 513, 516, 517–18
funding 521, 523
implementation 514–18
international assistance 521–23
meetings 513
objectives 513
post-shipment controls 514–15
SALW and 445, 459, 460–61
states parties 513, 520, 521
transit measures 516
transparency and reporting 518–21
treaty universalization 521
UAVs and 446
Ukraine war and 514, 516–17, 524
UNROCA and 473, 519–20
arms transfers:
1950–2022 trend 210
2022 developments 212–16
armed conflicts and 208, 216–23
control *see* **arms trade control**
conventional and nuclear weapons 214–16
Covid-19 and 212
definitions 211
financial data 232
future transfers: estimates 223
global trends 209–23
importers
  2018–22 developments 233–44
  Africa 209, 216–17, 233–38, 236
  Americas 209, 236, 238–39
  armed conflicts and 216

  Asia and Oceania 209, 236
  Eastern Mediterranean 221–23
  Europe 209–10, 236, 241
  major importers 207–208, 210
  Middle East 209, 236, 243–45
methodology 211
multilateral export control regimes 541–49
  see also specific regimes
overview 207–208
regional statistics 212
suppliers
  2018–22 developments 224–32
  major suppliers 207, 210, 224
survey 207–45
transparency
  regional mechanisms 476–78
  UNROCA 471–75, 519–20
Ukraine war and 209–10, 213–14, 218–21, 225, 229, 236–37, 242, 557–58
see also individual countries
ASEAN (Association of Southeast Asian Nations) 611–12
ASEAN Plus Three (APT) 612
ASEAN Regional Forum (ARF) 612
Bangkok Treaty (1995) 590–91
East Asia Summit (EAS) 612
HCOC and 481
Myanmar and 30, 40–41, 56
Aselsan 203
Asia and Oceania:
arms imports 209, 236, 239–41
arms industry 198–200
ATT states parties 520, 521
conflicts 36, 37–41, 63–64
Covid-19 pandemic 393
military expenditure 158, 159, 166, 167
  2013–22 table 170
  2022 181–87
  burden 171
see also individual countries
Asia-Pacific Economic Cooperation (APEC) 611
ASIS International 124
Aslin, Aiden 152
Asociata RALF 140
ATK Group 116
ATMIS (African Union Transition Mission in Somalia) 69, 72–74, 78, 81, 82, 92, 100, 102, 217, 632
AU-MVCM (AU Monitoring, Verification and Compliance Mission in Ethiopia) 69, 76, 92, 102, 638
Aushev, Yegor 507–508

Austin, Lloyd 343
Australia:
  2022 elections 185
  arms exports 238
  arms imports 241
    major importer 210, 233, 239
    Spain 231
    United Kingdom 231
    US 214, 224, 227, 241
  arms industry 198
  AUKUS 215–16, 340, 352–53
  BWC and 410
  China and 215, 241
  climate change 629
  Covid-19 pandemic 630
  geopolitics 184–85
  military aid to Ukraine 185, 218
  military expenditure 169, 182, 184–85
  naval deployments in North East Asia 13
  outer space and 498
  TPNW and 365
Australia Group 625
  2022 meeting 543
  chair 543
  geopolitics 512
  nature of regime 541
  outreach 543–44
  participants 543
  scope 542–43
Austria:
  CCW and 447
  EU arms trade control and 553
  HCOC and 479
  military expenditure 161, 163
  neutrality 161
  NPT Conference and 354, 357
  TPNW and 360–61
autonomous weapon systems (AWS):
  2022 proposals 466–69
  CCW and 463, 464–71
  challenges 436, 463–70
  debate 463–64
  IHL and 467, 468, 469
  outlook 469–70
  Ukraine war and 464–66
AwfulShred 493
AWS *see* **autonomous weapon systems**
Azerbaijan:
  cluster munitions 451, 453
  conflict fatalities 44
  Russian–Turkish Joint Monitoring Centre 95, 103
  see also **Nagorno-Karabakh conflict**

Backdoor malware 486
BAE Systems 119, 200, 204
Baker, James 23
ballistic missiles:
  North Korea 313–14, 480, 637
  proliferation 479–80
Bangkok Treaty (1995) 590–91
Bangladesh:
  conflict fatalities 36
  contribution to peace operations 81, 83
Barkhane, Operation 47, 87, 97, 630, 637
Bashir, President Omar al- 51, 141
Baykar 203
Behanzin, Francis 74
Belarus:
  arms exports: Angola 237
  arms imports: Russia 214–15
  arms trade control and 511
  biosecurity and 400
  cybersecurity and 506, 508
  EU arms embargo on 526, 533
  Lithuania and 356–57
  MTCR and 545
  political protests 122
  Russia and 214–15, 440–41
  Russian nuclear weapons in 356–57, 633
  trade sanctions on 512, 535–50
  Ukraine war and 18, 41, 440–41
Belgium:
  arms imports from US 214
  CCW and 447
  mpox 395
  SALW and 460
  TPNW and 365
  trade sanctions on Russia/Belarus 538
  US nuclear weapons in 258
Belt and Road Initiative (BRI) 123, 128, 134
Bencini, Leonardo 407
Benin:
  conflict fatalities 48
  contribution to peace operations 97
  Mali peace operation and 88
  mercenaries in 109
BestChange cryptoexchange 508
Bharat Electronics 199–200
Biden, President Joe:
  arms industry mergers and 196–97
  IPEF and 633
  Myanmar and 40
  NPT and 343
  nuclear posture 15, 252–53

Pakistan and 301
Russian relations 341–42, 630
Somalia and 633
Taiwan and 12
worldview 9
Xi Jinping meetings 346–47, 637
Bilateral Consultative Commission (BCC) 344, 605–606
Binance 506
BINUH (UN Integrated Office in Haiti) 102
Biodiversity Convention (CBD) 16, 17–18, 638
Biological and Toxin Weapons Convention (BWC, 1972) 571–72
  9th Review Conference 391–92, 407, 409–12, 637
  2021 activities 391
  Article V 397, 399, 402
  Article VI 401, 403
  Article X 411
  developments 406–12
  Eastern European Group 410
  First Committee of UNGA and 391, 408–409
  outlook 412
  PrepCom 406–408
  Russia and 391, 397–405, 410
  states parties 391, 406
  Ukraine and 399–402
biological weapons:
  allegations 391, 397–405, 408
  BWC *see* **Biological and Toxin Weapons Convention**
  Geneva Protocol (1925) 409
  Ukraine war and 397–402
  see also **Australia Group**
Bitdefender 505
Black Sea Grain Initiative 6, 44, 54, 634
Blackwater 110, 129, 136
Blinken, Anthony 347, 504
Boeing 196, 204
Boko Haram 49–50, 65, 66, 97, 173
Bolsonaro, President Jair 181
Borrell, Josep 369, 370
Bosnia and Herzegovina:
  cluster munitions 453, 454
  EUFOR Althea 102
  Florence Agreement (1996) 592, 624
  landmines 457
  military expenditure 163
  OHR 95, 96, 103
  OSCE Mission 103
Botswana: ATT reporting 519

Brazil:
  arms exports 237, 238
  arms imports 238
  arms industry 203, 204
  biological weapons and 403, 404
  cluster munitions 453
  conflict fatalities 34
  floods 630
  HEU 334
  military expenditure 181
  New Agenda Coalition 355n38
  Ukraine war and 535
British Association of Private Security Companies 124
Brown, Louise 139
Brown and Root Industrial Services 115
Bulgaria:
  cluster munitions 453, 454
  FDI screening and 552
Burhan, Fattah al- 59
Burkina Faso:
  ATT reporting 519
  BWC and 410
  conflict fatalities 48
  contribution to peace operations 83, 97
  coup d'état 52, 217, 636
  jihadist violence 31, 47, 97, 137
  Operation Barkhane 630
  PMSCs in 137
  Russia and 47
  US relations 217
Burundi:
  conflict 48, 75
  contribution to peace operations 217
  PMSCs in 132
BWC *see* **Biological and Toxin Weapons Convention**

CACI 129
CaddyWiper 493
Cambodia:
  cluster munitions 451, 453
  landmines 457
  Myanmar negotiations 40
Cameroon:
  violence 48, 51
  Wagner Group in 133
Canada:
  arms control: FDI screening 553
  arms imports 227, 231
  ATT and 514
  military aid to Ukraine 218

military expenditure 169, 175–76, 476
outer space and 497
Cayman Islands: arms control 553
CCW (Inhumane Weapons Convention, 1981) 574–76
  2022 meetings 445, 447
  AWS debate 463, 464–71
  consensus rule 444, 445, 447
  EWIPA and 449
  incendiary weapons 446
  landmines and 454
  overview 444
  protocols 574
  states parties 445
  tensions 435, 445
CEEAC (Economic Community of Central African States) 527, 596, 613
Central African Republic (CAR):
  arms embargo 511–12, 526–27, 532
  conflict 51
  conflict fatalities 48
  EUTM RCA 103
  HCOC and 482
  landmines 456
  MINUSCA 79–80, 81, 82, 83, 84–85, 91, 98, 99, 100, 102, 132, 139
  MISAC 92, 93, 102
  MOUACA 92–93, 102
  peace operations 71
  PMSCs in 121, 132, 133, 137–40, 238
    Wagner Group 49, 69, 85, 89, 98, 99, 110–11, 132–33, 138–39, 144, 145
  Russia and 137–40, 238
CEO Group 121
CFE (Treaty on Conventional Armed Forces in Europe, 1990) 437–38, 442
CFE-1A Agreement (1992) 589
Chad:
  cluster munitions 453, 454
  conflict fatalities 48
  jihadist violence 49–50, 51
chemical weapons:
  allegations 413–24
    Russian allegations 408
    Syria 392, 401, 413–20, 423
    Ukraine war 392, 398, 422–24
  CWC *see* **Chemical Weapons Convention**
  destruction 425–26
  disarmament 425–34
  Geneva Protocol (1925) 409
  Iran–Iraq War 542–43
  Navalny poisoning 392, 419–21
  UNSGM 431
  see also **Australia Group**, **OPCW**
Chemical Weapons Convention (CWC, 1993) 577–78
  5th Review Conference 392, 432–33
  25th anniversary 392, 425, 632
  2022 developments 392
  Article IX 420
  Article VIII 419
  Article X 424
  outlook 433–34
  states parties 425
  see also **OPCW**
Chesterfield Group 123
Chile:
  arms imports 238–39
  Australia Group membership 543
  AWS debate and 470–71
  biosecurity and 402
  cluster munitions 453
  landmines 457
  TPNW and 362
China:
  arms control: FDI screening 553
  arms embargoes and 511, 531
    CAR 527
    Haiti 511, 528–29, 636
    Somalia 528
    South Sudan 527
    Sudan 528
  arms exports 230
    Africa 233, 237
    Albania 230
    Angola 237
    major supplier 207, 210, 224
    Mali 238
    Nigeria 237–38
    Pakistan 239
    Serbia 230
    UAE 244
  arms imports 239, 240
    major importer 210, 233, 239
    regional tensions and 216
    Russia 227–28, 240
  arms industry 158, 198–99
  ATT reporting 519
  AUKUS and 215
  Australia and 215, 241
  Belt and Road Initiative 123, 128, 134
  biological weapon allegations and 400–401, 403, 404
  border disputes 37–38, 185, 241
  Bosnia and Herzegovina and 96
  chemical weapons 425–26, 427
  China–Africa Action Plan 129

cluster munitions 453
Covid-19 pandemic 3, 393, 394, 638
cyber governance and 507
drought 4
economic growth 9–10
Ethiopia and 55
EU arms embargo 533
human rights 635
India and 37–38, 185, 294, 299
IPEF and 633
Japanese relations 184, 638
JCPOA and 368
military expenditure 10, 11, 158, 167
  2022 182–83
  increase 169
  top spender 181–82
  UNMILEX and 476
  US comparisons 176
Myanmar and 55
North Korea and 53
NPT nuclear state 355
nuclear arms control
  NPT Review Conference 353, 356, 357
  US bilateral negotiations 339, 346–48
outer space and 496, 498
peace operations and 85, 98
PMSCs 105, 106, 108, 109, 123, 142
  Africa 106, 126–27, 128–31, 134–36
  geopolitical competition 128–31
  role 142
Russian relations 8–10
  biological weapon allegations and 397, 404
  energy supply 191
  nuclear arms control 346
  Xi–Putin meetings 346–47, 397, 630
soft power 11
Taiwan and 4, 11–12, 38, 225, 634, 638
temperatures 635
Uighurs 635
Ukraine war and 9, 42, 535
UNROCA and 473, 474
US relations 11–13
  arms control 341
  North East Asia 12–13
  nuclear arms control 339, 345–48
  Taiwan 4, 11–12
  Xi–Biden meetings 346–47, 637
see also **nuclear weapons**
China International Trust and Investment Corporation (CITIC) 136
China State Shipbuilding Corporation (CSSC) 433

Chinese Enterprises Association 136
chlorine 415, 417, 418, 432
CICA (Conference on Interaction and Confidence-building Measures in Asia) 613–14
CIFTA (Inter-American Convention Against the Illicit Manufacturing of and Trafficking in Firearms, Ammunition, Explosives, and Other Related Materials, 1997) 593
Cisco Talos Intelligence Group 505
CITAAC (Inter-American Convention on Transparency in Conventional Weapons) 477–78, 593
climate change:
  Australia 629
  Brazil 630
  diplomacy 16–18
  displacements and 51
  effects 3–4
  floods 3, 4, 51, 173, 630, 632, 633, 636
  food insecurity 635
  Horn of Africa 630
  IPCC report 630
  Paris Agreement (2015) 16, 630
  South Africa 632
  temperatures 634, 635
  UNFCC COP27 16–17, 637
  UNFCC COP28 17
  United States 630
  US–Chinese relations and 12
Cloudflare 505
Cluster Munition Coalition 452, 453
cluster munitions:
  2022 developments 451–54
  CCM (2010) 444, 451, 453, 454, 582–83, 635
  clearance and destruction 453
  Lausanne Action Plan 454
  Ukraine war 435, 444, 451–53, 462, 635
Cobham 198
COCOM (Coordinating Committee for Multilateral Export Controls) 547, 628
Collective Security Treaty (1992) 72, 612
Collective Security Treaty Organization (CSTO) 37, 69, 71–72, 77, 100, 102, 612, 629
Colombia:
  arms imports: Israel 232
  conflict 34, 36
  landmines 456
  MAPP/OEA 103

peace process 30, 60
UNVMC 102
Colonial Pipeline 503
Commonwealth of Independent States (CIS) 613
Commonwealth of Nations 606
Comoros: mercenaries in 109
Comprehensive Nuclear-Test-Ban Treaty (CTBT, 1996) 578–79
Comprehensive Nuclear-Test-Ban Treaty Organization (CTBTO) 606
Conference on Disarmament (CD) 384, 496, 603
Conflict Armament Research 539
conflict management:
  geopolitics 52–56
  overview 53–60
  peace processes 57–60
  regional organizations 55–56
  UN institutions 52–54
Conflict Management Research 461–62
Congo, Democratic Republic of the (DRC):
  arms embargo 511–12, 526, 527, 532
  cluster munitions 453
  conflict 30, 50–51, 629
  conflict fatalities 48
  EACRF-DRC 51, 69, 75–76, 81, 82, 94, 100, 102, 633
  landmines 456
  MONUSCO 50, 81–82, 83, 84, 86–87, 90–91, 99, 102, 631
  peace operations 69
  peace process 57
  PMSCs in 136, 140
    Wagner Group 99, 133, 144
  Rwanda and 76
Constellis 117
Control Risks 123, 129
Convention for the Supervision of the International Trade in Arms and Ammunition and Implements of War (1925) 562
Convention on the Physical Protection of Nuclear Material and Nuclear Facilities (1980) 573–74
conventional arms control:
  ammunition 459, 460–62
  CFE Treaty (1990) 437–38, 442, 587–88
  European agreements 437, 438
  overview 435–36
  transparency and 471–78
    HCOC 436, 479–82
    regional mechanisms 476–78
    UNROCA 471–75
  treaties 435
  Ukraine war and 435, 437–43
  see also **EWIPA**, **Wassenaar Arrangement** and specific treaties
Cossacks 116
Costa Rica: cyberattacks on 632
Côte d'Ivoire:
  ATT reporting 519
  conflict fatalities 48
  contribution to peace operations 97
  MINUSMA and 88
Cotton, Anthony 347
Council of Europe 420–21, 614
Council of the Baltic Sea States (CBSS) 614
Counter Ransomware Initiative 484, 505
counterspace: meaning 485
counterterrorism:
  Afghanistan 37
  Africa 106
  Mali 47–48, 56, 87, 97
  OPCW and 431–32, 433
  PMSCs and 107, 108, 129, 130, 146
Covid-19 pandemic:
  2022 update 393
  arms industry and 204–205
  arms transfers and 212
  deaths 393, 631, 632, 635
  effect 3, 167, 177, 391
  inflation and 164
  legacy 158, 159
  military expenditure and 165
  origins 394–95
  pandemic treaty 395
  semiconductor shortages 201
  vaccination 393
  see also individual countries
Croatia:
  arms imports: France 229
  cluster munitions 453
  Florence Agreement (1996) 592, 624
  landmines 457
  military expenditure 163
CSIC (China Shipbuilding Industry Corporation) 199
CSSC (China State Shipbuilding Corporation) 199
CTBT (Comprehensive Nuclear-Test-Ban Treaty,1996) 578–79, 606
CTSAMVN (Ceasefire and Transitional Security Arrangements Monitoring and Verification

Mechanism) 93, 103
Cuba:
  AWS debate and 464, 465, 470
  biosecurity and 400
  incendiary weapons and 447
  outer space and 495–96
  SALW and 459
Cubic Corporation 198
CWC *see* **Chemical Weapons Convention**
cyber governance:
  2022 developments 501–509
  Counter Ransomware Initiative 484, 505
  international cooperation 501, 503–508
    with Russia 503–504
    with Ukraine 504–508
  state–non-state cooperation 507–508
  Ukraine war and 501
  United Nations 501–503
  see also **cyberattacks**
cyberattacks:
  Counter Ransomware Initiative 484, 505
  FoxBlade malware 484, 488, 491, 492, 506
  IHL and 486
  OPCW: attacks on 429–30
  overview 483–84
  PMSCs and 122, 124, 125
  space–cyberspace nexus 483, 485–88, 495
  Ukraine war 483, 487, 488–94, 501, 502–503
    government and industry 491–92
    power facilities 493–94
    space assets 489–90, 630
    telecommunications 492–93
  United Nations and 487
  Viasat 486, 489–90, 630
  see also **cyber governance**
Cyprus:
  arms imports 223
  FDI screening and 552
  UNFICYP 102
Czechia:
  arms exports: Nigeria 238
  biosecurity and 401
  military aid to Ukraine 218, 219
  military expenditure 163
  NATO and 22

DA-ASAT tests 483, 497–98

Damiba, President Paul-Henri Sandaogo 137, 636
DarkSide 503
Dassault Aviation Group 200
democracy:
  EU and 536
  US perspective 9, 129, 141
demography 637
Denmark:
  military expenditure 161
  NSG and 547
displacement:
  Africa 173
  climate change and 51
  Ukraine war 19
Djibouti 217
Dmarket 506
Dominican Republic: military expenditure 180
Doomsday Clock 4
DPRK *see* **Korea, Democratic People's Republic of**
drought 3, 4, 396
dual-use goods:
  EU control 512, 537–38, 550–51
    sanctions on Russia/Belarus 536–38
  NSG and 546
  see also **Wassenaar Arrangement**
Duterte, President Rodrigo 79
Dyck Advisory Group (DAG) 124
DynCorp 129, 196

East African Community:
  EACRF-DRC 51, 69, 75–76, 81, 82, 87, 92, 94, 100, 102, 633
  peace operations 92
ECOMIB (ECOWAS Mission in Guinea-Bissau) 74
ECOMIG (ECOWAS mission in Gambia) 93
Economic Community of Central African States (CEEAC) 527, 596, 613
ECOWAS (Economic Community of West African States) 614–15
  conflict management 56
  ECOMIB 74
  ECOMIG 93, 102
  Mali and 141
  peace operations 92, 102, 128
  SALW Convention (2006) 595
  SSMGB 69, 74, 92, 93, 102, 630
Ecuador:
  landmines 457

political instability 34–35
Edge 202–203
Egypt:
   arms imports 243, 245
      conflict and 216
      France 221, 229, 245
      Germany 221
      Italy 230, 245
      Russia 227–28, 245
      South Korea 231, 245
      United States 245
   cluster munitions 453
   conflict fatalities 46
   contribution to peace operations 83
   EU arms embargo on 533
   MFO 95, 103
   New Agenda Coalition 355n38
   United States and 228, 245, 352
   UNROCA and 473
El Salvador:
   military expenditure 180
   state of emergency 631
   violence 34, 36
Elbit Systems 203
Embaló, President Umaro Sissoco 74
Embraer 204
Enmod Convention (1978) 572–73
ENOT Corp 116
environment:
   armed conflicts and 435, 450, 638
   degradation 16
   TPNW and 340, 362, 363, 366
Equatorial Guinea: PMSCs in 109
Erinys 129
Eritrea: Ethiopia and 51, 59–60
ESET 493, 505
Estonia:
   arms imports: US 243
   cyber governance 506
   military expenditure 163
   NATO and 22
   Ukraine war and 440–41
Ethiopia:
   AU-MVCM 69, 76, 92, 102, 638
   China and 55
   contribution to peace operations 80–81, 82, 89, 217
   EWIPA use 447–48
   landmines 457
   military expenditure 175
   peace process 57, 59–60
   Sudan and 80–81
   Tigray conflict 5, 51
      casualties 32, 33

ceasefire 30, 631, 635
fatalities 48, 633
geopolitics 55
major conflict 29
military expenditure and 175
peace agreement 637
Turkish weapons 204
EUAM Iraq (EU Advisory Mission in Iraq) 103
EUAM Ukraine (EU Advisory Mission in Ukraine) 103
EUBAM Libya (EU Integrated Border Management Assistance Mission in Libya) 103
EUBAM Rafah (EU Border Assistance Mission for the Rafah Crossing Point) 102
EUCAP Sahel Mali (EU Capacity Building Mission in Mali) 94–95, 103
EUCAP Sahel Niger (EU CSDP Mission in Niger) 102
EUFOR Althea (EU Military Operation in Bosnia and Herzegovina) 102
EULEX Kosovo (EU Rule of Law Mission in Kosovo) 102
EUMAM Ukraine (EU Military Assistance Mission in Support of Ukraine) 94, 96–97, 557
EUMCAP (EU Monitoring Capacity to Armenia) 94
EUMM Georgia (EU Monitoring Mission in Georgia) 94
EUMPM Niger (EU Military Partnership Mission in Niger) 94, 96–97
EUPOL COPPS (EU Police Mission for the Palestinian Territories) 102
Euratom 329, 615
Europe:
   armed conflicts 41–45
      Ukraine *see* **Ukraine war**
   arms imports 209–10, 236, 241
   arms industry 200–201
   ATT states parties 520
   CFE-1A Agreement (1992) 589
   CFE Treaty (1990) 437–38, 442, 587–88
   Covid-19 pandemic 393
   energy supply 635, 636
   military expenditure 159
      2013–22 table 170
      2022 187–92
      2022 growth rates 162
      2022 statistics 166
      burden 171

Ukraine war and 157, 160–65
see also individual countries
European Defence Agency (EDA) 615
European Security Academy 117
European Union 615–16
  arms embargoes 512, 525, 526
    table 533–34
  arms industry and 201
  arms trade control 550–58
    common position 555–58
    database 555–56
    dual-use items 512, 537–38, 550–51
    FDI screening 550, 551–54
    US cooperation 554–55
  ATT and 521, 522
  Australia Group and 543–44
  biosecurity and 401
  chemical weapons and 422
  conflict management 55–56
  cyber governance and 501, 504–505, 506
  EU–US Trade and Technology Council (TTC) 550, 554, 625–26
  HCOC and 481
  incendiary weapons and 447
  JCPOA and 368, 369–70
  military expenditure and 189
  military technology 242
  NSG and 546
  peace operations 94–95, 128
    EUAM Iraq 103
    EUAM Ukraine 103
    EUBAM Libya 103
    EUBAM Rafah 102
    EUCAP Sahel Mali 94–95, 103
    EUCAP Sahel Niger 102
    EUFOR Althea 102
    EULEX Kosovo 102
    EUMAM Ukraine 94, 96–97, 557
    EUMCAP 94
    EUMM Georgia 94
    EUMPM Niger 94, 96–97
    EUPOL COPPS 102
    EUTM Mali 94–95, 103
    EUTM Mozambique 103
    EUTM RCA 103
    EUTM Somalia 102
    table 102–103
  PESCO 616
  PMSCs 128–31
  Somalia and 73
  Trust Fund for Syria Missions and 413
  Ukraine war and 30
    arms transfers 557–58
    chemical weapons 422
    FDI screening 554
    military aid 218
    NPT Review Conference 358
    sanctions 9, 535–38, 551, 552, 630
    Wagner Group and 133–34
Eutelsat 489
EUTM Mali (EU Training Mission Mali) 94–95, 103
EUTM Mozambique (EU Training Mission Mozambique) 103
EUTM RCA (EU Training Mission in the CAR) 103
EUTM Somalia (EU Training Mission Somalia) 102
Evergreen Coast Capital 198
EWIPA:
  2022 developments 445, 447–50
  Political Declaration 449–50, 637
  Ukraine war and 435, 447–48
Executive Outcomes 115, 123, 127

Faaxxx 503
Fancy Bear 490
Faxtrod 503
Fedorov, Mykhailo 488, 498, 506, 507, 508
Financial Action Task Force (FATF) 606–607
Fincantieri 200
Finland:
  BWC and 410
  military expenditure 163, 189
  NATO accession 189, 225, 442, 632, 633
  sanctions on Russia/Belarus 538
  TPNW and 365
  Ukraine war and 189, 538
fissile material:
  2022 global stocks 330
  civil use 328–29
  Israel 323–25
  North Korea 309–11, 312
  NPT Review Conference and 357
  overview 247
  types 328–29
  see also **HEU; plutonium;** individual countries
Flank Document (1996) 588
floods 3, 4, 51, 173, 630, 633, 635, 636
Florence Agreement (1996) 592, 624
food insecurity:
  climate change and 635
  global instability and 34–35

increase 3
Ukraine war and 5–6, 164, 634
foreign direct investment (FDI) 550, 551–54
Foundation for Strategic Research (FRS) 481
FoxBlade malware 484, 488, 491, 492, 506
France:
  arms control negotiations 339
  arms exports
    2018–22 229
    Africa 233, 237
    Americas 238
    Angola 237
    Croatia 229
    Cyprus 223
    Egypt 221, 229, 245
    Europe 242
    Greece 221–23, 229
    India 200, 229, 239
    Indonesia 229, 241
    major supplier 207, 210, 211, 224
    Mali 238
    Middle East 243
    Nigeria 238
    Qatar 200, 229, 244
    UAE 244
  arms industry 200, 201, 204
  AWS debate 471
  biological weapon allegations and 403, 404
  counterterrorism
    Africa 130, 132–33
    Mali 47–48, 97, 140
  Covid-19 pandemic 393
  cyberattacks in 488, 490
  EU arms trade control and 553
  Gabon and 217
  HCOC and 481
  HEU stocks 330
  Iran and 368, 529–30
  Mali and 47–48, 87, 97, 140
  military expenditure 187
  mpox 395
  MTCR and 544
  NPT and 279–81, 354
  NPT nuclear state 355
  nuclear weapons 247, 279–83, 357
  Operation Barkhane 47, 87, 97, 630, 637
  outer space and 498
  PMSCs 124
  Russia and Navalny poisoning 420
  Syrian chemical weapons issue 419

  Takuba Task Force 47, 87, 97, 140, 634
  Türkiye and 222
  Ukraine war and 282, 422
  UNROCA and 473
Frontier Services Group (FSG) 136
Fu Cong 346
Fujitsu 199

G4S 117, 123, 129
G5 Sahel 30, 49, 56, 97, 616, 633
G7 (Group of Seven) 398, 544, 607–608
G20 42, 347–48, 637
Gabon:
  African arms embargoes and 527, 528
  ATT state party 513, 521
  France and 217
Gamaredon 492
Gambia:
  coup d'état 52
  ECOMIG 93
GardaWorld 123, 129
Gazprom 635
gender:
  Afghan women's rights 37, 638
  chemical weapons and 433
  NPT and 359
  OPCW and 431
  PMSC regulation and 149–50
  SALW control and 436, 459–60
  TPNW and 359, 362
General Dynamics 196
Geneva Conventions:
  Additional Protocol I (1977) 565
  Additional Protocol II (1977) 565
  Convention IV (1949) 564
  mercenaries: definition 112, 144, 152
Geneva Protocol (1925) 407, 409, 562–63
Genocide Convention (1951) 563–64
Genscher, Hans Dietrich 23
Georgia:
  biosecurity and 400
  cluster munitions 453
  EUMM Georgia 94
  NATO–Georgia Commission 619
  NATO membership 25–26
  Russian invasion (2008) 10, 121
Germany:
  arms exports 230
    Egypt 221
    Israel 230, 326–27
    major supplier 207, 210, 224
    Nigeria 238
    Singapore 241

Türkiye 223, 230
arms imports: US 214, 227, 242
arms industry 200, 201, 204
ATT and 513, 514–15, 523
CCW and 447
cluster munitions 453
contribution to peace operations 94
Covid-19 pandemic 393
cyberattacks in 488, 490
EU arms trade control and 553, 556
HEU 334
Iran and 368, 529–30
Mali peace operation and 49, 87, 88
military expenditure 157, 187, 187–88, 206, 242
mpox 395
MTCR and 545
NPT Review Conference and 356, 358
OPCW and 429
outer space and 487–88, 498
PMSCs 124
Russia and Navalny poisoning 420
TPNW and 365
Türkiye and 222–23
Ukraine war and 157
   military aid 188, 218, 219–20
   military expenditure 242
   NPT Review Conference 358
UNROCA and 473
US nuclear weapons in 258
Ghana:
biological weapon allegations and 403, 404
CAR arms embargo and 527
conflict fatalities 48
contribution to peace operations 82, 97
Global Initiative to Combat Nuclear Terrorism (GICNT) 607
Global Partnership against the Spread of Weapons and Materials of Mass Destruction 608
Göbel, Thomas 511
Google 505
Gorbachev, Mikhail 13, 355–56
Greece:
arms imports: France 221–23, 229
ATT reporting 519
cluster munitions 453
landmines 457
military expenditure 161
Grenada: cluster munitions 453
Griffiths, Philip 548
Grossi, Rafael 309, 358, 385, 387, 388, 631
Grundberg, Hans 57, 636

GUAM (Organization for Democracy and Economic Development) 620
Guatemala:
ATT reporting 519
conflict fatalities 34
Guinea:
conflict fatalities 48
PMSCs in 132
Guinea-Bissau:
cluster munitions and 454
coup d'état 52
ECOMIB 74
ECOWAS SSMGB 69, 74, 92, 93, 102, 630
landmines 457
Gulf Cooperation Council (GCC) 616
Guterres, António 54–55, 89, 410, 632, 635

Hadi, President Abdrabbuh Mansur 57
Haftar, Khalifa 119
Hague Code of Conduct against Ballistic Missile Proliferation (HCOC) 626
21st ARM 480–81
assessment 482
ballistic missile proliferation 479–80
cruise missiles and 480
objectives 479
origins 479
outreach 481
transparency mechanism 436, 479–82
Ukraine war and 480–81
UNGA Resolution 481–82
Haiti:
BINUH 102
conflict fatalities 34, 634
peace operation discussions 76–77
sanctions on gang members 54
UN arms embargo 511, 525, 528–29, 531, 532, 636
UNSC and 29–30
violence 30, 36, 180
Halliburton 129
Hanwha Aerospace 199
health security:
Covid-19 update 393
mpox 391, 395–96
overview 391
survey 393–96
see also specific diseases
Hecker, Siegfried 310
Hermetic Wipe 491

HEU:
    2022 facilities 334
    2022 global stocks 330
    AUKUS submarines 215, 352–53
    JCPOA and 372–75
    North Korea 310–11, 312
    NPT and 215
    production methodology 328
Hindustan Aeronautics 199–200
Honduras: conflict fatalities 34
Hua Xin Zhong An (HXZA) 135
Human Rights Council 139, 471
Human Rights Watch (HRW) 447, 451–52, 455
Hun Sen 40
Hungary: NATO and 22

ICANN 488, 507
Iceland: ATT reporting 519
ICRC (International Committee of the Red Cross):
    AWS and 468
    incendiary weapons and 447
    PMSCs and 112
    Ukraine war and 54
IGAD (Intergovernmental Authority on Development) 617
    CTSAMVM 93, 103
    peace operations 92
    Sudan peace process 59
improvised explosive devices (IEDs) 446, 454, 456
incendiary weapons 446–47
India:
    arms imports 239–40
        conflict and 216
        France 200, 229, 239
        Israel 231, 239
        major importer 210, 218, 233, 239
        regional tensions and 216
        Russia 202, 227–28, 239
        South Korea 239
        United Kingdom 239
        United States 239
    arms industry 198, 199–200
    AWS debate and 464, 465, 470, 471
    biological weapon allegations and 403, 404
    China and 37–38, 185, 294, 299
    cluster munitions 453
    conflicts
        Chinese border dispute 37–38, 185
        fatalities 36
        Kashmir 37
        Pakistan 61, 185, 216, 294, 301, 631
    contribution to peace operations 82
    Covid-19 393
    HEU stocks 330
    landmines 455, 456, 457
    military expenditure 158, 167, 169, 181–82, 185–86
    naval deployments in North East Asia 13
    nuclear weapons 247, 294–99
    outer space and 498
    political instability 34–35
    Russian relations 9, 191
    South Sudan arms embargo and 527
    Ukraine war and trade sanctions 535
    UNMOGIP 102
    UNROCA and 473
    Wassenaar Arrangement and 548
Indo-Pacific Economic Framework (IPEF) 633
Indonesia:
    arms imports 186, 229, 231, 241
    arms industry 198–99
    conflict: fatalities 36
    contribution to peace operations 83
    military expenditure 186
    political instability 34–35
Industroyer malware 493
INF Treaty (Intermediate-range and Shorter-range Missiles Treaty, 1987) 273, 342, 598–99
inflation 31, 34, 158, 163, 164, 177, 190, 194
Infraud Organization 503
inhumane weapons:
    Convention *see* **CCW**
    multilateral regulation 444–62
    see also specific types of weapons
Inter-American Defense Board 622
Intergovernmental Panel on Climate Change (IPCC) 630
International Atomic Energy Authority (IAEA) 604–605
    AUKUS and 352–53
    fissile material and 329
    JCPOA and 15, 340, 368, 369, 370, 371–77
    North Korea and 309, 310
    nuclear installations resolutions 384
    nuclear safety in wartime 339
    pillars of nuclear safety 385–86, 389
    Ukrainian nuclear installations and 339, 358, 378, 380–81, 383–89
    diplomacy 635, 638

missions to Ukraine 386–88
warnings 631
International Campaign to Ban Landmines (ICBL) 455
International Code of Conduct for Private Security Providers 106, 147, 148
International Conference on the Great Lakes (ICGLR) 527, 617
International Convention against the Recruitment, Use, Financing and Training of Mercenaries 111–12, 146
International Court of Justice (ICJ) 605
International Criminal Court (ICC) 608
  Rome Statute (1998) 580–82
  war crimes in Ukraine war 452
International Institute for Strategic Studies 546
International Labour Organization: PMSCs and 149
International Monetary Fund (IMF) 162, 164, 191, 192
International Monitoring Mission in Mindanao 69, 79, 95, 103, 634
International Network on Explosive Weapons (INEW) 449
International Raytheon Technologies 117
International Stability Operations Association (ISOA) 124
Iran:
  arms embargoes 525
    European Union 533
    United Nations 529–30, 532
  arms exports: Russia 42, 220, 221, 370–71, 540
  arms imports 42, 245
  biosecurity and 400, 402
  cluster munitions 453
  conflict fatalities 46
  HEU 330, 334
  human rights 370, 636
  Iran–Iraq War
    chemical weapons 542–43
    nuclear installations 379
  Israel and 373, 375, 379
  JCPOA
    2022 developments 14–15, 340, 368–77
    arms embargo and 529
    Comprehensive Safeguards Agreement 371, 375–77
    end of continuous monitoring 371–72
    enrichment activities 372–73
    heavy water 375
    nuclear fuel production 373–75
    prospects 377
    revival attempts 369–71
    US and 340, 368, 369, 370, 377, 634
  landmines 455
  military expenditure 193, 476
  NPT Conference 352
  PMSCs 117
  political protests 340, 370, 636, 638
  Russia and 340, 368, 401, 402
    arms embargo 529–30
    arms transfers 42, 220, 221, 245, 370–71, 540
  SALW and 459
  Saudi Arabia and 530
  Syria and 419
  UAE and 530
  Ukraine war and 220, 221, 340, 370
  United Kingdom and 530
  Yemeni conflict and 243, 244, 530
Iraq:
  Abu Ghraib prison 110, 113
  arms embargo 532
  biosecurity and 400, 402
  cluster munitions 453
  conflict fatalities 46
  EUAM Iraq 103
  Gulf War (1990–91) 379
  Iran–Iraq War
    chemical weapons 542–43
    nuclear installations 379
  landmines 457
  military expenditure 167
  NMI 95, 103
  PMSCs in 105, 107, 108, 110, 113, 115–16, 117, 120, 123, 127, 129
  SALW and 459
  UNAMI 102
  US attacks on nuclear installations 379
  violence 33, 45, 635
Ireland:
  biological weapon allegations and 401, 403, 404
  CCW and 447
  EWIPA control and 435, 445, 449, 637
  incendiary weapons and 447
  military expenditure 161
  New Agenda Coalition 355n38
  NPT Conference and 354
  TPNW and 362
  Wassenaar Arrangement and 548

Islamic State 50, 118, 432, 629
Islamic State in Iraq and the Levant (ISIL) 432, 532
Islamic State–Khorasan Province (ISKP) 37, 631
Islamic State–West Africa Province (ISWAP) 49–50, 173, 633
Israel:
  Abraham Accords 203
  arms exports 231–32, 232, 236, 237, 238
  arms imports 230, 239, 325, 326–27
  arms industry 202, 203
  cluster munitions 453
  Geneva Protocol (1925) and 409
  Iran and 373, 375, 379
  military expenditure 158, 193
  NPT and 352
  nuclear weapons 247, 323–27
  PMSCs 124
  UAE relations 203
  UNROCA and 473
  see also **Palestinian conflict**
Israel Aerospace Industries (IAI) 202
Itaguaí Construções Navais (ICN) 204
Italy:
  arms exports 224, 230, 241, 243, 245, 474
  arms imports: US 214
  arms industry 200
  BWC and 409–10
  Covid-19 410
  EU arms trade control and 553
  military expenditure 187
  mpox 395
  Ukraine war and 219, 538
  US nuclear weapons in 258

Jamaica: conflict fatalities 34
Japan:
  arms imports 216, 224, 239, 240
  arms industry 198, 199
  chemical weapons 425
  Chinese relations 184, 638
  geopolitical competition 129
  HCOC and 481
  HEU 334
  IPEF 633
  military expenditure 12, 157, 158, 181–82, 183–84, 214, 638
  North Korea and 240, 314, 638
  outer space and 498
  plutonium 332, 336
  regional tensions 216
  UNROCA and 473
JCC (Joint Control Commission) 95, 96, 103
JF-G5S (Joint Force of the G5 Sahel) 97
jihadism 30, 31, 33, 35, 47, 49–50, 137, 140, 634
Jordan:
  arms exports 238
  biosecurity and 400, 402
  conflict fatalities 46
  contribution to peace operations 83
  military expenditure 193
JPKF (Joint Peacekeeping Forces in Moldova) 95, 96

Kaboré, President Roch Marc 137
Karakaev, Sergei 267–68
Kazakhstan:
  Australia Group membership 543
  CSTO Collective Peacekeeping Forces 69, 71–72, 77, 100, 102, 629
  military expenditure 182
  NPT Conference and 354
  political protests 37
  TPNW and 362, 363
Kenya:
  African arms embargoes and 527, 528
  biological weapon allegations and 403, 404
  conflict fatalities 48
  contribution to peace operations 217
KFOR (Kosovo Force) 81, 95, 103
Khan, Imran 37, 240
Kim Jong Un 306–307, 308, 314
Kinshasa Convention (2010) 596
Kiribati: TPNW and 362, 363
Kmentt, Alexander 360
KNDS 201
Korea, Democratic People's Republic of (DPRK, North Korea):
  arms embargo 532
  ballistic missiles 313–14, 480, 637
  cluster munitions 453
  fissile material 309–11, 312
  Japan and 240, 314, 638
  Korean War 379
  nuclear arms control and 340
  sanctions 53
  South Korea and 216, 240, 314
  Ukraine war and 340, 382
  US attacks on nuclear facilities 379

see also **nuclear weapons**
Korea, Republic of (ROK, South Korea):
   arms exports 231
      Egypt 231, 245
      Europe 242
      financial value 232
      India 239
      Indonesia 186, 241
      Peru 474
      Philippines 241, 474
      Poland 199, 231, 242
   arms imports 241
      major importer 239, 240
      regional tensions and 216
      US 224, 227, 241
   arms industry 198, 199
   cluster munitions 453
   IPEF 633
   military expenditure 182, 184, 476
   NNSC in the Korean Peninsula 95, 103
   North Korea and 216, 240, 314
   outer space and 498
   US relations 224, 227, 241, 456
Kosovo:
   cluster munitions 453
   EULEX Kosovo 102
   KFOR 81, 95, 103
   OMIK 95, 103
   PMSCs in 115
   Serbian tensions 45
   UNMIK 102
Kotin, Petro 388
Krauss-Maffei Wegmann (KMW) 201
KRET 202
Kuwait:
   arms imports 224, 244, 474
   biosecurity and 402
   military expenditure 193
Kyivstar 492
Kyrgyzstan:
   conflict fatalities 36
   military expenditure 182
   Tajik conflict 37, 61, 635

landmines:
   2022 developments 454–58
   Afghanistan 455, 457–58
   APM Convention 444, 454, 457, 458, 579–80
   CCW and 454
   clearance and destruction 456–57
   use and production 455–56

Laos:
   cluster munitions 453
   military expenditure 186
Latvia:
   arms imports: US 243
   ATT reporting 519
   cybersecurity 491, 506
   military expenditure 163
   NATO and 22
   OSCE and 440
   Ukraine war and 440
Lavrov, Sergei 343
League of Nations 562
Lebanon:
   arms embargo 532
   biosecurity and 402
   cluster munitions 453
   conflict fatalities 46
   NPT Conference 352
   political instability 34
   UNIFIL 81, 82, 89, 102
Leonardo 200, 201, 204
Leyen, Ursula von der 9
Liberia: biosecurity and 400
Libya:
   arms embargo 530, 531, 532
   arms imports 233
   AU Mission 92, 102
   cluster munitions 451, 453
   conflict 46, 47
   EUBAM Libya 103
   landmines 455
   military expenditure 172
   PMSCs in 105, 110, 118, 119, 133, 144, 238
   Russia and 105, 238, 530
   UAE and 530
   UNSMIL 102
   Wagner Group in 144
Lithuania:
   arms exports: Angola 237
   arms imports: US 243
   ATT reporting 519
   Belarus and 356–57
   cybersecurity 491, 506
   military expenditure 161, 163
   NATO and 22
   Ukraine war and 440
Lobaye Invest 138
Lockheed Martin 196, 204, 205
London Club 546
Luanda process 75
Lukashenko, President Alexander 122, 440

Luxembourg: sanctions on Russia/ Belarus 538

M-Invest 141
Macron, President Emmanuel 279, 281, 440
Madagascar:
  conflict fatalities 48
  HCOC and 482
  PMSCs in 133
Malawi: CCW ratification 445
Malaysia:
  arms industry 198–99
  TPNW and 362
Maldives: ATT reporting 519
Mali:
  arms imports 238
  conflict 48, 97
  counterterrorism 47–48, 56, 87, 97, 140
  coup 49, 238
  EUCAP Sahel Mali 94–95, 103
  EUTM Mali 94–95, 103
  G5 Sahel and 49, 56, 633
  jihadist violence 47
  MINUSMA 81, 83, 87–89, 90–91, 98, 99
  MISAHEL 92, 102
  Operation Barkhane 47, 87, 97, 637
  peace operations 47–49, 69
  PMSCs in 140–41
  Russia and 47, 49, 140–41
  Task Force Takuba 47, 87, 97, 140, 634
  UN Multidimensional Integrated Stabilization in Mali 48
  Wagner Group in 49, 69, 87–88, 89, 98, 99, 110–11, 132–33, 140–41, 144, 238, 631
Malta: ATT reporting 519
Manalo, Enrique 458–59
MAPP/OEA (OAS Mission in Suport of the Peace Process in Colombia) 103
Marchenoir, Stéphane 139
Mauritania: cluster munitions 453
MBDA 200–201
Mexico:
  Australia Group membership 543
  AWS debate 470–71
  biological weapon allegations and 403, 404
  CCW and 447
  Haiti and 529
  military expenditure 179–80
  MTCR and 545
  New Agenda Coalition 355n38

NPT Conference and 354
TPNW and 362
violence 34, 36
Wassenaar Arrangement and 548
MFO (Multinational Force and Observers in the Sinai Peninsula) 95, 103
Microsoft 484, 488, 505–506
Middle East:
  armed conflicts 45–47, 64–65
  arms imports 209, 236, 243–45
  arms industry 202–203
  ATT states parties 520, 521
  conflict fatalities 46
  military expenditure 158, 159, 166, 167, 169, 171, 193–94
  NPT Review Conference and 350, 351–52
  PMSCs in 117–20
  UNTSO 102
  see also individual countries
military expenditure:
  Africa 166, 167
    2013–22 table 170
    2022 172–75
    burden 171
  Americas 158, 159, 166, 167
    2013–22 table 170
    burden 171
  Asia 158, 159, 166, 167
    2013–22 table 170
    burden 171
  Europe 157, 159
    2013–22 table 170
    2022 187–92
    2022 growth rates 162
    2022 statistics 166
    burden 171
    Ukraine war and 160–65
  global trends 3, 159–71
    2013–22 165–71
    burden 168–69, 171
  inflation and 163, 164
  information sharing 436
  Middle East 158, 159, 167
    2022 193–94
    2022 statistics 166
    burden 169, 171
  overview 157–58
  regional developments
    2013–22 160
    2022 172–94
    2022 statistics 166
    changes 174

top spenders 169–71
  table 168
Ukraine war and 157, 159, 160–65, 169, 187, 189
UNMILEX 471, 475–76
see also individual countries
Military Professional Resources Incorporated (MPRI) 115, 129
Minimal Risk Consultancy 123
Minsk Group 621
MINURSO (UN Mission for the Referendum in Western Sahara) 102
MINUSCA (UN Multidimensional Integrated Stabilization Mission in the CAR) 79–80, 81, 82, 83, 84–85, 91, 98, 99, 100, 102, 132, 139
MINUSMA (UN Multidimensional Integrated Stabilization Mission in Mali) 81, 83, 87–89, 90–91, 98, 99
MISAC (AU Mission for the CAR and Central Africa) 92, 93, 102
MISAHEL (AU Mission for Mali and the Sahel) 92, 102
Missile Technology Control Regime (MTCR) 626–27
  2022 meeting 545
  geopolitics 512
  HCOC and 479
  membership 544–45
  nature of regime 541
  objectives 543
  outreach 545–46
  scope 542, 544
  UAVs and 446
  Ukraine war and 541, 545
  Wassenaar Arrangement and 549
Mitsubishi Heavy Industries 199
MNJTF (Multinational Joint Task Force against Boko Haram) 97
MNJTF/AI (Multinational Joint Task Force/Accra Initiative) 97
Modise, Thandi 173
Moïse, President Jovenel 180
Moldova:
  JCC 95, 96, 103
  JPKF 95, 96
  OSCE Mission 103
  Russian tensions 44–45
Molnár, György 548
Montenegro:
  cluster munitions 453
  Florence Agreement (1996) 592, 624
Montreux Document 106, 112, 147, 148
MONUSCO (UN Organization Stabilization Mission in the DRC) 50, 81–82, 83, 84, 86–87, 90–91, 99, 102, 631
Mora, Enrique 370
Moran Security Group 132
Morocco:
  arms imports 232, 233, 236
  conflict 47
  MINURSO 102
MOTAPMs (mines other than APMs) 454
MOUACA (AU Observer Mission to the CAR) 92–93, 102
Mozambique:
  cluster munitions 453
  conflict fatalities 48
  EUTM Mozambique 103
  jihadism 30
  PMSCs in 121, 124, 132, 133
  SAMIM 50, 79, 81, 92, 93, 100, 103
  Wagner Group in 132
Mozart Group 117
mpox 391, 395–96
MTCR *see* Missile Technology Control Regime
Multinational Force and Observers in the Sinai Peninsula (MFO) 95, 103
Musk, Elon 498
MVM 121
Myanmar:
  ASEAN and 30
  conflict 29, 33, 36, 38–41, 61
  conflict management 56
  coup 38, 51
  EU arms embargo 533
  landmines 455, 456
  military expenditure 186
  UNSC and 29–30, 40–41, 54, 55

Nagorno-Karabakh conflict:
  Azeri victory 45
  cluster munitions 453
  continuing tensions 45
  EU conflict management 56
  interstate conflict 61
  OSCE arms embargo 525, 526
  OSCE PRCIO 103
  peace process 57
  PMSCs in 144
  reignition 7, 635
  Turkish weapons 203
  UAVs 214
Nairobi process 75
Nairobi Protocol (2004) 594

Nakamitsu, Izumi 397, 410
Nakasone, Paul 504
Namibia: BWC and 391, 406
NATO (North Atlantic Treaty Organization) 618–19
  arms imports 233, 242–43
  biological weapons/chemical weapons and 398
  cluster munitions and 452
  cyber governance 506
  Euro–Atlantic Partnership Council (EAPC) 618
  expansion 9, 22, 25–26
    Georgia 25–26
    Sweden and Finland 189, 225, 442, 632, 633
  Istanbul Cooperation Initiative (ICI) 618
  Mediterranean Dialogue 618–19
  military expenditure guidelines 161
  NATO–Georgia Commission 619
  nuclear weapons
    deployment in Europe 356–57
    Russian comparisons 271
    US weapons 258
  peace operations 94
    KFOR 81, 95, 103
    NMI 95, 103
    RSM 94, 95
    table 103
  PMSCs 109
  Russia and 9
    conventional arms control 437–38, 439
    NATO–Russia Council 619
    negotiations 342
    Ukraine war 22–24
  TPNW and 353, 365
  Ukraine and
    membership 25, 44
    NATO–Ukraine Commission 619
  Ukraine war and 22–24, 30, 55, 633
    arms transfers 225
    military aid 218–19
Naval Group 200, 204
Navalny, Alexei 392, 419–21
NCSIST (National Chung-Shan Institute of Science and Technology) 200
neo-liberalism 127
Nepal:
  contribution to peace operations 82
  political instability 35
Netherlands:
  arms imports 214, 225, 243, 474
  HEU 334
  military expenditure 242
  mpox 395
  OPCW and 429
  TPNW and 365
  trade sanctions on Russia/Belarus 538
  Ukraine war and 218, 242
  US nuclear weapons in 258
Neuberger, Anne 506
Neutral Nations Supervisory Commission (NNSC) in the Korean Peninsula 95, 103
New Agenda Coalition 355, 357
New START (2010) 600
  2022 developments 343–45
  arms number: table 344
  BCC 344, 605–606
  expiry date 343, 348
  prospects 348, 355
  Russian compliance 260, 267, 344–45, 634
  Ukraine war and 341
  US compliance 249, 344
New Zealand:
  CCW and 447
  outer space and 498
  TPNW and 362
NewSpace 545
Nexter 201
Nicaragua: biosecurity and 400
Niger:
  ATT reporting 519
  conflict 47, 50, 97
  conflict fatalities 48
  contribution to peace operations 97
  EUCAP Sahel Niger 102
  EUMPM Niger 94, 96–97
Nigeria:
  arms imports 217, 237–38
  conflict 29, 49–50, 217, 629
  conflict casualties 33, 48, 61, 633
  floods 173, 636
  HCOC and 480, 482
  military expenditure 167, 173
  PMSCs in 124, 132
NMI (NATO Mission in Iraq) 95, 103
NNSC (Neutral Nations Supervisory Commission) in the Korean Peninsula 95, 103
Non-Alignment Movement (NAM) 355, 406, 608–609
Non-Proliferation Treaty (NPT, 1968) 568–70

10th Review Conference 4, 14, 340, 634
   AUKUS and naval nuclear
      propulsion 352–53
   Middle East issue 350, 351–52
   NATO weapons 356–57
   proceedings 349–59
   risk reduction 354–56
   Russia/US statement 345
   Ukraine war and 349, 356, 357–58
11th Review Conference 359
Article VI 354, 355
France and 279–81
gender issues 359
HEU and 215
Iran and 14
New Agenda Coalition 355, 357
NSG and 547
nuclear states 345, 355, 546
outlook 359
TPNW and 340, 353–54
United Kingdom and 275
Nord Stream I & II 635, 636
NORINCO (China North Industries Group Corporation) 199
North Korea *see* **Korea, Democratic People's Republic of**
North Macedonia: OSCE Mission to Skopje 103
Northrop Grumman 196
Norway:
   arms imports 225, 242
   biological weapon allegations and 403, 404, 405
   CCW and 447
   cluster munitions 453
   TPNW and 365
novichok 392, 413, 420, 423
NPT *see* **Non-Proliferation Treaty**
nuclear arms control:
   2022 developments 13–15
   bilateral negotiations 339, 341–48
      Chinese involvement 339, 345–48
      prospects 348
   bilateral treaties 597–600
   Doomsday Clock 4
   Middle East 350, 351–52
   overview 339–40
   prospects 340
   Russia–US strategic stability dialogue 339, 341–43, 629
   Ukraine war and 339, 341, 342–43
   see also specific treaties
nuclear installations:
   1980 Convention 573–74

   IAEA pillars of nuclear safety 385–86, 389
   pre-2022 attacks 379
   Ukraine war and 378–89, 385–86
      assessment 389
      Chornobyl 378–81, 386–87, 388
      IAEA diplomacy 635, 638
      IAEA missions to Ukraine 386–88
      IAEA response 384–88
      Khmelnytsky 385, 388
      Rivne 383, 388
      South Ukraine 385, 387, 388
      Zaporizhzhia 381–83, 386, 387–88
Nuclear Suppliers Group (NSG) 627
   2022 meeting 546–47
   control list 547
   dual-use goods 546
   geopolitics 512
   nature of regime 541
   NPT and 547
   objectives 546
   participants 546
   scope 542
   transit shipments 547
   Ukraine war and 541
   Wassenaar Arrangement and 549
nuclear weapons:
   2023 statistics 248
   arms transfers 214–16
   China 247, 248
      2023 table 286
      air delivery 286, 287
      HEU 330, 334
      ICBMs 289–91
      intermediate-/medium-range ballistic missiles 291–92
      land-based missiles 286, 287–92
      modernization 247, 287–88, 290, 293, 347
      nuclear posture 13, 284–85
      plutonium 332, 336
      sea-based missiles 286, 292–93
      survey 284–93
      transparency issue 284
   definitions 271
   France 247, 248
      2023 table 280
      air delivery 280, 281–82
      HEU 330, 334
      modernization 281, 282, 283
      nuclear posture 279–81, 282, 357
      plutonium 332, 336
      sea-based missiles 280, 282–83
      survey 279–83

transparency 279
India 247, 248
  1974 tests 546
  2023 table 296
  air delivery 295, 296
  cruise missiles 299
  HEU 330, 334
  land-based missiles 295–98
  nuclear posture 294–95
  plutonium 336
  sea-based missiles 296, 298–99
  survey 294–99
Israel 247, 248
  2023 table 324
  air delivery 324, 325
  fissile material 323–25
  HEU 330
  land-based missiles 324, 326
  nuclear posture 323
  plutonium 332, 336
  sea-based missiles 324, 326–27
  survey 323–27
  transparency issue 323
Middle East 350, 351–52
North Korea 247, 248
  2023 table 319–22
  cruise missiles 316
  fissile material 306, 309–11, 312
  HEU 310–11, 312, 330, 334
  ICBMs 315–16, 631
  IRBMs 315
  land-based missiles 313–16, 319–21
  MRBMs 314
  nuclear posture 307–308, 635
  plutonium 309–10, 332, 336
  sea-based missiles 317–18, 321–22
  short-range ballistic missiles 313–14
  survey 306–22
  tests 12–13, 184, 306, 312–13, 314, 315, 316, 317
  warhead production 311–13
overview 247
Pakistan 247, 248
  2023 table 302
  air delivery 301–303, 302
  HEU 330, 334
  land-based missiles 302, 303–305
  nuclear posture 300–301
  plutonium 332, 336
  sea-based missiles 302, 305
  survey 300–305
Russia 247, 248
  2023 table 262–63
  air delivery 262, 266–67, 272–73

army weapons 273
Belarus and 633
HEU 330, 334
ICBMs 266, 267–69, 344
land-based missiles 262, 267–68
modernization 262–63, 267–68
non-strategic forces 262–63, 271–73
nuclear posture 261–65
plutonium 332, 336
sea-based 262, 268–69, 271–72
stockpile 260
strategic forces 262, 266–70
survey 260–73
transparency issue 260
Ukraine war and 13, 24–25, 42, 214–16
United Kingdom 247, 248, 274–78
  2023 table 276
  HEU 330, 334
  modernization 278
  nuclear posture 274, 275, 357
  personnel issues 277
  plutonium 332, 336
  sea-based missiles 275–78
  submarine replacement 275–77
  Trident 257, 274, 275, 276, 277
United States 247, 248
  2023 table 250
  air-delivery 250, 254–55
  deployment in Europe 258–59
  HEU 330, 334
  land-based missiles 250, 255–56
  modernization 252–53, 254–55, 256, 257, 258, 259
  non-strategic forces 250, 258–59
  nuclear posture 15, 252–53, 347, 636
  plutonium 332, 336
  sea-based missiles 250, 256–58
  stockpile 249
  strategic forces 250, 254–58
  survey 249–59
  warhead production 250, 253–54
see also **fissile material** and **nuclear arms control**
Nyagah, Jeff 75

Obama, President Barack 252
OCCAR (Organisation for Joint Armament Cooperation) 619
OECD (Organisation for Economic Co-operation and Development) 553–54, 609
Olive Group 123, 129
Oman: military expenditure 167, 193

OMIK (OSCE Mission in Kosovo) 95, 103
OPANAL (Agency for the Prohibition of Nuclear Weapons in Latin America and the Caribbean) 620
OPCW (Organisation for the Prohibition of Chemical Weapons) 609
   5th CWC Review Conference 432–33
   2022 developments 426–32
   Advisory Board on Outreach and Education 431
   Africa Programme 426–27
   Centre for Chemistry and Technology 392, 428, 433
   contested authority 392
   Covid-19 and 428–29
   cyberattacks on 429–30
   funding 428
   inspections 392, 429
   international cooperation 426–27
   mechanisms 413, 414
   Navalny poisoning 419–20, 421
   organization 427–28
   Scientific Advisory Board 430–31
   security challenges 429–30
   Syria and 392, 401, 413–20
   Ukraine war and 422–24
   working group on terrorism 431–32
Open Skies Consultative Commission (OSCC) 621
Open Skies Treaty (1992) 438, 590
Oracle 506
OrcShred 493
Organisation for Economic Co-operation and Development (OECD) 553–54, 609
Organisation of Islamic Cooperation (OIC) 610
Organization of American States (OAS) 621–22
   Inter-American Defense Board 622
   MAPP/OEA 103
   reporting arms transfers to 477, 593
Organization of the Black Sea Economic Cooperation (BSEC) 622
OSCE (Organization for Security and Cooperation in Europe) 620–21
   Joint Consultative Group (JCG) 621
   Latvia and 440
   Minsk Group 621
   Mission to Bosnia and Herzegovina 103
   Mission to Moldova 103
   Mission to Serbia 103
   Mission to Skopje 103
   Nagorno-Karabakh and arms embargo 525, 526
   PRCIO 103
   OMIK 95, 103
   peace operations 95, 103
   Presence in Albania 103
   role 7, 30, 55
   SMM in Ukraine 55, 69, 70, 77, 79, 94, 95, 98, 103, 631
   transparency of arms transfers and 471, 476–77
   Ukraine war and 7, 637
   Vienna Document 435, 437–41, 443, 477, 596–97
outer space:
   2022 developments 495–500
   counterspace 485–
   DA-ASAT tests 483, 497–98
   Draft Treaty 496
   government–companies cooperation 498–99
   IHL and 499
   overview 483
   PAROS 496–97
   space–cyberspace nexus 483, 485–88, 495
   Ukraine war and 484, 496
   UN working group 495–97
Outer Space Treaty (1967) 496, 499, 567–68

Pacific Islands Forum 622
Pakistan:
   arms imports 230, 239–40
   arms industry 198–99
   chemical weapons and 427
   cluster munitions 453
   conflicts 37
      fatalities 36, 631
      India 61, 185, 216, 294, 301, 631
   contribution to peace operations 82
   floods 633, 635
   HEU stocks 330
   landmines 455
   military expenditure 186
   MTCR and 545
   nuclear weapons 247, 300–305
   political instability 34–35, 37
   United States and 230, 301
   UNMOGIP 102

UNROCA and 473
Palestinian conflict:
  escalation 8
  EUBAM Rafah 102
  EUPOL COPPS 102
  fatalities 46–47
  Gaza ceasefire 634
Panama: CCW and 447
pandemic treaty 395
Papua New Guinea:
  conflict fatalities 36
  military expenditure 182
  PMSCs in 109
Paris Agreement (2015) 16, 630
Partial Test-Ban Treaty (PTBT, 1963) 566–67
Patriot 132
Pawn Storm 490
peace operations:
  2022 developments 7
  ad hoc coalitions 95–96
  arms transfers and 217
  closed operations 69, 77–79
  contributing countries 80–83
  geopolitical rivalries 98–99
  host country relations 99
  new operations 69, 71–77
  numbers 69, 71, 72, 73, 74
  overview 69–70
  personnel
    deployments 79–80
    fatalities 89–91, 92
    numbers 69, 74
  regional organizations 91–86
  regionalization 99–100
  table 101–103
  tensions 69–70, 98–100
  United Nations 84–91, 102, 128
    fatalities 89–91, 92
  way forward 98–100
  see also **African Union**, **Collective Security Treaty Organization**, **European Union**, **OSCE**, and specific operations and countries
peace processes:
  overview 57–60
  see also individual countries
Peace Research Institute Oslo (PRIO) 128
Peacebuilding Commission (PBC) 604
Peaceful Nuclear Explosions Treaty (PNET, 1976) 598
Pecsteen de Buytswerve, Marc 464
Pelindaba Treaty (1996) 591–92, 610

Pelosi, Nancy 11, 12, 347, 634
Peraton 196, 198
Perspecta 196
Peru:
  arms imports 474
  cluster munitions 453
PESCO (Permanent Structured Cooperation) 616
Petro, President Gustavo 36, 60
Philippines:
  arms imports 241, 474
  ATT state party 513, 521
  biosecurity and 400
  conflict fatalities 36
  IMT in Mindanao 69, 79, 95, 103, 634
  military expenditure 182, 186–87
  NPT Conference and 357
  peace process 38
Pinner, Shaun 152
pipelines 503, 635, 636
plastic pollution treaty 631
plutonium:
  2022 global stocks 332
  2022 reprocessing facilities 336
  Israel 323–25
  North Korea 309–10
  production methodology 328
PNET (Peaceful Nuclear Explosions Treaty, 1976) 598
Poland:
  arms imports 199, 214, 227, 231, 242
  cluster munitions 453
  contribution to peace operations 94
  cybersecurity 492, 506
  military expenditure 161, 188–89, 242
  NATO and 22
  Russian relations 231
  Ukraine war and 55, 218, 219, 242
population 637
populism 130
Portugal:
  military expenditure 161
  mpox 395
  temperatures 634
Prak Sokhon 40
Prestige ransomware 492
Prevention of an arms race in space (PAROS) 496–97 **Prigozhin, Yevgeny** 111, 131, 133, 134, 137–38, 141
Prince, Erik 136
private equity firms 198
private military and security companies (PMSCs):
  Africa 106, 126–42

INDEX 669

geopolitical shifts 127–31
key actors 134–36
recent activities 137–42
conflict zones 115–20, 137–42
definition 111–13, 115, 145–46
growth 107–25
human rights violations 109–11, 124, 132, 139, 143, 144
ICOCA 120, 124
issues 109–11
key actors 120–24, 134–36
mapping 113–15
Middle East and North Africa 117–20
numbers 114
overview 105–106
professional bodies 124
proxy actors 143–47
regulation 106, 143–52
  IHL 143–47
  recent case law 151–52
  self-regulation 124–25
  United Nations 147–51
see also individual companies
Proliferation Security Initiative (PSI) 627–28
Puerto Rico: conflict fatalities 34
Putin, President Vladimir:
arms exports: Belarus 214–25
Chinese relations
  nuclear arms control and 346
  Xi Jinping meetings 346–47, 397, 630
Macron meeting 440
military self-sufficiency 539
NPT and 343
nuclear posture 265
Ukraine war
  annexation laws 382, 636
  justification 20, 25
  mobilization 636
  nuclear threats 42, 344
  recognition of separatist states 630
US relations: nuclear arms control 341–42
Wagner Group and 111, 131
Western opinions 24

Qatar:
arms imports 200, 210, 218, 224, 229, 230, 233, 243, 244
biosecurity and 402
military expenditure 193
UNROCA and 473

Ramstein Group see Ukraine Defense Contact Group
RAND 132
Ransomeware 486
Rarotonga Treaty (1985) 587–88
Raytheon Technologies 196, 205
Reagan, President Ronald 13, 355–56
RECSA (Regional Centre on Small Arms in the Great Lakes Region, the Horn of Africa and Bordering States) 623
Redut-Antiterror/Centre R 132
refugees see **displacement**
Regional Cooperation Council 623
REvil 503
Rheinmetall 200, 206
Richard, Charles 347
ricin 432
ROK see **Korea, Republic of**
Roketsan 204
Romania:
cluster munitions 453
NATO and 22
Rome Statute (1998) 580–82
Rostec Group 202
Royal United Services Institute 539
RSB Group 116, 119, 132
RSM (Resolute Support Mission in Afghanistan) 94, 95
Russia:
2014 invasion of Crimea 18, 33, 163
  EU trade sanctions 536
arms control and
  AWS debate 464–65, 467, 470
  BWC 397–405, 410
  CCM 452
  CCW 445
  CFE Treaty 437–38
  cluster munitions 453, 462
  incendiary weapons 447
  MTCR 545
  SALW 459
  trade control 511
  Ukraine war and 435, 437–43, 464–66
arms embargoes and 511
  CAR 527
  EU 526, 533
  Iran 529–30
  Libya 530
  Somalia 528
  South Sudan 527–28
  Sudan 528

arms exports
  2018–22 227–29
  Africa 233, 237
  Algeria 236–37
  Belarus 214–15
  China 227–28, 240
  decline 228–29
  Egypt 227–28, 245
  Europe 242
  financial value 232
  India 202, 227–28, 239
  Iran 245
  major supplier 207, 210, 223, 224
  Middle East 243
  Nigeria 237–38
  Türkiye 225
  Ukraine war and 229, 236–37
arms imports
  Iran 42, 220, 221, 370–71, 540
  Ukraine war and 220–21
  US arms 539–40
arms industry 202
Belarus and 214–15, 356–57, 440–41, 633
biological weapons and 391, 397–405, 408
Bosnia and Herzegovina and 96
Burkina Faso and 47
CAR and 137–40
Chechen War 121
chemical weapons
  allegations 408
  Navalny poisoning 392, 419–21
  OPCW issues 427
  Syria 415, 418, 419
Chinese relations 8–10, 53–54
  biosecurity and 397
  energy supply 191
  Xi/Putin meeting 346–47, 397, 630
conflict fatalities 44
cybersecurity and 489–94, 501, 503–504, 506–508
decline 10
energy market 9, 191, 635
Ethiopia and 55
food production 6
foreign reserves 192
France and 420
Georgian war 10, 121
Germany and 420
HCOC and 480–81
Indian relations 9, 191
international conflict management and 54–5

Iran and 340, 368, 369, 401, 402, 529–30
landmines 455, 457
Mali and 47, 49, 140–41
military expenditure 10
  2022 190–92
  components 190–91
  increase 167, 187
  top spender 169
  UNMILEX and 476
Moldova and 44–45
Myanmar and 55
National Wealth Fund 191–92
NATO and 9
  conventional arms control 437–38, 439
  NATO–Russia Council 619
  negotiations 342
  Ukraine war 22–24
North Korea and 382
nuclear arms control
  bilateral negotiations 339
  bilateral treaties 597–600
  NPT nuclear state 355
  NPT Review Conference 349, 357
  Russia–US strategic stability dialogue 339, 341–43, 629
  TPNW 340
  Ukraine war and 13, 359
  see also individual bilateral treaties
Open Skies Treaty and 438
OSCE and 55
outer space and 495–96, 497, 498–99
peace operations and
  geopolitics 98–99
  MINUSCA 85
PMSCs 109
  Africa 106, 126–27, 131–34, 238
  concerns 31, 105, 110
  Middle East 117–19
  operations 121–22
  prisoner recruits 122
  proxy actors 143–47
  regulation 111, 146, 151
  state objectives 108
Polish relations 55, 231
Russian–Turkish Joint Monitoring Centre in Azerbaijan 95, 103
Saudi Arabia and 530
Stock Exchange 508
Sweden and. 420
Syria and 401, 402, 415, 418, 419
trade sanctions on: effect 512, 535–40
Turkish relations: energy supply 191
Ukraine and

INDEX 671

1994 Budapest Memorandum 18
2014 invasion 18, 33, 163, 536
2022 invasion *see* **Ukraine war**
United Kingdom and 420
UNROCA and 473
US relations
  biosecurity and 398–402
  CFE Treaty and 437
  cyber governance 484, 503–504
  deconfliction line 631
  Geneva Protocol (1925) and 409
  outer space and 497
  Russia–US strategic stability dialogue 339, 341–43, 629
  sanctions 630
  Ukraine war 5, 538, 630
Western relations 7–8, 98
Western sanctions 6, 7–8, 10
see also **New START** and **nuclear weapons**
Russian Electronics 202
Russian Helicopters 202
Rwanda:
  arms imports 474
  contribution to peace operations 82, 83, 94
  DRC and 76
Ryabkov, Sergei 342, 343

Saab 206
Saadouhe, Brahim 152
SADAT International Defense Consultancy 118, 144
SADC *see* **Southern African Development Community**
Sadr, Muqtada al- 635
Safarov, Farid 493
SALW (small arms and light weapons):
  2024 Review Conference 460
  achievements 460–61
  ammunition 459, 460–61
  arms embargoes and 527
  ATT and 445, 459, 460–61
  contentious issues 459–60
  ECOWAS Convention (2006) 595
  gender and 436, 459–60
  Kinshasa Convention (2010) 596
  Nairobi Protocol (2004) 594
  RECSA 623
  regulation 445
  UN POA 436, 445, 458, 459, 633
  UNROCA and 472, 475
SAMIM (SADC Mission in Mozambique) 50, 79, 81, 92, 93, 100, 103
sanctions *see* **trade sanctions**
Sandline International 109, 127
Sandworm 490, 492, 493, 506
Sao Tome and Principe: coup d'état 52
SAP 506
sarin 415
Saudi Arabia:
  arms imports 243–44
    conflict and 216
    major importer 210, 233
    Spain 231
    United Kingdom 210–11
    United States 224, 243–44
  arms industry 203, 204
  biosecurity and 402
  Iran and 530
  military expenditure 158, 167, 169, 193–94, 476
  PMSCs 119–20, 121
  Russia and 530
  Sudan and 30, 59
  UNROCA and 473
  Yemeni conflict and 57, 193, 216, 243, 244, 629
Saudi Arabian Military Industries (SAMI) 204
Sberbank 508
Schmid, Christian 96
Scholz, Olaf 188
Seabed Treaty (1971) 570–71
SEAL 117
Sednit 490
semiconductors 158, 201, 204, 206, 537
Semipalatinsk Treaty (2006) 595
Senegal: contribution to peace operations 83
Serbia:
  arms imports 230
  cluster munitions 453
  Florence Agreement (1996) 592, 624
  Kosovo and 45
  landmines 457
  OSCE Mission 103
Sewa Security Services 132
Seychelles:
  ATT reporting 519
  mercenaries in 109
Shanghai Cooperation Organisation (SCO) 623–24
Sherman, Wendy 342
Shoigu, Sergei 19, 272, 343
SICA (Central American Integration System) 624

Sierra Leone:
  biosecurity and 400
  PMSCs in 115
Singapore:
  arms imports: Germany 230, 241
  arms industry 198
  cluster munitions 453
  military expenditure 186
Skylogic 489
Slovakia:
  cluster munitions 453
  NATO and 22
Soaeres Damico, Flávio 465
Sofacy Group 490
SoloShred 493
Somalia:
  AMISOM 72–73, 78, 100, 632
  arms embargo 512, 528, 532
  ATMIS 69, 72–74, 78, 81, 82, 92, 100, 102, 217, 632
  cluster munitions 453
  conflict 30, 50
  conflict fatalities 48, 635, 637
  drought 4
  EUTM Somalia 102
  HCOC subscription 479
  PMSCs in 130, 132, 135–36
  political instability 34
  UNSOM 102
  US policy 633
Sophos 505
SORT (Strategic Offensive Reductions Treaty, 2002) 600
South Africa:
  arms exports 237, 238, 244
  biosecurity and 402
  cluster munitions 453
  contribution to peace operations 93
  election influences 133
  floods 632
  military expenditure 173–75
  New Agenda Coalition 355n38
  PMSCs 105, 123–24, 127, 129
  TPNW and 362
South Korea *see* **Korea, Republic of**
South Sudan:
  arms embargoes 511, 512, 525
    European Union 533
    United Nations 526, 527–28, 533
  cluster munitions 451, 453
  conflict fatalities 48
  contribution to peace operations 75
  CTSAMVM 93, 103
  floods 4, 51
  PMSCs in 123
  United Nations and 634
  UNMISS 81, 82, 84, 86, 102
  violence 51
Southern African Development Community (SADC) 624
  peace operation 92, 128
  Protocol on the Control of Firearms (2001) 594
  SAMIM 50, 79, 81, 92, 93, 100, 103
Soviet Union: nuclear arms control 13
space security *see* **outer space**
SpaceX 488, 498, 499
Spain:
  arms exports 224, 231, 238
  EU arms trade control and 553
  mpox 395
Sri Lanka:
  landmines 457
  military expenditure 182, 186
  political instability 35
SSMGB (ECOWAS Stabilisation Support Mission in Guinea-Bissau) 69, 74, 92, 93, 102, 630
START I & II 599
  see also **New START**
Stoltenberg, Jens 452
Stop Killer Robots 470–71
Strategic Offensive Reductions Treaty (SORT, 2002) 600
Strontium 490, 506
STTEP International 124
Sub-Regional Consultative Commission (SRCC) 624–25
Sudan:
  arms embargoes 512, 525
    European Union 533
    United Nations 526, 528, 533
  arms imports 233
  chemical weapons and 427
  cluster munitions 451, 453
  conflict 51
  conflict fatalities 48, 632
  diplomacy over 30
  Ethiopia and 80–81
  floods 4
  landmines 457
  peace process 57, 58–59, 60, 638
  PMSCs in 141–42
  political instability 35
  Russia and 141–42
  Saudi Arabia and 30, 59
  UNITAMS 58–59
  Wagner Group in 132, 141–42, 144

sulfur mustard 415, 430, 432
Sunak, Rishi 187
surveillance technology 108, 124, 525, 533, 534, 551
Sweden:
  arms industry 206
  biosecurity and 401
  EU arms trade control and 556
  Mali peace operation and 49, 88
  military expenditure 161
  mpox 395
  NATO accession 225, 442, 632, 633
  Russia and Navalny poisoning 420
  TPNW and 365
Switzerland:
  ATT and 514
  MTCR and 545
  outer space and 498
  PMSCs 112
  TPNW and 366–67
  Wassenaar Arrangement and 548
Syria:
  arms embargoes
    Arab League 525, 526, 534
    European Union 533
  arms imports 233
  biosecurity and 400, 402
  chemical weapons 392, 401, 413–20, 423
  cluster munitions 451, 453
  conflict 33, 46
    fatalities 46
    Islamic State and 629
    Kurds and 629
  CWC accession 413
  EWIPA use 447–48
  France and 419
  incendiary weapons 447
  international conflict management 53
  Iran and 419
  landmines 455
  NPT Conference 352
  peace process 57
  PMSCs in 105, 110, 117–18, 121, 133
  Russia and 401, 402, 415, 418, 419
  Türkiye and 203
  UNDOF 102
  United States and 629

Tactical Missiles Corporation 202
Taiwan:
  arms imports: US 225
  arms industry 198, 200
  Chinese tensions 4, 11–12, 38, 225, 634, 638
  military expenditure 182
  Pelosi visit 634
  US–Chinese tensions 4, 11–12
Tajikistan:
  cluster munitions 453
  conflict fatalities 36
  Kyrgyz conflict 37, 61, 635
  military expenditure 182
TakubaTask Force 47, 87, 97, 140, 634
Taliban 33, 37, 57, 185, 457–58, 638
Tambèla, Appolinaire Joachim Kyélem de 47
Task Force Yankee Ukraine 117
TASS 508
Tedros Adhamos Ghebreyesus 635
Thailand:
  arms industry 198–99
  conflict fatalities 36
  landmines 457
  military expenditure 186–87
  TPNW and 362
Thales 201, 204
Threshold Test-Ban Treaty (TTBT, 1974) 598
Thyssenkrupp 204
Tier 1 Group 121
Tlatelolco Treaty (1967) 586–87
Togo:
  conflict fatalities 48
  contribution to peace operations 83, 97
  military expenditure 175
Tokayev, President Kassym-Jomart 71–72
Touadéra, President Faustin-Archange 137–38
TPNW (Treaty on the Prohibition of Nuclear Weapons, 2017) 585–86
  1st Meeting of Parties 340, 354
    decisions 361–62, 633
    Declaration 364
    preparations 360–61
    proceedings 360–67
  environmental remediation 340, 362, 363, 366
  gender issues 362
  NPT and 340, 353–54
  outlook 366–67
  ratifications 361, 367
  time limits 361–62
  umbrella states 365–66
  victim assistance 340, 362, 363, 366
  Vienna Action Plan 362–64

Trade and Technology Council (TTC) 550, 554, 625–26
trade sanctions:
  European Union
    chemical weapons and 422
    Ukraine war 9, 535–38, 551, 552–53, 630
  North Korea and China 53
  Ukraine war and
    arms industry effect 205, 206
    bypassing 539–40
    categories 535
    EU sanctions 9, 535–38, 551, 552–53, 630
    impact 6, 7–8, 10, 22, 33–34, 164, 191, 512, 539–40
    JCPOA and 369
    multilateral export control regimes and 541–42
    United States 535, 536, 538, 630
  see also **arms embargoes**
Trinidad and Tobago: conflict: fatalities 34
Triple Canopy 129
Trojan malware 486
Trump, President Donald 15, 252, 368, 633
Truss, Elizabeth 187
Tshisekedi, President Félix 140
TTBT (Threshold Test-Ban Treaty, 1974) 598
Tunisia: military expenditure 172
Türkiye:
  arms exports 213, 238, 244, 474
  arms imports 222–23, 223, 225, 230
  arms industry 202, 203–204
  cluster munitions 453
  conflict fatalities 46
  France and 222
  geopolitical competition 129
  Germany and 222–23
  landmines 457
  military expenditure 194
  PMSCs 106, 117, 118, 143
  Russian energy supply 191
  Russian–Turkish Joint Monitoring Centre in Azerbaijan 95, 103
  Syria and 203
  Ukraine war and 54, 535
  UNROCA and 473, 474
  US nuclear weapons in 258
Turkish Aerospace 202, 203

UAVs 203, 204, 213, 214, 220, 223, 244, 446, 529, 530, 544, 548
Uganda:
  arms imports and conflict 217
  biosecurity and 400
  conflict fatalities 48
  contribution to peace operations 75, 217
  drought 4
  forces in DRC 75
  PMSCs in 124
Ukraine:
  1994 Budapest Memorandum 18
  2014 Russian invasion 18, 33
    effect on military expenditure 163
    EU trade sanctions 536
  arms exports: Nigeria 238
  arms imports 213–14, 241
    European Peace Facility 557–58
    major importer 218–21
    Türkiye 213
    United States 225–27
  biological weapons: allegations 397–405
  CCM and 452
  cluster munitions 453
  conflict fatalities 44
  contribution to peace operations 96
  cyber governance and 501, 504–508
  economy 192
  EUAM Ukraine 103
  EUMAM Ukraine 94, 96–97, 557
  food production 6
  Iran and 529–30
  landmines 457
  military aid to 192, 218–21
    arms industry and 201, 205
    Australia 185, 218
    Canada 218
    Germany 188
    types of weapons 219–21
    US 177–79, 205–206, 218, 219, 221
  military expenditure 169, 192
  NATO and 25, 44, 619
  nuclear installations 358, 378–89
  OSCE SMM in Ukraine 55, 69, 70, 77, 79, 94, 95, 98, 103, 631
  outer space and 498–99
  PMSCs in 110, 116–17, 121, 133
  Russian war *see* **Ukraine war**
  UNROCA and 473
  Wagner Group in 106, 111, 116–17, 122, 143, 144, 145–46

Ukraine Defense Contact Group (Ramstein Group) 205, 219, 632
Ukraine war:
  2022 developments 41–44
  arms control and 435, 437–43
  arms industry and 201, 205–206
  arms trade control and 511
    EU FDI screening 552–53
  arms transfers and 209–10, 213–14
    2022 218–21, 225
    Europe 242, 557–58
    Russian exports 229, 236–37
  ATT and 514, 516–17, 524
  AWS debate and 464–66
  biological weapon allegations 391, 397–402
  Black Sea Grain Initiative 6, 44, 54, 634
  casualties 19, 32, 33, 61
  Chasiv Yar attack 634
  chemical weapons allegations 392, 398, 422–24
  China and 9, 42, 535
  cluster munitions 435, 444, 451–53, 462, 635
  conflict category 29, 61
  conflict management 53–56
  cyberwarfare 483, 487, 488, 488–94, 501, 502–503, 630
  destruction 19–20
  effects 29
    economics 34
    Europe 7
    food supply 5–6, 164, 634
    global impact 3
    global instability 35
    humanitarian impact 632
    inflation 177
    OSCE SMM 70, 77
    peace operations 96, 98–99
  Engels air strike 267, 637
  European Union and
    arms transfers 557–58
    FDI screening 552–53, 554
  EWIPA use 447–48
  facts and figures 18–20
  France and 282
  HCOC and 436, 480–81
  incendiary weapons 446–47
  infrastructure destruction 19–20
  international conflict management 53–55
  internationalization of civil wars 33
  Iran and 370
  Kerch bridge attack 42, 636
  Kyiv attacks 632
  landmines 455
  Mariupol siege 41–42, 54, 631, 633
  mass graves 636
  media and 30
  military expenditure and 157, 159, 160–65, 169, 187, 189
  Moskva sinking 42, 632
  multilateral export control regimes and 541–42, 545, 547
  NPT Review Conference and 349, 356, 357–58
  nuclear arms control and 339, 341, 342–43
    TPNW 364
  nuclear installations and 339, 358, 378–89
    assessment 389
    Chornobyl 378–81, 386–87, 388
    IAEA diplomacy 635, 638
    IAEA missions to Ukraine 386–88
    IAEA response 384–88
    IAEA warnings 631
    Khmelnytsky 383, 388
    Rivne 383, 388
    South Ukraine 383, 387, 388
    Zaporizhzhia 381–83, 386, 387–88
  nuclear weapons threat 13, 24–25, 42, 214–16, 261–65, 344
  OSCE and 7, 637
  outer space and 484
  peace process 57
  PMSCs in 105, 106, 116–17
    case law 152
    Wagner Group 19, 106, 111, 116–17, 122, 143, 144, 145–46
  prospects 25–26
  refugees 630
  Russian annexations 382, 636
  Russian defeats 636, 637
  Russian false flag operations 507
  Russian goals 20–21
  Russian mobilization 636
  Russian paramilitary troops 190–91
  Russian strategic bombers 267
  Russian withdrawal from Kyiv 631, 632
  sanctions *see* **trade sanctions**
  significance 5
  space–cyberspace nexus 483
  Ukrainian defeats 633
  Ukrainian weapons 203
  UN and 9, 18–19, 31–32, 42, 49, 53, 70, 382, 448, 636
  United States and *see* **United States**

war crimes 452, 632, 636
Western involvement 20–24
   aid 21–22
   NATO 22–24
   sanctions *see* **trade sanctions**
Ukrtelecom 492–93
Ultra Electronics 198
UN Framework Convention on Climate Change (UNFCC) 16–17, 637
UNAMA (UN Assistance Mission in Afghanistan) 54, 102
UNAMI (UN Assistance Mission in Iraq) 102
UNASUR (Union of South American Nations) 625
UNDC (UN Disarmament Commission) 604
UNDOF (UN Disengagement Observer Force) 102
UNFICYP (UN Peacekeeping Force in Cyprus) 102
Unicc 503
UNIFIL (UN Interim Force in Lebanon) 81, 82, 89, 102
UNISFA (UN Interim Security Force for Abyei) 80, 81, 82, 89, 102
UNITAD 432
UNITAMS (UN Integrated Transition Assistance Mission in Sudan) 58–59
United Aircraft Corporation (UAC) 202
United Arab Emirates (UAE):
   arms exports: Mali 238
   arms imports 244, 474
   arms industry 202–203
   biological weapon allegations and 402, 403, 404
   geopolitical competition 129
   HCOC and 481
   Iran and 530
   Israeli relations 203
   Libya and 530
   MTCR and 545
   PMSCs 119–20
   Russia and 530
   Sudan peace process 59
   Yemeni conflict and 57, 216, 243, 629
United Engine Corporation (UEC) 202
United Kingdom:
   arms control 339, 553
   arms exports 224, 230–31
      competition 210–11
      India 239
      Indonesia 241
      Qatar 244
      Saudi Arabia 210–11
      United States 238
      UNROCA and 474
   arms imports 225, 240, 241
   arms industry 200, 204
   AUKUS 215–16, 340, 352–53
   AWS debate and 467
   biological weapon allegations and 403
   HEU stocks 330
   Iran and 529–30, 530
   Mali peace operation and 49, 87
   military expenditure 167, 187, 476
   mpox 395
   naval deployments in North East Asia 13
   NPT and 275, 547
   NPT nuclear state 355
   NSG and 547
   nuclear weapons 247, 257, 274–78, 357
   outer space and 495, 498
   PMSCs 105, 109, 123, 127, 129
   Russia and Navalny poisoning 420
   Sudan peace process 59
   Ukraine war and
      chemical weapons 423
      cyberattacks 490
      military aid 218, 219
      trade sanctions 535
   UNROCA and 473, 474
United Nations 601–603
   2030 Agenda for Sustainable Development 459
   ammunition control and 461–62
   chemical weapons and 431
   cluster munitions control 452
   cybersecurity and 484, 487, 501–503
   environmental protection in armed conflicts 435, 450, 638
   EWIPA control 449–50
   First Committee
      AWS debate 471
      BWC and 391, 408–409
      cyber governance 484
      IEDs and 454
      SALW 458
   global population report 637
   HCOC resolution 481–82
   High Commissioner for Human Rights 635
   Human Rights Council 139, 471
   international conflict management 53–55
   Mine Action Service (UNMAS) 461
   Myanmar and 19–30, 40–41, 54, 55

outer space and 483, 495–97
Pakistan and 635
plastic pollution treaty 631
PMSCs and 115, 124, 147–51
SALW POA 436, 445, 458, 459, 633
South Sudan and 634
Sudan peace process 59
TPNW and 365
UAVs and 446
Ukraine war and 9
   annexations 382, 636
   EWIPA use 448
   statistics 18–19
UNODA 407, 458, 601
Women and Peace and Security Agenda 459
World Food Programme 6, 630, 635
Yemen and 57–58, 636
see also **peace operations**, **United Nations Security Council** and **UNROCA**
United Nations Security Council 603
   armed conflicts and 29–30
   arms embargoes 525, 526–33
   biological weapon allegations and 391, 397–98, 401, 403–405
   conflict management 54
   DRC and 140
   effectiveness 7, 8
   Ethiopia and 55
   geopolitics and peace operations 98
   Haiti and 76–77
   Iran and: JCPOA 14–15
   Mali and 87
   Myanmar and 29–30, 40–41, 54, 55
   North Korea and 340
   P5 nuclear war statement (2022) 13–14, 261, 339, 341, 347–48, 355–56, 629
   Somalia and 50, 78
   Syria and 57
   TPNW and 353
   Ukraine war and 31–32, 42, 49, 53, 70
   see also **peace operations**
United Shipbuilding Corporation (USC) 202
United States:
   arms control and
     AWS debate 467, 468, 471
     CCM 452–53
     chemical weapons 392, 425–26, 433
     cluster munitions 453
     FDI screening 553
     Geneva Protocol (1925) 409
     landmines 435–36, 455, 456, 457, 633

     SALW 459
   arms embargoes and 512, 529–30
   arms exports
     2018–22 developments 224–27
     Africa 233
     Americas 238
     Angola 237
     Asia and Oceania 239, 240
     Australia 214, 224, 227, 241
     Baltic states 243
     Belgium 214
     Egypt 245
     Europe 242
     Germany 214, 227, 242
     India 239
     Israel 325
     Italy 214
     Japan 224, 240
     Kuwait 244
     major supplier 207, 210, 223
     Mali 238
     Middle East 243–44
     Morocco 236
     Netherlands 214
     Nigeria 238
     Qatar 224, 244
     Russia 539–40
     Saudi Arabia 224, 243–44
     South Korea 224, 227, 241
     United Kingdom 225, 240
     UNROCA and 474–75
   arms imports 216, 238, 474
   arms industry 158, 195–98
   arms trade control 549, 554–55
     transparency of arms transfers 474–75, 477
   AUKUS 215–16, 340, 352–53
   border control 121
   Burkina Faso and 217
   Chinese relations 11–13
     arms control 339, 341, 345–48
     North East Asia 12–13
     nuclear arms control 346–48
     nuclear assessments 284, 285, 287, 289, 290, 291–92, 293, 347
     Taiwan 4, 11–12
     Xi–Biden meetings 637
   climate change 630
   counterterrorism 37, 107, 129–30
   Covid-19 pandemic 164, 393, 394–95, 629, 632
   cyber governance and 488, 501, 503, 504–506
   democracy and 19, 129, 141

Egypt and 228, 245, 352
EU–US Trade and Technology Council (TTC) 550, 554, 625–26
Guam bases 291
Haiti and 529
India and 299
inflation 177
IPEF 633
Iran and
   arms embargo 529–30
   JCPOA 340, 368, 369, 370, 377, 634
Iraq: Gulf War 379
Israel and 323–24
Korean War 379
military expenditure 158, 167, 169, 176–79, 476
North Korea and 310–11, 315, 318, 379
NPT nuclear state 355
nuclear arms control
   bilateral negotiations 339
   bilateral treaties 597–600
   China and 346–48
   INF suspension 273, 342
   NPT Conference 352
   Russia–US strategic stability dialogue 339, 341–43, 629
   Soviet era 13
   TPNW 340, 365
   Ukraine war and 13
   see also individual bilateral treaties
Open Skies Treaty and 438
OSCE and 477
outer space and 497–98
Pakistan and 230, 301
PMSCs 105, 107, 109–10
   Africa 128–31
   geopolitical competition 128–31
   Iraq and Afghanistan 115–16
   operations 120–21
   regulation 113
   services 127
   use 117
Russian relations
   biosecurity and 397, 398–402
   CFE Treaty and 437
   cyber governance 484, 503–504
   deconfliction line 631
   Geneva Protocol (1925) and 409
   nuclear threats 24–25
   outer space and 497
   sanctions 630
   strategic stability dialogue 339, 341–43, 629
   Ukraine war and 5, 358, 630

Somalia and 633
South Korea and 224, 227, 241, 456
Sudan and 30, 59
Syria and 629
Ukraine war and 358, 503
   cyberattacks 490
   deconfliction line 631
   military aid 177–79, 205–206, 218, 219, 221
   Russian relations 5, 358, 630
   trade sanctions 535, 536, 538, 630
   Ukraine Defense Contact Group 632
   warnings 41
UNROCA and 472–73, 474–75
see also **New START** and **nuclear weapons**
UNMHA (Mission to Support the Hodeidah Agreement) 102
UNMIK (UN Interim Administration Mission in Kosovo) 102
UNMILEX (UN Report on Military Expenditure) 471, 475–76
UNMISS (UN Mission in South Sudan) 81, 82, 84, 86, 102
UNMOGIP (UN Military Observer Group in India and Pakistan) 102
UNODA (UN Office for Disarmament Affairs) 407, 458, 601
UNROCA (UN Register of Conventional Arms):
   assessment 475
   ATT and 473, 519–20
   format 519–20
   inaccuracies 436, 474–75
   objectives 471–72
   participation 472–73
   SALW and 472, 475
   transparency 471–75
UNSMIL (UN Support Mission in Libya) 102
UNSOM (UN Assistance Mission in Somalia) 102
UNTSO (UN Truce Supervision Organization) 102
UNVMC (UN Verification Mission in Colombia) 102
UralVagonZavod 202
uranium *see* **HEU**

Venezuela:
   biosecurity and 400
   conflict fatalities 34
   EU arms embargo 534

SALW and 459
Veritas Capital 198
Viasat 486, 489–90, 630
Vienna Document (2011) 435, 437–41, 443, 477, 596–97
Viet Nam:
 arms industry 198–99
 cluster munitions 453
 military expenditure 186
 MTCR and 545
Viinanen, Jarmo 350

Wagner Group:
 African operations 122, 130–33, 144
  sanctions against 133–34
 Burkina Faso 137
 CAR 49, 69, 85, 89, 98, 99, 110–11, 132–33, 138–39, 144, 145
 DRC 99, 133, 144
 human rights violations 110–11, 151
 landmine use 455
 Libya 144
 Mali 69, 87–88, 89, 98, 110, 110–11, 140–41, 238, 631
 Middle East 117–18, 119
 origins 111
 proxy role 105, 106, 144–47
 recruitment methods 144
 role 31, 142
 Sudan 132, 141–42, 144
 Syria 110
 Ukraine war 19, 106, 111, 116–17, 122, 143, 144, 145–46
Walesa, President Lech 23
Wang Yi 347
war crimes 23, 124, 143, 144, 151, 452, 580, 584, 608, 632, 636
Warsaw Pact 22
Wassenaar Arrangement (WA) 628
 2022 meeting 547–48
 chairing 548
 control lists 548
 Covid-19 and 548
 geopolitics 512
 MTCR and 549
 nature of regime 541
 NSG and 549
 origins 547
 Scholarship for Peace and Security 548–49
 scope 542, 547

Ukraine war and 541, 547
Western Sahara:
 cluster munitions 453
 MINURSO 102
WhisperGate 491
Wiper malware 486
Wittke, Albrecht von 461
Women and Peace and Security Agenda 459
World Bank 232, 632
World Food Programme 6, 630, 635
World Health Organization (WHO) 393–96, 632, 635

X-Agent 490
Xe Services 129
Xi Jinping, President 135, 346–47, 397, 630, 637

Yeltsin, President Boris 23
Yemen:
 arms embargo 533
 arms imports 233
 cluster munitions 451, 453
 conflict 45–46
  arms transfers and 216, 243, 244
  ceasefire 7, 30, 45–46, 57–58, 632, 636
  fatalities 46
  Iran and 243, 244, 530
  Saudi Arabia and 57, 193, 216, 243, 244, 629
  UAE and 57, 216, 243, 629
 EWIPA use 447–48
 landmines 457
 peace process 57–58, 60
 PMSCs in 119–20
 UNMHA 102
Yoon Suk-yeol, President 184

Zakharov, Valery 138
Zangger Committee 546, 628
Zelensky, President Volodymyr 25, 41, 44, 388, 637
Zhora, Victor 490, 493
Zimbabwe:
 biosecurity and 400
 EU arms embargo 534
 PMSCs in 133
Zlauvinen, Gustavo 349, 350, 357–58